PROPORTIONALI

Having identified proportionality as the main tool for limiting constitutional rights, Aharon Barak explores its four components (proper purpose, rational connection, necessity, and proportionality *stricto sensu*) and discusses the relationships between proportionality and reasonableness and between courts and legislation. He goes on to analyze the concept of deference and to consider the main arguments against the use of proportionality (incommensurability and irrationality). Alternatives to proportionality are compared and future developments of proportionality are suggested.

AHARON BARAK is a faculty member at the Interdisciplinary Center (IDC) Herzliya, Israel, and a visiting professor at Yale Law School. In 1975 he was appointed Attorney General of the State of Israel, becoming Justice of the Supreme Court of Israel in 1978 and serving as President from 1995 until his retirement in 2006. He has also served as a lecturer, professor and Dean of the Law School at the Hebrew University of Jerusalem.

CAMBRIDGE STUDIES IN CONSTITUTIONAL LAW

The aim of this series is to produce leading monographs in constitutional law. All areas of constitutional law and public law fall within the ambit of the series, including human rights and civil liberties law, administrative law, as well as constitutional theory and the history of constitutional law. A wide variety of scholarly approaches is encouraged, with the governing criterion being simply that the work is of interest to an international audience. Thus, works concerned with only one jurisdiction will be included in the series as appropriate, while, at the same time, the series will include works which are explicitly comparative or theoretical – or both. The series editors likewise welcome proposals that work at the intersection of constitutional and international law, or that seek to bridge the gaps between civil law systems, the US, and the common law jurisdictions of the Commonwealth.

Series Editors
David Dyzenhaus
Professor of Law and Philosophy, University of Toronto, Canada
Adam Tomkins
John Millar Professor of Public Law, University of Glasgow, UK

Editorial Advisory Board
T. R. S. Allan, Cambridge, UK
Damian Chalmers, LSE, UK
Sujit Choudhry, Toronto, Canada
Monica Claes, Maastricht, Netherlands
David Cole, Georgetown, USA
K. D. Ewing, King's College London, UK
David Feldman, Cambridge, UK
Cora Hoexter, Witwatersrand, South Africa
Christoph Moellers, Goettingen, Germany
Adrienne Stone, Melbourne, Australia
Adrian Vermeule, Harvard, USA

PROPORTIONALITY

Constitutional Rights and their Limitations

AHARON BARAK

Translated from the Hebrew by

DORON KALIR

CAMBRIDGE
UNIVERSITY PRESS

CAMBRIDGE UNIVERSITY PRESS
Cambridge, New York, Melbourne, Madrid, Cape Town,
Singapore, São Paulo, Delhi, Mexico City

Cambridge University Press
The Edinburgh Building, Cambridge CB2 8RU, UK

Published in the United States of America by Cambridge University Press, New York

www.cambridge.org
Information on this title: www.cambridge.org/9781107008588

First published in Hebrew by Nevo Publishing 2010

First published in English by Cambridge University Press 2012

A catalogue record for this publication is available from the British Library

ISBN 978-1-107-00858-8 Hardback
ISBN 978-1-107-40119-8 Paperback

CONTENTS

Table of conventions and international documents   *page* xvi
Table of constitutions and statutes   xvii
Table of cases   xix

Introduction   1

PART I   **Constitutional rights: scope and limitations**   17

1   Constitutional rights: scope and the extent of their
    protection   19

    A. The nature of the distinction   19
        1. Scope and protection   19
        2. The distinction in practice: the scope of freedom of expression and
            its protection   21

    B. The centrality of the distinction   22

    C. The distinction in comparative law   24

    D. Three stages of constitutional judicial review   26

    E. Absolute rights   27
        1. Are there absolute constitutional rights?   27
        2. The jurisprudence of absolute rights   29
        3. Absolute rights turned relative   31

    F. Relative rights   32
        1. The nature of the relative constitutional right   32
        2. Boundaries and limitations   32

    G. Constitutional rights: prima facie or definite?   37
        1. The problem presented   37
        2. The prima facie constitutional right: Alexy's view   38
        3. Definite constitutional rights that cannot be realized   39

    H. Is there a constitutional right to commit a proportional
        crime?   42

v

1. A constitutional right to steal? 42
2. The criticism and a response 43

2 Determining the scope of constitutional rights 45
   A. The right's scope is determined by constitutional
      interpretation 45
      1. Constitutional interpretation 45
      2. Constitutional interpretation: a generous view 69
   B. The right's scope and public interest 75
      1. The proper role of public interest considerations 75
      2. Public interest as part of proportionality 76
   C. The scope of constitutional rights and the rights of
      others 80
      1. The proper role of "rights of others" considerations 80
      2. The "rights of others" and constitutional rights conflict 81

3 Conflicting constitutional rights 83
   A. Resolving the constitutional conflict at the sub-
      constitutional level 83
      1. A model of constitutional conflict 83
      2. Conflicts between constitutional rights and the rule of law 86
   B. Conflict between rule-shaped constitutional rights 86
   C. Conflict between principle-shaped constitutional
      rights 87
      1. The scope and validity of the conflicting rights are not affected 87
      2. The effect on the realization of the conflicting rights 89
      3. Interpretive balancing between principle-shaped constitutional
         rights 92
      4. Constitutional validity 93
      5. Conflicting rights with no implementing legislation 94
      6. Conflicting rights which lead to a conflict between the legislation
         which defines their realization 96
   D. A conflict between a principle-shaped right and a
      rule-shaped right 97

4 Limitation of constitutional rights 99
   A. Limitation and amendment of rights 99
   B. Limitation on rights 101
      1. Infringement and limitation on rights 101
      2. De minimis constitutional limitations 103

3. Incidental limitations   105
4. Waiving constitutional rights   106

5   Limiting constitutional rights by law   107
  A. The legality principle   107
    1. Legal authority to limit a right   107
    2. The authorization chain   108
  B. Statutory limitations   110
    1. Limitation by statute   110
    2. Limitation according to statute   111
  C. The legality principle and common law   118
    1. The constitution and common law   118
    2. The common law and the limitation clause   121

PART II   **Proportionality: sources, nature, function**   129

6   The nature and function of proportionality   131
  A. The nature of proportionality   131
    1. Proportionality and its components   131
    2. Different methods of limiting constitutional rights   133
    3. The "silent constitution" and limitation of rights   134
    4. Specific limitation clauses   141
    5. General limitation clauses   142
    6. Hybrid limitation clauses   144
    7. The preferred regime: general, specific, or hybrid limitation clause?   145
  B. The formal role of proportionality   146
    1. Proportionality regarding validity and proportionality regarding meaning   146
    2. The constitutionality of limiting a constitutional right by a sub-constitutional law   147
    3. The reason behind the constitutional hierarchical relationship   149
    4. The effect on a constitutional right of a constitutional norm   152
    5. Limitation of a sub-constitutional norm by a lower sub-constitutional norm   155
    6. Limitation of a sub-constitutional norm by an equal-level norm   157
  C. The substantive role of proportionality   161
    1. Human rights and their limitation   161

2. Protecting human rights and recognizing the constitutionality of their limitations   165

3. Both the right and its limitations stem from a shared source   166

4. The limits on constitutional limitations   166

D. Limitation clause and the override   167

1. The nature of the override   167

2. The relationship between the limitation clause and the override   169

7 The historical origins of proportionality   175

A. Proportionality: in life and in the law   175

1. On the philosophical origins of proportionality   175

2. Proportionality and the Enlightenment   176

3. Proportionality as counter-formalism   177

4. The contribution of Carl Gottlieb Svarez   177

B. The development of proportionality in German public law   178

1. Proportionality in German administrative law, 1800–1933   178

2. The development of proportionality in German constitutional law post-Second World War   179

C. The migration of proportionality from German law to European law   181

1. European legal migration   181

2. Proportionality and the European Convention on Human Rights   183

3. Proportionality in the law of the European Union   184

D. From European law to Western European states' law   186

E. From European law to Canada, Ireland, and England   188

1. Canada   188

2. Ireland   190

3. United Kingdom   192

F. From Canada to New Zealand and Australia   194

1. New Zealand   194

2. Australia   195

G. From Canada and Germany to South Africa   197

H. Proportionality migrates to Central and Eastern Europe   198

I. Proportionality migrates to Asia and South America   199

1. Asia   199
2. South America   201

J.   Proportionality and international human rights law   202
1. International and national human rights law   202
2. Proportionality and the Universal Declaration of Human
   Rights   203
3. Proportionality and international humanitarian law   204

K.   Has proportionality arrived in America?   206

L.   Proportionality in Israel   208

8   The legal sources of proportionality   211
A.   Proportionality as a criterion for the realization of
     constitutional rights   211
1. The need for a constitutional entrenchment   211
2. The nature of the constitutional entrenchment   213

B.   Proportionality and democracy   214
1. The relationship between democracy and proportionality: basic
   assumptions   214
2. First assumption: democracy is of a constitutional status   214
3. Second assumption: democracy includes human rights   218
4. Third assumption: democracy is based on a balance between
   constitutional rights and the public interest   220
5. Fourth assumption: balancing through limitation clauses   221
6. Fifth assumption: limitation clauses are based on
   proportionality   222
7. An assessment of democracy as a source of proportionality   226

C.   Proportionality and the rule of law   226
1. The German approach   226
2. First assumption: the rule of law has a constitutional status   228
3. Second assumption: the rule of law includes human rights   230
4. Third assumption: the rule of law is based on a balance between
   constitutional rights and the public interest   232
5. Fourth assumption: the balancing is conducted through limitation
   clauses   232
6. Fifth assumption: limitation clauses are based on
   proportionality   233
7. An assessment of rule of law as a source of proportionality   234

D.   Proportionality as intrinsic to the conflict between legal
     principles   234

E. Proportionality and interpretation   238

F. Legal sources summary: is proportionality a logical
   necessity?   240

PART III   **The components of proportionality**   243

9   Proper purpose   245

A. The proper purpose as a component of
   proportionality   245
   1. The nature of the proper purpose and its sources   245
   2. Proper purpose as a threshold requirement   246

B. The elements of proper purpose   249
   1. The scope of the proper purpose   249
   2. The components of the proper purpose   251

C. The proper purpose's content and the state's democratic
   values   251
   1. Democracy's minimum requirements   251
   2. Pertinent democratic values   253
   3. General criteria for determining the proper purpose   257
   4. The categories of proper purposes   260

D. The urgency of proper purpose   277
   1. The problems with urgency   277
   2. Is "urgency" required?   278
   3. Criteria for determining urgency   279

E. Identifying the proper purpose   285
   1. The purposes of the limiting law   285
   2. Subjective or objective test?   286
   3. The correct solution for identifying the proper purpose   298

10   Rational connection   303

A. The nature of the rational connection test   303
   1. The content of the rational connection test   303
   2. The nature of the rational connection   305
   3. Rational connection and the means "designed to achieve" the proper
      purpose   306
   4. Rational connection and arbitrary means   307

B. The rational connection test and factual uncertainty   308
   1. The problem of factual uncertainty   308
   2. The certainty of the rational connection: rejection of extreme
      approaches   309

3. Determining the factual basis required for the existence of the rational connection   310
4. Rational connection and the test of time   312
5. Rational connection: a threshold test   315
C. Is the rational connection test essential?   315

11 Necessity   317
A. Characteristics of the necessity test   317
1. The content of the necessity test   317
2. The nature of the necessity test   320
3. The elements of the necessity test   323
4. The necessity test and the purpose's level of abstraction   331
B. Means "narrowly tailored" to fulfill the law's purpose   333
1. The metaphors of the cannon and the sparrows   333
2. Overinclusiveness   335
C. The necessity test: an evaluation   337
1. The "heart and soul" of the proportionality test?   337
2. Necessity: an important test   337

12 Proportionality stricto sensu (balancing)   340
A. The characteristics of proportionality stricto sensu   340
1. The content of the test   340
2. The nature of the proportionality stricto sensu test   342
3. Proper relation: a balancing test   343
4. The uniqueness of the test   344
B. The rule of balancing   345
1. The centrality of balancing   345
2. Balancing and validity   346
3. The nature of the balancing   348
4. Balancing based on the importance of the benefits and the importance of preventing the harm   349
C. The basic balancing rule   362
1. The elements of the basic balancing rule   362
2. The components of the basic balancing rule and its justification   363
3. Balanced scales   365
4. The basic balancing rule and specific balancing   367

5. Principled balancing   370

13 Proportionality and reasonableness   371
    A. From reasonableness to proportionality   371
    B. The components of proportionality and
       reasonableness   372
       1. The components of proportionality   372
       2. The components of reasonableness   373
    C. The relationship between proportionality and
       reasonableness   375
       1. Degree of detailing   375
       2. Balancing   377

14 Zone of proportionality: legislator and judge   379
    A. The application of proportionality to the three branches of
       government: the issue of judicial review   379
       1. Proportionality and the three branches of government   379
       2. Proportionality, judicial review, and democracy   381
       3. Proportionality and the separation of powers   384
    B. Discretion and the components of proportionality   400
       1. The decision to legislate   400
       2. Determining purposes   401
       3. Choosing the legislative means   405
       4. The rational connection test   405
       5. The necessity test   407
       6. The proportionality stricto sensu test (balancing)   413
    C. The zone of proportionality   415
       1. Its nature   415
       2. The zone of proportionality: legislator and judge   417
    D. Margin of appreciation   418
       1. Its nature   418
       2. The margin of appreciation and the zone of proportionality   419

15 Proportionality and positive constitutional rights   422
    A. Positive constitutional rights   422
       1. The nature of positive constitutional rights   422
       2. Positive constitutional rights in comparative law   423
       3. The legal source of positive constitutional rights   425
       4. Constitutional positive aspect and constitutional positive
          right   427

B. Positive constitutional rights and proportionality's components   429

1. Positive rights as relative rights   429

2. The proper purpose component   430

3. The rational connection component   432

4. The necessity component   433

5. The proportionality stricto sensu component   433

16 The burden of proof   435

A. The issue presented   435

B. The burden of proof: facts and law   436

C. The burden of persuasion and the burden of producing evidence   437

D. The first stage of constitutional review: a limitation of a constitutional right   437

E. The second stage of constitutional review: justification of the limitation of a right   439

1. The elements which make up the justification of the limitation of a right   439

2. Comparative analysis   439

F. The burden of persuasion during the second stage: on the party claiming the existence of a justification for the limitation   442

1. The burden of persuasion and the status of human rights   442

2. The counter-argument: the presumption of constitutionality   444

G. The burden of producing evidence during the second stage: on the party arguing that the limitation is justified   447

1. The basic approach   447

2. The burden during the second stage and the status of human rights   447

3. The burden of producing evidence and the burden of the claim that there is no less limiting alternative (necessity test)   448

4. The burden of producing the evidence and the unique nature of the judicial process in constitutional matters   449

PART IV **Proportionality evaluated**   455

17 Proportionality's importance   457

A. Proportionality and its critique   457

B. The emphasis on the need for rational justification   458
C. The need for structured discretion   460
   1. The importance of structured discretion   460
   2. Transparency   462
   3. Appropriate considerations in proper context   463
   4. A dialogue between the legislature and the judiciary   465
D. Proportionality and human rights theories   467
   1. Proportionality as a vessel for human rights theories   467
   2. Proportionality and liberalism   468
E. Proportionality, democracy, and judicial review   472
   1. Proportionality and democracy   472
   2. Proportionality and judicial review   473
   3. Kumm's approach   475
   4. Beatty's approach   476

18 The criticism on proportionality and a retort   481
A. The scope of the criticism on proportionality   481
B. Internal criticism   482
   1. The nature of the internal criticism   482
   2. The lack of a standard by which proportionality can be
      examined   482
   3. The lack of rationality   484
C. External criticism   487
   1. Too wide a judicial discretion   487
   2. Insufficient protection of constitutional rights   488
D. Lack of judicial legitimacy   490
   1. The nature of the criticism   490
   2. A retort   491

19 Alternatives to proportionality   493
A. Non-categorization-based alternatives   493
   1. Absolute rights   493
   2. Protecting the core of the constitutional right   496
   3. The dual model   499
B. The categorization-based alternatives   502
   1. Categorization within the human rights discourse   502
   2. The nature of thinking in legal categories   503
   3. Constitutional rights in categorized thinking   505

4. Categorization and the two-stage model   507

5. Categorization and balancing   508

6. Categorization and human rights in American constitutional law   509

20 The future of proportionality   528

A. Regarding the need for renewal   528

B. The proper purpose component – future developments   529

1. Different approaches to proper purpose   529

2. The proper approach: the hierarchy of constitutional rights with regard to the purpose's importance   531

3. Proper purpose and protection of constitutional rights   533

C. The rational connection component   539

D. The necessity component: future developments   540

E. The proportionality stricto sensu component: future developments   542

1. The nature of principled balancing formulas   542

2. Principled balancing formulas: a comparative survey   545

Bibliography   548
Index   593

TABLE OF CONVENTIONS
AND INTERNATIONAL DOCUMENTS

American Declaration of the Rights and Duties of Man (1948)   260
Declaration of the Rights of Man and of the Citizen (1789)   162, 255
European Convention for the Protection of Human Rights and Fundamental
      Freedoms (1950)   21, 25, 28, 35, 83, 122, 133, 134, 141, 159, 181, 182, 183, 188,
      190, 193, 199, 200, 210, 258, 419, 514, 531
   Protocol No. 2 (ETS No. 44), September 21, 1970   182
   Protocol No. 5 (ETS No. 55), December 20, 1971   182
   Protocol No. 8 (ETS No. 118), January 1, 1990   182
   Protocol No. 9 (ETS No. 140), October 1, 1994   182
   Protocol No. 11 (ETS No. 155), November 1, 1998   182
International Covenant on Civil and Political Rights (1966)   25, 113, 196, 200,
      204, 268, 269, 441
International Covenant on Economic, Social and Cultural Rights (1966)   25,
      200, 204, 260
Limburg Principles on the Implementation of the International Covenant on
      Economic, Social and Cultural Rights   204
Siracusa Principles on the Limitation and Derogation Provisions in the
      International Covenant on Civil and Political Rights   113, 204, 441
Treaty Establishing the European Coal and Steel Community (1951)   182
Treaty Establishing the European Atomic Energy Community (1957)   182
Treaty Establishing the European Economic Community (1957)   182
Treaty on European Union (1992)   182
Treaty Establishing the European Community (1997)   182
Treaty Establishing a Constitution for Europe (2004)   186
Treaty of Lisbon amending the Treaty on European Union and the Treaty
      Establishing the European Community (2007)   186
Universal Declaration of Human Rights (1948)   24, 27, 68, 121, 142, 143, 203,
      260, 262, 270

TABLE OF CONSTITUTIONS
AND STATUTES

Bar Law (1961)   402
Basic Law for the Federal Republic of Germany (1949)   52, 113, 135, 136, 139, 150,
    179, 214, 218, 227, 267, 379, 423, 473, 496, 532
Basic Law of the Hong Kong Special Administrative Region of the People's
    Republic of China   200
Basic Law: Freedom of Occupation   143, 148, 168, 169, 171, 172, 173, 210, 212,
    215, 222, 259, 267
Basic Law: The Government   110
Basic Law: Human Dignity and Liberty   26, 73, 91, 93, 94, 101, 118, 143, 148, 172,
    173, 174, 210, 212, 215, 219, 222, 224, 246, 254, 258, 259, 267, 360, 379, 423,
    426, 427
Basic Law: The Judiciary   91, 94, 385
Canadian Charter of Rights and Freedoms   26, 47, 60, 100, 101, 133, 142, 143,
    148, 150, 158, 167, 168, 173, 188, 189, 190, 202, 204, 215, 221, 222, 246, 258,
    279, 281, 337, 439, 440, 473
Charter of Human Rights and Responsibilities Act 2006   146
Civil Torts Law (Liability of the State) (2005)   318
Constitution of Albania   198
Constitution of India   141, 150, 200, 429
Constitution of Ireland   190, 191, 215
Constitution of Italy   215
Constitution of Moldova   199
Constitution of Poland   260
Constitution of Portugal   215, 228, 496
Constitution of Romania   199, 212
Constitution of South Korea   200
Constitution of Spain   216, 228, 473, 496
Constitution of Switzerland   143, 187, 188, 212, 269, 366, 496
Constitution of the Netherlands   149, 380
Constitution of the Republic of South Africa   26, 27, 33, 34, 73, 113, 118, 119, 122,
    126, 127, 132, 142, 144, 150, 151, 197, 198, 215, 216, 218, 219, 222, 229, 246,
    253, 257, 271, 273, 283, 360, 380, 422, 423, 425, 432, 441, 499, 532
Constitution of Turkey   212
Health Disciplines Act, RRO 1980   342
Human Rights Act 1998   66, 135, 136, 146, 152, 159, 193, 197, 348, 359, 397, 442,
    458, 465
Italian Civil Code   57

Law of Citizenship and Entry into Israel (Temporary Measure) (2003) 241, 251, 321
Law of Implementing Disengagement Program (2005) 308
Law of Legal Foundations (1980) 94, 95
Law of State Service (Discipline) (1963) 91, 92
Law to Postpone Service for Students Devoting Their Life to Torah Study (2002) 313
New Zealand Bill of Rights Act 1990 89, 157, 159, 194, 195, 360
Press Ordinance (1933) 73, 74
US Constitution 54, 70, 137, 227, 238, 256, 295, 422, 424, 426, 505, 509, 514, 523, 526
  Amendment I 31, 133, 138, 284, 294, 296, 297, 298, 299, 506, 507, 508, 514, 546
  Amendment XIII 295
  Amendment XIV 295
  Article I, § 9 114

TABLE OF CASES

A (FC) v. Secretary of State for the Home Department [2005] UKHL 71   524
A v. Secretary of State for the Home Department [2004] UKHL 56   334, 398, 473
A. D. M. Jabalpur v. S. Shuka, AIR 1976 SC 1207   232
Abrams v. United States, 250 US 616 (1919)   500
Academic Center of Law and Business v. Minister of Finance, HCJ 2605/05 [2009]   273, 416
Adalah – The Legal Center for the Rights of the Arab Minority v. Minister of Interior, HCJ 7052/03 [2006]   51, 134, 224, 322, 340, 407, 517
Adalah – The Legal Center for the Rights of the Arab Minority v. Minister of Defense, HCJ 8276/05 [2006] (2) IsrLR 352   32, 342
Allied Dunbar (Frank Weisinger) Ltd. v. Frank Weisinger [1988] 17 IRLR 60   192
Amod v. Multilateral Motor Vehicle Accidents Fund, 1998 (4) SA 753 (CC)   380
Andrews v. Law Society of British Columbia [1989] 1 SCR 143   282
Arlington Heights v. Metropolitan Housing Dev. Corp., 429 US 252 (1977)   302
Article 26 and Part V of the Planning and Development Bill 1999, In Re [2000] 2. IR 321   192
Article 26 and the Matrimonial Home Bill 1993, In Re [1994] IR 305   191
Article 26 of the Employment Equality Bill 1996, In Re [1997] 2 IR 321   192
Artico v. Italy, Eur. Ct. H. R., App. No. 6694/74 (1980)   424
Ashingdane v. United Kingdom, App. No. 8225/78, 7 EHRR 528 (1985)   135
Associated Provincial Picture Houses v. Wednesbury Corporation [1948] 1 KB 22   192, 373
Attorney-General of Quebec v. Quebec Association of Protestant School Boards *et al.* [1984] 2 SCR 66   100
August v. Electoral Commission, 1999 (3) SA 1 (CC)   430
Australian Capital Television Pty Ltd. v. Commonwealth (1992) 177 CLR 106   50, 106
Australian National Airways Pty Ltd. v. Commonwealth (1945) 71 CLR 29   69
Avni v. Prime Minister of Israel, HCJ 1384/98 [1998] IsrSC 52(5) 206   149
Baker v. State of Vermont, 744 A 2d 864 (1999)   425
Bartnicki v. Vopper, 532 US 514 (2001)   425
Barzilai v. Government of Israel, HCJ 428/86 [1986] IsrSC 40(3) 505   67, 232
BC Motor Vehicle Act, Re [1985] 2 SCR 486   60
BCGEU v. British Columbia [1988] 2 SCR 214   122
Beit Sourik Village Council v. Government of Israel, HCJ 2056/04 [2004] IsrSC 58(5) 807   342, 353, 414

Ben-Atiya v. Minister of Education, Culture and Sport, HCJ 3477/95 [1995] IsrSC
     49(5) 1   228
Bendix Autolite Corp. v. Midwesco Enterprises Inc., 486 US 888 (1988)   483
Botzer v. Macabim-Re'ut Regional Municipality, HCJ 7081/93 [1996] IsrSC 50(1)
     19   271
Boumediene *et al.* v. Bush, President of the United States *et al.*, 553 US 723
     (2008)   525
Burial Society v. Kestenbaum, CA 294/91 [1992] 46 (2) PD 464   277
BVerfGE 2, 380   229
BVerfGE 5, 585   218
BVerfGE 7, 198   238, 276
BVerfGE 14, 32   70
BVerfGE 28, 243   137
BVerfGE 34, 238   180
BVerfGE 39, 1   428
BVerfGE 45, 187   61
BVerfGE 53, 135   319
BVerfGE 55, 159   304
BVerfGE 88, 203   428
Campbell v. United Kingdom, App. No. 13590/88, 15 EHRR 137 (1993)   329
Canada (Attorney-General) v. JTI-Macdonald Corp. [2007] 2 SCR 610   340
Canadian Newspaper Co. v. Canada (Attorney-General) [1988] 2 SCR 122   329
Carmichele v. Minister of Safety and Security, 2001 (4) SA 938 (CC)   380
Certification of the Constitution of the Republic of South Africa, In Re, 1996 (4)
     SA 74 (CC)   216
Chadash-Ta'al Party v. Chairman of Knesset Election Committee Knesset, HCJ
     2257/04 [2004] IsrSC 58(6) 685   49, 54, 230
Chamberlain v. Surrey School District No. 36 [2002] 4 SCR 710   360
Chee Siok Chin v. Minister for Home Affairs [2006] 1 SLR 582   199
Chevron USA Inc. v. Natural Resources Defense Council Inc., 467 US 837
     (1984)   394
Chorev v. Minister of Transportation, HCJ 5016/96 [1997] IsrSC 51(4) 1   478
Chorherr v. Austria, App. No. 13308/87, 17 EHRR 358 (1994)   116
Christian Education South Africa v. Minister of Education, 2000 (4) SA 757
     (CC)   330
Christine Goodwin v. UK, Eur. Ct. H. R., App. No. 28957/95 (2002)   424
City of Cleburne v. Cleburne Living Ctr. Inc., 473 US 432 (1985)   510
Coetzee v. Government of the Republic of South Africa, 1995 (4) SA 631
     (CC)   335, 343
Commitment to Peace and Social Justice v. Minister of Finance, HCJ 366/03
     [2005] 104   422
Committee for the Commonwealth of Canada v. Canada [1991] 1 SCR 139   109
Contram Ltd. v. Ministry of Finance – Custom and VAT Department, HCJ
     164/97 [1998] IsrSC 52(1) 289   162, 218
Cooper v. Aaron, 358 US 1 (1958)   393
Council of Civil Service Unions v. Minister for the Civil Service [1985]
     AC 374   192, 373
Cox v. Ireland [1992] 2 IR 503   191

Craig v. Boren, 429 US 190 (1976)   510
Cunliffe v. Commonwealth (1994) 182 CLR 272   50, 196
Dagenais v. Canadian Broadcasting Corporation [1994] 3 SCR 835   247, 360
Dawood v. Minister of Home Affairs, 2000 (3) SA 936 (CC)   107, 114, 229
De Reuck v. Director of Public Prosecutions, 2004 (1) SA 406 (CC)   77
Decision No. 2007-555 DC (August 16, 2007)   132, 407
Decision No. 2008-562 (February 21, 2008)   132, 407
Decision No. 2009-580 (June 10, 2009)   132, 407
Dennis v. United States, 341 US 494 (1951)   491
Deshaney v. Winnebago County Department of Social Services, 109 S Ct 998 (1989)   425
Design 22 Shark Deluxe Furniture Ltd. v. Director of Sabbath Work Permits Department, Ministry of Labor and Social Affairs, HCJ 5026/04 [2005] (1) IsrLR 340   167
Diagoras Development Ltd. v. National Bank of Greece SA (1985) 1 CLR 581   393
District of Columbia v. Heller, 554 US 290 (2008)   207, 478
DK v. Crowley [2002] 2 IR 744   192
Doctors of Life International v. Speaker of the National Assembly, 2006 (6) SA 416 (CC)   216
Du Plessis v. De Clerk, 1996 (3) SA 850 (CC)   122
Dubois v. Queen [1985] 2 SCR 350   70
Edmonton Journal v. Alberta [1989] 2 SCR 1326   282
Edwards v. Attorney-General of Canada [1930] AC 124 (PC)   65
Egan v. Canada [1995] 2 SCR 513   396
Eisenberg v. Minister of Building and Housing, HCJ 6163/92 [1992–4] IsrLR 19   232
Euronet Golden Lines Ltd. v. Minister of Communication, HCJ 987/94 [1994] IsrSC 48(5) 412   209
Fay v. New York, 332 US 261 (1947)   49
FCC v. Beach Communications, 508 US 307 (1993)   293
Ferreira v. Levin NO, 1996 (1) SA 984 (CC)   44, 71, 438
Ford v. Attorney-General of Quebec [1988] 2 SCR 712   100, 170
Fox, Campbell & Hartley v. UK, App. No. 12244/86 (1991) 13 EHRR 157   424
Ganimat v. State of Israel, CrimA 537/95 [1995] IsrSC 49(3) 355   345
Ganimat v. State of Israel, HCJ 2316/95 [1995] IsrSC 49(4) 589   272
Ganor v. Attorney-General, HCJ 935/89 [1990] IsrSC 44(2) 485   373
Gaza Coast Regional Council v. Knesset of Israel, HCJ 1661/05 [2005] IsrSC 59(2) 481   245, 308, 311, 312, 403, 404
Ghaidan v. Mendoza [2004] 3 WLR 113   160
Golder v. United Kingdom, App. No. 4451/70, 1 EHRR 524 (1979–80)   134
Gompers v. United States, 233 US 604 (1914)   70
Gosselin v. Quebec (Attorney-General) [2002] 4 SCR 429; 2002 SCC 84   423
Gosselin (Tutor of) v. Quebec (Attorney-General) [2005] 1 SCR 238; 2005 SCC 15   361
Graham v. Florida, 560 US (2010)   175
Griswold v. Connecticut, 381 US 479 (1965)   55
Hanafin v. Minister for Environment [1996] 2 IR 321   215
Hand v. Dublin Corporation [1989] IR 26   192

Handyside v. United Kingdom, App. No. 5493/72, 1 EHRR 737 (1979)   184, 419
Hansen v. Queen, SC 58/2005 [2007] NZSC 7 (CA)   77
Harvey v. New Brunswick (Attorney-General) [1996] 2 SCR 876   410
Haughey v. Moriarty [1999] 3 IR 1   215
Heaney v. Ireland [1994] 3 IR 593   191
Hemed v. State of Israel, CA 5604/94 [2004] IsrSC 58(2) 498   374
Herbert v. Lando, 441 US 153 (1979)   361
Hill v. Church of Scientology [1995] 2 SCR 1130   124
HKSAR v. Hung Chan Wa (2006) 9 HKCFAR 614   199
HKSAR v. Lam Kwong Wai (2006) 9 HKCFAR 574   199
Hoffmann v. South African Airways, 2001 (1) SA 1   109
Hoffnung v. Knesset Speaker, HCJ 3434/96 [1996] IsrSC 50(3) 57   102, 103, 104
Huang v. Secretary of State for the Home Department [2007] UKHL 11   395, 398
Hunter v. Southam Inc. [1984] 2 SCR 145   47
Illinois State Board of Elections v. Socialist Workers Party, 440 US 173
    (1979)   411
Institute of Chartered Accountants v. Bevan [2003] 1 NZLR 154   195
International Transport Roth GmbH v. Secretary of State for the Home
    Department [2002] 3 WLR 344   399
Internationale Handelsgesellschaft mbH v. Einfurh- und Vorratsstelle für
    Getreide und Futtermittel, Case 11/70 [1970] ECR 1125   185
Israel Investment Managers Association v. Minister of Finance, HCJ 1715/97
    [1997] IsrSC 51(4) 367   68, 319, 396
Jackson v. City of Joliet, 715 F 2d 1200 (7th Cir. 1982)   424
Jackson v. Her Majesty's Attorney-General [2006] 1 AC 262   120
Jane Doe v. Disciplinary Court for Government Employees in Haifa, HCJ
    1435/03 [2003] IsrSC 58(1) 529   80
J. B. International Ltd. v. Auckland City Council [2006] NZRMA 401   195
Judgment 20.530 decided by the Constitutional Court of Peru on June 3,
    2005   201
Judgment ROL 519 decided by the Constitutional Court of Chile on June 5,
    2007   201
Judgment T-422 decided by the Constitutional Court of Colombia on June 16,
    1992   201
Juicio de Amparo en Revision 1659/2006, February 27, 2002   201
Kach Faction v. Knesset Speaker, HCJ 73/85 [1985] IsrSC 39(3) 141   385
Kelly v. UK, Eur. Ct. H. R., App. No. 30054/96 (2001)   424
Khumalo v. Holomise, 2002 (5) SA 401 (CC)   453
Kibbutz Hatzor v. Internal Revenue Service Officer, CA 165/82 [1985]
    IsrSC 39(2) 70   72
"Kol Ha'am" Company Ltd. v. Minister of the Interior, HCJ 73/53 [1953]
    IsrSC 7 871   73, 288
Korematsu v. United States, 323 US 214 (1944)   519
Kruger v. Commonwealth (1997) 190 CLR 1   50, 196
La'or v. Commission for Censorship of Movies and Plays, HCJ 14/86 [1987]
    IsrSC 41(1) 421   269
Lange v. Australian Broadcasting Corp. (1997) 189 CLR 520   50, 196
Laor v. Israel Film and Theatre Council, HCJ 14/86 [1987] IsrSC 41(1) 421   349

Lavigne v. Ontario Public Service Employees Union [1991] 2 SCR 211   310
Lavoie v. Canada [2002] 1 SCR 769   360
Lesapo v. North West Agricultural Bank, 2000 (1) SA 409 (CC)   310
Leung Kwok Hung v. HKSAR (2005) 8 HKCFAR 229   199
Levy v. Southern District Commissioner of Police, HCJ 153/83 [1984] IsrSC 38(2)
    393   544
Levy v. Victoria (1997) 189 CLR 579   50, 196
Litzman v. Knesset Speaker, HCJ 5131/03 [2004] IsrSC 59(1) 577   111
London Regional Transport v. Mayor of London and another [2001] EWCA
    Civ. 1491   463
Mahe v. Alta [1990] SCR 342   60
Majority Headquarters v. Israel Police, HCJ 2557/05 [2006] (2) IsrLR 399   272,
    422
Malone v. United Kingdom, App. No. 8691/79, 7 EHRR 14 (1984)   117
Manitoba Language Rights, Re [1985] 1 SCR 721   229
Marab v. IDF Commander in the West Bank, HCJ 3239/02 [2002] IsrSC 57(2)
    349   272
Marbury v. Madison, 5 US (1 Cranch) 137 (1803)   473, 526
Matatiele Municipality v. President of the Republic of South Africa, 2006 (5)
    SA 47 (CC)   450
Mathieu-Mohin and Clarfayt v. Belgium, App. No. 9267/81, 10 EHRR 1
    (1987)   135
McGinty v. Western Australia (1996) 186 CLR 140   50, 196
Meatrael v. Minister of Finance, HCJ 4676/94 [1996] IsrSC 50(5) 15   70, 169
Minister of Health v. Treatment Action Campaign, 2002 (5) SA 721 (CC)   432
Minister of Home Affairs v. Fisher [1979] 3 All ER 21   69
Minister of Home Affairs v. National Institute for Crime Prevention and the
    Re-integration of Offenders (NICRO), 2005 (3) SA 280 (CC)   270
Minister of Transport v. Noort [1992] 3 NZLR 260 (CA)   122, 440
Mohlomi v. Minister of Defence, 1997 (1) SA 124 (CC)   271
Moise v. Greater Germiston Transitional Local Council, 2001 (4) SA 491
    (CC)   441, 453
Moonen v. Film and Literature Board of Review (No. 2) [2002] 2 NZLR 754
    (CA)   195
Moonen v. Film and Literature Board of Review [2000] 2 NZLR 9 (CA)   159
Moseneke v. Master, 2001 (2) SA 18 (CC)   292
Movement for Quality Government in Israel v. Knesset, HCJ 6427/02 [2006]
    IsrSC 61(1) 619   23, 43, 250, 311, 403
Muhammad Bakri v. Israel Film Council, HCJ 316/03 [2003] IsrSC 58(1) 249   275
Murphy v. Independent Radio and Television Commission [1999] 1 IR 12   192
Myers v. United States, 272 US 52 (1926)   386
National Assembly Ltd. v. Attorney-General, HCJ 10203/03 (unreported decision
    of August 20, 2008)   20, 78
National Coalition for Gay and Lesbian Equality v. Minister of Home Affairs,
    2000 (2) SA 1 (CC)   304
Nationwide News Pty Ltd. v. Wills (1992) 177 CLR 1   50, 196
Neiman v. Central Election Board, Eleventh Knesset, EA 2/84 [1985] IsrSC 39(2)
    281   88

New York Times v. Sullivan, 376 US 254 (1963)   123
Newfoundland (Treasury Board) v. NAPE [2004] 3 SCR 381   270
Ng Yat Chi v. Max Share Ltd. (2005) 8 HKCFAR 1   199
Nixon v. Shrink Missouri Government PAC, 528 US 377 (2000)   207
Official Receiver and Trustee in Bankruptcy of Chan Wing Hing v. Chan Wing
    Hing and Secretary for Justice (2006) 9 HKCFAR 545   199
Om Kumar v. Union of India (2001) 2 SCC 386   201
Ozgur Gundem v. Turkey, Eur. Ct. H. R., App. No. 22492/93 (2000)   424
Personnel Administrator of Massachusetts v. Feeney, 442 US 256 (1979)   296
Plato Sharon v. Knesset Committee, HCJ 306/81 [1981] IsrSC 35(4) 118   385
Police v. Curran [1992] 3 NZLR 260 (CA)   440
Powerco v. Commerce Commission, HC Wellington, 9 June 2006,
    CIV-2005-485-1066   195
President of the Republic of South Africa v. Hugo, 1997 (4) SA 1 (CC)   115, 231
President of the Republic of South Africa v. Modderklip Boerdery (Pty) Ltd., 2005
    (5) SA 3 (CC)   430
President of the Republic of South Africa v. South African Rugby Football Union,
    2000 (1) SA 1 (CC)   380
President of the Republic of South Africa, In Re Ex Parte, 2000 (2) SA 674   107,
    229
Prince v. President of the Law Society of the Cape of Good Hope, 2002 (2)
    SA 794 (CC)   258, 330
Prinz v. United States, 521 US 898 (1997)   67
Progressive Enterprises Ltd. v. North Shore City Council [2006] NZRMA 72   195
Public Committee Against Torture in Israel v. Government of Israel, HCJ 769/02
    [2006] (2) IsrLR 459   205
Public Committee Against Torture in Israel v. Prime Minister, HCJ 5100/94
    [1999] IsrSC 53(4) 817; [1998–9] IsrLR 567   29
R. (Farrakhan) v. Secretary of State for the Home Department [2002] 3 WLR
    481   417
R. (ProLife Alliance) v. BBC [2003] 2 WLR 1403   398
R. (Razar) v. Secretary of State for the Home Department [2004] 2 AC 363   398
R. (Wilkinson) v. Inland Revenue Commissioners [2006] All ER 529   160
R. v. Big M Drug Mart Ltd. [1985] 1 SCR 295   69, 289
R. v. Brown [2002] 2 SCR 185   360
R. v. Butler [1992] 1 SCR 452   290
R. v. Chief Constable of Sussex, ex parte International Trader's Ferry Ltd. [1999]
    2 AC 418   375
R. v. Edwards Books and Art Ltd. [1986] 2 SCR 713   280, 306, 409
R. v. Goldstein [1983] 1 WLR 151   333
R. v. Keegstra [1990] 3 SCR 697   281
R. v. Lambert [2002] 2 AC 545   135
R. v. Lord Saville of Newdigate, ex parte A and B [1999] 4 All ER 860   363
R. v. MAFF, ex parte First City Trading [1997] 1 CMLR 250   376
R. v. Ministry of Defence, ex parte Smith [1996] QB 517   363
R. v. Nova Scotia Pharmaceutical Society [1992] 2 SCR 606   118
R. v. Oakes [1986] 1 SCR 103   165, 189, 222, 258, 303, 340, 343, 408, 440, 539

R. v. Secretary of State for the Environment, Transport and the Regions [2001]
   2 All ER 929   193
R. v. Secretary of State for the Home Department, ex parte Brind [1991]
   1 AC 696   192
R. v. Secretary of State for the Home Department, ex parte Daly [2001] 3 All
   ER 433   193, 376, 395
R. v. Sharpe [2001] 1 SCR 45   340
R. v. Therens [1985] 1 SCR 613   60, 122
Reference re Remuneration of Judges of the Provincial Court (PEI) [1997]
   3 SCR 3   217, 229
Reference re Same-Sex Marriage [2004] 3 SCR 608   361
Reference re Secession of Quebec [1998] 2 SCR 217   54, 215
Rekanat v. National Labor Court, HCJFH 4191/97 [2000] IsrSC 54(5) 330   272
RJR-MacDonald Inc. v. Canada (Attorney-General) [1995] 3 SCR 199   272
Rock v. Ireland [1997] 3 IR 484   192
Rocket v. Royal College of Dental Surgeons of Ontario [1990] 2 SCR 232   342
Rubinstein v. Minister of Defense, HCJ 3267/97 [1998–9] IsrLR 139   386
RWDSU v. Dolphin Delivery Ltd. [1986] 2 SCR 573   122
Ryan v. Attorney-General [1965] IR 294   191
S. v. Baloyi (Minister of Justice Intervening), 2000 (2) SA 425 (CC)   423
S. v. Bhulwana, 1996 (1) SA 388 (CC)   348
S. v. Jordan, 2002 (6) SA 642   291
S. v. Makwanyane, 1995 (3) SA 391 (CC)   319
S. v. Mambolo, 2001 (3) SA 409 (CC)   122
S. v. Manamela, 2000 (3) SA 1 (CC)   319
S. v. Mbatha, 1996 (2) SA 464 (CC)   304
S. v. Thebus, 2003 (6) SA 505 (CC)   122
S. v. Zuma, 1995 (2) SA 642 (CC)   48, 441
Sambamurthy v. State of Andhra Pradesh, AIR 1987 SC 66   229
Schneider v. State, 308 US 147 (1939)   500
Secretary of State for the Home Department v. E [2007] UKHL 47   524
Secretary of State for the Home Department v. JJ and others (FC) [2007]
   UKHL 45   524
Secretary of State for the Home Department v. MB [2007] UKHL 46   524
Senesh v. Broadcasting Authority, HCJ 6126/94 [1999] IsrSC 53(3) 817   274
Shalit v. Minister of the Interior, HCJ 58/68 [1969] IsrLR 23(2) 477   72
Shatil v. Mekorot-Israel National Water Co., CA 10078/03 [2007]   377
Shavit v. Rishon LeZion Jewish Burial Society, CA 6024/97 [1999] IsrSC 53(3)
   600   345, 479
Sheldrake v. DPP [2004] UKHL 43   160
Shelley v. Kraemer, 334 US 1 (1948)   125
Shtanger v. Speaker of the Knesset, HCJ 2334/02 [2003] IsrSC 58(1) 786   334
Singh v. Minister of Employment and Immigration [1985] 1 SCR 177   269
Slaight Communications Inc. v. Davidson [1989] 1 SCR 1038   375
Solicitor v. Law Society (2003) 6 HKCFAR 570   199
Soobramoney v. Minister of Health, 1998 (1) SA 765 (CC)   265
South African Association of Personal Injury Lawyers v. Heath, 2001 (1) SA 883
   (CC)   216

Sporrong and Lönnroth v. Sweden, App. No. 7151/75, 5 EHRR 35 (1982)   344
Stanford v. Kentucky, 492 US 361 (1989)   67
State of Israel v. Klein, LCRA 1127/93 [1994] IsrSC 48(3) 485   115
State of Madras v. V. G. Raw, AIR 1952 SC 196   201
Stephens v. West Australian Newspapers Ltd. (1994) 182 CLR 211   196
Sunday Times v. United Kingdom, App. No. 6538/74, 2 EHRR 245 (1980)   109,
    115, 189
Supreme Monitoring Committee for Arab Affairs in Israel v. Prime Minister of
    Israel, HCJ 1163/03 [2006] (1) IsrLR 105   110
Taylor v. New Zealand Poultry Board [1984] 1 NZLR 394 (CA)   194
Temple Mount Faithful v. Government of Israel, HCJ 7128/96 [1997] IsrSC 51(2)
    509   276
Tenufah Human Services v. Ministry of Labor and Welfare, HCJ 450/97 [1998]
    IsrSC 52(2) 433   45
Teri Oat Estates Ltd. v. U. T. Chandigarh (2004) 2 SCC 130   201
Terminiello v. Chicago, 337 US 1 (1949)   163
Texas v. Johnson, 491 US 397 (1989)   500
The Queen v. Jones [1986] 2 SCR 284   103
The State (M) v. Attorney-General [1979] IR 73   216
Theophenous v. Herald Weekly Time Ltd. (1995) 182 CLR 104   60
Thompson v. Oklahoma, 487 US 815 (1988)   67
Trinity Western University v. British Columbia College of Teachers [2001]
    1 SCR 772   360
Turner Broadcasting System Inc. v. FCC, 520 US 180 (1997)   206
Tzemach v. Minister of Defence, HCJ 6055/95 [1999] IsrSC 53(5) 241   272, 360,
    451
Union of India v. G. Ganayutham, AIR 1997 SC 3387   201
United Mizrahi Bank Ltd. v. Migdal Cooperative Village, CA 6821/93 [1995]
    IsrLR 1   47, 103, 220, 253, 317, 389, 435, 473
United States v. Cotroni [1989] 1 SCR 1469   322
United States v. Lovett, 328 US 303 (1946)   114
United States v. O'Brien, 391 US 367 (1968)   298
United States v. Playboy Entertainment Group, 529 US 803 (2000)   206
United States v. Then, 56 F 3d 464 (2nd Cir. 1995)   66
United States v. United Foods, 533 US 405 (2001)   206
United States, ex rel. Attorney-General v. Delaware & Hudson Co., 213 US 366
    (1909)   289
United States Railroad Retirement Board v. Fritz, 449 US 166 (1980)   293
Wakin, Re (1993) 73 ALJR 839   59
Wallace v. Jaffree, 472 US 38 (1985)   297
Webster v. Reproductive Health Services, 109 S Ct 3040 (1989)   425
West Virginia University Hospitals Inc. v. Casey, 499 US 83 (1991)   62
WIC Radio Ltd. v. Simpson [2006] SCR 41   361
Wolf v. Minister of Immigration [2004] NZAR 414   195
Ysursa v. Pocatello Education, 555 US 353 (2009)   206
Zana v. Turkey, App. No. 18954/91, 27 EHRR 667 (1999)   268

~

Introduction

This book reflects the constitutional theory developed following the Second World War. It reflects an expansion of the concept of constitutional law,[1] a blurring of the lines between constitutional and private law[2] as well as the development of purposive interpretation.[3] This modern constitutional theory also recognizes positive constitutional rights alongside the negative ones,[4] and stipulates a wider judicial review on the law's constitutionality.[5] It is based on the fundamental distinction between recognizing the scope of the constitutional rights and their limitations.[6] Two key elements in developing this modern constitutional theory are the

[1] See L. Weinrib, "The Postwar Paradigm and American Exceptionalism," in S. Choudhry (ed.), *The Migration of Constitutional Ideas* (Cambridge University Press, 2006), 83; M. Kumm, "Who's Afraid of the Total Constitution?," in A. J. Menendez and E. O. Ericksen (eds.), *Arguing Fundamental Rights* (Dordrecht: Springer, 2006).

[2] See D. Friedman and D. Barak-Erez (eds.), *Human Rights in Private Law* (2001); T. Barkhuysen and S. Lindenbergh (eds.), *Constitutionalisation of Private Law* (2006); D. Oliver and J. Fedtke (eds.), *Human Rights and the Private Sphere: A Comparative Study* (2007).

[3] A. Barak, *Purposive Interpretation in Law* (Sari Bashi trans., Princeton University Press, 2005), 83.

[4] See below, at 422.

[5] See E. McWhinney, *Judicial Review in the English-Speaking World* (University of Toronto Press, 1956); D. W. Jackson and C. N. Tate (eds.), *Comparative Judicial Review and Public Policy* (1992); A. Stone Sweet, *The Birth of Judicial Politics in France: The Constitutional Council in Comparative Perspective* (Oxford University Press, 1992); C. N. Tate and T. Vallinder (eds.), *The Global Expansion of Judicial Power* (1995); A. Stone Sweet, *Governing with Judges: Constitutional Politics in Europe* (Oxford University Press, 2000); M. Shapiro and A. Stone Sweet, *On Law, Politics and Judicialization* (Oxford University Press, 2002); R. Prochazka, *Mission Accomplished: On Founding Constitutional Adjudication in Central Europe* (Budapest: Central European University Press, 2002); T. Koopmans, *Courts and Political Institutions: A Comparative View* (Cambridge University Press, 2003); R. Hirsch, *Towards Juristocracy: The Origins and Consequences of the New Constitutionalism* (Cambridge, MA: Harvard University Press, 2004); V. Ferreres Comella, *Constitutional Courts and Democratic Values: A European Perspective* (New Haven, CT: Yale University Press, 2009). For a criticism of judicial review, see below, at 490.

[6] See below, at 19.

1

notions of democracy and the rule of law. The concept of proportionality stems from these two notions. This book seeks to analyze that concept.

Proportionality has different meanings in various contexts. This book focuses on one meaning in particular – the proportionality of a limitation applied within a democratic system, on a constitutional right by a law (a statute or the common law). For that, we must assume the very existence of such constitutional rights[7] and their legal origin (either explicitly or implicitly) in a constitutional text. The book examines the situations in which a law may limit such a right in a constitutionally recognized manner. The limitations that may be imposed on a constitutional right will be analyzed, as well as the limits of these limitations.

This is an analytical essay on the limitations of constitutional rights in a constitutional democracy.[8] The discussion must therefore include the

---

[7] See W. Newcomb Hohfeld, "Fundamental Legal Conceptions as Applied in Judicial Reasoning," in W. Wheeler Cook (ed.), *Fundamental Legal Conceptions as Applied in Judicial Reasoning and Other Legal Essays* (New Haven, CT: Yale University Press, 1919); H. L. A. Hart, *Essays on Bentham: Jurisprudence and Political Theory* (Oxford University Press, 1982), 162; R. Dworkin, *Taking Rights Seriously* (Cambridge, MA: Harvard University Press, 1977); D. Lyons (ed.), *Rights* (1979); J. Waldron (ed.), *Theories of Rights* (1984); J. Raz, *The Morality of Freedom* (Oxford: Clarendon Press, 1986); L. W. Summer, *The Moral Foundation of Rights* (Oxford University Press, 1987); C. Santiago Nino, *The Ethics of Human Rights* (Oxford University Press, 1991); J. Waldron, *Liberal Rights: Collected Papers 1981–1991*(Cambridge University Press, 1993); J. Raz, *Ethics in the Public Domain: Essays in the Morality of Law and Politics* (Oxford: Clarendon Press, 1994); M. H. Kramer, N. E. Simmonds, and H. Steiner, *A Debate over Rights: Philosophical Inquiries* (Oxford University Press, 1988); C. Wellman, *An Approach to Rights: Studies in the Philosophy of Law and Morals* (Dordrecht: Kluwer Academic Publishers, 1997); F. M. Kamm, "Rights," in J. Coleman and S. Shapiro (eds.), *The Oxford Handbook of Jurisprudence and Philosophy of Law* (Oxford University Press, 2002), 476; W. A. Edmundson, *An Introduction to Rights* (Cambridge University Press, 2004); G. W. Rainbolt, *The Concept of Rights* (Dordrecht: Springer, 2006); C. Gearty, *Can Human Rights Survive?* (Cambridge University Press, 2006); M. J. Perry, *Toward a Theory of Human Rights: Religion, Law, Courts* (Cambridge University Press, 2007); P. Eleftheriadis, *Legal Rights* (Oxford University Press, 2008).

[8] On constitutional democracy, see C. H. McIlwain, *Constitutionalism: Ancient and Modern* (Ithaca, NY: Cornell University Press, 1947); A. Sajo, *Limiting Government: An Introduction to Constitutionalism* (Budapest: Central European University Press, 1999); J. Elster and R. Slagstad (eds.), *Constitutionalism and Democracy* (1988); D. Greenberg *et al.* (eds.), *Constitutionalism & Democracy: Transition in the Contemporary World* (1993); L. Alexander (ed.), *Constitutionalism: Philosophical Foundations* (1988); J. Kis, *Constitutional Democracy* (Budapest: Central European University Press, 2003); W. F. Murray, *Constitutional Democracy: Creating and Maintaining a Just Political Order* (Baltimore, MD: Johns Hopkins University Press, 2007); M. Loughlin and N. Walker (eds.), *The Paradox of Constitutionalism* (2007); K. S. Ziegler *et al.* (eds.), *Constitutionalism and the Role of Parliament* (2007); P. Dobner and M. Loughlin, *The Twilight of Constitutionalism?* (Oxford University Press, 2010).

well-entrenched notion of democracy itself,[9] as well as of the rule of law.[10] Both are central to the understanding of constitutional limitations. Both are given a broad interpretation in these pages. The two are well connected in that the rule of law entails the law of rules and the rule of values underlying fundamental democratic ideals (such as the separation of powers and the independence of the judiciary). At the heart of these values we find constitutional rights, and their limitations. And at the heart of these limitations we find the concept of proportionality. A limitation on a constitutional right by law (statutory or common law) will be constitutionally permissible if, and only if, it is proportional. The constitutionality of the limitation, in other words, is determined by its proportionality.

Proportionality, therefore, can be defined as the set of rules determining the necessary and sufficient conditions for a limitation of a constitutionally protected right by a law to be constitutionally permissible. According to the four sub-components of proportionality, a limitation of a constitutional right will be constitutionally permissible if (i) it is designated for a proper purpose;[11] (ii) the measures undertaken to effectuate such a limitation are rationally connected to the fulfillment of that purpose;[12] (iii) the measures undertaken are necessary in that there are no alternative measures that may similarly achieve that same purpose with a lesser degree of limitation;[13] and finally (iv) there needs to be a proper relation ("proportionality *stricto sensu*" or "balancing") between the importance of achieving the proper purpose and the social importance of preventing the limitation on the constitutional right.[14]

Certain aspects of proportionality arise in circumstances that do not limit a constitutional right by statute. One of those aspects is the use of proportionality in interpretation. The interpreter often finds himself with a need to determine the scope of the governmental authority. This is true, for example, when the interpreter needs to determine the scope of a government minister's authority to provide or refuse a license as provided in a law. Regarding the question of authority, the interpreter must interpret the law's language along with its purpose. In determining the purpose, the interpreter should balance professional freedom with the public interest, which makes up the law's foundation and its purpose at a high level of abstraction. This balancing is carried out by interpretive analogy from

---

[9] See below, at 214.   [10] See below, at 226.
[11] For a discussion on this sub-component, see below, at 245.
[12] For a discussion on this sub-component, see below, at 303.
[13] For a discussion on this sub-component, see below, at 317.
[14] For a discussion on this sub-component, see below, at 340.

the proportionality *stricto sensu* element. This is interpretive balancing.[15] It differs from the all-encompassing proportionality which is discussed in this book. It is limited to only one of proportionality's elements – *stricto sensu* (balance). It deals with the interpretation (meaning) of the law and not with its constitutionality (validity).

The set of rules that make up proportionality are a legal construct which reflect a constitutional methodology justifying limitations on constitutional rights.[16] Proportionality's nature does not suggest a neutral approach towards constitutional rights. The concept of proportionality is not indifferent to the limitations of rights. On the contrary, it is based on the need to protect them. Indeed, the limitations that proportionality imposes on the realization of constitutional rights, as well as the rights themselves, draw their authority and content from the same source.[17] Thus, proportionality determines the proper level of protection for constitutional rights in a constitutionally rights-based democratic society. Proportionality emphasizes the importance of reason and justifying limitations on constitutional rights.[18]

This book is the product of both legal thought and legal practice. It reflects my considered views about proportionality over the years, including the comparative study of the subject. It also reflects the experience of judging. For twenty-eight years I served as a Justice on Israel's Supreme Court – first as an Associate Justice, then as a Vice-President, and finally as the Supreme Court President. Even before fully understanding the concept of proportionality, I ruled in accordance with its precepts. However, in the last fourteen years of my judicial career, I wrote dozens of Supreme Court opinions explicitly applying the concept of proportionality, as did my colleagues on the bench. This book is based on this judicial experience.

Although my judicial experience is limited to Israel's legal system, this book is not so narrow. On the contrary, it attempts to provide a universal understanding of the concept of proportionality in constitutional democracies. It reflects the law of many legal systems where proportionality is frequently applied. I am hopeful that countries with constitutional rights will be able to make use of this book in understanding their own approach towards proportionality. The same should apply to other legal systems – such as those of the United Kingdom, New Zealand, and

---

[15] See below, at 72. [16] See below, at 458. [17] See below, at 166.
[18] See *S. v. Makwanyane*, 1995 (3) SA 391, § 156. On the "culture of justification," see below, at 458.

Victoria, Australia – where human rights are not on a constitutional level, but the courts are still authorized to determine whether their limitation is proportional. Although such a determination does not render the law unconstitutional, it fully applies the rules of proportionality as analyzed in these pages.[19]

The goal of this book is not to describe the legal reality surrounding proportionality in various countries' constitutional law. The intention is not to compare the use of proportionality in different legal systems. Rather, the goal of this book is to present an analytical model of the legal institution dubbed proportionality. The appeal to comparative law is meant to substantiate the model presented herein. It is meant to show that this is not only a theoretical model disconnected from reality. It aims to convince that this theoretical model is accepted in comparative law, which draws from it and influences its development.

Every study of proportionality must recognize Alexy's influence.[20] His contribution to the understanding of the rules of proportionality and their development is very significant. This is particularly the case in civil law legal systems; but now also true in common law systems thanks to the excellent translation by Professor Julian Rivers of Alexy's book which deals with, amongst other matters, proportionality,[21] as well as Rivers' comprehensive introduction to that book.[22] While Alexy's influence is clear on many of this book's pages, the opinion herein diverges from him on some of the key issues relating to proportionality. It is sufficient to

---

[19] See below, at 72. See also D. Jenkins, "Common Law Declarations of Unconstitutionality," 7 *Int'l J. Const. L.* 183 (2009).

[20] See R. Alexy, *A Theory of Constitutional Rights* (J. Rivers trans., Oxford University Press, 2002 [1986]); R. Alexy, "Individual Rights and Collective Goods," in C. Nino (eds.), *Rights* (New York University Press, 1989), 168; R. Alexy, "Jurgen Habermas's Theory of Legal Discourse," 17 *Cardozo L. Rev.* 1027 (1996); R. Alexy, "On the Structure of Legal Principles," 13(3) *Ratio Juris* 294 (2000); R. Alexy, "Constitutional Rights, Balancing, and Rationality," 16(2) *Ratio Juris* 131 (2003); R. Alexy, "On Balancing and Subsumption: A Structural Comparison," 16(4) *Ratio Juris* 433 (2003); R. Alexy, "Balancing, Constitutional Review, and Representation, 3 *Int'l J. Const. L.* 572 (2005); R. Alexy, "Thirteen Replies," in G. Pavlakos (ed.), *Law, Rights, and Discourse: The Legal Philosophy of Robert Alexy* (Portland, OR: Hart Publishing, 2007), 345; R. Alexy, "On Constitutional Rights to Protection," 3 *Legisprudence* 1 (2009). For studies reviewing Alexy's work, see A. J. Menendez and E. O. Eriksen (eds.), *Arguing Fundamental Rights* (2006); G. Pavlakos, (ed.), *Law, Rights, and Discourse: The Legal Philosophy of Robert Alexy* (2007).

[21] R. Alexy, *A Theory of Constitutional Rights* (J. Rivers trans., Oxford University Press, 2002 [1986]), 200.

[22] J. Rivers, "A Theory of Constitutional Rights and the British Constitution", in Robert Alexy (ed.), *A Theory of Constitutional Rights* (Oxford University Press, 2002 [1986]), xvii.

mention a number of these departures: First, Alexy is of the opinion that, when two constitutional rights shaped as principles are in conflict, or when a constitutional right is in conflict with the public interest, a special constitutional rule is formed that operates on the constitutional sphere and reduces the scope of the constitutional right.[23] In my opinion, such a rule operates only on the sub-constitutional level (statutory or common law), and does not affect the scope of the constitutional right itself. Second, the balancing rule, according to Alexy, compares the importance of the purpose that the limiting law seeks to obtain to the harm (light, moderate, or serious) inflicted upon the constitutional right. Although we agree that the first part of the balancing equation should include the importance of the proper purpose, this should be balanced against the importance of preventing the limitation of the constitutional right. To me, constitutional rights are not of equal importance. The importance of the right in tipping the scale is determined not solely on the extent of the constitutional right's limitation, but rather according to the importance of preventing the harm caused by the limitation. Third, according to Alexy's proportionality concept, the same rule applies in protecting constitutional rights as it does in the protection of public interest.[24] My approach draws a distinction between these two notions. Fourth, according to Alexy, the application of proportionality considerations is preconditioned upon the right being shaped as a constitutional *principle*.[25] This is not my approach. Thus, proportionality considerations may apply even where the right is shaped as a constitutional rule. The legal source from which proportionality derives is not related to the way the right is phrased (as a rule or principle), but rather to considerations of democracy and the rule of law affecting the text's legal interpretation.

With the "migration" or "transplantation" of proportionality in constitutional law from its birthplace in Germany to many of the world's legal systems, the legal literature on the subject abounds. Many important books and essays are dedicated to it.[26] This raises the obvious question – is

---

[23] See below, at 38.   [24] See below, at 364.   [25] See below, at 286.

[26] See A. de Mestral, S. Birks, M. Both *et al.* (eds.), *The Limitation of Human Rights in Comparative Constitutional Law* (Montreal: Les Editions Yvon Blais, 1986); X. Philippe, *Le Contrôle de Proportionnalité dans les Jurisprudences Constitutionnelle et Administrative Francaises* (Economica-Presses Universitaires d'Aix-Marseilles, 1990); N. Emiliou, *The Principle of Proportionality in European Law: A Comparative Study* (London: Kluwer Law International, 1998); Evelyn Ellis (ed.), *The Principle of Proportionality in the Laws of Europe* (1999); D. M. Beatty, *The Ultimate Rule of Law* (Oxford University Press, 2004); G. Van der Schyff, *Limitation of Rights: A Study of the European Convention and the South African Bill of Rights* (Nijmegen, The Netherlands: Wolf Legal Publishers, 2005);

there a need for another book on proportionality? How is this book any different from the many that have preceded it? The answer is that this book is unique in the following four characteristics: First, it does not follow the pattern of analyzing proportionality in one legal system and then comparing it to another; rather, it creates a comprehensive analytical framework of the concept of constitutional proportionality, and it does so against a comparative background. Thus, the book contains a discussion of proportionality in constitutional law in general, while providing several examples from different legal systems in each sub-topic discussed.

Second, a fundamental part of the book's approach is the perception that the most central component of the proportionality analysis is proportionality *stricto sensu* or balancing.[27] This is the component that draws most of the criticism on the concept as a whole. The book attempts to respond to this criticism, while redesigning the balancing tests. For that reason, it places – on both sides of the scale – the term social importance.[28] This term focuses on the marginal social importance of achieving the law's proper purpose on the one hand, and the marginal social importance in preventing the harm to the right itself on the other. In addition, in discussing the limitations on rights, the book distinguishes between more and less important rights; as aforementioned not all rights were created equal. It is against this background that the suggestion is made to redefine the rules of balancing by adding – in between the basic balancing rule and ad hoc balancing – a principled balancing rule.

Third, this book emphasizes the methodological aspect of proportionality. To that end, it highlights the distinction between the first stage of the analysis, where the scope of the constitutional right is determined, and the second stage, where the justifications to limit the right are considered. It also notes the distinction between the constitutional nature of the right and the sub-constitutional nature of the limitation of that right. It develops an approach to special instances whereby two constitutional rights conflict. That approach is based on the notion that such a conflict

---

W. Sadurski, *Rights before Courts: A Study of Constitutional Courts in Postcommunist States of Central and Eastern Europe* (Dordrecht: Springer, 2005); C. B. Pulido, *El Principio de Proporcionalidad y los Derechos Fundamentales* (Madrid: Centro de Estudios Políticos y Constitucionales, 2007); E. T. Sullivan and R. S. Frase, *Proportionality Principles in American Law: Controlling Excessive Government Actions* (Oxford University Press, 2008);. H. Keller and A. Stone-Sweet (eds.), *A Europe of Rights: The Impact of the ECHR on National Legal Systems* (2008); G. Webber, *The Negotiable Constitution: On the Limitation of Rights* (Cambridge University Press, 2009).
[27] See below, at 340.   [28] See below, at 349.

will usually affect only the statutory or common law level; it will not, however, affect the scope of the conflicting constitutional rights. The book also draws a distinction between balancing as one of the components of proportionality (which is relevant to the examination of the constitutionality of laws which limit a constitutional right), and interpretative balancing (which is relevant for the examination of the interpretation of a law whose purpose includes conflicting principles).[29] It emphasizes the role of the public interest and the protection of the constitutional right in the framework of the balancing component and rejects the view that it can determine the scope of the constitutional rights. It distinguishes between a limitation of a constitutional right by statute and the common law.

Finally, the book examines several alternatives to proportionality, and analyzes the pros and cons of each.[30] According to the book's approach, proportionality suffers from many shortcomings; still, none of the alternatives is better – or even as good as – proportionality itself. Having said that, there are elements of proportionality that should be refined and improved. The book examines and develops some key ideas to do so. Should these improvements be implemented, they would not affect the uniqueness of the concept. However, they may bring the concept of proportionality closer to the approach practiced in the United States.

Any review of the proportionality of a law which limits a constitutional right is based on a three-stage inquiry. In the first stage, one should examine the scope of the protected right. This stage deals with the boundaries of the constitutional right. In the second stage, the question is whether there is a justification to limit the right – i.e., whether the constitutional right's limitation is proportional. It examines the extent of the rights protection. This examination deals with the application of the four components of proportionality. The third stage – which does not deal directly with proportionality – occupies itself with the remedy, should the court decide that one of the components failed. It thus deals with the consequences of the unconstitutionality of a disproportional limitation on a constitutional right. This book is mostly occupied with the second stage (the proportionality of a limiting law). It does not examine the third stage (remedy). It does review the central tenets of the first stage (the right's scope), which are conditions for the application of the rules of proportionality. Accordingly, the book proceeds as follows:

The first part of the book reviews the scope of the constitutional rights (the first stage). The first chapter deals with the basic distinction in modern

---

[29] See below, at 72.   [30] See below, at 493.

constitutional theory between the scope of the constitutional right[31] and the justification for its limitation.[32] From this basic distinction, the notions of "relative rights" and "absolute rights" may also be drawn. The chapter analyzes these notions and emphasizes that most constitutional rights are relative – rather than absolute – in nature. That relativity entails that limitations may exist on their legal realization. The chapter analyzes the characteristics of these limitations and concludes with the examination of the question of whether a relative constitutional right is a *prima facie* right or a definite right. The second chapter reviews the parameters for determining the scope of the constitutional right. These parameters are interpretive in nature.[33] The chapter briefly discusses constitutional purposive interpretation, while emphasizing both the importance of the constitutional text (either explicit or implicit) and the constitutional purpose. The discussion stresses the importance of a comprehensive comparative perspective to these questions. The approach here is that a constitutional right should be examined through a "wide lens," and that its scope should not be restricted due to considerations of either public interest or the constitutional rights of others. Both the public interest and the constitutional rights of others should be considered, but only in the next stage of the inquiry – that considering justifications for possible limitations on the right itself. The third chapter examines situations where one constitutional right conflicts with another. According to this approach, the solution to such a conflict is not on the constitutional level (the rights' scope is not affected by the conflict); rather, the solution is in the subconstitutional realm (that is, the constitutionality of the law limiting one constitutional right in order to protect the other may be affected).[34] The fourth chapter examines the conditions to determine that a law (statutory or common law) has in fact limited a constitutional right. Here, I review the distinction between limitations placed on a constitutional right and the amendment of a constitutional right.[35] The book's first part ends with the fifth chapter, which analyzes the principle of legality according to which a limitation on a constitutional right must be carried out by a law whose authority can be traced back to the constitution itself (the "authority chain"). The chapter then reviews the special issues which arise out of a common law limitation upon a constitutional right.[36]

The second part of the book examines more closely the nature, role, function, and origins of proportionality. The sixth chapter defines

---

[31] See below, at 19.   [32] See below, at 20.   [33] See below, at 45.
[34] See below, at 87.   [35] See below, at 99.   [36] See below, at 118.

proportionality and reviews several methods for the limitation of constitutional rights.[37] It examines situations where the constitution is silent
about such limitations and where it explicitly acknowledges that rights can
be limited by a law – but without saying anything else about the nature of
such a law or the conditions it should meet. The conclusion is that in both
situations such a law must be proportional. The chapter emphasizes the
close connection between the constitutional right and its limitations. It
highlights the importance of proportionality as the proper rule for evaluating both the justification for limitations on a constitutional right and
the protection of constitutional rights. The chapter ends with an analysis
of the "override" clause, which appears in several constitutional texts, and
its relationship with proportionality. The seventh chapter reviews the historical origins of proportionality.[38] It follows the concept's migration (or
transplantation) – from its beginnings in Germany to Continental Europe
and then on to the rest of the world. The eighth chapter examines the
legal sources of proportionality[39] and specifically reviews four of them,
namely: democracy, the rule of law, the shaping of a constitutional right
as a principle, and constitutional interpretation. After analyzing each of
these sources, my conclusion is that each may independently suffice to
provide legitimacy to the concept of proportionality – but none is able to
provide actual content to proportionality itself.

The third part is the book's main part: It examines each of the components of proportionality. The ninth chapter examines the "proper purpose" component.[40] It examines its nature, legal sources, and content.
The chapter differentiates between a purpose relating to the protection
of the constitutional rights of others and one relating to the protection
of the public interest, such as the continued existence of the state and its
existence as a democracy, national security interests, public order, justice, tolerance, sensitivity to the feelings of others, and the promotion of
objective constitutional values that reflect the subjective constitutional
rights. The chapter then examines the degree of urgency regarding proper
purposes and the ways to prove such in court. The tenth chapter examines
the "rational connection" component.[41] The chapter concludes with an
assessment of the importance of this component. The eleventh chapter
examines the "necessity" component. Here, the book reviews the nature
of this requirement, its elements and importance.[42] A considerable part of
the discussion is dedicated to the question of "overbreadth" coverage and

---

[37] See below, at 133.   [38] See below, at 175.   [39] See below, at 211.
[40] See below, at 245.   [41] See below, at 303.   [42] See below, at 317.

to situations where it is impossible to achieve the proper purpose without the use of overly broad means. The twelfth chapter examines the "proportionality *stricto sensu*" component.[43] This is the central component of proportionality. The book reviews the content of this component and the fact that it is based on balancing. Most of the chapter is dedicated to the nature of that balancing. It stresses that the required balance is between the marginal social importance of the benefit in fulfilling the law's proper purpose, and the marginal social importance in preventing the harm to the constitutional right. This therefore concerns the relative notion of social importance found on each side of the scale. In this regard, the book emphasizes the marginal nature of the examination of the competing social priorities. The question, therefore, is not, for example, how to compare the importance of national security to the importance of the sanctity of life; rather, what is the social importance in the marginal contribution to national security (as a result of such law) as compared with the social importance of the marginal harm caused to the constitutional right to life because of it. In considering the marginal social importance of fulfilling the proper purpose, one has to consider how urgent it is to obtain such a goal, as well as the probability of obtaining such a goal by other means. In determining the marginal social importance in preventing harm to the constitutional right one must consider the nature of the right, its place in the rights hierarchy, the degree of the intended limitation, and the probability of the occurrence of such a limitation. In that respect, the book suggests that not all rights are created equal in importance. Accordingly, it devised – based on Alexy – the following basic balancing rule: The more important it is to prevent marginal harm on the constitutional right, and the higher the probability such harm will occur, then the marginal benefit to the public interest (or to the protection of other persons' rights) required to justify such limits should be more socially important, more urgent, and more probable. Based on this basic rule of balancing, one can carry out *ad hoc* balancing in concrete cases, according to their specific facts. This chapter concludes with a review of the case of the "balanced scales." This occurs whenever both sides of the balance are of equal marginal social importance. In these cases, the social value in preventing harm to the constitutional right should prevail. The thirteenth chapter is dedicated to the examination of the relationship between proportionality and reasonableness.[44] At the outset it is noted that much of the examination depends on how one defines reasonableness. To the extent

---

[43] See below, at 340.   [44] See below, at 371.

that reasonableness is defined in terms of balancing between competing values, there is little distinction between reasonableness and proportionality. Chapter fourteen examines the role of the legislator, as well as that of the judge, regarding proportionality.[45] It is emphasized that every branch of government should respect the rules of proportionality. Each branch has its own role to fill, and its own discretion to exercise, within the rules of proportionality. Thus, for example, the constitutional role of the judiciary is to ensure that other branches of government abide by the applicable rules of proportionality. The constitutional roles of the legislator are many, and include a preliminary discretion whether to legislate at all; discretion as to the purposes it wishes to promote through that legislation, and discretion relating to the means that are required to obtain such purposes. Importantly, all these discretionary acts should abide by the rules of proportionality. To the extent that the legislator operates within the proportional realm of discretion – as long as it operates within the "proportionality zone" – there is no place for the judiciary to replace legislative discretion by judicial discretion. This result does not mean that the judiciary defers to the legislator; rather, it means that the judiciary recognizes the constitutionality of the legislator's actions while operating within its discretional boundaries. The chapter expands on this point, while examining the notion of deference. The chapter concludes with an assessment of the "margin of appreciation." The relevance of this term should be reduced and should only be used by international tribunals. It should play no role in national courts. Chapter fifteen is dedicated to positive rights and legislative omissions. It examines the role of proportionality when a positive constitutional right (like the duty to protect human dignity) is affected by legislative omission.[46] The chapter begins with an analysis of the notion of a "positive right," its origins, nature, and likely consequences. With this in mind, it examines the application of the rules of proportionality when a positive right is affected by an omission of the legislator. The conclusion is that there is nothing unique about the notion of a positive constitutional right in relation to a proportionality analysis. Thus, the application of proportionality to a legislative omission is identical to its application to a legislative action in the case of a negative constitutional right (like the duty not to affect human dignity). The sixteenth and last chapter of the third part is dedicated to the issue of the burden of proof.[47] The burden of proof (which includes both the burden of persuasion and the evidentiary burden) lies with the party arguing that

---

[45] See below, at 379.   [46] See below, at 429.   [47] See below, at 435.

a limitation has been placed on the constitutional right in the first stage of the constitutional examination ("Is there a limitation upon a constitutional right?"). In the second stage of the constitutional examination ("Is the limitation proportional?"), the burden lies with the party arguing that there is a justification for the limitation, i.e., that such a limitation is proportional. The uniqueness of the judicial process in public law is considered, as are the implications of such uniqueness on issues regarding the burden of proof.

The fourth part is dedicated to the assessment of the concept of proportionality. The seventeenth chapter examines the various arguments supporting proportionality.[48] It focuses on a number of principal arguments emphasizing the need for justification, structured discretion and its transparency, as well as the assistance proportionality provides in creating dialogue between the legislator and the judge. The chapter examines the connection between proportionality and constitutional rights theories. The argument developed is that proportionality, as an analytical structure, fits in well with most of the modern approaches to constitutional rights. The chapter concludes with an examination of the connection between proportionality, democracy, and judicial review of legislation. It is stressed that the concept of proportionality offers an important justification for judicial review in that it enforces constitutional legitimacy by opening the courts' doors for argument of good reasons which justify the limitation of rights. It also contributes to judicial objectivity.

The eighteenth chapter examines the main arguments against the use of proportionality (primarily, balancing) and their possible answers.[49] It examines the critique on proportionality from the standpoints of incommensurability and the lack of rationality ("internal" critiques). It is argued that the premise of both concepts is wrong, since the common ground for the balancing test is well founded and well recognized – the marginal social importance of the benefit in fulfilling the proper purpose as compared with the marginal social importance in preventing the harm to the constitutional right. In particular, the notion that proportionality's balancing act is "irrational" because it contains several elements of discretion is rejected. Alongside the "internal" critique, the "external" ones are considered. The arguments – that proportionality (mainly the balancing) provides the judge with too wide a discretion, that it does not grant sufficient protection to constitutional rights, and that it lacks legitimacy – are addressed and countered.

---

[48] See below, at 457.   [49] See below, at 481.

The nineteenth chapter considers proportionality's alternatives.[50] These alternatives include considering the rights as absolute while their scope is determined by the legislator;[51] an absolute protection of all rights within the constitutional core;[52] and the dualistic model.[53] Most of the chapter is dedicated to the assessment of the classification of constitutional rights practiced in the United States.[54] Thus, the American approach is analyzed and compared to the concept of proportionality. Most of the comparison focuses on the "strict scrutiny" review as exercised by the United States Supreme Court, and the conclusion that arises is that this is a difficult comparison due to the ambiguity in the strict scrutiny examination. This ambiguity exists mainly in relation to overinclusiveness coverage, particularly in situations where it is impossible to narrowly tailor the means by which the legislator can achieve the governmental interest. In that respect, an offer is made to reexamine the *Korematsu* case,[55] assuming that there exists an evidentiary basis regarding the claim that a large percentage (e.g., 10 percent or more) of American citizens of Japanese descent actually assisted the Japanese enemy in times of war. If, under these assumptions, it would be held – under the "strict scrutiny" test – that the law in question is constitutional, then it is clear that the concept of proportionality is more protective of human rights than the American doctrine, as it would still require the judges to examine the law through the eyes of the fourth component – proportionality *stricto sensu* – and to conduct the balancing accordingly. The result of this examination may be that the limitation of constitutional rights is not properly balanced and thus unconstitutional. Conversely, if, under these assumptions, it would be held – through the "strict scrutiny" test – that the law in question is unconstitutional, then it is clear that the concept of proportionality is less protective of constitutional rights, as it would perhaps still find the law to be constitutional under the balancing component. At the end of this chapter, a reexamination of the arguments against proportionality are carried out and the question to what extent – if any – they apply to the American categorization is asked. Despite all this, the conclusion is that, in the face of the many criticisms of proportionality – some of them justified – a better alternative has not been found yet.

---

[50] See below, at 493.   [51] See below, at 493.   [52] See below, at 496.
[53] See below, at 499.   [54] See below, at 502.
[55] *Korematsu* v. *United States*, 323 US 214 (1944).

The twentieth and last chapter in this part proposes several ideas for the future development of the concept of proportionality.[56] In relation to the "proper purpose" component, the need to provide limiting criteria for such a purpose is noted, as the German approach, which is satisfied by the fact that such a purpose is not contrary to the constitution itself, is insufficient. The suggestion to distinguish regarding the proper purpose, between those rights that rank higher in importance, and other rights, is made. When dealing with these more important rights – just like with the "strict scrutiny" test in the United States – the proper purpose required should be pressing or compelling. When dealing with the rest of the rights, it is sufficient for the social purpose to be designated as important. Furthermore, when examining such proper purposes I suggest the development of new rules to distinguish between cases in which the proper purpose is to protect another right and those where the proper purpose relates to the protection of the public interest. Concerning the "rational connection" component, it is suggested that the current probability test be adjusted in such a fashion that if the law in question limits a high-ranked constitutional right then the probability required to fulfill this purpose should be "substantial" (and not be satisfied with non-negligible probability). For all other rights, the probability required should be reasonable.

Most of the other suggestions are intended for proportionality *stricto sensu*.[57] It is proposed to recognize an intermediate level of balancing between the basic rule of balancing and specific (*ad hoc*) cases of balancing. This intermediate level is based upon principled balancing formulas. It stems from the basic rule, but also studies several typical cases, and then incorporates the data into several formulas of constitutional limitations (in a level of abstraction that is lower than the basic balancing, but higher than that of the concrete one). Such a level of abstraction will properly express the principle considerations that lie at the heart of both the right itself and the justification for its limitation. Accordingly, for example, in the conflict between the right to political free speech, on the one hand, and the protection of the public from the possible damage of "fighting words" or inciting speech, on the other, it may be determined that it would be possible to limit the right of free speech if, and only if, the purpose of protecting the public from the effect of such speech is pressing or compelling in order to prevent an imminent and severe harm to the public order. This principled balance approach is analyzed and compared

---

[56] See below, at 528. [57] See below, at 542.

to its American counterpart, while reviewing both the similarities and differences between the two.

I am neither a philosopher nor a political scientist. Rather, I am a judge and scholar of constitutional law. This book is not about the philosophy of law or of political theory. It is rather an analytical essay in constitutional law that deals with the doctrine of justifying the limitation of constitutional rights and its limits. It is meant to be read by legal scholars, judges, and practitioners interested in those issues. The aim is that the comparative study included in these pages enrich the reader and bring them closer to the methodology of proportionality and the justifiable limitations on constitutional rights.

I am grateful to the Interdisciplinary Center Herzliya, the Yale University Law School and the Faculty of Law at the University of Toronto, who opened their doors to me and provided me with the research environment which enabled the writing of this book. I would like to thank Rivka Weill, Barak Medina, Yigal Marzel, Suzie Navot, Gideon Sapir, and Amnon Reichman, who read through different parts of the Hebrew handwritten manuscript and provided me with helpful remarks. A special thanks to Doron Kalir who worked day and night in translating the Hebrew version of the book into English. I am grateful to Leehee Goldenberg for her work on the English version. A special thanks to Mattias Kumm who provided important remarks on the English version. A special thanks to my research assistants, Eran Davidi, Matan Guttman, Moran Glickstein, Lior Hadas, and Ori Kivity, who helped me in gathering the material and in using it, and to Esther Tammuz who co-ordinated the editing efforts. And as always I thank Elika without whom none of my ideas would see the light of day.

PART I

Constitutional rights: scope and limitations

1

Constitutional rights: scope and the extent of their protection

A. The nature of the distinction

1. Scope and protection

The modern theory of constitutional rights was formed after the Second World War.[1] It draws a fundamental distinction between the scope of the constitutional right,[2] and the extent of its protection.[3] The scope of the constitutional right marks the right's boundaries and defines its content; the extent of its protection prescribes the legal limitations on the exercise of the right within its scope. It defines the justifications for the right's limitation by a sub-constitutional law – e.g., statute or common law.[4] Following this distinction, the modern theory of constitutional rights is said to be based on a two-stage analysis.[5] In the first stage, the constitutional right's

---

[1] See L. Weinrib, "The Postwar Paradigm and American Exceptionalism," in S. Choudhry (ed.), *The Migration of Constitutional Ideas* (Cambridge University Press, 2006), 84.

[2] See G. Van der Schyff, *Limitation of Rights: A Study of the European Convention and the South African Bill of Rights* (Nijmegen, The Netherlands: Wolf Legal Publishers, 2005), 11; M. Cohen-Eliya and I. Porat, "American Balancing and German Proportionality: The Historical Origins," 8(2) *Int'l J. Const. L.* 263 (2010). For a critique of this approach, see G. C. N. Webber, *The Negotiable Constitutions: On the Limitation of Rights* (Cambridge University Press, 2009). For my criticism of Webber, see below, at 494.

[3] German methodology uses the expression "*Tatbestand*" or "*Schutzbereich*": see R. Alexy, *A Theory of Constitutional Rights* (Julian Rivers trans., Oxford University Press, 2002 [1986]), 196. For criticism of this distinction, see B. W. Miller, "Justification and Rights Limitations," in G. Huscroft (ed.), *Expounding the Constitution: Essays in Constitutional Theory* (Cambridge University Press, 2008), 93.

[4] For convenience in this text, I will primarily discuss statutory limitations. The analysis, however, should equally apply to other types of limitation, such as common law or regulations. As to the role of the common law in rights limitation, see below, at 118.

[5] See G. Van der Schyff, above note 2, at 11. See also S. Woolman and H. Botha, "Limitations," in S. Woolman, M. Bishop, and J. Brickhill (eds.), *Constitutional Law of South Africa*, 2nd edn. (Cape Town: Juta Law Publishers, looseleaf, 2002–), 3; P. W. Hogg, *Constitutional Law of Canada*, 5th edn., vol. II (Toronto: Thomson Carswell, 2007), 112. For a critique of this approach, see Webber, above note 2; Miller, above note 3. The third stage deals with

scope is determined,[6] and the area it covers is defined. Both the right's "positive" scope (i.e., what should be done to protect the right) and its "negative" scope (i.e., what should be done not to affect it) are determined.[7] The right's "core" is defined, as well as its "penumbra."[8] The right's content is prescribed. Finally, the right's boundaries – what separates it from other constitutional rights – are drawn. The second stage examines whether constitutional justifications exist to limit the realization of the right by a sub-constitutional law (e.g., by statute or common law). Specifically, this stage examines whether the legal system provides the constitutional right with full-scope protection or a more limited one. This stage examines the extent to which the right may be realized – either to its full extent or with limitations – at the sub-constitutional level. In this manner, the current theory of constitutional rights distinguishes between the boundaries of the constitutional right ("scope") and the limitations imposed upon its realization by law ("protection"). The right's boundaries determine its position in the universe of constitutional rights. They draw the entire spectrum of "the constitutional field"[9] and the "contours" of the constitutional right or its *Normbereich*. They define the human behavior covered by the right.[10] The limitations imposed upon a right assume it exists within defined boundaries. These limitations operate under the constitutional authorization to limit the realization of the constitutional right by a sub-constitutional law. The constitutional authorization of those limitations is often found in special constitutional provisions dubbed "limitation clauses."[11] At the heart of these limitation clauses lies the principle of proportionality.[12] Modern theory therefore distinguishes between the

---

remedies for the violation of constitutional rights. This stage is beyond the scope of this book.

[6] For a discussion of "scope-affecting considerations," see F. Schauer, *Playing by the Rules: A Philosophical Examination of Rule-Based Decision-Making in Law and in Life* (Oxford University Press, 1991), 89; A. S. Butler, "Limiting Rights," 33 *Victoria U. Wellington L. Rev.* 113, 117 (2002).

[7] On the distinction between the negative rights and the positive rights, see below, at 422.

[8] As used here, the distinction between the right's core and its penumbra is relevant only to the notion of "proportionality in its narrow sense" (balancing) (see below, at 362). It is not relevant to the notion of the right's scope overall; indeed, the right's penumbra is also a part of its scope.

[9] HCJ 10203/03 *The National Assembly Ltd.* v. *Attorney General* (unreported decision of August 20, 2008), para. 6 (Procaccia, J.).

[10] See K. Hesse, *Grundzüge, des Verfassungsrechts der Bundesrepublik Deutschland* (Heidelberg: C. F. Müller Verlag, 1999), § 310.

[11] For different types of "limitation clauses," see below at 141.

[12] See below, at 161.

constitutional right *per se* and its proportional limitations by a sub-constitutional law; between the constitutional right's clauses and constitutional limitation clauses (the latter allowing a sub-constitutional law to limit the realization of a constitutional right). This distinction is at the heart of the two-stage analysis, which consists of the determination of the right's scope, and the determination of the right's limitations. Therefore, the distinction is also known as the two-stage theory.

2.   *The distinction in practice: the scope of freedom of expression and its protection*

The distinction between the scope of the constitutional right and the extent of its implementation is clearly demonstrated by Article 10(1) of the European Convention for the Protection of Human Rights and Fundamental Freedoms.[13] The article reads:

> Everyone has the right to freedom of expression. This right shall include freedom to hold opinions and to receive and impart information and ideas without interference by public authority and regardless of frontiers. This article shall not prevent States from requiring the licensing of broadcasting, television or cinema enterprises.

Article 10(1) determines the scope of the right to freedom of expression. According to its interpretation, its scope is extremely broad, covering all forms of expression (such as books, paintings, and movies) and all forms of the expression's content (including racist hate speech, libel, or obscenity).[14] However, despite the right's broad scope, the convention contains a clause which allows for the limitation of the exercise of this freedom. Article 10(2) of the Convention, which is a special limitation clause, defines the circumstances under which it is justifiable to limit the right to freedom of expression:

> The exercise of these freedoms, since it carries with it duties and responsibilities, may be subject to such formalities, conditions, restrictions or penalties as are prescribed by law and are necessary in a democratic society, in the interests of national security, territorial integrity or public safety, for the prevention of disorder or crime, for the protection of health or morals, for the protection of the reputation or rights of others,

---

[13] Convention for the Protection of Human Rights and Fundamental Freedoms, November 4, 1950, 213 *UNTS* 222.

[14] See R. C. A. White and C. Ovey, *Jacobs, White and Ovey: The European Convention on Human Rights*, 5th edn. (Oxford University Press, 2010), 426.

for preventing the disclosure of information received in confidence, or for
maintaining the authority and impartiality of the judiciary.

Thus, according to the article, limitations may be imposed upon the exercise of the right to freedom of expression by a law in order to protect a person's reputation, to prevent an individual or group from hate speech, or to
restrict pornographic expression.[15] These limitations must be "necessary
in a democratic society," or, in other words, they must be proportional.[16]

B.   The centrality of the distinction

The modern distinction between the scope of a constitutional right and
the extent of its protection at the sub-constitutional level is of major
importance for several reasons.[17] First, it emphasizes the considerable
weight granted by the legal system to the individual's right and the need
to respect it. It demonstrates the need for a justification each time a limitation is imposed upon that right through statute or common law.[18] The
burden of proof of such a justification falls on the state.[19] Second, the distinction highlights the difference between the constitutional level, where
rights are determined and their scope is prescribed, and the sub-constitutional level, where the extent of the right's realization (application) is
determined and its limitations prescribed. Such a dichotomy between
the constituent body (which determines the constitutional nature of the
right, as well as the mechanism for amending its scope), and the legislative body (which determines the means for realizing these constitutional
rights) is of cardinal importance. In a constitutional democracy, this
dichotomy provides the individual or the minority with the shield to be
used against a possible tyranny of rights by the majority.[20] This dichotomy
may also assist in properly shaping the public discourse about constitutional rights and sets up boundaries regarding the areas wherein society's
daily politics can intervene. Third, the distinction between the scope of
the constitutional right and the extent of its protection properly exemplifies the twofold role of the modern constitutional judge – as an interpreter
of the constitutional rights and as an adherent of the constitutional rule

[15] *Ibid.*, at 429, 444.
[16] See Van der Schyff, above note 2, at 197.
[17] For criticism of this distinction, see Miller, above note 3; Webber, above note 2. For
criticism of Webber, see below, at 494.
[18] See below, at 458.   [19] See below, at 439.
[20] See R. Den Otter, *Judicial Review in an Age of Moral Pluralism* (Cambridge University
Press, 2009).

where limitations of such rights may not exceed those prescribed by the limitation clause (itself a part of the constitution). Fourth, the distinction correctly sets the parameters for the dialogue between the legislative and judicial branches.[21] Finally, the distinction sets forth an analytical framework to describe the scope of constitutional rights, and provides a structured and transparent way of thinking regarding the justification in limiting the realization of those constitutional rights through sub-constitutional law.[22]

One may question the legitimacy of including in the right's scope portions whose realization or protection cannot be justified. The response to this is that the extent of the right's realization or protection changes from time to time and from one issue to another, reflecting the needs of the time and place. Indeed, the extent of the right's protection only reflects the views of a given legal community at a given point in time. The scope of the right itself, on the other hand, reflects the fundamental principles upon which the community is built, as interpreted according to the rules of constitutional interpretation.[23] A change in the right's scope comes only via constitutional amendment or a change in the court's interpretation of the constitutional text. Contrary to a change in the right's scope – which must be reflected at the constitutional level – a change of the extent of the right's protection occurs at the sub-constitutional level. As such, social

---

[21] On the dialog between the two branches, see A. Barak, *The Judge in a Democracy* (Princeton University Press, 2006), 236–240. See below, at 465.

[22] See HCJ 6427/02 *The Movement for Quality Government in Israel* v. *The Knesset* [2006] IsrSC 61(1) 619, available in Hebrew at http://elyon1.court.gov.il/files/02/270/064/a22/02064270.a22.HTM, on the advantages provided by the distinction between the scope of the constitutional right and the extent of its protection: "The distinction [between the scope of the right] provides proper tools for legal analysis; it serves to clarify the analysis and refine the thought-process ... Here it sheds light on the fundamental division in human rights discourse between the scope of the protected right and the extent of its protection, or legal realization ... It is used as an analytical basis for the distinction between horizontal balancing (in the first stage of the constitutional analysis) and vertical balancing (in the second stage), between several intersecting human rights, and the balancing between those rights and other social values and interests ... It also assists drawing the line between the role of the court as interpreter of the right as it appears in the fundamental text (constitution, basic law, convention), and the court's role in reviewing the constitutionality of its infringement by a lower legal norm. Further, the distinction helps to examine legal doctrines, such as affirmative action, in that it examines whether they are properly examined within the scope of the constitutional right to equality, or whether they should be examined as a part the extent of its protection as proportionally prescribed by the limitation clause. Finally, it helps resolve controversies over the burden of persuasion." See below, at 460.

[23] On constitutional interpretation, see below, at 45.

change may lead to new laws, which protects the constitutional right according to society's current social understanding. Such change – as understood by the constitutional democracy approach – can only be carried out in accordance with the requirements prescribed by the limitation clause. In other words, they must be proportional. Such proportionality is achieved only if these changes are viewed on the one hand as limiting the right, but adhering to the justification required by the limitation clause on the other.

Therefore, the distinction between the scope of the constitutional right and the extent of its realization or protection is a distinction between the constitutional and sub-constitutional levels.[24] It is central to the understanding of all modern constitutional rights law. The distinction, however, does not constitute an analytical necessity. Even without it a full-scale framework of constitutional rights may exist. Think of a system breaking the two analytical stages down into one, creating, in essence, a single constitutional provision concurrently determining both the right's scope and the extent of its protection. Most legal systems today do not combine these two stages. They use the two-stage distinction between a constitutional right and its proportional limitation; between the question of the scope of the right and the question of its proper realization.[25] Some systems – the United Kingdom, New Zealand and Victoria (Australia) – distinguish between these two stages, although they are both at the sub-constitutional level. In addition, in these cases, the distinction between scope and protection may be relevant, as will be discussed in Chapter 6.[26]

C.   The distinction in comparative law

An early manifestation of the modern distinction between the right's scope and the extent of its protection can be found in the 1948 United Nations Universal Declaration of Human Rights.[27] The Declaration contains a list of human rights that seem, at first glance, absolute. But a

---

[24] Regarding the distinction between the scope of the constitutional right and its degree of protection, see R. Dworkin, *Taking Rights Seriously* (Cambridge, MA: Harvard University Press, 1977), 260; F. Schauer, "Categories and the First Amendment: A Play in Three Acts," 34 *Vand. L. Rev.* 265, 270 (1981); F. Schauer, *Free Speech: A Philosophical Enquiry* (Cambridge University Press, 1982), 89; F. Schauer, "The Boundaries of the First Amendment: A Preliminary Exploration of Constitutional Salience," 117 *Harv. L. Rev.* (2004); for a critique of the distinction, see Webber, above note 2.
[25] See S. Gardbaum, "Limiting Constitutional Rights," 54 *UCLA L. Rev.* 789 (2007).
[26] See below, at 131.
[27] Universal Declaration of Human Rights (1948).

general limitation clause relating to those rights appears at the end of the Declaration. Article 29(2) of the Declaration reads:

> In the exercise of his rights and freedoms, everyone shall be subject only to such limitations as are determined by law solely for the purpose of securing due recognition and respect for the rights and freedoms of others and of meeting the just requirements of morality, public order and the general welfare in a democratic society.

Therefore, a unique feature of the Declaration is the general scope of its limitation clause. The clause applies to each and every right mentioned therein. It provides a general meaning, regarding all constitutional rights, to the principle of proportionality.[28] A different approach is taken by the European Convention for the Protection of Human Rights and Fundamental Freedoms.[29] The Convention does not contain a general limitation clause, but rather several specific clauses, each of which applies to a different right. One of these clauses, specifically related to the right of freedom of expression, was discussed earlier.[30] This, and the other specific limitation clauses included in the Convention are based upon the principle of proportionality.[31]

Several conventions on rights have been signed since the 1950s.[32] An impressive number of constitutions were written by post-Second World War democracies, which include chapters on rights.[33] Each of these

---

[28] See below, at 142.

[29] The Convention for the Protection of Human Rights and Fundamental Freedoms, above note 13.

[30] See above, at 21.   [31] See below, at 141.

[32] Some of the key conventions include the Convention for the Protection of Human Rights and Fundamental Freedoms, above note 13; International Covenant on Civil and Political Rights (1966); International Covenant on Economic, Social and Cultural Rights, opened for signature December 19, 1966, 993 *UNTS* 3 (entered into force March 23, 1976).

[33] The new European national constitutions – post-Second World War and post-communist Europe – were considerably affected by the European Convention for the Protection of Human Rights and Fundamental Freedoms. See V. Ferreres Comella, *Constitutional Courts and Democratic Values: A European Perspective* (New Haven, CT: Yale University Press, 2009); Helen Keller and Alec Stone-Sweet (eds.), *A Europe of Rights: The Impact of the ECHR on National Legal Systems* (2008); R. Teitel, *Transitional Justice* (Oxford University Press, 2000); H. Schwartz, *The Struggle for Constitutional Justice in Post-Communist Europe* (University of Chicago Press, 2000); R. Prochazka, *Mission Accomplished: On Founding Constitutional Adjudication in Central Europe* (Budapest: Central European University Press, 2002); N. Singer and J. Singer (eds.), *Sutherland Statutes and Statutory Construction* (2007); W. Sadurski, *Rights Before Courts: A Study of Constitutional Courts in Postcommunist States of Central and Eastern Europe* (Dordrecht: Springer, 2008).

documents differentiates between the scope of the right and the extent of its realization.[34] Some of the documents contain general limitation clauses, while others contain specific ones; still others contain a combination of both. Noted examples of general limitation clauses include the Canadian Charter of Rights and Freedoms of 1982 (Article 1), the 1996 Constitution of the Republic of South Africa (Article 36) and the Israeli Basic Law: Human Dignity and Liberty (Article 8).[35] All the limitation clauses – whether general or specific – are manifestations of the notion of proportionality.

D.   Three stages of constitutional judicial review

The theoretical distinction between the scope of the constitutional right and the extent of its realization, or protection, leads to the conclusion that the judicial review of a statute's constitutionality should be conducted in three stages. The first stage examines whether the statute limits a constitutional right. To do so, the court must interpret the relevant article of the constitutional text as well as that of the statute allegedly limiting that right. The constitutional provision is interpreted according to rules of constitutional interpretation.[36] The statute is interpreted according to rules of statutory interpretation.[37] At the end of the first stage, the judge must determine whether the statute limits a constitutional right. If the answer is "no," the constitutional examination ends there and there is no need to proceed to the next stage. However, should the judge determine that the statute limits a constitutional right, the examination should continue on to the next stage.

The second stage of judicial review examines whether the limitation of the constitutional right is constitutional. Here, the judge examines whether

---

[34] See Gardbaum, above note 25.

[35] See the Canadian Charter of Rights and Freedoms, Part I of the Constitution Act 1982; Constitution of the Republic of South Africa No. 108 of 1996, Part 36; Israeli Basic Law: Human Dignity and Liberty, available at: www.knesset.gov.il/laws/special/eng/basic3_eng.htm.

[36] On constitutional interpretation, see below, at 45.

[37] On the distinction between constitutional interpretation and statutory interpretation, see A. Barak, *Purposive Interpretation in Law* (Sari Bashi trans., Princeton University Press, 2005), 339–370. Regarding statutory interpretation, see N. Maccormick and R. S. Summers, *Interpreting Statutes: A Comparative Study* (Aldershot: Dartmouth, 1991); W. N. Eskridge Jr., *Dynamic Statutory Interpretation* (Cambridge, MA: Harvard University Press, 1994); F. Bennion, *Statutory Interpretation: A Code*, 4th edn. (London: Butterworths, 2002); L. M. du Plessis, *Re-interpretation of Statutes* (Durban: Butterworths, 2002).

the limiting statute abides by the conditions set by the limitation clause – in other words, whether the limitations are proportional. This is the stage where the judge examines the justifications to not allow for the complete fulfillment of the right's scope. If the judge concludes that the limitation is proportional, the review ends there. Conversely, should the judge conclude that the limitation is not proportional, that the constitutional right has been violated, they must continue to the third and final stage.

The third stage examines the effects of the unconstitutionality of the statute. This is a remedial stage. A discussion of this stage is beyond the scope of this book.

E.   Absolute rights

1.   Are there absolute constitutional rights?

Most constitutional rights enjoy only partial protection. They cannot be realized to the full extent of their scope as their limitation can be justified. The extent of their protection is narrower than their scope. These rights will be referred to as relative rights.[38] Relative rights do not constitute the entire universe of constitutional rights. Modern constitutional law made several – albeit rare – exceptions to the partial protection rule, by recognizing a number of constitutional rights as absolute.[39] These rights cannot be limited. The extent of their protection or realization is equal to their scope as their limitation cannot be justified. Strictly speaking, every right – once its limitations are grasped to be constitutional in relation to a given set of facts – may be referred to as "absolute" in relation to that set of facts. But this is a truism, a trivialization of the notion of an absolute right, which will not be used here. The term is used in the sense that a right is absolute if, and only if, its scope is fully protected in the sub-constitutional dimension – i.e., that the extent of its protection or realization is equal to its scope. One example of such an absolute right is the widely accepted constitutional prohibition of slavery.[40] Another example can be found in Article 1(1) of the German Constitution (*Grundgesetz*), which reads:

> Human dignity shall be inviolable [*unantastbar*]. To respect and protect it shall be the duty of all state authority.

[38] They are also called qualified rights: see A. Kavanagh, *Constitutional Review under the UK Human Rights Act* (Cambridge University Press, 2009), 257.

[39] Also called unqualified rights: see Kavanagh, above note 38, at 257.

[40] See, e.g., US Const., Am. XIII § 1 ("Neither slavery nor involuntary servitude … shall exist within the United States."); Universal Declaration of Human Rights, above note 27,

The interpretation of this provision provides that the German constitutional right to human dignity cannot be limited. The German courts ruled that neither the need to protect other individual rights, nor the general public interest, can justify a limitation on that right. As such, the right to human dignity in Germany is absolute.[41] In a recent case, the German Constitutional Court examined the constitutionality of a 9/11-prevention-type statute. The statute allowed a state agency to order the interception and shooting down of a civilian passenger airplane if it is obvious that the plane was hijacked by terrorists and that it is about to crash in a location that would lead to the injury of innocent bystanders.[42] Importantly, the statute allowed for the shooting down of the plane even when there was tangible knowledge of innocent passengers being held hostage. The court held that the statute was unconstitutional, as it limited the innocent hostages' right to human dignity. Human dignity, the court reasoned, is an absolute right that cannot be limited.[43] Amongst other things, the absolute nature of the right dictates that humans should never be treated as merely a means to the end of protecting other humans. The statute in question violates the hostages' human dignity, as it turns the innocent hostages into human shields for other innocent people. Accordingly, it was held that the statute cannot stand.

Another example of an absolute right can be found in Article 3 of the European Convention for the Protection of Human Rights and fundamental freedoms. The article reads:

> No one shall be subjected to torture or to inhuman or degrading treatment or punishment.

This prohibition is absolute.[44] The public interest, or the rights of other individuals, cannot diminish the extent of its protection. Its scope is

---

at Art. 4; Convention for the Protection of Human Rights and Fundamental Freedoms, above note 29, at Art. 4(1); Slavery, Servitude, Forced Labour and Similar Institutions and Practices Convention of 1926 (Slavery Convention of 1926), 60 *LNTS* 253 (entered into force March 9, 1927), at Art. 1. See also Van Droogenbroeck, Report of 9 July 1980, Series B, No. 44.

[41] According to Alexy, even dignity is a relative right under the German *Grundgesetz*: Alexy, above note 3, at 62.

[42] See BVerfGE, February 15, 2006, BVerfGE 115.

[43] For the non-amendable facet of the absolute right of human dignity in Germany, see below, at 31. As to its non-amendability, see below, at 31.

[44] See W. Brugger, "May Government Ever Use Torture? Two Responses from German Law," 48 *Am. J. Comp. L.* 661 (2000); J. J. Paust, "The Absolute Prohibition of Torture and Necessary and Appropriate Sanctions," 43. *Valp. L. Rev.* 1535 (2009).

equal to its coverage. In a similar context, the Israeli Supreme Court was called upon to examine whether the state – through its secret service – may allow for the use of torture in interrogations of terrorist suspects. The court's answer was no. Writing for the court, I emphasized that:

> A reasonable interrogation is an interrogation without torture, without cruel or inhuman treatment of the suspect, and without degrading his person ... Human dignity entails the human dignity of the interrogated suspect. Such a conclusion is commensurate with basic principles of public international law ... These restrictions are "absolute" – they have no exceptions, and they require no balancing.[45]

2. The jurisprudence of absolute rights

The notion of absolute rights is not without controversy. Some legal commentators question the mere concept of a jurisprudentially recognized absolute right (i.e., a right without limitations).[46] There are those who believe that every right is relative; that even the most significant of rights can be limited.[47] Other scholars are of the opinion that there should be no principled objection to the recognition of absolute rights. Gewirth, for example, while basing his argument on Aristotelian ethics, provides the example of a mother's absolute right not to be tortured to death by her own son.[48] Gewirth asserts that such a right is absolute even in the extreme case where, as a result of the son's refusal to torture his mother to death, a group of terrorists would use a nuclear weapon against a large peaceful city. Indeed, the literature on this subject is vast and replete with examples of preventing catastrophes. Other writers deal with more conventional cases. A well-known example in this context is the "Trolley Problem."[49] Suppose you are the driver of a railway trolley whose brakes have failed. You are about to hit and fatally wound a group of five rail workers. This fatal accident can be completely avoided by pushing another workman, John Doe, onto the tracks – to his own certain death. Does Mr. Doe have an absolute right not to be pushed onto the tracks – and to his death – even

---

[45] HCJ 5100/94 *The Public Committee Against Torture in Israel* v. *Prime Minister* [1999] IsrSC 53(4) 817; [1998–9] IsrLR 567.

[46] J. J. Thomson, *The Realm of Rights* (Cambridge, MA: Harvard University Press, 1990); L. Zucca, *Constitutional Dilemmas: Conflicts of Fundamental Legal Rights in Europe and the USA* (Oxford University Press, 2007).

[47] See Alexy, above note 3, at 64.

[48] See A. Gewirth, "Are There Any Absolute Rights?," *Philosophical Quarterly* 31 (1981), 1.

[49] See generally, J. J. Thomson, "The Trolley Problem," 94 *Yale L. J.* 1395 (1985).

while recognizing that five other people would certainly lose their lives because of that? Suppose now that the trolley can change its course and divert to another spur of tracks, thus saving the group of five workmen; the only issue is that Mr. Doe is now standing on that spur of tracks and is unable to escape the coming trolley on time. Thus, a change of course would directly lead to the death of Mr. Doe. Does Mr. Doe have an absolute right, under these circumstances, not to be fatally injured, even at the price of five other lives? Is there a difference between the two cases? And how important is the size of the group about to be injured?

The examination of these questions – which, until recently, were considered theoretical in nature – has unfortunately turned very practical due to the increasing number of terrorist attacks on peaceful communities around the world. Do terrorists have an absolute constitutional right not to be tortured when their investigation may lead to many lives being saved? Do innocent hostages, kidnapped by terrorists, have an absolute constitutional right not to pay with their lives to save a larger number of people? These and many other questions await their answer, in both the legal and ethical spheres. In this book no attempt is made to contribute to this debate. Its only purpose is to add an additional dimension to the dispute. Much of the literature dealing with the jurisprudence of constitutional rights tends to ignore the basic distinction between the constitutional level (where the right's scope is determined) and the legislative level (where its limitations are set). A typical example is the question of whether a property owner has the right to prevent a fatally injured person's entry onto his premises, even if the latter action is likely to save that person's life. According to the constitutional right two-stage model, a solution to the problem can be found along the following lines: While the scope of a constitutionally protected right to property includes the right to refuse entry to any person, the legislator may conclude that the right should not be exercised – i.e., be limited under certain justified circumstances. One of these circumstances may be when a near-death experience may be avoided by entering the premises (despite the refusal of the owner). Here, again, the scope of the right is separate from the extent of the protection afforded by the legislator. If the limitations placed by the legislator on the right are proportional, the law would pass constitutional muster, and the owner would have no legal option to prevent the entry. Of course, one could argue against any justification of the limitation of the constitutional right to property. No attempt is made to solve that problem, but only to add an additional dimension to its analysis.

3. *Absolute rights turned relative*

Suppose a legal system wishes to turn an absolute right into a relative one. What methods are available for it to do so? One way, as I have previously mentioned, is the use of interpretive tools. That is the route chosen by the US Supreme Court when it approached the seemingly absolute First Amendment right of freedom of expression. What should a legal system do when it realizes, after applying its own interpretive rules, that this avenue is blocked – that the only plausible interpretive result leaves the right as absolute? The answer is that the remaining avenue open to that system is that of a constitutional amendment – a change to the constitutional text itself. While this avenue is available, at least in theory, in many legal systems, it does raise some difficulties. First, in some cases the text of the constitution provides that the absolute nature of the right is not amendable but rather "eternal."[50] In these circumstances, a constitutional amendment simply cannot occur. An entirely new constitution is required to achieve the desired result. An example of such an "eternal" absolute right can be found in the German Constitution. Bear in mind that Article 1(1) of the Constitution establishes the right to human dignity. According to Article 79(3), any amendment affecting "the principles laid down in Article 1 … shall be inadmissible."[51] Therefore, the absolute nature of this right cannot be changed even through constitutional amendment. Second, in some extreme cases, even without an express constitutional provision preventing such amendments, some courts have decided that some amendments can be viewed as so fundamentally contrary to the basic structure of the constitution itself that they may no longer be considered "fit" for the process of a constitutional amendment.[52] These are the "unconstitutional constitutional amendments," which require the promulgation of an entirely new constitution as the amendment of the

---

[50] On the eternal nature of the constitutional provisions, see S. Weintal, "'Eternal Provisions' in the Constitution: The Strict Normative Standard for Establishing New Constitutional Order" (unpublished PhD dissertation, Hebrew University of Jerusalem, 2005); Mads Andenas (ed.), *The Creation and Amendment of Constitutional Norms* (2000); J. R. Vile, *Contemporary Questions Surrounding the Constitutional Amending Process* (Santa Barbara, CA: Praeger Publishers, 1993).

[51] Art. 79(3) of the German *Grundgesetz*.

[52] On the notion of "unconstitutional constitutional amendments," see K. Gözler, *Judicial Review of Constitutional Amendments: A Comparative Study* (Bursa, Turkey: Ekin Press, 2008); S. Krishnaswamy, *Democracy and Constitutionalism in India: A Study of the Basic Structure Doctrine* (Oxford University Press, 2009); C. Schmitt, *Constitutional Theory* (Jeffrey Seifzer trans., Duke University Press, 2008) (1928).

current constitution is held unconstitutional. A discussion of this question is beyond the scope of this book.[53]

F.   Relative rights

1.   *The nature of the relative constitutional right*

The number of absolute rights is very small. The vast majority of constitutional rights are relative rights. A right is relative if it is not protected to the full extent of its scope. Justified limitations are thus placed on the right's full realization. Indeed, we can say that a right is relative whenever the extent of its protection is narrower than its entire scope. The right is relative in that limitations may be imposed on actions or omissions that are otherwise included within its scope. In other words, the right is relative in that, with the determination of its scope, the legal system creates a constitutional mechanism which allows for the imposition of limitations on the realization of that scope. Limitation clauses (both general and specific), and the principle of proportionality at their core, reflect the relativity of the right.[54]

2.   *Boundaries and limitations*

i.   Types of provisions

The notion of relative rights may encounter analytical difficulties whenever the constitutional provision defining that right also contains an internal modifying element. Does the mere existence of such an element

---

[53] See the Symposium on Unconstitutional Constitutional Amendment in 44 *Israel Law Review* (forthcoming 2011).

[54] See *International Transport Roth GmbH* v. *Secretary of State for the Home Department* [2002] 3 WLR 344: "Even rights which are not absolute ... can be interfered with only to an extent which is proportionate. However compelling the social goal, there are limits to how the individual's interest can legitimately be sacrificed"; HCJ 8276/05 *Adalah – The Legal Center for the Rights of the Arab Minority* v. *Minister of Defense* [2006] (2) IsrLR 352, para. 26: "The concept of a limitation clause is premised on the notion that human rights will always stand side-by-side with human duties; that we do not live on an island, but rather are a part of society; that the interests of that society may justify limitations on the rights humans have; and that therefore those rights are not absolute, but relative. The limitation clause reflects the view that human rights may be limited, but also that these limitations have their legal limits ... Indeed, human rights do not receive full legal protection according with their scope. The constitutional structure prevents the realization of the rights to their fullest extent." (Barak, P.).

turn the right into a relative one? Should this element be treated as an internal, specific limitation clause? Should the rules of proportionality apply to this element? Take, for example, the right to assemble as defined by the Constitution of the Republic of South Africa:

> Everyone has the right, peacefully and unarmed, to assemble, to demonstrate, to picket and to present petitions.[55]

Is this right to assemble – defined with the internal element of "peacefully and unarmed" – a relative right? The answer is naturally yes, as the general limitation clause included in the South African Constitution[56] – which applies to each of the enumerated human rights – applies to this right as well. But does the relativity of the right to assemble stem solely from the presence of the general limitation clause? Could we not say that the right is relative by virtue of its own provision? The answer to that question is no. The words "peacefully and unarmed" do not reflect a limitation on the constitutional right, but rather make up a part of its definition. According to this view,[57] there are two types of constitutional provisions relating to rights: The first includes constitutional provisions determining the boundaries of the right that contain internal qualifiers of the right's scope; the second includes constitutional provisions determining the circumstances in which the right – according to its determined scope – can be justifiably limited within the sub-constitutional level. The provision containing the expression "peacefully and unarmed" belongs to the first type. It determines the scope of the constitutional right, not its limitations. I will elaborate further on this distinction. I will begin with provisions determining the right's scope.

ii.   Provisions determining the right's scope

These provisions, according to their proper constitutional interpretation, define the right's scope. Naturally, these provisions are linked to the right's definition as it appears in the constitutional text and assist in the proper interpretation of such definitions.[58] They do not turn the right

---

[55] Constitution of The Republic of South Africa, Art. 17.
[56] *Ibid.*, Art. 36.
[57] For a different view, see Alexy, above note 3, at 185–192 (differentiating between immediate limitations, which can be found in the constitutional text, and mediate limitations, which can be found in the sub-constitutional level; both require use of the rules of proportionality).
[58] See I. Currie and J. de Waal, *The Bill of Rights Handbook*, 5th edn. (Cape Town: Juta Law Publishers, 2006), 186 ("Their purpose is definitional: defining the scope of the right

into a relative one. They do not prescribe limitations on the realization of the right within its proper boundaries through sub-constitutional provisions. Thus, the constitutional right to assemble in South Africa – a right which, according to its definition, can only apply to "peaceful and unarmed" activities – is not a relative right due to the qualifying text which appears as part of its defining provision. Such qualifications relate only to the determination of the right's boundaries and its proper scope. They do not relate to the ways in which the right can be realized, or to the extent of its protection. The same is true for Article 16 of the Constitution of the Republic of South Africa, which defines the right to freedom of expression (in subsection (1)), and then provides (in subsection (2)):

> The right in subsection (1) does not extend to—
>
> (a) Propaganda for war;
> (b) Incitement of imminent violence; or
> (c) Advocacy or hatred that is based on race, ethnicity, gender or religion, and that constitutes incitement to cause harm.

This provision narrows the scope of the constitutional right to freedom of expression in South Africa. It does not express an opinion on the issue of whether limitations may be placed on the ways in which that constitutional right may be realized. Such limitations may be imposed in accordance with the general constitutional limitation clause (which can be found in Article 36 thereof). The mere existence of the general limitation clause is what turns the right into a relative one. Accordingly, Article 16(2) is not a provision limiting the constitutional right to freedom of expression, but rather a provision that helps determine the right's scope. Such provisions should not be seen as "internal limitations" of the right,[59] but rather as "internal modifiers," "internal qualifiers,"[60] or "demarcations."[61] Importantly, they contain a part of the right's scope and not a part the extent of its protection.

more precisely than is the case with the textually unqualified rights"). In Germany, these orders are referred to as *grundrechtsimmanente grenzen*. See also Hesse, above note 10.

[59] See Gardbaum, above note 25, at 801. See also D. Meyerson, "Why Courts Should Not Balance Rights Against the Public Interest," 31 *Melb. L. Rev.* 801 (2007). For criticism of using the expression "internal limitations," see H. Cheadle, N. Haysom, and D. Davis (eds.), *South African Constitutional Law: The Bill of Rights* (2003), 701.

[60] See Woolman and Botha, above note 5, at 30. See also Butler, above note 6, at 120.

[61] See Currie and de Waal, above note 58, at 186. See also Butler, above note, at 117; G. Carpenter, "Internal Modifiers and Other Qualifications in Bills of Rights – Some Problems of Interpretation," 10 *SA Public Law* 260 (1995).

iii. Provisions which set forth limitations on the realization

Provisions that place limitations on the realization of the constitutional right – within its proper scope – through the use of sub-constitutional laws are termed provisions determining the extent of the right's protection. They turn any constitutional right to which they apply into a relative right. They do not affect the right's scope. They do not determine its boundaries. They do not define its reach. They do, however, create a constitutional possibility to limit the constitutional right through a sub-constitutional provision within the right's boundaries. These are the limitation clauses.

A prominent example of such a provision can be found in Article 10(2) of the European Convention for the Protection of Human Rights and Fundamental Freedoms discussed earlier.[62] Remember that this article specifies several constitutional limitations that may be placed on the realization of the right. These limitations do not affect the scope of the right, but rather affect the extent of its protection and the ways in which it can be realized. Sometimes these limitations are "general" – that is, they apply to all the rights included in a given constitution. Sometimes they are "specific," or "special" – that is, they apply to only one specific right.[63]

iv. The importance of the distinction

In most cases, the distinction between the two types of provisions – internal qualifying provisions and specific limitation clauses – is clear and straightforward, and therefore easy to implement. However, in some cases, the distinction is not so clear. This is important, as the distinction serves both theoretical and practical purposes. Theoretically, the distinction may assist in determining the nature of the right as absolute or relative. Practically speaking, the distinction may prove essential in several

---

[62] See above, at 21.

[63] See Currie and de Waal, above note 58, at 187: "A few rights ... are qualified by language that specifically demarcates their scope. Such qualifications can be termed demarcations of that right. Their purpose is definitional: defining the scope of the right more precisely than is the case with the textually unqualified rights ... Other textual qualifications of rights create criteria for the limitation of certain rights by the legislature. These are more properly called special limitations. Engaging in any form of limitation analysis ... assumes that an infringement of a right has been established. This means that reliance on a special limitation clause is a second-stage matter. At the first stage the person relying on the right has to show that an infringement has taken place. Once shown, at the second stage, the state or the person relying on the validity of legislation must show that the limitation of the right is justified either by reference to a special limitation clause or the general criteria of Art. 36." See also Cheadle, Haysom, and Davis, above note 59, at 701.

contexts. One such context involves the use of the balancing prescribed by the general limitation clause. As we shall see,[64] the rules of proportionality written into the general limitation clause require the balancing of several constitutional elements. Is the application of this balancing test appropriate when examining the internal qualifiers (which determine the right's scope)? In other words, can the balancing rules included in the general limitation clause also be used for the scope-determining qualifiers? Take the South African constitutional right to demonstrate "peacefully and unarmed." Bear in mind that this constitution also contains a general limitation clause. The question is, should the balancing and proportionality considerations used by the general limitation clause also be applied in determining the scope of the right itself? My answer to this question is in the negative. The general limitation clause – and the proportionality and balancing considerations used by it – should play no part in the interpretation of the internal qualifiers. The limitation clause applies if, and only if, a constitutional right is limited by a sub-constitutional law. The internal qualifier does not limit the constitutional right, but rather defines its scope more narrowly. Indeed, the examination of the internal qualifier's proper range is in its essence a question of constitutional interpretation. The question is what is the proper reach of the right, considering the factors at the basis of the right. The answer to the said question takes into consideration the reasons underlying the qualifying provision. This is an "internal" constitutional examination, relating to the essence of the right itself. It is not affected by external considerations, such as public interest considerations or the rights of other individuals.[65] It would be inappropriate, therefore, to either consider or balance, within the interpretive process of the qualifying provision which determines the right's scope, the same set of factors that are considered to be within the limitation clause's proportionality rules. There may be occasions where an interpretive inquiry would reveal two conflicting principles that reside side-by-side within the internal qualifying provision. In these cases, the interpretive examination of the qualifier may require a resolution of such a conflict through a balancing test. While this resolution does constitute an interpretive balancing act, it does not constitute – and should not be considered as – an application of the limitation clause. The issue of

---

[64] See below, at 343.
[65] See Woolman and Botha, above note 5, at 3: "The internal modifier is concerned with a determination of the content of the right and not with an analysis of competing rights or interests."

interpretive balancing and its relation to limitation clause balancing will be discussed in later chapters.[66]

Another practical context where the distinction between internal qualifying provisions and general limitation clauses plays a central role is in the evidentiary realm of the burden of proof. If the case at hand involves internal qualifying provisions, since they constitute a part of the right itself, the burden of proof (both the burden of persuasion and the burden of producing evidence) in the first stage of the constitutional examination – attempting to establish whether a right has been limited – lies with the party arguing that the right, within its proper scope (of which the internal qualifying is a part), was in fact limited.[67] The burden of proof shifts in the second stage of the examination to the party arguing that the limitation on that right is justified – that the limitation abides by all the requirements of the limitation clause, or in other words, it is proportional.[68]

G.   Constitutional rights: prima facie or definite?

1.   *The problem presented*

The distinction between the scope of a constitutional right and the extent of its justifiable limitation leads to difficulty when answering a basic question: is a constitutional right a definite right or a *prima facie* right? The answer to this question requires an examination of the concept of *prima facie* rights.[69] It directly relates to the problem of conflicting constitutional rights and to the attempt to resolve such conflicts.[70] A thorough discussion of these issues is beyond the parameters of this book. The discussion here will be limited to the part of the question relating to the constitutional right and its scope. No attempt will be made to confront the general jurisprudential claim that all constitutional rights are merely *prima facie* rights. The argument here is, rather, that, when a constitution defines a

---

[66] See below, at 72. See also Woolman and Botha, above note 5, at 3.
[67] See Woolman and Botha. above note 5, at 42; see also Currie and de Waal, above note 58, at 187.
[68] See below, at 439.
[69] On the jurisprudence of *prima facie* rights, see, e.g., D. Ross, *The Right and the Good* (Oxford University Press, 1930), 19, 28; J. Searle, "Prima Facie Obligations," in J. Raz (ed.), *Practical Reasoning* (Oxford University Press, 1978), 81; J. Raz, *The Morality of Freedom* (Oxford: Clarendon Press, 1986), 184; Schauer, above note 24, at 113.
[70] See below, at 83.

right ("scope"), and at the same time allows for the placement of justifiable limitations upon the realization of that right through sub-constitutional law ("the extent of its protection"), the existence of the power to limit the realization of the right, in and of itself, cannot turn the constitutional right into a *prima facie* right.

2.   *The prima facie constitutional right: Alexy's view*

Alexy[71] begins his discussion of constitutional norms with a distinction between rules and principles.[72] Constitutional principles, according to Alexy, consist of "optimization requirements ... norms which require that something be realized to the greatest extent possible given the legal and factual possibilities."[73] Those legal and factual possibilities are the rules of proportionality. Contrary to the principles, according to Alexy, constitutional rules "are norms which are always either fulfilled or not. If a rule validly applies, then the requirement is to do exactly what it says, neither more nor less."[74] Accordingly, a conflict between constitutional rights formed as rules is resolved either through the invalidation of one of the rules, or by reading an exception to it. Conversely, a conflict between competing constitutional rights formed as principles is resolved only when one of the principles is outweighed at the point of conflict, but not through invalidation.[75]

What is the status of each constitutional principle at the precise point of conflict? According to Alexy, it is only at that point that the conditions are set for one principle to outweigh the other. These conditions are set in accordance with the constitutional rules of proportionality, which prescribe the set of permitted limitations – both legal and factual – on these constitutional principles. These conditions reflect the recognition of a new constitutional rule. This is a derivative constitutional rule, created by both conflicting principles. At the precise point of conflict, this rule determines which principle should outweigh the other. As Alexy puts it:

> [T]he result of every correct balancing of constitutional rights can be formulated in terms of a derivative constitutional rights norm in the form of a rule under which the case can be subsumed.[76]

---

[71] On Alexy and his analytical contribution to the study of constitutional rights, see Introduction, above, at 5.
[72] Alexy, above note 3, at 47.
[73] *Ibid.* By "given the legal and factual possibilities," Alexy refers to the proportionality rules.
[74] *Ibid.*, at 48.   [75] *Ibid.*   [76] *Ibid.*, at 56.

According to Alexy's analysis, constitutional principles are not definitive. They are the reasons for the action and can be overcome with opposing reasons. The relationship between these reasons is determined by the factual and legal possibilities, namely, the proportionality of their realization in a given situation. Their use in a given case is always subject to the derivative rule – reflecting their legal and factual limitation – which overcomes them. It is through these assumptions that Alexy concludes that all constitutional rights formed as principles merely represent *prima facie* rights rather than definite ones. In his words:

> [P]rinciples can only ever be *prima facie reasons*. In and of themselves they can only create prima facie rights ... The route from the principle, that is, the prima facie right, to the definitive right runs by way of relation of preference. But establishing a preference relation is, according to the Law of Competing Principles, to create a rule. We can therefore say that whenever a principle turns out to be the dominant reason for a concrete ought-judgment, then the principle is a reason for a rule, which in turn is the definitive reason for the judgment. Principles in themselves are never definitive reasons.[77]

According to Alexy's approach, whenever a limitation on a *prima facie* constitutional right is proportional, the right itself is affected in that its scope is diminished. This *prima facie* scope, according to Alexy, is very wide, since "everything which the relevant constitutional principle suggests should be protected falls within the scope" of the right.[78] Alexy's approach to the determination of the *prima facie* scope of the right is, therefore, very broad. However, the constitutional derivative rule that is created as a result of the application of the proportionality rule narrows the right's otherwise broad scope. That narrowing, however, applies only in the situation's unique circumstances. In those circumstances the constitutional right no longer exists.

3.   *Definite constitutional rights that cannot be realized*

Unlike Alexy, I believe that limitations of principle-formed constitutional rights do not affect their scope, even in concrete cases. I do accept that, whenever two constitutional rights (which are formed as principles) conflict, a new constitutional derivative rule is created that reflects the proportional balance between those rights.[79] However, according to my

---

[77] *Ibid.*, at 60.   [78] *Ibid.*, at 210.
[79] On the conflict between constitutional rights, see below, at 83.

approach, this derivative constitutional rule can only operate within the sub-constitutional level. It affects only the realization of the constitutional right on the sub-constitutional level.[80] It has no effect at the constitutional level. It is unable to narrow the scope of the constitutional right itself. In other words, the effects of the derivative constitutional rule – which reflects the proportionality requirements set by the limitation clause – only operates at the level of the limiting statute or common law. It affects the constitutionality of the statute. It cannot have any effect on the scope of the right. This is true for all limitation clause (proportionality) rules. They do not operate at the constitutional level.

A key component of this approach is the understanding that a constitutional right is not a *prima facie* right, but rather, a definite right.[81] Take, for example, the right to freedom of expression. When considered within its entire scope, it is definite and complete. However, due to the need to protect the rights of others or public interest considerations, the right to freedom of expression cannot be realized to its fullest extent (divulging state secrets, for example, is illegal). But these limitations on the realization of the right do not operate at the constitutional level. The scope of the right has not changed. Rather, the limitations only operate at the sub-constitutional level. They can be found in statutes or common law that limits the extent of the protection of the right of one person in favor of promoting other constitutionally recognized principles. This is the effect – both factual and legal – of the proportionality requirements set by the limitation clause.

Alexy's approach, according to which there are only *prima facie* principle-formed constitutional rights, stems from his general perception of the principle. According to Alexy, a principle is an optimization requirement that may be realized to the greatest extent possible given the legal and factual possibilities.[82] The "legal and factual possibilities" mentioned by Alexy are the constitutional rules of proportionality. Therefore, the notion of proportionality, according to Alexy, must be seen as part of the very definition of a constitutional principle. The conclusion that every principle – and every constitutional right formed as a principle – is only a *prima facie* principle is a necessary conclusion.

This approach to the principles, however, is not analytically compelled.[83] According to my view, a legal norm formed as a principle is made up of fundamental values. These values in turn reflect ideals aspiring to be

---

[80] See below, at 89.   [81] See Zucca, above note 46, at 60.
[82] See Alexy, above note 3, at 47.
[83] The attempt to properly define the term "legal principle" has yielded voluminous literature. See, e.g., H. Avila, *Theory of Legal Principles* (Dordrecht: Springer, 2007); M. Sachs

realized to their maximum extent. In practice, however, at the sub-constitutional level, these ideals may not be realized to their full scope. The constitutional interpretation of these values shapes their scope in accordance with each underlying reason. The question of the realization of that right arises within the parameters of that right's predetermined scope. Again, these constitutional rights formed as principles at a high level of abstraction may be realized at the sub-constitutional level at varying degrees of intensity. This realization is not a part of the right's scope, but only part of the extent of its protection. The rules of proportionality define the extent of that realization. They do not form a part of the right's scope.

Therefore, according to this approach, the constitutional right formed as a principle is not a *prima facie* right, but a definite right. In some cases, the realization of such a right is affected by other principles – relating to other peoples' rights or to public interest considerations. However, in either case, the narrowing realization does not entail a diminished scope. This narrow realization or diminished protection (limitation) – as compared with the right's full scope – speaks only to the level of intensity in which the right is realized at the sub-constitutional level. That level does not affect the principle's scope. Thus, the options available for limiting the principle's realization do not turn the principle-formed right into a *prima facie* right,[84] though they may create a *prima facie* violation of the right.[85] Thus, the right is not *prima facie* but, rather, definite.

There are several advantages to this approach over Alexy's. First, it places the constitutional right on solid ground. The *prima facie* nature of the right, conversely, may hurt its social standing, its exemplary role, and its moral capability. Second, this approach prevents constant corrosion in the scope of constitutional rights. According to Alexy, the constitutional derivative rule that limits the constitutional right's scope operates only at the lowest level of abstraction. It reflects a case-by-case (*ad hoc*) balancing approach. However, it is well within the nature of the judicial process that case-by-case decisions are understood as providing guidance on a much higher level of abstraction, thus serving as precedents for future cases. Third, and finally, since the final results of the application of the proportionality rules are set at the sub-constitutional level, these results may

---

(ed.), *GG Grundgesetz Kommentar* (2007), 723; see Zucca, above note 46, at 7; Schauer, above note 24.

[84] See below, at 89.

[85] As to the burden of proof, see Chapter 16.

constantly be the subject of political debate and public discourse; they may change according to the day-to-day needs of society at any given period.

H.   Is there a constitutional right to commit a proportional crime?

1.   A constitutional right to steal?

Does it arise from the view presented that one has a constitutional right to steal? According to Alexy, the prohibition on committing criminal offenses – assuming they are proportional – excludes criminal activity from the scope of the constitutional right to private autonomy.[86] Accordingly, there is no constitutional right steal. This is not my approach. In my opinion, criminal activity can still be covered at the constitutional level, but properly – that is, proportionally – prohibited (limited) at the sub-constitutional level. In other words, if private autonomy constitutes a constitutional right, the act of stealing is part of that right (at the constitutional level), as it forms an action in accordance to one's private autonomy; such an act is forbidden, however, at the sub-constitutional level by a statute criminalizing the act that has been held to be proportional.

Does this analysis suggest the existence of a constitutional right to steal? The answer is that the only constitutional right is that of private autonomy. There is no separate constitutional right to steal. In Israel, the right to private autonomy is part of the constitutional right to human dignity. In other jurisdictions, it is a part of other constitutional rights such as the right to liberty. The prohibition on stealing, on the other hand, cannot be found in the constitutions themselves. Stealing is not a constitutional concept. If the prohibition on stealing was to appear as a rule in the constitutional text itself, the scope of the constitutional right to private autonomy would be diminished accordingly.[87] It could no longer be said that that activity be included as part of the right's scope. The same is true for every constitutionally mandated rule. However, in the absence

---

[86] I assume – together with Alexy, above note 3, at 223 – that a democratic constitution recognizes a general right to private autonomy (see Art. 2(1) of the German *Grundgesetz*). Such an assumption, however, is not universally shared and is theoretically disputed by some. See Dworkin, above note 24, at 266. A review of this dispute is not required to understand my argument, and is beyond the scope of this book.

[87] In a conflict between a constitutional rule (no stealing) and a constitutional principle (autonomy), the constitutional rule prevails. The scope of the constitutional principle is affected. See below, at 97.

of such a constitutional prohibition, the legal restriction on the act of theft is the product of a sub-constitutional law included in the criminal code. It is therefore in the legal area of criminal law that the concept of theft is created, and it is there that the concept's legal boundaries are set. It is criminal law that provides that stealing is prohibited. Accordingly, a constitutional right to human autonomy exists (at the constitutional level), but the availability to realize that right is limited. This limitation is formed *inter alia* within the criminal law prohibition on theft. We assume that that prohibition is proportional, and therefore the limitation on the right is constitutionally valid. The same analysis may apply not only to other criminal acts, but also to torts resulting in liability according to the law of torts, breaches of contracts sanctioned by contract law, and other types of behavior restricted by law. Importantly, all these limitations are not constitutional notions and do not operate at the constitutional level. Rather, they are notions created by the institutions of private and criminal law. The constitutional level deals with the notion of private autonomy (or other constitutional rights). Such constitutional rights cannot be realized when private law or criminal law so prescribe, so long as that prescription is proportional and therefore constitutional.

2. *The criticism and a response*

It can be argued that the approach described may lead to a trivialization of the concept of constitutional rights. I cannot agree. There may be cases in which such an impression is made, but this is only an initial impression. This impression, if it exists, cannot hold up to the overwhelming evidence – and social recognition – of scores of legislative determinations created precisely to properly limit the realization of these well-recognized constitutional rights. Such limitations serve as the backbone of every organized democracy. The question of the constitutionality of such legislative determinations is considered at the second stage of the judicial constitutional review, examining whether the legislation is proportional. But not only are constitutional rights not trivialized by the existence of such a system, they are in fact elevated to a more secure analytical basis in the system as a whole. Justice Ackermann of the South African Constitutional Court has responded to the trivialization arguments:

> I cannot … comprehend why an extensive construction of freedom would
> "trivialize" the charter, either in theory or in practice, or, more relevantly
> for our purpose, our present Constitution. It might trivialize a constitu-
> tion (it would indeed cause chaos) if it resulted in the regulation measures

being struck down. But that is not the consequence. An extensive construction merely requires the party relying thereon to justify it in terms
of a limitation clause. It does not trivialize a constitution in theory; in fact
it has the reverse effect by emphasizing the necessity for justifying intru-
sion into freedom. It does not trivialize a constitution in practice because
in the vast majority of cases dealing with regulatory matters, the justification is so obviously incontestable that it is taken for granted and never
becomes a live issue. In the borderline cases (and even in mundane regulatory statutes such cases may arise) there is no pragmatic reason why the
person relying on the measure ought not to justify it.[88]

[88] CCT 23/95 *Ferreira* v. *Levin NO*, 1996 (1) SA 984, § 82 (CC).

2

Determining the scope of constitutional rights

A. The right's scope is determined by constitutional interpretation

1. Constitutional interpretation

i. Purposive interpretation

The two-pronged analysis distinguishes between the scope of the constitutional right and the extent of the right's realization. How is the right's
scope determined? The answer is that the right's scope is determined by
the interpretation of the legal text in which the right resides. When the
right is within a constitutional text, the process is of constitutional interpretation.[1] There are several theories of constitutional interpretation.[2]

---

[1] See HCJ 450/97 *Tenufah Human Services* v. *Ministry of Labor and Welfare* [1998] IsrSC
52(2) 433, 440 ("When the claim before us relates to a limitation on a constitutional human
right, this Court has to make a determination as to the scope of that right, which can be
found in the text of the Basic Law. Such determination is made according to the rules of
constitutional interpretation that we have accepted. They are, in essence, the rules of purposive interpretation ... These rules are a part of our purposive-interpretation doctrine.
As with any other legal text, the constitutional text should also be interpreted according to the rules of purposive interpretation. With that, the special nature of the text may
influence its purposive interpretation ... The judge has to be sensitive to the fact that he is
interpreting a constitutional text; clearly, the interpretation of a regular legislative order
is different from the interpretation of a fundamental constitutional decree.") (Barak, P.).
On the definition of the Constitution in constitutional interpretation, see L. du Plessis,
"Interpretation," in S. Woolman, M. Bishop, and J. Brickhill (eds.), *Constitutional Law of
South Africa*, 2nd edn. (Cape Town: Juta Law Publishers, looseleaf, 2002–), para. 32–16.
[2] See S. Barber, *On What the Constitution Means* (Baltimore, MD: Johns Hopkins
University Press, 1984); L. Tribe and M. Dorf, *On Reading the Constitution* (Cambridge,
MA: Harvard University Press, 1991); C. Sampford and K. Preston (eds.), *Interpreting
Constitutions: Theories, Principles and Instruction* (Annandale, Australia: Federation
Press, 1996); A. Scalia, *A Matter of Interpretation: Federal Courts and the Law* (Princeton
University Press, 1997); K. Whittington, *Constitutional Interpretation. Textual Meaning,
Original Intent, and Judicial Review* (Lawrence, KS: University Press of Kansas, 1999); J.

The following pages will focus on what is considered the best theory of constitutional interpretation, the theory of purposive interpretation.[3]

Constitutional interpretation comprises part of the general theory of legal interpretation. Like any legal text, the constitution should be interpreted in accordance with its purpose. That purpose is a normative term. It is a judicial construction. It is a "legal institution." It is the *ratio juris*. It is the purpose the text was designed to achieve. It is the text's function. That purpose contains both the subjective purpose, regarding the intentions of the creators of the constitutional text, and the objective purpose, as to the understanding of the text based on its role and function. This interpretation, in turn, should take into account both the role and function played by the text at the time it was created, as well as its role and function at the time of interpretation. Purposive interpretation takes into account the special nature of the constitutional text.[4] This nature is derived from the constitution's legal status as the supreme law of the land, as well as from its unique role in shaping the nation's image across generations.[5]

This general approach of constitutional interpretation also applies, naturally, to the interpretation of constitutional rights. These rights are

---

Shaman, *Constitutional Interpretation: Illusion and Reality* (Westport, CT: Greenwood Press, 2001); J. Goldsworthy and T. Campbell (eds.), *Legal Interpretation in Democratic States* (Farnham, England: Ashgate, 2002); A. Barak, *Purposive Interpretation in Law* (Princeton University Press, 2005); J. Goldsworthy (ed.), *Interpreting Constitutions: A Comparative Study* (New York: Oxford University Press, 2006); S. Barber and J. Fleming, *Constitutional Interpretation: The Basic Questions* (New York: Oxford University Press, 2007); W. Murphy, J. Fleming, and S. Barber, *American Constitutional Interpretation* (Westbury, NY: Foundation Press, 2008); G. Letsas, *A Theory of Interpretation of the European Convention on Human Rights* (New York: Oxford University Press, 2009).

[3] The analysis in the text is based on A. Barak, *Purposive Interpretation in Law* (Princeton University Press, 2005). See also Du Plessis, above note 1, at para. 32–52.

[4] *Ibid.*, at 371.

[5] See also HCJ 6427/02 *The Movement for Quality Government in Israel* v. *The Knesset* [2006] IsrSC 61(1) 619 ("The special nature of the Basic Laws should be taken into account in their interpretation. These Basic Laws were meant to shape the image of the civic society and its aspirations throughout history; they were meant to determine the nation's most basic concepts, as well as to establish a foundation for its social values; they are seeking to set the nation's aspirations, commitments, and its long-term directions. Indeed, the Basic Laws were meant to guide human behavior for long. They reflect the events of the past; they lay a foundation for the present; and they are designed to set the future. They are at once a philosophy, politics, social sciences and law." (Barak, P.)); HCJ 1384/98 *Avni* v. *Prime Minister* [1998] IsrSC 52(5) 206 ("When we interpret a Basic Law we should fulfill the role of the constitutional norm. This norm determines both government and law. It shapes individual rights. By its very nature, it reflects the basic notions of its society, its legal system, and its governmental structure. It reflects the most fundamental political concept of the nation. It lays foundations for social values. It sets the nation's aspirations and directions. When interpreting a constitutional text, we should always note its special character." (Barak, P.)).

interpreted according to the reasons at their foundation as understood in the context of society's most fundamental values, the fundamentals of its existence, and with the basic principles shared by all constitutional rights.[6] As explained by Chief Justice Dickson of the Canadian Supreme Court in one of the first cases to interpret the Canadian Charter of Rights and Freedoms:[7]

> The task of expounding a constitution is crucially different from that of constructing a statute. A statute defines present rights and obligations. It is easily enacted and as easily repealed. A constitution, by contrast, is drafted with an eye to the future. Its function is to provide a continuing framework for the legitimate exercise of governmental power and, when joined by a Bill or a Charter of Rights, for the unremitting protection of individual rights and liberties. Once enacted, its provisions cannot easily be repealed or amended. It must, therefore, be capable of growth and development over time to meet new social, political, and historical realities often unimagined by its framers. The judiciary is the guardian of the constitution and must, in interpreting its provisions, bear these considerations in mind.[8]

The constitution itself, as well as the rights protected by it, enjoys a special status in the legal system. It fulfills a function no other norm in the system can realize.[9]

ii.   Purposive interpretation and the constitution's unique nature

The special status of the constitution affects its interpretation. What is the nature of such an interpretive effect?[10] What is the proper way to reconcile the notion that a constitution is, first and foremost, a legal text – and therefore should be interpreted according to the same rules and principles that apply to the interpretation of every other legal text – with

---

[6] See CA 6821/93 *United Mizrahi Bank Ltd.* v. *Migdal Cooperative Village* [1995] IsrLR 1 ("The scope of each constitutional right is determined by the process of its interpretation. This is constitutional interpretation. It is sensitive to the nature of the interpreted document in question. Indeed, 'it is the constitution that we are expounding ...'. Thus, the interpretation of a standard legislative provision is not the same as the interpretation of a basic constitutional provision ... Constitutional interpretation is directed by the criteria set by constitutional purpose ... Such constitutional purpose can be deduced from the language used by the text, its history, culture, and the nation's fundamental principles ... A constitutional provision was not created in a constitutional vacuum, and does not develop in a constitutional incubator. Rather, it serves as part of life itself." (Barak, P.)).

[7] Canadian Charter of Rights and Freedoms, Part I of the Constitution Act 1982.

[8] *Hunter* v. *Southam Inc.* [1984] 2 SCR 145.

[9] See D. Farber, "The Originalism Debate: A Guide for the Perplexed," 49 *Ohio St. L. J.* 1085, 1101 (1989).

[10] See Barak, *Purposive Interpretation in Law*, above note 3, at 371.

the notion that a constitution is also a unique legal text, requiring its own interpretive approach? The answer can be found within the concept of purposive interpretation. The process of purposive interpretation reflects, on the one hand, the notion of purposive unity applying to all legal texts, and, on the other hand, takes into account the unique nature of the constitutional text. Purposive interpretation of the constitution – as the purposive interpretation of every legal text – takes into account both the intention of the text's creators (subjective purpose) as well as the system's "intention" as a whole (objective purpose). Constitutional purposive interpretation does not subscribe to the notion that only the framers' intention – or any other creators of the constitutional text – should determine its interpretation. To the same extent, constitutional purposive interpretation rejects the notion that only the understanding of the text according to its values at the time of interpretation should determine the meaning of the constitutional text. Rather, constitutional purposive interpretation, with its holistic approach, takes into account both subjective and objective purposes when approaching the constitutional text. The constitutional purpose is therefore a synthesis between the study of the subjective purpose, as provided by the constitutional text and other external sources, and from the objective purpose, as provided again by the constitutional text and external sources. The special nature of the constitution is demonstrated by the internal relationship between its subjective and objective purposes, between the framers' intention and that of the system as a whole. Here, in case of a conflict the latter "intention" will have the upper hand.[11]

iii.   Constitutional text

a.   A constitutional text, not a metaphor   Constitutional interpretation is bound by the constitutional text.[12] As a rule, constitutional language is not different from the language used by other legal texts. Then again, a typical constitutional provision often contains more vague[13] or open-textured terms[14] than can be found in other legal texts. This is even

---

[11]   See *ibid.*, at 371. See also Du Plessis, above note 1, at para. 32–42.

[12]   See Barak, above note 3, at 373.

[13]   See *S. v. Zuma*, 1995 (2) SA 642, paras. 17 and 18 (CC); S. Magiera, "The Interpretation of the Basic Law," in C. Starck (ed.), *Main Principles of the German Basic Law* (Baden-Baden: Nomos Verlagsgesellschaft, 1983), 89.

[14]   See W. Brennan, "The Constitution of the United States: Contemporary Ratification," 27 *Tex. L. Rev.* 433 (1986); B. McLachlin, "The Charter: A New Role for the Judiciary," 29 *Alta. L. Rev.* 540, 545 (1991).

more so when the subject of the constitutional provision in question is the protection of a right.

Constitutional rights are often phrased as principles. They contain "majestic generalities."[15] They reflect national ideals seeking maximum realization. The synthesis of those ideals creates the purpose underlying all constitutional rights. But, if those ideals set its purpose, the language of the constitutional provision sets its interpretive limits. Constitutional language should not be interpreted in a manner that the text itself cannot tolerate. As noted in one case:

> The interpreter approaches an existing text, to which he gives meaning. He cannot create a new text. The interpreter cannot provide the text with an interpretive meaning that the text cannot tolerate. The limit of legal interpretation is the limit of the legal text, and the limit of that text is determined by the specific linguistic rules of that particular language … Thus, the interpretive process ends where the language ends … Every meaning provided by the interpreter must find an Archimedean anchor in the text itself … The text is not everything; we thus begin with the text but that does not conclude the interpretive process. Alongside the text, we examine the purpose. That purpose however, cannot be obtained unless it can be fulfilled by the text. The text, therefore, is always the framework within which the interpreter has to operate, and from which he may not depart … The limits of the interpretative process lie with the text.[16]

The text of a constitutional provision, which includes a principle-shaped norm cannot tolerate just any content. A constitution is not a metaphor. The constitutional text is not a non-binding recommendation.[17] It is not like clay in the sculptor's hands. The idea of constitutional amendments through judicial interpretation – rather than through the mechanisms set by the constitution itself – is merely a metaphor.[18]

b.   Explicit and implicit constitutional text   The term "constitutional text" entails both the constitution's explicit and implicit texts.[19] A constitutional text is explicit whenever its meaning may be conveyed through a dictionary definition of the text placed against the relevant legal context

---

[15] *Fay* v. *New York*, 332 US 261, 282 (1947) (Jackson, J.).
[16] HCJ 2257/04 *Chadash-Ta'al Party* v. *Chairman of Knesset Election Committee Knesset* [2004] IsrSC 58(6) 685, 703–701 (Barak, P.).
[17] See F. Schauer, "An Essay on Constitutional Language," 29 *UCLA L. Rev.* 797, 830 (1981).
[18] See S. Levinson (ed.), *Responding to Imperfection – The Theory and Practice of Constitutional Amendment* (Princeton University Press, 1995).
[19] See Barak, above note 3, at 104.

(both internal and external).[20] The implicit constitutional text, in contrast, is written with "invisible ink." It can be found "between the (constitutional) lines."[21] Take, for example, a constitution that includes chapters on both governmental powers and constitutional rights. That same constitution does not contain an explicit provision relating to separation of powers, the rule of law, or the independence of the judiciary. Despite the lack of such explicit provisions, one may persuasively argue that this constitution implicitly includes the principles of separation of powers, the rule of law, and judicial independence.[22]

The meaning of the constitutional text, therefore, includes the meaning of both its explicit and implicit portions. The implicit portion constitutes a part of the entire universe of the text, and should be treated the same as any other part of the explicit portion of the text.[23] Reasonable commentators and judges may differ as to the proper boundaries of implicit text. Take, for example, the following hypothetical. A constitution contains several electoral provisions expressing the principles of democratic and equal (i.e., based on the principle of one-person-one-vote) national elections. Does this constitution also imply a constitutional right to political freedom of expression? The High Court of Australia[24] answered this question in the positive.[25] The constitutional text does indeed speak to us both explicitly and implicitly. In a conflict between the explicit and the implicit portions of the constitutional text, the explicit text should always prevail. More accurately, when a certain constitutional matter can be addressed by an explicit constitutional text, there is no room to infer an implicit conflicting constitutional text.

The distinction between explicit and implicit texts should not be confused with the distinction between the core of the constitutional right and its penumbra. Both the right's core and its penumbra constitute part of the constitutional right, regardless of whether this has been established by the explicit text or deduced from the implicit part. The difference

---

[20] See F. R. Dickerson, *The Interpretation and Application of Statutes* (Boston: Little Brown & Co., 1975), 40.

[21] See Barak, above note 3, at 104.

[22] See below, at 238.

[23] See Barak, above note 3, at 105.

[24] See *Nationwide News Pty Ltd.* v. *Wills* (1992) 177 CLR 1; *Australian Capital Television Pty Ltd.* v. *Commonwealth* (1992) 177 CLR 106; *Theophanous* v. *Herald & Weekly Ltd.* (1994) 182 CLR 211; *Cunliffe* v. *Commonwealth* (1994) 182 CLR 272; *McGinty* v. *Western Australia* (1996) 186 CLR 140; *Lange* v. *Australian Broadcasting Corp.* (1997) 189 CLR 520; *Kruger* v. *Commonwealth* (1997) 190 CLR 1; *Levy* v. *Victoria* (1997) 189 CLR 579.

[25] See below, at 55.

between core and penumbra is not related to the content of the right or its scope; rather, it relates to the notion of the extent of the right's protection, or legal realization. Therefore, the correct analytical stage in which to distinguish between core and penumbra is when applying the rules of proportionality and not during the first constitutional stage – the analysis of the right's scope.

c.   **Explicit constitutional text: parent and child rights**   A constitutional right formed by explicit language as a principle is a "framing right."[26] It contains a bundle of rights.[27] In one of the cases, this kind of right was dubbed a "mother" right."[28] In order to determine the scope of matters where such parent (mother) right applies, an interpretive derivation is required. The result of such a derivation would be a series of "particular" rights, or – as I have named them – "daughter rights"[29] (or children rights). These are rights derived from the explicit text of the constitution as interpreted by its constitutional purpose. They provide a concretization of the parent rights framework. This concretization can be analyzed at several levels of abstraction. At the end of the interpretive process the judge arrives at a set of rules determining those concrete situations in which the constitutional right applies.[30]

It should be reemphasized that these child rights, which are derived from their parental constitutional rights, should also be considered a part of the explicit constitutional text. Remember that the process of arriving at such rights is that of constitutional interpretation. Accordingly, child rights are not implicit rights. They are explicit constitutional rights. By deriving them from their parental rights through interpretation we do

---

[26] See HCJ 7052/03 *Adalah – The Legal Center for the Rights of the Arab Minority* v. *Minister of Interior* (May 14, 2006, unpublished), para. 31 (Barak, P.), available in English at http://elyon1.court.gov.il/fileseng/03/520/070/a47/03070520. a47.pdf.

[27] See C. B. Pulido, *El Principio de Proporcionalidad y los Derechos Fundamentales* (Madrid: Centro de Estudios Políticos y Constitucionales, 2007).

[28] See *Adalah* v. *Minister of the Interior*, above note 26, at para. 31 (Barak, P.). In these pages I refer to the mother rights as parent rights, and the daughter rights as child rights.

[29] *Ibid.*

[30] *Ibid* ("The right to human dignity is, in its nature, a 'framing' or a 'mother' right. A central feature of such a right is that, according to its language, it does not specify the particular situations to which it applies. It has an 'open' application … The situations, to which it applies, therefore, may be deduced from interpreting the open-textured language of the Basic Law according to its constitutional purpose. These situations may, for convenience purposes, be classified in different categories or groups. Such categories may include the right to decent human living conditions; the right to completeness of body and mind; the right to good reputation; the right (of an adult) to adopt; and many other 'daughter' rights

not fill a gap (or "lacuna") in the constitutional text,[31] but rather, consider them to be part and parcel of the explicit constitutional text itself.

Alexy draws a distinction between constitutional rights whose scope can be directly deduced from the constitutional text and derivative constitutional rights, whose scope cannot be deduced directly from the constitution, although they are necessary in the application of the constitutional norm. The latter, indirectly deduced rights are what Alexy refers to as "clarifying rights."[32] For example, the German Constitution explicitly states that "research … shall be free."[33] From this general provision we can derive the more concrete right wherein a researcher has a right against any state influence in the receipt or conveying of scientific information.[34] According to this understanding, the daughter rights are derivative rights.

The distinction between direct and clarifying application, however, is not always easy to apply. Both the direct and clarifying application are applications stemming from the interpretive process applied to the explicit text of the constitution. In fact, the only possible realization of any parent constitutional right is through its child rights, whether this realization is deduced directly or indirectly (through clarification). Therefore, the parent right cannot apply to a concrete matter without the interpretive process – either conscious or sub-conscious – of deriving child – or even grand-child – rights in a descending level of abstraction, until the point has been reached where a constitutional rule applies to the specific matter at hand. Take the Israeli constitutional parent right to human dignity. At first glance, the right to human dignity does not name the specific situations to which it applies. Naturally, there are situations in which we can safely assume that "direct" interpretation will suffice, such as in the case of preventing personal humiliation. But we can also argue that

that may be derived from the 'mother' right … Of course, determining the exact scope of the daughter rights may raise serious interpretive difficulties. As long as these rights were not separated by the constitutional assembly from the right to human dignity and therefore stand on their own, there is no escape from deriving them through an interpretive process. Such an interpretive process is focused on the parent (mother) right of human dignity while attempting to determine the right's scope, derives several categories of situations from it. Such categorization would never exhaust the list of instances on which the parent (mother) right applies, and it is not meant to do so. All it attempts to do is to assist in understanding the framing right.").

[31] On gaps (lacunae) in a constitution, see below, at 56.
[32] See R. Alexy, *A Theory of Constitutional Rights* (Julian Rivers trans., Oxford University Press, 2002 [1986]), 33.
[33] See Basic Law for the Federal Republic of Germany, Art. 5(3).
[34] See Alexy, above note 32, at 34.

this personal humiliation is governed not directly by the general parent right to human dignity, but rather by the more concrete constitutional right – a "child" right – to be protected from personal humiliation. Such a child right may beget additional ("grand-child") rights, until a constitutional rule is formed that directly applies to the specific matter at hand. In principle, there is no difference between cases in which the child right is deduced directly from the parent right and those in which it is learned by way of clarification. Both child rights are well included within the scope of their parent right; both are deduced by the same interpretive process.

d. Explicit constitutional text: named and enumerated rights   The parent right has an explicit name. Human dignity, property, liberty, privacy – are all titles explicitly provided by many constitutions to define several constitutional rights. What is the proper name, however, of a child right? The constitutional text provides a name to the "framing" or parent right. It provides no such name to child rights; indeed, they should not be given a name as they are part and parcel of their parent rights. Their name is the same as their parent's. The fact that they have no name of their own, however, does not mean that they are not a part of the explicit constitutional text. They are not "unwritten" rights. They are not rights without an explicit constitutional reference. Their text is the text of the parent right. From the text's standpoint, they enjoy the same status as their parent right. They are enumerated rights.[35] The right has no specific name; yet it is still enumerated in the constitutional text. It is not an implicit right. It is an inseparable part of the parent right.

e. Implicit constitutional text   In addition to the explicit text, there is implicit constitutional text.[36] Whatever is implied by the constitutional text is a part of the constitution no less than what is stated explicitly by it. The implied part is written into the constitution, though it is written in invisible ink. It is not written "within" the lines of the constitutional text but "between" those lines. The implicit parts of the constitution can

---

[35] See R. Dworkin, "Unenumerated Rights: Whether and How Roe Should Be Overruled," 59 *U. Chi. L. Rev.* 381 (1992).

[36] See Barak, above note 3, at 373. See also W. Sinnott-Armstrong, "Two Ways to Derive Implied Constitutional Rights," in T. D. Campbell and J. Denys Goldsworthy (eds.), *Legal Interpretation in Democratic States* (Aldershot: Ashgate Publishing, 2002), 231; J. Kirk, "Constitutional Implications (I): Nature, Legitimacy, Classification, Examples," 24 *Melb. U. L. Rev.* 645 (2000); J. Kirk, "Constitutional Implications (II): Doctrines of Equality and Democracy," 25 *Melb. U. L. Rev.* 24 (2001).

be learned from the text, its structure,[37] and its internal architecture.[38] As Tribe has correctly noted:

> The Constitution's "structure" is (borrowing Wittgenstein's famous distinction) that which the text *shows* but does not directly *say*. Diction, word repetitions, and documentary organizing form (e.g., the division of the text into articles, or the separate status of the preamble and the amendments), for example, all contribute to a sense of what the constitution is about, that is as obviously "constitutional" as are the Constitution's words as such.[39]

In similar spirit, I wrote in one case:

> The meaning of a legal text cannot be solely deduced from its explicit portion. Rather, it also includes its implicit part. At times, that meaning can be determined by a single provision. Thus, for example, an explicit text relating to a positive result in one situation may lead to an interpretive negative conclusion in an opposite case, even though that opposite case was not covered explicitly by the provision. This kind of deduction may be achieved by looking at the text's entire structure and the totality of its provisions. For example, [in the Israeli legal system] we may find an implicit recognition of the principles of separation of powers, rule of law, and independent judiciary. The language of the constitutional text is not limited to words whose meaning may be found in a dictionary. The language of the text ... must also include its implied part, its structure, its organization, and the relationship between its provisions ... It may be argued that the implicit language of the text is written between the lines of the text in invisible ink.[40]

Accordingly, constitutional provisions specifying the authority of each of the three branches – the legislative, executive, and judicial branch – as

---

[37] See C. Black, *Structure and Relationship in Constitutional Law* (Baton Rouge, LA: Louisiana State University Press, 1969), 39; A. Stone, "The Limits of Constitutional Text and Structure: Standards of Review and the Freedom of Political Communication," 23 *Melb. U. L. Rev.* 668 (1999); A. Stone, "The Limits of Constitutional Text and Structure Revisited," 28 *Univ. of New South Wales L. J.* 50 (2005).

[38] On the architecture of the constitution and of rights, see F. Schauer, "Freedom of Expression Adjudication in Europe and the United States: A Case Study in Comparative Constitutional Architecture," in G. Nolte (ed.), *European and US Constitutionalism* (Cambridge University Press, 2005), 40; *Reference re Secession of Quebec* [1998] 2 SCR 217, para. 49.

[39] L. H. Tribe, *American Constitutional Law*, 3rd edn. (New York: Foundation Press, 2000), 40. See also D. Crump, "How Do Courts Really Discover Unenumerated Fundamental Rights?: Cataloging the Methods of Judicial Alchemy," 19 *Harv. J. L. & Pub. Pol'y* 795 (1995–1996).

[40] See *Chadash-Ta'al Party v. Chairman of Knesset Election Committee Knesset*, above note 16, at 703.

well as the provisions relating to constitutional rights may imply the existence of the constitutional principles of the separation of powers and an
independent judiciary.[41] Similarly, could the constitutional provisions
relating to democratic government imply a constitutional right to political speech? As noted earlier, the High Court of Australia was of the
opinion that they could.[42] In Canada, the Supreme Court had attempted
to develop (before the Charter was adopted) an implied Bill of Rights,
derived from the general structure of the constitution. Eventually this
attempt proved unsuccessful.[43] In the United States, Justice Douglas ruled
that several constitutional rights imply, in their penumbras, the constitutional right to privacy.[44] Indeed, the constitutional structure cannot add
words to the existing text, but it can assist in providing meaning to what
is written between the lines.[45] Tribe is right, therefore, to suggest that the
constitution is not merely its explicit language, but also "the spaces which
structures fill and whose patterns structures define."[46] He is also correct
to note that alongside the visible constitution we can find "the invisible
constitution."[47]

[41] See P. R. Verkuil, "The American Constitutional Tradition of Shared and Separated
     Powers: Separation of Powers, The Rule of Law and the Idea of Independence," 30 Wm.
     and Mary L. Rev. 301 (1989); M. D. Walters, "The Common Law Constitution in Canada:
     Return of Lex Non Scripta as Fundamental Law," 51 U. Toronto L. J. 91 (2001); J. Leclair,
     "Canada's Unfathomable Unwritten Constitutional Principles," 27 Queen's L. J. 389
     (2002); D. Mullan, "The Role for Underlying Constitutional Principles in a Bill of Rights
     World," New Zealand L. Rev. 9 (2004); P. Gerangelos, "The Separation of Powers and
     Legislative Interference," in P. Gerangelos (ed.), Judicial Process: Constitutional Principles
     and Limitations (Portland, OR: Hart Publishing, 2009).
[42] This is a part of the "Implied Bill of Rights" developed in Australia by the Court. See
     above note 24. See also Sinnott-Armstrong, above note 36, at 231; Stone, above note 37;
     A. Stone, "Rights, Personal Rights and Freedoms: The Nature of the Freedom of Political
     Communication," 25 Melb. U. L. Rev. 374 (2001).
[43] See P. W. Hogg, Constitutional Law of Canada, 5th edn., vol. II (Toronto: Thomson
     Carswell, 2007), 52. See also L. Weinrib, "The Supreme Court of Canada in the Age of
     Rights: Constitutional Democracy, the Rule of Law and Fundamental Rights under
     Canada's Constitution," 80 Can. Bar Rev. 699, 710 (2001).
[44] See Griswold v. Connecticut, 381 US 479 (1965). See also P. Kauper, "Penumbras,
     Peripherals, Emanations, Things Fundamental and Things Forgotten: The Griswold
     Case," 64 Mich. L. Rev. 235 (1965); L. Henkin, "Privacy and Autonomy," 74 Colum. L.
     Rev. 1410 (1974); R. Posner, "The Uncertain Protection of Privacy by the Supreme Court,"
     Sup. Ct. Rev. 173 (1979); B. Henly, "'Penumbra': The Roots of a Legal Metaphor," 15 Hast.
     Const. L. Q. 81 (1987); Sinnott-Armstrong, above note 36, at 231.
[45] See Black, above note 37, at 39.
[46] Tribe, above note 39, at 47.
[47] See L. H. Tribe, The Invisible Constitution (Oxford University Press, 2008). See also
     Mullan, above note 41.

An important distinction should be drawn between implied constitutional language and a gap in the constitutional text.[48] Implied constitutional language is part of the existing text, although it is invisible. A gap in the constitutional text presupposes the absence of any relevant language – whether explicit or implicit – governing the issue. It assumes an incomplete constitutional structure aiming to be completed. A constitutional gap exists whenever the constitution has aimed at solving the issue at hand but ultimately failed to do so. A constitutional gap means an imperfection in the constitutional structure, in a way that contradicts its constitutional purpose. The constitutional text may therefore be compared to a brick wall, where one (or more) of the bricks is missing.[49] The gap's filling is not done merely by an interpretive analysis of the existing constitutional text; rather, it requires, in addition, para-textual activity. "The problem of interpretation is to supply a meaning to the norm; that of lacunae is to supply the norm."[50] In interpretation, the judge gives meaning to an existing, explicit or implicit text that was created by others. In filling a gap, judges themselves create text (according to criteria set by law). These kinds of actions are familiar to several European legal systems regarding the notion of filling statutory gaps.[51]

An interesting question is whether the idea of a gap and its judicial filling applies to constitutions as well. Could one say that, in some cases, when the constitution is "silent" on a particular issue, it also creates a constitutional gap? Assuming that is the case, are judges allowed to fill such a gap? Can the Australian High Court's decisions on the implied constitutional right to political speech serve as a judicial example of a constitutional gap-filling in the area of constitutional rights? Does Justice Douglas' ruling – acknowledging the existence of a constitutional right to privacy as created by the penumbra of other explicit constitutional rights – open the door to constitutional gap-filling by the American courts?

---

[48] See Barak, above note 3, at 66.
[49] *Ibid.*, at 68.
[50] J. H. Merryman, "The Italian Legal Style III: Interpretation," 18 *Stan. L. Rev.* 583, 593 (1966).
[51] This is the case in Italy. See, e.g., Italian Civil Code, Art. 12 ("If a controversy cannot be decided by a precise provision, consideration is given to provisions that regulate similar cases or analogous matters; if the case still remains in doubt, it is decided according to the general principles of the legal order of the state."); see also the Italian Civil Code (Mario Beltaremo *et al.* trans., Oceana Publications Inc., 1969). See also Barak, above note 3, at 71; W. Canaris, *Die Feststellung von Lücken im Gesetz* (Berlin: Duncker und Humblot, 1983).

The Supreme Court of Switzerland was prepared to recognize a judicial role in constitutional gap-filling.[52] The court determined that new constitutional rights can be recognized by the court whenever these rights constitute a vital component of a democracy governed by the rule of law, or in areas where those rights were required as preconditions to the realization of other explicit constitutional rights.[53] Accordingly, the Swiss Supreme Court recognized the constitutional rights to property, life and liberty, as well as the constitutional freedom of expression and assembly.

Importantly, constitutional gaps should never be used as the first option. They do not apply, for example, where the legal issue may otherwise be resolved through the interpretation of the constitutional text (explicit or implicit). Thus, the judicial recognition of child rights[54] does not constitute a gap-filling activity, as these rights derive their content from the explicit language of a constitutional right. Accordingly, the Australian High Court decision recognizing the right to political freedom of expression should not be considered a gap-filling activity to the extent that such recognition was based on the implicit meaning of the existing constitutional text. Note that the distinction between explicit and implicit meaning on the one hand and the filling of a constitutional gap on the other is extremely important, for two reasons. First, providing meaning to a constitutional text – either explicit or implicit – falls well within the legitimate judicial activity of legal interpretation. Conversely, filling a constitutional gap does not fall within the purview of legal interpretation; as a result, it requires a special, separate source of legitimacy. Such a source does not currently exist in many of the Western legal systems.[55] Second, providing meaning to the text of a constitutional human right – either explicit or implicit – is done in accordance with the specific rules of legal

---

[52] See J. F. Aubert, *Traité de Droit Constitutionnel Suisse* (Neuchatel, Switzerland: Editions Ides et Calendes, 1967), 126; J. P. Muller, *Grundrechte: Besonderer Teil* (Cologne: Carl Heymanns Verlag, 1985), 287.

[53] See L. Wildhaber, "Limitations on Human Rights in Times of Peace, War and Emergency: A Report on Swiss Law," in A. de Mestral, S. Birks, M. Both *et al.* (eds.), *The Limitation of Human Rights in Comparative Constitutional Law* (Montreal: Les Editions Yvon Blais, 1986), 41, 44.

[54] See above, at 51.

[55] See Barak, above note 3, at 66. See also J. H. Merryman, "The Italian Legal Style III: Interpretation," 18 *Stan. L. Rev.* 583, 593 (1966); C. Perelman, *Le Problème des Lacunes en Droit* (Paris: Librairie Générale de Droit et de Jurisprudence, 1968); A. E. von Overbeck, "Some Observations on the Role of the Judge under the Swiss Civil Code," 37 *La. L. Rev.* 681 (1977); C. Canaris, *Die Feststellung von Lücken im Gesetz: Eine Methodologische Studie über Voraussetzungen und Grenzen der richterlichen Rechtsfortbildung Praeter Legem* (Berlin: Duncker und Humblot, 1983).

interpretation that apply to each legal system. The rules for filling a constitutional gap, in contrast, are para-interpretational. Each legal system that recognizes the judicial role of constitutional gap-filling is also required to produce a set of para-interpretational rules for that purpose. At the center of those rules is the notion of legal analogy (to the existing text of the constitutional rights), and, in cases where such analogy is unavailable, reference to the system's basic legal values.[56]

iv.   Constitutional purpose

a.   The nature of constitutional purpose   The process of purposive constitutional interpretation requires all available interpretive data – relating to either the subjective or the objective purpose of the constitutional text – to be examined at the same time.[57] There are no "stages" in the consideration of the "subjective" set of data and the "objective" set. Both are considered at the same time.

To begin, a constitutional text cannot be properly understood without taking into account the intent of its creators;[58] similarly, a constitutional text cannot be properly understood without considering its original understanding. Yet, the ultimate meaning of the constitutional text – while affected by both subjective and original understanding of the text – cannot be dominated by either. A vital component of the purpose of the constitutional text is its objective purpose. Purposive constitutional interpretation seeks to create a synthesis between the subjective and the objective data regarding the constitutional purpose.[59] The interpretive process does not call for a confrontation between the two sets of data, but rather to harmonize them.

What, then, should the interpreter do when the two sets of data do not align, when the subjective purpose points to one interpretative direction while the objective to another? According to purposive constitutional interpretation, in cases of a conflict between the two, the objective purpose – the understanding of the text at the time the interpretation is conducted – should prevail.[60] In other words, the objective purpose should be given more weight while balancing both sets of data. Only in that way can the constitution fulfill its most crucial social functions – the direction of

---

[56] *Ibid.*, at 71.   [57] *Ibid.*, at 385.

[58] See M. C. Dorf, "Integrating Normative and Descriptive Constitutional Theory: The Case of Original Meaning," 85 *Geo. L. J.* 1765 (1997).

[59] See Barak, above note 3, at 385.

[60] See Du Plessis, above note 1, at para. 32–43.

human behavior across generations of social change, and the provision of legal solutions to modern, evolving needs. The constitution must do all that, while properly balancing the past, the present, and the future of the society it governs. Indeed, the past may significantly affect the present, yet it should not determine it. The past may effectively direct the present, yet it should not enslave it. The basic concepts of society – which stem from the past and are intertwined in the legal and social history of a nation – should find their modern expression in the original constitutional text.[61]

Both the subjective purpose and the original understanding should be considered, though not be attributed a controlling weight, during the interpretation of the constitutional text.[62] This approach, considering past interpretations, while not according them a central interpretive role, is well accepted by many of the Western legal systems. This, for example, is

[61] See W. Brennan, "Construing the Constitution," 19 *UC Davis L. Rev.* 2, 7 (1985) ("We current Justices read the Constitution in the only way that we can: as Twentieth Century Americans. We look to the history of the time of framing and to the intervening history of interpretation. But the ultimate question must be, what do the words of the text mean in our time? For the genius of the Constitution rests not in any static meaning it might have had in a world that is dead and gone, but in the adaptability of its great principles to cope with current problems and current needs. What the constitutional fundamentals meant to the wisdom of other times cannot be their measure to the vision of our times. Similarly, what those fundamentals mean for us, our descendants will learn, cannot be the measure to the vision of their time."); see also M. Kirby, "Constitutional Interpretation and Original Intent: A Form of Ancestor Worship," 24 *Melb. U. L. Rev.* 1, 14 (2000) ("[I]n the kind of democracy which a constitution such as ours establishes, judges should make their choices by giving meaning to the words in a way that protects and advances the essential character of the polity established by the constitution. In Australia, this function is to be performed without the need constantly to look over one's shoulder and to refer to understandings of the text that were common in 1900 when the society which the Constitution addresses was so different. It is today's understanding that counts. Reference to 1900, if made at all, should be in the minor key and largely for historical interest. Not for establishing legal limitations. In my opinion, a consistent application of the view that the Constitution was set free from its founders in 1900 is the rule that we should apply. That our Constitution belongs to succeeding generations of the Australian people. That is bound to be read in changing ways as time passes and circumstances change. That it should be read so as to achieve the purposes of good government which the Constitution was designed to promote and secure. Our Constitution belongs to the 21st century, not to the 19th."); M. Kirby, "Australian Law – After 11 September 2001," 21 *ABR* 1, 9 (2001) ("Given the great difficulty of securing formal constitutional change, it is just as well that the High Court has looked creatively at the document put in its charge. Had this not been done, our Constitution would have remained an instrument for giving effect to no more than the aspirations of rich white males of the nineteenth century. Fortunately, we have done better than this."); *Re Wakin* (1993) 73 ALJR 839, 878. See also B. Wilson, "Decision-Making in the Supreme Court," 36 *U. Toronto L. J.* 227, 247 (1986).

[62] See Barak, above note 3, at 386.

the approach adopted in Canada. The Canadian Supreme Court grants little interpretive weight to either the constitution's original understanding or to its framers' intentions.[63] In one case, the Court examined section 7 of the Canadian Charter of Rights and Freedoms, which provides:

> Everyone has the right to life, liberty and security of the person and the right not to be deprived thereof *except in accordance with the principles of fundamental justice.*[64]

The issue was whether the notion of "fundamental justice" appearing in the constitutional text should be read as a procedural requirement or of substantial nature. One of the arguments in favor of the procedural aspect was that when the Charter was adopted this was the drafters' original intention. It was further demonstrated that the drafters deliberately chose to refrain from using the American term "due process," given the controversy surrounding it. In order to avoid such controversies and to assure the procedural – rather than the substantive – nature of the Canadian term, the drafters opted for an entirely new expression. And yet, the Canadian Supreme Court has decided to accord little weight to this subjective purpose. As Justice Lamer explained:

> Another danger with casting the interpretation of S. 7 in terms of the comments made by those heard at the Special Joint Committee Proceedings is that, in so doing, the rights, freedoms, and values embodied in the Charter in effect become frozen in time to the moment of adoption with little or no possibility of growth, development and adjustment to changing social needs. If the newly planted "living tree" which is the Charter is to have the possibility of growth and adjustment over time, care must be taken to ensure that historical materials … do not stunt its growth.[65]

A similar approach was expressed by the Australian High Court.[66] That court emphasized that it should not accord dispositive weight to the "dead

---

[63] See Hogg, above note 43, at 52.

[64] See Canadian Charter of Rights and Freedoms, above, at 7, Art. 7 (emphasis added).

[65] Re BC Motor Vehicle Act [1985] 2 SCR 486, 504; see also *R. v. Therens* [1985] 1 SCR 613, 623; *Mahe v. Alta* [1990] SCR 342, 369.

[66] See H. Patapan, "The Dead Hands of the Founders?: Original Intent and the Constitutional Protection of Rights and Freedoms in Australia," 25 *Fed. L. Rev.* 211 (1997). See also *Theophenous* v. *Herald Weekly Time Ltd.* (1995) 182 CLR 104, 106 ("[E]ven if it could be established that it was the unexpressed intention of the framers of the Constitution that the failure to follow the United States model should preclude or impede the implication of constitutional rights, their intention in that regard would be simply irrelevant to the construction of provisions whose legitimacy lay in their acceptance by the people. Moreover, to construe the Constitution on the basis that the dead hands of those who

hands" of the framers, who attempt to control the meaning of the constitution from their graves. This is also the approach adopted by the German
Constitutional Court. In one case, the court examined the question of
whether a mandatory sentence of life imprisonment without parole violates the constitutional right to human dignity. The court decided it does.
It concluded that inmates should have at least a trace of hope for a better future, and that to eliminate such hope would be unconstitutional.
It was argued that the framers' intention was to preserve mandatory
life sentences without parole, and that this punishment was intended as
a replacement of the death penalty. The court rejected this "subjective"
interpretation. The court explained:

> Neither original understanding nor the ideas and intentions of the fram-
> ers are of decisive importance in interpreting particular provisions of the
> Basic Law. Since the adoption of the Basic Law, our understanding of the
> content, function, and effect of basic rights has deepened. Additionally,
> the medical, psychological, and sociological effects of life imprisonment
> have become better known. Current attitudes are important in assess-
> ing the constitutionality of the imprisonment. New insights can influence
> and even change the evaluation of this punishment in terms of human
> dignity and the principles of a constitutional state.[67]

Summarizing the accepted interpretive approach in Germany, Professor
Kommers explains:

> [I]n Germany, original history – that is, the intentions of the framers – is
> seldom dispositive in resolving the meaning of the Basic Law. The court
> has declared that "the original history of a particular provision of the
> Basic Law has no decisive importance in constitutional interpretation."
> Original history performs, at best, the auxiliary function of landing sup-
> port to a result already arrived at by other interpretive methods. When
> there is a conflict, however, arguments based on text, structure, or tele-
> ology will prevail over those based on history.[68]

---

framed it reached from their graves to negate or constrict the natural implications of
its express provisions or fundamental doctrines would deprive what was intended to
be a living instrument of its vitality and adaptability to serve succeeding generations."
(Deane, J.)).
[67] German Constitutional Court, *In Re Life Imprisonment*, BVerfGE 45, 187 (translated into
English by D. Kommers). See also D. Kommers, *The Constitutional Jurisprudence of The
Federal Republic of Germany*, 2nd edn. (Durham, NC: Duke University Press, 1977), 307.
[68] See *ibid.*, at 42. See also K. H. Friauf, "Techniques for the Interpretation of Constitutions
in German Law," in *Proceedings of the Fifth International Symposium on Comparative
Law* (1968), 12; C. Starck, "Constitutional Interpretation," in *Studies in German
Constitutionalism: The German Contributions to the Fourth World Congress of the
International Association of Constitutional Law* (Nomos, 1995), 45; W. Bradford,

In these legal systems – Canada, Australia, Israel and Germany – neither the original understanding, nor the intent of the framers, occupies a central role in judicial consideration of constitutional interpretation.[69] Of course, neither is ignored; but they remain far from being the discussion's focal point.

This approach was not adopted in the United States. There is hardly a consensus regarding the proper weight to be accorded to past interpretations. Instead, in the United States, the competing notions of original intent of the founding fathers (also known as "intentionalism"), the original understanding of the terms used in the Constitution ("originalism"), and the "living constitution"[70] are all sources of an ongoing debate in academic writing and on the bench.[71] Indeed, the United States Supreme Court itself is – and has been for years – divided on this issue.[72] The entire corpus of American constitutional law finds itself in a state of crisis due

"Barbarians at the Gates: A Post-September 11th Proposal to Rationalize the Laws of War," 73 *Miss. L. J.* 639 (2004).

[69] See C. L'Heureux-Dubé, "The Importance of Dialogue: Globalization, the Rehnquist Court and Human Rights," in M. H. Belskey (ed.), *The Rehnquist Court: A Retrospective* (New York: Oxford University Press, 2002), 234.

[70] See below, at 65.

[71] The literature on the issue is vast. See, e.g., Tribe, above note 39, at 47–70 (and the sources cited therein); see also W. Kaplin, "The Process of Constitutional Interpretation: A Synthesis of the Present and a Guide to the Future," 42 *Rutgers L. Rev.* 983 (1990); M. Perry, "The Legitimacy of Particular Conceptions of Constitutional Interpretation," 77 *Va. L. Rev.* 669 (1991); R. Kelso, "Styles of Constitutional Interpretation and the Four Main Approaches to Constitutional Interpretation in American Legal History," 29 *Valp. U. L. Rev.* 121 (1994); S. J. Brison and W. Sinnot-Armstrong (eds.), *Contemporary Perspectives on Constitutional Interpretation* (1993); W. N. Eskridge, *Dynamic Statutory Interpretation* (Cambridge, MA: Harvard University Press, 1994); J. N. Rakove, *Original Meanings: Politics and Ideas in the Making of the Constitution* (New York: Vintage Books, 1996); A. Scalia, *A Matter of Interpretation: Federal Courts and the Law* (Amy Gutmann (ed.), Princeton University Press, 1997); D. J. Goldford, *The American Constitution and the Debate over Originalism* (Cambridge University Press, 2005); S. G. Calabresi (ed.), *Originalism: A Quarter-Century of Debate* (2007); J. O'Neil, *Originalism in American Law and Politics: A Constitutional History* (Baltimore, MD: Johns Hopkins University Press, 2007); S. D. Smith, "That Old-Time Originalism" (San Diego *Legal Studies* Paper No. 08–028); J. Greene, "On the Origins of Originalism," 88 *Tex. L. Rev.* 1 (2009); L. Alexander, "Simple-Minded Originalism," in G. Huscroft and B. Miller (eds.), *The Challenge of Originalism: Essays in Constitutional Theory* (forthcoming, 2011).

[72] See, e.g., *West Virginia University Hospitals Inc.* v. *Casey*, 499 US 83, 112 (1991) (Stevens, J. dissenting). See also M. C. Dorf, "Foreword: The Limits of Socratic Deliberation", 112 *Harv. L. Rev.* 4, 4 (1998); compare Justice Brennan's position, above note 61, to A. Scalia, "Modernity and the Constitution," in E. Smith (ed.), *Constitutional Justice under Old Constitutions* (The Hague: Kluwer Law International, 1995), 313, 315: "I do not worry about my old Constitution 'obstructing modernity,' since I take that to be its whole

to this lack of consensus. Without accord in the legal community about the proper role that original intent, original understanding, and current notions of constitutional interpretation should play in determining the meaning of constitutional provisions today, the entire constitutional system is hanging in the balance.[73] A crisis of this sort has been avoided in Canada, Australia, Germany and Israel. Hopefully, other constitutional legal systems will successfully avoid this dangerous situation, which may tear apart the legal system as well as focus all legal energy on the crisis.

According to the purposive constitutional interpretation approach, the intent of the framers or the original understanding should not be ignored; however, they should not be of higher status.[74] It is the objective – rather than the subjective – purpose that should be accorded most of the interpretive weight. The objective purpose properly reflects the basic modern notions of the legal system as it moves across history. This is how a constitution turns into a living document rather than remains stagnant parchment. This is how the present is not subjugated by the past. Indeed, constitutional interpretation is the process in which every generation expresses its own basic concepts as they were shaped against the nation's historical background.[75] This process is not limitless; it is not open-ended. The interpreter, providing meaning to the constitutional text, must work within a given social and historical framework. And, although the judge is sometimes accorded judicial discretion by the system, this discretion

purpose. The very objective of a basic law, it seems to me, is to place certain matters beyond risk of change, except through the extraordinary democratic majorities that constitutional amendment requires ... The whole *purpose* of a constitution – old or new – is to impede change, or, pejoratively put, to 'abstract modernity.'"

[73] That includes the approach of the founding fathers themselves, who wanted the Constitution to be interpreted according to its objective purpose. See, e.g., J. Powell, "The Original Understanding of Original Intent," 98 *Harv. L. Rev.* 885 (1985); R. Clinton, "Original Understanding, Legal Realism, and the Interpretation of 'This Constitution'," 72 *Iowa L. Rev.* 1177 (1987); C. A. Lofgren, "The Original Understanding of Original Intent?," 5 *Const. Comment.* 77 (1988); P. Finkelman, "The Constitution and the Intention of the Framers: The Limits of Historical Analysis," 50 *U. Pitt. L. Rev.* 349 (1989); H. Baade, "'Original Intent' in Historical Perspective: Some Critical Glosses," 69 *Tex. L. Rev.* 1001 (1991); S. Sherry, "The Founders' Unwritten Constitution," 54 *U. Chi. L. Rev.* 1127 (1994); W. Michael, "The Original Understanding of Original Intent: A Textual Analysis," 26 *Ohio N. U. L. Rev.* 201 (2000).

[74] For criticism of my approach, see S. Fish, "Intention Is All There Is: A Critical Analysis of Aharon Barak's Purposive Interpretation in Law," 29 *Cardozo L. Rev.* 1109 (2008). Regarding intentionalism, see L. Alexander, "Of Living Trees and Dead Hands: The Interpretation of Constitutions and Constitutional Rights," 22 *Can. J. L. & Juris.* 227 (2009).

[75] See T. Sandalow, "Constitutional Interpretation," 79 *Mich. L. Rev.* 1033, 1068 (1981).

is bounded by a limited set of values, traditions, history, and text that are unique to the system in which he operates. Indeed, the process of eliciting a constitutional purpose is based on fundamental concepts that seek to create a strong link to the constitutional past and grant it its due weight. The interpreter does not disconnect from the system's constitutional history. And, while the ultimate modern constitutional purpose is objective, its roots lie far in the constitutional past. "The constitutional provision was not legislated in a constitutional vacuum and does not develop in a constitutional incubator. Rather, it is a part of life."[76]

b.   Constitutional purpose and the protection of constitutional rights   There are those – such as Justice Scalia[77] – who argue that providing a modern meaning to the constitutional text contradicts one of the constitution's main functions, namely, the protection of individuals from the majority. According to this view, should the constitution be interpreted in accordance with current views it would only reflect the current majority's concept of what is right. These views, in turn, will affect individual rights that the majority seeks to limit. Accordingly, the constitution should be interpreted only in light of its original understanding in order to prevent such results. The response to this argument is that a current understanding of constitutional rights does not entail an adoption of the current majority's views on what is right. The process of the purposive interpretation of constitutional rights considers the most fundamental values of any given society, which reflect its long-standing views rather than its current, transient fads. At times, the judge may find it hard to disregard society's current trends and to continue reflecting on these fundamental views. At times, it will be harder to rely on well-established notions of history rather than to abide by current notions of public hysteria. Still, judges must perform their task, and indeed have been performing this task ever since the establishment of constitutional democracies. Judges will continue to do so while attempting to interpret their own constitutions. According to this interpretive process, each constitutional right should be accorded the same scope that best reflects the reasons justifying it. These reasons, in turn, reflect the legal system's movement across time well.

---

[76]   See *United Mizrahi Bank*, above note 6, at 235 (Barak, P.).
[77]   See A. Scalia, "Originalism: The Lesser Evil," 57 *U. Chi. L. Rev.* 849 (1989).

v.   "Living constitution" and "living tree"

One of the constitution's main functions is to enable each society to successfully confront its changing circumstances over time. When the constitution was first constituted, its framers sought to lay a foundation for a document that would govern society for generations to come. So as not to become tyrannical, however, this legal document also contains flexible mechanisms for future developments. This is the meaning of the metaphor about "a living constitution." The "life" of the constitution is not solely made up of the application of its old principles to new cases;[78] rather, the constitution's "life" also means pouring new content into old constitutional principles.[79] For the same reasons, the metaphor of "a living tree" is used in Canada.[80] But the image of a living tree also points to the metaphor's limitations: The "livelihood" of basic constitutional values is not an open invitation for the judge to change them at will. The subjective will of the constitution's creators should not be replaced by the subjective will of its interpreters. Rather, the changing content of constitutional values should reflect a change in the basic concepts of the society regarding its national creed. These changes reflect the history, tradition, and shared faith of each nation. They are not – and should not be considered as – an expression of the judge's personal ideas.

vi.   Comparative constitutional interpretation

Many democracies share basic values. Therefore, democracies can learn from one another.[81] Through comparative law, constitutional horizons may be broadened.[82] This is obviously the case when the constitutional

---

[78] For arguments against the concept of "living constitution," see, e.g., W. Rehnquist, "The Notion of a Living Constitution," 54 *Tex. L. Rev.* 693 (1976); R. Bork, *The Tempting of America: The Political Seduction of the Law* (New York: Touchstone, 1990), 163; Alexander, above note 71.

[79] See above, at 61 (Judge Deane).

[80] See *Edwards* v. *AG of Canada* [1930] AC 124, 136 (PC) (Lord Sankey) ("A constitution is a living tree capable of growth and expansion within its natural limits."). For this approach, see L. Walton, "Making Sense of Canadian Constitutional Interpretation," 12 *National Journal of Constitutional Law* 315 (2001); B. W. Miller, "Beguiled by Metaphors: The 'Living Tree' and Originalist Constitutional Interpretation in Canada," 22 *Can. J. L. & Jurisprudence* 331(2009).

[81] See generally S. Choudhry, "Globalization in Search of Justification: Toward a Theory of Comparative Constitutional Interpretation," 74 *Ind. L. J.* 819 (1999); A. Torres Pérez, *Conflicts of Rights in the European Union. A Theory of Supranational Adjudication* (Oxford University Press, 2009), 141.

[82] See A. Slaughter, "A Typology of Transjudicial Communication," 29 *U. Rich. L. Rev.* 99 (1994); G. P. Fletcher, "Comparative Law as Subversive Discipline," 46 *Am. J. Comp. L.*

text of one nation is influenced by another,[83] or by an international convention.[84] But this may also be the case, albeit to a lesser extent, without the direct or indirect influence of one democracy on another.[85] Legal systems may still learn from each other whenever their constitutions refer to

683 (1998); V. Jackson and M. Tushnet, *Comparative Constitutional Law* (New York: Foundation Press, 1999); S. Choudhry, "Globalization in Search of Justification: Toward a Theory of Comparative Constitutional Interpretation," 74 *Ind. L. J.* 819 (1999); K. Perales, "It Works Fine in Europe, So Why Not Here? Comparative Law and Constitutional Federalism," 23 *Vt. L. Rev.* 885 (1999); M. Tushnet, "The Possibilities of Comparative Constitutional Law," 108 *Yale L. J.* 1225 (1999); C. McCrudden, "A Part of the Main?: The Physician-Assisted Suicide Case and Comparative Law Methodology in the United States Supreme Court," in C. Schneider (ed.), *Law at the End of Life: The Supreme Court and Assisted Suicide* (Ann Arbor, MI: University of Michigan Press, 2000); C. McCrudden, "A Common Law of Human Rights? Transnational Judicial Conversations on Constitutional Rights," 20 *OJLS* 499 (2000); L. Weinrib, "Constitutional Concepts and Constitutional Comparativism," in V. Jackson and M. Tushnet (eds.), *Defining the Field of Comparative Constitutional Law* (Westport, CT: Praeger, 2002), 23; V. Jackson, "Constitutional Comparisons: Convergence, Resistance, Engagement," 119 *Harv. L. Rev.* 109 (2005); G. Sitaraman, "The Use and Abuse of Foreign Law in Constitutional Interpretation," 32 *Harv. J. L. & Pub. Pol'y* 653 (2009); V. Jackson, *Constitutional Engagement in a Transnational Era* (Oxford University Press, 2010), 114; T. Bingham, *Widening Horizons: The Influence of Comparative Law and International Law on Domestic Law* (Cambridge University Press, 2010).

[83] The primary example is the influence the American Constitution had on several legal systems, including those of Japan and Argentina. These situations can be referred to as "legal migrations." See also *United States* v. *Then*, 56 F 3d 464, 469 (2d Cir. 1995) (Calabresi, J., concurring) ("These countries are our 'constitutional offspring' and how they have dealt with problems analogous to ours can be very useful to us when we face difficult constitutional issues. Wise parents do not hesitate to learn from their children."). See also Jackson and Tushnet, above note 82, at 169. Another example is the influence the Canadian Charter has had on the constitutional law of South Africa. See, e.g., J. de Waal, "A Comparative Analysis of the Provisions of German Origin in the Interim Bill of Rights," 11 *SAJHR* 1 (1995); P. W. Hogg, "Canadian Law in the Constitutional Court of South Africa," 13 *SAPL* 1 (1998); H. Cheadle, "Limitation of Rights," in H. Cheadle, N. Haysom, and D. Davis (eds.), *South African Constitutional Law: The Bill of Rights* (Cape Town: Juta Law Publishers, 2002), 693. Yet another example is the influence the German Basic Law has had on the constitutional law of Spain and Portugal. See, e.g., J. Kokott, "From Reception and Transplantation to Convergence of Constitutional Models in the Age of Globalization – With Particular Reference to the German Basic Law," in C. Starck (ed.), *Constitutionalism, Universalism and Democracy – A Comparative Analysis: The German Contributions to the Fifth World Congress of the International Association of Constitutional Law* (Berlin: Nomos Verlagsgesellschaft, 1999), 71.

[84] See Human Rights Act 1998, section 2(1)(a): "A court or tribunal determining a question which has arisen in connection with a Convention right must take into account any judgment, decision, declaration or advisory opinion of the European Court of Human Rights."

[85] See, e.g., D. Kommers, "The Value of Comparative Constitutional Law," 9 *Marshall J. Practice & Procedure* 685 (1976).

shared democratic values.[86] Even in the absence of such shared reference, an interpretive influence is still available through the study of comparative constitutional law. However, such comparative inspiration should occur only when the two systems share an ideological framework and loyalty to the same basic constitutional values.[87] Similarly, the two systems should be examined in order to reveal any distinct historical or social factors that may render interpretational inspiration untenable.[88] However, when such limitations do not exist and a common constitutional basis is shared, a comparative-law interpretive inspiration may be helpful – whether the comparative source is another legal system or international law itself. Indeed, many international treaties contain well-established constitutional values and thus may prove helpful in the understanding of a particular constitutional text. Further, the rulings of international and

---

[86] HCJ 428/86 *Barzilai* v. *Government of Israel* [1986] IsrSC 40(3) 505 ("Since the establishment of the State of Israel, we have drawn extensively from the constitutional wells of the United States and England. The manner in which these legal systems treat many constitutional issues, including human rights, has been a major source of inspiration. With that, this type of learning should be controlled. Inspiration is useful if and only if the two systems share the same legal basis. Accordingly, a real comparison may happen only between institutions and processes that share common basis." (Barak, J.)) (available in English at http://elyon1.court.gov.il/files_eng/86/280/004/Z01/86004280.z01.pdf. In that case, I refused (in dissent) to accept constitutional interpretive guidance regarding the authority to provide a pre-trial pardon from either the authorities given to the English Crown or to the American President. I have noted the many differences between the Israeli system and these two legal institutions on that particular issue. See also F. Iacobucci, "The Charter: Twenty Years Later," 21 *Windsor Y. B. Access. Just.* 3 (2002).

[87] See, e.g., *Stanford* v. *Kentucky*, 492 US 361, 370 n.1 (1989) (referring to the "evolving standard of decency that marks the progress of a maturing society" as relating to the Eighth Amendment's ban on "cruel and unusual" punishment) ("We emphasize that it is *American* conceptions of decency that are dispositive, rejecting the contention of petitioners and their various *amici* (accepted by the dissent …) that the sentencing practices of other countries are relevant." (Scalia, J.)). While I agree with Justice Scalia that the final decision should be "American" in nature, I also agree with the dissent that, in the process of making that decision, a comparative interpretational inspiration may be of assistance – especially with countries whose treatment of constitutional human rights in general and the sanctity of human life in particular is quite similar to that of the United States. See also *Prinz* v. *United States*, 521 US 898 (1997); *Thompson* v. *Oklahoma*, 487 US 815 (1988).

[88] See, e.g., P. Legrand, "European Legal Systems Are Not Converging," 45 *Int'l & Comp. L. Q.* 52 (1996); M. Tushnet, "The Possibilities of Comparative Constitutional Law," 108 *Yale L. J.* 1225 (1999); M. Tushnet, "Some Reflections on Method in Comparative Constitutional Law," in S. Choudhry (ed.), *The Migration of Constitutional Ideas* (Cambridge University Press, 2006), 67; J. Bomhoff, "Balancing, the Global and the Local: Judicial Balancing as a Problematic Topic in Comparative (Constitutional) Law," 31 *Hastings Int'l & Comp. L. Rev.* 555 (2008).

local courts – interpreting those treaties – may provide guidance in the interpretation of a national constitutional text. In some cases, the constitution itself includes a provision incorporating – or allowing for the consideration of – comparative legal sources.[89]

It should be noted, however, that the rulings of foreign courts are never binding.[90] In fact, they are not even a "persuasive" source. Their authority should therefore not be compared to that of a Supreme Court ruling, which in most legal systems does not bind the Supreme Court itself. Indeed, the proper status of comparative legal materials is similar to that of a good book on the subject or a leading law-review article. Thus, the weight is determined more by the content of its discussion, than by an official measure.[91]

This measured approach towards the use of comparative constitutional law is not shared by all; in particular, the issue has created a deep

[89] See, e.g., South African Constitution, Art. 39(1)(b) and (c) ("When interpreting the Bill of Rights, a court, tribunal or forum … (b) must consider international law; and (c) may consider foreign law."); Spanish Constitution, Art. 10(2) ("The norms relative to basic rights and liberties which are recognized by the Constitution shall be interpreted in conformity with the Universal Declaration of Human Rights and the international treaties and agreements on those matters ratified by Spain.").

[90] See G. H. Patrick, "Persuasive Authority," 32 *McGill L. J.* 261 (1987).

[91] See HCJ 1715/97 *Israel Investment Managers Association* v. *Minister of Finance* [1997] IsrSC 51(4) 367, 403 ("Comparative law is a source of great importance to constitutional interpretation. To the extent that regulation in both systems is based upon shared basic assumptions, comparative inspiration may be of great value. Such comparison invigorates constitutional thinking and provides new theoretical horizons. It points to the potential that hides in the constitutional text; it sheds light on the legal arrangements practiced in other countries. It provides a mirror through which we can view ourselves in a clearer, brighter light. Indeed, the examination of comparative law provides the judge with confidence, in the sense that the solution he may provide has already been tried and tested in other places. With that, such comparative inspiration should not turn into automatic adaptation. The final decision is always 'domestic.' Further, comparative law has its own limitations. The legal system of each democracy reflects much of its society's attributes; ours are different from others. The weight of authority given by each legal system to certain considerations reflects its culture, its history, and its values – and these vary from one nation to another. Particular regulative arrangements often reflect local balances of power, or try to provide an answer to a specific, local issue. Finally, comparative analysis should never be limited to the technical comparison of similar provisions. Such comparison is of no value. A proper comparative study should examine the entire regulatory framework against the background of shared constitutional basic assumptions." (Barak, P.)). See also S. K. Harding, "Comparative Reasoning and Judicial Review," 28 *Yale J. Int'l L.* 409 (2003); S. Choudhry, "The Lochner Era and Comparative Constitutionalism," 2 *Int'l J. Const. L.* 1 (2004); S. Woolman, "Metaphors and Mirages: Some Marginalia on Choudhry's The Lochner Era and Comparative Constitutionalism and Ready-Made Constitutional Narratives," 20 (2) *SAPL* 281 (2005).

rift within the American legal system.[92] There, the "originalist" camp –
supporting the notion that the original understanding should govern
the interpretation of the constitutional text – strenuously opposes the
idea of considering any comparative or foreign law not part of such
understanding.[93] Despite that, the pattern in American law seems to
have moved in the direction of more openness towards foreign and comparative law.[94] It is hoped the Court will proceed in this direction.[95]

2. Constitutional interpretation: a generous view

i. Constitutional interpretation: generous, not expanding

A constitutional provision should be interpreted generously,[96] from a "substantive" rather than a "legalistic" approach, from a merit-based rather
than a "technical" or "pedantic" approach.[97] Even generous interpretation is still bound by the contours of the constitutional text.[98] Generous
interpretation does not entail an interpretive result. However, generous
interpretation may lead to either an expansive or a narrow interpretive
result. This is necessary, as what constitutes an "expansive interpretation"
of one constitutional provision may lead to a "limited interpretation" of
another.

---

[92] See above, at 62.

[93] See J. E. Khushal Murkens, "Comparative Constitutional Law in the Courts: Reflections
on the Originalists' Objections" (LSE *Legal Studies*, Working Paper No. 15/2008).

[94] See, e.g., V. C. Jackson, "Ambivalent Resistance and Comparative Constitutionalism:
Opening Up the Conversation on 'Proportionality', Rights and Federalism," 1 *U. Pa. J.
Const. L.* 583 (1999); J. Waldron, "Foreign Law and the Modern Ius Gentium," 119 *Harv.
L. Rev.* 129 (2005); M. Cohen-Eliya and I. Porat, "The Hidden Foreign Law Debate in
Heller: The Proportionality Approach in American Constitutional Law", 46 *San Diego
L. Rev.* 367 (2009).

[95] See S. Gardbaum, "The Myth and the Reality of American Constitutional Exceptionalism,"
107 *Mich. L. Rev.* 391, 408 (2008).

[96] See, e.g., *Minister of Home Affairs* v. *Fisher* [1979] 3 All ER 21, 25 ("A generous interpretation avoiding what has been called 'the austerity of tabulate legalism' suitable to
give to individuals the full measure of the fundamental rights and freedoms referred to."
(Lord Wilberforce)); in Canada, see *R.* v. *Big M Drug Mart* [1985] 1 SCR 295, 344 ("The
interpretation should be … a generous rather than legalistic one, aimed at fulfilling the
purpose of the guarantee and securing for the individual the full benefit of the Charter's
protection." (Dickson, J.)).

[97] See *Australian Nat'l Airways Pty Ltd.* v. *Commonwealth* (1945) 71 CLR 29, 81 ("we should
avoid pedantic and narrow construction in dealing with [such] an instrument of government" (Dixon, J.)).

[98] See Barak, above note 3, at 391.

ii.   Harmony-enhancing constitutional interpretation

Generous constitutional interpretation should provide a meaning that, more than any other, realizes the purpose of the constitutional text. This purpose reflects historical continuity and the modern fundamental constitutional concepts. It should achieve unity and constitutional harmony.[99] Further, generous interpretation is not solely limited to the meaning of the words in the historical-linguistic context in which they were created. Rather, it provides the constitution's language with a meaning reflecting both the historical context and the modern fundamental constitutional concepts.[100]

iii.   Generous interpretation of the constitutional right

The language of the constitutional text protecting rights should be interpreted according to its purpose from a generous point of view. Therefore, the text should be interpreted in a way that realizes the reasons underlying

[99] See Israeli Supreme Court, *United Mizrahi Bank*, above note 6, at 430 (Barak, P.); Barzilay, above note 86, at 595 (Justice Barak, dissenting) ("Every constitutional provision is but a brick in the entire constitutional structure. That structure is founded on each legal system's basic notions of law and society. Accordingly, the role of the judge-interpreter, while approaching a constitutional provision, is to create harmony between that provision and the foundations of constitutional law already existing in that system."); HCJ 4676/94 *Meatrael* v. *The Israeli Knesset* PD 50 (5) 15, 29 (1996) ("A proper interpretive concept regarding constitutional arrangements – even if they exist in separate documents – should always aspire towards constitutional unity. A constitutional norm does not stand on its own. It is always a part of a constitutional edifice. It is but one brick of an entire constitutional structure ... Each constitutional provision affects its constitutional surroundings. Thus, to interpret one constitutional provision is to interpret the entire constitutional framework. A single constitutional provision affects the understanding of the entire constitutional edifice, and that constitutional edifice, in turn, affects the understanding of the single provision ... Constitutional interpretation, therefore, should aspire to a result by which all the constitutional provisions – even when they are spread across several documents – should be integrated in a way providing constitutional harmony and systematic unity." (Barak, P.)). See also German Constitutional Court, BVerfGE 14, 32 ("A specific constitutional provision cannot be interpreted as a sole provision, unrelated to other constitutional provisions. The constitution contains an internal unity, and the understanding of each part directly relates to the understanding of other portions. As unity, the constitution reflects fundamental values and basic social determinations; each constitutional provision must abide by this unity principle."). See also *Dubois* v. *The Queen* [1985] 2 SCR 350, 365 ("Our constitutional charter must be construed as a system where 'every component contributes to the meaning as a whole, and the whole gives meaning to its parts' ... The courts must interpret each section of the Charter in relation to the others." (Lamer, J.)).
[100] See *Gompers* v. *United States*, 233 US 604, 610 (1914) ("The provisions of the Constitution are not mathematical formulas having their essence in their form, they are organic living institutions transplanted from English soil. Their significance is vital, not formal; it is to be gathered, not simply by taking the words and a dictionary, but by considering their origin and the line of their growth." (Holmes, J.)).

the right itself. It should reflect the full scope of the ideals that a particular right is seeking to achieve within a given society.[101] It should reflect the moral considerations underlying the right. These reasons change from time to time, and from one legal system to another. The interpretation of the constitutional text protecting a constitutional right should not include, as per its proper interpretation, tenuously related issues not reflecting the reasons for which it was made. Accordingly, for example, the right to freedom of expression should not be interpreted as including the right to commit perjury, or the right to issue threats, or the right to freedom of contract.[102] Rather, such interpretation should reflect the spectrum of reasons underlying the right's creation. For that reason, the right's scope should not be limited through interpretation merely due to public interest considerations,[103] or the rights of others.[104] These considerations should be taken into account in the second stage of the constitutional review. No such balancing should be conducted at the first stage.[105] For the same reasons, the right's scope should not be narrowed solely because the case at hand involves an "abuse of rights."[106] Even an abuse of rights presupposes the existence of the right itself, and that very existence should determine the right's scope. Of course, the abuse should be considered and will probably have consequences at a later stage, but has no place during the determination of the right's scope. The abuse is to be considered during the discussion of the extent of the right's protection and of its realization.

iv.   The relationship between the interpretation of the right
       and the interpretation of the limitation

According to a view found in the literature, the broad interpretation of a constitutional right should lead to the broad interpretation of the rules of proportionality contained in the limitation clause; narrow interpretation of the right, in turn, should lead to narrow interpretation of the rules of proportionality.[107] According to this view, once the right has been

---

[101] See L. H. Tribe and M. C. Dorf, "Levels of Generality in the Definition of Rights," 57 *U. Chi. L. Rev.* 1057 (1990).

[102] See F. Schauer, "Categories and the First Amendment: A Play in Three Acts," 34 *Vand. L. Rev.* 265 (1981); A. E. Sen, "Elements of a Theory of Human Rights Export," 32(4) *Philosophy and Public Affairs* 315 (2004).

[103] See below, at 75.   [104] See below, at 81.

[105] See CCT 23/95 *Ferreira* v. *Levin NO*, 1996 (1) SA 984 (CC), at para. 252 (Ackerman, J.).

[106] See G. Van der Schyff, *Limitation of Rights: A Study of the European Convention and the South African Bill of Rights* (Nijmegen, The Netherlands: Wolf Legal Publishers, 2005) 46.

[107] See, e.g., in Canada: Hogg, above note 43, at 54; in Israel, *Adalah* v. *Minister of the Interior*, above note 26, at para. 42 (Cheshin, J.).

interpreted broadly, the limitation should also receive a broad interpretation; similarly, once the right has been interpreted narrowly, the limitation should be interpreted narrowly. Another view argues for a broad interpretation of the right coupled with a narrow interpretation of its limitation.[108] A possible third view – for which no support was found – may advocate for a narrow interpretation of the right and a broad interpretation of the limitation.

None of these views can be supported. Both the constitutional rights and the proportionality found in the limitation clause should receive neither "narrow" nor "broad" interpretation. Rather, both should undergo the process of purposive interpretation. Such interpretation would enable the right to receive its due scope in accordance with its underlying reasons. Similarly, it would enable the limitation clause – and the elements of proportionality included therein – to be attributed its due interpretive scope in accordance with the same factors.

v.   Interpretive balancing

a.   The nature of the interpretive balancing   Generous interpretation may be exercised at different levels of abstraction.[109] At the most abstract level, it seeks to provide the constitutional text with the meaning which, more than any other, realizes the basic principles of the legal system in which the text was created.[110] At this level of abstraction, all legal texts share a similar purpose. This purpose may be referred to as the "normative umbrella" covering all legal texts that exist in a single legal universe. These are the very foundations on which the entire legal structure is built.[111] At the sub-constitutional level, whenever we examine a statutory provision, we observe that every legislative act is like "a creature living within its environment."[112] That legal environment contains not only the nearest statutory provisions, but rather "widening co-centric circles of accepted principles, shared basic purposes, and fundamental legal criteria."[113] The same should apply to constitutional provisions. The

---

[108]   See Van der Schyff, above note 106, at 31, 125.
[109]   See Barak, above note 3, at 90.
[110]   *Ibid.*, at 159.
[111]   See W. N. Eskridge Jr., "Public Values in Statutory Interpretation," 137 *U. Pa. L. Rev.* 1007 (1989); D. Oliver, *Common Values and the Public–Private Divide* (London: Butterworths, 1999).
[112]   See HCJ 58/68 *Shalit v. Minister of the Interior* [1969] IsrLR 23(2) 477 (Zussman, P.).
[113]   CA 165/82 *Kibbutz Hatzor v. Internal Revenue Service Officer* [1985] IsrSC 39(2) 70 (Barak, J).

constitution is enveloped by principles that reflect the nation's fundamental concepts,[114] as well as society's most entrenched values.[115] They contain an expression of the national ethos, the cultural heritage, the social tradition, and the entire historical experience of that nation.[116] In some cases, these principles are mentioned explicitly in the constitution.[117] In other cases, these principles are gleaned from sources external to the constitutional text.[118] These principles "envelop" the constitution and, in each case, "must be studied in light of that people's national way of life."[119] The different principles are often in a constant state of conflict. That conflict is resolved through the act of balancing.[120] This notion relates to the balancing of the conflicting basic principles while granting each their relative "weight" in the legal system reflecting their social importance. Over the last several decades, for example, the Israeli Supreme Court has dealt extensively with the notion of balancing conflicting principles. This judicial balancing was used, prior to the adoption of the judicial review of legislation, to assess the proper scope of executive power. *The People's Voice*[121] case demonstrates the potential of such use well. At issue was a provision of the 1933 Press Ordinance (enacted by the British during their mandate and still in effect at the time of the trial). According to that provision, the Minister of the Interior was authorized to shut down a

---

[114] See Tribe, above note 39, at 70; Walton, above note 80. See also R. Post, *Constitutional Domains: Democracy, Community, Management* (Cambridge, MA: Harvard University Press, 1995), 23.

[115] An express reference to "community values" in constitutional interpretation has been made in Australia. See A. Mason, "The Role of a Constitutional Court in a Federation: A Comparison of the Australian and the United States Experience," 16 *Fed. L. Rev.* 1 (1986); H. Patapan, "Politics of Interpretation," 22 *Syd. L. Rev.* 247 (2000).

[116] See Barak, above note 3, at 381.

[117] See Art. 39(I) of the 1996 Constitution of the Republic of South Africa ("When interpreting the Bill of Rights, a court, tribunal or forum – (a) must promote the values that underline an open and democratic society based on human dignity, equality and freedom ..."). See also Art. 1 of Israel Basic Law: Human Dignity and Liberty ("Fundamental human rights in Israel are founded upon recognition of the value of human beings, the sanctity of human life, and the principle that all persons are free"), available in English at www.knesset.gov.il/laws/special/eng/basic3_eng.htm.

[118] See Barak, above note 3, at 381; T. C. Grey, "Do We Have an Unwritten Constitution?," 27 *Stan. L. Rev.* 703 (1975).

[119] HCJ 73/53 *"Kol Ha'am" Company Ltd. v. Minister of the Interior* [1953] IsrSC 7 871 (Agranat, P.), available in English at http://elyon1.court.gov.il/files_eng/53/730/000/Z01/53000730.z01.pdf.

[120] See F. Iacobucci, "'Reconciling Rights': The Supreme Court of Canada's Approach to Competing Charter Rights," 20 *Sup. Ct. L. Rev.* 137 (2003), who prefers the term "reconciliation" over "balancing" in the context of a constitutional principles conflict.

[121] See *"Kol Ha'am" Company Ltd. v. Minister of the Interior*, above note 119 (Agranat, P.).

newspaper – either temporarily or permanently – if, in his sole discretion, "certain matter appearing in such newspapers ... [is] likely to endanger the public peace."[122] The daily *People's Voice* published an article critical of the Israeli government which was willing to send its troops to fight alongside American forces in the Korean War. In particular, the article stated that "the Israeli government may send its soldiers to die merely to serve the interests of American imperialism," and that "these soldiers would serve as 'cannon fodder' for the American fighting machine." Finally, the article claimed that "the majority of Israelis would not allow their leaders to trade with their sons' blood." After reading the piece, the Minister of the Interior decided to shut down the newspaper for several days. The newspaper petitioned the Supreme Court. Since, at the time, the judicial review of legislation had yet to be adopted, the constitutionality of the provision was never at issue. Rather, the issue was interpretative in nature. Specifically, the issue was the proper interpretation of a statutory provision allowing the Minister to shut down a newspaper. Within that provision, the court had to determine the specific causal connection between the notion of "likelihood" which is required to shut down the newspaper and the notion of "danger to the public peace." Justice Agranat held that the causal connection required by the provision should represent a proper balancing between the need to guarantee the public peace on the one hand, and the need to guarantee the right to freedom of speech on the other. The court then proceeded to conduct such a balancing, and concluded that the causal connection most fitting is that of "near certainty." In other words, the Minister can shut down a newspaper if (and only if), there was "near certainty" that a published piece would lead to the "endangerment of the public peace."[123]

The court did not use the balancing tool to determine the constitutionality of the statutory provision; rather, it used it to properly interpret the scope of executive authority as provided by a statutory provision. Through the act of balancing the court could arrive at the purpose underlying the statutory provision, not its constitutionality. The court used interpretive balancing. Following *The People's Voice*, the Israeli Supreme Court used interpretive balancing numerous times to assess the contours of the executive authority found in different statutory provisions.[124] Indeed, interpretive balancing may be used in every case that the purpose of the interpreted law is in question. Accordingly, interpretive balance should be applied to

[122] See Press Ordinance, Art. 19 (1933).
[123] See above, at 73.
[124] See A. Barak, "Human Rights in Israel," 39 *Isr. L. Rev.* 12 (2006).

the interpretation of any constitutional text, and in particular to the interpretation of a constitutional text relating to the protection of rights.

b.   Interpretive balancing and constitutional balancing   Interpretive balancing determines the objective purpose of law such as statutes or a constitution. It does so by balancing the conflicting principles underlying each norm. This balance is based upon the social importance ascribed to each conflicting principle. The interpretive balancing is relevant for the interpretation of a text the purpose of which is conflicting principles – not for the determination of its constitutionality. When determining the components of interpretive balancing there is no application of all the elements of proportionality used for the determination of the justification of the limitation of the constitutional right. However, the interpretive balancing is based on balancing, and may, through analogy, use the element of proportionality *stricto sensu* in the rules of proportionality.[125]

B.   The right's scope and public interest

1.   *The proper role of public interest considerations*

When attempting to determine the proper scope of a constitutional right, should public interest considerations be included? Take, for example, the right to freedom of expression: when attempting to determine its scope, should the interpreter take into account public interest considerations such as the protection of national security interests, the prevention of the publication of obscenities, or the solicitation of hate speech? The importance of these considerations is beyond dispute; but the issue here is when should they be considered? At what stage of the constitutional review?[126] The answer is clear in those cases where the legal system is based on a single-stage model of judicial review. In those situations, public interest considerations are taken into account in the single stage of the constitutional review.[127] But what is the case when the legal system has adopted a two-stage model, such as in Germany, Canada, South Africa, and Israel? As explained in Chapter 1, the two-stage model is based upon a distinction between the first stage of the constitutional review, where the scope

---

[125] See below, at 340.
[126] On the stages of constitutional review, see above, at 26.
[127] See R. H. Fallon, "Individual Rights and the Powers of Government," 27 *Ga. L. Rev.* 343, 361 (1993).

of the constitutional right is determined, and the second stage, where a determination is made as to the constitutionality of the justification of the limitations imposed on the right's realization.[128] Should public interest considerations be included in the first stage or the second or in both stages? Should public interest considerations affect the determination of the right's scope, or should consideration of these interests be postponed to the stage of justification of the discussion of the limitations imposed on the right's realization – in other words, to the discussion regarding proportionality?

2.   Public interest as part of proportionality

The proper location for public interest considerations is in the second stage of the constitutional review, as part of the discussion of the justification of the limitation on the constitutional right.[129] Thus, public interest considerations should be included, and receive their due attention, within the discussion of the rules of proportionality. As part of these rules, and in particular within the elements of "purpose" and "proportionality *stricto sensu*," public-interest considerations should be brought to bear. Accordingly, when a sub-constitutional law (such as statute or common law) attempts to limit the constitutional right to freedom of expression, public interest considerations should be included within the determination of the law's proportionality. In other words, they will be considered in the second stage of the constitutional review, determining the constitutionality of the limitations imposed on the right and its realization. Public interest considerations should not be included in the stage determining the scope of the constitutional right to freedom of expression itself.[130]

This is the approach of the German Constitutional Court which distinguishes between the elements constituting the right and the considerations applying to its limitations. Public interest considerations are not considered

---

[128] See above, at 26.

[129] C. Starck, "Constitutional Definition and Protection of Rights and Freedoms," in C. Starck (ed.), *Rights, Institutions and Impact of International Law According to the German Basic Law: The Contributions of the Federal Republic of Germany to the Second World Congress of the International Association of Constitutional Law* (Baden-Baden: Nomos Verlagsgesellschaft, 1987), 19, 25.

[130] See G. Erasmus, "Limitation and Suspension," in D. Van Wyk, J. Dugard, B. Villiers, and D. Davis (eds.), *Rights and Constitutionalism: The New South African Legal Order* (Oxford University Press, 1994), 629, 645 ("The balancing between the rights of an individual and the interests of society should not be invoked too early. It does not belong to this part of the investigation. Balancing only occurs once the state has demonstrated and identified those interests which will trigger the application of the limitation grounds."); see also Van der Schyff, above note 106, at 33.

when the right's scope is at issue, but they are brought to bear once the justification of the limitations is discussed. That way, individual liberty is maintained.[131] The same is true for the South-African Constitutional Court,[132] as well as for the Supreme Courts of New Zealand,[133] and Israel.[134]

[131] See N. Emiliou, *The Principle of Proportionality in European Law: A Comparative Study* (London: Kluwer Law International, 1996), 53 ("The doctrinal separation between the constituent elements of basic rights and their limits avoids the inclusion of public interest and welfare considerations directly in the element of basic rights themselves. In this way, the danger of arbitrarily restricting freedom by way of an *ad hoc* definition of basic rights is also avoided, ultimately ensuring optimal freedom.").

[132] See S. Woolman and H. Botha, "Limitations," in S. Woolman, M. Bishop, and J. Brickhill (eds.), *Constitutional Law of South Africa*, 2nd edn. (Cape Town: Juta Law Publishers, looseleaf, 2002-), Chapter 34, 20 ("The first stage of the analysis is generally understood to require the judge to determine the ambits of the right. The determination is made by asking what values underlie the right and then, in turn, what practices serve those values. The judge is not required to compare the importance of the values underlying the rights allegedly being infringed with the values said to underlie the policy or right or interest said to support the alleged infringement. This comparison is left for the second stage of the analysis under the limitation clause. It is under the limitation clause that we ask whether a party's interest in having a challenged law upheld is of sufficed import to justify the infringement of a right … [T]he determination made here is one of definition or demarcation, *not* balancing. We are asking what counts as protected assembly activity, *not* whether this kind of protected activity, when offset against some competing set of public or private interests, still merits protection. We are deciding what values animate and what practices are protected by a particular right. The problem of value conflict between a right and a law that limits the exercise of that right is played out at the next stage of the inquiry – the limitation clause."); see also *De Reuck* v. *Director of Public Prosecutions*, 2004 (1) SA 406 (CC), § 48 ("The respondents dispute that child pornography, as defined by the Act, is expression. Relying on the approach of the United States Supreme Court where certain categories of expression are unprotected forms of speech, the respondents argued such materials do not serve any of the values traditionally considered as underlying freedom of expression, namely, truth-seeking, free political activity and self fulfillment. This argument must fail. In this respect, our Constitution is different from that of the United States of America. Limitations of rights are dealt with under section 36 of the Constitution and not at the threshold level. Section 16(1) expressly protects the freedom of expression in a manner that does not warrant a narrow reading. Any restriction upon artistic creativity must satisfy the rigors of the limitation analysis.").

[133] See SC 58/2005 *Hansen* v. *The Queen* [2007] NZSC 7 (CA), § 22 ("The first question is the interpretation of the right. In ascertaining the meaning of the right, the criteria for justification are not relevant. The meaning of the right is ascertained from 'cardinal values' it embodies, collapsing the interpretation of the right and the S1 justification is insufficiently protective of the right. The later justification is according to a stringent standard, in which a party seeking to justify must show that the limit on a fundamental right is 'demonstrably justified' in a free and democratic society. The context for the application of S1 is then the violation of a constitutionality guaranteed right or freedom.").

[134] See *Adalah* v. *Minister of the Interior*, above note 26, at para. 21 ("public interest considerations should be taken into account, but this should be done only at the stage where the court is examining the limitation on the right (such as the right to freedom of expression),

This approach provides a better understanding of the notion of the constitutional right. It places the constitutional right as an ideal sought to be realized by the society in which it resides. This ideal may conflict with other ideals – or other interests – sought to be realized by the same society. This kind of conflict should not be resolved, however, by narrowing the scope of the ideals, but rather by limiting the way they are realized. The right itself, as a legal concept, should continue to exist in a pure form as an aspiration crossing dimensions of space and time. It should exist in a constant state of conflict with other opposing aspirations. Such a conflict is resolved through balancing at the sub-constitutional level.[135] Such balancing is governed by the rules of proportionality included in the limitation clause. The balancing between the ways in which the constitutional right is realized and the opposing aspiration does not affect or change the scope or the nature of the right itself. Rather, such balancing affects the realization of the right at the sub-constitutional level in a given society at a given time. Such an approach always provides society with the ideals it should aspire to fulfill, and strengthens the legal status of these ideals – even if they are never realized in practice. As such, the right's boundaries and powers are maintained even during catastrophes. Narrowing the means by which a right may be realized at any given time does not affect the right itself. In addition, a clear distinction between a constitutional right on the one hand and the public interest on the other will lead to a better, mutually productive public and constitutional discourse. The dividing lines between law and politics will prove clearer and more accurate. The different considerations

and not during the first stage, where the right's scope is being determined." (Barak, P.)). See also HCJ 10203/03 *The National Assembly Ltd.* v. *Attorney General* (unreported decision of August 20, 2008), para. 21 ("As a general rule, when we discuss limitations upon the realization of a protected human right, the balancing act is conducted between that protected right and other values and public interests. The same is true in this case, where the main justification for the limitation – or rather outright restriction – on political speech through paid advertisements is the doctrine of fairness. The balancing in this case is 'external,' between a constitutional human right and conflicting public-interest considerations. In principle, such balancing should be conducted within the contours of the limitation clause. Another view may lead to over-narrowing of the internal scope of the right itself, as the way to realize that right may no longer be protected. In addition, such an approach may create an analytic and practical blurring of the line between the stage in which the internal scope of the right is defined and the stage in which the proper amount of protection they deserve is determined, since the public-interest considerations that are weighed during the proper purpose stage will infiltrate into the very definition of the right. That, in turn, may lead to a heavier burden on those petitioners seeking to claim that the right has been infringed upon, since the examination of these public considerations would be removed into the first stage." (Beinish, P.)).

[135] See below, at 87.

will be presented clearly and most precisely, and the weight each is given will be evident – and thus easier to evaluate and criticize.[136]

This principled approach to the understanding of constitutional rights stems from the two-stage model.[137] This analytical model is based on the distinction between the scope of the right on the one hand, and the ways in which it may be realized on the other. It allows for an examination of the entire scope of the right in the first stage of the constitutional review, while imposing proportional limitations on the right in the second, sub-constitutional stage. It would be inappropriate and unfortunate if the same constitutional right would be affected twice – once during the first stage, when the scope of the right is narrowed, and the second time during the second stage, when further limitations are imposed on this already limited constitutional right.

One may critique this approach. First, it may be argued that this approach may lead to the undermining of the dignity of legislation, since every legislative act would ultimately infringe upon a constitutional right (so broadly defined). If, indeed, every such infringement would need to be examined by the courts, what would remain of the legislative institution?

It is agreed that human dignity should not displace legislative dignity.[138] The dignity of legislation is dear to anyone who holds democracy and human rights dear. But no contradiction exists between a generous approach to constitutional rights and the dignity of the legislation, just as no contradiction exists between judicial review on the validity of a statute and the dignity of that statute. Respect for the legislator and to statutes is demonstrated through respect for provisions of the constitution. The right relationship between the legislator and the judge is through constitutional dialogue rather than a monologue – either by the legislator or by the judge.[139]

Another argument is that this approach creates a burden on the second stage of the judicial review process (where the constitutionality of the limiting law is considered). That, in turn, may lead to the dilution of the protection granted to constitutional rights. According to this argument, the desire to provide adequate protection to constitutional rights through a more powerful limitation clause may lead to a restrictive approach to the scope of the right. Such a restrictive approach could be manifested

---

[136] See below, at 87.   [137] See above, at 26.

[138] See J. Waldron, *The Dignity of Legislation* (Cambridge University Press, 1999).

[139] See generally A. Barak, *The Judge in a Democracy* (Princeton University Press, 2006), 236–240.

through a consideration of the rights of other individuals as well as of the public interest. This argument was made by Hogg in relation to the proper analysis of the Canadian limitation clause.[140] It seems that the fears of restrictive interpretation are not well founded. They are surely least founded whenever the proportionality tests promulgated by the limitation clause are carefully applied by the courts in each case, with a close examination of both the right's scope and its limitation.

Finally, it can be argued that the approach described will open the litigation floodgates, creating an overwhelming burden for the courts. The factual premise to this argument is lacking. In any event, even if this should occur, the courts should, and will, find ways to properly respond to the new need. Restricting the scope of constitutional rights should not be the first option.

C. The scope of constitutional rights and the rights of others

1. The proper role of "rights of others" considerations

We have discussed one type of consideration – relating to the public interest – that should be considered during the second stage. What about another group of considerations – those relating to the rights of others? Should these be considered a part of the right's scope in the first stage, or, like public interest considerations, examined during the second stage – that of the justifications of the limitations? Take, for example, the right to freedom of expression. When determining this right's scope, should we take into account the right to privacy of others, or their right to enjoy a good reputation? Should such considerations limit the scope of the constitutional right to freedom of expression? The answer to this question is no – much like the answer provided to the question about public interest considerations, and for the same reasons. According to this approach, the scope of a constitutional right is determined by its interpretation. It reflects the underlying reasons of the right itself. It reflects the societal ideal expressed within that right. Such a scope should not be narrowed due to considerations of other people's rights.[141] Accordingly, the scope of the right to freedom of expression should not be narrowed due to considerations of other people's right to privacy or to enjoy a good reputation.

---

[140] See P. W. Hogg, "Interpreting the Charter of Rights: Generosity and Justification," 28 *Osgoode Hall L. J.* 817 (1990).

[141] See HCJ 1435/03, *Jane Doe. v. Disciplinary Ct. for Gov't Employees in Haifa* [2003] IsrSC 58(1) 529, 537 (Barak, P.). See below, at 87.

Therefore, a constitutional right to freedom of expression should include expressions that may be hurtful to other people's reputation, or even affect their privacy. These considerations, relating to the rights of others, are extremely important. They should not be ignored. They should be taken into account. The stage of reviewing such considerations, however, should not be within the determination of the right's scope; rather within the discussion of the possibilities of its realization. It should thus be a part of the second stage of the constitutional review. Such considerations constitute important elements that may affect the proportionality of the measures limiting the right.

The reasons behind this approach to consideration of the rights of others are quite similar to those discussed in relation to public interest considerations.[142] In both cases – the public interest and the rights of others – the correct approach would be, during the first stage of the constitutional review, to fully express the ideal underlying the right itself. Then, in the second stage, that same ideal should be confronted with other considerations – such as the one relating to the public interest or that of other people's rights – within the limitation clause requirements and the rules of proportionality they provide. Thus, the proper location of these considerations is not at the constitutional level, but rather at the sub-constitutional level. A sub-constitutional law (such as statute or common law) will be declared constitutional if the limitations it places on the right (on freedom of expression, for example) are proportional, whether those limitations were imposed to serve the public interest (such as national security considerations) or whether they were imposed for the protection of the right of others (as in the protection of another person's good reputation, or privacy). Indeed, the constitutional notion of freedom of expression should not be diluted by considerations that are not directly related to the right itself. However, a permissible constitutional limitation on that right would be recognized in order to serve other legitimate aims recognized by the legal system (such as considerations of public interest or the rights of others). Such permissible limitations would be executed through proportional means that would limit the right's realization in a proportional manner.

2.   The "rights of others" and constitutional rights conflict

The view just presented, according to which the scope of a constitutional right would only be determined according to reasons underlying its

---

[142] See above, at 75.

purpose, will inevitably lead to a conflict between several rights at the constitutional level. How can we resolve such a conflict? If we assume that the solution lies in narrowing the scope of the constitutional rights themselves, would that not amount to the narrowing of the scope due the right of others – a possibility we have just ruled out? True, such narrowing did not occur as a result of the interpretation of the right, but rather as a result of the rules relating to intra-constitutional rights conflict. But the result is the same: The scope of the constitutional right will be diminished due to the effect of other rights. What is the point then of preventing the right of others from entering through the "front door" of the constitutional interpretation analysis (in the first stage of the review), only to then allow it to enter through the "back door" (through the rules relating to constitutional rights conflicts)?

The answer is that the solution in both cases – the constitutional interpretation of rights scope and the conflict between constitutional rights – should use the same methodology. Accordingly, when the constitutional right to freedom of expression conflicts with the constitutional right to privacy or to good reputation, such conflict should *not* affect the scope of any of the rights involved. The solution to such conflict is not found at the constitutional level. Rather, the solution is at the sub-constitutional level. At that level, a limitation on the right to freedom of expression may be constitutional if it was meant to protect the reputation of a person or his privacy, and the degree of the limitation is proportional. This conclusion requires additional discussion, to which the next chapter is dedicated.

3

Conflicting constitutional rights

A. Resolving the constitutional conflict at the sub-constitutional level

1. A model of constitutional conflict

How should the legal system address conflicting constitutional rights?[1] The answer to this question is usually found within the system's process of legal interpretation.[2] Such interpretation examines the text as a whole. Considerations of analytical clarity, however, require us to draw a distinction between merely interpretive issues and conflict-of-rights issues; the former, in this context, deal with the meaning of the constitutional text; the latter examine its validity. Accordingly, a distinction is made between issues relating to the scope of constitutional rights – which are interpretive in nature, and may be resolved as part of purposive constitutional interpretation – and issues relating to the conflict between constitutional rights – which are not interpretive in nature, and therefore cannot be resolved within the confines of purposive interpretation but rather should be resolved by the constitutional rules relating to the validity of the rights.[3]

Regarding questions of constitutional validity, what is the proper way to address conflicting constitutional rights? The answer is that, when two principle-shaped[4] rights conflict, such a conflict should not

---

[1] See, e.g., C. Wellman, "On Conflicts Between Rights," 14 *Law and Philosophy* 271 (1995); P. Montague, "When Rights Conflict," 7 *Legal Theory* 257 (2001); F. M. Kamm, "Conflicts of Rights: Typology, Methodology, and Nonconsequentialism," 7 *Legal Theory* 239 (2001); E. Brems, "Conflicting Human Rights: An Exploration in the Context of the Right to a Fair Trial in the European Convention for the Protection of Human Rights and Fundamental Freedoms," 27 *Hum. Rts. Q.* 294 (2005); L. Zucca, *Constitutional Dilemmas: Conflicts of Fundamental Legal Rights in Europe and the USA* (Oxford University Press, 2007); E. Brems (ed.), *Conflicts Between Fundamental Rights* (2008).

[2] See A. Barak, *Purposive Interpretation in Law* (Princeton University Press, 2005), 74.

[3] *Ibid.*

[4] On principle-shaped rights, see above, at 40.

affect the validity of the rights[5] or their scope. Instead, such a conflict would affect their realization. The means by which a constitutional right may be realized are determined at the sub-constitutional level, as when a statute or the common law may limit one of the conflicting rights (or both). Such limitations on the conflicting rights are constitutional insofar as they comply with the proportionality requirements set by the limitation clause. Accordingly, a conflict between principle-shaped constitutional rights creates what Alexy calls a "derivative constitutional rule,"[6] which reflects the rules of proportionality. This new constitutional rule – as its name indicates – stems from the constitution, but in my approach, unlike that of Alexy, it operates only at the sub-constitutional level. It does not affect the scope of the rights involved; rather, it affects their realization. It deals with cases in which a constitutional right is limited by a sub-constitutional law (either a statute or the common law). It then determines the constitutionality of this limitation, or lack thereof. It does not determine the scope of the limited right. The derivative constitutional rule's determinations operate only at the sub-constitutional level.

The case is different when one (or both) of the conflicting laws is shaped as a rule.[7] Here, the conflict may affect the actual scope of the rights involved, or their validity. In these situations, no derivative constitutional rule is created; rather, the effect of the conflict is at the very constitutional level where the rights "reside." The conflict's resolution is determined by the rules of conflicting norms, which apply, in principle, at the constitutional level as well. According to these rules, when two legal norms conflict, the later norm prevails (*lex posterior derogat legi priori*), unless the earlier norm is specific to the matter at hand (*lex specialis derogat legi generali*).[8]

In order to fully understand my approach, it is worth examining a constitutional conflict between two constitutional rights shaped as principles more closely.[9] Take, for example, a conflict between Joe's right to privacy and Jane's right to freedom of expression. As a general rule, each of these constitutional rights – the right to privacy, freedom of expression, and others that may be involved – applies (vertically) *vis-à-vis* the state. Thus,

---

[5] See R. Alexy, *A Theory of Constitutional Rights* (Julian Rivers trans., Oxford University Press, 2002 [1986]) (1986), 54.
[6] On derivative constitutional rules, see above, at 38.
[7] On rule-shaped rights, see below, at 86.
[8] For these rules, see Barak, above note 1, at 75.
[9] See below, at 87.

Joe has a constitutional right (either positive[10] or negative[11]) *vis-à-vis* the state, and Jane has a constitutional right (either positive or negative) *vis-à-vis* the state. However, in most cases, Joe does not have a constitutional right *vis-à-vis* Jane and Jane does not have a constitutional right *vis-à-vis* Joe.[12] Joe is asking the state to protect his right to privacy *vis-à-vis* the state; concurrently, Jane is asking the state to protect her right to freedom of expression *vis-à-vis* the state. In this situation, the state is required to operate through one of its governmental branches – legislative, executive, or judicial – to resolve the conflict at hand. Once the state decides to act – regardless of the means it applies, its duty *vis-à-vis* Joe's right conflicts with its duty *vis-à-vis* Jane. In some cases, the rights involved are "negative" in nature; that is, one or both sides demand that the state refrain from limiting their rights. In those cases, the state must prevent the right from being limited. In other cases, the rights involved are "positive" in nature; that is, rights that should be protected by the state. In those cases, the state is required to actively defend the right in question.[13] The rights are "channeled" towards the state and it is asked to act to protect them. Such actions may be in the form of legislation, administrative action, or judicial decision. In all such cases, the action is at the sub-constitutional level. Whenever the state acts – through its organs – it may defend one constitutional right while limiting another; in such a case, a conflict will arise between those rights, within the state's legal zone of authority. This authority would be exercised at the sub-constitutional level, and the conflict is between rights expressed in laws found at the sub-constitutional level, such as legislation or common law. Assume, thus, that a statute protects Joe's right to privacy and limits Jane's right to freedom of expression. The constitutionality of this statute will be determined according to the rules of proportionality. The rules themselves are of constitutional status, as they originate in the constitutional limitation clause. A derivative constitutional rule is created, determining the proportionality of the

---

[10] On positive constitutional rights, see below, at 422.

[11] On negative constitutional rights, see below, at 422.

[12] A discussion relating to the "horizontal application" of constitutional rights – between the individuals themselves – is beyond the scope of this book. See generally Daniel Friedman and Daphna Barak-Erez (eds.), *Human Rights in Private Law* (2001); A. Sajo and R. Uitz, *The Constitution in Private Relations: Expanding Constitutionalism* (Utrecht, The Netherlands: Eleven International Publishing, 2005); Dawn Oliver and Jorg Fedtke (eds.), *Human Rights and the Private Sphere: A Comparative Study* (2007). See below, at 126.

[13] For the distinction between "positive" and "negative" constitutional rights, see below, at 422.

statute.[14] Such a determination operates at the sub-constitutional level in which the conflict takes place. Hence, the conclusion that a conflict between constitutional rights (shaped as principles) does not operate at the constitutional level and therefore does not affect the scope of the rights involved; rather, such a conflict operates at the sub-constitutional level and affects the extent of their realization.

2.   Conflicts between constitutional rights and the rule of law

Does this approach to a conflict between two principle-shaped constitutional rights violate the rule of law?[15] Is it not essential, from the viewpoint of the rule of law, to resolve a conflict of two constitutional rights at the constitutional level? The answer is that the rule of law is satisfied whenever the constitutional conflict is resolved through the use of the rules of proportionality, whose effects are felt at the sub-constitutional level. As for the constitutional level, it includes all of the conflicting constitutional principles. Indeed, our constitutional universe may be more complicated than it seems at first glance. The constitutional rights, containing the most fundamental values of society, reflect ideals competing for their maximum realization. Alas, the nature of human society is such that some of those ideals conflict. The way to resolve such a conflict is not through limiting the scope of one of the ideals (or eliminating it outright); rather, it is through the recognition of the constitutional co-existence of conflicting ideals.[16]

B.   Conflict between rule-shaped constitutional rights

How should the legal system address a conflict between two rule-shaped constitutional rights? A rule-shaped right is a right not made up of

[14] On derivative constitutional rights, see above, at 38.
[15] On the constitutional principle of the rule of law, see below, at 226.
[16] See *Jane Doe* v. *Disciplinary Court for Government Employee in Haifa*, HCJ 1435/03 [2003] IsrSC 58(1) 527, 538 ("One of the main characteristics of democracy is the wealth of rights, values, and principles, as well as the constant conflict between some of them. It has been suggested more than once that some of these rights, values, and principles are mirror images of each other, and are therefore in constant conflict. The resolution of such conflicts – which are not only a natural part of any democracy, but also nourish and provide it with much-needed vitality – is not through affecting the scope of such rights, values and interests such that the 'losing' ones would be removed from the constitutional discourse and from the reach of constitutional review. Rather, the solution of such conflicts should be through leaving the conflict at the constitutional level 'as is,' while determining the proper extent of the protection of the conflicting rights, values, and interests at the level of 'regular' legislation." (Barak, P.)).

principle-based components.[17] Usually, rule-shaped rights are also premised on principles; those principles, however, do not make up one of their
components. How should one resolve a conflict between two such rights?

The starting point to resolve a conflict between two rule-shaped rights
is to determine whether the conflict is genuine or imagined. A conflict
is genuine if it cannot be resolved once the interpretive process has been
completed. In cases where the conflict disappears after applying the interpretive process, or where one constitutional rule is recognized as the exception to the other, then the conflict is imaginary. However, when dealing
with a genuine conflict, the only possible result is that one constitutional
rule must be declared invalid (partly or completely). It is not possible to
leave both rules intact within the same legal system.[18] The determination
of which of the two rules would remain and which would be set aside
should be done in accordance with the specific rules governing each legal
system. In most systems, however, it is common to assume that the later
rule overrules the earlier one (*lex posterior derogat legi priori*), unless the
earlier rule is specific, in which case the specific prevails over the general
rule (*lex specialis derogat legi generali*).[19] Both these – and other – interpretive canons are based on the assumption that whenever two rule-based
rights conflict they cannot both remain in effect. Accordingly, one of the
rules loses its validity. These canons apply at every normative level. They
therefore also apply in a genuine conflict between constitutional rule-
shaped rights.

C. Conflict between principle-shaped constitutional rights

1. *The scope and validity of the conflicting rights are not affected*

How should the legal system address a conflict between two principle-
shaped constitutional rights? Principle-shaped rights consist of fundamental values that reflect ideals aspiring for their maximum realization.[20]
Those ideals may be realized, however, at different levels of intensity. They
do not lose their fundamental nature merely because they were not realized to their fullest extent. Take, for example, a case where the legal system
recognizes the right to freedom of expression as well as the right to good
reputation as constitutional rights. Assume now that these two rights are

---

[17] See above, at 86. [18] See Alexy, above note 5, at 54.
[19] See generally Barak, *Purposive Interpretation In Law*, above note 2, at 75.
[20] See above, at 40.

in conflict. How should the legal system resolve such a conflict between two principle-shaped constitutional rights?

The answer to this question is not simple. The starting point should always be that the conflict should not affect the validity or the scope of any of the constitutional rights involved. Moreover, the interpretive canons – regarding the later norm prevailing over the earlier norm and the specific norm prevailing over the general norm – do not apply to such conflicts either.[21] The result, therefore, is that both conflicting rights remain valid within the legal system, each according to their own scope. This is one of the major differences between a conflict of rule-shaped rights and a conflict of principle-shaped rights. A conflict between rule-shaped constitutional rights reflects a type of constitutional accident, after which one of the rights loses its full constitutional scope.[22] This is not the case when two principle-shaped constitutional rights conflict. This kind of conflict rarely reflects a constitutional accident. Rather, these conflicts are unavoidable, reflecting a perfectly natural state of affairs and expressing the very nature of those constitutional principles aspiring for maximum realization. These aspirations lead those principles to clash with other constitutional principles also aspiring to be fully realized.[23] Both constitutional rights, however, survive the clash unscathed at the constitutional level: both remain valid according to their original scope. They remain intact within the legal system's boundaries.[24]

---

[21] See *Jane Doe*, above note 16, at 537 ("In a state of (horizontal) conflict between two constitutional norms, which are equal in legal status and reflect separate values and principles, the interpretive cannon according to which a special norm overrides a general norm usually does not apply." (Barak, P.)).

[22] See above, at 86.

[23] See EA 2/84 Neiman v. *Central Election Board, Eleventh Knesset* [1985] IsrSC 39(2) 281, 308 ("Frequently the Judge … can find alongside one principle, its complete and opposite principle, and alongside the thesis lies the antithesis … The fundamental principles of the legal system may frequently march in pairs, with each principle pointing at a different direction." (Barak, P.)). See also B. Cardozo, *The Paradoxes of Legal Science* (New York: Columbia University Press, 1928), 62 ("We seem to see the working of a Hegelian philosophy of history whereby the tendency of every principle is to create its own antithesis.").

[24] See HCJ *Jane Doe*, above note 16, at 537 ("In a state of (horizontal) conflict between two constitutional norms, which are equal in legal status and reflect separate values and principles, the interpretive rule according to which a special norm overrides a general norm usually does not apply. The conflict should be resolved, therefore, through an examination of the nature of the infringement on each of the values and principles affected – while noticing the different infringement upon the core of the right or merely on its penumbra – and the affect of the conflict on the general norm setting." (Barak, P.)). See also D. Grimm, "Human Rights and Judicial Review in Germany," in D. M. Beatty (ed.), *Human Rights and Judicial Review: A Comparative Perspective* (London: Martinus

According to the analysis offered here, a conflict between two principle-shaped constitutional rights will not affect either their scope or their validity. Indeed, most legal systems acknowledge a situation where two constitutional rights overlap with regard to a certain human behavior while their provisions conflict with each other (at least in part). This legal situation – impossible in the case of rule-shaped constitutional rights – is natural to a conflict between two constitutional rights shaped as principles.[25]

What then is the conflict's resolution? The conflict is resolved not within the area of the constitutional right's scope or validity, but rather in the realization of the rights involved.[26] Only the extent of the right's protection is affected as a result of the conflict, and therefore the conflict's effects may be found only at the sub-constitutional level.[27]

2. *The effect on the realization of the conflicting rights*

How does a conflict between principle-shaped constitutional rights affect the realization of such rights? The answer to this question is found in the rules of proportionality within the limitation clause. These rules establish

Nijhoff Publishers, 1994), 267, 273 ("The value – or principle – of orientation means that the value embodied in a constitutional provision, particularly in a human right, has to be maximized as much as possible ... [I]f a collision between two or more constitutionally guaranteed values occurs, the question is not to determine which one prevails but to find a solution which leaves the greatest possible effect to both of them (*Prakische Konkordanz*).").

[25] See H. Cheadle, N. Haysom, and D. Davis (eds.), *South African Constitutional Law: The Bill of Rights* (2003), 700 ("Rights with competing claims can overlap. There is an overlap of the right of freedom of expression, the right to privacy, and the right to dignity in respect of defamatory speech. Claims based on these rights compete with each other. It is unnecessary, in a constitution with a limitation clause, to define the borders of the rights in such a way that the border of the right to freedom of expression ends where the right to dignity begins. In other words, it is not necessary to balance the competing claims of different rights at this stage of the analysis.").

[26] See A. S. Butler, "Limiting Rights," 33 *Victoria U. Wellington L. Rev.* 113, 122 (2002); S. Mize, "Resolving Cases of Conflicting Rights under the New Zealand Bill of Rights Act," 22 *New Zealand U. L. Rev.* 50, 63 (2006).

[27] See Cheadle, Haysom, and Davis, above note 25, at 700 ("It is more appropriate that competing claims arising from the overlap of rights be resolved by law rather than by an abstract balancing of rights to determine common and impermeable boundaries. The law can strike the balance between the competing claims arising from the rights, and that balance can be assessed under the proportionality analysis under the second stage of the enquiry. Instead of erecting walls between rights, one right may overlap with another and yet be limited by a law, whether statutory or common law, that not only gives effect to the other constitutional rights but justifies the limitation.").

a derivative constitutional rule[28] that operates solely at the sub-constitutional level. This kind of rule determines the result of the constitutional conflict, realized at the sub-constitutional level. The result may thus be found in the different areas of law where such realizations take place. Thus, for example, the result of a conflict between the constitutional right to freedom of speech (*vis-à-vis* the state) and the constitutional right to a good reputation (*vis-à-vis* the state) may be found within the law of torts, which prohibits libel and slander, with recognized exceptions. These laws provide one person with rights that may be used against another. Importantly, these areas of the law (such as tort law) do not provide – and cannot provide – constitutional rights, but only sub-constitutional rights.

To understand this argument, we must realize that it is the legislator that ultimately makes the decision of preferring one person's constitutional right *vis-à-vis* the state (e.g., to enjoy good reputation) over another person's constitutional right *vis-à-vis* the state (e.g., to freedom of expression). The same applies to the common law or to an administrative act. When a person makes the claim *vis-à-vis* the state that his or her constitutional rights were improperly limited, they in fact claim that such a limitation is unconstitutional. Such a claim is reviewed in accordance with the rules of proportionality. This review does not change the scope of the rights involved, but rather affects the extent of the right's protection – i.e., the ability to realize them in accordance with the proportionality rules found in the limitation clause. Take, for example, the claim that the law (statutory or common law) of libel is unconstitutional as it disproportionally limits the constitutional rights to freedom of speech, to enjoy good reputation, or to privacy (all *vis-à-vis* the state). These arguments are reviewed through the lens of proportionality rules. The results of this review operate only at the sub-constitutional level.

In the Israeli Supreme Court case of *Jane Doe*,[29] disciplinary proceedings were initiated against the defendant for the alleged sexual harassment of Jane Doe. Due to the defendant's medical condition, which may have been revealed during the hearings, the court ordered that the hearings be conducted in chambers (i.e., behind closed doors). The petitioner, Jane Doe, testified at one of the hearings. She also demanded to be present during all other hearings and to be granted full access to the court's transcripts and proceedings. The administrative tribunal – the trial-level

---

[28] On derivative constitutional rules, see above, at 39.
[29] See *Jane Doe*, above note 16.

court – refused, reasoning that the defendant's right to privacy should prevail over Jane Doe's interest in attending the hearings. Jane Doe petitioned the Israeli Supreme Court, which granted the petition and reversed the decision. According to the relevant Israeli statute, the Law of State Service (Discipline) (1963), the administrative tribunal may close its doors and not hold public hearings (i.e., hear arguments in chambers) "in order to protect morality."[30] The issue before the court was whether the concept of "protect[ing] morality" constituted a sufficiently good reason to prevent the petitioner from being present at the hearings. The Court held it did not. The judgment went on to explain that the petitioner's – here, Jane Doe's – constitutional right *vis-à-vis* the state to a public hearing (which may be derived from the Israeli Basic Law: The Judiciary[31]) prevails over the defendant's constitutional right to privacy *vis-à-vis* the state (which is explicitly recognized by the text of the Israeli Basic Law: Human Dignity and Liberty).[32] Therefore, the court concluded, the statutory language relating to the "protection of morality" cannot include incidents where the victim's right to a public hearing is limited. In my judgment, I wrote:

> We are dealing with an area in which the right to privacy and the principle of public hearings conflict. Such a conflict reflects a normal condition in a democratic society, where human rights constantly clash with each other (as in the case where the right to freedom of expression clashes with the right to enjoy a good reputation), and where human rights clash with values and fundamental principles of the society (as in the case where freedom of expression is in conflict with national security and safety considerations). Other than in the most extreme cases, this kind of conflict does not require a re-determination of the boundaries of the rights, values, and interests while invalidating the right, value, or interest that "lost" in the conflict. Thus, for example, we do not hold today that the right to freedom of expression does not entail an expression that may infringe upon another person's reputation. If we were to so hold, then we would significantly reduce the scope of both the constitutional rights and the values and principles that enjoy constitutional protection, and we would have created a legal framework where regular legislation that relates to good reputation would not abide by the constitutional limitations of such a right. This is an unwanted result, and it should be avoided – save for those rare cases in which we have no choice but to determine – at the constitutional level – the boundaries of each right.[33]

---

[30] Law of State Service (Discipline) (1963), § 41(b).
[31] See Art. 3 of Basic Law: The Judiciary.
[32] See Art. 7(a) of Basic Law: Human Dignity and Liberty.
[33] See *Jane Doe*, above note 16, at 537.

Later in that decision, this point was further elaborated:

> In such a conflict, we cannot say that one right prevails over the other, or
> that one right renders the other right void. Both rights continue to exist
> at the constitutional level in the Israeli legal system. Accordingly, the
> Israeli right to privacy includes the individual's right to privacy during
> court hearings; similarly, the (constitutional) principle of public hearing
> includes cases in which such publicity limits one's privacy. The resolution
> of this conflict – a solution that should be reached so that both parties, as
> well as the public as a whole, know how to plan their actions – is not found
> at the constitutional level; rather, such a solution can be found within the
> different legislative acts and their proper interpretation. These statutes
> limit both privacy and publicity. Their constitutionality is determined
> according to the provisions of the limitation clause.[34]

How, then, are such conflicts finally resolved? In order to answer that
question, a distinction between several types of cases must be made.

3.   Interpretive balancing between principle-shaped constitutional rights

The first typical case of conflicting constitutional rights may be exemplified by the facts of the Israeli Supreme Court case of *Jane Doe* discussed
earlier. There, Jane Doe (the alleged victim of a sexual harassment) asked
the court to realize her constitutional right to a public hearing *vis-à-vis*
the state, while the defendant relied on their constitutional right *vis-à-
vis* the state to privacy. Both relied on a statute – the Law of State Service
(Discipline) – which allows for non-public administrative hearings "in
order to protect morality."[35] The interpretation of this provision – like any
other statutory provision – was done as per its underlying purpose. This
purpose, the court noted, should have taken into account not only the
right to public hearings, but also the right to privacy.[36] Both those rights
are taken into account – in their full scope – while determining the statutory provision's purpose,[37] and because they are in a state of conflict the
interpreter has to balance between them. This is an interpretive balance.[38]
It considers each of the rights by taking into account their weight, in light

---

[34] *Ibid.*, at 539.   [35] See Art. 41(B) of the Law.

[36] More precisely, one does not take into account the (subjective) constitutional right but
rather the (objective) constitutional principles that reflect those rights; see below, at 276.

[37] See above, at 72.

[38] On interpretive balance, see above, at 72.

of the facts of the case. It reflects, by analogy, the balance drawn within the limitation clause's proportionality *stricto sensu*.[39] The purpose of this balancing, however, is not to determine the constitutionality of the statute; rather, it is designed to provide meaning to the statute in accordance with its purpose, where the purpose reflects a balance between the two conflicting rights. Accordingly, this is an interpretive balance. By using the said balancing, one is not applying the limitation clause. For example, there is no need to examine each of the limitation clause's components; whether the law has been created to serve a proper purpose is of no importance here. Similarly, the rational connection and necessary means (the "less damaging alternative") components should also not be considered. The only relevant component of proportionality to the interpretive balancing act is the component of proportionality *stricto sensu*.[40] This is solely an interpretive balance. Its "proportional" nature stems from the application – by analogy – of the rules relating to proportionality *stricto sensu*.

4. Constitutional validity

Let us assume now – and this is the second type of case relating to conflicting rights – that the defendant in *Jane Doe* (the alleged sexual harasser, whose medical condition was about to be published during the proceedings) argued that the statutory provision at issue, according to its proper interpretation, disproportionally limits his constitutional right to privacy and therefore is unconstitutional. This type of argument advances the analytical process from interpretive balancing to the examination of the limitation clause. In Israel, this kind of limitation clause can be found within Basic Law: Human Dignity and Liberty, which also establishes the constitutional right to privacy. This right to privacy has been limited, and the focal point of the discussion now moves to the rules of proportionality. These proportionality rules are the "instruments" designed by the legal system to resolve such conflicts. Within the framework of these proportionality rules, the court must balance between the defendant's right to privacy – a right limited by the statutory provision – and Jane Doe's right to a public hearing. This balancing is not interpretive. The result of this balance determines whether the statutory provision limiting the constitutional right is constitutional.

[39] On this type of balance, see below, at 341.
[40] See below, at 341.

5.   *Conflicting rights with no implementing legislation*

In the third situation, no legislation implementing one of the constitutional rights exists. Let's assume, for example, that there is no legislation implementing the right to a public hearing (and its exceptions). In this hypothetical case, *Jane Doe* argues that the constitutional right to a public hearing (which in Israel can be deduced from Basic Law: The Judiciary), which she possesses *vis-à-vis* the state, directly entitles her to be present in each of the hearings against the defendant and to review the court's transcripts. At the same time, the defendant argues that the right to privacy (which is established, in Israel, by Basic Law: Human Dignity and Liberty), which he possesses *vis-à-vis* the state, directly entitles him to prevent the complainant from attending the hearings or reviewing the court's transcript. How should such a conflict be resolved?

The first step of the examination requires that we rule out a "negative solution" scenario.[41] These are cases where the legislator has informed us of its view via a "speaking silence" or "informed silence." A negative solution is based on the notion that the legislative text exhausted the legislative purpose. The silence on a specific issue is therefore "informed"; it carries a specific meaning, which is, in most cases, a conscious choice not to regulate the matter at hand. If, indeed, the legislative silence constitutes a negative solution – which operates at the sub-constitutional level – then we have to examine the constitutionality of such an arrangement. Indeed, it is not only legislative provisions (explicit or implicit) which can be found unconstitutional: a legislative silence which is found to be a negative solution might also be found unconstitutional. A negative solution is based on silence that carries a message. It is a "speaking" silence, and its message may limit a constitutional right or prevent its proper protection. The constitutionality of such a negative solution will be determined according to the limitation clause's rules of proportionality. If, however, the legislative silence does not constitute a negative solution but rather a gap (or lacuna)[42] – or, in other words, the legislative silence was not informed – then the silence should be completed through the rules governing legislative gaps. In Israel, those rules are established by the Law of Legal Foundations, 1980, which provides:

> Where the court, faced with a legal question requiring a solution, could find no answer in a statute, the case law, or by analogy the court, shall

---

[41] For "negative solution," see Barak, above note 19, at 68.
[42] Regarding legislative gaps, see above, at 56.

decide the issue in light of the principles of freedom, justice, equity and peace of Israel's heritage.[43]

This is the legislative provision on which Israeli judges rely to complete a legislative gap. Accordingly, the judge's first step – after concluding that no other statutory or common law answers are readily available – is to examine possible analogies. An analogy is the natural way to fill a legislative gap. When a relevant analogy does not present itself, the next step would be to turn to the principles of liberty, justice, and integrity provided by Israel's historical legacy. Importantly, such judicial gap-filling should abide by the requirements presented by the limitation clause's proportionality rules. This is because, in Israel, such gap-filling is done in accordance with a sub-constitutional norm (the Law of Legal Foundations). In addition, this kind of gap-filling protects one constitutional right *vis-à-vis* the state while limiting another such right. Gap-filling, therefore, operates at the sub-constitutional level and is subject to the requirements presented by the limitation clause's rules of proportionality.

How should the legal system address a situation where the legislative silence is neither a negative solution nor a legislative gap? In this case, having exhausted all interpretive options, the judge in a common law system is entitled to exercise judicial lawmaking in developing the common law. These common law powers may result in the granting of a sub-constitutional right to one person and revoking it in respect of another. Importantly, however, this judicial creation is not limitless, but rather is limited by the limitation clause's proportionality rules. Indeed, since the effect of such common law rulings is at the sub-constitutional level, it should abide by the requirements set by the limitation clause's proportionality rules.[44]

Another important question is whether circumstances exist whereby the legislator – or the judge – is constitutionally required to act to protect a constitutional right adversely affected by the legislative silence. This issue will be discussed at a later stage during the discussion surrounding "positive" constitutional rights.[45] This analysis suggests that, in every case that we find a conflict between principle-shaped constitutional rights, its resolution should be conducted at the sub-constitutional – rather than the constitutional – level. This may manifest itself through primary legislation or delegated rulemaking, or through judicial gap-filling or judicial

---

[43] Law of Legal Foundations (1980), Art. 1 (translated by the present author).
[44] See below, at 121.   [45] See below, at 422.

lawmaking. Importantly, all these activities are conducted at the sub-constitutional level. All these should be proportional.

6.   Conflicting rights which lead to a conflict between the legislation which defines their realization

The fourth type of rights-conflict case involves a situation where a statute was enacted by the legislator, allowing for a limitation on one constitutional right – for example, the right to privacy – in order to protect another – for example, the right to a public judicial hearing. The constitutionality of this statute is not questioned. Assume now that another statute has been passed – whose constitutionality is again not in question – that enables a limitation on the right to a public hearing in order to protect the right to privacy. We are then faced with two conflicting statutory provisions: one enabling a limitation on the constitutional right to privacy in order to protect the constitutional right to public hearing, while the other allows for the reverse. How should such a conflict be resolved? Obviously, the interpreter must first attempt everything in their power to avoid such a conflict.[46] They must try to interpret both statutes as harmoniously co-existing within the system. What is the solution, assuming all such efforts have been exhausted and the two legislative provisions are still in conflict?

Once again we are dealing with a conflict at the sub-constitutional level. If both statutory provisions are structured as rule-shaped rights, the conflict would be viewed as a legislative-level conflict. However, if the rights are shaped as principles, the conflict between the two provisions will not be resolved at the legislative level, but rather, in most cases, at the sub-legislative level. That would ultimately be the level at which the normative arrangement is reduced to rules, rather than principles. Such a conflict would be resolved according to the canons that usually govern these situations, such as the rule later in time overriding the earlier rule, unless the earlier rule is more specific than the later, general rule.

This analysis raises the following question: have we not introduced – admittedly, through the "back door" – the same rules that apply to conflicts between rule-shaped rights to a conflict between principle-shaped rights? The answer is no. Both constitutional rights – in this case, privacy and disclosure – are left intact; their scope is not affected at the constitutional level. The only change is on the sub-constitutional level – here, the

---

[46] See Barak, above note 19, at 160.

legislative level, the administrative-act level, or the common law level – where the conflict is resolved. This level does not occupy itself with the scope of the constitutional rights, but only their realization.

D. A conflict between a principle-shaped right and a rule-shaped right

How should the legal system address a conflict between a rule-shaped right and a principle-shaped right? To answer this question, we must distinguish between two principal scenarios. In the first, both conflicting rights are at the constitutional level. In the second, one of the rights is at the constitutional level while the other is at the sub-constitutional level.

Let us begin with the conflict between two constitutional rights, one shaped as a rule while the other is shaped as a principle. As in all other cases, the first task the interpreter faces is to try and resolve the conflict in such a way that the two rights are able to harmoniously co-exist. Amongst other things, the interpreter may consider the possibility that the rule-shaped arrangement was meant to affect the right's realization, not its original scope, or that the rule was meant to serve as an exception to the principle. In this context, the interpreter may use interpretive balancing, while analogizing the balancing rules appearing in the proportionality *stricto sensu* component of the proportionality rules. The remainder of the proportionality components – such as proper purpose, rational connection, and necessary means (the "less damaging alternative") – do not apply and should not be considered here. But what is the case when such an interpretive attempt fails? What should the interpreter do when the rule-shaped constitutional right is ultimately interpreted as a norm designed to change the scope of the principle-shaped constitutional right? Which of the two constitutional rights should prevail? The answer is that in this type of conflict the normal interpretive canons, according to which the specific right should prevail over the general right, will usually apply; and, if the principle-shaped right is later in time, it may be interpreted as impliedly repealing the specific right that is rule-shaped. In this type of conflict, the limitation clause – and its rules of proportionality – does not apply. The scope of the constitutional rights is affected.

In the second scenario, we are dealing with a conflict of norms that are not at the same level. This is a conflict between a constitutional right (shaped as either a rule or a principle) and a statutory right (or an administrative act, or common-law-based right shaped as either a rule or a principle). In this type of case, the sub-constitutional right cannot affect the scope of the constitutional right. The constitutional validity of the sub-constitutional norm is determined in accordance with the requirements set by the limitation clause. Even if such a right abides by those requirements, its only effect would be at the sub-constitutional level, limiting the ways in which the constitutional right may be realized, not its scope.

Take, for example, the case of a principle-shaped constitutional right ("every person has the right to privacy"). Now assume that a statute sets a specific provision – shaped as a rule – relating to the right to public hearings. Such a determination may limit the right to privacy. However, this kind of provision may not affect the scope of the constitutional right to privacy. The provision does limit privacy, but this limitation would be constitutional if, and only if, it abides by all the requirements set by the limitation clause's rules of proportionality. The same would apply if the constitutional right is shaped as a rule while the sub-constitutional norm is shaped as a principle. Let us assume, for that matter, a rule-shaped constitutional provision relating exclusively to the right to public hearings. Let us further assume a principle-shaped legislative provision relating to the right to privacy. The statutory provision may not affect the scope of the constitutional provision. The constitutionality of such an act would be determined in accordance with the requirements set by the limitation clause.

4

Limitation of constitutional rights

A. Limitation and amendment of rights

A fundamental distinction exists between the amendment of a constitutional right and its limitation. The amendment of a constitutional right requires an amendment of the constitution, while a limitation of the right is possible with no constitutional change. The distinction stems from the more basic distinction between the right's scope and the extent of its protection. An amendment of a right entails a change – a narrowing or expansion – of its scope; such a change, in turn, affects the persons and institutions governed by the right, its content, or its application in terms of time and place. Thus, for example, a constitutional amendment would be a change in a constitutional provision – which currently applies to any person – according to which the provision would, from now on, apply only to citizens. Such a change is possible only through the mechanism of a constitutional amendment. Here, the proportionality of the constitutional change does not play a role. A statutory provision which intends to lead to such a change in the constitution is unconstitutional regardless of its proportionality. Conversely, a limitation of a constitutional right only narrows the ability to realize the right without changing the right's actual boundaries.[1] These limitations are constitutional only if they are proportional, as required by the limitation clause.

The distinction between a constitutional change (which requires a constitutional amendment) and the limitation of a constitutional right (through a proportional sub-constitutional law) is not always self-evident. The proper criterion to distinguish between the two should be objective in nature and not require an inquiry into the subjective intent of the law's creators. Naturally, the application of such an objective test may lead to substantial difficulties. Take, for example, the Canadian Supreme Court

---

[1] See E. Heinze, *The Logic of Constitutional Rights* (Burlington, VT: Ashgate Publishing, 2005), 13–26; B. Pieroth and B. Schlink, *Gdundrechte Staatsrecht II* (Heidelberg: C. F. Müller Verlag, 2006), 58.

case of *Quebec Protestant School Boards*.[2] There, the court was asked to examine the constitutionality of a Quebec statute that limited the acceptance of English-speaking students who studied English outside Quebec into English-speaking schools in Quebec, in an alleged violation of the Canadian Charter of Rights and Freedoms.[3] The Canadian Supreme Court held that the proposed change – through a statute – to the constitutional right cannot be considered a mere limitation whose constitutionality need be determined by the provisions of the limitation clause. Rather, the change should be seen as a complete denial of the constitutional right without following the rules required by the Charter for a constitutional amendment. Therefore, the court invalidated the statute and declared it unconstitutional; importantly, it did so without even examining whether the proposed change was as per the limitation clause. The court then added the following clarification:

> An Act of Parliament or of a legislature which, for example, purported to impose the belief of a state religion would be in direct conflict with Section 2(a) of the Charter, which guarantees freedom of conscience and religion, and would have to be ruled of no force or effect without the necessity of even considering whether such legislation could be legitimized by Section 1. The same applies to [the Quebec provision] in respect to Section 23 of the Charter.[4]

A more recent ruling by the Canadian Supreme Court emphasized that only a "complete denial" of the constitutional right would not be considered a mere "limitation" and therefore not examined through the lens of the limitation clause.[5] The decision was heavily criticized. Hogg argued that there is no rational basis to differentiate between a right's "denial" – whether partial or complete – and a right's limitation. In his opinion, any denial (partial or complete) should be considered a limitation whose constitutionality should be determined by the limitation clause.[6] It is hard to support such an approach.[7] With all the difficulties arising from the distinction between a constitutional change of a right and its limitation,

---

[2] *Attorney General of Quebec* v. *Quebec Association of Protestant School Boards et al.* [1984] 2 SCR 66.
[3] Canadian Charter of Rights and Freedoms, Part I of the Constitution Act 1982.
[4] See *Quebec Association of Protestant School Boards*, above note 2, at 88.
[5] See *Ford* v. *AG of Quebec* [1988] 2 SCR 712, 771.
[6] See P. W. Hogg, *Constitutional Law of Canada*, 5th edn., vol. II (Toronto: Thomson Carswell, 2007), 121.
[7] See also L. Weinrib, "The Supreme Court of Canada and Section One of the Charter," 10 *Sup. Ct. L. Rev.* 469, 479 (1988).

these difficulties should not deter us from using this analytically sound, constitutionally vital, distinction.

What should be the criterion to distinguish between a denial of right and a limitation thereof? The answer is that the proper criterion is the extent and the intensity of the change or the limitation, which is examined according to the results of the opposing norm and not its creators' intent. Take, for example, a legislative provision which provides that the right to freedom of occupation applies only to citizens. This is a denial of the right and not just a limitation. An examination of the proportionality of the provision according to the rules provided by the limitation clause will not suffice. In contrast, legislation restricting incitement speech, which leads to violence, or the publication of materials considered obscene, merely limits the constitutional right to freedom of speech; such provisions do not constitute a change of that right. Accordingly, such a limitation may be achieved through legislation as long as that legislation is proportional.

B. Limitation on rights

1. Infringement and limitation on rights

A limitation of a constitutional right by law also means its infringement by law.[8] Accordingly, several constitutions use these terms (limitation, infringement) interchangeably. In Israel, for example, the Basic Laws use the Hebrew equivalent of the term "infringement."[9] Conversely, the Canadian Charter of Rights and Freedoms uses the term "limits,"[10] which is also used by many other Western constitutions. There appears to be no difference between them. Accordingly, in this book, no distinction is made between a limitation on and an infringement of a constitutional right by law.[11] For convenience, this book uses the term "limitation."

---

[8] For a different view, see G. Webber, *The Negotiable Constitutions: On the Limitation of Rights* (Cambridge University Press, 2009). For a review of Webber's approach, see below, at 493.

[9] See Art. 8 of Basic Law: Human Dignity and Liberty, available in English at www.knesset.gov.il/laws/special/eng/basic3_eng.htm. But see the official English translation, which uses the term "violation," at *ibid*. That translation is wrong.

[10] Canadian Charter of Rights and Freedoms, § 1 ("The Canadian Charter of Rights and Freedoms guarantees the rights and freedoms set out in it subject only to such reasonable *limits* prescribed by law as can be demonstrably justified in a free and democratic society." (emphasis added)).

[11] The term "infringement" is often used in American legal discourse. See, e.g., F. Schauer, "Commensurability and Its Constitutional Consequences," 45 *Hastings L. J.* 785 (1994).

A limitation on a right occurs whenever a state action denies or prevents the right's owner from exercising it to its fullest scope. This is all that is required; accordingly, a limitation occurs whether the effect on the right is significant or marginal; whether the limitation is related to the right's core or to its penumbra; whether it is intentional or not; or whether it is carried out by an act or an omission (when there is a duty to positively protect the right[12]). Indeed, every limitation is unconstitutional unless it is proportional. Only when the statutory provision limiting the constitutional right is proportional – when it fulfills all the requirements of the limitation clause – can we say that the limitation is valid. Only then can the constitutional right peacefully co-exist with its limitation. When that same provision, however, does not abide by the proportionality rules set by the constitutional limitation clause, we conclude that the right has been violated. When the constitutional right can no longer co-exist with such a limitation; the solution must be an assertion that the limitation is invalid. We thus have to distinguish between a limitation that is proportional and therefore valid, and a limitation that is not proportional and therefore invalid. When the limitation is not valid, we say that the right has been violated (or breached).[13]

This seemingly straightforward analysis may lead to semantic conundrums. Take, for example, a provision limiting the constitutional right to equality. If the limitation is not proportional, and is therefore unconstitutional, we assert that the provision is discriminatory. Assume now that the provision, despite its limitation on the right to equality, is proportional and therefore constitutional. Is this provision therefore a "valid discrimination"? Or should the term "discrimination" be used only for those cases where the limitation is disproportional and therefore unconstitutional? If that is the case, how would we refer to a valid constitutional limitation on the right to equality? In one case, it was claimed, with regard to the limitation of equality, that "the distinction is no longer solely between equality (which is legal) and discrimination (which is illegal). We must now differentiate between the right to equality and the constitutional possibility of limiting such a right while fulfilling the requirements of the limitation clause."[14] What terminology should we

---

[12] See below, at 422.
[13] For a philosophical discussion, see J. Oberdiek, "Lost in Moral Space: On the Infringing/Violating Distinction and Its Place in the Theory of Rights," 23 *Law and Philosophy* 325–346 (2004); A. Botterell, "In Defense of Infringement," 27 *Law and Philosophy* 269–292 (2008).
[14] HCJ 3434/96 *Hoffnung* v. *Knesset Speaker* [1996] IsrSC 50(3) 57.

use in such a situation? One should not hesitate in calling this constitutional discrimination.

2. *De minimis constitutional limitations*

Every limitation of the constitutional right requires an examination as to its constitutionality. In that respect, there is no difference between a broad and a narrow limitation. Even a narrowly applied limitation – in terms of the number of people it applies to, its subject matter or the time and place in which it applies – requires a complete examination according to the proportionality rules set within the limitation clause. But, what about limitations so small that their effect is minimal? Does a *de minimis* limitation raise a constitutional problem?[15] In some legal systems, the accepted approach is that no constitutional examination is required when the limitation is trivial or insubstantial. The Canadian Supreme Court, for example, examined this question in the *Jones* case,[16] where the issue was a statutory provision relating to parents wishing to homeschool their children. The provision required parents to first apply to the state for approval of their proposed homeschooling curriculum. One of these parents, Jones, refused to apply for a permit as he did not recognize the authority of the state over the educational affairs of his child. As it turned out, had he applied for such a permit, he would have received one. Still, Jones claimed that the statutory provision violated his constitutional freedom of religion and therefore should be struck down. The court did not accept the argument, ruling that the statute was constitutional. Justice Wilson, in a separate opinion, ruled that the case did not even raise a constitutional issue, as the limitation on the right was "trivial."[17] A similar approach was adopted by the Israeli Supreme Court.[18]

[15] See M. Sachs (ed.), *Grundgesetz Kommentar* (2003), 64.

[16] *The Queen* v. *Jones* [1986] 2 SCR 284.

[17] *Ibid.*, at 313 ("[N]ot every effect of legislation on religious beliefs or practices is offensive to the constitutional guarantee of freedom of religion. Section 2(a) does not require the legislature to refrain from imposing *any burdens* on the practice of religion. Legislative or administrative action whose effect on religion is *trivial or insubstantial* is not, in my view, a breach of freedom of religion." (Wilson, J.)).

[18] See *United Mizrahi Bank Ltd.* v. *Migdal Cooperative Village*, CA 6821/93 [1995] IsrLR 1 at 237 ("[T]he constitutional prohibition applies to the infringement on the right to property. Every infringement violates the prohibition, and shifts the constitutional review to the limitation clause. At the same time, when the infringement on the right is trivial or minor – if it can be classified as *de minimis* – then it will not be regarded as an infringement and there is no need to embark upon the constitutional review of the second phase." (Barak, P.)); HCJ 3434/96 *Hoffnung* v. *Knesset Speaker* [1996] IsrSC 50(3)

This approach does not claim that a "trivial" limitation does not limit the right in question. It argues that this kind of *de minimis* limitation does not trigger – or require – constitutional review. Furthermore, the "minimal" nature of the limitation as well as its characterization as *de minimis* may change from one set of circumstances to another. Therefore, an answer is required as to the proper test for characterizing a limitation as "trivial" or "minimal." Noting the importance of this question, Justice Zamir of the Israeli Supreme Court observed:

> A question arises as to how we can measure a limitation and when we can consider it minimal. The answer depends, among others, on the nature of the right in question, the limitation's purpose, and the specific circumstances of each case. Accordingly, the answer may change from one case to another.[19]

A more general question, arising in this context, is whether the test for determining the minimal nature of the limitation should be objective – that is, reflecting the minimal nature of the limitation from the standpoint of the legal system as a whole – or should it be subjective – reviewing the limitation from the standpoint of the person affected by the limitation? The test should be made up of both objective and subjective elements. We should not forget that we are dealing with individual constitutional rights and limitations placed upon them by the state. Accordingly, it would be proper to examine the nature of the limitation from the subjective standpoint of the individual whose right was limited. However, this subjective test should also entail an objective component, such that, while considering the effects of the limitation, we should not take into account any exceptional attributes or unique circumstances of the specific person affected; rather, we should consider the limitation from the standpoint of a reasonable and typical person of the kind actually affected. Therefore, according to these tests, Justice Wilson's dissenting opinion in *Jones* may not correspond to the facts of the case. Indeed, from Mr. Jones' standpoint – and other reasonable persons of his kind, all belonging to a group of persons of deep religious faith – who was required, against his expressed belief, to appeal to state authorities in matters relating to the religious education of

---

57, 68 ("In order for the Court to strike down a law, the infringement in question cannot be minimal or trivial, but rather substantial and noticeable. This is the way this Court has acted in every legal issue. The Court does not tend to deal with insignificant matters: *de minimis non curat lex*. Accordingly, this Court would not examine a minimal infringement on the right." (Zamir, J.)).

[19] See *Hoffnung* v. *Knesset Speaker*, above note 18, at 68.

his own children, the requirement to appeal to the authorized authority is a limitation that is neither minimal nor trivial.[20]

3.   Incidental limitations

Incidental limitations occur whenever a statutory provision which according to its proper interpretation deals with one issue has an "incidental" effect of limiting a separate constitutional right, beyond its scope. Are incidental limitations on a constitutional right included in the same category as all other limitations? If so, the constitutionality of such a limitation should be examined within the rules of proportionality. If not, the issue of constitutionality does not arise and the rules of proportionality do not apply. This question cannot be given an inclusive answer. On the one hand, not every incidental limitation falls into the category of a constitutional "limitation." On the other hand, not every incidental limitation falls outside either. The answer is therefore case-specific and is largely dependant on the proper interpretation of the right in question.[21] Take, for example, freedom of occupation. Assume that a tax law provision is passed, raising taxes and therefore making it harder to realize that freedom. Such a provision would be considered a limitation on the constitutional right of freedom of occupation and therefore would have to be reviewed within the framework of the proportionality rules found in the limitation clause. The same is true for legislative provisions rendering the cost of employment more expensive or otherwise adversely affecting the ability of employers to realize their constitutional freedom. But what is the case when the same tax law provision also makes it harder to realize an occupation involving the freedom of expression (such as being a reporter)? Should we view that provision as limiting the freedom of expression? The answer is no. This is an example of an incidental limitation.[22] When the limitation is merely "incidental," it should not trigger a proportionality examination. However, the question of whether a limitation is "direct" or "incidental" is not always easily applicable. In fact, the very same limitation may be found to be "incidental" regarding one right

---

[20] See G. V. La Forest, "The Balancing of Interests under the Charter," 2 *Nat'l J. Const.* 134, 141 (1992) ("Mr. Jones' situation may have been trivial from the majority's point of view, but if Mr. Jones sincerely believed the law violated his religious convictions, that was good enough for me.").

[21] H. Cheadle, N. Haysom, and D. Davis (eds.), *South African Constitutional Law: The Bill of Rights* (2003), 700.

[22] *Ibid.*

(freedom of expression), and "non-incidental" or "direct" – and therefore triggering a proportional examination – in relation to another right (freedom of occupation).

4.   Waiving constitutional rights

Can a person unilaterally waive a constitutional right? Can an individual come to an agreement with the state waiving such a right? Is this waiver constitutional? Should such a waiver be examined in the first stage of the constitutional review (the right's scope stage) or during the second (the extent of its realization stage)? If the latter, should the waiver be proportional in accordance with the rules prescribed by the limitation clause? Can we say that the waiver is "according to the law"? All these are important questions; yet the constitutions themselves offer very little guidance, and neither the literature nor the courts have explored the issues sufficiently.[23] Uncertainty and confusion abound.[24]

Woolman is correct in saying that the waiver question should not be considered on its own; rather, the real question is whether, despite the waiver *vis-à-vis* the state to exercise a right to its fullest extent, the right has actually been limited. This question should be examined separately for each waived right. If the answer is that the waived right was not limited by the state in the first place, no constitutional issue arises and the inquiry ends. If, on the other hand, the waived right has been limited by the state, then the limiting actions taken by the state towards the waiving party would have to be examined in accordance with the proportionality requirements. Either way, there is no room for the creation of separate constitutional waiver rules.

[23] See Pieroth and Schlink, above note 1.

[24] See, e.g., K. Hopkins, "Constitutional Rights and the Question of Waiver: How Fundamental Are Fundamental Rights?," 16 *SAPL* 122 (2001); S. Woolman, "Application," in S. Woolman, M. Bishop, and J. Brickhill (eds.), Constitutional Law of South Africa, 2nd edn. (Cape Town: Juta Law Publishers, looseleaf, 2002–), 122 ("Whether the beneficiaries of constitutional rights can waive their rights is an underdeveloped and confusing area of constitutional law.").

5

Limiting constitutional rights by law

A.   The legality principle

1.   Legal authority to limit a right

In a constitutional democracy, a constitutional right cannot be limited unless such a limitation is authorized by law.[1] This is the principle of legality.[2] From here stems the requirement – which can be found in modern constitutions' limitation clauses, as well as in other international documents – that any limitation on a right be "prescribed by law." At the basis of this requirement stands the principle of the rule of law.[3] Every provision limiting a constitutional right must derive from a legal norm whose authority can be traced back – either directly or indirectly – to the constitution itself.[4] If this authority cannot be found, the limitation is unconstitutional. It can be said that in these matters the principle of legality – and the authorization it requires – is a threshold requirement. It is the legal "threshold" to the laws of proportionality. If the legality requirements are not satisfied, there is no need – and no reason – to examine the proportionality issue.

The legality principle requires legal authorization – which can be traced back to the constitution itself – to limit a constitutional right. This is the "authorization chain" requirement of having a "constitutional legal

---

[1] See G. Van der Schyff, *Limitation of Rights: A Study of the European Convention and the South African Bill of Rights* (Nijmegen, The Netherlands: Wolf Legal Publishers, 2005), 132.

[2] See O. M. Garibaldi, "General Limitations on Human Rights: The Principle of Legality," 17 *Harv. Int'l L. J.* 503 (1976).

[3] See, e.g., in South Africa, *Dawood* v. *Minister of Home Affairs*, 2000 (3) SA 936 (CC); in Germany, D. P. Currie, *The Constitution of the Federal Republic of Germany* (University of Chicago Press, 1994), 168; in Canada, P. W. Hogg, *Constitutional Law of Canada*, 5th edn., vol. II (Toronto: Thomson Carswell, 2007), 122.

[4] See *Pharmaceutical Manufacturers Association of South Africa: In re Ex parte Application of the President of the Republic of South Africa*, 2000 (2) SA 674 (CC).

pedigree."[5] This requirement represents a formal aspect of the rule-of-law principle. In addition to this formal requirement, the legality principle has been interpreted as requiring three other conditions:[6] first, in several legal systems an authorization of a general nature, or a "general application" authorization; second, accessibility to the law; and, third, clarity of the law. These requirements are based on a jurisprudential understanding of the principle of the rule of law.[7] It establishes additional requirements, which in turn represent the very essence of a constitutional democracy. These requirements are essential for the rule of law, not of men. This is what Rawls called "formal justice,"[8] and Fuller named "the inner morality of the law."[9] The list of these requirements is not final: it develops along with the understanding of the nature of law and its place in our society.[10] The legal basis for these requirements is in the interpretation of the word "law" in the limitation clause. We turn now to take a closer look at the principle of legality, as well as its underlying notion of the rule of law.[11]

2.   The authorization chain

i.   Normative validity stemming explicitly or implicitly from the constitution

The basic requirement in every constitutional democracy is that every limitation on a constitutional right be traced back to a valid legal norm. A valid legal norm means a norm that is a part of the hierarchical structure

---

[5] See Van der Schyff, above note 1, at 134; Garibaldi, above note 2, at 506.

[6] See, e.g., *Sunday Times* v. *United Kingdom*, App. No. 6538/74, 2 EHRR 245 (1980).

[7] On this aspect of the principle, see A. Barak, *The Judge in a Democracy* (Princeton University Press, 2006), 54. See also J. Raz, *The Authority of Law: Essays on Law and Morality* (Oxford: Clarendon Press, 1979), 210.

[8] See J. Rawls, *A Theory of Justice* (Cambridge, MA: Belknap Press of Harvard University Press, 1999), 235.

[9] See L. L. Fuller, *The Morality of Law* (New Haven, CT: Yale University Press, 1969), 33.

[10] See A. Barak, *Purposive Interpretation in Law* (Princeton University Press, 2006), 51.

[11] The proper location for the discussion of the principle of legality within these pages has been a source of much debate for me. On the one hand, the principle does not constitute a component of the proportionality rules themselves, and therefore should not appear in the third part of the book (dealing with those components). On the other hand, the legality principle is not a part of the right's scope either – the issue of the first part of the book. It does, however, form a part of the limitation clause. In this book, I have distinguished between the limitation of the right (which is discussed in the first part of the book), and the components of proportionality (discussed in the third). Due to the close proximity of the issue of legality to that of limitation of a right, I decided in favor of placing the legality discussion in the pages following the discussion on the limitation itself.

of the legal system. In other words, it should be based on a chain of authority starting with the constitution itself. The constitutional authorization for such a limitation may be explicit or implicit. The legislator's explicit authority to legislate stems from the provisions in the constitution about the legislative body's general authority to legislate. Without such explicit authority to limit a constitutional right, a valid implicit authorization may stem from the legal sources that have created the concept of proportionality.[12]

ii.   Limitation and violation

A legal provision limiting a constitutional right must constitute a part of the legal system's hierarchical structure. Regardless of its "distance" from the constitution, it must ultimately be connected to an authorization found therein. Conversely, when a provision limiting a constitutional right is not based on such an authorization chain, it constitutes a violation of both the constitution and the constitutional right itself. From a legal perspective, there is no authorization to limit the constitutional right.[13] Thus, for example, general policy considerations do not suffice to form a legal basis to limit a constitutional right – unless they are based on an authorization that may be traced back – directly or indirectly – to the constitution.[14] The same is true for an administrative regulation limiting constitutional rights. If these limiting administrative regulations are not authorized by a legal provision that is a part of the system's hierarchical structure (such as a statutory provision or a specific delegated power), these regulations cannot be considered a part of the authorization chain and thus should be invalidated. Therefore, when prisoners are prevented from sending mail from prison solely on the basis of the Department of Correction's regulations (without the ability to link those regulations to a hierarchical legal authority), the prisoner's constitutional right to freedom of expression is limited without proper legal basis.[15] This is not the case, however, if the same limitation is based on governmental discretion authorized by law, and the administrative regulations are meant only to serve as guidelines for the proper execution of this discretion. In such a case, the authority can be traced back to the enabling legislation and the regulations are seen merely as an aid in guiding the discretion.

[12] See below, at 211.
[13] For a discussion of cases where a legislative omission limited a positive right without an authorization chain, see below, at 430.
[14] See *Hoffman* v. *South African Airways*, 2001 (1) SA 1.
[15] See *Committee for the Commonwealth of Canada* v. *Canada* [1991] 1 SCR 139.

When no legal authority exists to limit a constitutional right, the proportionality of such a limitation is not at issue. Without legal authorization, the limitation is unconstitutional, regardless of its proportionality. A state actor operating in accordance with such unauthorized provision is deprived of the "normative umbrella" of the limitation clause. Accordingly, it may be found personally liable for these actions.

In Israel, the text of Basic Law: The Government provides that "[t]he Government is authorized to perform in the name of the State and subject to any law, all actions which are not legally incumbent on another authority."[16] Can such a constitutional provision serve as the legal authority for the limitation of constitutional rights? The answer is no. This kind of provision – and all similar provisions – may not be used as a source to limit any right – constitutionally or otherwise.[17]

B.   Statutory limitations

1.   Limitation by statute

Most cases of limitations on constitutional rights are based on statutes enacted by the legislative body. Typically, in these cases, all the legal elements required to properly execute the limitation of a right can be found in the statute itself. Take, for example, a statute determining that "no publication which may affect national security interests is allowed." Here, all the elements of the limitation on the right of freedom of expression are defined within the statute. The scope of the limiting provision is determined according to its interpretation. Such interpretation is performed in accordance with the standard rules of statutory interpretation.[18] The limiting statute may be formed as a rule or as a principle. The limitation of the constitutional right may be either implicit or explicit.

A limitation of a constitutional right by statute is valid only if the statute itself is valid. This is the case regardless of the type of justification provided for this limitation, or lack thereof. It is necessary, therefore, that the

---

[16] Basic Law: The Government (Art. 32).

[17] See HCJ 1163/03 *Supreme Monitoring Committee for Arab Affairs in Israel* v. *The Prime Minister of Israel* [2006] (1) IsrLR 105, 147 ("It has been held – and this case-law rule has been universally accepted – that the government is not authorized, by virtue of its residual power under the provisions of Section 32, to violate the basic rights of the individual ... The government's 'residual authority' may not serve as a legal source for affecting the liberty of any individual." (Cheshin, V.P.)).

[18] See Barak, above note 10, at 339.

limiting statute pass all the procedural hurdles required, for it to become a valid law. Thus, if a bill requires three readings to become a law (as is the case in Israel), a failure of any one of those votes should lead to the invalidation of the entire statute.[19] The same is true if the vote did not pass with the required majority, or if a required majority was obtained through fraud, as in the case of "double" votes (i.e., where one Member of Parliament votes for two).[20] Similarly, in a federal legal system a bill must abide by state or federal procedural requirements to become a valid law. A failure to abide by any of these requirements creates a break in the authorization chain, which in turn leads to the invalidation of the limiting statute. The question of proportionality, therefore, is not reached in those cases.

2.   Limitation according to statute

i.   The intensity of the statutory delegation

A limitation on a constitutional right is according to statute when the statute in question does not contain all the legal elements required to properly execute such a limitation. Many legal instances fall into this category. These "deficient" statutes differ in degree regarding the extent of the intensity in determining the elements of the sub-constitutional law. Some contain more of the required limitation elements, while others contain less; in all of these cases, the other limiting elements are found in a sub-statutory law (such as an executive or administrative regulation). Thus we can imagine a spectrum of "deficient" limiting statutes. On one end of the spectrum we find the limitations in which most of the legal fundamentals that make them up are detailed in the statute, with only minor elements left to be addressed by the sub-statutory norm. On the other end we find statutes that authorize a sub-statutory authority to decide most of the limiting elements. Between these two extremes we find many intermediate, or "hybrid," situations. Take, for example, a statutory provision requiring a license to practice certain occupations (physicians or lawyers, for example). Assume the provision also states that the executive branch – specifically, the department in charge of regulating such occupations – would determine the exact requirements needed to obtain such a license. In this example, the statutory provision contains

---

[19] See HCJ 5131/03 *Litzman* v. *Knesset Speaker* [2004] IsrSC 59(1) 577, available in English at http://elyon1.court.gov.il/files_eng/03/310/051/A04/03051310.a04.pdf.
[20] *Ibid.*

only some of the elements required for executing a limitation on the constitutional right (here, the right to freedom of occupation), while the rest of the elements required – the exact conditions for granting or refusing a license – are determined by administrative (or executive) regulations. The issue likely to arise in these situations is whether such a "minimal" statutory provision is sufficient to overcome the requirement that the limitation on a constitutional right be according to statute. These issues will now be examined.

ii.   Limitations on the statutory delegation's intensity

In principle, no constitutional issue arises when some of the elements required to properly execute a limitation on a constitutional right are found in a sub-statutory norm (such as regulations). However, the question arising from such a principled assertion is as follows: does the legislator have an unfettered discretion to determine the degree of intensity (or scope) of the elements making up the limitation appearing in both statutory and sub-statutory law? Is a legislative determination asserting that a constitutional right may be limited, while leaving the key elements of such a limitation to be determined by regulations, legal? Does it abide by the legality-principle requirement of the limitation clause?

The answer to this question changes from one legal system to another. Some legal systems support the view that primary arrangements regarding a limitation of constitutional rights must appear in the statute itself and not in a sub-statutory norm (the non-delegable doctrine). This is the case in the United States,[21] Germany,[22] Canada,[23] India,[24] and Israel.[25] Primary arrangements are arrangements setting the general policy as well as the leading principles.[26] The constitutional basis for this view is supported by the constitutional principles of separation of powers, the rule of law, and democracy itself. According to the separation of powers principle, the delegation of regulating authority to the executive branch is allowed, but only if the legislative branch determines the parameters

---

[21] See L. H. Tribe, *American Constitutional Law*, 3rd edn. (New York: Foundation Press, 2000), 977.

[22] See Currie, above note 3, at 132.

[23] See Hogg, above note 3, at 123.

[24] See M. P. Jain, *Indian Constitutional Law*, 5th edn., 2 vols. (London: LexisNexis Butterworths, 2003), 139.

[25] See S. Navot, *The Constitutional Law of Israel* (Alphen aan den Rijn, The Netherlands: Kluwer Law International, 2007), 73.

[26] *Rubinstein* v. *Minister of Defense*, HCJ 3267/97 [1998–9] IsrLR 139, 502 (Barak, P.).

within which the executive branch may operate.[27] The rule-of-law principle requires, in turn, that the legislative branch determine the principles or primary arrangements, while the administrative (or executive) branch only be allowed to determine, through regulations, the details of such arrangements ("secondary arrangements"). As for the notion of democracy, it requires that substantial resolutions be made through the duly elected representatives sitting in the legislative body, and not by delegation to non-elected officials.

The conclusion is that a statute which delegates to an administrative agency (or another executive body) the authority to limit a constitutional right without determining the primary arrangements relating to the content of said limitation is invalid. The nature of the limited right, its place in the hierarchy of rights, and the scope of the limitation are all of no consequence to this conclusion. Conversely, when the statute does determine the primary arrangements of the limitation, there is no legal objection to the secondary arrangements being determined either by regulations or through the exercise of other executive (or administrative) authority.

iii.   General authorization

Some constitutions require that limitations on constitutional rights rely on a law with "general application." The German Constitution, for example, requires that any limiting legislation "apply generally and not solely to an individual case."[28] This requirement, therefore, calls for the general application of the limiting legislation, rather than for a limited application to an individual case. A similar provision, influenced by its German counterpart, appears in the Constitution of the Republic of South Africa: "The rights in the Bill of Rights may be limited only in terms of law of general application."[29] Even when the limitation clause – whether included in a constitution or an international treaty – does not specify the requirement for "general" application, it has been at times interpreted that the "generality" requirement still applies.[30]

---

[27] Rubinstein, above note 26, at 504 (Barak, P.).

[28] Basic Law for the Federal Republic of Germany, § 19(1).

[29] Constitution of the Republic of South Africa, § 36(1).

[30] See, e.g., "The Siracusa Principles on the Limitation and Derogation Provisions in the International Covenant on Civil and Political Rights," § 15, in 7 *Hum. Rts. Q.* 3 (1985); A. C. Kiss, "Permissible Limitations on Rights," in L. Henkin (ed.), *The International Bill of Rights: The Covenant on Civil and Political Rights* (New York: Columbia University Press, 1981), 290, 308.

The "generality" requirement is consistent with – and is in fact a part of – the rule-of-law principle.[31] Some view the generality requirement as part of the separation of powers principle.[32] According to this explanation, a special legislative act dedicated to a specific individual, or to a specific matter, represents an undue intervention in matters of the executive branch (if the matter is of an administrative nature) or of the judicial branch (if the matter is of a judicial nature) without abiding by all the requirements justifying such a legislative intervention. This is the basis for the American constitutional prohibition on Bills of Attainder,[33] which are "legislative acts, no matter their form, that apply to either named individuals or easily ascertainable members of a group in such a way as to inflict punishment on them without a judicial trial."[34] Still others base the "generality" requirement on the principle of equality before the law. According to this view, a legislation arbitrarily limiting a constitutional right is unconstitutional as it does not fulfill the requirement that the constitutional right's limitation be prescribed by law.

The different explanations as to the analytical basis of the "generality" requirement lead, in most cases, to the same interpretive result – in most, but not all, cases. Take, for example, the equality rationale. If the main reason behind the "generality" requirement is to guarantee equality, then a specific statute (applying to a specific individual) may not limit, in some cases, equality itself. This is the case when legal justifications exist, according to the principle of equality itself, to provide different (legal) treatments to different members of a given community. The result would be different, in these cases, if the rationale behind the requirement was related to either the rule-of-law or the separation-of-powers principles.

In any event, it seems that subscribers to the different rationales behind the "generality" requirement would agree on the following three

---

[31] See *"National Recruitment" Ltd* v. *Attorney General*, HCJ 1023/03 [2007] ("The requirement to limit a right "by" a statute or "according to" a statute should be seen as a part of the rule-of-law principle – not only by its formal interpretation but also according to its substantial (narrow) meaning. Accordingly, in order to pass constitutional muster, a limiting legislation must comply with all the requirements of a valid, binding legal norm, including – but not limited to – publicity, accessibility, lack of ambiguity, and lack of arbitrariness." (Beinish, P.)); S. Woolman and H. Botha, "Limitations," in S. Woolman, M. Bishop, and J. Brickhill (eds.), *Constitutional Law of South Africa*, 2nd edn. (Cape Town: Juta Law Publishers, looseleaf, 2002–), 48; *Dawood* v. *Minister of Home Affairs*, above note 3.

[32] See Van der Schyff, above note 1, at 139. See also I. M. Rautenbach and E. F. J. Malherbe, *Constitutional Law*, 4th edn. (Durban: Butterworths, 2004), 349.

[33] See US Const., Art. I, § 9, cl. 3.

[34] *United States* v. *Lovett*, 328 US 303, 316 (1946).

propositions. First, the substance, and not the wording, of the limiting legislation is the deciding factor. What may appear as a "general" limitation according to its wording may turn out to be a law which applies to an individual in substance. Such limitations could not be considered "general" for purposes of the constitutional requirement. Second, the "generality" requirement is not satisfied whenever the limiting legislation applies to a known and easily identified group of people. The dividing line between a known and easily identified group (which violates the "generality" requirement) and a group that is not known and not easily identified may, however, be hard to establish in some cases. Third, in determining the line between individual law (prohibited by the requirement) and "general" law (required by the limitation clause), the interpreter may need to address the reasons behind the legislation.[35]

It may be claimed that, with the rise of the status of the constitutional right to equality, the generality requirement becomes less important. According to this claim, most cases where a law, limiting a constitutional right, is unconstitutional due to its lack of generality will also be unconstitutional due to its limitation of equality. However, the generality requirement retains its importance as a threshold requirement, for two reasons. First, not every case of "non-generality" stems from discrimination; second, if the limiting statute does not realize the generality requirement, there is no need to examine its proportionality. Surely, without generality's threshold requirements a limitation of equality does not suffice, and there is a need to examine the proportionality of equality's limitation. From here stems the importance of the generality requirement in legal systems where the principle of equality is developed.

iv.   "Accessible" authorization

Many legal systems share the notion that any law authorizing a limitation of a constitutional right must be "accessible" to the public.[36] It should be public domain. Accordingly, the statute should be published. A "secret law" or regulations with legislative powers promulgated behind closed doors are not accessible, and are therefore unconstitutional.[37]

---

[35] See Van der Schyff, above note 1, at 139.

[36] See *Sunday Times* v. *United Kingdom*, above note 6; *Dawood* v. *Minster of Home Affairs*, above note 31; *President of the Republic of South Africa* v. *Hugo*, 1997 (4) SA 1 (CC).

[37] LCRA 1127/93 *State of Israel* v. *Klein* [1994] IsrSC 48(3) 485, 515 ("The principle of public legislation is at the heart of hearts of the rule of law ... This element of the publication of statutory provisions penetrates deep into the kingdom of the rule of law in its substantive aspect – both in terms of content and value – which is the rule of law as steeped in the fundamental values of society and of the individual." (Cheshin, J.)).

A similar question arises regarding internal guidelines of the executive branch: if they are authorized by primary legislation, are they also required to abide by the publicity requirement? The answer is yes. The publicity requirement is satisfied if, and only if, these internal regulations are accessible to the public. Similarly, a judicial decision is considered "public" only if it is properly, and openly, published. This accessibility requirement is also aimed at any authorizing (or delegating) law. An individual directive, authorized by law, is not required to be public; only the authorizing law itself must be public and accessible. It would be sufficient for the individual directive to be brought to the attention of the person against whom it was issued. Some are of the opinion that legislation cannot limit rights retroactively. Retroactive (or retrospective) law is not accessible as the limitation did not exist when the action took place and was obviously not accessible.[38] It seems that a retrospective, or retroactive, law limiting a constitutional right is accessible if published properly. Its constitutionality should be determined, therefore, according to a set of well-determined legal criteria rather than a simple threshold test.

v.   Sufficiently clear authorization

Some courts have ruled that in order to satisfy the requirement of "prescribed by law" the limiting law should be "clear enough."[39] A limiting law, in other words, should be comprehensible to a reasonable reader (including, if need be, with the assistance of a professional to reach this comprehension). Otherwise, the statutory arrangement is the functional equivalent of a "secret law." The law is not a riddle. On the other hand, the more complex the issue is, the more complex the legal arrangement. The law is not a simple arithmetic equation, either. The clarity required is relative to the complexity of the issue at hand.[40] The proper criterion is that of reasonable understanding, one that would enable reasonable people to guide their future actions (even, if need be, with the help of a professional). The European Court of Human Rights noted this point in the *Sunday Times* case:

> [A] norm cannot be regarded as "law" unless it is formulated with sufficient precision to enable the citizen to regulate his conduct; he must be able – if need be with appropriate advice – to foresee, to a degree that is

[38] See, e.g., Currie, above note 3, at 169.
[39] See Van der Schyff, above note 1, at 140, 180, 245; Woolman and Botha, above note 31, at 49.
[40] See *Chorherr v. Austria*, App. No. 13308/87, 17 EHRR 358 (1994).

> reasonable in the circumstances, the consequences which a given action
> may entail. Those consequences need not be foreseeable with absolute cer-
> tainty; experience shows this to be unattainable. Again, whilst certainty
> is highly desirable, it may bring in its train excessive rigidity and the law
> must be able to keep pace with changing circumstances. Accordingly,
> many laws are inevitably couched in terms which, to a greater or lesser
> extent, are vague and whose interpretation and application are questions
> of practice.[41]

Accordingly, for example, if the statute determines the conditions under
which the government may legally eavesdrop, every informed person –
including the person to whom the government is secretly listening –
should be able to discern these conditions, even if he has no idea that his
own rights are limited in this way.[42]

Some legal systems adopted the doctrine of unconstitutional "vagueness." According to the doctrine, a statutory provision limiting a constitutional right is void if it is too "vague."[43] The doctrine of vagueness may
well be seen as an integral part of the general requirement of the constitutional limitation to be "clear enough." It is important to note that the level
of clarity required – or rather the level of lack of clarity that would render
the limiting provision void – would apply regardless of the degree of proportionality of the limiting provision. Accordingly, a provision is clear if
it sets a clear arrangement to the limitation of a constitutional right, even
if the limitation turns out not to be proportional. Clarity is separate from
proportionality. Clarity is a threshold requirement.

What is the level of clarity required by the constitution for the limiting provision? The answer may change from one legal system to the next.
However, generally speaking, the clarity required should not be such that
a mere initial reading would provide the exact contours of constitutional
limitation; such a requirement cannot be met by most constitutional democracies (assuming, *arguendo*, that they aimed at meeting such a requirement in the first place). Indeed, most initial readings are intuitive.[44] They
attach a substantial weight to the dictionary meaning of the legal text. The
legal system as a whole, however, is a much more nuanced and complex

---

[41] See *Sunday Times*, above note 6, at para. 49.
[42] See *Malone* v. *United Kingdom*, App. No. 8691/79, 7 EHRR 14 (1984).
[43] See generally Hogg, above note 3, at 125. See also, in the US, Note, "The Void-for-
Vagueness Doctrine in the Supreme Court," 109 *U. Pa. L. Rev.* 67 (1960); R. D. Cooter,
"Void for Vagueness: Introduction," 82 *Calif. L. Rev.* 487 (1994); J. Waldron, "Vagueness
in Law and Language: Some Philosophical Issues," 82 *Calif. L. Rev.* 509 (1994); J. E. Nowak
and R. D. Rotunda, *Constitutional Law*, 8th edn. (Eagan MN: West, 2010), 1280.
[44] See Barak, above note 10, at 39.

creature. Accordingly, the rules of statutory interpretation have evolved over hundreds of years. A legal text cannot be understood without the process of legal interpretation,[45] and no pre-interpretive understanding can stand.[46] Therefore, the clarity required is the clarity achieved after the interpretive process has been exhausted. Every text is clear and understandable – in relation to the legal issues in question – after the interpretive process has been completed. There is no text that is un-interpretable; there is no text which the process of legal interpretation does not render, at the end of the day, clear and lucid as to the legal issues in question. We may therefore conclude that the level of lack of clarity required to render the limiting provision unconstitutional is extreme. This occurs only in those (rare) cases where an educated reading of the provision, including the application of all the rules of statutory interpretation by a professional, still leaves the reader with serious doubt as to its legal meaning.[47] In those cases – and only in those cases – we should determine that the limiting provision is not clear enough.

C.   The legality principle and common law

1.   *The constitution and common law*

Most common law legal systems drafted their constitutions within the context of an existing – and sometimes long-standing – common law regime. It is only natural, therefore, that one of the first questions to arise in those systems was that of the proper relation between the common law – developed either prior to the constitution or post that date – and the constitution itself. Can a constitutional democracy tolerate the common law? Can the common law limit a constitutional right? Legislation limiting constitutional rights is constitutional – and valid – if it abides by the requirements of the limitation clause – in other words, if it is proportional. Can a court decision be treated the same way? Should the courts be asked to abide by the same requirements posed by the limitation clause? Should they be proportional? Constitutions sometimes determine that every state authority must respect constitutional rights.[48] If it is agreed that the judiciary is a state authority, it must respect constitutional rights.

---

[45] *Ibid.*, at 12.   [46] *Ibid.*

[47] See, in Canada, *R. v. Nova Scotia Pharmaceutical Society* [1992] 2 SCR 606.

[48] See Art. 1(2) of the German *Grundgesetz*; Art. 7(2) of the Constitution of the Republic of South Africa; Art. 11 of Basic Law: Human Dignity and Liberty.

When the court develops the common law in the field of private law it at times takes rights from one and gives them to the other. This is the case in contract law and tort. Such common law will usually limit an individual's rights *vis-à-vis* the state. Such limitation was carried out by a state authority – for example, the judiciary. If this limitation had been carried out through statute, it would be unconstitutional – unless it fulfills the requirements in the limitation clause. Should the common law which created these rights in private law – and therefore also limits those rights *vis-à-vis* the state – fulfill the requirement of the limitation clause?

Despite its significance, this book cannot give this issue its due treatment. Instead, the following pages will present an initial sketch of the major considerations involved. It begins by noting that providing a positive answer to the question – requiring common law decisions to abide by the requirements posed by the limitation clause – is essential to any legal system that would like to continue existing as a common law system. Indeed, if the common law, by developing rights between individuals, cannot limit an individual's constitutional right *vis-à-vis* the state, its function as a creative common law – which is separate from its role in statutory and constitutional interpretation – is severely harmed.

How could we ensure, therefore, the status of the common law as a viable source of law in a constitutional democracy?[49] Without an express constitutional directive,[50] the answer lies in legal tradition. In most common law systems, the rule of recognition – to use Hart's term[51] – accepts the authority of the common law to create new law. But what is the case when the legal system is governed by a formal constitution? What then is the legal source of common law authority? For some, the question should be reversed, as legal authority of the constitution

---

[49] See F. Michelman, "The Rule of Law, Legality and the Supremacy of the Constitution," in S. Woolman, M. Bishop, and J. Brickhill (eds.), *Constitutional Law of South Africa*, 2nd edn. (Cape Town: Juta Law Publishers, looseleaf, 2002–), 11-1.

[50] But see Constitution of the Republic of South Africa, Art. 8(3) ("When applying a provision of the Bill of Rights to a natural or juristic person in terms of subsection (2), a court (a) in order to give effect to a right in the Bill, must apply, or if necessary develop, the common law to the extent that legislation does not give effect to that right; and (b) may develop rules of the common law to limit the right, provided that the limitation is in accordance with Section 36(1)."); *ibid.*, Art. 39(2) ("When interpreting any legislation, and when developing the common law or customary law, every court, tribunal or forum must promote the spirit, purport and objects of the Bill of Rights."). On the South African constitutional view on this issue, see S. Woolman, "Application," in S. Woolman, M. Bishop, and J. Brickhill (eds.), *Constitutional Law of South Africa*, 2nd edn. (Cape Town: Juta Law Publishers, looseleaf, 2002–), Chapter 31, 1.

[51] See H. L. A. Hart, *The Concept of Law*, 2nd edn. (Oxford: Clarendon Press, 1994).

itself lies with the common law.[52] Thus, for example, an English court
has decided that the very concept of parliamentary sovereignty originated from the common law, and therefore the contours of this constitutional concept should be drawn by the courts.[53] Another view holds
that the common law can only draw its authority from constitutional
directives, whether they are explicit or implicit.[54] According to this

---

[52] See, e.g., O. Dixon, "The Common Law as an Ultimate Constitutional Foundation," in
O. Dixon, *Jesting Pilate* (Buffalo, NY: William S. Hein & Company, 1965), 203; R. Cooke,
"Fundamentals," *New Zealand L. J.* 158 (1988); T. R. S. Allen, "The Common Law as
Constitution: Fundamental Rights and First Principles," in C. Saunders (ed.), *Courts of
Final Jurisdiction: The Mason Court in Australia* (Sydney: Federation Press, 1996), 146;
M. D. Walters, "The Common Law Constitution in Canada: Return of Lex Non Scripta as
Fundamental Law," 51 *U. Toronto L. J.* 91 (2001); T. R. S. Allen, *Constitutional Justice: A
Liberal Theory of the Rule of Law* (Oxford University Press, 2001); T. Poole, "Questioning
Common Law Constitutionalism," 25 *Legal Studies* 142 (2005); M. Elliott, "United
Kingdom Bicameralism, Sovereignty, and the Unwritten Constitution," 5 *I. Con.* 370
(2007); S. Lakin, "Debunking the Idea of Parliamentary Sovereignty: The Controlling
Factor of Legality in the British Constitution," 28 *OJLS* 709 (2008); D. Edlin, *Judges and
Unjust Laws: Common Law Constitutionalism and the Foundations of Judicial Review*
(Ann Arbor, MI: University of Michigan Press, 2008).

[53] *Jackson v. Her Majesty's Attorney General* [2006] 1 AC 262; on parliamentary sover-
eignty, see T. R. S. Allen, "Parliamentary Sovereignty: Law, Politics, and Revolution," 113
L. Q. Rev. 443 (1997); N. MacCormick, *Questioning Sovereignty: Law, State and Nation
in the European Commonwealth* (Oxford University Press, 1999); Allen, above note 52.
Regarding the *Jackson* case, see J. Steyn, "Democracy, the Rule of Law and the Role of
Judges," *Eur. Hum. Rts. L. Rev.* 243 (2006); A. Young, "Hunting Sovereignty: Jackson v.
Attorney General," *PL* 187 (2006); J. Jowell, "Parliamentary Sovereignty under the New
Constitutional Hypothesis," *PL* 562 (2006); A. Tomkins, "The Rule of Law in Blair's
Britain," 26 *U. Queensland L. J.* 255 (2007); Elliott, above note 52.

[54] See *Pharmaceutical Manufacturers*, above note 4, at § 40 ("There is only one system of
law. It is shaped by the Constitution which is the supreme law, and all law, including
the common law, derives its force from the Constitution and is subject to constitutional
control ... Whereas previously constitutional law formed part of and was developed consistently with the common law, the roles have been reversed ... [T]he constitution is the
supreme law and the common law ... must be developed consistently with it, and subject
to constitutional control ... The common law supplements the provisions of the written Constitution but derives its force from it. It must be developed to fulfil the purposes
of the Constitution and the legal order that it proclaims ... There is, however, only one
system of law and within that system the Constitution is the supreme law with which all
other law must comply."); J. Goldsworthy, "The Myth of the Common Law Constitution,"
in D. E. Edlin (ed.), *Common Law Theory* (Cambridge University Press, 2007), 205; T.
Mullen, "Reflections on Jackson v. Attorney General: Questioning Sovereignty," 27 *Legal
Studies* 1 (2007); R. Ekins, "Acts of Parliament and the Parliament Acts," 123 *L. Q. Rev.* 91
(2007); T. Bingham, "The Rule of Law and the Sovereignty of Parliament," 19 *King's Law
Journal* 223 (2008); J. Goldsworthy, *Parliamentary Sovereignty: Contemporary Debates*
(Cambridge University Press, 2010).

view, parliamentary sovereignty does not draw its authority from the common law.[55]

The gap between these two approaches is considerable. Albeit, in practice, it is narrower than it first appears to be. Those of the first opinion limit the common law's power, compared to the constitution, to extreme cases where the constitution limits the law's essential elements as established in the common law.[56] Those of the second opinion are, at times, willing to recognize the limitations applicable to the constitution stemming from external principles. The gap between the two approaches is, therefore, expressed in the shaping of basic and essential principles that even the constitution must uphold.

It is therefore possible to conclude – as per both approaches – that in regular cases – those that do not fall into the category of basic and essential principles – the authority of the common law to limit the constitutional right as well as protect it should be found within the constitution itself, whether explicitly or implicitly. According to this approach, the common law's authority to limit and protect the constitutional right is found in the limitation clause (explicitly or implicitly). Indeed, the limitation clause may serve as the legal source for the continued power of the common law in a constitutional democracy.

2.   The common law and the limitation clause

i.   Common law as a law limiting constitutional rights

The limitation clause (either explicit or implicit) may be seen as the legal source of the common law's authority to limit and protect rights in a constitutional democracy. Indeed, many constitutional limitation clauses in common law systems provide that a limitation of rights is only valid if prescribed by "law," a term those systems consider to include the common law.[57] This view was initially espoused by the European Court of Human Rights in the *Sunday Times* case.[58] There, the House of Lords issued an injunction against the publication of a newspaper article relating to a

---

[55] See J. Goldworthy, *The Sovereignty of Parliament: History and Philosophy* (Oxford University Press, 1999); Goldsworthy, above note 54; Bingham, above note 54.

[56] See H. Woolf, "Droit Public – English Style," *PL* 57 (1995); S. Sedley, "Human Rights – A Twenty-First Century Agenda," *PL* 373 (1995); J. Laws, "Law and Democracy," PL 72 (1995).

[57] See Van der Schyff, above note 1, at 136. For the term "law" and its relation to common law in the Universal Declaration of Human Rights and other international conventions, see Garibaldi, above note 2; see also Barak, above note 7, at 155.

[58] *Sunday Times*, above note 6.

pending case in England. The injunction was based, among others, on the English common law concept of "contempt of court." The European Court was asked to decide whether such a common law concept may properly limit the constitutional right to freedom of expression, guaranteed by Article 10(1) of the European Convention for the Protection of Human Rights and Fundamental Freedoms. No one disputed that the English ruling had the effect of limiting the right; the only question before the European Court was whether this limitation is proper, that is, whether it abides by all the requirement of the Convention's specific limitation clause (Article 10(2)). The limitation clause determines that the limitation has to be "prescribed by law."[59] Is the common law included in that term? The European Court ruled that it was. As the Court explained:

> The Court observes that the word "law" in the expression "prescribed by law" covers not only statute but also unwritten law. Accordingly, the Court does not attach importance here to the fact that contempt of court is a creature of the common law and not of legislation. It would clearly be contrary to the intention of the drafters of the Convention to hold that a restriction imposed by virtue of the common law is not "prescribed by law" on the sole ground that it is not enunciated in legislation; this would deprive a common-law state which is Party to the Convention of the protection of Article 10(2) and strikes at the very roots of that state's legal system.[60]

Other courts in common law systems have reached similar results.[61] Referring to the limitation clause included in the *Constitution of the Republic of South Africa*, Judge Kriegler wrote:

> [The clause] draws no distinction between different categories of law of general application ... A rule of the common law which, for example, infringes on a person's right to privacy or human dignity can be saved if it meets the Section 33(1) requirements. And it is irrelevant whether such rule is statutory, regulatory, horizontal, or vertical, and it matters not whether it is founded on the XII Tables of Roman Law, a Placaet of Holland or a tribal custom.[62]

---

[59] For the entire wording of the provision, see above at 21.

[60] *Sunday Times*, above note 6, at para. 47.

[61] See, in Canada, *R. v. Therens* [1985] 1 SCR 613; *RWDSU v. Dolphin Delivery Ltd.* [1986] 2 SCR 573; *BCGEU v. British Columbia* [1988] 2 SCR 214; in New Zealand, *Minister of Transport v. Noort* [1992] 3 NZLR 260 (CA); P. Rishorth, G. Huscropft, S. Optican, and R. Mahoney, *The New Zealand Bill of Rights* (Oxford University Press, 2003). See also Hogg, above note 3, at 122; see, in South Africa, *S. v. Mambolo*, 2001 (3) SA 409 (CC); *S. v. Thebus*, 2003 (6) SA 505 (CC). See also Woolman and Botha, above note 31, at 51.

[62] *Du Plessis v. De Clerk*, 1996 (3) SA 850 § 136 (CC).

When the courts develop the common law by granting rights to one individual *vis-à-vis* another (e.g., contracts, torts), the state acts. This action affects the rights of individuals *vis-à-vis* the state. Thus, by developing a common law rule about libel, the courts are limiting the right to freedom of expression of the individual *vis-à-vis* the state.[63] The common law is a state action just as legislation is a state action. Both are "law," both may affect the constitutional rights of individuals *vis-à-vis* the state, and, in both cases, the constitutionality of those laws should be decided according to limitation clauses. In both cases, the law must be proportional. It does not seem right to me that, while a statute that limits the constitutional rights of the individual *vis-à-vis* the state is subject to proportionality requirements, a common law decision with the same effect is not subject to proportionality requirements.[64] One should note that my view is not based on the assumption that the constitutional rights operate *vis-à-vis* individuals (horizontally). It is based on the assumption that constitutional rights operate only *vis-à-vis* the state. However, when the common law is providing rights between individuals – rights that operate on the sub-constitutional level only – such common law activity affects also the constitutional rights of the individuals *vis-à-vis* the state. The limitation on their constitutional rights *vis-à-vis* the state is prescribed by common law. This common law must be proportional in order to be constitutional. One should note that the scope of the individual's constitutional right *vis-à-vis* the state is more expansive than the individual's right *vis-à-vis* another individual. The reason for this is that in determining the scope of the individual's constitutional right *vis-à-vis* the state, one should consider the rationale of the right's basis.[65] No balance should be made on the constitutional level between it and the considerations which justify the right's limitation (i.e., the public interest or the rights of others).[66] Balances should be made only when determining the constitutionality of the limitation of the constitutional right by a sub-constitutional law.[67] With regard to the determination of the common law right of one individual *vis-à-vis* another individual, the scope of the right is determined by the common law and is a product of the balancing between the rationale at the right's basis and the rationale at the basis of the constitutional rights of others or the public interest. Of course, the constitutionality of this

---

[63] See *New York Times* v. *Sullivan*, 376 US 254 (1963).
[64] As is the case in Canada: see Hogg, above note 3.
[65] See above, at 71.   [66] See above, at 75.   [67] See below, at 340.

balance is determined by the limitation clause. This sub-constitutional common law is constitutional only if it is proportional.

ii.   The difficulties in applying a limitation clause to common law

The application of the limitation clause's provisions to the common law is far from easy. Three main difficulties will be noted here. The first issue is that limitation clauses are mostly created – and then interpreted by courts – with limiting legislative provisions in mind – hence, the constitutional requirements of accessibility, clarity, proper purpose, and the use of proportional means to achieve those purposes. These requirements, as formal requirements, are foreign to the common law. The common law has rarely evolved in that manner in the past; the addition of such threshold requirements under a constitutional regime may impose a heavy burden on its development.[68] However, constitutional provisions may not be ignored, even when they impose "heavy burdens." The common law should not be given any "special treatment" compared with legislation.[69] The approach applied to legislation which limits the constitutional right must be applied with regard to case law limiting a constitutional right. Accordingly, the common law must abide by them. Therefore, amongst other conditions, common law judgments must be properly published; the law stemming from them must be clear and unequivocal; the purposes these rulings seek to advance must be proper; and the means used by those precedents to achieve those purposes must be proportional as well. The constitutional experience of several common law countries demonstrates that, despite the difficulties, such requirements are plausible.

The second difficulty in applying the limitation clause to the common law lies in the "presumption of legality" of executive action. This presumption is a basic principle of administrative law in many common law systems.[70] Does the presumption of legality support the idea that constitutional rights can be limited not only by statute but also by the common law precedents? The answer is that it does. The presumption of legality "fits in" well with common law limitations on constitutional rights. The reason for that is that, in common law systems, judicial decisions are a valid legal source. They are part and parcel of the prevailing

---

[68] See Hogg, above note 3, at 159.
[69] See Hill v. Church of Scientology [1995] 2 SCR 1130, where Justice Cory ruled that the rules of proportionality need to be used in a more flexible manner where the limitation of the constitutional right is done by the common law.
[70] See D. Foulkes, Administrative Law, 8th edn. (London: Butterworths, 1995), 53.

positive law. Common law has undergone major changes over the years in that respect.[71] Initially, general judicial rules of administrative law were viewed as merely statutory-interpretation products rather than an independent source of law. Thus, for example, the basic rules relating to fair hearing and conflict of interest were seen as deriving from the relevant statutory provisions. However, over the years, the close connection between the common law and legislation weakened, until it finally withered away. Common law has been recognized as an independent source of law, regardless of the accompanying legislation. And, since judges were no longer tied to any statutory provision in order to develop those rules, their authority no longer depended upon legislative delegation. Finally, with the constitutionalization of many of the common law legal systems, we now view the constitution itself as the legal source of the common law. Regarding the limitation clause, it is sufficient that the constitution is recognized as the legal source of the authority exercised by common law judges to continue developing general principles of administrative law. As such a legal source is constitutional, it can therefore also allow for the limitation of constitutional rights, whether explicitly or implicitly recognized. In that respect, the "presumption of legality" of executive actions must include the common law as a source of authority. In other words, the "presumption of legality" does not require that every executive action originate with a statutory authority; rather, such a presumption – much like the rule-of-law principle, of which it is a part – merely requires that every executive action must be legal (and is in fact presumed to be that way until shown otherwise). In a common law system, the term "law" encompasses the common law in addition to statutory law.

The third difficulty in applying the limitation clause to the common law lies in the notion that most constitutional rights are primarily directed at the state and not towards other individuals. That said, if the judicial branch is included within the state, the result may be that constitutional rights can operate between private parties to a legal dispute.[72] This result is achieved through the dual role played by the courts in a constitutional democracy: On the one hand, a court settles a private law dispute according to the rules of private law (contracts, torts, and the like). On the other hand, when doing so, the court may limit the constitutional right of one of the parties, which originally operated only *vis-à-vis* the state. Take the case of Joe Smith, who claims that a publication by Jane Doe damaged his

[71] See P. Craig, *Administrative Law*, 6th edn. (London: Sweet & Maxwell, 2008), 3.
[72] See *Shelley* v. *Kraemer*, 334 US 1 (1948).

reputation. This is a dispute within the confines of private law (here, the law of libel). Joe's right to privacy, as well as Jane's right to free speech, are both recognized within the spheres of private law, and therefore may be exercised against each other. None of these parties, however, has a constitutional right *vis-à-vis* the other. The constitutional rights operate usually *vis-à-vis* the state.[73] But now consider the role of the judicial branch. This branch's acknowledgment of one party's common law right to limit another's common law right – a valid acknowledgment within the confines of common law – may concomitantly constitute a limitation on one party's (or both) constitutional right *vis-à-vis* the state. The constitutionality of this limitation would have to be determined according to the rules of proportionality provided by the limitation clause. The result, in practice, is that the right of one party (Joe Smith) *vis-à-vis* another party (Jane Doe) within the confines of private law has turned – through the intervention of the judicial branch – into a constitutional right that may be exercised against another person.

The answer to the third difficulty is that, in my opinion, constitutional rights apply directly only *vis-à-vis* the state.[74] They do not apply directly to the relationships governed by private law. According to this point of view, Joe Smith cannot argue that Jane Doe has affected his constitutional right not to be defamed. All Joe Smith can argue is that his private law right *vis-à-vis* Jane Doe not to be defamed has been limited. However, the constitutional right of individuals *vis-à-vis* the state may affect the content of private law. The constitutional right *vis-à-vis* the state of freedom of expression may be limited by a common law rule on libel. In such a case, the common law limitation is constitutional only if it is proportional. A proportional common law creates direct rights between individuals. However, these rights are not constitutional, but rather sub-constitutional rights.[75] Those sub-constitutional rights are the offspring

---

[73] See above, at 85.

[74] But see *The Constitution of the Republic of South Africa*, Art. 8(2): "A provision of the Bill of Rights binds a natural or a juristic person if, and to the extent that, it is applicable, taking into account the nature of the right and the nature of any duty imposed by the right." See above, at 85.

[75] See M. Kumm and V. Ferreres Comella, "What Is So Special about Constitutional Rights in Private Litigation?: A Comparative Analysis of the Function of State Action Requirements and Indirect Horizontal Effect," in A. Sajo and R. Uitz (eds.), *The Constitution in Private Relations: Expanding Constitutionalism* (Utrecht, The Netherlands: Eleven International Publishing, 2005), 241; M. Kumm, "Who's Afraid of the Total Constitution?," in A. Menéndez and E. Eriksen (ed.), *Arguing Fundamental Rights* (Dordrecht: Springer, 2006), 113.

of the conflict between constitutional rights. Even if the constitution provides – as does the Constitution of the Republic of South Africa[76] – that
constitutional rights apply directly between individuals, such application
will need prescriptive content provided by sub-constitutional laws.[77] Such
laws will reflect the proportional limitation on the conflicting rights.
Thus, Joe Smith's constitutional right *vis-à-vis* Jane Doe under the South
African Bill of Rights to his good reputation will conflict with Jane Doe's
constitutional right *vis-à-vis* Joe Smith to freedom of expression. This
conflict will not be resolved on the constitutional level.[78] Rather, it will be
resolved on the sub-constitutional level (common law) that will fulfill the
proportionality requirement. Thus, though the horizontal application of
constitutional rights in South Africa creates a direct relationship among
individuals, this direct relationship is operative on the sub-constitutional
level. Therefore, there is no place for special constitutional remedies for
breach of those rights. The place for the remedies is on the sub-constitutional level (private law).

It follows, that the question of the vertical or horizontal application of
the constitutional rights do not affect the proposition that the limitation
clause (proportionality) applies to the common law. The common law is
sub-constitutional law. It establishes direct common law rights between
individuals. Those rights effect the individual constitutional rights *vis-à-
vis* the state. In order for that effect to be constitutional, it must be proportional. The provision of the limitation clause, that limits on constitutional
rights must be by law, and that the law must be proportional, applies also
to the common law. It applies to common law that grants power to the
state; it applies to common law that establishes rights and duties between
individuals. In both cases, the common law affects the rights of the individual *vis-à-vis* the state, and therefore must be proportional according to
the provisions of the limitation clause.

---

[76] See above, at 126.
[77] See *Khumalo* v. *Holomise*, 2002 (5) SA 401 (CC). See also S. Woolman, "Application," in S.
Woolman, M. Bishop, and J. Brickhill (eds.), *Constitutional Law of South Africa*, 2nd edn.
(Cape Town: Juta Law Publishers, looseleaf, 2002–).
[78] See above, at 89.

PART II

Proportionality: sources, nature, function

6

The nature and function of proportionality

A.   The nature of proportionality

1.   *Proportionality and its components*

At the foundation of the modern understanding of human rights is the distinction between the scope of the constitutional right (as determined by the constitution) and the justification for its limitation which determines the extent of its protection or realization (as determined by sub-constitutional norms).[1] In the first part of this book, the first component of the distinction was discussed – the scope of the constitutional right. It was emphasized that most constitutional rights are relative – there is justification for not realizing them to the full extent of their scope. The criterion by which such a realization is measured is that of proportionality. This part of the book examines the nature, role, and sources (both legal and historical) of proportionality. It is assumed that the constitutional right in question has been limited by a sub-constitutional law (such as a statute or the common law). The issue presented, therefore, is what is the basis – both formal and substantive – of this limitation? The answer is that this basis can be found in proportionality, located in the limitation clause (whether explicit or implicit) in the constitution.

Proportionality is a legal construction. It is a methodological tool. It is made up of four components: proper purpose, rational connection, necessary means, and a proper relation between the benefit gained by realizing the proper purpose and the harm caused to the constitutional right (the last component is also called "proportionality *stricto sensu*" (balancing)). These four components are the core of the limitation clause. They are crucial to the understanding of proportionality. The limiting law must uphold these four components in order to pass constitutional muster.

---

[1] See above, at 19.

These components render the otherwise abstract notion of proportionality into a more concrete, usable concept.

This aggregate approach – which requires all four components in each case that a constitutional right is limited – has been adopted by a significant number of countries. It reflects a structured approach to the notion of proportionality.[2] However, some legal systems have adopted a "softer" approach. Some emphasize only three of the four components – such as proper purpose, rational connection, and a proper relation between the fulfillment of the purpose and the damage to the constitutional right.[3] Others consider these tests to be recommendations rather than constitutionally mandated requirements.[4] The structured approach is the most suitable. It provides proportionality with concrete content and adequate protection to the limited constitutional rights.[5]

Typically, proportionality is described as a criterion determining the proper relation between the aims and the means. This description may be misleading. It may suggest that the only relevant factors in considering proportionality are the purposes and the means chosen to achieve it; this is not accurate. The means chosen are not only examined in relation to the purpose they were meant to achieve; they are also examined in relation to the constitutional right. They provide the justification for limiting the right. Only means that can sustain both examinations are proper means. Only when the social importance of the benefit in realizing the proper purpose is greater than the social importance of preventing the harm caused by limiting the right, can we say that such a limitation is proportional. Thus, proportionality examines the purpose of the means, the constitutional right, and the proper relationship between them.

The proper relationship between the social importance of the benefit in realizing the purpose and the social importance of preventing the harm caused to the constitutional right is expressed differently in different constitutions. In some cases, the constitutional text demands that the

---

[2] Regarding the structured approach, see below, at 460.

[3] This was the approach adopted in France. See Decision No. 2007–555 DC (August 16, 2007). Lately, however, it seems that the French Constitutional Court has adopted a new approach, requiring the necessary means test as well. See Decision No. 2008–562 (February 21, 2008); Decision No. 2009–580 (June 10, 2009).

[4] See, e.g., Constitution of the Republic of South Africa, Art. 36(1) (requiring the "taking into account of all relevant factors, including" these tests).

[5] See W. van Gerven, "The Effect of Proportionality on the Actions of Member States of the European Community: National Viewpoints from Continental Europe," in E. Ellis (ed.), *The Principle of Proportionality in the Laws of Europe* (Portland, OR: Hart Publishing, 1999), 37, 61.

limitation of the constitutional right be "necessary"[6] or "reasonable"[7] in a democratic society. These and other, similar terms have often been interpreted as the proportionality requirement. As President Chaskalson of the Constitutional Court of South Africa in the *Makwanyane* case well observed:

> The limitation of constitutional rights for a purpose that is reasonable and necessary in a democratic society involves the weighing up of competing values, and ultimately an assessment based on proportionality.[8]

2.   Different methods of limiting constitutional rights

There are several ways to limit a constitutional right. No unified approach has been adopted by all constitutions.[9] Instead, the relevant provisions set up in the different constitutions are usually a reflection of the unique historical background of each legal system. We are thus faced with a spectrum of constitutional solutions regarding limitations. On one end of the spectrum we might find a constitution defining several human rights without providing any mechanism for their limitation. Such is the case of the American Constitution in relation to the First Amendment rights of freedom of expression and free exercise of religion.[10] On the other end of the spectrum we might find a constitution which defines the rights in "absolute" terms alongside a general limitation clause which applies to all those rights. This is the approach adopted by Canada, South Africa, and Israel.[11] Between these two extremes are a plethora of constitutional arrangements. Some contain no general limitation clause, but rather a specific limitation clause for specific constitutional rights.[12] Some contain both general and specific limitation clauses.[13] Some contain no

---

[6] See Arts. 8–11 of the European Convention for the Protection of Human Rights and Fundamental Freedoms, November 4, 1950, 213 *UNTS* 222.

[7] See Section 1 of the Canadian Charter of Rights and Freedoms, Part I of the Constitutional Act 1982.

[8] *S. v. Makwanyane*, 1995 (3) SA 391 § 104.

[9] See A. Bleckmann and M. Bothe, "General Report on the Theory of Limitations on Human Rights," in A. L. C. de Mestral, *The Limitations of Human Rights in Comparative Constitutional Law* (Montreal: Les Editions Yvon Blais, 1986), 44; F. G. Jacobs, "The 'Limitation Clause' of the European Convention on Human Rights," in A. L. C. de Mestral, *The Limitations of Human Rights in Comparative Constitutional Law* (Montreal: Les Editions Yvon Blais, 1986), 22.

[10] See below, at 509.   [11] See below, at 142.

[12] See below, at 141.   [13] See below, at 144.

general limitation clause, with some rights accompanied by specific limitation clauses while other rights are not. Indeed, each legal system ultimately decides for itself which is the best way to either allow or prevent the limitation of constitutional rights. Every legal system has its own way of acknowledging the relativity of constitutional human rights.[14]

3.   The "silent constitution" and limitation of rights

i.   Implied (or judge-made) limitation clause

The inclusion of an express limitation clause in a constitution indicates the relative nature of the rights to which it applies. But is the opposite true as well? Does the non-inclusion of an express limitation clause (neither general nor specific) indicate the absolute nature of those rights? Are all rights included in constitutions without express limitation clauses – "silent constitutions" – absolute? Take, for example, Article 6(1) of the European Convention for the Protection of Human Rights and Fundamental Freedoms:[15]

> In the determination of his civil rights and obligations or of any criminal charge against him, everyone is entitled to a fair and public hearing within a reasonable time by an independent and impartial tribunal established by law.

This provision is interpreted as granting a right to access the courts in civil matters.[16] Can this right be limited? Note that Article 6(1) does

---

[14] See HCJ 7052/03 *Adalah – The Legal Center for the Rights of the Arab Minority* v. *Minister of Interior* (May 14, 2006, unpublished), available in English at http://elyon1.court.gov.il/fileseng/03/520/070/a47/03070520. a47.pdf, para. 53 ("These clauses may sometimes be found explicitly in the constitutional text, and are sometimes the result of common law developments ... Furthermore, in most cases, the constitutional right does not contain a specific limitation clause. In these cases, that right would be subject to the general limitation clause (applying to all constitutional rights), whether such a clause has been written into law or is merely a 'judicial' limitation clause ... In addition, in some cases we may observe a specific limitation clause designed to apply to only one right. In those cases, the constitutional right (or provision) in question would be subject to several, aggregated limitation clauses. Indeed, the right in question would have to abide by both the requirements of the specific limitation clause as well those presented by the general clause." (Barak, P.)). Available in English at http://elyon1.court.gov.il/files_eng/03/520/070/a47/03070520.a47.pdf.

[15] The European Convention for the Protection of Human Rights and Fundamental Freedoms, see above, at 6.

[16] See *Golder* v. *United Kingdom*, App. No. 4451/70, 11 EHRR 524 (1979–80); R. C. A. White and C. Ovey, *Jacobs, White and Ovey: The European Convention on Human Rights*, 5th edn. (Oxford University Press, 2010), 254.

not contain a specific limitation clause. The European Convention does not contain a general limitation clause. Despite that, it was held that the authority to limit the right to access is well recognized.[17] A similar approach was adopted regarding Article 3 of the First Protocol to the European Convention, which requires that the contracting states provide "free elections at reasonable intervals by secret ballot, under conditions which will ensure the free expression of the opinion of the people in the choice of the legislature." The European Court of Human Rights interpreted this provision as guaranteeing a general right to vote and to be elected. The court added, however, that these rights are not absolute and are bound by the implied limitation clause.[18] This kind of limitation may be aptly characterized as either implied or judge-made. The Basic Law for the Federal Republic of Germany also contains some rights unaccompanied by a limitation clause.[19] The courts pronounce that these rights contain implied or immanent limitations. Accordingly, some limitation clauses "may be found within the explicit text of the constitution, while others are the result of judicial enterprise."[20]

The view adopted by most legal systems is that the constitution's silence regarding limitation clauses (general or specific) does not render the constitutional rights absolute. This conclusion is interpretive in nature. This stems from the interpretation of the constitution as a whole.[21] The proper approach is to recognize those rights as part of the entire constitutional framework. They must, therefore, be interpreted in harmony with the constitution's other provisions. This kind of interpretation gives rise to a constitutionally implied or immanent limit to those rights, stemming from the very nature of those rights as part of the framework of a democratic society.[22] The relative nature of constitutional rights is inherent to

[17] See *ibid.*, 254. See also M. Eissen, "The Principles of Proportionality in the Case-Law of the European Court of Human Rights," in R. St. J. MacDonald, F. Mestscher, and H. Petzold (eds.), *The European System for the Protection of Human Rights* (Dordrecht: Kluwer Academic Publishers, 1993), 125; *Ashingdane* v. *United Kingdom*, App. No. 8225/78, 7 EHRR 528 (1985).

[18] *Mathieu-Mohin and Clarfayt* v. *Belgium*, App. No. 9267/81, 10 EHRR 1 (1987); see also White and Ovey, above note 16, at 527.

[19] See, e.g., Basic Law for the Federal Republic of Germany, Art. 4(1) (freedom of faith and conscience) and Art. 5(3) (freedom of arts and sciences; freedom of teaching).

[20] *Adalah*, above note 14, at para. 53 (Barak, P.); see also Bleckmann and Bothe, above note 9, at 107.

[21] On the comprehensive interpretive approach to the constitution, see below note 70, at 70.

[22] See *R. v. Lambert* [2002] 2 AC 545. See also D. Feldman, "Proportionality and the Human Rights Act 1998," in E. Ellis (ed.), *The Principle of Proportionality in the Laws of Europe* (Oxford: Hart Publishing, 1999), 117, 123.

democracy. Accordingly, a constitution striving to prevent the limitation of a human right must provide so explicitly. Thus, for example, the Basic Law for the Federal Republic of Germany provides, regarding the principle of human dignity (Article 1(1)):

> Human dignity shall be inviolable.[23]

Following the text of this provision, as well as the status granted to the right to human dignity by the Basic Law for the Federal Republic of Germany – a status preventing any future amendments to the right ("eternal provision")[24] – German court rulings have recognized the absolute nature of that right.[25] This, however, is the exception. In most cases, the interpretation provided by the courts to constitutional rights asserts their relative nature. The courts have acknowledged that constitutional rights are relative, in other words, they may be limited.

The prevailing view in comparative constitutional law is that, alongside explicit limitations, implicit limitations are recognized as well.[26] An implicit limitation on a constitutional right is treated in the same manner – and has the same constitutional status – as an explicit limitation. Both do not affect the scope of the right, but only the extent of its protection – the way the right is realized.[27] Therefore, the implicit limitation operates as a part of the two-stage structure of the constitutional analysis,

---

[23] The term "inviolable" was adopted by the official German translation of the following German original text: "Die Würde des Menschen ist unantastbar." In my opinion, this is an unfortunate translation. The same term appears in the translation of Art. 4(1), despite the fact that the original text uses a different term, providing that the freedoms of faith and conscience shall be "*uverletzlich*." Here the term "inviolable" is more appropriate. The proper translation of the first term, however, should be "sacrosanct" or "untouchable."

[24] Basic Law for the Federal Republic of Germany, Art. 79(3) ("Amendments to this Basic Law affecting the ... principles laid down in Articles 1 ... shall be inadmissible.").

[25] See above, at 31.

[26] See G. Van der Schyff, *Limitation of Rights: A Study of the European Convention and South African Bill of Rights* (Nijmegen, The Netherlands: Wolf Legal Publishers, 2005), 127 ("[A] limitation provision may be in written form or in unwritten form."). Robert Alexy, *A Theory of Constitutional Rights* (Julian Rivers trans., 2002 [1986]), 188; M. Rautenbach and E. F. J. Malherbe, *Constitutional Law*, 4th edn. (Durban: Butterworths, 2004), 315. For a different view, see I. Leigh, "Taking Rights Proportionately: Judicial Review, the Human Rights Act and Strasbourg" *PL* 265 (2002).

[27] For a different view, see A. Kavanagh, *Constitutional Review under the UK Human Rights Act* (Cambridge University Press, 2009), 262: "With respect to the so-called 'unqualified rights' there is no formal division into two different steps. However, in seeking to establish whether the right has been violated, the courts assess whether the alleged violation is so severe that it can be said to go beyond the scope of the right."

acting as an explicit limitation clause would.[28] The conclusion relating to the existence of an implicit limitation clause is interpretive in nature. The conclusion would be the opposite should the interpretive process point to a "negative solution" by the text.[29] In most legal systems, however, the very existence of an explicit limitation clause for some rights does not suggest a "negative solution" with regard to the existence of implicit limitation clauses to other rights. Furthermore, the constitution's silence regarding the existence of a limitation clause should not be interpreted as a gap – or lacuna – needing to be filled. The judicial recognition of an implicit limitation clause, therefore, is not a gap-filling activity. Those implicit clauses are written into the constitution with an invisible ink. They are implicit of the nature of the existing text. They are a part of the constitutional text.[30]

The components of the implicit limitation clause are not necessarily identical to those of the explicit limitation clause. The recognized approach is that the proportionality requirement applies both on explicit and implicit limitations. The main difference between the two can be found in the purposes justifying the limitation. In the absence of a special constitutional provision relating to "proper purposes," the legitimacy of the limitation is measured against the general provisions of the constitution, either explicit or implicit.[31] Accordingly, a constitutional right not accompanied by a limitation clause (neither general nor specific) can be limited to realize the purpose of protecting other human rights enumerated in the constitution. Similarly, a right may be limited to realize other purposes protected (either explicitly or implicitly) by the constitution. As the German Constitutional Court noted:

> Having due regard for the unity of the Constitution and the entire values protected by it, conflicting constitutional rights of third parties and other legal values of constitutional status ... are capable, in exceptional circumstances, of limiting unqualified constitutional rights.[32]

ii. Implied limitation clause in US constitutional law

The Bill of Rights included in the American Constitution contains a list of constitutional rights. On the surface, some of those rights seem abso-

---

[28] See Van der Schyff, above note 26, at 16.
[29] Regarding negative arrangements, see above, at 94.
[30] See above, at 53.
[31] See M. Sachs, *GG Verfassungsrecht II. Grundrechte* (Berlin: Springer, 2003), 71.
[32] BVerfGE 28, 243, cited in Alexy, above note 26, at 188. See also I. M. Rautenbach, *General Provisions of the South African Bill of Rights* (Durban: Butterworths, 1995), 83.

lute. A typical example is the First Amendment, which provides, among others:

> Congress shall make no law ... abridging the freedom of speech.[33]

This provision is not accompanied by an explicit limitation clause. Similarly, the Bill of Rights has no general limitation clause. Despite that, in a long and consistent line of cases, the US Supreme Court has ruled *inter alia* that the right to freedom of speech may be limited by an act of Congress, provided that such an act was designed to achieve a compelling state interest or a pressing public necessity or a substantial state interest, and the means designated by such an act were "necessary," that is, "narrowly tailored" to achieve those ends. Such acts were held to be constitutional.[34] How should those rulings be considered in relation to the right itself? Should it be seen as though it has determined the scope of the right to freedom of expression? This view asserts that the right is protected to its fullest extent; that extent (or scope), however, was narrowed by judicial interpretation. According to another view, these rulings had nothing to do with the scope of the right; rather, they have prescribed (judicial) limitations on the rights' realization. Thus, the scope of the right was not affected by the ruling, but rather they provided the criterion by which the right may be realized. This view asserts that the right to free speech is not protected to its fullest extent; instead, judicial limitations of this right were acknowledged by the system.

Admittedly, neither the American courts nor the literature has devoted significant importance to the distinction.[35] The literature in the United States tends to disregard the distinction between the two-stage model

---

[33] US Const., Am. I.

[34] See, e.g., Note, "Less Drastic Means and the First Amendment," 78 *Yale L. J.* 464 (1969); Note, "The First Amendment Overbreadth Doctrine," 83 *Harv. L. Rev.* 844 (1970); J. M. Shaman, "Cracks in the Structure: The Coming Breakdown of the Levels of Scrutiny," 45 *Ohio St. L. J.* 161 (1984); L. H. Tribe, *American Constitutional Law*, 2nd edn. (Mineola, NY: Foundation Press, 1988), 832; I. Ayers, "Narrow Tailoring," 43 *UCLA L. Rev.* 1781 (1995); E. Volokh, "Freedom of Speech, Permissible Tailoring and Transcending Strict Scrutiny," 144 *U. Pa. L. Rev.* 2417 (1996); A. Winkler, "Fatal in Theory and Strict in Fact: An Empirical Analysis of Strict Scrutiny in the Federal Courts," 59 *Vand. L. Rev.* 793 (2006); R. H. Fallon, "Strict Judicial Scrutiny," 54 *UCLA L. Rev.* 1267 (2007). See also below, at 510.

[35] See F. Schauer, "Categories and the First Amendment: A Play in Three Acts," 34 *Vand. L. Rev.* 265 (1981); F. Schauer, "A Comment on the Structure of Rights," 27 *Ga. L. Rev.* 415 (1993); F. Schauer, "The Boundaries of the First Amendment: A Preliminary Exploration of Constitutional Silence," 117 *Harv. L. Rev.* 1765 (2004); F. Schauer, "The Exceptional First Amendment," in M. Ignatieff (ed.), *American Exceptionalism and Human Rights*

(distinguishing the scope of the constitutional right from the extent of its realization) and the single-stage model (focusing on the right's scope only).[36] However, the issue has not yet been clarified in American literature. Several views exist as to the proper constitutional attitude. They all agree that the requirement relating to "a proper purpose" (and the concomitant requirement of compelling government interest) is case law. This legal approach is an important source of inspiration, in that the constitutional text relating to a constitutional right may be limited or affected without explicit textual authority to do so. It seems this is an interesting comparative law source which allows the recognition of implied (or judge-made) limitation on a constitutional right.[37]

iii. Constitutions determining that human rights can be limited "by law"

Human rights provisions in several constitutions are accompanied by provisions of specific limitation clauses allowing for the limitation of those rights "by law."[38] In most cases, these constitutions provide no additional guidance as to the conditions required for imposing such limitation.[39] The recognized interpretation is that the constitutional requirement for limitation "by law" also entails a "rule of law" component – in both the formal and substantive meaning of the term.[40] This requirement is based on the substantive test which provides it with the necessary legitimation. This "rule of law" notion may be reduced down, in essence, to the requirement of proportionality. As Professor Grimm observed:

> Laws could restrict human rights, but only in order to make conflicting rights compatible or to protect the rights of other persons or important community interests ... [A]ny restriction of human rights not only needs

---

(Princeton University Press, 2005), 29; F. Schauer, "Expression and Its Consequences," 57 *U. Toronto L. J.* 705 (2007); F. Schauer, "Balancing Subsumption, and the Constraining Role of Legal Text," in M. Klatt (ed.), *Rights, Law, and Morality Themes from the Legal Philosophy of Robert Alexy* (Oxford University Press, forthcoming 2011).

[36] See S. Gardbaum, "The New Commonwealth Model of Constitutionalism," 47 *Am. J. Comp. L.* 707 (2001); S. Gardbaum, "Limiting Constitutional Rights," 54 *UCLA L. Rev.* 789 (2007); S. Gardbaum, "The Myth and the Reality of American Constitutional Exceptionalism," 107 *Mich. L. Rev.* 391 (2008).

[37] See Van der Schyff, above note 26, at 127.

[38] See, e.g., Basic Law for the Federal Republic of Germany, Arts. 10(2), 12(1), 14(1).

[39] These provision are called "claw-back provisions"; see Rautenbach, above note 32, at 82, 84, 107.

[40] See Van der Schyff, above note 26, at 127.

a constitutionally valid reason but also to be proportional to the rank and importance of the right at stake.[41]

Accordingly, any limitation clause (either specific or general) that provides that the right may be limited "by law" is not an open invitation to the legislator to limit the right as it sees fit. The limitation must be proportional. It should serve a proper purpose. The means should be rational and necessary. The harm to the constitutional right must be proportional to the benefit gained from the limitation itself (proportionality *stricto sensu*).

What, then, is the added value of the requirement that a limitation be made "by law?" Is this requirement not redundant? Could we not argue that even in the absence of such a requirement any limitation of a constitutional right must be proportional? There are several possible answers. First, one may argue that the requirement of a "by law" limitation is designed to eliminate the purposive result of a "negative solution,"[42] according to which a limitation is not legally plausible. Despite the fact that this interpretation is erroneous, it is still possible that the court will provide this interpretation. In order to prevent the latter, an explicit provision was enacted which allows for the limitation of the constitutional right by a proportional sub-constitutional provision. Another possible explanation is that the term "law" indicates the desired level of the limiting norm as being a statute alone, emphasizing that a limitation cannot be imposed by either administrative regulations or case law. This explanation seems incorrect to me for two reasons: first, there is no reason to prevent regulations found within the law from limiting the constitutional right; second, in constitutions in civil law systems, there is no need to determine that a ruling by the court (which does not interpret a constitutional provision) cannot limit a constitutional right. The latter is obvious. Despite this, in common law constitutions, as well as in international treaties, it is inappropriate to limit the possibility of limiting the constitutional right by common law. Therefore, the expression "law" in the limitation clauses should be interpreted as encompassing the common law. Another view, proposed by Alexy, is that an explicit provision may provide the legislator

---

[41] D. Grimm, "Human Rights and Judicial Review in Germany," in D. M. Beatty (ed.), *Human Rights and Judicial Review: A Comparative Perspective* (Dordrecht: Martinus Nijhoff Publishers, 1994), 267, 275.

[42] On "negative solutions," see above, at 94.

with wider discretion (as to limiting the rights) than otherwise provided by a constitutional silence.[43] It is agreed that the legislator has very wide discretion in deciding whether to limit a constitutional right or not, and, if so, for what purpose and by what means.[44] But such a wide discretionary power exists regardless of an explicit constitutional provision allowing the legislator to do so "by law." The scope of that discretion, importantly, is not changed by such a provision.

4.   Specific limitation clauses

The most prevalent method of limiting constitutional rights in modern constitutions is by adopting several constitutional limitation clauses.[45] These are the specific limitation clauses. They provide special arrangements for each constitutional right (or group of rights). Thus, they provide both the purpose for which a limitation of a right is valid and the means by which such a purpose may be attained. This method was adopted by The European Convention for the Protection of Human Rights and Fundamental Freedoms,[46] and by most Western European constitutional democracies established after the Second World War such as Germany, Spain, Portugal, and Italy. The same is true for the constitution of India, as well the constitutions of countries part of the former Soviet Union such as Poland and the Czech Republic.[47] In many of the constitutional democracies established after the Second World War, which include specific limitation clauses, the courts have ruled that such clauses contain the proportionality requirement. Such was the case with the European Convention for the Protection of Human Rights and Fundamental Freedoms.[48] That was also the case in Germany, Spain, Portugal, Italy, Poland, the Czech Republic, Hungary, and, as of late, India.[49]

---

[43] See Alexy, above note 26, at 189.
[44] Regarding legislative discretion in limiting the rights, see below, at 400.
[45] See Bleckmann and Bothe, above note 9; Rautenbach and Malherbe, above note 26.
[46] See above, at 134.
[47] See W. Sadurski, *Rights before Courts: A Study of Constitutional Courts in Postcommunist States of Central and Eastern Europe* (Dordrecht: Springer, 2008); W. Osiatynski, *Human Rights and Their Limits* (Cambridge University Press, 2009).
[48] See Van der Schyff, above note 26, at 214.
[49] See below, at 200.

5.   *General limitation clauses*

The 1948 Universal Declaration of Human Rights[50] determines a list of human rights. It does not contain specific limitation clauses. However, the relative nature of the rights in the Declaration is preserved through the inclusion of a general limitation clause. This general clause applies to all the rights in the Declaration. Article 29(2) states:

> In the exercise of his rights and freedoms, everyone shall be subject only to such limitations as are determined by law solely for the purpose of securing due recognition and respect for the rights and freedoms of others and of meeting the just requirements of morality, public order and the general welfare in a democratic society.[51]

The Canadian Charter of Rights and Freedoms contains a general limitation clause that provides:

> The Canadian Charter of Rights and Freedoms guarantees the rights and freedoms set out in it subject only to such reasonable limits prescribed by law as can be demonstrably justified in a free and democratic society.[52]

The Canadian general limitation clause, in turn, influenced the South African Interim Constitution,[53] and eventually the Final Constitution.[54] Article 36 of the Constitution of the Republic of South Africa provides:

> (1) The rights in the Bill of Rights may be limited only in terms of law of general application to the extent that the limitation is reasonable and justifiable in an open and democratic society based on human dignity, equality and freedom, taking into account all relevant factors, including
>
> (a) The nature of the right;
> (b) The importance of the purpose of the limitation;
> (c) The nature and extent of the limitation;
> (d) The relation between the limitation and its purpose; and
> (e) Less restrictive means to achieve the purpose.
>
> (2) Except as provided in subsection (1) or in any other provision of the Constitution, no law may limit any right entrenched in the Bill of Rights.[55]

<hr/>

[50] UN General Assembly Res. 217A (III), UN Doc. A/810, 71.
[51] *Ibid.*
[52] Canadian Charter of Rights and Freedoms, Section 1, above note 7.
[53] See South Africa – Interim Constitution, Art. 33.
[54] See above, at 132.
[55] Constitution of the Republic of South Africa, Art. 36.

Israel, too, was influenced by the Canadian general limitation clause. Accordingly, the limitation clause included in Basic Law: Human Dignity and Liberty provides:

> There shall be no infringement of rights under this Basic Law except by a law befitting the values of the State of Israel, enacted for a proper purpose, and to an extent no greater than is required.[56]

A similar provision appears in the Israeli Basic Law: Freedom of Occupation.[57] In all of these constitutional texts, the rights appear to be of an absolute nature. Their relative nature is the result of reading them in conjunction with the general limitation clause.

All the general limitation clauses were interpreted by the courts as containing the proportionality requirement. Such is the case in relation to the Universal Declaration of Human Rights.[58] This is also the case regarding the Canadian Charter of Rights and Freedoms,[59] as well as with regard to the limitation clauses appearing in both the interim and final constitutions of South Africa.[60] The new Federal Constitution of Switzerland of 1999 has a general limitation clause expressly containing the principle of proportionality:

> 1. Restrictions on fundamental rights must have a legal basis. Significant restrictions must have their basis in a federal act. The foregoing does not apply in cases of serious and immediate danger where no other course of action is possible.
> 2. Restrictions on fundamental rights must be justified in the public interest or for the protection of the fundamental rights of others.
> 3. Any restrictions on fundamental rights must be proportionate.
> 4. The essence of fundamental rights is sacrosanct.[61]

Other constitutions, such as the Constitution of the Republic of Turkey, contain explicit references to the principle of proportionality. It provides that a limitation "shall not be in conflict with ... the principles of proportionality."[62] This is also the case with the Israeli Basic Law: Human Dignity and Liberty and Basic Law: Freedom of Occupation.

---

[56] Basic Law: Human Dignity and Liberty, Art. 8. The Ministry of Justice translation uses the term "violation" rather than "limitation" of rights; in my opinion, the latter term better reflects the original Hebrew.
[57] Basic Law: Freedom of Occupation, Art. 4.
[58] See above, at 142.   [59] See above, at 142.   [60] See above, at 142.
[61] Federal Constitution of Switzerland, Art. 36 available in English at www.admin.ch/org/polit/00083/index.html?lang=e/n.
[62] Constitution of the Republic of Turkey, Art. 13.

6. *Hybrid limitation clauses*

Different constitutions have adopted different arrangements to limit the rights they contain. There is no agreed-upon arrangement shared by all constitutions. In fact, some of the constitutions include both general and specific limitation clauses. This is the case, for example, with the Constitution of the Republic of South Africa.[63] These situations are dubbed "hybrid arrangements."[64]

Hybrid arrangements can raise serious issues in examining the relationship between the general limitation clause and specific limitation clauses.[65] These are interpretive questions. Both the general and specific limitation clauses make up a part of the constitution. They are of equal normative status. Accordingly, while applying constitutional purposive interpretation to these provisions we should make every effort to read them together harmoniously. We should not assume that one prevails over the other. It is important to note – as a basic premise – that the general limitation clause applies to all constitutional rights, including those accompanied by a specific limitation clause. In some cases, the specific limitation clause is used to set stricter or laxer conditions than those set out by the general limitation clause with regard to the limitation of a single right. In other cases, the specific clause is designed to clarify, or emphasize, the limitation condition of a certain right. When the proper interpretation of a specific limitation clause is that of providing stricter, or laxer, conditions for limitations, such interpretation should be given legal effect.[66] This result is consistent with standard canons of interpretation, according to which, when two rule-shaped constitutional norms of the same normative level conflict, the norm later in time will prevail over the former, unless the former consists of a specific law (*lex specialis*); when both norms are found in the same document, the specific norm should be given the interpretive preference as long as no other interpretation can be found. Accordingly, since the specific limitation clause is "specific law"

---

[63] Constitution of the Republic of South Africa, Arts. 9, 15(3), 26, 27, 30, 31 (special limitation clause), and Art. 36 (general limitation clause).

[64] See Van der Schyff, above note 26, at 128.

[65] See M. Rautenbach and E. F. J. Malherbe, *Constitutional Law*, 4th edn. (Durban: Butterworths, 2004); K. Iles, "Limiting Socio-Economic Rights: Beyond the Internal Limitations Clauses," 20 *SAJHR* 448, 458 (2004); S. Woolman and H. Botha, "Limitations," in S. Woolman, M. Bishop, and J. Brickhill (eds.), *Constitutional Law of South Africa*, 2nd edn. (Cape Town: Juta Law Publishers, looseleaf, 2002–).

[66] See Van der Schyff, above note 26, at 128; Rautenbach and Malherbe, above note 65.

in relation to the general limitation clause, in a case of conflict between them[67] the specific provision should prevail.

7. The preferred regime: general, specific, or hybrid limitation clause?

An interesting question is what arrangement is the best to limit constitutional rights? In terms of legal certainty, that best regime seems to be a general limitation clause. A general, comprehensive clause would enable the legal system to develop a general, comprehensive theory of rights limitation. True, a heavy burden would be placed on the judicial branch, which will have to play a significant role in developing a uniform approach to this complicated issue while reconciling the different constitutional cases. Another view considers the best approach in terms of the rights' protection. Here, the preferred approach is that of several specific limitation clauses.[68] By providing a unique arrangement for each right (or group of rights), the constituent authority may accurately reflect its views as to the relative importance of each right. Accordingly, the constitutional authority may "derive" a unique arrangement for limitation that takes into account each of the many complicated constitutional features of the specific right. Thus, for example, while general limitation clauses rarely include a detailed list of the proper purposes for which a limitation is justified, specific limitation clauses do contain such an account in many cases. The judicial task thus becomes easier, as purposes not included within the constitutional provision are eliminated. Accordingly, in most cases, the right itself is better protected.

The preferred constitutional regime is that of specific limitation clauses. Such an arrangement requires the constituent authority to consider each right separately. It further requires that same authority to examine each and every reason to limit the right separately and then to repeat the process regarding each of the rights included in the constitution. As such, the protection of each right would be more accurately and structurally defined and thus the extent of their protection – the ways in which they can be realized – would be easier to establish. Along with the specific clauses one may consider the inclusion of a general limitation clause expressing the

---

[67] Regarding genuine conflict, see above, at 87.

[68] See Alexy, above note 26, at 70. See also W. Sadurski, *Rights before Courts: A Study of Constitutional Courts in Postcommunist States of Central and Eastern Europe* (Dordrecht: Springer, 2008), 288.

concept of proportionality as an "umbrella concept" applying to all constitutional rights.

B. The formal role of proportionality

1. Proportionality regarding validity and proportionality regarding meaning

Proportionality is a central term in modern constitutional law. It serves different and various functions. Its meaning may change with the different roles it purports to fill. Thus, for example, the term proportionality as used in criminal law is not the same as the one used by administrative law and both terms differ from the term as used by international law. Moreover, even within one legal field – such as constitutional law – the understanding of the term proportionality has changed over the years.

This book focuses on analyzing proportionality as a criterion for resolving constitutional questions relating to conflicting norms that exist at different levels of the constitutional hierarchy. Within this general framework, this book examines a specific case of a superior norm (found within the constitution), which establishes a human right, and an inferior norm (found within a statutory provision, or the common law), which attempts to limit that right. Central to the analysis, therefore, is the question of the validity of the sub-constitutional norm in conflict with a constitutional norm establishing a human right. This book examines the relationship between a human right based in the constitution and a contradictory law located at a lower normative level, such as a statute or the common law. It does not discuss the application of proportionality in "institutional" constitutional arrangements, such as the three branches' structure and their mutual relationships. A different situation will be discussed where both the right and the limiting law are of equal normative status – both are prescribed by statute. Specifically, a situation where the court is authorized to declare the compatibility or incompatibility of the statutory norm limiting a statutory right with the requirements set by the limitation clause (based on proportionality), which can also be found in a statute, will be examined. This "non-constitutional" proportionality setting exists in England[69] and in Victoria, Australia.[70] Despite the fact that both norms exist at the same level of the constitutional hierarchy,

[69] See section 4(2) of the Human Rights Act 1998.
[70] See section 7 of the Charter of Human Rights and Responsibilities Act 2006.

the fact that the courts are authorized to determine the incompatibility of the limiting statute on the statutory right renders the analysis quite similar to that of a typical constitutional setting, where one norm is superior to the other.[71]

Proportionality has another significant role – its interpretive function. At the core of this interpretive function is the issue of providing meaning to legal norms, and in particular that of statutory interpretation. Within this role, proportionality is used as a criterion for providing meaning to the legislative norm. To achieve this, proportionality in its narrow sense (*stricto sensu*), or the notion of balancing, is used by analogy. This role is dubbed "interpretive balancing."[72]

2.   The constitutionality of limiting a constitutional right by a sub-constitutional law

i.   A limitation of a constitutional right

Constitutional limitation clauses do not apply in every situation where two norms are in conflict with each other. Rather, they apply in those situations where one of the conflicting norms contains a constitutional right. The limitation clause and the notion of proportionality on which it is based were designed to provide both the justification for limiting a constitutional human right and the boundaries of such a justification. They do so in light of the basic democratic, and rule of law, tenets according to which it is sometimes justified to limit one person's constitutional right to realize other public interests or to guarantee the rights of other persons. This justification does not apply – and therefore neither does the limitation clause – when the conflicting norms are not related to human rights. Thus, for example, where the higher norm sets up the structure of an executive body, or prescribes the manner in which an administrative agency operates – if these issues are unrelated to human rights – then the limitation clause is not triggered.

ii.   The limiting norm is sub-constitutional

The limitation clause in various constitutions – whether explicit or implicit[73] – are primarily designed to provide the conditions under which a

---

[71] The argument that, in UK law, the Human Rights Act 1998 creates a higher norm than other regular statute will not be discussed: see Kavanagh, above note 27, at 269.

[72] See above, at 72.

[73] For a distinction between an expressed and implied limitation clause, see above, at 134.

limitation of a constitutional right by a sub constitutional norm (e.g., statute, common law) would be justified and therefore valid. Thus, for example, in Israel the limitation clause provides:

> There shall be no infringement of rights under this Basic Law except by a law befitting the values of the State of Israel, enacted for a proper purpose, and to an extent no greater than is required.[74]

Similar provisions, emphasizing the constitutional nature of the right on the one hand, and the sub-constitutional nature of the limiting norm on the other, are found in other constitutions' limitation clauses.[75] Such provisions define the conditions under which a justification exists for limiting a constitutional right by a lower, sub-constitutional law. The limitation clause thus provides a constitutional foundation for the authority of both the legislator and the common law[76] to limit constitutional rights.

The constitutional limitation clause is based on the hierarchical relationship between the limited constitutional right and the limiting law. The limited right exists at the constitutional level. The limiting law – a statute or the common law – exists at the sub-constitutional level. The purpose for which the limitation was prescribed is either the public interest or the protection of a right. With this hierarchical background several questions arise. First, what is the reason for such a hierarchical relationship between the norms? Second, what is the law when the hierarchical order is not relevant and a constitutional right is limited by another constitutional norm? Third, what is the case when the hierarchical order is relevant and the right limited is at the sub-constitutional level and the limiting norm is found at a lower sub-constitutional level? Fourth, what is the law when the hierarchical order is not relevant – both norms are of equal normative status – and the norms exist only at the sub-constitutional level? Finally, what is the law when the hierarchical relationship is reversed – that is, the limited right exists at a sub-constitutional level and the limiting norm exists as either a constitutional norm or a higher sub-constitutional norm? Each of these issues will now be discussed briefly.

---

[74] Basic Law: Human Dignity and Liberty (Art. 8); Basic Law: Freedom of Occupation (Art. 4).
[75] See, e.g., Canadian Charter of Rights and Freedoms, Section 1; South African Constitution, Art. 36.
[76] See above, at 121.

3. *The reason behind the constitutional hierarchical relationship*

i. The constitutionality of a limitation

The basic assumption underlying every hierarchical legal order is that the constitution is the highest-level norm in the system. From this fundamental understanding stems the conclusion that, if conflict arises, the higher-ranking norm prevails over the lower-ranking norm in the hierarchical order: *lex superior derogt legi inferiori*. A lower norm cannot overcome a higher norm. Accordingly, a statute or the common law cannot limit a constitutionally protected human right.[77] As such, the proper status of human rights in the legal system is maintained. Sub-constitutional norms cannot legally limit those rights. One possible conclusion of this description is that every law attempting to limit a constitutional right is unconstitutional. Another possible conclusion is that the courts in a constitutional democracy (either every court in the system or a special court specifically designed for this role)[78] may pronounce the invalidity (or unconstitutionality) of a law limiting constitutional rights. This is often the case, but not always.[79] The same constitution which provides that no law can limit the rights it contains can also provide that under certain circumstances a limiting law can be constitutional, and therefore valid. The norm that has given may also take away, and *vice versa*.

This is the effect of the constitutional limitation clause. It is designed, formally speaking, to overcome the interpretive canon according to which a superior norm always prevails over an inferior norm.[80] Indeed, the formal role of the limitation clause (and the proportionality principle found at its center) is to enable the limitation of a constitutional right by a sub-constitutional law, without this limitation being considered

---

[77] This is the modern premise for judicial review as pronounced by Chief Justice Marshall in *Marbury* v. *Madison*, 5 US (1 Cranch) 137 (1803).

[78] See V. Ferreres Comella, *Constitutional Courts and Democratic Values: A European Perspective* (New Haven, CT: Yale University Press, 2009).

[79] See Art. 120 of the Constitution of The Netherlands: "The constitutionality of Acts of Parliament and Treaties shall not be reviewed by the courts." See *Constitutions of Europe: Texts Collected by the Council of Europe Venice Commission* (Leiden: Martinus Nijhoff Publishers, 2004), 1291.

[80] See HCJ 1384/98 *Avni* v. *Prime Minister of Israel* [1998] IsrSC 52(5) 206 ("In the relationship between regular legislation and Basic Law, the canon according to which the superior norm prevails over the inferior norm (*lex superior derogat inferiori*) applies. Of course, there is no restriction on providing, within the Basic Law itself, the conditions under which a legislative provision would be able to limit Basic Law provisions. The limitation clauses found in our Basic Laws do just that." (Barak, P.)).

unconstitutional and therefore invalid. Of course, this result can be achieved through interpretation, by recognizing an implicit or judge-made limitation. In order to avoid doubt regarding the latter, the explicit limitation clause comes into effect.

ii.   A limitation by a sub-constitutional law

The proportionality in the limitation clause examines the constitutionality of a limitation on a constitutional right caused by a sub-constitutional law. Constitutional limitation clauses, by their nature, deal with limitations on constitutional rights by a sub-constitutional law; this is true whether the limitation clause is explicit or implicit, whether the constitutional right is shaped as a principle or as a rule; whether the sub-constitutional law is shaped as a principle or a rule. In many cases, the sub-constitutional laws that can limit the right are combined under the term "law."[81] This term includes both statutes and the common law.[82] In civil law systems, the constitution may specify that the limiting norm has to be a statute.[83]

The limitation clause is a part of the constitution itself. Its normative status, therefore, is equal to that of the limited rights. For the right's limitation to be valid, the normative foundation of such a limitation must be found (expressly or impliedly) in the constitution itself.[84] A constitution that includes provisions establishing constitutional rights may also include provisions establishing the legal possibility of limiting such rights by a sub-constitutional law. The constitutional limitation clause fills that role. The clause enables a limitation on a constitutional right by a sub-constitutional law in a manner that would render the limitation constitutional. That is the essence of the proportional limitations, which provide a valid legal justification for the limitation of a constitutional right. Thus, reflecting the limited nature of the limitation clause: it does not alter the normative status of the limiting law; it does not turn the limiting law into a part of the constitution. The limiting law remains at its sub-constitutional level. The limitation clause, in turn, provides a protective "legal umbrella" to the limiting law. Thus, when the limitation is proportional,

---

[81] See, e.g., Canadian Charter of Rights and Freedoms, Section 1, above note 75; Constitution of the Republic of South Africa, Art. 36; European Convention on Human Rights, Arts. 8–10, above note 15; Constitution of India, Art. 13(2).

[82] See above, at 121.

[83] See Basic Law for the Federal Republic of Germany, Arts. 2(2), 8(2), 11(2), 14(1) ("*Gesetz*").

[84] See Alexy, above note 26.

the regular rules demanding the preference of a higher-ranking norm over a lower-ranking one would not apply; whenever the limitation is not proportional, however, the protective "umbrella" disappears and the usual rules – providing a preference to the higher-ranking norm – will apply. In such cases, the limiting law is unconstitutional. The proportionality of the limitation on a constitutional right provides the justification for such a limitation. When the justification disappears, the rationale for constitutional protection of the limitation goes along with it.

This formal function of the limitation clause – and the proportionality requirement at its center – leads to the conclusion that, when there is no limitation of a constitutional right by a sub-constitutional law, the limitation clause (and the proportionality requirement) would not apply. The limitation clause and the proportionality requirement at its center were designed to narrow the application of the rule according to which the higher-ranking norm is always superior to the lower-ranking norm. Without a conflict between two norms of a different constitutional status, and without the involvement of a human right, there is no room for the application of the limitation clause.

What is the case when a constitutional provision outside the limitation clause authorizes a state actor to limit a constitutional right? The *Hugo* case in South Africa illustrates this situation.[85] The Constitution of the Republic of South Africa grants the President of the Republic the authority to "pardon ... or reprieve ... offenders."[86] The President, exercising this power, decided to pardon women prisoners who were mothers to children under the age of twelve. The pardon did not apply to male prisoners in a similar situation. The argument before the court was whether this exercise of power was discriminatory. Assuming, for a moment, that the presidential decision is, indeed, discriminatory,[87] would the constitutional general limitation clause apply to such a decision? The answer is yes. The act of pardoning is authorized by the constitution, but does not – in and of itself – make up a part of the constitution. It therefore represents a sub-constitutional action by the state. The authority to pardon according to the constitution does not come with any guidelines for its application. The question, then, is whether the exercise of such authority is governed by the general limitation clause. This question can be described as an intra-constitutional interpretive question. Does the limitation clause apply in these

---

[85] *President of the Republic of South Africa and Another* v. *Hugo*, 1997 (4) SA 1 (CC).
[86] Constitution of the Republic of South Africa, Art. 84(2)(j).
[87] That assumption was not shared by most judges in the case.

types of situation? If the answer to that question is yes, then the next question is whether the specific constitutional provision relating to the power
to pardon prevents the application of the general limitation clause. The
only judge in *Hugo* willing to entertain that question was of the opinion
that the limitation clause should apply in these cases, and that no other
provision in the constitution prevents such a result.[88]

Does the analysis thus far suggest that the limitation clause is not
applicable – or has no legal significance – whenever the legal system does
not recognize the concept of judicial review of legislation? Strictly speaking, it is clear that a limitation clause may appear in the constitution without concomitant recognition by the legal system of judicial review. But,
while the constitutional restriction – on disproportional limitation – may
still apply, there would be no practical way to enforce it; the limiting statute would not be declared unconstitutional by the courts. That, however,
does not render the limitation clause entirely superfluous. It still serves
as a guiding light to all state actors, who are sworn to uphold the constitution and its provisions. It can also be used as a basis for a judicial
declaration of incompatibility between the limiting statute and the constitution, even when such incompatibility may not lead to a declaration of
invalidity.[89] Even without such a declaration, the limiting clause's value as
a guide is preserved. Through judicial review we can achieve institutional
restraint. In addition, the use of interpretive balancing would still apply
in the absence of judicial review.[90] Finally, the common law would continue to develop in accordance with the constitutional provisions, including its limitation clause.

4.   The effect on a constitutional right of a constitutional norm

i.   The norm that giveth may taketh away

Limitation clauses presuppose constitutional hierarchical orders.
According to this order, a right at the constitutional level is limited by a
sub-constitutional level law. What is the case, however, when a constitutional right is affected by another constitutional norm? The answer is that

---

[88] See *ibid.* (Mokgoro, J., concurring). The other judges were of the opinion that the right to
equality was never limited in the first place, and therefore did not consider the question.
[89] This is the case today in England; see the Human Rights Act 1998, section 4(2). It is
possible to claim that the authorized court can give a declaration regarding the incompatibility even when an explicit provision on this matter does not exist. See D. Jenkins,
"Common Law Declaration of Unconstitutionality," 7 *Int. J. Con. L.* 183 (2009).
[90] On interpretive balance, see above, at 72.

in these situations the limitation clause does not apply. There is no legal need for its use. As we have seen, the clause was designed to regulate a situation where a sub-constitutional norm can limit constitutional rights. This is the case when a statute or the common law affects a constitutional right. The limitation clause (express or implied) sets up the conditions under which a limitation may be constitutional; this is important, since without such a determination each and every limitation by a sub-constitutional norm would be deemed unconstitutional and therefore invalid. This problem is solved – and the limitation clause is not applicable – when the constitution itself (whether the original constitution or an amendment) affects a constitutional right. The same norm that has given may also take away.[91]

It is of course possible to critique the provision in the constitution which affects constitutional rights. The place for such criticism is not within the constitutional limitation clause. This is not its purpose. Its formal role is to allow the sub-constitutional norm to constitutionally limit the constitutional right. Its role is not to set the rules affecting the constitutional right in the constitution itself. A number of typical situations regarding this matter will be discussed herein.

ii.   Limitation clauses and internal modifiers

An important distinction is that between constitutional provisions establishing the scope of a constitutional right (either narrowly or widely) and constitutional provisions limiting the possibility of realizing the right within that scope.[92] The former kind of constitutional provisions are called "internal modifiers" or "internal qualifiers." The latter kind of constitutional provisions are called "limitations."[93] Limitations do not narrow the scope of the right. Rather, they allow for the limitation of the right within the framework of its scope.[94] Proportionality and constitutional limitation clauses are these kinds of constitutional provisions. The reason for including those provisions in the constitution is that the limitations themselves are posed by sub-constitutional norms. Without a constitutional (express or implied) foundation, no sub-constitutional norm would be able to limit a constitutional right. By providing such a foundation – or legal "umbrella" – to proportional limitations, the limitation

---

[91] Some constitutions do not allow any limitation of the right's "core": see below, at 496. Those provisions do not apply if the core was affected by a constitutional amendment. See Sachs, above note 31.

[92] For the distinction, see above, at 19.

[93] See above, at 19.   [94] See above, at 19.

clause overcomes the hierarchical problem of limiting a superior norm by an inferior one.

The limitation clause and proportionality are irrelevant to an examination of the "internal qualifiers."[95] These qualifiers are a part of the constitution itself. They do not present any issue relating to constitutional hierarchy. The only issue they do raise is interpretive in nature: What is the scope of the narrowing (or widening) provision? Limitation clauses, therefore, play no role in the interpretation of the internal qualifiers. However, the interpretive issues posed by the internal qualifiers may include – as part of the process of purposive constitutional interpretation – a need to balance two (or more) competing constitutional principles. This is an interpretive balance.[96] This balance, in turn, may be determined by considerations of proportional balancing. This is not the proportionality found at the center of the constitutional limitation clause. This is interpretive proportionality. It is based, by analogy, on proportionality *stricto sensu*.[97]

iii.   The limitation clause and the conflict of constitutional rights

The ways in which a conflict between constitutional rights should be resolved has been examined herein.[98] The conclusion was that, as far as the constitutional level is concerned, the constitutional limitation clause is not relevant. The reason for that is as follows. In an intra-constitutional conflict between two provisions, the issue of constitutional hierarchy is not triggered; therefore, the need to examine the requirements posed by the limitation clause for such a conflict is not triggered either. Thus, for example, there is no reason to examine whether the two conflicting rights serve a "proper purpose." There is also no point in reviewing whether the effect of one constitutional right by another was authorized "by law." All of those questions are irrelevant when the conflict is between two constitutional norms. Accordingly, there is no need to turn to the limitation clause. This use of the clause is reserved for those instances in which a sub-constitutional norm limits a constitutional right. It is not applicable when one constitutional norm conflicts with another constitutional norm. Accordingly, there is no place to examine – in relation to the constitutionality of the conflict – whether this conflict is proportional. The terms set

---

[95] See S. Gardbaum, "Limiting Constitutional Rights," 54 *UCLA L. Rev.* 789, 811 (2007).

[96] On interpretive balance, see above, at 72.

[97] See above, at 97.   [98] See above, at 83.

by the limitation clause may influence through analogy the interpretive balancing conducted in such cases, in order to assure unity and harmony within a given legal system. It should be emphasized that such an analogy is of an interpretive nature. It would mostly require the balancing component of proportionality *stricto sensu*.

iv.   Amendment of a constitutional right by another constitutional norm

The limitation clause – and the requirement of proportionality at its core – is relevant to an examination of a limitation of a constitutional right by a sub-constitutional norm. They are not relevant to an examination of an amendment of a constitutional right by another constitutional norm. The reason for this distinction is that, when the limitation of a constitutional right is performed by a sub-constitutional norm (statute or the common law), such a limitation requires constitutional authorization. Accordingly, a limitation that is not proportional is not protected by the limitation clause. This is not the case when the amendment is made by another constitutional norm. Such amendments need not be examined by the limitation clause. Both the amendment and the amending norms are of the same constitutional status. The same norm that has given may also take away. The constitutional limitation clause has no place in this discussion. Accordingly, a constitutional amendment performed in accordance with all the formal requirements demanded by the constitution is not obliged to abide by the requirements of the limitation clause. Such an amendment would be constitutional even if it is disproportional.[99] However, every interpretive effort should be made to eliminate such a conflict. Here the judge may well use interpretive balancing by analogy.[100]

5.   Limitation of a sub-constitutional norm by a lower sub-constitutional norm

What happens when the hierarchical order "descends" one level and both the limited and limiting norms operate at the sub-constitutional level? Take a right protected by statute and a limiting norm consisting of an administrative regulation or the common law; or take a right protected by an administrative regulation that is limited by the common law – what

---

[99] Such constitutional amendment may still be disqualified due to other considerations, such as the doctrine acknowledging "unconstitutional amendments." See above, at 31.
[100] On interpretive balancing, see above, at 72.

should then be the case? The answer to these – and similar – questions is not found within the confines of the constitutional limitation clause. This clause applies to cases where a constitutional right is limited. When the limitation does not relate to a constitutional right, the constitutional limitation clause does not apply.

Where, then, should we look for the solution in such situations? What might that solution be? Regarding the first case – where a right protected by a statute is limited by an administrative regulation – here one can think of two types of case. In the first, the limiting regulation was enacted in accordance with an authorization granted by the same statute that establishes the right itself. In the second, the limiting regulation and the limited right originate in two separate statutes. We begin with the first type. When the two norms originate from the same statute, we should examine the congruence between the statutory authorization and the regulation itself: Was the regulation promulgated in accordance with the powers granted by the statute? Such an examination is interpretive in nature. It entails a thorough examination of the context of the authorizing legislation, including the human rights context. That concludes the examination. In the second type of case – where the limiting regulation and the limited right originate from two separate statutes – we should conduct two separate examinations. We first examine whether the regulation was promulgated in accordance with the powers granted by the statute. If so, we move to our second examination. Here we look at the relationship between the two statutes – the one establishing the right and the other granting the authority to limit it. We are faced with two statutes of equal constitutional status. They conflict with each other. We may apply the standard canons of interpretation to such a conflict. However, we should make every interpretive effort to eliminate the conflict and provide an interpretive solution establishing unity and harmony within the legal system.[101]

In the second case, a right established by statute or a (properly promulgated) administrative regulation is limited by the common law. In such a case, the statute or the regulation should prevail, as the common law may not override a legislative provision or a properly promulgated administrative regulation. The true nature of the conflict should be examined carefully in this type of case. Such an examination is interpretive in nature.

To conclude, in both cases – where the limitation is either by administrative regulation or by common law – the issue is solved through

---

[101] See above, at 70.

interpretive means. These interpretive means would include an interpretive balancing between the conflicting norms.[102] In both cases, the limitation clause does not apply. It applies only in cases where the limited norm exists at the constitutional level and the limiting norm exists at the sub-constitutional level, while in the cases examined here, both norms operate at the sub-constitutional level. However, we may apply, by analogy, the balancing conducted with the proportionality *stricto sensu*.[103]

6.   Limitation of a sub-constitutional norm by an equal-level norm

The constitutional limitation clause applies when a constitutional right is limited by a sub-constitutional norm. Does it apply when a statutory right is limited by the provisions of another statute?

The answer to these – and similar – questions is that, whenever statutes conflict, the standard interpretive canons apply. Thus, for example, when these norms are shaped as rules, the later norm will prevail (*lex posteriori derogat legi priori*), unless the earlier norm constitutes a special law (*lex specialis derogat legi generali*).[104] The same is true in cases where one of the equal-level norms is shaped as a rule while the other is shaped as a principle.[105] However, when both norms are shaped as principles, we should first examine whether the solution can be found at the legislative level, or, where the conflict cannot be resolved at that level, the solution can only be found at the sub-legislative level.[106] As for two statutory rights that are in conflict, the earlier discussion – relating to two conflicting constitutional rights – may apply here as well, *mutatis mutandis*.[107] When two common law precedents are in conflict, the rules of *stare decisis* will apply. An examination of these rules is beyond the scope of this book. In none of these cases is the limitation clause triggered. Rather, the solution is interpretive in nature. Within the interpretive process, the interpreter may need to use interpretive balancing; in these cases, this can be done by analogy to the balancing used by the component of proportionality *stricto sensu*.[108]

A special case is that of a statute establishing a human right and providing instructions as to the proper limitation of such a right by another statute. This is the case with the New Zealand Bill of Rights Act of 1990.[109]

---

[102] See above, at 72.   [103] See above, at 72.
[104] See above, at 87.   [105] See above, at 97.
[106] See above, at 89.   [107] See above, at 87.   [108] See above, at 72.
[109] No. 109. A similar case is that of the State of Victoria in Australia; see Charter of Human Rights and Responsibilities Act 2006 (Vic.).

This Bill of Rights is entrenched in a statute. It is not governed by a constitutional (or other supra-legislative) provision.[110] The New Zealand
statutory provisions were essentially copied from the Canadian Charter
of Rights and Freedoms. New Zealand adopted the Canadian limitation clause, but changed it to reflect the different constitutional levels in
which the two clauses operate. Thus, the New Zealand limitation clause
provides:

> Subject to Section 4 of this Bill of Rights, the rights and freedoms con-
> tained in the Bill of Rights may be subject only to such reasonable limits
> prescribed by law as can be demonstrably justified in a free and demo-
> cratic society.[111]

Section 4 of the Bill of Rights Act states, in turn:

> No court shall, in relation to any enactment (whether passed or made
> before or after the commencement of this Bill of Rights)—
>
> (a) hold any provision of the enactment to be impliedly repealed or
>   revoked, or to be in any way invalid or ineffective; or
> (b) decline to apply any provision of the enactment
>
> by reason only that the provision is inconsistent with any provision of this
> Bill of Rights.[112]

Accordingly, in New Zealand (according to sections 4 and 5 of the Bill of
Rights Act), whenever a statute limits a statutory human right, even if the
limitation is disproportional, the limiting statute remains valid; it may
not be repealed or revoked. This is true both for limiting statutes enacted
before the *Bill of Rights Act* went into force as well as for later limiting
statutes.

What is the role of New Zealand's limitation clause? It seems that it
has a triple role. First, it can play a role whenever the conflict is between
a statutory provision and a common law precedent. New Zealand's
common law (to the extent it does not include its statutory-interpretation function) must abide by the requirements posed by the limitation
clause.[113] Second, the limitation clause has interpretive value. The use of
interpretive balancing is not eliminated by the provisions of section 4 of

---

[110] See P. Rishworth, G. Huscroft, S. Optican, and R. Mahoney, *New Zealand Bill of Rights*
(Oxford University Press, 2003); P. A. Joseph, *Constitutional and Administrative Law in
New Zealand*, 3rd edn. (Wellington: Brookers, 2007).
[111] New Zealand Bill of Rights, Art. 5 ("Justified Limitations"). See above note 109.
[112] *Ibid.*, Art. 4 ("Other Enactments Not Affected").
[113] See above, at 121.

the Bill of Rights Act.[114] Such interpretive balancing may assist in the continuing development of New Zealand's legislation – by means of statutory interpretation rules – in the spirit of the Bill of Rights. Indeed, a specific provision in the Bill of Rights Act requires that "[w]herever an enactment can be given a meaning that is consistent with the rights and freedoms contained in this Bill of Rights, that meaning shall be preferred to any other meaning."[115] This provision may encourage the development of new interpretive rules that will protect human rights more vigorously. Third, the statutory limitation clause may serve an important guiding function. It may guide the New Zealand legislator on how to act in a manner that would not disproportionally limit human rights included within the Bill of Rights. Accordingly, the clause may also serve a deterrent purpose, as it may deter Members of Parliament from supporting a disproportional legislation. While the limiting legislation may not stand trial in court – i.e., it would not be the subject of judicial review – it will certainly stand trial in the court of public opinion, hence the importance of the limitation clause.

Another case is that of the United Kingdom's Human Rights Act (HRA) of 1998.[116] The act gives effect in the United Kingdom to the legal rights established by the European Convention for the Protection of Human Rights and Fundamental Freedoms, including those with specific limitation clauses. In terms of interpretation, the HRA provides that "[s]o far as it is possible to do so, primary legislation and subordinate legislation must be read and given effect in a way which is compatible with the Convention's rights."[117] However, if such interpretation is not possible, the "validity, continuing operation, or enforcement" of the incompatible legislation would not be affected.[118] In these kinds of situation, if the court is "satisfied that the provision is incompatible with a Convention right," it may "make a declaration of that incompatibility."[119] That declaration may trigger an expedited legislative process which would "make such amendments to the legislation … necessary to remove the incompatibility."[120]

---

[114] See Rishworth, Huscroft, Optican, and Mahoney, above note 110, at 117. See also *Moonen* v. *Film and Literature Board of Review* [2000] 2 NZLR 9. On interpretive balancing, see above, at 72.

[115] New Zealand Bill of Rights Act, Art. 6, above note 109. See Rishworth, Huscroft, Optican, and Mahoney, above note 110.

[116] Human Rights Act 1998, c. 42 (Eng.).

[117] *Ibid.*, section 3(1).   [118] *Ibid.*, section 3(2)(b).   [119] *Ibid.*, section 4(2).

[120] *Ibid.*, section 10(2) ("Power to take remedial action").

What is the effect of the HRA? It seems that there is agreement on two conclusions. First, that the HRA has not authorized the courts in the UK to declare that a statute incompatible with the rights incorporated by the HRA is void. The law's validity is preserved. Second, in practice, the chances that the incompatible statute will persist is unlikely. In most cases when there has been a declaration of incompatibility, the statute has been amended by the legislator so as to make it compatible. The concern that, if that law was not changed, the European Court of Human Rights – to whom a claim by the losing side may be presented – will reach the same result may have led to the change in the UK's law. The constitutional status of the HRA is controversial.[121] This controversy concerns two developments which characterize the HRA. One, the development of special rules for the interpretation of statutes which are claimed as incompatible with the HRA.[122] These rules differ from the regular rules of statutory interpretation. They severely limit the cases when the court will have to declare a statute incompatible. Second, according to the regular rules for the conflict of statutes, in those cases when the statute which came after the HRA is incompatible with it, the court could determine that the provision within the HRA is impliedly repealed. This is not the case regarding the HRA. When the court determines the later statute to be incompatible[123] with the HRA, it cannot repeal the HRA's provision. All it can do is declare the incompatibility of the statute. These developments lead some to the conclusion that the HRA is at a higher normative level than an ordinary statute.

The controversy existing in UK law regarding the legal status of the HRA is not connected to the question of proportionality – and its four components – which also apply regarding the rights incorporated by the HRA and which are limited by statutes. The UK courts are required

---

[121] The literature on this subject is vast. Its analysis is beyond the scope of this book. For an analysis of the literature and the different opinions, see A. Lester and D. Pannick, *Human Rights Law and Practice* (London: Butterworths, 2004); A. Kavanagh, *Constitutional Review under the UK Human Rights Act* (Cambridge University Press, 2009); A. Young, *Parliamentary Sovereignty and the Human Rights Act* (Portland, OR: Hart Publishing, 2009).

[122] See *Ghaidan* v. *Mendoza* [2004] 3 WLR 113; *Sheldrake* v. *DPP* [2004] UKHL 43; *R. (Wilkinson)* v. *Inland Revenue Commissioners* [2006] All ER 529.

[123] This is also the case for a statute enacted before the HRA. Regarding this statute, it may be said that the HRA is weaker than a regular statute, because, according to the implied repeal rule, the older statute would be voided, yet the HRA prevents the declaration of voidability and replaces it with a declaration of incompatibility.

by the HRA to determine if a statute which limited the rights is incompatible with those rights. To do so, it must first establish the scope of the right set forth in the HRA (the first stage of the legal analysis), and, second, respond to the question whether the limitation is proportional (the second stage of the legal analysis). Within the framework of the second stage – the determination whether the limitation is proportional – the rules of proportionality and all its components will apply. It is similar to the constitutional balancing, other than the remedy (the third stage) which is not voiding but rather a declaration of incompatibility. The difference therefore is not with regard to the application of the rules of proportionality, but rather with regard to the remedy for the disproportional limitation of the right. Therefore, there is room to apply the rules of proportionality which apply to the relationship between constitutional rights and sub-constitutional law which limits the right, and also to the relationship between the rights incorporated by the HRA and the statute which limits them (whether it was enacted before or after the HRA).

C.   The substantive role of proportionality

1.   Human rights and their limitation

i.   Democracy: rights and obligations

Human rights constitute an essential part of modern democracies. We should never forget that these democracies were built atop the ruins of the Second World War and the Holocaust. Take human rights out of democracy, and democracy has lost its soul. Human rights are the crown jewels of democracy. A democracy without human rights is like an empty vessel.

Human rights are essential to democracy. However, democracy cannot exist when based only on human rights. A democratic society must acknowledge the possibility of limiting those rights.[124] There are two types of limitation.[125] The first type includes a limitation on one person's right in order to make way for the rights of another person. If one member of society may act as he pleases without any limitation, the rights of another member to do the same would be concomitantly limited. A principled recognition of both persons' freedom to act also requires the placing of

---

[124] See A. Barak, *The Judge in a Democracy* (Princeton University Press, 2006), 82.
[125] See below, at 253.

limitations on both persons' ability to exercise this freedom. This idea can be found as far back as the French Declaration of the Rights of Man and of the Citizen of 1789, which states:

> Liberty consists in the freedom to do everything which injures no one else; hence the exercise of the natural rights of each man has no limits except those which assure to the other members of the society the enjoyment of the same rights. These limits can only be determined by law.[126]

The second type of limitation on human rights in a democracy consists of limitations in favor of public interest considerations. In a democratic society, a human right may be limited to ensure the very existence of the state; to ensure its continued existence as a democracy; to ensure public health; to ensure public education; as well as several other national causes. These are the purposes for which a democratic society may limit the rights of its members.[127] In fact, the state may even impose duties, including the duty to sacrifice one's life for society.[128] This demonstrates the special nature of democracy, which is based on the idea that the state protects the rights of the individual, and the individual protects the state – its safety and peaceful existence.[129]

---

[126] Declaration of the Rights of Man and of the Citizen 1789, Art. 4.

[127] See below, at 256.   [128] See Osiatynski, above note 47.

[129] See HCJ 164/97 *Contrem Ltd.* v. *Minister of Finance* [1998] IsrSC 52(1) 289, 320 ("The state authority and the citizen do not stand against each other, on two sides of the wall; rather, they stand alongside each other, partners in the enterprise of the state ... The government (or, as I prefer to call it, the public service) must serve the public – to guarantee peace and legal order; to provide essential services; to protect the human dignity and liberty of each citizen; to create social justice. But at the same time, the same public service – which, in and of itself, is unable to provide all those services – must be received from the public in order to provide. The proper relationship between the public service and the public – in fact, the only possible relationship – is a relationship based on a mutual give and take. Accordingly, the same type of relationship should exist between the state agency and the citizen. A citizen may not assume, morally or practically, that he may demand – and receive – everything from the agency, while he owes nothing to the same. While he may have some rights *vis-à-vis* the state agency, he also has duties. This is the essence of the social contract between the members of the democratic society and themselves, and between them and their public service. This is the essence of the existence of the modern democratic state." (Zamir, J.); "Democracy does not only constitute human rights. Democracy is also made up of human duties. These entail duties towards other people, and duties towards the government. Indeed, democracy is based on a shared notion of national interests. The government is set up to serve the people. In order to do so, the government must be equipped with powers. Without those powers, the government would be unable to realize the public interest. Those governmental powers, in turn, create duties for individuals. These duties are imposed in order for the government to fulfill the national goals it aims to achieve in

ii. The relationship between human rights
and the public interest

Human rights are essential to democracy; at the same time their very existence presupposes a democratic regime. Thus, the existence of a democratic society and human rights is interrelated. To have a democracy, you must guarantee human rights; and to guarantee human rights, you must have a democracy.[130] "A constitution is not a recipe for suicide, and human rights are not a prescription for national annihilation ... Each nation's legislative provisions should be interpreted in a way that assumes each nation's continued existence. Human rights derive from that same existence, and therefore they should not become a weapon for the destruction of the democratic state."[131] To the same extent, "human rights should not be sacrificed on the altar of the state. Human rights are natural to humans, and they existed long before the birth of the modern democracy. Indeed, the protection of human rights also requires the adoption of a social and national framework that guarantees – and recognizes the importance of – such protection."[132] A democracy is based on mutual respect between the rights of the individuals and the public interest. Both human rights and the public interest constitute a part of the constitutional structure which both establishes the rights and enables their limitation.[133]

---

a democratic regime. They derive from that same shared notion of national interests, as well as the need to promote the liberty of every individual. They are based on the modern concept of the welfare state, and on social solidarity. They derive from the notion that considers the individual as someone who is shaped by his surroundings, and therefore includes, as part of his personality, a 'social facet.' From this 'social facet' comes the need to take the entire society into account. This same society may demand the individual – as a member of the society – to act to advance the public interest. Such a demand is the result of balancing between public needs and the individual rights." (Barak, P.)).

[130] Barak, above note 129, at 83, 84.

[131] EA 2/84 *Neiman* v. *Chairman of Central Election Committee for Eleventh Knesset* [1985] IsrSC 39(2) 225, 310 (Barak, J.) (based, in part, on *Terminiello* v. *Chicago*, 337 US 1, 36 (1949) (Jackson, J., dissenting)).

[132] Barak, above note 129, at 83, 84.

[133] CA 6821/93, *United Mizrahi Bank Ltd* v. *Migdal Cooperative Village* [1995] IsrLR 1, para. 89 ("Human rights exist within a social framework that enables their existence. They reflect the fundamental notion that human rights do not view the individual as living on their own, but rather as part of society, which in turn has national interests and goals. Human rights exist as part of the recognition that they should be kept together with the national framework. A limitation of those human rights is therefore allowed to maintain the social framework that protects those rights ... Alongside human rights we may find human obligations ... Indeed, the normative world entails both rights and obligations ... Alongside each person's right we find his obligations towards his fellow men,

iii.   The limitation clause as an instrument in shaping the proper relationship between human rights and their limitations

What is the proper relationship between the rights of the individuals and the public interest? When is it justified for the state to impose a limitation on a person's right towards his fellow citizens and towards the state? There is no agreed-upon answer to these questions. The answer changes from one legal system to another and from one period to another. It seems that the only agreed-upon principle is that the proper relationship between human rights and the public interest is the relationship that is deemed proper by a democratic society.

How, then, would a democracy determine that proper relationship? What is the instrument used for this determination when the human right is a constitutional right? The answer is found in the limitation clause – and in the proportionality which shapes it. Proportionality is the legal instrument by which the proper relationship between constitutional rights and their sub-constitutional law limitations is determined. It is a legal "institution." It is a legal construction. It provides the relevant considerations regarding the proper relationship between the constitutional right and its sub-constitutional limitation.[134] Proportionality and the limitation clause limit both the powers of the state and the rights of the individual.[135]

iv.   The centrality of proportionality and the limitation clause

The proportionality requirements set by the limitation clause are at the heart of the doctrine of human rights. Those requirements express the complexity of the modern constitutional right. Such a right was designed to let each member of society realize their wishes to the fullest extent; alas, such a realization is not possible without the limitation by law of other people's rights. In addition, we should acknowledge the possibility that no full realization

---

and his duty towards the society as a whole." (Barak, P.)). See also *Contram*, above note 129, at para. 346 ("The nature of life within a democratic society requires at times a limitation of human rights. Indeed, the protection of human rights is not possible without the limitation of human rights. A democratic regime does not entail unlimited human rights. Human rights are not a prescription for national annihilation. A central feature of a democratic regime is that it would only permit a limitation of human rights in order to promote human rights, and even then, only to the smallest extent possible. A democracy allows for limitations on human rights in order to enable the continued existence of a social framework guaranteeing human rights.". (Barak, P.)).

[134] See S. Woolman, "Riding the Push-Me Pull-You: Constructing a Test That Reconciles the Conflicting Interests Which Animate the Limitation Clause," 10 *SAJHR* 60, 77 (1994).

[135] See below, at 166.

of such rights would be possible due to the special needs of society at a given time and place – as those needs are reflected in sub-constitutional law (a statute or the common law). This point was noted in one case:

> The limitation clause … constitutes a central feature of human-rights protection. The role of the limitation is twofold. It at once protects human rights and enables their limitation. It demonstrates the relative nature of the rights … The limitation clause is the peg on which the constitutional system balances between the individual and the community, between the individual and society as a whole. It reflects the notion that alongside human rights we may find human obligations; that alongside each member's right stands their obligations towards their fellow man and towards society as a whole.[136]

Indeed, Robinson Crusoe never needed constitutional (or other) rights. The very existence of constitutional rights assumes the existence of a human society, as well as a limitation on the wants and needs of its members. Such limitations are set by the limitation clause – and the requirements of proportionality at its center. Proportionality, therefore, represents the notion that the individual lives within a society and is a part thereof; that the very existence of that society – its needs, as well as its tradition – may provide a justification to the limitation of human rights through laws that are proportional. Constitutional rights are rights of the individual as part of the society; accordingly, they may be limited by sub-constitutional laws serving proper social goals.

2.   Protecting human rights and recognizing the constitutionality of their limitations

The limitation clause – and the proportionality requirements at its center – fulfills a dual role in constitutional democracies: It both protects constitutional rights and provides a justification for their limitation. Chief Justice Dickson of the Canadian Supreme Court wrote in *Oakes* in relation to the Canadian limitation clause:

> It is important to observe at the outset that Section 1 has two functions: first, it constitutionally guarantees the rights and freedoms set out in the provisions which follow; and second, it states explicitly the exclusive justificatory criteria … against which limitations on those rights and freedoms must be measured.[137]

---

[136] *Mizrahi Bank*, above note 133, at 239.
[137] *R. v. Oakes* [1986] 1 SCR 103, 135.

Just like the Roman god Janus, the limitation clause has two faces: the protection and justification of limitation.[138]

3.   Both the right and its limitations stem from a shared source

The "two-face" metaphor may point to the central feature of the limitation clause: The constitutional right on the one hand, and its limitations (by sub-constitutional laws) on the other, are the two sides of the same constitutional idea. They stem from a common source and advance common values. As Chief Justice Dickson noted in *Oakes*:

> The underlying values and principles of a free and democratic society are the genesis of the rights and freedoms guaranteed by the Charter and the ultimate standard against which a limit on a right or freedom must be shown, despite its effect, to be reasonable and demonstrably justified.[139]

These ideas were echoed in *United Mizrahi Bank*:

> The constitutional right and its limitation stem from a common source … Both the right and its limitations are subservient to the fundamental principles on which the Basic Law is founded (Article 1), and its goals (Articles 1a, 2).[140]

The constitutional right is entrenched in the constitution, and the authority regarding its limitation is entrenched in the constitution. Moreover, the same constitutional principles justifying the recognition of constitutional rights equally justify the recognition of the legal possibility of justifying the limitation of those rights through sub-constitutional laws. As Woolman and Botha have noted, in the South African context:

> [T]he same values that inform our understanding of what constitutes a justifiable limitation on a right – openness, democracy, dignity, equality, and freedom – also flesh out the extension of the individual rights themselves.[141]

4.   The limits on constitutional limitations

The limitation clause expresses the notion of the relative – as opposed to absolute – nature of constitutional rights.[142] It does so by providing

---

[138] See J. Karp, "Criminal Law – Yanus of Human Rights: Constitutionalization and Basic Law: Human Dignity and Liberty," *Hapraklit* 42(1) 64 (1995).
[139] *Oakes*, above note 137, at 136.   [140] See above note 133.
[141] See Woolman and Botha, above note 65, at 2.
[142] *Mizrahi Bank*, above note 133, at 239.

constitutional status both to the right and to the power to limit its exercise by a sub-constitutional law. One of the most important features of the
limitation clause is that even the limitations have limits. As Alexy noted:

> The principled nature of constitutional rights gives rise not only to the
> idea that constitutional rights are limited and limitable in light of coun-
> tervailing principles, but also that their limiting and limitability is itself
> limited.[143]

The same idea was noted in the *Design* case:

> Human rights are not absolute; they may be limited. Albeit, those limita-
> tions have their own limits. Those boundaries are set by the limitation
> clause.[144]

This notion of "limits on limitations"[145] is of utmost importance. It lies
at the very foundation of constitutional democracy. It is the legal basis
for the limitation of the legislative power in relation to the limitation of
human rights. In the same way that human rights require a thorough
study, so too do their limitations.

D.   Limitation clause and the override

1.   *The nature of the override*

The Canadian Charter of Rights and Freedoms includes an override
clause. The clause states:

(1)   Parliament or the legislature of a province may expressly declare in
an Act of Parliament or of the legislature, as the case may be, that the
Act or a provision thereof shall operate notwithstanding a provision
included in section 2 or sections 7 to 15 of this Charter.

(2)   An Act or a provision of an act in respect of which a declaration made
under this section is in effect shall have such operation as it would have
but for the provision of this Charter referred to in the declaration.

(3)   A declaration made under subsection (1) shall cease to have effect
five years after it comes into force or on such earlier date as may be
specified in the declaration.

---

[143] Alexy, above note 26, at 192.
[144] HCJ 5026/04 *Design 22 Shark Deluxe Furniture Ltd.* v. *Director of Sabbath Work Permits
Department, Ministry of Labor and Social Affairs* [2005] (1) IsrLR 340, 353. See above, at
166.
[145] See B. Pieroth and B. Schlink, *Grundrechte, Staatsrecht II* (Berlin: C. F. Müller
Verlagsgruppe, 2006), 64.

(4) Parliament or the legislature of a province may re-enact a declaration made under subsection (1).

(5) Subsection (3) applies in respect of a re-enactment made under subsection (4).[146]

Influenced by that provision, and as part of a political compromise, the Israeli Knesset also constituted a special override provision in one of the Basic Laws. That provision, found in Basic Law: Freedom of Occupation, states:

> A provision of a law that violates freedom of occupation shall be of effect, even though not in accordance with Article 4, if it has been included in a law passed by a majority of the members of the Knesset, which expressly states that it shall be of effect, notwithstanding the provisions of this Basic Law; such law shall expire four years from its commencement unless a shorter duration has been stated therein.[147]

The override clause provides that, even if the "override" legislation is disproportional, it is still valid. In essence, it grants a statute fulfilling certain conditions "immunity" from judicial review.

Despite the similarities between the two provisions, the Israeli override clause seems to better protect human rights than its Canadian counterpart in the following ways. First, it applies only to one constitutional right – freedom of occupation – rather than to several rights included within the Canadian Charter. Despite this, even in Canada the clause does not apply to all constitutional rights. Second, in Israel, a majority of Members of Parliament is required to enact an "overriding"

---

[146] Canadian Charter of Rights and Freedoms, Section 33. For commentary and political background, see L. Weinrib, "Learning to Live with the Override," 35 *McGill L. J.* 541 (1990); P. H. Russell, "Standing Up for Notwithstanding," 29 *Alta. L. Rev.* 293 (1991); T. Kahana, "The Notwithstanding Mechanism and Public Discussion: Lessons from the Ignored Practice of Section 33 of the Charter," 43 *Can. Public Admin.* 225 (2001); T. Kahana, "Understanding the Notwithstanding Mechanism," 52 *U. Toronto L. J.* 221 (2002); T. Kahana, "What Makes for a Good Use of the Notwithstanding Mechanism?," 23 *Sup. Ct. L. Rev.* 191 (2004); P. W. Hogg, *Constitutional Law of Canada*, 5th edn., vol. II (Toronto, Thomson Carswell, 2007), 163. A similar provision was legislated in Victoria, Australia. Amongst other things, it determines (Art. 31(4)): "It is the intention of Parliament that an override declaration will only be made in exceptional circumstances." For a critique of the latter, see J. Debeljak, "Balancing Rights in a Democracy: The Problems with Limitations and Overrides of Rights under the Victorian Charter of Human Rights and Responsibilities Act 2006," 32 *Melb. U. L. Rev.* 422 (2008).
[147] Basic Law: Freedom of Occupation, Art. 8. Art. 4, mentioned in the text, is the general limitation clause providing: "There shall be no infringement of rights under this Basic Law except by a law befitting the values of the State of Israel, enacted for a proper purpose, and to an extent no greater than is required."

statute; such a requirement does not appear in Canada. Third, in Israel, such "overriding" legislation expires within four years of its enactment. The statute, in other words, has a limited lifespan ("sunset provisions"). In Canada, the statute is not limited in time; rather, the constitutional protection from judicial review is temporary – it expires after five years. The statute itself, however, continues to be in effect until otherwise ruled. Both systems allow for the renewal of these periods once they have expired.

2.   The relationship between the limitation clause and the override

i.   Legal and political limitations

The formal role of the override clause is similar to that of the limitation clause. Both have constitutional status. Both deal with the limitation of constitutional rights rather than their amendment. Both allow such limitation in a way rendering the limitation valid within the legal system. However, they are markedly different. The limitation clause expresses both the formal and substantial notions of democracy. It reflects a delicate balance between the sovereignty of the people – as reflected by legislation – and constitutional rights. One of the limitation clause's main features is the imposition of legal restraints – in the form of judicial review – on the legislative power of parliament in relation to disproportional limitations of constitutional human rights. In contrast to the limitation clause, the override clause only satisfies the formal notion of democracy. It was designed to provide the people – through its representatives – with the authority to override the proportionality requirements posed by the constitutional limitation clause over the legislator's legislative power. It turns the legal limitations on the legislator into political ones.[148]

---

[148] See HCJ 4676/94 *Meatrael* v. *Minister of Finance* [1996] IsrSC 50(5) 15, 26 ("The purpose of the override clause is to enable the legislator to realize its social and political ends, even if those limit the rights included in Basic Law: Freedom of Occupation and such limitation does not meet the requirements set by the limitation clause ... The override clause enables the legislator to achieve through legislation social and political ends without the fear that such legislation would be declared invalid by judicial review ... The override clause preserves the status of the Basic Law as a constitutional norm, while at the same time granting the legislator the powers to limit the rights therein included without the need to abide by the requirements set by the limitation clause; all that, without the need to amend the Basic Law itself." (Barak, P.)).

The override clause was initially formulated in Canada as a result of political compromise.[149] Today it is seen as a new constitutional institution,[150] striking a new balance between past and present, between the legislative and the judicial branches.[151] Indeed, the override clause creates a dialogue between the legislator and the judge. Some view it as a new form of "soft" constitutionalism,[152] providing a wanted response to the counter-majoritarian claim.[153] The main reason for that is that the override clause enables the legislator to override the constitutional limitations posed by the limitation clause with regard to human rights without a constitutional amendment. While it is true that the override clause may weaken the institution of judicial review, it does not eliminate it outright. In Canada it only applies to several Articles relating to human rights. It does not allow for institutional arrangements set by the constitution (such as the establishment of three branches of government) to be overridden. In addition, it does not apply to all human rights. For example, it does not apply to the constitutional right to vote or to be elected; it does not apply retroactively;[154] and it may not affect a *res judicata*, or a final judicial decision. It is time-sensitive. Finally, it requires that the legislator declare that they are aware that the limitation of the constitutional right is not proportional.[155]

Is the override clause worthy? Would it be proper to include it in the constitution? The answer differs from one democratic society to another and from one legal system to the next. One of the main issues to consider is what would be the alternative to the inclusion of an override clause, as well as how often it would actually be put to use by the legislator. We cannot compare a well-defined and, indeed, rare use of the clause – as

---

[149] See Hogg, above note 146, at 166.
[150] See Weinrib, above note 146 (referring to the override clause as the "new institutional hybrid").
[151] See P. C. Weiler, "Rights and Judges in a Democracy: A New Canadian Version," 18 *U. Mich. J. L. Reform* 51, 80 (1984); L. E. Weinrib, "Learning to Live with the Override," 36 *McGill L. J.* 541 (1990); S. Gardbaum, "The New Commonwealth Model of Constitutionalism," 49 *Am. J. Comp. L.* 707 (2001).
[152] See S. Gardbaum, "Limiting Constitutional Rights," 54 *UCLA L. Rev.* 789, 821 (2007); M. Tushnet, *Weak Courts, Strong Rights: Judicial Review and Social Welfare Rights in Comparative Constitutional Law* (Princeton University Press, 2008), 24; S. Gardbaum, "Reassessing the New Commonwealth Model of Constitutionalism," 8 *Int'l. J. Const. L.* 167 (2010).
[153] See Hogg, above note 146, at 174 (arguing that, following the Canadian override clause, "the American debate over the legitimacy of judicial review is rendered irrelevant.").
[154] See *Ford* v. *AG of Quebec* [1988] 2 SCR 712, 744.
[155] See Weinrib, above note 151, at 568.

done, for example, in Canada[156] – with a repeated, unlimited use of the clause,[157] or, worse yet, such a comprehensive use of the clause that would render all human rights superfluous.[158] In Israel, for example, as part of the national compromise relating to a new constitution, it would be possible to consider the inclusion of a general override clause, like the one currently appearing only within Basic Law: Freedom of Occupation. This might be a risky move; then again, what is the alternative?

ii. The relationship between the limitation clause and the override

The override clause assumes that a statute may limit a constitutional right disproportionally. Despite that, the legislator sees a need for this disproportional statute, and therefore the statute needs the constitutional protection (or "immunity") offered by the override. How would the legislator know that the act is disproportional? One way is through a judicial decision to that effect. Another is the fear of the likelihood of such a decision, even before it is handed down.

In both Canada and Israel, the requirements of proportionality apply to all constitutional rights. This is not the case with the override. It does not have a general application. A special issue may arise when one statutory limitation may affect several constitutional rights, some of which are governed by the override while others are not. Take, for example, a statutory provision limiting the constitutional right of freedom of occupation (which is governed in Israel by the override) which may simultaneously limit the right to property (which is not subject in Israel to the override). Assume that the limitation is disproportional for both constitutional rights involved. Recall that the override requires that the legislator declare that the statute "shall operate notwithstanding" the existence of a constitutional provision. Once such a declaration has been made, the override is triggered, but only in relation to the relevant constitutional rights (that is, those rights that the clause governs). This statute limits a constitutional right (the right to property) – to which the override does not apply – in a disproportional manner. Should we say that the statute is unconstitutional due to its disproportional limitation of a right which is not governed by the override?

---

[156] See Hogg, above note 146, at 165; Gardbaum, above note 132, at 178.
[157] See Gardbaum, above note 152, at 757.
[158] See Ford, above note 154.

This question was considered in Israel in the case of *Meatrael*.[159] At issue was an Act of Parliament that limited the freedom of occupation of several meat importers.[160] In Israel, the freedom of occupation is both a constitutional right and (the only) right governed by the override clause. For fear that the statute may be limiting the right disproportionally, and therefore may be declared unconstitutional,[161] the statute included a declaration that it "shall operate notwithstanding" the constitutional right to freedom of occupation.[162] The petitioner, in turn, argued that the statute limited their right to property – another recognized constitutional right in Israel, but one not governed by the override clause. Accordingly, the petitioner argued that the statute should be invalidated as it disproportionally limited a constitutional right not governed by the override clause. It was noted that the "overriding" act in question may be granted constitutional protection within the limits of Basic Law: Freedom of Occupation. It is not granted, for that reason alone, protection under Basic Law: Human Dignity and Liberty. Accordingly, there may be situations in which an "overriding" act may be protected from invalidation for the purposes of *Basic Law: Freedom of Occupation*, but invalid for purposes of the other Basic Law.[163]

Such an approach raises complex interpretive issues in all those cases – and there are many – in which the disproportional means used by the "overriding" legislative provision in question may limit more than one right. How should we determine the relationship between those limitations where, as in this case, some are protected by the override clause, while others are not? In the case, the following guidelines were provided:

> A proper interpretation would provide constitutional protection to an "overriding" legislative provision limiting not only the freedom of occupation but other constitutional rights [as well] … when the three following conditions are met: First, the limitation of other constitutional rights is incidental to, and naturally flows from, the limitation of the freedom of occupation. Second, the limitation of the freedom of occupation is the primary limitation, while the other limitations are secondary. Third, the limitation of other constitutional rights, in and of itself, is not substantial. Once these three conditions are met, the proper interpretive result – one which considers the entire constitutional framework as one unified

---

[159] *Meatrael*, above note 148.
[160] The act in question was titled the Import of Frozen Meat Law, SH 10 (1994). It is now titled the Law of Meat and Its Products, 1994.
[161] Following an *obiter dictum* by the Israeli Supreme Court in a previous case.
[162] See Art. 5 of the Import of Frozen Meat Law, above note 160.
[163] *Meatrael*, above note 148, at 29.

whole, and which seeks constitutional harmony – would be to provide the "override" legislative provision with general protection so that it would be valid beyond the mere provisions of Basic Law: Freedom of Occupation. Any other interpretive result would render the override clause superfluous, rendering any use thereof ineffective. A proper interpretation must refrain from such a result. However, the interpretive solution provided here also maintains the proper boundaries of Basic Law: Human Dignity and Liberty. It acknowledges the fact that this Basic Law does not contain an override clause, while protecting the rights included therein from a primary limitation that may arise as a result of the enactment of an "overriding" legislative provision.[164]

iii.   The limitations of the override clause

The override clause provides constitutional protection to any statute that either limits constitutional rights in a disproportional manner or is suspected of doing so. Does that necessarily mean that any deviation from the rules of proportionality, regardless of its scope, would provide constitutional protection to the statute in question? That question has been considered in the Canadian literature.[165] One view is that the general limitations included in the Canadian limitation clause – according to which all rights and freedoms set out in the Charter are "subject only to such reasonable limits prescribed by law as can be demonstrably justified in a free and democratic society"[166] – should also apply to the override clause, such that an act of parliament that places "unreasonable" limits on those constitutional rights would not be able to enjoy the protection of the override clause. The standard used under the limitation clause should be lower. This view was never adopted by the Canadian courts. Hogg noted – while relying on a series of cases by the Canadian Supreme Court – that the override clause only requires several formal conditions. Accordingly, in his approach, the proportionality requirements and the limitation clause may not apply to such conditions.[167]

The issue was also considered in Israel. According to the text of the Israeli override clause – "a legislative provision limiting the freedom

---

[164] Ibid., at 30.
[165] See Hogg, above note 146, at 170. See also D. J. Arbess, "Limitations on Legislative Override under the Canadian Charter of Rights and Freedoms: A Matter of Balancing Values," 21 Osgoode Hall L. J. 113 (1983); B. Slattery, "Canadian Charter of Rights and Freedoms – Override Clauses under Art. 33 – Whether Subject to Judicial Review under Art. 1," 61 Can. Bar Rev. 391 (1983).
[166] Canadian Charter of Rights and Freedoms, Section 1, above note 7.
[167] Hogg, above note 146, at 170.

of occupation shall remain in effect, even if it is not in accordance with
Article 4 of this Basic Law" – it is clear that the constitutional protection
would not be lifted merely because the act in question is disproportional.
In fact, according to its text, the Israeli override clause is triggered when
the "overriding" provision is disproportional. But what is the proper relationship between the override and the constitutional provisions relating to
the principles of the Basic Law,[168] as well as to its purposes?[169] In *Meatrael*
the argument that such "principles" may outweigh the provisions of the
override clause was not ruled out:

> Even if we assume, *arguendo*, that some basic values and purposes are
> so fundamental that even an "overriding" provision may not limit them,
> then these are obviously the same basic values and purposes upon which
> our entire constitutional structure – including our Basic Laws – is built.
> The limitation of such principles should be substantial and concrete …
> otherwise, the entire override clause would be rendered superfluous. This
> is not the case before us.[170]

Accordingly, it may be argued that the override is not helpful whenever
a similar constitutional amendment would be deemed unconstitutional.
The discussion regarding the question of whether every constitutional
amendment is constitutional is beyond the scope of this book. If the legal
system recognizes the legal possibility of "unconstitutional constitutional amendments,"[171] such recognition may limit the use of the override
clause. Thus, the override clause may not be used to bring in, through the
"back door," a new constitutional order that – had it been entered through
the "front door" of constitutional amendment – would have been deemed
unconstitutional.

---

[168] Israeli Basic Law: Human Dignity and Liberty, Art. 1: "Fundamental human rights in
  Israel are founded upon recognition of the value of the human being, the sanctity of
  human life, and the principle that all persons are free; these rights shall be upheld in the
  spirit of the principles set forth in the Declaration of the Establishment of the State of
  Israel."

[169] Israeli Basic Law: Human Dignity and Liberty, Art. 1A: "The purpose of this Basic Law
  is to protect human dignity and liberty, in order to establish in a Basic Law the values of
  the State of Israel as a Jewish and democratic state."

[170] *Meatrael*, above note 148, at 28.

[171] See above, at 31.

7

The historical origins of proportionality

A. Proportionality: in life and in the law

1. On the philosophical origins of proportionality

Proportionality is a worthy quality to possess in one's day-to-day life. It reflects life experience and careful reasoning.[1] It is an embodiment of the notion of justice and can therefore be found in the image of Lady Justice holding scales.[2] It is also an expression of rational thinking.[3] We demand of ourselves and others to act proportionally. We require that the punishment be proportional to the offense.[4] Therefore, an "eye for an eye" was considered a measured response.[5] In the Jewish religious sources we find the Golden Rule which says: "That which is hateful to you, do not do to your fellow."[6] The notion of proportionality has inspired thinkers throughout the generations.[7] The classical Greek notions of corrective justice (*justitia vindicativa*) and distributive justice (*justitia distributiva*) have also contributed to the development of proportionality as a rational

---

[1] See E. M. Thomas, *The Judicial Process: Realism, Pragmatism, Practical Reasoning and Principles* (Cambridge University Press, 2005), 337.

[2] See D. E. Curtis and J. Resnik, "Images of Justice," 96 *Yale L. J.* 1727, 1741 1987).

[3] See J. Raz, *Practical Reasons and Norms*, 2nd edn. (Oxford University Press, 1999), 95.

[4] See *Graham* v. *Florida*, 560 US (2010) (Slip. Op. at 8) ("The concept of proportionality is central to the Eighth Amendment. Embodied in the Constitution's ban on cruel and unusual punishments is the 'precept of justice that punishment for crime should be graduated and proportioned to [the] offense.'").

[5] See Exodus 21:23–25 ("But if any harm follow [when men strive together], then thou shalt give life for life, eye for eye, tooth for tooth, hand for hand, foot for foot, burning for burning, wound for wound, stripe for stripe."). The term appears several more times in the Jewish Bible. See M. Miller, *Eye for an Eye* (Cambridge University Press, 2006); M. J. Fish, "An Eye for an Eye: Proportionality as a Moral Principle of Punishment," 28 *OJLS* 57 (2008).

[6] Babylonian Talmud, Shabbat 31 a.

[7] For a discussion of proportionality in Christianity, see G. L. Hallet, *Greater Good: The Case for Proportionalism* (Washington, DC: Georgetown University Press, 1995).

concept.[8] Early Roman law recognized the notion as well.[9] By 1215, the Magna Carta had already recognized the principle in writing:

> For a trivial offence a free man shall be fined only in proportion to the degree of his offense, and for a serious offence correspondingly but not so heavily as to deprive him of his livelihood.[10]

The writings of St. Thomas Aquinas made a significant contribution to the development of the notion of proportionality.[11] During the Middle Ages, the international law doctrine of "Just War" made use of the term. According to the doctrine, there was a need to balance the overall utility of the war with the damage it may inflict.[12]

2.   Proportionality and the Enlightenment

The development of the concept of proportionality is inexorably linked to the Enlightenment of the eighteenth century and the notion of the social contract. These new developments viewed the relationships between citizens and their ruler in an entirely new light: It was the citizens who provided their ruler with powers – limited powers – and those powers were granted only if they would be used for the people's benefit, not the ruler's. These notions were echoed in the law. Thus, for example, Sir William Blackstone notes in his famous commentaries that the concept of civil liberty should be found only within "natural liberty so far restrained by

---

[8] See E. J. Weinrib, "Corrective Justice," 77 *Iowa L. Rev.* 403 (1992); I. Englard, *Corrective and Distributive Justice: From Aristotle to Modern Times* (Oxford University Press, 2009). On Plato and proportionality, see T. Poole, "Proportionality in Perspective," *New Zealand L. Rev.* 369 (2010).

[9] See K. Stern, "Zur Entstehung und Ableitung des Ubermassverbots," in P. Badura and R. Scholz (eds.), *Wege und Verfahren des Verfassungslebens: Festschrift fur Peter Lerche zum 65 Geburstag* (Munich: C. H. Beck, 1993). Regarding Cicero and proportionality, see Poole, above note 8.

[10] See G. R. C. Davis, *Magna Carta* (London: Trustees of the British Museum, 1963), 19.

[11] See T. Aquinas, *Summa Theologica II-II*. Qua estio 64, and 7.

[12] For the notion of Just War, see, e.g., J. Von Elbe, "The Evolution of the Concept of the Just War in International Law," 33 *Am. J. Int'l L.* 665 (1939); J. T. Johnson, *Ideology, Reason, and the Limitation of War: Religious and Secular Concepts, 1200–1740* (Princeton University Press, 1975); J. Johnson, *Just War Tradition and the Restraint of War* (Princeton University Press, 1981); J. Gardam, *Necessity, Proportionality and the Use of Force by States* (Cambridge University Press, 2004), 8; Y. Dinstein, *War, Aggression and Self-Defense*, 4th edn. (Cambridge University Press, 2005), 67.

human laws (and not farther) as is necessary and expedient for the general advantage of the public."[13]

The concept of proportionality is also linked to the notion of the liberal state, which emerged in Europe at the end of the nineteenth century. According to this notion, not every purpose that serves the public interest is justified when it also limits fundamental human rights. Finally, the development of the concept of proportionality is connected to some aspects of natural law.

3.   Proportionality as counter-formalism

During the end of the nineteenth century and the first half of the twentieth century, the development of the concept of proportionality was seen as part of the more general move in German law from the jurisprudence of concepts (*Begriffsjurisprudenz*) to the jurisprudence of interests (*Interessenjurisprudenz*). Proportionality has also shared several features with the realist trends in Continental European law, as well as with the then-nascent notion of legal positivism – although it should not be seen as emerging from either. At the center of development of the concept of proportionality stood the need for and the will to protect human rights from the powers of the state.[14]

4.   The contribution of Carl Gottlieb Svarez

The historical roots of proportionality as a public-law standard can be found in eighteenth-century German administrative law. According to most German commentators today, it was Carl Gottlieb Svarez (1746–1798) who, more than anyone else, contributed to the development of modern proportionality.[15] Svarez was the principal drafter of the Prussian Civil Code of 1794 (*Allgemeines Landrecht für die Preußishen*).

---

[13] W. Blackstone, *Commentaries on the Laws of England* (Oxford: Clarendon Press, 1765), 125.

[14] See M. Cohen-Eliya and I. Porat, "American Balancing and German Proportionality: The Historical Origins," 8 *Int'l J. Const. L.* 263 (2010).

[15] See L. Hirschberg, *Der Grundsatz Der Verhältnismäßigkeit* (Göttingen: Schwarz, 1980); K. Stern, "Zur Entstehung und Ableitung des Übermaßverbots," in P. Badura and R. Scholz (eds.), *Festschrift fur Peter Lerche zum 65 Geburtstag* (Munich: C. H. Beck, 1993), 165; D. P. Currie, *The Constitution of the Federal Republic of Germany* (University of Chicago Press, 1994), 307; A. Stone Sweet and J. Mathews, "Proportionality, Balancing and Global Constitutionalism," 47 *Colum. J. Transnat'l L.* 72 (2009).

In a series of lectures he gave between 1791 and 1792 (known as the *Kronprinzenvortage*), Svarez noted, in accordance with the principal tenets of the Enlightenment, that the state may only limit the liberty of one subject in order to guarantee the freedom and safety of others. More specifically, Svarez emphasized the "minimum relationship" that has to exist between the social hardship to be averted and the limitation on one's "natural freedom." As he wrote:

> Only the achievement of a weightier good for the whole can justify the state in demanding from the individual the sacrifice of a less substantial good. So long as the difference in weights is not obvious, the natural freedom must prevail … The [social] hardship, which is to be averted through the restriction of the freedom of the individual, has to be more substantial by a wide margin than the disadvantage to the individual or the whole that results from the infringement.[16]

Svarez viewed these requirements as expressions of both reasonableness and justice – principles dominant in a legal system which recognizes the natural right of the individual to freedom. Despite his substantial contribution to the concept, Svarez himself never used the term "proportionality" (*Verhaltnismassigkeit*) in his writings.[17]

B.   The development of proportionality in German public law

1.   *Proportionality in German administrative law, 1800–1933*

Proportionality as a positive legal concept – as opposed to Svarez' ideal social notion – began appearing in Prussian administrative law in the second half of the nineteenth century.[18] The term proportionality (*Verhältnismäßigkeit*) is first seen in German administrative law literature towards the end of the eighteenth century.[19] At the time, proportionality was discussed in the context of police laws (*Polizeirecht*), which served as the general framework of Prussian administrative law. The concept itself,

---

[16] See C. Gottlieb Svarez, *Vortrage über Recht und Staat* (Hermann Conrad and Gerd Kleinheyer (eds.), Cologne: Westdeutscher Verlag, 1960), 40. Translation taken from Stone Sweet and Mathews, above note 15, at 99.

[17] See G. Frumkin, "A Survey of the Sources of the Principle of Proportionality in German Law" (unpublished thesis, University of Chicago, 1991), 18 (on file with the author).

[18] See M. P. Singh, *German Administrative Law in Common Law Perspective*, 2nd edn. (Berlin: Springer, 2001).

[19] The first use of the term is usually attributed to Gunther Heinrich von Berg; see Frumkin, above note 17, at 17.

however, was mainly developed by the Supreme Administrative Court of Prussia (*Preußishes Oberverwaltungsgericht*).[20] In a long line of cases, the court ruled that police conduct was illegal because it was disproportional. One of those cases was that of a store owner who violated his store's liquor license several times. In response, the police ordered a closure of the entire store. The court overruled the police order, explaining that a complete closure was a disproportional sanction in the case, given the clear option of revoking the store's liquor license.[21] In another case, the court examined a property owner who built a fence on his property. The fence was not visible at night, creating a potential risk for pedestrians. The police, in response, ordered the owner to remove the entire fence. The court ruled against the police, suggesting that a less drastic measure was called for, such as requiring the owner to install proper lighting to eliminate the risk.[22] In 1928, Fleiner properly summarized the law of proportionality of the time, when he said: "You should never use a cannon to kill a sparrow."[23] The development of proportionality continued well into the beginning of the 1930s. It continued throughout the Weimar Republic, and ended with the rise to power of the Nazi party.

2.   The development of proportionality in German constitutional law post-Second World War

The Basic Law for the Federal Republic of Germany does not contain any explicit provision relating to proportionality.[24] Other than the absolute right to human dignity (*Würde des Menschen*),[25] all the rights mentioned by the Basic Law are relative. Some of the rights have no explicit limitation clauses, while others may only be limited "by law" (*durch Gesetz*).[26]

---

[20] For the historical development, see Singh, above note 18, at 16. See also K. Ledford, "Formalizing the Rule of Law in Prussia: The Supreme Administrative Law Court, 1876–1914," *Central European History*, vol. 37, No. 2 (2004), 203–224; see also Cohen-Eliya and Porat, above note 14.

[21] See 13 PrOVGE 424, 425, as cited by Frumkin, above note 17, at 23. See also Stone Sweet and Mathews, above note 15, at 101.

[22] See 13 PrOVGE 426, 427, as cited by Frumkin, above note 17, at 23. See also Stone Sweet and Mathews, above note 15, at 101.

[23] See F. Fleiner, *Institutionen des Deutschen Verwaltungsrechts* (Tübingen, 1928), 404.

[24] An explicit provision relating to proportionality does appear in some of the constitutions of Germany's States. See Currie, above note 15, at 308. See also Hirschberg, above note 15, at 2.

[25] See Basic Law for the Federal Republic of Germany, Art. 1(1): "Die Würde des Menschen ist unantsbar."

[26] See Art. 12(I) and 14(I) of the Basic Law.

Some contain their own specific limitation clause. Regardless, since the day it was established, the German Constitutional Court has been strict in following the notion that all rights included in the Basic Law – other than the right to human dignity – are bound by the concept of proportionality and all of its components. The meaning of this statement is that, in each case, the court must find a proper purpose and a rational connection between the means used by the limiting statute and the proper purpose, the absence of less intrusive means, and a proper balance between the limitation on the right and the benefit gained by the limiting statute.[27] The case of *Secret Tape Recordings* of 1973[28] may serve as a useful example. There, the Constitutional Court considered whether a recording made without the knowledge and consent of the speaker may serve as evidence in a court of law. The court ruled that the use of such a recording limits the right to the "free development of his personality," which is protected by Article 2(1) of the Basic Law. As to the constitutionality of such a limitation, the court said:

> It is not the entire sphere of private life which falls under the absolute protection of the basic right under Article 2(1) in conjunction with Article 1(1) of the Basic Law … The individual, as part of a community, rather has to accept such state interventions which are based on an overriding community interest under the strict application of the principle of proportionality, as long as they do not affect the inviolate sphere of private life.[29]

In a long line of cases, the German Constitutional Court emphasized the importance of proportionality. Similar developments followed in German administrative law[30] and in other fields of law.

The German approach to proportionality expanded beyond Germany. This is one of the prime examples of migration[31] – or transplantation[32] – of

[27] See Stern, above note 15.   [28] BVerfGE 34, 238.
[29] The English translation appears at S. Michalowski and L. Woods, *German Constitutional Law: The Protection of Civil Liberties* (Sudbury, MA: Dartmouth Publishing Co Ltd., 1999), 127.
[30] See Singh, above note 18, at 19.
[31] On the phenomenon, see J. Kokott, "From Reception to Transplantation to Convergence of Constitutional Models in the Age of Globalization – With Particular Reference to the German Basic Law," in C. Starck (ed.), *Constitutionalism, Universalism and Democracy – A Comparative Analysis: The German Contributions to the Fifth World Congress of the International Association of Constitutional Law* (Berlin: Nomos Verlagsgesellschaft, 1999), 71; S. Choudhry (ed.), *The Migration of Constitutional Ideas* (Cambridge University Press, 2006).
[32] See generally R. Sacco, "Legal Formants: A Dynamic Approach to Comparative Law (Installment II of II)," 39 *Am. J. Comp. L.* 343 (1991); A. Watson, *Legal Transplants: An Approach to Comparative Law*, 2nd edn. (Athens, GA: University of Georgia

constitutional models in the modern legal age. Indeed, it is possible to argue, together with Weinrib, that proportionality is the post-war paradigm of human rights protection.[33] Today, proportionality serves as a major component of the constitutional model shared by many democracies.[34] It consists – in the words of Law – of a part of the "generic constitutional law,"[35] and, within it, "generic constitutional analysis."[36] It is a part of the shared constitutional discourse, prevalent among jurists.[37] In some cases, after migrating to a new legal system, the concept of proportionality retained all of the components of the German approach. In other cases, the receiving legal system adopted only some components while rejecting others. Even within a given common component (e.g., balancing), different legal systems may give the component different meanings.[38] Many legal systems use proportionality today, while filling it with their own content. Still, the systems are very similar. We will now examine in further detail the migration or transplantation of the legal concept of proportionality.[39] A general depiction of the migration can be seen in Figure 1.

C. The migration of proportionality from German law to European law

1. European legal migration

Alongside the law of each of the European Union member states stands European law. For our purposes, this law is exemplified by the European Convention for the Protection of Human Rights and Fundamental

---

Press, 1993); J. Allison, "Transplantation and Cross-Fertilisation," in J. Beatson and T. Tridimas (eds.), *European Public Law* (Portland, OR: Hart Publishing, 1998). Regarding the transplantation of proportionality within legal transplant typologies, see M. Cohen, "Legal Transplant Chronicles: The Evolution of Unreasonableness and Proportionality Review of the Administration in the United Kingdom," 58 *Am. J. Comp. L.* 583 (2010).

[33] L. E. Weinrib, "The Postwar Paradigm and American Exceptionalism," in S. Choudhry (ed.), *The Migration of Constitutional Ideas* (Cambridge University Press, 2006), 84. See also Cohen-Eliya and Porat, above note 14, at 12.

[34] See V. Jackson, *Constitutional Engagement in a Transnational Era* (Oxford University Press, 2010), 60.

[35] See D. S. Law, "Generic Constitutional Law," 89 *Minn. L. Rev.* 652 (2005).

[36] *Ibid.*, at 693; J. Bomhoff, "Genealogies of Balancing as Discourse," 4 *Law and Ethics of Hum. Rights* 108 (2010).

[37] See Choudhry, above note 31.

[38] See Cohen-Eliya and Porat, above note 14.

[39] See Stone Sweet and Mathews, above note 15.

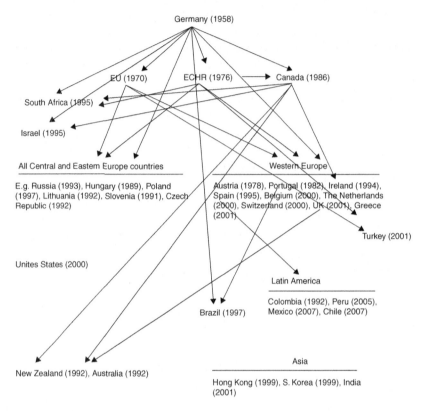

Figure 1   The migration of proportionality

Freedoms[40] and its amending protocols,[41] as well as several of the treaties establishing the European Union.[42] These documents, in turn, have established courts authorized to be the final interpreters of the

---

[40] The European Convention for the Protection of Human Rights and Fundamental Freedoms (1950).

[41] See Protocol No. 2 (ETS No. 44), September 21, 1970; Protocol No. 3 (ETS No. 45), September 21, 1970; Protocol No. 5 (ETS No. 55), December 20, 1971; Protocol No. 8 (ETS No. 118), January 1, 1990; Protocol No. 9 (ETS No. 140), October 1, 1994; Protocol No. 11 (ETS No. 155), November 1, 1998, http://conventions.coe.int/treaty/en/Treaties/Html/005.htm.

[42] See Treaty Establishing the European Coal and Steel Community (1951); Treaty Establishing the European Economic Community (1957); Treaty Establishing the European Atomic Energy Community (1957); Treaty on European Union (1992); Treaty Establishing the European Community (1997).

documents according to which they were established. Thus, the European Convention for the Protection of Human Rights and Fundamental Freedoms established the European Court of Human Rights, which sits in Strasbourg. The establishing treaties of the European Union are interpreted and operated by the European Court of Justice, which sits in Luxembourg. The relationships between the member states' courts and these European courts are complex and elaborate;[43] an examination of these relationships is beyond the scope of this book. Importantly, however, a reciprocal movement of ideas exists between the member states' courts and the European courts. Thus, legal doctrines developed by the European courts are often adopted by several of the member states, while doctrines developed by a member state court may later be adopted by the European courts.[44]

2.   Proportionality and the European Convention on Human Rights

The European Convention for the Protection of Human Rights and Fundamental Freedoms is the principal shared human rights text in Europe. The Convention recognizes a list of human rights. It does not explicitly recognize the concept of proportionality. Some of the rights are accompanied by a specific limitation clause, which determines the criterion according to which those rights may be limited.[45] This criterion requires that a limitation of a right be done only to the extent "necessary in a democratic society."[46] Other rights – not accompanied by a specific limitation clause – were also interpreted as relative rights,[47] other than the prohibition of torture.[48] According to the European Court of Human Rights, the concept of proportionality – with all its components, including

[43] See A. Torres Pérez, *Conflicts of Rights in the European Union: A Theory of Supranational Adjudication* (Oxford University Press, 2009).
[44] See Helen Keller and Alec Stone-Sweet (eds.), *A Europe of Rights: The Impact of the ECHR on National Legal Systems* (2008).
[45] Regarding "specific limitation clause," see above, at 141.
[46] See ECHR, Arts. 8, 9, 10, 11, above note 40. See also D. Shelton, *Regional Protection of Human Rights* (Oxford University Press, 2008), 226.
[47] See *Golder* v. *UK* (1979–80) 1 EHRR 524; T. R. S. Allan, "Legislative Supremacy and Legislative Intention: Interpretation, Meaning, and Authority," 63 *Cambridge L. J.* 685 (2004); J. Rivers, "Proportionality and Variable Intensity of Review," 65 *Cambridge L. J.* 174, 182 (2006).
[48] See ECHR, Art. 3. See above, at 40.

proportionality *stricto sensu* (balancing) – is a central feature of human rights according to the Convention.[49]

When was the first time that proportionality appeared in a judgment of the European Court of Human Rights? Somewhat surprisingly, an authoritative answer to this question is not readily available; it requires an intense historical survey which is beyond the scope of this book. According to Eissen,[50] the first decision to include a discussion of proportionality was in the case of *Handyside* in 1976.[51] In this freedom of expression case, the court ruled, *inter alia*:

> [E]very "formality," "condition," "restriction," or penalty imposed in this sphere must be proportionate to the legitimate aim pursued.[52]

The inspiration for this wording came from judgments of the German Constitutional Court relating to proportionality.[53]

3.   Proportionality in the law of the European Union

The term "proportionality" is not mentioned in the constituent documents that establish the law of the European Union. The concept was developed

---

[49] See R. Ryssdall, "Opinion: The Coming Age of the European Convention on Human Rights," *Eur. Hum. Rts. L. Rev.* 18 (1966); J. McBride, "Proportionality and the European Convention on Human Rights," in E. Ellis (ed.), *The Principle of Proportionality in the Laws of Europe* (Portland, OR: Hart Publishing, 1999), 23; Y. Arai-Takahashi, *The Margin of Appreciation Doctrine and the Principle of Proportionality in the Jurisprudence of the ECHR* (Oxford: Hart Publishing, 2002); S. Greer, "Constitutionalizing Adjudication under the European Convention on Human Rights," 23 *OJLS* 405 (2003); V. Jukka, *The European Court of Human Rights as a Developer of the General Doctrines of Human Rights Law: A Study of the Limitations Clauses of the European Convention on Human Rights* (Tampere, Finland: Tampereen yliopisto, 2003), 266; S. Greer, "'Balancing' and the European Court of Human Rights: A Contribution to the Habermas-Alexy Debate," 63 *Cambridge L. J.* 412 (2004); S. Greer, *The European Convention on Human Rights: Achievements, Problems and Prospects* (Cambridge University Press, 2006), 216; P. Van Dijk, F. Van Hoof, A. Van Rijn, and L. Zwaak (eds.), *Theory and Practice of the European Convention on Human Rights*, 4th edn. (2006), 335; H. Keller and A. Stone-Sweet (eds.), *A Europe of Rights: The Impact of the ECHR on National Legal Systems* (2008), 699; G. Letsas, *A Theory of Interpretation of the European Convention on Human Rights* (Oxford University Press, 2009).
[50] See M. Eissen, "The Principle of Proportionality in the Case-Law of the European Court of Human Rights," in R. St. J. MacDonald, F. Mestscher, and H. Petzold (eds.), *The European System for the Protection of Human Rights* (The Hague: Kluwer Law International, 1993), 125, 126.
[51] *Handyside* v. *United Kingdom*, App. No. 5493/72, 1 EHRR 737 (1979).
[52] *Ibid.*, para. 47.
[53] See Stone Sweet and Matthews, above note 15.

by the European Court of Justice. The Court of Justice developed the concept both in matters relating to review of EU institutions and in matters where a member state court referred a legal question to the Court of Justice to be determined in accordance with the principles of European law. This was done in light of the Court of Justice's recognition – following notions of French law – of general principles of law that exist alongside the formal written texts.[54] Among those general principles are the protection of human rights, the fulfillment of legitimate expectations,[55] the basic principles of natural justice and the principles of the rule of law. The concept of proportionality was given a central place among those principles.[56] According to most commentators, the concept was adopted by the European Court of Justice as influenced by German law.[57]

The concept of proportionality was initially explored by the European Court of Justice in a series of cases from the 1950s and 1960s. It was fully developed, however, in the 1970 in the case of *Internationale Handelsgesellschaft*.[58] The Advocate General on the case, Dutheillat de Lamonthe, thoroughly examined the concept of proportionality and found that it had roots in the documents establishing the European Union. The Court accepted his position. In that case, the Court examined a challenge to a direction of the European Economic Community that allegedly violated a human right. This approach was expanded early in the 1980s, when the court was willing to examine the congruence between the legislation of the member states and that of the EU.[59]

---

[54] See T. Tridimas, *The General Principles of EC Law* (Oxford University Press, 1999), 89; M. De S.-O.-l'E. Lasser, *Judicial Transformations: The Rights Revolution in the Courts of Europe* (Oxford University Press, 2009), 224.

[55] See R. Thomas, *Legitimate Expectations and Proportionality in Administrative Law* (Portland, OR: Hart Publishing, 2000).

[56] See J. Weiler and N. Lockhart, "'Taking Rights Seriously': The European Court and Its Fundamental Rights Jurisprudence – Part 1," 32 *Common Market L. Rev.* 51, 81 (1995); W. van Gerven, "The Effect of Proportionality on the Actions of Member States of the European Community: National Viewpoints from Continental Europe," in E. Ellis (ed.), *The Principle of Proportionality in the Laws of Europe* (1999), 37.

[57] See N. Emiliou, *The Principle of Proportionality in European Law: A Comparative Study* (London: Kluwer Law International, 1996).

[58] Case 11/70, *Internationale Handelsgesellschaft mbH v. Einfuhr- und Vorratsstelle für Getreide und Futtermittel* [1970] ECR 1125; J. Schwarze, *European Administrative Law* (London: Sweet & Maxwell Ltd., 1992), 708.

[59] See Emiliou, above note 57, at 134. See also G. de Burca, "The Principle of Proportionality and Its Application in EC Law," 13 *Y. B. Eur. L.* 105 (1993); T. Tridimas, "The Principle of Proportionality in Community Law: From the Rule of Law to Market Integration," 31 *Irish Jurist* 83 (1996); T. Tridimas, "Proportionality in Community Law: Searching for the Appropriate Standard of Scrutiny," in E. Ellis (ed.), *The Principle of Proportionality in*

In 2004, a draft of the Treaty Establishing a Constitution for Europe was accepted by representatives of twenty-five member states.[60] According to the draft, this attempt at a European Constitution contained a bill of rights. Those rights were phrased as "absolute"; however, some were accompanied by specific limitation clauses, and all were governed by a general limitation clause (Article 112(1) of the Treaty), which read:

> Any limitation on the exercise of the rights and freedoms recognized by this Charter must be provided for by law and respect the essence of those rights and freedoms. Subject to the principle of proportionality, limitations may be made only if they are necessary and genuinely meet objectives of general interest recognized by the Union or the need to protect the rights and freedoms of others.

Not all member states of the European Union approved this draft. Instead, the Treaty of Lisbon was prepared by the member states in 2007 and entered into force on December 1, 2009.[61] Article 3b(4) of the Lisbon Treaty reads: "Under the principle of proportionality, the content and form of Union action shall not exceed what is necessary to achieve the objectives of the Treaties." This ratified clause demonstrates the centrality of proportionality in EU law today. Further, the Lisbon Treaty gave effect to the Charter of Fundamental Rights, and to its general limitation clause.[62]

D.   From European law to Western European states' law

Following the evolution of the concept in Germany and in European law – as demonstrated both by the European Court of Justice and by the European Court of Human Rights – the concept began to gain traction in the law of Western Europe's states.[63] Thus, the concept of proportionality

the Laws of Europe (Portland, OR: Hart Publishing, 1999), 65; J. H. Jans, "Proportionality Revisited," 27(3) Legal Issues of European Integration 239 (2000); L. Moral Soriano, "How Proportionate Should Anti-Competitive State Intervention Be?," 28 Eur. L. Rev. 112 (2003); J. H. Jans, "Minimum Harmonisation and the Role of the Principle of Proportionality" (2007), available at www.ssrn.com/abstract=1105341/.

[60] See Treaty Establishing a Constitution for Europe (2004).
[61] See Treaty of Lisbon amending the Treaty on European Union and the Treaty Establishing the European Community (2007). For analysis, see P. Roza, "Rights and Their Limits: The Constitution for Europe in International and Comparative Legal Perspective," 23 Berkeley J. Int'l L. 223 (2005).
[62] See Art. 6(I) of the Treaty of Lisbon, above note 61.
[63] See Keller and Stone, above note 49; A. Bortoluzzi, "The Principle of Proportionality in Comparative Law: A Comparative Approach from the Italian Perspective," in P. Vinay Kumar (ed.), Proportionality and Federalism (Hyderabad: ICFAI University Press, 2009).

was accepted in Spain,[64] Portugal,[65] France,[66] Italy,[67] Belgium,[68] Greece,[69] and Switzerland.[70] Turkey underwent a similar process.[71] In some of these

[64] See Recurso de Amparo (Habeas Corpus) 66/1995 decided by the Constitutional Court of Spain on May 8, 1995; J. Barnes, "El Principio de Proporcionalidad: Estudio Preliminar," 5 *CDP* 15 (1998); J. Barnes, "Introducción a la Jurisprudencia Constitucional Sobre el Principio de Proporcionalidad en el Ambito de los Derechos y Libertades," 5 *CDP* 333 (1998); G. Ferreira Mendes, "O Principio da Proporcionalidade na Jurisprudencia do Supremo Tribunal Federal: Novas Leituras," *Repertorio IOB de Jurisprudencia*, v. 4, 23–24 (2000); J. Brage Camazano, *Los Límites a los Derechos Fundamentales* (Madrid: Dykinson 2004); C. Bernal Pulido, *El Principio de Proporcionalidad y los Derechos Fundamentales* (Centro de Estudios Políticos y Constitucionales, 2007); J. Barnes, "The Meaning of the Principle of Proportionality for the Administration," in Schäffer *et al.*, *Constitutional Principles in Europe*, Societas Iuris Publici, Europaei, Fourth Congress, Göttingen (2008).

[65] See 1976 Constitution S18 (2) 7th revision (2005); V. Canas, "Proporcionalidade," in *Dicionário Jurídico da Administração Pública*, vol. VI (1994); A. Leão, "Notas Sobre o Principio da Proporcionalidade ou da Proibição do Excesso," 5 *FDUP* 999 (2001); L. F. Colaco Antunes, "Interesse Público, Proporcionalidade e Mérito: Relevância e Autonomia Processual do Principio da Proporcionalidade," in *Estudos em Homenagem a Professora Doutora Isabel de Magalhaes Collaco*, vol. II (2002), 539; T. Ngcukaitobi, "The Evolution of Standing Rules in South Africa and Their Significance in Promoting Social Justice," 18 *SAJHR* 590 (2002); J. Reis Novais, *Os Principios Constitucionais Estruturantes da República Portuguesa* (Coimbra, Portugal: Coimbra Editora 2004), 161; I. Wolfgang Sarlet, "Constituição, Proporcionalidade e Direitos Fundamentais," 81 *BFD* 325 (2005).

[66] See X. Philippe, *Le Contrôle de Proportionnalité dans les Jurisprudences Constitutionnelle et Administrative Françaises* (Aix-en-Provence: Presses Universitaires d'Aix-Marseille, 1990); V. Goesel-Le Bihan, "Le Contrôle de Proportionnalité Exercé par le. Conseil Constitutionnel," 22 *Les Cahiers du Conseil Constitutionnel* 208 (2007).

[67] See D. U. Galetta, *Principio di Proporzionalita e Sindacato Giurisdizionale nel Diritto Administrativo* (Milan, 1998); A. M. Sandulli, *La Proporzionalita Dell'azione Administrativa* (Padova, Italy: Cedam, 1988).

[68] See M. Sakellaridou, "La Genealogie de la Proportionnalité" (Paper presented at the VIIth World Congress of the International Association of Constitutional Law, Athens, June 14, 2007); A. Rasson and R. Ryckeboer, "Le Principe de Proportionnalité dans la Jurisprudence de la Cour Constitutionnelle de Belgique," CDL-JU(2007)024.

[69] See S. Orfanoudakis and V. Kokota, "The Application of the Principle of Proportionality in the Case law of Community and Greek Courts: Similarities and Differences" (Paper presented at the VIIth World Congress of the International Association of Constitutional Law, Athens, June 14, 2007.

[70] A general provision about proportionality may be found in Art. 5(2) of the Federal Constitution of Switzerland: "State activities must be conducted in the public interest and be proportionate to the ends sought." A more specific provision, relating to human rights, can be found in Art. 36(3): "Any restrictions on fundamental rights must be proportionate."

[71] Thus, for example, Art. 13 of the Constitution of the Republic of Turkey, following a 2001 amendment, provides: "Fundamental rights and freedoms may be restricted only by law and in conformity with the reasons mentioned in the relevant articles of the Constitution without infringing upon their essence. These restrictions shall not be in conflict with the

countries, the concept of proportionality was explicitly included as part of a constitutional limitation clause in the chapter on human rights.[72]

E.   From European law to Canada, Ireland, and England

1.   Canada

Until the Canadian Charter of Rights and Freedoms of 1982,[73] the Canadian Supreme Court did not recognize the concept of proportionality as part of Canadian human rights law. Initially, the Canadian Constitution, included in the Constitution Act of 1867, did not include a chapter on human rights. In 1960, when the Canadian Bill of Rights was enacted, it was devised as a regular statute; the bill did not enjoy a constitutional status, and its interpretation did not include the concept of proportionality.[74] All that changed in 1982, when the Canadian Charter of Rights and Freedoms was constituted. The Charter is now constitutional. It contains an explicit provision rendering any legislation conflicting with the Charter as "of no force and effect,"[75] which the Canadian courts may declare and enforce.[76] Alongside the recognition of several human rights, Article 1 of the Charter includes a general limitation clause,[77] as follows:

> The Canadian Charter of Rights and Freedoms guarantees the rights and freedoms set out in it subject only to such reasonable limits prescribed by law as can be demonstrably justified in a free and democratic society.

What is the meaning of the requirement that human rights may be limited only in a "reasonable" manner, such that "can be demonstrably justified in a free and democratic society"? When reviewing this provision in 1985, Hogg referred to the European Convention for the Protection of Human Rights and Fundamental Freedoms and its interpretation by

---

letter and spirit of the Constitution and the requirements of the democratic order of the society and the secular Republic and the principle of proportionality." See also Y. Ogurlu, "A Comparative Study on the Principle of Proportionality in Turkish Administrative Law," *Kamu Hukuku Arşivi, Khuk* 5 (2003).

[72]   See Art. 13 of the Constitution of the Republic of Turkey (above note 71); Art. 5(2) of the Federal Constitution of Switzerland (above note 70).

[73]   Canadian Charter of Rights and Freedoms, Part I of the Constitution Act 1982.

[74]   See P. W. Hogg, *Constitutional Law of Canada*, 5th edn., vol. II (Toronto: Thomson Carswell, 2007), 24.

[75]   See Art. 52(1) of the Canadian Charter of Rights and Freedoms, above note 73.

[76]   See *ibid.*, Art. 24.

[77]   For the term "general limitation clause," see above at 142.

the European Court of Human Rights.[78] In particular, Hogg noted the *Sunday Times* case of 1979.[79] He added:

> In applying Section 1 of the Charter, Canadian courts will have to follow a reasoning process similar to that employed in the *Sunday Times* case. The word "reasonable" in Section 1 requires that a limit on Charter rights be rationally related to a legitimate purpose. The word "reasonable" also contains within it an idea of proportionality. In the *Sunday Times* case, the court acknowledged the legitimacy of the governmental purpose of protecting the courts from undue public pressure, but held that the suppression of all speech relating to ongoing litigation was a disproportionately severe restraint. The same kind of reasoning would be put under Section 1.[80]

Barely a year after Hogg's review, the Canadian Supreme Court issued its decision in *Oakes*.[81] Writing for the Court, Chief Justice Dickson provided an analysis of Article 1 and adopted a "form of proportionality test."[82] In particular, the Chief Justice ruled that "reasonable" limitations that can be "demonstrably justified in a free and democratic society" require a "sufficiently significant objective" and a proportional means used to achieve it. The "significant objective" must "relate to concerns which are pressing and substantial." The proportionality of the relationship will be determined through the following three tests. First, the means should be "rationally connected to the objective." Second, the means should impair "as little as possible" the right or freedom in question. Third, there should be a proportional relation between the effects on the rights of the means chosen and the objective identified as having sufficient importance.[83] Thus, the proportionality adopted by the Canadian Court closely followed the understanding of the European Court of Human Rights

---

[78] See P. W. Hogg, *Constitutional Law of Canada*, 2nd edn. (Toronto: Carswell, 1985), 687. Similarly, see B. Hovius, "The Limitation Clauses of the European Convention on Human Rights: A Guide for the Application of Section 1 of the Charter?," 17 *Ottawa L. Rev.* 213 (1985); B. Hovius, "The Limitations Clauses of the European Convention on Human Rights and Freedoms and Section 1 of the Canadian Charter of Rights and Freedoms: A Comparative Analysis," 6 *Y. B. Eur. L.* 105 (1987).

[79] *Sunday Times* v. *United Kingdom*, App. No. 6538/74, 2 EHRR 245 (1980).

[80] Hogg, above note 78, at 687.

[81] *R.* v. *Oakes* [1986] 1 SCR 103.   [82] *Ibid.*, at 136–137.

[83] For an analysis and criticism of the Canadian rulings on the issue, see Hogg, above note 78, and S. R. Peck, "An Analytical Framework for the Application of the Canadian Charter of Rights and Freedoms," 25 *Osgoode Hall L. J.* 1 (1987); R. M. Elliot, "The Supreme Court of Canada and Section 1 – The Erosion of the Common Front," 12 *Queen's L. J.* 277 (1987); L. E. Weinrib, "The Supreme Court of Canada and Section One of the Charter," 10 *Sup. Ct. L. Rev.* 469 (1988); R. P. Kerans, "The Future of Section One of the Charter," 23

in interpreting the European Convention for the Protection of Human Rights and Fundamental Freedoms.[84] The adoption of the principle of proportionality by Canadian constitutional law raised the question of its adoption by administrative law as well. That question has yet to be answered in Canada.[85]

2. Ireland

The Constitution of Ireland (1937) is familiar with judicial review of the constitutionality of statutes. It contains a chapter on fundamental rights; however, it does not contain a general limitation clause.[86] Specific limitation clauses[87] include the objective for which a limitation on the right is permissible. Several rights were allowed to be limited "in accordance with law." Several others, however, may be limited without an express

---

U. Brit. Colum. L. Rev. 567 (1988); P. G. Murray, "Section One of the Canadian Charter of Rights and Freedoms: An Examination at Two Levels of Interpretation," 21 *Ottawa L. Rev.* 631 (1989); N. Siebrasse, "The Oakes Test: An Old Ghost Impeding Bold New Initiatives," 23 *Ottawa L. Rev.* 99 (1991); R. Colker, "Section 1, Contextuality, and the Anti-Disadvantage Principle," 42 *U. Toronto L. J.* 77 (1992); A. Lokan, "The Rise and Fall of Doctrine under Section 1 of the Charter," 24 *Ottawa L. Rev.* 163 (1992); C. M. Dassios and C. P. Prophet, "Charter Section 1: The Decline of Grand Unified Theory and the Trend Towards Deference in the Supreme Court of Canada," 15 *Advocates' Quarterly* 289 (1993); L. E. Trakman, W. Cole-Hamilton, and S. Gatien, "R. v. Oakes 1986–1997: Back to the Drawing Board," 36 *Osgoode Hall L. J.* 83 (1998); D. Newman, "The Limitation of Rights: A Comparative Evolution and Ideology of the Oakes and Sparrow Tests," 62 *Sask. L. Rev.* 543 (1999); M. Rothstein, "Section 1: Justifying Breaches of Charter Rights and Freedoms," 27 *Man. L. J.* 171 (2000); T. Macklem and J. Terry, "Making the Justification Fit the Breach," 11 *Sup. Ct. L. Rev.* 575 (2000); J. A. Terry, "Section 1: Controlling the Oakes Analysis," *Law Society of Upper Canada Special Lectures* 479 (2001); C. D. Bredt, "The Increasing Irrelevance of Section 1 of the Charter," 14 *Sup. Ct. L. Rev.* 175 (2001); L. E. Weinrib, "The Charter's First Twenty Years: Assessing the Impact and Anticipating the Future" (Paper presented at the 2002 Isaac Pitblado Lectures, November 22 and 23, 2002); L. E. Weinrib, "Canada's Charter of Rights: Paradigm Lost?" 6 *Review of Constitutional Studies* 119 (2002); S. Choudhry, "So What Is the Real Legacy of Oakes? Two Decades of Proportionality Analysis under the Canadian Charter's Section 1," 34 *Sup. Ct. L. Rev.* 501 (2006); L. Tremblay and G. Webber, *The Limitation of Charter Rights: Critical Essays on R. v. Oakes* (Montreal: Thémis, 2009).

[84] See T. R. S. Allan, "Human Rights and Judicial Review: A Critique of 'Due Deference'," 65(3) *Cambridge L. J.* 671 (2006); A. Barak, "Proportional Effect: The Israeli Experience," 57 *U. Toronto L. J.* 369 (2007); D. Grimm, "Proportionality in Canadian and German Constitutional Jurisprudence," 57 *U. Toronto L. J.* 383 (2007).

[85] See G. Régimbald, "Correctness, Reasonableness, and Proportionality: A New Standard of Judicial Review," 31 *Man. L. J.* 239 (2005).

[86] On general limitation clauses, see above, at 142.

[87] On specific limitation clauses, see above, at 141.

limitation. The Constitution of Ireland does not expressly mention proportionality. Article 40(3) of the Constitution reads:

(1) The State guarantees in its laws to respect, and, as far as practicable, by its laws to defend and vindicate the personal rights of the citizen.
(2) The State shall, in particular, by its laws protect as best it may from unjust attack and, in the case of injustice done, vindicate the life, person, good name, and property rights of every citizen.

Interpreting this provision, the Supreme Court of Ireland has ruled that the Constitution also guarantees the protection of several rights not expressly mentioned by its text.[88] Naturally, the Constitution contains no provisions as to the limitation of these rights.

Proportionality was accepted by the Irish courts in the early 1990s, though initially this was done without explicit acknowledgment of the term.[89] Later on, the Irish Supreme Court referred explicitly to the concept of proportionality as then accepted by the European Court of Human Rights and the Supreme Court of Canada.[90] In the 1994 case of *Heaney*, Judge Costello of the Irish Supreme Court provided an analysis of proportionality in a manner resembling that of Chief Justice Dickson of the Canadian Supreme Court:

The objective of the impugned provision must be of sufficient importance to warrant overriding a constitutionally protected right. It must relate to concerns pressing and substantial in a free and democratic society. The means chosen must pass a *proportionality test*. They must: (a) be rationally connected to the objective and not arbitrary, unfair or based on irrational considerations; (b) impair the right as little as possible, and (c) be such that their effects on rights are proportional to the objective.[91]

Judge Costello relied on both the Canadian and the European Court of Human Rights' decisions when approaching the analysis of proportionality.[92] Since that decision, Irish courts often turn to proportionality within

---

[88] *Ryan v. AG* [1965] IR 294.
[89] See G. Hogan, "The Constitution, Property Rights and Proportionality," 32 *Irish Jurist* 373 (1997).
[90] See *Cox v. Ireland* [1992] 2 IR 503; *In Re Article 26 and the Matrimonial Home Bill 1993* [1994] IR 305, 326; J. M. Kelly, *The Irish Constitutions*, 4th edn. (G. Hogan and G. Whyte (eds.), Dublin: Butterworths, 2003), 1271.
[91] *Heaney v. Ireland* [1994] 3 IR 593, 607.
[92] See D. Costello, "Limiting Rights Constitutionally", in J. O'Reilly (ed.), *Human Rights and Constitutional Law: Essays in Honour of Brian Walsh* (Dublin: Round Hall Press, 1992), 173.

constitutional law.[93] The development in administrative law, however, was not as swift. Some of the difficulties in adapting proportionality to administrative law were related to the relationship between proportionality and the reasonableness requirement. Notwithstanding these difficulties, however, most commentators consider proportionality today as part of Irish administrative law as well.[94]

3.   United Kingdom

Much like in Ireland, the integration of the principle of proportionality into United Kingdom law was anything but straightforward.[95] Most difficulties, here too, stemmed from English law's wide recognition of the principle of reasonableness as it was adopted in the 1940s following the case of *Wednesbury*.[96] For many, proportionality seemed not only unwarranted, but potentially damaging. Several attempts to adopt proportionality were made during the 1970s and 1980s. These were met with great enthusiasm from some, and harsh criticism from others.[97] Thus, for example, in one mid-1980s case, Lord Diplock raised the possibility of accepting the concept, which was already adopted by several European states, but ultimately decided to leave the question open.[98] Another Judge saw proportionality as a dangerous option.[99] In another case, from 1991, the House of Lords was specifically asked to adopt the concept – and refused, although it did leave the door open for the future adoption of the principle.[100] Lord

---

[93] See Kelly, above note 90, at 1270. See also J. Casey, *Constitutional Law in Ireland* (Dublin: Round Hall Press, 2000), 388; *In Re Article 26 and the Employment Equality Bill 1996* [1997] 2 IR 321; *Rock* v. *Ireland* [1997] 3 IR 484; *Murphy* v. *Independent Radio and Television Commission* [1999] 1 IR 12; *In Re Article 26 and Part V of the Planning and Development Bill 1999* [2000] 2 IR 321; *DK* v. *Crowley* [2002] 2 IR 744.

[94] See *Hand* v. *Dublin Corporation* [1989] IR 26. For analysis, see G. Hogan and D. G. Morgan, *Administrative Law in Ireland*, 2nd edn. (Dublin: Round Hall Press, 1991), 531, 541; G. Hogan, "Judicial Review – The Law of the Republic of Ireland," in B. Hadfield (ed.), *Judicial Review: A Thematic Approach* (Dublin: Gill and Macmillan, 1995), 316, 336.

[95] See Cohen, above note 32.

[96] *Associated Provincial Picture Houses* v. *Wednesbury Corporation* [1948] 1 KB 223. See below, at 373.

[97] See A. Lester and J. Jowell, "Beyond Wednesbury: Substantive Principles of Administrative Law," 4 *PL* 368 (1987); G. de Burca, "The Influence of European Legal Concepts on UK Law: Proportionality and Wednesbury Unreasonableness," 3 *Eur. Public Law* 561 (1993).

[98] See *Council of Civil Service Unions* v. *Minister for the Civil Service* [1985] AC 374.

[99] See Judge Millet's opinion in *Allied Dunbar (Frank Weisinger) Ltd.* v. *Frank Weisinger* [1988] 17 IRLR 60, 65.

[100] See *R.* v. *Secretary of State for the Home Department, ex p. Brind* [1991] 1 AC 696.

Ackner noted that, so long as the European Convention for the Protection of Human Rights and Fundamental Freedoms was not part of the law of the United Kingdom, there is no legal basis for the adoption of proportionality in the United Kingdom. The legal literature, however, continued to examine the question.[101]

In 1998, the United Kingdom adopted the Human Rights Act (HRA) of 1998.[102] That Act gave effect, in the United Kingdom, to rights provided in the European Convention for the Protection of Human Rights and Fundamental Freedoms. The Act provided English courts with the authority to declare whether a provision of primary or subordinate legislation in England is compatible with those rights. Such a declaration may apply to laws adopted either before or after the HRA was adopted.[103] This Act had a profound effect on the legal landscape in the United Kingdom.[104] It also introduced proportionality into English law.[105] Accordingly, the relationship between the United Kingdom and the European concept of proportionality is clear and well established. Over time, the concept expanded to other fields of law, beyond those covered by the HRA. Today, the exact

---

[101] See, e.g., S. Boyron, "Proportionality in English Administrative Law: A Faulty Translation?," 12 *OJLS* 237 (1992); J. Laws, "Is the High Court of Justice the Guardian of Fundamental Constitutional Rights?," 59 *PL* (1993); G. de Burca, "Proportionality and Wednesbury Unreasonableness: The Influence of European Legal Concepts on UK Law," 3 *Eur. Public Law* 561 (1997); J. Jowell, "Restraining the State: Politics, Principle and Judicial Review," 50 *CLP* 189 (1997); J. Laws, "Wednesbury," in C. Forsyth and I. Hare (eds.), *The Golden Metwand and the Crooked Cord: Essays in Honour of Sir William Wade QC* (Oxford University Press, 1998), 185; P. Craig, "Unreasonableness and Proportionality in UK Law," in E. Ellis (ed.), *The Principle of Proportionality in the Laws of Europe* (Portland, OR: Hart Publishing, 1999), 85; Lord Hoffmann, "The Influence of the European Principle of Proportionality upon UK Law," in E. Ellis (ed.), *The Principle of Proportionality in the Laws of Europe* (Portland, OR: Hart Publishing, 1999), 107. For analysis of the dispute until that time, see Thomas, above note 1, at 78.

[102] Human Rights Act 1998, c. 42 (Eng.).

[103] *Ibid.*, at section 4.

[104] See S. Sedley, "The Last 10 Years' Development of English Public Law," 12 *Australian J. of Adm. L.* 9 (2004); A. Kavanagh, *Constitutional Review under the UK Human Rights Act* (Cambridge University Press, 2009); A. Young, *Parliamentary Sovereignty and the Human Rights Act* (Portland, OR: Hart Publishing, 2009). See above, at 159.

[105] See *R. v. Secretary of State for the Home Department, ex p. Daly* [2001] 3 All ER 433; *R. v. Secretary of State for the Environment, Transport and the Regions* [2001] 2 All ER 929; *Huang* v. Secretary *of State for the Home Department* [2007] UKHL 11; D. Feldman, "Proportionality and the Human Rights Act 1998," in E. Ellis (ed.), *The Principle of Proportionality in the Laws of Europe* (Oxford: Hart Publishing, 1999), 117; R. Clayton, "Regarding a Sense of Proportion: The Human Rights Act and the Proportionality Principle," 5 *Eur. Hum. Rts. L. Rev.* 504 (2001); T. Hickman, "The Substance and Structure of Proportionality," *PL* 694 (2008); Kavanagh, above note 104, at 233.

scope of proportionality in the United Kingdom has not yet been determined; a vigorous academic debate is taking place as to the concept's exact place in administrative law.[106]

F.   From Canada to New Zealand and Australia

1.   New Zealand

For many years, human rights were an integral part of New Zealand's common law. The courts creating those rights, however, were not familiar with the concept of proportionality. As with every other Commonwealth jurisdiction, in New Zealand, too, the view for many years had been that any legislation can overcome any rights recognized by the common law. The latter was challenged by Judge Robin Cooke, then the President of the Court of Appeal, both from the bench,[107] and in an article he published.[108] President Cooke wrote that ordinary legislation challenging the most basic common law human rights may be unconstitutional and may be invalidated by the courts. This approach, however, was not adopted by other judges. Instead, the efforts were directed at adopting a constitutional bill of rights. Spearheading the effort was the New Zealand government, headed by Palmer. This attempt, too, failed.[109] Instead, New Zealand adopted the Bill of Rights Act in 1990.[110] The Act incorporated many facets of the governmental proposals, while also making the necessary changes from constitutional charter to ordinary legislation. The new Bill of Rights Act adopted many parts of the Canadian Charter, including a general limitation clause:

> Subject to Section 4 of this Bill of Rights, the rights and freedoms contained in this Bill of Rights may be subject only to such reasonable limits prescribed by law as can be demonstrably justified in a free and democratic society.[111]

---

[106] See P. Craig, *Administrative Law*, 6th edn. (London: Sweet & Maxwell, 2008); Cohen, above note 32; T. Hickman, "The Reasonableness Principle: Reassessing Its Place in the Public Sphere," 63 *Cambridge L. J.* 166 (2004).

[107] See *Taylor* v. *New Zealand Poultry Board* [1984] 1 NZLR 394, 398; J. Caldwell, "Judicial Sovereignty – A New View," *New Zealand L. J.* 357 (1984).

[108] See R. Cooke, "Fundamentals," *New Zealand L. J.* 158 (1988).

[109] For the developments in New Zealand, see P. Rishworth, "The Birth and Rebirth of the Bill of Rights," in G. Huscroft and P. Rishworth (eds.), *Rights and Freedoms: The New Zealand Bill of Rights Act 1990 and the Human Rights Act 1993* (Wellington: Brookers, 1995), 1.

[110] New Zealand Bill of Rights Act 1990, No. 109.

[111] *Ibid.*, at Art. 5.

Section 4 of the Act, which is mentioned in the limitation clause, states that:
Section 4 of the Bill of Rights Act states, in turn:

> No court shall, in relation to any enactment (whether passed or made before or after the commencement of this Bill of Rights) … hold any provision of the enactment to be impliedly repealed or revoked, or to be in any way invalid or ineffective … by reason only that the provision is inconsistent with any provision of this Bill of Rights.

The adoption of the general limitation clause led to the adoption of the concept of proportionality in New Zealand law. Today, proportionality is a staple of human rights law in New Zealand.[112] As for administrative law, the question remains open as to whether proportionality replaced the notion of reasonableness, or whether the two exist side by side.[113]

2. Australia

The Australian Federal Constitution, which recognizes judicial review on the constitutionality of legislation, is mostly institutional in nature. It does not contain a separate bill of rights. Despite that, the Australian High Court recognized the political freedom of expression as an implied right

---

[112] See *Ministry of Transport v. Noort* [1992] 3 NZLR 260; *Moonen v. Film and Literature Board of Review* [2000] 2 NZLR 9; *Moonen v. Film and Literature Board of Review (No. 2)* [2002] 2 NZLR 754 (CA); *Institute of Chartered Accountants v. Bevan* [2003] 1 NZLR 154; *Wolf v. Minister of Immigration* [2004] NZAR 414; *Powerco v. Commerce Commission*, HC Wellington, June 9, 2006, CIV-2005–485–1066, Wild, J.; *Taylor v. Chief Executive Department of Corrections*, HC Wellington, September 11, 2006, CIV-2006–485–897, Clifford, J.; *J. B. International Ltd. v. Auckland City Council* [2006] NZRMA 401; *Progressive Enterprises Ltd. v. North Shore City Council* [2006] NZRMA 72; *Hansen v. R.* [2007] 3 NZLR 1 (CA); A. Butler, "Limiting Rights," 33 *Victoria University Wellington L. R.* 113 (2002); M. Taggart, "Administrative Law," *New Zealand L. Rev.* 75 (2006); J. Varuhas, "Keeping Things in Proportion: The Judiciary, Executive Action and Human Rights," 22 *New Zealand U. L. Rev.* 300 (2006); M. Taggart, "Proportionality, Deference, Wednesbury," *New Zealand L. Rev.* 423 (2008); P. A. Joseph, *Constitutional and Administrative Law in New Zealand*, 3rd edn. (Wellington: Brookers, 2007).

[113] See J. McLean, P. Rishworth, and M. Taggart, "The Impact of the New Zealand Bill of Rights on Administrative Law," in *The New Zealand Bill of Rights Act 1990* (Auckland: Legal Research Foundation, 1992), 62; P. A. Joseph, "The Demise of Ultra Vires – A Reply to Christopher Forsyth and Linda Whittle," 8 *Canterbury L. Rev.* 463 (2002); J. Varuhas, "Keeping Things in Proportion: The Judiciary, Executive Action and Human Rights," 22(2) *New Zealand U. L. Rev.* 300 (2006); J. Varuhas, "Powerco v. Commerce Commission: Developing Trends of Proportionality in New Zealand Administrative Law," 4 NZJPIL 339 (2006); M. Taggart, "Administrative Law," *New Zealand L. Rev.* 75, 83 (2006).

with a constitutional status.[114] The court held that the right is not absolute and that it may be limited with the help of proportionality. In reaching this conclusion, the court relied on the Canadian cases, *Oakes*[115] in particular. The Australian High Court referred to proportionality in other contexts as well.[116] The main issue in Australia, yet to be resolved, concerns proportionality's proper role in administrative law – the same issue that exists in the United Kingdom,[117] New Zealand,[118] and Ireland.[119]

In 2006, the state of Victoria enacted the Charter of Human Rights and Responsibilities Act.[120] The Act is primarily based upon the International Covenant on Civil and Political Rights. The Act also contains a general limitation clause, enacted after similar clauses appearing in the

---

[114] See *Nationwide News Pty Ltd.* v. *Wills* (1992) 177 CLR 1; *Australian Capital Television Pty Ltd.* v. *Commonwealth* (1992) 177 CLR 106; *Theophanous* v. *Herald & Weekly Ltd.* (1994) 182 CLR 104; *Stephens* v. *West Australian Newspapers Ltd.* (1994) 182 CLR 211; *Cunliffe* v. *Commonwealth* (1994) 182 CLR 272; *McGinty* v. *Western Australia* (1996) 186 CLR 140; *Lange* v. *Australian Broadcasting Corp.* (1997) 189 CLR 520; *Kruger* v. *Commonwealth* (1997) 190 CLR 1; *Levy* v. *Victoria* (1997) 189 CLR 579. For analysis, see G. Winterton, "The Separation of Judicial Power as an Implied Bill of Rights," in G. Lindell (ed.), *In Future Directions in Australian Constitutional Law* (Sydney: Federation Press, 1994), 185; L. Zines, *The High Court and the Constitution*, 5th edn. (Federation Press, 2008); G. Williams, *Human Rights under the Australian Constitution* (Oxford University Press, 1999); H. Patapan, *Judging Democracy: The New Politics of the High Court of Australia* (Cambridge University Press, 2001), 51.

[115] See *Oakes*, above note 81.

[116] See B. F. Fitzgerald, "Proportionality and Australian Constitutionalism," 12 *U. Tas. L. Rev.* 49 (1993); P. Bayne, "Reasonableness, Proportionality and Delegated Legislation," 67 *ALJ* 448 (1993); J. J. Doyle, "Constitutional Law: 'At the Eye of the Storm,'" 23 *U. West. Austl. L. Rev.* 15 (1993); H. Phun Lee, "Proportionality in Australian Constitutional Adjudication," in *Future Directions in Australian Constitutional Law* (Sydney: Federation Press, 1994), 126; R. Smyth, "The Principle of Proportionality Ten Years after GCHQ," 2 *Austl. J. Admin. Law* 189 (1995); J. Kirk, "Constitutional Guarantees, Characterisation and the Concept of Proportionality," 21 *Melb. U. L. Rev.* 1 (1997); P. Quirk, "Australian Looks at German Proportionality," 1 *U. Notre Dame Austl. L. Rev.* 39 (1999); A. Stone, "The Limits of Constitutional Text and Structure: Standards of Review and the Freedom of Political Communication," 23 *Melb. U. L. Rev.* 668 (1999). G. Villalta Puig, "Abridged Proportionality in Australian Constitutional Review: A Doctrinal Critique of the Cole v. Whitfield Saving Test for Section 92 of the Australian Constitution" (Paper presented at the VIIth World Congress of the International Association of Constitutional Law, Athens, June 14, 2007); B. Saul, "Australian Administrative Law: The Human Rights Dimension," in M. Groves and H. Phun Lee (eds.), *Australian Administrative Law: Fundamentals, Principles and Doctrines* (Cambridge University Press, 2007), 50; G. J. Appleby, "Proportionality and Federalism: Can Australia Learn from the European Community, the US and Canada?," 26 *U. Tas. L. Rev.* 1 (2007).

[117] See above, at 192.   [118] See above, at 194.   [119] See above, at 190.

[120] See Charter of Human Rights and Responsibilities Act 2006. See also J. Debeljak, "Balancing Rights in a Democracy: The Problems with Limitations and Overrides of

constitutions of Canada, New Zealand, and South Africa. It should be assumed that this limitation clause – which is structurally similar to the one in the Constitution of the Republic of South Africa – will be interpreted as adopting proportionality. Another Australian development is the enactment of the Human Rights Act of 2004, which applies to the Australian Capital Territory only. Those rights are not of a constitutional status.

G.   From Canada and Germany to South Africa

A general limitation clause appears in both South Africa's Interim Constitution of 1993 and its Final Constitution.[121] Both of those clauses were influenced by the limitation clause in the Canadian Charter on Rights and Freedoms.[122] It is no wonder, therefore, that in interpreting these clauses the South African Constitutional Court relies on the judgment of the Canadian Supreme Court. Analyzing the similarities between the two systems' limitation clauses, Woolman and Botha emphasized the central role of proportionality:

> Limitations analysis under the Charter and our Bill of Rights possesses such common features as … proportionality assessment that demands, at a minimum, that a rational connection exist between the means employed and the objective sought, that the means employed impair the right as "little as possible", and that the burdens imposed on those whose rights are impaired do not outweigh the benefits to society that flow from the limitation.[123]

In addition, the 1996 Constitution of the Republic of South Africa was influenced by German constitutional law.[124] It is important to note, however, that the manner in which proportionality is applied in South African constitutional law is not identical to the way it is used by Canada or

---

Rights under the Victorian Charter of Human Rights and Responsibilities Act 2006," 32 *Melb. U. L. Rev.* 422 (2008).

[121] See Art. 33 of the Interim Constitution of the Republic of South Africa; Art. 36 of the Constitution of the Republic of South Africa.

[122] See above, at 121.

[123] See S. Woolman and H. Botha, "Limitations," in S. Woolman, M. Bishop, and J. Brickhill (eds.), *Constitutional Law of South Africa*, 2nd edn. (Cape Town: Juta Law Publishers, looseleaf, 2002–), Chapter 34, 13.

[124] See J. de Waal, "A Comparative Analysis of the Provisions of German Origin in the Interim Bill of Rights," 11 *SAJHR* 1 (1995); L. Blaauw-Wolf, "The 'Balancing of Interests' with Reference to the Principle of Proportionality and the Doctrine of Guterabwagung – A Comparative Analysis," 14 *SAPL* 178 (1999).

Germany. The South African approach is less structured.[125] It grants more discretion to the legislator. Thus, the South African Constitutional Court has noted that the limitation clause is based on, among others, a careful balancing between the social benefits gained by the suggested limiting legislation and the damage caused by it to the human right in question.[126]

H.   Proportionality migrates to Central and Eastern Europe

With the collapse of communism in Central and Eastern Europe, the constitutional structure of those countries changed dramatically.[127] New constitutions were adopted. Special constitutional courts were established, heavily inspired – in structure and jurisdiction – by the model of the German Constitutional Court.[128] Judicial review of the constitutionality of legislation was recognized. And, importantly, each of the new constitutions included a main chapter dedicated to human rights.[129] Those rights are not absolute. They can be limited. Thus, the new Eastern and Central European constitutions contain limitation clauses. The typical model among these constitutions is that of a general limitation clause.[130] However, some countries adopted specific limitation clauses for some of the rights; while others adopted general limitation clauses that would apply only to those rights that the constitution specified as limitable.[131]

Very few of those Eastern and Central European constitutions refer explicitly to the concept of proportionality. Only a small number mention proportionality in the context of limitation of human rights.[132] Nonetheless, proportionality is well recognized today in the Eastern

---

[125]   See Constitution of the Republic of South Africa, Art. 36. See above, at 121.

[126]   See, e.g., *S. v. Makwanyane*, 1995 (3) SA 391, 431.

[127]   See R. G. Teitel, *Transitional Justice* (Oxford University Press, 2000); H. Schwartz, *The Struggle for Constitutional Justice in Post-Communist Europe* (University of Chicago Press, 2002).

[128]   See R. Prochazka, *Mission Accomplished: On Founding Constitutional Adjudication in Central Europe* (Budapest: Central European University Press, 2002); W. Sadurski, *Rights before Courts: A Study of Constitutional Courts in Postcommunist States of Central and Eastern Europe* (Dordrecht: Springer, 2008); V. Ferreres Comella, *Constitutional Courts and Democratic Values* (New Haven, CT: Yale University Press, 2009).

[129]   See W. Osiatynski, "Rights in New Constitutions of East Central Europe," 26 *Colum. Hum. Rts. L. Rev.* 111 (1994); A. Sajó (ed.), *Western Rights? Post-Communist Application* (1996). See also Sadurski, above note 128, at 163.

[130]   For general limitation clause, see above, at 142.

[131]   See Sadurski, above note 128, at 261.

[132]   See, e.g., Art. 17(1) of the Constitution of Albania ("[L]imitation of the rights and freedoms provided for in this Constitution may be established only by law, in the public

and Central European states.[133] A voluminous body of opinions relating to the proportional limitation of human rights has been developed by the courts in a number of countries, including Hungary,[134] Poland,[135] and Slovenia.[136] The constitutions of those states were heavily influenced by the European Convention for the Protection of Human Rights and Fundamental Freedoms, and the constitutional courts in those countries were influenced by the European Court of Human Rights.[137]

I.   Proportionality migrates to Asia and South America

1.   Asia

A few states in Asia have begun considering the concept of proportionality.[138] For example, proportionality was adopted in Hong Kong.[139]

---

interest or for the protection of the rights of others. A limitation shall be in proportion to the situation that has dictated it."); Art. 54(2) of the Constitution of Moldova ("The restrictions enforced must be in proportion to the situation that caused it, and may not affect the existence of that right or liberty."); Art. 53(2) of the Constitution of Romania, as revised in 2003 ("Such restriction shall only be ordered if necessary in a democratic society. The measure shall be proportional to the situation having caused it, applied without discrimination, and without infringing on the existence of such right or freedom.").

[133] See Sadurski, above note 128, at 266 ("The requirement that a restriction must remain in proper proportion to constitutionally mandated goals is perhaps the most powerful tool that the constitution of the region granted to constitutional courts.").

[134] See L. Solyom and G. Brunner, *Constitutional Judiciary in a New Democracy: The Hungarian Constitutional Court* (University of Michigan Press, 2000), 229, 239, 284; C. Dupré, *Importing the Law in Post-Communist Transitions: The Hungarian Constitutional Court and the Right to Human Dignity* (Portland, OR: Hart Publishing, 2003).

[135] See M. Wiącek, "The Principle of Proportionality in the Jurisprudence of the Polish Constitutional Tribunal," CDL-JU(2007)021.

[136] See A. Marjan Mavčič, "The Implementation of the Principle of Proportionality in the Slovenian Constitutional Case-Law" (Paper presented at the 6th Meeting of the Joint Council on Constitutional Justice, "Mini-Conference" on the Principle of Proportionality, May 30, 2007, available at www.venice.coe.int/docs/2007/CDL-JU(2007)017-e.pdf.

[137] See above, at 183.

[138] Proportionality was rejected in Singapore; see *Chee Siok Chin v. Minister for Home Affairs* [2006] 1 SLR 582.

[139] See S. N. M. Young, "Restricting Basic Law Rights in Hong Kong," 34 *Hong Kong L. J.* 110 (2004); *Solicitor v. Law Society* (2003) 6 HKCFAR 570; *Ng Yat Chi v. Max Share Ltd.* (2005) 8 HKCFAR 1; *Leung Kwok Hung and Others v. HKSAR* (2005) 8 HKCFAR 229; *Official Receiver and Trustee in Bankruptcy of Chan Wing Hing v. Chan Wing Hing and Secretary for Justice* (2006) 9 HKCFAR 545; *HKSAR v. Lam Kwong Wai* (2006) 9 HKCFAR 574; *HKSAR v. Hung Chan Wa* (2006) 9 HKCFAR 614.

This is, most likely, a result of the fact that both key international covenants – the International Covenant on Civil and Political Rights, and the International Covenant on Economic, Social, and Cultural Rights – are an integral part of Hong Kong's domestic law.[140] The highest court in Hong Kong, the Court of Final Appeal, has referred on a number of occasions to proportionality in the context of human rights limitations. These references have often been based on the European Convention for the Protection of Human Rights and Fundamental Freedoms and the European Court of Human Rights.

The 1987 Constitution of South Korea includes a special chapter dedicated to human rights.[141] This chapter includes, alongside several special limitation clauses, a general limitation clause.[142] The Constitutional Court of South Korea is authorized to review – and invalidate – the constitutionality of any law.[143] Using that authority, the Constitutional Court of South Korea has placed proportionality at the center of its constitutional analysis.[144]

The Constitution of India (1950) contains a special part dedicated to fundamental rights.[145] India's Supreme Court is authorized to conduct judicial review and to declare statutes that improperly limit those fundamental rights to be unconstitutional. The constitution does not contain a general limitation clause; rather, alongside the rights themselves the constitution provides specific limitation clauses. Those specific limitation clauses include the purposes for which restrictions may be imposed on those rights. They also state that those limitations must be "reasonable."[146] The Supreme Court established the criteria for determining the reasonableness of such restrictions.[147] While not mentioning proportionality by its name, the Court has concluded that the factors that should be considered within those criteria are similar to those constituting

---

[140] See Basic Law of the Hong Kong Special Administrative Region of the People's Republic of China, § 39; Y. Ghai, *Hong Kong's New Constitutional Order: The Resumption of Chinese Sovereignty and the Basic Law*, 2nd (ed.),(Hong Kong University Press, 1999); R. Wacks (ed.), *The New Legal Order in Hong Kong* (1999), 55.

[141] See Constitution of South Korea, Chapter 2 (Arts. 10–39).

[142] See *ibid.*, Art. 37(2).   [143] See *ibid.*, Art. 111(1).

[144] See CCC December 23, 1999 98HUNMA363; J. Hak-Seon, "L'application du Principe de Proportionnalité dans la Justice Constitutionnelle en Corée" (Paper presented at the VIIth World Congress of the International Association of Constitutional Law, Athens, June 14, 2007).

[145] See Constitution of India, Part III (Arts. 12–35).

[146] See *ibid.*, Art. 19(2)–(6).

[147] See T. T. K. Iyer, *Judicial Review of Reasonableness in Constitutional Law* (Madras: Madras Law Journal Office, 1979).

proportionality.[148] A significant change in approach can be seen in the late 1990s when the Supreme Court of India ruled, explicitly, that the constitutionality of legislation limiting a fundamental right shall be viewed through the lens of proportionality.[149] More recently, the court held that proportionality will also apply to the judicial review of administrative actions.[150]

2. South America

Following the infiltration of proportionality into Europe, in particular into Spain and Portugal, the concept began migrating to South America as well. As a result of Spanish influence – and, indirectly that of the German constitutional jurisprudence – proportionality began to emerge in Colombia,[151] Peru,[152] Mexico,[153] Chile,[154] and Argentina.[155] As a result of Portuguese influence – and, once again, indirectly influenced by German law – proportionality emerged in Brazil.[156] In all those

---

[148] An exception is the case of *State of Madras* v. *V. G. Raw*, AIR 1952 SC 196.

[149] See *Union of India* v. *G. Ganayutham*, AIR 1997 SC 3387.

[150] See *Om Kumar* v. *Union of India* (2001) 2 SCC 386; *Teri Oat Estates Ltd.* v. *U. T. Chandigarh* (2004) 2 SCC 130; A. Chugh, "Is the Supreme Court Disproportionately Applying the Proportionality Principle?," 8 SCC (J) 33 (2004), available at www.ebc-india.com/lawyer/articles/2004_8_33.htm; S. Felix, "Engaging Unreasonableness and Proportionality as Standards of Review in England, India and Sri Lanka," in H. Corder (ed.), *Comparing Administrative Justice Across the Commonwealth* (Cape Town: Juta Law Publishers, 2006), 95; T. Khaitan, "Beyond Reasonableness – A Rigorous Standard of Review for Article 15 Infringement," 50 *J. Indian L. Ins.* 177 (2008).

[151] See Judgment T-422 decided by the Constitutional Court of Colombia on June 16, 1992; M. J. Cepeda Espinosa, *Polémicas Constitucionales* (Bogota: Legis, 2007), 159.

[152] See Judgment 20.530 decided by the Constitutional Court of Peru on June 3, 2005; M. Carbonell and P. Grández (eds.,) *El Principio de Proporcionalidad en el Derecho Contemporáneo* (Lima: Palestra Editores, 2010).

[153] See *Juicio de Amparo en Revisión* 1659/2006, February 27, 2002; M. Carbonell (ed.), *El Principio de Proporcionalidad y protección de los Derechos Fundamentals* [*Proportionality Analysis and the Protection of Fundamental Rights*] (Mexico City: Comisión Nacional de los Derechos Humanos, 2008).

[154] See Judgment ROL 519 decided by the Constitutional Court of Chile on June 5, 2007; M. Carbonell (ed.), *El Principio de Proporcionalidad en la interpretación jurídica* (Santiago, UNAM & CECOCH, 2010).

[155] See L. Clérico, *El Examen de Proporcionalidad en el Derecho Constitucional* (Buenos Aires: Eudeba, 2009).

[156] See Direct Action of Unconstitutionality 1724 – Interim Measure decided by the Supreme Federal Court of Brazil on December 11, 1997; G. Ferreira Mendes, "O Princípio da Proporcionalidade na Jurisprudência do Supremo Tribunal Federal: Novas Leituras," 4 *Repertório IOB Jurisprudência: Tributária Constit. Adm.* 23 (2000); R. Camilo

countries, proportionality has only begun making its way into main-stream law. The concept has been criticized, by both commentators and judges. However, it seems that proportionality has an important status in South America's law.

J.   Proportionality and international human rights law

1.   International and national human rights law

Proportionality is a general concept of international law.[157] It serves several functions. It is a central feature of the laws of self-defense.[158] This aspect of proportionality is unique in that it comprises part of the relations between nations, a part of the body of rights and duties owed by one nation to another. This book, however, deals primarily with proportional limitations on human rights. Accordingly, this book focuses on the role of proportion-ality in international human rights law.[159] This examination is important, because of the mutual influence between international human rights law and the domestic human rights law of different states.[160] International law is indeed one of the main contributors to the shaping of domestic law – mostly

de Oliveira, "The Balancing of Values and the Compromising of the Guarantee of Fundamental Rights" (Paper presented at the VIIth World Congress of the International Association of Constitutional Law, Athens, June 14, 2007); A. Reis Freire, "Evolution of Constitutional Interpretation in Brazil and the Employment of Balancing 'Method' by the Brazilian Supreme Court in Judicial Review" (Paper presented at the VIIth World Congress of the International Association of Constitutional Law, Athens, June 14, 2007).

[157] See the entry for "Proportionality," in 7 *Encyclopedia of Public International Law* 396 (1984).

[158] See O. Schachter, "Implementing Limitations on the Use of Force: The Doctrine of Proportionality and Necessity," 86 *Am. Soc'y Int'l L. Proc.* 39 (1992); J. G. Gardam, "Proportionality and Force in International Law," 87 *Am. J. Int'l L.* 391 (1993); E. Cannizzaro, "The Role of Proportionality in the Law of International Countermeasures," 12 *Eur. J. Int'l. L.* 889 (2001); C. Wicker, *The Concepts of Proportionality and State Crimes in International Law* (Frankfurt: Lang Publishing Group, 2006); T. M. Franck, "On Proportionality of Countermeasures in International Law," 102 *Am. J. Int'l L.* 715 (2008). See also Gardam, above note 12.

[159] See A. L. Svensson-McCarthy, *The International Law of Human Rights and States of Exception* (The Hague: Kluwer Law International, 1998); N. Jayawickrama, *The Judicial Application of Human Rights Law: National, Regional and International Jurisprudence* (Cambridge University Press, 2002).

[160] See J. M. Ross., "Limitations on Human Rights in International Law: Their Relevance to the Canadian Charter of Rights and Freedoms," 6 *Hum. Rts. Q.* 180 (1984); F. Jacobs, "Limitation Clauses of the European Convention on Human Rights," in A. de Mestral, S.

constitutional law – relating to human rights. A classic example is Article 39(1) of the South African Constitution, which reads:

> When interpreting the Bill of Rights, a court, tribunal, or forum … (b) must consider international law.

Another example is Article 10(2) of the Spanish Constitution (1978), which reads:

> The principles relating to the fundamental rights and liberties recognized by the Constitution shall be interpreted in conformity with the Universal Declaration of Human Rights and the international treaties and agreements thereon ratified by Spain.

Simultaneously, the domestic constitutional law regarding human rights affects the developing understanding of international norms. We are faced, therefore, with the cross-migration of human rights law. The concept of proportionality, in turn, was developed in much the same way.

2. Proportionality and the Universal Declaration of Human Rights

Following the Second World War and the Holocaust, in 1948, the United Nations General Assembly adopted the Universal Declaration of Human Rights.[161] The Declaration contains a catalogue of human rights. Those rights are mostly phrased in "absolute" terms. However, the declaration has a general limitation clause:

> In the exercise of his rights and freedoms, everyone shall be subject only to such limitations as are determined by law solely for the purpose of securing due recognition and respect for the rights and freedoms of others and of meeting the just requirements of morality, public order and the general welfare in a democratic society.[162]

This general limitation clause has served as a template for other clauses (general and specific) later included in international treaties on human

Birks, M. Both et al. (eds.), The Limitation of Human Rights in Comparative Constitutional Law (Montreal: Les Editions Yvon Blais, 1986).

[161] Universal Declaration of Human Rights (1948).

[162] Ibid., Art. 29(2). See also E. l. A. Daes, "Restrictions and Limitations on Human Rights", in 3 Rene Cassin Amicorum Discipulorumque Liber 79 (1969); O. M. Garibaldi, "General Limitations on Human Rights: The Principle of Legality," 17 Harv. Int'l L. J. 503 (1976); T. Opsahl, "Articles 29 and 30: The Other Side of the Coin," in A. Eide and T. Swinehart (eds.), The Universal Declaration of Human Rights: A Commentary (Oxford University Press, 1992), 449; J. Morsink, The Universal Declaration of Human Rights, Origins, Drafting, and Intent (Philadelphia: University of Pennsylvania Press, 1999), 239.

rights.[163] Today proportionality is interpreted as being the main feature of these clauses.[164]

3. Proportionality and international humanitarian law

Together with international human rights law, another important source of international norms is international humanitarian law (IHL). The relationship between the two is that of a general and a specific law.[165] Thus, whenever the specific IHL is missing a norm that needs to apply to the

---

[163] See, e.g., International Covenant on Civil and Political Rights, opened for signature December 10, 1966, 999 *UNTS* 171 (entered into force March 23, 1976); International Covenant on Economic, Social and Cultural Rights, opened for signature December 19, 1966, 993 *UNTS* 3 (entered into force March 23, 1976); On these Covenants, see A. C. Kiss, "Permissible Limitations on Rights," in Louis Henkin (ed.), *The International Bill of Rights: The Covenant on Civil and Political Rights* (New York: Columbia University Press, 1981), 290; J. M. Ross, "Limitations on Human Rights in International Law: Their Relevance to the Canadian Charter of Rights and Freedoms," 6(2) *Hum. Rts. Q.* 180 (1984); "The Siracusa Principles on the Limitation and Derogation Provisions in the International Covenant on Civil and Political Rights," 7 *Hum. Rts. Q.* 3 (1985); "The Limburg Principles on the Implementation of the International Covenant on Economic, Social and Cultural Rights," 9 *Hum. Rts. Q.* 122 (1987); M. Nowak, *UN Covenant on Civil and Political Rights: CCPR Commentary* (Kehl am Rhein, Germany: Engel, 1993); M. Craven, *The International Covenant on Economic, Social and Cultural Rights: A Perspective on Its Development* (Oxford University Press, 1995); N. Jayawickrama, *The Judicial Application of Human Rights Law: National, Regional and International Jurisprudence* (Cambridge University Press, 2002), 182; S. Joseph, J. Schultz, and M. Castan, *The International Covenant on Civil and Political Rights: Cases, Materials and Commentary*, 2nd edn. (Oxford University Press, 2004); D. Shelton, *Regional Protection of Human Rights* (Oxford University Press, 2008), 226; M. Haas, *International Human Rights: A Comprehensive Introduction* (London: Routledge, 2008); A. Conte and R. Burchill, *Defining Civil and Political Rights: The Jurisprudence of the United Nations Human Rights Committee*, 2nd edn. (Farnham, UK: Ashgate Publishing, 2009).

[164] See Kiss, above note 163; "The Siracusa Principles on the Limitation and Derogation Provisions in the International Covenant on Civil and Political," above note 163; "The Limburg Principles on the Implementation of the International Covenant on Economic, Social and Cultural Rights," above note 163. Proportionality also applies within the normative regulation of the World Trade Organization. See Stone Sweet and Mathews, above note 15, at 153. See also A. Mitchell, "Proportionality and Remedies in WTO Disputes," 17 *Eur. J. Int'l L.* 985 (2006); H. Dreier, *GG Grundgesetz Kommentar* (Tübingen: Mohr Siebeck, 2006), 175; M. Andenas and S. Zleptnig, "Proportionality: WTO Law in Comparative Perspective," 42 *Tex. Int'l L. J.* 371 (2007); H. Xiuli, "The Application of the Principle of Proportionality in Tecmed v. Mexico," 6 *Chin. J. Int'l L.* 635 (2007).

[165] See *Legal Consequences of the Construction of a Wall in the Occupied Palestinian Territory*, Advisory Opinion, 2004 ICJ 136 (July 2004).

matter at hand, one would be "imported" from the general law of international human rights.[166]

IHL is meant to protect human rights in situations of armed conflict.[167] Naturally, these rights – like any other human rights – are not absolute. They may be limited. IHL determines the purposes for which the limitation of human rights during an armed conflict is justified. It also determines the means used to obtain such purposes. Those means are not unlimited either. IHL is based on balancing.[168] This balancing is conducted within the rules of proportionality.[169]

Accordingly, any limitation on a human right protected by IHL should be proportional. The actual content of that proportionality may change in accordance with the context of the legal question in which it arises. It seems that a general, uniform, customary rule has yet to be established regarding the application of proportionality in all situations in which human rights may be affected during an armed conflict. In addition, it seems that a common element to all proportionality requirements during armed conflict is proportionality *stricto sensu*, "the requirement that

---

[166] See HCJ 769/02 *Public Committee against Torture in Israel* v. *Government of Israel* [2006] (2) IsrLR 459, para. 18 (Barak, P.), available at http://elyon1.court.gov.il/files_eng/02/690/007/e16/02007690.e16.pdf.

[167] See D. Fleck and M. Bothe (eds.), *The Handbook of Humanitarian Law in Armed Conflicts* (1999); Y. Dinstein, *The Conduct of Hostilities under the Law of International Armed Conflict* (Cambridge University Press, 2004); J. M. Henckaerts and L. Doswald-Beck (eds.), *Customary International Humanitarian Law* (2005).

[168] See *Public Committee Against Torture*, above note 166, at para. 22 ("International law dealing with armed conflict is based on a delicate balance between two conflicting sets of considerations ... The first deals with humanitarian considerations relating to anyone who may be adversely affected by the armed conflict. These considerations are based upon the notions of human rights and human dignity. The other deals with the military considerations underlying the armed conflict itself. These considerations are based on military needs and the success-oriented military mission ... The balancing between these two sets of considerations is the very basis of the international law of armed conflict ... The upshot of this balancing is that human rights are protected by the laws of armed conflict, but not to their fullest extent. The same is true for the military needs. These may be achieved, but not to their fullest extent. Such balancing reflects the relative nature of human nature as well as the limits of military needs. The exact point of balancing is never fixed." (Barak, P.)).

[169] See *ibid.*, para. 42 ("The concept of proportionality is at the center of many international laws relating to armed conflict ... These laws are mostly of a customary nature ... The concept of proportionality is triggered both when a military activity is aimed at military targets and soldiers, and when it is aimed at civilians who take active part in military operations. During this military activity, innocent civilians may be hurt. The rule is that any damage caused to innocent civilians as an indirect result of a military action must be proportional." (Barak, P.)).

a proper proportional relationship exists between the military objective and the civilian harm."[170] Further analysis of IHL is beyond the scope of this book, whose content is devoted to the limitation of constitutional rights.

K.   Has proportionality arrived in America?

In several areas of American law one may find references to both proportionality and disproportionality. Thus, for example, Sullivan and Frase[171] cite numerous instances in which the term "proportional" is used by the federal courts. In addition, they point to several other instances that may also be explained in terms of proportionality. However, these commentators cannot point to a single instance in which the concept of proportionality in its entirety – including its four main components – is adopted by the American courts. This rule has an important exception: in a series of cases, Justice Breyer – in dissenting opinions – ruled that, in certain circumstances, the American Supreme Court had actually turned to a balancing test between competing interests, which included asking whether the limitation of a constitutional right is not proportional.[172] For example, Justice Breyer wrote in a campaign-finance-related case:

> In such circumstances – where a law significantly implicates competing constitutionally protected interests in complex ways – the Court has closely scrutinized the statute's impact on those interests, but refrained from employing a simple test that effectively presumes unconstitutionality. Rather, it has balanced interests. And in practice that has meant asking whether the statute burdens any one such interest in a manner out of proportion to the statute's salutary effects upon the others (perhaps,

---

[170] *Ibid.*, para. 44 (Barak, P.).

[171] See E. T. Sullivan and R. S. Frase, *Proportionality Principles in American Law: Controlling Excessive Government Actions* (Oxford University Press, 2009); A. Stone Sweet and J. Mathews, "All Things in Proportion? American Rights Doctrine and the Problem of Balancing," *Emory L. J.* (forthcoming, 2010); J. Blocher, "Categoricalism and Balancing in First and Second Amendment Analysis," 84 *N. Y. U. L. Rev.* 375 (2009). See also K. Sullivan, "Post-Liberal Judging: The Roles of Categorization and Balancing," 63 *U. Colo. L. Rev.* 293 (1992); V. C. Jackson, "Ambivalent Resistance and Comparative Constitutionalism: Opening Up the Conversation on 'Proportionality', Rights and Federalism," 1 *U. Pa. J. Const. L.* 583 (1998–1999); R. Singer, "Proportionate Thoughts About Proportionality," 8 *Ohio St. J. Crim. L.* 217 (2010).

[172] See *Turner Broadcasting System Inc.* v. *FCC*, 520 US 180 (1997); *United States* v. *Playboy Entertainment Group*, 529 US 803 (2000); *Bartnicki* v. *Vopper*, 532 US 514 (2001); *United States* v. *United Foods*, 533 US 405 (2001); *Ysursa* v. *Pocatello Education*, 555 US (2009).

but not necessarily, because of the existence of a clearly superior, less restrictive alternative).[173]

In another case, the American Supreme Court examined the scope of the Second Amendment to the American Constitution, which deals with the right to bear arms. Justice Breyer wrote in his dissent:

> [A]ny attempt *in theory* to apply strict scrutiny to gun regulations will *in practice* turn into an interest-balancing inquiry, with the interests protected by the Second Amendment on one side and the governmental public-safety concerns on the other, the only question being whether the regulation at issue impermissibly burdens the former in the course of advancing the latter. I would simply adopt such an interest-balancing inquiry explicitly. The fact that important interests lie on both sides of the constitutional equation suggests that review of gun-control regulation is not a context in which a court should effectively presume either constitutionality (as in rational-basis review) or unconstitutionality (as in strict scrutiny).[174]

Justice Breyer continued:

> Contrary to the majority's unsupported suggestion that this sort of proportionality approach is unprecedented ... the Court has applied it in various constitutional contexts.[175]

Proportionality components – with balancing between the benefits of fulfilling the law and the harm to the constitutional right in their center – have been recognized by American law in the past. Subjects wherein today the balancing is missing – such as freedom of expression – were formally regulated by the judicial approach which balances between benefit and harm. Therefore, the recognition of proportionality and the balancing at its center does not amount to the penetration of a foreign factor into American law.[176] However, Justice Breyer's approach, which recognizes proportionality and all of its components as a constitutional concept which can stand on its own and which applies in the different fields of the Bill of Rights, is an innovation in American constitutional law.[177] It

---

[173] *Nixon* v. *Shrink Missouri Government PAC*, 528 US 377, 402 (2000) (Breyer, J., dissenting).

[174] *District of Columbia* v. *Heller*, 554 US 290 (2008); see also S. Breyer, *Making Our Democracy Work: A Judge's View* (New York: Knopf, 2010), 159; M. Cohen-Eliya and I. Porat, "The Hidden Foreign Law Debate in Heller: The Proportionality Approach in American Constitutional Law," 46(2) *San Diego L. Rev.* 367 (2009).

[175] See *District of Columbia* v. *Heller*, 554 US 290 (2008), Chapter 3 (Breyer, J., dissenting).

[176] See Stone Sweet and Mathews, above note 171.

[177] As to proportionality in human administrative law, see G. Bermann, "The Principle of Proportionality," 26 *Am. J. Comp. L.* Sup. 415 (1977–1978).

will require a review of both the scope of the constitutional right as well as the justification for its limitation. Is American constitutional law ready for this change?[178]

L.   Proportionality in Israel

The four components that together make up the requirements of proportionality have played, for many years – albeit separately – an important role in the development of Israel's administrative law. That is the case for the requirement of a proper purpose; for the requirement of a rational connection; for the requirement of the least damaging alternative; and for the requirement of a proper balance between the harm caused to the human right and the benefit gained by the public interest. In some cases, each of these components stood on its own. In others, it served as a consideration of the reasonableness test, the standard according to which all administrative and executive actions are reviewed. While developing its own tests – such as that of reasonableness – the Israeli Supreme Court has digressed from English precedents such as *Wednesbury*.[179] Instead, the Court has placed the reasonableness of the administrative action as a stand-alone, independent test with the balancing of conflicting interests at its core.

For many years, these separate components have failed to form a single, unified administrative rule. The main sources for the creation of such a rule came from Israeli academia. The first to note proportionality as an independent cause of action was Segal. In an article he published in 1990,[180] Segal argued that "a review of Israeli Supreme Court cases … demonstrates that the Court has created a new cause of administrative review; this cause deals with the lack of proportionality between the means undertaken by the administrative agency and the damage it sought to prevent, or the purpose it sought to obtain."[181] Segal dubbed that

---

[178] See V. C. Jackson, "Ambivalent Resistance and Comparative Constitutionalism: Opening Up the Conversation on 'Proportionality', Rights and Federalism," 1 *U. Pa. J. Const. L.* 583, 616 (1998–1999); V. C. Jackson, "Being Proportional about Proportionality," 21 *Const. Comment.* 803, 842 (2004); Cohen-Eliya and Porat, above note 174; and see below, at 530.

[179] For *Wednesbury*, see above note 96.

[180] Z. Segal, "Disproportionality as a Cause of Action in Israeli Administrative Action," 39 *HaPraklit* 507 (1990).

[181] *Ibid.*, at 511.

"the cause of disproportionality."[182] Segal then turned to comparative law in order to further develop his opinion. He noted that, "in European law in general, and in French law in particular, this cause of action is a novel one. It began about twenty years ago, and now quickly develops to expand the judicial review of administrative action."[183] Four years later, in 1994, Zamir published a comprehensive article comparing Israel's administrative law to that of Germany.[184] In this article, Zamir introduced to the Israeli legal community for the first time the German notion of proportionality. He then expressed his opinion that the Israeli Supreme Court has neglected the use of proportionality.[185] He emphasized that the concept of proportionality was adopted by the court, but remained a "nameless stepchild" of the system,[186] as it always had to "hide" behind other causes of action, such as reasonableness or the balancing of interests. He then expressed the hope that this reason for action "would stand on its own two feet, as an independent cause of action, and would be able to be developed much like the other well-recognized causes."[187]

This hope was quickly realized. It was Zamir himself – this time, Justice Zamir of the Israeli Supreme Court – who recognized the cause of proportionality as an independent cause of action that may be argued against any executive or administrative action. As Justice Zamir wrote:

> Proportionality is an important legal concept, accepted by many nations and in many areas of law – in particular administrative law. It has also been used in Israeli law since its infancy, in several areas, sometimes originating in legislation and sometimes in the common law. Recently, however, proportionality was recognized by this court as a principle that guides and limits the administrative agency while it exercises its authority ... More concretely, proportionality is a wide-ranging and fundamental concept that until now, for some reason, has not received the weight and recognition it deserves in Israeli law.[188]

---

[182] *Ibid.*, at 512.   [183] *Ibid.*

[184] I. Zamir, "Israel's Administrative Law as Compared to Germany's Administrative Law," 2 *Mishpat U'Mimshal* [*Law and Government*] 109 (1994).

[185] *Ibid.*, at 132.   [186] *Ibid.*   [187] *Ibid.*, at 133.

[188] HCJ 987/94 *Euronet Golden Lines Ltd.* v. *The Minister of Communication* [1994] IsrSC 48(5) 412, 435. See also HCJ 3477/95 *Ben Atiyah* v. *Minister of Culture and Sports* [1995] IsrSC 49(5) 1, 10 ("The concept of proportionality has been accepted, as a matter of positive law, by Israel's legal system. It appears in several areas of law ... The concept of proportionality was first recognized by Israel's administrative law, but without calling it by its own name ... Recently, a more 'formal' recognition was granted to proportionality by the Israeli Supreme Court." (Barak, P.)).

These developments occurred mainly in the area of administrative law. Another important development, this time in constitutional law, occurred with the adoption of the two Basic Laws relating to human rights – Basic Law: Human Dignity and Liberty, and Basic Law: Freedom of Occupation. These two Basic Laws, which contain a list of constitutional human rights, adopted a general limitation clause.[189] Within that clause, the concept of proportionality is explicitly mentioned ("[the limitation shall be] to an extent no greater than is required"). In my opinion in the case of *United Mizrahi Bank* – a case that established the constitutional status of these Basic Laws – the sources of the concept of proportionality in Israel were noted:

> In the past we turned to the concept of proportionality as a cause of action in administrative law ... Now it has been granted a constitutional status. It is according to this concept that the constitutionality of legislation should be reviewed. The same has occurred in the laws of other nations: Proportionality began as an administrative law test. Today, this test is well received across the administrative laws of many of the European states ... It was developed in particular by the German administrative law ... [F]rom there, it migrated to the constitutional law of most of the European states, as well as other states outside Europe. It now serves, for example, as a main feature of Canadian law ... and also in South Africa, in accordance with its new constitution. Indeed, a review of the comparative law on proportionality demonstrates an attempt to render the test more concrete. It seems to me that we should learn from that comparative experience, common to Canada, Germany, the European Union and the European Court of Human Rights, as the concept of proportionality does not necessarily reflect a particular social history unique to a certain nation, or a particular stand on a constitutional issue. Rather, it reflects a comprehensive analytical view as to the proportionality of the law limiting a constitutional human right.

Following the comparative experience, proportionality in Israeli law is divided into four components; each of those assumed the interpretation adopted at the time by Canada, Germany, and judicial opinions interpreting the European Convention for the Protection of Human Rights and Fundamental Freedoms. Today, proportionality constitutes a central feature of Israeli law. It applies not only in constitutional law, but also in administrative law. It has become a central feature of the Israeli public discourse – which refers to the requirement of proportionality more than ever.

---

[189] See Basic Law: Human Dignity and Liberty, Art. 8; Basic Law: Freedom of Occupation, Art. 4.

8

The legal sources of proportionality

A. Proportionality as a criterion for the realization of constitutional rights

1. *The need for a constitutional entrenchment*

Any legal system wishing to adopt proportionality as a criterion for properly limiting constitutional rights through sub-constitutional law must provide a legal foundation for such an adoption.[1] It is insufficient to merely recognize proportionality as a key concept or to simply acknowledge its superiority over other limiting criteria. It would also be insufficient for the common law to recognize it, or even for statutory provisions to do so.[2] Rather, the only legal basis for the application of proportionality as a criterion for the limitation of constitutional rights by sub-constitutional law must be found in the constitution itself, either explicitly or implicitly. Indeed, in order to properly limit a constitutional right by a sub-constitutional law, the law establishing the limitation must rest on a constitutional foundation. What constitutes the constitutional basis of proportionality?

In Israel, the answer to this question appears straightforward. The Israeli Basic Laws contain, within their general limitation clauses, a specific provision stating that any limitation of the constitutional rights established therein must be by law "benefiting the values of the State of

---

[1] See L. Tremblay, "Normative Foundation of the Proportionality Principle in Constitutional Theory" (French) (EUI Working Papers LAW 2009/04); B. Schlink, "Der Grundsatz der Verhältnismässigkeit," in P. Badura and H. Dreier (eds.), *Festschrift 50 Jahre Bundesverfassungsgericht*, vol. II (Tübingen: Mohr Siebeck, 2001), 445, 447; C. B. Pulido, *El Principio de Proporcionalidad y los Derechos Fundamentales* (Centro de Estudios Políticos y Constitucionales, 2007), 505.

[2] When the rights are not part of the formal constitution, but embodied in statute or common law, proportionality may be recognized by statute or common law. The main question, as to statutory rights, will be the question of implied repeal: see A. Kavanagh, *Constitutional Review under the UK Human Rights Act* (Cambridge University Press, 2009), 294. See also above, at 159.

Israel, enacted for a proper purpose."[3] In addition, the limitation clauses must be "to an extent no greater than required." A similar provision may be found in several other constitutions. Take, for example, an amendment to the Austrian Constitution from 1988. While subsection (1) of the amended provision establishes a constitutional right to freedom, subsection (3) provides:

> The deprivation of personal liberty may be legally prescribed only if this is requisite for the purpose of the measure; deprivation of personal liberty may in any instance only occur if and inasmuch as this is not disproportionate to the purpose of the measure.

Similarly, the new Federal Constitution of Switzerland (2000) contains a general limitation clause (Article 36(3)), which includes the following specific language:

> Limitations of fundamental rights must be proportionate to the goals pursued.[4]

Another explicit provision relating to proportionality is found in Romania's Constitution (1991)[5] and in an amendment (2001) to the Constitution of the Republic of Turkey.[6] Some other constitutions have included within their limitation clauses (either general or specific) special provisions requiring that a limitation of a constitutional right be done in a manner that is "necessary" in a democratic society.[7] From the use of this term – "necessary" – the courts have deduced the proportionality requirement.[8]

While the mere existence of specific provisions in the constitution may advance our inquiry as to the legal foundation of the concept of proportionality, it fails to provide a complete answer. The reason for that is that the different terms used by the constitutional text – be it "necessary," "not beyond the required amount," "proportional," or others – require interpretation. The interpretive process raises several questions such as what does it mean to have a limitation that is "necessary," or "not beyond

---

[3] Basic Law: Human Dignity and Liberty (Art. 8); Basic Law: Freedom of Occupation (Art. 4).
[4] For analysis, see U. Hafelin, W. Haller, and H. Keller, *Schweizerisches Bundesstaatsrecht* (Zurich: Schulthess, 2008).
[5] See the Constitution of Romania, Art. 49(2).
[6] See the Constitution of Turkey, Art. 13.
[7] See above, at 141.   [8] See above, at 141.

what is required"? Similar questions arise when the constitutional text specifically uses the term "proportionality." What is the meaning of that provision? Is it the same as the one used by Canada, Germany, or South Africa? Maybe it is closer to the "reasonableness" requirement, adopted by the administrative laws of common law countries as well as in Israel? Maybe this is a unique proportionality, a *sui generis* for that specific legal system?

The question presented earlier remains unanswered: what is the legal basis of proportionality? What is the foundation of the concept in the constitutional law of the legal system that has adopted it? Beyond that, in some cases, the constitutions in question contain no explicit provisions relating to the proportional limitation of constitutional rights by sub-constitutional law. In other cases, all that those constitutions provide is that a limitation should be made only "by law," without referring to any other conditions.[9] Finally, some constitutions contain rights worded as absolute, without any additional guidance as to their limitation.[10] Despite that, all these constitutions were interpreted as requiring a proportional limitation – even without any explicit provision to that effect, or where the only provision available merely stated that the limitation should be prescribed "by law."[11] What was the constitutional foundation that such interpretations were based on? Indeed, the answer to the question of what is the constitutional basis of proportionality is critical to an understanding of the concept.

2.   *The nature of the constitutional entrenchment*

A review of the literature and judicial opinions relating to proportionality suggests that proportionality's constitutional basis may be explained by one of the following four views:

(a) Proportionality may be derived from the notion of democracy.
(b) Proportionality is a part of the rule of law.
(c) Proportionality is inherent to any conflict between legal principles.
(d) Proportionality is a likely outcome of harmonious interpretation of the entire constitution.

I review each of these below.

---

[9] See above, at 139.   [10] See above, at 134.   [11] See above, at 139.

B.   Proportionality and democracy

1.   *The relationship between democracy and proportionality: basic assumptions*

According to the first view, the requirement of proportional limitations of constitutional rights by a sub-constitutional law (e.g., a statute or the common law) is derived from an interpretation of the notion of democracy itself. The argument is based on five assumptions. First, the very notion of democracy is of a constitutional status. Second, the constitutional notion of democracy includes – other than the notions of representative democracy and majority rule – an element of human rights. Third, the constitutional notion of democracy is based on a balance between human rights on the one hand and the principles that representative democracy aims to achieve on the other. It is necessary, therefore, to prove that democracy is based upon a balance between human rights and their limitation. Fourth, that balance, required by the very nature of the notion of democracy, is performed through limitation clauses (general or specific, explicit or implicit), which renders the limitation of constitutional rights possible by a sub-constitutional law. Fifth, these limitation clauses, in order to properly fulfill their role, are based on the principle of proportionality. The principle of proportionality is based on the notion of democracy if and only if each of these five assumptions is correct. We turn now to an examination of these assumptions.

2.   *First assumption: democracy is of a constitutional status*

The view that proportionality is derived from the notion of democracy is based on the assumption that the notion of democracy is of a constitutional (supra-legislative) status. This is so because, if the notion of democracy is merely a reflection of the sub-constitutional reality, then it would not suffice to serve as a basis for a norm – or a criterion – operating at the constitutional level.

Does democracy have a constitutional status? Some constitutions explicitly state that the state is of a democratic nature. Thus, for example, the Basic Law for the Federal Republic of Germany provides that the Federal Republic of Germany is a democracy (*"ein demokratischer Bundesstaat"*).[12]

---

[12]   Basic Law for the Federal Republic of Germany, Art. 20(1).

A similar provision can be found in other constitutions.[13] The Canadian Charter of Rights and Freedoms declares that it "guarantees the rights and freedoms set out in it subject only to such reasonable limits prescribed by law as can be demonstrably justified in a free and democratic society."[14] A similar provision, relating to an "open and democratic society," appears in the Constitution of the Republic of South Africa.[15] In Israel, the democratic nature of the state was explicitly mentioned by the Basic Laws relating to human rights, which state that the purpose of these Basic Laws is "to establish in a Basic Law the values of the State of Israel as a Jewish and democratic state."[16]

What is the normative status of the constitutional determination that a state is "democratic," or that its values are those of a "democratic state," or that its rights may be limited in a manner "justified by a democracy"? These questions are interpretive in nature. The term "democracy," as it appears in a constitutional text, must be properly interpreted. Naturally, this interpretation may vary from one legal system to another, from one constitution to the next. Still, the judiciaries in most constitutional democracies adopted the view that the term "democratic" as it appears in the constitution is not merely of a declaratory nature; rather, it has a constitutional-operative meaning as well. It imposes, for example, obligations on the three branches of government. It also serves as an interpretive rule. Therefore, for example, it may be helpful when the question at issue is whether a referendum – which is not mentioned by the constitution – is an institution that is congruent with the constitution.[17] Similarly, it may be helpful when the question presented is: what are the circumstances under which a state belonging to a federation may withdraw from it?[18] The notion of democracy is also a source that may yield further powers not mentioned explicitly by the constitution itself, but which are intrinsic to its democratic nature.[19] In addition, the notion of democracy may

---

[13] See, e.g., the Constitution of Spain, Art. 1(1); Constitution of Italy, Art. 1; Constitution of Ireland, Art. 5; the Constitution of Portugal, Art. 2.

[14] The Canadian Charter of Rights and Freedoms, Section 1.

[15] Constitution of the Republic of South Africa, Art. 36(1).

[16] Israeli Basic Law: Human Dignity and Liberty (Art. 1a); Israeli Basic Law: Freedom of Occupation (Art. 2). On the relation between the values of the State of Israel as a democratic state and its values as a Jewish state, see A. Barak, "The Values of the State of Israel as a Jewish and Democratic State," in A. Maoz (ed.), *Israel as a Jewish and Democratic State* (forthcoming, 2011).

[17] *Hanafin v. Minister for Environment* [1996] 2 IR 321.

[18] *Reference re Secession of Quebec* [1998] 2 SCR 217.

[19] See *Haughey v. Moriarty* [1999] 3 IR 1.

encompass not only a formal but also a substantial facet. In that case, new human rights, not expressly enumerated by the constitution, may be recognized impliedly by the courts as stemming from the very notion of democracy.[20] Using such an approach, the Supreme Court of Ireland came to recognize the right to freedom of movement, although it is not specifically mentioned by the Irish Constitution.[21] Similarly, the High Court of Australia has recognized the right to freedom of political expression.[22]

The constitution does not always explicitly refer to the term "democracy." In those cases where it does not, should the notion of democracy still be accorded a constitutional status? The answer is yes. Several basic principles do not appear explicitly in a constitution, but they constitute an integral part of the document and are of constitutional status.[23] Even if those basic principles are not written expressly into the text of the founding democratic document, they appear impliedly between the lines.[24] They are implied by the constitutional text and the constitutional structure.[25] They constitute a part of the "invisible constitution."[26] Take, for example, the notion of the separation of powers. In most cases, the notion itself is not explicitly referred to in the constitutional text, but it is clearly impliedly included therein.[27] As I have noted elsewhere:

> The democratic value of separation of powers, and not just the de facto division of authority among the different branches, is itself a constitutional concept, superior to legislation. True, the constitution cannot contain an explicit provision recognizing the principle of separation of powers. Nevertheless, the principle of separation of powers is a constitutional principle. Such recognition is required by the purposive interpretation of the constitution. This principle might not be written in the lines of the constitution, but it is written between the lines. It is implicitly derived from the language of the constitution. It is a natural outgrowth

---

[20] See above, at 53.

[21] See *The State (M)* v. *Attorney General* [1979] IR 73.

[22] See above, at 50.

[23] See D. Mullan, "The Role for Underlying Constitutional Principles in a Bill of Rights World," *New Zealand L. Rev.* 9 (2004).

[24] See above, at 54.

[25] See *South African Association of Personal Injury Lawyers* v. *Heath*, 2001 (1) SA 883 (CC); *Doctors of Life International* v. *Speaker of the National Assembly*, 2006 (6) SA 416 (CC); S. Seedford and S. Sibanda, "Separation of Powers," in S. Woolman, M. Bishop, and J. Brickhill (eds.), *Constitutional Law of South Africa*, 2nd edn. (Cape Town: Juta Law Publishers, looseleaf, 2002–), 12–36.

[26] See L. H. Tribe, *The Invisible Constitution* (Oxford University Press, 2008).

[27] *Chairperson of the Constitutional Assembly: In re Ex parte Certification of the Constitution of the Republic of South Africa*, 1996 (4) SA 74 (CC).

of the structure of the constitution – which distinguishes between three branches of government and provides them each with a separate Basic Law – and all of its provisions.[28]

A similar approach was adopted by the Constitutional Court of South Africa, which stated:

> I cannot accept that an implicit provision of the Constitution has any less force than an express provision ... The Constitutions of the United States and Australia, like ours, make provision for the separation of powers by vesting the legislative authority in the Legislature, the executive authority in the Executive, and the judicial authority in the Courts. The doctrine of separation of powers as applied in the United States is based on inferences drawn from the structure and provisions of the Constitution, rather than an express entrenchment of the principle. In this respect, our Constitution is no different ... There can be no doubt that our Constitution provides for such a separation, and that laws inconsistent with what the Constitution requires in that regard, are invalid.[29]

Another fundamental principle often missing from the express text of most constitutions is the judiciary's independence (as opposed to the independence of the individual judges). The Supreme Court of Canada has held, nonetheless, that this basic principle is of a constitutional status.[30] Similarly, the principle of the rule of law rarely appears expressly in most modern constitutions. Still, many democratic constitutions consider this principle to be of constitutional status.[31] And, if this is the case for all those fundamental principles – which derive from the organizing principle of democracy itself – then surely the organizing principle itself, namely democracy, is considered an integral part of the constitution. This conclusion is supported by the constitutional structure and its separate parts – in particular, those relating to human rights, the right to vote, and the decisionmaking mechanisms of the elected body – which, combined, both constitute the notion of democracy and are affected by it.

My assumption, therefore, is that the notion of democracy is a constitutional- operative notion. Is it possible to derive from this notion the concept of proportionality? In order to answer this question in the affirmative, it is not enough to prove that the notion of democracy is of constitutional status. Rather, one must also establish – and this is the second assumption – that the constitutional notion of democracy entails

[28] A. Barak, *The Judge in a Democracy* (Princeton University Press, 2006), 44, 45.
[29] *Heath*, above note 25, at para. 20–22.
[30] See *Reference re Remuneration of Judges of the Provincial Court* (PEI) [1997] 3 SCR 3.
[31] See below, at 228.

a vital component of recognizing human rights. The second assumption will now be examined.

3. Second assumption: democracy includes human rights

The notion of democracy has many meanings. "There are many views of democracy – from popular democracy to western democracy; from a formal democracy to substantive democracy; and, within substantive democracy, there are different understandings as to the substance of democracy."[32] One of the key distinctions in that context is that between a formal democracy and a substantive democracy. The notion of formal democracy focuses on the sovereignty of the people, which is demonstrated mainly through free elections ("representative democracy"), which grant, in turn, the right to both vote and be elected to all, equally. The notion of substantive democracy emphasizes those special features that make democracy unique, like the principles of separation of powers, the rule of law, the independence of the judiciary, and the recognition of human rights.[33] Every constitution provides the notion of democracy with a meaning that best captures its purpose as appearing in that legal system. Most democratic constitutions today tend to interpret the notion of democracy expansively, in a fashion that entails both the formal and the substantive facets of democracy. Thus, for example, the German Constitutional Court has emphasized that the Basic Law for the Federal Republic of Germany is based upon the fundamental concept of free democracy, defined as follows:

> A regime governed by the rule of law and based on the self-declaration of all members of society in accordance with the majority rule, and on the notions of equality and liberty, which prevent any possibility of either rule by force or of an arbitrary and capricious tyranny.[34]

A similar approach was adopted by the Constitution of the Republic of South Africa:

---

[32] HCJ 164/97 *Contrem Ltd.* v. *Ministry of Finance – Custom and VAT Department* [1998] IsrSC 52(1) 289, 340 (Zamir, J.). See also R. A. Dahl, *On Democracy* (New Haven, CT: Yale University Press, 1998); T. Roux, "Democracy," in S. Woolman, M. Bishop, and J. Brickhill (eds.), *Constitutional Law of South Africa*, 2nd edn. (Cape Town: Juta Law Publishers, looseleaf, 2002–), 1: "Democracy is a noun permanently in search of a qualifying adjective."

[33] Regarding democracy's different aspects, see Barak, above note 28, at 23.

[34] BVerfGE 5, 585.

This Bill of Rights is a cornerstone of democracy in South Africa. It enshrines the rights of all people in our country and affirms the democratic values of human dignity, equality, and freedom.[35]

Roux has noted, in that context, that:

[N]o South African political system claiming to be democratic would be worthy of that name unless it respected the democratic values which the Bill of Rights affirms.[36]

A similar approach was adopted by the Israeli Basic Laws. For example, Article 1(a) of Basic Law: Human Dignity and Liberty reads:

The purpose of this Basic Law is to protect human dignity and liberty, in order to establish in a Basic Law the values of the State of Israel as a Jewish and democratic state.

Indeed, the link between democracy and human rights is inexorable.[37] The notion of democracy itself is rich and multi-faceted. We should not view democracy, therefore, from a single point of view. Democracy, rather, is multidimensional. While based on the notion of majority rule, it is made up of additional values – in particular that of human rights. Thus, democracy is based on the notion that each individual may enjoy certain rights, and that those rights may not be revoked by the majority despite having the alleged power to do so in accordance with the majority rule.[38]

---

[35] Constitution of the Republic of South Africa, Art. 7(1).
[36] Roux, above note 32, at 33; R. Dworkin, *A Bill of Rights for Britain* (London: Chatto & Windus, 1990), 35: "True democracy is not just statistical democracy, in which anything a majority or plurality wants is legitimate for that reason, but communal democracy, in which majority decision is legitimate only if it is a majority within a community of equals. That means not only that everyone must be allowed to participate in politics as an equal, through the vote and through freedom of speech and protest, but that political decisions must treat everyone with equal concern and respect, that each individual person must be guaranteed fundamental civil and political rights no combination of other citizens can take away, no matter how numerous they are or how much they despise his or her race or morals or way of life."
[37] See Barak, above note 28, at 24; Dworkin, above note 36, at 35; R. Dworkin, *Freedom's Law: The Moral Reading of the American Constitution* (Cambridge, MA: Harvard University Press, 1996); L. E. Weinrib, "The Supreme Court of Canada in the Age of Rights: Constitutional Democracy, the Role of Law and Fundamental Rights under Canada's Constitution," 80 *Can. Bar Rev.* 699, 701 (2001); W. Osiatynski, *Human Rights and Their Limits* (Cambridge University Press, 2009), 72; V. Ferreres Comella, *Constitutional Courts and Democratic Values: A European Perspective* (New Haven, CT: Yale University Press, 2009).
[38] See J. P. Muller, "Fundamental Rights in Democracy," 4 *Hum. Rts. L. J.* 131 (1983); J. Habermas, *Between Facts and Norms: Contributions to a Discourse Theory of Law and Democracy* (William Rehg trans., Cambridge, MA: MIT Press, 1996); C. R. Sunstein,

This link between democracy and human rights exists at the constitutional level, and it manifests itself in the interpretation given to the term "democracy" in various constitutions. The requirement that democracy be given not only its formal meaning but also its substantive meaning is, therefore, a constitutional requirement.[39]

As we have seen, at times the term "democracy" does not appear explicitly in the constitution. Little should be made of that, as the term is clearly implied by the text and structure of the constitution.[40] What is included in the implied term of democracy? The principled answer to this question is that the meaning and scope of the implied term of democracy is identical to that of its explicit term. Accordingly, even without an explicit mention of the term we should consider the implied notion of democracy to include both its formal and substantive facets, central to which are human rights.

4. Third assumption: democracy is based on a balance between constitutional rights and the public interest

Proportionality is derived from the notion of democracy, provided that the term is understood to encompass human rights, and is considered to have a constitutional status. While these are necessary conditions, they are not sufficient. Now, we should demonstrate that the same constitutional rights that form the notion of democracy can also be limited; in other words, that these rights are relative and not absolute. As we have seen, modern constitutional rights doctrines distinguish between the scope of the rights and the extent of their realization.[41] The constitutional rights are, therefore, relative. This relativity means that a constitutional license to limit those rights is granted where such a limitation may be justified to protect the public interest or the rights of others. When the constitutional rights are relative, both the right and the license to limit it are found in the constitution.

This phenomenon – of both the right and its limitation in the constitution – exemplifies the inherent tension between democracy's two fundamental elements. On the one hand is the right's element, which constitutes

Designing Democracy: What Constitutions Do (Oxford University Press, 2002); Van der Schyff, *Limitation of Rights: A Study of the European Convention and the South African Bill of Rights* (Nijmegen, The Netherlands: Wolf Legal Publishers, 2005), 143.
[39] See CA 6821/93 *United Mizrahi Bank Ltd.* v. *Migdal Cooperative Village* [1995] IsrLR 1, 228.
[40] See above at 214.   [41] See above at 19.

a fundamental component of substantive democracy. On the other hand is the people element, limiting those very rights through their representatives; these, too, constitute a fundamental component of the notion of democracy, though this time in its formal aspect. How can this tension be resolved? The answer is that this tension is not resolved by eliminating the "losing" facet from the constitution. Rather, the tension is resolved by way of a proper balancing of the competing principles. This is one of the expressions of the multi-faceted nature of democracy. Indeed, the inherent tension between democracy's different facets is a "constructive tension."[42] It enables each facet to develop while harmoniously co-existing with the others. The best way to achieve this peaceful co-existence is through balancing between the competing interests. Such balancing enables each facet to develop alongside the other facets, not in their place.[43]

5. Fourth assumption: balancing through limitation clauses

The key concept of the constitutional democracy is balancing – the balancing between the formal and substantive aspects of democracy.[44] Such balancing presupposes the simultaneous co-existence of both aspects, while determining the proper relationship between them. That balancing reflects the relative social value of each competing aspect when considered in proper context. When the relevant context is the tension between the formal facet of democracy and constitutional rights, that balancing is resolved through the use of limitation clauses (either general or specific, express or implied), which determine the required conditions under which a sub-constitutional law may limit a constitutional right. Thus, for example, the general limitation clause included in the Canadian Charter of Rights and Freedoms states:

> The Canadian Charter of Rights and Freedoms guarantees the rights and freedoms set out in it subject only to such reasonable limits prescribed by law as can be demonstrably justified in a free and democratic society.[45]

In interpreting the term "free and democratic society" which appears in the limitation clause, Chief Justice Dickson wrote:

---

[42] To use Roux's language; see Roux, above note 32, at 65.
[43] On the democratic justification for the balance, see S. Gardbaum, "A Democratic Defense of Constitutional Balancing," 4(1) *Law and Ethics of Hum. Rts.* 77 (2010).
[44] See Barak, above note 28, at 26.
[45] Canadian Charter of Rights and Freedoms, Section 1.

Inclusion of these words as the final standard of justification for limits on rights and freedoms refers the Court to the very purpose for which the Charter was originally entrenched in the Constitution: Canadian society is to be free and democratic. The Court must be guided by the values and principles essential to a free and democratic society which I believe embody, to name but a few, respect for the inherent dignity of the human person, commitment to social justice and equality, accommodation of a wide variety of beliefs, respect for cultural and group identity, and faith in social and political institutions which enhance the participation of individuals and groups in society.[46]

These words by the Chief Justice were taken into account when drafting the general limitation clause appearing in the Constitution of the Republic of South Africa:

The rights in the Bill of Rights may be limited only in terms of law of general application to the extent that the limitation is reasonable and justifiable in an open and democratic society based on human dignity, equality and freedom.[47]

In similar vein, the limitation clause of the Israeli Basic Laws reads:

There shall be no infringement of rights under this Basic Law except by a law befitting the values of the State of Israel, enacted for a proper purpose, and to an extent no greater than is required.[48]

The "values of the State of Israel," the criteria by which any limitation on constitutional rights established by these Basic Laws is measured, are determined in the "purpose provision" included in these same Basic Laws.[49] According to that provision, these are the values of the State of Israel "as a Jewish and democratic state."

6.   Fifth assumption: limitation clauses are based on proportionality

What is the criterion for a proper balance between the two facets of democracy? How can we balance majority rule with human rights? What is the criterion required by a democratic society to limit a constitutional right

---

[46] *R. v. Oakes* [1986] 1 SCR 103, 136.
[47] Constitution of the Republic of South Africa, Art. 36(1).
[48] Basic Law: Human Dignity and Liberty (Art. 8); Basic Law: Freedom of Occupation 1994 SH 90 (Art. 4).
[49] Basic Law: Human Dignity and Liberty (Art. 1a); Basic Law: Freedom of Occupation 1994 SH 90 (Art. 2).

by a sub-constitutional law? The answer to all these questions is that proportionality is a proper criterion. Importantly, this book does not argue that proportionality is the only criterion; my only claim at this point is that proportionality is a proper one. When a law limits a constitutional right, such a limitation is constitutional if it is proportional.[50] It is proportional if it is meant to achieve a proper purpose, if the measures taken to achieve such a purpose are rationally connected to the purpose and are necessary, and if the limiting of the constitutional right is proportional (*stricto sensu*). Each member of society constitutes an integral and equal part of that society. That society, in turn, is justified in limiting the right of each of its members if such a limitation was done for a proper purpose, through proper means, and while limiting the right proportionally – in other words, if the limitation is proportional. Indeed, each person's liberty is an expression of his or her autonomy as part of society. Such integration into society, however, also justifies the imposition of some limitations on this liberty – so long as those are proportional. As Chief Justice Dickson noted in *Oakes*:

> To establish that a limit is reasonable and demonstrably justified in a free and democratic society, two central criteria must be satisfied. First, the objective, which the measures, responsible for a limit on a Charter right or freedom are designed to serve, must be "of" sufficient importance to warrant overriding a constitutional protected right or freedom ... Second ... the party invoking Section 1 must show that the means chosen are reasonable and demonstrably justified. This involves "a form of proportionality test ..." Although the nature of the proportionality test will vary depending on the circumstances, in each case courts will be required to balance the interests of society with those of individuals and groups. There are, in my view, three important components of a proportionality test. First the measures adopted must be ... rationally connected to the objective. Second, the means ... should impair "as little as possible" the right or freedom in question ... Third, there must be a proportionality between the effects of the measures which are responsible for limiting the Charter right or freedom, and the objective which has been identified as of "sufficient importance." The more severe the deleterious effects of a measure, the more important the objective must be if the measure is to be reasonable and demonstrably justified in a free and democratic society.[51]

A similar approach was adopted by the South African Constitutional Court. In *Makwanyane*, the Court considered a challenge to the

---

[50] See Weinrib, above note 37, at 707.
[51] *Oakes*, above note 46, at 138.

constitutionality of a death-penalty statute. The Court held the statute unconstitutional because it was not proportional. As Chief Justice
Chaskalson noted:

> The limitation of constitutional rights for a purpose that is reasonable and
> necessary in a democratic society involves the weighing up of competing
> values, and ultimately an assessment based on proportionality ... which
> calls for the balancing of different interests.[52]

Indeed, if a law limits a constitutional right for an improper purpose, or
while using irrational means, or unnecessary ones – as others would not
impair the right as much – or that the social importance of preventing the
harm to the right is greater than the social importance of the benefit to
the public interest – when this is the result of the law, the limitation is not
justified in a democracy.

In a long series of cases, the Israeli Supreme Court has explained the
protection of human rights by way of a democratic justification. This is
also the type of reasoning used to justify the Israeli limitation clause. This
was demonstrated in *Adalah*, a case that examined the constitutionality of a statute restricting family unifications based on security reasons
(twenty-six of the non-Israeli spouses were involved in terrorist activities
in Israel).[53] Here, a majority of the Justices were of the opinion that the
statute in question, the Law on Citizenship and Entry to Israel (Interim
Provisions), 2003,[54] had in fact limited the right to human dignity, which
is constitutionally recognized in Israel by Basic Law: Human Dignity and
Liberty. In particular, the majority opined that the law limits the right
to human dignity of each Israeli spouse prevented from unifying with
their non-Israeli spouse living in the Occupied Territories, and that such
a limitation was not proportional, and therefore unconstitutional. This
view was based on considerations of democracy. As noted in that case:

> In reviewing the proportionality requirement (*stricto sensu*), we are
> reminded of the basic tenets on which our constitutional democracy is
> based, and the human rights enjoyed by all Israelis. These basic tenets
> include the notion that the cause may not always justify the means; that
> national security is not always paramount; and that the proper purpose
> of raising the level of national security may not justify a substantial injury

---

[52] *S. v. Makwanyane*, 1995 (3) SA 391, § 104.

[53] HCJ 7052/03 *Adalah – The Legal Center for the Rights of the Arab Minority* v. *Minister of Interior* (May 14, 2006, unpublished), available in English at http://elyon1.court.gov.il/fileseng/03/520/070/a47/03070520. a47.pdf.

[54] SH 544.

to the lives of thousands of Israelis. One of the main features of our democracy is that it places limits over the ability to limit human rights; that around each member of the society is a wall protecting his or her rights, and that the majority may not penetrate that wall ... [In this case,] the added degree of national security obtained by the law in question is achieved through both the elimination of the individual examination and the execution of a total restriction; these lead to an injury so severe to the family life and equality of thousands of Israeli citizens that such measures are disproportional. A democracy does not behave in that manner. A democracy does not impose a total restriction separating its citizens from their spouses, denying them the opportunity to lead a normal family life. A democracy does not impose an absolute restriction presenting its citizens with the option to live without their spouse, or to leave the country in order to lead a normal family life. A democracy does not impose an absolute restriction separating parents from their children. A democracy does not impose a total restriction discriminating between its citizens with regard to their family lives. Indeed, a democracy is required to relinquish the added measure of national security in order to achieve a greater measure – much greater – of equality and the right to family life. This is how a democracy behaves during times of peace. This is how it acts during times of terror. It is during these times in particular that the true nature of democracy is revealed ... It is during these tough times that Israel is experiencing that its democracy is being tested.[55]

Later on, in that same opinion, it was added:

Democracy and human rights cannot exist without some risk-taking ... Every democratic society is asked to balance between the need to defend the lives and security of its citizens, and the continuing need to protect and defend human rights. This "balance" does not mean that in order to protect human rights we must take risks that may cause injuries to innocent people. A society wishing to safeguard its democratic values, seeking to continue to keep its democratic nature in times of war and terror, is not entitled to prefer the right to life in any case in which such right conflicts with the protection of human rights. Rather, a democratic society is required to be engaged in the multifaceted task of balancing between the competing values. Such a balance, by its own nature, includes both components of risk and components of probability ... Naturally, unreasonable risks should not be taken. A democracy should not commit suicide in order to protect the human rights of its citizens. Democracy, rather, should defend itself and fight for its own existence and values. But such protection and such combat should be done in a manner that would not deny us our essential democratic nature.[56]

---

[55] See *Adalah* v. *Minister of Interior*, above note 53, at para. 93 (Barak, P.).
[56] *Ibid.*, para. 111 (Barak, P.).

Thus, proportionality provides a full account of democracy's multifaceted nature. Accordingly, it may be used as a proper criterion for the limitation of constitutional rights.

7.   An assessment of democracy as a source of proportionality

The conclusion that proportionality can be derived from the notion of democracy is based on five assumptions. All five appear legally sound. The last assumption – that limitation clauses are based upon proportionality – raises two separate questions. First, is proportionality the only way to guarantee the protection of constitutional rights? In other words, are there no other measures, other than proportionality, which guarantee the proper balancing between majority rule (the formal facet of democracy) and human rights (the substantive facet of democracy)? If the answer is that proportionality is the only way to guarantee a proper balance between the different facets of democracy, then a second question arises: What are the components of proportionality, and are all these components necessary to ensure its proper function? The discussion surrounding these questions will be held during the discussion of the pros and cons of proportionality.[57] For now, it is sufficient to say that, while proportionality is not the only way to realize constitutional rights, it is by far the best way available. This assertion requires proof – something I attempt to establish in the last part of this book.

C.   Proportionality and the rule of law

1.   The German approach

Many in the academic world in Germany – as well as the courts – are of the opinion that the concept of proportionality should be derived from the notion of *Rechtsstaat*.[58] This term is commonly translated into English as "the Rule of Law," and into French as "Etat de Droit."[59] All these

---

[57] See below, at 457 and below at 481.
[58] See K. Stern, "Zur Entstehung und Ableitung des Übermassverbots," in P. Badura and R. Scholz (eds.), *Wege und Verfahren des Verfassungslebens: Festschrift für Peter Lerche zum 65 Geburstag* (Munich: C. H. Beck, 1993), 165; H. Dreier, *GG Grundgesetz Kommentar* (Tübingen: Mohr Siebeck, 2006), 256.
[59] See R. Grote, "Rule of Law, Rechtsstaat and Etat de Droit," in C. Starck (ed.), *Constitutionalism, Universalism and Democracy – A Comparative Analysis* (Baden-Baden: Nomos, 1999), 269.

terms – which are not identical[60] – are complex. Much has been written about their meaning,[61] but the picture is not yet clear. Here, I focus on the German notion of *Rechtsstaat*.[62] This principle is mentioned in the Basic Law for the Federal Republic of Germany with regard to the constitutions of the states (*Länder*) that make up the German Federation (*Bund*).[63] The principle, however, is not explicitly mentioned with regard to constitutional rights at the federal level. The prevailing notion is that the principle of the rule of law is implied by the entirety of the Basic Law's provisions, and may also be derived directly from the notion of democracy mentioned explicitly by the Basic Law.[64]

This view – that the rule of law is one of the reasons for considering proportionality as a proper criterion for the constitutionality of

---

[60] See Van der Schyff, above note 38, at 5. See also L. Blaau, "The Rechtsstaat Idea Compared with the Rule of Law as a Paradigm for Protecting Rights," 107 *S. African L. J.* 76 (1990); E. W. Böckenförde, *State, Society and Liberty: Studies in Political Theory and Constitutional Law* (New York: Berg Publishing Ltd., 1991), 47; G. L. Neuman, "The US Constitutional Conception of the Rule of Law and the Rechtsstaatsprinzip of the Grundgesetz," in U. Battis, P. Kuing, I. Pernice, and A. Randeizhofer (eds.), *Das Grundgesetz im Prozess Europäischer und Globaler Verfassungsentwicklung* (Berlin: Nomos, 2000), 253.

[61] See J. Raz, *The Authority of Law: Essays on Law and Morality* (Oxford: Clarendon Press, 1979), 210; A. C. Hutchinson and P. J. Monahan, *The Rule of Law: Ideal or Ideology* (Toronto: Carswell, 1987); I. Shapiro (ed.), *The Rule of Law: Nomos XXXVI* (New York University Press, 1995); R. H. Fallon, "The Rule of Law as a Concept in Constitutional Discourse," 97 *Colum. L. Rev.* 1 (1997); R. A. Cass, *The Rule of Law in America* (Baltimore, MD: Johns Hopkins University Press, 2001); H. Botha, "The Legitimacy of Legal Orders (3): Rethinking the Rule of Law," 64 *Tydskrif vir Hedendaagse Romeins-Hollandse Reg* 523 (2001); M. Neumann (ed.), *The Rule of Law: Politicizing Ethics* (2002); J. M. Maravall and A. Przeworski (eds.), *Democracy and the Rule of Law* (2003); B. Z. Tamanaha, *On the Rule of Law: History, Politics, Theory* (Cambridge University Press, 2004); A. Czarnota, M. Krygier, and W. Sadurski (eds.), *Rethinking the Rule of Law after Communism* (2005); P. W. Hogg and C. F. Zwibel, "The Rule of Law in the Supreme Court of Canada," 55 *U. Toronto L. J.* 715 (2005); F. Michelman, "The Rule of Law, Legality and the Supremacy of the Constitution," in S. Woolman, M. Bishop, and J. Brickhill (eds.), *Constitutional Law of South Africa*, 2nd edn. (Cape Town: Juta Law Publishers, looseleaf, 2002–) ; T. R. S. Allan, "The Rule of Law, as Liberal Justice," 56 *U. Toronto L. J.* 283 (2006); P. Costa and D. Zolo (eds.), *The Rule of Law: History, Theory and Criticism* (2007); J. Waldron, "The Concept and the Rule of Law," 43 *Ga. L. Rev.* 1 (2008); M. Loughlin, *Foundations of Public Law* (Oxford University Press, 2010), 312; J. Goldsworthy, *Parliamentary Sovereignty: Contemporary Debates* (Cambridge University Press, 2010), 61.

[62] See Grote, above note 59; see Dreier, above note 58, at 175.

[63] See Basic Law for the Federal Republic of Germany, Art. 28(1) ("The constitutional order in the *Länder* must conform to the principles of a republican, democratic and social state governed by the rule of law …").

[64] See D. P. Currie, *The Constitution of the Federal Republic of Germany* (The University of Chicago Press, 1994), 309.

sub-constitutional law that limits constitutional rights – was also adopted by other legal systems.[65] Israel, too, has adopted a similar view.[66]

Is it appropriate to derive the concept of proportionality from the principle of the rule of law? In order to answer this question properly we should conduct a similar examination to the one we held in determining whether proportionality could be derived from the notion of democracy:[67] First, we have to examine whether the rule-of-law principle has a constitutional status. Second, we have to examine whether, as a constitutional principle, the rule of law includes a facet of human rights. Third, we have to examine whether the rule of law, as a constitutional principle, is based upon a balance between constitutional rights and their limitations. Fourth, we have to determine that such a balance is conducted through the use of limitation clauses (general or specific, explicit or implicit), which allow for the limitation of a constitutional right through sub-constitutional laws (statute or the common law). Fifth, we have to establish an opinion on whether limitation clauses, which advance the principle of the rule of law, are based on proportionality. These five questions will now be examined. Due to the similarity between the analysis of the different assumptions regarding the rule of law and the analysis of these same assumptions regarding democracy, an attempt will be made not to repeat things that have already been said.

2. First assumption: the rule of law has a constitutional status

The principle of the rule of law plays a central role in the laws of most modern democracies. However, does it have a constitutional status? This question has a simple, affirmative answer in those cases where the constitution itself declares that explicitly. Thus, for example, the Portuguese Constitution (1976) states explicitly that the Portuguese Republic is a democratic state "based on the rule of law" (*estado de direito*).[68] Similarly, the Spanish Constitution (1978) declares that Spain is a social and democratic state, "subject to the rule of law" (*estado de derecho*).[69] The

---

[65] See M. Fordham and T. de la Mare, "Identifying the Principle of Proportionality," in J. Jowell and J. Cooper (eds.), *Understanding Human Rights Principles* (Portland, OR: Hart Publishing, 2001), 27.

[66] See HCJ 3477/95 *Ben-Atiya v. Minister of Education, Culture and Sport* [1995] IsrSC 49(5) 1, 12.

[67] See above, at 213.   [68] Constitution of Portugal, Art. 2.

[69] Constitution of Spain, Art. 1(1).

Constitution of the Republic of South Africa declares that South Africa is a sovereign and democratic state founded, among others, on the values of "[s]upremacy of the constitution and the rule of law."[70] In those legal systems where the constitution refers explicitly to the rule of law, those provisions are viewed as having a constitutional operative effect and not merely of a declaratory nature.[71]

But what is the case when a constitution does not explicitly refer to the rule of law? The answer to this question varies from one legal system to another and from one court (supreme or constitutional) to the next. Thus, for example, the German Constitutional Court has recognized the principle of the rule of law (*Rechtsstaat*) as having constitutional status. The court arrived at this conclusion after reading the provisions of the Basic Law as one whole text,[72] while paying particular attention to Germany's democratic nature.[73] Similarly, the Supreme Court of Canada has determined that the principle of the rule of law is a fundamental principle having a constitutional status.[74] The Supreme Court of India has adopted a similar view, while noting that the rule of law is "clearly a basic and essential feature of the Constitution."[75] In the United States, Tribe has emphasized that the principle of the rule of law, while not explicitly mentioned by the American Constitution, is one of its basic tenets. He writes:

> The proposition that ours is a government of laws, not men – that we live under the "rule of law" – ... is a principle that, by just about any imaginable account, would have to be reckoned part of our Constitution.[76]

---

[70] Constitution of the Republic of South Africa, Art. 1(c); *Pharmaceutical Manufacturers Association of South Africa: In re Ex parte Application of the President of the Republic of South Africa*, 2000 (2) SA 674 § 40; F. Michelman, "The Rule of Law, Legality and the Supremacy of the Constitution," in S. Woolman, M. Bishop, and J. Brickhill (eds.), *Constitutional Law of South Africa*, 2nd edn. (Cape Town: Juta Law Publishers, looseleaf, 2002–), 11-1.

[71] See *Dawood* v. *Minister of Home Affairs*, 2000 (3) SA 936 (CC).

[72] See Dreier, above note 58, at 256; BVerfGE 2, 380 (403).

[73] See V. Götz, "Legislative and Executive Power under the Constitutional Requirements Entailed in the Principle of the Rule of Law," in C. Starck (ed.), *New Challenges to the German Basic Law* (Baden-Baden: Nomos, 1991), 141.

[74] See *Re Manitoba Language Rights* [1985] 1 SCR 721, 752; *Reference re Remuneration of Judges of the Provincial Court* (PEI) [1997] 3 SCR 3; M. D. Walters, "The Common Law Constitution in Canada: Return of Lex Non Scripta as Fundamental Law," 51 *U. Toronto L. J.* 91 (2001); M. Walters, "Written Constitutions and Unwritten Constitutionalism," in G. Huscroft (ed.), *Expounding the Constitution: Essays in Constitutional Theory* (Cambridge University Press, 2008), 245; see Goldsworthy, above note 61, at 277.

[75] *Sambamurthy* v. *State of Andhra Pradesh*, AIR 1987 S.C. 66.

[76] Tribe, above note 26, at 84. See also P. R. Verkuil, "The American Constitutional Tradition of Shared and Separated Powers: Separation of Powers, the Rule of Law and the Idea of Independence," 30 *Wm. and Mary L. Rev.* 301 (1989).

Is the rule of law a principle with constitutional status in Israel? The answer is yes. The Israeli legal system recognizes several basic constitutional principles which, although not written explicitly into the Basic Laws, are nevertheless written between their lines. One of these principles – alongside the separation of powers and the independence of the judiciary – is the principle of the rule of law.[77]

3.   Second assumption: the rule of law includes human rights

Much like the concept of democracy,[78] the principle of the "rule of law" has several meanings.[79] Its content may change in accordance with the user's tradition. All agree that the principle contains both formal aspects (the "formal rule of law") and jurisprudential aspects (the "jurisprudential rule of law"). Both aspects delineate the principle of legality. According to both aspects, formal and jurisprudential, the "rule of law" is "the law of rules."[80] This assertion immediately raises the difficult question of whether Hitler's Germany, or Apartheid South Africa, were legal systems governed by the rule of law. A negative answer to this question requires a more comprehensive understanding of the principle of the rule of law; one that demands, in addition to the formal and jurisprudential aspect, a substantive aspect of the principle.[81] This is the most controversial part of the rule of law. There is no consensus regarding its precise content; but those who agree that the rule of law includes a substantive aspect agree that one of the main tenets of the substantive aspect of the rule of law is the recognition and protection of human rights.

Such substantive aspects of the rule of law were adopted in Germany after the Second World War.[82] The constitutional view accepted in Germany is that the principle of a rule of law state (*Rechtsstaatsprinzip*), derived from the interpretation of the Basic Law, has a strong substantive aspect.[83] Such an approach was adopted by other democracies as well. Principles such as the separation of powers, the judiciary's independence and the right to access the courts (in both public and private matters) are

[77] See *Chadash-Ta'al Party* v. *Chairman of Knesset Election Committee Knesset*, above at 54.

[78] See above, at 218.   [79] See Barak, above note 28, at 51.

[80] See A. Scalia, "The Rule of Law as a Law of Rules," 56 *U. Chi. L. Rev.* 1175 (1989).

[81] See Blaau, above note 60.

[82] See Grote, above note 59, at 285; Dreier, above note 58, at 256. See also N. Emiliou, *The Principle of Proportionality in European Law: A Comparative Study* (London: Kluwer Law International, 1996), 40.

[83] See Grote, above note 59, at 270.

all considered derivatives of such a substantive rule-of-law principle.[84] The substantive aspect also includes the notion that the constitutional provisions apply to all state actions. Thus, for example, the view that a presidential pardon is an act of personal charity by the president may not be properly squared with the notion of a substantive rule of law. The granting (or denial) of a pardon are state actions, made by the president, and therefore the relevant constitutional provisions apply.[85] Similarly, any statutes enacted by parliament must comply with the provisions of the constitution; a law in conflict with the constitution is void, and the courts are authorized to declare it as such. Judicial review on the constitutionality of the statute, therefore, also derives from the substantive aspect of the rule-of-law principle. The same is true for the non-delegation doctrine, which prevents the legislator from delegating the task of promulgating primary arrangements to the executive branch.[86] Needless to say, the subordination of the executive branch to both the constitution and all the statutes enacted in pursuance thereof may also be derived from the substantive aspect of the rule-of-law principle. The constitutional basis for judicial review of administrative actions may also be derived from the substantive aspect of the rule of law. Also, if the executive branch violates its obligations under the constitution or under statute, the victims of such violations may be entitled to a remedy even if the executive action was carried out without fault (e.g., without negligence or intent). Finally, and above all, the substantive aspect of the rule of law strives to ensure several justice-related values, primarily the recognition and protection of human rights.[87] As Emiliou has correctly noted:

> Substantive rule of law requires the realization of a just legal order. Above all it subjects state power to substantive, definite and unamendable constitutional principles and material basic values. The emphasis of state activity should not be primarily on the establishment of a scheme of formal guarantee of freedom. It should rather be on the attainment, preservation and award of substantive justice within the sphere of the state and those spheres susceptible to state influence. The Grundgesetz does not consider the state as a value in itself. The state gains its value by securing the liberty of the people.[88]

[84] See Dreier, above note 58.
[85] See Currie, above note 64. See also *President of the Republic of South Africa* v. *Hugo*, 1997 (4) SA 1 (CC).
[86] See above, at 112.
[87] See U. Karpen, "Rule of Law," in U. Karpen (ed.), *The Constitution of the Federal Republic of Germany* (Baden-Baden: Nomos, 1988), 169, 178.
[88] Emiliou, above note 82, at 41.

The rule of law is not merely the law of rules. A similar view was adopted by the Supreme Court of India.[89] The Court premised the concept of judicial review on a rule of law foundation, and ruled that the rule of law means the rule of liberty. In Israel's legal culture the principle of the rule of law is understood as containing an element of the proper protection of human rights.[90]

4. Third assumption: the rule of law is based on a balance between constitutional rights and the public interest

The substantive aspect of the rule of law – much like the substantive aspect of democracy – is not made up entirely of the protection of constitutional rights.[91] Rather, the rule-of-law principle is a result of a proper balance between all its aspects. It is based, therefore, on a proper balance between constitutional rights and conflicting principles – including the public interest. This is the prevailing view today across modern constitutional democracies.[92] As Justice Khanna of the Indian Supreme Court has stated:

> Rule of law is now the accepted norm in all civilian societies ... Everywhere it is identified with the liberty of the individual. It seeks to maintain a balance between the opposing notions of individual liberty and public order.[93]

5. Fourth assumption: the balancing is conducted through limitation clauses

Much like the balancing between different aspects of democracy,[94] the balancing between the different aspects of the rule of law is conducted through the use of limitation clauses which determine the constitutionality of rights limitation by sub-constitutional laws. This result is not

---

[89] See M. P. Jain, *Indian Constitutional Law*, 5th edn. (Haryana, India: LexisNexis Butterworths Wadhwa, 2003), 9.

[90] HCJ 428/86 *Barzilai v. Government of Israel* [1986] IsrSC 40(3) 505, 622; HCJ 6163/92 *Eisenberg v. Minister of Building and Housing* [1992–4] IsrLR 19.

[91] See above, at 220.

[92] See Böckenförde, above note 60, at 66; Emiliou, above note 82, at 41; D. P. Kommers, *The Constitutional Jurisprudence of the Federal Republic of Germany*, 2nd edn. (Durham, NC: Duke University Press, 1997), 36.

[93] *A. D. M. Jabalpur v. S. Shuka*, AIR 1976 SC 1207, 1254, 1263.

[94] See above, at 221.

surprising, considering the close relationship between democracy and the rule of law.[95] Indeed, the formal and substantive aspects of democracy resemble the formal and substantive aspects of the rule of law. The main difference is in the level of abstraction, as the formal aspect of the rule of law is but one of formal democracy's components, while the substantive aspect of the rule of law is but one of substantive democracy's components.

6.   Fifth assumption: limitation clauses are based on proportionality

What should be the content of a limitation clause which properly balances the different aspects of the rule of law? The answer is that the sub-constitutional law limiting the constitutional right should be proportional. Generally, such an answer is warranted by the different aspects of the rule of law and those of the notion of democracy. If, indeed, proportionality may be derived from democracy,[96] it should also fit the principle of the rule of law. In a more specific sense, proportionality may be derived directly from the principle of the rule of law. The rule of law includes, as we have seen, both formal and substantive aspects, in a state of constant tension. The solution for this tension should be proportional, in that it should recognize both formal and substantive aspects while balancing both proportionally. Such a balance would have to recognize, on the one hand, the need to realize the will of the majority as expressed by the legislative body, and, on the other, the proportional limitations on such power by the majority.

Such an approach was adopted in Germany by constitutional commentators and the courts. According to this approach, proportionality is derived from the rule of law.[97] As Currie summarizes: "Proportionality is now commonly understood to be one aspect of the *Rechtsstaat* principle."[98] Such an approach is not limited to constitutional law, but can also be found in Germany's administrative law.[99]

---

[95] See above, at 221.   [96] See above, at 214.

[97] See Karpen, above note 87, at 177. See also J. Kokott, "From Reception and Transplantation to Convergence of Constitutional Models in the Age of Globalization – With Particular Reference to the German Basic Law," in C. Starck (ed.), *Constitutionalism, Universalism, and Democracy – A Comparative Analysis: The German Contributions to the Fifth World Congress of the International Association of Constitutional Law* (Berlin: Nomos Verlagsgesellschaft, 1999), 71, 98.

[98] Currie, above note 64, at 309. See also L. Hirschberg, *Der Grundsatz der Verhältnismässigkeit* (Göttingen: Schwarz, 1980).

[99] See also G. Nolte, "General Principles of German and European Administrative Law – A Comparison in Historical Perspective," 57 *Mod. L. Rev.* 191, 201 (1994); Emiliou,

234 PROPORTIONALITY: SOURCES, NATURE, FUNCTION

7. An assessment of rule of law as a source of proportionality

The remarks made regarding the concept of democracy as a legal source of proportionality[100] surely apply *mutatis mutandis* to the principle of the rule of law as a legal source of proportionality. Indeed, the close connection between democracy and the rule of law turns that principle into a special source of proportionality. The authority of proportionality exists due to, as well as is operated by, the very concept of democracy. According to this view, the principle of the rule of law adds nothing to proportionality. Naturally, however, in those legal systems that do not subscribe to the notion of a close connection between democracy (in both its formal and substantive aspects) and the rule of law (both formal and substantive), one should carefully separate considerations of democracy and considerations regarding the rule of law. Further, even if the rule of law serves as a legal source of proportionality, this alone does not mean that proportionality is the only way to realize the rule of law. However, it is the best way available. This assertion requires proof. The last part of this book will attempt to supply this proof.[101]

D. Proportionality as intrinsic to the conflict between legal principles

The third argument regarding proportionality focuses on the fact that most human rights are legally structured as principles rather than rules.[102] Similarly, the legal structure of many of the considerations justifying limitations on those rights – such as the public interest and the rights of others – is also that of principles. We are facing, therefore, a state

---

above note 82, at 41: "The underlying paradox of democracy based on the rule of law is that freedom requires the observance of certain rules; rules, however, threaten liberty. Ironically the state's very attempt to maximize freedom can result in the opposite effect of minimizing the freedom of the citizen. The answer of the liberal rule of law to this problem is to leave to the individual as much liberty as possible, guaranteed by basic rights, democratic participation and separation of state function. The principle of proportionality, which constitutes a substantive element of the rule of law has an important role to play in this context. Nobody should unduly restrict basic human rights; one should interfere with individual rights only if, and to the extent that it is, strictly necessary to satisfy a compelling public interest. Limits on individual freedom demand justification in terms of either community or individual values meriting legal protection (*Rechtsgüter*)." See also Grote, above note 59, at 290: "The Constitutional Court has explicitly linked the principle of proportionality to the concept of '*Rechtsstaat*'".

[100] See above, at 226.   [101] See below, at 457.   [102] See above, at 38.

of conflict between several constitutional principles. As previously mentioned, the solution to such a conflict is not through the declaration of one principle as the "victor," while excluding the other from the constitutional framework.[103] Rather, the solution lies in the proper balancing between the conflicting principles. Such balancing is the very foundation of the rules of proportionality. When the conflicting principles are of constitutional status, the concept of proportionality – which balances them – is of constitutional status as well.

This argument was made by Alexy, the most astute thinker in this field.[104] Alexy begins with the following premise:

> [P]rinciples are norms which require that something be realized to the greatest extent possible given the legal and factual possibilities. Principles are optimization requirements, characterized by the fact that they can be satisfied to varying degrees, and that the appropriate degree of satisfaction depends not only on what is factually possible but also on what is legally possible.[105]

Defining principles as such, Alexy next arrives at the conclusion that a conflict between principles – as opposed to a conflict between rules – requires the balancing of these conflicting principles. Such balancing is conducted based on the relative "weight" of these principles at the precise point of conflict.

How is balancing conducted at the precise point of conflict between principles? According to Alexy, it is conducted based on the rules of proportionality. This is not surprising, considering Alexy's view on the relationship between principles in general and the principle of proportionality:

> [T]here is a connection between the theory of principles and the principle of proportionality. This connection is as close as it could possibly be. The nature of principles implies the principle of proportionality and vice versa.[106]

---

[103] See above, at 87.

[104] See R. Alexy, "Individual Rights and Collective Goods," in C. Nino (ed.), *Rights* (New York University Press, 1992), 163; R. Alexy, "On the Structure of Legal Principles," 13 *Ratio Juris* 294 (2000); R. Alexy, *A Theory of Constitutional Rights* (J. Rivers trans., Oxford University Press, 2002 [1986]); R. Alexy, "Constitutional Rights Balancing and Rationality," 16 *Ratio Juris* 131 (2003).

[105] See Alexy, *A Theory of Constitutional Rights*, above note 104, at 47. See also above, at 87.

[106] See Alexy, *A Theory of Constitutional Rights*, above note 104, at 66.

According to Alexy, each of the three components of proportionality (rational connection, necessary means, and proportionality *stricto sensu*) is essential to an understanding of the constitutional principle, and, therefore, to the solution of the conflict between the several principles.

Alexy defines a principle as a legal norm requiring that some goal be realized to the greatest extent possible given the legal and factual possibilities. The taking into account of these "legal and factual possibilities" – which constitutes a part of the definition of the principle itself – reflects the notion of proportionality. Thus, taking into account the factual circumstances – which, again, are part of the definition itself – is reflected by the components of rational connection and of necessity. The rational connection component is required because, without a rational connection, the means used to achieve the proper purpose would have to be left out of the equation. The necessity component is required because, if we could use a means that would limit the right less, we should choose it over the one offered. In that way, other principles would be less limited. The legal possibilities are weighed by proportionality *stricto sensu*, which conducts the balance between the conflicting principles. As Alexy puts it:

> The principle of proportionality in its narrow sense, that is, the requirement of balancing, derives from its relation to the legally possible. If a constitutional rights norm which is a principle competes with another principle, then the legal possibilities for realizing that norm depend on the competing principle. To reach a decision, one needs to engage in a balancing exercise as required by the Law of Competing Principles. Since the application of valid principles, if indeed they are applicable, is required, and since their application in a case of competing principles requires a balancing exercise, the character of the constitutional rights norms as principles implies that when they compete with other principles, a balancing exercise becomes necessary. But this means that the principle of proportionality in its narrow sense can be deduced from the character of constitutional rights norms as principles.[107]

Alexy's approach to the concept of proportionality begins from his definition of the notion of principle. A separate definition of the principle is likely to lead to a different conclusion relating to proportionality.[108] According to my approach,[109] a principle is made up of fundamental values. These values reflect ideals seeking their maximum realization.

---

[107] *Ibid.*, at 67.
[108] See K. Möller, "Balancing and the Structure of Constitutional Rights," 3 *Int'l J. Const. L.* 453 (2007).
[109] See above, at 40.

They may not be realized. When one principle conflicts with another (for example, when freedom of expression conflicts with public order, or with one's right to enjoy a good reputation) a balance should be struck between the two. According to this approach, the act of balancing does not constitute a part of the definition of the notion of principle, but rather contains an external activity. Despite this, Alexy's approach is acceptable to the extent that he argues that a conflict between principles may explain the concept of proportionality. Indeed, our legal universe is full of conflicting principles, and nothing could be more natural than the constant search for the proper criterion to resolve those conflicts. Such criterion would be the product of the constant struggle, or conflict, between the different legal principles. Unlike Alexy, however, I do not see proportionality as part of the definition of the notion of a legal principle. Furthermore, I do not share the opinion that proportionality is the only way to resolve the conflict between legal principles.[110] Unlike Alexy, I am not of the opinion that proportionality affects the scope of the constitutional right.[111] Proportionality is aimed only at determining the constitutionality of the sub-constitutional law, namely, the realization of the right – not its scope. Common to this approach is Alexy's approach that proportionality is a key criterion in solving the constant conflicts between legal principles.

Unlike Alexy's approach, the one presented herein does not stem from a definition of a principle, and therefore does not affect the principle's scope but merely its realization, or the extent of the right's protection. In fact, as previously suggested, this approach recognizes that proportionality is not the only way to determine the extent of that protection; there are other ways to do so.[112] Accordingly, it is my task – my burden – to prove that proportionality is the best criterion to solve a conflict between constitutional principles – a conflict which is realized at the sub-constitutional level. This book will attempt to do so during the discussion in the last part of the book, in the part dedicated to an assessment of proportionality.[113]

A special issue arises as to those constitutional rights that are constructed as rules. The explanation offered for principles does not apply here. However, the concept of proportionality should apply even in those cases where the right is constructed as a rule and is limited by a sub-constitutional law.[114] The justification and the basis for that view do not arise from principle theory, but from one of the other explanations offered

---

[110] See Möller, above note 108.
[111] See above, at 41.   [112] *Ibid.*
[113] See below, at 457.   [114] See above, at 150.

earlier on, particularly the one dealing with the relation between proportionality and interpretation. This explanation will now be examined.

E.   Proportionality and interpretation

Democracy, the rule of law, and principle theory are not the only possible sources upon which to establish proportionality. Another source is the constitution itself and its interpretation.[115] This view has been adopted by several legal systems, including Germany, Canada, Spain, and Israel.

Constitutional interpretation approaches the text generously.[116] It aspires to achieve constitutional harmony. It adopts a holistic view of the constitution. The different parts of the constitution are deemed interconnected.[117] Together, they establish constitutional unity. This unity is based on fundamental values, and those values inspire the interpretation of the constitutional text. The fundamental provisions upon which the constitution is based create an objective hierarchy of values.[118] According to this hierarchical order, constitutional rights constitute the objective values upon which the constitution is built. These objective values – and the values that limit them – are a central feature of the objective constitutional structure.[119] As the German Constitutional Court noted in *Luth*:

> The Basic Law is not a value-neutral document ... Its section on basic rights establishes an objective order of values, and this order strongly reinforces the effective power of basic rights.[120]

The different values that together constitute the objective constitutional order tend to conflict with one another. For each principle, it is possible to find an opposing principle. This conflict's resolution is found not by emphasizing the distinguishing features of each principle, but by forming a synthesis between the different principles and creating internal har-

---

[115] See Pulido, above note 1, at 508.
[116] See above, at 69.
[117] See R. Smend, *Verfassung und Verfassungsrecht* (Munich: Duncker & Humblot, 1928). See also Kommers, above note 92, at 45; and above, at 70.
[118] See K. H. Friauf, "Techniques for the Interpretation of Constitutions in German Law," in *Proceedings of the Fifth International Symposium on Comparative Law* (1968), 12; below at 276.
[119] See D. Grimm, "The Protective Function of the State," in G. Nolte (ed.), *European and US Constitutionalism* (Cambridge University Press, 2005).
[120] BVerfGE 7, 198 (translated by Kommers, above note 92, at 363). See also below, at 276 and below, at 427.

mony between them. All these may be achieved by using the concept of proportionality. As noted by Hesse:

> The principle of constitutional unity requires an optimization of con-
> flicting values. The limitations on these values should be such that each
> value may achieve its own optimal effect. Accordingly, in each concrete
> case, those limitations must abide by the requirements of proportional-
> ity. Thus, these limitations should require no more than is necessary to
> achieve unity between the conflicting values.[121]

Indeed, resolving the conflict between the different constitutional rights – as well as between them and other competing constitutional values – through the concept of proportionality, helps maintain the unity of the constitution.

Alexy has opined that constitutional proportionality creates a deriva-tive constitutional rule that narrows, in each specific case, the constitu-tional scope of the conflicting principles.[122] Such an approach does not fully maintain the notion of constitutional unity, since the derivative constitutional rule keeps reducing the scope of the conflicting princi-ples. In contrast, my approach – which acknowledges the effect of the derivative constitutional rule only at the sub-constitutional level[123] – guarantees both maximum harmony and constitutional unity. The conflict between constitutional principles at the constitutional level creates no legal consequences at that level. Instead, the legal conse-quences occur only at the sub-constitutional level (statute or the com-mon law).[124]

The interpretive approach views proportionality as part of the consti-tution as a result of the interpretation of the entire constitution as a whole. At times proportionality may be derived directly from the explicit text of the constitution. At other times it may be derived from its implicit text. In both cases, however, we are dealing with a constitutional-level doctrine that stems from the desire to ensure constitutional unity and harmony.[125] The operative effect of proportionality, as mentioned, is not at the consti-tutional level but only at the sub-constitutional level. This kind of effect may determine the constitutionality of a sub-constitutional law trying to limit a constitutional right.

---

[121] K. Hesse, *Grundzüge des Verfassungsrechts der Bundesrepublik Deutschland* (Heidelberg: Die Deutsche Bibliotek, 1999), 23.
[122] See above, at 41.   [123] See above, at 41.   [124] See above, at 89.
[125] See D. M. Beatty, *The Ultimate Rule of Law* (Oxford University Press, 2004), 176.

What is the relationship between the view presented above and interpretive balancing?[126] The main difference between the two lies in the different roles assigned to constitutional proportionality on the one hand and interpretive balancing on the other. Constitutional proportionality determines the legislative validity or compatibility of a sub-constitutional law (a statute or the common law) that limits a constitutional right. It does so while fully developing the concept of proportionality and its components. Interpretive balance, on the other hand, deals not with the question of validity but with that of meaning. It provides meaning to the text of the legal norm. The balance it carries out uses, by analogy, only one of the components used by proportionality, that of proportionality *stricto sensu*. It has no interest in proportionality's other components.

The interpretive explanation is of considerable weight. However, it does not explain fully why proportionality should be preferred over other criteria that also strive to achieve constitutional unity. That issue will be discussed in the last part of the book.

F.   Legal sources summary: is proportionality a logical necessity?

Democracy, the rule of law, principle theory, and constitutional interpretation are all legal sources from which proportionality may be derived as a constitutional concept. When the conflicting principles are of constitutional status and a question arises as to the legal validity of the limiting sub-constitutional law, each of those four sources – and all four of them combined – can establish the constitutional status of proportionality.[127] This is of utmost importance, both to the rights involved and for constitutional democracies in general.

Can those four legal sources offer concrete content to the concept of proportionality? Could proportionality *stricto sensu*, for example, be derived from any of them? Alexy's answer to this question is in the affirmative. His answer is the by-product of his definition of the term principle. This term, according to Alexy, inherently contains the concept of proportionality.[128] I do not share this view.[128] According to my approach, the components of proportionality Alexy discusses are possible but not necessary and therefore the way one legal system understands proportionality may

---

[126] On interpretive balancing, see above, at 72.
[127] See Alexy, *A Theory of Constitutional Rights*, above note 104, at 69.
[128] See above, at 40.

inspire another legal system, but nothing more. Proportionality is not an inherent part of the idea of a principle. It is external to it. When constitutional principles conflict, the conflict's resolution is not a part of the principles, but rather it is external to them. The conflict is resolved at a sub-constitutional level. The third part of this book analyzes the different components of proportionality as they are understood across several legal systems. The fourth part will evaluate the concept of proportionality. According to this approach, proportionality is one possible criterion – but not the only one – for evaluating the limitations of constitutional rights. Still, of all the existing criteria, proportionality is the most appropriate. This is an assertion that needs to be proved.

PART III

The components of proportionality

9

Proper purpose

A. The proper purpose as a component of proportionality

1. *The nature of the proper purpose and its sources*

i. The nature of the proper purpose

One of the main characteristics of a constitutional democracy is that legal authorization to limit a constitutional right is not sufficient. Legality[1] does not equal legitimacy. Rather, a constitutional democracy requires, in addition to legality, a justification for the limitation on the constitutional right to be valid. In other words, the legitimacy component is required.[2] This element is made up of the proper purpose and the means to achieve that purpose, which limit the constitutional right in a proper manner. This chapter discusses the first of these – the proper purpose component of proportionality.

The element of proper purpose reflects a value-laden component. It reflects the notion that not every purpose can justify a limitation on a constitutional right. One of the unique features of a constitutional right is that it can be limited only to realize such purposes that can justify a limitation of a constitutional right.[3] The purposes that justify limitations on human rights are derived from the values on which society is founded. In

---

[1] Regarding legality, see above, at 107.

[2] See G. Van der Schyff, *Limitation of Rights: A Study of the European Convention and the South African Bill of Rights* (Nijmegen, The Netherlands: Wolf Legal Publishers, 2005), 141.

[3] See HCJ 1661/05 *Gaza Coast Regional Council* v. *Knesset of Israel* [2005] IsrSC 59(2) 481, 548 ("The question of whether the purpose is 'proper' is examined in the context of the limitation of the human right protected by the Basic Law. The question we should be answering is whether a limitation of a human right can be justified by the proper purpose of the legislation in question ... Accordingly, legislation limiting human rights satisfies the requirement of 'proper purpose' only if the purpose of such legislation provides sufficient justification to the specific limitation of human rights." (Barak, P.)).

a constitutional democracy, these values are democratic values.[4] Indeed, a proper purpose is one that suits the values of the society in a constitutional democracy.

ii.   The sources of the proper purpose

The proper purpose requirement necessitates a constitutional foundation. This constitutional foundation may be explicit or implicit.[5] Examples of an explicit foundation can be found in the Canadian Charter of Rights and Freedoms,[6] the Constitution of the Republic of South Africa,[7] and Israel's Basic Law: Human Dignity and Liberty.[8]

The constitutional foundation for the proper purpose requirement can also be implicit in the constitution's provisions. An implicit foundation is constitutionally valid just as an explicit foundation is.[9] Such an implicit foundation is evident from the principles of democracy and the rule of law. From the constitutional notion of democracy and the rule of law, one can deduce both the importance of the need to protect human rights, as well as the importance of the need to limit those same rights in order both to safeguard them and to satisfy the public interest.

2.   Proper purpose as a threshold requirement

i.   The reason for threshold requirements

The proper purpose component examines whether a law (a statute or the common law) that limits a constitutional right is for a purpose that justifies such limitation.[10] This examination is carried out without considering the scope of the suggested limitation on the constitutional right, the means used to achieve such a purpose, or the relationship between the benefit in achieving that purpose and the harm incurred by the constitutional right. Rather, this is a threshold examination. It focuses on the law's

---

[4] See Van der Schyff, above note 2, at 145.
[5] See above, at 53. See also Van der Schyff, above note 2, at 146.
[6] Canadian Charter of Rights and Freedoms, Part I of the Constitution Act 1982, Section 1 ("demostrably justified in a free and democratic society").
[7] Constitution of the Republic of South Africa, Art. 36 ("reasonable and justifiable in an open and democratic society based on human dignity, equality and freedom").
[8] See Israeli Basic Law: Human Dignity and Liberty, Art. 8 (befitting the values of the state of Israel, enacted for a proper purpose).
[9] See above, at 53.
[10] M. Kumm, "What Do You Have in Virtue of Having a Constitutional Right?: On the Place and Limits of the Proportionality Requirement" (New York University Law School, Public Law Research, Paper No. 06-41, 2006).

purpose rather than its consequences. Such an examination seeks to provide an answer to the threshold question of whether, in a constitutional democracy, a constitutional right can be limited to realize the purpose underlying the limiting law. The examination, therefore, does not conduct any balancing between the benefit to society should the law be allowed to proceed and the harm caused to the right due to that same law. Such balancing is conducted within other components of proportionality.

ii.   Hogg's opposing view

According to Hogg, "a judgment that the effects of the law were too severe would surely mean that the objective was *not* sufficiently important to justify limiting a Charter right."[11] Accordingly, Hogg concludes that the component of proportionality *stricto sensu*[12] is unnecessary, as the balancing between the benefit in realizing the purpose underlying the law and the harm caused to the right in question is carried out within the framework of the first component – that of a proper purpose:

> If the objective is sufficiently important, and the objective is pursued by the least drastic means, then it must follow that the effects of the law are an acceptable price to pay for the benefit of the law. I conclude, therefore, that an affirmative answer to the first step – sufficiently important objective – will always yield an affirmative answer to the fourth step – proportionate effect.[13]

iii.   A reply to Hogg

Hogg's view is unacceptable.[14] Nor is it accepted in comparative law.[15] We must differentiate between two questions: the first, what are the purposes that may justify, in a democracy, a limitation of a constitutional right; the other is whether a law designed to realize such a purpose properly balances between the benefit to society caused by the law and the harm it may cause to the constitutional right. In order to answer the first question we should set the proper criteria to examine which purposes would justify a limitation on a human right. These purposes are determined by

---

[11] P. W. Hogg, *Constitutional Law of Canada*, 5th edn., vol. II (Toronto: Thomson Carswell, 2007), 153.

[12] On proportionality *stricto sensu*, see below, at 340.

[13] Hogg, above note 11.

[14] See L. E. Trakman, W. Cole-Hamilton, and S. Gatien, "R. v. Oakes 1986–1997. Back to the Drawing Board," 36 *Osgoode Hall L. J.* 83 (1998). See also Justice Lamer in *Dagenais v. Canadian Broadcasting Corporation* [1994] 3 SCR 835.

[15] See, e.g., D. Grimm, "Proportionality in Canadian and German Constitutional Jurisprudence," 57 *U. Toronto L. J.* 383 (2007).

each society's values, and may vary, within a given society, from one right to another. In order to answer the second question we should determine whether the realization of the purpose underlying the law may justify the amount of harm caused to the constitutional right. Such criteria are determined by the other components of proportionality and those of proportionality *stricto sensu* in particular.[16]

Contrary to Hogg, the understanding of the proper purpose component as a threshold requirement protects human rights adequately. Such an approach draws a clear line between considerations that can justify limitations on human rights and considerations that cannot.[17] Beyond this line, no considerations should be examined, and the rest of proportionality's components would not be triggered. This approach may also be derived from considerations of separation of powers. Those considerations provide, in the present context, the granting of a wide discretion to the legislator in devising the purposes it seeks to realize.[18] When a court determines that a statute is unconstitutional by virtue of a limitation that failed to properly balance between the benefits caused by realizing the purpose and the harm caused to the right in question by the same legislation, then it would be wrong to assume that the purpose sought by the legislator, in and of itself, is unconstitutional. A court opinion rendering a law unconstitutional does not necessarily mean that the purpose chosen by the legislator is unconstitutional. That purpose may have been – and thus remains – proper, but such a purpose cannot be realized through the means chosen by the legislator, as these were disproportional with regard to the harm caused to the constitutional right in question. In these kinds of cases, therefore, it is not the purpose's nature giving rise to the constitutional issue, but rather the disproportionality of the means chosen to achieve that purpose. The lack of proportionality does not turn the purpose into an "improper" one; the conflict with the constitutional provision is not a matter of purpose but rather of the means chosen to achieve that purpose, means that limit the constitutional right in a disproportional manner.

Take, for example, a law limiting freedom of expression in order to protect national security. At this stage of the constitutional review, the only question requiring an answer is whether in principle we can – in light

[16] A similar (though not identical) distinction is drawn between the scope of the constitutional right and the extent of its protection. See below, at 340.

[17] See R. Pildes, "Dworkin's Two Conceptions of Rights," 29 *J. Legal Studies* 309 (2000).

[18] See below, at 401.

of the requirement that the law should serve a "proper purpose" – limit one person's right to freedom of expression in order to protect national security interests. A separate question – not considered at this stage – is: what is the scope of the limitation on freedom of expression that the purpose of national security can justify? An answer to this separate question requires a balancing between the benefits gained by the realization of the security purpose and the harm caused to the right in question. Such balancing, however, should not be conducted prematurely; it should not be carried out within the confines of the proper purpose component. Rather, it should be done in the next stages of proportionality, particularly the stage of proportionality *stricto sensu*.[19] Only at this later stage can we properly estimate the scope of a right's harm, and a balance be struck between that limitation and the benefits obtained by the limiting law. If at the end of the balancing process the result would be that no justification exists for this type of limitation on the right to freedom of expression, the purpose for which the law was enacted may still be "proper." Such a purpose would continue to be "proper" even if no means exist which would enable its complete realization.

A discussion of the constitutionality of the means while considering the appropriateness of the purpose chosen would be premature, and lack the required factual basis. Rather, we should first examine the legality of the law's purpose, while ignoring the means used to achieve that purpose. If there is no proper purpose, the law should be invalidated without further examination. Only after the law's purpose has been found to be "proper" can we continue to examine whether the means chosen to achieve that purpose are proper as well, and whether the relationship between the benefits of realizing the purpose and the harm caused to the right in question is proportional. Such an examination is not a part of the discussion of the law's purpose, but only its realization in practice.

B. The elements of proper purpose

1. The scope of the proper purpose

An examination of the purpose assumes the limitation of a constitutional right. Accordingly, the criteria used in determining the proper purpose should not be confused with that used for determining the right's scope. Moreover, the examination of the proper purpose does not include an

---

[19] See below, at 340.

examination of the extent of the limitation on the constitutional right. Indeed, the examination of the nature of the purpose is designed to answer the question of whether a constitutional democracy justifies a limitation on a constitutional right to realize that purpose. Here, two extreme views can be excluded:

> On the one hand, we should not deduce a presumption – in particular, a non-refutable presumption – wherein the purpose of each statute produced by the legislator is proper. If this was the accepted view the requirement for a proper purpose would turn into an exercise in futility ... But we should also object, on the other hand, to the view that a purpose is proper if and only if it does not limit any human right. This interpretation, too, turns the search for a proper purpose into an exercise in futility; the precise object of the examination is to determine which limitations on human rights are proper and which are not. An *ex ante* assumption that every limitation is not proper contradicts, therefore, the very essence of the search for a proper purpose, and therefore should not be adopted.[20]

Indeed, the issue in question is not whether a constitutional right can be limited. It is agreed upon that most rights are relative in nature and therefore can be limited.[21] Absolute rights are rare, and are only found in a limited number of constitutional rights such as the prohibition on slavery or torture.[22] The vast majority of constitutional rights are relative; i.e., they can be limited. The main difference between many Western constitutions lies in determining the exact protection granted to each of these constitutional rights. As far as the proper purpose component is concerned, the difference lies in determining which legal scenarios should be included within the "proper purposes" that may justify the limitation of a human right.

The discrepancy between the constitutions may be overstated. In fact, it is agreed upon that a limitation on one constitutional right may be justified – or, in other words, is for a "proper purpose" – if it was done in order to protect another constitutional right held by another.[23] Similarly, it is agreed upon that a right can be limited in order to prevent a national

---

[20] HCJ 6427/02 *The Movement for Quality Government in Israel* v. *The Knesset* (not yet published) [2006] (Barak, P.), available in Hebrew at http://elyon1.court.gov.il/files/02/270/064/a22/02064270.a22.HTM.

[21] For a different view, which assumes all rights are absolute, see G. Webber, *The Negotiable Constitutions: On the Limitation of Rights* (Cambridge University Press, 2009). For a critique of this approach, see below, at 494.

[22] See above, at 27.

[23] See R. Dworkin, *Taking Rights Seriously* (Cambridge, MA: Harvard University Press, 1977), 191.

calamity or social disaster.[24] Disagreement exists as to the precise probability by which such events should occur in order to justify the limitation, as well as to the scope of the protection to be granted to the public
interest beyond these obvious examples.

2. *The components of the proper purpose*

The question of when the purpose of a law limiting a constitutional right
is considered "proper" requires the examination of two related issues.[25]
First, we should examine the types of purpose that can justify limitations
imposed on constitutional rights. Second, we should examine the degree
of urgency required in realizing those proper purposes. The first issue is
related to the very nature of the purposes purporting to limit a constitutional right. It is meant to determine those purposes that constitute
the constitutional minimum below which no limiting law can exist. The
second issue relates not to the nature of the purpose but rather to its degree
of urgency. Without such a determination, no limiting law can exist in a
constitutional democracy. Each issue will now be reviewed separately.

C. The proper purpose's content and the state's democratic values

1. *Democracy's minimum requirements*

The proper purpose of a law limiting a constitutional right is derived from
the democratic values of the state; these values can be found (either explicitly
or implicitly[26]) in the constitution. From this determination we can conclude that a purpose conflicting with these constitutional provisions could
not be considered "proper" for purposes of constitutional review.[27] Thus, a
law whose only purpose is to discriminate is not for a proper purpose.[28] But
what are those democratic values for which realization constitutes a proper
purpose – despite placing limitations on the constitutional right?

---

[24] *Ibid.*
[25] See S. Woolman and H. Botha, "Limitations," in S.Woolman, M. Bishop, and J. Brickhill
(eds.), *Constitutional Law of South Africa*, 2nd edn. (Cape Town: Juta Law Publishers,
looseleaf, 2002–), 73.
[26] For an implied constitutional foundation, see above, at 53.
[27] See Grimm, above note 15. See also C. B. Pulido, *El Principio de Proporcionalidad y
los Derechos Fundamentales* (Madrid: Centro de Estudios Políticos y Constitucionales
2007), 696.
[28] See Grimm, above note 15.

Given the differences between the legal systems, it is no easy task to determine the democratic nature of each separately. However, since we are only dealing with the narrow issue of determining the constitutional minimum required in limiting human rights, there are many shared characteristics between the legal systems. As we have already seen,[29] the following two assumptions are shared by most Western legal systems.[30] First, it is essential for every constitutional democracy that the people be the ultimate sovereign.[31] This sovereignty is translated into practice through the conduct of free and equal elections, where the people elect those representatives who best reflect their opinions. Viewed in this way, a democracy can be identified with the notions of majority rule and the centrality of the legislative body, where the representatives of that majority operate. This is the formal aspect of democracy. It is of considerable importance. Without it, neither the regime nor the society can be seen as having a true democratic nature. The second assumption is that a democracy must recognize several principles, including separation of powers,[32] the rule of law (including the formal, jurisprudential, and substantive meaning of the term),[33] independence of the judiciary (both personal and institutional),[34] human rights, and other basic values allowing for the co-existence of different groups within a single democratic society. This is the substantive aspect of democracy, and it is of major importance. Without it, there is no democracy.

Democracy is a multi-faceted, complex phenomenon.[35] It should not be viewed as one-dimensional. Democracy is based, on the one hand, on the fundamental notion of the people – as represented by its elected representatives – and, on the other hand, on the notion of democratic values, including human rights as well as moral and social values.[36] Democracy has its own internal morality, without which the regime no longer remains democratic.[37] As I wrote in one case:

---

[29] See above, at 218.
[30] See A. Barak, *The Judge in a Democracy* (Princeton University Press, 2006), 23.
[31] *Ibid.*
[32] Regarding the separation of powers, see below, at 385.
[33] Regarding the rule of law, see above, at 226.
[34] Regarding judicial independence, see Barak, above note 30, at 76.
[35] See Barak, above note 30, at 23.
[36] See R. Post, "Democracy, Popular Sovereignty and Judicial Review," 86 *Cal. L. Rev.* 429 (1998).
[37] See R. Dworkin, *A Bill of Rights for Britain* (London: Chatto & Windus, 1990), 35; R. Dworkin, *Is Democracy Possible Here: Principles for A New Political Debate* (Princeton University Press, 2006), 131.

Democracy is not merely majority rule. Democracy is also the rule of fundamental values and human rights as expressed by the constitution. Democracy is a delicate balance between majority rule and fundamental values that control that majority. Democracy is not only "formal democracy" (which is primarily concerned with the election process of the representative institutions guaranteeing the majority rule). Democracy is also "substantive democracy" (which is primarily concerned with the protection of human rights) ... Remove majority rule from a constitutional democracy, and you have offended its very nature. Take fundamental-value rule away from a constitutional democracy, and you have offended its very existence.[38]

Democracy is premised, therefore, on the co-existence of both majority rule and the rule of democratic values.[39] Not every infringement on these aspects, however, necessarily renders the government non-democratic. Rather, we are dealing with a spectrum of factual circumstances, ranging from selective compliance with only those values that guarantee a minimal function of democracy, all the way to complete adherence to all democratic values. A state of "minimal democratic existence," therefore, is found at one end of the spectrum. This is the minimum threshold below which neither the society nor its government can claim to be democratic.

2.   Pertinent democratic values

i.   The protection of constitutional rights and the realization of the public interest

Of the many values underlying democracy, the most pertinent to the proper purpose component are constitutional rights on the one hand,[40] and the public interest (or the public good) on the other.[41] Constitutional rights are the rights embodied (expressly or impliedly) in the constitution *vis-à-vis* the state. In some instances, the constitution establishes the operation of these rights *vis-à-vis* other persons as well, in addition to their application to the state.[42] But these instances are rare. Most constitutions establish the individual's constitutional rights *vis-à-vis* the state and not *vis-à-vis* other individuals. It is generally agreed upon that the application of human rights *vis-à-vis* others is indirect rather than

---

[38] See CA 6821/93 *United Mizrahi Bank Ltd.* v. *Migdal Cooperative Village* [1995] IsrLR 1.
[39] See Barak, above note 30, at 23.
[40] See above, at 218.   [41] See above, at 218.
[42] See, e.g., the Constitution of the Republic of South Africa, Art. 8(2).

direct.[43] Those rights are aimed at the state authorities; who, in turn, when determining the laws which apply between individuals ("private law") should refrain from limiting the constitutional rights the individual has *vis-à-vis* them (negative rights) and should protect the individuals *vis-à-vis* the state (positive rights).[44] This determination of the law ("private law") is made through legislation, its interpretation, the filling of legislative gaps, and common law development.[45]

The public interest (or the public good) is the sum total of interests that do not constitute only constitutional rights. Considerations of public interest include the continued existence of the state, national security, public order, tolerance, protection of a person's feelings, and other interests that do not constitute constitutional rights. They are derived from – either explicitly or implicitly – the constitution itself.[46] One of democracy's unique features is that not every public interest consideration may justify a limitation on human rights – or, in other words, constitute a "proper purpose."

The distinction between a constitutional right and the public interest is far from trivial. An issue worth examining is at what point does a public interest – meant to protect the public – turn into a constitutional right. Take, for example, the public interest of national security, which includes the interest in the physical and mental well-being of the people of the state. Can this interest be "translated" into a constitutional right held by each resident of the state *vis-à-vis* the state to have their body and mind protected at all times? Does an individual have a right *vis-à-vis* the state for peace and security? The answer to this question is far from trivial; it may become even more complicated in those instances where a legal system recognizes a duty of the state to positively protect those rights.[47] How can we distinguish between the state's duty to protect human rights and its authority to guarantee the public interest? Take, for example, the right to life. The right of every person in a mature constitutional democracy is that the state should not limit their right to life.[48] Similarly, in every mature constitutional democracy the individual has the right that the state would protect their life.[49] Can we then conclude, from these two assumptions, that every person in a mature constitutional democracy

---

[43] See above, at 85.   [44] See below, at 422.
[45] See A. Barak, "Constitutional Human Rights and Private Law," in D. Friedmann and D. Barak-Erez (eds.), *Human Rights in Private Law* (Portland, OR: Hart Publishing, 2001), 13.
[46] See above, at 53.   [47] See below, at 422.
[48] Art. 2 of Israeli Basic Law: Human Dignity and Liberty, above note 8.
[49] Art. 4 of Israeli Basic Law: Human Dignity and Liberty, above note 8.

may have a right – *vis-à-vis* the state – to have his or her life protected through the war on terror, crime-fighting, or the enforcement of safe driving practices?

The distinction between protection of constitutional rights and public interest is of particular importance within the concept of proportionality in general, and the component of proper purpose in particular. The protection of a constitutional right, in and of itself, constitutes a "proper purpose." In contrast, not every interest included within the "public interest" may pass the threshold required to become a proper purpose.[50]

ii.   Protection of human rights

The protection of human rights is pertinent to the proper purpose for two reasons. First, the constitutional right itself is the object of limitation; second, the right is also an element of the proper purpose. This chapter focuses on the second reason. Indeed, it is accepted that, in a constitutional democracy, one such purpose, deemed proper in the context of limiting human rights, is the purpose of protecting human rights. A society seeking to protect one person's free will must also protect the free will of another person with opposite views. The legal system's recognition of both of their free wills requires, in turn, the imposing of limitations on both of their rights. The recognition of the rights of others, therefore, is a "proper purpose" for limiting a constitutional right. The Declaration of the Rights of Man and of the Citizen (1789) expresses the same idea by stating:

> Liberty consists in the freedom to do everything which injures no one else; hence the exercise of the natural rights of each man has no limits except those which assure to the other members of the society the enjoyment of the same rights. These limits can only be determined by law.[51]

In a mature constitutional democracy, the state has a double duty. First, it must refrain from limiting constitutional rights. This is the "negative" aspect (*status negativus*) of the constitutional right.[52] Second, it must maintain and protect the constitutional right. This is the positive aspect (*status positivus*) of the constitutional right.[53] Both of these aspects are within the purview of the state's duty. As the Constitution of the Republic of South

---

[50] See below, at 265.

[51] Declaration of the Rights of Man and of the Citizen, § 4 (1789).

[52] See Barak, above note 30, at 217.

[53] See D. P. Currie, "Positive and Negative Constitutional Rights," 53 *U. Chi. L. Rev.* 864 (1986); A. Mowbray, *The Development of Positive Obligations under the European Convention on Human Rights by the European Court of Human Rights* (Portland, OR:

Africa points out: "The state must respect, protect, promote and fulfill the rights in the Bill of Rights."[54] Thus, the state has a constitutional duty to protect human rights. But the state cannot fulfill that duty without limiting human rights. From here we may deduce the constitutional license to limit constitutional rights to protect the rights of others. Therefore, the fulfillment of the constitutional obligation to protect human rights is a proper purpose.

iii.   The public interest

Democracy consists not only of notions such as the people's sovereignty, separation of powers, the rule of law, the independence of the judiciary, and human rights. Rather, democracy also entails the realization of the fundamental principles essential to the shared existence of the people in a democracy. All these values, combined, represent the normative universe of democracy.[55] They draw their very existence from the culture of each society, from its history to its *raison d'être*. Therefore, the notion of "minimal democratic experience" must include several categories of worthy, or proper purposes, such as the continued existence of the state, the continued existence of its democratic nature, its national security and public order. These values, necessary to guarantee the continued shared existence of the people in a democracy, together constitute the public interest or the public good. The precise set of values included on that list is never fixed, and may change from time to time and from one constitutional society to another.

The scope of the public interest, and the categories which characterize it, are the main problems of the notion of proper purpose. In a constitutional democracy, not every value included in the public interest qualifies as a proper purpose for the limitation of a human right.[56] Doubts surround the scope of the category of the public interest. Too narrow an approach regarding the public interest may affect the existence of a democracy and its ability to protect human rights. Too wide an approach

---

Hart Publishing, 2004); D. Grimm, "The Protective Function of the State," in G. Nolte (ed.), *European and US Constitutionalism* (Cambridge University Press, 2005), 137; F. I. Michelman, "The Protective Function of the State in the United States and Europe: The Constitutional Question," in G. Nolte (ed.), *European and US Constitutionalism* (Cambridge University Press, 2005), 156. See also below, at 422.

[54] Art. 7(2).   [55] See above, at 251.

[56] See A. McHarg, "Reconciling Human Rights and the Public Interest: Conceptual Problems and Doctrinal Uncertainty in the Jurisprudence of the European Court of Human Rights," 62 *Mod. L. Rev.* 671 (1999). See also Kumm, above note 10.

may cause harm to human rights and to the notion of democracy itself. Therefore, it is important to establish general standards in the determination of the nature of the public interest. Additionally, it is important to determine the categories and sub-categories which realize it.

3. *General criteria for determining the proper purpose*

i. Comparative law

The criteria for determining the content of the proper purpose varies from one legal system to another. In some cases, the constitution itself may contain express provisions as to the content of the criteria. Thus, for example, the Constitution of the Republic of South Africa contains a general limitation clause, which states that the limitation on human rights should be "reasonable and justifiable in an open and democratic society based on human dignity, equality and freedom."[57] Naturally, such an intricate provision has raised some serious interpretive issues. As Woolman and Botha noted:

> Determining the meaning of this phrase is fraught with interpretive difficulties as old as political theory itself. There are, for starters, the tensions between democracy and rights, between equality and freedom, and the deeply contested nature of each of these terms.[58]

Woolman and Botha also provide some background to the criterion adopted by the Constitution of the Republic of South Africa for determining a proper purpose. They explain that the South African provision does not adopt many of the limitations used by other constitutions, such as national security, public interest, or public order. This omission was intentional, they explain; it reflects the accumulated experience of the Apartheid regime, during which opposition was suppressed on the basis of precisely those considerations which are now omitted from the Constitution. Instead, the Constitution has now chosen to refer in its general limitation clause to those fundamental values at the basis of every open and democratic society based on human dignity, equality, and liberty. As such, the legal system was forced to develop a substantive notion of the fundamental values adopted by the constitutional framework. This approach requires the harmonization of the different constitutional values

---

[57] Constitution of the Republic of South Africa, Art. 36(1).
[58] Woolman and Botha, above note 25, at 113.

and the relationships between them. As Justice Sachs of the Constitutional Court of South Africa stated:

> [L]imitation analysis under Section 36 is antithetical to extreme positions which end up setting the irresistible force of democracy and general law enforcement, against the immovable object of constitutionalism and protection of fundamental rights. What it requires is the maximum harmonization of all the competing considerations, on a principled yet nuanced and flexible case-by-case basis, located in South African reality yet guided by international experience, articulated with appropriate candour and accomplished without losing sight of the ultimate values highlighted by our Constitution.[59]

Often, the constitution provides a general statement that the limitations must be justified by the democratic nature of society. Thus, for example, Section 1 of the Canadian Charter of Rights and Freedoms requires limitations on constitutional rights to be "demonstrably justified in a free and democratic society."[60] In interpreting this provision, Chief Justice Dickson wrote:

> The Court must be guided by the values and principles essential to a free and democratic society which I believe embody, to name but a few, respect for the inherent dignity of the human person, commitment to social justice and equality, accommodation of a wide variety of beliefs, respect for cultural and group identity, and faith in social and political institutions which enhance the participation of individuals and groups in society. The underlying values and principles of a free and democratic society are the genesis of the rights and freedoms guaranteed by the Charter and the ultimate standard against which a limit on a right or freedom must be shown, despite its effect to be reasonable and demonstrably justified.[61]

A number of additional constitutions determine that the limitations be "necessary" in a democratic society.[62]

ii.   General criteria: Israeli law

The Israeli Basic Law: Human Dignity and Liberty contains a specific provision dedicated to "basic principles":

> Fundamental human rights in Israel are founded upon recognition of the value of the human being, the sanctity of human life, and the principle

---

[59] *Prince v. President of the Law Society of the Cape of Good Hope*, 2002 (2) SA 794, § 155.
[60] Section 1 of the Canadian Charter, above note 6.
[61] *R. v. Oakes* [1986] 1 SCR 103, § 64.
[62] See the Convention for the Protection of Human Rights and Fundamental Freedoms, November 4, 1950, 213 *UNTS* 222, Arts. 8–11, which determine, among others, that the

that all persons are free; these rights shall be upheld in the spirit of the principles set forth in the Declaration of the Establishment of the State of Israel.[63]

This provision, coupled with the Basic Law requirement that every law limiting constitutional rights must be in congruence with "the values of the State of Israel,"[64] assisted the Israeli Supreme Court in determining the general criterion for the proper purpose. The issue was raised in the *United Mizrahi Bank* case.[65] President Shamgar described the nature of the proper purpose as follows:

> A positive purpose from the point of view of human rights and society's values, including that of establishing a reasonable and fair balance between the rights of different people with inconsistent interests. A proper purpose is one that creates a foundation for living together, even if it entails a compromise in the area of granting optimal rights to each and every individual, or if it serves interests that are essential to the preservation of the state and society.[66]

In my own opinion in that case I wrote:

> The purpose is proper if it is intended to fulfill important social goals for the fulfillment of a social framework that recognizes the constitutional importance of human rights and the need to protect them.[67]

The Israeli Supreme Court adopted this approach in a long line of cases. Thus, for example, the Court ruled that a law's purpose would be recognized as proper if it demonstrates sensitivity to the notion of human rights within the overall social scheme. It was also noted by the Court that a purpose is proper if it was meant to create a foundation for the shared experience of individuals that is a part of the democratic experience, and to create a social framework to protect and advance human rights.[68]

---

limitation of the human rights discussed in these articles needs to be necessary. All of the Convention's member states use the same wording. See R. C. A. White and C. Ovey, *Jacobs, White and Ovey: The European Convention on Human Rights*, 5th edn. (Oxford University Press, 2010), 325.

[63] Israeli Basic Law: Human Dignity and Liberty (Art. 1); Israeli Basic Law: Freedom of Occupation (Art. 1).

[64] Art. 8 of Israeli Basic Law: Human Dignity and Liberty, above note 8; Art. 4 of Israeli Basic Law: Freedom of Occupation.

[65] See *United Mizrahi Bank*, above note 38.

[66] *Ibid.*, at 128.   [67] *Ibid.*, at 241.

[68] See *The Movement for Quality Government in Israel* v. *The Knesset*, above note 20, at para. 52 (Barak, P.).

4. *The categories of proper purposes*

i.   Specific purposes appearing in general and specific
limitation clauses

a.   Specified purposes in general limitation clauses   A general criterion for determining the notion of a proper purpose within a legal system must provide, with some degree of specificity, a number of categories (and sub-categories) that together constitute the proper purpose general criterion. Such specification may be useful on two levels. First, it determines those purposes that justify the limitation of human rights (positive determination). That, in turn, would reduce the friction and disagreements around that issue in any given legal system. Second, that degree of specificity may also inform us – through interpretation – which purposes should be excluded from consideration as being "proper" (negative determination). The list of the different categories, however, should never be closed. These categories change over time, according to the changes that the hosting democratic society is undergoing.

The most important example of categories and sub-categories of the types of purposes deemed "proper" appear in the Universal Declaration of Human Rights.[69] The Declaration's general limitation clause provides:

> In the exercise of his rights and freedoms, everyone shall be subject only to such limitations as are determined by law solely for the purpose of securing due recognition and respect for the rights and freedoms of others and of meeting the just requirements of morality, public order and the general welfare in a democratic society.[70]

This provision has inspired – and served as a model for – several international treaties as well as several constitutions.[71]

General limitation clauses specifying special purposes appear in several constitutions. Thus, for example, the Constitution of Poland (1997) contains a general limitation clause that specifies a list of proper purposes:

> Any limitation upon the exercise of constitutional freedoms and rights may be imposed only by statute, and only when necessary in a democratic state for the protection of its security or public order, or to protect

---

[69]   Universal Declaration of Human Rights (1948).
[70]   *Ibid.*, Art. 29(2).
[71]   See, e.g., International Covenant on Economic, Social and Cultural Rights, opened for signature December 19, 1966, 993 *UNTS* 3 (entered into force March 23, 1976); American Declaration of the Rights and Duties of Man (1948); P. Sieghart, *The International Law of Human Rights* (Oxford University Press, 1983), 85.

the natural environment, health or public morals, or the freedoms and rights of other persons. Such limitations shall not violate the essence of freedoms and rights.[72]

b. Explicit purposes in specific limitation clauses Most constitutions and treaties on human rights contain, along with the rights themselves, specific limitation clauses. Those limitation clauses are unique in that they specify those specific categories (and sub-categories) in which, for their fulfillment, constitutional rights may be limited. The European Convention on Human Rights is a good example.[73] The Convention contains no general limitation clause; however, some of the rights specified in the document are accompanied by specific limitation clauses. These specific limitation clauses list the purposes that may justify the limitation of specific rights recognized by the Convention. Thus, for example, Article 8(1) recognizes the right of any person to have "respect for his private and family life, his home and his correspondence." Article 8(2) specifies the instances in which such rights may be limited; this is when the limitation:

> [i]s necessary in a democratic society in the interests of national security, public safety or the economic well-being of the country, for prevention of disorder or crime, for the protection of health or morals, or for the protection of the rights and freedoms of others.

Similar purposes appear alongside the rights to freedom of thought, conscience and religion (Article 9); the right to freedom of expression (Article 10); and the right to freedom of peaceful assembly and to the freedom of association with others (Article 11). The prevailing view with regard to these provisions is that the list of express purposes therein is exhaustive, and no other implied purposes should be deduced or added to the list.[74] This is an interpretive conclusion. Each legal system may come to its own conclusions as to those specific limitation clauses in its constitutional interpretation process.

ii. Implicit purposes

At times the constitution contains no specific provisions regarding the category of proper purposes. This does not indicate that these constitutional rights are absolute. The constitution's silence should not be

---

[72] Constitution of the Republic of Poland, Art. 31(3).
[73] European Convention on Human Rights, above, at 62.
[74] White and Ovey, above note 62, at 309.

interpreted, in these instances, as a negative solution.[75] Rather, in most of these instances, the different categories of purposes may be implicitly derived from the constitutional text, and particularly from the provisions relating to the democratic nature of the state.[76] In some cases, a constitution may include several rights accompanied by explicit provisions relating to the type of cases in which their limitation would be justified, while several other rights included in the same constitution do not contain any such provisions. Here, too, the constitutional silence should not be interpreted as a negative solution. Finally, the implicit categories of proper purposes may vary from one legal system to another, and – over time – may change within a single legal system.

iii.   Protection of the rights of others

a. Explicit provisions   The agreed-upon approach is that the protection of the rights of others is a purpose that is "proper" – that is, a purpose that justifies the limitation of a constitutional right.[77] A specific provision to that effect appears, in some cases, in the general limitation clause itself. Such is the case, for example, with the Universal Declaration of Human Rights (1948).[78] Article 29(2) of the Declaration states that the rights enumerated therein may only be limited, *inter alia*, "for purposes of securing due recognition and respect for the rights and freedoms of others."

That same purpose may appear in specific limitation clauses. Thus, for example, the limitation clauses found in the rights appearing in Articles 8, 9, 10, and 11 of the European Convention on Human Rights[79] all state explicitly that the rights stated therein – the right to respect for a person's private and family life, his home and his correspondence (Article 8), the right to freedom of thought, conscience and religion (Article 9), the right to freedom of expression (Article 10), and the rights of freedom of assembly and association (Article 11) – may be limited, *inter alia*, for "the protection of the rights and freedoms of others."

b. Implied provisions   The constitution's silence regarding the protection of the rights of others as a proper purpose should not be interpreted

---

[75] See Sieghart, above note 71, at 103. See also above, at 56.
[76] See R. Alexy, *A Theory of Constitutional Rights* (Julian Rivers trans., Oxford University Press, 2002 [1986]), 82.
[77] See above, at 254; Van der Schyff, above note 2, at 151.
[78] Universal Declaration of Human Rights (1948).
[79] European Convention on Human Rights, above, at 62.

as a negative solution.[80] Without an explicit provision, the notion that constitutional rights may be limited to protect the rights of others should be deduced from the principled criteria and mainly from the democratic nature of the constitution. This justification is the easiest to defend. Indeed, he who wants to protect human rights must be prepared to limit those same rights. When human rights conflict, the right way to resolve such a conflict is not by narrowing the scope of the rights themselves (at the constitutional level) but by recognizing the possibility of limiting them at the sub-constitutional level,[81] when the justification for so doing is to protect the constitutional right of another.

c.   **The scope of the category**   The scope of the category regarding "the rights of others" is far from clear. One of the reasons for this is that the precise location of the line dividing a person's right from a person's interest is hard to prescribe accurately. In any event, what is clear is that the category regarding the limitation of a constitutional right in order to protect the rights of others includes all the other rights included in the constitution itself. The constitution grants individuals several rights *vis-à-vis* the state.[82] The state's duty towards that person may conflict with its duty towards others.[83] Thus, for example, the state's duty to protect one person's constitutional right[84] (such as privacy) may conflict with its duty not to limit another's constitutional right (such as freedom of expression). This conflict, as we have seen, occurs only at the sub-constitutional level.[85] According to this approach, a private-law statutory provision regulating individual rights – that is, granting certain rights to one person while limiting the rights of another – may find its constitutional justification in the protection it extends to the rights of others. Legislation in the fields of contracts, torts, and property, while taking from one, provides the same measure to another. While doing so, the state simultaneously limits one person's rights *vis-à-vis* the state while simultaneously fulfilling its duty to protect the rights of others *vis-à-vis* the state.

Should that consideration be limited only to a conflict between constitutional rights? What is the case, for example, with a law limiting a constitutional right in order to protect a right not included in the constitution?

---

[80] For a negative solution, see above, note 19, at 68.
[81] See above, at 89.
[82] See above, at 85.
[83] See above, at 85.
[84] For the notion of positive rights, see below, at 422.
[85] See above, at 89.

The answer is that the consideration regarding the protection of the rights of others is not limited to the protection of constitutional rights.[86] Rather, it applies to the protection of every right, whether it is included in the constitution or in a sub-constitutional law (such as a statute or the common law), and whether it was recognized when the constitution was ratified or at a later date. The justification for such an approach cannot rest with the special argument relating to the state's constitutional duty to protect the constitutional rights in conflict; but rather, with the more general notion of the criterion for proper purpose. Such criterion seeks "to take rights seriously." This "seriousness" is not limited to constitutional rights. The need to be sensitive to the vital role human rights play within the general social framework does not limit itself to constitutional rights alone; it also includes the notion that the protection of non-constitutional rights may justify the limitation of other rights, including constitutional rights. Indeed, a democracy seeks to protect not only those rights found in the constitution, but also those that remain outside that document. All human rights are precious to a democracy, regardless of their legal status. The constitutional recognition of some rights should not be interpreted as a negative solution for the legal system's recognition – at the sub-constitutional level – of the non-constitutional rights.[87] Such continued recognition justifies this consideration in the framework of the limitation of the constitutional right.[88] That said, the relative weight granted by the legal system to a non-constitutional right is different from the one provided to a constitutional right. This is particularly true in terms of the means taken to realize those rights, and the proper relationship – or proportionality – required between the potential benefits of those rights and the harm to the constitutional right in question. These matters, however, need not be considered during the discussion of the question of the proper purpose's threshold. They should not affect the recognition of the protection of a non-constitutional right as a possible justification for the limitation of a constitutional right.

In general, the scope of the category of the protection of the rights of others is immense.[89] Often it overlaps with other categories. Due to its wide application, some refer to it as a "catch-all" category.[90] Thus, for

---

[86] See Sieghart, above note 71, at 97; Van der Schyff, above note 2, at 255. See also A. M. Connelly, "The Protection of the Rights of Others," 5 *Hum. Rts. Rev.* 117 (1980).
[87] See above, at 68.   [88] Van der Schyff, above note 2, at 255.
[89] See Van der Schyff, above, note 2, at 255.
[90] See Sieghart, above note 71, at 97; Van der Schyff, above note 2, at 193.

example, the South African Constitutional Court examined a case where the petitioner claimed that his right to health was limited as he could not be connected to a dialysis machine (due to the shortage of such machines at the time). The court agreed that his right was limited; but was also of the opinion that this limitation was justified. This justification, the court explained, rested in part on the right of others to health.[91] The same is true in Israel, where the Supreme Court has recognized a possible limitation to the right to freedom of expression by allowing the consideration of an undue burden on the feelings on others.[92] Such justification may also be recognized as part of the more general category of the protection of the rights of others.[93]

iv. Public interest considerations

a. The nature of the public interest   I define public interest or public good as any consideration justifying a limitation of a constitutional right and which is not included within the category of the protection of the rights of others.[94] This category is made up of values and principles that society may consider as justifications for the limitation of a constitutional right.[95] It also demonstrates the notion that constitutional rights are not absolute.[96] While the very existence of this category is not in doubt, the precise details of its content are far from clear. A society striving to protect human rights – a society taking human rights seriously – should not allow every public interest consideration to justify a limitation of a constitutional right.[97] The benefits gained by satisfying the public interest (either substantive or procedural[98]), in and of themselves, are not sufficient to justify a limitation on constitutional rights. Despite that, even a society that takes rights seriously cannot protect human rights at all costs. The approach of *fiat lex pereat mundus* ("let justice be done, though

---

[91] *Soobramoney* v. *Minister of Health*, 1998 (1) SA 765 (CC).
[92] See below, at 275.   [93] See above, at 262.
[94] For a discussion of the term "public interest," see V. Held, *The Public Interest and Individual Interests* (New York: Basic Books, 1970); S. Greer, "Constitutionalizing Adjudication under the European Convention on Human Rights," 23(3) *OJLS* 405 (2003).
[95] See Van der Schyff, above note 2, at 141, 145, 183, 246.
[96] Regarding absolute rights, see above, at 27.
[97] See L. Weinrib, "The Supreme Court of Canada and Section 1 of the Charter," 10 *Sup. Ct. L. Rev.* 469 (1988).
[98] According to Ely's approach: see J. H. Ely, *Democracy and Distrust: A Theory of Judicial Review* (Cambridge, MA: Harvard University Press, 1980).

the world perish") is not accepted. Even Nozick, the great opponent of state intervention, was willing to recognize the notion of curtailing (or limiting) human rights in times of national disaster.[99] The same is true for Dworkin, who generally views rights as "trumps"[100] which trump the public interest, but who is willing to recognize the necessity of "preventing a catastrophe" or "to obtain a clear and major public benefit."[101] The consideration of the public interest must be of such a high level of social importance that society may see it as crucial enough to justify a limitation on its constitutional rights.[102] In addition, it must demonstrate the degree of urgency that would be required according to society's most fundamental values to limit a constitutional right. We will now examine the content of the notion of public interest; the urgency of that purpose will be discussed subsequently.[103]

The content of the public interest is derived from the constitution's basic principles, including the notions of democracy and the rule of law. The public interest must reflect the notions of justice and tolerance shared by society.[104] It should reflect democratic society's general approach towards the people, an approach that may justify, under certain circumstances, the limitation of a constitutional right granted to individuals who constitute a part of that same collective.[105] Without all of those, a constitutional right should not be limited. Note that determining the scope of the category of public interest is still a preliminary examination relating to the component of the proper purpose within proportionality. Accordingly, the other components are not considered at this stage. Rather, the element of the public interest – together with the concomitant requirement of urgency in its realization – constitutes a threshold issue for purposes of proportionality's analysis.

---

[99] R. Nozick, *Anarchy, State and Utopia* (New York: Basic Books, 1974), 30.

[100] See R. Dworkin, "Rights as Trumps," in J. Waldron (ed.), *Theories of Rights* (Oxford University Press, 1984), 153.

[101] Dworkin, above note 100, at 191.

[102] J. P. Müller, "Fundamental Rights in Democracy," 4 *Hum. Rts. L. J.* 131 (1983); L. Weinrib, "The Postwar Paradigm and American Exceptionalism," in S. Choudhry (ed.), *The Migration of Constitutional Ideas* (Cambridge University Press, 2006), 84, 96.

[103] See below, at 277.

[104] See Universal Declaration on Human Rights (Art. 29), above note 78. See also J. Rawls, *Political Liberalism* (New York: Columbia University Press, 1993); R. Dworkin, *Sovereign Virtue - The Theory and Practice of Equality* (Cambridge, MA: Harvard University Press, 2000).

[105] See A. Brudner, *Constitutional Goods* (New York: Oxford University Press, 2004).

The public interest category is never closed. The public interest develops as society itself advances throughout history. The concrete sub-categories that make up the notion of public interest will now be examined. I do not claim to cover all the sub-categories mentioned in the comparative literature.

b. The continued existence of the state as a democracy A sub-constitutional law (a statute or the common law) which strives to guarantee the continued existence of the state as a democracy is for a proper purpose.[106] This approach was expressed in Israel's Basic Law: The Knesset (Parliament). Article 7a of this Basic Law reads:

> A candidates' list shall not participate in the elections for the Knesset if its objects or actions, expressly or by implication, include one of the following:
> (1) Denying the existence of the State of Israel as a Jewish and democratic state;
> (2) Incitement to racism;
> (3) Support of armed warfare, by either enemy state or a terrorist organization, against the State of Israel.[107]

This is an expression of the State of Israel as a "defensive democracy," or a "militant democracy."[108] Similar provisions may be found in other constitutional texts. Thus, for example, the Basic Law for the Federal Republic of Germany provides:

> Parties that, by reason of their aims or the behavior of their adherents, seek to undermine or abolish the free democratic basic order or to endanger the existence of the Federal Republic of Germany shall be unconstitutional. The Federal Constitutional Court shall rule on the question of unconstitutionality.[109]

Even without such an express provision in the constitution, the argument that the state has to defend itself against forces who seek to undermine or

---

[106] Israeli Basic Law: Human Dignity and Liberty (Art. 1a); Israeli Basic Law: Freedom of Occupation (Art. 2).

[107] 1958 SH 69.

[108] For the term, see A. Sajó (ed.), *Militant Democracy* (2004); R. Miller, "Comparative Law and Germany's Militant Democracy," in R. Miller (ed.), *US National Security, Intelligence and Democracy* 229 (New York: Taylor & Francis, 2008); M. Thiel (ed.), *The 'Militant Democracy' Principle in Modern Democracies* (2009); R. Miller, "Balancing Security and Liberty in Germany," 4 *J. Nat'l Sec. L. & Pol'y* 369 (2010).

[109] German Basic Law, Art. 21(2).

to abolish its democratic nature does constitute a proper purpose. A number of constitutions have express articles to the effect that the democratic character cannot be changed through a constitutional amendment.[110] The Indian Supreme Court has developed the same doctrine. Thus, legislation which protects the democratic character of the regime is for a proper purpose, and legislation meant to harm the democratic regime is not for a proper purpose.

c. **National security**   It is widely accepted that the protection of national security interests constitutes a proper purpose, which may serve as justification for the limitation of constitutional rights,[111] as long as such protection satisfies the requirement of urgency.[112] Several constitutions expressly refer to the category of national security with regard to several rights, while not doing so with regard to others.[113] Here, too, the absence of an express constitutional provision relating to national security considerations should not be interpreted as a negative solution. The proper purpose of national security considerations is clearly implied by both the constitutional provisions and the need to protect the democratic nature of the state.[114] The line drawn between arguments relating to the continued existence of the state as a democracy and national security considerations may, in some cases, be too narrow to be noticed.[115]

The main issue with national security considerations is related not to their recognition as a legitimate proper purpose, but rather to the scope of national security.[116] Obviously, the term "national security" embodies actions taken by the state to fight its enemies – foreign and domestic – seeking to injure the civil population or national institutions. Here, too, the scope of the category may change from one legal system to another.

---

[110] See A. Barak, "Unconstitutional Constitutional Amendments," *Isr. L. Rev.* (forthcoming, 2011); see Art. 79(3) of the Basic Law of the Federal Republic of Germany; Art. 4 of the Constitution of the Republic of Turkey.
[111] See Van der Schyff, above note 2.
[112] See Van der Schyff, above note 2, at 147, 148, 251.
[113] See European Convention on Human Rights, Arts. 6(1), 8(2), 10(2), 11(2), above note 62; International Covenant on Civil and Political Rights (1966), Art. 12(3).
[114] See Van der Schyff, above note 2, at 147, 148, 251.
[115] *Zana* v. *Turkey*, App. No. 18954/91, 27 EHRR 667 (1997).
[116] See Van der Schyff, above note 2, at 147, 148, 251.

d. Public order The sub-category of public order is important. Without public order we cannot guarantee human rights. "Without order there is no liberty ... Democracy is not anarchy."[117] Having said that, it is necessary to carefully examine the scope of this sub-category.[118] The precise content of the term "public order" may vary from one constitution to another, from one society to the next, and even from one right to another.[119] Specific provisions relating to the proper purpose of the public order may be found in several international treaties,[120] as well as some constitutions.[121] In other instances, the courts have interpreted public order as an implied constitutional proper purpose.[122]

The scope of the term "public order" is interpreted according to the context in which it appears. It is widely accepted, however, that the prevention of crimes, the protection of minors' interests, and public health fall well within this sub-category. Beyond that, many of the considerations are more controversial. One of the most important aspects of the notion of proper purpose may be reflected in the meaning given to the sub-category of public order. In order to properly respect and protect human rights we must refrain from providing too wide a meaning to the possibility of limiting it through the notion of public order.

An interesting question in this context is whether considerations of administrative efficiency (or administrative convenience) are a proper purpose. Can national budgetary considerations be considered a proper purpose? Although several legal systems have looked into this issue, the answer is far from unequivocal at this stage. For example, the issue came up before the Supreme Court of Canada in the case of *Singh*,[123] where the court examined whether each person seeking the status of refugee in Canada must be granted a right to a hearing. The state argued that granting such a right to each of the thousands of potential refugees each year

[117] HCJ 14/86 *La'or* v. *Commission for Censorship of Movies and Plays* [1987] IsrSC 41(1) 421, 433–434 (Barak, P.).
[118] See Barak, above note 30, at 75.
[119] A. C. Kiss, "Permissible Limitations on Rights," in L. Henkin (ed.), *The International Bill of Rights* (New York: Columbia University Press, 1981), 290, 300.
[120] See Art. 29 of the Universal Declaration of Human Rights, above note 78; Arts. 12(3), 18(3) of the International Covenant on Civil and Political Rights, above note 113; Arts. 8(2), 10(2), 11(2) of the European Convention on Human Rights, above note 113.
[121] See the Federal Constitution of Switzerland (Art. 36(3); the Constitution of the Republic of Poland (Art. 31(3)).
[122] See above, at 53.
[123] *Singh* v. *Minister of Employment and Immigration* [1985] 1 SCR 177.

would impose too heavy a burden on the state's budget. The argument was rejected. In her opinion, Justice Wilson explained:

> I have considerable doubt that the type of utilitarian consideration brought forward by Mr. Bowie can constitute a justification for a limitation on the rights set out in the Charter. Certainly the guarantees of the Charter would be illusory if they could be ignored because it was administratively convenient to do so. No doubt considerable time and money can be saved by adopting administrative procedures which ignore the principles of fundamental justice but such an argument, in my view, misses the point of the exercise under Section 1. The principles of natural justice and procedural fairness which have long been espoused by our courts, and the constitutional entrenchment of the principles of fundamental justice in Section 7, implicitly recognize that a balance of administrative convenience does not override the need to adhere to these principles. Whatever standard of review eventually emerges under Section 1, it seems to me that the basis of the justification for the limitation of rights under Section 7 must be more compelling than any advanced in these appeals.[124]

Following *Singh*, however, the Canadian Supreme Court was willing to recognize some instances where there would be prohibitive costs,[125] or where a financial crisis was taking place,[126] such that a limitation of a constitutional right may be justified.

The South African Constitutional Court has also examined the issue. In *NICRO*[127] the court was called upon to determine the constitutionality of a statutory amendment that deprived convicted prisoners serving sentences that could not be substituted by a fine the right to participate in general elections (during the period of their incarceration). Here, too, the state argued that the restriction was intended to prevent logistical and budgetary constraints that would otherwise burden the election committee. That argument was rejected. Despite that, the Constitutional Court recognized that the consideration of the state's financial ability may be taken into consideration in some cases. The court quoted in that respect an earlier case in which it was held that:

> In the context of South African conditions and resources – political, social, economic and human … [what is reasonable in] one country with

---

[124] *Ibid.*, at para. 70.
[125] See Hogg, above note 11, at 140; M. P. Singh, *German Administrative Law in Common Law Perspective*, 2nd edn. (Berlin: Springer, 2001). 202.
[126] *Newfoundland (Treasury Board)* v. *NAPE* [2004] 3 SCR 381.
[127] *Minister of Home Affairs* v. *National Institute for Crime Prevention and the Re-Integration of Offenders (NICRO)*, 2005 (3) SA 280 (CC).

vast resources, does not necessarily justify placing an identical burden on
a country with significantly less resources.[128]

Still, the court in *NICRO* held that a complete denial of the right to
vote – which is a fundamental right guaranteed by the Constitution of
the Republic of South Africa – to an entire category of voters cannot be
justified through financial considerations; this was particularly true in
this case, where such a justification had not been properly established.
Other rulings of the South African Constitutional Court have repeated
the notion that mere considerations of administrative convenience or cost
saving would not justify, in and of themselves, limitations on constitutional rights. Thus, for example, the court held that the state's administrative inconvenience in defending claims against its security forces did
not justify a reduction in the statute of limitation period in these cases to
a mere six months. This curtailing of the period, the court ruled, unjustly
limits the right to access the courts.[129]

Similar questions have arisen in Israel. The Israeli Supreme Court had
to face – more than once – the issue of whether a constitutionally protected right may be limited due to financial considerations or those of
administrative convenience or cost-effectiveness. As I wrote elsewhere:

> A society that places human rights atop all other protected values must
> be also ready to pay for them. The rhetoric of human rights must be
> backed by a reality that places those rights at the top of the national con-
> siderations. The protection of human rights costs money and a society
> which respects those rights must be ready to carry the financial burden.
> And note: When a constitutional right is limited, the state cannot defend
> itself by claiming that it did not have enough resources to protect the
> right. Should we not hold elections merely because we cannot afford it?
> Should we eliminate the right to access the courts because it is financially
> burdensome?[130]

In one case, the state argued that it was not able to provide suitable access
to a school for a disabled student, as it would have been too costly. Rejecting
this claim, I wrote: "The guaranteeing of equal opportunities for the disabled is an expensive endeavor. However, a society based on the values
of human dignity, liberty, and equality is willing to pay that price."[131] In

---

[128] *Ferreira v. Levin*, 1996 (1) SA 984 (CC), § 133.
[129] *Mohlomi v. Minister of Defence*, 1997 (1) SA 124 (CC).
[130] See A. Barak, *Interpretation in Law: Constitutional Interpretation*, vol. III (Jerusalem: Nevo, 1994), 528.
[131] HCJ 7081/93 *Botzer v. Macabim-Re'ut Regional Municipality* [1996] IsrSC 50(1) 19, 27.

another case, Justice Dorner noted that "a basic right, by its own nature, has a social cost … The protection of basic human rights is not merely the interest of each member of the society, but also an interest of society as a whole; such protection determines the true nature of that society."[132] In another Israeli Supreme Court case, *Tzemach*,[133] the state argued that one of the reasons for preventing the shortening of the ninety-six-hour detention period for soldiers under military investigation to forty-eight hours is the lack of financial resources. Justice Zamir, addressing the claim, suggested that the answer would be dependent upon the "relative weight" of the right in question in relation to the resources required for its realization. He then added:

> Accordingly, what is that "relative weight"? This issue presents a challenge to Israeli society; such a society is measured, among others, according to the relative weight it assigns to personal liberties. Such "weight" should go beyond mere rhetoric, and beyond the law books; it should appear in the budget books, too. The protection of human rights comes at a cost. The society must be willing to pay a reasonable price for its protection on human rights.[134]

In another case dealing with age discrimination, I wrote:

> Human rights cost money. Guaranteeing equality costs money … This is a price both worthy and required in order to ensure our status as a human rights protecting society, which also respects equality.[135]

Accordingly, the Israeli Supreme Court has ruled that the police may not refrain from providing security to a demonstration merely because such a task would lead to a financial burden. "The saving of economic resources, in and of itself, may not serve as a justification for refraining from securing the demonstration."[136]

The conclusion arising from this line of "administrative efficiency" cases is that, because democratic societies assign great value to human rights, the starting point should always be that these rights should receive priority in the national budgetary process.[137] The more central the right is,

---

[132] HCJ 2316/95 *Ganimat v. State of Israel* [1995] IsrSC 49(4) 589, 629.

[133] HCJ 6055/95 *Tzemach v. Minister of Defence* [1999] IsrSC 53(5) 241.

[134] *Ibid.*, at 281.

[135] HCJFH 4191/97 *Rekanat v. The National Labor Court* [2000] IsrSC 54(5) 330, 355. See also HCJ 3239/02 *Marab v. IDF Commander in the West Bank* [2002] IsrSC 57(2) 349, 384 ("A society which desires both security and individual liberty must pay the price" (Barak, P.)) available at: http://elyon1.court.gov.il/files_eng/02/390/032/A04/02032390.a04.pdf.

[136] HCJ 2557/05 *Majority Headquarters v. Israel Police* [2006] (2) IsrLR 399, 414 (Barak, P.).

[137] See Weinrib, above note 97, at 486.

and the more severe the limitation on it is, the more priority should the right receive. However, administrative efficiency or budgetary constraints may not be ruled out as proper considerations to be weighed within the public interest. Indeed, when a similar argument was made before the Israeli Supreme Court – that economic efficiency, in and of itself, should never be considered a proper purpose for limitations of human rights – President Beinish rejected the argument and noted that it was "over inclusive since there are circumstances when an economic purpose would be deemed proper enough to justify limitations on a human right."[138] In those instances where the scope of the right includes an express reference to the state's economic means, such consideration should be taken into account.[139] The same is true in those cases where the state may grant benefits, as long as the purpose of the grant is not discriminatory.

e.   Tolerance   Can a constitutional right be limited by law in order to ensure social tolerance? Should tolerance be considered part of the public interest, and therefore justify a limitation of a human right? In Israel, the answer provided by the Supreme Court to this question was yes. The Israeli Supreme Court viewed tolerance as an important social value that may be a proper purpose for limiting a constitutional right.[140] Tolerance constitutes a part of the notion of democracy. It may, therefore, justify the limitation of a constitutional right. What is tolerance, and why may it be used as a justification for limiting individual rights?

Tolerance may be viewed as the demand that a person should respond properly to another person's opinion or behavior, despite the fact that that opinion or behavior is not acceptable to them.[141] Tolerance is an expression

---

[138]   HCJ 2605/05 *Academic Center of Law and Business* v. *Minister of Finance* [2009] (unpublished), available at: http://elyon1.court.gov.il/files_eng/05/050/026/n39/05026050.n39.pdf (para. 45, Beinisch, P.).

[139]   See, e.g., Constitution of the Republic of South Africa, Art. 26 :"(1) Everyone has the right to have access to adequate housing; (2) The state must take reasonable legislative and other measures, within its available resources, to achieve the progressive realization of this right."

[140]   Barak, above note 30, at 63.

[141]   See in general, M. Walzer, *On Toleration* (New Haven, CT: Yale University Press, 1997); L. C. Bollinger, *The Tolerant Society* (Oxford University Press, 1986); S. Mendus and D. S. Edwards (eds.), *On Toleration* (Oxford University Press, 1987); D. A. J. Richards, *Toleration and the Constitution* (Oxford University Press, 1989); R. Cohen-Almagor, *The Boundaries of Liberty and Tolerance: The Struggle against Kahanism in Israel* (Gainesville, FL: University Press of Florida, 1994); R. Cohen-Almagor, *The Scope of Tolerance: Studies on the Costs of Free Expression and Freedom of the Press* (London: Routledge, 2006).

of the personal autonomy of others, and of their freedom to be different. It contains an understanding of our society as pluralistic, a community where different people with different opinions live side-by-side, and where many people wish to express their separate opinions. Democratic regimes are based on the notion of tolerance. This means tolerance of opinions – and actions – expressed by others in the community. This might also mean the tolerance of intolerance. In a pluralistic society, tolerance may serve as the uniting force that facilitates co-existence. Indeed, tolerance may serve as both a means and an end. It serves as an important social purpose to which every democratic society should aspire. It serves as a means to balance between other social goals where those conflict with each other. Tolerance is a central value of social order. If every individual in a democracy would like to fulfill all of their desires, then the result would be that most wishes would never be fulfilled. Instead, modern society's life is based on the notions of mutual give-and-take. The tolerance sought is both by individuals towards other individuals and by individuals towards other groups. Similarly, this is the tolerance of groups towards other individuals, and tolerance of groups towards other groups.

Tolerance means respecting each individual's point of view; a consideration of the opinions and feelings expressed by every human being; and an attempt to understand others' opinions even if those opinions deviate from the norm. Tolerance means a myriad of opinions, ideas, and views co-existing in a single society. The essence of tolerance is the willingness to compromise; a compromise between the individual and the community, and a compromise between the different individuals in the community. This compromise does not mean the relinquishing of principles, but rather the relinquishment of the notion that all means may be used to achieve those principles. Despite such difficulties, we should not give up. Without tolerance, there is no liberty.

f.   Feelings   Can the protection of feelings constitute a proper purpose justifying a limitation on a constitutional right?[142] In the Israeli Supreme Court case of *Horev*,[143] the issue was considered. It was noted

---

[142]   H. L. A. Hart, *Law, Liberty, And Morality* (Stanford University Press, 1963), 35; I. Saban, "Offensiveness Analyzed: Lessons for Comparative Analysis of Free Speech Doctrines," 2 *Journal of International and Comparative Law at Chicago-Kent* 60 (2002); M. Pinto, "What Are Offences to Feelings Really About?: A New Regulative Principle for the Multicultural Era," 30 *OJLS* 695 (2010).

[143]   HCJ 5016/96 *Horev* v. *Minister of Transport* [1997] IsrSC 51(4) 1. See also HCJ 6126/94 *Senesh* v. *Broadcasting Authority* [1999] IsrSC 53(3) 817.

that including feelings as one of the sub-categories justifying limitations on human rights is a complex issue. On the one hand, it is only natural for a democratic society to consider the feelings of its members. "Society, after all, exists in order to express those feelings."[144] If a constitutional right may be justifiably limited due to harm to life or limb of another, why would it not be justifiable in the case of offending the feelings of another? On the other hand, it is only natural for a right – any right – to offend feelings. "If we allow this cause to justify limitations on human rights, we will find ourselves, in the end, questioning the entire framework of human rights. A comprehensive protection of the feelings of others may lead to serious harm – perhaps more serious than we could endure – to the very notion of human rights."[145]

How could we resolve such a complex issue? In Israel, the case law refused to adopt an "all or nothing" approach; rather, the approach adopted has been that an offense to the feelings may constitute a proper purpose, but only if the harm to feelings was so severe that it exceeded the "tolerance level" acceptable to society.[146] In one such case, Justice Proccacia characterized the nature of such an injury, "which shocks the very foundations of mutual tolerance in a democracy," as follows: "Such an offense may occur only when it relates to the very moral fabric that defines us as individuals and as a society; an offense that questions the very assumptions upon which we are based (as a democracy) in a way that may harm our national and social structure; and where providing the proper answer to that question would be either impossible or nearly so."[147]

Two issues should be noted in this respect: First, in some cases the feelings are protected within the scope of a constitutional right. Thus, for example, in those legal systems where human dignity is recognized as a constitutional right, protection of feelings may well be considered part of protecting human dignity. According to this line of thought, the notion

[144] See *Horev*, above note 143, at 44 (Barak, P.).
[145] *Ibid.*, at 45 (Barak, P.).
[146] See *Senesh*, above note 143, at 836, 839 ("Only severe offenses to feelings may justify a limitation on the freedom of expression and creation. Indeed, in a democratic regime we have to recognize the existence of a 'tolerance level' of respecting other people's feelings, by which all members of a society should abide, and that is derived from the notion of tolerance itself. Only if the offense in question surpasses this "tolerance level" could we justify, in a constitutional democracy, a limitation of the freedom of speech and creation … We are dealing, therefore, with such an injury that shakes the very foundations of mutual tolerance in our society." (Barak, P.)).
[147] HCJ 316/03 *Muhammad Bakri* v. *The Israel Film Council* [2003] IsrSC 58(1) 249, 279, available at http://elyon1.court.gov.il/files_eng/03/160/003/L15/03003160.l15.pdf.

of respect for feelings is merely a part of the well-recognized concept of protection of the rights of others. In addition, an offense to feelings may be viewed as interference with the public order.[148] Second, the "level of tolerance" may change in accordance with the right in question.[149]

g. Constitutional principles The purpose of a law limiting a constitutional right is proper if it seeks to realize constitutional principles. Among those we can include the separation of powers,[150] the rule of law,[151] and the independence of the judiciary.[152] Alongside these principles, the constitution also includes a set of principles that reflect the objective aspect of constitutional rights.[153] Indeed, constitutional rights are aimed, first and foremost, at the state. This is the "subjective" aspect of constitutional rights. But they have an additional aspect. They are also an expression of the objective principles of the constitution.[154] As the German Constitutional Court noted in *Lüth*:

> [T]he Basic Law is not a value-neutral document ... Its section on basic rights establishes an objective order of values, and this order strongly reinforces the effective power of basic rights. This value system, which centers upon dignity of the human personality developing freely within the social community, must be looked upon as a fundamental constitutional decision affecting all spheres of law. It serves as a yardstick for measuring and assessing all actions in the areas of legislation, public administration, and adjudication.[155]

---

[148] *Ibid.*, at 276.
[149] HCJ 7128/96 *Temple Mount Faithful* v. *Government of Israel* [1997] IsrSC 51(2) 509, 521 ("The 'level of tolerance,' which an offense to feelings has to exceed to be considered justifiable, is not set; it may change according to the circumstances. This level may depend, for example, regarding what is the protected interest standing *vis-à-vis* the feelings we wish to protect. If, for example, the protected interest is the right to freedom of speech, this level may be higher than in the case of the interest in obtaining financial gains." (Zamir, J.)); *Bakri*, above note 147, at 279 ("The 'level of tolerance' relating to the feeling of others is not a constant notion; this level may change from one liberty to another and from one value to another, according to the circumstances ... Thus, the level of tolerance justifying the limitation of the right to freedom of expression due to an offense to other people's feelings must be very high, and only extreme circumstances could justify such a limitation; otherwise, the right itself may become an empty shell, devoid of any real content." (Proccacia, J.)).
[150] See Barak, above note 30, at 35.   [151] See above, at 226.
[152] Regarding the independence of the judiciary, see Barak, above note 30, at 76.
[153] See above, at 39.
[154] See Alexy, above note 76, at 352. See also B. Pieroth and B. Schlink, *Grundrechte, Staatsrecht II*, § 76 (Heidelberg: Müller, 2006); K. Hesse, *Grundzüge des Verfassungsrechts der Bundesrepublik Deutschland* (Heidelberg: Die Deutsche Bibliotek, 1999), § 290.
[155] BVerfGE 7, 198. Translated by D. P. Kommers, *The Constitutional Jurisprudence of the Federal Republic of Germany*, 2nd edn. (Durham, NC: Duke University Press, 1997), 361, 363.

This approach has several implications.[156] For our purposes it means that a law limiting a constitutional right in order to realize an objective value derived from the subjective constitutional rights may be considered as doing so for a proper purpose. In many cases, this sub-category would parallel that of the protection of the rights of others. This is true in many cases, but not all. The objective values may extend beyond the areas where the individual has constitutional rights. Thus, for example, even constitutions recognizing human dignity as a right do not always recognize a (subjective) right to such dignity after death; but the objective value of human dignity may apply in that area for purposes of guaranteeing a proper burial.[157]

D. The urgency of proper purpose

1. The problems with urgency

For the purpose of a law limiting a constitutional right to be proper, two requirements must be met. First, the law's content should be proper, and, second, its urgency should be proper. The first requirement – relating to content – was examined in the previous pages. The urgency requirement will now be discussed. This requirement poses two separate issues. The first questions the status of urgency as an independent requirement: would the purpose requirement not be sufficient in itself, without the need to consider the urgency of the purpose as an independent and separate requirement? In particular, the claim is that it would be more appropriate to examine the issue of urgency during other stages of the proportionality test, in particular proportionality *stricto sensu* – the balancing between the benefits obtained by realizing the proper purpose and the harm caused to the constitutional right in question. It is only after we agree that urgency should be examined during the threshold stage of the proper purpose that we can move on the second issue, which tries to determine the precise criterion by which such urgency should be determined. For example, should the same degree of urgency be required for each constitutional right? If so what degree would that be? Perhaps the right solution is to require different degrees of urgency for each constitutional right? If

---

[156] One of which is related to the application of constitutional rights within private law; see above, at 39. Another is related to the duty of the state to affirmatively protect human rights rather than guard against their limitation. See below, at 422.
[157] CA 294/91 *Burial Society* v. *Kestenbaum* [1992] 46 (2) PD 464.

that is the case, what would then be the criterion for determining such varying degrees of urgency?

2.   Is "urgency" required?

A strong argument can be made that, if the purpose of the limiting law is proper, this is sufficient and no other requirement should be added – for example, urgency – to enable the realization of that purpose. According to this argument, the examination of the proper purpose is a threshold examination. This threshold examination should not include the degree of urgency in realizing that purpose while limiting a human right. This examination should only be conducted when examining the proportional relationship between the benefits in realizing the purpose and the harm caused to the constitutional right in question. According to that claim, during the balancing stage, we could examine the urgency of the purpose and the need for its realization. This is the approach adopted in German constitutional law.[158] There, the issue of the purpose's urgency is not examined during the first stage as a threshold question within the framework of the proper purpose. Rather, it is considered during the last stage of the examination, that of proportionality *stricto sensu*.

This approach, however, has been rejected in Canada[159] and South Africa.[160] In those legal systems, it was ruled that, during the threshold stage, it would be insufficient for the purpose to be proper in terms of its content only; rather, a certain degree of urgency is also required. According to that approach, there is no need to further examine the proportionality of the means used by the limiting law when the realization of the purpose of the limiting law is not urgent enough.

What is the proper approach? The issue is not free from doubt. On the one hand, we should acknowledge the close proximity between the examination of the purpose's urgency regarding the proper purpose and the examination of the urgency of the purpose in relation to the balancing within proportionality *stricto sensu*.[161] The importance of the purpose in relation to the balancing in the last stage includes, as a theoretical matter, an examination of how urgent the purpose really is.[162] On the other hand, it is worthwhile to examine the propriety of the purpose without the need

---

[158] See Grimm, above note 15.   [159] See below, at 279.
[160] See Woolman and Botha, above note 25, at 73.
[161] See below, at 340.   [162] See above, at 362.

to refer to the degree the constitutional right is limited. If the purpose is deemed improper due to a lack of urgency, what would be the point in "delaying" this discussion to the last stage of the examination? It would be much better to determine this issue during the threshold examination of a proper purpose. Still, we should be careful not to turn this threshold stage into a balancing examination – where a balance between the degree of urgency of the limiting law and the harm caused to the constitutional right in question is carried out.

3.   Criteria for determining urgency

i.   No single model

Comparative law reveals no uniform approach relating to the criterion by which the urgency of the purpose should be determined. Instead, several models are used. The differences between the different models can be explained by the varying structures of the provisions dealing with human rights in different constitutions, as well as the different starting points with respect to democracy and its values. Another major difference that may have led to the use of different models is related to the understanding of the concept of human rights: should they all be treated as equal, or are there rights that are considered more important than others? Here, the two main models will be examined. The first model uses a single, unified level of urgency. Thus, this model does not distinguish, regarding the level of urgency, between the different proper purposes or the different limited rights. Here, only a single level of urgency is set. This is the accepted model in Canada and South Africa. The second model does not determine a unified level of urgency; rather, it uses several levels while taking into consideration the importance of each limited right in question. This is the American model.

ii.   The first model: Canada and South Africa

a.   The Oakes test   The Canadian Charter of Rights and Freedoms contains a general limitation clause. The clause states that the rights and freedoms set out in the Charter are "subject only to such reasonable limits prescribed by law as can be demonstrably justified in a free and democratic society."[163] In *Oakes*, the Canadian Supreme Court provided

---

[163]   Canadian Charter of Rights and Freedoms, above note 6, Section 1.

an authoritative and comprehensive interpretation of this clause.[164] The Court established a unified examination for the urgency of the purpose of the limiting law; this examination is applicable, according to the Court, to each and every right and freedom set out in the Charter. According to this examination, a high degree of urgency is required for the purpose of a law limiting a constitutional right. The purpose should be of fundamental importance. It must be "pressing and substantial."[165] Regarding the level of urgency of the purposes limiting the constitutional right, the Court ruled in *Oakes* that:

> [T]he objective, which the measures responsible for a limit on a Charter right or freedom are designed to serve, must be of "sufficient importance to warrant overriding a constitutionally protected right or freedom." The standard must be high in order to ensure that objectives which are trivial or discordant with the principles integral to a free and democratic society do not gain Section 1 protection. It is necessary, at a minimum, that an objective relate to concerns which are pressing and substantial in a free and democratic society before it can be characterized as sufficiently important.[166]

The criterion set by the Court in *Oakes* has two distinct elements. First, it serves as a unified criterion, which applies as a minimum to all rights. Second, the criterion sets a high standard, which only the most urgent of purposes can realize. Each of these features will now be examined.[167]

b.   Uniform standard for the limitation of all rights   The Court in *Oakes* had established a uniform standard for the degree of urgency of the purpose of a norm limiting a constitutional right. All constitutional rights are equal in importance in that regard. Whatever the right, whatever the scope of its limitation, the standard remains the same with regard to the purpose of the limiting law. That uniform standard requires that the purposes of the limiting law be of sufficient importance and that they relate to concerns which are pressing and substantial in a free and democratic society.

The uniformity of the standard has been criticized. It was argued that a strict standard is not wanted,[168] and that the myriad of situations in which the standard should apply renders its uniform application nearly

---

[164]   See *Oakes*, above note 61.   [165]   *Ibid.*, at 136.   [166]   *Ibid.*, at 138.

[167]   See Weinrib, above note 102. See also R. M. Elliot, "The Supreme Court of Canada and Section 1 – The Erosion of the Common Front," 12 *Queen's L. J.* 277 (1987).

[168]   *R. v. Edwards Books and Art Ltd.* [1986] 2 SCR 713.

impracticable.[169] It is hard, the argument goes on, to compare cases in which the rights of an individual who faces proceedings initiated by the state are at stake (e.g., the rights of the accused in criminal cases) to cases where the state is called upon to fairly allocate its resources between several groups in the community. While the first group of cases may justify a uniform standard, it is much harder to justify such uniformity in the second group of cases. That group, the argument continues, should be left for the people to decide through democratic determination, through the legislative body, which should be reasonably free to choose between several polycentric considerations. Thus, for example, Justice La Forest emphasized the need to provide the legislator with "reasonable room to manoeuvre."[170]

It was held that the *Oakes* test – including the purpose's degree of urgency – is not decisive but should rather serve as a list of factors to be taken into account. The emphasis should be on the context in which the right appears, rather than an abstract examination of the right in question.[171] Chief Justice Dickson himself, who authored the *Oakes* opinion, joined this approach in another case where he wrote: "The application of the *Oakes* approach will vary depending on the circumstances of the case, including the nature of the interests at stake."[172] The need to consider circumstances, naturally, makes difficult the very existence of a uniform standard; in addition, it also questions the standard's high level. This aspect will now be examined.

c.   **Strict criterion setting a high standard**   The second aspect of the *Oakes* test relating to the degree of urgency of a law limiting a constitutional right is that the uniform standard "must be high." The threshold that the limiting law is required to pass is high. The requirement is that the limitation of a constitutional right must be justified by a fundamental need, which is "pressing and substantial in a free and democratic society." This strict requirement has set very high standards for the limitation of all rights; in fact, the standard was set so high that the Canadian courts could hardly meet it. Thus, soon after the *Oakes* decision was rendered, the Canadian

---

[169]   *RJR-MacDonald Inc. v. Canada (Attorney General)* [1995] 3 SCR 199. See also P. G. Murray, "Section One of the Canadian Charter of Rights and Freedoms: An Examination at Two Levels of Interpretation," 21 *Ottawa L. Rev.* 631 (1989); G. V. La Forest, "The Balancing of Interests under the Charter," 2 *Nat'l. J. Const. L.* 132 (1992).

[170]   See *Edwards*, above note 168, at 795; La Forest, above note 169, at 145.

[171]   See La Forest, *ibid.*, at 146.

[172]   *R. v. Keegstra* [1990] 3 SCR 697, 738.

Supreme Court held that a less strict approach was in order.[173] The reason for that decision was that the high standard set by the *Oakes* test may have prevented the realization of some important social and economic goals which, although they may not be "pressing and substantial," are certainly reasonable and therefore should be considered "proper." Thus, for example, Justice McIntyre stressed in *Andrews* that a more flexible standard is required: "To hold otherwise would frequently deny the community-at-large the benefits associated with sound social and economic legislation."[174]

Cracks were found in *Oakes*' "united front."[175] And, while *Oakes* was never formally overruled by the Canadian Supreme Court, it instead began to serve as the framework used to distinguish between several types of cases.[176] Thus, for example, it was stressed that the principles underlying the different rights may vary in terms of their weight depending on the constitutional circumstances in question. In that way, the context began to play a larger role in determining the constitutionality of the laws attempting to limit constitutional rights. As Justice Wilson noted in the *Edmonton Journal* case:

> One virtue of the contextual approach, it seems to me, is that it recognizes that a particular right or freedom may have a different value depending on the context. It may be, for example, that freedom of expression has greater value in a political context than it does in the context of disclosure of the details of a matrimonial dispute. The contextual approach attempts to bring into sharp relief the aspect of the right or freedom which is truly at stake in the case as well as the relevant aspects of any values in competition with it. It seems to be more sensitive to the reality of the dilemma posed by the particular facts and therefore more conductive to finding a fair and just compromise between two competing values under Section 1.[177]

What then remains of *Oakes*? Does the uniform examination still apply? Is the requirement that the proper purpose be of fundamental importance and relate to a concern that is "pressing and substantial" still valid? Or has a new paradigm begun – under the umbrella of the contextual approach – according to which different tests would apply to different circumstances?[178]

---

[173] See La Forest, above note 169, at 145.
[174] *Andrews* v. *Law Society of British Columbia* [1989] 1 SCR 143, 184.
[175] See Elliot, above note 167.
[176] M. Rothstein, "Justifying Breaches of Charter Rights and Freedoms," 27 *Man. L. J.* 171 (2000).
[177] *Edmonton Journal* v. *Alberta* [1989] 2 SCR 1326, 1355.
[178] See Murray, above note 169, at 636. See also P. Blache, "The Criteria of Justification under Oakes: Too Much Severity Generated Through Formalism," 20 *Man. L. J.* 437 (1991); A.

Whatever the case may be, the new developments pay – at the very least – lip service to *Oakes*, while the actual role of the proper purpose is not as central as it has been.[179] Hogg notes that there are few cases where the Supreme Court of Canada ruled that the purpose of the legislation does not realize the threshold that it itself has set:

> In practice ... the requirement of a sufficiently important objective has been satisfied in all but one or two of the Charter cases that have reached the Supreme Court of Canada. It has been easy to persuade the Court that, when the Parliament or Legislature acts in derogation of individual rights, it is doing so to further values that are acceptable in a free and democratic society, to satisfy concerns that are pressing and substantial and to realize collective goals of fundamental importance.[180]

d.   South Africa   The Constitution of the Republic of South Africa acknowledges that the rights included therein may be limited in some circumstances, including, *inter alia*, by taking into account "the importance of the purpose of the limitation."[181] Woolman and Botha refer to the Canadian *Oakes* case regarding the question of urgency, thus adopting the idea that the purpose should be "pressing and substantial."[182] The Constitutional Court, however, has yet to discuss that question. It is unlikely that the Court would follow in the footsteps of *Oakes*. The reason for this is that *Oakes* is based on the premise that all rights are equally important in the eyes of the constitution. No right is more important than another.[183] Accordingly, only one, unified standard is required. This is not the approach adopted by the Constitution of the Republic of South Africa. There, the general limitation clause specifically mentions the "nature of the right" as one of the factors to be taken into account when reviewing the proportionality of the limitation.[184] In addition, even assuming, *arguendo*, that the *Oakes* test would be adopted by the South African courts, the constitution itself holds that this factor – the importance of the purpose – is not the decisive factor, but is instead one of several

Lokan, "The Rise and Fall of Doctrine under Section 1 of the Charter," 24 *Ottawa L. Rev.* 163, 178 (1992).

[179] See M. Cohen-Eliya, "Limitation Clauses in Basic Laws on Human Rights, Considering the Right's Nature" (unpublished PhD dissertation, Hebrew University of Jerusalem, 2000) (on file with author).

[180] Hogg, above note 11, at 132.

[181] Constitution of the Republic of South Africa, Art. 36(1)(b).

[182] See Woolman and Botha, above note 25, at 75.

[183] See below, at 360.

[184] Constitution of the Republic of South Africa, Art. 36(1)(a).

considerations to be taken into account before determining the constitutionality of the limitation.[185]

e. **The second model: the United States**   The Bill of Rights contains
no explicit (general or specific) limitation clause. Despite the "absolute"
nature of some of the rights enumerated in the American Constitution,
the American Supreme Court has held, in a long line of cases, that these
rights can be limited.[186] The Court divides all constitutional rights into
three major categories,[187] with each category earning a separate degree
of urgency which characterizes it. Importantly, each category separately
examines the purpose of the limiting law and the means used by it to
realize that purpose. Only the first part – the purpose and the degree of
urgency required – is dealt with here.

The first category of rights relates to those rights which require "strict
scrutiny."[188] The rights included in this group are the fundamental rights,
such as the rights within the First Amendment freedom of political
speech, freedom of the press, the right to peacefully assemble, the free
exercise of religion, the right of movement within US borders, the right to
vote, and the right to equal protection of the laws in relation to a suspect
classification (based on either race or national origin). In order to justify
a limitation of one of those rights, the limiting legislative provision must
serve a "compelling state interest" (or a "pressing public necessity" or a
"substantial state interest"). The second category of rights is that of "intermediate scrutiny."[189] This group includes, among others, equal-protection
legislation relating to quasi-suspect classifications (based on gender or
age), the right to commercial freedom of speech, and the public forum
free-speech doctrine. In order to justify a limitation on rights included in
this category, the legislative provision in question must have an "important governmental objective." The third and final category is that of "minimal scrutiny" or "rational basis review."[190] This category applies to all the
other rights recognized by the Bill of Rights. Here, all the limiting legislative provision has to overcome to be justified is to show that it serves a
"legitimate governmental objective."

Accordingly, the American approach is characterized by a lack of a
uniform standard for examining the urgency of the proper purpose that

---

[185] *Ibid.*, Art. 36(1).   [186] See below, at 509.   [187] See below, at 509.
[188] Regarding this category, see below, at 510.
[189] Regarding this category, see below, at 511.
[190] Regarding this category, see below, at 511.

limits the constitutional right. According to the American approach, not all rights are of equal importance. Thus, a higher – and strict – standard was set in order to limit the rights with the higher social value. Indeed, few laws ever succeed in passing strict scrutiny. As Gunther noted, strict scrutiny is "strict in theory but fatal in fact."[191] Limiting rights in the second category, although not as hard, is also not a trivial matter – the standard is set quite high. Only the third category of the standard is set very low, and most legislative provisions pass the "rational connection" test and are thus able to limit the rights included in that group.

The comparative lesson to be learned from the American experience is important, though limited. It is important, as the lesson well demonstrates, that there is no need for a single uniform standard for the degree of urgency required for the limiting law; rather, separate standards may be set in accordance with the relative value of each limited right – since not all rights are of equal value.[192] Still, the lesson is limited, in that none of the categories includes the notion of balancing between the benefit gained by realizing the proper purpose and the harm caused to the constitutional right.[193] The concept of proportionality is built not only on the notion of a proper purpose, but also on the existence of a proportional relationship between the benefit gained by the realization of that purpose and the harm caused to the constitutional right. The very existence of this additional step – the examination of proportionality *stricto sensu* – may affect the standards that should be determined during the first stage of the constitutional review.

E.   Identifying the proper purpose

1.   *The purposes of the limiting law*

So far this book has focused primarily on constitutional interpretation in relation to the notion of proper purpose. It now turns from the constitutional to the sub-constitutional level. The examination will now consider how one could determine whether the limiting law, which operates at the

[191] See G. Gunther, "The Supreme Court 1971 Term – Foreword: In Search of Evolving Doctrine on a Changing Court: A Model for a Newer Equal Protection," 86 *Harv. L. Rev.* 1, 8 (1972); S. E. Gottlieb, "Compelling Governmental Interests: An Essential But Unanalyzed Term in Constitutional Adjudication," 68 *Boston University L. Rev.* 917 (1988); A. Winkler, "Fatal in Theory and Strict in Fact: An Empirical Analysis of Strict Scrutiny in the Federal Courts," 59 *Vand. L. Rev.* 793 (2006).
[192] See below, at 359.   [193] See below, at 508.

sub-constitutional level, successfully meets the requirements set out in the constitution with regard to the proper purpose. This discussion takes place at the sub-constitutional level. The question is whether the sub-constitutional law actually follows – and abides by – all the requirements presented by the constitutional provisions regarding the proper purpose. My goal here is to examine the criteria by which we may identify the purposes underlying the limiting law.

The identification of the purposes underlying the limiting law is not an easy task. In most cases, laws limiting constitutional rights do not appear before us with signs indicating their purpose. Moreover, even if such signs do exist – as in a "purpose clause"[194] – the issue is far from settled; the question of whether such a provision should serve as the final arbiter for the issue of purpose remains a valid one. Of the many issues arising from such a situation, two will be focused on. The first question is whether the purpose of a limiting law can be identified by the intentions of the creators of that law at the time it became a law ("subjective test"), or according to the meaning of the law's purpose at the time it is interpreted ("objective test"). Perhaps it should be identified in accordance with some combination of the two? If the answer to this first question entails a requirement to examine the subjective intent of the law's creators, then the second question becomes relevant: how can we identify the subjective purpose of the law's creators?

2.   Subjective or objective test?

i.   The issue defined

In most instances, the legislator's intent at the time of enactment and the purpose that the statute pursues are identical, or at the very least very similar. This is true in most cases, but not all. In some cases, there is a gap between the subjective purposes that the legislator intended the statute to serve at the time of its enactment and the objective purposes the statute realizes at the time of its interpretation.[195] Mostly, this is a function of the time that has passed between enactment and interpretation. An example of this phenomenon – which repeats itself in several legal systems – is

---

[194] See F. Bennion, *Statutory Interpretation: A Code*, 4th edn. (London: Butterworths, 2002).

[195] On the difference between subjective and objective purpose, see A. Barak, *Purposive Interpretation in Law* (Sari Bashi trans., Princeton University Press, 2005), 10.

the "Sunday Laws."[196] During their enactment, these laws – which restrict work or trade on Sundays – were intended to serve a religious purpose. Over the years, however, they were interpreted by the courts objectively as serving a social – rather than a religious – purpose, namely, to provide a mandatory day of rest for workers. Let us assume now that the old (religious) purpose is perceived today as unconstitutional, while the new (social) purpose is deemed constitutional. Which of the two is the relevant purpose for determining the constitutionality of the law?

This change, over time, to the statute's purpose raises a real difficulty in trying to identify the purpose of the limiting statute in terms of it being "proper." Does the original subjective purpose of the limiting law determine the issue of proper purpose, or is it the new, objective purpose? Also, perhaps we are looking at a dual requirement, in that both the subjective purpose at the time of enactment and the objective purpose during interpretation should be constitutionally "proper." With respect to the example of the Sunday Laws, in order to identify the proper purpose, should the original subjective (religious) purpose govern, or should the new objective (social) purpose govern? Perhaps both purposes should be considered? In order to answer this question, we should focus on two different aspects. The first is the interpretive aspect. Here, the question is how do we provide meaning to the legislative provision – should it be interpreted in accordance with its subjective or objective purpose? While discussing this aspect we do not examine issues of constitutionality. The second aspect is constitutional; it deals with the proper purpose as defined by the limitation clause. Here, the question is: what is the relevant legislative purpose to the issue of the constitutionality of the legislative provision? The first aspect relates to meaning. The second relates to validity.[197] Each of these aspects, beginning with the first, will be discussed below.

ii. The interpretive aspect

Different approaches were adopted by different legal systems with regard to the interpretive aspect. There are those who interpret laws according to their original intent (intentionalism) and there are those who interpret laws according to the original understanding (originalism). Others interpret law according to their objective purpose at the time of

---

[196] See Hogg, above note 11, at 136; L. H. Tribe, *American Constitutional Law*, 2nd edn. (Mineola, NY: Foundation Press, 1988), 1205.

[197] For the distinction, see Barak, *Purposive Interpretation*, above note 130.

interpretation.[198] According to the purposive method of interpretation, in certain instances, including laws which affect human rights, the law should be given a meaning most suitable to its objective purposes at the time the interpretation is made. The interpretation is dynamic.[199] The law is "always speaking."[200] As I explained elsewhere, through dynamic interpretation,

> [i]t is possible to give legislation a modern interpretation to suit modern needs. The language of the statute remains as before, but its meaning has changed to adapt the law to contemporary conditions. An example is a law passed by a nondemocratic regime. When the regime changes and democracy reigns, the law was interpreted according to democratic values, narrowing the gap between law and society. But beyond that, through interpretation and by understanding the text's (objective) purpose – new fundamental principles are introduced into the legal system.[201]

An example for that interpretive approach was provided by the Israeli Supreme Court, when interpreting legislation enacted during the British mandate over Palestine. In a long line of cases, the Court established the notion that the old legislation should be interpreted not in accordance with its old (non-democratic) intent, but rather in accordance with the values of the new, democratic State of Israel.[202] Accordingly, old British mandate legislation intended to curtail freedom of speech was interpreted not in light of its original intent, but according to the values of the State of Israel as a democracy at the time that the legislation was interpreted. Should the same approach apply to the identification of the purposes of the law in the constitutional context? This aspect will now be examined.

iii.   The constitutional aspect

In the context of the limitation clause, the subjective or objective nature of the purpose is not an interpretive matter. We are not dealing with the question of how to understand the old legislation. Rather, the matter concerns

[198] See Barak, *Purposive Interpretation*, above note 130; L. du Plessis, *Re-interpretation of Statutes* (Durban: Butterworths, 2002), 92; D. N. MacCormick and R. Summers, *Interpreting Statutes: A Comparative Study* (Aldershot: Dartmouth, 1991); K. Greenawalt, *Legal Interpretation. Perspectives from Other Disciplines and Private Texts* (New York: Oxford University Press, 2010).
[199] Regarding dynamic statutory interpretation, see W. N. Eskridge, *Dynamic Statutory Interpretation* (Cambridge, MA: Harvard University Press, 1994).
[200] Barak, above note 130, at 41; Bennion, above note 194, at 762.
[201] Barak, above note 130, at ___.
[202] HCJ 73/53 *"Kol Ha'am" Company Ltd.* v. *Minister of the Interior* [1953] *Selected Judgments* 1, 90, available at: http://elyon1.court.gov.il/files_eng/53/730/000/Z01/53000730.z01.pdf.

constitutionality. The issue is whether the constitutionality of a legislative provision, which was enacted (initially) for an improper subjective purpose, is determined by its historic purpose (which is not proper), or by its current objective purpose (which is proper), or whether the issue of constitutionality should be determined in accordance with both purposes.[203]

The starting point to answer this question must lie in the understanding that the criteria used for the interpretation of a limiting law are not identical to the criteria used to determine its constitutionality. Issues of meaning are not the same as issues of validity. When we interpret the statute purposively, we assume that the legislator acted in accordance with the constitution, and the only question before us is what is the message the statute meant to convey to members of society at the time of its interpretation? In that respect, we are assisted by an approach according to which, between two interpretations – assuming all other conditions are equal – we should always prefer the interpretation that is constitutional.[204] This is not the case, and this doctrine cannot be used, when we examine the constitutionality of the provision itself. When the issue of the statutory provision's constitutionality is on the line, the examination is focused on the question of whether that provision satisfies all the constitutionality requirements. In particular, the question is whether the constitutional validity of the limiting law should be determined by its (subjective) purposes at the time the law was created, by its (objective) purposes at the time of its interpretation, or according to both.

iv.   A survey of comparative law

a.   Canada   At first, the approach adopted by the Canadian Supreme Court in relation to the constitutionality of a statutory provision was that the original purpose envisioned by the legislator at the time of the enactment should prevail. One should not consider, using this approach, any social changes that took place after the legislation's enactment that may justify another purpose at the time of the law's interpretation. Thus, for example, in *Big M*,[205] the Court examined a Sunday Law (the "Lord's Day

---

[203] See J. Rivers, "Proportionality and Variable Intensity of Review," 65 *Cambridge L. J.* 174, 196 (2006).

[204] For an interpretation that matches the constitution, see below, at 445; *US ex rel. Attorney General* v. *Delaware & Hudson Co.*, 213 US 366, 407 (1909) ("It is elementary when the constitutionality of a statute is assailed, if the statute be reasonably susceptible of two interpretations, by one of which it would be unconstitutional and by the other valid, it is our plain duty to adopt that construction which will save the statute from constitutional infirmity.").

[205] *R.* v. *Big M Drug Mart Ltd.* [1985] 1 SCR 295.

Act"), which restricted the opening of businesses on Sundays. At the time of its enactment, the (subjective) purpose envisioned by the legislators was a religious one. This purpose was not perceived as "proper" at the time of the act's constitutional review; however, at the time of the review, the (objective) purpose of the law, which was social, was perceived as proper. The issue, however, was still unresolved: According to which purpose should the law's constitutionality be determined – the subjective or the objective one? The Canadian Supreme Court held that only the subjective purpose should be considered at a time when the constitutionality of the law is being examined. As Chief Justice Dickson noted: "Purpose is a function of the intent of those who drafted and enacted the legislation at the time, and not of any shifting variable."[206]

Not long after the *Big M* case was decided, however, the Canadian Supreme Court had an opportunity to reexamine the issue. In *Butler*,[207] the Court repeated its approach that the purpose's change over time should not be a determining factor; however, the Court added an important exception, according to which a "shift in emphasis" over time – as opposed to a shift in the purpose itself – may be considered by a court in determining the law's purpose. *Butler* dealt with a criminal restriction on the distribution of obscene materials. This restriction limited the freedom of speech. The historical purpose, envisioned by the legislators, was the advancement of moral values. The Court held that such a purpose is not proper. The Court continued to hold, however, that, according to modern social trends, this kind of restriction also serves the purpose of equality between the sexes – a proper purpose by all accounts. But, in his opinion, Justice Sopinka explained that the original purpose the law was intended to serve was, in fact, the prevention of the harm caused by obscene materials. The shift over time in what that damage actually consisted of was nothing more than a "shift in emphasis," according to him.

The same year (1992) that *Butler* was decided, the Canadian Supreme Court also decided *Zundel*.[208] There, the Court examined the constitutionality of a law prohibiting the publication of false information or news. Zundel, a Holocaust denier, was convicted of spreading false news. The Court held that the criminal prohibition limited the constitutional right to freedom of speech. The original purpose of the act was to protect senior officials – originally the monarchy and later the government – by protecting their reputation. This purpose, the Court held, could no longer be

---

[206] *Ibid.*, at 335.   [207] *R. v. Butler* [1992] 1 SCR 452.
[208] See *R. v. Zundel* [1992] 1 SCR 731.

considered "proper." The current purpose of the law, however, is to secure social harmony, which, according to the Court, was a proper purpose. Does the move from the original purpose into the new one constitute "shifting objectives" (which should not be considered by the Court), or merely a "shift in emphasis" (which may be considered)? The Court was divided in answering this question. The majority opinion, authored by Justice McLachlin, held that the move from the first purpose (protection of senior officials) to the second purpose (social harmony) should not be considered by the Court as it constitutes a shifting objective rather than merely a shift in emphasis. Accordingly, the law was declared unconstitutional. The dissent, by Justices Cory and Iacobucci, was of the opinion that the restriction in question has always had, as a primary purpose, the prevention of damage caused by the dissemination of false information. The only thing that the new purpose constitutes, according to this line of thought, is a shift in emphasis; and therefore, the law was constitutional.

Hogg explains the *Butler* exception by arguing that the Court is aiming at a purpose at the highest level of abstraction.[209] Here, he is definitely correct. But that might also miss the real issue. The issue is whether the purpose – read at its highest level of abstraction – is the subjective purpose, set at the time the provision was enacted. If this is the case, then viewing the purpose at a proper level of abstraction may be considered by the Court as a "shift in emphasis," and therefore permitted. However, if the Court were to view that different, higher level of abstraction as a new purpose, not considered earlier, then the result would be different. If that is the case, then this new purpose would constitute a "shift in purpose," and therefore its consideration would not be permitted by the Court, according to the approach in *Big M*.

b. South Africa The issue was examined in South African in the *Jordan* case.[210] There, the Constitutional Court reviewed the constitutionality of a criminal prohibition of running a brothel. The enactment of the prohibition, the Court held, was meant to protect a certain moral point of view. Such protection was deemed inappropriate at the time of the trial, as it did not take into consideration the values of a pluralistic society. Despite that, the Court (Justices O'Regan and Sachs) was of the opinion that the same law could be attributed a "modern" purpose, such as the regulation of the sex trade. In the Justices' view, this purpose is a proper one in a democratic society. A year earlier, in the *Moseneke*

---

[209] See Hogg above note 11, at 137. [210] *S. v. Jordan*, 2002 (6) SA 642.

case,[211] the same court reached a different result. There, the Court dealt with laws enacted during the Apartheid regime, which distinguished, for the purposes of handling the estates of intestate deceased persons, between black people and white people. The Constitutional Court has held that the law is so deeply grounded in the Apartheid past that no attempt should be made to salvage it by looking for a more modern, proper purpose.

The question yet to be resolved in South Africa is where precisely the line should be drawn between these two approaches. Is the degree of deviation from the proper essence of the purpose determinative? Woolman and Botha have warned, after quoting both opinions, that:

> [I]t must also remain on guard that less overt or pernicious forms of discrimination – or state support for particular traditions, religions or worldviews that marginalize smaller, more vulnerable groups – may be countenanced in the name of a new, ostensibly unproblematic purpose.[212]

c.   United States

aa.   The lack of a uniform solution   The American legal system does not provide a uniform solution to the question of whether the proper purpose, in relation to the constitutionality of a legislative provision, should be determined in accordance with subjective or objective tests.[213] As in the case of other constitutional law issues, the American approach is to break up the examination into three levels of scrutiny: minimal, intermediate, and strict.[214] The solution to the question varies with each level of scrutiny. Accordingly, it is impossible to speak about a uniform, all-encompassing theory of proper purposes, but rather each right is examined according to its special approach, the level of scrutiny derived from its location on the level of examination.

bb.   Minimal scrutiny   This level of scrutiny applies to all constitutional rights that are not included within the other two levels of scrutiny (intermediate and strict).[215] Thus, this category includes economic and property

---

[211] *Moseneke* v. *The Master*, 2001 (2) SA 18 (CC).

[212] See Woolman and Botha, above note 25, at 78.

[213] J. H. Ely, "Legislative and Administrative Motivation in Constitutional Law," 79 *Yale L. J.* 1205 (1970); P. Brest, "Palmer v. Thompson: An Approach to the Problem of Unconstitutional Legislative Motive," *Sup. Ct. Rev.* 95 (1971); L. A. Alexander, "Introduction: Motivation and Constitutionality," 15 *San Diego L. Rev.* 925 (1978).

[214] See above, at 284; see below, at 509.

[215] See above, at 284; see below, at 511.

rights, and the right not to be discriminated against when the discrimination is not based on a "suspect" classification – such as one based on race
or national origin – or a "quasi-suspect" classification – such as one based
on gender or age – is involved. When a law limits one of those rights, all
that is required for the law's purpose to be valid is that it serve a "legitimate governmental interest."[216]

Does American law require that the purpose in question be the one
envisioned at the time of the enactment? Or is it enough that the purpose is "proper" at the time the legislation is examined by the courts?
The answer, according to the US Supreme Court, is that only the existence of an objective legitimate purpose should be considered. As Justice
Rehnquist has observed:

> Where, as here, there are plausible reasons for Congress' action, our
> inquiry is at an end. It is, of course, "Constitutionally irrelevant whether
> this reasoning in fact underlay the legislative decision" because this Court
> has never insisted that a legislative body articulate its reasons for enacting
> a statute.[217]

Accordingly, it is sufficient that an objective legitimate purpose be assigned
to the legislative provision, regardless of whether this purpose was in fact
the one envisioned by the legislator at the time of enactment. Thus, in
order to successfully claim that the statute's purpose is not "proper," one
must deny the existence of every possible legitimate purpose. As Justice
Thomas has noted:

> [T]hose attacking the rationality of the legislative classification have the
> burden "to negative every conceivable basis which might support it." [B]
> ecause we never require a legislature to articulate its reasons for enacting
> a statute, it is entirely irrelevant for constitutional purposes whether the
> conceived reason for the challenged distinction actually motivated the
> legislature ... [A] legislative choice is not subject to courtroom fact-find-
> ing and may be based on rational speculation unsupported by evidence or
> empirical data.[218]

Only in a small number of cases has the legislation failed such a lenient
test.

---

[216] E. Chemerinsky, *Constitutional Law: Principles and Policies*, 3rd edn. (New York: Aspen
Publishers, 2006), 677.
[217] *United States Railroad Retirement Board v. Fritz*, 449 US 166, 179 (1980).
[218] *FCC v. Beach Communications*, 508 US 307, 315 (1993).

cc.   Strict and intermediate scrutiny   Strict scrutiny applies in cases of "suspect" discrimination (based on race or national origin), or in cases limiting fundamental First Amendment rights such as the freedom of expression (other than commercial freedom of speech and zoning restrictions regarding pornographic expression), and the freedom of religion, freedom of movement and the right to vote.[219] At this level of scrutiny, the legislation must satisfy the test of a "compelling state interest," a "pressing public necessity," or a "substantial state interest."[220] Intermediate scrutiny applies in cases of a "quasi-suspect" classification (based on gender or age), or in cases of commercial freedom of speech, or of zoning restrictions regarding pornographic expression. Here, the legislation in question must satisfy the "important governmental objective" test.[221]

In all these cases, one has to show – regarding the proper purpose – that the limitation of the right abides by all the requirements presented by that level of scrutiny, and particularly those terms relating to the component of purpose. Again, the issue arises: which purpose determines – the one that the legislator himself (as a subjective matter) envisioned at the time of the enactment, or the one that the provision actually fulfills, objectively? This question plays a special role when the legislation in question is related to equal-protection cases, relating to the right to equality before the law. In order to disqualify a law limiting the right to equality, is it enough to show that the original purpose of the law was to discriminate (and not to advance the relevant social interest), or is it enough to show that the law has a discriminate impact – that is, it actually discriminates?

The general question – relating to the relevance of the original intent of the legislation in the strict and intermediate levels of scrutiny – has no uniform answer. Rather, the answer varies according to the right in question, and, at times, within the boundaries of the right itself in accordance with judge-made distinctions created over the years. Here, the discussion will be limited to two rights included at the highest level of scrutiny, the strict scrutiny level. These are the prohibition of discrimination and the right to freedom of expression. Is the legislator's original intention relevant in examining the existence of a compelling state interest?

dd.   The relevance of intent in the limitation of equality   American history, more than any other factor, dictates the judicial treatment of this issue. Until the Civil War, slavery was prevalent in the South. After the

---

[219] See above, at 284; see below, at 510.
[220] See above, at 284; see below, at 510.
[221] See above, at 284; see below, at 511.

conclusion of the Civil War in 1865, the US Constitution was amended by the Thirteenth Amendment, which prohibited slavery. Three years later, in 1868, the Constitution was amended once again. The Fourteenth Amendment guaranteed, to "any person" within the United States, "the equal protection of the laws." The Supreme Court has held that the purpose of legislation attempting to limit equality should be reviewed at the highest level of scrutiny – strict scrutiny.[222] Accordingly, only a compelling state interest, a pressing public necessity, or a substantial state interest can satisfy the inquiry and justify a limitation on the right to equality (provided that other conditions are met[223]). The main reason – though not the only one – behind the Fourteenth Amendment, in this context, was the elimination of race-based discrimination.

How should legislative purposes which limit the right to equality be treated? In attempting to answer this question, American constitutional law has drawn a distinction between two sets of purposes which limit equality.[224] In the first, the alleged limitation of equality may be inferred directly from the legislative text (a limitation "on the face of the law"). This is the case, for example, when the provision in question makes race-based classifications. In the second set of cases, the law is "facially neutral," but its purpose, or impact, allegedly violates the right to equality.

According to the American approach, legislation creating a race-based classification is to be reviewed under the strict scrutiny test.[225] The provision can survive the test only if it can be proven – in relation to its purpose – that it was meant to achieve a compelling or substantial state interest, or a pressing public necessity. A subjective discriminatory purpose, therefore, may deny the existence of the required purpose.

How should a facially neutral provision be treated? In order to be reviewed under the strict scrutiny test, such a provision must satisfy the following conditions.[226] First, the subjective purpose of the law should be discriminatory; second, the impact of the law should also be discriminatory. Both conditions must be met in order for the law to be reviewed under strict scrutiny. If only one of the two conditions exists, the law is to be reviewed under minimal scrutiny.

---

[222] See Tribe, above note 196, at 145.   [223] See below, at 510.
[224] L. H. Tribe, *American Constitutional Law*, 3rd edn. (Mineola, NY: Foundation Press, 2000), 1502.
[225] R. H. Fallon, "Strict Judicial Scrutiny," 54 *UCLA L. Rev.* 1267 (2007).
[226] See Chemerinsky, above note 216, at 710.

296 THE COMPONENTS OF PROPORTIONALITY

When can we say that the provision's purpose is discriminatory? According to American law, a purpose is discriminatory whenever the legislator intended to discriminate, or, in other words, envisioned a discriminatory purpose. It is therefore insufficient that members of Congress envisioned a discriminatory impact, or that they were indifferent to the existence of a discriminatory purpose; instead, they had to have had the intent to discriminate. This was the position of the US Supreme Court in *Feeney.*[227] In that case, the court examined the constitutionality of a state's statute which afforded veterans an advantage in employee hiring. More than 98 percent of veterans are men. The law's effect, therefore, was discrimination against women in hiring. The Supreme Court has held that, despite the discriminatory effect, the purpose of the law cannot be seen as discriminatory since there was never a discriminatory intent behind it. As Justice Stewart wrote:

> "Discriminatory purpose" implies more than intent as volition or intent as awareness of consequences. It implies that the decisionmaker, in this case a state legislature, selected or reaffirmed a particular course of action at least in part "because of" not merely "in spite of," its adverse effects upon an identifiable group.[228]

ee. The relevance of intent in free speech cases The First Amendment right to freedom of expression has been comprehensively discusses by the US Supreme Court.[229] One of the basic distinctions drawn by the Court in this regard was that between a "content based" limitation on the freedom of expression, and a "content neutral" limitation. In the first case, when the limitation on the freedom of expression is related to the content of the speech, such as pornography, the limiting law is to be the subject of strict scrutiny. In the second case, when the limitation on freedom of expression is not related to the content of the speech – such as limitations on the time, place, and manner in which the speech is presented – then the limiting law would be the subject of intermediate, or at times minimal, scrutiny. The second category also includes laws that may be considered content based, but that their purpose is to achieve legitimate social goals (such as protection of the public order). Accordingly, legislation seeking

---

[227] *Personnel Administrator of Massachusetts* v. *Feeney*, 442 US 256 (1979).
[228] *Ibid.*, at 279.
[229] See Tribe, above note 196, at 785. See also T. I. Emerson, *The System of Freedom of Expression* (London: Vintage Books, 1970); F. Schauer, *Free Speech: A Philosophical Enquiry* (1982); H. Kalven, *A Worthy Tradition: Freedom of Speech in America* (Cambridge University Press, 1988); S. Shiffrin, *The First Amendment, Democracy and Romance* (Cambridge, MA: Harvard University Press, 1990).

to prevent the screening of pornographic movies near schools or churches is constitutional: Despite being content based, the purpose of the law is to regulate the secondary effects of the expression and not to regulate the expression itself.[230]

How should we determine whether the law limits freedom of expression based on its content? The US Supreme Court has distinguished between two sets of content based cases. In the first set of cases, the text of the legislative provision itself may teach us that the limitation of the freedom of expression is content based; these cases are termed facial content based. A law restricting the publication of pornographic materials falls well within that group. In the second set of cases, the text of the legislative provision in question is neutral; these cases are sometimes referred to as facial content neutral. Still, despite the facially neutral content, the purpose of the provision is still to limit freedom of expression due to the content of the expression itself. In both sets of cases, the legislative provision's purpose is controlling. In the first set of cases – facial content based – the purpose determines whether the law was primarily intended to limit the freedom of expression, or whether it was intended, instead, to regulate only the secondary effects of the expression. In the second set of cases – facial content neutral – the law's purpose determines whether it should be subject to strict scrutiny or to a lower level of scrutiny.

Whenever the law is subject to strict scrutiny review, it would survive such review only if it can be shown that it was enacted to serve a compelling or substantial state interest, or to serve another pressing public need. In order to answer the question whether these purposes are fulfilled, the legislative intent of the law's creators is also examined. As Justice Powell has noted: "[A] law will not pass Constitutional master if the ... purpose articulated by the legislature is merely a 'sham.'"[231] Tribe summarized the issue in the following way:

> In the first amendment context, the Supreme Court has been willing to inquire regarding – and to strike down executive and administrative actions on the basis of – what it determines to be improper motives or purposes.[232]

---

[230] See Chemerinsky, above note 216, at 937.
[231] *Wallace* v. *Jaffree*, 472 US 38, 64 (1985).
[232] See Tribe, above note 196, at 816.

This conclusion, however, is not free from doubt. There are many Supreme Court opinions – regarding both freedom of expression and other matters – that have ruled that the constitutionality of the legislative provision does not depend on the purpose or the motive behind its enactment.[233]

3. The correct solution for identifying the proper purpose

i. Identifying the proper purpose: a subjective-objective test

The basic premise before us is that a statutory provision limits a constitutional right. Such a provision is constitutional only if the limitation serves a proper purpose. The different standards used to determine what would constitute a proper purpose have already been discussed. The discussion now turns to the sub-constitutional level. I ask the question whether the examination of proper purpose is made in accordance with a subjective criteria (the legislator's intent at the time of the enactment was to fulfill those proper purposes), or in accordance with an objective criteria (the object of the statute, as it is interpreted by the judge at the time of the interpretation, was to fulfill those proper purposes), or some combination of the two. In attempting to answer this question, it is important to note that we are not dealing with the question of "what is the meaning of the limiting law?" The question is not interpretive in nature.[234] Rather, it asks whether the limiting law is proportional. The question is constitutional in nature. Thus, for example, it is certainly possible to deny consideration of the subjective purpose of the law in the context of its interpretation – taking into account only dynamic objective interpretation – while at the same time considering the subjective intent in the context of the law's constitutionality in order to determine the law's subjective purpose.

The right approach should be based on a combined test, so that the purpose of the limiting legislation would be considered proper only if it satisfies both the subjective and the objective tests.[235] This approach applies to all rights. Unlike American constitutional law, this approach does not distinguish between different groups of rights. Rather a purpose is proper

---

[233] *Ibid.*, at 819. See also *United States* v. *O'Brien*, 391 US 367 (1968); E. Kagan, "Private Speech, Public Purpose: The Role of Governmental Motive in First Amendment Doctrine," 63 *U. Chi. L. Rev.* 413 (1996).

[234] See above, at 72.

[235] See Pulido, above note 27, at 718. For a different approach, see Rivers, above note 203, at 196.

only if the legislator's intent at the time of the enactment was to fulfill the proper purpose and that the objective purpose of the legislation at the time of its interpretation still fulfills this proper purpose. Accordingly, if the legislative purpose – as it appears to the judge while deciding the constitutional issue – does not fulfill a proper purpose, the law would be unconstitutional regardless of the fact that the legislator may have had a proper purpose in mind.

ii.   Reasons supporting the combined test

At the foundation of my approach lies the notion that the requirements relating to proper purpose are aimed, first and foremost, at the creators of the limiting law. The legislator should enact laws limiting constitutional rights only if such laws serve proper purposes. When the legislator is aware, therefore, that the law's objective is not proper, it should avoid its legislation altogether. The legislator should not be able to rely on the hypothesis that, in the future, whenever such a law is brought before the court for constitutional review, the objective purpose gleaned from it would lead the court to conclude that it was enacted to serve a proper purpose. Indeed, a judicial recognition of such an "escape route" would release the legislator from the need to examine its own intentions, and may in fact incentivize the enactment of acts for improper purposes. Thus, for example, a legislator wishing to enact laws with discriminatory effects would simply enact "facially content neutral" laws, and thus achieve its improper purposes. Such a legislative option should not be allowed. If we take the notion of proper purpose seriously, we should not allow improper purposes which merely appear (in disguise) as proper purposes while using a neutral language. The truth behind the words should be exposed, and the legislator should be prevented from achieving any of its improper goals. As Tribe wrote, in the context of freedom of expression:

> If the first amendment requires an extraordinary justification of government action which is aimed at ideas or information that government does not like, the constitutional guarantee should not be avoidable by government action which seeks to attain that unconstitutional objective under some other guise.[235a]

Should the examination of the subjective intent suffice? The question arises in those instances where the legislator's initial (subjective) purpose has been proper. Why should we continue to examine, under these assumptions, the current (objective) purpose of the legislation? The answer

---

[235a] See Tribe, above, note 196 at 84.

is that each examination serves a different role. The examination of the
subjective intention at the time of the enactment is meant to prevent the
legislation of a law that may limit a constitutional right in order to serve
an improper purpose. The examination of the purpose at the time of the
interpretation is meant to ensure that the human rights in question are
protected for the duration of the law's existence and not only at its birth. It
is therefore insufficient that the statute was created through proper intentions. The same rule applies to all other components of proportionality,[236]
and this is the appropriate solution here as well. The approach is that the
law should sustain the requirements of proportionality for the entire duration of its existence.

iii.   Reasons against the combined test

There are three main arguments against the combined test. First, a
multi-member body such as a legislature does not have (and cannot
form) "intent." Rather, intent can only be ascribed to humans, as in the
examples of the intent of the drafter of a will, or the intent of a minister (or
secretary) in promulgating regulations. Such intent cannot be ascribed
to – and has no meaning in the context of – the legislative branch, where
a multi-member body attempts to reach a settlement on a contentious
policy issue. The same argument – the missing "intent" of a legislative
body – has also been raised in the interpretive context in addition to the
constitutional context. This argument cannot be accepted in the interpretive context[237] or in the constitutional context. The task of identifying legislative intent is complicated. The proposition that the personal
motives of each member of the legislative body are not relevant for the
inquiry is accepted; instead, it is the aggregate intention of the legislative
body as a whole that matters. That aggregate intention is the result of the
negotiations conducted by the separate members, and the settlement it
reflects. It is that collective will that brought about the law.[238] Indeed, in a
constitutional democracy with a proper political structure, the members
of the legislative body, collectively, devise a purpose.[239] If they reach an
agreement and if they constitute a majority, they would vote and enact

---

[236] See below, at 312 (regarding rational connection), at 331 (regarding necessity).
[237] Barak, *Purposive Interpretation in Law*, above note 195, at 132.
[238] *Ibid.*, at 133. See also R. Dworkin, *A Matter of Principle* (Oxford University Press, 1985), 48.
[239] See B. Bix, *Law, Language, and Legal Determinacy* (Oxford University Press, 1993), 183; K. Greenawalt, "Are Mental States Relevant for Statutory and Constitutional Interpretation?," 85 *Cornell L. Rev.* 1609 (2000).

a law which, in their opinion, is aimed at achieving that purpose. But such a purpose is identifiable and can be compared to the proper purpose ascribed to the law. If the two are not congruent, we can conclude that the law was enacted to serve an improper purpose. The refusal to accept the notion of legislative intent is much like a refusal to accept the notion of legislation at all. In many instances, the final legislative text is the product of long negotiations between members of the legislative body whose separate interests and motives are not always aligned with those of the act itself. But that is also precisely the reason why we should not search for those individual intents and motives when looking for the legislative intent. Despite this, getting from here to the conclusion that no legislative intention exists is a long road. The law's intent is the purpose that the law was meant to serve, and for which the law has achieved the proper majority.

The second argument against the combined test focuses on those laws that served, at the time of their enactment, an improper purpose, but may be now assigned with an (objective) proper purpose. In these types of laws, the argument goes, there is no point in examining the (subjective) legislative intent, since, even if the law is declared unconstitutional for that reason, the legislative body would be able to reenact it under the current (objective) purpose. There is no point, according to the argument, in declaring such a law as unconstitutional.[240] The response is that such a declaration is useful on two levels. First, it is not certain that the current purpose would gain the required majority in the legislative body in order to reenact the law. Second, if the law was declared unconstitutional due to its improper purpose, such a determination may well deter members of the legislative body from reenacting the same law, for fear that the court may find that the same purpose still underlies the current law, despite the attempt to conceal it behind the new (and legitimate) purpose.[241]

The third and final argument against the combined test is based on the evidentiary issues arising from the attempt to present the intent of a multi-member body such as the legislator. According to this argument, even if - arguendo - we can theoretically ascribe an intention to such a multi-member body, the actual identification of this intent is near to impossible. I cannot agree with this argument. There are several ways by

---

[240] See Tribe, above note 196, at 821.
[241] See T. Eisenberg, "Disproportionate Impact and Illicit Motive: Theories of Constitutional Adjudication," 52 *N. Y. U. L. Rev.* 36, 116 (1977).

which the intention of a multi-member body can be identified.[242] The US Supreme Court did not face many difficulties when attempting to identify this intent regarding the strict scrutiny test, where legislative intent plays a major role. Thus, for example, when the limited right in question was the right to equality before the law and the classification was "suspect" – that is, based on race (for example) – the courts concluded that the intention was discriminatory and therefore improper.[243] In addition, one can learn from the pre-legislative history, the legislative history, and the post-legislative history on the intent that was envisioned by the legislative body at the time the law was enacted. As Justice Powell wrote in *Arlington Heights*, which examined the ways in which such intent may be determined:

> Determining whether invidious discriminatory purpose was a motivating factor demands a sensitive inquiry into such circumstantial and direct evidence of intent as may be available. The impact of the official action – whether it "bears more heavily on one race than another" – ... may provide an important starting point. Sometimes a clear pattern, unexplainable on grounds other than race, emerges from the effect of the state action even when the governing legislation appears neutral on its face ... The evidentiary inquiry is then relatively easy. But such cases are rare ... The historical background of the decision is one evidentiary source, particularly if it reveals a series of official actions taken for invidious purposes ... The specific sequence of events leading up to the challenged decision also may shed some light on the decision-maker's purposes ... The legislative or administrative history may be highly relevant, especially where there are contemporary statements by members of the decision-making body, minutes of its meetings, or reports. In some extraordinary instances the members might be called to the stand at trial to testify concerning the purpose of the official action, although even then such testimony frequently will be barred by privilege.[244]

Naturally, the state can always present evidence to the contrary.

---

[242] See Tribe, above note 196, at 823.
[243] See Chemerinsky, above note 216, at 714.
[244] *Arlington Heights* v. *Metropolitan Housing Dev. Corp.*, 429 US 252, 266 (1977).

10

Rational connection

A. The nature of the rational connection test

1. The content of the rational connection test

What is required by the rational connection (fit, *geeignetheit*, appropriateness, suitability) test? The requirement is that the means used by the limiting law fit (or are rationally connected to) the purpose the limiting law was designed to fulfill. The requirement is that the means used by the limiting law can realize or advance the underlying purpose of that law; that the use of such means would rationally lead to the realization of the law's purpose. It is therefore required that the means chosen be pertinent to the realization of the purpose in the sense that the limiting law increases the likelihood of realizing its purpose. Accordingly, if the realization of the means does not contribute to the realization of the law's purpose, the use of such means would be disproportional. Consider the following examples:

(a) According to legislation in both Canada and South Africa, when an individual is in possession of an illegal drug it is presumed that the possession is for the purpose of trafficking. Both the Supreme Court of Canada[1] and the Constitutional Court of South Africa[2] have ruled that there is no rational connection between the purpose of the "war on drugs" and the legislative determination that the mere possession of a small amount of an illegal drug may promote the war on drugs.[3] As the legislation disproportionally limited the constitutionally protected right to the presumption of innocence, both laws were held unconstitutional. In the Canadian case, Chief Justice Dickson has noted that there should be a rational connection

---

[1] See *R. v. Oakes* [1986] 1 SCR 103.
[2] See *S. v. Bhulwana*, 1996 (1) SA 388.
[3] For criticism of that approach, see below, at 306.

between the possession of the illegal drug and the presumption that the possession was with the intent to sell.[4] Such a rational connection does not exist when the amount in question is either very small or negligible.

(b) In South Africa, the Constitutional Court examined a statute which established a presumption regarding unlawful weapons. According to the presumption, any person "present at or occupying" a premises "shall be presumed" to be in possession of the unlawful weapons found in the premises "until the contrary is proved."[5] The Court held the law to be unconstitutional because it disproportionally limits the constitutional right to the presumption of innocence. In particular, the Court noted that there is no rational connection between the purpose of the struggle against the illegal possession of weapons and one's random presence at the location where such unlawful weapons were found

(c) In South Africa, the Constitutional Court examined a statute which denied same-sex couples a number of benefits afforded to married couples. The Court ruled that the purpose of the law was proper, as it was meant to protect the traditional family structure. However, the Court ruled that there is no rational connection between that purpose and the means of denying the benefits.[6]

(d) In Germany, a statute prescribed that in order to receive a hunting permit adequate knowledge of the use of firearms was required. It was argued that the law was unconstitutional as it relates to hunting with eagles. The German Constitutional Court held that the limitation on the constitutional freedom to develop one's personality is disproportional, as no rational connection exists between the law's purpose (guaranteeing the community's protection from hunting weapons) and the means used by the law – the requirement of technical knowledge of firearms regarding hunting with eagles – which is connected to an activity that has nothing to do with firearms.[7]

---

[4] See *Oakes*, above note 1, at 142. For the approach in New Zealand, see *Hansen* v. *R.* [2007] 3 NZLR 1 (CA).

[5] See *S.* v. *Mbatha*, 1996 (2) SA 464.

[6] See *National Coalition for Gay and Lesbian Equality* v. *Minister of Home Affairs*, 2000 (2) SA 1 (CC), § 56.

[7] See BVerfGE 55, 159.

2. *The nature of the rational connection*

The rational connection test does not require that the means chosen be the only ones capable of realizing the limiting law's purpose.[8] There is no requirement that one means and no other realize the proper purpose. There may be cases where several means are used – and all are considered as having a rational connection to the purpose. Take, for example, the regulation of the legal profession, which can be regulated in different ways. One way is self-regulation; another is through a governmental agency. The fact that several options exist does not render the selected means one without a rational connection.

There is no requirement that the means chosen fully realize the purpose. A partial realization of the purpose – provided that this realization is not marginal or negligible – satisfies the rational connection requirement.[9] Therefore, the requirement is that the legislative means sufficiently advance the purpose limiting the constitutional right and that there be a fit between the means chosen and the proper purpose.[10]

The question raised by the rational connection test is not whether the means are proper and correct, or whether there are other, more proper and correct means; rather, the question is: are the means chosen by the limiting law capable of advancing the law's underlying purpose?[11] Thus, whenever the means chosen do not advance the purpose – or have no effect on it – they have failed the rational connection test. In these cases, we may conclude that the legislator "missed its target." Of course, when the means chosen harm the purpose – instead of advancing it – these too will fail the test. However, there is no efficiency requirement. In order to pass the rational connection test, the means can advance the purpose inefficiently.[12]

---

[8] See N. Emiliou, *The Principle of Proportionality in European Law: A Comparative Study* (London: Kluwer Law International, 1996), 28.

[9] See *ibid.*, at 26; C. B. Pulido, *El Principio de Proporcionalidad y los Derechos Fundamentales* (Madrid: Centro de Estudios Políticos y Constitucionales, 2007), 723. See also J. Rivers, "Proportionality and Variable Intensity of Review," 65 *Cambridge L. J.* 174, 189 (2006).

[10] In that sense, the requirement mimics that of the American "rational connection" test (which is used at the lowest level of constitutional scrutiny). See E. Chemerinsky, *Constitutional Law: Principles and Policies*, 3rd edn. (New York: Aspen Publishers, 2006), 685; A. Stone Sweet and J. Mathews, "All Things in Proportion?: American Rights Doctrine and the Problem of Balancing," *Emory L. J.* (forthcoming, 2011).

[11] See Rivers, above note 9, at 197.

[12] See H. Avila, *Theory of Legal Principles* (Dordrecht: Springer, 2007), 116.

With this is mind we can return to examine some of the aforementioned examples.[13] Take the statutory provision reversing the burden of proof in drug-possession cases. This provision satisfies the rational connection test, if only in part,[14] since the probability that a person in possession of an illegal substance may be related to drug trafficking is not trivial. The main difficulty with burden-reversing legislation has less to do with the test of rational connection and more to do with the other tests (which will be discussed in the following chapters).[15]

3.   Rational connection and the means "designed to achieve" the proper purpose

In some cases, it was held that in order to satisfy the rational connection requirement the means chosen must be designed to achieve the purpose of the limiting law. As Chief Justice Dickson has noted in *Oakes*, the legislative means has to be "carefully designed to achieve the objective in question."[16] This approach is correct if by "designation" we refer to the ability of the means to advance the purpose in question. This approach is not correct, however, if by "designation" we mean the selection of the most adequate means – that is, a means that would neither over-expand nor over-restrict the limitation imposed by the law.[17] That second meaning of "designation" is not related to the rational connection test, though it may lead to the conclusion that the purpose of the limiting law is not the one claimed by the state but rather a different purpose.[18] In any event, this second meaning of "designation" is related to necessity[19] and proportionality *stricto sensu*[20] tests, which will be discussed in the following chapters. Accordingly, it would be advisable, so as to avoid terminological confusion, not to use the term "designation" in relation to the rational connection test.

---

[13] See above, at 303.   [14] See Avila, above note 12, at 181.

[15] See V. Tadros and S. Tierney, "The Presumption of Innocence and the Human Rights Act," 67 *Mod. L. Rev.* 402 (2004); D. A. Hamer, "The Presumption of Innocence and Reverse Burdens: A Balancing Act," 66 *Cambridge L. J.* 142 (2007).

[16] See *Oakes*, above note 1, at para. 70. See also *R. v. Edwards Books and Art Ltd.* [1986] 2 SCR 713, 770: "The requirement of rational connection calls for an assessment of how well the legislative garment has been tailored to suit its purpose".

[17] See Rivers, above note 9, at 188.

[18] See J. Kirk, "Constitutional Guarantees, Characterisation and the Concept of Proportionality," 21 *Melb. U. L. Rev.* 1, 4 (1997).

[19] See below, at 317.   [20] See below, at 340.

4. Rational connection and arbitrary means

In *Oakes*, Chief Justice Dickson emphasized that "the measures adopted ... must not be arbitrary, unfair, or based on irrational connections."[21] This statement well reflects the essence of the rational connection test if it relates to the requirement that the means adopted would be rational. That said, it seems that the "fairness" requirement is not directly related to the rational connection test, or – in other words – that it should be considered at this point of the analysis. In theory, a means chosen by the limiting law may be unfair but still rationally connected to the purpose in question. The fairness of the means is certainly important. An unfair means may limit the right to equality; an unfair means may not satisfy the proper purpose requirement; and it may also fail the other requirements imposed by proportionality.[22] Despite all that, an unfair means may rationally lead to the realization of the proper legislative purpose.

A similar issue arises regarding the approach that an "arbitrary" means does not fulfill the requirements of the rational connection test. This is true in some cases, but is it always true? The arbitrary nature of the means may indicate that the purpose is not proper.[23] It is possible that it may not pass proportionality's other tests. Still, this does not mean that, in every case in which arbitrary means are used, it fails to advance the proper purpose. A more thorough examination should be conducted as to the reasons for the arbitrariness, as well as its consequences. Certain aspects of the arbitrariness lead to the conclusion that no rational connection exists between the purpose and its realization. Other aspects might not necessarily lead to the same conclusion. Importantly, only those aspects of the arbitrary means that relate to their ability to advance the purpose in question are pertinent to the rational connection test. Other aspects of arbitrariness can be examined at other stages of the constitutional review of proportionality.

The rational connection test is a factual test. It asks an empirical question regarding the ability of the means used by the limiting law to advance or realize the proper purpose. Thus, the unfairness or arbitrariness of the test are irrelevant *per se*.

---

[21] See *Oakes*, above note 1, at para. 70.
[22] See Kirk, above note 18, at 5.
[23] See *ibid.*, at 6.

B. The rational connection test and factual uncertainty

1. The problem of factual uncertainty

Uncertainty is a well-known condition in the law.[24] It has many facets. One of these is the uncertainty frequently encountered regarding the probability of the means chosen to realize the purpose. In many cases, the means are chosen through prognosis and according to the probabilities regarding social, economic, and political developments. The latter, however, hardly ever reach a level of certainty as to the issue of whether the means chosen would actually advance the purpose in question. Take, for example, the Israeli Supreme Court case of the *Gaza Coast Regional Council*.[25] Here, the Court examined the constitutionality of a law implementing the Israeli government's disengagement plan from the Gaza Strip.[26] The law ordered the evacuation of all Jewish settlements and settlers from that area. As such, the law limited the constitutional rights of the Israeli settlers to human dignity, to property, and to freedom of occupation. The settlers claimed that such a limitation is unconstitutional. In particular, it was argued that no rational connection exists between the evacuation and the security and national purposes prescribed by the law. The majority opinion in that case phrased the issue in question as follows:

> Is there a rational connection between the policy, national, and security purposes underlying the Disengagement Act and the means chosen by that Act – namely the evacuation of Israeli settlers? According to the petitioners, the required rational connection does not exist. They claim that the plan would not advance the benefits assumed to be gained by the Act, but rather would inflict serious harm on each of the Act's goals. Are the petitioners correct?[27]

Further explaining the issue relating to the rational connection test, the majority noted:

> The disagreement between the parties revolves around the probability of realizing the purposes underlying the disengagement plan. Regarding this complex issue, however, it seems that no one is arguing for complete

---

[24] See A. Vermeule, *Judging under Uncertainty* (Cambridge, MA: Harvard University Press, 2006).

[25] See HCJ 1661/05 *Gaza Coast Regional Council* v. *Knesset of Israel* [2005] IsrSC 59(2) 481.

[26] Law of Implementing Disengagement Program (2005).

[27] See *Gaza Coast Regional Council*, above note 25, at 572.

certainty. Rather, we are dealing with evaluations of policy, and national and security interests; these evaluations, in turn, depend on many external factors that cannot be controlled. These are a series of "polycentric" considerations – considerations without a single focal point but rather they are based on several variables and their varying effects. When approaching this type of considerations, it is impossible to determine a single probability standard, but rather to examine a series of variables.[28]

Is the lack of factual certainty sufficient to lead to the conclusion that no rational connection exists between the means and the purpose? Does the rational connection test require factual certainty? If not – what is the rational connection test's requirement?

2. The certainty of the rational connection: rejection of extreme approaches

One extreme approach is that the rational connection test should demand complete certainty in that the means chosen by the law lead to the realization of the proper purpose. This approach provides maximum protection to all human rights. Still, it should not be adopted.[29] It does not suit the modern notion of the functions filled by the political branches (the legislative and executive) in a constitutional democracy. These functions include the setting and implementation of social policy. This is the case even if such policy contains elements of uncertainty. If complete certainty was required for the successful implementation of policy we would be unable to achieve most of the economic, security, social, and national objectives of the state. We should always remember that, while human rights are central to democracy, they are not democracy's only component. Alongside the recognition of human rights, we should recognize other proper interests that the political authorities seek to advance.

Another extreme approach maintains that the rational connection test is satisfied every time the political branches (legislative and executive) are of the opinion that such a connection exists. Admittedly, such an approach would enable the political branches to fulfill their proper purposes. Still, this position should also not be adopted. It is not consistent with the place human rights occupy in a constitutional democracy. This status indicates that human rights may not be limited based on mere speculations that are out of touch with reality, the result of which may be

---

[28] *Ibid.*
[29] See Emiliou, above note 8, at 27. See also R. Alexy, *A Theory of Constitutional Rights* (Julian Rivers trans., Oxford University Press, 2002 [1986]), 417.

that of no contribution – or a marginal contribution, at best – of the means chosen to the realization of the proper purpose. And, while it is true that the will of the majority and its needs are central tenets in democracy, they are not its only tenet. Alongside the public interest are the individual's rights. Such rights may not be limited through mere speculations.

The conclusion which arises from this analysis is that the rational connection test is not based on the notion that the means chosen realize the proper purpose in complete certainty.[30] However, a marginal contribution alone will not suffice.[31]

3. Determining the factual basis required for the existence of the rational connection

The evaluation of the existence of a rational connection is based on the facts presented to the legislator and the legislator's evaluation based on those facts. The evaluation is also based on the shared life-experience of a given society, as well as on the knowledge provided by science.[32] Mainly, the test is based on logic and common sense. As Justice Wilson has noted:

> The *Oakes* inquiry into "rational connection" between objectives and means to attain them requires nothing more than showing that the legitimate and important goals of the legislature are logically furthered by the means government has chosen to adopt.[33]

At times, the text of the law is insufficient in order to evaluate the likelihood of the existence of the rational connection. "Rationality requires facts, suitability needs data."[34] Regarding this situation, I have noted that:

> We are required to examine the social reality which the law sought to change. Typical to these cases is the realization that the evaluation of the rational connection, or the "fit," largely depends on future events. These are cases where various variables may affect the actual fit of the means

[30] See D. P. Currie, *The Constitution of the Federal Republic of Germany* (University of Chicago Press, 1994), 72.
[31] See *Lesapo* v. *North West Agricultural Bank*, 2000 (1) SA 409 (CC).
[32] See Pulido, above note 9, at 727.
[33] See *Lavigne* v. *Ontario Public Service Employees Union* [1991] 2 SCR 211.
[34] See HCJ 366/03 *Commitment to Peace and Social Justice – An NGO* v. *Minister of Finance* [2005] 104, 163. (Levy, J.), available in English at http://elyon1.court.gov.il/files_eng/03/660/003/a39/03003660.a39.pdf.

chosen to the purpose in question, as well as the rational connection between them. That fit, or rational connection, is then examined according to the results they may achieve in practice.[35]

The burden of proof is on the party arguing that there exists a rational connection.[36] When the state is the one defending the constitutionality of a legislative provision, it is required to present the factual foundation to the court on which the legislator based its evaluations. Obviously, the opposite party may present any factual foundation which appears proper to them. Based on the determined factual foundation, the court will examine the probability of realizing the proper purpose through the arrangements available in the law. Here, the court acknowledges the wide discretion granted to the legislator in these matters. As I have noted elsewhere:

> [T]he judge should beware of applying complex considerations of economic or social policy, which frequently are the subject of controversy, require expertise and information, and may necessitate assumptions and hypotheses that in turn require additional assumptions. The safe and reasonable way will usually be to leave the matter to the legislature, which can obtain all the relevant information from experts and which can formulate a public policy that suits the issue in its entirety.[37]

As for the policy, economic, and security-based considerations at the foundation of the disengagement, the Israeli Supreme Court (majority opinion) has noted, in the *Gaza Coast Regional Council* case:[38]

> In an issue such as the one before us, the Court should assume that both the legislative and executive branches have weighed the entire spectrum of probability considerations, while consulting experts in all relevant fields available to them. These branches bear the national responsibility for these difficult decisions. This is their role in the triangle of the three branches of government. They, and not the courts, should decide on these issues. Of course, there will be exceptions – for example, when corruption is proved – where the courts will determine that national policy with such far-reaching implications, such as the disengagement plan, does not advance its purposes.[39]

35 See HCJ 6427/02 *The Movement for Quality Government in Israel* v. *The Knesset* [2006], para. 58 (Barak, P.), available in Hebrew at http://elyon1.court.gov.il/files/02/270/064/a22/02064270.a22.HTM.
36 See below, at 439.
37 See A. Barak, *Judicial Discretion* (New Haven, CT: Yale University Press, 1989), 183. See L. Fuller, "The Forms and Limits of Adjudication," 92 *Harv. L. Rev.* 353, 364 (1979).
38 See *Gaza Coast Regional Council*, above note 25.
39 See *Gaza Coast Regional Council*, above note 25.

The *Gaza Coast Regional Council* case is unique in terms of the wide discretion granted to the legislator. However, even in less extreme cases, the same principle should apply. Indeed, the legislator's discretion in determining its legislative prognosis is wide.[40] The fact that at times there is a mistake is not sufficient to justify judicial reversal. However, the discretion is not absolute. Although complete certainty is not required for the legislative prognosis, mere speculation is also insufficient. An appropriate factual foundation should be laid.

4. *Rational connection and the test of time*

At what point in time is the rational connection tested?[41] When should a rational connection exist between the means chosen by the limiting law and its proper purpose? Should the connection occur at the time of enactment (*ex ante*) or at trial (*ex post*)? Should the rational connection test requirement be satisfied at both times?

The examination of the rational connection should be continuous.[42] There is no determining point in time. Rather, every point of the limiting law's life is relevant; the rational connection must exist throughout the law's entire lifespan. The issue of constitutionality accompanies the law throughout its existence.[43] Regarding the date of the law's enactment, the law must fulfill the rational connection test – that is, the means determined by the limiting law, and which limit the constitutional right, should have a rational connection to the purpose the law was designed to achieve. There is no need to prove, with complete certainty, that the purpose of the law will actually be realized. All that is required is that the probability of realizing that purpose is not trivial, or theoretical. Such an examination is forward-looking (*ex ante*). The requirement cannot be that the purpose be immediately realized with the law's enactment, or that the probability of its realization be clear at that point. Rather, the legislative prognosis should be examined as to its future evaluations. Thus, even when the legislative purpose is not achieved upon enactment but it is assessed that it will be fulfilled at a time still pertinent to the law's existence, this is sufficient to establish that at that point in time the required rational connection exists. Conversely, if it is that the law's purpose will not be fulfilled

---

[40] See below, at 405.

[41] See Emiliou, above note 8, at 28.

[42] See *ibid.*, at 27. For an *ex ante* approach, see Pulido, above note 9, at 731.

[43] Regarding necessity, see below, at 331.

either at enactment or in the future, that is sufficient to rule out the existence of a rational connection.[44]

What should the result be when on enactment the law seems to have
satisfied the rational connection test, but later on during its constitutional
examination (*ex post*) it turns out that it does not satisfy that requirement
and that, in fact, there is no chance it would be relevant to the law's lifespan
in the future? In this situation, the correct determination is that rational
connection does not exist (from here on in). The fact that at the time of the
enactment an evaluation predicted that the existence of a rational connection does not render obsolete the need to examine whether that prediction
is proved correct. If once again it turns out that there is no chance at fulfilling the law's purposes, one should conclude that no rational connection exists. Conversely, should the examination reveal that in the future it
is still likely that the prediction be proved correct, we should refrain from
the determination that no rational connection exists. Rather, this question can be reexamined in the future. Similarly, if during the examination
it is resolved that the law cannot advance its own purposes – either now or
at any relevant period in the future – then the court may determine that
the law has failed the rational connection test.

An example for this state of affairs was provided by the Israeli Supreme
Court in the case of *The Movement for Quality in Government*.[45] In Israel,
a mandatory draft to the military is in effect for all 18-year-old men and
women. The Israeli Parliament enacted a law postponing military service for religious students who devote their life to study of the Torah. The
law contained a sunset provision, limiting its effect for five years.[46] The
Supreme Court examined the constitutionality of the law three years into
its enactment. It was argued that the law limits the constitutional right
to equality, and does not satisfy the requirements found in the limitation clause. The majority opinion accepted the claim that the law limits
the right to equality. Regarding the limitation clause, it was held that the
purpose the law was meant to serve was proper. What about the other
components of proportionality? The Court reviewed the test of rational
connection, and held:

> It should be examined whether the law satisfies the requirement of a
> rational connection (or "fit") between the integrated purposes of the
> law postponing military service and the means used for its fulfillment.

[44] See Emiliou, above note 8, at 26.
[45] See *The Movement for Quality Government in Israel*, above note 35.
[46] See Law to Postpone Service for Students Devoting Their Life to Torah Study (2002).

Such an examination should be done, in this context, not as a theoretical exercise but as a practical matter, tested by its actual results. Indeed, as a theoretical question examined at the time of the law's enactment, it is possible that the legislative arrangements may bring about the desired results … But such an advanced examination (*ex ante*) is insufficient. When the underlying purpose of the legislation is to lead to social change, which is not only a theoretical evaluation but rather is examined throughout the test of life, the fit between the means and ends should be examined through the results obtained … The test of the service-postponement law is its actual fulfillment, the real social change achieved by the law.[47]

In its opinion, the Court examined the fulfillment of the law's purposes and concluded that, according to the results on the day of the trial, there was no rational connection between the law's purposes and the means chosen for their realization. It was held that "the law's purposes were realized but to a negligible degree."[48] However, the Court was of the opinion that not enough time had passed in order to fully examine the existence of a rational connection. I wrote in my judgment:

The law postponing military service deals with a fundamental problem in Israeli society, which cannot be resolved with a stroke of a pen. It deals with a sensitive topic, requiring tolerance and consensus. It seeks to provide solutions that are neither easy nor simple to implement. It was enacted, specifically, as a temporary measure containing a sunset clause. The legislature asked for time to examine the fit between the law's purposes and the means chosen to advance them. We are dealing with a complex social issue. A waiting period of five years falls well within the legislative discretionary purview. All these factors require us to withhold our conclusions. We have to provide the executioners of this law with the opportunity to fix what they broke. We should enable Israeli society as a whole, and the Haredi faction in particular, to internalize the legislative arrangements set up by the law as well as their intended implementation. All these considerations indicate that we should withhold our judgment for a period of five years from the date of the enactment of the law. By then, the legislator should have carefully reviewed the ways of its actual realization. In particular, the legislator would have to have examined whether the time that has passed since this decision was rendered has changed the legislative landscape significantly.[49]

Accordingly, the petition was denied; while the Court announced that, "although we have ruled today that the petitions are denied – as at this

---

[47] See *The Movement for Quality Government in Israel*, above note 35, at paras. 63–64 (Barak, P.).
[48] *Ibid.*, para. 66 (Barak, P.).   [49] *Ibid.*, para. 68 (Barak, P.).

point we cannot render a decision as to the law's constitutionality – we also hold that if the current trend continues and no significant change occurs in the state of affairs, there is concern that the postponement law will become unconstitutional."[50]

5. Rational connection: a threshold test

The rational connection component – much like the proper purpose component – is a threshold test.[51] It is not a balancing test.[52] It does not balance between the proper purpose and the limitation of the right. Rather, it rules out instances where a law limits a constitutional right without advancing the purposes it is designed to achieve. It is based on factual probabilities – and therefore is considered a factual test, of a negative nature.[53] The rational connection test does not examine the relationship between the purpose and the limited constitutional right; rather, it deals with the relationship between the purpose in question and the means chosen to advance it. In other words, the probability question which the rational connection test is meant to deal with is the probability that the means used by the law fulfill the public interest, which is at the foundation of the law. The rational connection test was not designed, however, to provide an answer to the questions relating to the probability that if the means are used the constitutional right will be effected, or if the means are not used the public interest will be damaged.

C. Is the rational connection test essential?

Is the rational connection test essential? Can we do without it? If the test only rules out the cases where no rational connection exists between the limiting means determined by law and its proper purpose, then there is no real need for it.[54] The reason is that the necessity test – the lack of a lesser limiting alternative – can solve the same cases, since in this situation the lack of legislation would be considered a less limiting alternative. If there

---

[50] *Ibid.*, para. 70 (Barak, P.).   [51] See Rivers, above note 9, at 189.

[52] See M. Cohen-Eliya and I. Porat, "American Balancing and German Proportionality: The Historical Origins," 8 *Int'l J. Const. L.* 263 (2010).

[53] See Alexy, above note 29, at 398. See Pulido, above note 9, at 726.

[54] See J. Rivers, "A Theory of Constitutional Rights and the British Constitutions," in R. Alexy (ed.), *A Theory of Constitutional Rights* (Julian Rivers trans., Oxford University Press, 2002 [1986]); W. Sadurski, *Rights before Courts: A Study of Constitutional Courts in Postcommunist States of Central and Eastern Europe*, 2nd edn. (Dordrecht: Springer, 2008), 268.

is a need for legislation – that is, if there is no less limiting alternative (and the necessity test is satisfied) – then in any case a rational connection exists. Either way, the rational connection test may also be considered part of the "necessity" requirement.

It seems that the question of necessity of the rational connection test arises only regarding those cases where the means chosen by the limiting law do advance the law's purpose, but only to a very limited extent. In these cases the rational connection test stands on its own: through it we can examine whether the purpose presented as the legislative purpose is, indeed, the real purpose.[55] We will admit it is not that significant. Its entire purpose is to provide a quick solution in extreme cases where the incongruence between the means and the purpose is obvious, and by that to expedite the process of constitutional review.[56] Grimm was therefore right when he noted, in relation to the rational connection test, that "its function is to eliminate the small number of runaway cases."[57] Even this perhaps unimpressive contribution to the analytical process should not be discounted.

---

[55] See Kirk, above note 18, at 6; J. Jowell, "Beyond the Rule of Law: Towards Constitutional Judicial Review," *PL* 669, 679 (2000); A. Kavanagh, *Constitutional Review under the UK Human Rights Act* (Cambridge University Press, 2009), 235.

[56] See J. Schwarze, *European Administrative Law* (London: Sweet & Maxwell, 1992), 857.

[57] See D. Grimm, "Proportionality in Canadian and German Constitutional Jurisprudence," 57 *U. Toronto L. J.* 383, 389 (2007).

11

Necessity

A. Characteristics of the necessity test

1. *The content of the necessity test*

The next component of proportionality is the necessity test (*Erforderlichkeit*). It is also referred to as the requirement of "the less restrictive means." According to this test, the legislator has to choose – of all those means that may advance the purpose of the limiting law – that which would least limit the human right in question. This test was discussed in the *United Mizrahi Bank* case:

> A statute limits a fundamental right to an extent no greater than is required only if the legislator has chosen – of all the available means – that which would least limit the protected human right. The legislator, accordingly, should begin with the lowest "step" possible, and then proceed slowly upwards until reaching that point where the proper purpose is achieved without a limitation greater than is required of the human right in question.[1]

This test of proportionality is based on the premise that the use of the law's means – or the need to use such means – is required only if the purpose cannot be achieved through the use of other (hypothetical) legislative means that would equally satisfy the rational connection test and the level of their limitation of the right in question be lower. The necessity for the means determined by law stems therefore from the fact that no other hypothetical alternative exists that would be less harmful to the right in question while equally advancing the law's purpose. If a less limiting alternative exists, able to fulfill the law's purpose, then there is no need for the law. If a different law will fulfill the goal with less or no limitation of the human rights, then the legislator should choose this law. The limiting

[1] CA 6821/93 *United Mizrahi Bank Ltd.* v. *Migdal Cooperative Village* [1995] IsrLR 1. See also B. Pieroth and B. Schlink, *Gdundrechte Staatsrecht II* (Heidelberg: C. F. Müller Verlag, 2006), 68.

law should not limit the constitutional right beyond what is required to advance the proper purpose. Consider the following examples:

(a) In Israel, a recent statute – the Civil Torts Law (Liability of the State) 2005[2] – establishes, *inter alia*, that the State of Israel is not liable in torts for any damage caused by its security forces operating in conflict areas. This provision was meant to exclude the damages incurred during combat operations from the scope of regular tort law. The Supreme Court has held[3] that the statute limits the constitutional right to which Basic Law: Human Dignity and Freedom applies, beyond what is necessary. This is because it exempts from any liability in tort for damage incurred in a conflict zone, even for those damages not caused by combat activities. The Court recognized that the purpose of the law is proper, and that a rational connection exists between that purpose and the limiting statute; still, the necessity test could not be satisfied. The Court held that, in order to realize the statute's purpose, the legislator could have opted for a less limiting limitation of the constitutional right so as to provide the state with an exemption from tort liability for combat activities. The measure adopted by the legislator limits the constitutional right beyond what is necessary, as it exempts the state from any damage incurred in a conflict zone, including that caused by non-combat activities.

(b) In Israel, a statutory provision included in the Regulation of Investment Advice, Investment Marketing and Investment Portfolio Management Law, 1995,[4] required a license to manage investment portfolios. The requirement was applied retroactively to anyone who managed investment portfolios prior to the enactment of the statute. The license requirement included a mandatory test, applicable to anyone who had managed investment portfolios for less than seven years prior to the statute's coming into force. The Supreme Court held that this statute limited the constitutionally protected right of freedom of occupation of the veteran portfolio managers and that the limitation was for a proper purpose and satisfied the rational connection test. Still, the transitional provisions regarding the mandatory test for veteran managers failed to pass the necessity test. The Court ruled that

---

[2] Civil Torts Law (Liability of the State) (2005).
[3] HCJ 8276/05 *Adalah – The Legal Center for the Rights of the Arab Minority* v. *Minister of Defense* [2006] (2) IsrLR 352.
[4] Regulation of Investment Advice, Investment Marketing and Investment Portfolio Management Law, 5755–1995, SH 416.

the law's purpose could have been fulfilled while limiting the veteran portfolio managers' right to a much lesser extent, while taking into account their accumulated experience.[5]

(c) In the *Makwanyane*[6] case, the South African Constitutional Court examined the constitutionality of a statute recognizing the death penalty. The Court held the statute to be unconstitutional since it was disproportional. The Court held, *inter alia*, that the state failed to lift its burden in proving that the statute's purposes could not be achieved through a life sentence, which limits the constitutional right to life to a lesser extent.

(d) In South Africa, in the *Manamela* case,[7] the Constitutional Court examined a statute establishing a reverse onus in cases relating to the acquisition of stolen goods. In particular, the statute provided that anyone accused of acquiring stolen goods should bear the burden of proving that the goods were not stolen. The Court held that the purpose of the law – the protection of the community from dealing with stolen goods – was proper. Regarding the means used, it was ruled that the necessity test was not fulfilled as its purposes could have been achieved through a less limiting measure, such as limiting the scope to a particular category of high-value property.

(e) In Germany, food regulations prohibited the sale of certain candies that contained cocoa powder which were primarily made out of rice. Those regulations limited the constitutionally protected right of freedom of occupation of several candy manufacturers. The purpose of the regulation was to protect consumers from a mistaken purchase. The Constitutional Court held that the purpose was proper, and that a rational connection existed between that purpose and the limiting law. Still, the Court held that the means chosen by the legislator were disproportionate in that they were not necessary. The same purpose could have been achieved through a warning label on the product; a complete prohibition of its sale was therefore unnecessary. The alternative means – proper labeling – is equal in efficiency to the means chosen by the legislator in achieving the proper purpose, but the harm that such a measure would cause to the constitutional right would be of a much lesser extent.[8]

---

[5] HCJ 1715/97 *Israel Investment Managers Association* v. *Minister of Finance* [1997] IsrSC 51(4) 367.

[6] *S.* v. *Makwanyane*, 1995 (3) SA 391 (CC).

[7] *S.* v. *Manamela*, 2000 (3) SA 1 (CC).   [8] See BVerfGE 53, 135.

2. The nature of the necessity test

The necessity test is based upon the assumption that the law's purpose is a proper one. Thus, while examining the requirements of necessity, there is no room for an examination of the constitutionality of the law's purpose. Similarly, there is no room to question the wisdom behind establishing that purpose, or the very need to establish it. The necessity test relates to the means chosen by the legislator to achieve the purposes and not to the need to achieve those purposes. We assume that the means chosen by the legislator is a rational one; if the means chosen is irrational, there is no necessity in it.[9] The requirement established by the necessity test, therefore, is that, in order to achieve the law's purpose, rational means should be chosen such that the intensity of the realization is no less than that of the limiting law,[10] and those means limit the constitutional right to the lesser extent.[11]

The main point of the necessity test – which is an expression of the notion of efficiency, or, more specifically, of Pareto efficiency[12] – is that the law's purpose can be achieved through hypothetical means whose

[9] See Pieroth and Schlink, above note 1, at 67.
[10] See C. B. Pulido, *El Principio de Proporcionalidad y los Derechos Fundamentales* (Madrid: Centro de Estudios Políticos y Constitucionales, 2007), 737.
[11] See N. Emiliou, *The Principle of Proportionality in European Law: A Comparative Study* (London: Kluwer Law International, 1996), 30, 21: "The judicial standard against which a public measure is tested, is whether it could be substituted by another means which is 'milder' but 'equally effective' in achieving the ends pursued. 'Milder' is the measure which causes the least possible adverse repercussions on the legal status of the party concerned. A measure can be considered as 'equally effective' when it is suitable to achieve actually and with, at least, equal intensity the desired end." See also J. Rivers, "Proportionality and Variable Intensity of Review," 65 *Cambridge L. J.* 174, 198 (2006): "The test of necessity asks whether the decision, rule or policy limits the relevant right in the least intrusive way compatible with achieving the given level of realisation of the legitimate aim. This implies a comparison with alternative hypothetical acts (decisions, rules, policies, etc.) which may achieve the same aim to the same degree but with less cost to rights."
[12] See Rivers: above note 11, at 198: "The test of necessity thus expresses the idea of efficiency or Pareto-optimality. A distribution is efficient or Pareto-optimal if no other distribution could make at least one person better off without making any one else worse off. Likewise an act is necessary if no alternative act could make the victim better off in terms of right-enjoyment without reducing the level of realisation of some other constitutional interest." See also R. Alexy, *A Theory of Constitutional Rights* (J. Rivers trans., Oxford University Press, 2002 [1986]), 105, 398; D. M. Beatty, *The Ultimate Rule of Law* (Oxford University Press, 2004), 110. Regarding the Pareto efficiency test, see R. Cooter and T. Ulen, *Law and Economics*, 4th edn. (Reading, MA: Addison Wesley, 2003). For an analysis of the approach according to Pareto's necessity test, see Pulido, above note 10, at 737.

limitation of the protected right would be to a lesser extent. Accordingly, the necessity test does not require the use of means whose limitation is the smallest, or even of a lesser extent, if the means cannot achieve the proper purpose to the same extent as the means chosen by the law. The necessity test does not require a minimal limitation of the constitutional right; it only requires the smallest limitation required to achieve the law's purpose. At times, even the "smallest" limitation may be harsh. Indeed, the necessity test compares two rational means that equally realize the law's purpose. In this situation, the legislature should select the means whose limitation of the constitutional right is smallest. The necessity test is triggered only when the fulfillment of the purpose is possible through the use of several alternative rational means, each of which limits the constitutional right to a different extent. In this situation, the necessity test demands that the legislator choose the means which limit the constitutional right to the least extent.[13] In order to properly answer the question of whether the alternative means – which limit the right to a lesser extent – equally advance the purpose as the means chosen by the legislator, an understanding of both the purpose and the probability of its being achieved through the alternative means is necessary. An estimate is insufficient; the understanding should be of the concrete factual data, as well as of the probabilities and risks involved.

In *Adalah*, the Israeli Supreme Court reviewed the constitutionality of the Law of Citizenship and Entry into Israel (Temporary Measure) 2003, which, *inter alia*, established a blanket restriction on the unification of families where one of the spouses was Israeli and the other was a resident of either the West Bank or the Gaza Strip. The purpose of the statute was to protect national security interests; it was demonstrated to the Court that, on twenty-six occasions, the spouse who entered Israel from the Occupied Territories through the process of family unification assisted in the execution of a terrorist act. The Court held that the statute limited the Israeli spouse's constitutionally protected right to human dignity. The Court also held that the purpose of the statute was proper, and that the means chosen were suited to achieving that purpose. Was the necessity test met in this case? The petitioners argued that the proper purpose can be achieved through less limiting means – for example, an individual

---

[13] See *RJR-MacDonald Inc. v. Canada (Attorney General)* [1995] 3 SCR 199, § 96: "The minimal impairment requirement does not impose an obligation on the government to employ the least intrusive measures available. Rather, it only requires it to demonstrate that the measures employed were the least intrusive, in light of both the legislative objective and the infringed right."

review of each resident of the Occupied Territories who requests family unification with their Israeli spouse. The majority rejected the argument, holding that the blanket restriction satisfied the necessity test:

> We have seen that the law's objective was to reduce, as much as possible, the threat created by the foreign spouses arriving in Israel. With this understanding of the law's purpose, can we conclude that the individual review and the blanket restriction advance that purpose equally? In order to answer this question we should compare the blanket restriction, as is, and the most comprehensive process of individual review possible. However, a process of individual review could never achieve the degree of security achieved by a blanket restriction. Accordingly, in light of the fundamental value of human life that the law is meant to protect, it is clear that the blanket restriction will always be more efficient – from the standpoint of reducing the security threat to the lowest level possible – than the individual review. Our conclusion, therefore, is that, in the circumstances before us, the individual review does not fulfill the legislative purpose to the same extent as the blanket restriction. Therefore, there is no requirement in the framework of the less limiting means, to stop at this level and the legislator was allowed to choose the blanket restriction as it did.[14]

This principle is well illustrated in the case of *Cotroni*.[15] There, the Supreme Court of Canada examined the constitutionality of a statute which determined the rules of extradition. According to the said law, Canadian citizens could be extradited. It was claimed that this statute was unconstitutional. It was agreed that the statute limited the constitutional right of Canadian citizens to remain in Canada. The question arose whether extradition meets the requirements of the Canadian limitation clause. The Court held that the law fulfills the purpose requirements. The Court was divided, however, as to the requirement of the existence of less limiting means. The petitioners argued that, under the circumstances at hand – a Canadian conspiracy to distribute illegal drugs in the United States – less limiting means existed, namely, an indictment against the Canadian citizens in Canada. The majority opinion, however, written by Justice La Forest, held that, while it is true that this means limits the constitutional right to a lesser degree, it cannot fulfill the purposes of the extradition. The use of this means would raise evidentiary problems and therefore may weaken the war on illegal drugs and international co-operation. The

---

[14] See HCJ 7052/03 *Adalah – The Legal Center for the Rights of the Arab Minority* v. *Minister of Interior* (May 14, 2006, unpublished), available in English at http://elyon1.court.gov.il/fileseng/03/520/070/a47/03070520.a47.pdf, para. 89 (Barak, P.).

[15] See *United States of America* v. *Cotroni* [1989] 1 SCR 1469.

dissenting opinion, written by Justices Wilson and Sopinka, emphasized that, since the criminal conspiracy took place in Canada, it was possible to file the indictment in Canada.

The majority opinion was correct in this case. The alternative means that would limit the right to a lesser extent – the indictment in Canada – could not have advanced the law's purposes to the same extent as the more limiting means (extradition). Still, it is possible that the harm incurred by the constitutional right by using the legislative means is disproportionate to the benefit to the public interest caused by the use of alternative means. This is a serious question, but its examination is part of the next stage of the constitutional review – proportionality *stricto sensu*.[16]

3. The elements of the necessity test

i. The two elements of the necessity test

The necessity test includes two elements.[17] The first is the existence of hypothetical alternative means that can advance the purpose of the limiting law as well as, or better than, the means used by the limiting law; the second is that the hypothetical alternative means limit the constitutional right to a lesser extent than the means used by the limiting statute. If these two requirements are satisfied, we can conclude that there is no necessity in the limiting law. However, if a hypothetical alternative means that equally advances the law's purpose does not exist, or if this alternative means exists but its limitation of the constitutional right is no less than that of the limiting law, then we can conclude that the limiting law itself is necessary. The necessity test is met. Each of these elements will be examined separately.

ii. The first element: the existence of a hypothetical alternative means which equally advances the law's purpose

a. The nature of the first element The first element of the necessity test examines the question of whether alternative means can fulfill the law's purpose at the same level of intensity and efficiency as the means determined by the limiting law. If such an alternative does not exist, the law is necessary and the necessity test is met.[18] An alternative exists only

---

[16] Regarding that test, see below, at 340.
[17] See Pulido, above note 10, at 738.
[18] See J. Cianciardo, "The Principle of Proportionality: The Challenges of Human Rights," 3 *J. Civ. L. Stud.* 177 (2010), 179.

if the (hypothetical) means would advance the law's purpose at the same level of intensity as those determined in the limiting law. It is therefore required that the alternative means fulfill the law's purpose quantitatively, qualitatively, and probability-wise – equally to the means determined by the limiting law itself.[19]

b. The necessity test and external considerations

aa. The necessity test paradigm The necessity test presupposes both a law's given purpose and a given limitation of the constitutional right through the means that the law determines. Based on these two assumptions, the necessity test determines that, if alternative means can be used to achieve the law's purpose while imposing a lesser limitation on the constitutional right, those less limiting means should be used. Thus, the necessity test functions within the framework of the law's purposes and not by virtue of other purposes.

The same is true regarding the means. The necessity test examines the question of whether the law's purpose can be fulfilled through means which limit the constitutional right less – but no more. The necessity test assumes that the less limiting means has an identical effect to that chosen by the law in every respect. Accordingly, the necessity test is not met when the law's purpose can be fulfilled through means whose limitation of the constitutional right is lesser, but requires additional limitations or expenses. Those cases are discussed within the framework of proportionality *stricto sensu*.[20]

bb. Effect on factors external to the limited right A limiting law is necessary when the use of less limiting means will lead to a limitation of other rights which were not limited by the means set out in the law.[21] Similarly, the limiting law is necessary whenever the cost of the decrease in the limitation of the constitutional right must be borne by a new policy that the state does not favor, or is financed by a budget designed to advance other purposes. The limiting law is unnecessary only in cases where the fulfillment of the law's purpose is achieved through less limiting means, when all the other parameters remain unchanged. The necessity test cannot be used as a pretext for selecting a less limiting measure when the latter would lead to an expenditure of state funds, a re-ordering of the national budgetary priorities, or to further limitations on other rights of the same

---

[19] Pulido, above note 10, at 740.   [20] See below, at 340.
[21] See H. Dreier, *GG Grundgesetz Kommentar* (Tübingen: Mohr Siebeck, 2006), 259.

person or of the rights of others. Writing for the dissent in the *Manamela* case,[22] Justices O'Regan and Cameron of the Constitutional Court of South Africa have similarly noted:

> The problem for the Court is to give meaning and effect to the factor of less restrictive means without unduly narrowing the range of policy choices available to the Legislature in a specific area. The Legislature when it chooses a particular provision does so not only with regard to constitutional rights, but also in the light of concerns relating to costs, practical implementation, the prioritisation of certain social demands and needs and the need to reconcile conflicting interests. The Constitution entrusts the task of legislation to the Legislature because it is the appropriate institution to make these difficult policy choices. When a Court seeks to attribute weight to the factor of "less restrictive means" it should take care to avoid a result that annihilates the range of choice available to the Legislature.[23]

The majority in this case – Justices Madala, Sachs, and Yacoob – also adopted the same view:

> The duty of a court is to decide whether or not the legislature has overreached itself in responding, as it must, to matters of great social concern. As the minority judgment points out, when giving appropriate effect to the factor of "less restrictive means," the court must not limit the range of legitimate legislative choice in a specific area. The minority judgment also states that such legislative choice is influenced by considerations of cost, implementation, priorities of social demands, and the need to reconcile conflicting interests. These are manifestly sensible considerations that do not provoke disagreement.[24]

The necessity test is based on the assumption that the only change that should be brought about by the alternative means is that the limitation on the constitutional right would be of a lesser extent. The rest of the conditions as well as the rest of the operational results should not be altered. Thus, the goal advanced by the lesser limiting means should be the same goal at the foundation of the law's limitation. The financial means dedicated to the advancement of that proper purpose should not increase. The rights limited by the alternative means should be the same rights the original law limited, while the extent of the limitation is diminished.

What happens when these assumptions are not met? What if the reduction in the limitation of the constitutional right entails a limitation on other human rights of the same person, or a limitation on the rights of

---

[22] See *Manamela*, above note 7.
[23] *Ibid.*, at 95.   [24] *Ibid.*, at 43.

others not limited by the original arrangement? The answer to these questions is that they are not controlled by the framework of the necessity test, but rather within the framework of proportionality *stricto sensu*.[25]

If the purpose of the limiting law can be achieved while reducing the limitation on a constitutional right without additional expenses, one should conclude that the law is not necessary. But, whenever the new means, whose limitation of the constitutional right is of a lesser extent, require additional expense, we can no longer conclude that the means originally chosen are not necessary. They are necessary to achieving the law's purpose through the means provided by the legislator, and in order to prevent any additional expense. True, this leads to the further limitation of the human right, a limitation that could have been prevented were the state willing to accommodate the additional expense. But the state refuses. The issue, therefore, is whether the state's choice of avoiding the additional expense in order to prevent the further limitation of a human right is constitutional. The necessity test cannot assist us in attempting to resolve this issue; indeed, this discussion should be conducted within the framework of proportionality *stricto sensu*, which is based on balancing. The saying "human rights cost money"[26] – which highlights the need to protect human rights even if this entails a financial burden – is not meant to refer to the necessity test. It is part of the balancing considerations which apply within the framework of proportionality *stricto sensu*.

iii.   The second element: the hypothetical alternative means which limits the constitutional right to a lesser extent

a. The nature of the second element   The second element of the necessity test examines the question of whether the hypothetical alternative limits the constitutional right to a lesser extent than the limiting law. In order to examine the second element, we should compare the effect of the limiting law on the constitutional right in question and the effect of the hypothetical alternative on the same right. The requirement is that the alternative means limit that right to a lesser extent. This extent is determined, among others, by examining the scope of the limitation, its effect, its duration, and the likelihood of its occurrence. Such a comparison may lead to a simple conclusion where each component of the alternative limitation limits the right less than the original law. But what happens when by comparison it becomes clear that in a number of parameters it limits

---

[25] See Alexy, above note 12, at 400.
[26] See below, at 340.

the constitutional right more than the original limiting law and in other parameters it limits the constitutional right less? In these cases, we cannot say that the alternative limits the constitutional right in question to a lesser extent. The result, therefore, is that the law is considered necessary and the necessity test is met. The decision will be made in the framework of proportionality *stricto sensu*.

b. **"Limitation to a lesser extent": an objective test** How can we determine whether the means chosen by the legislator is the less limiting one? Should the test be of a subjective or an objective nature? The test for determining the constitutionality of the law – as compared to the question of its application to a specific case – must be objective. The comparison must be between two types of limitation of the right as viewed by a typical right-holder. Any special circumstances, unique to the right-holder who brought the case before the court, should play no role in the determination of the issue of the "lesser extent."[27] Personal circumstances should not be a factor in determining the constitutionality of a legislative act. Rather, this determination must be based upon objective observations of a typical right-holder. However, the right-holder's personal information may affect the legality of any sub-statutory state action, such as warrants and administrative actions made by virtue of the law in question.

The objective test is determined, largely, by the standard of common sense. According to this standard, a blanket restriction on a random freedom (such as freedom of occupation) would constitute a greater limitation on that right than a partial restriction on the use of that right. Therefore, the requirement to close a business during certain hours would constitute less of a limitation than the requirement to shut down that same business completely. A requirement to properly label a product so that it is clear that it is dangerous for consumption constitutes less of a limitation (on the protected right to freedom of occupation) than imposing a complete restriction on the sale of the same product. The application of the objective test is relatively clear in those instances where the means in question can be found on the same logical spectrum – from the lighter to the harsher limitation on the right.[28] As such, a life imprisonment sentence limits the right to life less than a death penalty, and a five-year sentence constitutes less of a limitation than a ten-year sentence on that same right. Imposing

[27] See Emiliou, above note 11, at 31.
[28] *Ibid.*, at 30. See also P. W. Hogg, *Constitutional Law of Canada*, 5th edn., vol. II (Toronto: Thomson Carswell, 2007), 146.

a limitation which applies to only part of a country's territory is less of a limitation than an imposition of the limitation obligation on the entire country. A short-term limitation is less limiting than a long-term limitation. A limitation that applies only to some individuals is less limiting than a limitation applicable to all. These are the easy cases; the application of the objective test becomes much harder when there is no clear logical spectrum.

The answer to the objective question – of whether the limitation imposed by the alternative means is of a lesser extent – is a determination of law (rather than fact). It is for the court to provide.[29] The legislator's belief that the limitation of the means chosen by the constitutional right is of a lesser extent than the limitation of a different means is not determinative. The court, in making its determination as to the objective question, should refrain from considering trivial (*de minimis*)[30] differences between the means. Whenever the court reaches a conclusion that a number of alternatives – including that determined by the law – satisfy the need to limit the constitutional right in a less restrictive fashion, it should leave the legislative choice intact.[31] However, that choice will be examined further on in the framework of the next stage of the examination – that of proportionality *stricto sensu*.

c.   **Complete restriction versus individual examination**   The limitation of a constitutional right is of a lesser extent if it requires an individual examination of the right-holder instead of a blanket restriction of the right's realization.[32] Therefore, acceptance into the police force on the basis of an individual examination would limit the constitutionally protected right to freedom of occupation less than a complete restriction on anyone who is over the age of thirty-five to do the same. In the same vein, it was held that an individual examination of prisoners' mail – based on specific security alerts – limits their right to privacy less than a general provision requiring an examination of all mail received

---

[29] See below, at 412.   [30] See above, at 103.   [31] See below, at 415.

[32] See P. Plowden and K. Kerrigan, *Advocacy and Human Rights: Using the Convention in Courts and Tribunals* (London: Routledge Cavendish, 2002), 133; P. Sales and B. Hooper, "Proportionality and the Form of Law," 119 *L. Q. Rev.* 426, 430 (2003); U. Hafelin, W. Haller and H. Keller, *Schweizerisches Bundesstaatsrecht* (Zurich: Schulthess, 2008). See also *Adalah* v. *Minister of the Interior*, above note 14, at para. 69 ("The need to choose the means that least limits the constitutional right frequently prevents the use of a complete restriction (or blanket ban). The reason for that is that in most cases, the use of individual examination may achieve the same purpose while using a means which limits the human right in question less." (Barak, P.)).

by prisoners.[33] Also, a general individual examination is more limiting than an individual examination based on advanced information or
some sort of categorization. Under this approach, revoking one's pass-
port based on an individual security check limits the person's right to
travel less than a total ban which prevents the granting of passports. The
same is true in cases where an exception is determined to the complete
restriction at issue. Thus, a total ban fails the necessity test if an individual examination fulfills the law's purpose to the same extent as a total
ban. The same is not true if the individual examination does not fulfill
the law's purpose to the same extent. Consider the following examples:

(a) A provision of the Canadian Criminal Code provided that, in cases of
    sexual assault, "if application is made by the complainant," the court
    "shall" grant an order directing that her identity (or any information
    that could disclose it) should not be published. The Supreme Court
    held that such a provision limits the constitutionally protected right
    to freedom of expression.[34] The Court examined whether the provi-
    sion is proportional. It was argued, in the context of the necessity test,
    that alternative means – based on an individual examination by the
    court in each case rather than a complete ban on publication – would
    limit the right to a lesser extent. The argument was rejected. The Court
    held that the law's purpose was to encourage complainants to come
    forward and turn to the police while providing them with complete
    protection from the potential trauma of public exposure. Only a total
    ban, the Court held, can accomplish such a goal. The granting of judi-
    cial discretion to the court reviewing such matters – although limit-
    ing the right to a lesser extent – would not accomplish that purpose,
    since complainants may then fear that the court will order that their
    identity be disclosed. As Justice Lamer has noted: "[A] discretionary
    provision under which the judge retains the power to decide whether
    to grant or refuse the ban on publication would be counterproductive,
    since it would deprive the victim of that certainty. Assuming that there
    would be a lesser impairment of freedom of the press if the impugned
    provision were limited to a discretionary power, it is clear, in my view,
    that such a measure would not, however, achieve Parliament's object-
    ive, but rather defeats it."[35]

---

[33] See *Campbell* v. *United Kingdom*, App. No. 13590/88, 15 EHRR 137 (1993).
[34] *Canadian Newspaper Co.* v. *Canada (Attorney General)* [1988] 2 SCR 122.
[35] *Ibid.*, para. 18.

(b) A South African statute prohibited corporal punishments in schools. Parents of children petitioned the Constitutional Court claiming the statute violated their religious freedoms as they had consented to such punishments, which were in line with their religious beliefs. The Court held that recognizing a new consent exception to the existing statutory ban would damage the law's policy, which was to unify educational methods throughout the country. The Court further held that creating a constitutionally compelled exception, as requested by the parent-petitioners, would not only hinder the advancement of the statute's purpose but would actually operate directly against it.[36]

(c) In South Africa, a provision of the Drugs and Drug Trafficking Act 140 of 1992 prohibited the use and possession of dangerous drugs, including cannabis. The ban included an exception for medical uses. The Constitutional Court examined whether a religious exception should be determined as well.[37] The petitioner in that case had wanted to become a lawyer, but his request was declined by the local law society due to two prior convictions for cannabis use. However, all parties agreed that the petitioner was in possession of the drug for religious reasons (the petitioner is a Rastafarian). He argued that the law in question limits his religious rights disproportionally: the disproportionality stemmed from the lack of an exception to the criminal ban regarding the possession and use of dangerous drugs for religious reasons. The justices had all agreed on the fact that the criminal ban has a proper purpose in the battle against drugs. It was also agreed that the ban limits the petitioner's freedom of religion. The question was whether the absolute ban went too far in restricting the religious freedoms of the petitioner. The justices were divided over whether such an exception would undermine the proper purpose of the prohibition (the prevention of illegal drug use). The majority held that this purpose could not be achieved through the establishment of the additional exception, since it would be virtually impossible in each case to review whether the user was actually a member of the Rastafari religion and, if so, whether the use was for religious purposes. The Court further held that without a proper licensing mechanism – unattainable in this case due to the structure of the religion and the lack of recognized institutions – it would not be possible to distinguish between the "island" of Rastafari use and the "ocean" of

[36] See *Christian Education South Africa v. Minister of Education*, 2000 (4) SA 757 (CC).
[37] See *Prince v. President of the Law Society of the Cape of Good Hope*, 2002 (2) SA 794 (CC).

use in general. The majority was correct regarding the necessity test. A different issue is whether the complete ban is proportional according to proportionality *stricto sensu*.

d.   The necessity test and the test of time   The rational connection requirement must be met both during the enactment of the limiting statute (*ex ante*) and during the constitutional review (*ex post*).[38] Should the same requirement apply to the necessity test? The answer is yes. Therefore, the necessity test must be satisfied during enactment as well as during a constitutional review of the limiting law by the courts.[39] The reason for this approach stems from the understanding that a limitation on the right in question is maintained throughout the law's life. The justification for limiting a constitutional right should be continuous rather than momentary. Thus, for example, if a technological breakthrough following the enactment of the limiting statute enables the advancement of its purpose at the same level of intensity but with a lesser limitation of the right, the legislator should take advantage of the advancement. A statute may otherwise lose its constitutionality, since it is no longer necessary.

4.   *The necessity test and the purpose's level of abstraction*

The necessity test examines the means the law uses to fulfill its purpose. It is required that the means both advance the law's purpose and limit the right in question less. From that premise we may infer the close relationship between the necessity test and the law's purpose. The necessity test focuses on the purpose and the ways in which it may be fulfilled. This focus leads to difficulties when the law has several purposes. These purposes may be at the same level of abstraction, or at several levels of abstraction. In both cases, the degree of necessity of the means chosen is derived from the manner in which the purpose is determined.[40]

An example may be the *Manamela* case,[41] decided by the Constitutional Court of South Africa. Here, the Court reviewed a statute establishing a reverse onus of proof in matters regarding stolen goods. The Court was divided. The majority held that the law was unconstitutional since it did

---

[38]   See above, at 312.

[39]   Regarding the requirement that the test is *ex ante*, see Pulido, above note 10, at 734.

[40]   See S. Woolman and H. Botha, "Limitations," in S.Woolman, M. Bishop, and J. Brickhill (eds.), *Constitutional Law of South Africa*, 2nd edn. (Cape Town: Juta Law Publishers, looseleaf, 2002–), 87.

[41]   See *Manamela*, above note 7.

not meet the necessity requirement. The dissent was of the opinion that the necessity test was met. Commenting on this division, Woolman and Botha[42] explained that this disagreement was caused by adopting a different understanding of the statute's purpose. The majority adopted a view of the statutory purpose at a high level of abstraction – the statute was meant to create tools to limit the market in stolen goods. Based on this purpose, it was held that the same purpose may be achieved through the use of less limiting means, such that the reverse-onus presumption would apply only in cases of high-value stolen goods.[43] The dissent, in contrast, viewed the purpose as a warning to the public not to partake in any activity related to the market in stolen goods. In order to fulfill that purpose there was a need to adopt the means chosen by the legislator – a less limiting means would not be able to fulfill that goal.

With this in mind, it is possible to conclude that the higher the purpose's level of abstraction, the more likely it is to find alternative means which limit the right to a lesser extent and which can fulfill the goal at the same level of efficiency. In contrast, the lower the level of abstraction, the harder it would be to render the means chosen by the legislator unnecessary.[44] In addition, a lower level of abstraction may raise difficult questions regarding the test of proportionality *stricto sensu*. This can be demonstrated through the Israeli Supreme Court case of *Adalah*.[45] Here, the legislator imposed a complete restriction on the unification of families in which one spouse resided in Israel and the other was a resident of the Occupied Territories. The reason for the total restriction was grounded in national security considerations. Among others, the Court examined the question of whether an individual examination of the security risk – rather than a blanket restriction – would equally advance the law's security purpose while limiting the right to family life to a lesser extent. In order to solve this question, the Court first had to determine the statute's purpose. In my opinion, I noted that the statute's purpose was "to reduce, as much as possible, the security risk posed by foreign spouses who choose to settle

[42] See Woolman and Botha, above note 40, at 87.
[43] See above, at 331.
[44] See P. W. Hogg, "Section 1 Revisited" 1 *National Journal of Constitutional Law* 1, 5 (1992): "If the objective has been stated at a high level of generality, it will be easy to think of other ways in which the wide objective could be accomplished with less interference with the [fundamental] right. If the objective has been stated at a low level of generality, perhaps simply restating the terms of the challenged law, it will be hard to think of other ways in which the narrow objective could be accomplished with less interference with the … right." See also Woolman and Botha, above note 40, at 87.
[45] *Adalah v. Minister of Interior*, above note 14.

down in Israel."[46] Having determined the statute's purpose in this manner, I concluded that the individual examination could not have advanced that purpose at the same level of intensity as the means chosen by the legislator – a complete ban on family unification. I then considered the possibility that the statute's purpose was not to reduce the security risk "as much as possible," but rather to reduce that risk only "somewhat."[47] With that as the provision's purpose, the alternative means – the individual examination – would suffice. I went on to determine which of those was the purpose designated by the statute, and I concluded that that purpose was to reduce the security risk "as much as possible." Accordingly, I concluded that the law satisfied the necessity test. I then moved on to examine whether this actual purpose ("as much as possible") satisfied the test of proportionality *stricto sensu*.[48]

This example indicates another conclusion pertinent to the necessity test. The level of abstraction in which the law's purpose should be examined – whether the law has one purpose or several purposes at the same level of abstraction – should be determined in accordance with the actual (real) purpose which underlies the law.[49] The question is not whether we can theoretically attribute a certain purpose to the law, but rather what was the actual purpose designated by the law. The court does not choose the law's purpose. The court, however, may examine the constitutionality of the means chosen by the law to achieve that purpose. When the law has several purposes, such an examination would be carried out in respect of the law's predominant purpose.

B.   Means "narrowly tailored" to fulfill the law's purpose

1.   The metaphors of the cannon and the sparrows

The necessity test requires that the means chosen be "narrowly tailored" to achieve the law's purpose. This notion was already expressed in 1911 by Fritz Fleiner, who famously wrote that the "police cannot shoot a sparrow with a canon" ("polizie soll nicht mit Kanonen auf Spatzen schießen").[50] Lord Diplock used a similar metaphor when he noted, in one of his cases, that one "must not use a steam hammer to crack a nut."[51] The Israeli

---

[46] *Ibid.*, para. 89 (Barak, P.).   [47] *Ibid.*, para. 90 (Barak, P.).
[48] See below, at 340.   [49] See above, at 331.
[50] F. Fleiner, *Institutionen des Deutschen Verwaltungsrechts* (Tübingen, 1928), 404.
[51] *R. v. Goldstein* [1983] 1 WLR 151, 155. Regarding this metaphor, see G. Wong, "Towards the Nutcracker Principle: Reconsidering the Objections to Proportionality," *PL* 92 (2000).

Supreme Court, in one of its opinions, repeated this metaphor, albeit slightly differently, when it asked whether "the legislator has used a cannon to hurt a fly."[52] All of these metaphors are meant to drive home the point that the means should fit the purpose. Whenever the purpose can be fulfilled through the use of less limiting means, this should be done. There is no sense in using a hammer when all you need is a nutcracker.[53]

The requirement that the means be "narrowly tailored" to achieve the law's purpose fails in two sets of circumstances. In the first, the means does not completely achieve the purpose and there are matters required to fulfill the purpose that are not covered by the means. This is the case of underinclusiveness. It is not related to the necessity test. Underinclusiveness may highlight an improper motive on the part of the legislator and thus affect the purpose component.[54] It may indicate that the principle of equality has been violated. It may affect the suitability of the means used to realize the law's purpose.[55] Either way, it does not affect the question of necessity. In the second set of circumstances, the means chosen achieve the law's purpose, but they are not "narrowly tailored" to fulfill that goal in that they limit the right in question beyond what is necessary. This is the case of overinclusiveness (or over-breadth). In the words of Justice Ngcobo, in cases of overinclusiveness the legislator has cast too wide a net.[56] This is the same as a cannon shooting a sparrow, or a hammer cracking a nut, all the while limiting once again the constitutional right in question. This aspect – the lack of being "narrowly tailored" – is pertinent to the necessity test.

---

[52] HCJ 2334/02 *Shtanger* v. *The Speaker of the Knesset* [2003] IsrSC 58(1) 786, 797 (Barak, P.).

[53] Some commentators are of the opinion that this metaphor belongs with the rational connection test. See, e.g., W. van Gerven, "The Effect of Proportionality on the Actions of Member States of the European Community: National Viewpoints from Continental Europe," in E. Ellis (ed.), *The Principle of Proportionality in the Laws of Europe* (1999), 37, 61. In some places, I have placed this metaphor within the framework of the third test of proportionality *stricto sensu*. See *Shtanger*, above note 52. The correct "location" of the metaphor is within the framework of the test of necessity. However, the metaphor itself is far from perfect. It does work well to demonstrate the waste of resources (on one side of the equation), but fails to demonstrate the over-damaging effect on the right in question (on the other).

[54] See J. Rubenfeld, "Affirmative Action," 107 *Yale L. J.* 427 (1997), 430; Rivers, above note 11, at 189. See also R. H. Fallon, "Strict Judicial Scrutiny," 54 *UCLA L. Rev.* 1267, 1327 (2007).

[55] See *A* v. *Secretary of State for the Home Department* [2004] UKHL 56.

[56] See *Prince*, above note 37, at para. 81.

2. Overinclusiveness

Overinclusiveness occurs whenever only a portion of the means, which limit the constitutional right, are required to achieve "full coverage" of the law's purpose; in other words, not all the measures adopted are required to achieve the law's purpose.[57] Instances of overinclusiveness are divided into two groups. The first group includes situations where it is possible to differentiate between the means not necessary to achieve the purpose (the "overinclusive" means) and the means required to achieve that purpose. Thus, the law's purpose may be achieved without the additional limitation on human rights caused by the "overinclusive" means. In these cases, overinclusiveness leads to the conclusion that the means are not necessary. The remedy may be the separation of those means necessary to achieve the purpose from those that are not. Here, the necessity test and the restriction on overinclusiveness merge; they are identical. An example of such a case is the South African case of *Coetzee*.[58] In that case, the Constitutional Court of South Africa reviewed the constitutionality of a provision which allowed for the imprisonment of judgment debtors. It was held that the provision limited the constitutionally protected right to freedom, and that such a limitation was beyond what was necessary since the law did not distinguish between those debtors who are able to pay and those who are not. The law's purpose was to create an enforcement mechanism for debtors who were able to pay off their debt. It was not meant to enforce a debt on someone who could not pay. In this case, it is possible to differentiate between the "overinclusive" means (an imprisonment of a debtor who is not able to pay) and the means necessary to fulfill the law (imprisonment of a debtor who is able to pay).

The second group of situations involving overinclusiveness is more complex. Here, separating the necessary means from the "overinclusive" ones is not possible. In other words, there is no way to fulfill the law's purpose without using overinclusive means. In these cases tension develops between the necessity test and the restriction on overinclusiveness. Which of the two requirements will prevail?[59] The answer is that the necessity test will prevail. As per the necessity test, overinclusiveness is prohibited only where it is not necessary. When the necessary and "overinclusive" means cannot be separated, overinclusiveness becomes necessary as well. In this

---

[57] See H. P. Monaghan, "Overbreadth," *Sup. Ct. Rev.* 1 (1981).

[58] *Coetzee v. Government of the Republic of South Africa*, 1995 (4) SA 631 (CC).

[59] Regarding this question in American law, see Fallon, above note 54, at 1328.

situation (overinclusiveness which cannot be separated), the examination of the limitation caused by the overinclusiveness should not be carried out in the framework of the necessity test but rather within the framework of proportionality *stricto sensu*.[60]

An example of this approach can be found in the *Adalah* case.[61] To ensure national security and to defend the state from acts of terror, a blanket ban on the unification of families was applied on couples where one spouse was Israeli and the other from the Occupied Territories. As a result of the total ban, the right of spouses from the Occupied Territories who pose no threat to the security of the State of Israel was severely limited. However, the Court held that it was impossible to distinguish between innocent spouses and spouses who pose a genuine threat to Israel's national security. The individual examination was held to be insufficient. Under these circumstances, the Israeli Supreme Court has held that the means chosen by the legislator, despite being overinclusive, still satisfy the necessity test. The results of the blanket ban and those of the individual examination were compared, as follows:

> A comparison between the two levels is not the examination required at this stage of the constitutional review. The question here is not whether the individual examination limits the rights of the Israeli spouse to a lesser extent than the complete restriction; rather, the question is whether the statutory purpose can be fulfilled through the use of the less-restrictive means. If the less-restrictive means fulfill the purpose to a level lesser than the means originally chosen by the legislator, then that alternative means cannot be considered necessary. The requirement as to the less-restrictive means applies only when those means advance the statutory purpose at the same level as the original. Thus, at this stage of the constitutional review, the question is not whether the individual examination limits the right of the Israeli spouse less than the blanket ban. Rather, the question is whether the individual examination fulfills the statutory purpose at the same level as the blanket ban. If the answer is in the affirmative – both means advance the purpose equally – then the legislator must choose this means. Conversely, if the individual examination does not fulfill the statutory purpose, then the means are unnecessary, the legislator is not obligated to choose it. The legislator must only select the means which fulfill the statutory purpose and which limit the constitutional right of the Israeli spouse the least.[62]

---

[60] See below, at 340.
[61] *Adalah* v. *Minister of Interior*, above note 14.
[62] *Adalah* v. *Minister of Interior*, above note 14, at para. 88 (Barak, P.).

Despite the overinclusiveness of the blanket restriction, it satisfies the necessity test in those cases where the necessary and the "overinclusive" means cannot be separated. In such a case, the necessity test does not require the adoption of partial inclusiveness. Still, the constitutionality of overinclusiveness will be determined within the framework of proportionality *stricto sensu*.

C.   The necessity test: an evaluation

1.   The "heart and soul" of the proportionality test?

Israeli case law has expressed the opinion that the necessity test or the demand for the least restrictive means constitutes the "heart" of the proportionality test. The "responsibility" for such an approach is, first and foremost, mine. In the *United Mizrahi Bank* case, I wrote:

> Of all the tests used within the proportionality test, the most important is the second test. The requirement that the statute limit the constitutional right in question as little as possible lies at the heart of the requirement of proportionality.[63]

This approach is accepted in comparative law as well. As Peter Hogg has noted in the context of the Canadian Charter of Rights and Freedoms:

> The requirement of least drastic means has turned out to be the heart and soul of Section 1 justification … [F]or the great majority of cases, the arena of debate is the … requirement of least drastic means.[64]

Is the special status of the necessity test justified?

2.   Necessity: an important test

There is no doubt that the necessity test is an important one. While the rational connection test examines the relationship between the means designated by the law and its purpose, the necessity test chooses between several rational alternative means, that which least limits the constitutional right. The necessity test inquires, while examining the law's prognosis and its factual background,[65] whether the law's purpose could have

[63] See *United Mizrahi Bank*, above note 1, at para. 95.
[64] See Hogg, above note 28, at 146.
[65] See J. Rivers, "A Theory of Constitutional Rights and the British Constitution," in R. Alexy (ed.), *A Theory of Constitutional Rights* (J. Rivers trans., Oxford University Press, 2002 [1986]).

been achieved through the use of less restrictive means to the constitutional right in question. Incidentally, it also examines if what was presented as the law's purpose is the law's true purpose. This examination has a value-laden aspect. However, the necessity test is not a balancing test.[66] Thus, for example, when the examination reveals that the less limiting means may limit another right of the person in question, or the rights of other people, or the public interest, then the necessity test does not help solve the dilemma before the court.[67] The same is true in those cases where the alternative, less limiting means are available, but the advancement of the law's purpose is lesser than that of the limiting law.[68] Here, too, the necessity test is of no assistance to the limited right.

Despite these "weaknesses" of the necessity test, and despite its limited protection of constitutional rights, the test is important. It is an important threshold test. Courts usually prefer to announce the lack of proportionality without resorting to any balancing tests. In that way, the courts avoid unnecessary conflict with the legislator, as their decision is perceived as a "factual" matter, without the need for balancing. Indeed, in those cases where the necessity test fails there is no need to continue the constitutional review and to arrive at the test of proportionality *stricto sensu*. In that sense and to that limited extent, the necessity test may indeed be considered the "heart" of proportionality. On the other hand, we should not try and include in the necessity test things it cannot contain. These should generally be left for the balancing test of proportionality *stricto sensu*. Judges should be honest with themselves. They must speak the truth[69] and the truth is that in many cases the judge reveals that an alternative means that limits the right in question to a lesser extent does exist; but upon further examination it turns out that these means may not achieve the

---

[66] See L. C. Blaau, "The Rechtsstaat Idea Compared with the Rule of Law as a Paradigm for Protecting Rights," 107 *South African L. J.* 76 (1990); J. Kirk, "Constitutional Guarantees, Characterisation and the Concept of Proportionality," 21 *Melb. U. L. Rev* 1, 7 (1997); B. Schlink, "Der Grundsatz der Verhältnismässigkeit," in P. Badura and H. Dreier (eds.), *Festschrift 50 Jahre Bundesverfassungsgericht*, vol. II (Tübingen: Mohr Siebeck, 2001), 445; J. Rivers, "Proportionality, Discretion and the Second Law of Balancing," in G. Pavlakos (ed.), *Law, Rights, and Discourse: The Legal Philosophy of Robert Alexy* (Portland, OR: Hart Publishing, 2007), 167, 171; M. Cohen-Eliya and I. Porat, "American Balancing and German Proportionality: The Historical Origins" 8 *Int'l J. Const. L.* 263 (2010).

[67] See above, at 323.   [68] See above, at 323.

[69] For a discussion of judicial integrity, see A. Barak, *Judicial Discretion* (New Haven, CT: Yale University Press, 1989). See also D. L. Shapiro, "In Defense of Judicial Candor," 100 *Harv. L. Rev.* 731 (1987); M. Shapiro, "Judges as Liars," 17 *Harv. J. L. & Pub. Pol'y* 155 (1994); A. Hirsch, "Candor and Prudence in Constitutional Adjudication," 61 *Geo. Wash. L. Rev.* 858 (1993).

law's purpose in full, or that in order to achieve those purposes in full the state has to change its national priorities or limit other rights. In those cases, the judge should rule that the law is necessary, and that the less limiting means cannot achieve the intended legislative purpose. Then, the judge must proceed to the next stage of the examination – and determine the constitutionality of the law within the framework of proportionality *stricto sensu*.[70] Thus, although the necessity test may no longer be seen as the "heart" of the proportionality requirement, it can definitely be considered as playing an important role in its application.

[70] G. Davidov, "Separating Minimal Impairment from Balancing: A Comment on R. v. Sharpe," 5 *Rev. Const. Stud.* 195 (2000).

12

Proportionality stricto sensu (balancing)

A. The characteristics of proportionality stricto sensu

1. The content of the test

The last test of proportionality is the "proportional result," or "proportionality *stricto sensu*" (*Verhältnismässigkeit im engeren Sinne*). This is the most important of proportionality's tests. What does the test require? According to proportionality *stricto sensu*, in order to justify a limitation on a constitutional right, a proper relation ("proportional" in the narrow sense of the term) should exist between the benefits gained by fulfilling the purpose and the harm caused to the constitutional right from obtaining that purpose. This test requires a balancing of the benefits gained by the public and the harm caused to the constitutional right through the use of the means selected by law to obtain the proper purpose. Accordingly, this is a test balancing benefits and harm. It requires an adequate congruence between the benefits gained by the law's policy and the harm it may cause to the constitutional right. As I have written on this test in *Adalah*:

> A proper purpose, a rational connection between the statute's purpose and provisions while using the least restrictive means which can still achieve the proper purposes – are all necessary conditions for the constitutionality of the limitation of human rights. These are insufficient conditions. A constitutional regime seeking to realize a regime of human rights is not satisfied by these. Rather, it also sets up a line which cannot be crossed by the legislator regarding the protection of human rights. It demands that the fulfillment of the proper purpose – by rational means that are least restrictive in achieving the purpose – cannot lead to a disproportional limitation of human rights.[1]

---

[1] HCJ 7052/03 *Adalah – The Legal Center for the Rights of the Arab Minority* v. *Minister of Interior* (May 14, 2006, unpublished), available in English at http://elyon1.court.gov.il/fileseng/03/520/070/a47/03070520. a47.pdf, para. 75 (Barak, P.); *R.* v. *Oakes* [1986] 1 SCR 103; *R.* v. *Sharpe* [2001] 1 SCR 45, 99; *Canada (Attorney General)* v. *JTI-Macdonald Corp.* [2007] 2 SCR 610, § 45.

Consider the following examples regarding the use of this sub-test:

(a) A provision in the Law of Citizenship and Entry into Israel (Temporary Order), 2003[2] sets a blanket restriction on the entry of spouses of Israeli citizens residing in the Occupied Territories (Gaza and the West Bank) into Israel. The reason behind this is national security.[3] The Israeli Supreme Court held that the restriction satisfies the proper purpose, rational connection, and necessity components.[4] Does the law satisfy the proportionality *stricto sensu* test? Five Justices (out of the eleven) were of the opinion that the test was not met, since the law "sets a disproportional relation between the measure of additional security in comparison to the former arrangement, which was based on individual examination ... and the additional harm to the constitutionally protected right to human dignity that the new measure creates."[5] Five of the remaining six Justices were of the opinion that the relation was proportional. The eleventh Justice held that the necessity test was not met.

(b) A provision in legislation relating to the Security Fence in the West Bank ordered the seizure of land – while compensating the owners – for the erection of the fence. The purpose of the fence's erection was national security. It was held that a rational connection exists between the erection of the fence and these national security considerations. Finally, it was held that no other means would have achieved this national-security-related goal with less restrictive effect. However, the Court held that the part of the fence at issue did not meet the proportionality *stricto sensu* test. As noted in my opinion: "There is no proportional relation between the degree of harm to the local residents and the security-related benefits yielded by the erection of the Security Fence in the precise location ordered by the military commander. The construction of the fence in that location would undermine the delicate balance between the commander's duty to guarantee national security and his duty to guarantee that the needs of the local residents are met. Our approach is based on the notion that the location chosen by the military commander for the Security Fence – which would separate the local residents from their farmlands – causes extensive harm

---

[2] Law of Citizenship and Entry into Israel (Temporary Measure) (2003).

[3] For the facts of the case, see above at 336.

[4] See above, at 321.

[5] *Adalah*, above note 1, at para. 75 (Barak, P.).

to those local residents while violating their rights in accordance with International Humanitarian Law."[6]

(c) Regulations promulgated in Ontario, Canada, following the enactment of the Canadian Health Disciplines Act[7] restricted dentists' advertisements. A dentist who broke this law was convicted and appealed to the Supreme Court. The Canadian Supreme Court held that the regulations limited the dentist's right to freedom of speech.[8] Regarding proportionality, the Court held that the regulations were promulgated for a proper purpose and that they met the rational connection test. The Court held that the benefits in ensuring professionalism and preventing irresponsible and misleading advertising are not proportional to the harm done to the freedom of expression.

2.   The nature of the proportionality stricto sensu test

The proportionality *stricto sensu* test is a result-oriented test. It equally applies to laws limiting constitutional rights shaped as rules and laws limiting constitutional rights shaped as principles. It applies whether the purpose of the limiting law is to protect another constitutional right or the public interest. Any law limiting a constitutionally protected right must meet the test of proportionality *stricto sensu*. This is a test that examines the result of the law and the effect it has on the constitutional right. This test compares the positive effect of realizing the law's proper purpose with the negative effect of limiting a constitutional right. This comparison is of a value-laden nature.[9] It is meant to determine whether the relation between the benefit and the harm is proper.

The moral nature of the test – as well as its importance – is well demonstrated by an example presented by Grimm.[10] Assume a law that allows the police to shoot a person (even if this shooting would lead to that person's death) if it is the only way to prevent that person from harming another's

---

[6] HCJ 2056/04 *Beit Sourik Village Council* v. *The Government of Israel* [2004] IsrSC 58(5) 807, 850.

[7] Health Disciplines Act, RRO 1980, section 37.

[8] See *Rocket* v. *Royal College of Dental Surgeons of Ontario* [1990] 2 SCR 232.

[9] See HCJ 8276/05 *Adalah – The Legal Center for the Rights of the Arab Minority* v. *Minister of Defense* [2006] (2) IsrLR 352, para. 107 ("proportionality 'in the value-laden sense,' [since] the main focus of this test is morality, and this focus should be reflected by its name" (Cheshin, J.)).

[10] See D. Grimm, "Proportionality in Canadian and German Constitutional Jurisprudence," 57 *U. Toronto L. J.* 383, 396 (2007). See also J. Kirk, "Constitutional Guarantees, Characterisation and the Concept of Proportionality," 21 *Melb. U. L. Rev.* 1, 9 (1997).

property. This law is designed to protect private property, and therefore its purpose is proper. The means chosen by the legislator are rational, since it advances the proper purpose. According to the provision's own words, it can only be triggered when no other means exist to protect the property without hurting a human life. Therefore, the law meets the necessity test as well. However, the provision is still unconstitutional because the protection of private property cannot justify the taking of human life.

3. Proper relation: a balancing test

At the foundation of the proportionality *stricto sensu* test is the requirement of proper relation between the benefit gained by the limiting law and the harm caused by it. The limitation on a constitutional right is not proportional *stricto sensu* if the harm caused to the right by the law exceeds the benefit gained by it. This is a balancing test. The term "balancing" has different meanings in different legal contexts.[11] In this book, "balancing" is an analytical process that places the proper purpose of the limiting law on one side of the scales and the limited constitutional right on the other, while balancing the benefit gained by the proper purpose with the harm it causes to the right.[12]

Comparative law understands proportionality *stricto sensu* as reflecting a balance between those two competing principles. This is the law as set out in rulings in South Africa,[13] Canada,[14] the United Kingdom,[15]

---

[11] R. H. Fallon, "Individual Rights and the Powers of Government," 27 *Ga. L. Rev.* 343, 346 (1993); R. H. Fallon, *Implementing the Constitution* (Cambridge, MA: Harvard University Press, 2001), 82; S. Gardbaum, "Limiting Constitutional Rights," 54 *UCLA L. Rev.* 789, 792 (2004); J. Bomhoff, "Balancing, the Global and the Local: Judicial Balancing as a Problematic Topic in Comparative (Constitutional) Law," 31 *Hastings Int. & Comp. L. Rev.* 555 (2008); J. Bomhoff, "Genealogies of Balancing as Discourse," 4 *Law and Ethics of Hum. Rts.* 108 (2010). See also footnote 14 in S. Gardbaum, "A Democratic Defence of Constitutional Balancing," 4(1) *Law and Ethics of Hum. Rts.* 78 (2010).

[12] R. Alexy, "On Balancing and Subsumption: A Structural Comparison," 16(4) *Ratio Juris* 433 (2003); F. Schauer, "Balancing Subsumption, and the Constraining Role of Legal Text," in M. Klatt (ed.), *Rights, Law, and Morality Themes from the Legal Philosophy of Robert Alexy* (Oxford University Press, forthcoming 2011).

[13] S. Woolman and H. Botha, "Limitations," in S.Woolman, M. Bishop, and J. Brickhill (eds.), *Constitutional Law of South Africa*, 2nd edn. (Cape Town: Juta Law Publishers, looseleaf, 2002–), 94. See also *S. v. Makwanyane*, 1995 (3) SA 391; *Coetzee v. Government of the Republic of South Africa*, 1995 (4) SA 631, 656.

[14] See *R. v. Oakes* [1986] 1 SCR 103. See also P. W. Hogg, *Constitutional Law of Canada*, 5th edn., vol. II (Toronto: Thomson Carswell, 2007).

[15] See *R (Razar) v. Secretary of State for the Home Department* [2004] 2 AC 363; *Huang v. Secretary of State for the Home Department* [2007] UKHL 11.

Ireland,[16] Germany,[17] Israel,[18] and the other countries that have adopted the concept of proportionality. The European Court of Human Rights expressed this notion in *Sporrong*:

> The Court must determine whether a fair balance was struck between the demands of the general interest of the community and the requirements of the protection of the individual's fundamental rights ... The search for this balance is inherent in the whole of the Convention.[19]

4. The uniqueness of the test

The first three components of proportionality deal mainly with the relation between the limiting law's purpose and the means to fulfill that purpose. This examination is conducted against the background of a claim that a constitutional right has been limited. However, the examination's focus is not the limited right, but rather the purpose and the means to achieve it. Accordingly, those tests are referred to as means-end analysis.[20] They are not based on balancing.

The test of proportionality *stricto sensu* is different.[21] It does not examine the relation between the limiting law's purpose and the means it takes to achieve it. Rather, it examines the relation between the limiting law's purpose and the constitutional right. It focuses on the relation between the benefit in fulfilling the law's purpose and the harm caused by limiting the constitutional right.[22] It is based on balancing. Noting the difference between the necessity test and that of proportionality *stricto sensu*, Rivers has written:

> It is vital to realize that the test of balance has a totally different function from the test of necessity. The test of necessity rules out inefficient human rights limitations. It filters out cases in which the same level of realization of a legitimate aim could be achieved at less cost to rights. By contrast, the test of balance is strongly evaluative. It asks whether the combination

---

[16] J. Casey, *Constitutional Law in Ireland* (Dublin: Round Hall Press, 2000), 313.

[17] N. Emiliou, *The Principle of Proportionality in European Law: A Comparative Study* (London: Kluwer Law International, 1996).

[18] See *Adalah*, above note 1.

[19] *Sporrong and Lönnroth* v. *Sweden*, App. No. 7151/75, 5 EHRR 35 (1982), § 69.

[20] See S. Woolman, "Riding the Push-Me Pull-You: Constructing a Test That Reconciles the Conflicting Interests Which Animate the Limitation Clause," 10 *SAJHR* 60, 89 (1994).

[21] M. Cohen-Eliya and G. Stopler, "Probability Thresholds as Deontological Constraints in Global Constitutionalism," 49 *Colum. J. Transnat'l L.* 102 (2010).

[22] See A. Kavanagh, *Constitutional Review under the UK Human Rights Act* (Cambridge University Press, 2009).

of certain levels of rights-enjoyment combined with the achievement of other interests is good or acceptable.[23]

B.   The rule of balancing

1.   The centrality of balancing

Balancing is central to life and law.[24] It is central to the relationship between human rights and the public interest,[25] or amongst human rights.[26] Balancing reflects the multi-faceted nature of the human being, of society generally, and of democracy in particular.[27] It is an expression

---

[23] J. Rivers, "Proportionality and Variable Intensity of Review," 65 *Cambridge L. J.* 174, 200 (2006).

[24] CrimA 537/95 *Ganimat* v. *State of Israel* [1995] IsrSC 49(3) 355, 397 ("The notion of 'balancing' controls us and everything that is around us. Planet Earth revolves around the sun 'to balance' between the gravitational forces pushing it towards the sun and the gravitational forces pulling it back to outer space. Each and every one of us is a kind of 'balance' between their father and mother and their respective families. The same is true for every living organism. The same is true of the legal universe: Every legal norm represents a balance between interests and forces pulling in different directions. This is true for all constitutions, for Basic Laws, for ordinary legislation, for regulations – every legal norm, whether general or individual. Every 'law' is ultimately a 'balance.' Every legal norm has its own 'balance.' Part of that 'balancing' is determined by the legislator; the other part is determined – as per the legislator – by the courts." (Cheshin, J.)).

[25] *Ibid.*, at 413 ("The history of Israeli case law is the history of finding the right balance between the individual and the general public. The main contribution of the Israeli Supreme Court to the development of Israeli law, since the establishment of the State of Israel, has been the recognition of human rights and the determination of the proper balance between those rights and the need to guarantee the public peace and safety. Once the Israeli Supreme Court has recognized those (natural) human rights, and granted them a superior legal status, it had to balance between those rights and the needs of the community as a whole. The Court's most important decisions in all legal fields – either private or public – emphasized the need to draw a balance between an individual and the public, between the individual and the community as a whole, between human rights and the need for public peace and safety" (Barak, P.)).

[26] CA 6024/97 *Shavit* v. *Rishon LeZion Jewish Burial Society* [1999] IsrSC 53(3) 600, 649 ("We are faced with two conflicting values ... How should this Court resolve such a conflict? The answer provided to this question, ever since the establishment of the State of Israel, is that the Court should put the conflicting values on either side of the legal scales. It should balance between the conflicting values and principles. It should determine between that balance according to the relative weight of the conflicting values at the point of determination. This is the way this Court has been working from its establishment and until this very day. This ... balancing ... applies in our public law ... Indeed, since the establishment of the State of Israel we have been dealing with balancing between conflicting values and interests." (Barak, P.)).

[27] See above, at 218.

of the understanding that the law is not "all or nothing." Law is a complex framework of values and principles, which in certain cases are all congruent and lead to one conclusion, while in other situations are in direct conflict and require resolution. The balancing technique reflects this complexity. At the constitutional level, balancing enables the continued existence, within a democracy, of conflicting principles or values, while recognizing their inherent constitutional conflict.[28] At the sub-constitutional level, balancing provides a solution that reflects the values of democracy and the limitations that democracy imposes on the majority's power to restrict individuals and minorities in it.

2. Balancing and validity

The discussion regarding balancing, followed by the discussion regarding the weight, is a metaphor.[29] The scales do not actually exist. The consideration regarding balancing is normative in nature. It assumes the very existence of conflicting principles. This is meant to resolve those conflicts. The solution is not by providing a permanent label of "weight" to each conflicting principle, but rather through shaping legal rules – the rules of balancing – that determine under which circumstances we may fulfill one principle while limiting another. Those balancing rules reflect the relation between the conflicting considerations at the foundation of the realization of each conflicting principle. They are evaluated according to their relative weight at the point of conflict. The solution to such a conflict is not through upholding the validity of one principle while denying any validity to the other; rather, the balancing approach reflects the notion that the legal validity of all of the conflicting principles is kept intact.[30] Their scope is preserved. The result of the conflict is not a change in the

---

[28] See above, at 87.

[29] See P. Kahn, "The Court, the Community and the Judicial Balance: The Jurisprudence of Justice Powell," 97 *Yale L. J.* 1 (1987); F. M. Coffin, "Judicial Balancing: The Protean Scales of Justice," 63 *N. Y. U. L. Rev.* 16, 19 (1988); R. H. Fallon, "Individual Rights and the Powers of Government," 27 *Ga. L. Rev.* 343 (1993); for the pros and cons of the balancing metaphor, see W. Winslade, "Adjudication and the Balancing Metaphor," in H. Hubien (ed.), *Legal Reasoning* (Brussels: Emile Bruylant, 1971), 403; D. E. Curtis and J. Resnik, "Images of Justice," 96 *Yale L. J.* 1727 (1987); I. Porat, "The Dual Model of Balancing: A Model for the Proper Scope of Balancing in Constitutional Law," 27 *Cardozo L. Rev.* 1393, 1398 (2006). Regarding this metaphoric discussion, see G. Lakoff and M. Johnson, *Metaphors We Live By* (University of Chicago Press, 1980).

[30] See above, at 87.

principles; it is in the possibility of the realization of the principle at the sub-constitutional level.

Balancing rules have different roles in the law. In the present context, it is important to distinguish between interpretive balancing and constitutional balancing.[31] In interpretive balancing, the balancing is used to determine the purpose of the interpreted law. It outlines its normative boundaries.[32] Constitutional balancing, in contrast, is designed to determine the constitutionality of a sub-constitutional law. It is not designed to interpret the sub-constitutional law, but rather to determine its validity. Constitutional balancing – and the balancing rules it develops – are meant to resolve the tension between the benefit obtained in the realization of the law's purpose, and the harm caused to the constitutional right. Thus, for example, the balancing rules are meant to determine the constitutionality of a sub-constitutional law (a statute or the common law) that realizes the constitutional right to free speech and therefore limits the constitutional right to privacy. Equally, the constitutional balancing rule determines the constitutionality of a sub-constitutional law that limits a constitutional right (such as free speech or privacy) in order to realize a public interest (such as national security). The conflicting principles exist at the constitutional level and operate at the sub-constitutional level; therefore, the balancing rule should also be found at the constitutional level.[33] The constitutional rules of balancing are "housed," therefore, within the limitation clause; more particularly, they can be found within the proportionality *stricto sensu* test. Whenever a country's constitution contains a specific limitation clause, the constitutional balancing rule can be found within that specific limitation clause; whenever a constitution does not contain an explicit limitation clause regarding rights conflicting amongst themselves or with the public interest, the constitutional balancing rule can be found within an implied, or judge-made, limitation clause.[34] Either way, the rules of proportionality *stricto sensu* are found in the constitution. They exist at a constitutional level. They determine whether a sub-constitutional law that limits a constitutional right satisfies the requirements of the limitation clause. If the answer to this question is yes, then the limitation of the constitutional right is constitutional,

---

[31] See above, at 72.
[32] Regarding interpretive balancing, see A. Barak, *Purposive Interpretation in Law* (Princeton University Press, 2005), 177.
[33] See above, at 72.   [34] See above, at 134.

and therefore valid. If the answer is no, then the limitation on the right is unconstitutional and therefore invalid.[35]

A special case is that found in the United Kingdom's Human Rights Act 1998 (HRA).[36] Regarding this law, both the right as well as the limiting law are found at the same normative level – this is at the statute level. Ostensibly there is no room to discuss this matter in this context. The reason for this is that the solution to the conflict between the right and its limitation could be found in the rules which regulate conflicting laws, according to which the law later in time prevails (*lex posterior derogat legi priori*), unless the earlier law is more specific (*lex specialis derogat legi generali*). This solution was denied in the HRA. The court has been authorized solely to determine if there is an incompatibility between the conflicting laws and, if such laws are incompatible, to give a declaration of incompatibility.[37] Under these legal regimes there is room to apply the rules of proportionality in general, and in particular the balancing element within them.[38][39]

3. *The nature of the balancing*

Whenever constitutional balancing is triggered – whenever a constitutional right is limited by a sub-constitutional law – the balancing rule asks us to place on one end of the scales the purpose that the sub-constitutional law attempts to advance, the probability that the benefit that would be gained from fulfilling this proper purpose would actually be realized, and the benefit that is gained by fulfilling the proper purpose, in accordance with its urgency (the scale of fulfilling the purpose). On the other end of the scale should be the limited constitutional right, the harm it incurs and the probability that such harm would actually occur (the scale of limiting the right). We should establish a normative rule which determines the relative weight of each side of the scale.[40] Based on this weight we could determine which end of the scale is heavier.[41] Thus, it is necessary to balance the scale of fulfilling the purpose with the scale of limiting the right. How do we conduct such a balance?

---

[35] Regarding balancing within the UK Human Rights Act of 1998, see above, at 159.
[36] Human Rights Act 1998, c. 42 (Eng.).
[37] See *ibid.*, section 4(2).   [38] See above, at 159.
[39] See Kavanagh, above note 22, at 307.
[40] Regarding the scale metaphor, see the opinion of Justice O'Regan of the Constitutional Court of South Africa in *S. v. Bhulwana*, 1996 (1) SA 388 (CC), § 18.
[41] F. Schauer, "Prescriptions in Three Dimensions," 82 *Iowa L. Rev.* 911 (1997).

At the center of the rules of balancing – and at the center of proportionality *stricto sensu* – is the search for legal rules that determine the conditions in which a limitation of a constitutional right by a sub-constitutional law are proportional *stricto sensu*. No one seriously suggests that such a conflict should be resolved through the toss of a coin. Everyone agrees that we should adopt a principled, normative approach to the conflict. The issue lies with the shaping of the normative approach to solve the balancing problem.

4. Balancing based on the importance of the benefits and the importance of preventing the harm

i. The social importance

The relevant rule according to which the weight of each of the scales should be determined is that of the social importance of the benefit gained by the limiting law and the social importance of preventing harm to the limited constitutional right at the point of conflict.[42]

The main issue is, of course, how should we determine the social importance of the benefits gained by the limiting law and the social importance of preventing harm to the limited constitutional right. The answer is that the determination is not scientific or accurate. The balancing between conflicting principles is not conducted through scientific instruments. Rather, it is derived, *inter alia*, from different political and economic ideologies, from the unique history of each country, from the structure of the political system, and from different social values. The legal system at issue should be observed as a whole. The assessment of the social importance of each of the conflicting principles should be conducted against the background of the normative structure of each legal system. This kind of balancing should be affected by the entire value structure of the particular legal system. We should consider the constitutional status of the

---

[42] HCJ 14/86 *Laor v. Israel Film and Theatre Council* [1987] IsrSC 41(1) 421, 434 (In order to determine this balance, the conflicting values should be given a weight. These expressions – "balancing," "weight" – are only metaphors. Behind them stands the notion that not all principles are equally important in the eyes of the community in which they reside. Without legislative directive, the Court should evaluate the relative social value associated with the different principles. Much like you cannot have a person without a shadow, you cannot have a principle without a weight. The determination of the balance based on weight means the assessment of the social importance of each of the principles at the point of conflict.) See also Kavanagh, above note 22, at 234; M. Cohen-Eliya and I. Porat, "American Balancing and German Proportionality: The Historical Origins" 8 *Int'l J. Const. L.* 263 (2010).

conflicting principles. Principles found in the constitution are *prima facie* of greater social importance than those external to the constitution. That is insufficient. The importance of principles – and the importance of the prevention of their harm – is not determined solely by their normative status. Principles at the same normative level can be considered to be of different social importance. These kinds of values may be influenced by both extrinsic and intrinsic factors.[43] The extrinsic factors are of a social nature. They reflect society's history and culture.[44] The intrinsic factors are of a normative nature.[45] They reflect the internal relations of the different principles. Thus, for example, a right that constitutes a precondition to another right may be considered more important.

ii.   Clarifying the scope of balancing

a.   Generally   On the surface, the task of comparing the benefits and harm seems almost impossible. How can we compare the benefits inherent in national security and the harm incurred to the right of freedom of speech? It is appropriate, therefore, at this early stage of the discussion, to define the issue more narrowly, or to clarify its scope properly. Such a clarification is two-pronged. First, it is important to note that the comparison is not between the importance of fulfilling the purpose of the limiting law and preventing the harm to the constitutional right. Rather, the comparison focuses only on the marginal effects – on both the benefits and the harm – caused by the law. In other words, the comparison is between the margins. Second, in order to conduct the balance properly we must consider the hypothetical proportional alternative to the limiting law. If, indeed, such an alternative exists, then the comparison between the marginal benefits and marginal harm is made in light of that proportional alternative. Although this alternative was not adopted by the limiting law itself, the lawmaker can still adopt it as an amendment to the limiting law. These two clarifications will now be examined in turn.

b.   First clarification: comparing the marginal benefit to the marginal harm   In determining the balancing we compare the weight of the social importance of the benefit gained by fulfilling the proper purpose and the weight of the social importance of preventing the harm that this fulfillment may cause to the constitutional right. This comparison focuses on the state of affairs prior to the law's enactment and the changes caused by

---

[43] See below, at 361.   [44] See below, at 361.   [45] See below, at 361.

the law. Accordingly, the issue is not the comparison of the general social importance of the purpose (security, public safety, etc.) on the one hand and the general social importance of preventing harm to the constitutional right (equality, freedom of expression, etc.) on the other. Rather, the issue is much more limited. It refers to the comparison between the state of the purpose prior to the law's enactment, compared with that state afterwards, and the state of the constitutional right prior to the law's enactment compared with its state after enactment. Accordingly, we are comparing the marginal social importance of the benefit gained by the limiting law and the marginal social importance of preventing the harm to the constitutional right caused by the limiting law. The question is whether the weight of the marginal social importance of the benefits is heavier than the weight of the marginal social importance of preventing the harm. This approach to proportionality was applied by the Israeli Supreme Court in *Adalah*.[46] Before the legislation of the Law of Citizenship and Entry Into Israel (Temporary Measure) 2003, the unification of an Israeli spouse and their spouse from the Occupied Territories was prevented when an individual security check raised questions regarding whether the spouse from the Occupied Territories was a security threat. The law revoked this arrangement, as under it, at least twenty-six spouses involved in terrorist activities were permitted to enter Israel. In order to remedy this situation, the new law imposed a blanket ban on family unification for a period of one year (with an option to extend). When presenting the issue of whether the law's regulatory framework is proportional *stricto sensu*,[47] I wrote:

> The issue before us is not the national security of the residents of Israel or the respect of the human dignity of the Israeli spouses. The issue is not about life, or quality of life. Rather, the issue before us is much narrower. Does the additional security achieved by the transition from the strictest individual examination possible by law of the non-Israeli spouse to a blanket restriction on entry into Israel have an adequate relation (that is, is proportional) to the additional harm caused to the human dignity of the Israeli spouse as a result of such a transition?[48]

In a similar vein, Grimm has noted:

> It is rarely the case that a legal measure affects a fundamental right altogether. Usually, only a certain aspect of a right is affected. For

---

[46] See *Adalah*, above note 1.
[47] Regarding the necessity component in *Adalah*, see above, at 321.
[48] *Ibid.*, para. 91 (Barak, P.).

instance, a law may regulate not all speech but, rather, commercial speech regarding certain products and in certain media. The weight of the aspect of the right that has been regulated in relation to the right at large must be determined carefully. The same is true for the good in whose interest the right is restricted. Rarely is one measure apt to give full protection to a certain good. Only certain aspects of this good will be affected in a salutary way. The importance of these aspects in view of the good at large must be carefully determined, as well as the degree of protection that the measure will render.[49]

Take, for example, a statute limiting the right to freedom of occupation by imposing a ban on the sale of a product that may be dangerous to public health. While determining the proper balancing point between obtaining the benefits and preventing the harm, the question is not one of what is the balance between the weight of the social importance of the principle of public health and the weight of the social importance of the principle of freedom of occupation; rather, the issue is much narrower in scope: what is the balance between the weight of the marginal social importance of the benefit to public health achieved by imposing the restriction and the weight of the marginal social importance of preventing the harm to freedom of occupation that is caused as a result of the restriction.

The issue, therefore, focuses on the constitutionality of the weight of the marginal social importance of the benefit and harm. In most cases, the analysis presupposes a state of affairs whose constitutionality is not at issue. From that premise stems the question of whether the change brought by the new law – in the narrow scope in which it occurs – is constitutional. Obviously this narrow scope may become wider if the current state of affairs is unconstitutional and the constitutional argument applies to the existing condition as well. In a case such as this we should once again narrow the scope of the review as much as possible so that it applies to the analysis only from the point where no argument exists regarding its constitutionality.

c. **Second clarification: considering a proportional alternative** A close examination of the comparison of the weight of the marginal social importance of the benefits gained by the limiting law and the marginal

[49] Grimm, above note 10, at 396. See also S. J. Heyman, *Free Speech and Human Dignity* (New Haven, CT: Yale University Press, 2008), 70: "[B]alancing seeks to determine which right has more weight. This determination should be made at the margin – that is, instead of asking whether freedom of speech or, say, the right to privacy has greater value in general, one should ask (1) how much the value of privacy would be affected by the speech at issue, and (2) how much the value of free speech would be impaired by regulations to protect privacy."

social importance of preventing the harm to the constitutional right teaches us that in most cases the scope of the comparison is even narrower. Thus far, we have compared the state of affairs before the law was enacted to that state afterwards. However, we must recall that, while examining the necessity test, possible hypothetical alternatives were examined.[50] At times included within those alternatives are alternatives that would be able to gain the main marginal social benefit while causing less harm to the constitutional right. These alternatives do not meet the necessity test as they do not fulfill fully the purpose of the limiting law.[51] These alternatives can be reintroduced into the constitutional discussion within the test of proportionality *stricto sensu*, if one of those alternatives, if enacted into law, can meet the requirements of the proportionality *stricto sensu* test. Accordingly, the starting point for the comparison in this type of situation is not just the state of affairs prior to the law but also the state of affairs should the hypothetical alternative solution be adopted by law. Thus, on the first scale – that of "fulfilling the proper purpose" – we place the marginal social importance of the benefits gained by rejecting the possible alternative and adopting the proposed law, while on the scale of "harming the constitutional right" we place the marginal social import- ance of preventing the harm caused to the constitutional right from reject- ing the possible alternative and adopting the proposed law. The question examined in this scenario is which has the heavier weight on the scales.

An example of such marginal benefit and harm can be found in the Israeli Supreme Court case of *Beit Sourik*.[52] There, the Court examined the legality of a decision by the Israeli government to erect a Security Fence in the West Bank. The purpose of erecting the fence was the preven- tion of the entry of terrorists into Israel or Israeli settlements within the Occupied Territories. The Court held, first, that the order which permitted the fence's erection – which limited the rights of the local Arab residents – had a proper purpose. As for the means, the Court held that there was a rational connection between the fulfilling of the security purpose and the means chosen. In addition, it was held that several alternatives offered to the Court as to the location of the fence – despite causing less harm to the local Arab residents – could not have achieved the same degree of

[50] See above, at 326.

[51] J. Rivers, "Proportionality, Discretion and the Second Law of Balancing," in G. Pavlakos (ed.), *Law, Rights, and Discourse: The Legal Philosophy of Robert Alexy* (Portland, OR: Hart Publishing, 2007).

[52] HCJ 2056/04 *Beit Sourik Village Council* v. *The Government of Israel* [2004] IsrSC 58(5) 807.

security that the order sought to promote. Accordingly, the Court held that the law met the necessity test as well. But doubts arose in relation to proportionality *stricto sensu*. What comparison should be made here? Is it a comparison between the state of affairs that existed before the issuance of the executive order and the one that existed afterwards, while comparing the marginal measure of security obtained by the fence and the marginal measure of harm caused to the local Arab residents? Or, perhaps the correct comparison was to the alternatives proposed to the Court? True, these alternatives did not satisfy the requirements of necessity, since they did not offer the same degree of additional security as achieved by the proposed fence. Still, it was held that, if that alternative had been chosen by the Israeli government, it would have satisfied the requirements of proportionality *stricto sensu*. Accordingly, the Court determined that the proper basis for comparison should not be between the state of affairs *ex ante* and *ex post*, but rather between the state of affairs after the realization of the alternative and the state of affairs after the issuance of the order. As I wrote in my opinion:

> The third test of proportionality determines that the harm caused to the individual from the means chosen by the administrative authority to fulfill its purposes must be proportional to the benefits brought about by that means. This is the test of the proportional means (or proportionality *stricto sensu*). That test is usually applied in "absolute terms," that is while directly comparing the benefits gained by the executive action and the harm caused by it. In some cases the same test may be applied "relatively," that is while comparing the executive action with an alternative measure which could not yield the same level of benefits produced by the original executive action. Thus, the original action would be disproportional according to the third test in cases where a small reduction of the benefits gained by the original action, such as the adoption of the alternative means, would guarantee a significant reduction of the harm caused to the constitutional right by the original means ... The real issue before us is whether the additional advantage to national security gained by adopting the approach expressed by the military commander ... is proportional to the harm that adopting such an opinion would cause ... Our answer is that the choice made by the military commander as to the route of the separation fence is disproportional. The disparity between the security measures required by the military commander's opinion and the security measures gained by the alternative route is much smaller than the significant disparity that exists between a fence separating local residents from their land and a fence that does not create such a separation, or whose separation is so small that it can be lived with.[53]

[53] *Ibid.*, at 840, 851–852.

It is obvious that this basis for comparison exists only if the alternative itself is proportional. If the alternative itself is not proportional – and no other proportional alternative exists – then we must return to the comparison between the marginal benefit and marginal harm caused by the legislation, without considering a possible alternative.

What, then, is the role of the alternative? Obviously, it does not render the need to determine an "adequate relation" between benefit and harm redundant. Of course it cannot "bypass" the issues of balancing and weight. The alternative's importance is that it narrows the scope of the balancing actions. The issue is no longer how to compare between the social importance of the marginal benefit gained by fulfilling the purpose by means of the law (as compared to the state of affairs *ex ante*) and the marginal social importance of preventing the harm to the constitutional right caused by the law (as compared to the state of affairs *ex ante*). The required comparison, rather, is much narrower: it is between the alternative and the limiting law. We must ask whether the limiting law is proportional (*stricto sensu*) when compared with the alternative. The solution to this question takes into consideration only a very limited set of marginal benefits and the prevention of the marginal harm, therefore making the determination of the weight and the balance much simpler.

It is understood that the basic premise must be that the alternative is proportional. The examination of this basic premise requires a comparison between that alternative and the state of affairs before the law came into effect. We begin this examination with the test of necessity, where we compare the purpose the law fulfills and the purpose fulfilled by the alternative law. When the result of this comparison is that the alternative cannot completely fulfill the original purpose, the examination of the necessity test ends. The examination may continue within the test of proportionality *stricto sensu*. Here, we also examine the "advancing the purpose" scale. Thus, the question is whether the social importance of the marginal benefits of the alternative option (compared with the state of affairs before the law was enacted and without a viable alternative) is greater than the social importance of preventing the marginal harm caused by the law within the scale of "harming the right" (compared with the state of affairs before the legislation was enacted and without the existence of an alternative). If the result is that the alternative is not proportional, the alternative should not be considered. If the alternative is proportional, then the issue is whether the limiting law is proportional when compared with the alternative.

An alternative can only be considered if it stands on its own. It must be practical rather than theoretical, real rather than imaginary. It must advance the same purposes that the law sought to advance, although not completely. The limitation of the constitutional right should be of a lesser extent than the law's limitation. These requirements are not easy to fulfill. In some cases, no suitable alternative exists; either because it is not practical and real, or because it is not proportional. However, when a proportional, practical alternative is available, it should serve as the basis of the proportionality examination of the limiting law. When this comparison is conducted by the court, it should assume that this alternative will be adopted by the lawmaker. The court should ask itself if the transition from this alternative to the law is proportional *stricto sensu*. If the answer is in the negative, then the legislation at issue is unconstitutional. However, despite the unconstitutionality of the law, the legislator is not facing a dead end. The legislator is not required to return to the drawing board, to its position before the limiting law was introduced. Rather, the legislator can reduce the "damage" of the unconstitutionality. It can do so by legislating the alternative. That way, benefits will be gained and the harm reduced in comparison to the situation before the law's enactment. It should be noted that the degree of the benefits obtained would probably be less than that obtained by the original law. However, this partial fulfillment should satisfy the legislator's policy considerations.

An argument can be made that the examination of the alternative will make the constitutional review more complicated, since, instead of one examination which focuses on the limiting law and the changes it proposes, despite the situation *ex ante*, two examinations are now executed: the first compares the alternative with the state of affairs that existed *ex ante*, before the limiting law; and the other compares the limiting law with the alternative. Indeed, this critique does carry some weight. However, the very existence of an alternative option is of great importance. It assists in conducting the constitutional examination within proportionality *stricto sensu* in that it provides an answer to the question of the proper relation between the benefits and harm. This assistance is mainly expressed by answering the questions of weight and importance of the conflicting principles. This alleviation is derived from the narrowing of the questions to be resolved: the questions of benefits and harm are "divided" into sublevels, and that, in turn, eases the receipt of an answer to the questions of weight and importance.

d. The importance of the clarification

The two-pronged clarification above does not turn balancing into a factual problem.[54] It cannot negate the value-laden discretion of the balance. However, the scope of the legal issues in question – as well as the principles discussed – is made clearer. The clarification allows us to realize that the value-laden issue before the decisionmaker (be it a legislator, a judge, or the executive branch) is not as "expansive" as the balancing between the general principles of security, liberty, life, privacy, and freedom of expression. Rather, the clarification helps us to understand that the balance is much narrower in scope and that it balances between the marginal social importance of the benefits gained by one principle (beyond the proportional alternative) and the marginal social importance of preventing the harm to the constitutional right (beyond the proportional alternative). That, in turn, helps us to realize the rational nature of the balancing[55] as well as its structural integrity.[56] In addition, this can assist in responding to critics of the proportionality *stricto sensu* balancing test.[57] The limits of judicial discretion are drawn more clearly and therefore contribute to the justification of balancing as a judicial measure aimed at protecting constitutional rights and justifying the act of judicial review itself.[58]

iii. The marginal social importance of the "advancing the purpose" scale

a. The purpose On one end of the scales we find the purpose that the law seeks to realize. This purpose is proper, after it meets the threshold requirements regarding the proper purpose[59] when determining the importance of the purpose, we should focus on the importance of the marginal benefits in its fulfillment compared to the situation prior thereto or to the possibility of the realization of an alternative.[60] Thus, when the purpose is the protection of human rights, the marginal social importance of that purpose is determined in accordance with the protection that these rights received prior to the legislation and that they received following that law. The same is true for purposes designed to satisfy the public

---

[54] For a different opinion, see D. M. Beatty, *The Ultimate Rule of Law* (Oxford University Press, 2004), 170. See also below, at 477.
[55] See below, at 485. [56] See below, at 460.
[57] See below, at 481. [58] See below, at 473.
[59] See above, at 246. [60] See above, at 352.

interest. The social importance of these purposes is determined as per the marginal social importance gained by their fulfillment compared with the previous situation or with an alternative. Thus, the marginal social importance of fulfilling that purpose is influenced by the harm caused to other human rights or to the public interest should the law's purpose not be realized. The larger the harm incurred, the more important the goal of preventing this harm becomes.

b.   The probability of fulfillment   In order to answer the question of whether the marginal social importance of the benefit gained from fulfilling the purpose justifies the marginal social importance in preventing the harm to the constitutional right, we must examine the probability of its realization should the proposed law pass constitutional muster.[61] This probability is conditional on factual data, as well as an evaluation (prognosis) regarding the likelihood of fulfillment of that proper purpose. In *Adalah*,[62] the Israeli Supreme Court examined this question regarding probability:

> The proper approach to the issue is at the level of the risks and the probability of their realization, as well as their impact on society as a whole. The questions that must be raised are those regarding probability. The question is what is the probability that human lives will be lost should we continue with the regime of individual examinations, compared with the probability that human lives will be lost if we move on to a regime of a blanket restriction, and whether this additional probability is equivalent to the increase in harm caused to the rights of some Israeli citizens.[63]

Thus, in determining the weight of fulfilling the law's purpose (whether it is the protection of another right or fulfilling the public interest) we should first consider the probability of the purpose's actual occurrence.[64] The weight of an important purpose, whose realization is urgent and the probability of its actual occurrence is high, is not equal to the weight of a similarly important purpose, whose realization is also urgent but whose probability of occurrence is extremely low.

iv.   The marginal social importance of the "limiting of the right" scale

a.   The considerations in question   The social importance of the "limiting of the right" scale is determined by the social importance of

---

[61] See R. Alexy, *A Theory of Constitutional Rights* (J. Rivers trans., Oxford University Press, 2002 [1986]), 44. See also Rivers, above note 51.

[62] *Adalah*, above note 1.   [63] *Ibid.*, para. 110 (Barak, P.).

[64] See above, at 308.

the limited right as well as the importance in preventing its limitation. Here, too, the social importance is determined according to the principles underlying the limited right as well as the social importance of preventing this limitation. The weight of the limitation of the right is not determined abstractly but rather is determined in the context of the marginal social importance in preventing the harm to the constitutional right. At the center of the "limiting the right" scale lies the constitutional right itself. The weight of the marginal social importance in preventing the harm to the right is derived from its social importance and is affected by the scope of the limitation and the probability of its realization. Each of these considerations will now be examined in more detail.

b. The social importance of the right   Are all constitutional rights equal in their social importance? Are there rights that are more important than others? Should we simply conclude that all rights are equal in social importance since their normative status is the same? The answer is that we should distinguish between constitutional status and social weight. The constitutional status of a right is determined through constitutional interpretation. Without a constitutional instruction to the contrary, the assumption is that all constitutional rights enjoy the same constitutional status.[65]

Rights of equal normative status are not necessarily rights of equal social importance. The social importance of a right – and, as a result, its weight in comparison to other rights – is derived from its underlying reasons and the importance of these reasons within society's fundamental understanding of rights.[66] The understanding that constitutional rights are not all of equal social importance and weight is accepted in Israeli case law. As noted in the *Horev* case:

> Regarding the protection of constitutional rights from prospective limitations, not all rights are equal. For example, the right to human dignity is not equal to the right to own property. Moreover, within each right there are different levels of protection for different parts of the right. For example, the protection granted to political speech would be greater than that granted to commercial speech.[67]

---

[65] Regarding the constitutional status of the United Kingdom Human Rights Act 1998, see above, at 159.

[66] See J. Rivers, "Proportionality and Discretion in International and European Law," in N. Tsagourias (ed.), *Transnational Constitutionalism: International and European Perspectives* (Cambridge University Press, 2007), 118; C. B. Pulido, "The Rationality of Balancing," 92 *Archiv für Rechts- und Sozial Philosophie* 195 (2007).

[67] HCJ 5016/96 *Horev* v. *Minister of Transport* [1997] IsrSC 51(4) 1, 49.

A similar approach was advanced by Justice Zamir in the *Tzemach* case:

> Personal freedom is a constitutional right of the first order, it is also a precondition for the exercise of other fundamental rights. A limitation of the right to personal freedom – like throwing a rock into still water – creates ripples which limit other rights; not only the right to freedom of movement, but also the freedom of speech, the right to privacy, the right to personal property and other rights. As Section 1 of Basic Law: Human Dignity and Liberty teaches us, "[f]undamental human rights in Israel are founded upon recognition of the value of the human being, the sanctity of human life, and the principle that all persons are free." Only a free person can fully and appropriately realize their constitutional rights. And personal freedom, more than any other right, is that which makes a person free. Therefore, the denial of personal liberty is an extremely harsh limitation.[68]

A comparative law survey confirms the assumption that many legal systems accept the approach that differentiates between the different rights as to their relative social importance. Thus, for example, in American law this differentiation forms the basis for the noted distinction between three levels of scrutiny.[69] Similarly, the 1996 Constitution of the Republic of South Africa states that, in reviewing the constitutionality of a limiting law, the court must take into account "the nature of the right."[70] According to the approach accepted in South Africa, the rights to dignity, equality, and liberty are considered central to South African society.[71] Several court decisions in New Zealand adopted a similar approach.[72] However, a contrary opinion can also be found in comparative law, according to which all constitutional rights are equal in social importance. This is, for example, the approach adopted in the constitutional law of both Germany[73] and Canada.[74]

---

[68] HCJ 6055/95 *Tzemach* v. *Minister of Defence* [1999] IsrSC 53(5) 241, 261.

[69] See above, at 284.

[70] Constitution of the Republic of South Africa, Art. 36(1)(a).

[71] See Woolman and Botha, above note 13, at 70.

[72] See S. Mize, "Resolving Cases of Conflicting Rights under the New Zealand Bill of Rights Act," 22 *New Zealand U. L. Rev.* 50 (2006).

[73] See Grimm, above note 10, at 395. Not everyone agrees with that approach; for a discussion, see L. Blaauw-Wolf, "The Balancing of Interest with Reference to the Principle of Proportionality and the Doctrine of Guterabwagung – A Comparative Analysis," 14 *SAPL* 178 (1999).

[74] See *Dagenais* v. *Canadian Broadcasting Corporation* [1994] 3 SCR 835; *Trinity Western University* v. *British Columbia College of Teachers* [2001] 1 SCR 772; *Lavoie* v. *Canada* [2002] 1 SCR 769; *R.* v. *Brown* [2002] 2 SCR 185; *Chamberlain* v. *Surrey School District No.*

Not all constitutional rights are equal in their social importance. The social importance of a constitutional right – as well as the marginal social importance of preventing its limitation – is determined by the society's fundamental perceptions. These perceptions are shaped by the culture, history, and character of each society. They are derived from the constitution's purposes. Such considerations can be dubbed "external" considerations. With these, we can find other considerations, of a more "internal" nature. These are considerations related to the internal relations between different constitutional rights. Thus, for example a right used as a precondition for the realization or act of another right is understood as more socially important.[75] From this premise we may deduce the increased social importance of the right to life, to human dignity, to equality, and to political speech – all of which constitute preconditions to the realization of other rights. The distinction regarding the importance of a right may also apply within the rights themselves (as opposed to between the different rights). Thus, the marginal social importance of preventing harm to the right to political speech is unlike the marginal social importance in preventing harm to the right to commercial speech. From that premise we can also derive the marginal social importance of the social rights which, at their most basic level, are meant to provide minimal living conditions to the members of a given community.

Thus, the marginal social importance of a constitutional right is determined from different perspectives. Rights that advance the legal system's most fundamental values and that contribute to the personal welfare of each member of the community[76] differ from rights that rely upon general welfare considerations as their only justification. Similarly, "suspect" rights, which historically have been limited by the majority for improper reasons, differ from rights that are not "suspect" in that way.[77] The different perspectives at times suit one another. In other cases, they point in different directions. We must assume that, with time, it will be possible to establish more specific criteria on this matter.

---

36 [2002] 4 SCR 710; *Reference re Same-Sex Marriage* [2004] 3 SCR 608; *Gosselin (Tutor of)* v. *Quebec (Attorney General)* [2005] 1 SCR 238; *WIC Radio Ltd.* v. *Simpson* [2006] SCR 41.

[75] C. B. Pulido, "The Rationality of Balancing," 92 *Archiv für Rechts- und Sozial Philosophie* 195 (2007). See *Tzemach*, above note 68, at 261.

[76] *Herbert* v. *Lando*, 441 US 153 (1979).

[77] See R. Dworkin, *Taking Rights Seriously* (Cambridge, MA: Harvard University Press, 1977), 266.

c.   The intensity of the limitation of the right   The weight assigned to the "limitation of the right" scale is derived not only from the marginal social importance of the right, but also from the scope of the right's limitation, its intensity, and its size. The limitation's acuteness influences its weight. A limitation of one right (the limited right) differs from a limitation on additional rights (in addition to the limited right); similarly, a limitation on the right's core differs from a limitation on the right's penumbra; a temporary limitation differs from a permanent one.

d.   The probability of the right's limitation   Much as the probability of achieving the proper purpose is an important factor in determining the weight of the marginal social importance of the benefit it involves, the probability of the occurrence of a limitation on the constitutional right is an important factor to consider in determining the weight of the marginal social importance of preventing the harm that may be suffered by that right. A limitation whose probability of occurrence is high differs from a limitation whose probability of occurrence is much lower. In the legal literature, this aspect of the "limiting the right" scale is not emphasized. The reason for this is that, in most cases, the probability of the realization of the limitation is certain. When the limiting law is legislated, the limitation occurs instantaneously. This is true in most cases, but not all. In those cases where the occurrence of the limitation is not certain, the amount of uncertainty – in other words, the probability of its realization – may affect the weight of the right's limitation. A law determining certain conditions in which a constitutional right should not be realized differs from a law that provides the executive branch with discretion relating to the statutory authority to limit that same right.

C.   The basic balancing rule

1.   The elements of the basic balancing rule

The fundamental measure for the balancer – whether done by legislators, members of the executive branch, or judges – is the marginal social importance of the competing scales. The terms used in that process are those of marginal social importance. The marginal social importance of the benefits gained by the legislation should be compared with the marginal social importance of preventing the harm to the right in question. The rules of balancing should reflect such comparison. As noted earlier, in determining the marginal social importance of each side of the scales we should factor in the probability of both achieving the desired purpose[78] as well as the probability of the occurrence of an actual harm to the protected right in question.[79]

The basic balancing rule seeks to determine a legal rule that reflects all the elements of balancing between a law limiting a constitutional right and its effect on the constitutional right. It should reflect both ends of the scales as well as their relationship. It should apply in cases where both of the scales carry a constitutional right (such as a law limiting the freedom of expression in order to better protect the right to privacy), as well as in cases where the societal benefit scale carries public interest considerations (such as a law limiting the freedom of expression in order to better protect national security interests). Thus, such a balancing rule should reflect the marginal social importance of the benefits created by the limiting law (either to the individuals involved or to the public at large) as well as the marginal social importance in preventing the harm caused to the limited right in question; it should also consider the probability of the occurrence of each. Such a basic balancing rule would be found within the constitutional limitation clause (either explicit or implicit).

2. The components of the basic balancing rule and its justification

Against this background, it is possible to determine the content of the basic balancing rule: The higher the social importance of preventing the marginal harm to the constitutional right at issue and the higher the probability of such an additional marginal harm occurring, then the marginal benefits created by the limiting law – either to the public interest or to other constitutional rights – should be of a higher social importance and more urgent and the probability of its realization should be higher. Therefore, we cannot justify a serious and certain limitation of a socially important constitutional right in the fulfillment of a minimal social benefit, to the public interest or to the protection of other less important constitutional rights, whose probability is low. As Justice Zamir of the Israeli Supreme Court noted in *Tzemach*:

> The more important the limited right and the more severe the limitation on that right, the more robust a public interest consideration is required in order to justify the limitation.[80]

---

[78] See above, at 358.   [79] See above, at 362.

[80] *Tzemach*, above note 68, at 273. See also the opinion of Lord Bingham in *R. v. Ministry of Defence, ex parte Smith* [1996] QB 517, 554; opinion of Lord Woolf in *R. v. Lord Saville of Newdigate, ex parte A and B* [1999] 4 All ER 860, 871.

Such an approach is on a par with the approach developed by Alexy with regard to the substantive law of balancing:

> The greater the degree of non-satisfaction of, or detriment to, one principle, the greater must be the importance of satisfying the other.[81]

In the constitutional context, Alexy's approach is focused on the importance of fulfilling the proper purpose and the prevention of the harm to the right. Thus, the constitutional balancing rule, as per Alexy, should compare between "the degree of importance of satisfying one principle and the satisfaction/non-satisfaction (non-infringement/infringement) of the other."[82] Later, Alexy opines that the substantive law of balancing "identifies what is significant in balancing exercises, namely the degree of intensity of non-satisfactions of, or detriment to, one principle versus the importance of satisfying the other."[83]

Despite the obvious similarities and the influence of Alexy's approach on mine, it is important to mention the differences between my approach and that of Alexy. Alexy does not consider the marginal social importance of the limited right but only the degree of its limitation. Not so with my approach. My approach considers both the marginal social importance of the proper purpose and that of the limited constitutional right. The basic balancing rule expresses the society's understanding of the marginal social importance of the principles it seeks to advance, while evaluating the content and urgency of these principles, and the probability of their realization, as well as the marginal social importance and probability of harming the constitutional human rights that same society seeks to protect. This balancing rule expresses the understanding that, in a democracy, a proper purpose – in and of itself – is not enough to justify the use of any means of having it realized. This matter was discussed in one of my opinions:

> A review of the third test – proportionality *stricto sensu* – brings us back to the very foundations on which our constitutional democracy is based and the human rights Israelis enjoy. These foundations include the notion that the end does not always justify the means; that national security is not a sacred principle above all else; that the proper purpose of increased security measures cannot justify a harsh limitation on the lives of thousands of Israeli citizens. Our democracy is characterized by the fact that its ability to place a limitation on protected human rights is carefully

[81] See Alexy, above note 61, at 102.
[82] Alexy, above note 61, at 105.
[83] *Ibid.*

restricted. It is based on the recognition that each person enjoys a wall surrounding them which protects their rights, which cannot be breached by the majority.[84]

The basic rule of balancing thus provides a set of general constitutional criteria; these criteria, in turn, determine the scope – and set up the boundaries – of the state's ability to realize its proper purposes and to limit its constitutional rights. The basic balancing rule therefore "takes rights seriously" in that the public interest is insufficient as an excuse to limit a constitutional right. It is required that the public interest be so important that it justifies the limitation of the constitutional right at issue. In that respect, the basic balancing rule can be viewed as a "shield" of constitutional rights.[85] The basic balancing rule is able to prevent harm to socially important constitutional rights that constitute – to use a Dworkinian term – "trumps."[86] However, the basic rule is a rule of balancing. Dworkin's notion of "rights as trumps" is not based on the concept of balancing; in fact, it is meant to prevent it. The only claim here is that the same basic balancing rule that is proposed herein may lead to many of the same results achieved by viewing those socially valued rights as "trumps."

3.   Balanced scales

What should be the case when the scale is completely balanced?[87] In these cases, the marginal social importance of preventing the harm to the constitutional right is equal to the marginal social importance of the benefit in fulfilling the public interest or protecting another constitutional right. In these cases, does the limiting law satisfy the requirements of the test of proportionality *stricto sensu*? The cases where this has occurred are very few; but what is the solution for such cases?

It could be argued that the solution is procedural in nature. The burden of persuasion to prove proportionality, including proportionality *stricto*

---

[84] *Adalah*, above note 1, at para. 93 (Barak, P.).
[85] To adopt a term used by Schauer; see F. Schauer, "A Comment on the Structure of Rights," 27 *Ga. L. Rev.* 415, 430 (1993).
[86] On rights as trumps, see Dworkin, *Taking Rights Seriously*, above note 77, at 184; R. Dworkin, "Rights as Trumps," in J. Waldron (ed.), *Theories of Rights* (Oxford University Press, 1984), 153; B. Friedman, "Trumping Rights," 27 *Ga. L. Rev.* 435 (1992); D. T. Coenen, "Rights as Trumps," 27 *Ga. L. Rev.* 463 (1992).
[87] See V. De Silva, "Comparing the Incommensurable: Constitutional Principles, Balancing, and Rational Decision," 31 *OJLS* 1 (2011).

sensu, lies with the party arguing for the proportionality of the limitation as a whole. When the scales are balanced, the conclusion should be that the interested party has failed to lift that burden and we have a proven limitation of a constitutional right while a justification for this limitation was not proven. Here, the law must be declared unconstitutional. This claim is wrong. The burden of persuasion is relevant to the factual aspect of the case; it does not concern issues of law. Completely balanced scales present, first and foremost, a legal issue. The court already has all the facts at this point. Some of those facts have been proved through standard evidentiary tools. Others were demonstrated through presumptions, including the presumption that the burden of persuasion to show the proportionality of the limiting law (i.e., a proper purpose, rational connection, necessity, and proportionality *stricto sensu*) lies with the party arguing in favor of a proportional limitation. Now we face the legal issue: what is the rule of balanced scales?

At times, one can argue that the solution to the question appears in the very text of the limitation clause. Take, for example, the Israeli limitation clause. According to its wording, constitutional rights cannot be limited unless such a limitation is made by a law that satisfies several conditions. Relevant to our discussion is the condition that the legislation can only limit the right "to an extent no greater than is required." The argument would therefore be that once the scales are equal, the limitation at issue is "no greater" than is required, since it is "equal to" what is required. According to this line of thought, in Israel, whenever the two ends of the scales are equal in weight the legislation satisfies the requirements of proportionality *stricto sensu*. Such a "textual" approach raises some difficulties and is therefore doubtful. Take, for example, the limitation clause appearing in Switzerland's Federal Constitution:

> Limitation of fundamental rights must be proportionate to the goals pursued.[88]

Is the proportionality requirement posed by this provision satisfied whenever the two ends of the scales are balanced?

The solution is not found within textual arguments. Nor is it found within general doctrines of proportionality. Instead, the solution is found in accordance with the views adopted by each constitutional democracy. For this matter, we should distinguish between two sets of cases. In the first set of cases, both scales carry constitutional human rights, and the

---

[88] Federal Constitution of Switzerland, Art. 36(3).

marginal social importance of the benefit gained from the protection of one right is equal to the marginal social importance of preventing harm caused to the other right. It could be argued that in that state of affairs there is no reason not to leave the limiting law intact, since its limitation of one constitutional right is equal to its protection of another. In this situation, the legislative discretion should remain. The role of the courts as defenders of human rights is fulfilled.[89]

In the second set of cases, one scale carries the marginal social importance of the benefit gained to the public interest, while the other carries the marginal social importance of preventing harm caused to the constitutional right. In this type of case, is the limitation of the constitutional right for the sake of the public interest justified?[90] In one type of constitutional democracy, human rights may gain a special status such that whenever the scales are completely balanced the scale with the human right should prevail. When in doubt, liberty prevails (*in dubio pro libertate*).[91] A different constitutional democracy may determine that human rights may be important but even more so is the public interest. In that type of a democracy, whenever the scales are balanced the scale carrying the public interest prevails. When the scales are balanced, the legislator prevails.[92] In light of the central status occupied by human rights in constitutional democracies, and in light of the court's special role in protecting those rights, the issue of the balanced scales should be resolved in favor of the constitutional rights, that is, in favor of liberty.

4. *The basic balancing rule and specific balancing*

i. Basic and specific balancing

The basic rule of balancing provides a general rule which allows for the resolution of situations where on the one hand we encounter a marginal benefit to the public interest or to another constitutional right, and on the other hand we encounter a marginal harm caused to the constitutional right. This basic rule is applied to the circumstances of each specific case. This rule should guide the person conducting the balance on how to

---

[89] On the role of the courts as defenders of human rights, see A. Barak, *The Judge in a Democracy* (Princeton University Press, 2006), 83.
[90] C. B. Pulido, "The Rationality of Balancing," 92 *Archiv für Rechts- und Sozial Philosophie* 195, 207 (2007); De Silva, above note 87.
[91] See Alexy, above note 61, at 384. See also M. Kremnitzer, "Constitutional Principles and Criminal Law," 27 *Isr. L. Rev.* 84, 88 (1993).
[92] *Ibid.*, at 410. See De Silva, above note 87.

resolve the issue of conflict at the point of friction in a specific case. Thus, alongside the basic rule of balancing there is always specific or concrete balancing. These rules are "sensitive" to the case's facts.[93] This is an *ad hoc* balancing. The basic rule of balancing is based on a generalization with a high level of abstraction. The specific rules are based on a low level of abstraction.

Based on the basic rule of balancing, a legal rule that reflects the specific balancing is derived.[94] This constitutes a derivative constitutional rule.[95] This would be a rule at a much lower level of abstraction, which would balance the relevant data relating to the proper purpose, its marginal social importance, its degree of urgency, and the probability of its fulfillment within each specific case; it would also balance all the relevant data relating to the limited right, its marginal social importance, the degree of the harm it is likely to suffer and its probability as derived from the basic rule of balancing within each specific case.

ii. The legal status of the specific balancing rule

The specific balancing rule is derived from the basic balancing rule. Much like the basic balancing rule, the specific balancing rule is a constitutional rule. It is of constitutional status as it is directly derived from the interpretation of the constitutional limitation clause (either explicit or implicit). The effect of the specific rule of balancing – much like the effect of the basic rule itself – is at the sub-constitutional level.[96] It is meant to determine whether a sub-constitutional law, such as a statute or the common law, which limits a constitutional right under certain circumstances, is constitutional. Thus, the specific rule of balancing does not affect the scope of the constitutional right.[97] If, as a result of its application, the specific rule ends up protecting the constitutional rights of others, this result does not mean that the rule has widened the constitutional scope of those rights in any way. The specific rule of balancing only operates at the sub-constitutional level, where the rights are realized and exercised.

As its name indicates, the specific rule of balancing only applies to a specific set of circumstances. Clearly, it can be reapplied to a similar set

---

[93] P. Sales and B. Hooper, "Proportionality and the Form of Law," 119 *L. Q. Rev.* 426 (2003).
[94] Regarding this rule, see above, at 89.
[95] Regarding derivative constitutional rules, see above, at 39.
[96] See above, at 89.
[97] For a different approach, see Alexy, above note 61, at 60.

of circumstances. It can also be applied by way of interpretive analogy[98] in other cases where circumstances are not identical, but bear substantial similarities to the initial case. The specific rule of balancing always stands alongside the basic rule of balancing, and reflects its fulfillment regarding a specific constitutional context. The specific rule of balancing does not change the scope of the limited right. It affects its realization. It operates only on the sub-constitutional level.[99]

iii.   The specific balancing rule and the doctrine of "praktische Konkordanz"

Much like the basic rule of balancing, the specific rule of balancing applies both when the limitations on constitutional rights are balanced against other rights or against the public interest. The discussion of the first set of cases – balancing two constitutional rights – has been extensively developed in German constitutional law through the doctrine of "*praktische Konkordanz.*"[100] According to that doctrine, the importance of both sides of the scale should be recognized. The weight of the first scale (containing the first constitutional right) should not overtake the second scale (containing the other constitutional right). Instead, the balance should be conducted while trying to satisfy both rights, so that the limitation on the first right is equal to the limitation on the other. The approach was developed in German constitutional law specifically to address constitutional rights with no limitation clause of their own. The German courts realized that the lack of a limitation clause does not create a constitutional vacuum, or "absolute" rights. Instead, the rights can still be balanced against each other. Each of these balances is specific. It takes into account the circumstances of each case brought before the court. It applies a specific rule of balancing. This rule operates in accordance with two basic assumptions. First, there are constitutional rights on both sides of the scale; and second, those constitutional rights are equal in importance.

---

[98]   On interpretive analogies, see above, at 75.

[99]   See above, at 89.

[100]   For a discussion of the doctrine, see T. Marauhn and N. Ruppel, "Balancing Conflicting Human Rights: Konrad Hesse's Notion of 'Praktische Konkordanz' and the German Federal Constitutional Court," in E. Brems (ed.), *Conflicts Between Fundamental Rights* (Mortsel, Belgium: Intersentia, 2008), 273.

5. *Principled balancing*

The basic rule of balancing operates at the highest level of abstraction. The specific rule of balancing operates at the lowest level of abstraction. The transition from one rule to another is sharp. There is room to consider the recognition of an intermediate balancing rule, between the two existing levels of abstraction. This balancing rule would also be of a principled nature – a principled balancing. This will be reviewed at a later stage.[101]

---

[101] See below, at 542.

13

Proportionality and reasonableness

A. From reasonableness to proportionality

What is the relationship between proportionality and reasonableness? Are the two completely different concepts or do they overlap? Are there aspects of proportionality that do not constitute a part of reasonableness, and aspects of reasonableness that do not constitute a part of proportionality?[1] These questions arise where a constitutional right[2] is limited by a sub-constitutional law. The same issues also appear in contexts where no constitutional rights are involved.[3] The focus is only on the first set of cases. These arose in many common law countries, where reasonableness was recognized long before proportionality. When proportionality "knocked on the door" of those legal systems, it was met by the concept of reasonableness.[4] Courts across several legal systems have ruled that, in light of the use of reasonableness to review the legality – and the constitutionality – of administrative actions, there is no need to recognize proportionality. The rationale provided was that, if the two concepts were identical, then reasonableness should suffice; and, if the two were not identical, reasonableness was preferable. Either way, there was no room for proportionality. This approach was changed with regard to the constitutionality of statutes limiting constitutional rights. The proportionality rule is now recognized as per the examination of the constitutionality of legislation which limits constitutional rights. It is also recognized where a sub-statutory law (e.g., administrative actions, regulations, executive orders) limits constitutional rights. The reason for that is that, if the constitutionality

---

[1] See N. Emiliou, *The Principle of Proportionality in European Law: A Comparative Study* (London: Kluwer Law International, 1996), 37; P. Craig, *Administrative Law*, 6th edn. (London: Sweet & Maxwell, 2008), 635.

[2] In the UK and New Zealand the question arises when a statutory right is limited by another statute. See above, at 157.

[3] In addition, they appear in several other contexts. See Craig, above note 1.

[4] See above, at 192. See also M. Taggart, "Proportionality, Deference, Wednesbury," *New Zealand L. Rev.* 423 (2008).

of legislation limiting constitutional rights is reviewed according to the requirements of proportionality, then the constitutionality of any other sub-statutory action that limits constitutional rights in accordance with a statutory authorization should also be reviewed in accordance with the same principle. This makes perfect sense: if the statute is unconstitutional because its limitation of the human right is disproportional, clearly all other sub-legislative actions authorized by the statute limiting the constitutional right are illegal, as they were executed without proper authorization. If the legislation is constitutionally valid since it is proportional, then the authorization it grants to sub-statutory actions should also be proportional. Either way, the constitutional or statutory validity of the sub-statutory action will be determined in accordance with the principle of proportionality. However, the issue of the proper relationship between the two concepts – proportionality and reasonableness – remains in the context of the limitation of constitutional rights. Does the recognition of the concept of proportionality render the concept of reasonableness redundant, or can the two live side-by-side?

B.   The components of proportionality and reasonableness

1.   *The components of proportionality*

Legislation limiting a constitutional right is constitutionally valid if it is proportional. Proportionality includes four components: a proper purpose; a rational connection between the advancement of the law's purpose and the means chosen by the law to limit the constitutional right; a necessary relationship between the realization of the law's purpose and the means chosen; and a proportional *stricto sensu* (balancing) relationship between the marginal social importance of the benefits gained by achieving the law's purpose and the marginal social importance in preventing the harm to the constitutional right.

2. The components of reasonableness

i. When is an action reasonable?

What is reasonableness?[5] What are its components? There is no consensus on this matter.[6] The conventional wisdom is that reasonableness is determined on a case-by-case basis, in accordance with each case's special circumstances. While this statement is undoubtedly true, what are the circumstances relevant to the determination of reasonableness? How do they affect the concept of reasonableness? Similarly, the aphorism "an action is reasonable if it was done by a reasonable person" does not advance this discussion. Who is the "reasonable person"? When is a person's behavior "reasonable"? Some argue that the "reasonable person" is the court itself. This too does not advance the understanding of reasonableness. I have been a judge and have always asked myself about how I should act so that my actions are reasonable. Not all my actions are reasonable. How would I know when I acted "reasonably"? How should I act to ensure my actions were reasonable? Indeed, "reasonableness is not personal; it is substantive. It is not the decisionmaker's reasonableness that renders the decision reasonable; rather, the decision's reasonableness turns its maker into a reasonable person."[7] It has been more than forty years since Professor Stone noted that reasonableness belongs to "categories of illusory reference."[8] Indeed, in many cases we use reasonableness in a circular manner.

In the United Kingdom, the courts developed the *Wednesbury* test[9] to help in defining the proper boundaries of reasonableness within administrative law. In particular, the courts were hesitant to intervene unless the unreasonableness was extreme, "so outrageous in its defiance of logic or accepted moral standards that no sensible person who had applied his mind to the question to be decided could have arrived at it."[10] But when would "simple" unreasonableness turn into "extreme" unreasonableness?

[5] See A. Barak, *The Judge in a Democracy* (Princeton University Press, 2006), 248. Regarding reasonableness in private law, see M. Moran, *Rethinking the Reasonable Person: An Egalitarian Reconstruction of the Objective Standard* (Oxford University Press, 2003). See also H. Avila, *Theory of Legal Principles* (Dordrecht: Springer, 2007), 105; W. Sadurski, "'Reasonableness' and Value Pluralism in Law and Politics," in G. Bongiovanni, G. Sartor, and C. Valentini (eds.), *Reasonableness and Law* (Dordrecht: Springer, 2009), 129; B. Schlink, "Der Grundsatz der Verhältnismässigkeit," in P. Badura and H. Dreier (eds.), *Festschrift 50 Jahre Bundesverfassungsgericht*, vol. II (Tübingen: Mohr Siebeck, 2001), 451.
[6] See T. R. Hickman, "The Reasonableness Principle: Reassessing Its Place in the Public Sphere," 63 *Cambridge L. J.* 166 (2004).
[7] HCJ 935/89 *Ganor* v. *The Attorney General* [1990] IsrSC 44(2) 485 (Barak, J.).
[8] See J. Stone, *Legal System and Lawyers' Reasoning* (Stanford University Press, 1968), 263.
[9] *Associated Provincial Picture Houses* v. *Wednesbury Corporation* [1948] 1 KB 223.
[10] *Council of Civil Service Unions* v. *Minister for the Civil Service* [1985] AC 374, 410 (Lord Diplock).

A proper answer to that question cannot be found. The cases have also resorted, ultimately, to a form of circular reasoning. We are back, then, to square one: when can we conclude that an action is reasonable? What are the components of reasonableness? As noted herein, no consensus has ever been reached on this issue. The notion of "reasonableness" has many varieties in several contexts, even within administrative law.[11]

ii.   Reasonableness as a balance between
conflicting principles

I believe we can advance the discussion regarding reasonableness – and break the vicious cycle – by acknowledging that "reasonableness is not a physical or metaphysical concept. Rather, reasonableness is a normative concept. It is achieved through an evaluative – rather than a descriptive – process. Reasonableness is not bound by deductive logic. Rather, it is determined by the identification of the relevant considerations and their balancing in accordance with their weight."[12] Pursuant to Sadurski, we may refer to this form of reasonableness as "reasonableness in the strong sense."[13]

Thus, we can no longer understand reasonableness as existing "on its own." Rather, "reasonableness is, in all cases, a result of the relationship between all the relevant factors and their proper assigned weights. The notion of reasonableness assumes a pluralistic approach, which recognizes the relevance of several proper considerations and seeks to balance between them by assigning a 'proper weight' to each within their internal relationships ... This 'proper weight' of the relevant factors is determined in accordance with their ability to advance the objectives that underlie the action (or the decision), when reasonableness is at issue. Indeed, a 'proper weight' is not a natural phenomenon inherent within those relevant factors. It is not determined by a logical deduction either ... Rather, a 'proper weight' is an evaluation of to what extent those relevant factors advance the goals that the action (or decision) was meant to achieve."[14] As MacCormick has noted:

---

[11] See Craig, above note 1, at 618. See also M. Bobek, "Reasonableness in Administrative Law: A Comparative Reflection on Functional Equivalence," in G. Bongiovanni, G. Sartor, and C. Valentini (eds.), *Reasonableness and Law* (Dordrecht: Springer, 2009), 311.

[12] CA 5604/94 *Hemed* v. *State of Israel* [2004] IsrSC 58(2) 498, 506 (Barak, P.).

[13] See Sadurski, above note 5, at 129.

[14] See *Ganor*, above note 7, at 513–514 (Barak. J.).

What justifies resort to the requirement of reasonableness is the existence of a plurality of factors required to be evaluated in respect of their relevance to a common focus of concern.[15]

Therefore, a decision is reasonable if it was reached after giving the proper weight to the different factors that should have been considered, and if it properly balances between the relevant factors.[16] At the heart of reasonableness lies the notion of balancing.[17]

C. The relationship between proportionality and reasonableness

1. Degree of detailing

The relationship between proportionality and reasonableness in the context of the constitutional rights is based on the definitions of these notions.[18] Any change in the definition of reasonableness would obviously change the understanding of its relationship with the concept of proportionality. Take reasonableness as defined by the English courts in *Wednesbury*, a definition based on the notion of "extreme" unreasonableness. According to this standard, a decision is unreasonable only when it contains "something so absurd that no sensible person could ever dream that it lay within the powers of the authority."[19] Such a definition of the concept of reasonableness, however, is not structured. It is not founded on consecutive analytical steps. It does not distinguish between the lack of a rational connection, necessity, and balancing. In the words of Chief Justice Dickson of the Canadian Supreme

---

[15] N. MacCormick, "On Reasonableness," in C. Perelman and R. van der Elst (eds.), *Les Notions à Contenu Variable en Droit* (Brussels: Emile Bruylant, 1984), 131, 136.

[16] See R. Alexy, "The Reasonableness of Law," in G. Bongiovanni, G. Sartor, and C. Valentini (eds.), *Reasonableness and Law* (Dordrecht: Springer, 2009), 5.

[17] See Barak, above note 3, at 249: M. Hunt, *Using Human Rights Law in English Courts* (Oxford: Hart Publishing, 1997), 217; D. Feldman, "Proportionality and the Human Rights Act 1998," in E Ellis (ed.), *The Principle of Proportionality in the Laws of Europe* (Oxford: Hart Publishing, 1999), 127; A. Kavanagh, *Constitutional Review under the UK Human Rights Act* (Cambridge University Press, 2009), 248.

[18] On the relationship in administrative law, see M. Cohen, "Legal Transplant Chronicles: The Evolution of Unreasonableness and Proportionality Review of the Administration in the United Kingdom," 58 *Am. J. Comp. L.* 583 (2010).

[19] See *Wednesbury*, above note 9, at 229. Over time this approach was "softened." See Craig, above note 1, at 617; Taggart, above note 4, see also *R. v. Chief Constable of Sussex, ex parte International Trader's Ferry Ltd.* [1999] 2 AC 418, 452.

Court, when comparing the concepts of reasonableness according to *Wednesbury* and proportionality:

> [U]nreasonableness rests to a large extent on unarticulated and undeveloped values and lacks the same degree of structure and sophistication of analysis.[20]

In some cases, the *Wednesbury* version of reasonableness does not even recognize balancing.[21] Such reasonableness is sometimes dubbed reasonableness "in the weak sense."[22] Often it is undistinguishable from the rational connection component of proportionality. A decision is reasonable if a rational connection exists between its objective and the means chosen to fulfill it. Accordingly, the way reasonableness should be considered differs from the way proportionality should be considered.[23] In the *Daly* case,[24] Lord Stein raised three ways in which the *Wednesbury* test differs from proportionality:

> First, the doctrine of proportionality may require the reviewing court to assess the balance which the decision maker has struck, not merely whether it is within the range of rational or reasonable decisions. Secondly, the proportionality test may go further than the traditional ground of review inasmuch as it may require attention to be directed to the relative weight accorded to interests and considerations. Thirdly, even the heightened scrutiny test developed in *R. v. Ministry of Defence, Ex p Smith* ... is not necessarily appropriate to the protection of human rights.[25]

In his judgment, Lord Stein has noted that the three components of proportionality are criteria "which are more precise and more sophisticated than the traditional grounds of review."[26] He further emphasized:

> [T]he intensity of review is somewhat greater under the proportionality approach ... [T]he intensity of the review, in similar cases, is guaranteed by the twin requirements that the limitation of the right was necessary in a democratic society, in the sense of meeting a pressing social need, and the question whether the interference was really proportionate to the legitimate aim being pursued.[27]

[20] *Slaight Communications Inc. v. Davidson* [1989] 1 SCR 1038, 1074.
[21] See A. Lester and J. Jowell, "Beyond Wednesbury: Substantive Principles of Administrative Law," 4 *PL* 368 (1987); G. de Burca, "Proportionality and Wednesbury Unreasonableness: The Influence of European Legal Concepts on UK Law," 3 *Eur. Public Law* 561 (1997). See also J. Varuhas, "Keeping Things in Proportion: The Judiciary, Executive Action and Human Rights," 22 *New Zealand U. L. Rev.* 300 (2006).
[22] See Sadurski, above note 5, at 131.
[23] See *R. v. MAFF, ex parte First City Trading* [1997] 1 CMLR 250.
[24] See *R. v. Secretary of State for the Home Department, ex parte Daly* [2001] 3 All ER 433. Regarding this case, see Kavanagh, above note 17, at 243.
[25] *Ibid.*, at para. 27.   [26] *Ibid.*   [27] *Ibid.*

With this in mind, one can question whether there is any sense in continuing to rely on *Wednesbury* whenever proportionality applies. This question has yet to be determined in English law.[28] The same is true for other legal systems that adopted *Wednesbury*, such as New Zealand.[29]

This book will focus on the relationship between reasonableness and proportionality in accordance with the definition of reasonableness adopted by Israeli law (reasonableness "in the strong sense"[30]). According to this definition, what is the difference between reasonableness and proportionality in the context of the protection of constitutional rights (the second stage of the constitutional review)? At first glance, it seems that proportionality is structured, transparent, and focused on the justification for the limitation of the constitutional right.[31] Reasonableness lacks all of these.[32] However, there are no inherent restrictions on the development of the concept of reasonableness – and, indeed, it should be developed in that direction – so that the use of reasonableness be transparent, structured, and focused on the justification for the limitation of the constitutional right.[33] Thus, for example, it could be argued that whenever no rational connection exists between the means chosen to advance the purpose and the proper purpose itself, those means are unreasonable. Similarly, means would be considered unreasonable if there are other means that can advance the law's purpose to the same extent, while being less restrictive – that is, causing less harm – to the constitutional right.[34] As long as those notions are left undeveloped, we can also view proportionality as stemming from the concept of reasonableness, and constituting one of its many applications.

2.   Balancing

A close examination of proportionality (according to its common definition) and reasonableness "in the strong sense" (as we have defined

---

[28] See Craig, above note 1, at 618. Craig, "Unreasonableness and Proportionality in UK Law," in E. Ellis (ed.), *The Principle of Proportionality in the Laws of Europe* (Portland, OR: Hart Publishing, 1999); J. Jowell, "Administrative Justice and Standards of Substantive Judicial Review," in A. Arnull, P. Eeckhout, and T. Tridimas (eds.), *Continuity and Change in EU Law: Essays in Honour of Sir Francis Jacobs* (Oxford University Press, 2008), 172.

[29] See Taggart, above note 4.

[30] See above note 374.   [31] See below, at 460.

[32] See *Daly*, above note 24, at para. 27.

[33] See M. Bobek, "Reasonableness in Administrative Law: A Comparative Reflection on Functional Equivalence," in G. Bongiovanni, G. Sartor, and C. Valentini (eds.), *Reasonableness and Law* (Dordrecht: Springer, 2009), 311, 323.

[34] See CA 10078/03 *Shatil v. Mekorot-Israel National Water Comp.* (March 19, 2007, unpublished), para. 25 (Levi, J.).

it[35]) shows a significant similarity between the two situations where the marginal social importance of the benefits gained by achieving the law's purpose have to be evaluated against the marginal social importance of preventing the harm caused to a constitutional right.[36] In that case, the similarity between reasonableness and proportionality is expressed through the balancing component.[37] As Alexy has noted: "Reasonable application of constitutional rights requires proportionality analysis. Proportionality analysis includes balancing."[38] Indeed, the central component of proportionality is proportionality *stricto sensu*.[39] At the heart of that component lies the notion of balancing between conflicting principles.[40] The main component of reasonableness is also the balancing between competing principles. Is there a difference between the two? The "technique" of balancing is identical in both concepts. The person conducting the balance must place, on one end of the scales, the marginal social importance of achieving one principle, and, on the other, the marginal social importance of preventing the harm to the other principle. If such a "technique" would be applied to a conflict between the principles, then both the manner in which we think about reasonableness and proportionality and the result of the two analyses would be the same. To be precise, the argument is not that reasonableness and proportionality are identical. The claim is much more limited. It relates solely to a situation where the advancement of a law's purpose will limit a constitutional right. The argument does not extend beyond those circumstances. But, in such a state of affairs, when we consider the relationship between the means limiting a constitutional right and the law's purpose for which they were chosen, there appears to be no difference between proportionality and reasonableness.[41] It is possible that, in other situations, where the limitation of constitutional rights is not at stake, the result would be different.[42]

---

[35] See above, at 374.　　[36] See Emiliou, above note 1, at 37.
[37] See Kavanagh, above note 17, at 243.
[38] See Alexy, above note 16, at 14.
[39] See above, at 340.　　[40] See above, at 343.
[41] There should be no difference as to deference: see below, at 396.
[42] See Taggart, above note 4, at 43 (distinguishing between rights and public wrongs). See also Emiliou, above note 1, at 37 (arguing that proportionality applies only in those limited circumstances where the relation between a purpose and the means to achieve it are concerned, while reasonableness applies in a much wider array of cases and is not limited to the goal-means scenario).

14

Zone of proportionality: legislator and judge

A. The application of proportionality to the three branches of government: the issue of judicial review

1. Proportionality and the three branches of government

Constitutional human rights and the rules of proportionality limiting them apply to all branches of government. The Basic Law for the Federal Republic of Germany provides that "[t]he following basic rights shall bind the legislature, the executive, and the judiciary."[1] A similar provision exists in other constitutions.[2] Thus, the legislative branch, the executive branch, and the judicial branch are all bound by the constitution. The discussion in this chapter begins with the duties of the legislative branch. In a constitutional democracy, legislation lies with the legislator. The power to legislate is wide in scope. However, it is not limitless. In a constitutional democracy, the legislator is not omnipotent, but rather has its own limitations. One of the most important limitations arises when a legislator seeks to limit a constitutional right. The said limitation must satisfy the constitutional requirements of proportionality.[3] These requirements limit the scope of the legislative discretion when the legislator limits a constitutional right. Accordingly, we may conclude that the members of the legislative branch want to know, should know, and are entitled to know, the limits of their legislative powers. This information is not directly related to judicial review. Even if a constitution specifically orders that the "constitutionality of Acts of Parliament ... shall not be reviewed

---

[1] Art. 1(3) of the Basic Law for the Federal Republic of Germany (1949). available in English at https://www.btg-bestellservice.de/pdf/80201000.pdf.

[2] See Art. 8(1) of the Constitution of the Republic of South Africa; Art. 11 of Basic Law: Human Dignity and Liberty, available at www.knesset.gov.il/laws/special/eng/basic3_eng.htm.

[3] S. Gardbaum, "Limiting Constitutional Rights," 54 *UCLA L. Rev.* 789, 810 (2007); S. Gardbaum, "A Democratic Defense of Constitutional Balancing," 4(1) *Law and Ethics of Hum. Rts.* 77 (2010).

by the courts,"[4] the legislator is still obligated, by its constitutional duty, to enact statutes limiting constitutional human rights in a manner which satisfies proportionality's requirements. The legislator must, therefore, refrain from disproportional legislation. The legislator is obligated to protect human rights,[5] to act in accordance with the rules of proportionality, and to maintain legislative restraint – even if the legislation's proportionality is not subject to judicial review, but rather only to public review (through the political process).

The executive branch must respect all recognized constitutional rights.[6] If its actions can limit those rights, they should satisfy the requirements of proportionality. The organs of the executive branch want to know, should know, and are entitled to know, the limits of their executive powers. This is true whether or not there is judicial review of legislation. The actions of the executive branch at the sub-constitutional level, which limit constitutional rights, must satisfy the requirements of proportionality.

The judiciary is subject to the requirements of proportionality.[7] Every judge-made sub-constitutional law which limits a constitutional right is bound by the rules of proportionality. Therefore, every development of the common law must be conducted in accordance with the rules of proportionality.[8] While fulfilling its function in conducting judicial review on the constitutionality of sub-constitutional laws (e.g., statutes, regulations, or common law), the judiciary must guarantee that this sub-constitutional law will satisfy the requirements of proportionality.

The conclusion is as follows. The rules of proportionality are uniform. They apply to each of the three branches of government. They do not change in accordance with the branch of government that operates within them. The rules of proportionality that apply to the legislative and executive branches – branches that operate at the sub-constitutional

---

[4] Constitution of The Netherlands, Art. 120. See *Constitutions of Europe: Texts Collected by the Council of Europe Venice Commission* (Leiden, The Netherlands: Brill, 2004), 1291. See also G. Van der Schyff, *Judicial Review of Legislation: A Comparative Study of the United Kingdom, The Netherlands and South Africa* (Dordrecht: Springer, 2010), 22.

[5] See K. Ewing, "The Parliamentary Protection of Human Rights," in K. S. Ziegler, D. Baranger, and A. W. Bradley (eds.), *Constitutionalism And the Role of Parliaments* (Portland, OR: Hart Publishing, 2007), 253.

[6] *President of the Republic of South Africa* v. *South African Rugby Football Union*, 2000 (1) SA 1 (CC).

[7] See above, at 121.

[8] See above, at 121. See also *Amod* v. *Multilateral Motor Vehicle Accidents Fund*, 1998 (4) SA 753 (CC); *Carmichele* v. *Minister of Safety and Security*, 2001 (4) SA 938 (CC); S. Woolman, "Application," in S. Woolman, M. Bishop, and J. Brickhill (eds.), *Constitutional Law of South Africa*, 2nd edn. (Cape Town: Juta Law Publishers, looseleaf, 2002–), 57.

level and limit constitutional rights – are the same rules of proportionality that apply to the judicial branch, which operates at the sub-constitutional level and creates new law, or exercises judicial review over the creation of new law by the other branches. This last activity (judicial review of sub-constitutional laws) is the basis and focus of this book. In this framework, the examination will focus on parliament's legislative activities, rather than on executive regulations or sub-statutory (and sub-constitutional) actions. This chapter now examines this element of judicial review.

2. Proportionality, judicial review, and democracy

Proportionality is pertinent to judicial activity in several different contexts. The discussion here is limited to the judicial review of statutes limiting constitutional human rights. The focus of the discussion is the examination of the scope of judicial discretion,[9] when there is a judicial review of the constitutionality of statutes. Naturally, a precondition for such a discussion is the recognition of judicial review. If judicial review is not recognized by the legal system, there is obviously no point in discussing the scope of a judicial discretion which does not exist.[10]

Judicial review of the constitutionality of statutes is one of the hallmarks of modern democracies. It bloomed significantly after the Second World War. It was perceived as one of the most important lessons of the rise of Nazism to power, and as one of the means of preventing this from ever recurring.[11] However, there is no single model of judicial review,[12] and

---

[9] On the concept of judicial discretion as used in this book, see A. Barak, *Judicial Discretion* (New Haven, CT: Yale University Press, 1989). See also M. Iglesias Vila, *Facing Judicial Discretion: Legal Knowledge and Right Answers Revisited* (Dordrecht: Springer, 2001).

[10] Our discussion does apply, however, *mutatis mutandis*, to cases where both the right and its limitation operate at the sub-constitutional level, but the courts can declare that this kind of limitation is incompatible with the right. See above, at 159.

[11] A. Barak, *The Judge in a Democracy* (Princeton University Press, 2006), 229. See also D. M. Beatty (ed.), *Human Rights and Judicial Review: A Comparative Perspective* (1994); C. Neal Tate and T. Vallinder (eds.), *The Global Expansion of Judicial Power* (1995); B. Ackerman, "The Rise of World Constitutionalism," 83 *Va. L. Rev.* 771 (1997); A. Stone Sweet, "Why Europe Rejected American Judicial Review and Why It May Not Matter," 101 *Mich. L. Rev.* 2744 (2003); M. Tushnet, "Alternative Forms of Judicial Review," 101 *Mich. L. Rev.* 2781 (2003).

[12] See Barak, above note 11, at 229. See also S. Gardbaum, "The New Commonwealth Model of Constitutionalism," 49 *Am. J. Comp. L.* 707 (2001); V. Ferreres Comella, *Constitutional Courts and Democratic Values: A European Perspective* (New Haven. CT: Yale University Press, 2009).

the institution often finds itself subject to harsh criticism.[13] Every society
has to make its own mind up as to the adoption of judicial review, and, if
so, according to which model. The selection of a particular model of judicial review often reflects a society's specific political, historical, and social
heritage, as well as its political power struggles. With this in mind, it is
common to distinguish between "strong" and "weak" judicial review.[14]

This book is not the proper forum to examine fundamental questions
relating to judicial review, such as whether the institution of judicial
review is appropriate for a constitutional democracy, or what is the proper
model of judicial review to adopt.[15] However, it is essential to understand
that, once a legal system has chosen – either explicitly or implicitly – to
recognize the institution of judicial review of the constitutionality of statutes, the critique leveled at the adoption of judicial review in the first place
should not emerge again when judicial review is applied. The opinion that
there is no room for judicial review in the system cannot be persuasively
argued against the actual exercise of judicial discretion within judicial
review once such a concept has been recognized by the legal system. Once
a legal system has opted to recognize judicial review, and such review is
exercised in accordance with the rules of proportionality, the contours
of that institution can no longer be shaped by arguments relating to the
preliminary issue of whether judicial review should be recognized by that
system in the first place.[16] This conclusion relates, primarily, to the criticism against the "non-democratic" or "counter-majoritarian" nature of
the institution of judicial review; specifically, it was argued that the judicial discretion used by the courts while exercising judicial review should
be limited in light of those traits. The same conclusion applies to those
who claim that judges should defer to the legislative branch because they
lack a "democratic foundation." This argument should also be rejected at
this stage. Once a society has made a decision – explicitly or implicitly – to

---

[13] See below, at 474.
[14] For this term, see M. Tushnet, *Weak Courts, Strong Rights: Judicial Review and Social Welfare Rights in Comparative Constitutional Law* (Princeton University Press, 2008), 18.
[15] See Barak, above note 11, at 229. See below, at 474.
[16] See J. Jowell, "Judicial Deference: Servility, Civility or Institutional Capacity?," *PL* 592 (2003); J. Jowell, "Judicial Deference and Human Rights: A Question of Competence," in P. Craig and R. Rawlings (eds.), *Law and Administration in Europe: Essays in Honour of Carol Harlow* (Oxford University Press, 2003), 67; T. R. S. Allan, "Common Law Reason and the Limits of Judicial Deference," in D. Dyzenhaus (ed.), *The Unity of Public Law* (Portland, OR: Hart Publishing, 2004), 289; T. R. S. Allan, "Human Rights and Judicial Review: A Critique of 'Due Deference,'" 65 *Cambridge L. J.* 671 (2006).

adopt judicial review, its exercise by the courts is a reflection of the people's will, and thus in effect not only embraces basic notions of democracy but actually entrenches them. The same "we the people" who adopted the constitution also adopted the institution of judicial review. Considerations of "counter-majoritarian difficulty" or "lack of sufficient democratic foundation" should not affect the actual exercise of judicial review. Rather, judicial review should be exercised in a way that would allow the judges the full ability to inquire whether the other branches – who limited a constitutionally protected human right – have properly followed the requirements of proportionality as prescribed by the constitution's "we the people."

Accordingly, while examining the scope of judicial discretion in relation to proportionality, there is no room for arguments relating to the democratic nature (or lack thereof) of the institution of judicial review.[17] Much like the member of the legislative or executive branch that must follow the requirements of proportionality whenever a statute limits a constitutional right, the member of the judicial branch must follow the exact same requirements when exercising judicial review of that same legislation. Whenever a statute limits a constitutional right, the legislative, executive, and judicial branches – all founded by the same constitutional document – must respect the same rights and operate in accordance with the same rules as dictated by the principle of proportionality. The legislator, the member of the executive, and the judge may not relieve themselves from that duty, which is based in the constitution itself, even if they wanted to.[18] Moreover, a possible judicial "fear" that certain judicial review decisions may be "overruled" by new legislation or by a future constitutional amendment should not affect the application of the rules of proportionality in any given case.[19] Judges must judge, legislators legislate, and constitutional assemblies author constitutions or amend them. If the legislator wishes to change the result of a certain court decision – whether sitting as a legislator or in its special capacity as a constitutional assembly (to the extent such capacity exists) – this is its democratic responsibility. The existence of one should not affect the other. Of course, one may criticize judicial review and argue for its abolition. However, so long as judicial review is recognized (explicitly or implicitly), the judges – like the legislators and executives – should be faithful to its existence.

---

[17] See Jowell, above note 16; Jowell, above note 16.
[18] *RJR-MacDonald Inc. v. Canada (Attorney General)* [1995] 3 SCR 199, § 136.
[19] See, however, R. Post and R. Siegel, "Roe Rage: Democratic Constitutionalism and Backlash," 42 *Harvard Civil Rights–Civil Liberties Law Review* 373 (2007).

3. Proportionality and the separation of powers

i.   Proportionality and discretion

Every governmental authority must apply the rules of proportionality whenever a sub-constitutional law (such as a statute) limits a constitutional right. Should this premise lead us to the conclusion that the scope of discretion exercised by each of these authorities is equal when it comes to the application of proportionality?[20] The answer is no. The components of proportionality – proper purpose, rational connection, necessity, and proportionality *stricto sensu* (balancing) – do not always lead to the same solution. In many cases, each governmental authority is given the discretion to choose between a number of alternatives. This discretion exists, naturally, if all the alternatives considered are constitutional.[21] The scope of the discretion itself, within those constitutional alternatives, may vary from one governmental authority to another. Thus, for example, the legislative branch may face a choice between two proportional alternatives limiting constitutional rights: The first advances a less important social purpose while limiting a constitutional right whose prevention is less socially important; the other advances a more important social purpose while limiting a constitutional right whose prevention is more socially important. Let us assume that, when facing such a choice, the legislator chooses one of the two options. The court now has to determine the constitutionality of that option. In this matter, the court may exercise its own discretion, as for example with regard to the question of whether the prevention of the limitation on the right in question may be more socially valuable than the advancement of the proper purpose. As the example demonstrates, the type and scope of discretion exercised by each of the two branches in this case are different. The scope of each branch of government is determined in accordance with its proper role within the concept of the separation of powers. As correctly noted by Rivers: "[A] theory of discretion must be co-extensive with the doctrine of proportionality if

---

[20]   The question was raised by Rivers: see J. Rivers, "Proportionality and Discretion in International and European Law," in N. Tsagourias (ed.), *Transnational Constitutionalism: International and European Perspectives* (Cambridge University Press, 2007), 107, 108.

[21]   Regarding the definition of discretion in general, see Barak, above note 9, at 7. Compare with K. C. Davis, *Discretionary Justice: A Preliminary Inquiry* (Baton Rouge, LA: Louisiana State University Press, 1969); D. J. Galligan, *Discretionary Powers: A Legal Study of Official Discretion* (Oxford: Clarendon Press, 1986); M. Iglesias Vila, *Facing Judicial Discretion: Legal Knowledge and Right Answers Revisited* (Dordrecht: Springer, 2001).

the separation of powers is not to collapse."[22] Therefore, what is the role of each of the governmental authorities in relation to proportionality while adhering to the concept of separation of powers?

ii.   Separation of powers: checks and balances

The modern concept of separation of powers is based on three elements. First, there is the distinction between the three branches of government: the legislative branch, the executive branch, and the judicial branch. Each branch has its own function. The main function of the legislative branch is legislation; the main function of the executive branch is execution; and the main function of the judicial branch is judging. The relationship between each branch and its main function is determined (either explicitly or implicitly) by the constitution. Second, in accordance with the constitutional framework, each branch fulfills its main function according to its own approach and while exercising discretion without the intervention of the other branches. This independence in the exercise of discretion does not mean that the other branches estrange the branch exercising its discretion. The opposite is true: all three branches operate with mutual respect; each also respects the role fulfilled by the others within the constitutional framework and the concept of the separation of powers. The third element is the notion of checks and balances between the three branches. The balance points out the interdependence between the branches. Thus, for example, in Israel the Committee for the Selection of Judges is made up of nine members, with representatives appointed by each of the three branches of government.[23] The "check" function indicates the authority to review and supervise the operations of one branch by the others. These checks and balances allow each branch to have "independence, with defined mutual supervision by the other branches."[24] Separation of powers is not based on complete separation and lack of interdependence between the branches; the opposite is true. Separation of powers means mutual checks and balances between the different branches. "Not walls separating the three branches, but bridges that provide checks and balances."[25]

These three elements of separation of powers are not intended to advance governmental efficiency. Rather, they are meant to ensure individual

---

[22] See Rivers, above note 20, at 108.
[23] See Art. 4 of Basic Law: The Judiciary.
[24] HCJ 306/81 *Plato Sharon* v. *The Knesset Committee* [1981] IsrSC 35(4) 118, 141 (Shamgar, J.).
[25] HCJ 73/85 *Kach Faction* v. *Knesset Speaker* [1985] IsrSC 39(3) 141, 458 (Barak, J.).

liberty. "The purpose was not to avoid friction, but, by means of the inevitable friction incident to the distribution of governmental powers among three departments, to save the people from autocracy."[26] "The separation of powers is not an end in itself. It was not meant to guarantee efficiency. The purpose of the separation of powers is advancing personal liberty and preventing the concentration of too much power at the hands of a single governmental branch in such a way that it may trample on such liberty."[27] The meaning of the principle of the separation of powers is not that each governmental branch can deviate from its authority or execute it illegally, without the other branches being permitted to intervene. Rather, the meaning of the principle is that each branch is free to operate in its field as long as it does so in accordance with the constitutional requirements. Separation of powers is not a license granted by the constitution to each of the branches to violate the law.

Who should determine if the branch in question has operated lawfully? Obviously, each branch, on its own, should review its own actions and ensure that they fall well within its authority. But what is the case when a dispute arises as to the lawfulness of the action in question? How should such a dispute be resolved? Here, the notion of "checks," which characterizes the principle of separation of powers, may provide the answer. According to this notion,[28] whenever a question arises as to the proper interpretation of the constitutionality of an action undertaken by a governmental branch, such a question should ultimately be resolved by the judicial branch. A constitutional democracy does not allow the legislative

---

[26] *Myers* v. *United States*, 272 US 52, 293 (1926) (Brandeis, J.).

[27] HCJ 3267/97 *Rubinstein* v. *Minister of Defense* [1998–9] IsrLR 139, 178–179, relying on *Meyers* v. *United States*, above note 26.

[28] For the different views, see L. Fisher, *Constitutional Dialogues: Interpretation as Political Process* (Princeton University Press, 1988); W. D. Popkin, "Foreword: Nonjudicial Statutory Interpretation," 66 *Chi.-Kent L. Rev.* 301 (1990); S. Gant, "Judicial Supremacy and Nonjudicial Interpretation of the Constitution," 24 *Hastings Const. L. Q.* 359 (1997); L. Alexander and F. Schauer, "On Extrajudicial Constitutional Interpretation," 110 *Harv. L. Rev.* 1359 (1997); A. Ides, "Judicial Supremacy and the Law of the Constitution," 47 *UCLA L. Rev.* 491 (1999); E. A. Hartnett, "A Matter of Judgment, Not a Matter of Opinion," 74 *N. Y. U. L. Rev.* 123 (1999); J. T. Molot, "The Judicial Perspective in the Administrative State: Reconciling Modern Doctrines of Deference with the Judiciary's Structural Role," 53 *Stan. L. Rev.* 1 (2000); N. Kumar Katyal, "Legislative Constitutional Interpretation," 50 *Duke L. J.* 1335 (2001); T. W. Merril and Kristin E. Hickman, "Chevron's Domain," 89 *Geo. L. J.* 833 (2001); K. E. Whittington, "Extrajudicial Constitutional Interpretation: Three Objections and Responses," 80 *N. C. L. Rev.* 773 (2002); L. Kramer, *The People Themselves: Popular Constitutionalism and Judicial Review* (Oxford University Press, 2006).

or the executive branches the final word as to the legality – or constitutionality – of their own actions; indeed, the notion of separation of powers does not grant each branch "absolute power" over its own domain; rather, according to the principle of "checks" that is the hallmark of the modern understanding of the separation of powers, the judiciary is the sole governmental branch entrusted by the constitution with the task of having the final word as to the legality – and constitutionality – of the actions taken by other branches of government.[29] Any other solution would seriously impede democracy. The very existence of the principle of separation of powers requires the creation of a mechanism for resolving questions of the legality and constitutionality of actions undertaken by each branch of government. Such a mechanism for resolving those issues cannot "reside" within either the legislative or executive branches, since such "residence" may grant those branches "absolute powers." It is required, therefore, that the mechanism be external to the governmental branch – legislative or executive – that has allegedly acted beyond its authority or powers, and has committed an illegal or unconstitutional act. This mechanism must be independent of those branches, and should operate objectively in accordance with one consideration alone – protecting the constitution. This mechanism is found within the judicial branch. There is no better branch to fulfill the role of checking the other branches. The independence of the judges; the fact that the judges "represent" no one but the constitution; the fact that they are not politically accountable and their professional training as authorized interpreters of the law – makes the judiciary the most suited to the role of providing "checks" on the other branches of government in accordance with the principle of the separation of powers. Indeed, most constitutions provide the judicial branch (either expressly or implicitly) with the power to resolve disputes and, therefore, incidentally to determine according to which law those disputes should be resolved. It is in this context that Chief Justice Marshall authored his most memorable quote: "It is emphatically the province and duty of the Judicial Department to say what the law is."[30]

iii.   Discretion of the judicial branch

a.   **Discretion**   The principle of separation of powers holds that the main function of the judicial branch is judging. At the heart of judging lies

---

[29] See G. M. Pikis, *Constitutionalism – Human Rights – Separation of Powers: The Cyprus Precedent* (Leiden, The Netherlands: Brill, 2006), 93.
[30] *Marbury* v. *Madison*, 5 US (Cranch) 137, 177 (1803).

conflict resolution.[31] What is the judge's discretion in this case and what is the relation to the legislator's discretion? In this context, judicial discretion is defined herein as the power – granted to the judge by law – to choose from a number of legal options.[32] According to this definition, judicial discretion is not a mental or psychological state of mind; rather, it is a legal situation which allows the judge to choose between several legally valid options. The very existence of judicial discretion, according to my definition, is not free of doubt: there is a doctrinal dispute about the issue,[33] whose examination is beyond the scope of this book. Therefore, the discussion here begins with the assumption that in certain circumstances the judge is empowered to decide between several alternatives as to the law's content on the issues, as well as regarding its application on the facts of the case.[34]

Thus, the objects of judicial discretion are the facts, the law, and the application of the law to the facts.[35] The distinction between law and facts is difficult,[36] and the issue does not need to be examined here. The chapter begins with the premise that a fact is anything absorbed by any of the five senses, as well as a person's mental state. According to this approach, facts also include evaluations as to the probability of the realization of certain risks or rewards related to the conflict's resolution. Therefore, the question of the probability that a certain legislative means achieves its desired goal is a factual one. In contrast, the question of whether this probability satisfies the requirements of proportionality is a question of law. The discussion begins with the judge's discretion regarding facts.

b.   The facts

aa.   "Historical" facts and "social" facts   Determining the pertinent facts is done through the factual framework presented to the court. Some

---

[31] See Barak, above note 11, at 173. See also H. L. A Hart, "The Courts and Lawmaking: A Comment," in M. G. Paulsen (ed.), *Legal Institutions Today and Tomorrow: The Centennial Conference Volume of the Columbia Law School* (New York: Columbia University Press, 1959), 41.

[32] See Barak, above note 9, at 7. See also Vila, above note 21; M. Klatt, "Taking Rights Less Seriously: A Structural Analysis of Judicial Discretion," 20 *Ratio Juris* 506 (2007).

[33] Barak, above note 9, at 27.

[34] Barak, above note 9, at 12. See also J. Frank, *Courts on Trial – Myth and Reality in American Justice* (Princeton University Press, 1949); C. E. Wyzanski, "A Trial Judge's Freedom and Responsibility," 65 *Harv. L. Rev.* 1281 (1952); J. Stone, *Social Dimensions of Law and Justice* (London: Stevens, 1966), 678; J. Cueto-Rua, *Judicial Methods of Interpretation of the Law* (New Orleans: Louisiana State University Press, 1981).

[35] Barak, above note 9, at 12.

[36] J. H. Wigmore, *Evidence in Trials at Common Law*, vol. 1 (Boston: Little Brown & Co. Law and Business, 1983), 31.

of these facts are "historical," and provide an answer to the question "what happened?" Other facts are "social," and provide answers to questions of social policy at the foundation of the conflict.[37] Both are presented to the court in accordance with the rules of evidence adopted by each legal system. The rules of evidence do not always enable a wide enough presentation of the pertinent social facts. It is appropriate that, whenever a court examines the constitutionality of a law, the rules of evidence recognized by that system will provide it with complete information regarding the social aspects of its ruling. There is no reason to prevent the social facts available to the legislator from being presented to the court.[38]

bb.   Polycentric facts   Information about the historical facts is fairly straightforward and easy to understand; judges are used to this. In contrast, information about social facts may be more complex and much harder to grasp and to understand; it requires a professional background. Still, this should not prevent it from being presented to the court. If a judge can

---

[37] H. M. Hart and A. M. Sacks, *The Legal Process: Basic Problems in the Making and Application of Law* (Foundation Press, 1958), 384; Professor Horowitz differentiates between "social" facts and "historical" facts: see D. L. Horowitz, *The Courts and Social Policy* (Washington, DC: Brookings Institution Press, 1977), 45; see also K. L. Karst, "Legislative Facts in Constitutional Litigation," *Sup. Ct. Rev.* 75 (1960); for the situation in the United States, see C. M. Lamb, "Judicial Policy-Making and Information Flow to the Supreme Court," 29 *Vand. L. Rev.* 45 (1976); for the experience accumulated on this matter in the German Constitutional Court, see H. Baade, "Social Science Evidence and the Federal Constitutional Court of West Germany," 23 *J. of Politics* 421 (1961); for the different methods in the formation of policy considerations and their place in court, see L. H. Mayo and E. M. Jones, "Legal-Policy Decision Process: Alternative Thinking and the Predictive Function," 33 *Geo. Wash. L. Rev.* 318 (1964); R. A. Daynard, "The Use of Social Policy in Judicial Decision-Making," 56 *Cornell L. Rev.* 919 (1971); A. S. Miller and J. A. Barron, "The Supreme Court, The Adversary System, and the Flow of Information to the Justices: A Preliminary Inquiry," 61 *Va. L. Rev.* 1187 (1975); Note, "Social and Economic Facts," 61 *Harv. L. Rev.* 692 (1948). See also H. Wolf Bikle, "Judicial Determination of Questions of Fact Affecting the Constitutional Validity of Legislative Action," 38 *Harv. L. Rev.* 6 (1925); P. A. Freund, "Review of Facts in Constitutional Cases," in E. Cahn (ed.), *Supreme Court and Supreme Law* (Bloomington, IN: Indiana University Press, 1954), 47; J. E. Magnet, "Jurisdictional Fact, Constitutional Fact and the Presumption of Constitutionality," 11 *Man. L. J.* 21 (1981); K. C. Davis and R. J. Pierce, *Administrative Law Treatise,* § 10.5, 4th edn. (New York: Aspen Publishers, 2002); P. W. Hogg, *Constitutional Law of Canada,* 5th edn., vol. II (Toronto: Thomson Carswell, 2007), 808. See also Barak, above note 9, at 14.

[38] CA 6821/93 *United Mizrahi Bank Ltd.* v. *Migdal Cooperative Village* [1995] IsrLR 1, 247 (Barak, P.). See also J. Webber, *Evidence in Charter Interpretation: A Comment on BC Teachers' Federation* v. *AG BC,* 23 *Carswell Practice Cases* (2d) 245 (1988); J. Kiedrowski and K. Webb, "Second Guessing the Law-Makers: Social Science Research in Charter Litigation," 19 *Can. Pub. Pol'y* 379 (1993); A. Lamer, "Canada's Legal Revolution: Judging in the Age of the Charter of Rights," 28 *Isr. L. Rev.* 579, 581 (1994).

learn healthcare issues, engineering standards, and military operations in order to hand down a ruling in private-law cases regarding medical malpractice, negligence in construction, and the negligence of military commanders, they can learn similar matters of healthcare, engineering, and military operations presented in order to prevent such negligence in the future.[39] If members of the legislative body learn this social data from professionals who assist parliamentary committees, judges can also learn those issues through the information presented to them.

By the same token, the court can learn the issues involved in cases presenting polycentric problems,[40] that is, problems that originate with complex considerations of social or economic policy that require certain assumptions which, in turn, require additional assumptions. If a member of the legislative or executive branch can reach a decision regarding polycentric issues, a member of the judiciary should be able to examine whether or not those decisions are lawful. If a judge presiding over a commission of inquiry can determine findings and make recommendations based on polycentric data, he can also rule within the judicial process. If an administrative judge in France, as a part of the Conseil d'Etat, can express their opinions as to a polycentric bill pending before the legislative chamber, they can also rule in accordance with the same law. If a supreme – or constitutional – court can rule on polycentric issues while exercising abstract judicial review, it can do the same while exercising concrete judicial review.[41]

cc. Institutional limitations   In principle, there is no reason why the same factual framework presented to the legislative or executive branch would not be presented to the judicial branch as well. The difficulty is not in the judges' ability to digest the facts; it is not personal; rather, it is institutional.[42] The claim is that the court is not a legislative body. Not all the relevant sides are presented to the court. "Third parties" that may well

---

[39] See G. Davidov, "The Paradox of Judicial Deference," 12 *Nat'l J. Const. L.* 133, 140 (2000).

[40] On the polycentric problem, see L. Fuller, "The Forms and Limits of Adjudication," 92 *Harv. L. Rev.* 353 (1979); J. W. F. Allison, "Fuller's Analysis of Polycentric Disputes and the Limits of Adjudication," 53 *Cambridge L. J.* 367 (1994); H. Petersen and H. Zahle, *Legal Polycentricity: Consequences of Pluralism in Law* (Sudbury, MA: Dartmouth Publishing Group, 1995).

[41] For the distinction between abstract and concrete judicial review, see V. Ferreres Comella, above note 12, at 66.

[42] See Jowell, above note 16, at 80. See also L. Steyn, "Deference: A Tangled Story," *PL* 346, 350 (2005); J. Rivers, "Proportionality and Variable Intensity of Review," 65 *Cambridge*

be affected by the outcome of the judicial process are not always parties to the legal proceedings before the court. This institutional limitation should not be overstated. The court does not have to determine social policy or prioritize social needs. It should examine the constitutionality of these determinations made by the two other branches – the legislative and executive. Therefore, these institutional limitations should not prevent the court from fulfilling its judicial role.

c.   The law

aa.   Judicial discretion in determining the law   In the context of proportionality, the law manifests itself in three dimensions. First is the scope of the constitutional right. The means available to the judiciary is constitutional interpretation.[43] Second is the limitation of the constitutional right by a sub-constitutional law. This limitation is determined by the interpretation of the sub-constitutional law.[44] Third is the rules of proportionality determined by the constitution. These rules are those which arise from the language of the constitutional text (either explicit or implicit).[45] In all three dimensions – interpretation of the constitutional right, interpretation of a limiting law, the application of the rules of proportionality – there may be judicial discretion. Such discretion exists when the judge is authorized to choose between several legal options.[46] Indeed, every interpretive system is based, to a varying degree, on the exercise of judicial discretion.[47] The construct of the rules of proportionality is also based on discretion.[48]

Judicial discretion is never unlimited.[49] These limitations are procedural and substantive. Procedural limitations require the judge to act fairly, objectively, impartially, and equally towards all parties. The judge should provide reasoning for the court's opinion.[50] Substantive limitations

---

L. J. 174, 177 (2006); J. A. King, "Institutional Approaches to Judicial Restraint," 28 *OJLS* 409, 422 (2008).

[43] See above, at 45.   [44] See above, at 155.

[45] See above, at 53.   [46] See Barak, above note 9, at 173.

[47] A. Barak, *Purposive Interpretation in Law* (Princeton University Press, 2005), 207.

[48] See above, at 211.

[49] See Barak, above note 9, at 20; Barak, above note 11, at 210. See also B. N. Cardozo, *The Growth of the Law* (New Haven, CT: Yale University Press, 1924), 60–61; M. Cappelletti, "The Law-Making Power of the Judge and Its Limits: A Comparative Analysis," 8 *Monash U. L. Rev.* 15 (1981); H. L. A. Hart, *The Concept of Law*, 2nd edn. (Oxford: Clarendon Press, 1994), 252.

[50] Barak, above note 9, at 22; Barak, above note 11, at 210. See also C. E. Clark, "The Limits of Judicial Objectivity," 12 *Am. U. L. Rev.* 1 (1963); G. G. Christie, "Objectivity in the

require the judge to exercise judicial discretion in a rational, coherent, and consistent manner.[51] The judge should always take into consideration that they operate within a given legal system,[52] as well as the need to fit into that legal system. The judge should take the various institutional limitations into account[53] as well as attempt to reach the best solution possible. Even when judges are behind closed doors and "by themselves," they are always a part of their community, their legal system, and their judicial tradition.[54]

bb. Legislative interpretation and judicial discretion   How much weight should the judge ascribe to the law's legislative interpretation? What is the proper relationship between legislative interpretation and the interpretation provided by the judge to the same law?[55] The answer lies with the principle of the separation of powers. The law's interpretation is for the judge to decide: The interpretation given by the legislative, or constituent, body to the meaning of legislation or the constitution cannot bind the judge who interprets these. Binding the judiciary to the same

Law," 78 *Yale L. J.* 1311 (1969); T. Nagel, "The Limits of Objectivity," in S. McMurrie (ed.), *The Tanner Lectures on Human Values* (University of Utah, 1980), 77; O. M. Fiss, "Objectivity and Interpretation," 34 *Stan. L. Rev.* 739 (1982); H. T. Edwards, "The Judicial Function and the Elusive Goal of Principled Decisionmaking," *Wis. L. Rev.* 837 (1991); K. Greenawalt, *Law and Objectivity* (Oxford University Press, 1992); H. Li Feldman, "Objectivity in Legal Judgment," 92 *Mich. L. Rev.* 1187 (1994); J. L. Coleman and B. Leiter, "Determinacy, Objectivity, and Authority," in A. Marmor (ed.), *Law and Interpretation: Essays in Legal Philosophy* (Oxford University Press, 1995), 203; A. Marmor, "Three Concepts of Objectivity," in A. Marmor (ed.), *Law and Interpretation: Essays in Legal Philosophy* (Oxford University Press, 1995), 177; N. Stavropoulos, *Objectivity in Law* (Oxford: Clarendon Press, 1996); A. Marmor, "An Essay on the Objectivity of Law," in B. Bix (ed.), *Analyzing Law: New Essays in Legal Theory* (Oxford: Clarendon Press, 1998), 3.

[51] Barak, above note 9, at 160; Barak, above note 11, at 210. See also R. Alexy and A. Peczenik, "The Concept of Coherence and Its Significance for Discursive Rationality," 3 *Ratio Juris* 130 (1990); K. Kress, "Coherence," in D. Patterson (ed.), *A Companion to the Philosophy of Law and Legal Theory* (Wiley-Blackwell, 1996), 533; N. MacCormick, "Coherence in Legal Justification," in A. Peczenik, L. Lindahl, and B. van Roermund (eds.), *Theory of Legal Science* (, 1984), 235; A. Peczenik, "Coherence, Truth and Rightness in the Law," in P. J. Nerhot (ed.), *Law, Interpretation and Reality: Essays in Epistemology, Hermeneutics and Jurisprudence* (Dordrecht: Kluwer Academic Publishers, 1990); J. Raz, "The Relevance of Coherence," 72 *Boston U. L. Rev.* 273 (1992).

[52] L. L. Fuller, *Anatomy of the Law* (Westport, CT: Greenwood Press, 1968), 94.

[53] Barak, above note 9, at 172.

[54] S. Breyer, "Judicial Review: A Practicing Judge's Perspective," 19 *OJLS* 153, 158 (1999).

[55] Barak, above note 11, at 35.

interpretation as the other governmental authorities violates the principle of the separation of powers.[56]

Can the judge ascribe some weight to the interpretation provided by other governmental branches while exercising interpretive discretion? If so, precisely how much weight? Can the judge say: "A specific legal question may have several reasonable (i.e., lawful) interpretations; there is a 'zone of reasonable interpretation.' The other branch's suggested interpretation lies within that zone. I must choose that particular interpretation, even if I would have chosen a different interpretation"? The answer to this question is complex. On the one hand, it is clear that the judge cannot disregard the interpretation of other governmental authorities. The respectful relationship between the branches justifies a review of the interpretation suggested by another branch of government. On the other hand, the judge may not reject his or her own interpretive conclusion in favor of another interpretive view merely because it was proposed by another branch of government.

According to the rules of administrative law, every decision, which lies within the zone of reasonableness, made by a governmental authority is binding on the judge. That conclusion is derived from the principle of the separation of powers. The "zone of reasonableness" is a zone of governmental authority, where responsibility for the governmental action taken – in accordance with the principle of the separation of powers – lies with the state actor who performs it. This is not the case in relation to the law's interpretive "zone of reasonableness." Here, the principle of the separation of powers requires that the judge – and, within the framework of the judicial branch, the Supreme Court or the Constitutional Court – will determine whether the interpretation appears proper. The question the court should discuss is not whether the interpretation offered by the executive branch is reasonable; the question should be what the proper interpretation of the law is.

In addition to the separation of powers, such a result is also supported by pragmatic interpretive considerations. The interpreter-judge must

---

[56] See above, at 387; see also *United Mizrahi Bank*, above note 38, at 225; *Cooper* v. *Aaron*, 358 US 1, 18 (1958); Alexander and Schauer, above note 28. The Supreme Court of Cyprus has ruled that any attempt by the legislator to appropriate the final authority to interpret the law is illegal. See *Diagoras Development Ltd.* v. *National Bank of Greece SA* (1985) 1 CLR 581. Any attempt by the legislator to take for itself the final authority in interpretation of the law is illegal. See G. M. Pikis, *Constitutionalism – Human Rights – Separation of Powers: The Cyprus Precedent* (Leiden, The Netherlands: Brill, 2006), 93.

strive for harmony within the legislative and constitutional frameworks.[57] The judge must strive for normative unity. The judge who interprets a single law within the system interprets them all. The interpretive enterprise aims at achieving normative harmony and uniformity.[58] This harmony and unity, however, will never be achieved if every single item of legislation stands on its own or is interpreted in accordance with the reasonableness of the interpretation offered by other governmental branches. In order to achieve such harmony, the laws and the constitution should be seen as one system. The ultimate responsibility for the law's interpretation lies with the courts. That responsibility cannot be abandoned, or delegated. Any other approach would lead to anarchy within the system.[59]

In American administrative law, courts follow the *Chevron* doctrine.[60] According to *Chevron*, whenever interpretive discretion exists regarding the legislative provision and provided the administrative agency has exercised that discretion reasonably, the court will defer to the agency's statutory interpretation. "[T]he court does not simply impose its own construction on the statute ... Rather, if the statute is silent or ambiguous with respect to the specific issue, the question for the court is whether the agency's answer is based on a permissible construction of the statute."[61] The literature on *Chevron*, be it supportive or critical, is rich.[62] According to the approach herein, the *Chevron* doctrine is misplaced, since it undermines the judicial function "to say what the law is."[63]

iv.   Applying the law to the facts

a.   Judicial review   The core concept of proportionality is the examination of whether a sub-constitutional law (such as statute) limiting a constitutional right is proportional. The primary decision is made by the

---

[57] See above, at 70.   [58] See above, at 70.

[59] Regarding the claim about chaos, see L. Alexander and F. Schauer, "On Extrajudicial Constitutional Interpretation," 110 *Harv. L. Rev.* 1359 (1997); for a critique of this claim, see K. E. Whittington, "Extrajudicial Constitutional Interpretation: Three Objections and Responses," 80 *N. C. L. Rev.* 773, 786 (2002).

[60] See *Chevron USA Inc.* v. *Natural Resources Defense Council Inc.*, 467 US 837 (1984).

[61] *Ibid.*, at 843 (Justice Stevens).

[62] See K. C. Davis and R. J. Pierce, *Administrative Law Treatise*, 3rd edn. (New York: Aspen Publishers, 1994), 109; C. R. Sunstein, "Law and Administration after Chevron," 90 *Colum. L. Rev.* 2071 (1990); T. W. Merrill, "Judicial Deference to Executive Precedent," 101 *Yale L. J.* 969 (1991–1992); R. J. Pierce, 'Chevron and Its Aftermath: Judicial Review of Agency Interpretation of Statutory Provisions," 41 *Vand. L. Rev.* 301 (1998). See also C. R. Farina, "Statutory Interpretation and the Balance of Power in the Administrative State," 89 *Colum. L. Rev.* 452 (1989).

[63] *Marbury* v. *Madison*, above note 30, at 177.

legislator and reflects what appears appropriate to the legislator. The legislator determines the legislative framework, including the proper purpose, the means, and the limitation of the constitutional right. Judicial review is not meant – and should not be used – to replace this legislative framework with a new judicial framework.[64] Rather, the object of judicial review is much narrower: It is designed to examine the constitutionality of the original framework – that and nothing more. Thus, the judge should not be examining a different legislative framework that may appear more appealing to the court; rather, the judge should examine only the legislative framework determined by the legislator. The basic premise of judicial review is that the legislative function should be fulfilled by the legislator. Thus, the court does not substitute the legislator's considerations with its own. The court does not put itself in the legislator's shoes. The court does not ask itself what means it would have chosen if it were a part of the legislative body.[65] The court exercises judicial review. It examines the constitutionality of the law, not its wisdom.[66] The question is not whether the law in question is beneficial, efficient, or justified. The question is whether the law is constitutional. Both a "socialist" and a "capitalist" legislator may enact different and opposed laws, but both laws would still be proportional. Nationalization and privatization might both occur in this framework. Both market capitalism and a socialist economy may well exist within them. As long as these actions – which limit constitutional rights – satisfy the requirements of proportionality, they are all constitutional.

b.   Caution in exercising judicial review   Declaring a law unconstitutional due to its disproportional limitation of a constitutional right is a serious matter. A judge would not make such a declaration lightly. Such an act requires respect and judicial caution. These requirements are derived from the principle of the separation of powers. However, none of those considerations justify leaving intact a disproportional limitation on a constitutional right. I have elaborated on this issue in one of my opinions:

> Judicial restraint does not equal judicial stagnation. Judicial restraint should not lead to judicial paralysis. Thus, when the legislator limits

---

[64] See *R. v. Secretary of State for the Home Department, ex parte Daly* [2001] 3 All ER 433 (Lord Stein).

[65] See *Huang v. Secretary of State for the Home Department* [2007] 2 AC 167 (Lord Bingham).

[66] See T. Hickman, "The Substance and Structure of Proportionality," *PL* 694 (2008).

a human right that is constitutionally protected and the limitation is not proportional, the judge has no option but to take a very clear stand. Just as we are not free to render a legislative act invalid merely because we, as judges, would not have enacted that same law were we sitting as members of the legislative branch, nor are we free not to declare a law unconstitutional merely because the legislator was of the opinion that it should be enacted. We, the judges, have a constitutional duty of safeguarding the constitutional criteria by which the constitutionality of a law is measured; we must ensure that those criteria are met in each and every case.[67]

c. Judicial review and judicial "intervention"   In many cases, courts use the term "intervention" to describe judicial activity.[68] Thus, the court asks whether it should "intervene" in a certain matter. The use of the term raises considerable issues. Whether the judge rules that the law is constitutional or unconstitutional, in both cases the court has "intervened." The key issue, therefore, is not "intervention" or "non-intervention," but rather proportionality versus disproportionality; constitutionality or unconstitutionality. A court that leaves a limitation on a constitutional right untouched must only do so if it believes that the limitation is proportional and not because it prefers not to "intervene" in the legislator's discretion. A court holding that a certain limitation on a constitutional right is disproportional – and therefore that the legislative provision is unconstitutional – does not do so because it is "intervening" in the legislative discretion, but, rather, because it is of the opinion that the limitation is disproportional.

d. Judicial review and judicial deference   Courts in several jurisdictions have adopted the notion that they should defer to the decisions made by the executive[69] or legislative branches.[70] The legal literature on

---

[67] HCJ 1715/97 *Israel Investment Managers Association v. Minister of Finance* [1997] IsrSC 51(4) 367, 389.

[68] In Israel alone, the Supreme Court has mentioned the term over 2,000 times in the past decade.

[69] D. J. Mullan, "Deference: Is It Useful Outside Canada?," in H. Corder (ed.), *Comparing Administrative Justice Across the Commonwealth* (Cape Town: Juta Law Publishers, 2006), 42.

[70] D. J. Solove, "The Darkest Domain: Deference, Judicial Review, and the Bill of Rights," 84 *Iowa L. Rev.* 941 (1999). See, for example, the opinion of Justice Sopinka in the ruling of the Supreme Court of Canada in *Egan v. Canada* [1995] 2 SCR 513; see also R. A. Schapiro, "Judicial Deference and Interpretive Coordinacy in State and Federal Constitutional Law," 85 *Cornell L. Rev.* 656 (2000).

the issue of deference is vast.[71] Deference would not have been an issue had the accepted meaning of the term "deference" been that the judicial branch must respect opinions issued by the other two branches of government, and treat those decisions with all seriousness and caution.[72] Dyzenhaus dubbed this approach "deference as respect."[73] Those requirements seem obvious, and are derived from the principle of separation of powers.[74] But the notion of deference includes more than that; it is this "addition" that poses difficulties. This addition, as explained by

[71] See A. Scalia, "Judicial Deference to Administrative Interpretations of Law," Duke L. J. 511 (1989); J. Vining, "Authority and Responsibility: The Jurisprudence of Deference," 43 *Admin. L. Rev.* 135 (1991); D. Dyzenhaus, "The Politics of Deference: Judicial Review and Democracy," in M. Taggart (ed.), *The Province of Administrative Law* (Portland, OR: Hart Publishing, 1997), 279; C. Hoexter, "The Future of Judicial Review in South African Administrative Law," 117 *S. Afr. L. J.* 484 (2000); R. Edwards, "Judicial Deference under the Human Rights Act," 65 *Mod. L. Rev.* 859 (2002); P. Soper, The Ethics of Deference: Learning from Law's Morals (Cambridge University Press, 2002); P. Sales and B. Hooper, "Proportionality and the Form of Law," 119 *L. Q. Rev.* 426 (2003); H. Corder, "Without Deference, With Respect: A Response to Justice O'Regan," 121 *S. Afr. L. J.* 438 (2004); P. Craig, "Judicial Review, Intensity and Deference in EU Law," in D. Dyzenhaus (ed.), *The Unity of Public Law* (Portland, OR: Hart Publishing, 2004), 335; R. Clayton, "Judicial Deference and Democratic Dialogue: The Legitimacy of Judicial Intervention under the Human Rights Act 1998," *PL* 33 (2004); C. E. Wells, "Questioning Deference," 69 *Mo. L. Rev.* 903 (2004); R. Pushaw, "Defending Deference: A Response to Professors Epstein and Wells," 69 *Mo. L. Rev.* 959 (2004); J. R. De Ville, "Deference as Respect and Deference as Sacrifice: A Reading of Bato Star Fishing v. Minister of Environmental Affairs," 20 *SAJHR* 577 (2004); A. Young, "Ghaidan v. Godin-Mendoza: Avoiding the Deference Trap," *PL* 23 (2005); F. Schauer, "Deferring," 103 *Mich. L. Rev.* 1567 (2005); R. Thompson, "Community Law and the Limits of Deference," *Eur. Hum. Rts. L. Rev.* 24 (2005); H. Corder, "Despair to Deference: Same Difference?," in M. Taggart and G. Huscroft (eds.), *Inside and Outside Canadian Administrative Law: Essays in Honour of David Mullan* (University of Toronto Press, 2006), 327; M. J. Beloff, "The Concept of 'Deference' in Public Law," 11 *Jud. Rev.* 213 (2006); R. E. Schiller, "The Era of Deference: Courts, Expertise, and the Emergence of New Deal Administrative Law," 106 *Mich. L. Rev.* 399 (2007); M. Taggart, "Proportionality, Deference, Wednesbury," 2008 *New Zealand L. Rev.* 423 (2008); A. Kavanagh, "Deference or Defiance?: The Limits of the Judicial Role in Constitutional Adjudication," in G. Huscroft (ed.), *Expounding the Constitution – Essays in Constitutional Theory* (Cambridge University Press, 2008), 184. See also Solove, above note 70; Schapiro, above note 70; Davidov, above note 39; Steyn, above note 42; King, above note 42; Allan, above note 16; Jowell, above note 16; Jowell, above note 16; Allan, above note 16; Rivers, above note 42; Rivers, above note 20; S. Gardbaum, "A Democratic Defense of Constitutional Balancing," 4 *Law and Ethics of Hum. Rts.*, 78 (2010); R. Dixon, "The Supreme Court of Canada, Charter Dialogue, and Deference," 47 *Osgoode Hall L. J.* 235 (2009).

[72] See above, at 395. See also Solove, above note 70, at 943.

[73] Dyzenhaus, above note 16.

[74] See above, at 395.

Dyzenhaus, relates more to "deference as submission."[75] Although there
is no accepted legal definition of the term deference,[76] it seems that in the
present context – the proportionality of a limitation on a constitutional
right – we can define deference as a situation where a judge adopts an
opinion expressed by another branch of government (either the legislative or executive) regarding the components of proportionality when,
without this expression, the judge would not have adopted that opinion.[77]
The three most common justifications for this deference are: the lack of
democratic legitimacy for judging; the lack of institutional capacity; and,
finally, judicial wisdom.[78] None of these justifications is proper. Judging
enjoys full democratic legitimacy,[79] as it is derived directly from the constitution. Similarly, the institutional structure allows the judiciary to
receive information regarding the different considerations in the same
way this information is presented to other branches of government. Of
course, the judge does not set social policy. That assertion, however, has
nothing to do with deference and everything to do with the principle of
separation of powers and the scope of the court's authority within that
principle. Finally, judicial wisdom cannot replace constitutional duty.
There is no room for deference (according to the definition herein).[80] It
seems that the notion is redundant in both instances: if the opinion of the
other branch – be it the legislative or executive – regarding the components of proportionality is lawful without deference, the judge should act
according to it while disregarding deference; if the opinion of the legislative or executive branch regarding the components of proportionality
is unlawful without deference, the judge should reject that opinion with

---

[75] Dyzenhaus, above note 71.

[76] H. P. Monaghan, "Marbury and the Administrative State," 83 *Colum. L. Rev.* 1, 4 (1983).
See also Allan, above note 16, at 291.

[77] P. Horwitz, "Three Faces of Deference," 83 *Notre Dame L. Rev.* 1061, 1072 (2008).

[78] See Edwards, above note 71; Steyn, above note 42; Kavanagh, above note 71; Taggart,
above note 71.

[79] See *A v. Secretary of State for the Home Department* [2004] UKHL 56, para. 42: "The
Attorney General is fully entitled to insist on the proper limits of judicial authority, but
he is wrong to stigmatize judicial decision-making as in some way undemocratic." (Lord
Bingham).

[80] See *RJR-MacDonald Inc.* v. *Canada (Attorney General)* [1995] 3 SCR 199; *R (ProLife
Alliance)* v. *BBC* [2003] 2 WLR 1403; *Huang* v. *Secretary of State for the Home Department*
[2007] UKHL 11; D. M. Beatty, *The Ultimate Rule of Law* (Oxford University Press,
2004), 156. See also Allan, above note 16; Allan, above note 16; Corder, above note 71;
Solove, above note 70; Beloff, above note 71; Kavanagh, above note 71; Hoexter, above
note 71.

no relation to deference. Either way, the notion of deference should have no place;[81] it has no place when the question is the proportionality of a limitation on a constitutional right.[82] The relevant question is the constitutionality of the opinion of the legislative or executive branch, and not the issue of deference. Accordingly, there is no room to argue that there are certain categories of cases, like national security or emergencies,[83] where the judge should exercise deference to the legislative or executive authority.[84] Once again, should the opinion expressed by the legislative or executive branch fall within the "zone of proportionality,"[85] then it should be adopted by the judicial branch. This is not because the judge deferred his opinion but because the opinion is lawful.

What is the case when both sides of the scale are of equal weight?[86] In such a case, the determination should not be based on considerations of judicial deference. One possible rule in such situations is that in case of doubt the right should prevail (*in dubio pro libertate*). Another possible rule is that when in doubt the limiting law should prevail. Either way, the rule is not based on the notion of deference.

The approach that a judge should defer to the legislative or executive branches does not fit a constitutional democracy. It limits the principle of the separation of powers. It is a judicial tool without rules[87] or a proper legal foundation.[88] It provides the judge with discretion where discretion is unwarranted, and denies judicial discretion when it should be exercised.

[81] There are those who are of the opinion that judicial deference should be exercised in certain circumstances. See, e.g., Rivers, above note 20; Rivers, above note 42. See also M. Hunt, "Sovereignty's Blight: Why Contemporary Public Law Needs the Concept of 'Due Deference,'" in N. Bamforth and P. Leyland (eds.), *Public Law in a Multi-Layered Constitution* (Portland, OR: Hart Publishing, 2003), 337. There are those who based the deference on the lack of institutional ability: Jowell, above note 16; Jowell, above note 16; Rivers, above note 20; Steyn, above note 42.

[82] Compare with Craig, above note 71.

[83] See F. D. Ni Aolain and O. Gross, "A Skeptical View of Deference to the Executive in Times of Crisis," 41 *Isr. L. Rev.* 545 (2008).

[84] For such a determination, see *International Transport Roth GmbH v. Secretary of State for the Home Department* [2002] 3 WLR 344.

[85] On the zone of proportionality, see below, at 415.

[86] For a discussion of this issue, see above, at 365.

[87] See Solove, above note 70, at 945; Edwards, above note 71, at 863.

[88] See Solove, above note 70, at 945; Beloff, above note 71; Kavanagh, above note 71; Davidov, above note 39.

B.　Discretion and the components of proportionality

1.　*The decision to legislate*

i.　Legislative discretion

The legislator enjoys a very wide discretion in deciding whether or not to legislate. The scope of such legislative discretion is one of the widest in constitutional democracies. This expresses the very notion of representative democracy: the peoples' representatives decide whether and when they would like to regulate and whether and when they would like to refrain from doing so. However, this discretion is not absolute. The authority to legislate is found in the constitution. The same constitution that grants the discretion may, in certain cases, require that the legislator use it. The same source which enabled the legislator to refrain from legislating may also require it to legislate. Thus, whenever an individual has a positive constitutional right (*status positivus*) *vis-à-vis* the legislature, a constitutional duty to legislate (*Schutzpflicht*) is imposed on the legislature; and the decision not to legislate may limit such a right. This argument is discussed in Chapter 15.[89] In this context, a legislative decision not to legislate – to deny legislation on the issue – is constitutional if such a decision is proportional. However, even when a duty to legislate exists, the legislator still enjoys a very wide discretion *within* the bounds of that duty.

ii.　Judicial discretion

As a rule, the courts do not demand that the legislator legislate. Importantly, however, this does not stem from the notion of judicial deference. Similarly, this approach does not render the legislative decision to legislate – or not to legislate – a non-justiciable issue. Rather, it expresses the judicial recognition that the legislative decision not to legislate is constitutionally valid. It reflects the judicial understanding that no legal right exists for the individuals, and therefore no corresponding duty applies to the legislator, to create laws. However, there is an exception to this rule with regard to positive human rights. The scope of that exception and the judicial discretion it provides to judges will be discussed in Chapter 15.

---

[89] See below, at 422.

2. Determining purposes

i.   Legislative discretion

A legislator exercising its discretion to legislate must set its legislative purposes. This is one of the legislator's main functions. This is the legislator's "national responsibility" in determining the national goals and in defining the purposes for which legislation is required. This discretion is limited by constitutional provisions (explicit or implicit) requiring that those purposes be proper.[90] The legislator cannot choose an improper legislative purpose. This limitation is not too difficult to uphold. In the majority of cases, the legislator enjoys a wide discretion in determining the legislative purposes. Thus, for example, the legislator can enact a law that is required, in the legislator's opinion, for national security purposes. This is a proper purpose – so long as the proper factual framework was presented to the legislator to justify this conclusion.[91] The factual framework should also establish the degree of urgency in achieving the legislative purpose, as well as the prognosis of its fulfillment (i.e., the probability it would actually occur). Based on this factual framework the legislator enjoys a wide discretion in determining the legislative purpose, its degree of urgency, and the probability that the purpose is actually achieved. Such a probability – the prognosis of fulfilling the purpose – falls within the legislator's wide discretion. Even if it turns out, at the end of the judicial review process, that the probability of fulfilling the statutory purpose was lower than required to justify such a limitation of the constitutional human right – a question to be examined during the proportionality *stricto sensu* stage of the review – this would not affect a judicial determination as to the purpose being proper. The purpose is proper – and its selection is well within the wide legislative discretion – even if the probability of its occurrence does not justify a limitation on the constitutional right. The judicial purpose's appropriateness is detached from the issue of its means or the balancing between the purpose's fulfillment and the harm it may cause.

The wide scope of the legislative discretion in determining the goals is derived from the constitution. In most cases, the constitution sets a wide parameter for legislative activity. From that premise we may also deduce that the setting of social policy should be given, among others, to the

---

[90] See above, at 245.
[91] C. E. Borgmann, "Rethinking Judicial Deference to Legislative Fact-Finding," 84 *Ind. L. J.* 1 (2009).

legislator. A useful example was provided in the Israeli Supreme Court
case of *Stanger*.[92] There, the Court examined whether the purpose behind
the Israeli Bar Law of 1961[93] – the statute regulating the practice of law in
Israel – is proper. In my opinion I wrote:

> There may be several models that can be used to regulate and supervise
> the practice of law. The choice between those models belongs to the legis-
> lative branch. Each model has its own advantages and disadvantages. The
> role of determining the proper arrangement is the legislator's as part of
> the notion of the separation of powers. However, this legislative discre-
> tion is bound by constitutional restraints. These are not politically char-
> acterized ideological restraints. A constitution is neither a capitalistic
> manifesto nor a socialist one … The legislator (Knesset) is free to choose
> the model it sees fit when exercising its power to determine the legisla-
> tion that would apply to the regulation and supervision of the practice of
> law. However, this freedom has its constitutional limits which should be
> upheld.[94]

Naturally, each constitution has its own structure. In some cases, the
constitution may prefer one social or political viewpoint or another and
these preferences may, in turn, impose further limitations on the "regular" legislator. In other cases, the limitations are so burdensome on the
legislator that suggestions arise to amend the constitution in order to
remove those limitations. At times this may also affect the scope of existing constitutional rights. Such an amendment is not required to fulfill the
requirements of proportionality.[95] It may, however, face a claim that the
amendment is unconstitutional.[96] An examination of this claim is beyond
the scope of this book.[97]

In some cases, the constitution, in a special limitation clause attached
to a specific right, determines that the limitation of the right is possible if
it was done to advance a special purpose.[98] Can this deny other purposes?
Is that a negative solution with regard to other purposes? The answer to
this question is interpretive in nature. When the constitutional provision
is interpreted as denying any other purpose, the legislator must examine in each case whether the proposed legislation falls within the zone of
purposes which, according to the constitution, can be limited in order
to be fulfilled. Without said special limitation, the principal rules apply.
According to these rules, whenever the statute limiting the constitutional

[92] HCJ 2334/02 *Stanger* v. *Knesset Speaker* [2003] IsrSC 58(1) 786.
[93] Bar Law (1961).   [94] See *Stanger*, above note 92, at 794.
[95] See above, at 155.   [96] See above, at 31.
[97] See above, at 31.   [98] See above, at 141.

right is meant to advance another right (whether constitutional or not), this legislation should be seen as being enacted for a proper purpose.[99] This is not the case whenever the limiting legislation is aimed at advancing the public interest. In these types of cases the solution varies from one legal system to another.[100]

ii. Judicial discretion

What is the judge's role in determining the legislative purposes? What is the scope of judicial discretion in those cases? The judge's role is to examine whether the purposes chosen by the legislator satisfy the constitutional requirements of a proper purpose.[101] The judge therefore must determine whether the content of the purpose set by the legislation, which limits a constitutional right, satisfies the requirements of the proper purpose, including the urgency requirement. Whenever a constitution is based on specific limitation clauses,[102] the judge must interpret the constitution's specific requirements regarding the purposes which justify a limitation on a constitutional right. The judge must then establish whether the limiting law satisfies these requirements.

The judge's discretion is directed towards determining the constitutionality of the purpose underlying the limiting legislation. Judicial discretion is not directed at the wisdom of the proposed legislative purpose, or at legislative consistency. The legislator can exercise its power to legislate laws that are unwise as well as inconsistent as long as they are proportional. Issues of wisdom, efficiency, consistency, fairness, and morality relating to the legislative purpose are pertinent only if they affect the law's proportionality. A statute may be proportional even if the solution it proposes is unwise, inefficient, or inconsistent.

The judge does not determine the legislative purpose. That is chosen by the legislator. The judge's role is to review that choice. Policy determinations are the role of the legislator; the constitutionality of the legislator's determination is for the judge to decide.[103] A useful example of this idea was offered by the Israeli Supreme Court in the case of *Gaza Coast*

---

[99] See above, at 255.   [100] See above, at 256.
[101] See above, at 249.   [102] See above, at 141.
[103] HCJ 6427/02 *The Movement for Quality Government in Israel* v. *The Knesset* (2006, not yet published), available in Hebrew at http://elyon1.court.gov.il/files/02/270/064/ a22/02064270.a22.HTM ("We may think of several solutions that reflect several approaches about balance and compromise between the conflicting social purposes. It is the role of the political branches to choose between those solutions. This is not the role of the judicial branch. The question before us is not whether other purposes could

Regional Council.[104] In that case, the Court examined legislation that formed the legal framework for the Knesset's decision to evacuate all of the Jewish settlers from the Gaza Strip. In particular, the Court examined whether the purpose underlying the relevant legislation – the Law to Implement the Evacuation Plan, 2005 – was proper. The Court was divided over that issue. The majority opinion stated:

> The question before us is not what we would have decided were the issues presented to us as members of the legislative body (the Knesset). We are not authorized to resolve the issue since – as this Court has been ruling ever since it was established, in hundreds of judicial opinions – we do not replace the discretion granted to the legislative (and executive) branch with our own. The Court's examination does not relate to the wisdom or efficiency of the legislative (or executive) decision, but only to its constitutionality or legal validity. Accordingly, we cannot rule on "who is right" in the bitterly contested issues before us. The only question on which we are authorized to, and must, provide an answer is derived from the constitutional framework before us. And the question is this: Whether the purposes underlying the current Knesset Law are proper purposes as required by the constitutional limitation clause.[105]

The Court operates well within its "classic" role. It examines whether the purposes set by the legislator pass the constitutional threshold of proper purpose once a limitation of human rights is considered. As Rivers has noted while discussing the notion of purposes and the limitation imposed by the constitution on their scope:

> be offered, or other compromises made, that would be just as appropriate – or even more appropriate – with regard to the legislative choice. Rather, the question before us is whether the purposes chosen by the legislator – those purposes that reflect the legislative choice on how to solve the social issue confronting it – are proper ... The question of drafting ultra-orthodox Yeshiva students is a complex social issue of national implications and the proper forum to resolve that issue is the legislative body. The Israeli legislator – the Knesset – has established several purposes in that context. It could have established other purposes. But the question before us today is not whether the purposes that the Knesset has established are the most appropriate purposes. The question before us is whether the purposes established by the Knesset, operating together, fall within the range of options allowed by the legislative discretion. The question before us is not whether the purposes chosen by the Knesset are wise and valuable. The question before us is whether those purposes, operating together, fall within the range of proper purposes that the legislator may choose. My answer to this question is yes, regardless of my own opinion as to these purposes. We are dealing with a fundamental social issue; we are facing a complicated social policy issue. The Knesset has the responsibility for shaping such policy." (Barak, P.).

[104] HCJ 1661/05 *Gaza Coast Regional Council* v. *Knesset of Israel* [2005] IsrSC 59(2) 481.

[105] *Ibid.*, at 570.

> The function of the court is simply to filter out those cases in which public bodies limit rights for the sake of public interest incapable ever of justifying that limitation.[106]

This approach is not based on judicial "non-intervention" or judicial deference towards the legislator. Rather, it is derived from the constitution. It is an expression of the principle of separation of powers. The legislator enjoys wide discretion in choosing the purpose, and the judge's "non-intervention" is an expression of the constitutionality of this legislative choice. An important judicial role is to locate the legislative purpose which underlies the legislation.[107] The legislator has determined it; the judge has to expose it.[108]

3. Choosing the legislative means

Once the legislator has chosen the purposes it wishes to fulfill through the legislation, it should determine the means to achieve those goals. The scope of the legislative discretion in selecting these means, however, is narrower than the discretion in choosing the legislative purposes. This is because, once the purposes are selected, the means that the legislator can select from are limited to only those means that satisfy the requirements of proportionality. The judicial role in respect of the means is to examine their proportionality. The court does not examine which means it would have selected to fulfill the legislative purpose were the judge a member of the legislative body; rather, the court's task is to review whether the means selected by the legislator are proportional – whether they satisfy the tests of proportionality. The scope of the legislative discretion varies in each of the tests and the same is true for the scope of the judicial discretion. Each of these tests will now be discussed, beginning with that of rational connection.

4. The rational connection test

i. Legislative discretion

The rational connection test determines that the means selected by the legislator should fit the purposes chosen – that is, that their use leads to the fulfillment of the legislative purpose. The requirement is not for the complete and absolute potential of achieving each of the legislative goals,

---

[106] Rivers, above note 42, at 196.
[107] See above, at 249.   [108] See above, at 285.

but rather for a contribution to further those purposes – which cannot be marginal.[109] It is required that a factual framework be presented to the legislator from which one may assert the existence of a rational connection. In most cases, this requirement for a rational connection provides the legislator with considerable discretion.[110] Legislation is a forward-looking institution. It is based on a prognosis of the occurrence of future events, as well as on evaluations of how things may – or may not – occur in the future. Moreover, the legislative purposes may be achieved, in most cases, in several ways; the probability of actually achieving the goals by these ways is not certain, but far from marginal. The existence of several ways to achieve the same legislative purpose stems, among others, from the existence of a number of variables and the selection of any one of these – in light of the information the legislator has – would still satisfy the requirements of the rational connection test. The choice between those elements should be left to the legislator.

ii.   Judicial discretion

Judicial review examines whether a rational connection exists between the law's purposes and the means selected for their fulfillment. In order to do so, the court examines the factual framework, which served as the legislative prognosis, presented to the legislator. The court must determine, according to the test of common sense, whether this factual framework establishes the rational connection. In light of the myriad means available to advance the law's purposes as well as the many variables that may be selected by the legislator to do so, it is natural to assume that the scope of judicial discretion in these matters is extremely narrow.[111] Only when the lack of rational connection can be deduced from all of the factual data presented should the court determine that the requirements of the rational connection test have not been met. Therefore, there are very few precedents – in most legal systems – where the court has accepted the claim that no rational connection exists between the legislation and the means selected to advance its purposes.[112]

---

[109]   See above, at 305.
[110]   See H. Avila, *Theory of Legal Principles* (Dordrecht: Springer, 2007), 118. See also Rivers, above note 42, at 195.
[111]   See H. Dreier, *GG Grundgesetz Kommentar* (Tübingen: Mohr Siebeck, 2006), 262; C. Bernal Pulido, *El Principio de Proporcionalidad y los Derechos Fundamentales* (Madrid: Centro de Estudios Políticos y Constitucionales 2007), 733.
[112]   See above, at 316.

5. The necessity test

i. Legislative discretion

a. The scope of the legislative discretion The necessity test requires the legislator to choose, from the variety of means available to fulfill the legislative purposes, the means that would least harm constitutional human rights.[113] Due to this requirement, the legislator is not free to choose whichever means it considers proper; rather, it can only select those means that fulfill the legislative purposes while harming the constitutional rights the least. Does the very existence of this legislative duty – which expresses the necessity test – coincide with the notion of legislative discretion? Should we not simply conclude that the necessity test denies the legislator's discretion in selecting the means?[114]

The answer to that question is no. The denial of the legislative discretion occurs very rarely, if ever. The reason for that is that the legislator determines the statutory purposes it is interested in fulfilling. This can be determined according to its discretion, at different levels of intensity. Assuming that both options satisfy the necessity test – the legislator is free to choose between any of them.[115]

Take, for example, the Israeli Supreme Court case of *Adalah*.[116] There, the legislator asserted that the statutory purpose was to mitigate, "as much as possible," the national security threat stemming from the spouses of Israeli citizens who reside in the Occupied Territories. With this assertion in mind, an individual examination could not have satisfied the necessity test. The legislator is permitted to determine a different purpose. It can demand that the security threat should only be "somewhat" mitigated; if that were the case, an individual examination would have satisfied the necessity test.[117] The purpose that the legislator wants to fulfill is within its

---

[113] See above, at 317.

[114] Such an approach has been adopted in France in the past, where the court ruled that the necessity test should not be considered part of the judicial review of the constitutionality of legislation. See Decision No. 2007–555 DC (August 16, 2007). Recently, the French Constitutional Court has changed its approach. According to the current approach, the necessity test is now included within constitutional proportionality. See Decision No. 2008–562 (February 21, 2008); Decision No. 2009–580 (June 10, 2009).

[115] See Dreier, above note 111, at 259.

[116] HCJ 7052/03 *Adalah – The Legal Center for the Rights of the Arab Minority* v. *Minister of Interior* (May 14, 2006, unpublished), available in English at http://elyon1.court.gov.il/fileseng/03/520/070/a47/03070520. a47.pdf. Regarding the facts of the case, see above, at 351.

[117] See above, at 331.

legislative discretion; and the necessity test operates within that realm of discretion. As Rivers has noted:

> [I]t does not rule out any level of achievement of any legitimate end. For example, it works even in the case of a legislature seeking near-perfect protection for national security, simply asking, given this level of national security, is privacy restricted to the least extent possible? Thus it still leaves as much discretion as a legislature could reasonably want. It allows every level of achievement of every permissible end.[118]

Moreover, legislation is always forward looking. Different means may fulfill it. Thus, for example, one legislative means may be more expensive, but quicker to fulfill the legislative purpose; another may be cheaper, yet slower to achieve the same purpose. The probability of fulfilling the purpose may also vary between one legislative means and the other. All these factors provide the legislator with considerable discretionary power; only the proper factoring of all the elements can provide an accurate picture as to the actual scope of the harm caused to the constitutional right. It is possible that this factoring may also not lead to a clear decision as to the way the legislator should choose. In this state of affairs the legislator enjoys considerable discretion. This is the zone of legislative discretion.[119] Thus, for example, the regulation and supervision of the practice of law – which limits the (constitutionally protected) right to freedom of occupation of every lawyer – may be done in several ways. The role may be assigned to either the executive or judicial branch; an independent statutory agency may be established; the agency's structure may be determined in several ways. All these options satisfy the necessity test and the legislator can choose any one of them.[120]

b.   The least reasonably limiting means   The necessity test originally held that the legislator must select the means that would harm the constitutional right the least. Chief Justice Dickson of the Canadian Supreme Court used the term "as little as possible" while establishing the necessity test in *Oakes*.[121] Similar language was adopted in the Israeli Supreme Court case of *United Mizrahi Bank*: "Other means, whose limitation on

---

[118] J. Rivers, "Proportionality and Discretion in International and European Law," in N. Tsagourias (ed.), *Transnational Constitutionalism: International and European Perspectives* (Cambridge University Press, 2007).
[119] See below, at 415.
[120] See *Stanger*, above note 92, at 797.
[121] *R. v. Oakes* [1986] 1 SCR 103, 134.

the human right is the smallest."[122] Since the Canadian courts first exercised the necessity test, however, that standard has been amended to include the reasonableness requirement.[123] Thus, for example, in *Edwards*, decided soon after *Oakes*, Chief Justice Dickson noted that the limitation should be "as little as reasonably possible."[124] A similar wording of the necessity test was adopted in South Africa.[125] A similar change also occurred in Israel.

Why was reasonableness added?[126] The reason behind the addition of reasonableness in the present context is to identify the domain of the legislative discretion.[127] It was meant to acknowledge that, in most cases, there is uncertainty as to the likelihood of the actual achievement of the legislative purposes through the use of the means selected to do so. In many cases, this factual uncertainty prevents the legislator from pointing out a single legislative means that may fulfill the necessity test. Thus, a domain of situations, which fulfill the legislative purposes with the least harm, is created. Within this domain, the decision to select the preferred means is the legislator's. As Justice McLachlin of the Canadian Supreme Court has noted:

> As the second step in the proportionality analysis, the government must show that the measures at issue impair the right of free expression as little *as reasonably possible* in order to achieve the legislative objective. The impairment must be "minimal", that is, the law must be carefully tailored so that rights are impaired no more than necessary. The tailoring process seldom admits of perfection and the courts must accord some leeway to the legislator. If the law falls within a range of reasonable alternatives, the courts will not find it overbroad merely because they can conceive of an alternative which might better tailor objective to infringement.[128]

Indeed, it is not enough to point to the means that would harm the constitutional right less than others. For such a means to satisfy the necessity test it should be shown that use of the less harmful means would not affect the likelihood that the legislative purpose would ultimately be achieved. Often such a probability-related, forward-looking requirement

---

[122] *United Mizrahi Bank*, above note 38, at 242.
[123] See above, at 282.
[124] *R. v. Edwards Books and Art Ltd.* [1986] 2 SCR 713, 772.
[125] *S. v. Makwanyane*, 1995 (3) SA 391, para. 107.
[126] For a criticism of such an addition, see W. Sadurski, "'Reasonableness' and Value Pluralism in Law and Politics," in G. Bongiovanni, G. Sartor, and C. Valentini (eds.), *Reasonableness and Law* (Dordrecht: Springer, 2009), 129.
[127] See above, at 407.
[128] *RJR-MacDonald Inc.*, above note 18, at para. 160.

is hard to satisfy due to evidentiary issues. Ultimately, in most instances the decision of which means to select is the result of the evaluation of several options. These are part of the legislator's discretion. Below are two instructive examples from the Canadian Supreme Court:

(a) A Canadian law prescribed that, once convicted of an illegal or corrupt practice pursuant to the Elections Act, a person shall be disqualified from running as a candidate for office for a period of five years. It was argued that such a provision limits the constitutional right to be elected in a disproportionate manner. The reason for that was that the five-year disqualification period does not limit the right in the least restrictive manner. The Canadian Supreme Court assumed a limitation on the constitutional right. As for the necessity test, the Court examined the length of the disqualification period and ruled that the period selected by the legislator factored in the assumption that the candidate would not be able to run for office at the next election. Furthermore, the disqualification period was fixed and did not change from one election cycle to another – a choice that was intended to ensure certainty and to allow for the regaining of public trust in the fairness of the election process. The Court held that there was no room to intervene in the legislative choice of a five-year disqualification period. Writing for the Court, Justice La Forest noted that "[t]his court has on several occasions asserted its unwillingness to second-guess the legislature in choosing between acceptable options."[129]

(b) The Canadian Retail Business Holiday Act prohibited the sale of goods by stores on Sunday. The act included an exception, according to which stores could open on Sunday if they were closed on Saturday, had no more than seven employees and had less than 5,000 square feet of retail space to serve the public. It was argued that the act disproportionally limited the constitutionally protected right to freedom of religion because, among others, the exception does not apply to *all* stores closed on Saturday. The Canadian Supreme Court held that the act limits the right to freedom of religion. Regarding the necessity test, the Court held that the act satisfies its requirements. The Court closely examined the parameters of the exception and compared them to a hypothetical legislative alternative that would have excluded all stores closed on Saturday. Writing for the Court, Chief Justice Dickson asserted: "I do not believe there is any magic

---

[129] *Harvey v. New Brunswick (Attorney General)* [1996] 2 SCR 876, § 47.

in the number seven as distinct from, say, five, ten, or fifteen employees as the cut-off point for eligibility for the exemption. In balancing the interests of retail employees to a holiday in common with their family and friends against the Section 2(a) interests of those affected the legislature engaged in the process envisaged by Section 1 of the Charter. A 'reasonable limit' is one which, having regard to the principles enunciated in *Oakes*, it was reasonable for the legislature to impose. The courts are not called upon to substitute judicial opinions for legislative ones as to the place at which to draw a precise line."[130]

Legislation is not an exact science. The fulfillment of statutory purposes is always subject to uncertainty. As a result, drawing an exact line is not possible. There are a range of possibilities and a zone of legislative discretion. Therein, the legislator can choose from several means, all of which satisfy the requirements of the necessity test. The choice is for the legislator alone, and the court will not substitute the legislative discretion with its own.[131] This approach is not an expression of judicial deference. Rather, it is an expression of the constitutionality of the legislative discretion and of the lack of judicial discretion.

c. "Only an unimaginative judge could not find a less restrictive means"   Justice Blackmun's well-known view on this goes as follows:

> [F]or me, "least drastic means" is a slippery slope ... A judge would be unimaginative indeed if he could not come up with something a little less "drastic" or a little less "restrictive" in almost any situation, and thereby enable himself to vote to strike legislation down.[132]

This statement is correct as far as it relates to judicial imagination. However, it does not accurately reflect the necessity test.[133] This is for two reasons. First, Justice Blackmun does not ask the right question. We have already seen that the question to be asked by the court is not the following hypothetical question:[134] "Are there any other reasonable means that may harm the constitutional right to a lesser degree than the proposed legislation?" Rather, the question that should be asked by the court is a specific, practical one: "Are there other means that may harm the constitutional

---

[130]   *R. v. Edwards Books*, above note 124, at para. 147.
[131]   See above, at 331.
[132]   *Illinois State Board of Elections* v. *Socialist Workers Party*, 440 US 173, 188 (1979).
[133]   G. Davidov, "Separating Minimal Impairment from Balancing: A Comment on R. v. Sharpe," 5 *Rev. Const. Stud.* 195 (2000).
[134]   See above, at 323.

right to a lesser degree, but also fulfill the legislative purpose to the same extent as the measure chosen by the legislature?" An answer to this question considers the probability of achieving the statutory purpose through the means chosen by the legislator, as well as the factual uncertainty connected to such a situation. Second, Justice Blackmun does not consider the realm of legislative discretion; he also fails to consider the possibility of several reasonable possibilities, the option of choosing from them is provided exclusively to the legislator.

ii.   Judicial discretion

Of the options available to the legislator, which all satisfy the requirements of the rational connection test, it should choose that option which harms the constitutional right the least. The legislator should stop at the stage of the normative "ladder" where its purpose is fulfilled, while the right suffers the least restrictive harm.[135] The party who argues that their constitutional right has been disproportionally limited bears the burden of showing (pleading) an alternative, which would harm the right less but which would still fulfill the legislative purpose at the same level of intensity.[136] Once that claim has been raised, the state would bear the burden of persuading the court that such a means either does not exist or, if it does, that it cannot advance the legislative purpose to the same extent.[137] Judicial discretion in these instances is not wide. The court should examine, based on the factual framework presented to it, whether an alternative exists that would fulfill the legislative purpose to the same extent as the chosen legislative means, but which would also cause less harm to the constitutional right. This decision is based, among others, on the prognosis as to the likelihood that the legislative purposes would actually be achieved while using the means chosen. In many cases, such a prognosis is a matter of uncertainty, which in turn enables the existence of several options that are likely to achieve the goal while harming the right to a lesser degree. The choice between those options is provided to the legislator and not to the judge.[138]

Once an alternative means that would advance the legislative purposes at the same level of intensity as the means proposed by the legislator is presented to the court, the answer to the question of whether such alternative means would harm the constitutional right to a lesser or greater

---

[135]   See above, at 317.   [136]   See below, at 442.
[137]   See Pulido, above note 111, at 759.
[138]   See Rivers, above note 118, at 120.

extent than the means chosen by the legislator is for the court to decide. Indeed, the determination of which option is the least restrictive is the result of judicial constitutional interpretation.[139] Take, for example, a law designed to address public order issues which requires that all retail businesses shut down at a certain hour and which imposes a criminal sanction of imprisonment for failing to do so. The legislator, in this case, avoided setting a sanction such as revoking a business license, either temporarily or permanently – thinking that the harm of such a measure to the constitutionally protected right of freedom of occupation would be greater than a criminal sanction of imprisonment. The question of which of the two measures limits the constitutional right the least is a legal question. As such, the final answer to it should be provided by the court.

6.   The proportionality stricto sensu test (balancing)

i.   Legislative discretion

As we have seen, the legislator enjoys considerable discretion with regard to the constitutional requirements of rational connection and necessity. What is the scope of the legislative discretion with regard to the test of proportionality *stricto sensu*? The answer is that this discretion is narrower than that of the other sub-tests. This discretion does not include the ability to determine whether the limitation on the right in question is proportional *stricto sensu*; such a determination would be made by the courts. What is left, then, for the legislator to decide?

Even before legislating, the legislator should examine whether the legislative purposes can be achieved through proportional means (*stricto sensu*). In most cases, the legislator has several goals and several proportional means to achieve them. Thus, for example, the legislator may face the two following proportional options. In the first, the increase in the public benefit would not be as great but the harm caused to the constitutional right would also not be as great; in the second, the increase in the public benefit would be greater but at a cost of more harm caused to the constitutional right. Both of these options are proportional (*stricto sensu*). In this situation, the legislator has the discretion to choose between the two options.[140] Naturally, we assume that both options satisfy the requirements posed by the proper purpose, necessity, and rational connection

---

[139] See above, at 328.
[140] Rivers, above note 118, at 108; Rivers, above note 42, at 191; R. Alexy, *A Theory of Constitutional Rights* (J. Rivers trans., Oxford University Press, 2002 [1986]).

tests. Another situation that the legislator may face is where only one legislative option exists – which allows for a certain addition to the public security at a certain cost to the right. In this state of affairs the legislative discretion is limited only to the question of whether it should legislate or not.[141] If the legislator chooses to legislate, this can only be done if that legislative option is proportional *stricto sensu*.

ii.   Judicial discretion

The role of the court is to examine whether the legislator's choice is proportional (*stricto sensu*). Once the court reaches the conclusion that the means is proportional (*stricto sensu*), it must determine it as so. This is not an expression of judicial "non-intervention." Neither is it an expression of judicial deference to the legislator. It is simply a judicial declaration that the legislator has acted constitutionally. If the court has concluded that the means is not proportional, it should so determine it. This is a part of its role. The national-constitutional responsibility, as part of the principle of the separation of powers, to review the proper balance between the additional social benefit gained by fulfilling the legislative purpose and the additional harm caused to the constitutional right is ultimately in the hands of the courts.[142] The fact that the legislator was of the opinion that the balance it struck was proportional (*stricto sensu*) does not decide the case. As I noted in one national-security-related case in the Israeli Supreme Court:

> The question is not whether the route of the Separation Fence is proportional according to the view of the military commander. The test in this context is not a subjective examination of the views held by the military commander. The question is not whether the military commander was of the opinion, *bona fide*, that the harm to the right is proportional. Rather, the test is objective. The question is whether, according to the accepted legal standards, the route of the Separation Fence satisfies the requirements of proportionality. This is a legal question, where the court has the professional expertise ... The military commander is the expert on the military nature of the route of the Separation Fence. We are the experts on its humanitarian aspects. The military commander determines where the fence route should pass, either on the mountaintop or in the valley; this is his expertise. We, the judges, examine whether the harm caused by this route to the local residents is proportional. This is our expertise.[143]

---

[141] Regarding the legislator's discretion on this matter, see above, at 400.

[142] Jowell, above note 16, at 78, 81.

[143] HCJ 2056/04 *Beit Sourik Village Council* v. *The Government of Israel* [2004] IsrSC 58(5) 807, 845.

This is true for all types of public interest considerations. It applies whether the considerations are of national security or are social or economic. Whatever the considerations involved, the court has to decide – according to its discretion – whether the marginal social importance of the increase in benefits gained by the public interest is proportional to the marginal social importance of the harm caused to the constitutional right. The judge is not an expert on national security; then again, once the pertinent considerations have been presented, they become an expert in balancing those considerations against the constitutional right.

C.   The zone of proportionality

1.   Its nature

Legislation involves the exercise of legislative discretion. When the act of legislation (or of not legislating) limits a constitutional right, such an act must be proportional. The requirement of proportionality does not entail the removal of legislative discretion; rather, it merely reduces it. The legislator still enjoys a very wide discretion as to whether to legislate at all. Once the decision to legislate has been made, the legislator enjoys a wide discretion as to the legislation's purposes. This wide discretion becomes narrower once the issue becomes the legislative means through which the purposes should be advanced. In this context, the discretion is considerably wide in selecting means that satisfy both the rational connection test and the necessity test – in other words, as long as no other option that fulfills the legislative purpose while causing less harm to the constitutional right exists. This discretion becomes narrower once the question becomes the proper relation between the marginal social importance of achieving that legislative goal and the marginal social importance of preventing the harm to the constitutional right at issue (proportionality *stricto sensu*).

Accordingly, the constitutional requirement that legislation always be proportional does not eliminate legislative discretion. However, it does limit the scope of the discretion. This reduction is not significant and the legislator still enjoys a very wide discretion as to the proper purposes; a considerable discretion in choosing the rational means which will fulfill it, and in selecting the means least restrictive to the right. However, the legislative discretion regarding the proportional relation between achieving the purpose and harming the right in question is reduced.

The conclusion which arises from this analysis is that proportionality recognizes the zones of legislative discretion which satisfy the proportionality requirements. These zones become smaller and smaller the further ahead the legislative process moves. They are most expansive during the first stage – when the legislator must decide whether to legislate or not – and when selecting the proper purpose. Once the purpose has been selected, expansive zones are derived from this for the selection of rational means, and significant zones are derived for the selection of means that are least restrictive to the human right. Once this choice is fulfilled, a rather narrow zone is derived from these zones regarding the proper relation between the marginal social importance of fulfilling the legislative purpose and the marginal social importance of preventing harm to the constitutional right.

These varying zones of legislative discretion are the areas in which the legislator has the leeway to operate. This is the zone of proportionality.[144] This is the zone of legislative discretion.[145] It is the result of the legislative discretion in deciding to legislate, in selecting the legislative purposes and the means that legally limit the constitutional right. As President Beinish of the Israeli Supreme Court has noted:

> When several options are available to the legislator and each may satisfy the requirements of proportionality, the legislator enjoys a legislative leeway dubbed by this Court "the zone of proportionality," in which the legislator may choose whatever option it sees fit. The limits of this legislative leeway, however, are determined, in each specific case, by the court in accordance with the nature of the interests and rights at issue.[146]

The zone of proportionality is determined in accordance with the interpretation provided by the court to the proportionality requirements. It is derived from the alternatives made available by proportionality. A legislative action taken outside the zone of proportionality entails a failure to meet the requirements of proportionality as they were interpreted by the court as part of the constitutional limitation clause. Accordingly, the zone of proportionality describes a normative reality determined by the rules of proportionality and which is derived from that reality. We should not understand the zone of proportionality as a reduction in the number of requirements demanded by proportionality. Once a legislative provision

---

[144] Compare with Gardbaum, above note 3.

[145] See Rivers, above note 42, at 182. See also M. Fordham and T. de la Mare, "Identifying the Principles of Proportionality," in J. Jowell and J. Cooper (eds.), *Understanding Human Rights Principles* (Portland, OR: Hart Publishing, 2001), 27, 83.

[146] HCJ 2605/05 *Academic Center of Law and Business* v. *Minister of Finance* (2009, unpublished), available in English at: http://elyon1.court.gov.il/files_eng/05/050/026/n39/05026050.n39.pdf, para. 46 (Beinisch, P.).

deviates from the zone of proportionality, the law becomes disproportional as it will not satisfy one of the requirements of proportionality. This
is true whether the deviation from the zone of proportionality was significant or marginal.

2.   The zone of proportionality: legislator and judge

The boundaries of the zone of proportionality are the lines separating the
legislator from the judge:[147] "The setting of the national policy and turning it into legislation is the role of the legislative branch; the review of the
constitutionality of the legislation if it disproportionally limits constitutional human rights is the role of the judicial branch."[148] The boundaries
of the zone of proportionality are an expression of the principle of the
separation of powers. The zone of proportionality is the legislator's kingdom; keeping the boundaries intact is the judge's kingdom. Within the
zone of proportionality the legislator is free to choose whether to legislate
and what purpose it wishes to achieve, and to select any means it wishes
to utilize in order to fulfill that purpose. The judge has no opinion about
those choices. The judge's only role is to maintain the boundaries of proportionality and to prevent the selection of disproportional means.

Within the zone of proportionality, legislative discretion is at its widest
when it makes a decision whether or not to legislate and at its narrowest
when determining whether the means selected to advance the legislative
purpose establish an appropriate relation between the purpose and the
limited constitutional right (proportionality *stricto sensu*). While maintaining the boundaries of the zone of proportionality, judicial discretion
stands in reverse correlation to legislative discretion. Thus, judicial discretion is at its narrowest when addressing the legislator's decision as to
whether or not to legislate; it is at its widest when addressing the decision whether the means satisfy the requirements of proportionality *stricto
sensu*.

It is worth once again noting that the notion of the zone of proportionality does not reflect an approach endorsing "non-justiciability" of
legislative determinations, or the deference of the judge to the legislator.
Similarly, it is not based on the assumption that a limitation is not proportional but the court will not intervene on the matter. The opposite

---

[147]   R. v. *Edwards Books*, above note 124, at 872. See also *R. (Farrakhan)* v. *Secretary of State
for the Home Department* [2002] 3 WLR 481, 502.

[148]   *Adalah*, above note 116, at para. 78 (Barak, P.).

is true: by its very definition, the notion of the zone of proportionality assumes that any legislative action within its boundaries is constitutional – and it is precisely for that reason that the court "intervenes" by reviewing the legislation and determining that it is constitutional. The terminology of the zone of proportionality is derived from the notion of the separation of powers. The court leaves intact only those limitations on constitutional rights that it finds to be proportional; in those instances, the court does not do so because it wishes "not to intervene" or due to considerations of judicial deference, but because it is constitutional.

D.   Margin of appreciation

1.   Its nature

The European Court of Human Rights has developed the notion of the "margin of appreciation." The term was accepted by the European Court of Justice, and from there has "migrated" to Inter-American human rights law and the Human Rights Commission of the United Nations. Despite these developments, there is still no consensus in the literature as to the exact nature of the term. Arai-Takahashi defined it as follows:

> The term "margin of appreciation" refers to the latitude a government enjoys in evaluating factual situations and in applying the provisions enumerated in international human rights treaties.[149]

The doctrine thus provides a margin of appreciation to the national actors – the three branches of government. It is based, among others, on the notion that, while no agreement exists at the European (or international) level as to the relative social importance of the public interest or of human rights, a certain weight should be accorded to the opinion of the state against which it was argued that its legislation has disproportionally limited a human right protected by international treaties. Thus,

---

[149] Y. Arai-Takahashi, *The Margin of Appreciation Doctrine and the Principle of Proportionality in the Jurisprudence of the ECHR* (Oxford: Hart Publishing, 2002), 2; H. Yourow, *The Margin of Appreciation Doctrine in the Dynamics of European Human Rights Jurisprudence* (Dordrecht: Martinus Nijhoff Publishers, 1996); G. Letsas, *A Theory of Interpretation of the European Convention on Human Rights* (Oxford University Press, 2009). For a comprehensive list of the literature on this matter, see Arai-Takahashi, above note 149.

for example, in *Handyside*,[150] the English court convicted Handyside for publishing obscene material; the obscene material consisted of the British version of "The Little Red Schoolbook," a then-widely publicized guidebook that contained twenty-six pages on sex for schoolchildren. The European Court of Human Rights examined whether Handyside's right to freedom of expression (which is protected by Article 10(1) of the European Convention on Human Rights[151]) was limited disproportionally by the English courts. The question before the Court was whether the restriction imposed by the United Kingdom satisfied the requirements of Article 10(2)'s limitation clause. The Court thus examined whether the English legislation was an expression of a "pressing social need" that may justify a limitation on the freedom of expression for reasons of "public morals," as determined in Article 10(2). In answering this question, the Court ruled:

> [I]t is not possible to find in the domestic law of the various Contracting States a uniform European conception of morals. The view taken by their respective laws of the requirements of morals varies from time to time and from place to place, especially in our era which is characterized by a rapid and far-reaching evolution of opinions on the subject. By reason of their direct and continuous contact with the vital forces of their countries, State authorities are in principle in a better position than the international judge to give an opinion on the exact content of these requirements as well as on the "necessity" of a "restriction" or "penalty" intended to meet them ... [I]t is for the national authorities to make the initial assessment of the reality of the pressing social need implied by the notion of "necessity" in this context. Consequently, Article 10 para. 2 leaves to the Contracting States a margin of appreciation. This margin is given both to the domestic legislator ("prescribed by law") and to the bodies, judicial among others, that are called upon to interpret and apply the laws in force.[152]

Based on this view, the court decided that there was no violation of Article 10(1).

2. *The margin of appreciation and the zone of proportionality*

The notion of the zone of proportionality examines the constitutionality of a limitation on a human right from a national standpoint.[153] It

---

[150] *Handyside* v. *United Kingdom*, App. No. 5493/72, 1 EHRR 737 (1979).
[151] Convention for the Protection of Human Rights and Fundamental Freedoms, November 4, 1950, 213 *UNTS* 222.
[152] *Handyside*, above note 152, at para. 48.
[153] See above, at 415.

determines the framework of factual and normative data from which the legislator may derive a valid limitation on a human right. The doctrine of the "margin of appreciation" examines the constitutionality of the limitation of a right from the standpoint of the international community. It determines the framework of factual and normative data whose existence allows the international community to provide considerable weight to the factual and normative determinations made by contracting state actors. Against this background, we may consider several of the similarities and differences between the two concepts.

First the similarities. Both concepts deal with the factual and normative data whose existence allows for a limitation on a human right. Both deal, therefore, with the factual data on which the national law is based, as well as the prognosis of their occurrence. Similarly, the two doctrines deal with the relative importance of the marginal social benefit added by fulfilling the law's purposes in relation to the marginal social benefit of preventing the harm caused to the constitutional right.

The difference between the two concepts may be seen, among others, in that the zone of proportionality deals with the factual and normative data that are relevant at the national level. The margin of appreciation, in contrast, deals with factual and normative data relevant to international law treaties, such as the European Convention on Human Rights.[154] In some cases there are major differences between these legal systems. In particular, there are differences in the way each legal system balances the marginal social importance of the benefit to the public interest with the marginal social importance of preventing the harm to the constitutional right as part of proportionality *stricto sensu*. The zone of proportionality reflects this balancing as conducted within the particular national legal system.[155] It is derived from the principle of the separation of powers. The margin of appreciation, in contrast, reflects the line separating the discretion exercised by the state actor – the legislator, the executive, or the judge – and that of the international judge. It is not related to the principle of the separation of powers, but rather is derived from the special relationship of international law treaties (such as the European Convention on Human Rights) to the national law. Accordingly, the concept of the margin of appreciation would apply in the relations between the national judge and the international judge, while the zone of proportionality is not relevant in examining the relationship between the different courts within a single legal system.

[154] Rivers, above note 42, at 175.   [155] See above, at 415.

Against this background of similarities and differences between the two concepts, we may ask what is the proper role of the "margin of appreciation" within a national (domestic) legal system? First, the study of the concept is of major importance, as it may explain and clarify much of the international law decisions and rulings that can also apply locally. It may also contribute to the analysis of comparative law.[156] But these contributions conclude the role of the concept of margin of appreciation for the national (domestic) judge.[157] While ruling on domestic issues, the judge should only base his or her decisions on the notion of the "zone of proportionality." At the basis of such a decision is that legal system's notion of the proper balance between the public interest and individual human rights.

[156] On the role of comparative law in constitutional interpretation, see above, at 65.
[157] Rivers, above note 42, at 175.

15

Proportionality and positive constitutional rights

A. Positive constitutional rights

1. *The nature of positive constitutional rights*

The classic approach to constitutional rights contends that their role – as well as their original function – is to protect the individual from acts of government.[1] They were originally intended to prevent the government from harming individuals and therefore those rights were dubbed "negative" or rights of "inaction" (*status negativus*). Therefore, the textual expression of these rights has often included such terms as "there shall be no limitation of …",[2] "Congress shall make no law …",[3] and everyone has the right "not to be deprived of freedom arbitrarily or without just cause."[4]

Over the years it became clear that the understanding of rights as negative was not comprehensive enough. The need to recognize the double role the government had regarding constitutional rights was emphasized: On the one hand, it should avoid any limitation of constitutional rights; this is the negative aspect. On the other hand, that same government must protect those rights. That is the positive aspect. This protection has two main features. First, the government has to proactively ensure that individuals are able to exercise their constitutional rights. Thus, for example, the government must protect demonstrators of political speech from a hostile crowd.[5] The second element is the state's duty to prevent other individuals from limiting constitutional rights.

---

[1] See D. Grimm, "The Protective Function of the State," in G. Nolte (ed.), *European and US Constitutionalism* (Cambridge University Press, 2005), 138; R. Alexy, *A Theory of Constitutional Rights* (J. Rivers trans., Oxford University Press, 2002 [1986]).

[2] *Ibid.*

[3] US Const., Am. I.

[4] Art. 12(1)(a) of the Constitution of the Republic of South Africa, 1996.

[5] HCJ 2557/05 *Majority Headquarters* v. *Israel Police* [2006] (2) IsrLR 399, 412 (Barak, P.); see HCJ 366/03 *Commitment to Peace and Social Justice* v. *Minister of Finance* [2005]

With these understandings in mind, the recognition of positive constitutional rights (*status positivus*) began taking shape. The content of these rights is the state's duty to actively protect the individual. Thus, the wording used to express this new breed of rights included terms such as "entitled to protection …";[6] "Marriage and the family shall enjoy the special protection of the state."[7]

2. *Positive constitutional rights in comparative law*

Today, the recognition of positive constitutional rights is widespread in constitutional democracies.[8] The scope of that recognition varies from one constitution to another. The most extensive recognition – which applies to all constitutional rights – can be found in the Constitution of the Republic of South Africa. Article 7(2) of that Constitution states:

> The state must respect, protect, promote, and fulfill the rights in the Bill of Rights.[9]

"Respect" refers to the state's duty not to violate constitutional rights; this is the negative aspect of the right. "Protect" refers to the protection of the said rights; this is the positive aspect of the right.[10] Finally, "fulfill" refers to the requirement to exercise the state's duties under the existing framework of constitutional rights; for example, the duty to adopt reasonable legal measures, within the existing means, to advance the fulfillment of several social and economic rights.[11] Germany, too, recognizes positive constitutional rights (*Schutzpflicht*) as applicable to all protected constitutional rights.[12] Therefore, it is possible in both these legal systems to

---

104, 119, available in English at http://elyon1.court.gov.il/files_eng/03/660/003/ a39/03003660.a39.pdf.

[6] Art. 4 of Basic Law: Human Dignity and Liberty.

[7] Art. 6(1) of the Basic Law for the Federal Republic of Germany.

[8] See *Gosselin* v. *Quebec (Attorney General)* [2002] 4 SCR 429, 2002 SCC 84.

[9] Constitution of the Republic of South Africa, Art. 7(2); for interpretation and discussion, see L. M. du Plessis, "Interpretation," in S. Woolman, M. Bishop, and J. Brickhill (eds.), *Constitutional Law of South Africa*, 2nd edn. (Cape Town: Juta Law Publishers, looseleaf, 2002–), para. 32–120.

[10] See *S.* v. *Baloyi (Minister of Justice Intervening)*, 2000 (2) SA 425 (CC).

[11] See, e.g., the Constitution of the Republic of South Africa, the right to access to housing (Art. 26), the right to health care, food, water, and social security (Art. 27), and the right to education (Art. 29). See also S. Liebenberg, "The Interpretation of Socio-Economic Rights," in S. Woolman, M. Bishop, and J. Brickhill (eds.), *Constitutional Law of South Africa*, 2nd edn. (Cape Town: Juta Law Publishers, looseleaf, 2002–).

[12] See K. Hesse, *Grundzüge des Verfassungrechts der Bundesrepublik Deutschland* (Heidelberg: C. F. Müller Verlag, 1999), § 350; M. Sachs, *GG Verfassungsrecht II*.

examine both the negative and the positive aspects of each protected constitutional right.

In most legal systems, however, there is no complete overlapping of the positive and negative aspects. The basic distinction between the positive and negative aspects of a right is well recognized by most of those systems, which also recognize several positive rights. This is the legal situation prescribed by the European Convention on Human Rights.[13] In its decisions, the European Court of Human Rights has recognized[14] a state's duty to investigate homicides;[15] to provide a suspect with explanations for their arrest;[16] to provide legal services to poor defendants;[17] to provide proper gender recognition to those who have undergone sex reassignment surgery;[18] as well as the allocation of reasonable police resources to protect information-gathering organizations from those who attempt, unlawfully and forcefully, to prevent them from fulfilling their role.[19] The same is true for many other constitutions which recognize social and economic rights, often framed as positive rights by the constitutions themselves.[20]

Several legal systems interpret their constitutions so as not to include positive rights. This is the case, for example, in the United States, where the accepted interpretive approach is that the American Bill of Rights includes only negative constitutional rights.[21] The US Supreme Court has

---

Grundrechte (Berlin: Springer, 2003), 44; D. Grimm, "The Protective Function of the State," in G. Nolte (ed.), *European and US Constitutionalism* (Cambridge University Press, 2005); H. Dreier, *GG Grundgesetz Kommentar* (Tübingen: Mohr Siebeck, 2006), 265; B. Pieroth and B. Schlink, *Grundrechte Staatsrecht II* (Heidelberg: C. F. Müller Verlag, 2006), § 58; D. P. Kommers, "Germany: Balancing Rights and Duties," in J. Goldsworthy (ed.), *Interpreting Constitutions: A Comparative Study* (Oxford University Press, 2006), 83; J. Barnes, "The Meaning of the Principle of Proportionality for the Administration," in Schäffer *et al.* (eds.), *Constitutional Principles in Europe* (Societas Iuris Publici, Europaei, Fourth Congress, Göttingen, 2008).

[13] A. Mowbray, *The Development of Positive Obligations under the European Convention on Human Rights by the European Court of Human Rights* (Portland, OR: Hart Publishing, 2004).

[14] *Ibid.*, at 2.

[15] *Kelly* v. *UK*, Eur. Ct. H. R., App. No. 30054/96 (2001).

[16] *Fox, Campbell & Hartley* v. *UK*, App. No. 12244/86, 13 EHRR 157 (1991).

[17] *Artico* v. *Italy*, Eur. Ct. H. R., App. No. 6694/74 (1980).

[18] *Christine Goodwin* v. *UK*, Eur. Ct. H. R., App. No. 28957/95 (2002).

[19] *Ozgur Gundem* v. *Turkey*, Eur. Ct. H. R., App. No. 22492/93 (2000).

[20] S. Fredman, *Human Rights Transformed: Positive Rights and Positive Duties* (Oxford University Press, 2008); H. Shue, *Basic Rights: Subsistence, Affluence and US Foreign Policy*, 2nd edn. (Princeton University Press, 1996), 155.

[21] See, e.g., *Jackson* v. *City of Joliet*, 715 F 2d 1200, 1203 (7th Cir. 1982) ("[The Bill of Rights] is a charter of negative rather than positive liberties … The men who wrote the Bill of

refused to interpret it as imposing duties on the state to positively act to protect individuals.[22] These decisions have been severely criticized.[23]

3. The legal source of positive constitutional rights

i. The constitutional text and its interpretation

The literature on positive constitutional rights is vast. One of the major contributors to this trend is the growing interest in constitutionally protected social and economic rights; these rights, in their very essence, are positive rights. Another reason for the growing interest in positive rights is the growing number of dangers posed to individual members of the community by non-state actors. Thus, for example, the dangers stemming from modern technology – such as the collection of personal data by private companies – is sometimes greater than similar dangers imposed by the government itself. Moreover, the growing trend of privatization in economies across the globe often releases states from their negative duties, in most cases without imposing similar duties on the private actor that replaces them. In order to properly protect individuals against these developments, it is necessary to recognize positive duties on the state in areas where only negative duties have previously been recognized.[24] However, to the extent that we are seeking to provide a constitutional status to those positive duties we must look for their source in the constitution. This source could be a general constitutional provision, such as the one found in Article 7(2) of the Constitution of the Republic of South Africa that grants a positive constitutional aspect to all the rights included in the Constitution.[25] But, even without a general constitutional

---

Rights were not concerned that Government might do too little for the people but that it might do too much to them." (Posner, J.)). State constitutions may include positive rights: see *Baker* v. *State of Vermont*, 744 A 2d 864 (1999).

[22] See S. F. Kreimer, "Allocational Sanctions: The Problem of Negative Rights in a Positive State," 132 *U. Pa. L. Rev.* 1293 (1984); M. Tushnet, "An Essay on Rights," 62 *Tex. L. Rev.* 1363 (1984); L. H. Tribe, "The Abortion Funding Conundrum: Inalienable Rights, Affirmative Duties, and the Dilemma of Dependence," 99 *Harv. L. Rev.* 330 (1985); *Deshaney* v. *Winnebago County Department of Social Services*, 109 S Ct 998 (1989); *Webster* v. *Reproductive Health Services*, 109 S Ct 3040 (1989).

[23] See D. P. Currie, "Positive and Negative Constitutional Rights," 53 *U. Chi. L. Rev.* 864 (1986); S. A. Bandes, "The Negative Constitution: A Critique," 88 *Mich. L. Rev.* 2271 (1989). See also C. R. Sunstein, *The Second Bill of Rights: FDR's Unfinished Revolution and Why We Need It More Than Ever* (New York: Basic Books, 2004), 1.

[24] See Grimm, above note 1, at 147.

[25] See above, at 423.

provision, a positive constitutional status may be recognized through specific provisions, such as Article 4 of Israel's Basic Law: Human Dignity and Liberty.[26]

What happens when the constitution contains neither a general provision relating to the positive aspect of the rights nor a specific one? What does the "constitutional silence," in relation to the positive aspect of constitutional rights mean? Take, for example, a provision of Basic Law: Human Dignity and Liberty, according to which "all persons are free to leave Israel."[27] Obviously, the provision imposes a negative duty on the state to refrain from preventing anyone from leaving Israel; but does it also impose a positive duty upon the state to actively enable someone to leave?

The answer to this question is interpretive in nature. As we have seen,[28] in the United States, the Supreme Court concluded that the Bill of Rights should be interpreted as containing only negative rights. This interpretive conclusion was supported by the expressly negative language of many of the rights in the Bill of Rights (notably, "Congress shall make no law ..."[29]). But what is the answer when the wording – even in the US Constitution – is neutral, such as the right to counsel – "the accused shall enjoy the right ... to have the assistance of counsel for his defense"?[30]

When a constitution contains no express provision relating either directly to positive constitutional rights or to the positive aspect of existing negative rights, the next step is to examine whether the constitution contains any relevant implied provisions.[31] The mere fact that, in some cases, several specific provisions include an explicit statement relating to the existence of a positive aspect of the constitutional right should not be interpreted as a "negative solution" with respect to the existence of other positive aspects of rights across the constitution. Every right should be interpreted in accordance with its own underlying reasons.[32]

Thus we return to the question: what is the legal source for recognizing the positive constitutional rights or their positive aspects? One answer is that the constitutional "silence" on the matter is a gap (lacuna) which requires judicial filling.[33] This approach would be of no use in those legal

---

[26] See above, at 423.
[27] Art. 6(a) of Basic Law Human Dignity and Liberty, above note 6.
[28] See above, at 424.   [29] US Const., Am. I.
[30] US Const., Am. IV. See Currie, above note 23, at 873.
[31] Regarding implied constitutional provisions, see above, at 53.
[32] Regarding negative solutions, see above, at 68.
[33] Regarding gap and gap-filling, see above, at 56.

systems where such judicial gap-filling is not recognized. At times the positive aspects of rights may be derived from the right to equality, such as through affirmative action.[34] But what is the case when these sources are to no avail?

ii. The objective nature of values as a source for the positive aspect of constitutional rights

Constitutional rights are not merely subjective rights *vis-à-vis* the state. They also constitute objective constitutional values,[35] which, in turn, may be used as a source for imposing a duty upon the state to act.[36] Thus, for example, the objective value of freedom of expression imposes on the state not only the duty not to limit that freedom but also the duty to actively protect it. Similarly, the subjective constitutional right to life creates an objective value of bodily integrity, from which one may derive the conclusion that the constitutional right to life is not merely a subjective right with a negative aspect but also a right with an objective aspect.[37] Take, for example, the right to privacy. In Israel, according to Basic Law: Human Dignity and Liberty: "all persons have the right of privacy and intimacy."[38] The negative aspect of the right demands that the state not take any action which would limit those individual rights. The positive aspect of these same rights imposes a duty on the state to prevent any limitation on those rights by third parties. This is especially true whenever the limitation is known to the state, but the state refrains from protecting privacy.

This approach is interpretive in its essence. It can provide the wording of the constitutional rights with a positive meaning and therefore recognize the positive aspect. This can only be applied where the wording of the constitutional right is neutral; but what happens when the constitutional text is clearly negative? How can the objective values extract a positive aspect from the negative text? Surely such values cannot create a positive constitutional right whenever such a right does not exist.

4. Constitutional positive aspect and constitutional positive right

Does every positive constitutional aspect mean the existence of a positive constitutional right? Could a positive aspect be recognized without

---

[34] See Fredman, above note 20, at 3.   [35]   See above, at 276.

[36] See the first abortion decision by the German Constitutional Court, BVerfGE 39, 1.

[37] See Grimm, above note 1, at 147.

[38] Art. 7(A) of Israeli Basic Law: Human Dignity and Liberty, above note 6.

recognizing a positive right? Take, for example, the German Constitutional Court's first abortion case.[39] The German legislator had determined that, as long as the abortion was performed within the first twelve weeks of the pregnancy by an authorized physician and with the woman's consent, no criminal responsibility was involved. The German Constitutional Court ruled that the law was unconstitutional in that it violated the fetus' human dignity. Thus, the legislator was required to reenact the law in a way that would guarantee the fetus' human dignity by imposing proper criminal sanctions. The petition was filed by the members of parliament as part of an abstract judicial review process.[40] The Court's decision did not state that the fetus enjoys a constitutional right as the decision never dealt with the issue of whether or not fetuses may be the subject of legal rights and duties.

Is this a case where the state is bound by a constitutional duty while no individual may claim an opposite constitutional right? The answer is in the negative. Opposite the state's constitutional duty stands the individual's constitutional right.[41] A separate issue is the possible remedies for non-performance of that duty. Would the legislator's duty to legislate and the individual's constitutional right to demand this legislation be recognized? This issue has yet to be resolved by the German courts.[42] According to my approach, the answer to this question is positive.

Do these questions – whether a duty exists without a right, or whether there is a duty to legislate – suggest that positive constitutional rights are fundamentally different – "genetically" – from negative rights? This issue has led to an intense discussion particularly in the context of social and economic constitutional rights. It has been argued that in light of the special nature of the positive constitutional rights – in particular, the direct relationship between the state's duty and the national resources – those rights are not justiciable.[43] The argument here was that it would be inappropriate for the judges to require the legislator to perform actions

---

[39] See BVerfGE 39, 1. Subsequently, there arose the second abortion case: BVerfGE 88, 203.

[40] Regarding the abstract judicial review process in German constitutional law, see D. Kommers, *The Constitutional Jurisprudence of the Federal Republic of Germany*, 2nd edn. (Durham, NC: Duke University Press, 1997), 13. Regarding judicial review in European constitutional courts, see V. Ferreres Comella, *Constitutional Courts and Democratic Values: A European Perspective* (New Haven, CT: Yale University Press, 2009), 66.

[41] See Alexy, above note 1, at 301; Grimm, above note 1, at 153.

[42] See Grimm, above note 1, at 153.

[43] See E. Palmer, *Judicial Review, Socio-Economic Rights and the Human Rights Act* (Portland, OR: Hart Publishing, 2007), 26; D. Barak-Erez and A. M. Gross (eds.), *Exploring Social Rights: Between Theory and Practice* (2007).

that would change the allocation of national resources. Thus, for example, the Constitution of India establishes,[44] in its fourth part, several duties to be imposed on the state; it then states that these duties are not enforceable by any court.[45] This is not the only approach. Many legal systems do recognize positive constitutional rights – either social, economic, or others – as well as their justifiability. Those rights suffer no genetic defect. However, they do, at times, justify a special attitude by the state. One of the instances where such a special attitude is required by positive constitutional rights is the application of the constitutional rules of proportionality. This application will now be discussed.

B. Positive constitutional rights and proportionality's components

1. Positive rights as relative rights

Positive constitutional rights are, like the majority of negative constitutional rights, relative rights.[46] Thus, avoiding a positive constitutional duty – much like imposing a limitation on a negative right – does not automatically render the omission unconstitutional. The omission is unconstitutional and one could move on to the stage of constitutional remedies, only where the omission is disproportional. Indeed, the two-stage model[47] applies to positive constitutional rights as well. During the first stage we examine whether the omission by the state actor limits the constitutional right. If the answer to this question is yes, we proceed to examine, during the second stage, whether the omission was justified. The rules of proportionality determine whether such a justification exists.

The determination that an omission is disproportional in relation to a positive right is reached much in the same way as the determination that a limitation on a negative right was disproportional. First, one has to establish the scope of the positive constitutional right in question. That task is achieved through the process of constitutional interpretation, and the rules of constitutional interpretation apply.[48] The positive constitutional

---

[44] See Constitution of India, Chapter 4, Arts. 36–51.

[45] *Ibid*. Art. 37 ("The provisions contained in this Part shall not be enforceable by any court, but the principles therein laid down are nevertheless fundamental in the governance of the country and it shall be the duty of the State to apply these principles in making laws.").

[46] Regarding relative rights, see above, at 32.

[47] Regarding the two-stage model, see above, at 19.

[48] See above, at 45.

right, much like the negative one, is interpreted from a generous view-point.[49] The scope of the positive constitutional right may conflict with the scope of another constitutional right – whether positive or negative. The resolution of the conflict is not through the limitation of the scope of the positive constitutional right; rather, the solution is found at the sub-constitutional level (a statute or the common law).[50]

The examination of a limitation on a negative right does not proceed to the second stage unless it is first established that the limitation was imposed "by law." This is an application of the principle of legality: a "chain of authorization" must be established all the way up to the constitution.[51] Do the same requirements apply to positive rights? The answer to this question is yes. In order for the legislator's omission (in protecting the positive right) to be justified, this justification must be based upon a legal provision, which is "by law." If the positive rights were limited by the state without any legislative provision, the state would be unable to justify its omission.[52] Thus, the limitation clause is able to provide a justification to the state's omission only where that omission is not complete (i.e., a complete evasion of the duty to protect the right) but rather partial (i.e., some protection was offered but, according to the argument, it is insufficient).

Assuming the omission limits a positive constitutional right in accordance with a law – and the burden falls on the party so arguing[53] – then the constitutional review moves to the second stage, that of justification. Here, the burden lies with the party arguing for this justification.[54] That party must present the factual framework that would allow the court to conclude that the inaction of the relevant state actor, in these circumstances, was proportional. This issue will now be examined.

2. The proper purpose component

The examination of proportionality regarding the omission in fulfilling the positive constitutional right begins with the purpose component.

---

[49] See above, at 69. [50] See above, at 89. [51] See above, at 108.
[52] See S. Liebenberg, "The Interpretation of Socio-Economic Rights," in S. Woolman, M. Bishop, and J. Brickhill (eds.), Constitutional Law of South Africa, 2nd edn. (Cape Town: Juta Law Publishers, looseleaf, 2002–), 55; S. Woolman and H. Botha, "Limitations," in S.Woolman, M. Bishop, and J. Brickhill (eds.), Constitutional Law of South Africa, 2nd edn. (Cape Town: Juta Law Publishers, looseleaf, 2002–), 60; President of the Republic of South Africa v. Modderklip Boerdery (Pty) Ltd., 2005 (5) SA 3 (CC); August v. Electoral Commission, 1999 (3) SA 1 (CC).
[53] See below, at 437. [54] See below, at 439.

Much like in negative rights,[55] positive rights, too, require that the limitation be done to advance a proper purpose. The question is whether the reason for not protecting the constitutional right is proper. This examination is conducted according to the same criteria that guide the examination of a limitation on negative rights. Thus, for example, if the only reason offered for the omission is a desire not to protect the right in question, this is not a proper purpose. But, if the reason was either to protect the rights of others or to protect national security interests – these could serve as proper purposes, so long as the proper factual framework has been laid to establish the degree of urgency of the omission as well as its prognosis. Every legal system has its own proper purpose tests. Thus, the prevention of the limitation of a negative right is a proper purpose for not having protected a positive right.

The legislative omission should be examined in accordance with the proper purpose test only if the omission is "partial" – that is, there is a legislative provision designed to protect the positive right, but this legislation is not sufficiently protective. When no legislation exists, its absence cannot be justified. The move to the justification stage – e.g., the justification relating to the proper purpose – occurs only when a legislative provision protecting the constitutional right exists, but the claim is that this legislation is not enough and therefore limits the positive constitutional right disproportionally. The party arguing that the omission is constitutional must show that the avoidance of taking further steps to protect the positive right was for a proper purpose. The scope of the discretion granted to the legislator in this context is very wide: it applies both to the question of whether to enact further legislation at all, as well as to the question of the proper purpose of the said legislation, and what means should be selected to fulfill it.[56]

The judicial discretion in these matters is extremely narrow.[57] This is true both for judicial discretion in examining the question of whether the legislator should have enacted additional legislation at all and in reviewing the issue of the appropriateness of the legislative purposes. This narrow judicial discretion is not the result of judicial deference to the legislator;[58] rather, the scope of the judicial discretion is directly derived from the wide discretion granted to the legislator. With regard to the negative rights,

---

[55] See above, at 245.
[56] See Grimm, above note 1, at 150.
[57] See above, at 403.
[58] Regarding judicial deference, see above, at 396.

the limitation can be prevented by simply avoiding such legislation; with regard to positive rights, an elimination of the legislative omission may be obtained in many ways. The choice between those is in the hands of the legislator, and well within its discretion.[59]

3.   The rational connection component

The rational connection test that applies in the context of negative rights applies to positive rights as well. In both cases, the means selected by the legislator must fit the chosen purposes.[60] There is no need to prove certainty as to the completion of the purposes. All that is required is to prove more than a minimal probability that the purposes will be fulfilled, even if only partially.[61] In the context of positive rights, the requirement is for a rational connection between the insufficient legislation (the "relative" or "partial" omission) and the proper purpose underlying the insufficient legislation.[62] In most cases, this requirement is not too difficult to satisfy. In some cases, however, avoiding the protection of the constitutional right does not contribute to the fulfillment of the proper purpose. Take, for example, the South African case of *Treatment Action Campaign*.[63] In that case, decided in the Constitutional Court of South Africa, the state violated its positive duty to take reasonable steps to ensure medical services within its financial means.[64] This was expressed, for example, in that the state refused to accept as a gift drugs that could prevent the infection of children with the HIV virus from their mothers. Such an omission, the South African Constitutional Court ruled, cannot satisfy the requirement of a rational connection since it cannot fulfill, in any way, the proper purpose.

The legislator enjoys a considerable discretion regarding the rational connection component; this is true for negative rights[65] and positive rights. The judicial discretion here is extremely limited; this is true for both negative rights[66] and positive rights.

[59]   See Grimm, above note 1, at 150.
[60]   See above, at 303.   [61]   See above, at 305.
[62]   See Grimm, above note 1, at 150.
[63]   *Minister of Health* v. *Treatment Action Campaign*, 2002 (5) SA 721 (CC).
[64]   The positive right in question appears in Art. 27 of the Constitution of the Republic of South Africa.
[65]   See above, at 405.   [66]   See above, at 406.

4. The necessity component

The necessity component imposes on the legislator the duty to select from all the means available to advance the proper purpose – those that would advance that purpose while least limiting the constitutional right.[67] The necessity test imposes, on the legislator, the duty to choose a hypothetical legislative alternative that would advance the legislative purpose to the same degree, while limiting the constitutional rights less. This test operates regarding both negative and positive rights. Accordingly, to satisfy this test, there should be no possible alternative which would fulfill the proper purposes to the same extent while providing better protection to the positive constitutional right. If that additional protection of the positive constitutional right requires the additional limitation of the (negative) rights of others or the limitation of the public interest beyond what is required by the legislator (as stated by the proper purpose), then the test has been satisfied. Much like negative rights, the same is true for positive rights: the legislative discretion is considerable. It determines the proper means.

5. The proportionality stricto sensu component

Proportionality *stricto sensu* is a balancing component.[68] It balances between the marginal social importance to the public interest or another constitutional right gained by fulfilling the legislative purpose against the marginal social importance of the prevention of the harm to the constitutional right. The basic rule of balancing states that the more important the prevention of the marginal harm to the constitutional right and the greater the probability of its occurrence, then it is required that the marginal benefits to the public interest or to another constitutional right must be of greater social importance and more urgency and the probability of their occurrence must be greater.[69]

This basic rule of balancing also applies in balancing the fulfillment of the public interest or another constitutional right and the non-fulfillment of the positive constitutional right. Thus, in its positive form, the basic balancing rule requires that the more important the marginal protection

---

[67] See above, at 317.
[68] See above, at 343.
[69] See above, at 362.

of the positive constitutional right and the greater the chances of fulfilling that right, then the requirement that the marginal benefits to the public interest or to another constitutional right by avoiding the enactment of legislation should be more socially important and more urgent, and the probability of their occurrence greater.

An example of the application of the proportionality *stricto sensu* component to positive rights can be found in the German Constitutional Court's first abortion case.[70] There, the Court reviewed a law that provided, among others, that there is no criminal responsibility involved when an abortion is performed during the first twelve weeks of the pregnancy, by a certified physician, and with the consent of the pregnant woman. The Court held that the law limited the protection granted by the Basic Law to the life of a person in accordance with Article 2(2) of the Basic Law.[71] This limitation was meant to enable the pregnant woman to practice her right to freely develop her personality in accordance with Article 2(1).[72] The Court then balanced the social importance of taking action to protect the life of the fetus and the social importance of allowing the mother to freely develop her personality.[73] The Court concluded that the protection of the life of the fetus was more important, and therefore ruled:

> In the ensuing balancing process ... the decision must come down in favor of the preeminence of protecting the fetus' life over the right of self-determination of the pregnant woman. Pregnancy, birth, and child-rearing may impair the woman's [right of self-determination] as to many personal developmental potentialities. The termination of pregnancy, however, destroys prenatal life. Pursuant to the principle of carefully balancing competing constitutionally protected positions ... [the state] must give the protection of the unborn child's life priority.[74]

That decision was later revised.[75] However, the principle regarding the application of proportionality *stricto sensu* as to the omission of adequately protecting such a right – has not changed.

---

[70] 39 BVerfGE 1 (1975).
[71] Art. 2(2) states, according to its formal translation: "Every person shall have the right to life and physical integrity ..."
[72] Art. 2(1) states, according to its formal translation: "Every person shall have the right to free development of his personality ..."
[73] Grimm, above note 1, at 151.
[74] Translation by D. Kommers, *The Constitutional Jurisprudence of the Federal Republic of Germany*, 2nd edn. (Durham, NC: Duke University Press, 1977), 339.
[75] See 88 BVerfGE 203 (1993). See also Kommers, above note 74, at 349.

16

The burden of proof

A. The issue presented

A petitioner argues before the court[1] that a constitutional right was disproportionally limited by law. Who bears the burden of proof in this matter? This issue does *not* relate to proving the law. Rather, it is related to proving the facts upon which the claim – that the right has been disproportionally limited – rests. The question relates to issues of the burden of persuasion and the burden of producing evidence. The constitutional approach is based upon the two-stage model.[2] At the first stage, the question examined is, when a constitutional right has been limited, who bears the burden during this stage? Does the burden lie with the party arguing that the right has been limited,[3] or with the party claiming no such limitation has occurred?[4] At the second stage, the question is whether such a limitation is justified, and therefore valid. The answer to that question lies within the rules of proportionality in the limitation clause. Who bears the burden of proof (both the burden of persuasion and the burden of producing the evidence) during this stage? Does it lie with the party arguing for the justification, or with the party arguing that no such justification exists?

---

[1] In most cases, issues of burden of proof arise in "vertical-type" litigation where an individual files a claim against a state actor. However, the same type of issues may arise in more conventional, "horizontal-type" litigation where an individual brings a suit against another individual or a corporation in a civil court. In Israel, the seminal *United Mizrahi Bank* case was the of the latter type, where a bank was sued in a civil court. See CA 6821/93 *United Mizrahi Bank Ltd.* v. *Migdal Cooperative Village* [1995] IsrLR 1.

[2] See above, at 26.

[3] Note that the person who makes that argument is most likely the person whose right was limited, but it could also be another person who has standing.

[4] See M. Kazazi, *Burden of Proof and Related Issues: A Study on Evidence before International Tribunals* (London: Kluwer Law International, 1996), 42; J. Kokott, *The Burden of Proof in Comparative and International Human Rights Law* (London: Kluwer Law International, 1998), 36.

B.   The burden of proof: facts and law

The burden of proof plays a role regarding the facts. It is irrelevant regarding legal issues. The court knows the law (*iura novit curia*). One can argue that the "burden of proof" on issues of law rests with the court itself, as in the old Latin saying: "Just provide me with the facts, and I will provide you with the law" (*da miti facta, dato tibi ius*). Further, the court cannot "pass on" its "burden" to any of the parties. The burden of proof issue is not relevant in the context of whether the limited right is constitutionally protected or not. This is an issue of law, and therefore the notion of burden of proof does not apply. The same is true regarding the right's scope and the interpretation of the legislative provision that, according to the argument, has limited the right. Similarly, the burden of proof plays no role in deciding whether a limitation on a right occurred "by law,"[5] or whether the purpose, according to which the right has been limited, is proper or not.[6] All these issues are matters of law, relating either directly to the constitutional interpretation of the limitation clause or to the statutory interpretation of the legislative provision that has limited the constitutional right. In matters of legal interpretation, the notion of the burden of proof plays no role. Therefore, the issue of burden of proof is not raised in relation to the interpretation of constitutional provisions relating to proportionality. The scope of these and similar provisions are a matter for the court.

When does the notion of the burden of proof become relevant in these matters? The burden is relevant whenever the application of the law is predicated on a fact. Thus, for example, the very notion of a limitation on a constitutional right requires a limitation. The term "limitation" is a legal term[7] whose interpretation and scope are matters for the court, and therefore there is no application of the burden of proof; the actual events that led to the result of the argued limitation are issues of fact, and, therefore, the burden of proof applies. Similarly, proportionality is a matter of law; therefore, there is no application of issues of the burden of proof. Then again, the events that lead to the conclusion that the limitation has been proportional – these events are matters of facts, where the burden of proof is applicable.

This chapter does not deal with legal interpretation, but rather with proving facts. In particular, this chapter deals with the burden of proof within these facts. Who bears that burden? Does it lie with the party

---

[5] See above, at 107.   [6] See above, at 245.
[7] See above, at 101.

arguing that a limitation has occurred, or with the person arguing that no such limitation has occurred? Does the burden lie with the party arguing for a justification of the said limitation, or with the party arguing that no such justification exists?

C.   The burden of persuasion and the burden of producing evidence

The term "burden of proof" or "onus of proof" is an aggregate term that consists of two separate burdens: the burden of persuasion and the burden of producing evidence. The burden of persuasion is the burden of one party to persuade the court that the facts presented entitle that party to a right claimed against the other party. The question of whether that party has lifted the burden of persuasion is examined at the end of the judicial process. If, at the end of the process, the two ends of the factual scales are completely balanced, then the party who brought the suit has failed to lift the burden of persuasion. The burden of producing evidence, in contrast, may shift from one party to the next during the judicial process; this is the burden of producing the facts and presenting them to the court.

D.   The first stage of constitutional review: a limitation of a constitutional right

The first stage examines the limitation on the constitutional right. Such an examination requires two separate inquiries. The first relates to the scope of the constitutional right at issue: what are its boundaries, what is included in the right, and what is external to it. This inquiry relates to the interpretation of the constitutional right in accordance with the rules of constitutional interpretation.[8] This is an inquiry of a legal nature and the issue of the burden of proof plays no part. The second examination is whether the law has limited a constitutional right. This inquiry requires, naturally, the limiting law to be provided with a meaning. This is carried out through the rules of statutory interpretation.[9] This too is for the court to decide. However, the second inquiry is not limited to an interpretation of the limiting law. It also contains the issue of the limitation itself, namely, whether the law has actually limited the constitutional right. "Limitation"

---

[8] See above, at 45.
[9] On statutory interpretation, see A. Barak, *Purposive Interpretation in Law* (Sari Bashi trans., Princeton University Press, 2005), 339.

in this context means that the owner of the right is unable to exercise
the right to its fullest extent, that is, to the extent it would be available
should the limitation not occur.[10] The decision that a limitation actually
took place must be based on a comparison between the constitutional text
(relating to the right's scope) and the limiting law (relating to the limitation's scope). When the comparison is of an abstract nature – sometimes
referred to as an "abstract review" – these are the only components of the
comparison. In many constitutional democracies, however, most of the
judicial comparisons are not merely abstract; rather, they are of a concrete
nature – these are concrete reviews, based on the occurrence of a concrete
(alleged) limitation.[11] This concrete limitation, in turn, is based on a specific set of facts. Who, then, bears the burden of proof (i.e., both the burden of persuasion and the burden of producing evidence) regarding the
existence of facts which establish the existence of a concrete limitation on
a constitutional right? The answer is that, during the first stage of the constitutional review, the burden of proof lies with the party claiming that
such a limitation has occurred. As Justice Ackerman of the South African
Constitutional Court has noted:

> The task of interpreting ... fundamental rights rests, of course, with the
> courts, but it is for the applicants to prove the facts upon which they rely
> for their claim of infringement of a particular right in question.[12]

Similarly, I noted in the Israeli case of *United Mizrahi Bank*:

> It seems that there is no dispute over the proposition that at the first stage
> of the constitutional review – establishing that a limitation on a consti-
> tutional human right has occurred – the burden of persuasion lies with
> the party arguing that such a limitation has occurred. The presumption
> is that the legislative provision is constitutional ... The party seeking to
> refute that presumption bears the burden of doing so.[13]

---

[10] See above, at 101.
[11] On abstract review, concrete review, and the comparison between them, see L.
Favoreu, "Constitutional Review in Europe," in L. Henkin and A. J. Rosenthal (eds.),
Constitutionalism and Rights: The Influence of the United States Constitution Abroad (New
York: Columbia University Press, 1990); A. Brewer-Carias, *Judicial Review in Comparative
Law* (Cambridge University Press, 1989); V. Ferreres Comella, *Constitutional Courts and
Democratic Values: A European Perspective* (New Haven, CT: Yale University Press, 2009).
[12] CCT 23/95 *Ferreira v. Levin NO*, 1996 (1) SA 984 (CC), § 44. See M. Chaskalson, G.
Marcus, and M. Bishop, "Constitutional Litigation," in S. Woolman, M. Bishop, and
J. Brickhill (eds.), *Constitutional Law of South Africa*, 2nd edn. (Cape Town: Juta Law
Publishers, looseleaf, 2002–), 3–7.
[13] See *United Mizrahi Bank*, above note 1, at para. 84.

This approach[14] is based on the view that the party initiating a claim against another should prove his argument. It may, of course, be based on the special approach regarding the presumption of constitutionality that applies on every law;[15] that presumption places the burden of proof on the party arguing that the limitation of their constitutional right exists.

E.   The second stage of constitutional review: justification of the limitation of a right

1.   The elements which make up the justification of the limitation of a right

The second stage of the constitutional review focuses on the existence – or lack thereof – of a justification for the limitation on the right. The basic approach is that human rights found in the constitution are not "absolute"; rather, they are relative.[16] They may be limited. This limitation is constitutional only if it has a legal justification. The justification is found in the rules of proportionality, which are a part of the limitation clause.[17] The question we now face is who bears the burden of establishing the different components of proportionality. This question relates only to the factual aspects of these components. The question did not create many difficulties in most legal systems. It has been established that the burden of proof (both the burden of persuasion and the burden of producing evidence) lies with the party arguing for the justification.[18]

2.   Comparative analysis

i.   Canada

The human rights in the Canadian Charter of Rights and Freedoms are usually formulated in absolute terms. Thus, for example, Section 2 of the Charter reads:

---

[14] P. W. Hogg, *Constitutional Law of Canada*, 5th edn., vol. II (Toronto: Thomson Carswell, 2007), 117; S. Woolman and H. Botha, "Limitations," in S.Woolman, M. Bishop, and J. Brickhill (eds.), *Constitutional Law of South Africa*, 2nd edn. (Cape Town: Juta Law Publishers, looseleaf, 2002–).

[15] Regarding that presumption, see below, at 444.

[16] See above, at 27.

[17] Regarding the limitation clauses, see above, at 141.

[18] See below, at 439–444.

Everyone has the following fundamental freedoms:

(a) freedom of conscience and religion;
(b) freedom of thought, belief, opinion and expression, including freedom of the press and other media of communication;
(c) freedom of peaceful assembly; and
(d) freedom of association.

The relative nature of those rights, that is, the constitutional ability to lawfully limit them, stems from the general limitation clause appearing in Section 1 of the Charter:

> The Canadian Charter of Rights and Freedoms guarantees the rights and freedoms set out in it subject only to such reasonable limits prescribed by law as can be demonstrably justified in a free and democratic society.

By virtue of this constitutional structure – rights phrased as "absolute" and the general limitation clause which turns them into "relative" rights – the Canadian case law has deduced the notion of a two-stage constitutional review. It is agreed that the party arguing that a limitation has occurred bears the burden of proof during the first stage. But who bears the burden during the second stage of the constitutional review? The question was raised and decided in the *Oakes* case.[19] As Chief Justice Dickson wrote:

> The onus of proving that a limit on a right or freedom guaranteed by the Charter is reasonable and demonstrably justified in a free and democratic society rests upon *the party seeking to uphold the limitation*. It is clear from the text of Section 1 that limits on the rights and freedoms enumerated in the Charter are exceptions to their general guarantee. The presumption is that the rights and freedoms are guaranteed unless the party invoking Section 1 can bring itself within the exceptional criteria which justify their being limited. This is further substantiated by the use of the word "demonstrably" which clearly indicates that the onus of justification is on the party seeking to limit.[20]

Oakes is good law in Canada in that respect; all Canadian courts act according to it.[21] The same approach is followed in New Zealand.[22]

[19] See *R. v. Oakes* [1986] 1 SCR 103. For the case analysis, see above, at 303.
[20] *Ibid.*, para. 66 (Dickson, C.J.) (emphasis added).
[21] See Hogg, above note 14, at 117.
[22] *Police* v. *Curran* [1992] 3 NZLR 260 (CA); *Minister of Transport* v. *Noort* [1992] 3 NZLR 260, 283 (CA); P. Rishworth, G. Huscroft, S. Optican and R. Mahoney, *The New Zealand*

ii.   South Africa and the International Covenant on Civil and Political Rights

The Bill of Rights of the 1996 Constitution of the Republic of South African is based upon the two-stage doctrine. Who bears the burden during the second stage? The South African Constitutional Court has ruled that the burden of proof – both the burden of persuasion and the burden of producing evidence – lies with the party arguing for the existence of a justification.[23]

A similar approach was adopted by the International Covenant on Civil and Political Rights of 1966.[24] According to Article 12 of the Siracusa Principles on the Limitation and Derogation of Provisions in the International Covenant on Civil and Political Rights (1984), the "burden of justifying a limitation upon a right guaranteed under the Covenant lies with the state."[25]

iii.   European Convention on Human Rights and Fundamental Freedoms

The European Convention on Human Rights and Fundamental Freedoms[26] is mostly based upon the two-stage doctrine. Thus, for example, Article 8(1) (right to respect for privacy and family life), Article 9(1) (freedom of thought, conscience, and religion), and Article 10(1) (freedom of expression) define the rights included therein. The concomitant provisions – Articles 8(2), 9(2), and 10(2), respectively – are special limitation

---

Bill of Rights (Auckland: Oxford University Press, 2003), 68; A. S. Butler, "Limiting Rights," 33 *Victoria U. Wellington L. Rev.* 113, 116 (2002).

[23] *S. v. Makwanyane*, 1995 (3) SA 391 § 102: "[I]t is for the legislature, or the party relying on the legislation, to establish this justification, and not for the party challenging it to show that it was not justified"; *S. v. Zuma*, 1995 (2) SA 642 (CC); *Moise v. Greater Germiston Transitional Local Council*, 2001 (4) SA 491 § 19: "It is also no longer doubted that, once a limitation has been found to exist, the burden of justification under section 36(1) rests on the party asserting that the limitation is saved by the application of the provisions of the section. The weighing up exercise is ultimately concerned with the proportional assessment of competing interests but, to the extent that justification rests on factual and/or policy Considerations, the party contending for justification must put such material before the Court." See also Woolman and Botha, above note 14, at 34–44; Chaskalson, Marcus, and Bishop, above note 12, at 3–7.

[24] Adopted by the UN General Assembly in December 1966, entered into force March 1976.

[25] See Principle 12A of "The Siracusa Principles on the Limitation and Derogation Provisions in the International Covenant on Civil and Political Rights," 7 *Hum. Rts. Q.* 3 (1985).

[26] Convention for the Protection of Human Rights and Fundamental Freedoms, November 4, 1950, 213 *UNTS* 222.

clauses stating that those rights may not be limited unless such limitations are prescribed by law and are necessary in a democratic society; the special limitation clauses also prescribe the special social values that should be protected in the case of such limitations (such as the "interests of public safety," "the protection of public order, health or morals," or "the protection of the rights and freedoms of others").

According to the accepted view, once the party has met the burden of proof as to the limitation of the right (first stage), the burden is shifted to the other party to justify this limitation, in accordance with Articles 8(2), 9(2), and 10(2) (second stage).[27] In that respect, the distinction between the burden of persuasion and the burden of production of evidence plays no role.

iv.   England

In 1998, the United Kingdom adopted the Human Rights Act. The Act incorporates the European Convention on Human Rights and Fundamental Freedoms into UK law. The Act states (in section 4) that, whenever a court is satisfied that a provision of primary legislation is incompatible with a Convention right, it may make a declaration of incompatibility. The Act goes on to establish a review process based on the two-stage doctrine. The burden lies, first, with the party arguing that their right was limited. Once that burden has been met, the burden of justification shifts to the party arguing that such a limitation is compatible with the provisions of the Human Rights Act.[28]

F.   The burden of persuasion during the second stage: on the party claiming the existence of a justification for the limitation

1.   The burden of persuasion and the status of human rights

In the absence of explicit legislative provisions, the rules relating to the burden of persuasion are based on case law. They are designed to provide an answer to the question of who should bear the consequences of not

---

[27] See Kokott, above note 4, at 230, 232.
[28] See M. Supperston and J. Coppel, "Judicial Review after the Human Rights Act," 3 *Eur. Hum. Rts. L. Rev.* 301, 326 (1999); M. Fordham and T. De La Mere, "Identifying the Principles of Proportionality," in J. Jowell and J. Cooper (eds.), *Understanding Human Rights Principles* (Oxford: Hart Publishing, 2001), 27; A. Kavanagh, *Constitutional Review under the UK Human Rights Act* (Cambridge University Press, 2009), 254; A. Lester and D. Pannick, *Human Rights Law and Practice*, 2nd edn. (London: Butterworths, 2004),

persuading the court, at the end of the proceedings, of the correctness of the claim. The examination of this case law through a comparative perspective shows that no universal rule has been adopted in this context. Moreover, according to Wigmore, a universal rule regarding the burden of persuasion is not merely non-existent, but also cannot exist:

> The truth is that there is not and cannot be any one general solution for all cases. It is merely a question of policy and fairness based on experience in the different situations.[29]

Similarly, James, Hazard, and Leubsdorf have agreed that no *a priori* test exists in that context; the burden is determined according to considerations of policy, fairness, and convenience.[30]

In examining the issue of the burden of persuasion regarding the justification of a limitation of constitutional rights, the decisive factor is the protection of human rights. Indeed, constitutional democracies are designed to protect human rights[31] and the protection of human rights is the function of constitutions in general and the bill of rights contained therein in particular.

The realization of this duty is expressed in different ways. One way is to impose the burden of persuasion to justify a limitation on a constitutional right on the party arguing for the existence of this justification. Thus, if at the end of the day the scales are balanced, and the facts presented for and against a justification are of equal weight, all that remains is the constitutional limitation itself. If, indeed, the main purpose of a constitutional democracy is the protection of human rights, this concern should also be reflected in the case of a factual tie. Thus, at the end of the day, once the factual scales are balanced, the court should rule against the limitation on the right and not in its favor.[32]

Alongside this fundamental notion of judicial policy are several other considerations of fairness and convenience. The factual data used to justify the limitation of constitutional rights are found, in most cases, with governmental authority which is the typical respondent in these types of cases. The legislative branch is presented with – or at least should be

---

91: "Where the right is not absolute but is subject to exceptions, it is for the respondent to show that there is a justification for a *prima facie* breach."

[29] See J. H. Wigmore, *Evidence in Trials at Common Law* (Boston: Little Brown & Co. 1981), §§ 2487–2488.

[30] See F. James, G. C. Hazard, and J. Leubsdorf, *Civil Procedure*, 5th edn. (Foundation Press, 2001), 421; J. W. Strong (ed.), *McCormick on Evidence*, 6th edn. (West Publishing Co., 2006), 565.

[31] See above, at 218.   [32] See above, at 365.

presented with – those factual findings that may justify the limitation in a concrete case on a human right. The individuals directly harmed by that limitation – and who claim that their right has been unduly limited – have no appropriate tools, in most cases, to gather that information and to present it to the court.

2.   The counter-argument: the presumption of constitutionality

i.   The burden of persuasion: on the party arguing against constitutionality

The foundation on which the approach that the burden of persuasion relating to the justification of the limitation on a constitutional right lies with the party arguing in favor of such justification rests with the notion that in a constitutional democracy, constitutionally protected rights are of the utmost importance. Against this argument one may argue that the constitution itself is equally important. The importance of the constitution may be expressed, among others, by the presumption of constitutionality. According to that presumption, every legislative provision is presumed to be validly enacted within the powers granted by the constitution. Such a presumption is also the reason behind the unanimously accepted notion[33] that during the first stage of the constitutional review – when the argument that a right has been limited is presented – the burden of persuasion lies with the party arguing that a limitation has occurred. The claim is that such constitutional logic should not stop at the first stage; it should also apply to the second stage, in which the justification claim is raised. The argument, then, is that the presumption of constitutionality should apply to all stages of the constitutional review. Accordingly, there is no point in distinguishing between the limitation-on-the-right stage and the justification-for-that-limitation stage; both stages should be treated as one for the purposes of the burden of proof. Is that the correct approach?

ii.   On the presumption of constitutionality

It is often said that constitutional democracies adopt the presumption of constitutionality.[34] The presumption applies in several contexts. The

---

[33] See above, at 437.
[34] See J. Eliot Magnet, "The Presumption of Constitutionality," 18 *Osgoode Hall L. J.* 87 (1980); H. Burmester, "The Presumption of Constitutionality," 13 *Fed. L. Rev.* 277 (1983); A. S. Butler, "A Presumption of Statutory Conformity with the Charter," 19 *Queens L. J.* 209 (1993).

most important of these is the interpretive context.[35] Thus, the presumption of constitutionality is a part of the objective purpose of each legislative provision.[36] Accordingly, a presumption is that the law's purposes do not conflict with the constitution.[37] If the interpreter faces two plausible interpretations, according to which one is constitutionally valid and the other is not, the interpreter must choose the constitutionally valid interpretation. As Justice Lamer of the Canadian Supreme Court has noted:

> [This] Court ... should not ... interpret legislation that is open to more than one interpretation so as to make it inconsistent with the Charter and hence of no force or effect.[38]

Another context where the presumption of legality applies is in the constitutional review of legislative provisions, in particular those cases where the legal issue may be resolved through the interpretive process. Here, the approach is that in those cases where the court can resolve the legal issue through interpretation it should do so rather than use the more extreme measure of declaring the law unconstitutional. This preference is based on the presumption of constitutionality.[39] This interpretive approach leads to a situation where the constitutionality of the legislative provision remains intact – or, in other words, the law is "saved" – through use of the interpretive process.[40]

The third context in which the presumption of constitutionality is said to apply is that of a burden of persuasion in relation to facts demonstrating the unconstitutionality of a law. Here, too, there is no dispute as to the application of the presumption with regard to demonstrating the facts on which the limitation on the constitutional right is based. The only doubt is in relation to the application of the presumption to proving the facts on which the justification for such a limitation is based. Should the presumption apply in this context?

iii. The presumption of constitutionality and the justification of the limitation of constitutional rights

The presumption of constitutionality cannot be properly used to justify the imposition of the burden of persuasion with the party arguing against

---

[35] See Hogg, above note 14, at 117.
[36] Regarding the objective purpose of legislation, see Barak, above note 9, at 148.
[37] See *ibid.*, at 358.
[38] *Slaight Communication* v. *Davidson* [1989] 1 SCR 1038, 1078.
[39] See Barak, above note 9, at 258.
[40] See A. Vermeule, "Saving Constructions," 85 *Geo. L. J.* 1945 (1997).

the existence of a justification for the limitation on a constitutional right. The reason for that is the central status of the protection of human rights within a constitutional democracy. This central status should justify the conclusion that the presumption has fulfilled its role once the burden of persuasion has been imposed on the person arguing that a limitation occurred during the first stage of the review. It is not appropriate – from the standpoint of the constitutional protection of human rights – to continue to impose that burden on the same party, now arguing that no justification exists for the limitation it proved earlier.[41] This is even more so in cases where the law in question preceded the constitution, and the presumption of constitutionality is artificial in the context of evidentiary burdens. The presumption of constitutionality is, therefore, the presumption of the non-limitation of the constitutional right; it does not apply to the matter of the justification of the limitation.

As we have noted, the presumption of constitutionality's existence is undisputed. It is the scope of the presumption's application that raises doubts. The presumption of constitutionality is judge-made law. Therefore, whenever it is not appropriate to apply the presumption, it should not be applied. One of those situations is whenever a limitation on a constitutional right is at issue. In these cases, the person arguing that the limitation is constitutionally justified must present the court with the factual framework upon which such an argument is based. In contrast, the presumption may well be applied to justify the imposition of a burden on the party arguing that their constitutional right has been limited, such that this party would be required to present the factual framework supporting this claim to the court. Once such a factual framework has been established, the burden has been lifted. Now the burden shifts to the party arguing that a justification exists for imposing such a limitation; that party must present the court with the factual framework upon which such justification rests. The presumption of constitutionality would be of no support at this stage. It has already been rebutted. It may only be of assistance during the first stage. Once that stage has been exhausted, so has the presumption.

---

[41] See Hogg, above note 14, at 120: "In Charter cases, the constitutional contest is between a government and an individual, who asserts that a right has been violated. In that context, it is not appropriate to tilt the scale in favor of the government. There should be no special obstacle placed in the way of an individual who seeks to vindicate a Charter right."

G.   The burden of producing evidence during the second stage: on the party arguing that the limitation is justified

1.   The basic approach

The basic approach is that, during the second stage of the constitutional review – the stage relating to the justification for limiting the constitutional right – there is no point in distinguishing between the burden of persuasion and the burden of producing evidence. Both burdens lie with the same party – the one arguing that the limitation has been justified. This approach is based on the central status of human rights, as well as on the access advantage the state enjoys to the factual data that may justify the means chosen and on the state's special status as a party to the legal proceedings within public law.

2.   The burden during the second stage and the status of human rights

Once the burden has been lifted during the first stage of the constitutional review, and the party arguing that a constitutional right has been limited has presented the court with a proper factual framework to support that claim, it is appropriate that the party arguing that a justification exists for such a limitation should be required to bear the burden of proof. In this context, there is no point in distinguishing between the burden of persuasion and the burden of producing evidence.[42] This approach is based, first and foremost, on the constitutional value of protecting human rights. If we are interested in providing this value with the proper treatment, it is necessary that the party that has limited the constitutional right justify that limitation. The imposition of the said burden – be it the burden of persuasion or the burden of producing evidence – on the person claiming the lack of a justification devalues the constitutional protection of those rights.

This general argument, which applies both to the burden of persuasion and to the burden of producing evidence, is reinforced due to the following claim, unique to the burden of producing evidence when the defendant is the state. The state, which legislated the law limiting the constitutional right, possesses all the information required to present a factual framework to the court justifying the limitation. We may therefore

---

[42] See above, at 437.

reasonably assume that the state was in possession of that same information at the time the legislation was adopted. In any event, it cannot be disputed that the state enjoys much better access to the information than any party claiming that their right has been limited. Therefore, we should not demand that the party – whose constitutional right has been limited and who has presented the court with the factual framework supporting that claim – now brings evidence to persuade the court that such a limitation has no justification. Often that party has no access, within their available means, to information that may support the existence – or non-existence – of such a justification. Furthermore, in most cases the justification – if it exists – was made with the full knowledge of the state, which limited the constitutional right, since the limitation was based on that justification in the first place. Accordingly, it is appropriate that the burden of producing evidence of the justification of the limitation be imposed on the state that has limited the constitutional right.[43]

3. The burden of producing evidence and the burden of the claim that there is no less limiting alternative (necessity test)

The necessity test requires that no less restrictive means exist such that they would advance the legislative purpose to the same extent while limiting the constitutional right less.[44] Who should bear this burden? Several Justices of the Israeli Supreme Court have opined that the burden in this matter should lie with the party arguing that less limiting alternatives exist.[45] Thus, for example, President Shamgar wrote in the case of *United Mizrahi Bank*:

> The party claiming the existence of less severe alternatives beyond the margin of possibilities adopted by the legislation bears the burden of producing the evidence … [T]he State presents the path chosen by it, and of course the considerations underlying that choice. However, it does not have to, and cannot, of its own initiative, present the endless range of other possibilities that could have been pursued to achieve the same objective. This is something that is completely unfeasible. The party asserting the

---

[43] See Woolman and Botha, above note 14, at 44: "One obvious ground for placing the burden of justification on the state where it seeks to uphold a law that limits a right is that the state will often possess unique, if not privileged, access to the information a court requires when attempting to determine whether a limitation is justified." See Chaskalson, Marcus, and Bishop, above note 12, at 3–7.
[44] See above, at 317.
[45] For a discussion of the necessity, see above, at 317.

existence of another course of action, which is less grave, fairer, more reasonable, and which can justify the intervention of the court to invalidate
the conditions authorizing the legislation, as these arise from section 8,
bears the burden of producing the evidence, and if he does not point out
the existence of such alternatives, we will be compelled to conclude that
the path chosen by the legislature does not exceed the proper extent.[46]

In the context of the necessity test we should distinguish between the burden to make a claim – the burden of pleading – and the burden to produce evidence to substantiate the said claim.[47] The proposition that the party
arguing that their rights were unduly limited should also identify the alternative means that may advance the legislative purpose to the same extent
while restricting the constitutional right less is acceptable. Indeed, the state
should not bear the burden of dealing with the "infinite set of possibilities
by which that same legislation may have been carried out." Thus, the party
arguing that a proper alternative exists should point to "a clear and certain
alternative"; if that were not the requirement, we may be facing incompre-
hensible situations. However, we should not conclude that the party arguing
for the existence of an alternative should also bear the evidentiary burden of
producing the evidence to establish such an alternative. Rather, the burden
of producing the evidence – as opposed to the burden of pleading – should
be imposed on the party arguing that there is no possibility of advancing
the proper purpose to the same extent with the proposed alternative, an
alternative that, according to the claim, limits the constitutional right less.
This information is usually at the hands of the state; it has already been
examined by the state and established the legislative provision that limited
the constitutional right. Thus, the state is the one that should be tasked with
the burden of presenting that information to the court.

4. The burden of producing the evidence and the unique nature of the judicial process in constitutional matters

The judicial proceedings relating to a private-law dispute are characteristically different from the judicial proceedings relating to a public-law

---

[46] See *United Mizrahi Bank*, above note 1, at para. 85.
[47] For a similar distinction in a different context, see F. James, "Burdens of Proof," 47 *Va. L. Rev.* 51, 59 (1961): "It is often said that the party who has the burden of pleading a fact must prove it. This is in large part true … though not infallible … The burden of proof does not follow the burden of pleading in all cases. Many jurisdictions for example require a plaintiff to plead non-payment of an obligation sued upon but not to require him to prove it." See also R. Belton, "Burdens of Pleading and Proof in Discrimination Cases: Toward a Theory of Procedural Justice," 34 *Vand. L. Rev.* 1205 (1981).

dispute. In a typical private-law dispute, two private parties stand before the court; both may argue that their rights have been breached by the other party. While the parties to the judicial process must act in good faith towards each other, no special duty – such as a duty of loyalty or heightened good faith – is owed by one party to the other. The situation is different in a public-law dispute. Here, on one side stands an individual claiming that his right was unduly limited by the state; while on the other side stands typically the very same state actor which applied the limitation, and which is now arguing before the court that the limitation is justified and therefore legally valid. The state, unlike a private actor, has both a duty of loyalty and a heightened level of good faith towards the citizens it is meant to serve. The individual, too, has duties to the state, including the duty to act fairly in some situations; however, the individual's duties – and their scope – are different, and are often lesser in scope than the special duties the state has towards individuals.[48] Justice Sachs of the Constitutional Court of South Africa expressed this unique position of the state as a party to constitutional litigation involving the constitutionality of the limiting statute:[49]

> [T]he Constitution requires candour on the part of government. What is involved is not simply a matter of showing courtesy to the public and to the courts, desirable though that always is. It is a question of maintaining respect for the constitutional injunction that our democratic government be accountable, responsive and open. Furthermore, it is consistent with ensuring that the courts can function effectively, as section 165(4) of the Constitution requires ... The notion that "government knows best, end of enquiry", might have satisfied Justice Stratford CJ in the pre-democratic era. It is no longer compatible with democratic government based on the rule of law as envisaged by our Constitution ... [F]ar from the foundational values of the rule of law and of accountable government existing in discreet categories, they overlap and reinforce each other. Openness of government promotes both the rationality that the rule of law requires, and the accountability that multi-party democracy demands. In our constitutional order, the legitimacy of laws made by Parliament comes not from awe, but from openness.

This difference may be manifested through the issue of the burden of production of evidence. Due to the special duty owed by the state to its citizens and the general duty of fairness (or a higher level of good faith)

---

[48] See A. Barak, *The Judge in a Democracy* (Princeton University Press, 2006), 222.
[49] *Matatiele Municipality* v. *President of the Republic of South Africa*, 2006 (5) SA 47 (CC), paras. 107, 109, 110.

owed by the state to the public, the result should be that the burden of persuasion, relating to the facts justifying a limitation on a constitutional right, be placed with the state rather than the private party to a public-law proceeding. Indeed, if the information relating to the existence – or non-existence – of a justification for the limitation is at the hands of the government, it should also be its duty to present that information to the court. This duty can be derived, in this context, from general principles of public law.[50]

The special nature of the public-law dispute is also expressed in other parts of the proceedings, in particular those relating directly to the judge's role. The judge's role in deciding a private-law dispute differs from that of deciding a public-law dispute.[51] One expression of this special role of the courts, in the context of the burden of producing evidence, can be seen in those instances where the factual framework presented to the court during the second stage of the constitutional review (the justification of the limitation of the right stage) is incomplete. This situation may exist for many reasons. Thus, for example, the public authority may be negligent in presenting the factual framework justifying the limitation. The state may – in breach of its obligation – intentionally refrain from presenting the entire factual framework as it would like the court to declare the legislation unconstitutional. If the burden of producing evidence would, in these instances, lie with the party arguing that their rights were unduly limited, it is more than likely that that party would not be able to lift that burden due to financial or other limitations. In these cases – and in many others – the court finds itself in a situation where a proper factual foundation to prove a limitation on a right was laid, but an insufficient factual framework was presented to justify that limitation. In this type of situation, how should the judge rule?

The special character of the proceedings affects the court's behavior. In the framework of the proceedings the constitutionality of a legislative provision is determined. This is an extremely significant determination. This determination applies to parties well beyond those involved in the specific controversy before the court. It also affects the rule of law, as well

[50] See M. Taggart, "Proportionality, Deference, Wednesbury," *New Zealand L. Rev.* 423 (2008); Chaskalson, Marcus, and Bishop, above note 12, at 3–25.

[51] See HCJ 6055/95 *Tzemach v. Minister of Defence* [1999] IsrSC 53(5) 241, 268: "I am doubtful that precedents relating to the burden of proof that originated in criminal law and private law cases should apply in the same way to public-law disputes." See also A. Chayes, "The Role of the Judge in Public Law Litigation," 89 *Harv. L. Rev.* 1281 (1976); O. M. Fiss, "Foreword: The Forms of Justice," 93 *Harv. L. Rev.* 1 (1979).

as the notion of the validity of the administrative (or executive) action in that system. It affects the scope of the protection offered by the legal system to the constitutional rights. For all those reasons, it would not be proper for the court to rule on constitutionality based merely on the requirements of the burden of proof (be it either the burden of persuasion or the burden of producing evidence). As Justice Zamir of the Israeli Supreme Court has noted:

> If the petitioner was successful in raising a substantial doubt as to the validity of the state actor's considerations, or the reasonableness of the administrative decision itself, but could not produce enough evidence such that the court would be able to conclusively determine that the decision was legally valid or invalid, the court is not obligated to deny the petition merely due to lack of evidence. Instead, the court can initiate and require the state to provide answers to several additional questions, or to produce certain evidence – all as deemed necessary by the court. This evidence may include affidavits, documents, or other exhibits. This is one of the main differences between a public-law dispute and a civil-law or a criminal-law dispute. This difference stems, first and foremost, from the nature of the administrative process: Such a process deals with a decision adopted by a state actor – a public agency operating on behalf of the people and for the people; therefore, the people have a principled right to know both the facts and the reasons that led to the decision. Second, this difference stems from the very notion of the rule of law: In an administrative proceeding, the court should not only rule on a dispute between two parties, but also in order to protect and maintain the notion of the rule of law. According to this notion, if a substantial doubt is raised as to the legal validity of an administrative decision such a doubt must be examined in order to make sure that no legally invalid decision remains on the books. From here, we can also derive the difference in the attitude towards the burden of proof between administrative proceedings and civil-law or criminal-law proceedings. In an administrative proceeding, more than in a civil-law or criminal-law proceeding, the court may intervene in order to further establish the factual framework presented to it, such that it would be able to rule as to the validity of the administrative decision. For that reason, in an administrative proceeding, once a substantial doubt has been raised during the initial phase as to the validity of the decision, the subject of the burden of proof, in most cases, does not arise during the next phases of the proceedings.[52]

Accordingly, if the state is a party to the proceedings and it refrains from presenting the court with a full factual framework as to the justification of the limitation on a constitutional right, the court can use its own powers to

---

[52] See *Tzemach*, above note 51.

demand the production of this evidence by the state.[53] The constitutionality of the legislation should not be determined by the state's omission to produce evidence to justify it.[54] With this is mind, it is easy to understand the court's willingness to examine some of the facts on its own, including social and legislative facts,[55] as well as the court willingness to use judicial notice.[56]

What should the court do when, at the end of the proceedings, after exhausting all the procedural options available to it in order to receive the maximum factual data, the court is still not presented with enough factual data to rule on the matter? What should the court do when all the possible factual data has been presented to it, but, after reviewing all the facts, the factual scales are balanced? In both of those types of cases, due to the central role of the limited human right, the court's decision should be against the party claiming a justification for the limitation of the human right.[57] When a justification is not fully established, the limitation on the right is not constitutional.

Justice Zamir of the Israeli Supreme Court has noted that, whenever the factual framework presented to the court is "so feeble that the court cannot establish any concrete findings on it as required to rule on the issue of the validity of the administrative action,"[58] then, in those cases, the issue of the burden of proof should be influenced by the special nature of the administrative proceeding:

---

[53] See *Khosa* v. *Minister of Social Development*, 2004 6 SA 505 (CC), para. 18: "Even in those cases where the view is taken that there is nothing to be said in support of challenged legislation, a court, in order to exercise the due care required of it when dealing with such matters, may well require the assistance of counsel. In this case it should have been apparent to the respondents that the declaration of invalidity of the impugned legislation could have significant budgetary and administrative implications for the state. If the necessary evidence is not placed before the courts dealing with such matters their ability to perform their constitutional mandate will be hampered and the constitutional scheme itself put at risk. It is government's duty to ensure that the relevant evidence is placed before the court." (Mokgoro, J.).

[54] See Woolman and Botha, above note 14, at 44: "[T]he Constitutional Court has, on a number of occasions, stated that the failure by the government to offer any support for a limitation does not relieve a court of the duty to inquire into its justifiability".

[55] See Hogg, above note 14, at 806; K. C. Davis, "Facts in Lawmaking," 80 *Colum. L. Rev.* 931 (1980); A. Woolhandler, "Rethinking the Judicial Reception of Legislative Facts," 41 *Vand. L. Rev.* 111 (1988).

[56] Regarding the doctrine of judicial notice, see S. L. Phipson, *Phipson on evidence*, 15th edn. (2000), 33. Regarding judicial knowledge in the process of the constitutional review of the law, see Hogg, above note 14, at 808.

[57] See *Moise* v. *Greater Germiston Transitional Local Council*, 2001 (4) SA 491.

[58] See *Tzemach*, above note 51, at 268.

The issue of the burden of proof may be influenced by considerations of the rule of law, by the presumption of constitutionality, by the social importance of the limited right and the scope and the size of the limitation at issue, by the efficiency of the administration and by other public-interest considerations.[59]

It seems that, if at the end of the day the court is not convinced that there exists a justification for the limitation of the right, then the court should hold that the limitation could not satisfy the requirement posed by the proportionality tests; therefore, the limitation is unconstitutional. Neither the presumption of constitutionality nor the presumption of legality applies at this stage of the review. The administration's efficiency, as well as other public interest considerations cannot produce, in and of themselves, a valid justification for a limitation on a constitutionally protected right, or even impose the burden of showing such a justification on the party arguing that their right was unduly limited. However, such considerations may affect the remedies for such a limitation; those remedies are outside the scope of this book.

[59] *Ibid.*, at 269.

PART IV

Proportionality evaluated

17

Proportionality's importance

A.   Proportionality and its critique

Since the end of the Second World War, proportionality has been widely received. It is now a part of many a legal system.[1] It is a manifestation of the migration, or transplantation, of laws. This trend has also continued into the beginning of the twenty-first century. Indeed, we now live in the age of proportionality. As balancing is found at proportionality's foundation we can also say that we live in the age of balancing.[2] However, proportionality is often highly criticized. In particular, the criticism is aimed at the component of proportionality *stricto sensu*. The latter is based on balancing between conflicting principles. This balancing is contested. Although in our private lives we are constantly balancing between conflicting principles, there are many critics of this balance when it is conducted by the courts and aimed at the review of the law's constitutionality. This part of the book will examine the various arguments in favor of proportionality and against it, while reviewing some of its possible alternatives.[3] At the examination's foundation are proportionality *stricto sensu* and the balancing at its core. The arguments presented here, therefore, apply equally to constitutional and interpretive balancing.[4] I am not of the opinion that proportionality is the only necessary condition, or even a *conditio sine qua non*, to the existence of a constitutional review. I am not of the opinion that the only rational way to reach a judicial decision is through proportionality. Further, I do not believe that, if we forego the notion of proportionality, the result would be that all constitutional rights would be absolute. Instead, my approach is based on the argument that,

---

[1] See above, at 181.
[2] See T. A. Aleinikoff, "Constitutional Law in the Age of Balancing," 96 *Yale L. J.* 943 (1987); S. Gardbaum, "A Democratic Defense of Constitutional Balancing," 4(1) *Law and Ethics of Hum. Rts.* 77 (2010).
[3] See A. Stone Sweet and Jud Mathews, "Proportionality Balancing and Global Constitutionalism," 47 *Colum. J. Transnat'l L.* 72 (2008).
[4] Regarding the distinction, see above, at 72.

of all the options available to ensure human rights in a pluralistic, democratic society, proportionality is the best available option. The approach
herein to proportionality, in other words, is a proportional approach.

B.   The emphasis on the need for rational justification

Proportionality – and the act of balancing at its foundation – emphasizes the need to rationally justify a limitation of a constitutionally protected right.[5] It also requires a constant examination of this justification's
existence. It establishes, in effect – to use Mureinik's term – a "culture of
justifications."[6] Democracy is based on human rights. Any limitation on
human rights requires a legal justification.[7] As Justice Ackerman of the
Constitutional Court of South Africa has well observed:

> In reaction to our past, the concept and values of the constitutional state,
> of the "regstaat", and the constitutional right to equality before the law
> are deeply foundational to the creation of the "new order" referred to in
> the preamble. The detailed enumeration and description in [the general
> limitation provision] of the criteria which must be met before the legis-
> lature can limit a right entrenched in [the Bill of Rights] emphasize the
> importance, in our new constitutional state, of reason and justification

---

[5] See J. Kirk, "Constitutional Guarantees, Characterisation and the Concept of
Proportionality," 21 *Melb. U. L. Rev.* 1, 20 (1997); J. M. Shaman, *Constitutional
Interpretation: Illusion and Reality* (Westport, CT: Greenwood Press, 2001), 44; M.
Kumm, "Political Liberalism and the Structures of Rights: On the Place and Limits of
the Proportionality Requirement," in G. Pavlakos (ed.), *Law, Rights and Discourse: The
Legal Philosophy of Robert Alexy* (Portland, OR: Hart Publishing, 2007), 131; V. Jackson,
Constitutional Engagement in a Transnational Era (Oxford University Press, 2010), 63;
M. Kumm, "The Idea of Socratic Contestation and the Right to Justification: The Point of
Rights-Based Proportionality Review," 4 *Law and Ethics Hum. Rts.* 140 (2010).

[6] See E. Mureinik, "A Bridge to Where? Introducing the Interim Bill of Rights," 10 *SAJHR*
31, 32 (1994); D. Dyzenhaus, "Law as Justification: Etienne Mureinik's Conception of Legal
Culture," 14 *SAJHR* 11, 27 (1998); A. Butler, "Limiting Rights," 33 *Victoria U. Wellington
L. Rev.* 113, 116 (2002); J. Jowell, "Judicial Deference and Human Rights: A Question of
Competence," in P. P. Craig and R. Rawlings (eds.), *Law and Administration in Europe: Essays
in Honour of Carol Harlow* (Oxford University Press, 2003), 67, 69; M. Hunt, "Sovereignty's
Blight: Why Contemporary Public Law Needs the Concept of 'Due Deference,'" in N.
Bamforth and P. Leyland (eds.), *Public Law in a Multi-Layered Constitution* (Portland, OR:
Hart Publishing, 2003), 340; M. Taggart, "Proportionality, Deference, Wednesbury," *New
Zealand L. Rev.* 423 (2008); M. Cohen-Eliya and I. Porat, "Proportionality and the Culture
of Justification," 59 *Am. J. Comp. L.* (forthcoming, 2011).

[7] D. Feldman, "Proportionality and the Human Rights Act 1998," in F. Ellis (ed.), *The
Principle of Proportionality in the Law of Europe* (Oxford: Hart Publishing, 1999), 117;
E. Den Otter, *Judicial Review in an Age of Moral Pluralism* (Cambridge University Press,
2009); A. Kavanagh, *Constitutional Review under the UK Human Rights Act* (Cambridge
University Press, 2009), 234.

when rights are sought to be curtailed. We have moved from a past characterized by much which was arbitrary and unequal in the operation of
the law to a present and a future in a constitutional state where state [or
private] action must be such that it is capable of being analyzed and justified rationally.[8]

Indeed, the theory behind proportionality is not intended to merely cat-
egorize a case into a group which solves the problem. Rather, proportionality is aimed at a constant review of the existence of a rational justification
for the limitation imposed on the right, while taking into consideration
each case's circumstances.

This justification is not merely a matter for the courts to reflect upon.
Each of the three branches of government must consider this justification as well.[9] Accordingly, before a law limiting a constitutional right
is enacted, the members of the legislative body must be persuaded that
the limitation is justified. The same is true for the executive and judicial branch's decisions. Proportionality establishes a uniform analytical
framework for any state action that may affect constitutional rights. Even
if there is no judicial review or if this review is limited in nature, there is
still a need for a rational justification of a limitation of a constitutional
right.[10] Proportionality ensures constitutional uniformity in the search
for a justification for the limitation placed on a constitutional right.
However, proportionality fully acknowledges the different scope of discretion provided to each of the three governmental branches.[11] Moreover,
the scope of the said governmental discretion varies from one branch to
another and may also change in accordance to the proportionality component at issue. Thus, for example, the widest discretion regarding the
purpose component is given to the legislative branch.[12] On the other hand,
the widest discretion regarding the balance between the marginal social
importance in fulfilling the purpose and the marginal social importance
of preventing harm to the constitutional right in relation to proportionality *stricto sensu*, given to the judicial branch.[13]

Proportionality is a framework based on a structured method of
thought. It determines the information which should be considered
which includes the proper purpose of the limiting law, its rational connection to the means used by the law, the law's necessity, and the marginal social importance of the purpose of the limiting law as compared

---

[8] *S. v. Makwanyane*, 1995 (3) SA 391, § 156.
[9] See S. Woolman, "Riding the Push-Me Pull-You: Constructing a Test That Reconciles the
Conflicting Interests Which Animate the Limitation Clause," 10 *SAJHR* 31 (1994).
[10] See above, at 379.   [11] See above, at 400.
[12] See above, at 401.   [13] See above, at 414.

to the marginal social importance of preventing the harm to the right. Proportionality is based on the reasons underlying each constitutional right, as well as the justifications for their limitation. These reasons and those justifications in and of themselves, however, are extrinsic to the concept of proportionality. Proportionality is unable to resolve those issues. Indeed, the answers to those questions may be found elsewhere in the laws of each legal system. The governmental branch conducting the balance in each particular case – be it the legislative, executive, or judicial branch – may learn about those issues from sources extrinsic to the concept of proportionality itself.

Due to its limited scope and structured nature, proportionality should not be identified with any "right-wing" or "left-wing" social theories.[14] Proportionality should not be seen as being in favor of, or against, any liberal or communitarian doctrines.[15] Rather, proportionality is a "tool." It is a legal construction. It is a legal methodology.[16] Proportionality's focus on the issue of the rational justification of the limitation of the right serves the notion of a constitutional democracy well.

C.   The need for structured discretion

1.   The importance of structured discretion

Proportionality is based on the notion of structured discretion.[17] A person applying proportionality must think in stages.[18] First, they must distinguish between questions relating to the right's scope and those relating

---

[14] See J. M. Shaman, "Constitutional Interpretation: Illusion and Reality," 41 *Wayne L. Rev.* 135, 154 (1995).

[15] See S. Shiffrin, "Liberalism, Radicalism, and Legal Scholarship," 30 *UCLA L. Rev.* 1103 (1982); compare with Kumm, above note 5. See also R. F. Nagel, "Liberals and Balancing," 63 *U. Colo. L. Rev.* 319 (1992). See below, at 467.

[16] See above, at 394.

[17] See P. Craig, "Unreasonableness and Proportionality in UK Law," in E. Eliss (ed.), *The Principle of Proportionality in the Laws of Europe* (Oxford: Hart Publishing, 1999), 85; D. M. Beatty, *The Ultimate Rule of Law* (Oxford University Press, 2004), 172; J. Rivers, "Proportionality and Variable Intensity of Review," 65 *Cambridge L. J.* 174, 176 (2006); L. Weinrib, "The Postwar Paradigm and American Exceptionalism," in S. Choudhry (ed.), *The Migration of Constitutional Ideas* (Cambridge University Press, 2006), 84, 96; P. Craig, *Administrative Law*, 6th edn. (London: Sweet & Maxwell, 2008), 637; Kavanagh, above note 7, at 255.

[18] See M. Fordham, "Common Law Proportionality," 7 *Judicial Review* 110, 112 (2002).

to the justification of limits on its realization and its protection.[19] Next, during the stage of justification of the limitation of the right and its protection, they should distinguish between the threshold question regarding a proper purpose[20] and questions relating to the means selected to advance that purpose,[21] as well as the relation between the fulfillment of the purpose and the harm caused to the constitutional right.[22] In other words, once the threshold requirement of proper purpose has been satisfied, the focus shifts to the three sub-questions relating both to the rational connection of the means selected by the legislator to advance its proper purpose, the necessity of the law, and the balance struck between the advancement of this purpose and the harm caused to the right in question. The first two questions – the "suitability" of the means and their necessity – are related to the relation between the proper purpose and the means chosen to advance it. The third question – that of proportionality *stricto sensu* – is related to the balance between advancing the purpose and limiting the constitutional right. The balance is performed according to the basic balancing rule[23] and the specific balancing rule.[24] On the basis of those components, the justification of limiting a constitutional right should be analyzed.

The structured nature of the discretion involved in proportionality has many advantages.[25] For one, it allows the person conducting proportionality analyses to think analytically, not to skip over things which should be considered, and to consider them in their time and place.[26] Proportionality also encourages the use of comparative-law analysis, since it can easily demonstrate whether a proper basis for comparison exists.[27] While these advantages apply to any exercise of proportionality's structured discretion by the three branches of government, they particularly apply in the

---

[19] See above, at 19. See also M. Khosla, "Proportionality: An Assault on Human Rights?: A Reply," 8(2) *I. Con.* 298 (2010).

[20] See above, at 245.   [21] See above, at 303 and 317.

[22] See above, at 340.   [23] On the basic rule, see above, at 362.

[24] On the specific balancing rule, see above, at 367.

[25] See H. Dreier, *GG Grundgesetz Kommentar* (Tübingen: Mohr Siebeck, 2006), 262. In accordance with Art. 36 of the South African Constitution, those advantages are lost in that legal system.

[26] See C. Bernal Pulido, "On Alexy's Weight Formula," in A. J. Menéndez and E. O. Eriksen (eds.), *Arguing Fundamental Rights* (Dordrecht: Springer, 2006), 101, 106; A. Attaran, "A Wobbly Balance – A Comparison of Proportionality Testing in Canada, the United States, the European Union and the World Trade Organization," 56 *University of New Brunswick L. J.* 260 (2007).

[27] See Jackson, above note 5.

context of exercising legislative discretion. Indeed, the structured nature of proportionality's discretion is predominantly designed to assist members of the legislative body to "think constitutionally," as required by the constitutional nature of legislative action. Thus, while considering legislation intended to limit a human right, the legislators must examine whether such legislation satisfies the requirements posed by the limitation clause. The same is true for an executive action that may limit a constitutional right. Finally, the structured nature of the discretion may assist the judges in "thinking constitutionally," as required by the constitutional nature of the judicial task in a constitutional democracy. While in most instances the structured nature of the discretion is mentioned in the context of judicial activity, it is important to note that proportionality in general, as well as the structured nature of its discretion in particular, is available to anyone required to act proportionally. This is first and foremost the legislator. Beside the legislator stands the judge, who is assisted by discretion's structured nature while dealing with human rights in general, and while determining the proportionality of their limitation in particular.

2.   Transparency

The structured nature of the discretion exercised by proportionality provides additional advantages. One of those is transparency.[28] A person reviewing a decision obtained based on structured discretion – be it a legislative decision to legislate, or a judicial decision as to the constitutionality of legislation – can both recognize and follow the stages and the reasons leading to the decision. The decision is no longer a "closed book." Rather, everything is out in the open – on the face of the decision. Accordingly, it should be fairly easy to identify the legislator's considerations; it would be possible to know why a law has been enacted and why specific legislative measures were adopted. It becomes possible to examine the reasons behind the legislation, as well as the factual framework underlying it. The

---

[28] F. Michelman, "Foreword: Traces of Self-Government," 100 *Harv. L. Rev.* 4, 34 (1986); J. Kirk, "Constitutional Guarantees, Characterisation and the Concept of Proportionality," 21 *Melb. U. L. Rev.* 1, 20 (1997); M. Sachs, *GG Verfassungsrecht II Grundrechte* (Berlin: Springer, 2003), 71; V. C. Jackson, "Being Proportional about Proportionality," 21 *Const. Comment.* 803, 830 (2004); F. M. Coffin, "Judicial Balancing: The Protean Scales of Justice," 63 *N. Y. U. L. Rev.* 16 (1988); T. Poole, "Tilting at Windmills?: Truth and Illusion in the Political Constitution," 70 *Mod. L. Rev.* 250, 268 (2007); for a critique of this approach, see V. C. Jackson, "Ambivalent Resistance and Comparative Constitutionalism: Opening Up the Conversation on 'Proportionality', Rights and Federalism," 1 *U. Pa. J. Const. L.* 583, 621 (1999).

same is true for the judicial branch. The process of judicial decisionmaking becomes open to the reader. The reasons at the decision's foundation are provided, as well as their relative weight. Thus, those decisions are better explained and understood. Moreover, it becomes much easier to properly criticize those decisions. It can be expected.[29] As Sadurski has observed:

> A judge engaged in the act of weighing and balancing of competing con-stitutional goods discloses the elements of his reasoning to the public. It is, to use an admittedly imperfect analogy, as if a cook in an elegant restaurant first revealed to the customers all the ingredients and then showed the guests, step by step, all the stages of the preparation of the dish before it lands on their tables.[30]

This transparency may point out both difficulties faced by the judge in obtaining the result at issue; it also demonstrates the thought-process behind the decision, eliminating any notion of a "mechanical" approach in reaching it. All these enhance the public's trust in the courts as well as in democracy itself.

The said transparency is important in a democratic system. It allows for the understanding of the decision's foundation. Understanding yields appreciation, even when the result is disputed. Transparency is the basis for educated public discourse, as well as for a constitutional dialogue between the legislative and judicial branches.[31] It allows for informed criticism of the decision. It prevents conflicts of interest and the consider-ation of irrelevant or unethical issues – if the decisionmaker is exposed to them. It leads to faith in the decisionmakers' integrity. Of course, trans-parency cannot guarantee that these results can be achieved in all cases; it is always possible to hide one's ulterior motives so that even transparency cannot expose them. However, transparency is a major contribution to the notion of fairness and integrity in the decisionmaking process. That contribution, in and of itself, is of major value.

3. Appropriate considerations in proper context

Another advantage offered by the structured nature of proportionality's discretion is that appropriate considerations are taken into account in

---

[29] *London Regional Transport and another* v. *The Mayor of London and another* [2001] EWCA Civ. 1491, §§ 57–58.

[30] W. Sadurski, "'Reasonableness' and Value Pluralism in Law and Politics," in G. Bongiovanni, G. Sartor, and C. Valentini (eds.), *Reasonableness and Law* (Dordrecht: Springer, 2009), 129, 139.

[31] See below, at 465.

their proper context. Even without discretion's structured nature it can be guaranteed that only the relevant considerations be taken into account. The structured element ensures that those pertinent considerations are weighed in their proper context.[32] They guarantee, therefore, that considerations relating to the public interest or to the rights of others are considered only during the second stage of the analysis – regarding the justification of the limitation on the constitutional right – and not during the first stage – when determining the scope of the right.[33] They ensure that considerations of proper purpose are taken into account only as an independent, threshold requirement rather than during the examination of the means required to fulfill as well as to harm the constitutional right.[34] They ensure that the balancing between the conflicting principles will occur only during the last stage of proportionality, during the examination of proportionality *stricto sensu*.[35]

The importance of allowing for the appropriate considerations in the proper context is significant. Take, for example, the right to family life *vis-à-vis* the interest of national security.[36] If the two collide "too early," it is quite certain that the national security interest would prevail, since in general the notion of life is superior to the notion of family life. But, if we properly distinguish between the interpretive matter of whether the right to family life constitutes a part of the right to human dignity (the issue of the right's scope) and the matter of justification whether the balance between fulfilling security and preserving family life (the issue of proportionality *stricto sensu*), then a proper framework is established to examine the balance between them. Such a framework does not provide a general and permanent answer to the issue of the balance between national security and the right to family life. But such a framework would be able to resolve the issue at hand, which is the appropriate balance between the marginal social importance of the security measure of imposing a blanket restriction on family unification (compared with a proportional alternative) and the marginal social importance of preventing the separation between spouses of the same family, or between those spouses and their children. Instead of a general discussion examining which is constitutionally superior – life or family life – we are provided with a much more specific discussion, examining the proportionality of the marginal social importance gained by the interest of national security following

---

[32] See Kavanagh, above note 7, at 256.
[33] See above, at 76.   [34] See above, at 246.
[35] See above, at 340.   [36] See above, at 350.

the imposition of the blanket restriction as compared with the marginal social importance of preventing harm caused to those family members who are the subject of such blanket restriction.

4. A dialogue between the legislature and the judiciary

A structured and transparent discretion fosters open dialogue between the legislative and judicial branches.[37] Prior to the adoption of a bill, the legislator must ensure that there is a justification for limiting a constitutional right. It must be satisfied that its purposes are proper, that the means selected to advance those purposes are proper, and that the limitation of the constitutional right is proportional. In that context, the legislator must examine the factual framework that serves as the basis of its assertion[38] that the means selected are rational[39] and that they are necessary to advance the proper purpose.[40] The legislative branch is aware of the need

[37] Regarding the dialogue between the legislative and judicial branches, see A. Barak, *The Judge in a Democracy* (Princeton University Press, 2006), 226. See also F. I. Michelman, "Foreword: Traces of Self-Government – The Supreme Court 1985 Term," 100 *Harv. L. Rev.* 4 (1986); B. Friedman, "Dialogue and Judicial Review," 91 *Mich. L. Rev.* 577 (1993). P. W. Hogg and A. A. Bushell, "The Charter Dialogue between Courts and Legislatures (Or Perhaps the Charter of Rights Isn't Such a Bad Thing after All)," 35 *Osgoode Hall L. J.* 75 (1997); C. P. Manfredi and J. B. Kelly, "Six Degrees of Dialogue: A Response to Hogg and Bushell," 37 *Osgoode Hall L. J.* 513 (1999); P. W. Hogg and A. A. Bushell, "Reply to Six Degrees of Dialogue," 37 *Osgoode Hall L. J.* 529 (1999); K. Roach, *The Supreme Court on Trial: Judicial Activism or Democratic Dialogue* (Toronto: Irwin Law, 2001); C. Mathen, "Constitutional Dialogue in Canada and the United States," 14 *Nat'l J. Const.* L. 403 (2003); J. Goldsworthy, "Judicial Review, Legislative Override and Democracy," 38 *Wake Forest L. Rev.* 451 (2003); J. Waldron, "Some Models of Dialogue between Judges and Legislators," 23 *Supreme Court Law Review* (2nd) 7 (2004); R. Clayton, "Judicial Deference and Democratic Dialogue: The Legitimacy of Judicial Intervention under the Human Rights Act 1998," *PL* 33 (2004); T. Hickman, "Constitutional Dialogue, Constitutional Theories and the Human Rights Act 1998," *PL* 306 (2005); L. Tremblay, "The Legitimacy of Judicial Review: The Limits of Dialogue between Courts and Legislatures," 3 *I. Con.* 617 (2005); K. Roach, "Dialogue or Defiance: Legislative Reversals of Supreme Court Decisions in Canada and the United States," 4 *Int'l J. Const. L.* 347 (2006); C. P. Manfredi, "The Day the Dialogue Died: A Comment on Sauvé v. Canada," 45 *Osgoode Hall L. J.* 105 (2007); J. Debeljak, "Parliamentary Sovereignty and Dialogue under the Victorian Charter of Human Rights and Responsibilities: Drawing the Line between Judicial Interpretation and Judicial Law-Making," 33 *Monash U. L. Rev.* 9 (2007); M. Tushnet, *Weak Courts, Strong Rights: Judicial Review and Social Welfare Rights in Comparative Constitutional Law* (Princeton University Press, 2008), 31; A. Torres Pérez, *Conflicts of Rights in the European Union: A Theory of Supranational Adjudication* (Oxford University Press, 2009), 103; A. Young, *Parliamentary Sovereignty* (Portland, OR: Hart Publishing, 2009), 115; Kavanagh, above note 7.
[38] See above, at 401.   [39] See above, at 405.
[40] Regarding principled balancing, see below, at 343.

to balance between the marginal social importance of the benefits gained by the legislation and the marginal social importance of preventing harm to the constitutional right. The basic balancing rule[41] directs the legislative discretion.

These data are presented to the judiciary when it convenes to consider the constitutionality of that same legislation. The opinion produced by the court expresses the judge's thought process. It highlights the data which lead it to the decision that the law's purpose is proper or not. It explains how conclusions were reached regarding the other component of proportionality. When the conclusion is that the legislation is unconstitutional, the reasons behind that conclusion are clear.

The court's ruling that the legislation is unconstitutional is not the end of the road. The dialogue between the two branches – which began with the legislation and continued with the determination that the legislation is unconstitutional – persists. The matter is then returned to the legislator. The transparency of the judicial decision allows the legislator to understand what should be done to continue fulfilling that law's purposes. The legislator has several options. First, assuming the court declared the purpose to be improper, it can modify the legislative purpose accordingly. That, in turn, would require the selection of new means to advance that purpose. Second, should the court approve of the purpose but declare the means disproportional, the legislator may select other, more proportional measures to advance it. The legislator may choose other ways. In any event, all these options are open to the legislator because now, after the judicial opinion has been produced, it is fully aware of what is constitutionally valid and what is not.

If the legislator continues to insist on its original opinion, and sees no room to change it, the dialogue does not come to a close. The option available for the legislator is to take steps to amend the constitution.[42] Most constitutional rights are not "eternal." They can be amended. The dialogue between the legislator and the judge now moves on to a higher constitutional level, regarding constitutional amendment. At times, the constitution amendment is politically complex, and at other times it is easily obtained. This difficulty or ease cannot harm the basic idea at the dialogue's foundation. When a constitutional amendment is not possible

---

[41] See above, at 362.

[42] An examination of the questions regarding constitutional amendments is beyond the scope of this book. See A. Barak, "Unconstitutional Constitutional Amendments," *Isr. L. Rev.* (forthcoming, 2011).

(legally or politically), the option of a new constitution becomes relevant. An interesting question is whether in such a case the dialogue comes to an end.

Thus, proportionality encourages an open dialogue between the different branches of government.[43] We are no longer dealing with two separate monologues or with a dialogue between deaf participants. Rather, we come across an interaction between the different branches of government, such that each branch is fully aware of, and fully comprehends, the actions taken by the other. In that way, each branch is encouraged to be more considerate of the other. All this is due to the fact that all three branches operate according to the framework of a uniform normative method, well recognized by each branch and common to all.

D. Proportionality and human rights theories

1. Proportionality as a vessel for human rights theories

There are many theories regarding human rights and their limitations.[44] Most of those theories can be found within proportionality. The concept of proportionality is not based upon – or committed to – any particular human rights theory. Rather, it may serve as a vessel for many – even opposing – theories about human rights. The reason for that relates to the very nature of the concept. Proportionality is an analytical and legal tool. It is fed by extrinsic data. Through different degrees of intensity relating to the requirements of proper purpose, rational connection, necessity, or proportionality *stricto sensu*, one is able to incorporate most current human rights theories into the concept of proportionality. However,

---

[43] R. A. Edwards, "Judicial Deference under the Human Rights Act," 65 *Mod. L. Rev.* 859, 867 (2002).

[44] See J. Waldron, "Introduction," in J. Waldron (ed.), *Theories of Rights* (Oxford University Press, 1984), 1; J. Rawls, *A Theory of Justice* (Cambridge, MA: Belknap Press of Harvard University Press, 1999); R. Dworkin, "Rights as Trumps," in J. Waldron (ed.), *Theories of Rights* (Oxford University Press, 1984), 153; J. Raz, *The Morality of Freedom* (Oxford: Clarendon Press, 1986); R. H. Pildes, "Avoiding Balancing: The Role of Exclusionary Reasons in Constitutional Law," 45 *Hastings L. J.* 711 (1994); R. H. Pildes, "Why Rights Are Not Trumps: Social Meanings, Expressive Harms and Constitutionalism," 27 *J. Legal Studies* 725 (1998); J. Waldron, "Pildes on Dworkin's Theory of Rights," 29 *J. Legal Studies* 301 (2000); R. H. Pildes, "Dworkin's Two Conceptions of Rights," 29 *J. Legal Studies* 309 (2000); G. Letsas, *A Theory of Interpretation of the European Convention on Human Rights* (Oxford University Press, 2007), 99; K. Möller, "Two Conceptions of Positive Liberty: Towards an Autonomy-Based Theory of Constitutional Rights," 29(4) *OJLS* 757 (2009).

proportionality is not "neutral." It is meant to protect both the human rights and the public interest at the same time. It allows the imposition of certain restrictions on constitutional rights, but ensures that those limitations are properly justified.[45] Accordingly, proportionality is not equally suitable to all theories of human rights. There are some theories that are more compatible with proportionality than others. Thus, for example, proportionality is well suited to Alexy's theory of principle-shaped rights. As we have seen,[46] according to Alexy, a principle always strives for optimal realization, in accordance with the available factual and legal possibilities – that is, in accordance with the rules of proportionality. The relationship between Alexy's theory of constitutional rights (shaped as principles) and proportionality is therefore both direct and necessary.[47] Proportionality is also compatible with communitarian approaches to human rights. These theories are based on the recognition of a proper balance between individual rights and the public interest.[48] But is proportionality compatible with liberal approaches? I turn now to examine this question.

2.   Proportionality and liberalism

i.   The general argument

In an important article, Kumm examines the extent to which proportionality provides a proper response to the issue of the right's structure in accordance with liberal theories.[49] In general, liberal theories in the present context represent the notion that individual rights are principally superior to the public interest; accordingly, a special justification is required to limit those rights to support that interest. In that respect, Kumm examined one of proportionality's common criticisms, according to which it does not adequately accommodate this liberal theory. As Kumm writes:

---

[45] See above, at 166.   [46] See above, at 38.   [47] See above, at 39.

[48] See M. J. Sandel (ed.), *Liberalism and its Critics* (1984); M. J. Sandel, *Democracy's Discontent: America in Search of a Public Philosophy* (Cambridge, MA: Belknap Press of Harvard University Press, 1996); S. Mulhall and A. Swift, *Liberals and Communitarians* (Malden, MA: Wiley-Blackwell, 1996).

[49] M. Kumm, "Political Liberalism and the Structures of Rights: On the Place and Limits of the Proportionality Requirement," in G. Pavlakos (ed.), *Law, Rights, and Discourse: The Legal Philosophy of Robert Alexy* (Portland, OR: Hart Publishing, 2007), 131, 141. Compare with R. Mullender, "Theorizing the Third Way: Qualified Consequentialism, the Proportionality Principle, and the New Social Democracy," 27(4) *J. L. & Soc'y* 493 (2000).

Liberal political rights are widely perceived as having special weight when competing with policy goals. The idea is expressed, for example, by Ronald Dworkin's conception of rights as trumps and the corollary distinction between principles and policies, or by what Rawls calls the "priority of the right over the good", or by Habermas' description of rights as firewalls. Ultimately these ideas can be traced back to a theory, perhaps most fully developed by Immanuel Kant, grounded in the twin ideals of human dignity and autonomy viewed as side-constraints on the pursuit of the collective good. Yet nothing in the account of rights as principles prioritises rights. Rights and policies compete on the same plane within the context of proportionality analysis.[50]

Kumm then analyzes this liberal criticism, while distinguishing between three approaches of prioritizing rights over the public interest. He examines each of these and its relation to proportionality. We will follow in Kumm's footsteps.

ii. The prioritization of rights and the approach of liberal antiperfectionism

Liberal approaches to human rights are based on the notion that no individual should be forced to adopt a certain way, directed by the government, to pursue his or her own happiness (the "good life"). The determination as to those issues should be left in the hands of the individual. That is the basis of the notion that the state cannot enforce a certain type of the "good life" on its citizens; in fact, the state's views in this context should be irrelevant. In any event, such views by the state should never be used in order to justify a limitation placed on individual rights. Due to its "negative" character, this notion is also known as the concept of "excluded reasons."

Kumm indicates[51] that this perception of liberalism is not in conflict with the concept of proportionality. In fact, proportionality endorses such a perception in presenting the requirement for a proper purpose.[52] Simply put, excluded reasons may not be used to form a proper purpose. While the protection of the rights of others is always a proper purpose, the mere protection of the public interest does not satisfy, in and of itself, the threshold requirement of a proper purpose.[53] Thus, exceptional reasons are required to justify a limitation on human rights for reasons relating to

[50] Kumm, above note 49, at 141–142.
[51] *Ibid.*, at 143.
[52] See R. Alexy, "Thirteen Replies," in G. Pavlakos (ed.), *Law, Rights, and Discourse: The Legal Philosophy of Robert Alexy* (Portland, OR: Hart Publishing, 2007), 333, 341.
[53] See above, at 256.

the public interest, and the nature of those exceptional reasons is determined by the rules of proportionality. The reasons themselves are derived from considerations extrinsic to proportionality itself.[54] To the extent that a constitutional democracy would like to adopt this liberal antiperfectionist approach, it may well do so through the concept of proportionality. Accordingly, the tests of proportionality would only be applied in their proper context; therefore, the notion of "excluded reasons" not only does not contradict proportionality, it actually complements it.

iii.   The prioritization of rights and liberal anticollectivism

According to this aspect of the liberal approach, the individual right should be prioritized over the collective good. Such prioritization does not necessarily translate into turning the public interest into an excluded reason. Rather, the public interest is a relevant consideration, but the right should also be given a proper weight, reflecting the centrality of the notions of both human dignity and autonomy in the system.

According to Kumm,[55] this liberal concept is also entirely compatible with proportionality.[56] The public interest – the "common good" – is also a legitimate consideration within proportionality; however, that consideration alone cannot suffice to provide a justification for a limitation of a constitutional right. That is for two reasons. First, proportionality requires special circumstances in order to consider the public interest as the justification for the limitation. Second, the public interest is never considered on its own, as proportionality also requires that the means selected to advance that interest comply with the other components of proportionality. Both of these requirements affect the weight accorded to considerations of the public interest whenever it conflicts with a constitutional right. Again, the actual content of these requirements is determined by considerations extrinsic to proportionality itself; yet proportionality ultimately reflects what a democratic society would deem as fair and appropriate considerations.

iv.   The prioritization of rights and liberal anticonsequentialism

In contrast with the previous two liberal concepts, Kumm admits that proportionality is incompatible with the concept of anticonsequentialist

---

[54] See Shiffrin, above note 15, at 1211.
[55] Kumm, above note 49, at 148.
[56] See Alexy, above note 52, at 341.

liberalism.[57] This is because proportionality, ultimately, is built upon a consequentialist method of thinking. It does not support a mere deontological view of rights. Thus, proportionality places certain boundaries on the limitation of rights even in those cases where such limitations are meant to achieve desired consequences. According to the Kantian notion of deontological rights, the saving of three lives cannot be justified by sacrificing the life of a fourth; such a conclusion may not always be achieved when using proportionality analysis.

v. Deontological concepts and proportionality

Kumm is correct in noting that proportionality is not a solution for a liberal deontological approach. Proportionality is based on a balance which compares the relative values of principles while considering the consequences of either advancing or limiting them. A deontological approach, in contrast, does not take consequences into account.[58] It is theoretically possible to argue – as Alexy has done[59] – that deontological approaches also conduct a balance, but that the right's end of the scales would always be granted infinite weight such that it would always prevail over the end of the scales consisting of achieving the legislative purpose. This is an admission that proportionality cannot really operate in a deontological environment. Indeed, proportionality may only be operable when the right in question is relative, that is, when it is not protected to the fullest extent of its scope.[60] Whenever a right is absolute – which is the essence of the anticonsequentialist concept – there is no room for proportionality. Similarly, there is no place for proportionality whenever the public interest is perceived as absolute. Indeed, proportionality can only operate when the weights of the conflicting principles at issue are larger than zero and smaller than infinity. It is only between those two extremes that proportionality can properly conduct a meaningful balance. But, in the extreme cases, beyond that range, proportionality cannot be utilized; the only solution to these cases may be found outside the concept of proportionality. A separate question is whether a liberal deontological concept can apply such that it would not be indifferent to the consequences in any given case.[61] Thus, for example, would a deontological approach not

[57] See Kumm, above note 49, at 152.
[58] *Ibid.*, at 153.
[59] See Alexy, above note 52, at 344.
[60] See above, at 32.
[61] See Kumm, above note 49, at 154.

take consequences into account even in a case of a fatal catastrophe? If the answer to this question is that it would, then proportionality – and the act of balancing on which it is based – may be said to be compatible with deontological approaches as well. This would not be the case if deontological approaches would refuse, under all circumstances, to take consequences into account. If that is the case, then there is no alternative but to admit that proportionality is incompatible with this particular liberal concept.

E. Proportionality, democracy, and judicial review

1. Proportionality and democracy

The legal source of proportionality is found (directly or indirectly) in the constitution.[62] By basing itself on this notion, proportionality gains not only a legal source for its constitutional status but also a substantive justification for its operation. If proportionality is derived from democracy and the rule of law (including the formal and substantive meanings of the terms), then democracy and the rule of law are also the justifications for the concept of proportionality.[63] Indeed, democracy, the rule of law, and human rights are inseparable. Without democracy and the rule of law there are no human rights, and without human rights there is no democracy and rule of law.[64] This relationship between democracy, the rule of law, and human rights is based on the understanding that when a number of legal conditions are met, the limitation of human rights is not undemocratic. Hence, here one may also derive the notion that human rights are not absolute.[65] The limitation of human rights is compatible with democracy and the rule of law if there is a proper justification for limiting a constitutional right, namely, a proper balance is struck between the rights on the one end and the reasons for their limitation on the other. Note that it is not claimed herein that proportionality is the *only* way to determine the proper balance between the public interest and constitutional rights. Nor is it claimed, at this stage,[66] that proportionality is the *best* way in a democracy to determine the proper balance between individual rights and the public interest. All that is argued at this stage is that there is a meaningful,

---

[62] See above, at 211.
[63] See Gardbaum, above note 2; Jackson, above note 5, at 90.
[64] See Barak, above note 37, at 81.
[65] See above, at 27.
[66] See below, at 526.

inherent connection between proportionality and democracy and the rule of law, and that this is enough to establish proportionality's key role in a constitutional democracy.

2. Proportionality and judicial review

Most democracies recognize judicial review of the constitutionality of a law limiting a constitutional right.[67] In most cases, such recognition is the result of an explicit constitutional provision.[68] In rare cases – such as in the United States[69] and Israel[70] – the recognition is the result of the judicial interpretation of implicit constitutional provisions. The justification for judicial review on the constitutionality of legislation – much like the justification for proportionality itself[71] – can be traced back to the notion of democracy itself. According to that approach, if the constitution is democratic, then the judicial review found (explicitly or implicitly) in the constitution is also democratic.[72] That same view also holds that democracy does not manifest itself solely through majority rule. Democracy, rather, also consists of the recognition of human rights. Thus, when the court holds that a legislative provision is unconstitutional due to its undue limitation of a human right, it actually fulfills the constitution and democracy.[73]

---

[67] See D. W. Jackson and C. N. Tate (eds.), *Comparative Judicial Review and Public Policy* (1992); C. N. Tate and T. Vallinder (eds.), *The Global Expansion of Judicial Power* (1995); A. Stone Sweet, *Governing with Judges: Constitutional Politics in Europe* (Oxford University Press, 2000); M. Shapiro and A. Stone Sweet, *On Law, Politics and Judicialization* (Oxford University Press, 2002); R. Procházka, *Mission Accomplished: On Founding Constitutional Adjudication in Central Europe* (Budapest: Central European University Press, 2002); R. Hirschl, *Towards Juristocracy: The Origins and Consequences of the New Constitutionalism* (Cambridge, MA: Harvard University Press, 2004); M. Tushnet, *Weak Courts, Strong Rights: Judicial Review and Social Welfare Rights in Comparative Constitutional Law* (Princeton University Press, 2008); M. De S.-O.-l'E. Lasser, *Judicial Transformations: The Rights Revolution In The Courts Of Europe* (Oxford University Press, 2009); V. Ferreres Comella, *Constitutional Courts and Democratic Values: A European Perspective* (New Haven, CT: Yale University Press, 2009); V. Jackson, *Constitutional Engagement in a Transnational Era* (Oxford University Press, 2010).

[68] See, e.g., Basic Law for the Federal Republic of Germany, Art. 93; Constitution of Spain, Art. 161; Constitution of the Republic of Poland, Art. 188; Canadian Charter of Rights and Freedoms, Section 52(1).

[69] *Marbury v. Madison*, 5 US (1 Cranch) 137, 177 (1803).

[70] See CA 6821/93 *United Mizrahi Bank Ltd. v. Migdal Cooperative Village* [1995] IsrLR 1.

[71] See above, at 214.

[72] See *United Mizrahi Bank*, above note 70, at para. 80 (Barak, P.).

[73] See *ibid.*; *A v. Secretary of State for the Home Department* [2004] UKHL 56, para. 42: "[T] he function of independent judges charged to interpret and apply the law is universally

Not everyone agrees with the proposition that judicial review is a democratic institution.[74] The literature on the issue is vast.[75] The critics of judicial review argue that there is no proof that constitutional rights are better under judicial review than under legislative supremacy. They also argue that judges exercising judicial review of legislation lack democratic legitimacy. A full examination of those claims is beyond the scope of this

recognised as a cardinal feature of the modern democratic state, a cornerstone of the rule of law itself … [The Attorney General] is wrong to stigmatise judicial decision-making as in some way undemocratic." (Lord Bingham).

[74] See J. Waldron, *Law and Disagreement* (Oxford: Clarendon Press, 1999); M. J. Perry, "Protecting Human Rights in a Democracy: What Role for the Courts?," 38 *Wake Forest L. Rev.* 635 (2003). As to justification of judicial review under the United Kingdom Human Right Act 1998, see Kavanagh, above note 7, at 338.

[75] See A. M. Bickel, *The Least Dangerous Breach: The Supreme Court at the Bar of Politics* (Indianapolis, IN: Bobbs-Merrill, 1962); J. H. Ely, *Democracy and Distrust: Theory of Judicial Review* (Cambridge, MA: Harvard University Press, 1980); R. M. Dworkin, *Freedom's Law: The Moral Reading of the American Constitution* (Oxford University Press, 1999); D. J. Solove, "The Darkest Domain: Deference, Judicial Review, and the Bill of Rights," 84 *Iowa L. Rev.* 941 (1999); M. V. Tushnet, *Taking the Constitution away from the Courts* (Princeton University Press, 2000); B. Friedman, "The Counter-Majoritarian Problem and the Pathology of Constitutional Scholarship," 95 *Nw. U. L. Rev.* 933 (2001); B. Friedman, "The Birth of an Academic Obsession: The History of the Countermajoritarian Difficulty, Part Five," 112 *Yale L. J.* 153 (2002); C. F. Zurn, "Deliberative Democracy and Constitutional Review," 21 *Law and Philosophy* 467 (2002); L. B. Tremblay, "General Legitimacy of Judicial Review and the Fundamental Basis of Constitutional Law," 23 *OJLS* 525 (2003); A. Harel, "Rights-Based Judicial Review: A Democratic Justification," 22 *Law and Philosophy* 247 (2003); L. McDonald, "Rights, 'Dialogue' and Democratic Objections to Judicial Review," 32 *Fed. L. Rev.* 1 (2004); L. G. Sager, *Justice in Plainclothes: A Theory of American Constitutional Practice* (New Haven, CT: Yale University Press, 2006); L. D. Kramer, *The People Themselves: Popular Constitutionalism and Judicial Review* (Oxford University Press, 2006); J. Jowell, "Parliamentary Sovereignty under the New Constitutional Hypothesis," 3 *PL* 562 (2006); J. Waldron, "The Core of the Case Against Judicial Review," 115 *Yale L. J.* 1346 (2006); Y. Eylon and A. Harel, "The Right to Judicial Review," 92 *Yale L. Rev.* 991 (2006); R. Bellamy, *Political Constitutionalism: A Republican Defense of the Constitutionality of Democracy* (Cambridge University Press, 2007); W. Waluchow, *A Common Law Theory of Judicial Review: The Living Tree* (Cambridge University Press, 2007); L. Alexander, "Constitutions, Judicial Review, Moral Rights, and Democracy: Disentangling the Issues," in G. Huscroft (ed.), *Expounding the Constitution: Essays in Constitutional Theory* (Cambridge University Press, 2008), 119; R. H. Fallon, "The Core of an Uneasy Case for Judicial Review," 121 *Harv. L. Rev.* 1693 (2008); D. S. Law, "A Theory of Judicial Power and Judicial Review," 97 *Geo. L. J.* 723 (2009); V. Ferreres Comella, *Constitutional Courts and Democratic Values* (New Haven, CT: Yale University Press, 2009); G. Webber, *The Negotiable Constitution: On the Limitation of Rights* (Cambridge University Press, 2009; A. Walmen, "Judicial Review in Review: A Four-Part Defense of Legal Constitutionalism: A Review Essay on Political Constitutionalism," 7(2) *Int'l J. Const. L.* 329 (2009); Den Otter, above note 7.

book. I will examine two responses to those claims, one by Kumm[76] and the other by Beatty.[77]

3. Kumm's approach

Kumm emphasizes proportionality's uniqueness. He does not concern himself with the interpretation of the constitutional right. His theory does not examine – as the accepted approach in the United States does – the specific case's belonging to a predetermined category. Proportionality is unique in that it examines the justification of the limitation of a constitutional right in a given case:

> Courts engage public reason, reasons that can serve to justify acts of public authorities that place burdens on people without their explicit consent.[78]

This way of thinking is dubbed by Kumm as the Rational Human Right Paradigm (RHRP).[79] According to Kumm's approach:[80]

> Both judicial review of legislation and electoral accountability of the legislator give institutional expression to co-original and equally basic commitments of liberal-democratic constitutionalism. An equal right to vote gives expression to a commitment of political equality. A right to contest decisions by public authorities before gives expression to a commitment of liberty as non-domination not to be subject to laws that you might not reasonably have consented to. Both are central pillars of constitutional legitimacy.

According to his approach:

> Judicial review is not just a legitimate option. Liberal democracy without judicial review would be incomplete and deficient.[81]

Kumm finds an interesting relationship between Socratic contestation and thinking according to proportionality. According to his approach:

> The point of judicial review ... is to legally institutionalize a practice of Socratic contestation. Socratic contestation refers to the practice of

---

[76] See M. Kumm, "Democracy Is Not Enough: Rights, Proportionality and the Point of Judicial Review" (New York University Public Law and Legal Theory, Working Papers. Paper 118, 2009); A. Harel and T. Kahana, "The Easy Core Case for Judicial Review" 2 J. Legal Analysis 227 (2010).

[77] M. Beatty, *The Ultimate Rule of Law* (Oxford University Press, 2004).

[78] Kumm, above note 76, at 3.

[79] *Ibid.*, at 6.   [80] *Ibid.*, at 4.

[81] *Ibid.*, at 6.

critically engaging authorities, in order to assess whether the claims they make are based on good reasons.[82]

According to my approach, there is a deep relationship between democracy and human rights and the judicial review of a law's constitutionality. Through judicial review the individual's right is protected *vis-à-vis* the majority's power. As such, judicial review fulfills the constitution. Just as the constitution is based on the limitation of the majority's power, so is judicial review. Just as the constitution is countermajoritarian so is judicial review. Kumm's approach that at the constitution's foundation are the majority and the individual's powers is accepted herein. One of these is expressed in elections. The other is expressed by the courts.[83] Kumm writes:[84]

> The question is not what justifies the "Countermajoritarian" imposition of outcomes by non-elected judges. The question is what justifies the authority of a legislative decision, when it can be established with sufficient certainty that it imposes burdens on individuals for which there is no plausible justification. The judicial practice of Socratic contestation, structured conceptually by the RHRP and the proportionality test, and institutionally protected by rules relating to independence, impartiality and reason-giving, is uniquely suitable to give expression to and enforce this aspect of constitutional legitimacy. Constitutional legitimacy does not stand only on one leg.

4. Beatty's approach

i. The approach presented

In his book, *The Ultimate Rule of Law*,[85] Beatty argues that proportionality guarantees judicial objectivity and provides the main justification for the exercise of judicial review. Judicial objectivity is ensured by proportionality by turning legal questions – which have a wide judicial discretion – into factual questions. As Beatty puts it:

---

[82] *Ibid.*, at 4.

[83] See S. Freeman, "Constitutional Democracy and the Legitimacy of Judicial Review," 9 *Law and Philosophy* 327 (1990); J. Raz, "Rights and Politics," 71 *Ind. L. J.* 27 (1995); Harel, "Rights-Based Judicial Review," above note 75; Eylon and Harel, above note 75; Harel and Kahana, above note 76; see also Kavanagh, above note 7, at 338.

[84] Kumm, above note 76.

[85] D. M. Beatty, *The Ultimate Rule of Law* (Oxford University Press, 2004).

> [P]roportionality offers judges a clear and objective test to distinguish coercive action by the state that is legitimate from that which is not. When they stick to the facts, the personal sympathies of the judges towards the parties in the case never come into play.[86]

Beatty elaborates:

> With its focus on the particulars of each act of government, proportionality transforms questions that in moral philosophy are questions of value into questions of fact. It stimulates a distinctive kind of discourse that operates, in Habermas's terms, in an intermediate zone between facts and norms. In deciding whether a law on abortion, or sex discrimination, or housing, or health care, is constitutional or not, everything turns on the facts. Whether a state can legitimately punish women who abort their fetuses, or treat people differently on the basis of their religion or sex, or withhold resources they need to survive, depends entirely on the factual details of each case. Strict abortion laws can be justified in societies such as Ireland whose religious traditions equate pre- and post-natal life. Some forms of discrimination may be tolerated in the home that could not be practiced on the street. The resources each person can legitimately claim from the state vary directly with the affluence of their communities and the number of people who are in need.[87]

ii. A critique of Beatty's approach

Beatty's book made an important contribution to the understanding of human rights as well as of judicial review on legislation limiting those rights.[88] It clarifies the important role played by proportionality in protecting human rights. It emphasizes the centrality of proportionality in the field of human rights protection, and supports the recognition of judicial review on the constitutionality of limiting legislation. However, Beatty's argument – that proportionality transforms questions of law into questions of fact and therefore guarantees the judicial objectivity of the judicial decision regarding proportionality – is insufficiently supported.[89] This is particularly so because of proportionality *stricto*

---

[86] *Ibid.*, at 166.   [87] *Ibid.*

[88] For an evaluation of Beatty's book, see V. C. Jackson, "Being Proportional about Proportionality," 21 *Const. Comment.* 803 (2004).

[89] See Jackson, above note 88, at 821. See also G. C. N. Webber, "The Cult of Constitutional Rights Reasoning" (Paper presented at the VIIth World Congress of the International Association of Constitutional Law, Athens, June 14, 2007); Stone Sweet and Mathews, above note 3.

sensu. It is not factual in any way. True, this test is also based on a factual framework; but its main findings are legal. It is based on balancing. Indeed, the determination of whether the advancement of the social purpose may be properly balanced against the harm to the human right reflects a value-based determination as to the marginal social importance of the benefits gained by fulfilling that social purpose as well as the marginal social importance of the benefits gained by preventing the harm caused to the constitutional right. These determinations are not factual. These are legal determinations.[90] Value-based judgments do not provide the judge with full, unbounded discretion; in fact, judicial discretion is well bounded, and in some cases extremely so. However, I cannot accept the argument that the judge has no element of discretion in making a determination on those issues.[91] Proportionality cannot guarantee complete objectivity. In fact, each of proportionality's components entails an element of judicial discretion which must be exercised with an element of judicial subjectivity. But proportionality limits judicial discretion. It emphasizes the justification requirement, the structured nature of judicial discretion, its transparency, the need to realize the basic balancing rule and the concrete balancing. All those significantly limit the scope of the judicial discretion and its subjective aspects. As Justice Breyer wrote in *Heller* in reference to proportionality:

> [A]pplication of such an approach, of course, requires judgment, but the very nature of the approach – requiring careful identification of the relevant interests and evaluating the law's effect upon them – limits the judge's choices.[92]

The judge is no longer required to determine which interest is more important – human dignity or national security.[93] Proportionality clarifies and redefines the legal issues requiring judicial determination. That legal issue is the balance between the marginal social importance of the benefits gained by the public interest and the marginal social importance of preventing the harm to the right due to the said limitation in solving the fact that the judges cannot exercise complete discretion;

---

[90] See Jackson, above note 88, at 825.
[91] HCJ 5016/96 *Chorev* v. *Minister of Transportation* [1997] IsrSC 51(4) 1.
[92] *District of Columbia* v. *Heller*, 554 US 570, 719 (2008) (Breyer, J., dissenting).
[93] See above, at 350.

nor can they consider any consideration they see fit. The judges cannot impose their own values upon the society in which they operate. They should balance between the different interests in accordance with what they view as the best interests of the society of which they are a member.

Even when discretion is used, in exceptional cases, subjectively,[94] this subjectivity is meant to achieve the proper balance and not to advance one's personal worldview. Although this judicial subjectivity[95] is recognized, it

[94] CA 6024/97 *Shavit v. Rishon LeZion Jewish Burial Society* [1999] IsrSC 53(3) 600; [1998–9] IsrLR 658: "I do not deny that at some point, subjective elements become a consideration in the judicial decision-making process ... I am not disregarding the 'opinionated' aspects of the judicial opinion. However, it is essential to remember that the subjective considerations part is very small. Most of the judge's work is dictated by a complex framework of objective considerations. These originate in the founding documents and have been determined in case law as well as being shared by all judges. The decision is always value-laden. That does not mean that said judgment is subjective. Most value-laden judgments are objective, and pre-determined by the legal system's most fundamental values. A professional judge may well arrive at those value judgments while properly differentiating between the objective considerations and his own subjective approaches. This is the way judicial decisions have been made throughout history. The difficulties involved in producing a judicial decision, the 'opinionated' nature, in some cases, of the decision, or the need for a subjective determination in some cases – do not deny the special status gained by values and principles in the system, as well as the need to balance between them at the point of conflict. We no longer wish to return to the period of the jurisprudence of pure notions (*Begriffsjurisprudenz*) in which the conclusion appeared, seemingly independently, from objective considerations. We prefer a jurisprudence of principles (*Interessenjurisprudenz*) and jurisprudence of values (*Wertungsjurisprudenz*), where an 'opinionated' decision is required ... We prefer substance over form. All these can be obtained through an objective resolution, which while not completely subjective, is still 'opinionated.' In any event, this should be a trend, while recognizing that in some cases there is no solution other than subjective decisions. This 'price' is well worth paying in order to guarantee justice in the law."

[95] See A. Barak, *Judicial Discretion* (New Haven, CT: Yale University Press, 2006), 18. B. N. Cardozo, *The Nature of the Judicial Process* (Whitefish, MT: Kessinger Publishing LLC, 1921), 89; T. Nagel, "The Limits of Objectivity," in S. M. McMurrin (ed.), *The Tanner Lectures on Human Values* (Salt Lake City, UT: University of Utah Press, 1979), 77; K. Greenawalt, *Law and Objectivity* (Oxford University Press, 1992); N. Stavropoulos, *Objectivity in Law* (Oxford University Press, 1996); T. R. Machan, *Objectivity: Recovering Determinate Reality in Philosophy, Science, and Everyday Life* (Aldershot: Ashgate Publishing, 2004); R. Badinter and S. Breyer, *Judges in Contemporary Democracy: An International Conversation* (New York University Press, 2004), 275; G. Pavlakos, "Two Concepts of Objectivity," in G. Pavlakos (ed.), *Law, Rights, and Discourse: The Legal Philosophy of Robert Alexy* (Portland, OR: Hart Publishing, 2007), 83; M. H. Kramer, *Objectivity and the Rule of Law* (Cambridge University Press, 2007); L. Alexander,

is meant to achieve the proper solution determined according to objective considerations.[96] Thus, complete objectivity can never be achieved within the framework of proportionality, but the same is true for any of its proposed alternatives.[97]

"Legal Objectivity and the Illusion of Legal Principles," in M. Klatt (ed.), *Rights, Law, and Morality: Theme from the Legal Philosophy of Robert Alexy* (forthcoming, Oxford University Press, 2010).

[96] See R. Dworkin, "Pragmatism, Right Answers, and True Banality," in M. Brint and W. Weaver (eds.), *Pragmatism in Law and Society* (1991), 359; A. Barak, *Purposive Interpretation in Law* (Princeton University Press, 2005), 202.

[97] C. B. Pulido, *El Principio de Proporcionalidad y los Derechos Fundamentales* (Madrid: Centro de Estudios Políticos y Constitucionales, 2007), 70.

18

The criticism on proportionality and a retort

A. The scope of the criticism on proportionality

Proportionality is under constant attack.[1] The criticism against proportionality is primarily aimed at its balancing component, proportionality *stricto sensu*. This balancing has been referred to as "the *enfant terrible* of modern judging."[2] The criticism on judicial balancing does indeed abound.[3] The criticism can be divided into two main categories.[4] The first is internal criticism, examining proportionality from within. The second is external criticism, examining proportionality from a larger legal context. Each of these critiques will be referred to individually. This chapter strives to provide a satisfactory retort. In any event – and that, at the end of the day, is the very basis of my replies – the suggested alternatives are no better. In fact, their defects exceed those of proportionality.

---

[1] L. Henkin, "Infallibility under Law: Constitutional Balancing," 78 *Colum. L. Rev.* 1022 (1978); S. Tsakyrakis, "Proportionality: An Assault on Human Rights?," 7 *I. Con.* 468 (2003); I. Porat, "The Dual Model of Balancing: A Model for the Proper Scope of Balancing in Constitutional Law," 27 *Cardozo L. Rev.* 1393 (2006); G. Webber, *The Negotiable Constitution: On the Limitation of Rights* (Cambridge University Press, 2009); S. Tsakyrakis, "Proportionality: An Assault on Human Rights?: A Rejoinder to Madhav Khosla," 8(2) *I. Con.* 307 (2010).

[2] P. M. McFadden, "The Balancing Test," 29 *B. C. L. Rev.* 585, 586 (1988). For an analysis of the critique and a retort, see A. Stone Sweet and J. Mathews, "Proportionality Balancing and Global Constitutionalism," 47 *Colum. J. Transnat'l L.* 72 (2008).

[3] Webber, above note 1. At the core of this critique is the dispute between Alexy and Habermas. Regarding this dispute, see S. Greer, "'Balancing' and the European Court of Human Rights: A Contribution to the Habermas-Alexy Debate," 63 *Cambridge L. J.* 412 (2004). For the opinion of the parties to the dispute, see J. Habermas, *Between Facts and Norms: Contributions to a Discourse Theory of Law and Democracy* (Cambridge, MA: The MIT Press, 1996), 256; R. Alexy, "Jürgen Habermas's Theory of Legal Discourse," 17 *Cardozo L. Rev.* 1027 (1996); R. Alexy, *A Theory of Constitutional Rights* (J. Rivers trans., Oxford University Press, 2002 [1986]), 44; R. Alexy, "Constitutional Rights, Balancing, and Rationality," 16 *Ratio Juris* 131 (2003); R. Alexy, "On Balancing and Subsumption: A Structural Comparison," 16 *Ratio Juris* 433 (2003).

[4] See T. A. Aleinikoff, "Constitutional Law in the Age of Balancing," 96 *Yale L. J.* 943, 972 (1987).

B.   Internal criticism

1.   *The nature of the internal criticism*

The internal criticism on proportionality can be described from two separate viewpoints.[5] The first focuses on the lack of standards by which proportionality *stricto sensu* can be determined; the second focuses on the non-rational nature of the balancing component on which proportionality *stricto sensu* is based. A closer look, however, reveals that these two viewpoints are, in fact, two different aspects of the same argument. According to this claim, the balancing act – on which proportionality is based – is nothing but a manifestation of intuition and improvisation.[6] It has neither consistency nor coherence.[7] It lacks accuracy. In fact, it is based on a false sense of a scientific method which stems from the unsuccessful use of balancing and weight metaphors.[8] These arguments will be addressed in turn.

2.   *The lack of a standard by which proportionality can be examined*

i.   The issue of incommensurability

The main point of this line of criticism is that in order to balance between competing principles they should be based on a common denominator. This common denominator is impossible to find since the conflicting principles do not have a common denominator. They are incommensurable.[9] Therefore, the entire edifice of balancing rests on a false premise,

---

[5] See C. B. Pulido, *El Principio de Proporcionalidad y los Derechos Fundamentales* (Madrid: Centro de Estudios Políticos y Constitucionales 2007), 163.

[6] S. E. Gottlieb, "The Paradox of Balancing Significant Interests," 45 *Hastings L. J.* 825, 850 (1994).

[7] See McFadden, above note 2.

[8] D. L. Faigman, "Madisonian Balancing: A Theory of Constitutional Adjudication," 88 *Nw. U. L. Rev.* 641 (1994).

[9] On the issues of incommensurability and incomparability, see D. Luban, "Incommensurable Values, Rational Choice, and Moral Absolutes," 38 *Clev. St. L. Rev.* 65 (1990); R. Chang (ed.), *Incommensurability, Incomparability, and Practical Reason* (1997); M. D. Adler and E. A. Posner, *Cost–Benefit Analysis: Legal, Economic and Philosophical Perspectives* (University of Chicago Press, 2000); H. Mather, "Law-Making and Incommensurability," *McGill L. J.* 345 (2002); F. D'Agostino, *Incommensurability and Commensuration: The Common Denominator* (Aldershot: Ashgate Publishing, 2003). See the symposium on this subject held at the University of Pennsylvania Law School and published in M. Adler, "Symposium: Law and Incommensurability: Introduction," 146 *U. Pa. L. Rev.* 1168 (1998). See also F. Schauer, "Commensurability

and is therefore destined to fail.[10] In referring to balancing, Justice Scalia
has noted:

> [T]he scale analogy is not really appropriate, since the interests on both
> sides are incommensurate. It is more like judging whether a particular
> line is longer than a particular rock is heavy.[11]

According to this approach, for the balancing to be successful there must
be a hierarchy of principles. Alas, this hierarchy simply does not exist.[12]
All attempts to establish one have failed.[13] In this situation there is no
room to conduct any kind of balancing. The balancing metaphor remains
empty, with no substantial content.

ii.   A retort

I accept the premise that in order to conduct a balance, a common
denominator is required.[14] This common denominator does not have to
be quantitative. All that is required is that a shared basis for evaluating
the result of the balance exists.[15] The development of the common law
is nothing but the continuous historical process of balancing between

and Its Constitutional Consequences," 45 *Hastings L. J.* 785 (1994); J. Waldron, "Fake
Incommensurability: A Response to Professor Schauer," 45 *Hastings L. J.* 813 (1994);
C. R. Sunstein, "Incommensurability and Valuation in Law," 92 *Mich. L. Rev.* 779
(1994); J. Raz, *Engaging Reason: On the Theory of Value and Action* (Oxford University
Press, 1999), 46; J. Bomhoff and L. Zucca, "The Tragedy of Ms. Evans: Conflicts and
Incommensurability of Rights," 2 *Eur. Const. L. Rev.* 424 (2006); G. C. N. Webber,
"The Cult of Constitutional Rights Reasoning" (Paper presented at the VIIth World
Congress of the International Association of Constitutional Law, Athens, June 14, 2007).
S. Tsakyrakis, "Proportionality: An Assault on Human Rights?," 7(3) *I. Con.* 468 (2009);
P. Veel, "Incommensurability, Proportionality, and Rational Legal Decision-Making,"
4 *Law and Ethics Hum. Rts.* 176 (2010); V. De Silva, "Comparing the Incommensurable:
Constitutional Principles, Balancing, and Rational Decision," 31 *OJLS* (forthcoming, 2011).

[10] See L. B. Frantz, "Is the First Amendment Law?: A Reply to Professor Mendelson," 51 *Cal.
L. Rev.* 729 (1963); L. Zucca, *Constitutional Dilemmas: Conflicts of Fundamental Legal
Rights in Europe and the USA* (Oxford University Press, 2007), 85. See also Henkin, above
note 1; Aleinikoff, above note 4; Webber, above note 1, at 89.

[11] *Bendix Autolite Corp.* v. *Midwesco Enterprises Inc.,* 486 US 888, 897 (1988).

[12] See G. La Forest, "The Balancing of Interests under the Charter," 2 *Nat'l. J. Const. L.* 132,
134 (1992).

[13] See R. Pound, "A Survey of Social Interests," 57 *Harv. L. Rev.* 1 (1943); E. B. McLean,
"Roscoe Pound's Theory of Interests and the Furtherance of Western Civilization," 41 *Il
Politico* 5 (1976).

[14] See Pound, above note 13, at 2.

[15] See J. M. Shaman, "Constitutional Interpretation: Illusion and Reality," 41 *Wayne
L. Rev.* 135, 152 (1995); R. Posner, *Law, Pragmatism, and Democracy* (2003), 363; R.
Alexy, "The Reasonableness of Law," in G. Bongiovanni, G. Sartor, and C. Valentini

competing principles. If this balancing is possible within the confines of the common law, there is no reason to assume it is not so in constitutional law. At the foundation of the constitutional balance lie the marginal social importance in fulfilling one principle and the marginal social importance in preventing the harm to another principle.[16] Accordingly, whenever the two ends of the scale contain constitutional rights, a balancing is carried out between the marginal social importance gained by the protection of one constitutional right and the marginal social importance gained by preventing more harm to the other constitutional right. When the public interest is on one side of the balance (such as national security or public safety) and on the other side we find a constitutional right (such as freedom of expression or human dignity), the comparison is between the marginal social importance of the benefits gained by advancing the public interest and the marginal social importance of the benefits gained by preventing the harm to the constitutional right. Thus, a shared base – or a common denominator – exists; it is in the form of the marginal social importance in fulfilling the public purpose and the marginal social importance in preventing the harm to the constitutional right. The question is whether the marginal social importance of the benefits to one constitutional principle is important enough to justify the marginal social importance in preventing the harm caused to the other. This contextual presentation of the issue provides the common denominator – the relative social importance – required to conduct the balance. The metaphors of balancing and weight thus receive substantive content.[17]

3.   The lack of rationality

i.   The nature of the criticism

The argument is that any act of balancing between competing interests is based entirely on intuition and improvisation.[18] It lacks any rational

---

(eds.), *Reasonableness and Law* (Dordrecht: Springer, 2009), 5; F. Schauer, "Balancing, Subsumption and the Constraining Role of Legal Text," in M. Klatt (ed.), *Rights, Law, and Morality: Themes from the Legal Philosophy of Robert Alexy* (Oxford University Press, 2009); Waldron, above note 9. See also Gottlieb, above note 6.

[16] See above, at 350. See also R. H. Fallon, "Foreword: Implementing the Constitution," 111 *Harv. L. Rev.* 54, 85 (1998).

[17] See Pulido, above note 5, at 789; De Silva, above note 9. For criticism, see Tsakyrakis, above note 9, at 474.

[18] See above, at 483.

foundation.[19] It is not based on any rigorous criteria.[20] In addition, it lacks an objective component and instead relies entirely on subjective considerations of the person conducting the balance (be it a legislator, judge, or a member of the executive branch[21]). Therefore, similar cases receive different solutions and therefore the notion of balancing is arbitrary.[22]

ii. A retort

The argument that proportionality lacks a rational basis has not been left unanswered. The answer is that balancing is carried out in accordance with rational standards.[23] Of course, the act of balancing may in some cases confer a limited measure of discretion upon the person conducting it (be it the legislator, the judge,[24] or a member of the executive branch). But, the very existence of the element of discretion does not render the act irrational.[25] So long as the discretion operates within well-defined rational standards, the decision reached through them is rational. Indeed, the rationality of the act of balancing is derived from the existence of a rational justification for the balancing act and cannot be denied merely through discretion's existence. As Kumm has argued,[26] proportionality

---

[19] See Habermas, above note 3, at 259. See also B. Pieroth and B. Schlink, *Grundrechte Staatsrecht II* (Heidelberg: C. F. Müller Verlag, 2006), 66. For an analysis of the argument and the retort, see Pulido, above note 5, at 163.

[20] See C. B. Pulido, "The Rationality of Balancing," 92 *Archiv für Rechts- und Sozial Philosophie* 195 (2007).

[21] See D. S. Bogen, "Balancing Freedom of Speech," 38 *Md. L. Rev.* 387, 388 (1979); B. Neuborne, "Notes for a Theory of Constrained Balancing in First Amendment Cases: An Essay in Honor of Tom Emerson," 38 *Case W. Res. L. Rev.* 576 (1988); B. Schlink, "Der Grundsatz der Verhältnismßssigkeit," in P. Badura and H. Dreier (eds.), *Festschrift 50 Jahre Bundesverfassungsgericht*, vol. II (Tübingen: Mohr Siebeck, 2001), 445.

[22] See C. R. Ducat, *Modes of Constitutional Interpretation* (1978), 128.

[23] See D. P. Kommers, "Germany: Balancing Rights and Duties," in J. Goldsworthy (ed.), *Interpreting Constitutions: A Comparative Study* (Oxford University Press, 2006), 161; E. T. Feteris, "The Rational Reconstruction of Weighing and Balancing on the Basis of Teleological-Evaluative Considerations in the Justification of Judicial Decisions," 21(4) *Ratio Juris* 481 (2008); J. Bomhoff, "Balancing, the Global and the Local: Judicial Balancing as a Problematic Topic in Comparative (Constitutional) Law," 31 *Hastings Int'l. & Comp. L. Rev.* 555 (2008). See also Alexy, above note 3, at 101; Schauer, above note 9; Pulido, above note 5, at 707.

[24] See above, at 414.

[25] See R. Alexy, "Constitutional Rights Balancing and Rationality," 16 *Ratio Juris* 131 (2003); Alexy, above note 3, at 134.

[26] See M. Kumm, "Democracy Is Not Enough: Rights, Proportionality and the Point of Judicial Review" (New York University Public Law and Legal Theory, Working Papers. Paper 118, 2009); M. Kumm, "The Idea of Socratic Contestation and the Right to Justification: The Point of Rights-Based Proportionality Review," 4 *Law and Ethics Hum, Rts.* 140.

reflects a rational human right paradigm: it imposes on public authorities the burden to justify a limitation on a constitutional right in terms of public reason. It provides a structure for the assessment of public reasons. Kumm points out that reasoning about rights means reasoning about how a particular value relates to the exigencies of the circumstances. It requires general practical reasoning as it applies to a particular context.

The rational justification for the balancing act is found in the basic rule, according to which a proper balance compares between the marginal social importance of the benefits gained by fulfilling the public interest or protecting another constitutional right and the marginal social importance of the benefits gained by preventing the harm to the constitutional right as a result.[27] The said balancing is not based upon logical syllogism. The lack of syllogism does not mean a lack of rationality. Subjective components of exercising discretion do not deny rationality.

There are those who claim that the concept of balancing presents itself as (or at least creates a façade of having) scientific accuracy; while it is actually based on judicial subjectivity.[28] This argument cannot be accepted.[29] As for the "façade," it should be noted that it was never argued that the act of balancing is scientific, or that it completely eliminates judicial discretion. Rather, the judicial discretion exercised in the process of balancing is always limited and is never arbitrary.[30] Thus, even where subjective elements are used, these operate within limited confines and only in order to achieve proper purposes.[31] Moreover, judicial discretion must fulfill general principles of judicial coherence and judicial consistency. It must respect the principle of *stare decisis*. It must reflect the fundamental values of the legal system.[32] It is transparent and open to criticism and review by the legal community. In fact, balancing brings – rather than confusion – a sense of order and method into constitutional law analysis. It forces the judge to identify the relevant principles and to provide a justification for the right's limitation. It requires the judge to deal with the marginal social importance. It forces the judge to expose, both to themselves and to others, their train of thought. It allows for both independent, internal criticism as well as external review.[33]

---

[27] See above, at 350.
[28] See Zucca, above note 10, at 88; Alienkoff, above note 4.
[29] See A. Barak, *The Judge in a Democracy* (Princeton University Press, 2006), 174.
[30] See above, at 391.   [31] See above, at 391.
[32] See K. Greenawalt, *Law and Objectivity* (Oxford University Press, 1992), 206.
[33] See Barak, above note 29, at 172. See also F. M. Coffin, "Judicial Balancing: The Protean Scales of Justice," 63 *N. Y. U. L. Rev.* 16, 25 (1988): "Open balancing restrains the judge and minimizes hidden or improper personal preferences by revealing every step in the

The act of balancing is not merely a judicial technique. It is also a mental process. It is an expression of the complexity of human nature, as well as the complexity of human relations. The law is not an "all or nothing" approach. The law is a complex system of principles, which in some cases all point in the same direction while in other cases are in a state of conflict and require judicial resolution. The rule of balancing expresses this complexity.[34]

C.   External criticism

1.   Too wide a judicial discretion

i.   The nature of the criticism

The argument here is that proportionality – and, in particular, the balancing conducted within proportionality *stricto sensu* – provides the judge with too wide a discretion.[35] As a result, judicial certainty is damaged[36] as there is no way to predict the results in advance.[37]

ii.   A retort

I agree that, in some cases, there is no possibility of conducting a balance without a component of judicial discretion.[38] There is no way to solve this conflict without judicial discretion. The critique should prove that the discretion exercised by judges in a balance is wider than that granted to them in the proposed alternatives for resolving conflicts between competing principles. That is not the argument offered. A more adequate argument would show that the use of this seemingly too wide a discretion leads to negative effects. This kind of proof was not given and it is unlikely that it

---

thought process; it maximizes the possibility of attaining collegial consensus by responding to every relevant concern of disagreeing colleagues; and it offers a full account of the decision-making process for subsequent professional assessment and public appraisal."

[34] See Barak, above note 29, at 173. See also F. Michelman, "Foreword: Traces of Self-Government," 100 *Harv. L. Rev.* 4, 34 (1986).

[35] See M. V. Tushnet, "Anti-Formalism in Recent Constitutional Theory," 83 *Mich. L. Rev.* 1502, 1508 (1985); I. Porat, "The Dual Model of Balancing: A Model for the Proper Scope of Balancing in Constitutional Law," 27 *Cardozo L. Rev.*1393 (2006). See also Faigman, above note 8, at 648.

[36] See M. B. Nimmer, "The Right to Speak from Times to Time: First Amendment Theory Applied to Libel and Misapplied to Privacy," 56 *Cal. L. Rev.* 935, 939 (1968).

[37] See L. B. Frantz, "The First Amendment in the Balance," 71 *Yale L. J.* 1424, 1441 (1962).

[38] See V. C. Jackson, "Being Proportional about Proportionality," 21 *Const. Comment.* 803, 835 (2004).

exists. Indeed, even the American model – based on categorization[39] – is based on judicial discretion.[40] It was never demonstrated that such categorization reduces the discretion, or that it leads to more judicial certainty, or provides a better opportunity to predict the results. As noted, proportionality makes transparent legal decisions. Categorization tends to be less transparent. The reasons underlying the categorical choice are typically not made explicit. Today, most constitutional democracies use balancing, and there is no proof that their judicial discretion is wider than that used by American judges. Finally, it was never demonstrated that the legal certainty in the United States is greater than that offered by those countries using balancing.

2.   Insufficient protection of constitutional rights

i.   The nature of the criticism

Several commentators, reflecting different opinions, have criticized proportionality for not providing enough protection to human rights.[41] One type of criticism derives from an understanding of rights which is critical to the concept of balancing. According to that criticism, rights should not be balanced away based on proportionality considerations. There are those, like Dworkin, who deem rights to be "trumps," which prevail over policy relating to the public interest.[42] According to this view, only in extreme and special circumstances, which require a unique justification, can a right be limited. Habermas views rights as firewalls, which protect the individual from the community.[43] These approaches are quite suspicious of the concept of proportionality. In fact, they view proportionality as a tool for limiting human rights rather than as an instrument designed to protect them.[44] The second type of criticism claims that, even

---

[39] See below, at 502.

[40] See Posner, above note 15, at 375; Shaman, above note 15, at 141.

[41] See Webber, above note 1; Tsakyrakis, above note 1.

[42] See R. Dworkin, *Taking Rights Seriously* (Cambridge, MA: Harvard University Press, 1977), 184–205; R. Dworkin, "Rights as Trumps," in J. Waldron (ed.), *Theories of Rights* (Oxford University Press, 1984), 153. For an analysis of this approach, see B. Friedman, "Trumping Rights," 27 *Ga. L. Rev.* 435 (1992); D. T. Coenen, "Rights as Trumps," 27 *Ga. L. Rev.* 463 (1992); J. Waldron, "Pildes on Dworkin's Theory of Rights," 29 *J. Legal Studies* 301 (2000); R. Pildes, "Dworkin's Two Conceptions of Rights," 29 *J. Legal Studies* 309 (2000).

[43] See Habermas, above note 3, at 258.

[44] See E. C. Baker, "Limitations on Basic Human Rights – A View from the United States," in A. de Mestral, S. Birks, M. Both *et al.* (eds.), *The Limitation of Human Rights in Comparative Constitutional Law* (Montreal: Les Editions Yvon Blais, 1986).

if on the level of political morality proportionality provides the right kind of structure, courts are likely to cave in under pressure if their only ground to resist public authorities claiming that something is necessary and appropriate in the face of majority public policy concerns is a highly indeterminate proportionality structure. It is frequently argued that the categorization used in the American model provides more robust protection to human rights than the two-stage proportionality model which distinguishes between the scope of the right and the extent of its protection. This argument rests on the assumption that, whenever the protection of the constitutional right depends on a specific balancing process, considerations relating to the public interest will usually prevail over individual (or minority) rights.[45] This argument is said to apply primarily during times of national emergency,[46] but may also apply during quiet periods when an individual right conflicts with the public interest. As Niemmer has noted:

> It is too much to expect that our judges will be entirely untouched, consciously or otherwise, by such strong popular feelings – feelings that have more than once reached a point of national hysteria – when they come to engage in the "delicate and difficult task" of weighing competing interests. Thus at the very time when the right of freedom of speech becomes crucial, the scales may become unbalanced.[47]

Gunther even went so far as to suggest that balancing is equal to "abdication of the judicial responsibility for the protection of civil liberties,"[48] whereas Webber claimed that judicial balancing limits the very idea of a constitution.[49]

ii.   A retort

Regarding the first type of criticism, my answer is that there is nothing in the methodology of proportionality which contradicts a liberal antiperfectionist or anticollectivist democratic tradition.[50] Proportionality is a legal framework that must be filled with content. It allows for different

---

[45] See Ducat, above note 22, at 179.
[46] See J. H. Ely, "Flag Desecration: A Case Study in the Roles of Categorization and Balancing in First Amendment Analysis," 88 *Harv. L. Rev.* 1482, 1501 (1975); L. H. Tribe, *American Constitutional Law* 2nd edn. (Mineola, NY: Foundation Press, 1988), 793.
[47] See Nimmer, above note 36, at 940.
[48] See G. Gunther, "In Search of Judicial Quality on a Changing Court: The Case of Justice Powell," 24 *Stan. L. Rev.* 1001, 1005 (1972). See also McFadden, above note 2, at 636.
[49] See Webber, above note 1, at 101.
[50] See above, at 469 and 470.

levels of protection, according to the principles and values of each legal system. Thus, for example, each system determines its own content with regard to the threshold test of the proper purpose. This could establish a high standard (as in Canada[51]) or a low standard (as in Germany[52]). The same is true for the threshold requirement of the rational connection test and the necessity requirement; different levels may be established by different countries. The balancing, which is performed as part of proportionality *stricto sensu*, reflects the importance that each legal system ascribes to the marginal social benefits gained by fulfillment of the proper purpose and the marginal social importance of preventing the harm caused to the constitutional right in question.[53] This marginal importance varies from one legal system to another and from one period to the next. There is no reason to assume *a priori* that this justification is "weaker" in systems that have adopted proportionality. Indeed, the component of proportionality *stricto sensu* may well incorporate the notions of "rights as trumps," or "rights as firewalls." As for the second type of criticism, it requires a comparison between the protection of constitutional rights under proportionality and their protection under proportionality's alternatives. This comparison will be carried out in Chapter 19, mainly by comparing proportionality to the American categorization. The conclusion there is that the claim that human rights are better protected in the United States than in legal systems where the proportionality regime applies is without merit.

D.   Lack of judicial legitimacy

1.   *The nature of the criticism*

According to this argument, balancing between competing interests is the legislator's job.[54] Accordingly, a judge performing that task is "trespassing" on legislative territory.[55] The judge, according to this argument,

---

[51] See above, at 281.   [52] See below, at 529.

[53] See above, at 350.

[54] See Shaman, above note 15, at 155; Webber, above note 1.

[55] See Frantz, above note 37, at 1443; Aleinikoff, above note 4, at 984; McFadden, above note 2, at 641; Henkin, above note 1, at 104. See also B. Schlink, "Der Grundsatz der Verhältnismässigkeit," in P. Badura and H. Dreier (eds.), *Festschrift 50 Jahre Bundesverfassungsgericht*, vol. II (Tübingen: Mohr Siebeck, 2001), 445, 461; I. Porat, "Why All Attempts to Make Judicial Review Balancing Principled Fail" (Paper presented at the VIIth World Congress of the International Association of Constitutional Law, Athens, June 14, 2007); C. Ducat, *Modes of Constitutional Interpretation* (1978), 119.

turns himself into a super-legislator,[56] thus violating the principle of the separation of powers.[57] Hence, one may deduce the need to avoid judicial balancing or that it should be conducted, if at all, only in the most extreme of circumstances.[58] In essence, this argument is about judicial democratic "deficiency." Another argument, in the same vein, is that the court lacks the institutional capacity to conduct the balance. The judge's point of view – due to the inherent nature of the judicial process – is too narrow. His ability to deal with empirical data is limited.[59]

2.   A retort

The formal reply to the argument about the lack of judicial legitimacy in conducting the balance is that the authority to exercise judicial review, as well as the authority to balance between competing principles (within the limitation clause), is anchored in the constitution. The court did not take on this authority for itself. It was granted to the court by the constitution (either explicitly or implicitly). In the same manner by which the constitution conferred upon the legislator the power to legislate, it also provided the judge with the authority to review that legislation.[60]

In addition to this formal answer, there is another, more substantive reply that directly deals with the assumption at the criticism's foundation – that the very nature of the institution of judicial review is undemocratic. The substantive answer, therefore, focuses on this basic premise of the criticism. This expansive topic cannot be fully examined within the confines of this book. Chapter 17 provides a partial examination of the subject. In essence, judicial review of the constitutionality of legislation is an expression of the democratic nature of the constitution. From the said democratic character of the constitution, as well as from the legislator's duty to fulfill the constitution's provisions, stems the judiciary's role as the constitution's defender and a protector of human rights, such that those rights would not be unduly limited by the legislator.[61] According to

---

[56] See Ducat, above note 22, at 130.

[57] See McFadden, above note 2, at 588.

[58] See *Dennis* v. *United States*, 341 US 494, 525 (1951).

[59] See Porat, above note 35.

[60] For a criticism of this argument, see Webber, above note 1; J. Waldron, *Law and Disagreement* (Oxford University Press, 1999), 255.

[61] See J. Paul Muller, "Fundamental Rights in Democracy," 4 *Human Rights Law Journal* (1983); S. Gardbaum, "A Democratic Defense of Constitutional Balancing," 4(1) *Law and Ethics of Hum. Rts.* 77 (2010).

my approach, proportionality generally and balancing in particular are an important judicial tool for protecting a democratic constitution. The legislator, too, conducts balancing while adopting legislation. By doing so, the legislator is looking to reflect the very balanced approach adopted by – and inherent to – the constitution. However, it would be inappropriate to provide the legislator with the last word on the constitutionality of the balance it has conducted. This is the foundation for the institution of judicial review. According to that notion, the institutional structure of the court, its independence, and its distance from day-to-day political pressures, put judicial balancing closer than any other type of balancing to the balancing required by the constitution.[62] Further, the court is fully equipped, both professionally and ethically, to perform the task. In that context, as noted earlier, there is no room for judicial deference.[63] Finally, I could not find any other approach – other than proportionality (and its balancing core) – that would be able to guarantee both the appropriate status of the legislature and the appropriate status of human rights in the system.[64] Accordingly, the real issue is not whether we should adopt proportionality or another method to review legislation's constitutionality. The real question is whether to have judicial review of the law's constitutionality or to have no review at all. The real matter is not whether proportionality – with balancing at its core – is an appropriate method. The only relevant question is whether the institution of judicial review is proper. To that question the reply is a resounding "yes." Judicial review protects and defends democracy, by both the formal and substantive meanings of the term, and protects human rights.[65] The power of the legislature to legislate is not absolute. It is subject to the limitations imposed by constitutional human rights. The courts protect those rights through judicial review. Kumm has emphasized that the constitutional legitimacy of the legislature is enforced not only through the people's vote, but also through the judicial review of independent judges.[66]

---

[62] See above, at 491; V. Ferreres Comella, *Constitutional Courts and Democratic Values: A European Perspective* (New Haven, CT: Yale University Press, 2009).

[63] See above, at 396.

[64] See Pulido, above note 5, at 205.

[65] See above, at 473.   [66] See Kumm, above note 26.

19

Alternatives to proportionality

Proportionality is a legal tool designed to resolve conflicts between constitutional rights, or conflicts between constitutional rights and the public interest. It is not the only tool designed to provide such solutions. Other legal tools also seek to provide solutions to these conflicts. This chapter will review some of these alternatives, particularly the alternative referred to as "categorization," which is frequently used by American courts. Before categorization is reviewed, however, several other alternatives are presented.

A. Non-categorization-based alternatives

1. *Absolute rights*

i.   The nature of the alternative

Webber proposed an alternative to proportionality.[1] According to his approach, the scope of constitutional rights is determined as per their interpretation. This scope is supplemented by limitations constructed by the legislator. Those limitations are a part of the constitutional right. They do not limit it. Rather, they determine its content in accordance with the community's views at a given time. These views are expressed through legislation, which expresses the people's will. The legislator operates in accordance with the limitation clause. According to this clause, the legislator must demonstrate the justification for the right as it exists in a free and democratic society. The legislator, in other words, is the one to determine the boundaries of the right. Once these boundaries are set (in accordance with the right's proper interpretation and the limitations set by legislation), the right becomes absolute. Thus, neither proportionality nor the balancing at its core has a place. Indeed, the legislator is not bound

---

[1] See G. C. N. Webber, *The Negotiable Constitution: On the Limitation of Rights* (Cambridge University Press, 2009), 1087, 1088.

by proportionality. Accordingly, the role of the judicial branch is to examine whether or not the use of legislative discretion was arbitrary.

At the core of Webber's approach is the notion that a constitutional right's content reflects a continuing process. This content expresses the ongoing negotiation between members of society, as reflected by limitations imposed on the right by the legislator from time to time. Those legislative limitations thus become a part of the right. The judicial role, to the extent it exists, is very limited. Thus proportionality and the notion of balancing are "foreign" to this concept of a democratic process.

ii.   Assessment of the alternative

Webber's alternative – as well as his negative approach to proportionality and balancing – is predicated on his own view of constitutional rights. This view, however, seems unfounded. The accepted and proper view considers constitutional rights as a shield to protect individuals from the tyranny of the majority, as reflected by the legislator. Webber, in contrast, views the scope of constitutional rights as determined by the legislator – the very same body that expresses that type of tyranny of the majority. The limitations on the power to legislate, according to Webber, are limited. It seems that, according to Webber, there is no room for a constitutional bill of rights; there is no real need to limit the legislative power regarding human rights; there is no need for judicial review of the constitutionality of legislation limiting constitutional rights; and therefore, obviously, there is no need for proportionality – or the balancing at its core – to set boundaries for the limitations of constitutional rights. Webber's approach not only presents an alternative to proportionality, it is an alternative to the entire accepted notion of constitutional rights.

Webber's perception of the constitution – as an ongoing process of negotiations between society's members, which is determined by the legislator – renders the constitutional bill of rights devoid of its powers to protect the individual from the tyranny of the majority. What appears to be a right at the constitutional level is, in fact, a right operating at the sub-constitutional level. The tasks of both interpreting the scope of the right and setting its limits are provided to the legislator, and to the legislator alone. The cancellation of the accepted two-stage approach (a constitutional level and a legislative level) creates a single level that, in fact, is of a sub-constitutional level. And, while it is true that the legislator is not permitted to change the wording of the constitutional right, it is otherwise permitted to act as it pleases.

Webber's approach is unique, and very original. A similar approach was not found in any constitution or in the comparative literature. Even systems that do not accept the concept of proportionality, such as the United States, do not grant the legislator as wide a discretion as Webber advocates. Similarly, neither Habermas, Nozik, nor Dworkin – all brought forward by Webber in support of his criticism of proportionality – have ever adopted Webber's approach. Clearly, any legal system that would adopt such an approach is seriously risking undermining the constitutional nature of its rights. Therefore, Webber does not offer any real alternative to proportionality and balancing; instead, he presents an alternative to the constitutional nature of the bill of rights.

There is a close connection between Webber and Waldron's approaches.[2] They both deny judicial review of a statute's constitutionality. As already mentioned in Chapters 16 and 17, judicial review is proper. However, Webber's approach is more extreme than Waldron's. It seems that Webber provides the legislator with powers (through the interpreting of the scope of constitutional rights) which according to Waldron require a constitutional amendment. Waldron does not oppose what he refers to as weak judicial review as it exists in his opinion in England (through a declaration of incompatibility),[3] which it seems that Webber opposes. Webber's approach is therefore characteristically extreme. It does not take human rights seriously. Nor does it take democracy seriously, as it does not protect the individual's right *vis-à-vis* the public – a protection found in democracy's foundation.

Webber's approach is based on the notion of absolute human rights. This absolutism operates *vis-à-vis* the judicial branch. It does not operate *vis-à-vis* the legislator. The legislator is authorized to limit those rights. Webber emphasizes time and again his notion that the legislator's

---

[2] See J. Waldron, "The Core of the Case Against Judicial Review," 115 *Yale L. J.* 1346 (2006). See also R. Bellamy, *Political Constitutionalism: A Republican Defense of the Constitutionality of Democracy* (Cambridge University Press, 2007).

[3] See Waldron, above note 2, at 1355. See also A. Kavanagh, *Constitutional Review under the UK Human Rights Act* (Cambridge University Press, 2009), 416, who argues that under the UK Human Rights Act judicial review is of a strong form. See above, at 160. Waldron noted that judicial review of legislation in Canada is not proper despite the existence of the override clause: Waldron, above note 2, at 1356. This approach has been criticized: see J. Goldsworthy, "Judicial Review, Legislative Override, and Democracy," 38 *Wake Forest L. R.* 451 (2003); D. Dyzenhaus, "The Incoherence of Constitutional Positivism," in G. Huscrot (ed.), *Expounding the Constitution: Essays in Constitutional Theory* (Cambridge University Press, 2008), 138, 140. This criticism is justified. The justification or criticism of constitutional review is related to the legislator's power and not to his ability, or lack thereof, to use the said power.

limitations constitute a development of the right rather than its limitation. This distinction, however, renders the difference between the development of and the limitation of a right nearly superfluous. It seems that,
in most cases where courts have declared legislative provisions unconstitutional for their disproportional limitation of a constitutional right,
Webber would have understood these as the development of the constitutional right. The absoluteness of the constitutional right according to
Webber is trivial at best.[4] Such a view, in practice, is not that different
from that which considers every constitutional right as absolute if the
courts have agreed that its limitation was proportional.

2.   *Protecting the core of the constitutional right*

i.   The nature of the alternative

While Webber's "absolute rights" alternative to proportionality seeks to
turn all rights into absolutes, the "protection of the right's core" alternative views only the right's "core" as an absolute. Anything within that
"core," according to this alternative, cannot be limited. This is protected
to the full extent of its scope. Proportionality applies only to what is not
included in the core. The historical origin of this approach can be found
in German law.[5] Article 19(2) of the Basic Law for the Federal Republic of
Germany reads (in its official translation):

> In no case may the essential content (*Wesensgehalt*) of a basic right be
> encroached upon.

Following the German example, several constitutions have adopted similar provisions, including the constitutions of Turkey,[6] Portugal,[7] Spain,[8]
and the Federal Constitution of Switzerland.[9]

---

[4] See above, at 27.

[5] See L. Wildhaber, "Limitations on Human Rights in Times of Peace, War and Emergency:
A Report on Swiss Law," in A. de Mestral, S. Birks, M. Both *et al.* (eds.), *The Limitation of
Human Rights in Comparative Constitutional Law* (Montreal: Les Editions Yvon Blais,
1986); R. Alexy, *A Theory of Constitutional Rights* (J. Rivers trans., Oxford University
Press, 2002 [1986]), 192; M. Sachs, *GG Verfassungsrecht II Grundrechte* (Berlin: Springer,
2003), 734; G. Van der Schyff, "Cutting to the Core of Conflicting Rights: The Question
of Inalienable Cores in Comparative Perspectives," in E. Brems (ed.), *Conflicts Between
Fundamental Rights* (Mortsel, Belgium: Intersentia, 2008), 131.

[6] Constitution of the Republic of Turkey, Art. 13.

[7] Constitution of Portugal, Art. 18(3).

[8] Constitution of Spain, Art. 53(1).

[9] Federal Constitution of Switzerland, Art. 36(4).

The application of each of those provisions requires a determination, for each constitutional right, of the right's core (or its nuclear substance) and which parts constitute the penumbra. Such a determination should be based on the values and principles that the right is meant to advance.[10]

An important question in this context is whether the test of the limitation is subjective or objective.[11] According to the objective test, the question of the right's core is determined from the viewpoint of the legal system as a whole, while considering the potential victims of the limitation. According to this approach, the right's core is affected in cases where the right loses much of its significance in relation to all, or the vast majority of, a given community. Thus, for example, a statute prohibiting a police officer from killing another person under certain circumstances does not limit the core of the right to life of the general public. According to the subjective test, the question of the right's core is determined from the viewpoint of the victim – the limited person. According to this approach, the right's core is limited when the right has lost its significance in relation to the specific individual.

There are those who believe that no comprehensive answer should be given to the question of subjective versus objective tests. According to this approach, the answer varies in accordance with the right's nature.[12] Thus, for example, the core of the right to life should be determined by an objective test, while the core of the right to bodily integrity should be determined by a subjective test.

ii. The rules of proportionality and the right's core

Does proportionality play any role in determining whether a limitation pertains to the right's core?[13] Opinions on this issue vary.[14] Some are of the opinion that the restriction imposed on limiting a right's core

---

[10] See E. Orucu, "The Core of Rights and Freedoms: The Limit of Limits," in T. Campbell (ed.), *Human Rights: From Rhetoric to Reality* (New York: Basil Blackwell, 1986), 187.

[11] See Alexy, above note 5, at 192; Sachs, above note 5, at 735. See also G. Van der Schyff, *Limitation of Rights: A Study of the European Convention and the South African Bill of Rights* (Nijmegen, The Netherlands: Wolf Legal Publishers, 2005), 164; B. Pieroth and B. Schlink, *Gdundrechte Staatsrecht II* (Heidelberg: C. F. Müller Verlag, 2006), 70.

[12] See Pieroth and Schlink, above note 11.

[13] See Van der Schyff, above note 11, at 164. See also J. Rivers, "Proportionality and Variable Intensity of Review," 65 *Cambridge L. J.* 174 (2006).

[14] See Van der Schyff, above note 11, at 167; Sachs, above note 5, at 735. See also K. Hesse, *Grundzüge des Verfassungsrechts der Bundesrepublik Deutschland* (Heidelberg: Die Deutsche Bibliotek, 1999), § 333.

creates an "absolute" constraint on the possibility of limiting that right. According to that opinion, proportionality plays no role in determining the nature of this limitation; any limitation of the right's core, in and of itself, is equivalent to an amendment to the right.[15] The prohibition of the effect on the rights core applies even if the limitation is proportional.[16] Others believe that the restriction on limiting the right's core is not "absolute" but rather "partial," and is derived from its context. According to this approach, the rules of proportionality determine whether the limitation was "authorized," and therefore the said determination would be the result of the balance struck between conflicting values and principles.[17]

The difference in opinions between these two approaches is, to a large extent, artificial. It seems that those who favor the "absolute" approach to the notion of the right's core find it difficult to define the exact contours of that "core." At the end of the day, they may consider a limitation to be of the right's core only when such a limitation is disproportional.[18]

iii.   Assessment of the alternative

Is this approach proper? It seems that the answer is no.[19] As the comparative law experience has shown, legal systems have difficulties defining the "core." At the end of the day, it seems that the "core" is best understood in terms of proportionality.[20] If that is the case, why not simply determine that the rules of proportionality should apply to limitations on every part of the right, core and penumbra alike? The difference between a limitation on the right's core and its penumbra is expressed through the rules of proportionality, in particular proportionality *stricto sensu*. South Africa's 1993 Interim Constitution included a provision prohibiting a limitation on the right's core,[21] but that provision was removed from the (permanent) 1996 Constitution of the Republic of South Africa.

---

[15] For the distinction between limitation and amendment, see above, at 99.

[16] See M. Medina Guerrero, *La Vinculación Negativa del Legislador a los Derechos Fundamentales* (Madrid: McGraw-Hill, 1996), 165.

[17] See Wildhaber, above note 5, at 41, 56.

[18] See Rivers, above note 13, at 187.

[19] See Van der Schyff, above note 11, at 167; Wildhaber, above note 5, at 55.

[20] As Hesse put it, the restriction on limitation of the right's core has been derived from the *praktische Konkordanze*. See K. Hesse, *Grundzüge des Verfassungsrechts der Bundesrepublik Deutschland* (Heidelberg: Die Deutsche Bibliotek, 1999), § 333.

[21] Art. 33(1)(b).

3.   The dual model

i.   The nature of the alternative

The right's "core" alternative distinguishes between limitations pertaining to the core of each right and those pertaining to its penumbra. The right's core is protected in an absolute manner. Proportionality may not apply to it. It is only outside the contours of the right's core that proportionality may apply. Another view, with apparent similarities, is Porat's "dual model."[22] Much like the "core model," Porat distinguishes within every right, between a situation where proportionality can apply and a situation where the right is absolutely protected such that proportionality cannot apply. However, the "dual model" and the "right's core" model are different. The core model seeks to characterize the limitation placed on the constitutional right – whether it pertains to the right's core or to its penumbra. The dual model seeks to characterize the nature of the conflict which led to the limitation, while remaining indifferent to the issue of whether said limitation pertains to the right's core or penumbra. What are these considerations?

The dual model is a synthesis between two theoretical paradigms, one proposed by Raz[23] and the other by Kelman.[24] Porat distinguishes between two types of conflict: a first-order conflict and a second-order, or exclusionary, conflict. First-order conflicts are characterized by the fact that they are conflicts between a constitutional right and a limited-resources interest (such as a budget). A second-order conflict typically takes the form of a constitutional right conflicting with an interest that should not be taken into consideration at all. According to the dual model, the first conflict is resolved through balancing between the conflicting interests. The second conflict is not resolved through balancing but rather through the preference of the right over the conflicting interest. The conflicting interest is completely "excluded" from consideration.

Porat demonstrates the dual model's application to the American Bill of Rights. He examines, among others, the right to freedom of expression.[25] A first-order conflict exists whenever the right to freedom of expression clashes with a public interest which limits the right for reasons that are

---

[22] See I. Porat, "The Dual Model of Balancing: A Model for the Proper Scope of Balancing in Constitutional Law," 27 *Cardozo L. Rev.* 1393.

[23] See J. Raz, *Practical Reasons and Norms*, 2nd edn. (Oxford University Press, 1999).

[24] See M. Kelman, "Market Discrimination and Groups," 53 *Stan. L. Rev.* 833 (2001).

[25] See Porat, above note 22, at 1417.

content-neutral. This conflict is resolved through balancing.[26] A second-order conflict exists between freedom of expression and the public interest limiting it for content-related reasons. This conflict is not resolved through balancing.[27]

ii. Assessment of the alternative

Porat's dual model is interesting. Although it seeks to explain the role of proportionality in American law, it can be given a more general application. However, it seems that, in principle, the model can be located within the concept of proportionality itself. Thus, a first-order conflict finds its place in the component of proportionality *stricto sensu* (balancing). Similarly, each case of a conflict between two constitutional rights – a conflict that according to the dual model raises a first-order conflict – would be resolved (on the sub-constitutional level) through the rules of proportionality, and in particular through proportionality *stricto sensu*. A second-order conflict can also be easily incorporated into proportionality, this time through the proper purpose requirement. Thus, considerations related to the actual content of the speech – which, according to Porat, render the balance moot – may simply be referred to as considerations that do not constitute a proper purpose and therefore do not require any balancing.

What, then, is the contribution of the dual model? In the context of first-order conflicts, the model recognizes the need for balancing and therefore easily integrates into proportionality. The difference between proportionality and the dual model may arise regarding second-order conflicts. Take, for example, a limitation on the right to freedom of expression for reasons of national security. This is a second-order conflict. According to the dual model, there is no room for balancing. National security considerations are not part of the considerations that can be considered. In contrast, according to proportionality, these considerations may constitute, under the right circumstances, a proper purpose, and thus are "fair game" for balancing. The constitutionality of a limitation due to such considerations, therefore, would be determined in accordance with proportionality. In some cases, this limitation is constitutional, while in others it would be declared unconstitutional. This is the framework that is proper. Indeed, some national security considerations are

---

[26] Through the doctrine of "time, place, and manner." See *Schneider* v. *State*, 308 US 147 (1939).

[27] See *Abrams* v. *United States*, 250 US 616 (1919); *Texas* v. *Johnson*, 491 US 397 (1989).

worthy of balancing; in contrast, under the dual model, they should never be balanced. Furthermore, even if one were to argue that in rare cases the dual model would be willing to recognize the need to consider them, then the conclusion must be that there is no justification for a separate model external to proportionality. Instead of developing rules to distinguish between conflicts of the first and second order, it would make more sense to simply apply the traditional rules of proportionality.

An interesting approach in this regard is Meyerson's. She too differentiates between first-order considerations and second-order considerations. According to her approach, second-order considerations should be softened. The softening is expressed by the fact that not every second-order consideration is one that should not be considered. Those second-order considerations which can be considered should be given a "light" weight. In her opinion, this is the case where constitutional rights conflict with a public interest. The public interest should be given less weight in the balance. As a result of this, only in special cases will the public interest overcome the constitutional right:[28]

> I want to suggest that we should see a bill of rights as a source of second-order or reweighting reasons. Such reasons would instruct judges not to exercise their own judgement as to what the balance of reasons requires, but rather to assign a greater weight to rights and a lesser weight to the public interest than they would ordinarily think they deserve. Such an approach would acknowledge that bills of rights do not exclude consideration of the public interest, but would also build into rights adjudication a "systematic bias" against permitting the infringement of rights. The public interest is therefore a "viable opponent" – as required by the non-absolute character of rights – but one operating with a handicap. I will call this the "reweighting approach". Whereas the balancing model sees a bill of rights as merely adding rights to the overall mix of reasons which judges are obliged to consider at the first-order level, the reweighting approach sees a bill of rights as operating at the second-order level – as an instruction to depart from the weights which judges would accord if they were operating at the first-order level.

This approach "improves" the dual model. It can be expressed in the framework of the basic balancing rule. Within this rule it can be determined that the relative social importance of preventing the limitation of the constitutional right should be given more weight than the relative social importance in advancing the public interest. I am not convinced

---

[28] D. Meyerson, "Why Courts Should Not Balance Rights against the Public Interest." 31 *Melb. U. L. Rev.* 873 (2007), 883.

this approach is justified. It is sufficient to consider the relative social importance, without adding additional considerations regarding the relative weight. Every legal system will give its own weight – reflecting its history and tradition – to its constitutional rights.

B.   The categorization-based alternatives

1.   Categorization within the human rights discourse

Proportionality's critics, as a standard for the limitation of rights, do not limit themselves to criticism alone. Some point to alternatives that they believe to be more proper. As we have seen, Webber, for example, offers to replace judicial proportionality with legislative construction.[29] Another alternative was offered by Schlink, who suggests that, in cases involving judicial review of the constitutionality of legislation (as opposed to the constitutionality of administrative acts), proportionality should be narrowed so that it does not contain the component of proportionality *stricto sensu*.[30] But, if the executive branch is subject to proportionality when it limits constitutional rights, why should the legislative branch not be subject to the same need for justification? The major threats to constitutional rights come from legislation that authorizes the executive to limit constitutional rights. If these limitations are free from judicial review, the whole idea of the judicial review of legislation collapses.

The most important alternative offered to proportionality, by far, is that of categorization. This alternative is used in many areas of American constitutional law. What is this alternative, and are its advantages greater than its disadvantages? Is it preferable to proportionality? This question is posed to anyone engaged in the adoption of a new constitution. Does categorization have any significance in a constitution which has explicitly recognized proportionality as the standard by which a right's limitation should be measured? The answer to this question is complex. Obviously, in those legal systems which recognize the concept of proportionality, categorization cannot replace proportionality. The latter would require a constitutional amendment. However, categorization can still affect the interpretation of rights and the constitutional limitation clause. Such an

---

[29] See above, at 493.

[30] See Schlink, "Der Grundsatz der Verhältnismässigkeit," in P. Badura and H. Dreier (eds.), *Festschrift 50 Jahre Bundesverfassungsgericht*, vol. II (Tübingen: Mohr Siebeck, 2001), 445.

effect may manifest itself in different contexts. Thus, for example, it may affect the scope of the rights.[31] It may also affect the answer to the interpretive question of whether the public interest or the rights of others, which conflict with the protected constitutional right, should be considered part of providing meaning to the scope of the protected rights. Categorization may also affect the question of whether proportionality should be structured or flexible.[32] It is relevant for the different sub-tests of proportionality. It can be quite influential in providing an answer to the question – if the question is recognized by a given legal system – whether proportionality *stricto sensu* should be used as a standard for limiting constitutional rights. Even if the answer to this question is yes, categorization may still affect the actual application of proportionality *stricto sensu*.[33] What is categorization? What is the difference between categorization and proportionality in general, and balancing in particular? Does categorization provide better protection to human rights than proportionality? Should it be preferred at a time when a new constitution is adopted, or during the process of interpreting an existing constitution? These questions will now be discussed in greater detail.

2. *The nature of thinking in legal categories*

Thinking in categories is one of the earliest forms of human thought. One of the main characteristics of ancient law was thinking in categories. The classification of factual circumstances into a legal category (such as "property" or "marriage") determined the legal outcome. The transition from the ancient to the modern legal period is thus sometimes perceived as a move from thinking in categories ("status") to thinking in more open terms ("contract").[34]

Thinking in categories has, therefore, been an integral part of the development of the law. In recent centuries, however, another form of legal thinking – one relating to interests, or values – began developing. Soon, tension arose between these two forms of legal thought. Both categorization and value-related thinking have been very influential in the development of legal thinking. In Europe, for example, the tension between the two models of legal thinking led to the concomitant development of "concept jurisprudence" (*Begriffsjurisprudenz*)[35] and "interest jurisprudence"

---

[31] See below, at 513.   [32] See above, at 460.   [33] See above, at 340.

[34] See H. Maine, *Ancient Law* (London: John Murray, 1861), 141.

[35] See E. Patterson, *Jurisprudence: Men and Ideas of the Law* (New York: Foundation Press, 1953), 459; J. Stone, *Province and Function of Law: Law As Logic, Justice and Social*

(*Interessenjurisprudenz*).[36] A similar tension began to emerge in American law as well. As Morton Horowitz observed: "Nothing captures the essential difference between the typical legal minds of nineteenth and twentieth-century America quite as well as their attitude towards categories."[37] This kind of tension can still be observed in today's legal thinking around the world.

What does "thinking in categorization terms" mean? Thinking in categories is a form of interpretive thinking. It seeks to resolve all legal questions through the use – and within the boundaries – of a predetermined legal category.[38] In essence, this is a formalistic type of thinking, focusing on classifications and attributions. Thus, the legal text is divided into several categories, and each category is further divided into sub-categories.[39] Each category and sub-category has its own well-defined realm of operation. The main legal issue thus becomes the identification of the proper category, and then the application of the factual framework to that proper, pre-determined legal category. Once a category has been chosen, the accompanying set of legal rules will automatically apply. Legal development occurs in the move from one category to another, by creating new categories, or by modifying and amending the understanding of existing categories.

Thinking in legal categories does not require the exclusion of policy considerations. Instead, policy considerations have been part of the considerations that led to the creation – and final shape – of each legal category. Those considerations help set the category's boundaries. Once these boundaries have been set, however, there is no need to reexamine the policy considerations that formed the category in the first place. It is enough to apply the category – a result of the original policy considerations – in order to solve the legal problem. Accordingly, an examination

---

Control, A Study in Jurisprudence (Sydney, Australia; Assoc. General Publication Pty Ltd., 1961), 162; J. Stone, *Legal System and Lawyers' Reasoning* (Stanford University Press, 1968), 227.

[36] See J. Bomhoff, "Balancing, the Global and the Local: Judicial Balancing as a Problematic Topic in Comparative (Constitutional) Law," 31 *Hastings Int. & Comp. L. Rev.* 571 (2008).

[37] See M. J. Horwitz, *The Transformation of American Law: 1870–1960* (Oxford University Press, 192), 17.

[38] See F. Schauer, "Categories and the First Amendment: A Play in Three Acts," 34 *Vand. L. Rev.* 265 (19981); K. M. Sullivan, "Post-Liberal Judging: The Roles of Categorization and Balancing," 62 *U. Colo. L. Rev.* 293 (1992); J. Blocher, "Categoricalism and Balancing in First and Second Amendment Analysis," 83 *N. Y. U. L. Rev.* 375 (2009).

[39] See Schauer, above note 38, at 282.

of the policy considerations underlying the category would only take place when a new legal development is considered, either by changing the scope of existing categories or in creating new ones. Accordingly, thinking in categories may be creative thinking. Such creativity is expressed through a constant reexamination of the scope, the status, and the application of existing categories, as well as the creation of new ones.

3. Constitutional rights in categorized thinking

i. Every right constitutes its own category

Thinking in categories can be applied to every legal field. It also applies to the field of constitutional law. It holds a special place in the field of constitutional rights. Thus, categorization seeks to classify each human right, or a specific part of it, as its own independent category. It seeks to resolve every question relating to such rights through the interpretation of the legal text creating it. It attempts to prevent a situation where one constitutional right (the first category) conflicts with another constitutional right (the second category).[40] However, it may view several rights, each of which is an independent category, as sub-categories of a single broader category.

The distinction between the scope of the right and the extent of its realization has already been discussed,[41] as has the distinction between narrowing the scope of the right and limiting its realization.[42] These distinctions are interpreted differently in categorization thinking. The reason for that is that all the provisions – whether relating to expanding or narrowing the right's scope, or regarding the protection of or the limitation of a right – are found within the constitutional text that shapes the right itself.[43]

With this in mind, it is widely accepted today that the US Constitution's Bill of Rights is based substantially – but not exclusively[44] – on the notion of legal categorization.[45] Every right in the American Bill of Rights makes

---

[40] See R. H. Fallon, "Individual Rights and the Powers of Government," 27 *Ga. L. Rev.* 343, 362 (1993).

[41] See above, at 19.   [42] See above, at 99.

[43] See S. Gardbaum, "Limiting Constitutional Rights," 54 *UCLA L. Rev.* 789, 807 (2007).

[44] See A. Stone Sweet and J. Mathews, "All Things in Proportion? American Rights Doctrine and the Problem of Balancing," *Emory L. J.* (forthcoming, 2011).

[45] See F. Schauer, "The Exceptional First Amendment," in M. Ignatieff (ed.), *American Exceptionalism and Human Rights* (Princeton University Press, 1980), 29; F. Schauer, "Categories and the First Amendment: A Play in Three Acts," 34 *Vand. L. Rev.* 265, 282

up an independent category. However, not everyone agrees with this view. Gardbaum, for one, is of the opinion that the basic structure of the American Bill of Rights is no different than that typically found in other constitutional democracies.[46] For example, in America, rights are shields from – as opposed to trumps over – the public interest. In America, as elsewhere, protection of the right is done in two stages. First, the right's scope is determined, followed by the extent of its protection. Despite the similarities between the legal systems which Gardbaum has pointed out, the methodological difference between the American legal system and other systems is substantial; in essence, this difference may be summed up as thinking in legal categories.[47] In the United States, the categorical attributes of the right determines the level of constitutional scrutiny; that level of scrutiny, in turn, determines the limitations that may be placed on the rights at issue. These limitations are mostly not determined by specific (or *ad hoc*) balancing.[48] The second stage of American constitutional review does not include specific balancing. Gardbaum argues that American judges often turn to balancing within each category. However, to him "balancing" is very broadly defined,[49] encompassing any limitation on the exercise of the right, including limitations that do not apply proportionality *stricto sensu*.

ii.   Example: freedom of expression in the First Amendment

The First Amendment to the American Constitution states, regarding freedom of expression:

> Congress shall make no law ... abridging the freedom of speech, or of the press.

Thinking in legal categories would consider this text as forming a category of freedom of speech. Thus, every legal question related to freedom of

---

(1981); V. C. Jackson, "Ambivalent Resistance and Comparative Constitutionalism: Opening Up the Conversation on 'Proportionality', Rights and Federalism," 1 *U. Pa. J. Const. L.* 583, 605 (1999); M. Kumm and V. Ferreres Comella, "What Is So Special About Constitutional Rights in Private Litigation?: A Comparative Analysis of the Function of State Action Requirements and Indirect Horizontal Effect," in A. Sajó and R. Uitz (eds.), *The Constitution in Private Relations: Expanding Constitutionalism* (The Hague: Eleven International Publishing, 2005), 241, 286.

[46] See S. Gardbaum, "The Myth and the Reality of American Constitutional Exceptionalism," 107 *Mich. L. Rev.* 391 (2008).

[47] See above, at 505.

[48] On specific balancing, see above, at 367.

[49] See Gardbaum, above note 43, at 792.

speech should be considered – and find its interpretive solution – within the First Amendment's text. The significant number of cases dealing with, and attempting to interpret, this portion of the First Amendment demonstrates the complexity of the questions the amendment raises. Obviously, such a legal state of affairs places a heavy burden on anyone attempting to resolve these interpretive questions. This interpretive task is especially burdensome in those cases where the judge attempts, on the one hand, to be loyal to the constitutional text, while, at the same time, providing an answer to many new situations left uncovered by the "thin" constitutional text.

Gardbaum seeks to distinguish, within American constitutional law, between the scope of the right and the limitations imposed on its realization. He attempts to determine, through the substantive body of judicial decisions, the content of the First Amendment. At the end of the day, Gardbaum limited himself to those situations where the question was whether some form of expression can be prevented due to its content:

> The right to be free from intentional, content-based regulation of non-economic speech or expressive conduct that does not constitute fraud, obscenity, fighting words, or a clear and present danger unless the regulation necessary to promote a compelling governmental interest.[50]

Such language is worthy of praise. However, it does not blur the basic methodological distinction between the American approach and those of other constitutional democracies. Such a distinction is based on the fact that the American approach views freedom of expression as an independent category. The categorical nature of the reference determines, in turn, the level of constitutional scrutiny. This scrutiny does not contain, in most cases, the conduct of specific balancing.

4. Categorization and the two-stage model

Can categorization be reconciled with the two-stage model? The answer depends, first and foremost, on the constitutional text itself. Whenever the constitutional text explicitly determines two stages in a constitutional arrangement, then all forms of interpretive thinking – including categorization – recognize the existence of those two stages. The question focuses on the constitutional text which does not differentiate between the two

---

[50] *Ibid.*, at 807.

stages. The First Amendment is an example of this. What should the solution be in those cases?

It seems that this question has no clear answer. According to Gardbaum's definition, it is possible to say that the First Amendment is based solely on a single stage. The limitation clause – which determines the circumstances in which the right can be limited without affecting its scope – is "integrated" into the definition of the right itself. However, Gardbaum acknowledges that this is not the only view possible. Other views of the American First Amendment approach may well include a clear distinction between the scope of the right and questions relating to the extent of its protection. According to those views, the American approach may well be reconciled with the two-stage model.[51]

5. Categorization and balancing

Methodologically speaking, thinking in legal categories stands in sharp contrast to legal thinking based upon specific, or *ad hoc*, balancing.[52] This was true in the nineteenth and twentieth centuries and remains true today. The focus on categories was meant, among others, to prevent the use of specific balancing in each case. The characterization of a set of facts as being attributed to a certain category led to a legal solution, without the need to conduct a specific balancing within that category. Legal categorization accepts the notion of principled balancing to the extent that it operates at the interpretive level determining the scope of the categories in question and their boundaries.[53] At the core of each legal category is the interpretive balance that preceded its creation.[54]

Take, for example, the right to freedom of speech. Categorization recognizes that in order to determine the boundaries of the right to freedom of speech we should properly balance between the principles underlying the right and the principles opposing it.[55] The result of such a principled balance would lead, for example, to taking a stand on the question of whether the right to freedom of speech may cover instances of racist

---

[51] *Ibid.*, at 609. See also Schauer, above note 38; Schauer, above note 45.

[52] Regarding specific balancing, see above, at 367.

[53] See M. B. Nimmer, "The Right to Speak from Times to Time: First Amendment Theory Applied to Libel and Misapplied to Privacy," 56 *Cal. L. Rev.* 935 (1968); R. H. Fallon, "Individual Rights and the Powers of Government," 27 *Ga. L. Rev.* 343 (1993).

[54] See E. Chemerinsky, *Constitutional Law: Principles and Policies*, 3rd edn. (New York: Aspen Publishers, 2006), 539.

[55] See Stone Sweet and Mathews, above note 44; Blocher, above note 38.

speech or obscenity. Similarly, a principled balance would determine the answer to the question of in what circumstances would the right to enjoy good reputation prevail over another's right to freedom of speech. But, once the contours of the category – in this example, the contours of the right to freedom of speech regarding its content – are determined, there is no room for additional balancing. Once again, no specific (*ad hoc*) balancing is conducted to determine the result of a specific case when freedom of speech was affected because of its content.

The obvious result is that the main factor which differentiates between legal categorization and proportionality is proportionality *stricto sensu*. The act of balancing, which is the very foundation of proportionality *stricto sensu*, separates and distinguishes proportionality as a method of legal thinking from legal categorization. In particular, the distinguishing factor is the conduct of specific (*ad hoc*) balancing, relating directly to the circumstances of each and every case separately. Specific balancing is the basis of the main difference between the two modes of constitutional thought. The rest of proportionality's components (proper purpose, rational means, and the lack of a less restrictive alternative) may well be considered a part of categorization as well. This will be demonstrated through a review of the American approach to constitutional rights in greater detail.

6. Categorization and human rights in American constitutional law

i. American categorization

a. Three categories The US Constitution's Bill of Rights mostly contains no limitation clauses, whether general or specific. Most rights enumerated in the Bill of Rights are expressed in absolute terms and each right constitutes its own category. However, the similarities between the enumerated rights enabled the development of three categories, to which most rights may be attributed. These three categories are typified by the different levels of judicial scrutiny attached to each of them.[56] The three categories are: rights whose limitation invites strict scrutiny; rights whose limitation invites intermediate scrutiny; and rights whose limitation invites minimal scrutiny. Each of these super categories will be examined briefly. Along with those three categories there are additional categories,

---

[56] See L. H. Tribe, *American Constitutional Law*, 2nd edn. (New York: Foundation Press, 1998), 769. See also Chemerinsky, above note 54, at 539.

but these will not be dealt with here. Similarly, there is an understanding – expressed by only a small number of justices – that there is no room for this strict division of categories.[57] Even in the framework of the categories dealt with here, the analysis is very brief – perhaps too brief. The American literature on the subject is voluminous, and extremely varied. Summarizing each of the views presented in the literature is a task far beyond the contours of this book. All that can be done here is to provide a quick "X-ray image" of the issue, while examining its comparison to proportionality. It is obvious that the analysis here does not do the complexity of the issue any justice, and may not even present it accurately enough; nor does it do any justice to the American approach, which is made up of a vast array of rules and exceptions that are nearly impossible to summarize as needed for this book. In addition, the analysis herein refers to the American law currently in use. A historical review is not offered. This review teaches that in the past there was room for balancing within the judicial review of a limitation of a constitutional right.[58] Finally, even in today's approach, there are judicial voices, a minority, which recognize the balancing.[59]

b.   Strict scrutiny   The first category is the category of rights known in American law as fundamental rights. This category includes rights such as freedom of political speech, the rights to demonstrate and to associate, the freedom to exercise religion, the freedom to move freely within US borders, and the right to elect representatives. In addition to these fundamental rights, this category also entails any government action relating to "suspect classification" based on race or national origin. Any attempt to regulate (that is, to limit) those rights would invite a judicial "strict scrutiny" – the most stringent level of constitutional review.[60] This review applies to both the purposes underlying the limiting legislation as well as the means selected to fulfill that purpose. As for the purposes, precedent determines that a law limiting one of the rights in this category would be declared unconstitutional unless it was enacted to justify a compelling governmental (or state) interest, a pressing public necessity, or a substantial state interest. The means used to achieve the purpose should be

---

[57] See *Craig* v. *Boren*, 429 US 190, 211–212 (1976) (Stevens, J.); *City of Cleburne* v. *Cleburne Living Ctr Inc.*, 473 US 432 (1985) (Marshall, J.).

[58] See Stone Sweet and Mathews, above note 44; Blocher, above note 38.

[59] See Stone Sweet and Mathews, above note 44; Blocher, above note 38.

[60] See G. Gunther, "In Search of Judicial Quality on a Changing Court: The Case of Justice Powell," 24 *Stan. L. Rev.* 1001, 1005 (1972); I. Ayres, "Narrow Tailoring," 43 *UCLA L. Rev.*

"necessary." This means that they should be "narrowly tailored" to achieve the compelling interest at stake.[61] The "narrowly tailored" requirement is two-pronged: first, that there is no other means that would be less restrictive of the right in question;[62] and, second, that those means are not "too wide," a prohibition on overinclusiveness or overbreadth.[63]

c. **Intermediate scrutiny** The second category,[64] that of "intermediate" scrutiny, includes: the right to equality – in those cases where the limitation was based upon "quasi-suspect" classifications such as gender or age; the limitation of the right to freedom of commercial speech; and the right to speech in a public forum. Legislation included in this category would pass constitutional muster if it was designed to achieve an important governmental objective. The means used to fulfill the purpose must reveal a substantial relation between the purpose and the means used for its realization.

d. **Minimal scrutiny** The last category[65] – "minimal" scrutiny – applies to the remaining constitutional rights. It includes, for example, any limitation of equality which is not based on suspect or quasi-suspect

---

1781 (1995); E. Volokh, "Freedom of Speech, Permissible Tailoring and Transcending Strict Scrutiny," 144 *U. Pa. L. Rev.* 2417 (1995); G. White, "The First Amendment Comes of Age: The Emergence of Free Speech in Twentieth-Century America," 95 *Mich. L. Rev.* 299 (1996); P. J. Rubin, "Reconnecting Doctrine and Purpose: A Comprehensive Approach to Strict Scrutiny after Adarand and Shaw," 149 *U. Pa. L. Rev.* 1 (2001); S. Goldberg, "Equality Without Tiers," 77 *S. Cal. L. Rev.* 481(2004); G. Robinson and T. Robinson, "Korematsu and Beyond: Japanese Americans and the Origin of Strict Scrutiny," 68 *L. and Contemp. Probs.* 29 (2005); G. E. White, "Historicizing Judicial Scrutiny," 57 *South Carolina L. Rev.* 1 (2006); A. Winkler, "Fatal in Theory and Strict in Fact: An Empirical Analysis of Strict Scrutiny in the Federal Courts," 59 *Vand. L. Rev.* 793 (2006); S. Siegel, "Origin of the Compelling State Interest Test and Strict Scrutiny," 48 *Am. J. Legal Hist.* 355 (2006); A. Winkler, "Fundamentally Wrong about Fundamental Rights," 23 *Const. Comment.* 227 (2006); R. H. Fallon, "Strict Judicial Scrutiny," 54 *UCLA L. Rev.* 1267 (2007); I. Ayres and S. Foster, "Don't Tell, Don't Ask: Narrow Tailoring After Grutter and Gratz," 85 *Tex. L. Rev.* 517 (2007); R. Barnett, "Scrutiny Land," 106 *Mich. L. Rev.* 1479 (2008); Stone Sweet and Mathews, above note 44.

[61] See Ayres, above note 60.

[62] See G. M. Struve, "The Less-Restrictive-Alternative Principle and Economic Due Process," 80 *Harv. L. Rev.* 1463 (1967); Note, "Less Drastic Means and the First Amendment," 78 *Yale L. J.* 464 (1969).

[63] See Note, "The First Amendment Overbreadth Doctrine," 83 *Harv. L. Rev.* 844 (1970). As to underinclusiveness, see above, at 334.

[64] See Chemerinsky, above note 54, at 540.

[65] *Ibid.*

classifications; and rights such as the right to movement outside the country. According to American precedent, it is sufficient that the legislation was designed to achieve a legitimate governmental purpose. There is no need to examine the purpose's urgency. Regarding the means, they must have a rational basis. This rational basis is determined while considering the possible results and alternatives.[66]

e.   **Categories with no ad hoc balancing**   A review of each of the three categories as they are understood in contemporary American jurisprudence[67] shows that the limitation of a constitutional right is not based upon any specific, or *ad hoc*, balancing between the marginal social benefits in fulfilling the legislative purpose and the marginal social harm caused to the constitutional right. As for principled balancing, such balancing is conducted – but only during the process of creating a new category or amending an existing one. This balancing, however, is no longer conducted once the category has been established. There is no more balancing. This is even more so in the case of minimal scrutiny. All that is required by this level of review is that the legislative means have a rational basis. This basis does not require a balancing between the benefit and the harm. It is similar, in many ways, to the sub-test of proportionality – that of rational connection.[68] That test, too, is not based on the act of balancing.[69]

The intermediate level of scrutiny demands a substantial relation between the purpose and the means. This requirement is not based on a balancing between the benefits gained by fulfilling the purpose and the harm to the constitutional right. This test, to some degree, is similar to proportionality's rational connection test, although it demands a higher level of connection.

Finally, at the strict scrutiny level, the legislative means must be narrowly tailored, or "necessary" in order to achieve the "compelling" legislative purpose at hand. There are significant similarities between the

---

[66] Regarding the rationality requirement in this context, see H. A. Linde, "Due Process of Lawmaking," 55 *Neb. L. Rev.* 197 (1976); R. W. Bennett, "'Mere' Rationality in Constitutional Law: Judicial Review and Democratic Theory," 67 *Cal. L. Rev.* 1049 (1979); F. I. Michelman, "Politics and Values or What's Really Wrong with Rationality Review?," 13 *Creighton L. Rev.* 487 (1979).

[67] See Stone Sweet and Mathews, above note 44.

[68] See M. Cohen-Eliya and I. Porat, "American Balancing and German Proportionality: The Historical Origins," 8(2) *Int'l J. Const. L.* 263 (2010).

[69] See above, at 315.

phrasing of this requirement and that of proportionality's test of necessity.[70] This requirement, as well, is not based on any act of balancing between the benefits gained by the public interest and the harm caused to the individual right.[71] This category is based on a principled-interpretive balancing which determined the category's boundaries. Once the category's boundaries have been set, no additional balancing should be conducted within the category's boundaries.

ii. Protecting human rights: categorization versus proportionality

a. The potential for protection and its realization Proportionality and categorization – which of the two provides human rights with the greater level of protection?[72] The answer to this question can be given at two levels. The first is the theoretical-methodological level.[73] This level examines the theoretical potential within each of the two models in relation to the level of protection they provide to constitutional human rights (through legislation or case law). This level of protection will determine, in turn, the boundaries of governmental discretion when a constitutional right is limited.[74] The second level is the empirical level.[75] This level examines the actual manner in which the theoretical underpinnings were utilized in a given legal system. Most of the examination is dedicated to the first level, but a few comments regarding the second level will be made as well.

b. The scope of a constitutional right The scope of the constitutional right – to differentiate from its realization at the sub-constitutional level[76] – is determined through interpretation of the constitutional text. This is well known to legal systems that have adopted proportionality, as well as to the American legal system which has adopted categorization. On a theoretical level, there is no reason for the scope of any given right to differ from one system to another. Thus, for example, from a principled-theoretical standpoint there is no reason to assume that the scope of the right to freedom of expression in Canada, South Africa, Israel,

---

[70] See above, at 317. [71] See above, at 338.
[72] See K. M. Sullivan, "Post-Liberal Judging: The Roles of Categorization and Balancing," 62 U. Colo. L. Rev. 293 (1992); R. F. Nagel, "Liberals and Balancing," 63 U. Colo. L. Rev. 319 (1992).
[73] See Schauer, above note 45, at 31.
[74] See above, at 400. [75] See Schauer, above note 45, at 31.
[76] For the distinction, see above, at 19.

or according to the European Convention for the Protection of Human Rights[77] would be different from the scope of the right as determined by the First Amendment to the US Constitution. But, in practice, the scope is different.[78] Several types of speech have been excluded from the right as interpreted by the American system, while they are still regarded as part of the right by those legal systems that adopted proportionality. Thus, for example, hate speech,[79] obscenity,[80] incitement to illegal action,[81] and intentional (or reckless) defamation of a public figure,[82] are excluded from the scope of the right to freedom of speech as the First Amendment is interpreted. In contrast, all of these do make up a part of the rights in those legal systems that have adopted proportionality.

An interesting question is whether this narrowing of the right's scope is connected to the method of legal categorization which characterizes American law. The answer to this questions tends to be positive. The categorization approach, as part of the principled-interpretive balance it conducts, seeks to provide every right with a clear and well-defined scope such that it would not conflict with other constitutional rights. Each category is independent. There is no room, within a given category, to conduct a specific (or *ad hoc*) balancing. This approach – which reduces the possibility of a conflict between two (or more) constitutional rights – leads to an interpretive result that leaves some aspects of the right's penumbra outside its recognized scope.

---

[77] Convention for the Protection of Human Rights and Fundamental Freedoms, November 4, 1950, 213 *UNTS* 222.

[78] See D. Kretzmer, "Freedom of Speech and Racism," 8 *Cardozo L. Rev.* 445 (1987). See also Schauer, above note 38; D. Kommers, "The Jurisprudence of Free Speech in the United States and the Federal Republic of Germany," 53 *S. Cal. L. Rev.* 657 (1979–80); R. Errera, "The Freedom of the Press: The United States, France and Other European Countries," in L. Hegkin and A. Rosenthal (eds.), *Constitutionalism and Rights: The Influence of the United States Constitution Abroad* (New York: Columbia University Press, 1990); B. Jurgen, "Freedom of Speech and Flag Desecration: A Comparative Study of German, European and United States Laws," 20 *Denv. J. Int'l L. & Pol'y* 471 (1991–1992); K. Greenawalt, "Free Speech in the United States and Canada," 55 *Law and Contemp. Probs.* 5 (1992); K Boyle. "Hate Speech – The United States Versus the Rest of the World," 53 *Me. L. Rev.* 487 (2001); M. Rosenfeld, "Hate Speech in Constitutional Jurisprudence: A Comparative Analysis," 24 *Cardozo L. Rev.* 1532 (2003); F. Schauer, "Freedom of Expression Adjudication in Europe and the United States: A Case Study in Comparative Constitutional Architecture," in G. Nolte (ed.), *European and US Constitutionalism* (Cambridge University Press, 2005), 31; R. Sedler, "An Essay on Freedom of Speech: The United States Versus the Rest of the World," Michigan State L. Rev. 377 (2006); E. Barendt, *Freedom of Speech*, 2nd edn. (Oxford University Press, 2007).

[79] See Chemerinsky, above note 54, at 1001.

[80] *Ibid.*, at 1017.   [81] *Ibid.*, at 987.   [82] *Ibid.*, at 540.

c. **Limitations on realizing the right's scope**   Legal systems do not consider all constitutional rights as absolutes. The rules of proportionality, and, in the United States, the different levels of scrutiny, limit the realization of the right to its fullest scope. How do the two methods compare in this realm?

It seems that all would agree that the minimal level of scrutiny, adopted by American law regarding a number of rights, enables the imposition of more substantial limitations on those rights in this category than would be permitted under proportionality. At this level of scrutiny, it is sufficient that the purpose is a legitimate government interest and that the means selected to achieve that interest have a rational basis.[83] The proper purpose requirement matches that required by German constitutional law,[84] albeit, it is a narrower demand than required by other legal systems which practice proportionality.[85] Regarding the means, the American requirement seems to be quite similar to proportionality's rational connection test.[86] Proportionality, on the other hand, is not satisfied with this. Rather, proportionality requires that the means be necessary (that no less restrictive alternative exists),[87] and that a proper relation exists between the marginal social benefits in fulfilling the law's purposes and the marginal social harm it would cause to the right in question.[88] These two requirements, which are part and parcel of proportionality, are not required in the minimal scrutiny test. Thus, the rights included in this category – such as the limitation of equality (not including suspect and quasi-suspect classifications), and the right to travel outside the country – receive less protection by American law than that offered by those countries that have adopted proportionality.[89]

A similar conclusion is reached regarding intermediate scrutiny. Here, too, the level of protection offered by American law is narrower than that offered by countries that have adopted proportionality. This category entails, *inter alia*, protection of the right to equality (when the classifications are based on gender or age), the right to commercial speech, and freedom of speech in a public forum. This category requires that the legislation's purpose be an important governmental interest and that the means selected should bear a substantial relation to fulfilling the purpose.

[83] See R. C. Farrell, "Successful Rational Basis Claims in the Supreme Court from the 1971 Term through Romer v. Evans," 32 *Ind. L. Rev.* 357 (1999).

[84] See below, at 529.   [85] See above, at 289.

[86] See above, at 303.   [87] See above, at 317.   [88] See above, at 350.

[89] See Stone Sweet and Mathews, above note 44, at 45 ("[R]ational basis review leads American judge to abdicate their duty to protect rights.").

The American requirement regarding the important governmental purpose is stricter than the requirement in German law, which is satisfied with a legislative purpose that does not contradict the constitution.[90] Then again, the American requirement falls short of the requirements posed by other countries that have adopted proportionality.[91] The main difficulty, however, concerns the means. The American substantial relation requirement falls short of proportionality's necessity test.[92] Most importantly, the American test does not demand a proper relation between the marginal social benefit gained by the limiting legislation and the marginal social harm caused to the right in question. It has no balancing. From a holistic point of view it seems to provide less protection to the rights included within it than that offered by those legal systems that have adopted proportionality.

d.   The issue with regard to strict scrutiny   The most complicated comparison is that between the level of protection offered to the rights included within the first tier of protection – strict scrutiny – and that offered by proportionality. The difficulty is two-fold. First, it stems from the lack of clarity regarding the conditions of the strict scrutiny review; and, second, from the difficulty in comparing the actual fulfillment of the different requirements which have arisen in the case law. The first difficulty is theoretical; the second is pragmatic. Due to the sheer amount of American case law and literature on the subject, the difficulties are evident.

The discussion begins with the theoretical comparison. Strict scrutiny requires, in terms of the legislation's proper purpose, that the limiting legislation be a compelling state interest, or that its fulfillment be a pressing public necessity or a substantial state interest. This is a very high level requirement. Only some of the countries that have adopted proportionality have a similar requirement. In Canada, for example, a similar requirement exists which demands that the legislation's purpose must fulfill a pressing public necessity or a substantial state interest.[93] However there is a difference between this requirement in Canadian and American law, this difference is concerns the "seriousness" with which the requirement is actually applied. While American courts have taken the proper purpose

---

[90]   See below, at 529.
[91]   See above, at 289.
[92]   See above, at 317.
[93]   See above, at 279.

requirement extremely seriously, in Canada, conversely, its application depends on the circumstances of the case. A plausible explanation is that in the United States this requirement appears only with regard to strict scrutiny (that is, with regard to only a few of the rights protected by the Constitution), whereas in Canada the same requirement applies to all constitutional rights.

More difficult still is the comparison of the means used by the legislator. American law requires, with regard to the strict scrutiny review, that the means be narrowly tailored, or necessary to fulfill the legislation's purpose.[94] This condition, again, is two-fold: first, that there is no other means that are less restrictive;[95] and, second, that those means are not overbroad.[96] Comparing these requirements and proportionality's tests reveals that the first requirement regarding no other means being less restrictive, is quite similar to the necessity requirement imposed by proportionality's test.[97] The difference with regard to the necessity test focuses on the requirement regarding overbreadth.[98] Both proportionality and strict scrutiny would agree that, if there is overbreadth, then part of the limitation of the constitutional right is not necessary to fulfill the legislative purpose. In this case, the means are unconstitutional according to strict scrutiny and proportionality.

What should happen when it is not possible to separate the overbreadth and the necessary breadth?[99] What about when the overbreadth is inherent to the subject in such a manner that the law's purposes cannot be fulfilled without overbreadth. An example is the Israeli Supreme Court case of *Adalah*.[100] There, in order to prevent the aiding and abetting of terrorist activity aimed at Israel, the Israeli government imposed a complete ban on family unification with spouses residing in the Occupied Territories. This restriction also applied, naturally, to spouses who had never aided or abetted any terrorists and who – according to the best

---

[94] See Ayers, above note 60. See also I. Ayres and S. Foster, "Don't Tell, Don't Ask: Narrow Tailoring after Grutter and Gratz," 85 *Tex. L. Rev.* 517 (2007).

[95] See Note, above note 62. See G. Feldman, "The Misuse of the Less Restrictive Alternative Inquiry in Rule of Reason Analysis," 58 *Am. U. L. Rev.* 561 (2009).

[96] See Note, above note 62. I will not discuss the underinclusive case.

[97] See above, at 326.

[98] See H. Paul Monaghan, "Overbreadth," *Sup. Ct. Rev.* 1 (1981).

[99] See above, at 395.

[100] See HCJ 7052/03 *Adalah – The Legal Center for the Rights of the Arab Minority* v. *Minister of Interior* (May 14, 2006, unpublished), available in English at http://elyon1.court.gov.il/fileseng/03/520/070/a47/03070520. a47.pdf.

available intelligence – were not likely to do so in the future. This is, by
any measure, "overbroad" coverage. To prevent it, an individual examination was necessary. It was demonstrated to the Court that within the
individual examination it was impossible to identify which spouses had
the "potential" to aid and abet. In this type of situation, overbreadth is
virtually inevitable.

How do the two methods solve this situation? According to proportionality, all the requirements of the second (necessity) test have been met,
and therefore, despite its overbreadth, the measure would continue on the
course of constitutional review and would now have to satisfy the requirements of proportionality *stricto sensu*. In some cases, therefore, the legislation would be held constitutional – if a proper relation exists between
the marginal social benefits gained by the legislation and the marginal
social harm caused to the right in question. In other cases, however, the
law would be declared unconstitutional. In any event, such a determination would be made in accordance with the requirements of the proportionality *stricto sensu* test.

What is the American approach to the issue? The answer is not free
from doubt.[101] If under American law the necessity requirements are
met – when the overbroad portion cannot be separated from the rest of
the means – then the legislation passes constitutional muster and there
is no need to continue the process of judicial review. This is not the case
with proportionality: here, satisfying the necessity test is but one of the
requirements to pass constitutional muster.[102] According to proportionality, after passing the necessity test, the test of proportionality *stricto sensu*
still remains, this test demands a balance between the marginal social
benefits in fulfilling the law's purposes and the marginal social harm to
the constitutional right. Then the conclusion – based on the assumption
that, with inseparable overbreadth, the necessity requirement of the strict
review is fulfilled – is that the protection of constitutional right according to proportionality is stronger. Legislation deemed constitutional in
American law after the necessity test must still pass another review (proportionality *stricto sensu*) according to proportionality, and may still be
found unconstitutional. As such, the right in question is guaranteed better protection.

The result according to American law is different when the necessity
requirement is not fulfilled in the case of overbreadth which cannot be

---

[101] See Fallon, above note 60, at 1328.
[102] See above, at 340.

separated. According to this assumption, the legislation is not constitutional as it has not passed the necessity test and therefore there is no room
for additional examinations. This is not the case according to proportionality. According to proportionality, the necessity requirement is fulfilled
and the legislation's fate is once again decided by proportionality *stricto
sensu*. The conclusion is as follows: assuming the overbreadth which cannot be separated does not satisfy the necessity requirement according
to strict scrutiny, the protection of the constitutional right according to
this level of scrutiny is stronger in American law than according to proportionality. Legislation which, after the necessity test, has been found
unconstitutional in American law must still pass the proportionality
stricto sensu test, after which it may be found constitutional.

Take, for example, the case of *Korematsu*.[103] There the court reviewed
the constitutionality of an executive order, issued during the Second
World War, which forbade all American citizens of Japanese descent from
remaining in certain areas, as determined in the order, which included
the west coast of the United States. The reason the order was issued was
military necessity stemming from the concern that American-Japanese
were more likely to co-operate with Japan – with whom the US was at war.
No individual examination was conducted. The petitioner violated the
order; he was indicted and convicted, and he appealed to the US Supreme
Court. All nine Justices agreed that the order was "suspect," as the classification was based upon race and that strict scrutiny of the order was
needed. Most of the Justices (six) accepted the government's argument
that this order was necessary at a time of war and therefore that the con-
viction should be affirmed. The dissent was of the opinion that the order
was unconstitutional. Today, it is widely accepted that the majority opinion was incorrect. The reason behind this is the striking lack of evidence
supporting the military necessity argument presented by the government
at the time of the trial.[104]

Let us assume, then, for argument's sake, a hypothetical situation
where military necessity was proved to the court. Let us further assume
that it was shown that every fifth American of a certain descent is actively
conspiring to co-operate with the enemy. Assume that it has been proven
that there is no way to identify those citizens suspected of collaborating
and that there is no other means to prevent the danger they represent save

---

[103] See *Korematsu* v. *United States*, 323 US 214 (1944).
[104] See Chemerinsky, above note 54, at 698.

for a blanket restriction on the entire group. Under those circumstances, would such an executive order pass constitutional muster? A review of the American literature on the subject does not yield a clear answer.

Fallon has thoroughly reviewed the concept of strict scrutiny. In particular, Fallon examined the question discussed earlier relating to overbreadth which cannot be narrowly tailored to achieve the compelling government interest at issue. Fallon, too, noted that no clear approach could be found in American case law to this question. However, Fallon raised the possibility that in those circumstances the legislation would not be declared unconstitutional, but rather the proportionality of its limitation would be examined. As he wrote:

> It is imaginable, if only barely, that even the smallest element of underinclusiveness or overinclusiveness could condemn a statute subject to strict scrutiny. But if any underinclusiveness, and perhaps especially any overinclusiveness, is permissible, the question inevitably arises: How much under- or overinclusiveness is tolerable, and how much is too much?
>
> Although the Supreme Court has seldom if ever said so expressly, the need to answer this question would appear to require an inquiry analogous to those that other countries' courts conduct in assessing "proportionality" – a term that I invoke here to emphasize similarity, not to claim identity. In determining whether a particular degree of statutory under- or overinclusiveness is tolerable, a court must judge whether the damage or wrong attending an infringement on protected rights is constitutionally acceptable in light of the government's compelling aims, the probability that the challenged policy will achieve them, and available alternative means of pursuing the same goals.[105]

If Fallon's approach were to be adopted by the American Supreme Court, it would be possible to say that the level of protection granted to human rights by the American strict scrutiny level of review is similar, in theory at least, to the one offered by those countries that have adopted proportionality.[106] But what if Fallon is wrong? What if, under this set of circumstances, the limiting legislation would uphold the requirements of the strict scrutiny review without any review of its proportionality? If that were the solution, then the level of protection offered by proportionality is greater than that offered by the American strict scrutiny.

So far the comparison between proportionality and strict scrutiny has been solely theoretical. This comparison lacks a practical aspect. According to the conventional wisdom in the United States, once a

---

[105] See Fallon, above note 60, at 1330.
[106] See Stone Sweet and Mathews, above note 44.

legislative provision is categorized as falling into the purview of strict scrutiny, it is most likely destined to fail the constitutional review. It is in that context that Gunther commented that "strict scrutiny is strict in theory but fatal in fact."[107] This is not always the case according to the tests of proportionality.

iii.   Categorization and criticism of proportionality

a.   Categorization and the internal critique of balancing   At the foundation of proportionality's criticism is the critique of proportionality *stricto sensu*. This test anchors the balancing between the marginal social benefits gained by the limiting legislation and the marginal social harm caused by it to the constitutional right.[108] This criticism can be divided into internal and external criticism. The internal criticism, which opens this discussion, focuses on the issue of incommensurability and its lack of a rational basis,[109] and continues on to the claim that it stems from intuition and improvisation and subjective judging.[110] Could the same arguments be made against categorization? Categorization is not based upon specific (*ad hoc*) balancing; therefore, the internal critique, assuming it is aimed at that act of balancing, is not relevant to categorization. However, categorization is based upon principled balancing.[111] Such balancing is of an interpretive nature (interpretive balancing).[112] It determines the scope of the category. Accordingly, any criticism of this type of balancing within proportionality may well be aimed at that same type within the categorization. Thus, for example, it is possible to argue that categorization's view, according to which the right to free speech does not include obscenities or incitement to commit illegal acts, is merely the result of an interpretive-principled act of balancing between the principle of free speech and other competing principles. Thus, if a specific balancing is not plausible, neither is principled balancing, which gives the principle of free speech very little, if any, weight. Similarly, the claims regarding a lack of rationality and the subjective judiciary can also be raised against

---

[107] See G. Gunther, "The Supreme Court, 1971 Term – Foreword: In Search of Evolving Doctrine on a Changing Court: A Model for a Newer Equal Protection," 86 *Harv. L. Rev.* 1, 8 (1972). Not everyone agrees with this description: see S. E. Gottlieb, "Compelling Governmental Interests: An Essential But Unanalyzed Term in Constitutional Adjudication," 68 *Boston University L. Rev.* 917 (1988). See also Winkler, above note 60.

[108] See above, at 350.   [109] See above, at 482.   [110] See above, at 512.

[111] See Stone Sweet and Mathews, above note 44.

[112] On interpretive balancing, see below, at 522.

the principled-interpretive balancing at categorization's foundation. The answers provided within proportionality to those arguments also apply to categorization. However, the criticism applies more vigorously to proportionality than to categorization, since for proportionality this criticism applies – to a different degree – in every single case, whereas for categorization the criticism applies only to the creation of the category (or to the modification of its scope).

b.   Categorization and the external critique on balancing

aa.   Too wide a judicial discretion   One of the arguments against proportionality is that it provides judges with too wide a discretion.[113] Is categorization spared this criticism? The answer, in principle, is no. If the criticism against proportionality is aimed at determining the proper legislative purpose by the judge, the same arguments may be raised against determining the compelling state interest or similar notions within the contours of categorization. The same is true for judicial discretion regarding the rational connection test and the necessity test; both of these apply to categorization, mostly at the same intensity.

But what about judicial discretion as it applies to balancing? Categorization entails no specific balancing act, but it does include a principled-interpretive balancing that determines the limits of the category. Is the judicial discretion available during the concrete balancing wider than that available during the principled-interpretive balancing? From the standpoint of the trial judge, the answer is yes. In those systems where categorization applies, the category is provided to the trial court as a given, a finished product that cannot be reevaluated. Thus, the trial judge has no discretion as to the principled-interpretive type of balancing; obviously, the judge has no discretion as to specific balancing either, since this type of balancing does not exist within categorization. This is not the case according to proportionality. Here, the trial judge may exercise discretion while conducting a specific balance. Thus, the discretion exercised at the trial level is narrower with categorization than it is with proportionality.

Does the same conclusion apply to the highest court in the system? Is the discretion used by the highest court for balancing within categorization narrower than that used within proportionality? This question has no simple answer. The proposition that the highest court may exercise

---

[113] See above, at 487.

some discretion as to balancing is acceptable.[114] However, this discretion is of a limited nature. It is limited by past precedents; it is limited by judicial tradition; and it is limited by the values upon which that legal system is based. Is this discretion wider than that exercised by the American Supreme Court justices with regard to categorization? American Supreme Court justices, who are allowed to overturn their own precedents, can use judicial discretion whenever they approach the creation of a new category or the setting of new contours in an existing category.[115] Such discretion is based on the conduct of a principled-interpretive balance. In several notable cases, the American Supreme Court was asked to change the structure of existing constitutional categories. Thus, for example, much of the feminist movement for equal rights was focused on "upgrading" the level of scrutiny relating to gender-based classifications from intermediate to strict. The same is true for age-based classification. These struggles over the proper place in the hierarchy of constitutional scrutiny often mirror the social struggles in the United States. It is very difficult to evaluate the scope of the discretion provided to American justices in comparison to the discretion granted to other supreme and constitutional court judges in applying proportionality *stricto sensu*. It is difficult, for example, to evaluate the loyalty demonstrated by the American Supreme Court to past precedents in comparison with the loyalty to precedents demonstrated by judges of proportionality courts. I doubt that these can be quantified. It seems we are left with nothing more than mere speculations.

bb.   Lack of sufficient protection on human rights   Another criticism of proportionality argues that the balance that underlies it weakens the protection granted to human rights. According to this argument, the protection granted to constitutional rights by the American categorization approach – in particular, the protection provided by the strict scrutiny review – provides greater protection than that offered by proportionality. This argument, however, is far from describing the normative reality. The picture is much more complex and does not allow for an unequivocal answer. A precise reply requires an examination of each and every right – both on the theoretical level, as well as on the practical level.[116]

---

[114] See above, at 414.

[115] See Stone Sweet and Mathews, above note 44.

[116] See E. J. Eberle, *Dignity and Liberty: Constitutional Visions in Germany and the United States* (Santa Barbara, CA: Praeger Publishers, 2001); M. Arden, "Human Rights in the Age of Terrorism," 121 *L. Q. Rev.* 604 (2005); E. J. Eberle, *European and US Constitutionalism* (Georg Nolte (ed.), 2005); P. E. Quint, "The Most Extraordinarily

It has been argued that categorization may provide human rights with better protection than proportionality particularly during national emergencies. The reason for this is that, during times of national emergency, judges tend to ascribe more weight to arguments favoring national security as opposed to those favoring individual rights. In contrast, the argument goes on, thinking in categories is immune to these considerations. Both parts of this argument are far from being factually sustainable.[117] Thus, for example, the Israeli Supreme Court has provided ample protection to constitutional rights during periods of extremely trying national emergency, all while using proportionality *stricto sensu* (balancing).[118] The same is true for the English House of Lords.[119] In contrast, American courts, despite the use of different categories, found this protection troublesome at times of national emergency,[120] although, at the end of

Powerful Court of Law the World Has Ever Known – Judicial Review in the United States and Germany," 65 *Md. L. Rev.* 152 (2006); J. B. Hall, "Taking 'Rechts' Seriously: Ronald Dworkin and the Federal Constitutional Court of Germany," 9 *German L. J.* 771 (2008); A. Baker, "Proportional, Not Strict, Scrutiny: Against a US 'Suspect Classifications' Model under Article 14 ECHR in the UK," 56 *Am. J. Comp. L.* 847 (2008); see Stone Sweet and Mathews, above note 44.

[117] See S. Boyne, "The Future of Liberal Democracies in a Time of Terror: A Comparison of the Impact on Civil Liberties in the Federal Republic of Germany and the United States," 11 *Tulsa J. Comp. & Int'l L.* 111 (2003); R. J. Krotoszynski Jr., "A Comparative Perspective on the First Amendment: Free Speech, Militant Democracy, and the Primacy of Dignity as a Preferred Constitutional Value in Germany," 78 *Tul. L. Rev.* 1549 (2004); M. Rosenfeld, "Judicial Balancing in Times of Stress: Comparing the American, British, and Israeli Approaches to the War on Terror," 27 *Cardozo L. Rev.* 2079 (2006); K. Roach, "Must We Trade Rights for Security?: The Choice Between Smart, Harsh, or Proportionate Security Strategies in Canada and Britain," 27 *Cardozo L. Rev.* 2151 (2006); R. A. Kahn, "The Headscarf as Threat: A Comparison of German and US Legal Discourses," 40 *Vand. J. Transnat'l L.* 417 (2007); T. Poole, "Recent Developments on the 'War on Terrorism' in Canada," 7 *Hum. Rts. L. Rev.* 633 (2007).

[118] See A. Barak, "The Role of a Supreme Court in a Democracy, and the Fight Against Terrorism," 58 *U. Miami L. Rev.* 125 (2003); A. Barak, "Human Rights in Times of Terror – A Judicial Point of View," 28 *Legal Studies* 493 (2008).

[119] See *A (FC)* v. *Secretary of State for the Home Department* [2004] UKHL 56; *A (FC)* v. *Secretary of State for the Home Department* [2005] UKHL 71; *Secretary of State for the Home Department* v. *E* [2007] UKHL 47; *Secretary of State for the Home Department* v. *JJ and others (FC)* [2007] UKHL 45; *Secretary of State for the Home Department* v. *MB* [2007] UKHL 46. See also M. Navoth, "Torture Versus Terror: The Israeli and British Cases," 1 *Isr. J. Foreign Affairs* 69 (2007).

[120] See H. H. Koh, "Setting the World Right," 115 *Yale L. J.* 2350 (2006); O. M. Fiss, "The War Against Terrorism and the Rule of Law," 26 *OJLS* 235 (2006); D. Cole, "The Poverty of Posner's Pragmatism: Balancing Away Liberty After 9/11," 59 *Stan. L. Rev.* 1735 (2007); S. Reinhardt, "Weakening the Bill of Rights: A Victory for Terrorism," 106 *Mich. L. Rev.* 963 (2008).

the day, the movement has been positive towards human rights.[121] The war on terror – one of the judicial hallmarks of the late twentieth and the beginning of the twenty-first century – does not point to any principled advantage gained by the use of categorization over proportionality in terms of human rights protection. In fact, the opposite seems to be true. Proportionality has demonstrated its ability to protect human rights particularly in the dark hours of the war on terror.

cc. Denying judicial legitimacy The argument is that the act of balancing, which is at the core of proportionality, is one of the main characteristics of legislation and therefore should not be performed by judges.[122] Categorization, the argument continues, is more typical of judging as it is devoid of the feature of specific balancing. It seems, once again, that both parts of the argument are not substantiated. Balancing is typical of both legislating and judging. The common law is based on the balancing between competing principles, and its entire being is based on judging. Thinking in categories, on the other hand, is often used by legislators as well. Thus, both balancing and categorization may well be considered an integral part of the tasks performed by each of the two branches – the judicial and the legislative.[123]

It is interesting to note that the legitimacy of judicial review is most often under attack in the United States, which applies categorization.[124] This is not the case in most legal systems that have adopted proportionality, including the balancing at its foundation.[125] In fact, in these countries, the use of judicial review seems to be spreading.[126] Countries that

---

[121] See *Boumediene et al. v. Bush, President of the United States et al.*, 553 US 723 (2008).

[122] See above, at 490.

[123] See Stone Sweet and Mathews, above note 44.

[124] See above, at 473.

[125] See A. Stone Sweet, *Governing with Judges: Constitutional Politics in Europe* (Oxford University Press, 2000); M. M. Shapiro and A. Stone Sweet, *On Law, Politics, and Judicialization* (Oxford University Press, 2002); T. Koopmans, *Courts and Political Institutions: A Comparative View* (Cambridge University Press, 2003); R. Hirschl, *Towards Juristocracy: The Origins and Consequences of the New Constitutionalism* (Cambridge, MA: Harvard University Press, 2004).

[126] See A. R. Brewer-Carías, *Judicial Review in Comparative Law* (Cambridge University Press, 1989); D. W. Jackson and C. Neal Tate (eds.), *Comparative Judicial Review and Public Policy* (1992); D. M. Beatty (ed.), *Human Rights and Judicial Review: A Comparative Perspective* (1994); C. N. Tate and T. Vallinder (eds.), *The Global Expansion of Judicial Power* (1995); R. Hirschl, *Towards Juristocracy: The Origins and Consequences of the New Constitutionalism* (Cambridge, MA: Harvard University Press, 2004); R. Hirschl, "The New Constitutionalism and the Judicialization of Pure Politics Worldwide," 75 *Fordham*

were unwilling to adopt the institution of judicial review in the past are now changing their constitution in order to allow it. That was the case, for example, with most countries of the former Soviet Union.[127] The same is true in France, which in 2008 adopted full judicial review of the constitutionality of legislation not only prior to its publication ("preview") but also after being published ("review").[128] It seems that there is a growing trend according to which the notion of a constitutional democracy entails both a written constitution and an acknowledgment of the institution of judicial review. This development may be explained in two ways. First, the US Constitution contains no explicit provision relating to judicial review of a law's constitutionality. The adoption of judicial review there was done through the courts.[129] This is not the case for those constitutions that have adopted proportionality. In those constitutions, a specific provision relating to judicial review is an integral part of the constitutional text. Second, despite its formal provisions on the matter, the US Constitution is, in practice, very difficult to amend. This, again, is not the case with many of the proportionality-related constitutions. These may be relatively easily amended in comparison to their American counterpart. Both of those explanations are not directly related to thinking in categories or to the conduct of balancing.

iv.   Categorization as an alternative to proportionality?

While proportionality may not be able to provide fully convincing replies to all of its criticisms, the same conclusion may apply to categorization as well. Each method has its advantages and disadvantages.[130] Each method has developed as part of a very distinct set of historical and social circumstances. It can be assumed that the two methods will draw closer in

---

L. Rev. (2006); V. Ferreres Comella, *Constitutional Courts and Democratic Values: A European Perspective* (New Haven, CT: Yale University Press, 2009).

[127] See R. G. Teitel, *Transitional Justice* (Oxford University Press, 2000); H. Schwartz, *The Struggle for Constitutional Justice in Post-Communist Europe* (University of Chicago Press, 2002); R. Prochazka, *Mission Accomplished: On Founding Constitutional Adjudication in Central Europe* (Budapest: Central European University Press, 2002); W. Sadurski, *Rights before Courts: A Study of Constitutional Courts in Postcommunist States of Central and Eastern Europe* (Dordrecht: Springer, 2008).

[128] See Loi Constitutionnelle No. 2008-724 du 23 Juillet 2008 des institutions de la Vème République.

[129] See *Marbury v. Madison*, 5 US 137 (1803).

[130] See V. C. Jackson, "Ambivalent Resistance and Comparative Constitutionalism: Opening Up the Conversation on 'Proportionality', Rights and Federalism," 1 *U. Pa. J. Const. L.* 583, 605 (1999).

the future.[131] Indeed, the first signs of this trend may already be emerging, as some American courts have begun adopting some aspects of proportionality.[132] Still, it seems that it is too early to properly evaluate this trend. It might be the case, as Schauer argues, that proportionality courts will adopt some aspects of the American system.[133] Indeed, both proportionality and categorization are a part of the legal architecture.[134] Each reflects the society in which it was developed, and each is shaped and influenced by extrinsic legal developments. It is therefore hard to assess what the future holds for each. In any event, every legal system must strive to improve and further develop the methods it uses. Some of the ways to do just that will now be examined.

---

[131] On the general trends in this context, see V. Jackson, *Constitutional Engagement in a Transnational Era* (Oxford University Press, 2010). See also Stone Sweet and Mathews, above note 44.

[132] See above, at 206.   [133] See Schauer, above note 45, at 32.

[134] See Schauer, above note 45, at 49.

20

The future of proportionality

A. Regarding the need for renewal

Proportionality is not perfect; yet none of the suggested alternatives – with categorization as the central one – ensures a more appropriate arrangement. We should therefore focus on proportionality and ways to improve it. Indeed, by now it has been several decades since proportionality was first introduced to the Western legal systems. During this period, no significant changes have occurred in its components or its understanding as a constitutional tool. It seems that the time is ripe, therefore, for a reexamination. It is in this context that the subjects which require a reconsideration are raised, in order to refresh and develop the doctrine of proportionality.

When considering improvements to proportionality, it is important to make use of the legal and judicial experience provided by comparative law. Obviously, of particular interest are those legal systems that have adopted proportionality; it is appropriate that they learn from each other's perspective, but this is insufficient. The American academic literature and case law are of particular interest. The difference between proportionality and the American system of categorization in relation to the protection of human rights can be reduced to the issue of specific (*ad hoc*) balancing, or proportionality *stricto sensu*.[1] Other than in this component, however, the two methods are in fact quite similar. That is also the main reason for the two methods drawing closer in recent decades, at least with respect to the portions in which they are similar.[2]

In this final chapter, each of proportionality's components will be examined. The main subjects which require further development in each

---

[1] See S. Gardbaum, "The Myth and the Reality of American Constitutional Exceptionalism," 107 *Mich. L. Rev.* 391 (2008). See above, at 508.

[2] See generally, V. Jackson, *Constitutional Engagement in a Transnational Era* (New York: Oxford University Press, 2010), 60.

of these components will be discussed. The discussion begins with the proper purpose, that is, the purpose justifying a limitation on a constitutional right. This requirement is common to all legal systems, and therefore development in this area may be of particular interest. The chapter then turns to a review of the components of rational connection and necessity and examines whether these components can bear a "heavier burden" of value-laden content and therefore "relieve the burden" from proportionality *stricto sensu*. Finally, the different aspects in the development of the consideration regarding that last component – proportionality *stricto sensu* will be examined.

B. The proper purpose component – future developments

1. Different approaches to proper purpose

i. The spectrum of approaches

A review of comparative law reveals several approaches to the proper purpose component. The focus herein is on those instances where the proper purpose relates to the public interest. Instances where the proper purpose constitutes an individual right will be dealt with separately.[3] Regarding those cases where on one side of the scales we have a constitutionally protected right limited by law and on the other we have a public interest whose fulfillment led to the limitation, we can differentiate between several principled approaches. On one end of the spectrum is German constitutional law, according to which, in the absence of a specific constitutional provision on this matter, the only thing the proper purpose needs to satisfy is the fairly undemanding requirement of not running contrary to the constitution.[4] On the other end of the spectrum is the approach adopted by the Canadian Supreme Court in *Oakes*, according to which in order to satisfy the requirement that the purpose be "sufficiently important" it must "relate to concerns which are pressing and substantial in a free and democratic society."[5]

Between these two ends of the spectrum are the approaches that have been adopted in different countries. For example, in South Africa opinions are divided on this matter. Some are of the opinion that the Canadian

---

[3] See below, at 533.
[4] See D. Grimm, "Proportionality in Canadian and German Constitutional Jurisprudence," 57 *U. Toronto L. J.* 383, 388 (2007).
[5] R. v. *Oakes* [1986] 1 SCR 103, § 69.

Oakes test[6] should be adopted, while others are satisfied suggesting a "compelling purpose," or one that carries "substantial" weight.[7] In Israel, it has been stated that a purpose is proper only if it corresponds with the values of the State of Israel and if it shows particular sensitivity to the role of human rights in the Israeli legal system.[8] American law distinguishes between three categories of rights.[9] In the first category, which includes the most fundamental rights, the legislative purpose must serve a compelling state interest (or a pressing public necessity, or a substantial state interest). In the second category (the middle one), which includes the "intermediate" rights, the court requires that the legislative purpose in question serve "an important" governmental interest. Finally, in the third category (the lowest one), the rest of the constitutional rights are included. To limit the rights in this category all that is required is that the legislation be legitimate.

ii. A threshold requirement based on a justification

The key similarity between all these approaches is that the requirement for a proper purpose is a threshold requirement.[10] There is no *ad hoc* balancing. The scope of the limitation on the constitutional right in question is not at issue while determining the "appropriateness" of the law's purpose. This is the proper approach. It reflects the proper relation between the constitutional right and the public interest. This relation means that the very existence of a public interest, in and of itself, would not suffice in justifying a limitation on a constitutional right. The public interest must be of a special character in order to examine the nature of the limitation and decide whether it is constitutional. In that sense, all legal systems have accepted the approach that rights are shields used by individuals to protect themselves from the tyranny of the majority.[11]

A key question is where should such a threshold requirement be located. In some cases, the solution may be found in the constitution itself. It may specify those instances in which the public interest may

---

[6] See S. Woolman and H. Botha, "Limitations," in S. Woolman, M. Bishop, and J. Brickhill (eds.), *Constitutional Law of South Africa*, 2nd edn. (Cape Town: Juta Law Publishers, looseleaf, 2002–), 75.
[7] See H. Cheadle, "Limitation of Rights," in H. Cheadle, N. Haysom, and D. Davis (eds.), *South African Constitutional Law: The Bill of Rights* (Cape Town: Juta Law Publishers, 2002), 693, 710.
[8] See *Adalah – The Legal Center of the Rights of the Arab Minority* v. *Minister of Defence*, HCJ 8276/05 [2006] (2) IsrLR 352.
[9] See above, at 509.   [10] See above, at 508.
[11] See F. Schauer, "A Comment on the Structure of Rights," 27 *Ga. L. Rev.* 415, 443 (1993).

justify imposing a limitation on a protected right. Thus, for example, the European Convention for the Protection of Human Rights and Fundamental Freedoms[12] explicitly states that the right to freedom of expression may be limited in order to protect national security interests.[13] Such a provision, however, only begins the inquiry; it does not direct us in understanding what level of national security threat would justify the limitation on the freedom of expression. Similarly, in the same provision it provides that the right to freedom of expression may only be limited by provisions that are "prescribed by law and are necessary in a democratic society."[14] Can that provision direct the interpreter as to the importance of the limiting purpose as a threshold requirement, or does it relate to other components of proportionality, once the threshold requirement has been satisfied?

We are, then, back to square one: what is the proper threshold level to be satisfied to justify the imposition of a limitation of a constitutional right? Further, should this level be uniform, as suggested by the Canadian Supreme Court in *Oakes*? Or should the level instead vary in accordance with the social importance of the right, as the American Supreme Court has held? If we opt for a uniform level, then what should that level be? If the levels vary, then what are those different levels?

2.   *The proper approach: the hierarchy of constitutional rights with regard to the purpose's importance*

i.   A hierarchy of rights based on historical experience

It appears that the best approach is to establish a hierarchy of rights in relation to the legislative purpose in question. Moreover, that hierarchy should include only two levels of constitutional rights. The first level would consist of all the "fundamental" or "high-level" rights; the other level would consist of all the other rights.

As an initial matter, the approach that all constitutional rights are equal in importance in relation to the requirement of proper purpose, and that therefore a uniform approach should be established for the requirement, cannot be accepted. The main concern is that, should such a uniform approach be adopted, the threshold level required would be far too low for all the protected rights. Such is the case, for example, in Germany, where

---

[12] European Convention for the Protection of Human Rights and Fundamental Freedoms (1950).
[13] *Ibid.*, Art. 10(2).   [14] *Ibid.*

the only requirement for the law's purpose to satisfy is that it would not be in conflict with the constitution. Such an easy-to-satisfy requirement is not sufficient to justify the placing of a limitation on a constitutionally protected human right, as it does not acknowledge the special role constitutional rights have within the system of a constitutional democracy. Having said that, however, the issue of a too-low uniform requirement may be resolved through the adoption of a much more demanding standard. That was the solution, for example, adopted by the Canadian Supreme Court in *Oakes*. But experience has shown that the courts found it nearly impossible to apply such a high threshold requirement. In fact, over the years the courts have gradually reduced this high threshold level, turning it, in practice, into an even lower requirement. More importantly, not all rights are created equal; not all rights are equal in their social value.[15] True, all constitutional rights are of equal constitutional status; but the same constitutional status does not render them of the same social value. Thus, my position on the need for two levels of constitutional rights rests on both a practical and a theoretical (or normative) reasoning.

What is the nature of those separate levels of constitutional rights? In this context, it is recommended that each legal system adopt its own solution; each country should determine for itself which rights are "fundamental" to its own democracy and which rights are not. It is not logic, but rather historical experience, that should be the decisive factor here. According to the historical experience of both the United States[16] and South Africa,[17] it would be only natural to consider equality – and in particular equality on the basis of race – as a right of the highest order. Similarly, based on Europe's historical account, it would only be natural to consider the right to human dignity as a right of the highest order in post-Second World War Germany.[18] It seems to me that Israel ascribes the highest level of importance to human dignity as its people were victims of the violation of human dignity in the Second World War.

ii.   The importance of the purpose requirement as derived
from the hierarchy of rights

Once a hierarchy of rights has been determined, it is time to set the threshold level of the purpose's importance. The American legal system may be of guidance in this matter. It seems that the first two levels of scrutiny are

---

[15] See above, at 359.   [16] US Const., Am. XIV.
[17] Constitution of the Republic of South Africa, Arts. 1, 7, 36.
[18] Basic Law for the Federal Republic of Germany, Art. 1.

proper, whereas the third (the minimal one) is not. Regarding the constitutional rights of the highest level, it is appropriate to adopt an arrangement similar to the "strict scrutiny" used in American law. It should be
required that the law's purpose be either "compelling" or "pressing."
This would properly express the high degree of social importance placed
by these systems on those fundamental rights. In addition, in order to
succeed, as the Canadian experience has taught us, such a requirement
should be reserved for a relatively small number of rights that are considered by that society to be of the highest order.

The rest of the rights should be grouped into the second level. Here, the
requirement should be that the law's purpose be "important." This is the
requirement posed by the American "intermediate scrutiny" level. Such a
demand balances the need not to require too high a threshold while, at the
same time, according the proper weight to those rights in a constitutional
democracy. Indeed, a lower requirement – such as the "legitimate purpose" requirement posed by the minimal level of scrutiny in the United
States would represent too low a threshold for limiting rights in a constitutional democracy.

3.   Proper purpose and protection of constitutional rights

i.   The conventional wisdom

When two constitutional rights conflict (such as the right to privacy with
that of freedom of expression), the solution is found at the sub-constitutional level (a statute or common law).[19] Thus, proportionality operates at
the sub-constitutional level. It applies in any case where a constitutional
right has been limited. As for the reason behind the limitation on the right
in question (such as the freedom of expression), there is usually no distinction between a case where the limitation was caused by the fulfillment of
the public interest (such as national security interests) and that of a limitation caused by the need to advance another person's right (such as the
right to privacy of another person):[20] in both cases, the law's purpose must
be proper; a rational connection must exist between the means selected
to fulfill the law's purpose and the purpose; that no alternative means
exist which equally fulfill the law's purposes while being less restrictive to
the right; and that there is a proportional relation between the marginal

---

[19]   See above, at 89.
[20]   See R. Alexy, "Individual Rights and Collective Goods," in C. Nino (eds.), *Rights* (New
York University Press, 1992), 163.

social benefits gained by fulfilling the law's purposes and the marginal
social harm caused by limiting the right in question.

This approach stems from the fundamental understanding that proportionality applies whenever a constitutional right (such as the freedom
of expression) conflicts with an opposing principle, and it is irrelevant
whether said opposing principle was meant to serve the public interest
(as in national security considerations) or the right of another person (as
in the right to privacy). Contributing to this notion is the understanding
that the distinction between the public interest and other people's rights
are blurred. Thus, some of the issues that were once perceived as part of
the public interest (such as education, medical services, and the environment) are now understood as individual rights.[21] Moreover, often a limitation on one person's right is intended to fulfill a person's right which in
terms of its magnitude and influence is similar to those of the state itself,
to the extent that it would be justified to view such rights as part of the
public interest rather than as an individual right. Finally, in many cases,
considerations of the public interest and individual rights are conflated to
a point that it is hard to see where one begins and the other ends. In light
of all of these developments, the current prevailing approach – according
to which a limitation on a constitutional right should be treated in the
same manner whether it protects another constitutional right or furthers
the public interest – is both justified and appropriate. However, although
this approach is clear and proper, it is time to refine it in several respects,
so that the special importance of the constitutional right protected will
be reflected in the justification of the limitation of another constitutional
right.

ii.   Disadvantages of the conventional wisdom

Most constitutional rights are shaped as principles. According to Alexy, a
principle strives for optimization subject to factual and legal possibilities.
Is the opposing public-interest consideration (such as national security
considerations or public order) also a principle seeking optimization?
Alexy's answer is positive,[22] but it is doubtful that this is indeed the case.
Rivers correctly noted, when referring to public interest considerations,
that:

> [T]hey cannot be optimisation requirements in the same sense as rights,
> since legislatures are under no obligation to optimise them or even pursue

---

[21]   See above, at 254.

[22]   See Alexy, above note 20.

that at all. One could accept that they are unenforceable optimisation requirements on account of a lack of a relevant cause of action. But even under constitutional systems which permit legal actions to ensure the general constitutionality of a measure, courts never consider whether legislatures have pursued the public interest to the greatest possible extent. Thus, public interests have to be construed as optimisation permissions, and principles must be redefined as optimisation requirements or permissions. Only rights correlate to optimisation requirements in the strict sense.[23]

Indeed, we cannot properly compare protection of the public interest (such as national security) as a justification for placing a limitation on a human right (such as freedom of expression), and the case of protecting another constitutional right (such as the right to privacy) as a justification for the same limitation. Take, for example, legislation limiting a public interest (such as the level of national security) in order to elevate – that is, to better protect – the normative level of a constitutional right (such as the freedom of expression). Should the limitation on the public interest satisfy all the requirements of proportionality? Would the limiting law be declared unconstitutional merely because the (elevated) level of protection granted to the right in question by the limiting law may be obtained through the use of a means that would be less restrictive to the public interest in question? Would the balancing test of proportionality *stricto sensu* apply in the same way to this kind of limitation – that is, a limitation on the public interest in order to protect a constitutional right? Should we not say that, when we have constitutional rights on both sides of the scales, then the requirements of proportionality should address both, while, when on one end of the scales we have a constitutional right and on the other a consideration of the public interest, then proportionality would only apply to a limitation on a constitutional right?[24]

It is believed that we should distinguish between two situations. One way of reasoning such a distinction would be to follow the Dworkinian approach which distinguishes between principles and policies.[25] While Dworkin adamantly opposed letting a judge balance between limitations on a constitutional right and fulfilling social policies, he never opposed

---

[23] J. Rivers, "Proportionality, Discretion and the Second Law of Balancing," in G. Pavlakos (ed.), *Law, Rights, and Discourse: The Legal Philosophy of Robert Alexy* (Portland, OR: Hart Publishing, 2007), 167, 168.

[24] See D. Meyerson, "Why Courts Should Not Balance Rights against the Public Interest," 31 *Melb. U. L. Rev.* 873 (2007).

[25] See R. Dworkin, *Taking Rights Seriously* (Cambridge, MA: Harvard University Press, 1977), 22.

granting a judge the authority to balance between two competing constitutional rights. Rawls, too, has recognized the need to allow a judge to balance between two conflicting constitutional rights. Obviously, this does
not mean we must go the distance with either Dworkin or Rawls; rather,
we can adopt the distinction while applying it in a more reserved fashion.
Another justification may be that supplied by Rivers,[26] who argues that
the legislator is under no obligation to seek the optimization of the public
interest, while it does have a constitutional obligation to seek an optimization for constitutional rights. This obligation reflects the "positive" aspect
of constitutional rights, which mostly deals with the level of protection
granted to those rights rather than with preventing the imposition of
limitations on them.[27] The prevailing notion[28] is that the legislative duties
are not exhausted by merely complying with the negative aspect of those
rights. Rather, the legislator must also satisfy the "positive" duties relating to those same rights. Against this background, it should be clear why
the status of a constitutional right – which requires the legislator to abide
by both positive and negative duties – is quite different to that of a public
interest consideration, which does not require the same of the legislator. It
may also be the case that the justification for the distinction between the
high level of protection granted to individual rights and the lower level of
protection granted to the public interest relates to the scope of legislative
discretion applied to each. Thus, for example, the scope of the discretion
that the legislator may exercise in relation to his duties with respect to the
constitutional right is much narrower than the discretion it may use with
regard to the advancement of the public interest. And, while all those differences do not affect the need to apply proportionality to both sides of the
scales whenever two constitutional rights are weighed against each other,
they may well affect a more subtle application of the requirements of proportionality in those cases where against the constitutional right stands a
consideration of the public interest.

iii.   Proper purpose: protection of a constitutional right as a
justification for the limitation of a constitutional right

Proportionality requires that the limiting law be enacted for a proper
purpose.[29] This requirement is an expression of the understanding that

---

[26] See Rivers, above note 23.
[27] *Ibid.*, at 168.
[28] See above, at 422.
[29] See above, at 245.

a limitation on a constitutional right may not be taken for granted. The constitutional right is meant to protect the individual from the tyranny of the majority. Not every consideration of the public interest may serve as a legitimate justification for limiting a human right. Rather, the public interest consideration must be sufficiently unique to justify such a limitation. Those considerations apply, naturally, when the legislative purpose was meant to serve the public interest (such as national security).

But what is the case when the legislative purpose is designed to advance not the public interest but rather another constitutional right? What should be the essence of the requirement for a "proper purpose" where on both sides of the scales we have constitutional rights? It seems to me that the proper answer is that whenever the purpose of a limiting legislation on one constitutional right (such as the right to privacy) is to advance another constitutional right (such as the right to enjoy good reputation), this alone should provide sufficient justification for the limitation of the (first) right. In other words, the very purpose of advancing another constitutional right, in and of itself, is a proper purpose in a constitutional democracy. This conclusion is clearly valid in those cases where the right the legislator wishes to promote has a constitutional status. But this insight should apply to other rights at the sub-constitutional level. No other demands should be placed on such a limitation. Such recognition would express the high level of social importance placed upon the promotion of any right (here, the right to enjoy a good reputation) in a constitutional democracy.

Of course, in the framework of proportionality *stricto sensu* (balancing), more weight should be given to the constitutional right than to the protection of the sub-constitutional right. The reason for this is that protection of the constitutional right has more significant social importance than the protection of the sub-constitutional right. However, there is room to take into account, within the balancing, the scope of the limitation of one right and the scope of the protection of the other right. Therefore, it will at times be possible to justify a small limitation of a constitutional right to provide the sub-constitutional right with comprehensive protection.

iv.   The duty to prevent the limitation of one
right while protecting another

Proportionality's tests (rational connection, necessity, and proportionality *stricto sensu*) are all derived from the notion of a constitutional duty not to limit a constitutionally protected right (such as freedom of expression).

This duty, however, is not absolute. In some instances, a constitutional right may be limited. The different tests posed by proportionality examine these instances from different angles. They provide public interest considerations (such as national security) with ample weight. However, they do not consider the advancement of the public interest to be a constitutional duty. National security considerations are for the executive branch to consider. An individual has no constitutional right to enjoy a higher (or lower) level of national security.

The situation is different when the limitation on the constitutional right was imposed to fulfill the protection of another constitutional right. The rules of proportionality not only examine the scope of the limitation placed on the limited constitutional right, but also the scope of the protection of the protected constitutional right. Take, for example, a law which limits the right to freedom of expression in order to increase the protection of a person's right to enjoy privacy. Both duties exercised by the legislator in this type of case – the duty not to limit the freedom of speech, and the duty to protect the individual's right to enjoy a good reputation – are part of the legislator's duties. The rules of proportionality must first examine whether the limitation on the freedom of expression is proportional in relation to the protection provided to the right to privacy and then examine whether the protection of a good reputation is proportional in relation to the limitation imposed on the right to freedom of expression.

These two examinations should yield similar, or at least compatible, results. If not, the following situation may occur. A statute will be enacted limiting the right of freedom of expression in order to protect the right to privacy. The statute will be declared constitutional. Another statute protecting the right to freedom of expression while limiting the right to privacy would also be held constitutional. Both statutes are constitutional, as the legislator acted in both of them within the zone of proportionality.[30] Closer examination of both provisions, however, would reveal that they are in conflict. This is an undesirable result. The notions of constitutional harmony and coherence require a holistic examination that leads to a symmetrical result in all cases – whatever the viewpoint may be. The sub-constitutional level at which the rules of proportionality apply should guarantee that the result is identical from every viewpoint. Another way to guarantee such harmony would be through the use of sub-constitutional rules relating to conflicts between two legislative provisions. This solution, however, is not desired. The solution chosen must

---

[30] See above, at 415.

be one that achieves constitutional harmony regardless of the viewpoint taken.

This approach should apply, naturally, when two rights at the same level of social importance and which share the same limitation clause are in conflict. However, the application should be the same when the two rights are not at the same level of social importance and even if each has its own limitation clause. True, the specific solution in each case may vary in accordance with the social importance of the right, as well as the wording of the specific limitation clause in question; yet the principled approach – according to which we should aspire to achieve harmonious results and prevent, to the greatest extent possible, conflicts between the several legislative provisions appearing in different laws, as well as between several provisions of the same legislative act – should apply to this type of case as well.

C. The rational connection component

The rational connection test requires that the means selected to advance the law's purpose would be rationally connected to that same purpose.[31] It reflects a probability test. The degree of probability required is low. All that is required is that the contribution of the means to the fulfillment of the legislative purpose is more than minimal, and that the probability that the legislative purpose is actually achieved is not merely theoretical.[32] This requirement is too low. The level of probability that should be required to satisfy the rational connection test should reflect the relative social importance of the marginal benefits gained by achieving the law's purpose in comparison with the social importance of the marginal benefits gained by preventing the harm caused to the constitutional right in question. But what is the proper level of probability that should be required? This question finds very little guidance in the comparative literature. It seems that most legal systems did not address the rational connection component. As a result, most of the interesting questions relating to probabilities have been "removed" to the later component of proportionality *stricto sensu*. It seems that a call for analytical development of the rational connection component is in order. What is the appropriate direction of such development?

---

[31] See above, at 303.
[32] See above, at 305.

On the one hand, being satisfied by a level of probability which is merely beyond minimal is not proper; on the other hand, it seems that the demand for a high level of probability – such as "near certainty" of the realization of the purpose should the means selected by the legislator be implemented – is also unwarranted.[33] One should not impose levels of probability that simply do not fit the social realities in a modern constitutional democracy.[34] What, then, is the proper level of probability?

It seems that the proper development in the rational connection component should comport itself to the proposed developments in the proper purpose component.[35] In the context of the proper purpose I have suggested a hierarchy of rights that reflects the limited right's social importance. This hierarchy would include two levels. The first would include those fundamental rights perceived by the legal system to be the most important rights. The rest of the rights should be included in the second level. Regarding the rights at the first level, the suggestion is that the purpose which would justify the limitation should be compelling or pressing. As for the rights at the second level, the purpose in question should be "important."

What is the level of probability required to fulfill the "compelling" or "pressing" purpose (for those more important rights) and the "important" purpose (for the rest of the rights)? Regarding the "compelling" or "pressing" purpose, it is proper to demand that the probability of its fulfillment be "substantial"; as for the "important" purpose, it is proper to demand that the required probability be "reasonable." With the help of these two levels of probability, the value-laden character of this component would increase; the nature of the legislative purpose would be expressed as well as the nature of the limited right; and the burden currently placed on proportionality *stricto sensu* would be significantly diminished.

D. The necessity component: future developments

The necessity component – or the least restrictive means component – demands that the means selected by the law to fulfill the law's purpose be necessary.[36] The meaning of this requirement is that there are no other means capable of fulfilling the law's purpose to the same degree and

---

[33] The "near certainty" test is more appropriate for review in the context of proportionality *stricto sensu* than in the context of the rational connection test. See above, at 315.
[34] See above, at 315.   [35] See above, at 536.   [36] See above, at 317.

whose limitation of the constitutional right is of a lesser extent. A similar component exists in the American strict scrutiny test,[37] which demands that the limiting legislation be "narrowly tailored." The meaning of that requirement – like the necessity component – is that the law should use the less drastic or intrusive means, which is overinclusive.

A review of the American case law on the subject reveals that this requirement is difficult for the legislation to satisfy.[38] This is a natural result as this test constitutes the constitutional right's very last resort: If this test is satisfied, the limitation on the right is constitutional. There is no additional examination of the balancing between the harm to the right and the benefit to the public interest. In contrast to American law, however, a review of the case law of the necessity test as part of proportionality reveals a much more complex picture. In several legal systems, the necessity test serves as the main test to determine the constitutionality of the limiting legislation.[39] Other legal systems (such as France[40]) had in the past refused to recognize the requirement at all. Still others have focused on the requirement of proportionality *stricto sensu* as the main tool to examine constitutionality, rendering the necessity test a less vital part of the review process. It is hard to explain such a diverse set of results. Seemingly, we could have expected a much more uniform approach. Be the explanation as it may, it seems that additional thought is required as to the more uniform application of this component in the future.

In the framework of this reconsideration of the necessity test, it is important to preserve the test as a threshold requirement.[41] It is not a balancing test.[42] Thus, if the proposed alternative – which leads to less harm to the constitutional right – does not fulfill the legislative purpose, the law is necessary. The law is not necessary only in those cases where the proposed alternative would limit the constitutional right to a lesser extent and fulfill the legislative purpose to the same degree as the limiting legislation. In reviewing the proposed legislative alternatives the court must apply an objective test. Indeed, in attempting to resolve the constitutional issue – either through the necessity test or through the proportionality *stricto*

---

[37] See above, at 511.   [38] See above, at 520.
[39] P. W. Hogg, *Constitutional Law of Canada*, 5th edn., vol. II (Toronto: Thomson Carswell, 2007), 146.
[40] See above, at 407.
[41] In that context, I regret the fact that in the South African Constitution the necessity test appears only as one of several substantive considerations to be weighed in reviewing the constitutionality of limiting legislation.
[42] See above, at 338.

sensu component – the judge should never step outside the boundaries of the analytical framework. Each test should be applied in accordance with its conditions. Only thus can the judicial branch create a coherent and structured approach to all of proportionality's tests.

E.   The proportionality stricto sensu component: future developments

1.   The nature of principled balancing formulas

i.   A principled balance as implementing the basic balancing rule

The basic rule of balancing provides normative content to the balancing at the heart of proportionality *stricto sensu*.[43] It operates at the highest level of abstraction and therefore requires a concrete application on a case-by-case basis. This application is done through specific (or *ad hoc*) balancing.[44] The move from the highest level of abstraction to the lowest is a particularly sharp transition. This situation is not desirable.[45] The basic rule of balancing is too abstract. It does not specifically relate to many of the aspects in which the particular right in question becomes a special object of either limitation or protection. It does not contain the required focus on the reasons underlying the creation of those rights, and thus does not directly relate to the reasons that justify their limitation or protection. It also does not include a proper roadmap of all the considerations that would justify the protection of a constitutional right. In contrast, the specific rule of balancing is at too low a level of abstraction. It only relates to the case at hand, and lacks a more general viewpoint of the system as a whole.

With this in mind, the question arises whether there is room for a third rule of balancing. This rule would be located between the basic balancing rule (which is the most abstract) and the specific balancing (which is the most concrete). This intermediate-level rule would present a principled balancing, in a way that would implement or apply the basic rule of balancing into several principled rules or principled formulas of balancing. As such, those formulas would be phrased in a lower level of abstraction than the basic rule of balancing, but at a higher level of abstraction than the

---

[43] See above, at 362.
[44] See above, at 367.
[45] J. King, "Institutional Approaches to Judicial Review," 28 *OJLS* 409, 435 (2008).

specific rule of balancing.[46] This intermediate level of abstraction would express the principled consideration which underlies the constitutional right and the justification of its limitation. What should the nature of this intermediate level be? How similar should it be to specific balancing? What are its justifications? I turn to these questions now.

ii.   The structure of the principled balancing formula

The principled balancing formula must, first and foremost, fulfill the basic balancing rule. That basic rule of balancing compares the marginal social importance of the benefit gained by the limiting law and the marginal social importance of preventing the harm to the constitutional right. The principled balancing formula would translate this abstract notion into a formula comparing the marginal social importance of the specific limited right on the one end and the marginal social importance of the specific legislative purpose on the other. It would determine the conditions that the limiting law must satisfy for the limitation to be proportional *stricto sensu*. The principled formula will reflect the main normative considerations that justify marginal harm to the constitutional right in question in order to gain the marginal benefits for another right, or for the public interest as a whole. One end of the scales consists of considerations relating to the marginal social importance of the right, to the scope of the suggested limitation, and to the probability that such a limitation would actually occur. The other end of the scales – that of the legislative purpose – would reflect considerations relating to the marginal social importance of the purpose as interpreted against the background of its content and the degree of urgency in its realization, the probability of its realization and the harm that would be incurred should the purpose not be realized, and the probability of the occurrence of such damage.[47]

Take, for example, a statute limiting the right to political speech. This right is of a fundamental nature. Assume that the reason for the limitation is the protection of the public from racist political speech. The principled balancing formula that applies to a conflict between the right to freedom of political speech and the right to be protected from the effects of racist speech may determine that a limitation of the right in these circumstances would be justified only in those instances where the purpose of protecting

---

[46]   M. Cohen-Eliya and G. Stopler, "Probability Thresholds as Deontological Constraints in Global Constitutionalism," 49 *Colum. J. Transnat'l L.* 102 (2010); A. Barak, "Principled Balancing," 4 *Law and Ethics of Hum. Rts.* 1 (2010).

[47]   On probability tests in American law, see J. S. Masur, "Probability Thresholds," 92 *Iowa L. Rev.* 1293 (2007).

the public from the effects of such speech is "pressing" or "compelling" in order to prevent imminent and severe harm to public order. This example demonstrates how the principled balancing formula operates at a lower level of abstraction than that of the basic rule of balancing, yet one that is still higher than specific balancing. It operates at that level of abstraction which expresses the reasons underlying the creation of the right itself, the justifications for its limitation, and the reasons for its protection.

Principled balancing formulas and specific balancing should exist concomitantly. One is not intended to replace the other.[48] Specific balancing fulfills the principled balancing formulas according to the circumstances of each specific case. It implements the principled balancing formulas – which, in turn, are based on the basic balancing rule – on a case-by-case basis. The principled balancing formulas "reflect a general legal norm, which sets a constitutional principle that applies on a set of similar circumstances." The notion of basic balancing may apply in this way to every situation where a constitutional right has been limited.

There are many constitutional rights, each with their own aspects. There are many considerations of the public interest, each with its own aspects. Principled balancing formulas must reflect this diversity.[49] Several principled balancing formulas should be established, therefore, in order to guarantee said reflection. Thus, for example, principled balancing formulas relating to political speech should not be the same as those relating to commercial speech; formulas relating to prior restraint should not be identical to those relating to *ex post facto* restrictions; those relating to minimal infringements should be markedly different from those relating to substantial limitations; a law whose purpose is the protection of life differs from a law whose purpose is preserving one's privacy.

The number of principled balancing formulas relating to constitutional rights is much higher than the number of constitutional rights. Each constitutional right may be accompanied by a number of principled balancing formulas that reflect its social importance, the scope of the harm it would suffer should the purpose of the limiting law be achieved, and the probability that such a limitation would occur. In addition, the balancing formula reflects the social importance of the law's purpose, the degree of its urgency, the harm that may be caused to another right (either of the individual that is harmed, or of another person) or to the public interest

---

[48] See S. Gardbaum, "Limiting Constitutional Rights," 54 *UCLA L. Rev.* 789, 804 (2007).

[49] See HCJ 153/83 *Levy* v. *Southern District Commissioner of Police* [1984] IsrSC 38(2) 393, 400 ("The diversity of circumstances requires a diversity of balancing points. There should not be a single standard by which all problems should be evaluated.").

should the law's purpose not be advanced, the probability that such harm would be caused to the public interest under those circumstances, and finally the probability of gaining the benefits intended by the limiting law should the limitation be imposed on the constitutional right at issue.

2. Principled balancing formulas: a comparative survey

i. The lack of principled balancing formulas

A review of the comparative constitutional law on the issue of principled balancing formulas leads to the conclusion that, other than American and Israeli law,[50] very little attention has been paid by most legal systems to the development of principled balancing formulas. What might be the reason for this lack of interest? It is possible that it stems from the prevailing notion – across many a legal system – that all constitutional rights – the rights limited and the rights protected – are of equal social importance.[51] According to this notion, when a constitutional right is limited in order to protect another constitutional right, all that needs to be examined is the type of limitation imposed on the right – a light, moderate, or serious[52] limitation; and, according to the answer to this question, to examine the importance of advancing the law's purpose. Thus, the identical importance of the limited rights and the right protected has prevented the abstraction of the notion of balancing beyond the concrete cases. The social value of the fulfillment of the legislative purpose is always considered, but it seems that those legal systems found it difficult to recognize principled balancing formulas whenever one end of the scales – the end pertaining to the right's limitation – cannot "rise" above the level of the circumstances of the specific case. Indeed, Alexy emphasizes that all the balancing process examines is which of the conflicting principles – all having equal stature in theory – has more weight in the specific case at hand:

> [A]bstract weights only have an influence on the outcome of balancing if they [the principles] are different. If they are equal, which in the case of competing constitutional rights is often the case, the only relevant factor is their concrete importance.[53]

---

[50] See A. Barak, *The Judge in a Democracy* (Princeton University Press, 2006), 170; A. Barak, "Human Rights in Israel," 39 *Isr. L. Rev.* 12 (2006).

[51] See S. Greer, *The European Convention on Human Rights: Achievements, Problems and Prospects* (Cambridge University Press, 2006), 218.

[52] See R. Alexy, *A Theory of Constitutional Rights* (Julian Rivers trans., Oxford University Press, 2002 [1986]).

[53] *Ibid.*, at 406.

The same reasoning may also explain the German approach, according to which whenever two constitutional rights are in conflict – assuming they are equal in their social importance – they should be balanced only through "*praktische Konkordanz*."[54]

This explanation, however, is not satisfactory.[55] This is for two reasons. First, several legal systems have developed an approach according to which not all rights are equal in social importance.[56] Accordingly, a principled standard is required to determine the balancing between these rights. Second, even if all constitutional rights are of equal social importance, there is still room for principled balancing formulas for those cases where the (equal) rights conflict with the public interest. Principled balancing – as derived from the basic rule of balancing – is the correct approach to be adopted. Is that the reason it has been adopted by the American legal system? This question will now be examined.

ii.   Principled balancing in American constitutional law

The role of principled balancing within American constitutional law is different from the suggested role of principled balancing formulas within proportionality *stricto sensu*. In American law, principled balancing is used as an interpretive standard to determine the scope of the constitutional right.[57] For example, the US Supreme Court has ruled that the First Amendment right to freedom of expression does not apply to several depictions of racist hate speech or obscenities.[58] Such an interpretive conclusion is the result of interpretive balancing[59] whose purpose is to determine the boundaries of freedom of expression as a constitutional right. The Supreme Court thus considered the purposes underlying the right to freedom of expression, balanced between them, and ruled that the right should not protect racist hate speech and obscenities. That is the reason that this kind of balancing is dubbed "definitional balancing," as it defines

---

[54] See above, at 369.
[55] G. C. N. Webber, "The Cult of Constitutional Rights Reasoning" (Paper presented at the VIIth World Congress of the International Association of Constitutional Law, Athens, June 14, 2007).
[56] See above, at 360.
[57] See A. Stone Sweet and J. Mathews, "All Things in Proportion? American Rights Doctrine and the Problem of Balancing," *Emory L. J.* (forthcoming, 2011).
[58] See E. Chemerinsky, *Constitutional Law: Principles and Policies* (New York: Aspen Law & Business, 2006), 986.
[59] On interpretive balancing, see above, at 72.

the scope of the right.[60] Once the right's boundaries have been defined, there is no longer a need for this interpretive (or definitional) balancing. Similarly, no additional balancing is required or conducted within those well-defined boundaries. Thus, for example, the strict scrutiny review[61] – which applies to all political speech – examines whether the limitation was meant to serve a compelling or pressing governmental interest, and whether the legislative means have been narrowly tailored to achieve such a purpose. None of those requirements demands a balancing.[62] Thus, a "proportionality leaning" scholar or judge should be extremely cautious in relying on American jurisprudence on this issue as useful comparative material. One should always remember that, in the United States, once the right has been narrowed (or redefined) according to the interpretive balancing which has been conducted, it is no longer the subject of additional balancing. Further, a legal system applying proportionality should be extremely careful when using the American precedents on the subject for the following reason: if such a system were to adopt the American approach of initially narrowing the right's scope through the use of interpretive balancing, it would still need to continue and reduce the extent to which the right is protected through the use of principled balancing as required by both proportionality in general and proportionality *stricto sensu* in particular. Thus, by relying on the American approach, the constitutional right at issue may well be affected twice: first, through the narrowing of its scope (by using the American interpretive balancing), and, second, by reducing the extent to which the right is protected (by using proportionality's principled balancing as developed by Israeli law).

---

[60] M. B. Nimmer, "The Right to Speak from Times to Time: First Amendment Theory Applied to Libel and Misapplied to Privacy," 56 *Cal. L. Rev.* 935, 944 (1968).

[61] See above, at 510.

[62] See above, at 508.

BIBLIOGRAPHY

Ackerman, B. "The Rise of World Constitutionalism," 83 *Va. L. Rev.* 771 (1997)

Adler, M. "Symposium: Law and Incommensurability: Introduction," 146 *U. Pa. L. Rev.* 1168 (1998)

Adler, M. and Posner E. *Cost-Benefit Analysis: Legal, Economic and Philosophical Perspectives* (University of Chicago Press, 2000)

Aleinikoff, T. "Constitutional Law in the Age of Balancing," 96 *Yale L. J.* 943 (1987)

Alexander, L. "Constitutions, Judicial Review, Moral Rights, and Democracy: Disentangling the Issues," in G. Huscroft (ed.), *Expounding the Constitution: Essays in Constitutional Theory* (Cambridge University Press, 2008)

"Introduction: Motivation and Constitutionality," 15 *San Diego L. Rev.* 925 (1978)

"Legal Objectivity and the Illusion of Legal Principles," in M. Klatt (ed.), *Institutional Reason: The Jurisprudence of Robert Alexy* (forthcoming, Oxford University Press, 2011)

"Of Living Trees and Dead Hands: The Interpretation of Constitutions and Constitutional Rights," 22 *Can. J. L. & Juris.* 227 (2009)

"Simple-Minded Originalism," in G. Huscroft and B. Miller (eds.), *The Challenge of Originalism: Essays in Constitutional Theory* (forthcoming, 2011)

Alexander, L. and Schauer, F. "On Extrajudicial Constitutional Interpretation," 110 *Harv. L. Rev.* 1359 (1997)

Alexy, R. *A Theory of Constitutional Rights* (Julian Rivers trans., Oxford University Press, 2002 [1986])

"Constitutional Rights, Balancing, and Rationality," 16 *Ratio Juris* 131 (2003)

"Individual Rights and Collective Goods," in C. Nino (ed.), *Rights* (New York University Press, 1992)

"Jürgen Habermas's Theory of Legal Discourse," 17 *Cardozo L. Rev.* 1027 (1996)

"On Balancing and Subsumption: A Structural Comparison," 16 *Ratio Juris* 433 (2003)

"On the Structure of Legal Principles," 13 *Ratio Juris* 294 (2000)

"The Reasonableness of Law," in G. Bongiovanni, G. Sartor, and C. Valentini (eds.), *Reasonableness and Law* (Dordrecht: Springer, 2009)

"Thirteen Replies," in G. Pavlakos (ed.), *Law, Rights, and Discourse: The Legal Philosophy of Robert Alexy* (Portland, OR: Hart Publishing, 2007)

Alexy, R. and Peczenik, A. "The Concept of Coherence and Its Significance for Discursive Rationality," 3 *Ratio Juris* 130 (1990)

Allan, T. R. S. "Common Law Reason and the Limits of Judicial Deference," in D. Dyzenhaus (ed.), *The Unity of Public Law* (Portland, OR: Hart Publishing, 2004)

    Constitutional Justice: A Liberal Theory of the Rule of Law (Oxford University Press, 2001)

    "Human Rights and Judicial Review: A Critique of 'Due Deference'," 65(3) *Cambridge L. J.* 671 (2006)

    "Legislative Supremacy and Legislative Intention: Interpretation, Meaning, and Authority," 63 *Cambridge L. J.* 685 (2004)

    "Parliamentary Sovereignty: Law, Politics, and Revolution," 113 *L. Q. Rev.* 443 (1997)

    "The Common Law as Constitution: Fundamental Rights and First Principles," in C. Saunders (ed.), *Courts of Final Jurisdiction: The Mason Court in Australia* (Sydney: Federation Press, 1996)

    "The Rule of Law, as Liberal Justice," 56 *U. Toronto L. J.* 283 (2006)

Allison, J. "Fuller's Analysis of Polycentric Disputes and the Limits of Adjudication," 53 *Cambridge L. J.* 367 (1994)

    "Transplantation and Cross-Fertilisation," in J. Beatson and T. Tridimas (eds.), *European Public Law* (Portland, OR: Hart Publishing, 1998)

Andenas, M. (ed.), *The Creation and Amendment of Constitutional Norms* (BIICL, 2000)

Andenas, M. and Zleptnig, S. "Proportionality: WTO Law in Comparative Perspective," 42 *Tex. Int'l L. J.* 371 (2007)

Appleby, G. "Proportionality and Federalism: Can Australia Learn from the European Community, the US and Canada?," 26 *U. Tas. L. Rev.* 1 (2007)

Aquinas, T. *Summa Theologica II-II.* Qua estio 64, and 7

Arai-Takahashi, Y. *The Margin of Appreciation Doctrine and the Principle of Proportionality in the Jurisprudence of the ECHR* (Oxford: Hart Publishing, 2002)

Arbess, D. J. "Limitations on Legislative Override under the Canadian Charter of Rights and Freedoms: A Matter of Balancing Values," 21 *Osgoode Hall L. J.* 113 (1983)

Arden, M. "Human Rights in the Age of Terrorism," 121 *L. Q. Rev.* 604 (2005)

Attaran, A. "A Wobbly Balance – A Comparison of Proportionality Testing in Canada, the United States, the European Union and the World Trade Organization," 56 *University of New Brunswick L. J.* 260 (2007)

Aubert, J. *Traité de Droit Constitutionnel Suisse* (Neuchatel, Switzerland: Editions Ides et Calendes, 1967)

Avila, H. *Theory of Legal Principles* (Dordrecht: Springer, 2007)

Ayres, I. "Narrow Tailoring," 43 *UCLA L. Rev.* 1781 (1995)

Ayres, I. and Foster, S. "Don't Tell, Don't Ask: Narrow Tailoring after Grutter and Gratz," 85 *Tex. L. Rev.* 517 (2007)

Baade, H. "'Original Intent' in Historical Perspective: Some Critical Glosses," 69 *Tex. L. Rev.* 1001 (1991)

"Social Science Evidence and the Federal Constitutional Court of West Germany," 23 *J. of Politics* 421 (1961)

Badinter, R. and Breyer, S. *Judges in Contemporary Democracy: An International Conversation* (New York University Press, 2004)

Baker, A. "Proportional, Not Strict, Scrutiny: Against a US 'Suspect Classifications' Model under Article 14 ECHR in the UK," 56 *Am. J. Comp. L.* 847 (2008)

Baker, E. "Limitations on Basic Human Rights – A View from the United States," in A. de Mestral, S. Birks, M. Both *et al.* (eds.), *The Limitation of Human Rights in Comparative Constitutional Law* (Montreal: Les Editions Yvon Blais, 1986)

Bandes, S. "The Negative Constitution: A Critique," 88 *Mich. L. Rev.* 2271 (1989)

Barak, A. "Constitutional Human Rights and Private Law," in D. Friedmann and D. Barak-Erez (eds.), *Human Rights in Private Law* (Portland, OR: Hart Publishing, 2001)

"Human Rights in Israel," 39 *Isr. L. Rev.* 12 (2006)

"Human Rights in Times of Terror – A Judicial Point of View," 28 *Legal Studies* 493 (2008)

Interpretation in Law: Constitutional Interpretation, vol. III (Jerusalem: Nevo, 1994)

Judicial Discretion (New Haven, CT: Yale University Press, 1989)

"Principled Balancing," 4 *Law & Ethics of Human Rights* 1 (2010)

"Proportional Effect: The Israeli Experience," 57 *U. Toronto L. J.* 369 (2007)

Purposive Interpretation in Law (Princeton University Press, 2006)

The Judge in a Democracy (Princeton University Press, 2006)

"The Role of a Supreme Court in a Democracy, and the Fight Against Terrorism," 58 *U. Miami L. Rev.* 125 (2003)

"The Values of the State of Israel as a Jewish and Democratic State," in A. Maoz (ed.), *Israel as a Jewish and Democratic State* (forthcoming, 2011)

"Unconstitutional Constitutional Amendments," *Isr. L. Rev.* (forthcoming, 2011)

Barak-Erez, D. and Gross, A. (eds.), *Exploring Social Rights: Between Theory and Practice* (Portland, OR: Hart Publishing, 2007)

Barber, S. *On What the Constitution Means* (Baltimore, MD: Johns Hopkins University Press, 1984)

Barber, S. and Fleming, J. *Constitutional Interpretation: The Basic Questions* (New York: Oxford University Press, 2007)

Barendt, E. *Freedom of Speech*, 2nd edn. (Oxford University Press, 2007)

Barkhuysen, T. and Lindenbergh, S. (eds.), *Constitutionalisation of Private Law* (Oegstgeest, The Netherlands: Brill, 2006)

Barnes, J. "El Principio de Proporcionalidad: Estudio Preliminar," 5 *CDP* 15 (1998)

"Introducción a la Jurisprudencia Constitucional Sobre el Principio de Proporcionalidad en el Ambito de los Derechos y Libertades," 5 *CDP* 333 (1998)

"The Meaning of the Principle of Proportionality for the Administration," in Schäffer *et al.* (eds.), *Constitutional Principles in Europe* (Societas Iuris Publici, Europaei, Fourth Congress, Göttingen, 2008)

Barnett, R. "Scrutiny Land", 106 *Mich. L. Rev.* 1479 (2008)

Bayne, P. "Reasonableness, Proportionality and Delegated Legislation," 67 *ALJ* 448 (1993)

Beatty, D. (ed.), *Human Rights and Judicial Review: A Comparative Perspective* (Martinus Nijhoff Publishers, 1994)

The Ultimate Rule of Law (Oxford University Press, 2004)

Bellamy, R. *Political Constitutionalism: A Republican Defense of the Constitutionality of Democracy* (Cambridge University Press, 2007)

Beloff, M. "The Concept of 'Deference' in Public Law," 11 *Jud. Rev.* 213 (2006)

Belton, R. "Burdens of Pleading and Proof in Discrimination Cases: Toward a Theory of Procedural Justice," 34 *Vand. L. Rev.* 1205 (1981)

Bennett, R. W. "'Mere' Rationality in Constitutional Law: Judicial Review and Democratic Theory," 67 *Cal. L. Rev.* 1049 (1979)

Bennion, F. *Statutory Interpretation: A Code*, 4th edn. (London: Butterworths, 2002)

Bermann, G. "The Principle of Proportionality," 26 *Am. J. Comp. L. Sup.* 415 (1977–1978)

Bickel, A. *The Least Dangerous Breach: The Supreme Court at the Bar of Politics* (Indianapolis, IN: Bobbs-Merrill, 1962)

Bingham, T. "The Rule of Law and the Sovereignty of Parliament," 19 *King's Law Journal* 223 (2008)

Widening Horizons: The Influence of Comparative Law and International Law on Domestic Law (Cambridge University Press, 2010)

Bix, B. *Law, Language, and Legal Determinacy* (Oxford University Press, 1993)

Blaau, L. "The Rechtsstaat Idea Compared with the Rule of Law as a Paradigm for Protecting Rights," 107 *S. African L. J.* 76 (1990)

Blaauw-Wolf, L. "The Balancing of Interest with Reference to the Principle of Proportionality and the Doctrine of Guterabwagung – A Comparative Analysis," 14 *SAPL* 178 (1999)

Blache, P. "The Criteria of Justification under Oakes: Too Much Severity Generated Through Formalism," 20 *Man. L. J.* 437 (1991)

Black, C. *Structure and Relationship in Constitutional Law* (Baton Rouge, LA: Louisiana State University Press, 1969)

Blackstone, W. *Commentaries on the Laws of England* (Oxford: Clarendon Press, 1765)

Bleckmann, A. and Bothe, M. "General Report on the Theory of Limitations on Human Rights," in A. L. C. de Mestral (ed.), *The Limitations of Human Rights in Comparative Constitutional Law* (Montreal: Les Editions Yvon Blais, 1986)

Blocher, J. "Categoricalism and Balancing in First and Second Amendment Analysis," 84 *N. Y. U. L. Rev.* 375 (2009)

Bobek, M. "Reasonableness in Administrative Law: A Comparative Reflection on Functional Equivalence," in G. Bongiovanni, G. Sartor, and C. Valentini (eds.), *Reasonableness and Law* (Dordrecht: Springer, 2009)

Böckenförde, E. W. *State, Society and Liberty: Studies in Political Theory and Constitutional Law* (New York: Berg Publishing Ltd., 1991)

Bogen, D. "Balancing Freedom of Speech," 38 *Md. L. Rev.* 387 (1979)

Bollinger, L. *The Tolerant Society* (Oxford University Press, 1986)

Bomhoff, J. "Balancing, the Global and the Local: Judicial Balancing as a Problematic Topic in Comparative (Constitutional) Law," 31 *Hastings Int'l & Comp. L. Rev.* 555 (2008)

"Genealogies of Balancing as Discourse," 4 *Law & Ethics of Hum. Rights* 108 (2010)

Bomhoff, J. and Zucca, L. "The Tragedy of Ms Evans: Conflicts and Incommensurability of Rights," 2 *Eur. Const. L. Rev.* 424 (2006)

Borgmann, C. "Rethinking Judicial Deference to Legislative Fact-Finding," 84 *Ind. L. J.* 1 (2009)

Bork, R. *The Tempting of America: The Political Seduction of the Law* (New York: Touchstone, 1990)

Bortoluzzi, A. "The Principle of Proportionality in Comparative Law: A Comparative Approach from the Italian Perspective," in P. Vinay Kumar (ed.), *Proportionality and Federalism* (Hyderabad: ICFAI University Press, 2009)

Botha, H. "The Legitimacy of Legal Orders (3): Rethinking the Rule of Law," 64 *Tydskrif vir Hedendaagse Romeins-Hollandse Reg* 523 (2001)

Botterell, A. "In Defense of Infringement," 27 *Law and Philosophy* 269 (2008)

Boyle, K. "Hate Speech – The United States Versus the Rest of the World," 53 *Me. L. Rev.* 487 (2001)

Boyne, S. "The Future of Liberal Democracies in a Time of Terror: A Comparison of the Impact on Civil Liberties in the Federal Republic of Germany and the United States," 11 *Tulsa J. Comp. & Int'l L.* 111 (2003)

Boyron, S. "Proportionality in English Administrative Law: A Faulty Translation?," 12 *OJLS* 237 (1992)

Bradford, W. "Barbarians at the Gates: A Post-September 11th Proposal to Rationalize the Laws of War," 73 *Miss. L. J.* 639 (2004)

Brage Camazano, J. *Los Límites a los Derechos Fundamentales* (Madrid: Dykinson, 2004)

Bredt, C. "The Increasing Irrelevance of Section 1 of the Charter," 14 *Sup. Ct. L. Rev.* 175 (2001)

Brems, E. "Conflicting Human Rights: An Exploration in the Context of the Right to a Fair Trial in the European Convention for the Protection of Human Rights and Fundamental Freedoms," 27 *Hum. Rts. Q.* 294 (2005)

Brennan, W. "Construing the Constitution," 19 *UC Davis L. Rev.* 2 (1985)

"The Constitution of the United States: Contemporary Ratification," 27 *Tex. L. Rev.* 433 (1986)

Brest, P. "Palmer v. Thompson: An Approach to the Problem of Unconstitutional Legislative Motive," *Sup. Ct. Rev.* 95 (1971)

Brewer-Carías, A. *Judicial Review in Comparative Law* (Cambridge University Press, 1989)

Brems, E. (ed.), *Conflicts between Fundamental Rights* (Mortsel, Belgium: Intersentia, 2008)

Breyer, S. "Judicial Review: A Practicing Judge's Perspective," 19 *OJLS* 153, 158 (1999)

Making Our Democracy Work: A Judge's View (New York: Knopf, 2010)

Brison, S. and Sinnot-Armstrong, W. (eds.), *Contemporary Perspectives on Constitutional Interpretation* (Westview Press, 1993)

Brudner, A. *Constitutional Goods* (New York: Oxford University Press, 2004)

Brugger, W. "May Government Ever Use Torture? Two Responses from German Law," 48 *Am. J. Comp. L.* 661 (2000)

Burmester, H. "The Presumption of Constitutionality," 13 *Fed. L. Rev.* 277 (1983)

Butler, A. "A Presumption of Statutory Conformity with the Charter," 19 *Queens L. J.* 209 (1993)

"Limiting Rights," 33 *Victoria U. Wellington L. Rev.* 113 (2002)

Calabresi, S. (ed.), *Originalism: A Quarter-Century of Debate* (Regnery Publishing, 2007)

Caldwell, J. "Judicial Sovereignty – A New View," *New Zealand L. J.* 357 (1984)

Canaris, C. *Die Feststellung von Lücken im Gesetz: Eine Methodologische Studie über Voraussetzungen und Grenzen der richterlichen Rechtsfortbildung Praeter Legem* (Berlin: Duncker und Humblot, 1983)

Canas, V. "Proporcionalidade," in *Dicionário Jurídico da Administração Pública*, vol. VI (1994)

Cannizzaro, E. "The Role of Proportionality in the Law of International Countermeasures," 12 *Eur. J. Int'l. L.* 889 (2001)

Cappelletti, M. "The Law-Making Power of the Judge and Its Limits: A Comparative Analysis," 8 *Monash U. L. Rev.* 15 (1981)

Carbonell, M. (ed.), *El Principio de Proporcionalidad en la Interpretación Jurídica* (Santiago: UNAM & CECOCH, 2010)

El Principio de Proporcionalidad y Protección de los Derechos Fundamentales [*Proportionality Analysis and the Protection of Fundamental Rights*] (Mexico City; Comisión Nacional de los Derechos Humanos, 2008)

Carbonell, M. and Grández, P. (eds.), *El Principio de Proporcionalidad en el Derecho Contemporáneo* (Lima: Palestra Editores, 2010)

Cardozo, B. *The Growth of the Law* (New Haven, CT: Yale University Press, 1924)

The Nature of the Judicial Process (Whitefish, MT: Kessinger Publishing LLC, 1921)

The Paradoxes of Legal Science (New York: Columbia University Press, 1928)

Casey, J. *Constitutional Law in Ireland* (Dublin: Round Hall Press, 2000)

Cass, R. *The Rule of Law in America* (Baltimore, MD: Johns Hopkins University Press, 2001)

Cepeda Espinosa, M. *Polémicas Constitucionales* (Bogota: Legis, 2007)

Chang, R. (ed.), *Incommensurability, Incomparability, and Practical Reason* (Cambridge, MA: Harvard University Press, 1997)

Chaskalson, M., Marcus, G., and Bishop, M., "Constitutional Litigation," in S. Woolman, M. Bishop, and J. Brickhill (eds.), *Constitutional Law of South Africa*, 2nd edn. (Cape Town: Juta Law Publishers, looseleaf, 2002–)

Chayes, A. "The Role of the Judge in Public Law Litigation," 89 *Harv. L. Rev.* 1281 (1976)

Cheadle, H. "Limitation of Rights," in H. Cheadle, N. Haysom, and D. Davis (eds.), *South African Constitutional Law: The Bill of Rights* (Cape Town: Juta Law Publishers, 2002)

Cheadle, H., Haysom, N., and Davis, D. (eds.), *South African Constitutional Law: The Bill of Rights* (2002)

Chemerinsky, E. *Constitutional Law: Principles and Policies*, 3rd edn. (New York: Aspen Publishers, 2006)

Choudhry, S. "Globalization in Search of Justification: Toward a Theory of Comparative Constitutional Interpretation," 74 *Ind. L. J.* 819 (1999)

"So What Is the Real Legacy of Oakes? Two Decades of Proportionality Analysis under the Canadian Charter's Section 1", 34 *Sup. Ct. L. Rev.* 501 (2006)

"The Lochner Era and Comparative Constitutionalism," 2 *Int'l J. Const. L.* 1 (2004)

The Migration of Constitutional Ideas (Cambridge University Press, 2006)

Christie, G. G. "Objectivity in the Law," 78 *Yale L. J.* 1311 (1969)

Chugh, A. "Is the Supreme Court Disproportionately Applying the Proportionality Principle?," 8 *SCC (J)* 33 (2004)

Cianciardo, J. "The Principle of Proportionality: The Challenges of Human Rights," 3 *J. Civ. L. Stud.* 177 (2010)

Clark, C. "The Limits of Judicial Objectivity," 12 *Am. U. L. Rev.* 1 (1963)

Clayton, R. "Judicial Deference and Democratic Dialogue: The Legitimacy of Judicial Intervention under the Human Rights Act 1998," *PL* 33 (2004)

"Regarding a Sense of Proportion: The Human Rights Act and the Proportionality Principle," 5 *Eur. Hum. Rts. L. Rev.* 504 (2001)

Clérico, L. *El Examen de Proporcionalidad en el Derecho Constitucional* (Buenos Aires: Eudeba, 2009)

Clinton, R. "Original Understanding, Legal Realism, and the Interpretation of 'This Constitution'," 72 *Iowa L. Rev.* 1177 (1987)

Coenen, D. "Rights as Trumps," 27 *Ga. L. Rev.* 463 (1992)

Coffin, F. "Judicial Balancing: The Protean Scales of Justice," 63 *N. Y. U. L. Rev.* 16 (1988)

Cohen, M. "Legal Transplant Chronicles: The Evolution of Unreasonableness and Proportionality Review of the Administration in the United Kingdom," 58 *Am. J. Comp. L.* 583 (2010)

Cohen-Almagor, R. *The Boundaries of Liberty and Tolerance: The Struggle against Kahanism in Israel* (Gainesville, FL: University Press of Florida, 1994)

The Scope of Tolerance: Studies on the Costs of Free Expression and Freedom of the Press (London: Routledge, 2006)

Cohen-Eliya, M. "Limitation Clauses in Basic Laws on Human Rights, Considering the Right's Nature" (unpublished PhD dissertation, Hebrew University of Jerusalem, 2000)

Cohen-Eliya, M. and Porat, I. "American Balancing and German Proportionality: The Historical Origins," 8 *Int'l J. Const. L.* 263 (2010)

"Proportionality and the Culture of Justification," 59 *Am. J. Comp. L.* (forthcoming, 2011)

"The Hidden Foreign Law Debate in Heller: The Proportionality Approach in American Constitutional Law," 46 *San Diego L. Rev.* 367 (2009)

Cohen-Eliya, M. and Stopler, G. "Probability Thresholds as Deontological Constraints in Global Constitutionalism," 49 *Colum. J. Transnat'l L.* 102 (2010)

Colaço Antunes, L. "Interesse Público, Proporcionalidade e Mérito: Relevância e Autonomia Processual do Principio da Proporcionalidade," in *Estudos em Homenagem a Professora Doutora Isabel de Magalhães Collaço* 539 (vol. II, 2002)

Cole, D. "The Poverty of Posner's Pragmatism: Balancing Away Liberty after 9/11," 59 *Stan. L. Rev.* 1735 (2007)

Coleman, J. and Leiter, B. "Determinacy, Objectivity, and Authority," in A. Marmor (ed.), *Law and Interpretation: Essays in Legal Philosophy* (Oxford University Press, 1995)

Colker, R. "Section 1, Contextuality, and the Anti-Disadvantage Principle," 42 *U. Toronto L. J.* 77 (1992)

Connelly, A. "The Protection of the Rights of Others," 5 *Hum. Rts. Rev.* 117 (1980)

Conte, A. and Burchill, R. *Defining Civil and Political Rights: The Jurisprudence of the United Nations Human Rights Committee*, 2nd edn. (Farnham, UK: Ashgate Publishing, 2009)

Cooke, R. "Fundamentals," *New Zealand L. J.* 158 (1988)

Cooter, R. "Void for Vagueness: Introduction," 82 *Calif. L. Rev.* 487 (1994)

Cooter, R. and Ulen, T. *Law and Economics*, 4th edn. (Reading, MA: Addison Wesley, 2003)

Corder, H. "Despair to Deference: Same Difference?," in M. Taggart and G. Huscroft (eds.), *Inside and Outside Canadian Administrative Law: Essays in Honour of David Mullan* (University of Toronto Press, 2006)

"Without Deference, With Respect: A Response to Justice O'Regan," 121 *S. Afr. L. J.* 438 (2004)

Costa, P. and Zolo, D. (eds.), *The Rule of Law: History, Theory and Criticism* (Springer Publishing, 2007)

Costello, D. "Limiting Rights Constitutionally", in J. O'Reilly (ed.), *Human Rights and Constitutional Law: Essays in Honour of Brian Walsh* (Dublin: Round Hall Press, 1992)

Craig, P. *Administrative Law*, 6th edn. (London: Sweet & Maxwell, 2008)

"Judicial Review, Intensity and Deference in EU Law," in D. Dyzenhaus (ed.), *The Unity of Public Law* (Portland, OR: Hart Publishing, 2004)

"Unreasonableness and Proportionality in UK Law," in E. Ellis (ed.), *The Principle of Proportionality in the Laws of Europe* (Portland, OR: Hart Publishing, 1999)

Craven, M. *The International Covenant on Economic, Social and Cultural Rights: A Perspective on Its Development* (Oxford University Press, 1995)

Crump, D. "How Do Courts Really Discover Unenumerated Fundamental Rights? Cataloging the Methods of Judicial Alchemy," 19 *Harv. J. L. & Pub. Pol'y* 795 (1995–1996)

Cueto-Rua, J. *Judicial Methods of Interpretation of the Law* (New Orleans: Louisiana State University Press, 1981)

Currie, D. "Positive and Negative Constitutional Rights," 53 *U. Chi. L. Rev.* 864 (1986)

The Constitution of the Federal Republic of Germany (University of Chicago Press, 1994)

Currie, I. and de Waal, J. *The Bill of Rights Handbook*, 5th edn. (Cape Town: Juta Law Publishers, 2006)

Curtis, D. and Resnik, J. "Images of Justice," 96 *Yale L. J.* 1727 (1987)

Czarnota, A., Krygier, M., and Sadurski, W. (eds.), *Rethinking the Rule of Law after Communism* (Central European University Press, 2005)

D'Agostino, F. *Incommensurability and Commensuration: The Common Denominator* (Aldershot: Ashgate Publishing, 2003)

Daes, E. "Restrictions and Limitations on Human Rights," in *3 Rene Cassin Amicorum Discipulorumque Liber* 79 (1969)

Dahl, R. *On Democracy* (New Haven, CT: Yale University Press, 1998)

Dassios, C. and Prophet, C. "Charter Section 1: The Decline of Grand Unified Theory and the Trend Towards Deference in the Supreme Court of Canada," 15 *Advocates' Quarterly* 289 (1993)

Davidov, G. "Separating Minimal Impairment from Balancing: A Comment on R. v. Sharpe," 5 *Rev. Const. Stud.* 195 (2000)

"The Paradox of Judicial Deference," 12 *Nat'l J. Const. L.* 133 (2000)

Davis, G. *Magna Carta* (London: Trustees of the British Museum, 1963)

Davis, K. C. *Discretionary Justice: A Preliminary Inquiry* (Baton Rouge, LA: Louisiana State University Press, 1969)

"Facts in Lawmaking," 80 *Colum. L. Rev.* 931 (1980)

Davis, K. C. and Pierce, R. *Administrative Law Treatise*, 4th edn. (New York: Aspen Publishers, 2002)

Daynard, R. "The Use of Social Policy in Judicial Decision-Making," 56 *Cornell L. Rev.* 919 (1971)

De Burca, G. "Proportionality and Wednesbury Unreasonableness: The Influence of European Legal Concepts on UK Law," 3 *Eur. Public Law* 561 (1997)

"The Influence of European Legal Concepts on UK Law: Proportionality and Wednesbury Unreasonableness," 3 *Eur. Public Law* 561 (1993)

"The Principle of Proportionality and Its Application in EC Law," 13 *Y. B. Eur. L.* 105 (1993)

De Oliveira Camilo, R. "The Balancing of Values and the Compromising of the Guarantee of Fundamental Rights" (Paper presented at the VIIth World Congress of the International Association of Constitutional Law, Athens, June 14, 2007)

De S.-O.-l'E. Lasser, M. *Judicial Transformations: The Rights Revolution in the Courts of Europe* (Oxford University Press, 2009)

De Silva, V. "Comparing the Incommensurable: Constitutional Principles, Balancing, and Rational Decision," 31 *OJLS* (forthcoming, 2011)

De Ville, J. "Deference as Respect and Deference as Sacrifice: A Reading of Bato Star Fishing v. Minister of Environmental Affairs," 20 *SAJHR* 577 (2004)

De Waal, J. "A Comparative Analysis of the Provisions of German Origin in the Interim Bill of Rights," 11 *SAJHR* 1 (1995)

Debeljak, J. "Balancing Rights in a Democracy: The Problems with Limitations and Overrides of Rights under the Victorian Charter of Human Rights and Responsibilities Act 2006," 32 *Melb. U. L. Rev.* 422 (2008)

"Parliamentary Sovereignty and Dialogue under the Victorian Charter of Human Rights and Responsibilities: Drawing the Line Between Judicial Interpretation and Judicial Law-Making," 33 *Monash U. L. Rev.* 9 (2007)

Den Otter, E. *Judicial Review in an Age of Moral Pluralism* (Cambridge University Press, 2009)

Dickerson, F. *The Interpretation and Application of Statutes* (Boston: Little Brown & Co., 1975)

Dinstein, Y. *The Conduct of Hostilities under the Law of International Armed Conflict* (Cambridge University Press, 2004)

    War, Aggression and Self-Defense, 4th edn. (Cambridge University Press, 2005)

Dixon, O. "The Common Law as an Ultimate Constitutional Foundation," in O. Dixon, *Jesting Pilate* (Buffalo, NY: William S. Hein & Company, 1965)

Dixon, R. "The Supreme Court of Canada, Charter Dialogue, and Deference," 47 *Osgoode Hall L. J.* 235 (2009)

Dorf, M. "Foreword: The Limits of Socratic Deliberation," 112 *Harv. L. Rev.* 4 (1998)

    "Integrating Normative and Descriptive Constitutional Theory: The Case of Original Meaning," 85 *Geo. L. J.* 1765 (1997)

Doyle, J. "Constitutional Law: 'At the Eye of the Stor'," 23 *U. West. Austl. L. Rev.* 15 (1993)

Dreier, H. *GG Grundgesetz Kommentar* (Tübingen: Mohr Siebeck, 2006)

Du Plessis, L. *Re-interpretation of Statutes* (Durban: Butterworths, 2002)

    "Interpretation," in S. Woolman, M. Bishop, and J. Brickhill (eds.), *Constitutional Law of South Africa*, 2nd edn. (Cape Town: Juta Law Publishers, looseleaf, 2002–)

Ducat, C. *Modes of Constitutional Interpretation* (1978)

Dupré, C. *Importing the Law in Post-Communist Transitions: The Hungarian Constitutional Court and the Right to Human Dignity* (Portland, OR: Hart Publishing, 2003)

Dworkin, R. *A Bill of Rights for Britain* (London: Chatto & Windus, 1990)

    A Matter of Principle (Oxford University Press, 1985)

    Freedom's Law: The Moral Reading of the American Constitution (Cambridge, MA: Harvard University Press, 1996)

    Is Democracy Possible Here?: Principles for a New Political Debate (Princeton University Press, 2006)

    "Pragmatism, Right Answers, and True Banality," in M. Brint and W. Weaver (eds.), *Pragmatism in Law and Society* 359 (1991)

    "Rights as Trumps," in J. Waldron (ed.), *Theories of Rights* (Oxford University Press, 1984)

    Sovereign Virtue – The Theory and Practice of Equality (Cambridge, MA: Harvard University Press, 2000)

    Taking Rights Seriously (Cambridge, MA: Harvard University Press, 1977)

    "Unenumerated Rights: Whether and How Roe Should Be Overruled," 59 *U. Chi. L. Rev.* 381 (1992)

Dyzenhaus, D. "Law as Justification: Etienne Mureinik's Conception of Legal Culture," 14 *SAJHR* 11 (1998)

"The Incoherence of Constitutional Positivism," in G. Huscrot (ed.), *Expounding the Constitution: Essays in Constitutional Theory* (Cambridge University Press, 2008)

"The Politics of Deference: Judicial Review and Democracy," in M. Taggart (ed.), *The Province of Administrative Law* (Portland, OR: Hart Publishing, 1997)

Eberle, E. *Dignity and Liberty: Constitutional Visions in Germany and the United States* (Santa Barbara, CA: Praeger Publishers, 2001)

European and US Constitutionalism (Georg Nolte ed., 2005)

Edlin, D. *Judges and Unjust Laws: Common Law Constitutionalism and the Foundations of Judicial Review* (Ann Arbor, MI: University of Michigan Press, 2008)

Edwards, H. "The Judicial Function and the Elusive Goal of Principled Decisionmaking," *Wis. L. Rev.* 837 (1991)

Edwards, R. "Judicial Deference under the Human Rights Act," 65 *Mod. L. Rev.* 859 (2002)

Eisenberg, T. "Disproportionate Impact and Illicit Motive: Theories of Constitutional Adjudication," 52 *N. Y. U. L. Rev.* 36 (1977)

Eissen, M. "The Principles of Proportionality in the Case-Law of the European Court of Human Rights," in R. St. J. MacDonald, F. Mestscher, and H. Petzold (eds.), *The European System for the Protection of Human Rights* (Dordrecht: Kluwer Academic Publishers, 1993)

Ekins, R. "Acts of Parliament and the Parliament Acts," 123 *L. Q. Rev.* 91 (2007)

Eliot Magnet, J. "The Presumption of Constitutionality," 18 *Osgoode Hall L. J.* 87 (1980)

Elliot, R. "The Supreme Court of Canada and Section 1 – The Erosion of the Common Front," 12 *Queen's L. J.* 277 (1987)

Elliott, M. "United Kingdom Bicameralism, Sovereignty, and the Unwritten Constitution," 5 *I. Con.* 370 (2007)

Ely, J. *Democracy and Distrust: A Theory of Judicial Review* (Cambridge, MA: Harvard University Press, 1980)

"Flag Desecration: A Case Study in the Roles of Categorization and Balancing in First Amendment Analysis," 88 *Harv. L. Rev.* 1482 (1975)

"Legislative and Administrative Motivation in Constitutional Law," 79 *Yale L. J.* 1205 (1970)

Emerson, T. *The System of Freedom of Expression* (London: Vintage Books, 1970)

Emiliou, N. *The Principle of Proportionality in European Law: A Comparative Study* (London: Kluwer Law International, 1996)

Englard, I. *Corrective and Distributive Justice: From Aristotle to Modern Times* (Oxford University Press, 2009)

English, R. and Havers, P. (eds.), *An Introduction to Human Rights and the Common Law* (2000)

Erasmus, G. "Limitation and Suspension," in D. Van Wyk, J. Dugard, B. Villiers, and D. Davis (eds.), *Rights and Constitutionalism: The New South African Legal Order* (Oxford University Press, 1994)

Errera, R. "The Freedom of the Press: The United States, France and Other European Countries," in L. Hegkin and A. Rosenthal (eds.), *Constitutionalism and Rights: The Influence of the United States Constitution Abroad* (New York: Columbia University Press, 1990)

Eskridge, W. *Dynamic Statutory Interpretation* (Cambridge, MA: Harvard University Press, 1994)

"Public Values in Statutory Interpretation," 137 *U. Pa. L. Rev.* 1007 (1989)

Ewing, K. "The Parliamentary Protection of Human Rights," in K. S. Ziegler, D. Baranger, and A. W, Bradley (eds.), *Constitutionalism and the Role of Parliaments* (Portland, OR: Hart Publishing, 2007)

Eylon, Y. and Harel, A. "The Right to Judicial Review," 92 *Yale. L. Rev.* 991 (2006)

Faigman, D. "Madisonian Balancing: A Theory of Constitutional Adjudication," 88 *Nw. U. L. Rev.* 641 (1994)

Fallon, R. "Foreword: Implementing the Constitution," 111 *Harv. L. Rev.* 54, 85 (1998)

Implementing the Constitution (Cambridge, MA: Harvard University Press, 2001)

"Individual Rights and the Powers of Government," 27 *Ga. L. Rev.* 343 (1993)

"Strict Judicial Scrutiny," 54 *UCLA L. Rev.* 1267 (2007)

"The Core of an Uneasy Case for Judicial Review," 121 *Harv. L. Rev.* 1693 (2008)

"The Rule of Law as a Concept in Constitutional Discourse," 97 *Colum. L. Rev.* 1 (1997)

Farber, D. "The Originalism Debate: A Guide for the Perplexed," 49 *Ohio St. L. J.* 1085 (1989)

Farina, C. "Statutory Interpretation and the Balance of Power in the Administrative State," 89 *Colum. L. Rev.* 452 (1989)

Farrell, R. "Successful Rational Basis Claims in the Supreme Court from the 1971 Term through Romer v. Evans," 32 *Ind. L. Rev.* 357 (1999)

Favoreu, L. "Constitutional Review in Europe," in L. Henkin and A. J. Rosenthal (eds.), *Constitutionalism and Rights: The Influence of the United States Constitution Abroad* (New York: Columbia University Press, 1990)

Feldman, D. "Proportionality and the Human Rights Act 1998," in E. Elis (ed.), *The Principle of Proportionality in the Laws of Europe* (Oxford: Hart Publishing, 1999)

Feldman, G. "The Misuse of the Less Restrictive Alternative Inquiry in Rule of Reason Analysis," 58 *Am. U. L. Rev.* 561 (2009)

Feldman, H. "Objectivity in Legal Judgment," 92 *Mich. L. Rev.* 1187 (1994)

Felix, S. "Engaging Unreasonableness and Proportionality as Standards of Review in England, India and Sri Lanka," in H. Corder (ed.), *Comparing*

Administrative Justice Across the Commonwealth (Cape Town: Juta Law Publishers, 2006)

Ferreira Mendes, G. "O Princípio da Proporcionalidade na Jurisprudência do Supremo Tribunal Federal: Novas Leituras," 4 *Repertório IOB Jurisprudência: Tributária Constit. Adm.* 23 (2000)

Ferreres Comella, V. *Constitutional Courts Democratic Values: A European Perspective* (New Haven, CT, and London: Yale University Press, 2009)

Feteris, E. "The Rational Reconstruction of Weighing and Balancing on the Basis of Teleological-Evaluative Considerations in the Justification of Judicial Decisions," 21(4) *Ratio Juris* 481 (2008)

Finkelman, P. "The Constitution and the Intention of the Framers: The Limits of Historical Analysis," 50 *U. Pitt. L. Rev.* 349 (1989)

Fish, M. "An Eye for an Eye: Proportionality as a Moral Principle of Punishment," 28 *OJLS* 57 (2008)

Fish, S. "Intention Is All There Is: A Critical Analysis of Aharon Barak's Purposive Interpretation in Law," 29 *Cardozo L. Rev.* 1109 (2008)

Fisher, L. *Constitutional Dialogues: Interpretation as Political Process* (Princeton University Press, 1988)

Fiss, O. "Foreword: The Forms of Justice," 93 *Harv. L. Rev.* 1 (1979)

"Objectivity and Interpretation," 34 *Stan. L. Rev.* 739 (1982)

"The War Against Terrorism and the Rule of Law," 26 *OJLS* 235 (2006)

Fitzgerald, B. "Proportionality and Australian Constitutionalism," 12 *U. Tas. L. Rev.* 49 (1993)

Fleck, D. and Bothe, M. (eds.), *The Handbook of Humanitarian Law in Armed Conflicts* (Oxford University Press, 1999)

Fleiner, F. *Institutionen des Deutschen Verwaltungsrechts* (Tübingen, 1928)

Fletcher, G. "Comparative Law as Subversive Discipline," 46 *Am. J. Comp. L.* 683 (1998)

Fordham, M. "Common Law Proportionality," 7 *Judicial Review* 110 (2002)

Fordham, M. and de la Mare, T. "Identifying the Principle of Proportionality," in J. Jowell and J. Cooper (eds.), *Understanding Human Rights Principles* (Portland, OR: Hart Publishing, 2001)

Foulkes, D. *Administrative Law*, 8th edn. (London: Butterworths, 1995)

Franck, T. "On Proportionality of Countermeasures in International Law," 102 *Am. J. Int'l L.* 715 (2008)

Frank, J. *Courts on Trial – Myth and Reality in American Justice* (Princeton University Press, 1949)

Frantz, L. "Is the First Amendment Law?: A Reply to Professor Mendelson," 51 *Cal. L. Rev.* 729 (1963)

"The First Amendment in the Balance," 71 *Yale L. J.* 1424 (1962)

Fredman, S. *Human Rights Transformed: Positive Rights and Positive Duties* (Oxford University Press, 2008)

Freeman, S. "Constitutional Democracy and the Legitimacy of Judicial Review," 9 *Law and Philosophy* 327 (1990)

Freund, P. "Review of Facts in Constitutional Cases," in E. Cahn (ed.), *Supreme Court and Supreme Law* (Bloomington, IN: Indiana University Press, 1954)

Friauf, K. "Techniques for the Interpretation of Constitutions in German Law," in *Proceedings of the Fifth International Symposium on Comparative Law* (1968)

Friedman, B. "Dialogue and Judicial Review," 91 *Mich. L. Rev.* 577 (1993)

  "The Birth of an Academic Obsession: The History of the Countermajoritarian Difficulty, Part Five," 112 *Yale L. J.* 153 (2002)

  "The Counter-Majoritarian Problem and the Pathology of Constitutional Scholarship," 95 *Nw. U. L. Rev.* 933 (2001)

  "Trumping Rights," 27 *Ga. L. Rev.* 435 (1992)

Friedman, D. and Barak-Erez, D. (eds.), *Human Rights in Private Law* (Hart Publishing, 2001)

Frumkin, G. "A Survey of the Sources of the Principle of Proportionality in German Law" (unpublished thesis, University of Chicago, 1991) (on file with the author)

Fuller, L. *Anatomy of the Law* (Westport, CT: Greenwood Press, 1968)

  "The Forms and Limits of Adjudication," 92 *Harv. L. Rev.* 353 (1979)

  The Morality of Law (New Haven, CT: Yale University Press, 1969)

Galetta, D. *Principio di Proporzionalita e Sindacato Giurisdizionale nel Diritto Administrativo* (Milan, 1998)

Galligan, D. *Discretionary Powers: A Legal Study of Official Discretion* (Oxford: Clarendon Press, 1986)

Gant, S. "Judicial Supremacy and Nonjudicial Interpretation of the Constitution," 24 *Hastings Const. L. Q.* 359 (1997)

Gardam, J. *Necessity, Proportionality and the Use of Force by States* (Cambridge University Press, 2004)

  "Proportionality and Force in International Law," 87 *Am. J. Int'l L.* 391 (1993)

Gardbaum, S. "A Democratic Defense of Constitutional Balancing," 4(1) *Law and Ethics of Hum. Rts.* 77 (2010)

  "Limiting Constitutional Rights," 54 *UCLA L. Rev.* 789 (2007)

  "Reassessing the New Commonwealth Model of Constitutionalism," 8 *Int'l. J. Const. L.* 167 (2010)

  "The Myth and the Reality of American Constitutional Exceptionalism," 107 *Mich. L. Rev.* 391 (2008)

  "The New Commonwealth Model of Constitutionalism," 47 *Am. J. Comp. L.* 707 (2001)

Garibaldi, O. M. "General Limitations on Human Rights: The Principle of Legality," 17 *Harv. Int'l L. J.* 503 (1976)

Gerangelos, P. "The Separation of Powers and Legislative Interference," in P. Gerangelos (ed.), *Judicial Process: Constitutional Principles and Limitations* (Portland, OR: Hart Publishing, 2009)

Gewirth, A. "Are There Any Absolute Rights?," *Philosophical Quarterly* 31 (1981)

Ghai, Y. *Hong Kong's New Constitutional Order: The Resumption of Chinese Sovereignty and the Basic Law*, 2nd edn. (Hong Kong University Press, 1999)

Goesel-Le Bihan, V. "Le Contrôle de Proportionnalité Exercé par le Conseil Constitutionnel," 22 *Les Cahiers du Conseil Constitutionnel* 208 (2007)

Goldberg, S. "Equality Without Tiers," 77 *S. Cal. L. Rev.* 481 (2004)

Goldford, D. *The American Constitution and the Debate over Originalism* (Cambridge University Press, 2005)

Goldsworthy, J. (ed.), *Interpreting Constitutions: A Comparative Study* (New York: Oxford University Press, 2006)

"Judicial Review, Legislative Override and Democracy," 38 *Wake Forest L. Rev.* 451 (2003)

Parliamentary Sovereignty: Contemporary Debates (Cambridge University Press, 2010)

"The Myth of the Common Law Constitution," in D. E. Edlin (ed.), *Common Law Theory* (Cambridge University Press, 2007)

The Sovereignty of Parliament: History and Philosophy (Oxford University Press, 1999)

Goldsworthy, J. and Campbell, T. (eds.), *Legal Interpretation in Democratic States* (Farnham, England: Ashgate, 2002)

Gottlieb, S. "Compelling Governmental Interests: An Essential But Unanalyzed Term in Constitutional Adjudication," 68 *Boston University L. Rev.* 917 (1988)

"The Paradox of Balancing Significant Interests," 45 *Hastings L. J.* 825 (1994)

Gottlieb Svarez, C. *Vorträge über Recht und Staat* (Hermann Conrad and Gerd Kleinheyer eds., Cologne: Westdeutscher Verlag, 1960)

Götz, V. "Legislative and Executive Power under the Constitutional Requirements Entailed in the Principle of the Rule of Law," in C. Starck (ed.), *New Challenges to the German Basic Law* (Baden-Baden: Nomos 1991)

Gözler, K. *Judicial Review of Constitutional Amendments: A Comparative Study* (Bursa, Turkey: Ekin Press, 2008)

Greenawalt, K. "Are Mental States Relevant for Statutory and Constitutional Interpretation?," 85 *Cornell L. Rev.* 1609 (2000)

"Free Speech in the United States and Canada," 55 *Law & Contemp. Probs.* 5 (1992)

Law and Objectivity (Oxford University Press, 1992)

Legal Interpretation: Perspectives from Other Disciplines and Private Texts (New York: Oxford University Press, 2010)

Greene, J. "On the Origins of Originalism," 88 *Tex. L. Rev.* 1 (2009)

Greer, S. "'Balancing' and the European Court of Human Rights: A Contribution to the Habermas–Alexy Debate," 63 *Cambridge L. J.* 412 (2004)

"Constitutionalizing Adjudication under the European Convention on Human Rights," 23 *OJLS* 405 (2003)

The European Convention on Human Rights: Achievements, Problems and Prospects (Cambridge University Press, 2006)

Grey, T. "Do We Have an Unwritten Constitution?," 27 *Stan. L. Rev.* 703 (1975)

Grimm, D. "Human Rights and Judicial Review in Germany," in D. M. Beatty (ed.), *Human Rights and Judicial Review: A Comparative Perspective* (Dordrecht: Martinus Nijhoff Publishers, 1994)

"Proportionality in Canadian and German Constitutional Jurisprudence," 57 *U. Toronto L. J.* 383 (2007)

"The Protective Function of the State," in G. Nolte (ed.), *European and US Constitutionalism* (Cambridge University Press, 2005)

Grote, R. "Rule of Law, Rechtsstaat and Etat de Droit," in C. Starck (ed.), *Constitutionalism, Universalism and Democracy – A Comparative Analysis* (Baden-Baden: Nomos, 1999)

Gunther, G. "In Search of Judicial Quality on a Changing Court: The Case of Justice Powell," 24 *Stan. L. Rev.* 1001 (1972)

"The Supreme Court 1971 Term – Foreword: In Search of Evolving Doctrine on a Changing Court: A Model for a Newer Equal Protection," 86 *Harv. L. Rev.* 1 (1972)

Haas, M. *International Human Rights: A Comprehensive Introduction* (London: Routledge, 2008)

Habermas, J. *Between Facts and Norms: Contributions to a Discourse Theory of Law and Democracy* (W. Rehg trans., Cambridge, MA: MIT Press, 1996)

Hafelin, U., Haller, W., and Keller, H. *Schweizerisches Bundesstaatsrecht* (Zurich: Schulthess, 2008)

Hak-Seon, J. "L'application du Principe de Proportionnalite dans la Justice Constitutionnelle en Corée" (Paper presented at the VIIth World Congress of the International Association of Constitutional Law, Athens, June 14, 2007)

Hall, J. "Taking 'Rechts' Seriously: Ronald Dworkin and the Federal Constitutional Court of Germany," 9 *German L. J.* 771 (2008)

Hallet, G. *Greater Good: The Case for Proportionalism* (Washington, DC: Georgetown University Press, 1995)

Hamer, D. "The Presumption of Innocence and Reverse Burdens: A Balancing Act," 66 *Cambridge L. J.* 142 (2007)

Harding, S. "Comparative Reasoning and Judicial Review," 28 *Yale J. Int'l L.* 409 (2003)

Harel, A. "Rights-Based Judicial Review: A Democratic Justification," 22 *Law and Philosophy* 247 (2003)

Harel, A. and Kahana, T. "The Easy Core Case for Judicial Review," 2 *J. Legal Analysis* 227 (2010)

Hart, H. L. A. *Law, Liberty, and Morality* (Stanford University Press, 1963)

The Concept of Law, 2nd edn. (Oxford: Clarendon Press, 1994)

"The Courts and Lawmaking: A Comment," in M. G. Paulsen (ed.), *Legal Institutions Today and Tomorrow: The Centennial Conference Volume of the Columbia Law School* (New York: Columbia University Press, 1959)

Hart, H. and Sacks, A. *The Legal Process: Basic Problems in the Making and Application of Law* (Foundation Press, 1958)

Hartnett, E. "A Matter of Judgment, Not a Matter of Opinion," 74 *N. Y. U. L. Rev.* 123 (1999)

Heinze, E. *The Logic of Constitutional Rights* (Burlington, VT: Ashgate Publishing Company, 2005)

Held, V. *The Public Interest and Individual Interests* (New York: Basic Books, 1970)

Henckaerts, J. and Doswald-Beck, L. (eds.), *Customary International Humanitarian Law* (Cambridge University Press, 2005)

Henkin, L. "Infallibility under Law: Constitutional Balancing," 78 *Colum. L. Rev.* 1022 (1978)

"Privacy and Autonomy," 74 *Colum. L. Rev.* 1410 (1974)

Henly, B. "'Penumbra': The Roots of a Legal Metaphor," 15 *Hast. Const. L. Q.* 81 (1987)

Hesse, K. *Grundzüge des Verfassungrechts der Bundesrepublik Deutschland* (Heidelberg: C. F. Müller Verlag, 1999)

Heyman, S. *Free Speech and Human Dignity* (New Haven, CT: Yale University Press, 2008)

Hickman, T. "Constitutional Dialogue, Constitutional Theories and the Human Rights Act 1998," *PL* 306 (2005)

"The Reasonableness Principle: Reassessing Its Place in the Public Sphere," 63 *Cambridge L. J.* 166 (2004)

"The Substance and Structure of Proportionality," *PL* 694 (2008)

Hirsch, A. "Candor and Prudence in Constitutional Adjudication," 61 *Geo. Wash. L. Rev.* 858 (1993)

Hirschberg, L. *Der Grundsatz Der Verhältnismäßigkeit* (Göttingen: Schwarz, 1980)

Hirschl, R. "The New Constitutionalism and the Judicialization of Pure Politics Worldwide," 75 *Fordham L. Rev.* 721 (2006)

Towards Juristocracy: The Origins and Consequences of the New Constitutionalism (Cambridge, MA: Harvard University Press, 2004)

Hoexter, C. "The Future of Judicial Review in South African Administrative Law," 117 *S. Afr. L. J.* 484 (2000)

Hoffmann, Lord "The Influence of the European Principle of Proportionality upon UK Law," in E. Ellis (ed.), *The Principle of Proportionality in the Laws of Europe* (Portland, OR: Hart Publishing, 1999)

Hogan, G. "Judicial Review – The Law of the Republic of Ireland," in B. Hadfield
    (ed.), *Judicial Review: A Thematic Approach* (Dublin: Gill & Macmillan,
    1995)
    "The Constitution, Property Rights and Proportionality," 32 *Irish Jurist* 373
    (1997)
Hogan, G. and Morgan, D. *Administrative Law in Ireland*, 2nd edn. (Dublin: Round
    Hall Press, 1991)
Hogg, P. "Canadian Law in the Constitutional Court of South Africa," 13 *SAPL* 1
    (1998)
    Constitutional Law of Canada, 2nd edn. (Toronto: Carswell, 1985)
    Constitutional Law of Canada, 5th edn., vol. II (Toronto: Thomson Carswell,
    2007)
    "Interpreting the Charter of Rights: Generosity and Justification," 28 *Osgoode
    Hall L. J.* 817 (1990)
    "Section 1 Revisited" (1992) 1 *National Journal of Constitutional Law* 1
Hogg, P. and Bushell, A. "Reply to Six Degrees of Dialogue," 37 *Osgoode Hall L. J.*
    529 (1999)
    "The Charter Dialogue between Courts and Legislatures (Or Perhaps the
    Charter of Rights Isn't Such a Bad Thing After All)," 35 *Osgoode Hall L. J.*
    75 (1997)
Hogg, P. and Zwibel, C. "The Rule of Law in the Supreme Court of Canada," 55 *U.
    Toronto L. J.* 715 (2005)
Hopkins, K. "Constitutional Rights and the Question of Waiver: How Fundamental
    Are Fundamental Rights?," 16 *SAPL* 122 (2001)
Horowitz, D. *The Courts and Social Policy* (Washington, DC: Brookings Institution
    Press, 1977)
Horwitz, M. *The Transformation of American Law: 1870–1960* (Oxford University
    Press, 1992)
Horwitz, P. "Three Faces of Deference," 83 *Notre Dame L. Rev.* 1061 (2008)
Hovius, B. "The Limitation Clauses of the European Convention on Human Rights:
    A Guide for the Application of Section 1 of the Charter?," 17 *Ottawa L. Rev.*
    213 (1985)
    "The Limitations Clauses of the European Convention on Human Rights and
    Freedoms and Section 1 of the Canadian Charter of Rights and Freedoms: A
    Comparative Analysis," 6 *Y. B. Eur. L.* 105 (1987)
Hunt, M. "Sovereignty's Blight: Why Contemporary Public Law Needs the Concept
    of 'Due Deference,'" in N. Bamforth and P. Leyland (eds.), *Public Law in a
    Multi-Layered Constitution* (Portland, OR: Hart Publishing, 2003)
    Using Human Rights Law in English Courts (Oxford: Hart Publishing, 1997)
Hutchinson, A. C. and Monahan, P. J. *The Rule of Law: Ideal or Ideology?* (Toronto:
    Carswell, 1987)
Iacobucci, F. "'Reconciling Rights': The Supreme Court of Canada's Approach to
    Competing Charter Rights," 20 *Sup. Ct. L. Rev.* 137 (2003)

"The Charter: Twenty Years Later," 21 *Windsor Y. B. Access. Just.* 3 (2002)

Ides, A. "Judicial Supremacy and the Law of the Constitution," 47 *UCLA L. Rev.* 491 (1999)

Iglesias Vila, M. *Facing Judicial Discretion: Legal Knowledge and Right Answers Revisited* (Dordrecht: Springer, 2001)

Iles, K. "Limiting Socio-Economic Rights: Beyond the Internal Limitations Clauses," 20 *SAJHR* 448 (2004)

Iyer, T. *Judicial Review of Reasonableness in Constitutional Law* (Madras: Madras Law Journal Office, 1979)

Jackson, D. and Tate, C. (eds.), *Comparative Judicial Review and Public Policy* (Greenwood Press, 1992)

Jackson, V. "Ambivalent Resistance and Comparative Constitutionalism: Opening up the Conversation on "Proportionality," Rights and Federalism," 1 *U. Pa. J. Const. L.* 583 (1999)

"Being Proportional about Proportionality," 21 *Const. Comment.* 803 (2004)

"Constitutional Comparisons: Convergence, Resistance, Engagement," 119 *Harv. L. Rev.* 109 (2005)

Constitutional Engagement in a Transnational Era (Oxford University Press, 2010)

Jackson, V. and Tushnet, M. *Comparative Constitutional Law* (New York: Foundation Press, 1999)

Jacobs, F. "The 'Limitation Clause' of the European Convention on Human Rights," in L. C. Armand de Mestral, *The Limitations of Human Rights in Comparative Constitutional Law* (Montreal: Les Editions Yvon Blais, 1986)

Jain, M. *Indian Constitutional Law*, 5th edn. (Haryana, India: LexisNexis Butterworths Wadhwa, 2003)

James, F. "Burdens of Proof," 47 *Va. L. Rev.* 51, 59 (1961)

James, F., Hazard, G. C., and Leubsdorf, J. *Civil Procedure*, 5th edn. (Foundation Press, 2001)

Jans, J. "Minimum Harmonisation and the Role of the Principle of Proportionality" (2007), available at www.ssrn.com/abstract=1105341/

"Proportionality Revisited," 27 *Legal Issues of European Integration* 239 (2000)

Jayawickrama, N. *The Judicial Application of Human Rights Law: National, Regional and International Jurisprudence* (Cambridge University Press, 2002)

Jenkins, D. "Common Law Declaration of Unconstitutionality," 7 *Int. J. Con. L.* 183 (2009)

Johnson, J. *Just War Tradition and the Restraint of War* (Princeton University Press, 1981)

Ideology, Reason, and the Limitation of War: Religious and Secular Concepts, 1200–1740 (Princeton University Press, 1975)

Joseph, P. A. *Constitutional and Administrative Law in New Zealand*, 3rd edn. (Wellington: Brooker's, 2007)

"The Demise of Ultra Vires – A Reply to Christopher Forsyth and Linda Whittle," 8 *Canterbury L. Rev.* 463 (2002)

Joseph, S., Schultz, J., and Castan, M. *The International Covenant on Civil and Political Rights: Cases, Materials and Commentary*, 2nd edn. (Oxford University Press, 2004)

Jowell, J. "Administrative Justice and Standards of Substantive Judicial Review," in A. Arnull, P. Eeckhout, and T. Tridimas (eds.), *Continuity and Change in EU Law: Essays in Honour of Sir Francis Jacobs* (Oxford University Press, 2008)

"Beyond the Rule of Law: Towards Constitutional Judicial Review," *PL* 669 (2000)

"Judicial Deference and Human Rights: A Question of Competence," in P. Craig and R. Rawlings (eds.), *Law and Administration in Europe: Essays in Honour of Carol Harlow* (Oxford University Press, 2003)

"Judicial Deference: Servility, Civility or Institutional Capacity?," *PL* 592 (2003)

"Parliamentary Sovereignty under the New Constitutional Hypothesis," 3 *PL* 562 (2006)

"Restraining the State: Politics, Principle and Judicial Review," 50 *CLP* 189 (1997)

Jukka, V. *The European Court of Human Rights as a Developer of the General Doctrines of Human Rights Law: A Study of the Limitations Clauses of the European Convention on Human Rights* (Tampere, Finland: Tampereen yliopisto, 2003)

Jurgen, B. "Freedom of Speech and Flag Desecration: A Comparative Study of German, European and United States Laws," 20 *Denv. J. Int'l L. & Pol'y* 471 (1991–1992)

Kagan, E. "Private Speech, Public Purpose: The Role of Governmental Motive in First Amendment Doctrine," 63 *U. Chi. L. Rev.* 413 (1996)

Kahana, T. "The Notwithstanding Mechanism and Public Discussion: Lessons from the Ignored Practice of Section 33 of the Charter," 43 *Can. Public Admin.* 225 (2001)

"Understanding the Notwithstanding Mechanism," 52 *U. Toronto L. J.* 221 (2002)

"What Makes for a Good Use of the Notwithstanding Mechanism?," 23 *Sup. Ct. L. Rev.* 191 (2004)

Kahn, P. "The Court, the Community and the Judicial Balance: The Jurisprudence of Justice Powell," 97 *Yale L. J.* 1 (1987)

Kahn, R. A. "The Headscarf as Threat: A Comparison of German and US Legal Discourses," 40 *Vand. J. Transnat'l L.* 417 (2007)

Kalven, H. *A Worthy Tradition: Freedom of Speech in America* (Cambridge University Press, 1988)

Kamm, F. M. "Conflicts of Rights: Typology, Methodology, and Nonconsequentialism," 7 *Legal Theory* 239 (2001)

Kaplin, W. "The Process of Constitutional Interpretation: A Synthesis of the Present and a Guide to the Future," 42 *Rutgers L. Rev.* 983 (1990)

Karp, J. "Criminal Law – Yanus of Human Rights: Constitutionalization and Basic Law: Human Dignity and Liberty," 42(1) *Hapraklit* 64 (1995)

Karpen, U. "Rule of Law," in U. Karpen (ed.), *The Constitution of the Federal Republic of Germany* (Baden-Baden: Nomos, 1988)

Karst, K. "Legislative Facts in Constitutional Litigation," *Sup. Ct. Rev.* 75 (1960)

Kauper, P. "Penumbras, Peripherals, Emanations, Things Fundamental and Things Forgotten: The Griswold Case," 64 *Mich. L. Rev.* 235 (1965)

Kavanagh, A. *Constitutional Review under the UK Human Rights Act* (Cambridge University Press, 2009)

"Deference or Defiance?: The Limits of the Judicial Role in Constitutional Adjudication," in G. Huscroft (ed.), *Expounding the Constitution – Essays in Constitutional Theory* (Cambridge University Press, 2008)

Kazazi, M. *Burden of Proof and Related Issues: A Study on Evidence before International Tribunals* (London: Kluwer Law International, 1996)

Keller, H. and Stone-Sweet, A. (eds.), *A Europe of Rights: The Impact of the ECHR on National Legal Systems* (2008)

Kelly, J. *The Irish Constitutions*, 4th edn. (G. Hogan and G. Whyte eds., Dublin: Butterworths, 2003)

Kelman, M. "Market Discrimination and Groups," 53 *Stan. L. Rev.* 833 (2001)

Kelso, R. "Styles of Constitutional Interpretation and the Four Main Approaches to Constitutional Interpretation in American Legal History," 29 *Valp. U. L. Rev.* 121 (1994)

Kerans, R. "The Future of Section One of the Charter," 23 *U. Brit. Colum. L. Rev.* 567 (1988)

Khaitan, T. "Beyond Reasonableness – A Rigorous Standard of Review for Article 15 Infringement," 50 *J. Indian L. Ins.* 177 (2008)

Khosla, M. "Proportionality: An Assault on Human Rights?: A Reply," 8(2) *I. Con.* 298 (2010)

Khushal Murkens, J. "Comparative Constitutional Law in the Courts: Reflections on the Originalists' Objections" (LSE Legal Studies, Working Paper No. 15/2008)

Kiedrowski, J. and Webb, K. "Second Guessing the Law-Makers: Social Science Research in Charter Litigation," 19 *Can. Pub. Pol'y* 379 (1993)

King, J. "Institutional Approaches to Judicial Review," 28 *OJLS* 409 (2008)

Kirby, M. "Australian Law – After 11 September 2001," 21 *ABR* 1 (2001)

"Constitutional Interpretation and Original Intent: A Form of Ancestor Worship," 24 *Melb. U. L. Rev.* 1 (2000)

Kirk, J. "Constitutional Guarantees, Characterisation and the Concept of Proportionality," 21 *Melb. U. L. Rev.* 1 (1997)

"Constitutional Implications (I): Nature, Legitimacy, Classification, Examples," 24 *Melb. U. L. Rev.* 645 (2000)

"Constitutional Implications (II): Doctrines of Equality and Democracy," 25 *Melb. U. L. Rev.* 24 (2001)

Kiss, A. "Permissible Limitations on Rights," in Louis Henkin (ed.), *The International Bill of Rights: The Covenant on Civil and Political Rights* (New York: Columbia University Press, 1981)

Klatt, M. "Taking Rights Less Seriously: A Structural Analysis of Judicial Discretion," 20 *Ratio Juris* 506 (2007)

Koh, H. "Setting the World Right," 115 *Yale L. J.* 2350 (2006)

Kokott, J. "From Reception and Transplantation to Convergence of Constitutional Models in the Age of Globalization – With Particular Reference to the German Basic Law," in C. Starck (ed.), *Constitutionalism, Universalism and Democracy – A Comparative Analysis: The German Contributions to the Fifth World Congress of the International Association of Constitutional Law* (Berlin: Nomos Verlagsgesellschaft, 1999)

The Burden of Proof in Comparative and International Human Rights Law (London: Kluwer Law International, 1998)

Kommers, D. "Germany: Balancing Rights and Duties," in J. Goldsworthy (ed.), *Interpreting Constitutions: A Comparative Study* (Oxford University Press, 2006)

The Constitutional Jurisprudence of the Federal Republic of Germany, 2nd edn. (Durham, NC: Duke University Press, 1997)

"The Jurisprudence of Free Speech in the United States and the Federal Republic of Germany," 53 *S. Cal. L. Rev.* 657 (1979–1980)

"The Value of Comparative Constitutional Law," 9 *Marshall J. Practice & Procedure* 685 (1976)

Koopmans, T. *Courts and Political Institutions: A Comparative View* (Cambridge University Press, 2003)

Kramer, M. *Objectivity and the Rule of Law* (Cambridge University Press, 2007)

Kreimer, S. "Allocational Sanctions: The Problem of Negative Rights in a Positive State," 132 *U. Pa. L. Rev.* 1293 (1984)

Kremnitzer, M. "Constitutional Principles and Criminal Law," 27 *Isr. L. Rev.* 84 (1993)

Kress, K. "Coherence," in D. Patterson (ed.), *A Companion to the Philosophy of Law and Legal Theory* (Wiley-Blackwell, 1996)

Kretzmer, D. "Freedom of Speech and Racism," 8 *Cardozo L. Rev.* 445 (1987)

Krishnaswamy, S. *Democracy and Constitutionalism in India: A Study of the Basic Structure Doctrine* (Oxford University Press, 2009)

Krotoszynski, R. "A Comparative Perspective on the First Amendment: Free Speech, Militant Democracy, and the Primacy of Dignity as a Preferred Constitutional Value in Germany," 78 *Tul. L. Rev.* 1549 (2004)

Kumar Katyal, N. "Legislative Constitutional Interpretation," 50 *Duke L. J.* 1335 (2001)

Kumm, M. "Democracy Is Not Enough: Rights, Proportionality and the Point of Judicial Review" (New York University Public Law and Legal Theory, Working Papers. Paper 118, 2009)

"Political Liberalism and the Structures of Rights: On the Place and Limits of the Proportionality Requirement," in G. Pavlakos (ed.), *Law, Rights, and Discourse: The Legal Philosophy of Robert Alexy* (Portland, OR: Hart Publishing, 2007)

"The Idea of Socratic Contestation and the Right to Justification: The Point of Rights-Based Proportionality Review," 4 *Law & Ethics Hum. Rts.* 140 (2010)

"What Do You Have in Virtue of Having a Constitutional Right? On the Place and Limits of the Proportionality Requirement" (New York University Law School, Public Law Research, Paper No. 06–41, 2006)

"Who's Afraid of the Total Constitution?," in A. Menéndez and E. Eriksen (eds.), *Arguing Fundamental Rights* (Dordrecht: Springer, 2006)

Kumm, M. and Ferreres Comella, V. "What Is So Special about Constitutional Rights in Private Litigation?: A Comparative Analysis of the Function of State Action Requirements and Indirect Horizontal Effect," in A. Sajó and R. Uitz (eds.), *The Constitution in Private Relations: Expanding Constitutionalism* (The Hague: Eleven International Publishing, 2005)

Kramer, L. *The People Themselves: Popular Constitutionalism and Judicial Review* (Oxford University Press, 2006)

L'Heureux-Dubé, C. "The Importance of Dialogue: Globalization, The Rehnquist Court and Human Rights," in M. H, Belskey (ed.), *The Rehnquist Court: A Retrospective* (New York: Oxford University Press, 2002)

La Forest, G. "The Balancing of Interests under the Charter," 2 *Nat'l. J. Const. L.* 132 (1992)

Lakin, S. "Debunking the Idea of Parliamentary Sovereignty: The Controlling Factor of Legality in the British Constitution," 28 *OJLS* 709 (2008)

Lakoff, G. and Johnson, M. *Metaphors We Live By* (University of Chicago Press, 1980)

Lamb, C. "Judicial Policy-Making and Information Flow to the Supreme Court," 29 *Vand. L. Rev.* 45 (1976)

Lamer, A. "Canada's Legal Revolution: Judging in the Age of the Charter of Rights," 28 *Isr. L. Rev.* 579 (1994)

Lasser, M. *Judicial Transformations: The Rights Revolution in the Courts of Europe* (Oxford University Press, 2009)

Law, D. "A Theory of Judicial Power and Judicial Review," 97 *Geo. L. J.* 723 (2009)

"Generic Constitutional Law," 89 *Minn. L. Rev.* 652 (2005)

Laws, J. "Is the High Court of Justice the Guardian of Fundamental Constitutional Rights?," 59 *PL* (1993)

"Law and Democracy," *PL* 72 (1995)

"Wednesbury," in C. Forsyth and I. Hare (eds.), *The Golden Metwand and the Crooked Cord: Essays in Honour of Sir William Wade QC* (Oxford University Press, 1998)

Leão, A. "Notas Sobre o Princípio da Proporcionalidade ou da Proibição do Excesso," 5 *FDUP* 999 (2001)

Leclair, J. "Canada's Unfathomable Unwritten Constitutional Principles," 27 *Queen's L. J.* 389 (2002)

Ledford, K. "Formalizing the Rule of Law in Prussia: The Supreme Administrative Law Court, 1876–1914," *Central European History*, vol. 37, No. 2 (2004)

Legrand, P. "European Legal Systems Are Not Converging," 45 *Int'l & Comp. L. Q.* 52 (1996)

Leigh, I. "Taking Rights Proportionately: Judicial Review, the Human Rights Act and Strasbourg," *PL* 265 (2002)

Lester, A. and Jowell, J. "Beyond Wednesbury: Substantive Principles of Administrative Law," 4 *PL* 368 (1987)

Lester, A. and Pannick, D. *Human Rights Law and Practice*, 2nd edn. (London: Butterworths, 2004)

Letsas, G. *A Theory of Interpretation of the European Convention on Human Rights* (Oxford University Press, 2009)

Levinson, S. (ed.), *Responding to Imperfection – The Theory and Practice of Constitutional Amendment* (Princeton University Press, 1995)

Liebenberg, S. "The Interpretation of Socio-Economic Rights," in S. Woolman, M. Bishop, and J. Brickhill (eds.), *Constitutional Law of South Africa*, 2nd edn. (Cape Town: Juta Law Publishers, looseleaf, 2002–)

Linde, H. "Due Process of Lawmaking," 55 *Neb. L. Rev.* 197 (1976)

Lofgren, C. "The Original Understanding of Original Intent?," 5 *Const. Comment.* 77 (1988)

Lokan, A. "The Rise and Fall of Doctrine under Section 1 of the Charter," 24 *Ottawa L. Rev.* 163 (1992)

Loughlin, M. *Foundations of Public Law* (Oxford University Press, 2010)

Luban, D. "Incommensurable Values, Rational Choice, and Moral Absolutes," 38 *Clev. St. L. Rev.* 65 (1990)

MacCormick, N. "Coherence in Legal Justification," in A. Peczenik, L. Lindahl, and B. van Roermund (eds.), *Theory of Legal Science* (1984)

"On Reasonableness," in C. Perelman and R. van der Elst (eds.), *Les Notions à Contenu Variable en Droit* (Brussels: Emile Bruylant, 1984)

Questioning Sovereignty: Law, State and Nation in the European Commonwealth (Oxford University Press, 1999)

MacCormick, N. and Summers, R. *Interpreting Statutes: A Comparative Study* (Aldershot: Dartmouth, 1991)

Machan, T. *Objectivity: Recovering Determinate Reality in Philosophy, Science, and Everyday Life* (Aldershot: Ashgate Publishing, 2004)

Macklem, T. and Terry, J. "Making the Justification Fit the Breach," 11 *Sup. Ct. L. Rev.* 575 (2000)

Magiera, S. "The Interpretation of the Basic Law," in C. Starck (ed.), *Main Principles of the German Basic Law* (Baden-Baden: Nomos Verlagsgesellschaft, 1983)

Magnet, J. "Jurisdictional Fact, Constitutional Fact and the Presumption of Constitutionality," 11 *Man. L. J.* 21 (1981)

Maine, H. *Ancient Law* (London: John Murray, 1861)

Mak, C. *Fundamental Rights in European Contract Law: A Comparison of the Impact of Fundamental Rights on Contractual Relationships in Germany, The Netherlands, Italy and England* (Alphen aan den Rijn, The Netherlands: Kluwer Law International, 2008)

Manfredi, C. "The Day the Dialogue Died: A Comment on Sauvé v. Canada," 45 *Osgoode Hall L. J.* 105 (2007)

Manfredi, C. and Kelly, J. "Six Degrees of Dialogue: A Response to Hogg and Bushell," 37 *Osgoode Hall L. J.* 513 (1999)

Marauhn, T. and Ruppel, N. "Balancing Conflicting Human Rights: Konrad Hesse's Notion of 'Praktische Konkordanz' and the German Federal Constitutional Court," in E. Brems (ed.), *Conflicts Between Fundamental Rights* (Mortsel, Belgium: Intersentia, 2008)

Maravall, J. and Przeworski, A. (eds.), *Democracy and the Rule of Law* (Cambridge University Press, 2003)

Marjan Mavčič, A. "The Implementation of the Principle of Proportionality in the Slovenian Constitutional Case-Law" (Paper presented at the 6th Meeting of the Joint Council on Constitutional Justice, "Mini-Conference" on the Principle of Proportionality, May 30, 2007, available at www.venice.coe.int/docs/2007/CDL-JU(2007)017-e.pdf

Marmor, A. "An Essay on the Objectivity of Law," in B. Bix (ed.), *Analyzing Law: New Essays in Legal Theory* (Oxford: Clarendon Press, 1998)

"Three Concepts of Objectivity," in A. Marmor (ed.), *Law and Interpretation: Essays in Legal Philosophy* (Oxford University Press, 1995)

Mason, A. "The Role of a Constitutional Court in a Federation: A Comparison of the Australian and the United States Experience," 16 *Fed. L. Rev.* 1 (1986)

Masur, J. "Probability Thresholds," 92 *Iowa L. Rev.* 1293 (2007)

Mathen, C. "Constitutional Dialogue in Canada and the United States," 14 *Nat'l J. Const. L.* 403 (2003)

Mather, H. "Law-Making and Incommensurability," *McGill L. J.* 345 (2002)

Mayo, L. and Jones, E. "Legal-Policy Decision Process: Alternative Thinking and the Predictive Function," 33 *Geo. Wash. L. Rev.* 318 (1964)

McBride, J. "Proportionality and the European Convention on Human Rights," in E. Ellis (ed.), *The Principle of Proportionality in the Laws of Europe* (Portland, OR: Hart Publishing, 1999)

McCrudden, C. "A Common Law of Human Rights? Transnational Judicial
    Conversations on Constitutional Rights," 20 *OJLS* 499 (2000)
    "A Part of the Main?: The Physician-Assisted Suicide Case and Comparative
    Law Methodology in the United States Supreme Court," in C. Schneider
    (ed.), *Law at the End of Life: The Supreme Court and Assisted Suicide* (Ann
    Arbor, MI: University of Michigan Press, 2000)
McDonald, L. "Rights, 'Dialogue' and Democratic Objections to Judicial Review,"
    32 *Fed. L. Rev.* 1 (2004)
McFadden, P. "The Balancing Test," 29 *B. C. L. Rev.* 585 (1988)
McHarg, A. "Reconciling Human Rights and the Public Interest: Conceptual
    Problems and Doctrinal Uncertainty in the Jurisprudence of the European
    Court of Human Rights," 62 *Mod. L. Rev.* 671 (1999)
McLachlin, B. "The Charter: A New Role for the Judiciary," 29 *Alta. L. Rev.* 540
    (1991)
McLean, E. "Roscoe Pound's Theory of Interests and the Furtherance of Western
    Civilization," 41 *Il Politico* 5 (1976)
McLean, J., Rishworth, P., and Taggart, M. "The Impact of the New Zealand Bill of
    Rights on Administrative Law," in *The New Zealand Bill of Rights Act 1990*
    (Auckland: Legal Research Foundation, 1992), 62
Medina Guerrero, M. *La Vinculación Negativa del Legislador a los Derechos
    Fundamentales* (Madrid: McGraw-Hill, 1996)
Mendus, S. and Edwards, D. (eds.), *On Toleration* (Oxford University Press, 1987)
Merrill, T. "Judicial Deference to Executive Precedent," 101 *Yale L. J.* 969
    (1991–1992)
Merrill, T. and Hickman, K. "Chevron's Domain," 89 *Geo. L. J.* 833 (2001)
Merryman, J. "The Italian Legal Style III: Interpretation," 18 *Stan. L. R.* 583 (1966)
Meyerson, D. "Why Courts Should Not Balance Rights against the Public Interest,"
    31 *Melb. U. L. Rev.* 873 (2007)
Michael, W. "The Original Understanding of Original Intent: A Textual Analysis,"
    26 *Ohio N. U. L. Rev.* 201 (2000)
Michalowski, S. and Woods, L. *German Constitutional Law: The Protection of Civil
    Liberties* (Sudbury, MA: Dartmouth Publishing Co. Ltd., 1999)
Michelman, F. "Foreword: Traces of Self-Government – The Supreme Court 1985
    Term," 100 *Harv. L. Rev.* 4 (1986)
    "Politics and Values or What's Really Wrong with Rationality Review?," 13
    Creighton L. Rev. 487 (1979)
    "The Protective Function of the State in the United States and Europe:
    The Constitutional Question," in G. Nolte (ed.), *European and US
    Constitutionalism* (Cambridge University Press, 2005)
    "The Rule of Law, Legality and the Supremacy of the Constitution", in S.
    Woolman, M. Bishop, and J. Brickhill (eds.), *Constitutional Law of South
    Africa*, 2nd edn. (Cape Town: Juta Law Publishers, looseleaf, 2002)

Miller, A. and Barron, J. "The Supreme Court, the Adversary System, and the Flow of Information to the Justices: A Preliminary Inquiry," 61 *Va. L. Rev.* 1187 (1975)

Miller, B. "Beguiled by Metaphors: The 'Living Tree' and Originalist Constitutional Interpretation in Canada," 22 *Can. J. L. & Jurisprudence* 331(2009)

"Justification and Rights Limitations," in G. Huscroft (ed.), *Expounding the Constitution: Essays in Constitutional Theory* (Cambridge University Press, 2008)

Miller, M. *Eye for an Eye* (Cambridge University Press, 2006)

Miller, R. "Balancing Security and Liberty in Germany," 4 *J. Nat'l Sec. L. & Pol'y* 369 (2010)

"Comparative Law and Germany's Militant Democracy," in R. Miller (ed.), *US National Security, Intelligence and Democracy* (New York: Taylor & Francis, 2008), 229

Mitchell, A. "Proportionality and Remedies in WTO Disputes," 17 *Eur. J. Int'l L.* 985 (2006)

Mize, S. "Resolving Cases of Conflicting Rights under the New Zealand Bill of Rights Act," 22 *New Zealand U. L. Rev.* 50 (2006)

Möller, K. "Balancing and the Structure of Constitutional Rights," 3 *Int'l J. Const. L.* 453 (2007)

"Two Conceptions of Positive Liberty: Towards an Autonomy-Based Theory of Constitutional Rights," 29(4) *OJLS* 757 (2009)

Molot, J. "The Judicial Perspective in the Administrative State: Reconciling Modern Doctrines of Deference with the Judiciary's Structural Role," 53 *Stan. L. Rev.* 1 (2000)

Monaghan, H. "Marbury and the Administrative State," 83 *Colum. L. Rev.* 1 (1983)

"Overbreadth," *Sup. Ct. Rev.* 1 (1981)

Montague, P. "When Rights Conflict," 7 *Legal Theory* 257 (2001)

Moral Soriano, L. "How Proportionate Should Anti-Competitive State Intervention Be?," 28 *Eur. L. Rev.* 112 (2003)

Moran, M. *Rethinking the Reasonable Person: An Egalitarian Reconstruction of the Objective Standard* (Oxford University Press, 2003)

Morsink, J. *The Universal Declaration of Human Rights, Origins, Drafting, and Intent* (Philadelphia: University of Pennsylvania Press, 1999)

Mowbray, A. *The Development of Positive Obligations under the European Convention on Human Rights by the European Court of Human Rights* (Portland, OR: Hart Publishing, 2004)

Mulhall, S. and Swift, A. *Liberals and Communitarians* (Malden, MA: Wiley-Blackwell, 1996)

Mullan, D. "Deference: Is It Useful Outside Canada?," in H. Corder (ed.), *Comparing Administrative Justice Across the Commonwealth* (Cape Town: Juta Law Publishers, 2006)

"The Role for Underlying Constitutional Principles in a Bill of Rights World," *New Zealand U. L. Rev.* 9 (2004)

Mullen, T. "Reflections on Jackson v. Attorney General: Questioning Sovereignty," 27 *Legal Studies* 1 (2007)

Mullender, R. "Theorizing the Third Way: Qualified Consequentialism, the Proportionality Principle, and the New Social Democracy," 27(4) *J. L. & Soc'y* 493 (2000)

Müller, J. "Fundamental Rights in Democracy," 4 *Hum. Rts. L. J.* 131 (1983)
  Grundrechte: Besonderer Teil (Cologne: Carl Heymanns, Verlag, 1985)

Mureinik, E. "A Bridge to Where? Introducing the Interim Bill of Rights," 10 *SAJHR* 31 (1994)

Murphy, W., Fleming, J., and Barber, S. *American Constitutional Interpretation* (Westbury, NY: Foundation Press, 2008)

Murray, P. "Section One of the Canadian Charter of Rights and Freedoms: An Examination at Two Levels of Interpretation," 21 *Ottawa L. Rev.* 631 (1989)

Nagel, R. "Liberals and Balancing," 63 *U. Colo. L. Rev.* 319 (1992)

Nagel, T. "The Limits of Objectivity," in S. M. McMurrin (ed.), *The Tanner Lectures on Human Values* (Salt Lake City, UT: University of Utah Press, 1979)

Navot, S. *The Constitutional Law of Israel* (Alphen aan den Rijn, The Netherlands: Kluwer Law International, 2007)

Navoth, M. "Torture Versus Terror: The Israeli and British Cases," 1 *Isr. J. Foreign Affairs* 69 (2007)

Neuborne, B. "Notes for a Theory of Constrained Balancing in First Amendment Cases: An Essay in Honor of Tom Emerson," 38 *Case W. Res. L. Rev.* 576 (1988)

Neuman, G. "The US Constitutional Conception of the Rule of Law and the Rechtsstaatsprinzip of the Grundgesetz," in U. Battis, P. Kuing, I. Pernice, and A. Randeizhofer (eds.), *Das Grundgesetz im Prozess Europäischer und Globaler Verfassungsentwicklung* (Berlin: Nomos, 2000)

Neumann, M. (ed.), *The Rule of Law: Politicizing Ethics* (Ashgate Publishing, 2002)

Newman, D. "The Limitation of Rights: A Comparative Evolution and Ideology of the Oakes and Sparrow Tests," 62 *Sask. L. Rev.* 543 (1999)

Ngcukaitobi, T. "The Evolution of Standing Rules in South Africa and Their Significance in Promoting Social Justice," 18 *SAJHR* 590 (2002)

Ni Aolain, F. and Gross, O. "A Skeptical View of Deference to the Executive in Times of Crisis," 41 *Isr. L. Rev.* 545 (2008)

Nimmer, M. "The Right to Speak from Times to Time: First Amendment Theory Applied to Libel and Misapplied to Privacy," 56 *Cal. L. Rev.* 935 (1968)

Nolte, G. "General Principles of German and European Administrative Law – A Comparison in Historical Perspective," 57 *Mod. L. Rev.* 191 (1994)

Note, "Less Drastic Means and the First Amendment," 78 *Yale L. J.* 464 (1969)

"Social and Economic Facts," 61 *Harv. L. Rev.* 692 (1948)

"The First Amendment Overbreadth Doctrine," 83 *Harv. L. Rev.* 844 (1970)

"The Void-for-Vagueness Doctrine in the Supreme Court," 109 *U. Pa. L. Rev.* 67 (1960)

Nowak, J. and Rotunda, R. *Constitutional Law,* 8th edn. (Eagan MN: West, 2010)

Nowak, M. *UN Covenant on Civil and Political Rights: CCPR Commentary* (Kehl am Rhein, Germany: Engel, 1993)

Nozick, R. *Anarchy, State and Utopia* (New York: Basic Books, 1974)

Poole, T. "Tilting at Windmills? Truth and Illusion in the Political Constitution," 70 *Mod. L. Rev.* 250 (2007)

O'Neil, J. *Originalism in American Law and Politics: A Constitutional History* (Baltimore, MD: Johns Hopkins University Press, 2007)

Oberdiek, J. "Lost in Moral Space: On the Infringing/Violating Distinction and Its Place in the Theory of Rights," 23 *Law and Philosophy* 325 (2004)

Ogurlu, Y. "A Comparative Study on the Principle of Proportionality in Turkish Administrative Law," *Kamu Hukuku Arşivi, Khuk* 5 (2003)

Oliver, D. *Common Values and the Public–Private Divide* (London: Butterworths, 1999)

Oliver, D. and Fedtke, J. (eds.), *Human Rights and the Private Sphere: A Comparative Study* (Routledge-Cavendish, 2007)

Opsahl, T. "Articles 29 and 30: The Other Side of the Coin," in A. Eide and T. Swinehart (eds.), *The Universal Declaration of Human Rights: A Commentary* (Oxford University Press, 1992)

Orfanoudakis, S. and Kokota, V. "The Application of the Principle of Proportionality in the Case Law of Community and Greek Courts: Similarities and Differences" (Paper presented at the VIIth World Congress of the International Association of Constitutional Law, Athens, June 14, 2007)

Orucu, E. "The Core of Rights and Freedoms: The Limit of Limits," in T. Campbell (ed.), *Human Rights: From Rhetoric to Reality* (New York: Basil Blackwell, 1986)

Osiatynski, W. *Human Rights and Their Limits* (Cambridge University Press, 2009)

"Rights in New Constitutions of East Central Europe," 26 *Colum. Hum. Rts. L. Rev.* 111 (1994)

Palmer, E. *Judicial Review, Socio-Economic Rights and the Human Rights Act* (Portland, OR: Hart Publishing, 2007)

Patapan, H. *Judging Democracy: The New Politics of the High Court of Australia* (Cambridge University Press, 2001)

"Politics of Interpretation," 22 *Syd. L. Rev.* 247 (2000)

"The Dead Hands of the Founders?: Original Intent and the Constitutional Protection of Rights and Freedoms in Australia," 25 *Fed. L. Rev.* 211 (1997)

Patrick, G. "Persuasive Authority," 32 *McGill L. J.* 261 (1987)

Patterson, E. *Jurisprudence: Men and Ideas of the Law* (New York: Foundation Press, 1953)

Paust, J. "The Absolute Prohibition of Torture and Necessary and Appropriate Sanctions," 43. *Valp. L. Rev.* 1535 (2009)

Pavlakos, G. "Two Concepts of Objectivity," in G. Pavlakos (ed.), *Law, Rights, and Discourse: The Legal Philosophy of Robert Alexy* (Portland, OR: Hart Publishing, 2007)

Peck, S. "An Analytical Framework for the Application of the Canadian Charter of Rights and Freedoms," 25 *Osgoode Hall L. J.* 1 (1987)

Peczenik, A. "Coherence, Truth and Rightness in the Law," in P. J. Nerhot (ed.), *Law, Interpretation and Reality: Essays in Epistemology, Hermeneutics and Jurisprudence* (Dordrecht: Kluwer Academic Publishers, 1990)

Perales, K. "It Works Fine in Europe, So Why Not Here? Comparative Law and Constitutional Federalism," 23 *Vt. L. Rev.* 885 (1999)

Perelman, C. *Le Problème des Lacunes en Droit* (Paris: Librairie Générale de Droit et de Jurisprudence, 1968)

Perry, M. "Protecting Human Rights in a Democracy: What Role for the Courts?," 38 *Wake Forest L. Rev.* 635 (2003)

  "The Legitimacy of Particular Conceptions of Constitutional Interpretation," 77 *Va. L. Rev.* 669 (1991)

Petersen, H. and Zahle, H. *Legal Polycentricity: Consequences of Pluralism in Law* (Sudbury, MA: Dartmouth Publishing Group, 1995)

Philippe, X. *Le Contrôle de Proportionnalité dans les Jurisprudences Constitutionnelle et Administrative Francaises* (Aix-en-Provence: Presses Universitaires d'Aix-Marseille, 1990)

Phipson, S. *Phipson on Evidence*, 15th edn. (2000)

Phun Lee, H. "Proportionality in Australian Constitutional Adjudication," in *Future Directions in Australian Constitutional Law* (Sydney: Federation Press, 1994)

Pierce, R. 'Chevron and Its Aftermath: Judicial Review of Agency Interpretation of Statutory Provisions," 41 *Vand. L. Rev.* 301 (1998)

Pieroth, B. and Schlink, B. *Grundrechte Staatsrecht II* (Heidelberg: C. F. Müller Verlag, 2006)

Pikis, G. *Constitutionalism – Human Rights – Separation of Powers: The Cyprus Precedent* (Leiden: Brill, 2006)

Pildes, R. "Avoiding Balancing: The Role of Exclusionary Reasons in Constitutional Law," 45 *Hastings L. J.* 711 (1994)

  "Dworkin's Two Conceptions of Rights," 29 *J. Legal Studies* 309 (2000)

  "Why Rights Are Not Trumps: Social Meanings, Expressive Harms and Constitutionalism," 27 *J. Legal Studies* 725 (1998)

Pinto, M. "What Are Offences to Feelings Really About? A New Regulative Principle for the Multicultural Era," 30 *OJLS* 695 (2010)

Plowden, P. and Kerrigan, K. *Advocacy and Human Rights: Using the Convention in Courts and Tribunals* (London: Routledge Cavendish, 2002)

Poole, T. "Proportionality in Perspective," *New Zealand L. Rev.* 369 (2010)

"Questioning Common Law Constitutionalism," 25 *Legal Studies* 142 (2005)

"Recent Developments on the 'War on Terrorism' in Canada," 7 *Hum. Rts. L. Rev.* 633 (2007)

Popkin, W. "Foreword: Nonjudicial Statutory Interpretation," 66 *Chi.-Kent L. Rev.* 301 (1990)

Porat, I. "The Dual Model of Balancing: A Model for the Proper Scope of Balancing in Constitutional Law," 27 *Cardozo L. Rev.* 1393 (2006)

"Why All Attempts to Make Judicial Review Balancing Principled Fail" (Paper presented at the VIIth World Congress of the International Association of Constitutional Law, Athens, June 14, 2007)

Posner, R. *Law, Pragmatism, and Democracy* (Cambridge, MA: Harvard University Press, 2003)

"The Uncertain Protection of Privacy by the Supreme Court," *Sup. Ct. Rev.* 173 (1979)

Post, R. *Constitutional Domains: Democracy, Community, Management* (Cambridge, MA: Harvard University Press, 1995)

"Democracy, Popular Sovereignty and Judicial Review," 86 *Cal. L. Rev.* 429 (1998)

Post, R. and Siegel, R. "Roe Rage: Democratic Constitutionalism and Backlash," 42 *Harvard Civil Rights–Civil Liberies Law Review* 373 (2007)

Pound, R. "A Survey of Social Interests," 57 *Harv. L. Rev.* 1 (1943)

Powell, J. "The Original Understanding of Original Intent," 98 *Harv. L. Rev.* 885 (1985)

Procházka, R. *Mission Accomplished: On Founding Constitutional Adjudication in Central Europe* (Budapest: Central European University Press, 2002)

Pulido, C. *El Principio de Proporcionalidad y los Derechos Fundamentales* (Madrid: Centro de Estudios Políticos y Constitucionales, 2007)

"On Alexy's Weight Formula," in A. J. Menéndez and E. O. Eriksen (eds.), *Arguing Fundamental Rights* (Dordrecht: Springer, 2006)

"The Rationality of Balancing," 92 *Archiv für Rechts- und Sozial Philosophie* 195 (2007)

Pushaw, R. "Defending Deference: A Response to Professors Epstein and Wells," 69 *Mo. L. Rev.* 959 (2004)

Quint, P. "The Most Extraordinarily Powerful Court of Law the World Has Ever Known – Judicial Review in the United States and Germany," 65 *Md. L. Rev.* 152 (2006)

Quirk, P. "Australian Looks at German Proportionality," 1 *U. Notre Dame Austl. L. Rev.* 39 (1999)

Rabello, A. and Sercevic, P. (eds.), *Freedom of Contracts and Constitutional Law* (Hebrew University of Jerusalem, 1998)

Rakove, J. *Original Meanings: Politics and Ideas in the Making of the Constitution* (New York: Vintage Books, 1996)

Rasson, A. and Ryckeboer, R. "Le Principe de Proportionnalité dans la Jurisprudence de la Cour Constitutionnelle de Belgique," CDL-JU(2007)024

Rautenbach, I. M. *General Provisions of the South African Bill of Rights* (Durban: Butterworths, 1995)

Rautenbach, I. and Malherbe, E. *Constitutional Law*, 4th edn. (Durban: Butterworths, 2004)

Rawls, J. *A Theory of Justice* (Cambridge, MA: Belknap Press of Harvard University Press, 1999)

Political Liberalism (New York: Columbia University Press, 1993)

Raz, J. *Engaging Reason: On the Theory of Value and Action* (Oxford University Press, 1999)

Practical Reasons and Norms, 2nd edn. (Oxford University Press, 1999)

"Rights and Politics," 71 *Ind. L. J.* 27 (1995)

The Authority of Law: Essays on Law and Morality (Oxford: Clarendon Press, 1979)

The Morality of Freedom (Oxford: Clarendon Press, 1986)

"The Relevance of Coherence," 72 *Boston University L. Rev.* 273 (1992)

Régimbald, G. "Correctness, Reasonableness, and Proportionality: A New Standard of Judicial Review," 31 *Man. L. J.* 239 (2005)

Rehnquist, W. "The Notion of a Living Constitution," 54 *Tex. L. Rev.* 693 (1976)

Reinhardt, S. "Weakening the Bill of Rights: A Victory for Terrorism," 106 *Mich. L. Rev.* 963 (2008)

Reis Freire, A. "Evolution of Constitutional Interpretation in Brazil and the Employment of Balancing 'Method' by Brazilian Supreme Court in Judicial Review" (Paper presented at the VIIth World Congress of the International Association of Constitutional Law, Athens, June 14, 2007)

Reis Novais, J. *Os Princípios Constitucionais Estruturantes da República Portuguesa* (Coimbra, Portugal: Coimbra Editora, 2004)

Richards, D. *Toleration and the Constitution* (Oxford University Press, 1989)

Rishworth, P. "The Birth and Rebirth of the Bill of Rights," in G. Huscroft and P. Rishworth (eds.), *Rights and Freedoms: The New Zealand Bill of Rights Act 1990 and the Human Rights Act 1993* (Wellington: Brooker's, 1995)

Rishworth, P., Huscropft, G., Optican, S., and Mahoney, R. *The New Zealand Bill of Rights* (Oxford University Press, 2003)

Rivers, J. "A Theory of Constitutional Rights and the British Constitution," in R. Alexy (ed.), *A Theory of Constitutional Rights* (J. Rivers trans., Oxford University Press, 2002 [1986])

"Proportionality and Discretion in International and European Law," in N. Tsagourias (ed.), *Transnational Constitutionalism: International and European Perspectives* (Cambridge University Press, 2007)

"Proportionality and Variable Intensity of Review," 65 *Cambridge L. J.* 174 (2006)

"Proportionality, Discretion and the Second Law of Balancing," in G. Pavlakos (ed.), *Law, Rights, and Discourse: The Legal Philosophy of Robert Alexy* (Portland, OR: Hart Publishing, 2007)

Roach, K. "Dialogue or Defiance: Legislative Reversals of Supreme Court Decisions in Canada and the United States," 4 *Int'l J. Const. L.* 347 (2006)

"Must We Trade Rights for Security? The Choice Between Smart, Harsh, or Proportionate Security Strategies in Canada and Britain," 27 *Cardozo L. Rev.* 2151 (2006)

The Supreme Court on Trial: Judicial Activism or Democratic Dialogue (Toronto: Irwin Law, 2001)

Robinson, G. and Robinson, T. "Korematsu and Beyond: Japanese Americans and the Origin of Strict Scrutiny," 68 *L. and Contemp. Probs.* 29 (2005)

Rosenfeld, M. "Hate Speech in Constitutional Jurisprudence: A Comparative Analysis," 24 *Cardozo L. Rev.* 1532 (2003)

"Judicial Balancing in Times of Stress: Comparing the American, British, and Israeli Approaches to the War on Terror," 27 *Cardozo L. Rev.* 2079 (2006)

Ross, D. *The Right and the Good* (Oxford University Press, 1930)

Ross, J. "Limitations on Human Rights in International Law: Their Relevance to the Canadian Charter of Rights and Freedoms," 6 *Hum. Rts. Q.* 180 (1984)

Rothstein, M. "Justifying Breaches of Charter Rights and Freedoms," 27 *Man. L. J.* 171 (2000)

Roux, T. "Democracy," in S. Woolman, M. Bishop, and J. Brickhill (eds.), *Constitutional Law of South Africa*, 2nd edn. (Cape Town: Juta Law Publishers, looseleaf, 2002–)

Roza, P. "Rights and Their Limits: The Constitution for Europe in International and Comparative Legal Perspective," 23 *Berkeley J. Int'l L.* 223 (2005)

Rubenfeld, J. "Affirmative Action," 107 *Yale L. J.* 427 (1997)

Rubin, P. "Reconnecting Doctrine and Purpose: A Comprehensive Approach to Strict Scrutiny after Adarand and Shaw," 149 *U. Pa. L. Rev.* 1 (2001)

Russell, P. "Standing Up for Notwithstanding," 29 *Alta. L. Rev.* 293 (1991)

Ryssdall, R. "Opinion: The Coming Age of the European Convention on Human Rights," *Eur. Hum. Rts. L. Rev.* 18 (1966)

Saban, I. "Offensiveness Analyzed: Lessons for Comparative Analysis of Free Speech Doctrines," 2 *Journal of International and Comparative Law at Chicago-Kent* 60 (2002)

Sacco, R. "Legal Formants: A Dynamic Approach to Comparative Law (Installment II of II)," 39 *Am. J. Comp. L.* 343 (1991)

Sachs, M. (ed.), *GG Grundgesetz Kommentar* (Munich: C. H. Beck, 2007)

GG *Verfassungsrecht II Grundrechte* (Berlin: Springer, 2003)

Sadurski, W. "'Reasonableness' and Value Pluralism in Law and Politics," in G. Bongiovanni, G. Sartor, and C. Valentini (eds.), *Reasonableness and Law* (Dordrecht: Springer, 2009)

  Rights before Courts: A Study of Constitutional Courts in Postcommunist States of Central and Eastern Europe (Dordrecht: Springer, 2008)

Sager, L. *Justice in Plainclothes: A Theory of American Constitutional Practice* (New Haven, CT: Yale University Press, 2006)

Sajó, A. (ed.), *Militant Democracy* (Utrecht, The Netherlands: Eleven International Publishing, 2004)

  Western Rights? Post-Communist Application (Kluwer Law International, 1996)

Sajó, A. and Uitz, R. (eds.), *The Constitution in Private Relations: Expanding Constitutionalism* (Utrecht, The Netherlands: Eleven International Publishing, 2005)

Sakellaridou, M. "La Généalogie de La Proportionnalité" (Paper presented at the VIIth World Congress of the International Association of Constitutional Law, Athens, June 14, 2007)

Sales, P. and Hooper, B. "Proportionality and the Form of Law," 119 *L. Q. Rev.* 426 (2003)

Sampford, C. and Preston, K. (eds.), *Interpreting Constitutions: Theories, Principles and Instruction* (Annandale, Australia: Federation Press, 1996)

Sandalow, T. "Constitutional Interpretation," 79 *Mich. L. Rev.* 1033 (1981)

Sandel, M. *Democracy's Discontent: America in Search of a Public Philosophy* (Cambridge, MA: Belknap Press of Harvard University Press, 1996)

  (ed.), *Liberalism and Its Critics* (New York University Press, 1984)

Sandulli, A. *La Proporzionalita Dell'azione Administrativa* (Padova, Italy: Cedam, 1988)

Saul, B. "Australian Administrative Law: The Human Rights Dimension," in M. Groves and H. Phun Lee (eds.), *Australian Administrative Law: Fundamentals, Principles and Doctrines* (Cambridge University Press, 2007)

Scalia, A. *A Matter of Interpretation: Federal Courts and the Law* (Princeton University Press, 1997)

  "Judicial Deference to Administrative Interpretations of Law," *Duke L. J.* 511 (1989)

  "Modernity and the Constitution," in E. Smith (ed.), *Constitutional Justice Under Old Constitutions* (The Hague: Kluwer Law International, 1995)

  "Originalism: The Lesser Evil," 57 *U. Chi. L. Rev.* 849 (1989)

  "The Rule of Law as a Law of Rules," 56 *U. Chi. L. Rev.* 1175 (1989)

Schachter, O. "Implementing Limitations on the Use of Force: The Doctrine of Proportionality and Necessity," 86 *Am. Soc'y Int'l L. Proc.* 39 (1992)

Schapiro, R. "Judicial Deference and Interpretive Coordinacy in State and Federal Constitutional Law," 85 *Cornell L. Rev.* 656 (2000)

Schauer, F. "A Comment on the Structure of Rights," 27 *Ga. L. Rev.* 415 (1993)

"An Essay on Constitutional Language," 29 *UCLA L. Rev.* 797 (1981)

"Balancing Subsumption, and the Constraining Role of Legal Text," in M. Klatt (ed.), *Rights, Law, and Morality Themes from the Legal Philosophy of Robert Alexy* (Oxford University Press, forthcoming, 2011)

"Categories and the First Amendment: A Play in Three Acts," 34 *Vand. L. Rev.* 265 (1981)

"Commensurability and Its Constitutional Consequences," 45 *Hastings L. J.* 785 (1994)

"Deferring," 103 *Mich. L. Rev.* 1567 (2005)

"Expression and Its Consequences," 57 *U. Toronto L. J.* 705 (2007)

Free Speech: A Philosophical Enquiry (Cambridge University Press, 1982)

"Freedom of Expression Adjudication in Europe and the United States: A Case Study in Comparative Constitutional Architecture," in G. Nolte (ed.), *European and US Constitutionalism* (Cambridge University Press, 2005)

Playing by the Rules: A Philosophical Examination of Rule-Based Decision-Making in Law and in Life (Oxford University Press, 1991)

"Prescriptions in Three Dimensions," 82 *Iowa L. Rev.* 911 (1997)

"The Boundaries of the First Amendment: A Preliminary Exploration of Constitutional Silence," 117 *Harv. L. Rev.* 1765 (2004)

"The Exceptional First Amendment," in M. Ignatieff (ed.), *American Exceptionalism and Human Rights* (Princeton University Press, 1980)

Schiller, R. "The Era of Deference: Courts, Expertise, and the Emergence of New Deal Administrative Law," 106 *Mich. L. Rev.* 399 (2007)

Schlink, B. "Der Grundsatz der Verhältnismäßigkeit," in P. Badura and H. Dreier (eds.), *Festschrift 50 Jahre Bundesverfassungsgericht*, vol. II (Tübingen: Mohr Siebeck, 2001)

Schmitt, C. *Constitutional Theory* (Jeffrey Seifzer trans., Duke University Press, 2008)

Schwartz, H. *The Struggle for Constitutional Justice in Post-Communist Europe* (University of Chicago Press, 2002)

Schwarze, J. *European Administrative Law* (London: Sweet & Maxwell, 1992)

Searle, J. "Prima Facie Obligations," in J. Raz (ed.), *Practical Reasoning* (Oxford University Press, 1978)

Sedler, R. "An Essay on Freedom of Speech: The United States Versus the Rest of the World," *Michigan State L. Rev.* 377 (2006)

Sedley, S. "Human Rights – A Twenty-First Century Agenda," *PL* 373 (1995)

"The Last 10 Years' Development of English Public Law," 12 *Australian J. of Adm. L.* 9 (2004)

Seedford, S. and Sibanda, S. "Separation of Powers," in S. Woolman, M. Bishop, and J. Brickhill (eds.), *Constitutional Law of South Africa*, 2nd edn. (Cape Town: Juta Law Publishers, looseleaf, 2002–)

Segal, Z. "Disproportionality as a Cause of Action in Israeli Administrative Action," 39 *HaPraklit* 507 (1990)

Sen, A. "Elements of a Theory of Human Rights Export," 32(4) *Philosophy and Public Affairs* 315 (2004)

Shaman, J. *Constitutional Interpretation: Illusion and Reality* (Westport, CT: Greenwood Press, 2001)

"Cracks in the Structure: The Coming Breakdown of the Levels of Scrutiny," 45 *Ohio St. L. J.* 161 (1984)

"Constitutional Interpretation: Illusion and Reality," 41 *Wayne L. Rev.* 135 (1995)

Shapiro, D. "In Defense of Judicial Candor," 100 *Harv. L. Rev.* 731 (1987)

Shapiro, I. (ed.), *The Rule of Law: Nomos XXXVI* (New York University Press, 1995)

Shapiro, M. "Judges as Liars," 17 *Harv. J. L. & Pub. Pol'y* 155 (1994)

Shapiro, M. and Stone Sweet, A. *On Law, Politics and Judicialization* (Oxford University Press, 2002)

Shelton, D. *Regional Protection of Human Rights* (Oxford University Press, 2008)

Sherry, S. "The Founders' Unwritten Constitution," 54 *U. Chi. L. Rev.* 1127 (1994)

Shiffrin, S. "Liberalism, Radicalism, and Legal Scholarship," 30 *UCLA L. Rev.* 1103 (1982)

The First Amendment, Democracy and Romance (Cambridge, MA: Harvard University Press, 1990)

Shue, H. *Basic Rights: Subsistence, Affluence and US Foreign Policy*, 2nd edn. (Princeton University Press, 1996)

Siebrasse, N. "The Oakes Test: An Old Ghost Impeding Bold New Initiatives," 23 *Ottawa L. Rev.* 99 (1991)

Siegel, S. "Origin of the Compelling State Interest Test and Strict Scrutiny," 48 *Am. J. Legal Hist.* 355 (2006)

Sieghart, P. *The International Law of Human Rights* (Oxford University Press, 1983)

Singer, N. and Singer, J. (eds.), *Sutherland Statutes and Statutory Construction* (Thomson West, 2007)

Singer, R. "Proportionate Thoughts about Proportionality," 8 *Ohio St. J. Crim. L.* 217 (2010)

Singh, M. *German Administrative Law in Common Law Perspective*, 2nd edn. (Berlin: Springer, 2001)

Sinnott-Armstrong, W. "Two Ways to Derive Implied Constitutional Rights," in T. D. Campbell and J. Denys Goldsworthy (eds.), *Legal Interpretation in Democratic States* (Aldershot: Ashgate Publishing, 2002)

Sitaraman, G. "The Use and Abuse of Foreign Law in Constitutional Interpretation," 32 *Harv. J. L. & Pub. Pol'y* 653 (2009)

Slattery, B. "Canadian Charter of Rights and Freedoms – Override Clauses under Art. 33 – Whether Subject to Judicial Review under Art. 1," 61 *Can. Bar Rev.* 391 (1983)

Slaughter, A. "A Typology of Transjudicial Communication," 29 *U. Rich. L. Rev.* 99 (1994)

Smend, R. *Verfassung und Verfassungsrecht* (Munich: Duncker & Humblot, 1928)

Smith, S. "That Old-Time Originalism" (San Diego Legal Studies Paper No. 08-028)

Smyth, R. "The Principle of Proportionality Ten Years after GCHQ," 2 *Austl. J. Admin. Law* 189 (1995)

Solove, D. "The Darkest Domain: Deference, Judicial Review, and the Bill of Rights," 84 *Iowa L. Rev.* 941 (1999)

Solyom, L. and Brunner, G. *Constitutional Judiciary in a New Democracy: The Hungarian Constitutional Court* (University of Michigan Press, 2000)

Soper, P. *The Ethics of Deference: Learning from Law's Morals* (Cambridge University Press, 2002)

Starck, C. "Constitutional Definition and Protection of Rights and Freedoms," in C. Starck (ed.), *Rights, Institutions and Impact of International Law According to the German Basic Law: The Contributions of the Federal Republic of Germany to the Second World Congress of the International Association of Constitutional Law* (Baden-Baden: Nomos Verlagsgesellschaft, 1987)

"Constitutional Interpretation", in *Studies in German Constitutionalism: The German Contributions to the Fourth World Congress of the International Association of Constitutional Law* (Nomos, 1995), 45

Stavropoulos, N. *Objectivity in Law* (Oxford: Clarendon Press, 1996)

Stern, K. "Zur Entstehung und Ableitung des Übermaßverbots," in P. Badura and R. Scholz (eds.), *Wege und Verfahren des Verfassungslebens: Festschrift fur Peter Lerche zum 65 Geburstag* (Munich: C. H. Beck, 1993)

Steyn, J. "Democracy, the Rule of Law and the Role of Judges," *Eur. Hum. Rts. L. Rev.* 243 (2006)

Steyn, L. "Deference: A Tangled Story," *PL* 346 (2005)

Strong, J. (ed.), *McCormick on Evidence*, 6th edn. (West Publishing Company, 2006)

Stone Sweet, A. *Governing with Judges: Constitutional Politics in Europe* (Oxford University Press, 2000)

"Why Europe Rejected American Judicial Review and Why It May Not Matter," 101 *Mich. L. Rev.* 2744 (2003)

Stone, A. "Rights, Personal Rights and Freedoms: The Nature of the Freedom of Political Communication," 25 *Melb. U. L. Rev.* 374 (2001)

"The Limits of Constitutional Text and Structure: Standards of Review and the Freedom of Political Communication," 23 *Melb. U. L. Rev.* 668 (1999)

"The Limits of Constitutional Text and Structure Revisited," 28 *Univ. of New South Wales L. J.* 50 (2005)

Stone, J. *Legal System and Lawyers' Reasoning* (Stanford University Press, 1968)

Province and Function of Law: Law as Logic, Justice and Social Control, A Study in Jurisprudence (Sydney, Australia Assoc. General Publication Pty Ltd., 1961)

Social Dimensions of Law and Justice (London: Stevens, 1966)

Stone Sweet, A. and Mathews, J. "All Things in Proportion? American Rights Doctrine and the Problem of Balancing," 60 *Emory L. J.* (forthcoming, 2011)

"Proportionality Balancing and Global Constitutionalism," 47 *Colum. J. Transnat'l L.* 72 (2008)

Struve, G. "The Less-Restrictive-Alternative Principle and Economic Due Process," 80 *Harv. L. Rev.* 1463 (1967)

Sullivan, E. and Frase, R. *Proportionality Principles in American Law: Controlling Excessive Government Actions* (Oxford University Press, 2009)

Sullivan, K. "Post-Liberal Judging: The Roles of Categorization and Balancing," 63 *U. Colo. L. Rev.* 293 (1992)

Sunstein, C. *Designing Democracy: What Constitutions Do* (Oxford University Press, 2002)

"Incommensurability and Valuation in Law," 92 *Mich. L. Rev.* 779 (1994)

"Law and Administration after Chevron," 90 *Colum. L. Rev.* 2071 (1990)

The Second Bill of Rights: FDR's Unfinished Revolution and Why We Need It More Than Ever (New York: Basic Books, 2004)

Supperston, M. and Coppel, J. "Judicial Review after the Human Rights Act," 3 *Eur. Hum. Rts. L. Rev.* 301 (1999)

Svensson-McCarthy, A. L. *The International Law of Human Rights and States of Exception* (The Hague: Kluwer Law International, 1998)

Tadros, V. and Tierney, S. "The Presumption of Innocence and the Human Rights Act," 67 *Mod. L. Rev.* 402 (2004)

Taggart, M. "Administrative Law," *New Zealand L. Rev.* 75 (2006)

"Proportionality, Deference, Wednesbury," *New Zealand L. Rev.* 423 (2008)

Tamanaha, B. *On the Rule of Law: History, Politics, Theory* (Cambridge University Press, 2004)

Tate, C. and Vallinder, T. (eds.), *The Global Expansion of Judicial Power* (New York University Press, 1995)

Teitel, R. *Transitional Justice* (Oxford University Press, 2000)

Terry, J. "Section 1: Controlling the Oakes Analysis," *Law Society of Upper Canada Special Lectures* (2001), 479

Thiel, M. (ed.), *The "Militant Democracy" Principle in Modern Democracies* (Ashgate Publishing, 2009)

Thomas, E. *The Judicial Process: Realism, Pragmatism, Practical Reasoning and Principles* (Cambridge University Press, 2005)

Thomas, R. *Legitimate Expectations and Proportionality in Administrative Law* (Portland, OR: Hart Publishing, 2000)

Thompson, R. "Community Law and the Limits of Deference," *Eur. Hum. Rts. L. Rev.* 24 (2005)

Thomson, J. *The Realm of Rights* (Cambridge, MA: Harvard University Press, 1990)

"The Trolley Problem," 94 *Yale L. J.* 1395 (1985)

Tomkins, A. "The Rule of Law in Blair's Britain," 26 *U. Queensland L. J.* 255 (2007)

Torres Pérez, A. *Conflicts of Rights in the European Union: A Theory of Supranational Adjudication* (Oxford University Press, 2009)

Trakman, L., Cole-Hamilton, W., and Gatien, S. "R. v. Oakes 1986–1997: Back to the Drawing Board," 36 *Osgoode Hall L. J.* 83 (1998)

Tremblay, L. "General Legitimacy of Judicial Review and the Fundamental Basis of Constitutional Law," 23 *OJLS* 525 (2003)

"Normative Foundation of the Proportionality Principle in Constitutional Theory" (French) (EUI Working Papers LAW 2009/04)

"The Legitimacy of Judicial Review: The Limits of Dialogue Between Courts and Legislatures," 3 *I. Con.* 617 (2005)

Tremblay, L. and Webber, G. *The Limitation of Charter Rights: Critical Essays on R. v. Oakes* (Montreal: Thémis, 2009)

Tribe, L. *American Constitutional Law* 2nd edn. (Mineola, NY: Foundation Press, 1988)

American Constitutional Law, 3rd edn. (New York: Foundation Press, 2000)

"The Abortion Funding Conundrum: Inalienable Rights, Affirmative Duties, and the Dilemma of Dependence," 99 *Harv. L. Rev.* 330 (1985)

The Invisible Constitution (Oxford University Press, 2008)

Tribe, L. and Dorf, M. "Levels of Generality in the Definition of Rights," 57 *U. Chi. L. Rev.* 1057 (1990)

On Reading the Constitution (Cambridge, MA: Harvard University Press, 1991)

Tridimas, T. "Proportionality in Community Law: Searching for the Appropriate Standard of Scrutiny," in E. Ellis (ed.), *The Principle of Proportionality in the Laws of Europe* (Portland, OR: Hart Publishing, 1999)

The General Principles of EC Law (Oxford University Press, 1999)

"The Principle of Proportionality in Community Law: From the Rule of Law to Market Integration," 31 *Irish Jurist* 83 (1996)

Tsakyrakis, S. "Proportionality: An Assault on Human Rights?," 7(3) *I. Con.* 468 (2009)

"Proportionality: An Assault on Human Rights?: A Rejoinder to Madhav Khosla," 8(2) *I. Con.* 307 (2010)

Tushnet, M. "Alternative Forms of Judicial Review," 101 *Mich. L. Rev.* 2781 (2003)

"An Essay on Rights," 62 *Tex. L. Rev.* 1363 (1984)

"Anti-Formalism in Recent Constitutional Theory," 83 *Mich. L. Rev.* 1502 (1985)

"Some Reflections on Method in Comparative Constitutional Law," in S. Choudhry (ed.), *The Migration of Constitutional Ideas* (Cambridge University Press, 2006)

Taking the Constitution Away from the Courts (Princeton University Press, 2000)

"The Possibilities of Comparative Constitutional Law," 108 *Yale L. J.* 1225 (1999)

Weak Courts, Strong Rights: Judicial Review and Social Welfare Rights in Comparative Constitutional Law (Princeton University Press, 2008)

Van der Schyff, G. "Cutting to the Core of Conflicting Rights: The Question of Inalienable Cores in Comparative Perspectives," in E. Brems (ed.), *Conflicts Between Fundamental Rights* (Mortsel, Belgium: Intersentia, 2008)

Judicial Review of Legislation: A Comparative Study of the United Kingdom, The Netherlands and South Africa (Dordrecht: Springer, 2010)

Limitation of Rights: A Study of the European Convention and the South African Bill of Rights (Nijmegen, The Netherlands: Wolf Legal Publishers, 2005)

Van Dijk, P., Van Hoof, F., Van Rijn, A., and Zwaak, L. (eds.), *Theory and Practice of the European Convention on Human Rights*, 4th edn. (Intersentia Publishing, 2006)

Van Gerven, W. "The Effect of Proportionality on the Actions of Member States of the European Community: National Viewpoints from Continental Europe," in E. Ellis (ed.), *The Principle of Proportionality in the Laws of Europe* (Portland, OR: Hart Publishing, 1999)

Varuhas, J. "Keeping Things in Proportion: The Judiciary, Executive Action and Human Rights," 22 *New Zealand U. L. Rev.* 300 (2006)

"Powerco v. Commerce Commission: Developing Trends of Proportionality in New Zealand Administrative Law," 4 *NZJPIL* 339 (2006)

Veel, P. "Incommensurability, Proportionality, and Rational Legal Decision-Making," 4 *Law & Ethics Hum. Rts.* 176 (2010)

Verkuil, P. "The American Constitutional Tradition of Shared and Separated Powers: Separation of Powers, the Rule of Law and the Idea of Independence," 30 *Wm. and Mary L. Rev.* 301 (1989)

Vermeule, A. *Judging under Uncertainty* (Cambridge, MA: Harvard University Press, 2006)

"Saving Constructions," 85 *Geo. L. J.* 1945 (1997)

Vile, J. R. *Contemporary Questions Surrounding the Constitutional Amending Process* (Santa Barbara, CA: Praeger Publishers, 1993)

Villalta Puig, G. "Abridged Proportionality in Australian Constitutional Review: A Doctrinal Critique of the Cole v. Whitfield Saving Test for Section 92 of the Australian Constitution" (Paper presented at the VIIth World Congress of the International Association of Constitutional Law, Athens, June 14, 2007)

Vining, J. "Authority and Responsibility: The Jurisprudence of Deference," 43 *Admin. L. Rev.* 135 (1991)

Volokh, E. "Freedom of Speech, Permissible Tailoring and Transcending Strict Scrutiny," 144 *U. Pa. L. Rev.* 2417 (1996)

Von Elbe, J. "The Evolution of the Concept of the Just War in International Law," 33 *Am. J. Int'l L.* 665 (1939)

Von Overbeck, A. "Some Observations on the Role of the Judge under the Swiss Civil Code," 37 *La. L. Rev.* 681 (1977)

Wacks, R. (ed.), *The New Legal Order in Hong Kong* (Hong Kong University Press, 1999)

Waldron, J. "Fake Incommensurability: A Response to Professor Schauer," 45 *Hastings L. J.* 813 (1994)

"Foreign Law and the Modern Ius Gentium," 119 *Harv. L. Rev.* 129 (2005)

"Introduction," in J. Waldron (ed.), *Theories of Rights* (Oxford University Press, 1984)

Law and Disagreement (Oxford: Clarendon Press, 1999)

"Pildes on Dworkin's Theory of Rights," 29 *J. Legal Studies* 301 (2000)

"Some Models of Dialogue between Judges and Legislators," 23 *Sup. Ct. L. Rev.* (2nd) 7 (2004)

"The Concept and the Rule of Law," 43 *Ga. L. Rev.* 1 (2008)

"The Core of the Case Against Judicial Review," 115 *Yale L. J.* 1346 (2006)

The Dignity of Legislation (Cambridge University Press, 1999)

"Vagueness in Law and Language: Some Philosophical Issues," 82 *Calif. L. Rev.* 509 (1994)

Walmen, A. "Judicial Review in Review: A Four-Part Defense of Legal Constitutionalism: A Review Essay on Political Constitutionalism," 7(2) *Int'l J. Const. L.* 329 (2009)

Walters, M. D. "The Common Law Constitution in Canada: Return of Lex Non Scripta as Fundamental Law," 51 *U. Toronto L. J.* 91 (2001)

"Written Constitutions and Unwritten Constitutionalism," in G. Huscroft (ed.), *Expounding the Constitution: Essays in Constitutional Theory* (Cambridge University Press, 2008)

Walton, L. "Making Sense of Canadian Constitutional Interpretation," 12 *National Journal of Constitutional Law* 315 (2001)

Waluchow, W. *A Common Law Theory of Judicial Review: The Living Tree* (Cambridge University Press, 2007)

Walzer, M. *On Toleration* (New Haven, CT: Yale University Press, 1997)

Watson, A. *Legal Transplants: An Approach to Comparative Law*, 2nd edn. (Athens, GA: University of Georgia Press, 1993)

Webber, G. "The Cult of Constitutional Rights Reasoning" (Paper presented at the VIIth World Congress of the International Association of Constitutional Law, Athens, June 14, 2007)

   The Negotiable Constitution: On the Limitation of Rights (Cambridge University Press, 2009

Webber, J. "Evidence in Charter Interpretation: A Comment on BC Teachers' Federation v. AG BC," 23 *Carswell Practice Cases* (2d) 245 (1988)

Weiler J. and Lockhart, N. "'Taking Rights Seriously': The European Court and Its Fundamental Rights Jurisprudence – Part 1," 32 *Common Market L. Rev.* 51, 81 (1995)

Weiler, P. C. "Rights and Judges in a Democracy: A New Canadian Version," 18 *U. Mich. J. L. Reform* 51 (1984)

Weinrib, E. "Corrective Justice," 77 *Iowa L. Rev.* 403 (1992)

Weinrib, L. "Canada's Charter of Rights: Paradigm Lost?," 6 *Review of Constitutional Studies* 119 (2002)

   "Constitutional Concepts and Constitutional Comparativism," in V. Jackson and M. Tushnet (eds.), *Defining the Field of Comparative Constitutional Law* (Westport, CT: Praeger, 2002)

   "Learning to Live with the Override," 36 *McGill L. J.* 541 (1990)

   "The Charter's First Twenty Years: Assessing the Impact and Anticipating the Future" (Paper presented at the 2002 Isaac Pitblado Lectures, November 22 and 23, 2002)

   "The Postwar Paradigm and American Exceptionalism," in S. Choudhry (ed.), *The Migration of Constitutional Ideas* (Cambridge University Press, 2006)

   "The Supreme Court of Canada and Section One of the Charter," 10 *Sup. Ct. L. Rev.* 469 (1988)

   "The Supreme Court of Canada in the Age of Rights: Constitutional Democracy, the Role of Law and Fundamental Rights under Canada's Constitution," 80 *Can. Bar Rev.* 699 (2001)

Weintal, S. "'Eternal Provisions' in the Constitution: The Strict Normative Standard for Establishing New Constitutional Order" (unpublished PhD dissertation, Hebrew University of Jerusalem, 2005)

Wellman, C. "On Conflicts Between Rights," 14 *Law and Philosophy* 271 (1995)

Wells, C. "Questioning Deference," 69 *Mo. L. Rev.* 903 (2004)

White, G. E. "Historicizing Judicial Scrutiny," 57 *South Carolina L. Rev.* 1 (2006)

   "The First Amendment Comes of Age: The Emergence of Free Speech in Twentieth-Century America," 95 *Mich. L. Rev.* 299 (1996)

White, R. and Ovey, C. *Jacobs, White and Ovey: The European Convention on Human Rights*, 5th edn. (Oxford University Press, 2010)

Whittington, K. "Extrajudicial Constitutional Interpretation: Three Objections and Responses," 80 *N. C. L. Rev.* 773 (2002)

   Constitutional Interpretation. Textual Meaning, Original Intent, and Judicial Review (Lawrence, KS: University Press of Kansas, 1999)

Wiącek, M. "The Principle of Proportionality in the Jurisprudence of the Polish Constitutional Tribunal," CDL-JU(2007)021

Wicker, C. *The Concepts of Proportionality and State Crimes in International Law* (Frankfurt: Lang Publishing Group, 2006)

Wigmore, J. *Evidence in Trials at Common Law* (Boston: Little Brown & Co., 1981) *Evidence in Trials at Common Law*, vol. 1 (Boston: Little Brown & Co., 1983)

Wildhaber, L. "Limitations on Human Rights in Times of Peace, War and Emergency: A Report on Swiss Law," in A. de Mestral, S. Birks, M. Both *et al.* (eds.), *The Limitation of Human Rights in Comparative Constitutional Law* (Montreal: Les Editions Yvon Blais, 1986)

Williams, G. *Human Rights under the Australian Constitution* (Oxford University Press, 1999)

Wilson, B. "Decision-Making in the Supreme Court," 36 *U. Toronto L. J.* 227 (1986)

Winkler, A. "Fatal in Theory and Strict in Fact: An Empirical Analysis of Strict Scrutiny in the Federal Courts," 59 *Vand. L. Rev.* 793 (2006) "Fundamentally Wrong about Fundamental Rights," 23 *Const. Comment.* 227 (2006)

Winslade, W. "Adjudication and the Balancing Metaphor," in H. Hubien (ed.), *Legal Reasoning* (Brussels: Emile Bruylant, 1971)

Winterton, G. "The Separation of Judicial Power as an Implied Bill of Rights," in G. Lindell (ed.), *Future Directions in Australian Constitutional Law* (Sydney: Federation Press, 1994)

Wolf Bikle, H. "Judicial Determination of Questions of Fact Affecting the Constitutional Validity of Legislative Action," 38 *Harv. L. Rev.* 6 (1925)

Wolfgang Sarlet, I. "Constituição, Proporcionalidade e Direitos Fundamentais," 81 *BFD* 325 (2005)

Wong, G. "Towards the Nutcracker Principle: Reconsidering the Objections to Proportionality," *PL* 92 (2000)

Woolf, H. "Droit Public – English Style," *PL* 57 (1995)

Woolhandler, A. "Rethinking the Judicial Reception of Legislative Facts," 41 *Vand. L. Rev.* 111 (1988)

Woolman, S. "Application," in S. Woolman, M. Bishop, and J. Brickhill (eds.), *Constitutional Law of South Africa*, 2nd edn. (Cape Town: Juta Law Publishers, looseleaf, 2002–) "Metaphors and Mirages: Some Marginalia on Choudhry's The Lochner Era and Comparative Constitutionalism and Ready-Made Constitutional Narratives," 20(2) *SAPL* 281 (2005) "Riding the Push-Me Pull-You: Constructing a Test that Reconciles the Conflicting Interests Which Animate the Limitation Clause," 10 *SAJHR* 60 (1994)

Woolman, S. and Botha, H. "Limitations," in S. Woolman, M. Bishop, and J. Brickhill (eds.), *Constitutional Law of South Africa*, 2nd edn. (Cape Town: Juta Law Publishers, looseleaf, 2002–)

Wyzanski, C. E. "A Trial Judge's Freedom and Responsibility," 65 *Harv. L. Rev.* 1281 (1952)

Xiuli, H. "The Application of the Principle of Proportionality in Tecmed v. Mexico," 6 *Chin. J. Int'l L.* 635 (2007)

Young, A. "Ghaidan v. Godin-Mendoza: Avoiding the Deference Trap," *PL* 23 (2005)

"Hunting Sovereignty: Jackson v. Attorney General," *PL* 187 (2006)

Parliamentary Sovereignty and the Human Rights Act (Portland, OR: Hart Publishing, 2009)

Young, S. "Restricting Basic Law Rights in Hong Kong," 34 *Hong Kong L. J.* 110 (2004)

Yourow, H. *The Margin of Appreciation Doctrine in the Dynamics of European Human Rights Jurisprudence* (Dordrecht: Martinus Nijhoff Publishers, 1996)

Zamir, I. "Israel's Administrative Law as Compared to Germany's Administrative Law," 2 *Mishpat U'Mimshal* [*Law and Government*] 109 (1994)

Ziegler, K. (ed.), *Human Rights and Private Law: Privacy as Autonomy* (Hart Publishing, 2006)

Zines, L. *The High Court and the Constitution*, 5th edn. (Federation Press, 2008)

Zucca, L. *Constitutional Dilemmas: Conflicts of Fundamental Legal Rights in Europe and the USA* (Oxford University Press, 2007)

Zurn, C. "Deliberative Democracy and Constitutional Review," 21 *Law and Philosophy* 467 (2002)

INDEX

abortion law and right to life, 428, 434
absolute rights, 27–32
  as alternative to proportionality,
    493–496
  jurisprudence of, 29–30
  nature of, 27–29
  relativization of, 31
accessibility requirement for
    limitations on constitutional
    rights, 108, 115–116
Ackermann, Lourens, 43, 438, 458
Ackner, Lord, 193
aims and means, determining
    relationship between, 132
Alexy, R.
  on balancing, 6, 11, 364, 378
  on "by law" limitation requirements,
    140
  on conflicts between constitutional
    rights, 84, 235–237
  on deontological concepts and
    proportionality, 471
  human rights theory of, 468
  influence of, 5–6
  on interpretation and
    proportionality, 239
  on limits on limitations, 167
  logical necessity, on proportionality
    viewed as, 240
  on parent and child rights, 52
  on *prima facie* versus definite nature
    of constitutional rights, 38–39,
    40, 41
  proportional crime, on
    constitutional right to commit,
    42

  on public interest considerations,
    534
  on reasonableness, 378
alternatives to proportionality,
    8, 14, 493–527.
    See also categorization-based
    alternatives to proportionality
  absolute rights, 493–496
  dual model, 499–502
  non-categorization based, 493–502
  protection of constitutional right's
    core, 496–498
amendment distinguished from
    limitation of constitutional
    rights, 99–101, 155
American doctrine, 14
Arai-Takahashi, Y., 418
Argentina, proportionality in,
    201–202
Aristotle, 29
Asia, proportionality in, 199
Australia
  democracy, constitutional status of,
    216
  distinguishing scope of right and
    extent of its protection in, 24
  historical development of
    proportionality in, 195–197
  implicit constitutional right to
    political freedom of expression
    in, 50, 55, 56, 57
  non-constitutional proportionality
    in, 146
  original purpose or intent,
    consideration of, 60
authorization chain, 107–110, 430

balancing (proportionality *stricto
sensu*), 11. *See also*
interpretive balancing
"advancing the purpose" scale,
357–358
Alexy on, 6, 11
basic balancing rule, 362–370
categorization and, 508–509,
512–513
centrality to concept of
proportionality, 7
as component of proportionality, 3
constitutional, 75
constitutional balancing and
interpretive balancing
distinguished, 347–348
content of balancing test, 340–342
critiques of proportionality
chiefly aimed at, 481,
521. *See also* critiques of
proportionality
definitional balancing, 546
equally balanced scales, cases
involving, 365–367
future development and
improvements to concept of,
542–547
future development of, 15
Hogg on lack of necessity of, 247
importance of, 345–346, 457
legislative and judicial discretion
regarding, 413–415
"limiting the right" scale, 358–362
marginal benefit compared to
marginal harm, 350–352
nature of, 342–343, 348–349
necessity test differentiated, 344
positive constitutional rights and,
433–434
principled balancing, 370, 521,
542–547
proper relationship between benefit
and harm, measuring, 343–
344, 349–362
proportional alternative,
considering, 352–356
reasonableness as, 373, 374–375

relative rights, scope provisions
versus limitation clauses
regarding, 36–37
scope, clarification of, 357
social importance of, 349–350
specific balancing rule, 367–369, 544
structured discretion, as part of, 461
unique capacities of balancing test,
344–345
urgency of proper purpose and, 278
validity of conflicting principles in,
346–348
Beatty, D. M., 476–480
Beinish, Dorit, 273, 416
Belgium, proportionality in, 186–188
Biblical law, proportionality in, 175
Blackmun, Harry, 411
Blackstone, Sir William, 176
Botha, H., 166, 197, 257, 283, 292, 332
Brazil, proportionality in, 201–202
Breyer, Stephen, 206–207, 478
burden of proof, 12, 435–454
burden of persuasion and burden
of producing evidence
encompassed in, 437
in comparative law, 439–442
distinguishing scope of right
and extent of its protection,
importance of, 22
facts and law, 436–437
judicial procedure and, 449–454
justification of limitation of right
and, 439–442
limitation of constitutional right
and, 437–442
necessity test and, 448–449
on party claiming existence of
justification for limitation,
442–446
on party claiming that limitation is
justified, 447–454
presumption of constitutionality
and, 444–446
for rational connection, 311
relative rights, scope provisions
versus limitation clauses
regarding, 37
valuation of human rights and, 447

Cameron, Edwin, 325
Canada
Australia, migration of concept of
proportionality to, 195–197
balancing in, 360
balancing test in, 342, 343
burden of proof in, 439–440
democracy, constitutional status of,
215, 217
distinction between scope of right
and extent of its protection in,
26
equal-level sub-constitutional
norms, reconciling, 158
historical development of
proportionality in, 188–190
implicit constitutional rights in, 55
interpretation and proportionality
in, 238
Israel influenced by, 210
limitation of constitutional rights in,
99, 101, 103, 133
limitations clause in, 142, 143, 221
necessity in, 322, 329, 337
New Zealand, migration of concept
of proportionality to, 194–195
original purpose or intent,
consideration of, 60
override clause in, 167–169, 170–171,
173
proper purpose in, 246, 258, 269–
270, 278, 279–283, 289–291,
516, 529, 531, 532, 533
protection of constitutional rights
in, 490
purposive interpretation in, 47
rational connection in, 303
rule of law in, 229
scope of constitutional rights in, 513
South Africa, migration of concept
of proportionality to, 197–198
statutory limitation in, 112
zone of proportionality, legislators
and judges operating within,
409, 410–411
categorization-based alternatives to
proportionality, 502–527
balancing and, 508–509, 512–513

constitutional rights in, 505–507
critiques of proportionality and,
521–526
intermediate scrutiny and, 511, 512,
515
minimal scrutiny and, 511, 512, 515
nature of thinking in legal
categories, 503–505
proper purpose and, 515–517
proportionality compared to
categorization, 513–521
strict scrutiny and, 510–511, 512,
516–521
two-stage model and, 507–508
Central and Eastern Europe,
proportionality in, 198–199,
526
Chaskalson, M., 133, 224
checks and balances, concept of,
385–387
Chile, proportionality in, 201–202
clarity requirement for limitations
on constitutional rights, 108,
116–118
Colombia, proportionality in, 201–202
common law and proportionality,
118–127, 371
comparative law
on burden of proof, 439–442
interpretation, 65–69
positive constitutional rights in,
423–425
proper purpose, general criteria for
determining, 257–258
proportionality studied according
to, 4–5, 7, 16
concept jurisprudence to interest
jurisprudence, historical shift
from, 177, 503
conflicts between constitutional rights,
9, 83–98. *See also* principle-
shaped rights, conflicts
between
analytical framework for
addressing, 83–86
constitutional validity and, 83, 86,
87–89
interpretive balancing and, 73–75

conflicts between constitutional
rights (*cont.*)
interpretive differences
distinguished, 83
limitation clauses and, 154–155
mixed conflicts between principle-
shaped and rule-shaped rights,
84, 97–98
negative solution to, 94–96
new constitutional derivative rule
created by, 39
proportionality as intrinsic to,
234–238
reasonableness as balance between
conflicting principles,
374–375
rights of others, scope of
constitutional rights in relation
to, 80–82
rule of law, conflicts between rights
and, 86
rule-shaped rights, conflicts
involving, 84, 86–87, 97–98, 157
scope issues distinguished, 83,
87–89
scope of protection of constitutional
rights and, 263–265
sub-constitutional level, resolution
at, 83–86, 90, 96–97
consequentialist nature of
proportionality, 470
constitutional aspect of proper
purpose, 288–289
constitutional balancing, 75
constitutional basis for proportionality
in a legal system, 211–213, 246
constitutional interpretation.
See interpretation
constitutional principles, as public
interest consideration, 276
constitutional rights, 8–9.
See also absolute rights;
conflicts between
constitutional rights;
limitations on constitutional
rights; positive constitutional
rights; protection of

constitutional rights; relative
rights
amendment distinguished from
limitation, 99–101, 155
in categorized thinking, 505–507
complementary nature of
limitations and, 166
democracies, importance in,
161–162, 163, 164–165, 218–220
determining scope of, 9, 45–82
categorization versus
proportionality and, 513–514
concept of constitutional text and.
See constitutional text
conflicts between rights
distinguished from scope
issues, 83, 87–89
interpretation of text as means of,
45. *See also* interpretation
public interest considerations
and, 75–80, 81
rights of others and, 80–82
distinguishing scope of right and
extent of its protection, 9,
19–44
absolute rights and, 27–32
in comparative law, 24–26
freedom of expression in ECHR
and, 21–22
importance of, 22–24
judicial review and, 26–27
prima facie versus definite nature
of rights and, 37–42
proportional crime,
constitutional right to commit,
42–44
relative rights and, 27–29, 32–37
two-stage theory of, 19–21
naming and enumerating, 53
parent and child rights, 51–53
prima facie versus definite nature of,
37–42
proportionality of limitations
applied to. *See* proportionality
public interest considerations
balanced with. *See* public
interest considerations

realization of scope, limitations on, 515–516

rule of law, inclusion of human rights in, 230–232

social importance of, 359–361

state rather than individuals, directed at, 125–127, 253, 263

theories of human rights, proportionality as vessel for, 467–472

two-stage theory of, 19–21, 507–508

waiver of, 106

constitutional status of democracy, 214–218

constitutional status of rule of law, 228–230

constitutional text

common law, relationship to, 118

explicit, 49–53

implicit, 49–51, 53–58

as living document, 64–65

naming and enumerating rights in, 53

non-metaphorical nature of, 48–49

original purpose or intent, consideration of, 58–64, 69

parent and child rights in, 51–53

positive constitutional rights, legal source of, 425–427

purposive interpretation and unique nature of, 48

subjective versus objective interpretation of, 58–59, 63

constitutional validity, 83, 86, 87–89, 346–348

Cooke, Robin, 194

Cory, Peter, 291

Costello, D., 191

counter-formalism, 177

criminal activity, proportional, constitutional right to commit, 42–44

critiques of proportionality, 13, 457–458, 481–492

balancing central to, 481, 521

categorization and, 521–526

constitutional rights, insufficient protection of, 488–490, 523–525

external criticism, 487–492, 522–526

internal criticism, 482–487, 521–522

judicial discretion, width of, 487–488, 522–523

judicial legitimacy, lack of, 490–492, 525–526

rationality, lack of, 484–486

standards, lack of, 482–484

Currie, D. P., 233

Czech Republic, limitation clauses in, 141

de minimis limitations, 103–105

Declaration of the Rights of Man and of the Citizen, limitation of rights in, 162, 255–257

deference, judicial, 396–399, 417

definitional balancing, 546

democracy

constitutional rights and public interest considerations, balancing, 220–221, 253–257

constitutional status of, 214–218

continued existence of state as, as public interest consideration, 267–268

formal and substantive aspects of, 218, 221–222, 252

importance of human rights and human rights limitations to, 161–162, 163, 164–165, 218–220, 221–222

judicial review and, 381–383, 473

as legal source of proportionality, 2, 214–226, 472–473

limitation clauses as means of balancing aspects of, 221–222

proper purpose and, 251–257

rule of law as value of, 252

tolerance as central to, 274

transparency and, 463

denial of constitutional right
distinguished from limitation,
101
deontological concepts and
proportionality, 471–472
Dickson, Brian, 47, 165, 166, 189, 191,
221, 223, 258, 281, 303, 306, 307,
375, 408, 410, 440
Diplock, Lord, 192, 333
discretion
judicial, 387–388
application of law to facts,
394–399
balancing and, 414–415
critique of proportionality based
on width of, 487–488, 522–523
decision to legislate and, 400
facts, determination of, 388–391
law, determination of, 391–394
legislative interpretation and,
392–394
necessity and, 412–413
positive constitutional rights and,
431, 432
proper purpose and, 403–405
rational connection and, 406
at widest and narrowest, 417
legislative
balancing and, 413–414
decision to legislate and, 400,
415–417
necessity and, 407–412
positive constitutional rights and,
431, 432, 433
proper purpose and, 401–403
rational connection and, 405–406
structured discretion,
proportionality as means of, 462
at widest and narrowest, 417
proportionality and, 384–385
structured, 460–467
Dorner, Dalia, 271–272
Douglas, William O., 56
Dworkin, R., 266, 365, 488, 495, 535
Dyzenhaus, David, 397

Eastern and Central Europe,
proportionality in, 198–199,
526

Emiliou, N., 231
ends and means, determining
relationship between, 132
English law. See United Kingdom
Enlightenment, proportionality in,
176, 178
equality, right to, 115, 294–296
European Convention for the
Protection of Human Rights
and Fundamental Freedoms
(ECHR), 183–184
burden of proof in, 441–442
Central and Eastern European
nations influenced by, 199
distinction between scope of right
and extent of its protection in,
21–22, 25
as exemplar of European law, 181
Hong Kong influenced by, 200
Israel influenced by, 210
limitation clauses in, 35, 134, 141
margin of appreciation and, 419
positive constitutional rights in, 424
proper purpose in, 261, 262, 531
scope of constitutional rights in, 514
torture, absolute prohibition of, 28
UK Human Rights Act effecting,
193, 442
European Court of Human Rights
on balancing test, 344
on clarity requirement for
limitations on constitutional
rights, 116
on common law, 121
on concept of proportionality, 183
on implied limitation clauses, 135
on margin of appreciation, 418, 419
on positive constitutional rights, 424
European Court of Justice
development of concept of
proportionality by, 184–186
on margin of appreciation, 418
European law, 181
Canada, migration of concept of
proportionality to, 188–190
development and migration of legal
principles in, 181–183
Ireland, migration of concept of
proportionality to, 190–192

shift from jurisprudence of concepts
    to jurisprudence of interests
    in, 503
UK, migration of concept of
    proportionality to, 192–194
Western European states, migration
    of concept of proportionality
    to, 186–188
European Union, concept of
    proportionality in law of,
    184–186
excluded reasons, concept of, 469–470
executive branch
    application of proportionality to,
        380
    rational justification,
        proportionality as means of,
        459–460
    structured discretion,
        proportionality as means of,
        462
expression, freedom of. *See* freedom of
    expression

facts
    application of law to, 394–399
    burden of proof and, 436–437
    historical facts and social facts,
        388–389
    judicial determination of, 388–391
    polycentric facts, 389–390
    rational connection and factual
        uncertainty problem, 308–315
Fallon, R. H., 520
feelings, protection of, as public
    interest consideration, 274–276
Fleiner, Fritz, 179, 333
formal and substantive aspects
    of democracy, 218, 221–222, 252
    of rule of law, 232–233
founding purpose or intent,
    consideration of, 58–64, 69
France
    European law, migration of concept
        of proportionality from,
        186–188
    general principles of law, concept
        of, 185
    judicial review in, 526

methodological approach to
    proportionality in, 132 n. 3
necessity test in, 541
polycentric facts, judicial
    determination of, 390
zone of proportionality, legislators
    and judges operating within,
    407 n. 114
Frase, R., 206
freedom of expression
    Australia, implicit constitutional
        rights in, 50, 55, 56, 57, 216
    in categorized thinking, 506–507,
        508
    conflict of rights involving, 84, 90
    ECHR, distinguishing scope of right
        and extent of its protection in,
        21–22
    interpretive balancing in, 31
    interpretive balancing of, 73–75
    legal basis required for limitation
        of, 109
    national security limitations
        on, 248
    necessity test and, 329
    prima facie versus definite nature
        of, 40
    principled balancing and, 543
    proper purpose and, 248, 290,
        296–298, 531
    public interest considerations and,
        75
    rights of others and, 80
    in United States, 31, 133, 546
freedom of occupation
    balancing test and, 352
    incidental limitations on, 105
    necessity test and, 319, 328
freedom of religion
    necessity test and, 330, 410
    Sunday laws, 287, 289, 410
    in United States, 133
Fuller, L., 108

Gardbaum, S., 506–507, 508
general authorization requirement for
    limitations, 108, 113–115
general limitation clauses, 142–143,
    145, 260–261

generous approach to constitutional
    interpretation, 69–71
Germany
    absolute rights in, 27, 31
    alternatives to proportionality in,
        496
    balancing test in, 343, 360, 369, 546
    democracy in, 214, 218
    general authorization requirement
        for limitations in, 113
    historical origins of proportionality
        in. See under historical
        origins and development of
        proportionality
    interpretation and proportionality
        in, 238
    limitations clauses in, 135–136, 137,
        141
    necessity in, 319
    original purpose or intent,
        consideration of, 61
    parent and child rights in, 52
    positive constitutional rights in, 423,
        428, 434
    proper purpose in, 15, 267, 276, 278,
        515, 516, 529, 531
    protection of constitutional rights
        in, 490
    public interest considerations in, 76
    rational connection in, 304
    rule of law in, 226–228, 229, 230, 233
    statutory limitation in, 112
    zone of proportionality in, 379
Gewirth, A., 29
Golden Rule, 175
good reputation, right to enjoy, 80, 90
Greece, proportionality in, 186–188
Greek philosophy, proportionality in,
    175
Grimm, D., 139, 342, 351

Habermas, J., 495
Hazard, G. C., 443
Hesse, K., 239
historical origins and development of
    proportionality, 10, 175–210
    in Asia, 199
    in Australia, 195–197

in Canada, 188–190
in Central and Eastern Europe,
    198–199
counter-formalism, 177
Enlightenment period, 176, 178
in European law, 181
German law, origins in, 6, 178–181
    administrative law, 177, 178–179
    Brazil influenced by, 201–202
    Central and Eastern Europe
        influenced by, 198
    constitutional law, 179–181
    European law, migration to, 181
    Israel influenced by, 210
    shift from jurisprudence of
        concepts to jurisprudence of
        interests, 177
    South Africa influenced by,
        197–198
    Svarez's contribution to
        proportionality concept,
        177–178
in international law
    human rights law, influence of
        national law on, 202
    humanitarian law, 204–205
    national and international human
        rights law, mutual influence
        of, 202
    Universal Declaration of Human
        Rights and development of
        proportionality, 203–204
in Ireland, 190–192
in Israel, 208–210
in New Zealand, 194–195
pre-modern philosophical origins,
    175–176
in South Africa, 197–198
in South America, 201–202
in UK, 192–194
in United States, 206–208
Western European states, migration
    of concept of proportionality
    to, 186–188
Hogg, P. W., 173, 188, 247–249, 283,
    291, 337
Hong Kong, proportionality in, 199
Horowitz, Martin, 504

human dignity, right of, 27, 61, 277, 360, 427, 428

human rights. *See* constitutional rights

humanitarian international law, 204–205

Hungary, proportionality in, 141, 199

hybrid limitation clauses, 144–145

Iacobucci, Frank, 291

incidental limitations, 105–106

India
    historical origins and development of proportionality in, 200
    limitations clauses in, 141
    positive constitutional rights in, 429
    proper purpose in, 268
    rule of law in, 229, 232
    statutory limitation in, 112

individualism and proportionality, 470

infringement and limitation on constitutional rights, 101

Inter-American human rights law, margin of appreciation in, 418

interest jurisprudence, historical shift from concept jurisprudence to, 177, 503

internal modifiers, 153–154

international law
    burden of proof in, 441
    Hong Kong, development of proportionality in, 200
    humanitarian law, 204–205
    national and international human rights law, mutual influence of, 202
    Universal Declaration of Human Rights and development of proportionality in, 203–204

interpretation, 45–82.
    See also interpretive balancing
    comparative, 65–69
    concept of constitutional text and. *See* constitutional text
    conflicts between constitutional rights distinguished from, 83
    determining scope of constitutional rights by, 45
    generous approach to, 69–71

    as legal source of proportionality, 238–240
    legislative interpretation and judicial discretion, 392–394
    limitation and right, relationship between interpretation of, 71–72
    modern meaning, application of, 64–65
    original purpose or intent, consideration of, 58–64, 69
    proper purpose, interpretive aspect of, 287–288
    purposive, 46–48, 58
    "strict scrutiny" review in U.S., 14, 15, 284, 294, 295, 297
    subjective versus objective, 58–59, 63

interpretive balancing, 3
    conflict of principle-shaped constitutional rights and, 92–93
    constitutional balancing distinguished, 347–348
    constitutional interpretation and, 240
    defined, 147
    determining scope of constitutional rights and, 72–75
    in distinguishing scope and extent of protection of constitutional rights, 31
    between equal-level sub-constitutional norms, 157
    internal modifiers and, 153–154

Ireland, proportionality in, 190–192, 216, 343

Israel
    balancing test in, 341, 343, 351, 353–355, 358, 359
    burden of proof in, 438, 448, 452, 453
    conflicts between rights in, 90–95
    constitutional basis for proportionality in, 211
    democracy in, 215, 219, 224–226
    distinction between scope of right and extent of its protection in, 26

Israel (*cont.*)
historical origins and development
of proportionality in, 208–210
interpretation and proportionality
in, 238
interpretive balancing in, 73–75
judicial review, 473
legality principle in, 110
limitation of constitutional rights in,
101, 103, 104, 133
limitations clause in, 143, 148, 222
necessity in, 318–319, 321, 332, 336,
337
overinclusiveness of means in,
515–517
override clause in, 168, 171, 172–173
positive constitutional rights in, 426,
427
principled balancing and, 545–547
private autonomy, as constitutional
right in, 42
proper purpose in, 246, 258–259,
267, 271–272, 273, 274, 278, 288,
530
protection of constitutional rights
in, 524
public interest considerations in, 77
rational connection in, 308, 311, 313
reasonableness in, 208
rule of law in, 230, 232
scope of constitutional rights in, 513
statutory limitation in, 111, 112
zone of proportionality, legislators
and judges operating within,
402, 403, 407, 408, 414
Italy, proportionality in, 141, 186–188

James, F., 443
Japanese-Americans interned during
WWII, 14, 516
Jewish law, proportionality in, 175
judiciary, judges, and proportionality.
See zone of proportionality,
legislators and judges operating
within
Just War doctrine, 176

Kant, Immanuel, 469, 471
Kelman, M., 499

Khanna, Hans Raj, 232
Kommers, D., 61
Korematsu case, reexamination of, 14,
516
Kriegler, Johann, 122
Kumm, M., 468–471, 475–476, 485,
492

La Forest, Gérard, 322, 410
Lamer, Antonio, 60, 329, 445
Latin America, proportionality in,
201–202
law
burden of proof and, 436–437
facts, application to, 394–399
judicial determination of, 391–394
least reasonably limiting means
requirement, 408–412
legal sources of positive constitutional
rights, 425–427
legal sources of proportionality, 10,
211–241
conflicts between legal principles,
proportionality as intrinsic to,
234–238
constitutional basis for
proportionality in a legal
system, importance of
establishing, 211–213
democracy, 2, 214–226, 472–473
interpretation, 238–240
logical necessity, proportionality
viewed as, 240–241
rule of law, 3, 226–234
legality principle, 9, 107–110, 430
legislators and proportionality.
See zone of proportionality,
legislators and judges operating
within
legitimacy distinguished from legality,
245
less restrictive means requirement.
See necessity
Leubsdorf, J., 443
lex posteriori derogat priori, 157, 348
lex specialis derogat generali, 157, 348
lex superior derogat legi inferiori, 149
liberalism and proportionality, 177,
468–472

life, right to, 428, 434, 497
limitation clauses
  common law and, 121–127
  conflicts between constitutional
    rights and, 154–155
  constitutional validity in conflict of
    rights cases, 93
  democracy, balancing formal and
    substantive aspects of, 221–222
  explicit purposes in specific
    limitation clauses, 261
  general, 142–143, 145, 260–261
  hybrid, 144–145
  implied or silent, 134–141
  importance of, 164–165
  overrides and, 167–174
  preferred regime in, 145–146
  proportionality as basis for,
    222–226, 233
  protective nature of, 165–166
  relationship between right and
    limitation, shaping, 164
  relative rights, as part of, 35
  rule of law, balancing aspects of,
    232–233
  specific, 141, 145, 261
  specific purposes in general
    limitation clauses, 260–261
  types of, 133–134
limitations on constitutional rights,
    9, 99–106. See also means of
    limitation
  accessibility requirement, 108,
    115–116
  amendment distinguished, 99–101,
    155
  authorization chain for, 107–110,
    430
  balancing test and "limiting the
    right" scale, 358–362
  burden of proof and, 437–442
  "by law" requirement, 139–141, 430
  clarity requirement, 108, 116–118
  common law and, 118–127
  complementary nature of rights and,
    166
  by constitutional norms, 151–152
  de minimis limitations, 103–105
  defined, 102

  democracies, importance in,
    161–162, 163, 164–165,
    221–222
  denial of right distinguished, 101
  general authorization requirement,
    108, 113–115
  hierarchical relationship between
    limited right and limiting law,
    148–152
  incidental limitations, 105–106
  infringement and, 101
  internal modifiers distinguished,
    153–154
  interpretation of limitation and
    right, relationship between, 9
  legality principle regarding, 9,
    107–110, 430
  limited nature of, 166–167
  methods of limitation, 133–134
  normative validity of, 108, 146
  proportionality in.
    See proportionality
  as public interest considerations,
    162–163
  rights of others, limitations allowing
    for, 161
  statutory limitations, 110–118
  by sub-constitutional laws. See sub-
    constitutional norms

MacCormick, N., 374
Madala, Tholie, 325
Magna Carta, 176
margin of appreciation, 418–421
Marshall, Thurgood, 387
McIntyre, William Rogers, 282
McLachlin, Beverley, 291, 409
means of limitation
  aims and means, determining
    relationship between, 132
  arbitrary or unfair means, 307
  choice of, 305–307
  hypothetical alternative means
    equally advancing law's
    purpose, 323–326
  hypothetical alternative means
    limiting constitutional right to
    lesser extent, 326–331
  legislative choice of, 405

means of limitation (*cont.*)
  narrowly tailored to fulfill law's
    purpose, 333–337
  overinclusiveness of, 335–337,
    517–520
  rational connection of means of
    limiting law to proper purpose.
    See rational connection
Mexico, proportionality in, 201–202
Meyerson, D., 501
migration or transplantation of
  laws, proportionality as
  manifestation of, 457
mother and child rights, 51–53

narrow tailoring of means to fulfill
  law's purpose, 333–337
national security. *See also* terrorism
  freedom of expression, limitations
    on, 248
  as public interest consideration, 268
natural law, proportionality in, 177
necessity, 10, 317–339
  balancing test differentiated, 344
  burden of proof and, 448–449
  complete restriction versus
    individual examination of,
    328–331
  as component of proportionality, 3
  content of necessity test, 317–319
  elements of necessity test, 323–331
  future development and
    improvements to necessity test,
    540–542
  hypothetical alternative means
    equally advancing law's
    purpose, 323–326
  hypothetical alternative means
    limiting constitutional right to
    lesser extent, 326–331
  importance of necessity test,
    337–339
  least reasonably limiting means
    requirement, 408–412
  as legal source of proportionality,
    240–241
  legislative and judicial discretion
    regarding, 407–413

narrow tailoring of means to fulfill
  law's purpose, 333–337
nature of necessity test, 320–323
overinclusiveness of means, 335–337
Pareto efficiency, as expression of,
  320
positive constitutional rights and,
  433
proper purpose's level of abstraction
  and, 331–333
of rational connection test, 315–316
structured discretion, as part
  of, 461
test of time and, 331
as threshold test, 541
negative solution to conflict of rights,
  94–96
Netherlands, no judicial review of
  constitutional issues in, 149
  n. 79
New Zealand
  Australian law influenced by, 197
  balancing in, 360
  burden of proof in, 440
  distinguishing scope of right and
    extent of its protection in, 24
  equal-level sub-constitutional
    norms, reconciling, 157–159
  historical development of
    proportionality in, 194–195
  public interest considerations in, 77
  reasonableness in, 377
normative validity of limitations, 108,
  146
Nozick, R., 266, 495

objective versus subjective.
    See subjective versus objective
obscene materials, restrictions on, 290,
  419, 546
occupation, freedom of. *See* freedom of
  occupation
O'Regan, Kate, 291, 325
original purpose or intent,
    consideration of, 58–64, 69
overinclusiveness of means, 335–337,
  517–520
override clauses, 167–174

Palmer, Geoffrey, 194
parent and child rights, 51–53
Peru, proportionality in, 201–202
Poland, proportionality in, 141, 199, 260
political theory
    liberalism and proportionality, 177, 468–472
    neutrality of proportionality regarding, 460
    theories of human rights, proportionality as vessel for, 467–472
popular sovereignty, as democratic value, 252
Porat, I., 499–500
Portugal, proportionality in, 141, 186–188, 201–202, 228, 496
positive constitutional rights, 12, 422–430
    balancing and, 433–434
    in comparative law, 423–425
    legal source of, 425–427
    nature of, 422–423
    necessity and, 433
    objective nature of values and, 427
    positive constitutional aspect and, 427–429
    proper purpose and, 430–432
    rational connection and, 432
    relative nature of, 429
positivism, legal, 177
Powell, Lewis F., 302
praktische Konkordanz, doctrine of, 369, 546
presumption of constitutionality and burden of proof, 444–446
presumption of legality of executive action, 124
principle, concept of, 234–238
principle-shaped rights, conflicts between, 83–86, 87–97
    effectuating legislation, conflict between, 96
    effectuating legislation, conflicting rights without, 94–96
    equal-level sub-constitutional norms, 157

interpretive balancing, 92–93
    legislative realization of, 90
    limitation clause, constitutional validity of, 93
    proportionality as intrinsic to, 234–238
    realization of rights, effect on, 89–92
    scope and validity of rights not affected by conflict, 87–89
principled balancing, 370, 521, 542–547
privacy rights, 56, 80, 84, 90–95, 427
private autonomy, as constitutional right, 42–43
Proccacia, Ayala, 275
proper purpose, 10, 245–302
    abstraction, level of, 331–333
    balancing test and "advancing the purpose" scale, 357–358
    categorization-based alternatives to proportionality and, 515–517
    in comparative law, 257–258
    as component of proportionality, 3, 245–249
    components of, 251
    constitutional aspect of, 288–289
    constitutional foundation of, 246
    democratic requirements and values, 251–257
    explicit purposes in specific limitation clauses, 261
    future development and improvements to, 529–539
    future development of, 15
    general criteria for determining, 255–257
    hierarchy of rights regarding purpose's importance, 531–533
    Hogg on, 247–249
    identification of, 285–302
    implicit purposes, 261–262
    interpretive aspect of, 287–288
    legislative and judicial discretion regarding, 401–405
    multiple purposes, 331–333
    nature of, 245
    necessity and, 331–333
    positive constitutional rights and, 430–432

proper purpose (*cont.*)
protection of constitutional rights
and, 253, 262–265, 533–539
public interest considerations,
253–257, 265–277
rational connection of means of
limiting law to. *See* rational
connection
scope of, 249–251
specified purposes in general
limitation clauses, 260–261
structured discretion, as part of, 461
of sub-constitutional limiting law,
285–286
subjective or objective test for,
286–298
as threshold requirement for
proportionality, 246–249,
530–531
urgency of, 277–285
proportional crime, constitutional
right to commit, 42–44
proportionality, 1–16, 131–174,
457–480
aims and means, determining
relationship between, 132
alternatives to, 8, 14, 493–527.
See also alternatives to
proportionality
appropriate considerations in proper
context, allowing for, 463–465
burden of proof and, 12, 435–454.
See also burden of proof
in common law, 123, 127
in comparative law, 4–5, 7, 16
components of, 3, 10–13, 131.
See also balancing; necessity;
proper purpose; rational
connection
conflicts of rights and, 9, 83–98.
See also conflicts between
constitutional rights
critiques of, 13, 457–458, 481–
492. *See also* critiques of
proportionality
defined, 2–3, 102–103
dialogue between legislature and
judiciary, allowing, 465–467
different uses of term, 146

formal role of, 146–161
future development and
improvements to, 528–529
historical background, 10, 175–210.
See also historical origins and
development of proportionality
human rights theories, as vessel for,
467–472
importance of, 164–165
internal modifiers and, 153–154
in interpretation, 3, 147
legal sources of, 10, 211–241.
See also legal sources of
proportionality
liberalism and, 177, 468–472
limitation clauses, as basis for,
222–226, 233
methodological approach to, 7, 8,
132–133
migration or transplantation of laws,
as manifestation of, 457
nature of, 131–146
non-constitutional, 146
of normative validity, 146
political theory and. *See* political
theory
positive constitutional rights and,
12, 422–430. *See also* positive
constitutional rights
as protective of constitutional rights,
4
public interest considerations and,
76–80
rational justification, as means of,
458–460
reasonableness and, 11, 371–378.
See also reasonableness and
proportionality
social repercussions of, 132,
463–465
stricto sensu. See balancing
structured discretion, need for,
460–467
substantive role of, 161–167
transparency and, 462–463
zone of, 12, 379–421. *See also* zone of
proportionality, legislators and
judges operating within
protection of constitutional rights

core of right, 496–498
explicit protections, 253–257,
    262–265
implicit protections, 262–263
limitations as protective, 165–166
as proper purpose, 253, 262–265,
    533–539
proportionality as protective, 4
scope of, 263–265
sufficiency critique, 488–490,
    523–525
public interest considerations
constitutional principles as, 276
democracies balancing
    constitutional rights with,
    220–221, 253
democracy, continued existence of
    state as, 267–268
feelings, protection of, 274–276
liberalism and proportionality,
    468–472
limitations as, 162–163
national security as, 268
nature of, 265–267
proper purpose and, 253–257,
    265–277
public order as, 269–273
rule of law and balance of
    constitutional rights with, 232
scope of constitutional rights and,
    75–80, 81
tolerance as, 273
public law principles and state's burden
    to produce evidence, 451
public order, as public interest
    consideration, 269–273
purposive interpretation, 46–48, 58

rational connection, 10, 303–316
arbitrary or unfair means, 307
burden of proof regarding, 311
as component of proportionality, 3
content of, 303–304
"designed to achieve proper
    purpose" requirement, 306
determining existence of, 310–312
extreme approaches to, 309–310
factual uncertainty, problem of,
    308–315

future development and
    improvements to, 539–540
future development of, 15
legislative and judicial discretion
    regarding, 405–406
means chosen, 305–307
nature of, 303–307
necessity of, 315–316
positive constitutional rights and,
    432
structured discretion, as part of, 461
test of time and, 312–315
as threshold test, 315
Rational Human Right Paradigm
    (RHRP), 475
rational justification, 458–460,
    484–486
Rawls, John, 108, 469, 536
Raz, J., 499
realism in Continental European law,
    177
reasonableness and proportionality, 11,
    371–378
balancing, reasonableness as, 373,
    374–375
common law countries' recognition
    of, 192, 208, 371
components of reasonableness,
    373–374
definition of reasonableness, 373,
    375
least reasonably limiting mean
    requirement, 408–412
relationship between, 375–378
Rehnquist, William, 293
relative rights, 32–37
defined, 27–29, 32
importance of distinction between
    provision types, 35–37
limitation clauses, 35
positive constitutional rights as, 429
scope provisions, 33–34
types of provisions leading to, 32–33
religion, freedom of. See freedom of
    religion
rights. See constitutional rights, and
    specific rights and freedoms,
    e.g. freedom of expression
Rivers, Julian, 5, 344, 384, 408, 534

Roman law, proportionality in, 176

Romania, proportionality in, 212

rule of law
authorization chain as formal aspect of, 108
"by law" limitations requirements, 139
conflicts between constitutional rights and, 86
constitutional rights and public interest considerations, balancing, 221
constitutional status of, 228–230
as democratic value, 252
formal and substantive aspects of, 232–233
German theories regarding, 226–228
human rights included in, 230–232
as legal source of proportionality, 3, 226–234
limitation clauses as means of balancing aspects of, 232–233
limitation clauses, proportionality as basis for, 233

rule-shaped rights, conflicts involving, 84, 86–87, 97–98, 157

Sachs, Albie, 258, 291, 325, 450

Sadurski, W., 374, 463

Scalia, Antonin, 64

Schlink, B., 502

scope of constitutional rights.
See constitutional rights

Segal, Z., 208

separation of powers, 384–399, 417–418

Shamgar, Meir, 259, 448

silence, legislative, 94–96

silent or implied limitation clauses, 134–141

slavery, prohibition of, 27

Slovenia, proportionality in, 199

South Africa
alternatives to proportionality in, 498
Australian law influenced by, 197
balancing in, 360
balancing test in, 343
burden of proof in, 438, 441, 450
common law and limitation clause in, 122, 127
conflicts between rights in, 89 n. 25
democracy in, 215, 217, 218
distinction between scope of right and extent of its protection in, 26
general authorization requirement for limitations in, 113
historical development of proportionality in, 197–198
international human rights law influencing, 203
limitation of constitutional rights in, 133, 151–152
limitations clause in, 142, 143, 144, 222
necessity in, 319, 325, 330–331, 335
positive constitutional rights in, 423, 425, 432
proper purpose in, 246, 255, 257, 265, 270, 278, 283–284, 291–292, 529, 532
public interest considerations in, 77
rational connection in, 303–304
relative rights in, 33
rule of law in, 229, 230
scope of constitutional rights in, 513
zone of proportionality, legislators and judges operating within, 409

South America, proportionality in, 201–202

South Korea, proportionality in, 200

sovereignty of the people, as democratic value, 252

Spain
alternatives to proportionality in, 496
European law, migration of concept of proportionality from, 186–188
international human rights law influencing, 203
interpretation and proportionality in, 238

limitations clauses in, 141
rule of law in, 228
South America, migration of concept
of proportionality to, 201–202
specific balancing rule, 367–369, 544
specific limitation clauses, 141, 145, 261
specified purposes in general
limitation clauses, 260–261
speech, freedom of. *See* freedom of
expression
stare decisis, 157
state rather than individuals,
constitutional rights directed
at, 125–127, 253, 263
state's burden of producing evidence,
449–454
state's continued existence as
democracy, as public interest
consideration, 267–268
statutory limitations on constitutional
rights, 110–118
stealing, proportional, constitutional
right to commit, 42–44
strict scrutiny review in U.S., 14, 15,
284, 294, 295, 297, 510–511, 512,
516–521, 541
stricto sensu proportionality.
See balancing
structured discretion, 460–467
sub-constitutional norms
equal-level norm, limitation by,
157–161
hierarchical relationship between
limited right and limiting law,
150–152
limitations on constitutional rights
by, 147–148, 150–152
lower sub-constitutional norm,
limitation by, 155–157
proper purpose of, 285–286
subjective versus objective
constitutional text, interpretation of,
58–59, 63
necessity test, "limitation to a lesser
extent" element of, 327–328
positive constitutional rights,
objective nature of values as
legal source of, 427

proper purpose test, 286–298
substantive and formal aspects
of democracy, 218, 221–222, 252
of rule of law, 232–233
Sullivan, E., 206
Sunday laws, 287, 289, 410
Svarez, Carl Gottlieb, 177–178
Switzerland, proportionality in, 57,
143, 186–188, 212, 366, 496

terrorism
innocent civilians, counter-terrorist
actions leading to harm to, 28
protection of constitutional rights
and, 524
torture, prohibition of, 29, 30
test of time, 312–315, 331
theft, proportional, constitutional
right to commit, 42–44
St. Thomas Aquinas, 176
Thomas, Clarence, 293
tolerance, as public interest
consideration, 273
torture, prohibition of, 28, 29, 30
transparency, 462–463
transplantation or migration of
laws, proportionality as
manifestation of, 457
Tribe, L. H., 54, 55, 229, 299
"Trolley Problem," 29
Turkey, proportionality in, 143,
186–188, 212, 496
two-stage theory of constitutional
rights, 19–21, 507–508

uncertainty, factual, and rational
connection, 308–315
United Kingdom
balancing test in, 343, 348
burden of proof in, 442
common law and constitution in,
120, 122
distinguishing scope of right and
extent of its protection in, 24
ECHR, Human Rights Act effecting,
193, 442
equal-level sub-constitutional
norms, reconciling, 157

United Kingdom (*cont.*)
  historical development of
    proportionality in, 192–194
  margin of appreciation in, 419
  non-constitutional proportionality
    in, 146
  protection of constitutional rights
    in, 524
  reasonableness in, 192, 373, 375
United Nations Human Rights
    Commission, on margin of
    appreciation, 418
United States
  American doctrine compared to
    proportionality, 14
  balancing in, 360
  Bills of Attainder, constitutional
    prohibition on, 114
  categorization approach in.
    See categorization-based
    alternatives to proportionality
  comparative constitutional law in,
    69
  concept of proportionality in,
    206–208
  freedom of expression in, 31, 133,
    546
  implicit constitutional right to
    privacy in, 56
  implied limitations clause in,
    137–139
  intermediate scrutiny in, 511, 512,
    515, 533
  Japanese-Americans interned
    during WWII in, 14, 516
  judicial discretion in, 488, 523
  judicial review, 473
  legislative interpretation and
    judicial discretion in, 392–394
  minimal scrutiny in, 511, 512,
    515
  original purpose or intent,
    consideration of, 61, 69
  positive constitutional rights
    concept rejected in, 424, 426
  principled balancing and, 545–547
  proper purpose in, 284–285, 292,
    530, 532

protection of constitutional rights
    in, 489, 490, 524
  rule of law in, 229
  statutory limitation in, 112
  strict scrutiny in, 14, 15, 284, 294,
    295, 297, 510–511, 512, 516–521,
    541
Universal Declaration of Human
    Rights
  distinguishing scope of right and
    extent of its protection in, 24
  general limitations clause in, 142, 143
  historical development of
    proportionality in international
    law and, 203–204
  proper purpose in, 260, 262
  urgency of proper purpose, 277–285

vagueness, unconstitutional, 117
validity, constitutional, 83, 86, 87–89,
    346–348

waiver of constitutional rights, 106
Waldron, J., 495
war on terror. *See* terrorism
Webber, G. C. N., 489, 493–496, 502
Wigmore, J., 443
Wilson, Bertha, 103, 104, 269–270, 282,
    310
Wittgenstein, Ludwig, 54
Woolman, S., 106, 166, 197, 257, 283,
    292, 332

Yacoob, Zak, 325

Zamir, I., 104, 209–210, 272–274, 360,
    363, 452, 453
zone of proportionality, legislators and
    judges operating within, 12.
    See also discretion
  absolute rights, jurisprudence of,
    29–30
  application of proportionality
    to branches of government,
    379–381
  balancing test and, 413–415
  checks and balances, concept of,
    385–387

common law and limitation of
    rights, 118–127
conflict of rights
    conflict between effectuating
        legislation resulting
        from, 96
    legislative silence regarding,
        94–96
    resolved at legislative level, 90
decision to legislate, 400
dialogue between legislature and
    judiciary, proportionality
    allowing, 465–467
distinguishing scope of right
    and extent of its protection,
    importance of, 22, 26–27
judicial deference, 396–399, 417
judicial intervention, 396
judicial legitimacy, critique of
    proportionality based on lack
    of, 490–492, 525–526
judicial procedure and burden of
    proof, 449–454

judicial review, 381–383, 394–399,
    473–480, 502
margin of appreciation and, 418–421
means of limitation, legislative
    choice of, 405
nature of, 415–417
necessity and, 407–413
proper purpose and, 401–405
public interest considerations and,
    79–80
rational connection and, 405–406
rational justification,
    proportionality as means of,
    459–460
separation of powers, 384–399,
    417–418
statutory limitations, 110–118
"strict scrutiny" review in U.S., 14,
    15, 284, 294, 295, 297
structured discretion,
    proportionality as means of,
    462, 465–467
transparency, importance of, 462

Printed in Great Britain
by Amazon

36855239R00354

The Complete Tofu Cookbook

Camille Oger

weldon**owen**

CONTENTS

Foreword 6
Introduction 7
Practical Advice 12
Preparing Tofu 14

Basic Recipes

Soy Milk (& Okara) 24
Firm Tofu 27
Silken Tofu 30
Silken Tofu with Citrus 31
Tofu Skins 32
Tofu Pudding (method 1) 34
Tofu Pudding (method 2) 36

China & Taiwan

Tofu Types & Uses 42
Everyday Fried Rice 48
Egg Tofu 49
Cold Tofu with Green Onion 50
Sautéed Tofu in Lettuce Cups 52
Cold Tofu with Century Eggs 54
"Thousand-Layer" Tofu 56
Tofu Honeycomb Soup 58
Bok Choy & Tofu Soup.....................60
Chinese Cabbage Sautéed with
Fermented Tofu 62
Tofu Noodle Salad...........................64
Sweet & Sour Tofu...........................66
Mung Bean Noodles Braised
with Tofu & Veggies..........................68
Sichuan-Style Mapo Tofu 70
Tofu Pot Stickers 72
Crispy Salt & Pepper Tofu................75
Steamed Stuffed Yuba......................76
3-Cup Tofu......................................77
Spicy Tofu with Peanuts 78
Red-Cooked Tofu.............................80
Sichuan-Style Braised Tofu...............82
Tofu Pudding Yunnan Style..............83
Rice Porridge with Sweet Potato 84
Breakfast Noodles 86
Tofu Stir-fry with Black Beans...........88
Pressed Tofu with Garlic Chives.......90
Tofu Pudding with Adzuki Beans 92
Five-Spice Pressed Tofu 94
Almond Tofu 95
Almond Tofu with Longan Fruit........96

Japan

Tofu Types & Uses 103
Cold Tofu with Ginger
& Green Onion...............................108
Cold Tofu with Natto 110
Zen Salad with Tofu Sauce 112
Very Simple Fried Tofu...................113
Melting Fried Tofu 114
Miso Soup with Tofu & Wakame......116
Miso Soup with Fried Tofu
& Daikon 118
Buddhist Broth...............................120
Grilled Miso Tofu 122
Grilled Tofu 124
Tofu Fritters with Vegetables..........126
Tofu Fermented in Miso 128
Salty-Sweet Fried Tofu Pockets.......130
Sushi in Tofu Pockets 132
Noodle Soup with Fried Tofu 134
Panfried Tofu with Nori 136
Kyoto-Style Tofu Hot Pot................138
Sautéed Minced Tofu 139
Tofu Rice Bowl with
Scrambled Eggs.............................140
Soba Noodles with Fresh Yuba.......142
Okara with Vegetables 144
Peanut Tofu 145
Edamame Tofu...............................146
Walnut Tofu 147
Walnut Tofu with Persimmon 148
Sesame Tofu...................................150
Tofu Mochi 152

Korea

Tofu Types & Uses 158
Deep-Fried Stuffed Chiles..............162
Herbed Tofu Canapés....................164
Panfried Tofu with Egg...................166
Caramelized Sesame Tofu 168
Spiced Stew with Very
Tender Tofu 169
Steamed Tofu with Sautéed Kimchi ...170
Broth with Potatoes & Tofu 172
Veggie Tofu Cakes 174
5-Color Rice Bowl (Bibimbap)........176
Sushi Rolls with Tofu &
Crunchy Veggies............................179
Spicy Braised Tofu 182

Korean Miso Stew 183
Mushroom & Tofu Hot Pot................184
Little Tofu Pockets with
Multicolor Rice................................186
Iced Noodle Soup with Soy Milk 188
Zucchini-Tofu Dumplings................190

Southeast Asia

Tofu Types & Uses 197
Lemongrass Tofu 200
Tofu Terrine, Vietnamese Style 201
Vegetarian Noodle Bowl (Bún) 202
Tofu & Veggie Sandwich (Bánh Mi)...204
Braised Yuba 206
Vegan Spring Rolls 208
Tofu Pudding with Ginger Syrup 211
Philippine-Style Braised Tofu..........212
Tofu Pudding with Syrup Pearls......214
Clear Soup with Egg Tofu 216
Egg Tofu Stir-fried with
Thai Veggies....................................217
Thai-Style Stir-fried
Rice Noodles (Pad Thai).................218
Tofu, Galangal & Coconut
Milk Soup..220
Tofu Stir-fry with Green
Peppercorns 222
Red Curry Tofu Stir-fry 224
Coconut Green Curry 226
Braised Tofu with Pineapple 228
Multicolor Indonesian Salad 230
Balinese Curry with Tofu
& Tempeh 232
Braised Tofu & Tempeh
Javanese Style................................234
Tofu Stir-Fry with Balinese Sauce....235
Savory Spiral Cookies.....................236
Tofu Puffs with Crunchy Veg
& Spiced Sauce 238
Tofu & Tempeh Satay with Peanut
Sauce 240
Spicy Tofu Sambal 242
Laotian Tofu Salad (Larb) 243

Burma

Tofu Types & Uses 248
Shan Country Yellow Tofu 250
Burmese Tofu...................................253
Burmese Tofu & Noodle Salad.........254
Burmese Tofu Salad 256
Burmese Tofu Curry........................258
Fried Tofu, Burmese Style 260
Burmese Twice-Fried Tofu..............262
Shan Noodles with Warm
Tofu Cream......................................264
Burmese Tofu Crackers 267

India

Spiced Tofu Pakora 272
Tofu Curry with Bell Peppers..........273
Vegan Butter Chicken.....................274
Tofu & Spinach Curry......................276
Tofu Curry with Green Peas 278
Black Pepper Tofu Curry 280
Tofu Tikka Masala...........................281
Tofu Tikka 282

Elsewhere

Tofu Types & Uses 288
Tofu-Olive Canapés.........................292
Crispy Deep-Fried Tofu...................294
Vegan Tzatziki 296
Wheat-Free Tabbouleh....................297
Tofu with Chilled
Apple-Mushroom Broth 298
Pink Radish Velouté 300
White Asparagus, Crème Fraîche
& Tofu 302
Lacto-Fermented Tofu.....................303
Soy-Ginger Lacto-Fermented Tofu..304
Vegan Greek Salad..........................306
Sesame-Breaded Tofu.....................308
Summer Veggie &
Sesame-Breaded Tofu Wrap 310
Mango-Avocado Salad with

Sesame-Breaded Tofu &
Chimichurri 312
Vegan Potato Salad.........................314
Mediterranean-Marinated Tofu.......315
Watermelon Salad with
Marinated Tofu 316
Tomato & Tofu Salad with
Date Dressing 318
Endive Salad with
Miso-Fermented Tofu 320
Arugula, Fig & Smoked Tofu Salad ..322
Warm Salad of Buckwheat, Roasted
Carrots & Lacto-Fermented Tofu.....324
Vegan Mayonnaise 326
Vegan Tartar Sauce 326
Tofu Nuggets 327
Vegan Pissaladière.........................328
Eggplant Stuffed with
Smoked Tofu...................................330
Vegan Leek Tart 332
Vegan Shakshuka 334
Orange-Braised Tofu & Fennel........336
Roasted Butternut with Sage, Tofu,
Pecans & Coffee 338
Green Peas with Smoked Tofu 340
Vegan Stuffed Mushrooms..............342

Panfried Tofu with Barbecue Sauce.343
Tofu Burger with Barbecue Sauce ...344
Pasta with Vegetarian Bolognese....346
Spinach & Tofu Lasagna 348
Spaghetti with Tofu-Artichoke
Cream...350
Lentils with Smoked Tofu 352
Strawberry Protein Smoothie 354
Pear-Matcha Smoothie 354
Tofu French Toast 356
Hazelnut, Chocolate & Silken
Tofu Tart 358
Vegan Caramel Flan.......................360
Almond "Tofu" with Cherries
& Black Pepper 361
Vegan Lemon Cake 362
Light Coffee Mousse 364
Vegan Apricot Clafoutis 366
Tofu Pudding with Red Fruit Coulis..368
Vegan Chocolate Mousse 369

Bibliography 370
Ingredient Index............................372
Recipe Index..................................380
Useful Addresses...........................383

FOREWORD

The Complete Tofu Cookbook was first published in France in 2019. It is now available in the English language to the American public.

This is the most comprehensive tofu cookbook created to date. It is pure joy to visit tofu culture through its pages featuring China, Taiwan, Japan, Korea, Southeast Asia, Burma, India, and other parts of the world. This is more than a tofu cookbook; it is an adventure in traditions and cultures. Add to this a distinctly French love for the art of making exquisite food, and you have a historical breakthrough in preparing tofu!

Various Asian traditions are described to highlight the unique craftsmanship handed down through generations of making tofu. The step-by-step recipes provide clear and detailed instructions, while the beauty of the finished dishes is highlighted through masterful photography.

The history of tofu in the United States dates back to the late 1800s but at that time the ingredient was almost unknown to the non-Asian population. I grew up in the San Francisco Bay Area in the 1950s, and my parents were fond of Chinese food. I remember eating dishes that on the menu included "soybean curd." This was my first encounter with tofu.

It was not until 1975 that my interest in tofu really blossomed. That was when I met William Shurtleff and Akiko Aoyagi, who published *The Book of Tofu* that same year. Akiko and William toured the United States to promote the consumption of soyfoods, including tofu, tempeh, and miso. By 1978 the number of non-Asian tofu manufacturing facilities in the United States had grown from zero to nearly 300,

and the first Soy Crafters Conference was held in Colorado. My Swedish wife and I attended this conference, and this inspired us to start Sweden's first tofu manufacturing facility in 1980. By the late 1990s, this company, Aros Sojaprodukter, was selling seven varieties of tofu and a soybean frozen dessert called Tofu-Line Glass.

In 1993 we moved from Sweden to California and continued to develop and produce new lines of soyfood. By this time, soyfoods had expanded exponentially in the United States. At most natural food stores and in natural food sections of supermarkets, one could find a large variety of soyfoods, including soy milk, soy yogurt, marinated tofu, baked tofu, and numerous Asian specialties with approachable English labels. Companies such as Soyfoods of America, Quong Hop, Island Spring, Tofutti Brands, Mori-Nu, Azumaya, and House Foods dotted the burgeoning natural foods landscape.

I have been preparing and enjoying tofu dishes in my home for decades and have a well-stocked library of tofu cookbooks. But *The Complete Tofu Cookbook* is unique. It far surpasses anything I have seen in the past. The curious reader will find intriguing preparations and ingredients, flavors, and spices that will inspire cooking experiences well beyond their expectations. Camille Oger's contribution to the world of soyfoods will bring joy to the art of preparing tofu in ways we never imagined in the West in 1975!

TED NORQUIST, PHD
FOUNDER WHOLESOY & CO
SONOMA, CALIFORNIA
2020

INTRODUCTION

IS THIS A VEGETARIAN COOKBOOK?

In Western countries, tofu is invariably associated with a vegetarian diet. This is not necessarily the case in Asia. This book, however, does offer only vegetarian and vegan recipes, as I find this is the best way to not exclude anyone. An omnivore can eat vegetarian, while the reverse is not possible. Not using meat products is also a way of getting around a number of religious bans, whether one is a Catholic observing Lent, or an adherent of Islam, Judaism, Hinduism, Buddhism, or another belief system that discourages the eating of pork, beef, or meat in general. If I can encourage people who eat meat every day to eat a little less, that's good for them. But please don't see this as a militant position. That is not the purpose of this book; its purpose is simply to present an often misunderstood and underestimated ingredient, to offer inspiration to those who sometimes lack it when mealtime comes around (myself included), and to give a little insight into other cultures, countries, and cuisines.

I am neither vegetarian nor vegan. I know the flavors of meat, fish, and eggs; I know what consistency they give to the dishes. So I won't tell you "it tastes like meat!" or "it has the same texture as with cream and eggs!" if that's not the case. There is nothing more frustrating than a substitute ingredient that does not perform well. No, tofu is not and never will be meat. In some recipes, it can be surprisingly deceptive (believe me, I'm the first one surprised, every time), but that's not the purpose of tofu. The meat/tofu dichotomy is pretty nonsensical anyway, and it's largely a Western perspective. The fact that tofu is not meat does not mean that it is "less than" or uninteresting; it has very special qualities in cooking that meat does not have. If there is one thing to remember about Asian cultures when it comes to tofu, it is that it is a normal everyday ingredient, and that it is not restricted to a particular population (like vegetarians). Tofu is for everyone!

WHAT IS TOFU?

"Tofu" is a Japanese word meaning "bean curd." For readers who still regard tofu as a mysterious, even suspicious, ingredient, know that it is actually a very simple product that has many points in common with fresh cheese. It is based on a legume: yellow soybeans. Soybeans are soaked and then mashed, mixed with water, and pressed to extract an off-white liquid known as soy milk. This is cooked, then curdled with the help of various coagulants. Traditionally, the coagulant used was *nigari*, a seawater precipitate rich in minerals such as magnesium and calcium chlorides. Modern-day manufacturers simply add magnesium chloride or calcium sulfate. Other coagulating agents are glucono-delta-lactone (GDL), a food additive that also plays a role in curing and pickling, or even just lemon juice or vinegar. (Turn to page 8 for more details on all these coagulants.) This coagulation process separates the soy milk into two distinct elements: "whey" and "curds" of proteins and lipids – in chemistry, we'd call the curds a "gel". This process works much the same way with animal milk as it does with soy milk.

To create what we call "firm" tofu, the soy milk curd is molded and pressed in order to squeeze out the whey, then cut into tidy blocks, rinsed in cold, clean water, and sold bathing in this water. In the US, most tofu is pasteurized to extend its shelf life. The texture of tofu can vary greatly depending on the coagulating agent used; it can be quite spongy and airy, denser and smoother, or rather gel-like. So-called "silken" tofu, on the other hand, is the result of soy milk coagulating directly in a mold, without pressing – a process similar to the way yogurt is made. There are many subtle variations in the manufacturing process that can yield a wide variety of results, which will be described in detail throughout this book.

Tofu is more or less white in color. Its color depends on several factors. First, the whiteness of the finished tofu is linked to the variety of soybeans used, and the color will be more or less bright white depending on the soybeans' content of beneficial plant nutrients such as anthocyanins, isoflavones, and polyphenols. In an industrial setting, you can force the whiteness of the soybean by playing with its pH during soy milk extraction. Next, the richer the tofu is in calcium and proteins, the denser it will be, dispersing light better, and therefore taking on a whiter appearance.

INVESTIGATING SOY

Some people tend to feel rather distrustful of soy, the raw material for tofu. This legume is interesting from a nutritional point of view because it is rich in protein, vitamin K, iron, magnesium, phosphorus, potassium, manganese, zinc, and copper. However, since it contains plant-based dietary estrogens it is sometimes accused of being an endocrine disruptor. There is no scientific consensus on this question at present; the many studies carried out on soy and soy products give varied, and sometimes even completely contradictory, outcomes. The wide divergence of conclusions can be explained quite simply: some studies are carried out on animals, others on humans; the subjects belong to different ethnic groups, who tend to consume differing amounts of soy and have been shown to derive less or more health benefits from it; the subjects' prior hormonal conditions can cause variations in the results; and finally, different

studies focus on distinct types of soy (different varieties of soybean, processed or unprocessed soy products).

Historically, the principal concern about soy's health effects centered around its isoflavone content. Researchers wondered whether these phytoestrogens, or "plant estrogens," could influence hormone receptors and cause either estrogenic or anti-estrogenic activity. However, the effects of plant estrogens in the human body have proven to be much weaker than the effects of our hormones. According to the Harvard School of Public Health, results of recent, well-designed human population studies indicate that soy has either a beneficial or neutral effect on human health.

In this context, the right approach is to encourage moderation. We'll read in one place that soy calms hot flashes, fights osteoporosis, and protects against hormone-related cancers, we'll read elsewhere that it encourages hormone-related cancers and thyroid problems. Do not panic: there is no risk in eating tofu in moderation several times a week. Like everything, you shouldn't abuse it and eat a couple of pounds a day. If you stick to reasonable portions (consumption of about four ounces per day three times a week is considered prudent), you can safely take advantage of the many benefits of soy. Soybeans are indeed one of the rare plants to offer complete proteins containing the nine amino acids essential to our bodies, and they are rich in polyunsaturated fatty acids, fiber, vitamins, and minerals while being low in saturated fat.

COAGULANTS

As mentioned previously, nowadays the main coagulants used commercially to curdle soy milk are magnesium chloride, calcium sulfate, and glucono-delta-lactone (GDL). Each gives a different texture to the final product and influences its taste. These additives are not risky to our health and are sold freely.

Tofu ingredients: yellow soybeans (1), magnesium chloride (2), calcium sulfate (3), and glucono-delta-lactone (4).

Magnesium chloride, the coagulant most commonly used in Japan and France, contributes a slightly bitter flavor and produces a less elastic gel, creating a fairly firm tofu with a rough and slightly spongy texture. To counter the bitterness of magnesium chloride, you can mix a pinch of licorice powder into your soy milk (or an amount equivalent to 0.2 percent of the total volume); not only will its flavor be sweeter, but your tofu will keep a little better.

Calcium sulfate, the most common coagulant used in the United States and China, results in a sweeter-tasting tofu and produces a more elastic and less firm gel. After pressing, we are left with a denser, softer, smoother, and whiter tofu.

Glucono-delta-lactone is particularly used in Japan for making silken tofu and in Southeast Asia and China for a snack called *dòuhuā,* known here as tofu pudding. GDL creates an extra-fine gel consistency similar to that of jelly. The resulting tofu has a flexible, elastic, and fragile flan-like texture.

Calcium chloride and magnesium sulfate are other chemical compounds that can work as coagulants, as can simple lemon juice, vinegar, or another acidic ingredient. Seawater and fermented whey are also traditional tofu coagulants in some countries. The three products mentioned above give the best results, however. To obtain a precise consistency or flavor, you can use them alone or mix them. These coagulants are easily found in organic markets or online, on sites dedicated to brewing beer or making tofu.

INTOLERANCES & ALLERGIES

Some people are convinced they can't stand silken tofu – even though they have no problem digesting firm tofu. They sometimes blame certain coagulating agents. These remain behind in silken tofu, which is not pressed, whereas they are partially removed with the extracted liquid when firm tofu is pressed. Obviously, some people might not be able to tolerate a particular additive; in that case, they must identify and avoid the offending ingredient. Magnesium chloride is known for its laxative effects, but the amounts used to make tofu (firm or silken) are not typically enough to have a significant impact. However, if you have the impression that this coagulant does not work for you, make sure to choose a silken tofu made with calcium sulfate or glucono-delta-lactone (GDL).

Also bear in mind that a suspected food intolerance is sometimes an illusion. I myself believed for years that silken tofu didn't agree with me; one very bad experience had nearly obliterated my desire to ever taste it again. However, I did go back and try it again, and have eaten it repeatedly since. I have tested all the coagulants, I have eaten it cooked and uncooked, and I have not been sick. It was, in fact, a case of food poisoning that one time. Unfortunately, this can happen if tofu is not stored carefully and is then eaten uncooked. Tofu is more fragile than it might seem; it must be kept refrigerated and used by the expiration date on the package. If tofu is removed from its package and stored in the refrigerator, keep it immersed in water and covered. The water should be changed each day to keep the tofu fresh. One to five days is usually the maximum time tofu will remain fresh under these conditions.

Tofu textures: firm tofu (1), pressed (super firm) tofu (2), medium tofu (3), and firm silken tofu (4).

TOFU HAS NO FLAVOR?

All styles of tofu have at least one flavor: that of soy. It is a little reminiscent of hazelnut, but very delicate. That said, there are many different styles of tofu that can have other flavors and aromas. Some are known for their blandness, others for their strong taste. But in general, the most widely known one is plain fresh tofu, which is particularly mild in flavor. This impression is reinforced by its simple white appearance and by the fact that it is not salty, sweet, or fatty. It is not uncommon to hear people criticizing tofu for its lack of flavor, sometimes even with a certain vehemence. There's something special about it: It's one of the few foods that causes some people to complain both that it is perfectly tasteless and that they hate it. Which doesn't really make sense. How can someone develop such an aversion to something whose flavor they do not perceive?

If you think about it, most foods that have little flavor are generally appreciated or at least tolerated by everyone, because they do not have a characteristic off-putting flavor – rice, white cheese, chickpeas.... Take the potato. It has no strong aromas, but I have never met anyone who hates potatoes. A plain, salt-free, fat-free boiled potato is at least as bland as a block of tofu. You will often be told that the potato is different because it can be transformed in a thousand ways, all delicious. Guess what? Tofu can too. Except that Westerners have a few centuries of experience with potatoes, and very little with tofu. The categorical rejection of tofu by some Westerners is in my opinion a posture, a stubborn prejudice, an admission of ignorance, or a silly food phobia.

Ironically, tofu is a food that is not supposed to trigger passions. In traditional Chinese medicine, it is a "cold" food. The blandness of fresh tofu is seen as an advantage, a culinary "white page," like that of white rice or wheat flour, which can be exploited in many ways – by marinating it to give it different flavors, by cooking it with spices, aromatics,

and various condiments.... Its neutrality makes it versatile; it goes with all vegetables, all fruits – it goes with everything. It's an inexhaustible source of culinary diversity. The possibilities are only limited by your imagination, because everything is possible, from sweet to salty, or a combination of the two.

As you will see in the coming sections of recipes originating in different countries, there are types of tofu that are not bland at all. Chinese fermented tofu have a taste, smell, and appearance similar to traditional European cheeses. The flavored tofus found in Asia and in France have well-developed, very distinctive aromas, such as smoked tofu or five-spice tofu. These products are very interesting to use in cooking but play a smaller role than fresh natural tofu, because their unique flavors can limit ways of cooking them. Finally, taste is not just a matter of aromas and flavors. It's also a story of textures, and there are endless texture variations in the world of tofu. If your mind immediately goes to picture a white block, firm and smooth, you need to expand your thinking. Here is an overview of tofu textures, which can help you find your way around and identify your favorite types of tofu by their specific consistencies.

TOFU TEXTURES

Tofu can take on a variety of textures: firmer or less firm and smoother or less smooth. Labeling practices, which vary from one brand to another and from one country to another, are meant to guide consumers, but in practice can be confusing. In addition, some packages are especially enigmatic, when they are imported products labeled in foreign languages. So here I try to classify the textures of tofu in a way that lets you know what you are looking at when you're shopping for tofu.

The firmness of a tofu product depends mainly on two very different things. First there is its density, which in turn depends on its water content and can be guessed at

FIRM TOFU (per 3½ ounces)		
Pre-pressed (super firm)	200+ Calories	Extremely dense and firm, generally smooth and supple.
Extra firm	145+ Calories	Very high density, very firm and solid tofu.
Very firm	125–145 Calories	Nice density, firm and solid tofu.
Firm	105–125 Calories	Basic firm tofu.
Medium	80–105 Calories	Basic firm tofu in Japan. Can be rather spongy (if made with magnesium chloride), crumbles easily. May be rather flexible (if made with calcium sulfate), firmer, and more crumbly.
Soft	55–80 Calories	Common in Asian grocery stores. Made with magnesium chloride, it is spongy, very tender, and fragile. With calcium sulfate, it is more flexible and holds together better.
SILKEN TOFU (per 3½ ounces)		
Extra firm	60–75 Calories	Quite solid, can be handled without great difficulty if it is made with calcium sulfate or GDL. Less fine and less flexible texture if made with magnesium chloride.
Firm	55 Calories	Basic silken tofu. If made with calcium sulfate, will have a flan-like texture, can be handled with care. If made with magnesium chloride, it has a more creamy texture, but reluctant to hold together. With GDL expect an extra-fine texture, almost jelled.
Soft	45 Calories	Texture of very fragile custard or firm yogurt. Chinese dòuhuā, (tofu pudding) falls into this category.
Extra-soft	44 Calories maximum	Extremely fragile, does not hold together regardless of the coagulant used. The curd can be gathered but never pressed. Generally sold in tubes in Korean grocery stores (sundubu).

by the number of calories indicated on the packaging – no matter what country the tofu comes from, this label is required. The more calories a tofu has, the denser it is, and therefore lower in water in proportion to its weight. The most caloric tofu is the firmest. Then, the firmness of tofu also depends on another crucial element: its porosity. The coarser and airier the texture of a tofu, the less firm it will be when compared to a smoother and less porous tofu, even when the two have an equivalent density.

The determining factor in denseness and porosity is the coagulant that was used to make the tofu. Magnesium chloride makes a tofu with an airy, somewhat spongy texture. Calcium sulfate makes a smoother and more flexible tofu that holds together better even at equivalent density. Finally, glucono-delta-lactone (GDL)

makes a tofu with an extra-fine texture, less porous and therefore even firmer at comparable density. Now, the coagulant used is indicated in the list of ingredients on the packaging. The full name may be listed – for example, "glucono-delta-lactone"; an abbreviation or acronym may be used, like "GDL." To make matters more complex, each tofu-producing country has its own conception of firmness. For example, Japanese firm tofu is much less solid than Chinese firm tofu, which is in turn much less dense than super firm vacuum-packaged tofu. So, here is a basic table in which I have tried to standardize the different degrees of tofu firmness according to density and porosity. I have separated tofu into two main categories: so-called "firm" tofu (which is pressed into a block) and so-called silken tofu (which is not pressed but molded

TYPE OF TOFU	PRIMARY USE
Pressed (super firm)	Sautéed, braised, grated, poached in a salad.
Extra firm	Braised, fried, sautéed, boiled, grilled.
Firm	Uncooked, braised, fried, sautéed, boiled, grilled.
Medium	Uncooked, crumbled, mixed, braised, boiled, soups and stews.
Soft	Uncooked, crumbled, mixed, boiled, fried dishes, soups and stews.
Extra firm silken tofu	Uncooked, mixed, desserts, soups and stews.
Firm silken tofu	Uncooked, mixed, desserts, soups and stews.
Soft silken tofu and tofu pudding (dòuhuā)	Uncooked, mixed, smoothies, sauces, desserts, soups and stews.
Extra-soft silken tofu	Uncooked, mixed, smoothies, sauces, desserts, soups and stews.

directly into its container, and which is therefore much more fragile, with a generally finer texture).

In order to have a game plan, I will use Western tofu standards as a reference in all the recipes in this book. When I talk about firm tofu without further details, it will be basic firm tofu made with magnesium chloride. If I specify that it is soft firm tofu, the coagulating agent is, on the other hand, calcium sulfate. For silken tofu, the mention of "firm" refers to the most common firmness of silken tofu in the West. If I specify that it is extra fine silky tofu, this means that the coagulating agent is GDL, which creates a perfectly smooth texture, quite supple but fragile, close to a jelly.

PRACTICAL ADVICE

CHOOSING TOFU

Anyone can eat tofu and enjoy it – if it's a good product and it is treated properly. And that's where we have our work cut out for us. You must learn to choose, prepare, and cook your tofu just like any other food. Westerners are not educated about

tofu at home, and so many styles of tofu are available – which does not make the neophyte's task any easier. We weren't trained to recognize the right ones, taught what kind of tofu is made for what. So, here is a guide to help you see the field more clearly. Of course, we all have personal preferences and constraints, so I advise you to see what is available to you locally and to test various types of tofu for yourself. Do not hesitate to visit Asian groceries, which offer a wide choice of products, from the firmest to the most tender. And don't forget that a good tofu is always found in the fresh section: the only exception is shelf-stable silken tofu, found in Tetra Pak containers, which can be stored in a cupboard for up to a year.

HANDLING TOFU

Firm, extra firm, and pressed tofu are easy to work with because they are solid. They are easy to remove from their packaging, drain, and cut. The other types of tofu are much more fragile and must be treated with care and precision. Blocks of medium and soft tofu can be damaged from the slightest jostling; from the moment you buy them, you must transport them without banging or bumping them, as you would delicate pastries or ripe fruit. The best way to get them out of their packaging while keeping them whole is to stand in front of your sink, open the wrapping completely and put one hand on the tofu block, then turn the packaging over to let the whey drain into your sink, holding the tofu back with your hand. You can then gently place the tofu on a cutting board and cut it to your liking. Tofu artisans often unmold their tofu in a large water bath to avoid damaging it and hold it in their hand while cutting, still in the water. However, this precaution is not needed with smaller tofu blocks.

Silken tofu does not bathe in its whey; it fills its mold completely. This means it can be removed more easily from the mold directly onto a plate or cutting board. To make sure it comes out easily from its mold, pass the blade of a knife around the sides before turning it over and gently squeezing the packaging if necessary. If you cut it into slices or pieces, for example to eat it cold, transfer it with the flat edge of a large knife. If you use silken tofu or soft tofu in a stew, such as the famous *mápó dòufu,* always make sure to use the back of your wooden spoon to mix the preparation so as not to damage the cubes, which are very fragile.

PREPARING TOFU

Before cooking, tofu can be treated in different ways to adjust its taste and texture. A few tips will let you really take advantage of tofu's great versatility.

FIRMING UP TOFU

Method 1: pressing
Block tofu should always be drained before cooking. If it's extra firm or pressed tofu, it will be solid enough for sautéing in a frying pan or wok. All you will need to do is pat it dry with paper towels. Medium to firm tofu will need to be firmed up for some recipes. The simplest and most effective method to get your tofu texture

a little denser is to wrap it with several layers of paper towel, place it on a plate, and weight it with another plate for 30 minutes, 1 hour, or more depending on the desired firmness. The block will give up some water and lose volume, but will gain solidity. In each of the recipes in this book, you will find details on the recommended pressing method, when needed. The technique is always very simple and does not require any special equipment – simply plates, cutting boards, even bowls filled with fruit.

Method 2: saltwater bath
Some tofus are too fragile to be pressed. This is true of soft tofu and extra firm silken tofu, which would be crushed under any weight and is even too fragile to be wrapped in paper towels without damage. To firm them up a bit before cooking them, perhaps in a stew, just give them a saltwater bath. To do this, dissolve ¼ cup of salt in 1 quart of boiling water. Cut your tofu as desired

Using the inclined plane method to drain and firm up tofu in a manufacturing workshop in Japan.

(into cubes, slices, or so on, depending on the recipe) and gently place it in the water – ideally, use a large and shallow container that you can place the tofu into without damaging it. Let it soak for 15 minutes, then carefully remove it from the water and place it on several layers of paper towels. Let drain another 15 minutes.

You can also do a saltwater soak for firmer tofu: hot salt water flushes out excess moisture from the surface of the tofu by tightening its structure. It also keeps it soft inside. Plus, tofu absorbs salt well, so it is in effect pre-salted. Finally, if you sauté or fry it, it will be crisper on the outside. Do not hesitate to apply this treatment to your tofu whenever you want, even if the recipe does not specify it; it will never hurt.

Method 3: the inclined plane
To drain your tofu effectively, wrap a cutting board with a clean cloth and lay your block of tofu on top. Tilt the board as much as possible (without letting the tofu slide off – it's up to you to find the right angle), directing the lowest side toward your sink to collect the liquid. Leave the tofu like this for at least 1 hour.

MARINADES
Before cooking, tofu can be treated in different ways to adjust its taste and texture. A few tips will let you really take advantage of tofu's great versatility.

Brown the tofu in advance
By browning slices or cubes of tofu in a frying pan for a few minutes on each side, you create a crust on the surface that does a fabulous job of absorbing sauces and marinades. Many Asian recipes require this step, especially before braising the tofu. You can also fry a block in an oil bath (the Japanese call it *atsuage*; see recipe on page 113), or you can even buy ready-fried tofu, available in the refrigerated case at Asian groceries.

Freeze the tofu beforehand
This may seem surprising, but freezing tofu radically changes its consistency. There are two basic methods for this: the Japanese version and the Chinese version. The Japanese method is to drain a block of firm tofu, wrap it in a cloth, place it in a box, and freeze it overnight for 24 hours. Then let it thaw in the fridge, after running it under warm water to remove the cloth wrapper – or immersing it in a large warm saltwater bath. Drain on several layers of paper towel for at least 15 minutes, and it will be ready to be cut into pieces and marinated. During the freezing and thawing process, tofu releases a lot of water; when it stays overnight in the fridge, small ice crystals form inside, giving it a slightly more spongy texture that absorbs marinades beautifully. A unique form of tofu is found in Japanese grocery stores, which takes this process to the extreme: freeze-dried tofu, called *kōyadōfu*. Rehydrate it in a bowl of water, squeeze it by hand to drain the excess water, and then marinate it as desired.

The Chinese method is to encourage the formation of ice crystals in the tofu in order to leave visible holes after thawing. This produces a more fragile but very absorbent tofu. To do this, slice a block of firm tofu, place it directly on a plate, in a plastic bag, or in an airtight container, and leave it in the freezer for 24 to 48 hours. Then leave it to thaw in the refrigerator or in a cool place on a plate covered with several layers of paper towel. You can also speed up thawing by dipping the tofu slices in a large, warm salt-water bath. Drain the slices on several layers of paper towel for at least 15 minutes. Then they will absorb marinade at an impressive speed!

Infusions
Firm tofu can be flavored by infusions; this is how you make five-spice pressed "tofu (see page 94). For this technique, we simmer a block or pieces of tofu in a spicy and fragrant concoction for about thirty minutes. You can use the spices of your choice instead of the traditional Chinese.

CRUMBLE & MIX

You almost always see tofu called for in the same form in most recipes: cut into cubes or slices. In fact, there are many other things you can do with it. It is interesting to run a few cubes of medium to firm tofu through a blender or small food processor. By pulsing in short bursts, we can observe each stage of its transformation, and all the different consistencies that appear suggest new ideas. First the tofu is coarsely chopped, then finely, and then begins form a paste that can be mixed with a little water to achieve a perfectly smooth and homogeneous cream.

Fairly soft and spongy tofu can simply be crumbled by hand. Rough, hand-torn pieces are sometimes what we are looking for, rather than a clean cut with a knife. Coarsely shredded tofu has a better texture for breading or a sauce to cling to.

STORING TOFU

Despite its clean white appearance and style of packaging that suggests an aseptic product, fresh tofu is as fragile as cheese. It must be refrigerated. Check the expiration date before buying tofu, and stick to it. If you've started a package of firm tofu without finishing it, you can keep the rest for two days in the refrigerator – it should soak in a liquid, whether it's whey or fresh water. Firm tofu can also be frozen without any problem, whole in its unopened or opened box, drained and placed in an airtight container or a freezer storage bag. When frozen, it turns yellowish and a bit translucent, but don't worry – it hasn't gone off. It will go back to its normal color once thawed. Its time in the freezer will even give it a superpower: that of absorbing marinades (see page 16). Silken tofu loses its smoothness in the freezer; it will take on some chewiness and can no longer be used in recipes that highlight its creamy texture. It can still be used in soups, broths, and stir-frys.

OTHER SOY PRODUCTS & TOFU DERIVATIVES

To make tofu, you need yellow soybeans. After they have been soaked in water, you can make soy milk. This can easily be done at home (see page 24), and is also preferable to industrial soy milk, which will likely not be concentrated enough to make a good tofu, and will sometimes contain additives (sugar, preservatives, thickeners). Freshly pressed and cooked soy milk is very good, try it! You can also use it in cooking. After pressing ground soybeans and water to extract the "milk" that will be used to make tofu, you end up with dry soybean pulp, or *okara*. This can be used in cooking, in particular to make a delicious little Japanese dish simmered and served as an accompaniment or as a starter, called *unohana* (see page 144). You will also find in this book an absolutely delicious recipe from Korea that uses unfiltered soy milk: *kongguksu*, a noodle soup garnished with soy, pine nuts, and sesame (see page 188).

There are a multitude of types of tofu with different consistencies, as well as derivatives based on tofu or soy milk that are commonly used in the different cuisines of the Far East. You will discover them in detail in this book in sections devoted to each country. The amazing skin of soy milk, or *yuba*, will open up unexpected possibilities in the kitchen. Tofu fermented in brine, or *dòufǔrǔ*, will add flavor to your wok-fried vegetables and sauces. Pressed tofu in all its forms, including fabulous noodles, will allow you to use tofu in previously unthinkable ways. Tofu puffs will absorb the liquid in your soups, broths, and casseroles beautifully, or if you grill or fry it, will offer a crisp surface and airy interior. The world of tofu is much larger than you might think at first glance, and it's a lot of fun.

OTHER TYPES OF "TOFU"

It's not just all about yellow soybeans. You can also make tofu with black soybeans (though this is rare) or edamame, which are immature yellow soybeans and have a pretty green color. Some people even try making tofu with other legumes. Not all of them work, and the results are quite variable. However, by changing the method, you can do wonders with chickpeas or pigeon peas. This is what the Burmese do. Their yellow tofu is very different from soy tofu and it is a real wonder to discover in the chapter devoted to Burma (see page 245).

Then, there are many so-called "tofus" that are not really tofus. They are given this name in their countries of origin because of their block shape, but the resemblance stops there. They are based on nuts and oilseeds, like almonds, sesame, or peanuts. These ingredients are finely ground with water to obtain vegetable "milks." Instead of adding a coagulating agent, they may be thickened using kudzu, the starch from the roots of *Pueraria montana*, a vine of the legume family, or set using agar-agar, a vegetable substitute for gelatin made

Pressed tofu can take many forms.

from different species of red algae. The resulting thick paste is then molded and cooled. They form solid blocks with a more or less flexible consistency, and give off pleasant and delicate aromas of the almonds, peanuts, or other nuts and seeds used to make them. They are generally eaten cold; they are perfect as a starter with salty condiments, and delicious as a dessert with a sweet sauce or even fruit. You will find different recipes of this type in the pages dedicated to China and Japan.

TOFU BASICS

Soy
Tofu is usually made from yellow soybeans, although black soybeans can also be used. There are a huge number of varieties of yellow soybeans in Asia, each with its unique advantages for a specific use. In the West, the choice is much more limited. The most important thing is to choose good fresh Asian soybeans (available in Korean and Japanese grocery stores) or untreated fresh soybeans (in organic stores). The soybeans should be bright and unblemished, uniform in color and size.

Water
Tofu is above all a story of water. This is the ingredient that the tofu artisans I have met in China, Japan, and Korea paid the most attention to. The water should be very soft and very pure. Use a soft mineral water or filtered water.

The coagulant
Coagulants can be found in several forms. Food-grade magnesium chloride in crystals is common because it is sold in most organic stores and in pharmacies. It also exists in liquid form. *Nigari* is the traditional Japanese version, made from evaporated seawater. Calcium sulfate and glucono-delta-lactone (GDL) can be ordered online in powder form without any problem. I recommend using magnesium chloride or calcium sulfate to make firm tofu, and GDL to make silken tofu.

Equipment
Few utensils are really essential for making tofu. At the very least you will need a large, heavy-based pot, a smaller pot, a stand blender (not a hand blender), a wooden spatula, a large chinois or fine sieve, cheesecloth, a ladle, and a tofu pressing box. This tofu pressing box can be replaced by other things: a cheese mold, a plastic takeout container you've saved, or a colander and a small plate. You will also need a few heavy items to press the tofu, such as full cans of beans or tomatoes.

Yellow soybeans.

Black soybeans.

Basic recipes

SOY MILK
(& Okara)

Making soy milk at home is a little time consuming and it will require you to wash some dishes, but it is so good! Homemade soy milk is generally the best choice for making tofu, because you'll have just the right amount and it will contain no additives. In addition, you will get *okara,* or pressed soybean pulp, which you will also find useful in the kitchen.

🕐 prep **20 min**　🕐 soak **10 hr**　🕐 cook **15 min**　🍴 vegan

For 2 quarts soy milk
• 1 cup dried yellow soybeans • 2 qt filtered water

Rinse the soybeans well and soak them in a large bowl with five times their volume of tap water. Let them soak at room temperature for at least 8 hours in summer and up to 10 hours in winter. Once rehydrated, they should open easily when you squeeze one with your fingers. Drain, then rinse them again several times.

In a large, heavy-based pot, bring 5 cups of filtered water to boil over medium-high heat. While it is heating, whirl the rehydrated beans in a blender with 2 cups of filtered water. The mixture should look like a milkshake. Add this mixture to the boiling water, lower the heat, and rinse out the blender with ½ cup of filtered water and add this to the pot. Heat the mixture over low heat for a few minutes until it begins to foam. Watch it carefully, so it doesn't overflow! Turn off the heat, use a skimmer to remove excess foam, and stir to incorporate the rest.

Place a chinois or other fine-mesh strainer lined with cheesecloth in another pot set in your sink. Have at hand a tool for pressing, such as a potato masher or a pestle. A wooden spoon could do the trick. Pour the hot mixture into the cheese-cloth-lined strainer. When it is full, wait for the level to drop and continue to pour.

When all of the soy milk has passed through the cheesecloth, gather all the corners of the fabric in one hand and twist the fabric to form a bag – if it's too hot, let it cool for a moment. Press the bag with against the strainer your potato masher, pestle, or wooden spoon to extract the last drops of liquid. Open the fabric, lightly spread out the remaining solid pulp, add ½ cup of filtered water, and mix with a wooden spoon. Squeeze the cheesecloth again by hand to extract a little more liquid.

(continued)

The white juice in your pot is your soy milk (still raw), in a perfect quantity to make firm tofu. It can also be used in other recipes. The dry pulp in your cheesecloth, called *okara,* can be used in cooking: you can add it to your pie dough, cookies, and other baked goods, or make it into a delicious little Japanese dish called *uno-hana* (see page 144). It must definitely be cooked before being consumed.

To cook your soy milk, heat it over low heat in its pot, covered (a clear lid is ideal for keeping an eye on it, because it tends to overflow if it gets too hot). Bring to a gentle simmer and let cook for 5 minutes. You can drink it, refrigerate it for up to 3 days, or immediately continue with the recipe opposite to make firm tofu.

Notes To make silken tofu, follow the steps above but make a more concentrated milk using only 1½ quarts of filtered water. For an even richer soy milk, use 2¼ cups of soybeans.

By covering soy milk, you can prevent a film from forming on its surface. If it seems more convenient, do not cover it, but be sure to remove the solid elements from the surface using a skimmer.

Many tofu makers recommend not stirring soy milk while heating, so as not to give it a burnt flavor (the bottom always burns a little, even on very low heat). I don't stir it either. To make cleanup easier, just use a nonstick pan.

FIRM
TOFU

Once you've made your soy milk, it's not a great deal more effort to make firm tofu. You just have to coagulate the milk and then press it. For coagulation, you can use magnesium chloride to create a rather spongy and rigid tofu, or calcium sulfate for a more dense and flexible tofu.

🕐 prep **20 min**   🕐 press **15 min**   🌱 vegan

For 1 block firm to medium tofu (12–16 oz)
- 2 qt soy milk
- 1 tsp (6 g) magnesium chloride in crystals or scant ½ tsp (6 g) calcium sulfate in powder
- 7 Tbsp filtered water

If you've just made your soy milk, it will be very hot in the pan. Turn off the heat and let it cool for 2 minutes without removing the lid. Otherwise, heat 2 quarts of soy milk over low heat in a pot covered with a clear lid (so you can keep an eye on it). When the milk comes to a gentle simmer, continue cooking for 5 minutes, keeping watch so that the milk does not overflow. Turn off the heat and let cool for 2 minutes without removing the lid.

Meanwhile, prepare your coagulant: in a small bowl, combine the crystals or the powder with 7 tablespoons of filtered water and stir to mix. Place a tofu pan – or other perforated pan, or colander – in your sink and line the inside with a generous length of cheesecloth, letting it hang over the sides of the pan.

Stir the soy milk vigorously using a wooden spatula, making a Z shape six to eight times. Pour a third of the coagulant into the pot, stirring again to distribute it throughout the milk, then stop the spatula in the center of the pot. When the milk is no longer moving, take out the spatula while holding it vertically, so as not to move the milk. Distribute another third of the coagulant over the milk with a teaspoon; do not mix. Cover the pot and wait for 3 minutes. Add the rest of the coagulant with the teaspoon, trying to distribute it evenly over all the milk. Use a spatula to gently turn the top layer of the mixture (going ¾ inch deep), then cover and wait for 3 minutes if you are using magnesium chloride, or 6 minutes for calcium sulfate.

(continued)

Artisanal firm tofu making.

Uncover the pot; the milk should be completely curdled. With a ladle, carefully scoop out as much whey as possible and use it to moisten the cheesecloth lining the mold. With the ladle, carefully scoop up the curd and place it in the cheesecloth. Squeeze out the excess whey by slightly lifting the cheesecloth. When all the curd is settled in the mold, fold the cheesecloth over and place the mold lid on top. If you are using a colander, place a small plate over it.

To make semi-firm tofu, weight the lid with a 1-pound weight and let drain for about 15 minutes. For firm tofu, use a 3-pound weight and drain for 15–20 minutes. After pressing, the volume of the tofu should be reduced by half for medium-firm tofu, and by two-thirds for firm tofu. It will firm up further as it cools; do not overpress it.

Fill a bowl with cold water and unmold the tofu into it. Leave it in the water for about 5 minutes to firm up. Slide a plate under the tofu and take it out of the water. Let it sit for a few hours in a cool place, covered with a cloth, before using. If you do not intend to use it within 8 hours, place it in the refrigerator in an airtight container, covered with water. Change the water every 2 days; the tofu should keep for up to 1 week.

Note If you are not up for making your own soy milk, you can buy it commercially. Ideally, choose the fresh soy milk that is sold in Chinese, Japanese, and Korean grocery stores. If you buy a domestic brand, be careful: it should not contain any thickeners, preservatives, or additives, and above all should not be sweet. Also make sure it is rich enough: it should contain at least 1.8 grams of fat and 3.6 grams of protein per 100 ml.

SILKEN TOFU

To make a good Japanese-style silken tofu, with a very fine, smooth, and almost custard-like texture, ideally you need to use glucono-delta-lactone or calcium sulfate as a coagulant. This tofu is in no hurry; we are not going to help it along by curdling the soy milk. The milk must set while remaining whole. It is a good idea to reuse the plastic trays from store-bought tofu to mold your silken tofu; this type of tofu, being quite fragile, does best in small containers. They must be small enough to place in a steamer basket. Butter dishes or small glass ramekins are also recommended.

🕐 prep **5 min**   🕐 cook **15 min**   🌱 vegan

For about 1½ pounds of silken tofu

- ½ tsp (2 g) glucono-delta-lactone (GDL) or ¼ tsp (2 g) calcium sulfate • 2 tsp filtered water
- 3 cups concentrated soy milk, cold or at room temperature

Heat water for steaming in a large pot. When the water comes to a boil, lower the heat slightly to keep it steaming steadily. In a small bowl, mix the GDL or calcium sulfate and the 2 teaspoons of filtered water.

Stir the soy milk to check its consistency; if it is not completely smooth, strain it through a cheesecloth-lined colander. Combine the soy milk and the coagulant. Mix well and pour into the molds to a depth of 1–2½ inches. Place the molds in a steam basket and partially cover the pot, leaving the lid askew so as to minimize condensation. Cook until the tofu is set – a 1-inch depth will require about 6 minutes.
The tofu is ready when it jiggles when shaken, like custard. If you tilt the mold, the tofu may slide slightly. To make sure it's cooked, insert a toothpick in the center; it should leave a small visible hole on the surface. If the tofu cooks for a little too long, it will be all right. If you are not sure whether it is ready, it is better to leave it in the steamer basket for too long than not long enough.

Carefully remove the steamer basket from the pot and let cool for a few minutes. Remove the molds from the basket and allow them to cool completely at room temperature before placing them in the fridge for at least 4 hours. The silken tofu will keep for 3 days.

To unmold the tofu, let it warm up slightly at room temperature for 15 minutes, then slip the blade of a knife along the sides of the mold. Place a plate on top and turn plate and mold over together.

SILKEN TOFU
WITH CITRUS

It is somewhat rare to find flavored tofus in Japan. The vast majority of the products available are natural. Some artisans, however, offer versions with a light scent, including silken tofu with yuzu (a mandarin orange hybrid). The recipe is very simple and can be made with other citrus fruits of your choice: orange, lemon, Buddha's hand, citron, bergamot orange...

🕐 prep **5 min**   🕐 cook **15 min**   🌱 vegan

For about 1½ pounds of silken tofu
- ½ tsp (2 g) glucono-delta-lactone (GDL) or ¼ tsp (2 g) calcium sulfate • 2 tsp filtered water
- 3 cups concentrated soy milk, cold or at room temperature
- organic or untreated citrus fruit of your choice

Heat water for steaming in a large pot. When the water comes to a boil, lower the heat slightly to keep it steaming steadily. In a small bowl, mix the GDL or calcium sulfate and the 2 teaspoons of filtered water. Set aside.

With the finest grater possible (small Japanese graters are ideal), remove 1½ teaspoons zest from your chosen citrus. Be sure to remove only the colorful skin and not the bitter white pith. The zest should be extremely fine; if needed, chop it further.

Stir the soy milk to check its consistency; if it is not completely smooth, strain it through a cheesecloth-lined colander. Combine the soy milk and zest, mixing well. Leave to infuse for a few minutes. Stir again, then add the coagulant. Mix well and pour into small molds (such as ramekins, butter dishes, or leftover tofu trays) to a thickness of 1–2½ inches. Place the molds in a steam basket and partially cover the pot, leaving the lid askew so as to minimize condensation. Cook until the tofu is set – a 1-inch depth will require about 6 minutes.

The tofu is ready when it jiggles when shaken, like custard. If you tilt the mold, the tofu may slide slightly. To make sure it's cooked, insert a toothpick in the center; it should leave a small visible hole on the surface. If the tofu cooks for a little too long, it will be all right. If you are not sure whether it is ready, it is better to leave it in the steamer basket for too long than not long enough.

Carefully remove the steamer basket from the pot and let cool for a few minutes. Remove the molds from the basket and allow them to cool completely at room temperature before placing them in the fridge for at least 4 hours. The silken tofu will keep for 3 days. To unmold the tofu, let it warm up slightly at room temperature for 15 minutes, then slip the blade of a knife along the sides of the mold. Place a plate on top and turn plate and mold over together.

TOFU
SKINS
(Yuba)

Like milk of animal origin, soy milk is very rich in protein and quite rich in fats, especially if it is concentrated. When you heat it up, it behaves similarly: a film or skin forms on its surface. This skin is a concentrate of proteins and fats, very popular in China, Taiwan, Vietnam, and Japan. It is easy to create this skin, but more difficult to handle it, because it sticks to itself like plastic wrap – but even worse. Ideally, you'll use highly concentrated homemade soy milk for this recipe, or rich fresh soy milk purchased from a Chinese, Korean, or Japanese grocery.

🕐 prep + cook **30 min** 🌱 vegan

For 4 servings
- 1 qt rich soy milk (see page 24)

Heat the soy milk over low heat, using a frying pan rather than a saucepan, to expose as much of the milk surface to the air as possible. When a skin forms on the surface, pass the blade of a knife along the sides of the pan to loosen this "skin" cleanly. With a pair of chopsticks, collect it and place it on a plate, trying to fold it neatly.

Repeat this operation as many times as necessary. If your soy milk is concentrated enough, it will not stop forming this skin on the surface as long as it is heated. Divide the tofu skin among 4 small separate bowls. Clean your chopsticks from time to time as you work. If you are not comfortable handling chopsticks, you can use a plastic spatula, the handle of a spoon, or any other smooth and flat utensil to collect the *yuba*. The Japanese craftsmen I met also do it by hand – beware, it's hot – or even with pliers.

Note Use a nonstick frying pan for easier cleanup! Even at very low heat, the soy milk sticks to the bottom of the pan.

TOFU
PUDDING
(Dòuhuā)

Delicious *dòuhuā*, of Chinese origin but adopted in much of Asia, is a kind of tofu custard with a wonderfully smooth texture, somewhat similar to silken tofu. It is very fragile and breaks as soon as you insert a spoon into it. Prepared in wide pans, *dòuhuā* is served with a large, flat spatula to make beautiful, thick layers in a bowl. It is seasoned with a salty sauce and all kinds of condiments (see the recipe for Yunnan-style tofu pudding on page 83) or enjoyed with sweet toppings (see the recipe for tofu pudding with red fruit coulis, page 368). This recipe makes it easy achieve a successful tofu pudding at home.

🕐 prep **2 min**　🕐 rest **1 hr**　🕐 cook **10 min**　🌱 vegan

For 4 servings
• Scant 1 tsp (6 g) calcium sulfate • 1½ tsp cornstarch or potato starch
• ⅓ cup water • 1 qt homemade soy milk (see page 24)

In a small bowl, mix the calcium sulfate, starch, and water.

In a large nonstick pot over medium-low heat, bring the soy milk to a boil. Turn off the heat as soon as it boils and remove the foam on its surface with a skimmer.

Stir the calcium sulfate mixture again and pour it into a large bowl or pot. Immediately pour over the soy milk. Do not stir. Cover the container with a clean kitchen towel and a lid. Let the preparation set for about 1 hour.

Use a shallow ladle or large, flat spoon to divide the tofu pudding among bowls, and enjoy with a savory or sweet condiment.

TOFU
PUDDING
(Dòuhuā)

Many *dòuhuā* recipes call for using cornstarch as a thickener. It's not necessary if you're making very rich soy milk like this. The royal version of tofu pudding! For savory accompaniments, see page 83; for sweet toppings, see page 368.

🕐 prep **40 min**   🕐 soak **8–10 hr**   🕐 cook **5–10 min**   🌱 vegan

For 4 servings
• 1¼ cup dried yellow soybeans • 5¼ cups filtered water (+ 2 Tbsp)
• 1½ tsp (6 g) glucono-delta-lactone (GDL) or scant ½ tsp (6 g) calcium sulfate

Rinse the soybeans well and soak them in a large bowl with five times their volume of tap water. Let them soak at room temperature for 8 hours in summer or 10 hours in winter. Once rehydrated, they should open easily when you squeeze one with your fingers. Drain, rinse thoroughly, and place the beans in a blender. Blend them quite finely, then add 1 quart of filtered water and mix again for a few minutes. Place a chinois or other fine-mesh strainer lined with cheesecloth in a pot set in your sink. Pour the soy liquid into the cheesecloth, then rinse the sides of the blender with the remaining 1¼ cups filtered water and pour it into the cheesecloth as well. Squeeze the cheesecloth to extract all the liquid. Reserve the dry pulp (*okara*) if desired.

Rinse the cheesecloth thoroughly to clean it and repeat the straining process once or twice if needed to achieve perfectly smooth soy milk. Bring the milk to a boil over low heat, skimming off the foam as needed. Use a nonstick pan for this, if possible, as soy milk tends to burn and stick to the bottom. Do not stir it while it is heating, as scraping the burnt milk from the pan bottom will give the milk a burnt taste.

Mix the GDL or calcium sulfate with 2 tablespoons of filtered water. Pour this mixture into a large container (bowl or pot), then pour over the boiling soy milk. Do not stir. Cover and let set for at least 20 minutes. Use a large, flat spoon to divide among bowls, and serve with the sauces and condiments of your choice.

China
&
Taiwan

豆腐

Tofu manufacturing in an artisan workshop in the north of China.

THE BIRTHPLACE OF TOFU

The Chinese are the undisputed masters of tofu; they are also its inventors. At least that's what we assume, because we don't have written proof of the existence of tofu before 950. While several theories point to the north of the country as the birthplace of tofu, and describe its invention an accident, others argue that its creation was inspired by other peoples who had already mastered the coagulation of milk, such as the Mongols or certain Indian ethnic groups. During the Sung dynasty (960–1279), tofu became a common staple among the lower social classes. The secret of its success is that it was nourishing, filling, and cost less than mutton. This poor man's dish began to appeal to the rich as well, during the Ming dynasty (1368–1662); prized for its delicacy, it quickly became a staple food of all Chinese people, including the nobility.

Though Buddhist and Taoist monks were strictly vegetarians, this was not the case for the rest of the population. Traditionally, the Chinese are fond of meat products but refrain from eating meat at certain times of the year, especially around the lunar new year. While this practice has certainly contributed to making tofu such a popular product, this is not is not the only reason. Its low cost and high availability probably played a role in its success. And the Chinese have developed a taste for this versatile ingredient with varied textures, as sophistication in tofu has progressed. It must be said that with more than a millennium of expertise today – some historians think that we could even be close to two millennia – the Chinese have not only acquired an exceptional tofu-making mastery, but have also developed a real culture linked to this product.

TOFU CULTURE

Chinese tofu is really different from Western tofu. Or rather, the many types of Chinese tofu. Look at the tofu section of a good Chinese grocery, and you will be surprised. The choice is immense, even in tiny hole-in-the-wall shops, and the many forms that this ingredient can take will probably be foreign to you for the most part. These long brown strands over here are tofu. Just like these light beige leaves that look like super-dense lasagna. These little golden puffs, these are tofu too.

Truly, I invite Westerners to check out the products sold in Chinese groceries. And I invite domestic tofu manufacturers to copy these products. We would gain in quality and variety. Without even getting into the most specialized forms of Chinese tofu, the basic products themselves are really different from what we make. Firm tofu has several variations, none of which is as coarse and compact as the typical supermarket "firm" tofu.

Moreover, the various Chinese tofus available in the West – some of which are made domestically by Chinese-founded companies (and supplying only Asian businesses, not regular organic groceries) – are just a sample. When visiting China and Taiwan, you really grasp the idea of what tofu culture means. It's a bit like observing the culture of bread in France. Tofu is everywhere, its shapes are endlessly varied, many are handcrafted, and not a day goes by without seeing this all-important food. It's there at the table, it's in grandma's shopping bag as she returns from the market, it's in every corner store, on television...tofu is there. It is essential, and it is so much a part of everyday life that locals do not notice it, do not necessarily think about it. They will start thinking about it the day they find themselves in a foreign context where, for the first time, they will be confronted with its absence or its pitiful presence. Look at French people traveling, who complain about the lack of good bread. For the Chinese, it's the same story with good tofu, good rice, and other staples of their diet.

For a foreign visitor who is not used to tofu, its omnipresence in China and Taiwan is confusing, surprising. Especially if it is a

Tofu in all its forms
is a regular sight in
Chinese market stalls.

visitor who believes that tofu is off-putting or uninteresting. He'll stumble
across old-fashioned factories, chimneys
smoking early in the morning, windows
fogged up by the steam from large tubs
full of soy milk. He'll smell the nutty scent
of cooked beans, he'll see wood fires
crackling even now in the 21st century.
He'll see styles of tofu that he has never
seen, and that he probably won't see
anywhere else. Tofus drying in the sun
on the street. Furry tofus that are fuzzy
like little soft white stuffed animals. Tofus
made just like the world's most beloved
cheeses, runny, blue in places, or down-
right blackened, with molds to see,
touch, smell, and taste. Stinky tofus that
you can smell from 100 yards away. And
so many other forms of tofu that are less
extreme, theoretically less remarkable,
but still quite delicious, surprising, and
different from what we know. If you are

even a little interested in tofu, a trip to
China or Taiwan is a goldmine of discov-
eries and revelations.

ONE DOESN'T RULE OUT
THE OTHER

Your attention please: just because there
is a lot of tofu in China doesn't mean
that Chinese people are all vegetarians. In fact, the Chinese overwhelm-
ingly tend to be big fans of meat (more
so than, for example, the Taiwanese).
The consumption of meat products has
been increasing as the middle class has
grown and become richer. At the same
time, a fraction of young Chinese people – rather well-off and educated ones
– have become vegetarians or vegans
in recent years, exactly as in the West –
not for religious or cultural reasons, but
for personal, ethical, and environmental

reasons. However, they remain few in number. In a study by researchers at Jiao Tong University in Shanghai in 2016, only 0.77 percent of the 4,004 people interviewed were vegetarian (including 0.12 percent vegan). You might try to argue that perhaps this sample is not representative of the population, but as it turns out, Shanghai is one of the Chinese cities where there are the *most* vegetarians. The Chinese really love meat.

The fact is that, in China, even though tofu is a staple for vegetarians monks and is linked to specific vegetarian practices in the rest of the population, it is also and above all a product for everyone, whether omnivore, vegan, flexitarian, and so on. Tofu does not exist in opposition to meat. On the contrary: it rubs shoulders with it, it highlights it, it completes it. Don't expect, when you order a tofu dish in a restaurant, that it is devoid of meat: most of the time there will be both in the pot, wok, and bowl. These two foods coexist easily, because with their different tastes and textures, they fulfill different culinary roles.

Some Chinese tofu dishes are 100 percent vegetarian, but they are not defined or perceived as such. People don't even think about it. There is no meat in the recipe for cold tofu with green onions, for example, but that does not make it a dish for vegetarians – and this is especially true since vegetarian practices in China and Taiwan prohibit the use of green onions and all bulbous plants, because they are killed when plant is harvested. It's similar to how there is no meat in tabbouleh, but that does not mean that the people who eat it are vegetarians or that this dish is reserved for folks who don't eat meat products. That's just the nature of recipe, that's all, and omnivores don't think about it when they eat it. They don't feel like they're depriving themselves or that something is missing (unless you are seriously addicted to meat!).

In Taiwan, things are a little different. A significant portion of the population is part-time vegetarian – not only around the lunar new year – and they are doing it voluntarily and consciously, whether for religious or personal reasons. There are many vegetarian restaurants; it's common to frequent them once a week, with people telling themselves that they're vegetarian on Thursdays, on weekends, for a week a month, or when they need a cleanse. This discipline is much more common and visible than in China, even if it exists there too. In vegetarian restaurants, there is plenty of tofu – but not only tofu. Tofu is not the obvious solution to a meatless diet, the way we regard it in the West. It is only part of the answer. And it doesn't have the label "product for vegetarians" that it has in France. You can eat tofu on meatless days, but you can eat it on meat-eating days as well.

Tofu is an essential foodstuff in China and Taiwan precisely because it is not reserved for a certain population, or for a particular dietary regime. Or maybe it's the other way round: tofu is an essential food there, therefore it is not just intended for a particular population – much like rice throughout Asia, or like potatoes in Europe. In any case, there is nothing special, alternative, or marginal about tofu. It is commonplace. And sometimes it is exceptional. Like a potato: nothing is more unremarkable than a potato. But a beautifully cooked, high-quality potato is amazing. Tofu in itself can be unusual, or the way it is prepared can be. It may be hard to imagine this from where we're sitting, due to our cultural poverty when it comes to tofu. The pages that follow will help you better understand the different types of tofu we find in China and Taiwan. And keep in mind that this is only a small sampling...

TOFU TYPES & USES

FIRM TOFU

It is rather simplistic to want to make generalizations, especially in a country as vast as China, where, in terms of tofu, everything exists – each nuance of texture, density, and taste. Overall, though, we can consider that what is called "firm tofu "in this country is firmer than what is found in Japan and Korea under the same name – Taiwanese tofus represent a middle ground. This firmness is partly due to the fact that Chinese tofus are often more supple and less spongy – the more pronounced use of calcium sulfate in the production of firm tofu gives denser textures, with an equivalent soy content and caloric intake. It can also be due to the fact that they are often pressed more, in order to prepare the tofu for stir-frying. Firm tofus can be fried, sautéed, and braised, among other cooking techniques. Firm tofu is an extremely common everyday product in China and is very inexpensive.

SILKEN TOFU

Silken tofu found in China really is silken. No doubt invented by the Japanese, it must have been adopted by the Chinese, who call it "smooth tofu," huádòufu, because of its fine and slippery texture, slightly elastic but fragile, a bit like a well-set custard. It has a certain firmness, although it is not pressed but rather molded directly in its container (seen in the way that it does not bathe in water but comes in the same size as its packaging). Its taste is very mild, without any bitterness, thanks to generally being set with calcium sulfate or glucono-delta-lactone. Also, it is rich and creamy, being made from a more concentrated soy milk than is used to make firm tofu. There are several degrees of firmness found in silky tofus; the most tender are difficult to handle, but the densest can be manipulated with care. Silken tofus are excellent served cold or uncooked, with only a few condiments, but also work wonders in soups and some stews. They can be very carefully fried, resulting in a crispy exterior and melting interior.

TOFU PUDDING

Tofu pudding, called dòuhuā, is the jewel in the crown. Extremely smooth, even gelatinous if it is made with glucono-delta-lactone, it is very fragile and melting despite its solid appearance. It is also called dòufunǎo, or "tofu-brain," in reference to its consistency. It may be eaten warm or cold, sweet or savory, depending on the region and the season. Prepared in impressively large containers, it is dished up in layers that servers are careful not to break; with a few expert strokes of a large flat spoon, your bowl is full of a delicate tofu that breaks into pieces as soon as you touch it. It is light and slides down your throat just like that. It is a popular breakfast dish, ideal for starting the day.

PRESSED TOFU

Pre-pressed tofu is neither spongy nor silky; it contains very little water because it has been pressed to extract as much as possible, offering exceptional firmness and density. It is called dòugān, literally "dry tofu," or su ji, meaning "vegetarian chicken," when it comes as sausage rolls. Its texture, though, is not really that of meat. It is more reminiscent of certain cheeses, in particular scamorza – but unlike cheese, pressed tofu does not melt during cooking because it is not fatty. Its unique consistency lets it take on various forms: blocks, sheets, rolls, noodle-like strands...it holds up very well to stir-frying, but can also be used in stews and various other preparations. It is often found flavored with five-spice (see page 94), but you can also find a plain version, sometimes labeled super firm.

There is a very wide variety of tofu in China: firm tofu (1), pressed tofu (2 and 3), silken tofu (4), tofu pudding (5), stinky tofu (6) and fermented tofu (7).

FLAVORED TOFU

In China, tofu is generally not flavored before being molded. It may be flavored afterward. This is the case with five-spice pressed tofu (see page 94), which is flavored by steeping, and with smoked tofu, or *xiāng gān*, which is pressed and traditionally smoked over burning wood or herbs. Not only does this treatment give good flavor to the tofu, but it also helps it keep longer. Tofu can also be flavored in the same way as Chinese tea leaf eggs, by steeping in a solution of tea, soy sauce, and spices. While flavored pressed tofu is widespread – especially the five-spice version – fresh tofu (silken or firm) is generally kept plain, for a simple reason: the sauces and condiments used in Chinese cuisine bring plenty of flavor. Also, a fairly neutral base allows you to do what you want in the kitchen. And, of course, a good tofu made with good soy can be a pleasure in itself; its fine aroma is appreciated, there is no need to hide it.

FERMENTED TOFU

In China, as in Taiwan, fermented tofu is a whole world in itself, which feels completely insane and disconcerting for a French person like myself, since it certainly mirrors our obsession with cheeses (plus, tofu and cheese making processes are almost identical, and the results can be very similar in appearance and flavor). Most fermented tofus are regional specialties that you will probably never find abroad, just like unpasteurized French artisanal cheeses. Some fermented tofus show visible mold in various colors, from yellow to pink, blue-green, and black; they also vary in texture, becoming runny and creamy. A very cute tofu variety typical of Hui cooking is called *máodòufu*, which can be translated as "furry tofu" or "hairy tofu." Tofu cubes are covered with molds that form long, very fine filaments reminiscent of angora wool.

Other fermented tofus are visually less impressive, such as "tofu cream" or *dòufǔrǔ*, which is very easily found abroad. These are small tofu cubes that have fermented in the open air before being put in a jar in brine. The "white" version is cream to beige in color, while the "red" version, which tends to be used in braised dishes because of its full-bodied and boozy flavor, is a very beautiful dark red. There are fermented tofus flavored with chile or herbs, for example. *Dòufǔrǔ* reminds one of cheese because of its creamy consistency and its strong and very salty taste. The white version can be used uncooked as a condiment, or used in cooking: it is used in particular to flavor vegetables stir-fried in a wok. A jar of it is inexpensive, lasts a long time, and can be kept for years; it is an item to taste if only out of curiosity.

STINKY TOFU

Taiwan has built a solid reputation for smelly tofu because the one they have is particularly odorous – it's really just called that, *chòudòufu*, which is to say, "stinky tofu." Fermented in a solution that generally includes dried shrimp, you can smell it from afar as you approach Taiwanese night markets. It is sold prepared in different ways, mainly fried or cooked in a soup that is in itself an olfactory poem: stinky tofu, curds of goose blood (known as "blood tofu"), mustard pickles, and pork tripe. Take a whiff of that. Taiwan does not, however, have monopoly on in-your-face tofu. It is a specialty in many Chinese regions, each locality having its specialty. In Yunnan, for example, fermentation is spontaneous and takes place in the open air. Small squares of hand-molded tofu are stored for a few days in shelves on wooden trays, until they develop an odor that is completely bearable. They are then grilled and served with sauce of cilantro, chili, and Sichuan pepper.

Máodòufu (literally "furry tofu") is covered with molds that form long, very fine filaments.

FRIED TOFU

There are several ways to fry tofu. The easiest way is to fry pieces of tofu – firm to extra firm, even super firm pressed tofu – in oil to make what is called *zhádòufu*. The interior remains intact, but a crisp golden crust forms on the outside. It happens to be porous and therefore can absorb sauces and marinades. Tofu can be fried at home or bought ready-made; it is eaten hot with a light sauce, or used in all kinds of preparations. In Chinese and Korean cuisines, it is common to fry tofu before using it in many recipes, as you will see. Not only is it a way to give it a fairly solid external structure, but it also lets it soak up the good flavors of a braise, for example.

TOFU PUFFS

Tofu puffs are another form of fried tofu, with a radically altered consistency. It is called *dòupào* or *dòubŭ*, which means "pea bubble," in reference to the soybeans and to its airy interior. Outside, it looks rather yellow and slightly spongy; inside, it is fully honeycombed and fairly dry, so it absorbs liquid beautifully. It's a typical ingredient in some Buddhist dishes, like the famous Buddha's delight. This form of tofu is also very popular in Southeast Asia, especially in Malaysia and Indonesia.

TOFU SKINS

Tofu skin is not really tofu, but it is often made by the same producers, because its raw material is the same: soy milk. When soy milk is heated, a skin forms on its surface that is made up of about 50 percent protein, 25 percent fat, and 12 percent carbohydrate (among other components). Similar to the skin you get from heating whole milk, it's an excellent health food, popular in China and Taiwan, called *fŭpí* (*yuba* in Japanese). You can eat it fresh and tender, or dry it; its texture allows for it to take on various shapes: sheets, rolls, knots…. It is traditionally used in vegetarian Buddhist cuisine because it is a good substitute for meat thanks to its rich protein and its particular mouthfeel. It's an ingredient you'll always find in Taiwanese vegetarian restaurants and dishes for the lunar new year.

It is not uncommon to come across tofu drying in large baskets in the street.

EVERYDAY FRIED RICE

(Chăofàn)

There are very formal fried rice recipes in China. And then there are all the other fried rice "happenings" that we don't even really talk about, which are essentially a practical and popular way to use up leftovers or make a coherent dish with a few fresh but motley ingredients. The tiny lady I stayed with in Yunnan would have me fry rice almost every day with the ingredients she had on hand. Part of a head of cabbage? Perfect. A tomato, an egg? Great. Well, I put a little tofu in too, and a little green onion. It was always delicious, whatever the mixture. Here is a recipe for you...

🕐 prep **10 min** 🕐 cook **5 min** 🌢 vegetarian 🍴 4 servings

• 1 clove of garlic, minced • 2 green onions, thinly sliced • 1 shallot, thinly sliced
• 1 small carrot, diced • 4 oz napa cabbage, coarsely sliced • 4 shiitake mushrooms, thinly sliced
• 4 oz five-spice pressed tofu, diced • 1 egg, beaten • 2½ cups leftover rice
• 1 Tbsp light soy sauce • 1 Tbsp black vinegar • Vegetable oil • Salt

Pour a little oil around the sides of a wok heated over high heat; it will run down to the bottom of the wok anyway, but at least the sides won't stick. Quickly stir-fry the garlic, green onion, and shallot. Add the carrot, salt lightly, and continue to stir-fry, stirring for about 1 minute. Quickly scoop the vegetables out of the wok, leaving as much oil behind as possible, and set them aside close at hand.

Add a little more oil to the wok if needed, then add the cabbage. Stir-fry for 1 minute, then add the mushrooms and tofu, salt lightly, and continue cooking for 1 minute. Scoop out and set aside with the carrots.

Lightly oil the wok again if needed and pour the beaten egg into the wok, salt lightly, and cook for 30 seconds without stirring. Add the rice to the forming omelet and mix quickly by breaking up the rice with a spatula. The omelet will break up as well.

Return all the reserved vegetables to the wok and vigorously stir and toss all the ingredients. Add the soy sauce and vinegar, plus a little water if the rice seems too dry. Mix well and turn off the heat. Taste and adjust the seasoning, and serve hot.

EGG
TOFU
(Dàn dòufu)

The Chinese may call this dish literally "egg tofu," but it is not a real tofu. The name derives from the fact that the final dish looks like tofu and is used in the same way. Plus, it does contain a lot of soy. The catch is that it is not coagulated and pressed soy milk, but a steamed custard made of egg and soy milk. This preparation, which can replace extra firm silken tofu or flexible medium tofu in many recipes, is very popular in Japan, Thailand, Malaysia.... It is quite easily found in tubes in Asian grocery stores, but it's much better homemade – and at least that way we know exactly what's in it.

⏱ prep **10 min**   ⏱ cook **20 min**   🥚 vegetarian

For one 7-inch square pan
- 6 eggs • 2 cups soy milk, homemade or not
- ½ tsp salt • Vegetable oil

Line your pan with parchment paper greased with vegetable oil. Mix the eggs, soy milk, and salt, stirring until you have a homogeneous mixture. Strain the mixture through a chinois or other fine-mesh strainer into the pan. Steam for 15–20 minutes; a knife blade inserted in the "tofu" should come out clean. If you used a smaller pan, the tofu will be thicker and the cooking time may be longer.

Let cool completely before cutting into slices. You can keep the egg tofu in the refrigerator for 4 days without any problem.

COLD TOFU
WITH GREEN ONION
(Xiǎocōng bàn dòufu)

Cold tofu is a classic in China, very refreshing in summer. People eat it uncooked to appreciate its smooth texture and season it with a salty, spicy, and tangy sauce as well as fresh herbs and sesame seeds, although the ingredients vary from region to region. This recipe requires a tofu with a very fine texture, coagulated with calcium sulfate, like a flexible medium tofu or extra firm silken tofu. This is nothing like typical store-bought silken tofu; it is finer, firmer, and more flexible, and therefore easy to handle – with care. It is found in the fresh section of Chinese and Japanese food markets.

◷ prep **5 min** ● vegan ⚖ **4 servings**

- 7–10 oz flexible soft to medium tofu or extra firm silken tofu
- A few cilantro leaves • 1 green onion, thinly sliced

For the sauce
- 2 Tbsp light soy sauce • 2 Tbsp sesame oil • 2 Tbsp water • 2 tsp black vinegar
1–2 red chiles, thinly sliced, or 1–2 tsp chile oil
- 1 Tbsp toasted white sesame seeds • 1 tsp sugar • 1 clove garlic, minced
- 1 tsp minced root ginger • 2–3 sprigs cilantro, thinly sliced

Gently unmold the tofu and cut it into ¾-inch cubes. With the blade of a large, wide knife, place the tofu cubes in a large serving bowl or divide them among 4 individual bowls. You can also choose to keep the tofu in a single block to share, or to divide it into 4 small blocks.

In a bowl, combine all the sauce ingredients. Pour it over the tofu, add the cilantro leaves and green onion, and serve immediately.

Note To firm up your tofu before cutting it, you can dissolve ¼ cup of salt in 1 quart of boiling water and soak your block for 15 minutes, then drain it for at least 15 minutes on paper towels.

SAUTÉED TOFU
IN LETTUCE CUPS
(Shēng cài bāo)

This recipe is said to come from the ancient village of Fangcun, which is today in the city of Canton (Guagnzhou), known for its lettuce production. One doesn't necessarily associate green salad with China, and yet many varieties are found there – China is the world's top lettuce producer. In Fangcun, and more particularly in Kengkou, lettuce is celebrated in a festival every year; it is thanks to this celebration that *shēng cài bāo* was created. The idea is to wrap various ingredients in a lettuce leaf with a little sauce. There are hundreds of different interpretations of the idea, yielding extremely varied recipes. Here is a very crunchy and colorful vegan version with a light sauce, to eat as a snack, as an aperitif, or as a starter.

🕐 prep **25 min**   🕐 cook **15 min**   🌱 vegan

For 12–15 cups
- 1 tsp minced root ginger • 1 small carrot, julienned or diced
- 1 small handful edamame • 3 black mushrooms, fresh or rehydrated, diced
- 3 shiitake mushrooms, fresh or rehydrated, diced • 2 red chiles, thinly sliced, or ½ red bell pepper, diced
- 4 oz flexible firm tofu, coarsely chopped • 2 Tbsp Shaoxing rice wine • 2 Tbsp light soy sauce
- 2 green onions, thinly sliced • 2 Tbsp sesame oil • 2 hearts of Little Gem lettuce or 1 head escarole or iceberg lettuce • Vegetable oil • Salt, white pepper

Heat a wok over high heat and add a little vegetable oil, then the ginger. Brown for 15 seconds, then add the carrot. Salt lightly and stir-fry very briefly, stirring. Add the edamame and continue cooking for 30 seconds. Scoop them out of the wok, leaving as much oil behind as possible, and set aside in a bowl.

Add a little more oil to the wok if needed. In the same way, sauté the mushrooms and the chile (or the bell pepper). Add the tofu, rice wine, and soy sauce. Stir well, add the green onions, and stir-fry for another 30 seconds. Place in the bowl with the carrot. Toss together all the ingredients in the bowl. Season with salt (if needed) and pepper, and add the sesame oil. Toss again.

Separate your lettuce leaves. The small leaves of the heart are particularly practical and attractive for this recipe, but large leaves cut in half will also work. Fill the small leaves with the vegetable and tofu mixture like little boats. For a large leaf cut in half or a whole medium leaf, place a heaping tablespoon of filling on it, roll it up, and fasten it with a toothpick to keep the roll closed. Serve the little boats and rolls nicely arranged on a large platter.

COLD TOFU
WITH CENTURY EGGS
(Pídàn dòufu)

Century eggs and cold tofu form a classic culinary marriage in China and Taiwan – a marriage that terrifies Westerners. However, these eggs are delicious and absolutely not spoiled. They have changed texture and color by being preserved for several weeks to several months in a mixture of clay, salt, rice hulls, ash, and quicklime. The pH of the egg increases considerably during the process (becoming more basic); the whites turn amber to brown, translucent and brittle like a jelly; and the yolk takes on a melting texture and fabulous colors varying from deep black to green and blue. They are very good, and not weird at all. The rich taste and amazing consistency of the eggs go amazingly well with humble tofu.

🕐 prep **10 min**   🕐 cook **15 min**   🌱 vegetarian   👤 **4** servings

- 10 oz flexible soft to medium tofu or extra firm silken tofu
- 2 century eggs • 1–2 Tbsp soy sauce
- 1–2 tsp sesame oil • 1 green onion, thinly sliced

Carefully unmold the tofu in your hand over the sink to drain it. Place it on a plate and cut it into slices or cubes, or keep it whole. Peel the eggs and cut them in half, then cut each of the 2 halves in three wedges. Arrange them around the tofu. Drizzle with soy sauce and sesame oil, add the green onion and serve right away as a starter.

Note You will find century eggs (or hundred-year eggs) made from duck or chicken eggs in the refrigerated section of Asian groceries. Be careful not to confuse them with fertilized eggs – that's another story...

"THOUSAND-LAYER" TOFU

(Qiānyè dòufu)

"Thousand-layer" tofu is badly named. Personally, instead of "thousand-layer" I would rather call it "thousand-hole" tofu. It has a striking appearance, with a honeycomb texture that would seem to have required work, but the technique is in reality as easy as pie. It is simply frozen, then thawed. Ta-da! The ice crystals that form in the tofu leave holes as they melt. Besides the visual effect and the fun consistency, thousand-layer tofu has the advantage of absorbing sauces, marinades, and broths really well, just like a sponge. This lets it work wonders in many dishes, and it can replace firm tofu in most of the recipes in this book. It can also be fried.

🕐 prep **1 min**   🕐 set **24 hr**   🌱 vegan

For 1 block thousand-layer tofu
- **1 block firm tofu**

All firm tofus are suitable for this purpose. Extra firm or super firm pressed tofus are too dense.

Drain your tofu block and cut it into slices slightly thinner than ½ inch thick. Place them in a plastic bag and place in the freezer for 24–48 hours. When the slices are frozen through to the center, take them out of the bag and let them thaw in the refrigerator or in a cool place on a plate covered with several layers of paper towels.

The thawed tofu can be eaten uncooked with a sauce, or cooked – braised, fried, simmered, marinated.... It will absorb sauces particularly well.

TOFU
HONEYCOMB
SOUP
(Fēngcháo dòufu tāng)

When you cook firm tofu for a while in a simmering water bath, you slowly alter its composition and structure. It will lose firmness, and its small holes will widen to form "honeycomb tofu," as it is called in southeastern China. Its sweet flavor (it loses all trace of the flavor of its coagulating agent) and its extremely fragile and tender texture are appreciated in various recipes, in particular soups that shine with their finesse and simplicity – like this one.

⏲ prep **5 min**   ⏲ soak **1 night**   ⏲ cook **1 hr 15 min**   ◉ vegan   ♨ **4** servings

• 4 dried shiitake mushrooms • 10 oz firm tofu • ¼ cup Shaoxing rice wine
• ¾-inch piece root ginger, thinly sliced • 2 green onions
• Salt or mushroom powder • ⅓ cup edamame or green peas, fresh or frozen
• White pepper • 1 Tbsp sesame oil

The day before, rehydrate the mushrooms in 1 quart of cold water (you can do it the same day, but the broth will have less flavor). The next day, strain the mushroom-soaking water and pour it into a pot. Remove the stems from the mushrooms, slice the caps, and add them to the pot.

Cut the tofu in half lengthwise and then into slices a little less than ½ inch thick. Place them in a second pot and cover them with water. Bring to a boil over high heat, then lower the heat and simmer for 15 minutes. Drain the water, keeping the tofu in the pot, cover with water again, and cook in the same way. Repeat the operation a third time. The tofu will become more and more fragile, so be careful.

Transfer the drained tofu to the mushroom water. Add the rice wine, ginger, and the white parts of the green onions, left whole (slice the green parts thinly, and reserve for garnishing). Bring to a boil over high heat, then salt the water or add mushroom powder to taste. Lower the heat, cover, and let simmer for 30 minutes. Remove the ginger and the green onion. Add the edamame or peas and return to a boil. Taste and adjust the seasoning. Serve in bowls, adding to each some of the reserved sliced green onions and a drizzle of sesame oil.

Note You can use thousand-layer tofu (see page 56) for this recipe. It is already honeycombed and therefore will not need to be cooked several times; add it directly to the soup, which can be ready in just 15 minutes!

BOK CHOY & TOFU
SOUP
(Qīng cài dòufu tāng)

The Japanese do not have a monopoly on blandness; it is also appreciated in China. It is not a boring or depressing blandness, it is rather a moment of rest – and I would go so far as to say tenderness – for our taste buds, which are often overworked. This soup perfectly illustrates this idea: the vegetable is fresh and crunchy, the tofu is soft, the broth is mild, refined, made with almost nothing. It's good and it's very healthy.

🕐 prep **5 min**   🕐 cook **5 min**   🌱 vegan   ⚖ **4** servings

- 8 oz baby bok choy • 10 oz flexible medium tofu
- 1 tsp minced root ginger • 2 tsp sesame oil • 1 tsp salt

Separate the boy choy leaves, and rinse. Cut the tofu into ¾-inch cubes or into rectangles ½ inch thick.

Bring 1 quart of water to a boil. Add the tofu, bok choy, and ginger, then let boil for 2 minutes. Add sesame oil and salt to taste (add salt gradually, tasting as you go – you may not need a whole teaspoon). Mix well and serve hot.

CHINESE CABBAGE
SAUTÉED WITH FERMENTED TOFU
(Dòufǔrǔ càixīn)

Vegetables stir-fried with a little fermented tofu are an essential dish in China. The idea is that more or less all vegetables are suitable for this preparation, but leafy cabbages like flowering Chinese cabbage (*choy sum* or *yu choy*), water spinach (bindweed), and eggplant are the most common. If you can't find flowering Chinese cabbage, available in the vegetable section of Chinese grocery stores, you can replace it with Chinese broccoli (*gai lan*) or broccoli rabe (rapini), broccolini, or something similar.

🕐 prep **5 min** 🕐 cook **5 min** 🌱 vegan 🍴 **4** servings

• 10 oz flowering Chinese cabbage (*choy sum* or *yu choy*) • 2 Tbsp peanut oil
• 2 cloves garlic, thinly sliced or minced • 1 Tbsp water • 1 Tbsp Shaoxing rice wine
• 2 cubes white fermented tofu (*dòufǔrǔ*), crushed into a purée • 1 pinch white pepper

Prepare your cabbage: keep the thinnest and most tender bunches whole, separate the larger ones. If some stems are very thick and fibrous, you can cut them in half lengthwise. Peel the ends of any woody stems, much as you would asparagus. You can cut all the cabbage stems in half crosswise to shorten them, or keep them long.

Blanch the cabbage in a pot of boiling water for 30–40 seconds, then immediately immerse in a bowl of ice water to stop cooking. Drain well, pressing lightly to extract the moisture.

Heat your wok over very high heat, then add the oil. Add the cabbage and stir-fry for about 2 minutes. Spread it up the sides of the wok and put the garlic, water, rice wine, crushed tofu in the center. Stir this to make a sauce; when it comes to a boil, stir and toss it with the cabbage, then turn off the heat. Sprinkle with white pepper and serve at once.

TOFU NOODLE
SALAD
(Liángbàn gān sī)

Pre-pressed tofu is found in blocks in Chinese grocery stores; it can be plain or five-spice flavor. It can also found in the form of sheets and strips resembling noodles. These tofu "noodles" are tough, firm, but flexible – much less delicate than actual noodles, in fact. There are many ways to cook them, but it's common to eat them cold, as a salad, with carrots and celery – or other vegetables of your choice. It's very good in summer, as a starter to share or as an accompaniment to other dishes, and is full of protein.

🕐 prep **10 min**   🕐 cook **5 min**   🌱 vegan   🍽 **4 servings**

• 8 oz tofu noodles (plain or five-spice) • A few stalks of Chinese celery (or 1 rib of celery), julienned • 1 large carrot, spiralized, shredded, or julienned • 1 clove garlic, minced • 2 Tbsp sesame oil • 2 Tbsp light soy sauce • 1 Tbsp rice vinegar • 1 tsp sugar • 1 Tbsp toasted white sesame seeds

Cut the base of the tofu noodles to separate them if needed (they are sometimes joined on one side) and cut them down to size if they are too long. Blanch for 1 minute in a large pot of boiling salted water, along with the celery and carrot. Drain and rinse with cold water.

In a serving bowl, combine the garlic, sesame oil, soy sauce, rice vinegar, and sugar. Add the tofu noodles and vegetables to the bowl and toss. Serve sprinkled with sesame seeds.

Note   You can add chile oil to your salad dressing if you like a little spice.

SWEET & SOUR
TOFU
(Suān tián dòufu)

The original sweet-and-sour sauce recipe, called *gūlōuyuhk* in Cantonese and made with pork and with ingredients not widely found in Western countries, has undergone all kinds of changes over time. Even in its region of origin, it has become a "fusion" dish, with the addition of pineapple, bell peppers, and tomatoes. This tofu version corresponds to the modern standard of the dish, but revisits a basic principle of the traditional recipe: frying in two batches, for a crispy result. For the sauce, I preferred to avoid ketchup, widely used in Chinese restaurants in the West; sweet and savory plum sauce (see Note) is closer to the original recipe.

🕐 prep **20 min**   🕐 cook **20 min**   🌱 vegetarian   🍴 4 servings

- 14 oz flexible medium to firm tofu or very firm to extra firm tofu
- 1–2 eggs, beaten • 6 Tbsp cornstarch, tapioca flour, or potato starch
- 1 clove garlic, minced • 1 tsp minced root ginger
- 1 green onion, cut into ¾-inch lengths
- ½ green bell pepper, cut in 1½-inch triangles
- ½ red bell pepper, cut in 1½-inch triangles
- 15-oz can chunk pineapple or ½ fresh pineapple, cubed • Peanut oil • Salt

For the sauce
- 2 Tbsp Shaoxing rice wine
- 3 Tbsp plum sauce
- 1 tsp cornstarch, tapioca flour, or potato starch mixed with 3 Tbsp water

With your hands, tear the tofu into rough bite-sized pieces. You can cut it with a knife, but tearing it leaves it rougher and gives the sauce something to cling to. Blot the tofu dry with paper towels. Heat oil for deep-frying in a deep fryer or heavy pot.

Sprinkle the pieces of tofu with salt, then dip them in the lightly salted beaten egg and dredge with cornstarch. Fry in batches until they start to brown. Transfer with a skimmer to a rack set on a baking sheet lined with paper towels and let rest, well spaced out, for 10–15 minutes. Reserve the frying oil.

Heat the oil again. Dip the tofu pieces a second time in the egg and dredge again with starch. Fry until the pieces are perfectly golden and crisp. Transfer them to the rack, and prepare the rest of the dish immediately.

Heat a wok over high heat. Add a little peanut oil, then add the garlic, ginger, and the white part of the green onion. Stir-fry for 15 seconds, then add the bell peppers and stir-fry for 30 seconds. Add the pineapple, green onions, rice wine, and mix. Then add the plum sauce and the green part of the green onion, and the corn-starch slurry. Mix well. As soon as the sauce has thickened, remove the wok from the heat. Arrange the fried tofu on a platter and cover it with the hot vegetables and sauce.

Note Plum sauce (sometimes called "sweet-and-sour sauce") may be found in Asian groceries and well-stocked supermarkets. Some brands offer a good quality product, without preservatives, MSG, or other additives; read the ingredients carefully before choosing.

MUNG BEAN NOODLES
BRAISED
WITH TOFU & VEGGIES
(Dòufu Fěnsī bāo)

Braised dishes made with mung bean noodles (also called cellophane noodles or glass noodles) are common in China and neighboring countries. All kinds of combinations of ingredients are possible; the noodles, which have a slippery and interestingly elastic texture, do not really have much flavor of their own, so they lend themselves to many dishes. They will absorb the flavors of the broth, vegetables, spices, and aromatics they cook with. Normally this type of dish is prepared in a terra-cotta pot, but enameled cast iron also works very well.

🕐 prep **20 min** 🕐 cook **10 min** 🍃 vegan 🍴 **4 servings**

- 8 dried shiitake mushrooms • 8 oz mung bean noodles • 14 oz firm to extra firm tofu
- 2 cloves garlic, minced • 2 thin slices root ginger, julienned
- 1 green onion, thinly sliced • 1 carrot, julienned
- 1 baby bok choy, leaves separated and coarsely sliced • 2 Tbsp light soy sauce
- 2 Tbsp Shaoxing rice wine • Vegetable oil • Salt

Soak the mushrooms and the noodles in separate bowls of water for about 15 minutes. Cut the tofu in half lengthwise and then into slices a little less than ½ inch thick. Blot the slices dry with paper towels.

Heat a frying pan or wok over medium-high heat, add some oil, and brown the tofu slices on both sides. Remove it to a plate, leaving as much oil behind as possible. In the still-hot oil, stir-fry the garlic, ginger, and green onion for 30 seconds. Add the carrot, stir, then add the bok choy. Stir-fry briefly, season with salt, toss, and turn off the heat.

In a cast-iron pot, layer the drained noodles, then the vegetables and tofu. Score the mushroom caps and stand them up in the pot, stem down. Add a little salt, soy sauce, rice wine, and 2 cups of the mushroom-soaking water. Place over medium heat, cover, and simmer for 5 minutes, or until the noodles are tender. Taste and adjust the seasoning if needed, and serve at once.

SICHUAN-STYLE
MAPO TOFU
(Mápó dòufu)

This dish has a funny backstory. It was created at the end of the nineteenth century in Chengdu, Sichuan, by a restaurant owner nicknamed Mápó ("má" for *mázi*, which means "pockmark", and "pó" for *pópo*, which means "grandmother"). Granny Pockmark, aka Mápó, real name Chen Liu, cooked many dishes based on rice and tofu. Until the day she invented a ground beef and tofu stew (in some versions, at the request of her customers). Huge success: beef was rare in small canteens at the time and made the dish famous. The recipe has become more and more spicy over time. Today it is based on fermented black beans, or *dòuchǐ*, and fava (or broad) beans fermented with chile, a Sichuan specialty called *là dòubànjiàng*. As the chile is fermented, it does not taste that strong. You can also add a good dose of Sichuan pepper. Here is the recipe – without beef.

⏱ prep **20 min** ⏱ cook **10 min** 🌱 vegan 🍲 **4 servings**

- 28 oz flexible medium or soft tofu, or extra firm silken tofu
- 3 Tbsp fermented fava bean paste with chile (*là dòubànjiàng*)
- 1 Tbsp fermented black soybeans (*dòuchǐ*) • 1½ tsp minced root ginger
- 3 cloves garlic • 1 Tbsp red chile flakes (optional) • 2 Tbsp light soy sauce
- 2 garlic chives, thinly sliced • 1 Tbsp cornstarch or potato starch mixed with 3 Tbsp water
- 1 Tbsp sesame oil • ½ Tbsp Sichuan peppercorns, toasted and ground • Vegetable oil
- Salt • Steamed rice, for serving

Cut the tofu into ¾-inch cubes and gently add them to a large pot filled with cold water. Add ½ teaspoon salt, bring to a boil, reduce the heat, and simmer for 3 minutes. Drain the tofu gently in a colander. Set aside.

Roughly chop the spicy fermented fava beans and fermented black soybeans on a board with a knife. Heat a wok over high heat and add a little oil. Reduce the heat, scrape the beans into the wok, and stir-fry for 1 minute. Add the ginger and garlic and stir-fry for 30 seconds, then add the chile flakes. Pour 2½ cups of water into the wok, mix, and bring to a boil over high heat. Gently add the tofu cubes and soy sauce. Adjust the heat as needed to simmer for 8 minutes. Add half of the garlic chives and half of the cornstarch slurry to the wok. Wait 30 seconds, then pour in the rest. Gently mix with the back of a spatula, so as not to crush the tofu. Taste and season with salt, if needed. Let the sauce thicken, add the sesame oil, and mix. Serve sprinkled with Sichuan pepper and the rest of garlic chives, accompanied with rice.

TOFU
POT STICKERS
(Dòufu guōtiē)

The hardest part about making Chinese dumplings is to get the dough right. The rest is very easy. The folding does take a little while, but boy is it good! To simplify your life, I advise you to buy ready-made dumpling wrappers, available in the fresh case or the frozen aisle of Asian groceries (see Note, page 74). Then you can feast on these airy, crisp-on-the-bottom dumplings, called *jiān jiǎo* or *guōtiē*, which are the inspiration of Japanese *gyōza* (hence the very close names). You can stuff the *guōtiē* with just about anything you want; this vegan recipe calls for tofu, cabbage, and green onions.

🕐 prep **45 min** 🕐 cook **20 min** 🌱 vegan

For 40 dumplings
- 7 oz napa cabbage or pointed cabbage, coarsely chopped
- 10 oz extra-firm tofu, chopped • 4 green onions, thinly sliced
- 2 cloves garlic, minced • 1 tsp minced root ginger
- 1 Tbsp sesame oil • 1 Tbsp light soy sauce
- 1 Tbsp Shaoxing rice wine • 1 tsp cornstarch or potato starch
- 40 dumpling wrappers • Salt, white pepper • Vegetable oil

For the sauce
- 3 Tbsp light soy sauce • 3 Tbsp black vinegar • ½ tsp julienned root ginger

Put the cabbage in a bowl and sprinkle it with 1 teaspoon salt. Mix well with your hand and let drain for 15 minutes.

Meanwhile, combine the ingredients for the stuffing: tofu, green onions, garlic, ginger, sesame oil, soy sauce, rice wine, and cornstarch. Use your hands to squeeze the cabbage and remove excess water. You can rinse it briefly and squeeze again if you find it too salty. Add it to the stuffing, and mix. Taste and season with salt, if needed, and pepper.

(continued)

Place 1½–2 teaspoons of stuffing in the center of each disc of dough. Pick up each disc with two hands and fold it over itself while holding it by the ends. Make a pleat in the center of the dough on the side in front of you, and two pleats on either side of the central fold. This will give the ravioli a curved shape, much like a pretty, very chic croissant. Glue together the dough edges; to do this, dip your finger in a bowl of water, wet the edges of the dough, and pinch them together firmly all along their entire length, especially at the ends.

If this is too complicated, you can simply make half-moons by folding the dough disc over on itself and gluing the edges together flat. Place the folded dumplings on a sheet of parchment paper, taking care that they do not touch each other.

To make the sauce, combine the soy sauce, vinegar, and ginger in a bowl and stir to mix. Set aside.

Place a large frying pan over medium heat, add some vegetable oil, and when the oil is shimmering arrange the ravioli in the oil, all on the same side, in concentric circles without crowding (you will probably need to do this in 2 or 3 batches). Brown them for a few minutes on one side only. When they are golden on the bottom, add ¼ cup of water to the pan, pouring it down the sides of the pan. Cover, lower the heat slightly, and cook for another 3–5 minutes.

The water should evaporate and the ravioli will be fully cooked. If the water evaporates too quickly, add a little more. If, on the other hand, there is too much water left and the dumplings become too soft, remove the excess water, cook uncovered, and adjust the amount of water for the next batch. Serve the dumplings hot as you go along, accompanied with the sauce.

Note When purchasing dough rounds, be sure to buy dough for *gyoza, mandu,* and other *guōtiē*, which is egg-free. The egg yolk dough used to make wontons is thicker and won't pleat as well.

CRISPY
SALT & PEPPER
TOFU
(Jiāo yán dòufu)

When they talk about "salt and pepper" in China, they're usually thinking of Sichuan peppercorns – in Cantonese and Taiwanese cuisine, however, they are referring to white pepper. There are many variations of salt and pepper recipes, more or less saucy, more or less spicy, with different herbs.... Here is a rather dry version (made without broth), which of course includes tofu. The tofu becomes very crisp when it is fried twice.

🕐 prep **10 min** 🕐 cook **20 min** 🌱 vegan 🍴 **4** servings

- 1 lb flexible firm or medium tofu • 3 Tbsp cornstarch, tapioca flour, or potato starch • ¾ tsp salt
- ¾ tsp ground white or Sichuan peppercorns • 2 cloves garlic, minced
- 1 tsp minced root ginger • 1 green onion, thinly sliced • 1–2 red or green chiles, thinly sliced
- 1 Tbsp Shaoxing rice wine • Peanut oil • Steamed rice for serving

Cut the tofu into ¾-inch cubes. Place them on paper towels and blot dry. Heat oil for deep-frying into a deep fryer or heavy pot. Dredge the tofu cubes in cornstarch on all sides, and fry until crisp. Do this in several batches to avoid crowding. Place the fried tofu as it's ready on a rack set on a baking sheet lined with paper towels.

Combine the salt and pepper in a bowl. Heat a wok over high heat, add a little peanut oil, and then add the garlic, ginger, the white part of the green onion, and the chile. Stir-fry for about 10 seconds, then add the rice wine and the fried tofu and stir-fry for a few moments. Add the salt and pepper and the green part of the green onion and sauté for another 1 minute, stirring. Serve hot with rice.

Note When using Sichuan peppercorns, green or red, pick out any black seeds that may remain (you can tell higher-quality brands by the fact that they contain no gritty seeds or stray twigs). Toast them for a few moments in a dry pan and grind them to a powder before using.

STEAMED
STUFFED YUBA
(Fu pei gyun)

Stuffed rolled tofu skins (*yuba*) are a classic dim sum dish. They are usually stuffed with pork, sometimes shrimp, and possibly vegetables, and are then cooked in water, steamed, panfried, or deep-fried. This vegetarian recipe shows a simple, delicious, and very healthy way to use *yuba* to make delicious rolls as a starter or a main dish. Dried tofu skins are sometimes labeled "bean curd sheets."

🕐 prep **30 min**   🕐 cook **20 min**   🌢 vegetarian

For 8 pieces
• 4 dried shiitake mushrooms • 10 oz extra firm tofu, diced • 2 small carrots, grated or julienned • 2 green onions, thinly sliced • 4 oz bamboo shoots, julienned • 2 tsp cornstarch or potato starch • 1 Tbsp Shaoxing rice wine • Salt and pepper • 2–4 dried tofu skins, cut into eight 8-inch squares • 1 egg white, beaten • Peanut oil

For the sauce
• 1 tsp minced garlic • 1 Tbsp Shaoxing rice wine • 2 Tbsp light soy sauce • 1 cup mushroom soaking water • 1 Tbsp sesame oil • 1 tsp cornstarch or potato starch mixed with 1 Tbsp water

Rehydrate the mushrooms by placing them in a bowl and covering them with cold water. When they are softened, squeeze them to drain, remove the stems, and slice the caps. Strain and reserve the soaking water.

Mix all the stuffing ingredients in a large bowl: mushrooms, tofu, carrot, bamboo shoots, cornstarch, rice wine. Season with salt and pepper.

Place a square of yuba on your work surface. Moisten it with a damp cloth to soften. Place 3 heaping tablespoons of stuffing on the sheet an inch from the edge nearest you. Pack the stuffing into a sausage shape, leaving room on the sheet at both ends of the sausage. With a brush, apply egg white to all the edges of the sheet. Fold in both sides to contain and compact the stuffing, then roll forward (the folding and rolling is identical to that of spring rolls). Repeat the procedure until you have no more stuffing. Heat an inch or so of peanut oil in a frying pan or wok, and fry the rolls until golden.

Prepare the sauce: in a wok or a frying pan, combine the garlic, rice wine, soy sauce, and reserved mushroom water, and simmer for a few minutes. Add the sesame oil and the cornstarch slurry, and let the sauce thicken. Remove from the heat.

Place 2 to 3 rolls in a soup dish. Pour a quarter or a third of the sauce over them. Steam for 8–10 minutes. Repeat the procedure with the rest of the rolls and the sauce. Serve the rolls hot as they are ready.

3-CUP
TOFU
(Sān bēi dòufu)

This recipe is the vegan version of three-cup chicken, *sān bēi jī*, which is one of the most popular Taiwanese dishes. Pleasantly scented with Thai basil leaves, it owes its name to the fact that it is cooked with a cup of soy sauce, a cup of sesame oil, and a cup of Shaoxing rice wine. The tofu variant is quite common in Taiwan, with a large part of the population being part-time vegetarians – the Taiwanese people make a conscious and willing choice to not eat meat every day.

| ⏱ prep **5 min** | ⏱ cook **20 min** | 🌱 vegan | 👥 **4** servings |

- 14 oz firm tofu • 4 Tbsp sesame oil • 2 cloves garlic, thinly sliced
- ¾-inch piece root ginger, thinly sliced • 1 Tbsp sugar
- 4 Tbsp soy sauce • 4 Tbsp *mijiu* or Shaoxing rice wine
- 1 small handful Thai basil leaves • Vegetable oil • Steamed rice for serving

Cut the tofu into 1-inch cubes and blot dry with paper towels. Heat a wok or frying pan over high heat, add a little vegetable oil, and brown the tofu cubes. Set aside.

Heat a Dutch oven or casserole pan over medium heat, and add the sesame oil, garlic, and ginger. Let cook for a few moments, then add the sugar, soy sauce, and rice wine. Mix well, add the tofu, cover, and simmer for 5 minutes. Stir again, add the basil, cover, and simmer for 1 minute more. Serve hot with rice.

SPICY TOFU
WITH PEANUTS
(Gōngbǎo dòufu)

Like many Chinese dishes, the origin of *gōng bǎo* chicken (*gōng bǎo jī dīng*) is uncertain and controversial. The story that the Chinese like – probably because it flirts with legend – links this recipe to Dīng Bǎozhēn (1820–1886), who was the governor of Sichuan at the end of the Qing dynasty. He bore the title of *Gōngbǎo* and adored chicken cooked like this, to the point where they ended up baptizing this preparation in his honor. Whether it is true or not, the dish offers the typical Sichuan flavors: there are dried chile – from varieties that are less spicy and larger than Thai chiles – and Sichuan peppercorns, as well as peanuts, black vinegar, and sesame oil. Here is a vegan version of the recipe, with pre-pressed tofu replacing the meat.

🕐 prep **10 min** 🕐 cook **10 min** 🌱 vegan 🍴 **4** servings

- 1 lb pressed tofu (plain or five-spice) • 1 handful unsalted peanuts
- 10 dried Sichuan chiles • 1–2 tsp Sichuan pepper (whole husks, no seeds) • 3 cloves garlic, minced
- 1 Tbsp minced root ginger • 4 green onions, white parts chopped, green parts thinly sliced
- Vegetable oil • Steamed rice, for serving

For the marinade

- 1 pinch salt • 2 tsp soy sauce • 1 tsp Shaoxing rice wine

For the sauce

- 2 Tbsp sugar • 1 tsp cornstarch • 1 Tbsp water • 1 tsp light soy sauce
- 1 tsp dark soy sauce • 1 Tbsp black vinegar • 1 tsp sesame oil

Cut the tofu into ¾-inch squares that are ¼ inch thick, and mix them with the marinade ingredients in a large bowl. In another bowl, combine all the ingredients for the sauce.

Heat a wok over medium-high heat, add a little vegetable oil, heat until shimmering, and then add the peanuts. Stir-fry, stirring constantly for 1–2 minutes. Transfer them to a bowl nearby, leaving the oil in the wok.

Add a little more oil to the wok if needed, then add the chiles and Sichuan peppercorn. Stir-fry until the chiles are a little puffy and the oil is fragrant. Add the tofu and its marinade, and stir-fry for 2–3 minutes. Add the garlic, ginger, and green onion, toss, and continue to stir-fry for 2 minutes. Pour the sauce into the wok, mix well, and add the peanuts. When the sauce has thickened, turn off the heat, garnish with green onions, and serve at once with rice.

Note To reduce the heat of the chiles, make
a slit and remove the seeds (wear gloves!).
You can also use a smaller amount.

RED-COOKED
TOFU
(Hóngshāo dòufu)

The term "*hóngshāo*" is associated with several quite different recipes with varying main ingredients. It is translated as "red cooked" or "red braised," but these dishes are not necessarily red. Nor are they spicy. In this case, *hóngshāo* tofu is not really red, and not at all spicy. Tofu is first fried or sautéed and then braised with garlic, ginger, green onions, oyster sauce, and often some vegetables. It's very simple and quick to do, and really good.

🕐 prep **10 min** 🕐 cook **5 min** 🌱 vegan 👤 **4** servings

- 1¼ cups water or unsalted vegetable stock • 1 Tbsp vegetarian oyster sauce
- 1 Tbsp light soy sauce • 1 tsp dark soy sauce • 1 Tbsp Shaoxing rice wine
- ½ tsp sugar • ½ tsp salt • 1 tsp cornstarch or potato starch • 1 Tbsp water
- 14 oz flexible medium to firm tofu, or firm to extra firm tofu • 2 cloves garlic, thinly sliced
- 1 tsp minced root ginger • 3–5 black wood ear mushrooms, cut into 1-inch cubes
- ½ red bell pepper, cut into 1-inch cubes • ½ yellow or green bell pepper, cut into 1-inch cubes
- 1 green onion, chopped crosswise • Vegetable oil • Steamed rice, for serving

In a bowl, combine the water or broth, the oyster sauce, soy sauces, rice wine, sugar, and salt. Set aside. In a small bowl, combine the cornstarch and water. Set aside.

Cut the tofu in half lengthwise, then into slices a little less than ½ inch thick. Blot dry with paper towels. Set a wok or frying pan over high heat, add a little oil, and when the oil is shimmering brown the tofu on both sides.

Add the garlic, ginger, mushrooms, and the soy sauce mixture. Shake the wok a little to make sure the tofu doesn't stick. Bring to a boil over high heat, then reduce the heat to medium, cover, and simmer for 5 minutes. Some of the liquid should evaporate. Continue cooking uncovered if you find there is still too much liquid.

Raise the heat to high and add the bell peppers and green onions. Gently mix with the back of a spatula so as not to break up the tofu. Add the cornstarch slurry, mix again, and heat until slightly thickened. The sauce should coat the tofu and vegetables nicely. If it's too dry, add water. If it is too runny, let simmer for a few more moments, uncovered. Taste and adjust the seasoning. Serve hot with rice.

SICHUAN-STYLE
BRAISED TOFU
(Jiācháng dòufu)

China is a big country with different dialects, and Chinese people don't always understand one another. The words *jiā cháng*, which can have multiple meanings, are understood by the majority of the country to mean "home-style," along the lines of a family dish. But in Sichuan, they are taken very differently: the inhabitants of this province see in them the evocation of flavors typical of *their* home" "Sichuan-style." Some Sichuanese diplomatically note that this is the same thing, since the ingredients they use for their recipe are found in every family cupboard. Anyway, here is the version of this "Sichuan-style" tofu dish. It is braised in a spicy fermented fava bean paste sauce (*là dòubànjiàng*), a wonderful condiment that should be used in everything.

⏱ prep 5 min ⏱ cook 5 min 🌱 vegan 🍽 4 servings

- 5 oz bamboo shoots • 14 oz firm to extra firm tofu • 1 Tbsp minced garlic
- 1 tsp minced root ginger • 1–2 Tbsp fermented fava bean paste with chile (*là dòubànjiàng*)
- 1 Tbsp Shaoxing rice wine • 1 tsp sugar • 1–3 medium-spicy red chiles, thinly sliced (optional)
- 1¼ cups water • 1–2 Tbsp light soy sauce • 1 Tbsp sesame oil
- 3 green onions, thinly sliced • 1 tsp cornstarch or potato starch mixed with 1 Tbsp water
- Vegetable oil • Steamed rice, for serving

Cut the bamboo shoots into lengths of 1–1½ inches. Slice these in the direction of the grain. Cut the tofu into rectangles or triangles ¼ inch thick. Blot dry with paper towels. If you have time, you can press and drain the tofu for 30 minutes before cutting it.

Brown the tofu in an oiled wok or frying pan. You can fry it in an inch of vegetable oil if you prefer. Reserve on a plate.

Set a wok over high heat, add 1–2 tablespoons of vegetable oil, and stir-fry the garlic and ginger for 30 seconds. Add the bean paste and the bamboo shoots, and stir-fry for a few moments, then add the rice wine, the sugar, and the chiles. Put the tofu in the wok and add the water. Mix and bring to a boil. Reduce the heat to a bare simmer and gently braise for about 10 minutes, until three-quarters of the liquid is gone.

Taste, add a dash of soy sauce if it need salt. Add the sesame oil, cornstarch slurry, and three-quarters of the green onions, and mix well. Serve hot, sprinkled with the remaining green onion, with rice.

TOFU PUDDING
YUNNAN STYLE
(Hóng yóu dòuhuā)

In Yunnan, as in Sichuan – as well as in northern China – tofu pudding is eaten salty – as opposed to the south of the country and Southeast Asia, where it is sweetened. The specialty of Yunnan and Sichuan is to make a spicy version served with an array of toppings, which is absolutely delicious. The perfectly smooth, silky, and melting tofu pudding slides into the mouth and mixes with the crisp and crunchy textures of the aromatics. It's sweet and strong, fresh and salty, healthy and delicious. Here is the recipe that is served every morning at the food stands in the city of *Shāxī*, accompanied by delicious crispy and fluffy long doughnuts called *yóutiáo*.

🕐 prep **5 min** 🕐 cook **15 min** 🌱 vegan 🍽 4 servings

- 28 oz tofu pudding (homemade or not) • 4 Tbsp vegetable oil • 1 tsp minced garlic
- 1 tsp minced root ginger • 4 tsp fried shallots • 4 tsp crushed toasted peanuts
- 4 tsp crushed toasted sesame • 4 tsp Sichuan chile oil • 4 tsp soy sauce • 4 tsp black vinegar
- 4 tsp light soy sauce • 2 green onions, thinly sliced • 1 handful cilantro leaves, coarsely chopped
- 4 tsp medium-spicy Korean red chile flakes (*gochugaru*)
- A few pinches of Sichuan peppercorns, toasted and ground

Place the tofu pudding, in its container or other suitable container, in a steam basket and heat it with steam for about 15 minutes.

In a small pot over medium-low heat, warm half of the vegetable oil with the garlic. Gently cook the garlic until it is golden to almost brown, but don't let it burn. Remove from the heat and let cool. Do the same with the rest of the vegetable oil and the ginger. These two scented oils will be used in the tofu serving bowls (garlic and fried ginger included). You can prepare larger quantities, they keep well. Serve the tofu pudding warm in bowls, covered with all of the above-listed toppings and sauces. Each diner can arrange it to taste: more or less salty, spicy, peppery, and so on. Eat with a small (or large) spoon.

Note   You can find tofu pudding in the refrigerator case section of Chinese groceries – look for "tofu pudding," "tofu flan," or "*douhua*" made with glucono-delta-lactone (GDL) – or, prepare it yourself (see pages 34 and 36).

RICE PORRIDGE
WITH
SWEET POTATO
(Xīfàn)

Chinese rice porridge, or congee, which is called *zhōu* or *jūk* (among other names) in China, and *xīfàn* in Taiwan, is a classic breakfast dish. Very sweet, easy to digest, and nourishing – without being heavy – this dish is made from rice cooked for a while in a large amount of water. Depending on the region and the family, the end result may be thicker or thinner, with more or less texture. Quite bland in itself, porridge is accompanied with many toppings, usually leftovers from the previous day, pickles, soy sauce, and fermented tofu. Here is the recipe for Taiwanese *xīfàn*, which has the very nice habit of including sweet potatoes. An excellent dish to start – or finish – the day.

prep **10 min** • cook **10 min** • vegan • **4** servings

- 1 cup rice • 7½ cups water • 10 oz orange-fleshed sweet potatoes
- 1–2 green onions, thinly sliced • 3 thin slices root ginger, thinly sliced
- 1½–3 cubes of white fermented tofu (*dòufǔrǔ*), plain or spicy • Soy sauce • Salt

Rinse the rice several times and drain it. Place it in a Dutch oven or casserole pan with water. Bring to a boil, then lower the heat and simmer for 30 minutes, partially covered. Stir from time to time and make sure the rice isn't sticking to the pan bottom.

Meanwhile, halve or quarter the sweet potato lengthwise depending on its diameter, then cut into ¾-inch wedges. Steam these for 15 minutes. Transfer the sweet potato to the pot with the rice for the last 5 minutes of cooking. Turn off the heat and let stand for 5 minutes. Place the green onions, ginger, fermented tofu, soy sauce, and salt in separate bowls. Serve the porridge in individual bowls and let each diner choose toppings to taste.

Note You can also offer sesame oil, leftovers from the previous day, and pickles at the table to garnish the porridge.

BREAKFAST
NOODLES
(Dòuhuā mǐxiàn)

A typical breakfast in Yunnan usually includes rice noodles, extra fine and light silken tofu (tofu pudding), or both. *Mǐxiàn* are quite special rice noodles: they are thick, round, and fermented. Oddly, they are reminiscent of Japanese udon due to their slippery and somewhat elastic texture, though they are not made in the same way at all. They are used to make the favorite dish of the people of Kunming to start the day, called *dòuhuā mǐxiàn*, literally "rice noodles with tofu pudding." The dishes doesn't just include noodles and tofu; it is a spicy ground pork dish, served with a multitude of herbs and condiments. I offer here a vegan version.

🕐 prep **5 min** 🕐 cook **15 min** 🍃 vegan 🍲 **4** servings

- 14 oz tofu pudding or silken tofu • 4 tsp Korean red chile paste (*gochujang*)
- 10 oz dried rice noodles (thick) or 4 portions of fresh rice noodles
- 4 tsp crushed toasted peanuts • 4 tsp Sichuan chile oil
- 4 Tbsp light soy sauce • 4 tsp dark soy sauce
4 Tbsp mustard pickles, minced (*suāncài*)
- 2 green onions, thinly sliced • 1 handful cilantro leaves, coarsely chopped

Place the tofu pudding, in its container or other in suitable container, in a steam basket and heat it with steam for about 15 minutes.

In a bowl, dilute the chile paste with a little water to achieve the consistency of ketchup.

Cook the rice noodles according to package directions. Rinse them thoroughly with cold water to stop the cooking, shaking them in a colander. (When ready to eat, you can immerse them briefly in simmering water to warm them up, or eat them cold.)

Serve the rice noodles in large bowls or soup plates, topped with warm tofu and the above-listed toppings to your liking – the quantities shown opposite are just a suggestion. Mix the contents of your bowl before eating.

Notes Mustard pickles are found in Chinese and Vietnamese groceries; they are sold in sachets in brine.

You can find tofu pudding in the fresh section of Chinese groceries – look for "tofu pudding," "tofu flan," or "*douhua*" made with glucono-delta-lactone (GDL) – or prepare it yourself (see pages 34 and 36).

TOFU STIR-FRY
WITH BLACK BEANS
(Chǐ zhī dòufu)

Very good, very simple, ultra-fast, this recipe requires only a few ingredients and has flavors that we are really not used to. It's the fermented black soybean that's responsible, and we're thankful. Widely used in China and elsewhere in Asia, it is salted, generally dried, and used to make amazing and delicious sauces. Will you like it? I'll take that bet. You can easily find fermented black soybeans in Asian groceries and well-stocked supermarkets. In Mandarin, they are called *dòuchǐ*.

⏱ prep **5 min** ⏱ cook **5 min** ◉ vegan ♨ 4 servings

- 14 oz firm to extra firm tofu • 2 cloves garlic, thinly sliced
- 2 Tbsp dried fermented black beans, rinsed • 2 green onions, coarsely chopped
- 1 Tbsp Shaoxing rice wine • ½ Tbsp light soy sauce • 1 pinch white pepper
- 1 pinch sugar • 1 tsp cornstarch or potato starch mixed with 1 Tbsp water • Vegetable oil
- Steamed rice, for serving

Cut the tofu in half lengthwise, then into slices about ¼ inch thick. Blot dry with paper towels. Set a wok over high heat, add some oil, then brown the tofu on both sides. Reserve it on a plate.

Add a little more oil to the wok if needed and stir-fry the garlic, black beans, and the white parts of the green onions for 1 minute. Add the tofu, rice wine, soy sauce, white pepper, sugar, and the green part of the green onions. Stir-fry gently to avoid breaking up the tofu.

Add the cornstarch slurry and continue stirring until the sauce has thickened and coats the tofu nicely. Serve hot with rice.

PRESSED TOFU
WITH GARLIC CHIVES
(Jiǔcài chǎo dòu gān)

Here is a really easy and very tasty recipe. Garlic chive stems (with or without flower buds at the end) have an aroma very similar to that of wild garlic shoots, but stronger. If you love garlic, you're going to fall in love. If you don't like it, go your merry way. The pre-pressed tofu is, as the name suggests, already flavored with five-spice – but not spicy. So there is no need to add all kinds of aromatics, sauces, or herbs and spices to this little stir-fry dish: you can settle for a little salt or a dash of soy sauce.

🕐 prep **5 min**   🕐 cook **2 min**   🌱 vegan   🍴 **4** servings

- 5 oz garlic chive stems (1 bunch)
- 7 oz five-spice pressed tofu
- Vegetable oil • Steamed rice, for serving (optional)

If the bases of the garlic chives are too fibrous, remove them. Cut the rest into 1½-inch lengths, keeping the flower buds if there are any. Cut the tofu into slices about the same length and ¼ inch thick.

Heat a wok or frying pan over high heat, pour in a little oil, and add the tofu. Stir-fry for 30 seconds–1 minute. Add the garlic chives and stir-fry for 30 seconds–1 minute. Taste and season with salt, and mix.

Serve with rice, or as an accompaniment to other dishes.

Note   Be careful not to confuse long green onions (*Allium fistulosum*, or *cōng*) and garlic chives (*Allium tuberosum*, or *jiǔcài*). Also be careful not to confuse the leaves and stems!

TOFU PUDDING
WITH ADZUKI BEANS
(Hóngdòu dòuhuā)

In Taiwan, they eat tofu pudding topped with brown sugar syrup and sprinkled with peanuts, taro balls, oats, tapioca pearls (boba), herb jelly, and beans of all kinds.... Here is a basic recipe, with sweet adzuki beans and syrup. You are free to add other ingredients. I personally love candied palm fruits, even if they are incongruous in Taiwan – on the other hand they are very common in Malaysia and Thailand. As for adzuki, it is better to cook them yourself than to buy the canned version. This is what I had the misfortune to do to save time, and the beans were too firm. They are better overcooked.

🕐 prep **5 min** 🕐 soak **1 nuit** 🕐 cook **2 hr** 🌱 vegan 👥 **4** servings

• ½ cup adzuki beans • 1 pinch salt • ½ cup sugar • 28 oz tofu pudding (homemade or not)
For the syrup
• 1¼ cups water • ⅓ cup brown sugar • 3 thin slices root ginger (optional)

Soak the beans overnight in 1½ cups of water. In a pot over high heat, bring them to a boil in their soaking water. Drain, discarding this water, and return the beans to the pot with 1½ cups fresh water and a pinch of salt.

Bring the beans a boil again, then reduce the heat to the lowest possible setting and cook, covered, stirring occasionally, until the beans are tender, about 2 hours (or, 15 minutes in a pressure cooker). Drain if needed, return the beans to the pot, and mix in the sugar. It will melt and make the beans look shiny. Let cool.

While the beans are cooking, prepare the syrup. Pour the water into a small pot and bring to a boil. Add the brown sugar, reduce the heat to low, and melt, stirring. Remove from the heat and let cool.

Serve the tofu pudding chilled in bowls, top with as much adzuki as you like, and drizzle with a little syrup. You can serve the tofu pudding warm if you prefer, steamed for a few minutes to heat it up, drizzled with warm syrup.

Notes The quantities of syrup and adzuki in this recipe are quite generous; you can apportion them as you like. Leftovers will keep in the refrigerator for 1 week.

You can find tofu pudding in the refrigerator case section of Chinese groceries – look for "tofu pudding," "tofu flan," or "*douhua*" made with glucono-delta-lactone (GDL) – or, prepare it yourself (see pages 34 and 36).

FIVE-SPICE
PRESSED TOFU
(Wǔxiāng dòugān)

Pre-pressed five-spice tofu, recognizable by its smooth, brown exterior and its fine, very dense interior texture, is easy to find in any Chinese grocery, in the fresh section. Depending on the brand, it can be thick or thin, large or small, light or dark. If you prefer to make it at home, no problem: here is the recipe.

🕐 prep **5 min**　🕐 cook **15 min**　🌱 vegan

For 4 blocks pressed tofu
- 4 blocks firm or extra firm tofu (each 12 oz)
- 2 cups water • ½ cup dark soy sauce • ¼ cup Shaoxing rice wine • ½ tsp five-spice powder
- 1 tsp sugar • 3–4 thin slices root ginger

Start by pressing your tofu. Drain the tofu and wrap it in cheesecloth or paper towels. Place it between two large cutting boards, in a cool place where its liquid can drain away without causing damage. Put a weight on top – for example, a mixing bowl. Every hour or two, as the tofu becomes denser, you will be able to increase the pressure and add more and more weight. You can fill your bowl with fruit, stones, whatever you want, as long as the weight increases gradually: otherwise, you will just mash your tofu into porridge. See how it reacts and adapt accordingly. Depending on the pressure applied, it will take you 6–12 hours – or more – before you have a pressed tofu worthy of the name. It will only have a third of its original volume.

Cut each block of tofu into quarters. Place all the remaining ingredients except the tofu in a pot, and bring to the boil. Lower the heat, add the tofu, and simmer for 30 minutes. The tofu should be covered with liquid.

Preheat the oven to 350°F. Cover a plate with paper towels, place the pressed tofu on the paper, and bake for 15 minutes. Turn the tofu blocks over and bake for another 15 minutes, or until the surface of the blocks has dried. Let cool. You can use your pressed tofu at once, or keep it in the fridge in an airtight container for about 1 week.

Notes　Five-spice powder, very common in Chinese grocery stores, consists of ground cinnamon, cloves, fennel seeds, Sichuan peppercorns, and star anise. You can buy good whole spices, briefly roast them, and grind them yourself for a more fragrant result.

If you have a tofu press, pressing will be even easier.

ALMOND
TOFU
(Xìngrén dòufu)

Almond tofu has a misleading name: it is not made with sweet almonds but with bitter almonds, or more precisely a nonpoisonous bitter almond substitute, in this case the pits of Chinese plums – similar to how Italian amaretti cookies are made with "bitter almond" flavor from apricot kernels. These peeled "almonds" are found in some Chinese groceries. If you can't find them, you can still use regular almonds plus bitter almond flavor or extract, but it won't really be the same.

⏱ prep **10 min**   ⏱ soak **24 hr**   ⏱ cook **10 min**   🌱 vegan

For 1 lb almond tofu
- 4 oz bitter almonds, chopped
- 2¼ cups filtered water (or soft mineral water)
- 2 tsp agar-agar powder
- 1 Tbsp confectioners' sugar
- 1 pinch salt

Soak the almonds in a large bowl of water for 24 hours. Drain them and use a blender to blend them with the filtered water for several minutes, grinding them as finely as possible. Place a chinois or other fine-mesh strainer lined with cheesecloth over a pot. Pour the almond milk through the strainer. Squeeze the cheesecloth to extract the last drop. The remaining almond pulp (a sort of bitter almond "*okara*") can be used in recipes for pie dough, cookies, and so on.

Sprinkle the almond milk with agar-agar and mix with a whisk. Heat over low-medium heat, continuing to whisk to dissolve the agar-agar. Bring to a boil, whisking all the while. Turn off the heat, add the sugar and salt, and mix until they are dissolved.

Pour the mixture through a strainer into a rectangular glass mold with moistened sides. Let cool to room temperature, then cover and place in the refrigerator until the "tofu" is cool and firm. Unmold by placing a plate or a cutting board on the mold and turning mold and plate over, then cut into cubes with a knife.

Note   You can make a more robust almond tofu (this one is quite delicate) by replacing half of the water with soy milk, or even plain milk.

ALMOND TOFU
WITH LONGAN FRUIT
(Lóngyǎn xìngrén dòufu)

Longan is a delicious fruit, very common in southeast China and Southeast Asia, reminiscent of lychee. It is about the same size but its skin is light brown and smoother. When you peel it, you find white flesh of a similar consistency, with a big pit inside. The pulp, sweet and fragrant, tastes like honey. It is common to pair this fruit with almond tofu; this lovely tone-on-tone dessert is refreshing and ready in five minutes (if you have almond tofu already prepared; see page 95). You can replace canned longans with fresh fruit and homemade syrup, but it will take more effort and you will have to work around the pits.

🕐 prep **5 min** 🌱 vegan 🍴 **4** servings

- 14–16 oz almond tofu, diced
- 1 can longan fruit in light syrup

Divide the diced almond tofu and the longan fruits among dessert cups. Drizzle with light syrup, and serve chilled.

Japan

豆腐

Tofu fabrication in a workshop in Japan.

THE OTHER LAND OF TOFU

While Japan may not display the same exceptional variety of tofu forms as China, it is unequivocally the country that produces and eats the most after it. The Land of the Rising Sun should also have the nickname Soybean Nation: it's the world's leading consumer with 54 pounds per adult each year on average, in the form of tofu, *nattō*, soy sauce, miso, and others. Japanese tofu has a very long history, the beginnings of which are rather vague. The exact date of tofu's invention in China is unknown, but it is believed to have been introduced to Japan by Chinese Buddhist monks who came to teach, or to have been brought in from China by Japanese monks. Indeed, monks made many exchanges between the two countries between the eighth and twelfth centuries, and the first mention of tofu in Japan dates from 1182.

In China, tofu was a dish for the poor at the beginning of its history, while in Japan, tofu immediately seduced the upper classes – those who traveled to and interacted with China. In addition, it was very chic among the aristocracy at that time to cultivate a stripped-down simplicity, demanded by Buddhism (and perhaps snobbery), and tofu seemed to be the ideal food for expressing that. It was undoubtedly the Buddhist monks, numerous and in contact with the people, who popularized it among the poorest populations, and it could therefore have spread among the upper and lower classes simultaneously.

One peculiarity of Japan is that a government effort emerged in the ninth century to impose the vegetarian regime on all of its population, after an initial decree in this direction was made in the seventh century. In this context, tofu and other soy products had a forced but very real success, becoming pillars of the diet. Certainly, the Japanese found every possible loophole to allow them to continue eating animals. The consumption of fish and birds not being prohibited, they reclassified unrelated species into these two categories, such as dolphins, whales, and even game – hares, hinds, wild boars…. In fact, it was mainly the raising of domestic animals as a food source that was prohibited. Each culture has its own definition of vegetarian diet, you see.

Most classic Japanese tofu recipes date from the fifteenth century, when Japan began to grow soybeans on a large scale and this ingredient became widespread. Grilled tofu, or *yakidōfu*, dates back to that time, as does Kyoto-style tofu hot pot (*yūdōfu*), grilled tofu with miso (*tōfu dengaku*) or l'*oden*, Japanese hot pot. All are still widely enjoyed today. To put a little variety in their daily meals, the Japanese also invented at this time and in the following century forms of tofu that did not exist in China, like cold-dried tofu (*kōyadōfu*), *aburaage*, and *inariage*, the two main forms of Japanese fried tofu, as well as silken tofu. So you see they really did develop a unique tofu culture, with their own recipes and their own products, which explains the obvious differences between the Chinese and the Japanese approach to tofu.

IN PRAISE OF BLANDNESS

One of the peculiarities of the Japanese is to cultivate blandness, more than any other people, even if the Chinese can sometimes do it too. In addition to their appreciation of rather extreme aromatic mildness, the Japanese have a weakness for tender textures; tofu is ideal for this, especially if you keep it as is, in its simplest expression: white, plain, self-sufficient or almost so. While most Asian cuisines use the blandness of tofu as a blank canvas to transform with lots of spices and sauces – much as they willingly transform its texture – the Japanese have a real soft spot for tofu that simply resembles tofu. They are ready to pay top yen for an artisanal tofu that they will savor with a tiny spoon, appreciating the delicate aromas of the soybeans that have been rigorously selected for this specific use. Unfortunately, traditional tofu workshops have become rare. Colossal tofu factories – the largest in the world are

Firming tofu with the inclined board method.

people who have perfected it for close to a millennium, at least; yes, their tofu really is better, and yes, it is really good. It is the natural result of spending a few centuries working on the question.

NOT JUST FOR THE LADIES

For all its blandness and delicacy, tofu is not considered a "girly" food in Japan. Certainly, women who are healthy conscious will often prefer it to meat because it is less fatty and caloric, and is easy to digest, but the men don't feel that their virility is tested by eating tofu. Every day at the supermarket, you can see big muscular fellows or construction workers buying a block of tofu and some vegetables to make a little evening meal. A lot of guys who have something to prove – or inveterate meat-eaters – would see this as a strange paradox, a sissified behavior in these seemingly masculine men, as if food had a gender, and as if wanting to eat healthy was a confession that one is not a "real man." What a funny idea – especially since the Japanese are not the least macho guys on earth, they just like to eat tofu. Most tofu artisans, like chefs, have always been men, by the way.

Tofu has no gender or social class in Japan. It may be showing a generational divide, however: although it is far from unpopular, it is consumed much more by older people than by young people, unless they are part of the small vegetarian or vegan fringe of the population. The Japanese diet is changing at this time, becoming fattier, sweeter, and richer in meat products, but tofu has not said its last word. It is still considered a daily ingredient and is mass produced; simultaneously, in craft workshops and large restaurants, it is prized as an exquisite delicacy. Its forms are certainly less varied than in China – which wins the prize in this field – but they are numerous. Here are the most common.

in Japan – largely replaced them during the twentieth century.

Between this religious heritage, a quest for blandness, and a culture of "cleanliness," tofu has become a fundamental element of the Japanese diet. And while the consumption of meat and dairy products has skyrocketed in Japan, tofu is not about to disappear. Not only is it not necessarily opposed to meat – the two can be married – but it remains very inexpensive, widely available, and particularly easy to stock (square boxes, a Japanese passion), store, and cook. And then, it just pleases people. It is a little surprising from a Western point of view because we do not particularly want to taste the tofu *we* produce with a tiny spoon. And that's normal. But a very good tofu made with very good Japanese soybeans does not have the same taste or texture at all. You have to be a little humble and remember that we have only a few decades of experience in making tofu, compared with a

TOFU TYPES & USES

FIRM TOFU

In Japan, firm tofu is called *momen dōfu*, or "cotton tofu." When it is traditionally made in presses covered with cheese-cloth, the cloth leaves an impression on the surface of the finished block, hence the term "cotton" – referring to the texture of the tofu and not to the cloth used for its production. Japanese people traditionally don't use woks or frying pans, so their firm tofu doesn't need to be as solid as in other countries; instead, it is often simmered, crumbled, or mashed, or deep-fried in a large amount of oil. To fry it in the pan, you'll want to squeeze it for an hour to drain the excess water. Japanese firm tofu often has a slight bitter flavor due to the *nigari* that is used to coagulate the soy milk (see page 6). This coagulating agent also gives it a fairly spongy texture, generally, although there is a wide range of consistencies to satisfy all types of customers. The tofu shelf of any Japanese supermarket seems fairly uniform at first glance – all of these perfectly arranged blocks are the same color – but it actually contains a world of nuances.

SILKEN TOFU

The origin of silken tofu is unknown; however, we know that the first documented silken tofu was produced in Japan by pouring soy milk into small lacquered wooden molds. The coagulant, *nigari*, was then poured directly into the molds with the milk, which was allowed to set without stirring and without pressing. The second known form of silken tofu, produced in larger containers, was invented in a Tokyo restaurant as early as 1703, and then gradually spread. Very fragile and therefore difficult to transport, it was a dish reserved for the aristocracy. You will sometimes read that Japanese silken tofu is called *kinugoshi dōfu* (literally "tofu pressed into silk") because they used this fabric to make it, as opposed to the cotton of *momen dōfu*. This is a mistake: silken tofu is by definition not pressed – and firm tofu may have been pressed into silk, especially in China, as we can read in the book of traditional Chinese medicine *Bencao Gangmu*, completed in 1578. The idea of "silk" refers to its fine and slippery texture. However, the *nigari* used in Japan did not achieve the ideal consistency of silken tofu, until chemists got involved. This is where the story of modern Japanese silken tofu, the one we know today, began.

Very popular in China, the coagulant calcium sulfate, which produces a softer tofu with a finer texture, has been used in Japan for making silken tofu only since the Second World War. The firmer and more elastic consistency of this new product, with an equal content of water and protein, made it possible to manufacture pressed silken tofu, or *softo dōfu*, relatively solid but smooth and delicate. This is the one I classify as a soft, tender tofu. The great revolution of silken tofu came a little later, in the 1960s, with the use of glucono-delta-lactone, which makes a silken tofu that is super fine, super slippery, firm and elastic, even jelled (and therefore not very fragile), and easily transportable. It quickly established itself on the Japanese market and elsewhere in Asia. It is eaten uncooked, fresh, with a few condiments and sauces.

GRILLED TOFU

This Japanese specialty, called *yakidōfu*, dates back to the fifteenth century; traditionally, blocks of firm tofu are skewered and grilled over coals. In factories, the process is less poetic but gives a similar result: the tofu is slightly blackened on the surface, taking on a little grill flavor. This surface cooking gives it a certain solidity; it works best in hot pots and other broth dishes. It can also be eaten as is, if you have grilled it yourself, with a little soy sauce and grated ginger.

FREEZE-DRIED TOFU

Frozen tofu is a Chinese invention; blocks of firm tofu were once buried under the snow in winter to give the tofu a very special honeycomb texture. The Japanese have developed another form of frozen tofu of their own: freeze-dried tofu, or *kōyadōfu*. Usually, when a food is dried, it is exposed to warm temperatures to evaporate the water in it. In traditional freeze-drying, the food is repeatedly frozen and thawed, until all the water is extracted and the food is completely dried. In the coldest regions of Japan, this technique was mastered very early to preserve food and make it lighter. The first mentions of freeze-dried tofu by the Buddhist monks of Mount Kōya date back to the beginning of the seventeenth century. Before being cooked, this tofu is rehydrated by covering it with hot water and letting it swell. It can then be pressed firmly, but gently, by hand to squeeze out the excess water, then simmered, added to soups and broths, marinated, stir-fried, deep-fried.... It can replace other tofus in most recipes, but it has a very different texture. More spongy and dense, it does and admirable job of absorbing liquid and flavors.

FRIED TOFU

Japanese fried tofu is a little different from its Chinese counterpart. It exists in several forms, the simplest of which is without doubt inspired by the Chinese *zhádòufu*. In Japanese, it is called *atsuage*, literally "thick fried," or *namaage*, which means "raw fried." The technique is to take a block of firm tofu, press it for an even firmer texture and to drain some of its water, then deep-fry it in oil until a golden crust forms on the outside. Fried tofu can be purchased or prepared at home; it is eaten hot with a sauce and some condiments, or used like firm tofu in other preparations: soups, stews, and so forth. Similar products can be found outside of Japan in organic markets, generally under names like "tofu cutlets" or "bean curd strips." We Westerners treat fried tofu like a meat replacement, because we assume that we cannot be happy in life if we do not eat something that resembles meat.

FRIED TOFU POCKETS

Aburaage (literally "fried in oil") is another Japanese specialty. It is firm tofu cut into thin slices and fried twice: first in an oil bath at around 250°F, then in another at 350–400°F. This somewhat special treatment gives it an airy texture like that of Chinese tofu puffs; but since *aburaage* are narrow and elongated, they end up being hollow inside, forming a sort of fried tofu pocket. There are many ways to use these in the kitchen. You can, for example, take advantage of their thinness to make strips to garnish miso soup, or make use of the pocket and stuff them with all kinds of things, including rice. Generally, since these little puffs absorb liquid so well, they end up being marinated, simmered, or added to broths.

TOFU PUDDING

Tofu pudding is called *oboro dōfu* in Japanese, which could be translated as "tofu mist" or "cloud tofu." It is not as common as in China and Southeast Asia, and not necessarily as smooth: it can be coagulated with *nigari* and therefore take on a fairly lumpy texture. In any case, it is delicate, watery, and savored with a spoon with salty condiments and soy sauce. It is not common in Japan to eat it sweet, whereas this is the norm in many parts of Asia.

Yakidōfu (grilled tofu) is a Japanese specialty dating back to the fifteenth century. The process has become enormously industrialized since then.

YUBA

The skin that forms on the surface of heated soy milk, called *yuba* in Japanese, is mentioned in Chinese and Japanese texts from the sixteenth century. It is probably much older. In Japan, you can make it at home or buy it fresh or dried. While these products are fairly common, they remain associated, in their craft form, with certain regions. The city of Nikko in particular, dotted with Buddhist temples, is a *yuba* mecca. Many restaurants offer it in all its forms: fresh, fried, with noodles, in curry, in soup...

OKARA

The leftover pulp of soybeans that have been pressed to make soy milk are never thrown away in Japan. As in China and Korea, it is an ancient food, since it has been associated with tofu production since tofu's inception. However, its commercial potential is limited because it does not keep long. Humans consume significantly less *okara* than they produce in the great tofu nations, so most *okara* is used to feed livestock, including pigs and dairy cows. Much of the *okara* is also composted as fertilizer, and only a small fraction of the production is used in cooking. The most common Japanese *okara* dish, called *unohana no iri ni* – or simply *unohana* – is a typical small stewed dish, served cold. Besides the soybean pulp, it contains vegetables; the ingredients are braised in a mild broth until the liquid is completely absorbed.

Many products are derived from soy milk or tofu production: fresh *yuba* (1), dried *yuba* (2) and *okara* (3) .

COLD TOFU
WITH GINGER
& GREEN ONION
(Hiyayakko)

Japanese silken tofu, which is finer, firmer, and more flexible than what we find sold in Western organic grocery stores, is very delicate, so be careful when handling it. It can also found in individual serving portions ideal for this recipe: all you have to do is unmold them and accompany them with bright flavors that wake up bland and modest tofu. The Japanese call these ingredients with a strong "*yakumi*" flavor. Among them, the great classics are green onions, grated ginger, yuzu citrus zest, *myōga* (Japanese ginger), wasabi, minty *shiso* leaf…. Salt-rich condiments are also welcome, especially soy sauce and pickled plum. Cold tofu with these flavors is a Japanese summertime classic.

prep **5 min** vegan **4** servings

- 7 oz firm extra-fine silken tofu
- 1 green onion, thinly sliced
- 1 tsp very finely grated root ginger
- 4 tsp soy sauce

Unmold the tofu onto a plate and cut it into 4 small blocks. Place each block in a saucer. Arrange a quarter of the green onion and ginger on each, and drizzle each with 1 teaspoon soy sauce. Serve cold.

COLD TOFU
WITH NATTO
(Hiyayakko no nattō)

Soy + soy + soy = love. This recipe boasts soybeans in three totally different forms: tofu, soy sauce, and *nattō* (fermented soybeans that take on a rich flavor and a nice slippery texture, great for health). There is also a little pickled plum and okra, a vegetable appreciated by the Japanese and often paired with *nattō* because they have a similarly sticky texture. You can serve this cold tofu as a starter; soy's umami has a reputation for piquing the appetite, and the variety of textures will give you a very fun, cute, and surprising start to a meal for tofu neophytes.

⏱ prep **5 min**   🌱 vegan   🍴 **4** servings

- 7 oz firm extra-fine silken tofu • 1 can *nattō* (Japanese fermented soybeans)
- 2 tsp soy sauce • 1 pickled plum (*umeboshi*), puréed
- 2 okra, thinly sliced

Unmold the tofu and cut it into 4 small blocks. Place each block in a saucer. In a bowl, combine the *nattō*, soy sauce, pickled plum, and okra slices. Divide this topping among the 4 tofu blocks. Enjoy with a small spoon, drizzled with a little more soy sauce if needed.

Note *Nattō* is found in Japanese grocery stores (and sometimes Korean, Chinese, etc.) in the frozen section, usually in batches of 3 boxes. Let it thaw in the box in the refrigerator overnight, then stir it vigorously with a pair of chopsticks. It will take on a slightly mousse-like texture and make long, sticky threads. It's strange, but it's normal.

ZEN SALAD
WITH TOFU SAUCE
(Shiraae)

This salad, which originates from Zen vegetarian cuisine, can be made with many different vegetables, but one thing remains constant: its very tasty sauce is made with tofu, sesame, and miso. Its consistency is not liquid but rather thick; some people like it a more diluted, others like it thicker, but it generally stays somewhere between a paste and a smooth or rough cream. It's not just a seasoning, but one of the main ingredients in this recipe. This unfamiliar way of using tofu opens up many possibilities for those who lack the inspiration to cook it.

prep **10 min** • press **30 min** • cook **5 min** • vegan • **4 servings**

- 4 oz firm tofu • 2 tsp white sesame paste (*nerigoma* or tahini)
- 1 tsp sugar • 1 tsp white miso paste • 4 oz fresh mushrooms (*shimeji*, shiitake, enoki...)
- 1¾ oz konjac root (see Note) • 1 small carrot, julienned • 2 handfuls fresh spinach
- 1 Tbsp white sesame seeds, toasted • Salt

If you use Japanese firm tofu, which is richer in water than regular firm tofu, wrap it with paper towels and place it between two plates for about 30 minutes to drain it. Pound it with a wooden spoon or mortar to reduce it to a coarse paste. Add the sesame paste, sugar, white miso, and a little salt, and stir until you get a homogeneous mixture.

If you are using small mushrooms (*shimeji* or enoki), cut the base of their stems and separate them; if you are using shiitake, remove their stems and slice caps into $1/16$-inch slices. Blanch them in boiling water for 2–3 minutes, then run them under cold water and drain well. Squeeze to extract as much water as possible.

Cut the konjac root into $1/16$-inch slices, and boil them for 2 minutes to neutralize the odor. Drain. Blanch the carrot for 2 minutes and drain it. Blanch the spinach leaves for about 30 seconds, then run them under cold water, drain, and squeeze to extract as much water as possible.

Mix all the vegetables with the tofu paste. Add a little water if you prefer a more diluted consistency. Serve and sprinkled with toasted sesame seeds.

Note Konjac is a starchy root used in Asian cooking in root form, as noodles, or as a thickening powder.

VERY SIMPLE
FRIED
TOFU
(Atsuage)

There are several types of fried tofu in Japan, some of which you can buy ready-made at the supermarket. *Inariage*, fried twice at different temperatures, is very fine and has a puffed texture, becoming almost empty inside, a sort of tofu pocket. As for *atsuage*, it keeps its density because it is fried only once, as a block; it's just fried on the outside. Whereas making *inariage* at home is quite complex and technical, there is nothing simpler than making *atsuage*. *Atsuage* can be used in many ways: it can be served at once, still hot, with a few condiments, or used later as an ingredient. For example, you can marinate it in a sauce or broth, garnish a soup or a salad...

🕐 prep **5 min**   🕐 press **2 hr**   🕐 cook **10 min**   🌱 vegan

For 1 block tofu
• 1 block firm tofu • Oil for deep-frying

Wrap the tofu in paper towels and place it between two plates for 1 hour. Now change the paper towels, reposition the tofu, and place an additional weight on top: another plate, for example. Leave it for another 1 hour.

Heat oil for deep-frying to 350°F. Cut the block in half crosswise and fry the two blocks for about 10 minutes, until they are evenly golden. Drain on a wire rack.

You can cut the blocks into bite-size pieces and serve hot with a little thinly sliced green onion, grated ginger, and a drizzle of soy sauce, or marinate them to use in another dish.

MELTING FRIED TOFU
(Agedashi tōfu)

This fried tofu is extremely delicate; crusty on the outside, melty in the middle. *Agedashi tōfu* is served in a clear sweet-and-savory sauce with finely grated white radish and green onion, so it's not bland at all. On the contrary, it is one of the favorite dishes of Westerners in *izakaya* and other Japanese restaurants, because it offers, with very few elements, an extraordinary variety of textures and flavors. Simple, refined, exquisite.

🕐 prep **10 min** (+ traditional dashi **1 hr**)   🕐 cook **10 min**   🌱 vegan   🍽 4 servings

- ¹/₈ oz (3 g) kombu seaweed or ¾ tsp kombu dashi powder • 1 cup water
- ¼ cup soy sauce • ¼ cup mirin rice wine
- 1 lb extra-firm silken tofu or flexible soft to medium tofu
- ¼ cup potato starch • 2 inches daikon radish, finely grated
- 1 green onion, thinly sliced • Oil for deep-frying

First prepare your soup base, or dashi: cut or break the kombu into pieces, and put it in a saucepan with the water. Let steep for at least 1 hour, then heat over low heat, covered. Just before boiling, when small bubbles form on the surface of the kombu, remove the seaweed pieces from the pan. The scented water that remains will be your dashi. If you're in a hurry, you can use instant dashi and just add the powder to the same amount of heated water.

Combine the dashi, soy sauce, and mirin in a small saucepan. Bring to a boil, then turn off the heat. Set aside.

Cut the tofu into large cubes or rectangles about 1½ inches square (you need some thickness to the tofu to end up with a variety of textures). Plan on 3 pieces per person. Lay the cubes on several layers of paper towel and let them drain for 10 minutes.

Heat oil for deep-frying to 340°F. Dust the tofu with potato starch on all sides. You can use a brush for this. Fry the tofu as soon as the oil is ready (if it sits, the starch coating will become gummy), in batches of 4 to prevent crowding. Gently remove each piece when the outside is just crisp. They should not brown, or barely. It takes a few minutes. Place them on a wire rack and continue until you run out of tofu.

Divide the sauce among 4 bowls and add 3 pieces of fried tofu per bowl. Top with grated daikon and sprinkle with chopped green onion. Serve at once.

Note To firm up your tofu before cutting it, you can dissolve ¼ cup of salt in 1 quart of boiling water, remove from the heat, and soak your block for 15 minutes, then drain it for at least 15 minutes on paper towels.

MISO SOUP
WITH TOFU & WAKAME
(Tofu to wakame no misoshiru)

Miso soup is a basic element of the Japanese meal. Seventy-five percent of Japanese people consume it at least once a day. Miso, a fermented soybean paste, is diluted in a clear broth – dashi – and garnished with all kinds of vegetables, tofu, seaweed, and more. Depending on the region, the type of miso will vary and so will the other ingredients; there are hundreds of possible variations on miso soup. Here is one of the most common recipes.

🕐 prep **5 min** (+ traditional dashi **1 hr**) 🕐 cook **10 min** 🌱 vegan

For 4 bowls
• ¼ oz (8 g) kombu seaweed or 2 tsp kombu dashi powder • 3⅓ cups water
• 1 Tbsp dried wakame seaweed • 5 oz soft, flexible or medium-firm tofu
• 3 Tbsp white miso paste or mixed miso paste • 2–3 green onions

First prepare your soup base, or dashi: cut or break the kombu into pieces, and put it in a saucepan with the water. Let steep for at least 1 hour, then heat over low heat, covered. Just before boiling, when small bubbles form on the surface of the kombu, remove the seaweed pieces from the pan. The scented water that remains will be your dashi. If you're in a hurry, you can use instant dashi and just add the powder to the same amount of heated water.

While the kombu is steeping, rehydrate the wakame in a bowl of water. Cut the tofu into ½-inch cubes. Slice the green onion.

When the dashi is ready, add the tofu and the drained wakame to the pan and continue cooking over low heat for 1–2 minutes. Put the miso in a ladle filled with dashi or in a chinois or other fine-mesh strainer, and gently swirl it in the pan to dissolve it into the soup. Remove from the heat. Serve at once in small soup bowls, garnished with a little green onion.

Notes The higher the quantity of rice in miso (this is the case with white miso), the more alcohol it contains, which makes its aroma volatile. It is therefore advised to add it at the end of cooking and not to reheat it.

If you can't find tender or medium-firm tofu, you can replace it with regular firm tofu, or extra-firm silken tofu (available in some Asian groceries). Regular tofu will be a little firmer than soft tofu, and extra-firm silken tofu will be a little more delicate.

MISO SOUP
WITH FRIED TOFU & DAIKON
(Aburaage to daikon no misoshiru)

Fried tofu pockets, which are called *aburaage* in Japan, are often used in miso soup. They are cut into simple strips and allowed to absorb the delicious broth. Crunchy vegetables are favorite additions that provide texture variety. Daikon radish works very well, but you can also try small sweet turnips, okra slices, leafy greens...

⏱ prep **5 min** (+ traditional dashi **1 hr**) ⏱ cook **15 min** 🌱 vegan

For 4 bowls
• 3¹/₃ cups water • ¼ oz (8 g) kombu seaweed or 2 tsp kombu dashi powder
• 4 oz fried tofu pockets (*aburaage*) • 4 oz daikon radish
• Boiling water • 3 Tbsp *hatchō miso* (red miso paste made with 100% soybeans)
• 2 green onions

First prepare your soup base, or dashi: cut or break the kombu into pieces, and put it in a saucepan with the water. Let steep for at least 1 hour, then heat over low heat, covered. Just before boiling, when small bubbles form on the surface of the kombu, remove the seaweed pieces from the pan. The scented water that remains will be your dashi. If you're in a hurry, you can use instant dashi and just add the powder to the same amount of heated water.

Pour boiling water over the fried tofu and squeeze it by hand to drain out the excess water and oil. Flatten it again, cut it in half lengthwise, then slice it into slices ⅛ inch thick. Cut the daikon into slices ⅛ inch thick and then into half-moons or quarters, depending on the diameter. Thinly slice the green onion.

Put the miso in a ladle filled with dashi or in a chinois or other fine-mesh strainer, and gently swirl it in the saucepan to dissolve it into the soup. Add the daikon and continue cooking the dashi with miso and daikon over low heat for 5–10 minutes. Add the fried tofu strips to the pan, cook for another 2 minutes, and serve in bowls garnished with a little green onion.

BUDDHIST
BROTH
(Kenchinjiru)

This simple and healthful vegan soup, a legacy of Buddhist culinary traditions in Japan, is comforting during the cold season. Very popular in the Japanese mountains, it can be prepared with any autumn and winter vegetable: turnip, taro root, burdock root, winter squash or pumpkin.... In some regions, it is enriched with a little miso.

🕐 prep **30 min** (+ traditional dashi **1 hr**) 🕐 cook **15 min** 🌱 vegan 👥 **4** servings

- ¼ oz (8 g) kombu seaweed or 2 tsp kombu dashi powder • 3 dried shiitake mushrooms
- 7 oz firm tofu • 4½ oz konjac root (see Note, page 112) • 7 oz daikon radish
- 1 carrot • 5 oz lotus root • 1 Tbsp sesame oil • 3 Tbsp sake
- 2 Tbsp soy sauce • 2 green onions, sliced on the diagonal • Salt

First prepare your soup base, or dashi: cut or break the kombu into pieces, and put it in a saucepan with the water. Let steep for at least 1 hour, then heat over low heat, covered. Just before boiling, when small bubbles form on the surface of the kombu, remove the seaweed pieces from the pan. The scented water that remains will be your dashi. If you're in a hurry, you can use instant dashi and just add the powder to the same amount of heated water.

While the kombu is steeping, rehydrate the mushrooms in 1 cup of cool water. Wrap the tofu in paper towels, place it on a plate, and place another fairly heavy plate over it while you prepare the other ingredients.

Cut the konjac into slices 1/16 inch thick, and boil for 2 minutes to neutralize their odor. Drain and set aside. Peel the daikon and carrot and cut them into half-moons 1/16 inch thick. Clean the lotus root if needed and cut it into half-moons ⅛ inch thick.

When the mushrooms are rehydrated, gently squeeze them to extract excess water. Cut them in half or in quarters, depending on their size. Strain their soaking water through a coffee filter and add it to the dashi. Tear the tofu into pieces similar in size to the vegetables.

In a casserole pan over medium heat, heat the sesame oil and add the carrot, daikon, lotus root, and konjac. Stir to coat all the vegetables with oil. Your goal is to cook them until fragrant but not browned. Add the mushrooms and tofu, and stir again. Add the dashi and simmer for 10 minutes, skimming regularly. Add the sake and salt to taste, then cook until the vegetables are tender. Add the soy sauce at the end of cooking. Serve garnished with green onion.

GRILLED
MISO TOFU
(Tōfu dengaku)

This very easy recipe is a classic in Japan: they have eaten tofu in this way since the fifteenth century. The tofu is covered with a sweet and savory miso sauce and then broiled or, ideally, grilled. The flavor of the sauce is strong enough to transform the pale tofu. The type of miso used (depending on the region of Japan, it may be white miso, red miso, or any nuance in between) will give a more or less full-bodied result. White miso is the mildest and sweetest, and red miso is the strongest. The version of red miso called *hatchō miso*, popular around Nagoya and made only from soybeans and no barley or other grains, has the advantage of being gluten-free, for those interested.

🕐 prep **10 min** 🕐 press **30 min** 🕐 cook **5 min** 🌱 vegan 🍽 **4** servings

• 7 oz firm tofu • ¼ cup miso paste of choice • 3 Tbsp sugar
• 2 Tbsp mirin rice wine
• 2 Tbsp sake • 2 tsp white sesame seeds

If you use Japanese firm tofu, which has a higher water content than typical firm tofu, wrap it in paper towels and place it between two plates for around 30 minutes to drain. Cut it into slices about ½ inch thick.

Combine the miso, sugar, rice wine, and sake in a small saucepan. Heat over low heat, stirring constantly (red miso is very sticky and will take a while to loosen up – you can dilute it slightly with a small amount of water, if needed). Simmer the mixture for about 3 minutes while continuing to stir.

Preheat a broiler or grill. Place your tofu slices on a broiler pan or in a grill basket, and brush them thickly with the miso sauce on one side. Place them under the broiler or on the grill for 3–4 minutes, or until the miso tofu begins to caramelize and lightly brown in places. Serve sprinkled with sesame seeds.

GRILLED
TOFU
(Yakidōfu)

The tofu that the Japanese consider "firm" is actually quite tender. Its delicate texture crumbles easily and it can therefore fall apart when cooked in broth, as is the case with *nabe*, a kind of Japanese "fondue." When grilled, tofu stiffens up, which is why grilled tofu (*yakidōfu*) is often used in *nabe* instead of uncooked tofu. In addition, if tofu is barbecued, it takes on a particularly pleasant grilled-smoked taste. You can use this tofu in many of the recipes in this book; it will be ideal for herbed tofu canapés (see page 164) or Korean mushroom and tofu hot pot (see page 184).

prep **5 min**   press **1 hr**   cook **10–20 min**   vegan

For 1 large block tofu
- 1 large block firm tofu

Cut your tofu in half crosswise. Wrap it in paper towels and place it between two plates to drain for at least 1 hour.

Preheat a grill or broiler. Place the two blocks of tofu on several skewers or in a grilling basket or place them on a broiler pan and grill or broil them on both sides until their surface is colored, or even slightly blackened (it should not be fully charred, but well grilled).

TOFU FRITTERS
WITH VEGETABLES
(Ganmodoki)

Ganmodoki ("*ganmo*" to their friends) come from vegetarian Buddhist cuisine; their name literally means "pseudo-goose" because they are said to taste like poultry. This is not true, but at the same time the monks who gave them this name had no idea, since they did not eat goose. Anyway. These little fritters have an extraordinary texture due to the addition of *yama imo*, or Japanese yam, in the dough. This finely grated root has a unique gluey consistency that gives fabulous flexibility to the donut dough. It is found in Japanese grocery stores. Otherwise, potato can give a result that is somewhat different but close enough. You can serve these fritters as is, in a clear broth, or with Japanese mustard (*karashi*).

🕐 prep **20 min**   🕐 press **30 min**   🕐 cook **15 min**   🌱 vegetarian

For 12 pieces
- 14 oz firm tofu • ½ carrot, grated
- 2 Tbsp Japanese sweet potato or potato, finely grated (into a pulp)
- 1 green onion, thinly sliced • 2 shiitake mushrooms, thinly sliced
- 1 egg white • 2 Tbsp black sesame seeds • 1 Tbsp potato starch
- ½ tsp salt • Oil for deep-frying
- Broth, soy sauce, and/or Japanese mustard (*karashi*) for serving

Wrap the tofu in paper towels and place it between two plates to drain for 30 minutes. Pound it in a mortar or mix it until you get a smooth paste. Add the carrot, yam, green onion, mushrooms, egg white, half the sesame seeds, the potato starch, and salt and mix well.

Heat oil for deep-frying to 340–350°F. Form small oval balls of tofu dough, stick a pinch of sesame seeds on top, and immerse them in the oil 4 at a time at most, to prevent crowing. Fry until the fritters are golden brown. Drain on a wire rack.

Serve in small bowls with a little broth or simply with a little soy sauce and Japanese mustard – beware, it is strong!

TOFU
FERMENTED IN MISO
(Tōfu no misozuke)

For those who find tofu bland, here is something to change your mind: by letting it ferment in a miso-based mixture, you can develop aromas and textures similar to those of cheese. Miso-fermented tofu can be enjoyed on its own, in slices with bread and red wine, or used to garnish salads. In Japan, where this recipe came into being – it comes from Fukuoka, and the first written mention dates back to 1782 – it is tasted in small quantities, accompanied by sake, as a delicacy with a rich flavor.

🕐 prep **15 min**   🕐 press **1 hr 15 min**   🕐 aging **2 weeks**   🌱 vegan

For 1 block tofu (12 oz)
• 12 oz firm or extra-firm tofu • 8 oz mixed miso paste
• ¼ cup sake • 3 Tbsp mirin rice wine • 1 large square gauze or cheesecloth

Press your block of firm tofu to drain it: place it on a cutting board slightly raised on one side and place another fairly heavy board on top. You can place a pan on top for more weight, and therefore more pressure. Leave it for at least 1 hour, then wrap it in a clean cloth or paper towels for 15 minutes. (You can also use extra-firm tofu, well drained and simply wrapped in paper towels for 30 minutes.) Blot dry the entire surface of the tofu as much as possible, then wrap it in a double layer of gauze or cheesecloth.

In a bowl, mix the miso, sake, and mirin. Choose an airtight glass or clear plastic container barely larger than the block of tofu (ideally, the wrapped tofu will have a mere 1/16 inch margin on each side once placed in the container). Coat the bottom and sides of the container with the miso mixture, Be generous, especially in the corners. Place the wrapped tofu in the container, pressing hard to expel the air. Spread the rest of the miso mixture on top of the wrapped tofu. Make sure that it is fully coated and that there are no air bubbles. Close the container and place it in the refrigerator.

Once a week, check that the tofu does not show any trace of mold on its surface. If there are only a few spots of mold on the outside of the gauze, don't panic; remove them with the blade of a clean knife and sprinkle a little salt on the area. Ideally, avoid handling the tofu; the transparent container allows you to look without touching. After 2 weeks, the tofu will already have taken on flavor and changed color and texture. And after 2 months – that is the pinnacle!

Note   Make sure your container is clean and perfectly dry. Work with clean hands or with sterile gloves. If you have any doubts – an unpleasant odor, pungent taste, mold on the surface of the tofu, and so on – start fresh and do not consume the dubious tofu.

SALTY-SWEET
FRIED TOFU POCKETS
(Inariage)

In the frozen section of Japanese groceries (and sometimes in other Asian groceries that have a fairly wide selection of products), you find fried tofu called *aburaage*. It is first fried at a low temperature, then in hotter oil, which gives it a spongy texture similar to the puffed tofu that the Chinese call *dòubu* and the Malays call *tau pok*. *Aburaage* has the distinction of being fried in thin slices, resulting in a sort of large pocket. It is used in many Japanese recipes. Some recipes require you to cook it beforehand to obtain seasoned *aburaage*, which is called *inariage*. Here's how to do it.

🕐 prep **5 min** (+ traditional dashi **1 hr**)　🕐 cook **20 min**　🌱 vegan

For 12 pieces
• ⅛ oz (3 g) kombu seaweed or ¾ tsp kombu dashi powder • 1 cup water
• 6 frozen fried tofu pockets (*aburaage*), thawed • 1 qt boiling water • ¼ cup sugar
• 2 Tbsp mirin rice wine • 2 Tbsp sake • 3–4 Tbsp soy sauce

First prepare your soup base, or dashi: cut or break the kombu into pieces, and put it in a saucepan with the water. Let steep for at least 1 hour, then heat over low heat, covered. Just before boiling, when small bubbles form on the surface of the kombu, remove the seaweed pieces from the pan. The scented water that remains will be your dashi. If you're in a hurry, you can use instant dashi and just add the powder to the same amount of heated water.

Place the 6 pieces of *aburaage* flat between 2 sheets of plastic wrap and roll with a rolling pin (without pressing too hard). Cut the 6 pieces in half crosswise.

In a heatproof mixing bowl, pour 1 quart of boiling water over the 12 pieces of *aburaage*. Leave them for 2 minutes, then drain in a colander and pour a good amount of cold water over. Squeeze by hand (gently but firmly) to drain the excess water.

In a saucepan, combine the dashi, sugar, mirin, sake, and soy sauce. Add the l'*aburaage* and place an *otoshibuta* (the small wooden Japanese lids that you put on food), a pan lid that is too small for the pan, or a dessert plate directly on the *aburaage* to weight it down and keep it in the liquid. Bring to a simmer over medium heat and cook for about 15 minutes, until 90 percent of the liquid is gone. Let cool.

Your *inariage* is now ready for making sushi in a tofu pocket (*inarizushi*), fried tofu noodles (*kitsune udon*), and other dishes.

SUSHI IN TOFU POCKETS
(Inarizushi)

This recipe does not require you to be a sushi master; *inarizushi* is commonly prepared at home to fill the *bentō* lunchboxes of Japanese children. The dish consists of seasoned rice, usually garnished with sesame, seaweed, or other ingredients, served in a small pocket of salty-sweet fried tofu. You can use the ready-made *inarizushi* bags found in Japanese grocery stores, or the homemade version (see page 130), larger in size.

🕐 prep **15 min** (+ traditional dashi **1 hr**) 🕐 cook **40 min** 🌱 vegan

For 12–16 pieces
• 4 Tbsp rice vinegar • 1–2 Tbsp sugar • 1–1½ Tbsp salt • 2 cups sushi rice
• 2¼ cups water or dashi (see miso soup recipe, page 116) • 2 Tbsp white sesame seeds
• 12 pieces homemade *inariage* (see page 130) or 16 pieces store-bought *inarizushi* pockets
For the *hijiki* seaweed
• ⅓ oz (10 g) dried *hijiki* seaweed • 5 Tbsp dashi • 1 tsp sugar
• 1 tsp soy sauce • 1 tsp sake • 1 tsp mirin rice wine

Soak the *hijiki* in a large bowl of water for about 30 minutes.

Combine the rice vinegar, sugar, and salt to season the rice. Set aside. Rinse the rice and swish it with your hand in clear water several times until it no longer gives up any starch. Drain, then put it in a saucepan and add the water or dashi. Heat over high heat, covered, for 13–15 minutes, then over low heat for 5–6 minutes. Turn off the heat and let stand without touching the lid for another 10 minutes. Gently mix with a spatula to aerate the rice without crushing it, while sprinkling it with the seasoned rice vinegar. Let it cool down.

Drain the *hijiki* and mix it with the 5 tablespoons dashi, the sugar, soy sauce, sake, and mirin in a small saucepan, and simmer over medium heat until the liquid has evaporated.

Combine the rice, *hijiki,* and sesame seeds. Press the *inariage* to drain the excess sauce and reserve it in a bowl. Wet your hands with this sauce and press together enough rice (firmly, but without crushing it) to fill a piece of *inariage*. Carefully open an *inariage* pocket and fill it with rice. Repeat until you have used up all your rice and *inariage*. Serve at room temperature. No need for soy sauce, everything is already seasoned.

Note The seaweed that the Japanese call *hijiki* is found in dried form in Japanese grocery stores. It's an ultra-classic ingredient of *inarizushi*. You can replace it with mushrooms, edamame or other legumes, or just use white rice sprinkled with sesame or *furikake*, the Japanese seaweed-and-sesame sesaoning blend for rice.

NOODLE SOUP
WIHT FRIED TOFU
(Kitsune udon)

Here's an essential Japanese dish: you can eat it all over the country, all year round, and aside from few details it will always be the same. Of course, the broth will be a little more clear in Kansai – this cook will cut his fried tofu into triangles, while his neighbor prefers rectangles – but the recipe maintains a rare consistency at the national level. The fat wheat noodles (*udon*) with seasoned fried tofu (*inariage*) and broth are so popular that you can even suck down a bowl at full speed on the station platform before jumping on the train. For those who prefer it, substitute soba noodles for udon.

prep **10 min** (+ traditional dashi **1 hr**) cook **10 min** vegan

For 4 bowls
• 4 portions dried or precooked udon noodles • 8 pieces homemade *inariage* (see page 130)
• 1 qt dashi (see miso soup recipe, page 116) • 2 Tbsp mirin rice wine • 2 tsp sugar
• 2 Tbsp light soy sauce • 1 Tbsp salt • 2 green onions, thinly sliced

Immerse the udon in a large pot of boiling water. Heat them through as indicated on the packaging, stirring with chopsticks to separate them. Drain and rinse in cold water to remove the excess starch.

In a small frying pan, heat up the *inariage* in its juices. In a saucepan, combine the dashi, mirin, sugar, soy sauce, and salt. Turn off the heat just before it comes to a boil.

Divide the noodles among 4 bowls, then the hot broth (it will reheat the noodles). Place 2 pieces of *inariage* in each bowl and garnish with a little green onion.

PANFRIED TOFU
WITH NORI
(Tōfu no isobe maki)

This very simple and healthy recipe based on tofu, nori, and soy sauce is surprisingly delicious. It makes a good starter or can be eaten as a main dish with a little rice. If you add to that a small portion of vegetables and some miso soup, you will have a complete Japanese menu according to the rules of the game.

prep **5 min** • cook **10 min** • vegan • **4 servings**

- 12 oz firm tofu • 3 Tbsp potato starch
- 3 Tbsp soy sauce • 1 Tbsp sugar • 2 Tbsp sake
- 2 Tbsp water • 2 sheets nori seaweed • Vegetable oil

Cut the tofu into slices about 3/8 inch thick. Blot dry with paper towels and dust with starch to coat them on all sides.

In a bowl, combine the soy sauce, sugar, sake, and water.

In a frying pan over medium-high heat, heat a little oil. Brown the tofu on both sides. Add the sauce and swirl it in the pan, turning the tofu over so that it is completely coated. Remove from the heat.

Cut the nori into strips the entire length of the sheets about 1 inch wide. Take the tofu out of the pan and wrap each piece with a strip of nori. Serve hot with the sauce.

KYOTO-STYLE
TOFU HOT POT
(Yudōfu)

This dish is an edifying example of Japanese modesty or culinary snobbery – it all depends on your point of view. Its name literally means "hot water tofu." This Kyoto specialty consists of tofu cooked in a kombu-flavored broth and served with a few little condiments. And that's all. Extremely simple and stripped down, this recipe demands very good ingredients – an excellent fresh tofu, competition-level kombu, and best-quality soy sauce.

prep **5 min** | soak **2 hr–1 night** | cook **10 min** | vegan | **4** servings

- ¾ oz (20 g) kombu seaweed • ½ cup soy sauce • 2 Tbsp sake • 2 tsp mirin rice wine
- 21 oz medium-firm tofu • 2 pinches salt • 1 small bunch Japanese parsley (*mitsuba*)
- 2 green onions, thinly sliced • 1 tsp finely grated root ginger

With a clean cloth, gently wipe the surface of the kombu to remove any impurities – without removing the white powder, which is concentrated umami flavor. In a casserole pan or Dutch oven, place the kombu in 5 cups of water and let it soak for at least 2 hours and up to overnight.

Meanwhile, prepare the sauce by combining the soy sauce, sake, and mirin in a small saucepan. Bring to a simmer, turn off the heat, and set aside.

Cut the tofu into 8 large squares and gently place them in the water with the kombu. Lightly salt the water. Heat over medium-low heat until you see the tofu move due to the small bubbles forming in the water. Add the parsley and serve at once with the sauce.

Eat the tofu hot, dipped in the sauce with a little green onion and ginger.

SAUTÉED MINCED
TOFU
(Tōfu soboro)

Sautéed minced chicken is a simple and very common preparation in Japan; it is often used to garnish *bentō*. It is also the main ingredient of delicious *soborodon*, a bowl of rice topped with this famous chicken, vegetables, and scrambled eggs. The vegan version of this poultry preparation, which we can call *tōfu soboro* if we compare it to meat, or *iridōfu* if we compare it to a scrambled egg, is surprisingly rich in taste, and its texture does not leave one to imagine that it is tofu. Something to serve to reluctant carnivores.

🕐 prep **5 min** 🕐 cook **20 min** 🌱 vegan

For 4 portions
• 14 oz extra-firm tofu • ½ cup soy sauce
• ¼ cup sake • ¼ cup mirin rice wine • 3 Tbsp sugar
• 2 tsp finely grated root ginger • Vegetable oil • Steamed rice for serving

Heat a frying pan over medium heat and add a little oil. Crumble the tofu with your fingers, add it to the pan, and mix in the rest of the ingredients. Continue to crush and crumble the tofu with a spatula for a few minutes. Add a little water if necessary: the liquid should not completely disappear. Taste, adjust the seasoning if necessary, and serve with rice.

TOFU RICE BOWL
WITH SCRAMBLED EGGS
(Soborodon)

Four colors for a savory bowl: the light brown of sautéed tofu, the bright yellow of scrambled eggs, the bright green of blanched peas, and the neon pink of marinated ginger (*beni shōga*). This vegan version of a classic Japanese chicken dish creates an illusion, both visually and in the mouth, and is prepared much faster than it looks.

🕐 prep **5 min** 🕐 cook **35 min** 🌱 vegan

For 4 bowls
- 1½ cups sushi rice • 4 oz snow peas or sugar snap peas • 4 eggs
- 2 tsp soy sauce • 1 tsp sugar • 1 tsp mirin rice wine
- 4 portions *soboro* tofu, still warm in its juices (see page 139)
- 4 tsp red-pickled ginger, julienned (*beni shōga*) • Vegetable oil • Salt

Rinse the rice and swish it with your hand in clear water several times until it no longer gives up any starch. Drain, then put it in a saucepan with just enough water to cover your fingers when you lay your hand flat on the rice. Heat over high heat, covered, for 13–15 minutes, then over low heat for 5–6 minutes. Turn off the heat and let stand without touching the lid for another 10 minutes. Gently mix with a spatula to aerate the rice without crushing it.

Cut the peas on the diagonal ⅛ inch thick. Blanch them in a pan of boiling salted water for 20–30 seconds, then drain and immerse them in an ice water bath. Drain and set aside.

Break the eggs into a large bowl and add the soy sauce, sugar, mirin, and a pinch of salt. Take several chopsticks in one hand (5 is a good number) and use them to mix and beat the eggs without incorporating air. Heat a large frying pan over medium heat, add a little oil, and pour in the eggs. With your chopsticks, scramble the eggs as they cook until they are no longer sticky but not too dry.

Divide the rice among 4 bowls, and decoratively arrange the lukewarm *soboro* tofu with its juices, snow peas, and scrambled eggs over the rice. Add a little pink ginger, and serve at once.

SOBA NOODLES
WITH FRESH YUBA
(Yuba soba)

The film that forms on the surface of soy milk when you heat it is called *yuba*. In Japan, most small traditional tofu workshops also sell *yuba*, since the raw material is the same as for tofu. This skin, rich in proteins and vitamins, can be used fresh, tender, and creamy, or can also be found sold in dried form. For this soba (buckwheat noodle) recipe, very popular in Tochigi prefecture, you can use rehydrated dried yuba...but fresh yuba is so much better!

prep **5 min** · cook **35 min** · vegan

For 4 bowls
- 4 tsp sugar • 3 Tbsp mirin rice wine • ²/₃ cup soy sauce
- 1 qt rich soy milk (see page 24) • 4 portions soba noodles
- 1 qt dashi (see miso soup recipe, page 116) • 2 tsp sake
- 1 sheet nori seaweed, cut into matchsticks • 2 green onions, thinly sliced • 1 tsp wasabi

Combine the sugar and mirin in a saucepan and heat over medium heat, stirring. When the sugar is completely dissolved, add the soy sauce and continue to heat. When it comes to a simmer, remove from the heat and let cool.

Heat the soy milk over low heat in a sauté pan, in order to expose as much surface area as possible to the air. With a pair of chopsticks, collect the film that forms on the surface of the milk as it heats up. If your soy milk is concentrated enough, it will not stop forming this film on the surface as long as you continue to heat it. Place the fresh yuba on a plate, trying to fold it neatly. Form 4 small separate heaps.

Cook your soba noodles as directed on the package. Rinse them thoroughly in cold water so that they don't stick together.

Combine the mirin mixture with the dashi and sake. Heat until simmering. Serve the soba in 4 bowls with the yuba, nori, green onions, and a little wasabi. The sauce, hot or cooled, is normally served in small jugs and poured over the noodles by diners at the table.

Notes For a gluten-free version, use 100 percent buckwheat soba.

You can replace the sauce in this recipe with udon soup (see page 134).

OKARA
WITH VEGETABLES
(Unohana)

Okara is the solid residue that remains after pressing soybeans. After extracting all their juice, or soy milk, you end up with a pulp that is still a little damp (but not too damp), and which is packed with vitamins and fiber. Don't throw it out! It is an appreciated ingredient in tofu-producing countries, and can be used to make a lot of things. This simple dish is one of many recipes to make if you have l'*okara* – which is more and more easily found in outside of Japan, whether in Asian grocery stores or organic markets, in the fresh section.

⏱ prep **10 min** (+ traditional dashi **1 hr**) ⏱ cook **25 min** 🌱 vegan 🍴 **4 servings**

• ⅛ oz kombu seaweed or ½ tsp kombu dashi powder • 1 cup water • 2 dried shiitake mushrooms • 8 green beans • 2 green onions • 1 Tbsp sesame oil • 1 Tbsp neutral vegetable oil • 1 small carrot, julienned • 4 oz *okara* (see page 24) • 2 Tbsp sake • 1 tsp sugar • 1 Tbsp mirin rice wine • 1–2 Tbsp light soy sauce • Salt

First prepare your soup base, or dashi: cut or break the kombu into pieces, and put it in a saucepan with the water. Let steep for at least 1 hour, then heat over low heat, covered. Just before boiling, when small bubbles form on the surface of the kombu, remove the seaweed pieces from the pan. The scented water that remains will be your dashi. If you're in a hurry, you can use instant dashi and just add the powder to the same amount of heated water.

Rehydrate the mushrooms in a bowl of warm water. Cut the green beans in half lengthwise, then in half again crosswise. Blanch them in a pan of salted water for 1 minute. Rinse them in cold water, drain, and set aside. Drain the shiitakes (reserve 7 tablespoons of their soaking water, filter it, and add it to the dashi), remove their stems and cut the caps into slices about 1/16 inch thick. Slice the green onion.

In a pan over medium heat, combine the two oils, add the mushrooms and the carrot, and sauté them for 2 minutes, stirring. Add the okara and brown it with the vegetables for another 1–2 minutes. Add the dashi, sake, sugar, mirin, soy sauce, and a little salt to taste. Mix and adjust the seasoning if necessary.

Simmer for about 20 minutes, mixing from time to time. When the liquid is absorbed, add the beans and the green onion. Mix and let cool. Serve at room temperature. It's even better the next day (keep in the fridge and serve without reheating).

PEANUT
TOFU
(Jīmāmidōfu)

Like all nut "tofus", *jīmāmidōfu* is not, strictly speaking, tofu. It is made from peanuts and has an extremely firm and elastic texture – when you insert a spoon in it, it stays upright on its own. Particularly appreciated in the Okinawa archipelago in the south of Japan, it is traditionally prepared a little like almond tofu, which is quite a laborious process. Similar results are easily obtained with peanut butter, water, and a fabulous natural thickener, kudzu (or *kuzu*, or Japanese arrowroot). Peanut tofu can be eaten salted with soy sauce and wasabi, or sweetened with caramel sauce – but you can be as inventive as you like, try dicing it and adding it to vegetable or fruit salads.

🕐 prep **5 min** (+ chill **1 night**) 🕐 cook **20 min** 🌱 vegan

For 6–8 portions
- ¼ cup unsweetened, unsalted peanut butter
- 2²/₃ cups water • 5½ Tbsp kudzu root starch • ½ tsp salt

Mix the peanut butter and the water until you get a perfectly homogeneous consistency. Add the kudzu and salt, and mix again. In a saucepan over medium heat, heat the mixture, stirring constantly with a wooden spatula until it thickens. Turn the heat down as low as possible and continue to stir for about 10 minutes, or until the dough has thickened to the point where it does not seem pourable.

Immediately transfer the dough into a rectangular glass mold with moistened sides. Smooth the surface with wet fingers. Let cool to room temperature, then cover with plastic wrap and place in the refrigerator until the "tofu" is cool and firm. Cut portions with a knife after wetting the blade, and serve salted as a starter, or sweetened as a snack or dessert with the caramel sauce from the tofu mochi recipe (see page 152).

Notes Kudzu root starch can be found in organic markets, Japanese groceries, and online. It is sometimes called "Japanese arrowroot," but regular arrowroot will *not* work as a substitute to achieve the same consistency.

For a sweet version of peanut tofu, add 2 tablespoons of honey or agave syrup.

EDAMAME
TOFU
(Uguisudōfu)

This fresh edamame (green soybean) tofu is a beautiful pale green. It is not real tofu, although it is possible to make "real" tofu with edamame in the same way as with mature soybeans. However, *usuguisudōfu* is easier and faster to make, performs better, and requires less material. Edamame are common in the frozen section of Asian groceries and well-stocked supermarkets; you can replace them with fresh fava beans or lima beans in season.

🕐 prep **5 min**   🕐 cook **35 min**   🌱 vegan

For 6–8 portions
• ½ cup frozen edamame, thawed • 2²/₃ cups water
• 5½ Tbsp kudzu root starch (see Note, page 145) • ¼ tsp salt • Wasabi and soy sauce, for serving

In a food processor, blend the edamame, water, kudzu, and salt until you get a perfectly smooth mixture.

In a saucepan over medium heat, heat the mixture, stirring constantly with a wooden spatula, until it thickens. Turn the heat down as low as possible and continue stirring for about 10 minutes, or until the dough has thickened to the point where it does not seem pourable.

Immediately transfer the dough into a rectangular glass mold with moistened sides. Smooth the surface with wet fingers. Let cool to room temperature, then cover with plastic wrap and place in the refrigerator until the "tofu" is cool and firm. Cut portions with a knife after wetting the blade, and serve as a starter with a little wasabi and soy sauce.

WALNUT
TOFU
(Kurumidōfu)

This *Tōhoku* specialty is made from Japanese walnuts (*kurumi*), also called heart nuts, which may be hard to come by in your local market but may be ordered online. Their flavor is much more pronounced than that of regular walnuts, but you can substitute regular walnuts here. Tofu made from regular walnuts will have a more subtle aroma than the Japanese version, but is still very pleasant – at least, if you like nuts and delicate flavors. Like other nut tofus, it can be eaten sweet or savory.

🕐 prep **5 min** (+ chill **1 night**) 🕐 cook **20 min** 🌱 vegan

For 6–8 portions
- ½ cup walnuts, finely chopped • 2²/₃ cups water
- 5½ Tbsp kudzu root starch (see Note, page 145) • ½ tsp salt

Toast the walnut pieces in a dry pan until they have a pleasant aroma. In a food processor, combine them with half of the water and blend until you get a smooth texture. Rinse down the sides of the workbowl with the rest of the water, add the kudzu and salt, and continue to blend for 1 minute.

Transfer the mixture to a saucepan and heat over medium heat, stirring constantly with a wooden spatula, until it thickens. Turn the heat down as low as possible and keep stirring until the dough has thickened to the point where it no longer seems pourable.

Immediately transfer the dough into a rectangular glass mold with moistened sides. Smooth the surface with wet fingers. Let cool to room temperature, then cover with plastic wrap and place in the refrigerator until the "tofu" is cool and firm. Cut portions with a knife after wetting the blade, and serve salted as a starter, or sweetened as a snack or dessert.

WALNUT TOFU
WITH PERSIMMON
(Kurumidōfu to kaki)

I've never seen this recipe in Japan, but it must surely exist. The two iconic flavors of fall, walnut and persimmon, are an obvious marriage. The natural sugar of the fruit is enough to make this very simple assembly a dessert in itself. By using both non-astringent persimmons, which are eaten firm, and astringent persimmons, which are eaten overripe, even runny, you can obtain an amazing range of textures.

🕐 prep **10 min**   🌱 vegan   👥 **4** servings

- 4 portions walnut tofu
- 1 large nonastrigent persimmon (such as Fuyu), firm
- 1 large astringent persimmon (such as Hachiya), overripe and squishy
- Fleur de sel sea salt

Place the walnut tofu portions in saucers. Peel the firm persimmon like an apple and dice it. Halve the soft persimmon and scoop out the flesh with a small spoon into a bowl.

In each saucer, arrange one-fourth of the diced firm persimmon around the walnut tofu. Pour over one-fourth of the soft persimmon flesh and juice. Sprinkle with a little fleur de sel, and serve.

SESAME
TOFU
(Gomadōfu)

Sesame "tofu" is the most common of the seed and nut tofus. These are not real tofus but preparations based on oilseeds (sesame, peanuts, etc.) that Japanese people enjoy a bit like silken tofu. Their texture is generally very firm, very dense, and pretty elastic, even a little sticky, and their flavor is delicate but pleasant. They can be eaten as a starter, as a dessert, or as a snack, and they may be accompanied with sweet or savory sauces and condiments.

🕐 prep **5 min** (+ chill **1 night**) 🕐 cook **20 min** 🌱 vegetarian

For 6–8 portions
- ½ cup white or black sesame paste, or tahini
- 2 Tbsp sake • 2²/₃ cups water or dashi (see miso soup recipe, page 116)
- 6 Tbsp kudzu root starch • ½ tsp honey or agave syrup
- ½ tsp salt • Wasabi and soy sauce or caramel sauce (see page 152), for serving

Mix the sesame paste, sake, and water or dashi until you get a perfectly homogeneous consistency. Add the kudzu, honey, and salt, and mix again. In a saucepan, heat the mixture over medium heat, stirring constantly with a wooden spatula, until it thickens. Turn the heat down as low as possible and continue stirring for about 10 minutes, or until the dough has thickened to the point where it no longer seems pourable.

Immediately transfer the dough to a rectangular glass mold with moistened sides. Smooth the surface with wet fingers. Let cool to room temperature, then cover with plastic wrap and place in the refrigerator until the "tofu" is cool and firm. Cut portions with a knife after wetting the blade and serve salted as a starter, with a little wasabi and soy sauce, or sweet for dessert with caramel sauce.

Note Kudzu can be found in organic markets, Japanese groceries, and online. It is sometimes called "Japanese arrowroot," but regular arrowroot will *not* work as a substitute to achieve the same consistency.

TOFU MOCHI

(Tōfu dango)

Dango is a sweet confection (that is to say, sweet for Japanese people – therefore hardly sweet to the rest of us) based on rice flour, similar to mochi – white, dense, and elastic. To make the original *dango* (mitarashi dango), you need two different types of rice flour; for the tofu version, one is enough. They are shaped into little balls, threaded on skewers, and eaten with caramel sauce. A fun and easy activity, perfect for children.

🕐 prep **20 min**　🕐 cook **5 min**　🌱 vegan

For 6 skewers
- 4 oz extra-fine silken tofu • 2 tsp sugar
- ²/₃ cup glutinous rice flour (*shiratamako*)

For the sauce
- 5 Tbsp sugar • 1 Tbsp soy sauce • 1 Tbsp mirin rice wine
- 4 Tbsp water • 1 tsp potato starch mixed with 1 tsp water

In a mixing bowl, mash the tofu and mix it by hand with the sugar and rice flour. Very gradually add a small amount of water until you get the perfect consistency: a completely smooth, firm paste that does not stick to your fingers.

Form a sausage with the dough and divide it into three parts, then again into three parts, then into two parts. Form small balls by rolling the dough between your palms. It's a bit like playdough – kids love it.

Heat a large pot of water; when it comes to a boil, immerse the balls. When they rise to the surface, count for 1 minute, then take them out using a skimmer and immerse them in a bowl of ice water. Thread the balls onto small bamboo skewers, 3 by 3.

To make the sauce, combine the sugar, soy sauce, rice wine, and water in a small saucepan and bring to a boil, stirring. Add the starch slurry, mix well, and turn off the heat as soon as the sauce has thickened. Serve the *dango* skewers generously brushed with sauce.

Note The sticky rice flour needed for this recipe can be found in Japanese grocery stores. It has nothing to do with Vietnamese sticky rice flour, which cannot replace it. The skewers are even better if you grill or broil them for a few minutes on the barbecue or under the broiler before covering them with sauce.

Korea

두부

Preparing tofu in a workshop in Korea.

A PARTICULAR METHOD

Korean firm tofu is so close to Japanese that you can mistake the two; in general, it is slightly firmer, but its appearance is in all respects similar to that of its Japanese counterpart. On the other hand, its traditional method of preparation is a little more laborious. The soybeans are first soaked for 8–10 hours, then they are ground. This raw soybean paste is placed on a very solid cheesecloth lying flat above a basin, then sprinkled with boiling water; the water and the dough are mixed vigorously, and gradually until soy milk begins to pass through the cheesecloth in droplets. A mousse forms, due to the saponin present in the soybeans. The process is repeated as many times as necessary to extract all the juice from the soybeans and keep only the dry pulp, called *biji*, in the cheesecloth.

The soybean juice, or soy milk, collected in the basin is still raw. It is poured into a traditional large, thick iron pot called a *gamasot*, covered, and heated slowly for about 1 hour. At this stage it is never uncovered, because contact with air causes a solid film, *yuba*, to form on its surface. This protein-rich film, which the Chinese and Japanese love, is not appreciated in Korea, where it is considered as an undesirable effect of heating soy milk. When the contents of the *gamasot* come to a boil, seawater is added to it. It is rich in magnesium chloride, a coagulating agent. Seawater is a common traditional ingredient for making tofu in many countries. However, it has been largely abandoned almost everywhere in favor of magnesium chloride crystals. In Korea, however, it is still widely used among tofu artisans.

With the addition of seawater, the soy milk begins to coagulate in the center of the *gamasot*, revealing a whey slightly tinged with green; at this stage, it is important not to stir, so as not to break up the curd that we want to keep intact and as large as possible. Very carefully, with a large ladle, the curd is scooped up from the center of the *gamasot* with its whey and set aside.

They will be eaten as is, or cooked. This extremely tender, unpressed tofu that bathes in its own whey is one of a kind; the Koreans call it *sundubu*. The rest of the curd will be poured into a wooden mold covered with cheesecloth and pressed until you get a block of firm tofu.

MORE MARGINAL THAN IN CHINA & JAPAN

While tofu is inevitable and omnipresent in China and Japan, it is rarer in Korea. It is an everyday foodstuff, found in all supermarkets and traditional markets, and it appears on the menus of the great majority of restaurants; still, it is not eaten daily and rarely cooked in large quantities. Koreans consume on average three times less tofu than the Japanese. However, Korean tofu is excellent. Artisanal *sundubu* in particular is a delight; tender, supple, it is so mild that it almost seems sweet, highlighting the slight hazelnut flavor of soybeans. This sweetness is due to an ingredient that is usually missing in tofu that has been coagulated with magnesium chloride: salt. Naturally present in seawater, it is a fabulous flavor enhancer for soybeans and a welcome bitterness corrector for the slight bitter flavor of magnesium chloride. A good fresh *sundubu* can be eaten alone, hot or warm, in its whey, with a spoon, without needing absolutely anything. It's simply a treat.

There are fewer types of tofu and tofu products in Korea than in China and Japan. Tofu was introduced on the Korean peninsula between the tenth and twelfth centuries and quickly adopted by Buddhist monks, who practice for the most part a vegetable-based diet (they eat honey and see no harm in it, so you can't qualify them as vegans) or vegetarian diet (some consume dairy products). On the other hand, the rest of the population is very attached to the consumption of meat and seafood; it's difficult today to be a strict vegetarian in Korea unless all your friends are monks. Tofu is appreciated but pales in comparison to the beef, pork, or chicken that the Koreans devour with passion; tofu is often eaten as a side dish, or it is used as an ingredient in certain dishes that also contain meat products. Outside of Buddhist cuisine, it is rare for a tofu dish not to contain any traces of fish sauce, meat broth, or the like.

SPICY HOT TOFU... OR SUGAR SWEET TOFU

In Korea, tofu (like almost all other foods) is very commonly associated with chile. At first, I thought the chile pepper was used to spice up the tofu. But after a while, I started wondering if the tofu was there to tone down the chile. Korean cuisine has become so hot in recent times that tofu, like rice, seems to be one of the few mild elements of the meal that somewhat dampen the almost permanent fire. Even the Buddhists eat everything spicy. There really is no refuge for diners who can't take it. I still wanted to offer Korean recipes without hot pepper in this chapter, because this use of chiles, which has become systematic fairly recently, seems to me not only exaggerated, but grotesque. Most of the chefs with whom I raised the subject in Seoul and in the provinces also found this current escalation unpleasant.

It's all the more unfortunate to mask the taste of Korean tofu when it is a hand-crafted product. I ate very good tofus in China and Japan, which could be eaten alone and enjoyed as is, but the best plain tofu of my life was one I tasted in Korea, in the Chodang district or "tofu village" of the city of Gangneum. The craftsman who prepared it before my eyes, Mr. Kim, advised me to eat his *sundubu* without adding anything. And this fabulous product was enough in itself. In cities like Los Angeles or other places with a sizable Korean population, you should be able to find high-quality sundubu at Korean markets or possibly buy it from a restaurant. It may also be labeled "soon tofu" or "extra soft Korean tofu."

TOFU TYPES & USES

FIRM TOFU

Korean firm tofu can take on a fairly large range of textures. Brands often classify these textures by degree of firmness (extra-firm, firm, medium, etc.) or by use (for soups, for frying, etc.). In general, Korean tofu is a little more firm than Japanese tofu and a little less firm than Chinese tofu; for frying or sautéing you will want to press it in order to drain our some of the water and make its texture more dense and solid.

UNPRESSED TOFU

Unpressed soy milk curd is a type of tofu, even if it doesn't look like it. We are used to seeing block tofu, but this type has not undergone any pressing and has not been molded; the curd is clearly visible and bathes in its own whey, looking like little clouds. This extra-tender tofu, called *sundubu* or "soft tofu," is full of water and therefore very low in calories – around 30 to 40 calories per 100 grams (4 ounces). Traditionally, it is made with seawater, whose magnesium chloride serves as a coagulating agent. The salt of the seawater imparts a slightly salty flavor to the tofu, which is very pleasant. Factory-produced *sundubu* is coagulated with magnesium chloride, calcium sulfate, glucono-delta-lactone (GDL), or a mixture of the three, often giving a clearly more gelled and brittle texture. It is compressed in cylindrical or rectangular packages, since the curd tends to agglomerate into a texture similar to that of an extremely soft silken tofu. *Sundubu* is mainly used in soups and stews.

Different types of Korean tofu: silken tofu (1), firm tofu (2), unpressed tofu, the famous *sunbudu* (3) and fried tofu pockets (4).

SILKEN TOFU

Silken tofu did not exist in Korea until the twentieth century, but it was established there during the Japanese occupation, from 1910 to 1945. Today it is widely available in supermarkets in the typical Japanese forms. Since the Japanese had an important influence on the production of tofu in Korea, certain distinctions became blurred; silken tofu can be confused or hybridized with unpressed Korean tofu (*sundubu*), creating in-between versions, sold in rectangular packages or tubes. These may be more or less gelatinous – some can hold their shape despite their great fragility. Japanese-style silken tofu can serve as a substitute for *sundubu*, even if these are fundamentally very different products: silken tofu is by definition appreciated for its smooth texture, while *sundubu* on the contrary is prized for its clearly visible curd with a soft, springy consistency.

FRIED TOFU POCKETS

Japanese fried tofu pockets (*inariage* in Japanese, *yubu* in Korean) have been adopted by Koreans and can be used in a variety of ways: they can be cut into strips and sautéed, fried, or added to soups, their spongy texture absorbing broths well. They can also be marinated in a sweet-and-salty sauce to make delicious little rice pockets with multicolored ingredients inspired by Japanese *inarizushi*, called *yubuchobap* in Korean. Ready-to-use *yubuchobap* kits are widely available in Korean and Japanese grocery stores, and even in some general Asian groceries.

DEEP-FRIED
STUFFED CHILES
(Gochu twigim)

The Koreans are among the peoples who adore chile; they are able to revel in dishes that would send Europeans to the hospital. To make these delicious stuffed peppers, Koreans use different varieties; some are strong, others are sweet. I chose to use Padrón peppers, a small variety from Spain, as a substitute. Padróns are mostly mild, but one in ten has some heat to it. They are very similar – in looks and in flavor – to Korean *kkwari-gochu*, a.k.a. shishitos, another good choice. You can replace them with mild mini bell peppers, or large hot peppers if extreme spiciness doesn't scare you.

○ prep **45 min**   ○ cook **50 min**   ◉ vegetarian

For 30–40 pieces
• 30–40 Padrón peppers or other green chiles • Oil for deep-frying
For the stuffing
• 10 oz firm tofu • 1 small carrot, finely chopped • 1 small zucchini, finely chopped
• ½ onion, finely chopped • 1 green onion, thinly sliced • 1 egg • 1 tsp minced garlic • 1 tsp salt
For the coating
• 1 cup flour • 2 Tbsp potato starch • 1 cup ice water
For the sauce
• 4 Tbsp soy sauce • 4 Tbsp rice vinegar • 1 Tbsp lemon juice

If you are using Korean firm tofu, which has a higher water content than typical firm tofu, wrap it in paper towels and let it drain between two plates for 1 hour.

Slit each pepper down its side and remove the seeds. Set aside.

Crumble the tofu in a bowl and mix it with the remaining stuffing ingredients.

Fill all the peppers with stuffing, packing it in well. Prepare the coating at the last minute by briefly mixing all the ingredients with a few strokes of a pair of chopsticks. Lumps can (and should) remain.

Heat oil for deep-frying to about 350°F. Dip the peppers in the coating and fry them in batches of 5 to prevent crowding. When the coating is crisp, transfer to a wire rack to drain. For extra crisp and nicely golden peppers, fry them a second time.

Prepare the sauce by combining the ingredients. Serve the hot peppers with the sauce.

HERBED TOFU CANAPÉS
(Pa ganghwe)

People often say that Japanese cuisine is the prettiest. But the Koreans have a completely exquisite sense of geometry. Their presentations are unlike any other. They like to wrap long foods, even tying knots. *Ganghwe* is the name for dishes in which herbs and stems are wrapped and tied around other foods. In this case, I used tender spring onions (*pa*) for this lovely starter, so it's called *pa gangwhe*. It's extremely easy to do, but makes quite an impression. In addition, it is delicious and super healthy. You can replace the spring onion with other herbs of your choice: cilantro, parsley, chives...

🕐 prep **20 min**   🕐 cook **5 min**   🌱 vegetarian

For 15 pieces
• 10 oz firm tofu or grilled tofu (see pages 27 and 124) • 1–2 large mild chiles or ¼ red bell pepper
• 2 eggs • 15 tender green onions, chives, or long sprigs of parsley or cilantro • Salt • Vegetable oil
For the sauce
• 2 Tbsp Korean red chile paste (gochujang) • 1 Tbsp sesame oil
• 1 Tbsp sugar • 2 tsp soy sauce • 2 tsp water • 1 tsp rice vinegar
• 1 tsp minced garlic • 1 tsp toasted white sesame seeds

If you are using firm, non-grilled tofu, wrap it in paper towels and let it drain between two plates for 1 hour. Cut it into 1 by 2–inch rectangles about ¼ inch thick. Cut the chiles or bell peppers into 1- by ½-inch rectangles.

Beat the eggs with a pinch of salt using a pair of chopsticks, without incorporating air and frothing them up. Pass them through a chinois or other fine-mesh strainer to get a homogeneous mixture. Place a large frying pan over low heat and oil it lightly. Pour in half the mixture and spread it over the entire surface. Cook for 1–2 minutes, until the egg is cooked without browning. No need to flip this "pancake omelet," it is so fine that it cooks fully by heating on one side. Transfer to a platter and repeat with the rest of the eggs. Cut the "pancake omelettes" to the same dimensions as the tofu.

Blanch the green onions in a saucepan of salted water. As soon as they become flexible and change color, drain and immerse them in an ice-water bath. Separate the green onions to take only one leaf at a time. On each rectangle of tofu, place a rectangle of omelette and a rectangle of chile or bell pepper, then wrap a leaf of green onion around it, making several turns. Tuck in the end of the green onion on the back side of the canapé. Repeat to use up all of the ingredients. Arrange on a serving platter.

Combine all the ingredients for the sauce except the sesame seeds, sprinkle the sesame on top, and serve with the canapés.

PANFRIED TOFU
WITH EGG
(Dubu jeon)

The word *jeon* is often translated as "pancake," as this is the form that this Korean dish usually has. But sometimes, *jeon* are simply ingredients that are dredged in a mixture of flours, dipped into beaten egg, and then fried. Less crisp than breading – there are no bread crumbs involved – the result is nonetheless quite delicious. Tofu cooked this way, brown on the outside, soft on the inside, is an easy-to-prepare starter or side dish that everyone likes. Enjoy it while it's hot, dipped in a spicy sauce.

prep 10 min • **cook 10 min** • vegetarian • **4 servings**

- 14 oz firm tofu • A few sprigs of dill • ¼ cup all-purpose flour
- 1 Tbsp rice flour • 1 Tbsp potato starch
- 2 eggs • ½ tsp garlic powder • Salt and pepper • Vegetable oil

For the dipping sauce
- 2 Tbsp soy sauce • 1 Tbsp sesame oil • 1 Tbsp Korean red chile flakes (*gochugaru*)
- 1 green onion, thinly sliced • 1 tsp white sesame seeds

Cut the tofu into 1½- to 2-inch squares a scant ½ inch thick. Place them on paper towels and blot dry. You can also wrap thew tofu in paper towels and press between 2 plates to drain, if you prefer a firmer texture.

Cut the dill into small sprigs to garnish the tofu. Mix the two flours and the starch and place on a plate. Beat the eggs without frothing them and pour into a deep plate. Sprinkle a little garlic powder, salt, and pepper over the tofu.

Place a large pan over medium heat and oil generously. Dredge each piece of tofu in the flour mixture, then immediately dip it in the egg, add a sprig of dill on one side, and place it in the pan right away. Repeat to use all the tofu.

Brown tofu on both sides. Let pieces drain on a wire rack or on paper towels while you prepare the dipping sauce by mixing all the ingredients. Serve the panfried tofu hot with its sauce.

CARAMELIZED
SESAME
TOFU
(Dubu gangjang jorim)

Fans of sweet-and-salty sauces will love this very simple little dish of panfried tofu in a caramelized soy sauce. In Korea, they use malt syrup, which has a strong sweet flavor and gives the sauce a nice sheen, or rice syrup, less sweet and just as shiny. Malt syrup, available in Asian groceries, was made from barley, but nowadays it's often corn-based, so you can also use corn syrup. Or, you can replace these syrups with honey, agave syrup, or even maple syrup if that calls to you.

🕐 prep **5 min**   🕐 cook **10 min**   🌱 vegan   🍴 **4** servings

- 7 oz firm tofu • 1 clove garlic, minced
- 1 Tbsp soy sauce • 1 Tbsp Korean malt syrup (*mulyeot*), corn syrup, or rice syrup
- 1 tsp black sesame seeds, toasted • Vegetable oil

Cut the tofu into slices a scant ½ inch thick. Or, if you prefer, cut it into ¾-inch cubes. Place on paper towels and blot dry. Place a frying pan over medium heat, add a little oil, and brown the tofu on all sides.

Lower the heat and add the garlic, soy sauce, and malt syrup. Mix to coat all the tofu pieces with sauce. Serve sprinkled with sesame seeds.

SPICED STEW
WITH VERY TENDER TOFU
(Sundubu jjigae)

This stew – close to a soup, with plenty of goodies in it–- is red in color but less spicy than it looks. It is mellowed by the most tender tofu that exists, the Korean *sundubu*. This tofu is actually not even solid, because it is not pressed; the commercial version has an extremely smooth and fragile custard texture. It is found in flexible cylindrical tubes in the fresh section of Korean grocery stores. If you can't find it, replace the *sundubu* with regular silken tofu.

🕐 prep **20 min**   🕐 cook **15 min**   🍴 vegetarian

For 4 bowls
• 4 dried shiitake mushrooms • 2 cloves garlic, minced • 1 small onion, thinly sliced
• 2 Tbsp Korean red chile flakes (*gochugaru*) • 1 Tbsp soy sauce
• 2 cups dashi (see miso soup recipe, page 116) • 1 lb *sundubu* tofu
• 1 bunch enoki mushrooms, roughly separated • 4 oz oyster mushrooms or *shimeji*, separated
• 1 Tbsp sesame oil • 2 green onions, thinly sliced • Salt and pepper • Vegetable oil

Rehydrate the mushrooms in a bowl of warm water. When they are tender, remove and discard the stems and slice the caps. Reserve 7 tablespoons of the mushroom-soaking water. Place a Dutch oven or casserole pan over medium heat, add a little oil, and quickly brown the garlic, onion, chili powder, and soy sauce while stirring. Add the dashi and mushroom-soaking water and bring to a boil for 2–3 minutes. Season with salt to taste, and mix.

Carefully cut the *sundubu* packaging and try to cut it into thick slices, crushing it as little as possible. Add it to the stew, along with the mushrooms. Simmer for a few minutes, until the mushrooms are tender. Add sesame oil and pepper and serve sprinkled with the green onions.

Note   Koreans gladly crack two eggs directly into the pot when serving, to enrich the stew.

STEAMED TOFU
WITH SAUTÉED KIMCHI
(Dubu kimchi)

Kimchi, the fermented cabbage they eat daily in Korea, keeps for quite a while but loses its crispness and becomes acidic at some point. It's usually this "old" kimchi that is sautéed – it's not as pleasant to eat raw, but is very good cooked. It is served with slices of boiled or steamed tofu; this is a favorite *ahnju* – a dishes that accompanies booze. It's also one of the healthiest.

prep **15 min** | cook **10 min** | vegan | **4 servings**

- 8 oz vegetarian kimchi, coarsely sliced • 2 green onions, thinly sliced
- 1 tsp minced root ginger • 1 clove garlic, minced • 1 Tbsp soy sauce • 1 tsp sugar
- 14 oz firm tofu • Boiling water, as needed • 1 small onion, thinly sliced
- 1 tsp sesame oil • 1 tsp white sesame seeds • Vegetable oil • Pepper

In a large bowl, combine the kimchi, half the green onions, the ginger, garlic, soy sauce, and sugar. Let stand for 10–15 minutes.

Cut the tofu into 2 blocks. Place them in 1 quart of boiling water and cook over medium heat for 5 minutes. (You can also steam them for 5–10 minutes, if you prefer.) Carefully remove the tofu from the water, drain, and cut into slices about ¼ inch thick.

In an frying pan over medium-high heat, heat a little oil. Sauté the onion for a few moments, then add the kimchi mixture. Sauté until the liquid released by the kimchi is almost completely gone. Remove from the heat. Season with pepper, add the sesame oil, and mix again.

For a starter to be shared, place the stir-fried kimchi in the center of a platter, sprinkled with sesame seeds and the rest of the green onion, and surrounded with tofu slices. Or, if you prefer, you can distribute the tofu and the kimchi directly onto diners' plates.

BROTH
WITH POTATOES & TOFU
(Gamjaguk)

No, Koreans do not make everything spicy. Some preparations are very mild, like this clear soup made with three times nothing - mainly tofu, potatoes and green onion. You can make it a whole meal of it, enriching it with other vegetables, mushrooms, sweet potato noodles, beaten eggs, and even...chile. Well, in fact they really do make everything spicy.

🕐 prep **5 min** 🕐 cook **10 min** 🌱 vegan

For 4 bowls
- 2–3 medium potatoes • 7 oz firm tofu • 2 green onions
- 1 qt dashi (see miso soup recipe, page 116)
- 1 Tbsp soy sauce • Salt and pepper

Cut the potatoes into half-moons a scant ¼ inch thick. Cut the tofu in half lengthwise, then into ¼-inch-thick slices. Slice the green onion very thinly on the diagonal.

Add the potatoes and tofu, and season with salt and pepper to taste. Bring to a boil again and cook for about 5 minutes, until the potatoes are tender but not falling apart. Add the soy sauce and green onion, mix, and serve.

VEGGIE
TOFU CAKES
(Dubu yachae jeon)

By mixing tofu, vegetables, eggs, and flour, you get a fabulous dough. You could make it into one large pancake the size of a pan, but smaller sizes are easier to prepare, serve, and eat. What's more, they are very cute. Crispy on the outside, soft on the inside, and dotted with multicolored vegetables, these patties are an effective trick to get your most recalcitrant friends eat tofu and vegetables. If one already likes tofu and vegetables, it's even better.

🕐 prep **20 min** 🕐 cook **10 min** 🌱 vegetarian

For about 12 pieces
• 1 lb firm or medium tofu • 2 green onions, thinly sliced • 1 small carrot, coarsely chopped
• ½ zucchini, coarsely chopped • ⅓ cup all-purpose flour • 2 Tbsp rice flour
• 1 Tbsp potato starch • 1 tsp salt • 2 eggs
• 1 red chile, thinly sliced • Vegetable oil • Dipping sauce (see page 166)

In a mixing bowl, crumble the tofu with your hands. It's kinda fun. Mix with the green onion, carrot, zucchini, flours, starch, salt, and eggs. If you use regular tofu, which is firmer than Korean tofu, add a little water to form a thick paste, with a fairly consistent texture but not completely homogeneous.

In frying pan over medium-high heat, heat a little oil. Dollop a large tablespoonful of dough into the pan and add a slice of chile on top. Repeat with the rest of the dough, in batches. Don't crowd the little cakes together as they will spread slightly.

When the cakes are browned on the first side, flip them over and flatten them slightly with a spatula. Brown on the other side, and serve hot with the dipping sauce.

5-COLOR
RICE BOWL
(Bibimbap)

In Korea, the color composition of food is a dietary principle. The presence of five main colors (green, red, yellow, white, and black) within a meal, representing the five elements, is a sign of balance. Bibimbap is really perfect in this respect: it is a complete and healthy dish consisting of a rice base topped with a beautiful variety of colorful ingredients containing all the vitamins, fiber, protein, and minerals that we need. The toppings can change according to taste and season; tofu is not common there, as Koreans prefer beef, but it is easily accommodated. All the elements of the bowl must be mixed before eating, making a meal is both pleasant and playful.

🕐 prep **30 min** 🕐 cook **50 min** 🌱 vegetarian 🍴 **4 servings**

- 2 cups sushi rice • 10 oz firm tofu • 7 oz spinach
- 2 cloves garlic, minced • 2 tsp sesame oil
- 2 tsp white sesame seeds, toasted • 2 small zucchini
- 1 large carrot • 6 shiitakes or other brown mushrooms • 2 sheets nori seaweed
- 4 egg yolks (optional) • Vegetable oil • Salt and pepper

For the gochujang sauce

- ⅓ cup Korean red chile paste (gochujang) • 2 Tbsp water
- 1 Tbsp sugar • 1 Tbsp sesame oil
- 2 tsp soy sauce • 1 clove garlic, minced

Rinse the rice several times, then drain. Put it in a saucepan, add 2¼ cups of water, and cover. (The lid must remain in place for the entire cooking process.) Let stand for 10 minutes, then bring to a boil over high heat. As soon as it boils, turn the heat down as low as possible. Cook until all the water has been absorbed, 7–8 minutes. Turn off the heat and let stand for 10 minutes, still covered. Aerate the rice by mixing it gently with a spatula, and keep warm.

Blanch the spinach for about 2 minutes in a pot of boiling salted water. Drain and press firmly with a spatula to squeeze out the excess water. Put the spinach in a bowl and add 1 half of the garlic, 1 teaspoon of the sesame oil, 1 teaspoon of the sesame seeds, and salt and pepper to taste. Mix.

(continued)

Cut the zucchini into half-moons and cook briefly over medium heat in a lightly oiled pan with the remaining garlic. Add 1 teaspoon of the sesame oil and salt to taste, and mix.

Cut the tofu into strips 2 inches long and ¼ inch thick. Blot dry with paper towels, salt them, and sauté briefly in a hot oiled pan without letting them color too much.

Cut the carrot into matchsticks and, in an oiled pan over medium heat, cook until tender, without letting it color too much. Season with salt and pepper, and set aside. Slice the mushroom caps and cook them in the same way. Tear the nori sheets into small pieces.

Mix all the ingredients for the gochujang sauce.

Divide the rice among 4 large individual serving bowls, then garnish it artistically with one-quarter of each of the filling elements. Place a raw egg yolk in the middle of each serving, if using, and sprinkle with the rest of the sesame seeds. You can add a little gochujang sauce directly into each bowl, or serve it separately so that diners can add it to suit their taste.

Note In order for the vegetables to keep their color without burning, cook them over fairly moderate heat and cover after 2 minutes.

SUSHI ROLLS
WITH TOFU &
CRUNCHY VEGGIES
(Kimbap)

The Korean word *kimbap* means "rolled rice with seaweed." Originally, it was a simple rice roll seasoned with sesame oil and salt. In the twentieth century, under the influence of Japanese cuisine and its famous *maki* sushi rolls, *kimbap* gained a garnish of vegetables, eggs, and meat – but also exists in vegetarian and even vegan versions. Convenient for takeout, it is now the best-selling fast food in Korea; its great strength is that it gets the thumbs-up from all generations. However, it holds a special place in Korean hearts and minds as a childhood treat because it is inextricably linked to *sopung*, the school field trips that all schoolchildren eagerly await.

🕐 prep **1 hr** 🕐 cook **50 min** 🍴 vegan 🍽 4 servings

- 3¼ cups sushi rice • 2½ cups water • ½ cucumber
- 7 oz Korean yellow pickled radish (*danmuji*) • 7 oz firm tofu • 7 oz spinach
- 1 clove garlic, minced • 3½ Tbsp sesame oil • 2 tsp white sesame seeds, toasted
- 2 carrots • 7 sheets nori seaweed • 1 Tbsp rice vinegar • Vegetable oil • Salt and pepper

Rinse the rice several times, then drain. Put it in a saucepan, add the water, and cover. (The lid must remain in place for the entire cooking process.) Let stand for 10 minutes, then bring to a boil over high heat. As soon as it boils, turn the heat down as low as possible. Cook until all the water has been absorbed, 7–8 minutes. Turn off the heat and let stand for 10 minutes, still covered.

Transfer the rice to a large bowl and aerate it by gently mixing in 2 tablespoons of the sesame oil, 1 tablespoon of the vinegar, and 1 teaspoon salt.

Cut the cucumber in half lengthwise, scoop out the seeds, and cut the flesh into strips ¼ inch thick. Sprinkle with salt and let drain. Cut the yellow radish into strips ¼ inch thick.

Cut the tofu into strips a scant ½ inch thick, then brown them in a lightly oiled pan. Season with salt and pepper, and set aside.

(continued)

Blanch the spinach for about 2 minutes in a large pot of boiling salted water, then rinse under cold water, drain, and press them firmly to drain the water. Season with the garlic, ½ tablespoon of the sesame oil, and a sprinkling of sesame seeds, salt, and pepper.

Cut the carrot into 1/16-inch-thick strips. Cook very briefly in an oiled skillet over medium heat, covered. The carrot should not brown. Season with salt and pepper.

Put all the ingredients around your workspace. On a *maki* mat, place a sheet of seaweed even with the bottom of the mat. Take one-seventh of the rice and distribute it in a thin and even layer over about two-thirds of the sheet. The sheet should be covered with rice to the side edges, but the top of the sheet should be left uncovered. Place some of the five toppings one at a time on the rice. Roll up tightly, then wet the end of the seaweed with a little water to adhere the end and close the roll.

Continue to use up the remaining ingredients. When all the rolls are ready, brush them with sesame oil, cut crosswise into rounds a scant 2 inch thick, and sprinkle with sesame seeds.

Notes To handle sticky rice more easily, wet your fingers. Warm rice is easier to spread than cold rice, and much nicer to eat!

If you have any leftover toppings, slice them and eat with your *kimbap*.

Don't store *kimbap* in the refrigerator, as the rice will harden. Keep it for up to 2 hours at room temperature, covered, and cut it into slices at the last moment.

Wipe the blade of your knife often as you cut the rolls, for clean cuts.

SPICY
BRAISED TOFU
(Dubu jorim)

This tofu braised in a spicy sweet-and-salty sauce, with caramelized onion and sesame, is delicious with rice. The recipe is completely vegan, but it certainly has appeal for carnivores: the dense texture of the tofu and the bold flavors of the sauce sweep away all prejudices about vegetable-based cuisine. Nothing bland, boring, or austere on this plate!

🕐 prep **5 min** 🕐 cook **20 min** 🌿 vegan 🍴 **4** servings

- 1 lb firm tofu • 1 small onion, diced • 1 clove garlic, minced
- 2 green onions, thinly sliced • 1 Tbsp soy sauce • 1 tsp salt
- 1 tsp sugar • 1 Tbsp Korean red chile flakes (*gochugaru*)
- ½ cup water • 1 tsp sesame oil • 1 tsp white sesame seeds • Vegetable oil

Cut the tofu in half lengthwise, then into slices a scant ½ inch thick. Place them on paper towels and blot dry. Place a frying pan over medium heat, heat a little oil, and brown the tofu on both sides. Transfer the tofu to a plate, keeping the oil in the pan.

Add a little more oil to the pan if needed, then add the onion, garlic, and the white parts of the green onions. When they are golden, or even a little crispy, add the soy sauce, salt, sugar, chili flakes, and water. Mix well. When the sauce has thickened a little, add the tofu and braise it for a few moments while mixing. Add the sesame oil and the green parts of the green onions, and mix again. Serve hot, sprinkled with sesame seeds.

KOREAN MISO
STEW
(Doenjang jjigae)

Doenjang is the Korean equivalent of Japanese miso: a fermented soybean paste. It is used to make soups, sauces, and stews (*jjigae*). *Doenjang* stew is a very common recipe in Korea, particularly appreciated during the cold season. You can put all kinds of ingredients in it; this tofu and vegetable version is a classic that never disappoints. You can easily find *doenjang* in most Asian groceries.

🕐 prep **45 min**   🕐 cook **50 min**   🌱 vegan   ♟ **4** servings

- 1 lb firm or medium tofu • 1 zucchini • 4 oz daikon radish • ½ onion • 2 green onions
- ¼ cup fermented soybean paste (*doenjang*)
- 1 Tbsp Korean red chile flakes (*gochugaru*) • 1 qt water (or rice-rinsing water)
- 1 Tbsp instant vegetarian dashi • 2 cloves garlic, minced • 1 Tbsp rice vinegar
- Vegetable oil • Steamed rice, for serving

Cut the tofu and the zucchini into ½-inch cubes. Cut the daikon into ½-inch squares that are about $1/16$ inch thick. Thinly slice the onion and the green onions.

In a Dutch oven or casserole pan over medium-high heat, heat a little oil and sauté the soybean paste and chili flakes for a few moments, stirring to prevent burning.

Gradually add the water and the powdered dashi, stirring to dilute the soybean paste. Add the daikon and boil over high heat for 5 minutes. Add the tofu, garlic, onion, and zucchini. Boil for another 6 minutes. Add the green onion and vinegar, cook for another 1 minute, and serve very hot in bowls, accompanied with rice.

Note   When you rinse the rice to remove its starch, you get cloudy water called *ssaldde-umul*, which can be used in cooking. *Doenjang* stew is eaten with rice, so if you like, reserve the starchy water to make your broth.

MUSHROOM & TOFU
HOT POT
(Dubu busut jeongol)

Formerly reserved for the nobility, this fondue has become a popular dish. The pot is served at the table and shared by the guests; this type of meal is particularly warming. This is especially true as the pot is still boiling – the sort of thing you need to withstand the Korean winter chill. Rich in protein, *jeongol* is more nourishing than you might think, and is eaten with other small dishes and rice.

🕐 prep **45 min**   🕐 cook **50 min**   🌱 vegetarian   👥 4 servings

- 1 lb mixed fresh mushrooms (shiitake, oyster, king oyster, enoki, *shimeji*...)
- 1 carrot • 14 oz firm, medium-firm, or grilled tofu (see pages 27 and 124)
- 1 large handful bean sprouts (soybean or mung bean)
- 2 Tbsp perilla oil or sesame oil • A few garlic chives • Steamed rice, for serving

For the stock base
- ½ onion, thinly sliced • Shiitake stems • 1 Tbsp instant vegetarian dashi or a large piece of kombu
- 2 Tbsp Korean red chile flakes (*gochogaru*), or your favorite
- 7 Tbsp water • 2 Tbsp soy sauce • 1 tsp sugar • 1 tsp salt

Separate mushrooms that are attached at the base. Clean them and trim the bottoms of the stems if needed. Cut the largest oyster mushrooms in half, set aside the shiitake stems and chop the caps, cut the king oyster mushrooms into 1/16-inch-thick strips.

Slice the carrot into 2-inch sections, then cut the sections into 1/16-inch strips. Cut the tofu into squares or rectangles whose sides are 1 or 2 inches long by a scant ½ inch thick. Arrange all these ingredients and the bean sprouts nicely in a Korean hot pot – a good-sized Dutch oven or casserole pan can do the trick, as long as it is not too deep.

In a saucepan, combine all the ingredients for the stock base and simmer for about 10 minutes. In the hot pot, add water to reach the top of the vegetables (without covering them). Bring to a boil, skim, and then add the stock base. When the liquid boils again, lower the heat and simmer for 15–20 minutes. Add more salt if needed. Add the oil and the garlic chives cut into 2-inch lengths. Mix and serve very hot with rice.

LITTLE TOFU POCKETS
WITH MULTICOLOR RICE
(Yubuchobap)

Yubuchobap is the Korean equivalent of *inarizushi* (see page 132), and in my opinion it is even better. In a triangular pocket of fried tofu, you find rice mixed with crunchy vegetables and delicious daikon pickle (*danmuji*). Sweet, salty, tangy, these plump triangles are irresistible. Kids love them; this is what they put in their *dosirak* (Korean *bentō*) for picnics. Already seasoned fried tofu pockets are found in Korean groceries in the fresh aisle, generally sold in packs of 14. If you are a family of 4, buy at least 2...

⏱ prep **45 min**   ⏱ cook **30 min**   🌱 vegan

For 28 pieces
• 1 cup rice • 1 cup water • 1 tsp salt • 2 Tbsp rice vinegar
• 1 medium carrot, diced • 4 oz yellow pickled daikon radish (*danmuji*), diced
• 3 green onions or 1 spring onion, chopped • 2 Tbsp white sesame seeds, toasted
• 2 Tbsp black sesame seeds, toasted • 28 triangular fried tofu pockets (*yubu*)

Rinse the rice several times, then drain. Put it in a saucepan with the water and let it sit for 10 minutes. Cover (the lid must remain in place for the entire cooking process) and bring to a boil over high heat. As soon as it boils, turn the heat down as low as possible and cook until all the water has been absorbed, 7–8 minutes. Turn off the heat and let stand for 10 minutes, still covered. Transfer the rice to a bowl and aerate it by mixing gently with the salt dissolved in the rice vinegar.

Mix the uncooked vegetables and the white and black sesame seeds with the warm rice. Gently squeeze the pockets of fried tofu to drain any excess moisture. With a teaspoon, generously fill the pockets with the colorful rice, packing as you go (without forcing it, so as not to tear the fried tofu). Serve at room temperature.

Note Don't put *yubuchobap* in the refrigerator, the rice will dry out and harden! They should be eaten within 2 hours of cooking the rice.

ICED NOODLE SOUP
WITH SOY MILK
(Kongguksu)

Westerners are not used to eating cold soups, and even less so if there are noodles in it. But in Korea, they love it. This becomes understandable when you experience the extreme summer temperatures of this country. Nothing like a broth filled with ice cubes when the heat is oppressive! There are all kinds of noodle soups to eat cool, even iced, but the richest, the smoothest, the most delicate of all is undoubtedly *kongguksu*. It is made with fine wheat noodles in a thick soy milk, sesame, and pine nut broth. It's a real treat. The secret to success is to make your own soy milk with good quality soy – same as making tofu. The more fluid the milk, the lighter the soup will be.

prep **20 min** (+ soak **12 hr**) cook **25 min** vegan

For 4 bowls
- 1 cup dried yellow soybeans • ¼ cup pine nuts • ¼ cup white sesame seeds, toasted
- 12 oz fine wheat noodles (*somyeon* or *somen*) • Soy milk • 2 tsp salt
- ½ cucumber, julienned • 1 tomato, quartered • 12 ice cubes

To make the soy milk, soak the soybeans in a large bowl with five times their volume of water overnight. Drain and rinse them, then place them in a large heavy-bottomed saucepan, a casserole pan, or a Dutch oven with 1 quart of water. Cook for 15 minutes over high heat, then cover and simmer for 8 minutes over medium-low heat.

Drain the beans and place them in a blender to mix them. Add 2 cups of cold water, the pine nuts, and the sesame seeds, and blend until you get a perfectly smooth and creamy texture. Add 1 cup of water and blend again. When the liquid seems to stop moving, add another 1 cup of water and mix again. Place in the fridge.

Cook the noodles according to package directions. Rinse them in cold water, stirring them in a colander to remove excess starch. Divide the noodles among 4 large bowls.

Take the soy milk from the refrigerator and add 1 cup of very cold water. Mix until bubbles form. Pour the soy milk into the bowls. Add the uncooked vegetables to garnish the noodles and place a few ice cubes in the soup. Serve with salt alongside – in Korea, everyone adds salt to suit their own taste for this dish. Let diners season their own bowls, mix everything together, and enjoy.

Notes You can replace the tomato with chunks of watermelon – very, very good! Koreans like to add half a hard-boiled egg per bowl. This soup is even better sprinkled with a little toasted black or white sesame seeds – I also like to add a good dose of pepper. Leftover soy milk will keep in the refrigerator for up to 2 days.

ZUCCHINI-TOFU DUMPLINGS
(Hobak mandu)

Korean dumplings are called *mandu*. You will find almost-identical preparations all along the Silk Road – the Uyghurs call them *manta*, the Kazakhs call them *mänti*, the Turks call them *mantı*, for just a few examples. You can steam them, fry them, or boil them, and more or less all garnishes are possible. Mild and delicate zucchini *mandu* are particularly pleasant to eat in summer. The variety of zucchini used in Korea, which is also found in China, is long with bright green skin, somewhat resembling the trombetta or zucchetta zucchini, very common in the southern French region around Nice. You can use any type of summer squash for this recipe. Dumpling wrappers are available in packages of 40 to 50 in the fresh or frozen departments of Asian grocery stores.

🕐 prep **45 min**   🕐 cook **50 min**   🌱 vegan

For 40 pieces
• 2 small white zucchini, cut into matchsticks • 1 Tbsp sesame oil • 7 oz extra-firm tofu, crumbled • 2 green onions, thinly sliced • 1 Tbsp soy sauce • 40 round dumpling wrappers • Salt
For the sauce
• 2 Tbsp soy sauce mixed with 2 Tbsp rice vinegar

Place the julienned zucchini in a bowl and sprinkle with 2 teaspoons of salt. Mix well and let drain for 15 minutes. Gently press the zucchini with your hands to extract excess water. Don't worry about saltiness – a lot of the salt will drain off with the water. If not, rinse the zucchini lightly and squeeze again.

In a large frying pan over medium-high heat, heat the sesame oil and sauté the zucchini for a few moments. The goal is not to brown it, but to dry it out and add flavor. Don't let the squash brown. When it no longer releases water, place it in a bowl and let cool. Add the crumbled tofu, green onions, and soy sauce; taste and correct the seasoning if needed. With your hands, toss these ingredients together well to make a stuffing.

On each dumpling wrapper, place 1 large teaspoonful of stuffing in the center. Wet the edges of the wrapper and close it flat, pressing the edges together firmly to form a half-moon. Repeat to use all the wrappers. As you go, place them on parchment paper, as they might stick to a plate.

Place a sheet of perforated parchment paper in a large steaming basket and heat a couple of inches of water for steaming in a wok. Place a maximum of 10–12 *mandu* in the basket; they should not touch one another. When the water comes to a boil, cover the dumplings and place over the water to steam for 15–20 minutes. Repeat as many times as needed to cook the rest of the *mandu*. You can also stack several baskets – but beware, those at the top do not cook as well as those at the bottom, so you have to rotate them.

Serve the dumplings hot, as they are ready, with the sauce.

Southeast Asia

Đậu hũ

เต้าหู้

Tauhu

តៅហ៊ូ

Tahu

ເຕົ້າຮູ້

Taho

A market in Southeast Asia.

A CHINESE IMPORT

The spread of tofu in Southeast Asia is very poorly documented. We know that it was brought centuries ago by Chinese immigrants – and probably, in some countries at least, by Buddhist monks who came to teach in monasteries – but the exact dates are not known. What we know thanks to linguistics is that tofu was introduced to this region of the world by people from the Chinese provinces of Fujian and Guangdong. The terms used to talk about tofu are all similar and clearly derived from a dialect spoken in these regions: it is called *đâu hủ* in Vietnam, *tahu* in Indonesia, *tauhu* in Malaysia and Singapore, *taohu* in Thailand and Laos, *tawhou* in Cambodia, and *taho* in the Philippines.

Nevertheless, these very similar words designate very different products. Over the centuries, each country has developed its own peculiarities in terms of tofu, even if the lines of demarcation are becoming increasingly blurry. The continuous influence of China, then of Japan (which has financed the construction of tofu factories in contemporary times), the ethnic diversity, and the presence of large Chinese communities integrated for multiple generations within these countries make any classification all the more difficult.

A FIRMER TOFU

Still, there are some obvious differences from one country to another: when we talk about *taho* in the Philippines, for example, we're talking about tofu pudding that is eaten sweet with syrup and not the firm tofu, which is more rare here and goes by the name *tokwa*. The similar term *taukwa* pops up in Indonesia and Malaysia, where it designates extra-firm tofu, as opposed to "classic" firm tofu. Furthermore, each country has its own nuances of texture. As a general rule, the farther south you go, the denser the "firm" tofu – which helps it keep longer. More water-rich products quickly go bad

in hotter and more humid climates, especially in the absence of efficient modes of refrigeration. Firmness also ensures that the tofu will hold up well in cooking, especially in stir-fry recipes. For the same reasons, it is also common throughout Southeast Asia to use tofu that comes already fried in a block. It forms a fine puffed crust but remains intact inside, like Japanese *atsuage*.

Traditionally, there is no silken tofu in Southeast Asia, although globalization is gradually changing this situation. Tofu pudding, on the other hand, is very common throughout this region of the world and is still sold by street vendors, mainly in the morning. Other types of tofu that originated in China, such as tofu puffs, have been integrated into daily life by extremely varied populations. In most countries in Southeast Asia, firm (or extra-firm) tofu has long since found a place in local recipes. This is less true in Thailand, where tofu was only used by the Chinese community until the 1930s. It is now readily used in all kinds of recipes as a meat substitute, but it does not appear in traditional Thai dishes, only Thai-Chinese ones. It's a similar story in the Philippines, but even more so: firm (or extra-firm) tofu is not commonly used outside the Chinese community there. It is still that community, centuries after the introduction of this product, that makes it, consumes it, and appreciates it.

VIETNAM: A PARTICULAR CASE

Vietnam was the first country in Southeast Asia to adopt tofu. Since ancient texts were largely lost or destroyed during the wars that ravaged Indochina and then Vietnam for decades in the twentieth century, it is difficult to give a precise date the introduction of tofu as a new product. Some historians, however, situate it between the tenth and twelfth centuries, a period of political stability during which Buddhism became the official religion of the kingdom, favoring exchanges between Chinese and Vietnamese monks. This centuries-old introduction would explain the particular culture of tofu that has developed in Vietnam, with a large number of varied and unique products, which are an integral part of local cuisine.

Very early on, the Vietnamese adopted tofu as an everyday food, practical and inexpensive, and gave it forms that were not found elsewhere. It used to be freshly made every morning in small neighborhood workshops; no tofu factory existed until the early twentieth century. Many of them used acidified soybean "whey" – obtained by pressing the curds to form tofu – as a coagulating agent. These ancient workshops, their particular production methods, and some of the

products they offered until the end of the colonial era – notably a tofu shaped in logs and not in rectangular blocks, made in a special mold and developing a kind of skin on the outside – are increasingly rare today. In the twentieth century, Vietnamese tofu exceptionalism was somewhat lost, no doubt more because of war than globalization. Its consumption is also decreasing, but it remains significant.

THE FOOD
OF POVERTY

In Vietnam as in Laos, Cambodia, Malaysia, and Indonesia, the success of tofu is chalked up to several possible explanations. It is pretty easy to produce, it is nutritious, and above all, it doesn't cost a lot: more than anything, it is the food of the poor. Less expensive than meat, it is a source of protein available at a lower cost, even if it is not being used as a meat replacement. As in China, there is nothing unusual about cooking meat products and tofu together in much of Southeast Asia. Just look at the number of recipes that combine tofu and pork, beef, or seafood, not to mention fish sauce.

During certain religious festivals, however, particularly in the context of Buddhism and Taoism, food austerity is recommended and meat is prohibited. Tofu, *yuba*, and other soy products can replace it, but this is not systematic. Vegetarian stir-fried noodles are usually just made with vegetables; we they don't try to squeeze tofu in everywhere, and the meat can be removed without a substitute being swapped in. Certain vegetarian populations, like some of the Hindus of Southeast Asia – not all, it is complicated – use tofu more widely; this is obvious in Bali, where tofu and tempeh are the main sources of protein for those who do not consume meat products. In Malaysia, the Indian Muslim community has also incorporated this ingredient into hybrid recipes blending elements of South Asian and Southeast Asian cuisines.

In short, it is difficult to generalize when we talk about food practices in such populous and varied countries; the bottom line is that tofu is widely found throughout Southeast Asia, and it is generally a common product, integrated into many recipes, not necessarily a substitute for meat products – but sometimes yes... If Vietnam is the country that has developed the most specific versions of tofu, we find in other nations of the region several particular or recurring types – some of which are available in the West.

TOFU TYPES & USES

EXTRA-FIRM TOFU

There are various textures, more or less flexible or firm, but overall, the tofus from this region of the world are firmer than those from countries farther north, such as Japan, Korea, and much of China. In Indonesia, Malaysia, and the Philippines, extra-firm tofu is called *taukwa* or *tokwa*. Firmer tofu has the advantage of keeping longer, it is denser and therefore more caloric, and it holds its shape very well during cooking. In the Philippines, firm tofu is a product that was introduced centuries ago by the Chinese but it has never really entered into daily life for the rest of the population. In Malaysia, Singapore, and Indonesia, it is much more common and integrated into a large number of typical local recipes. *Mee goreng mamak*, a stir-fried noodle dish typical of the Indian Muslim community in Malaysia, contains extra-firm tofu, squid, and mutton or beef broth, as well as tomatoes, boiled potatoes, and prawn crackers, among other ingredients.

FRIED TOFU

Fried tofu is extremely popular throughout Southeast Asia. Whole blocks are immersed in oil until they form a crust on the outside, which helps them hold up better during subsequent cooking. This type of tofu is commonly used in well-known stir-fry recipes such as pad Thai; in noodle soups, such as the famous *laksa* of Bogor; in curries...it is suitable for all uses. Fried tofu is often dyed with turmeric or gardenia flowers, which give it a bright yellow color on the outside; the interior remains white.

TOFU PUFFS

Puffed tofu is a staple throughout Southeast Asia. Cut into cubes and fried until it has an airy texture, it absorbs broths and sauces particularly well, and is therefore often added to these types of preparation. Tofu puffs are found, for example, in the Chinese-Thai noodle soup with pink broth called *yen ta fo*; in many recipes of the Chinese communities of Singapore and Malaysia, such as *bak kut teh*, a broth made with pork, spices and medicinal herbs; or in various versions of *rojak*, a typical Indonesian salad that can mix fruit, uncooked vegetables, meat, seafood – and many other amazing things. Tofu puffs are also made into small veggie sandwiches and stuffed donuts sold by street vendors in Singapore and Malaysia. These delicious snacks have been adopted by everyone, including people you wouldn't instinctively associate with tofu, such as Christians and Muslims.

EGG TOFU

Brought by the Chinese, this "tofu" is not really tofu: it is, rather, an extremely thin flan made from eggs and soy milk. It is fragile and its texture tends towards gelatinous, like extra-firm glucon-delta-lactone silken tofu. Impossible to confuse them, however, because they are not at all alike. Egg tofu is yellow and is usually sold in cylindrical tubes. Although it is quite delicate, it is often used in stir-fry dishes, but also in soups and various other preparations.

TOFU PUDDING

Tofu pudding is a "must" in all of Southeast Asia. Sold in stalls or by street vendors, especially in the morning, it is more or less firm or smooth depending on the coagulant used, and is always served sweet. In the Philippines, they add a very dark brown sugar syrup called *arnibal* and sago or tapioca pearls; in Thailand, they like it with fruit and milk; in Vietnam, depending on the region, it might be accompanied by jasmine or ginger syrup, coconut water, sugar.... In Indonesia, Malaysia, and Singapore, syrup is often flavored with pandan leaf. Tofu pudding can be enjoyed cold, at room temperature, or a little warmer depending on regional preferences.

FERMENTED TOFU

Traditionally, fermentations are never uniform; these products are linked to particular terroirs, and we find different kinds of fermented tofus throughout Southeast Asia. Chinese *dòufǔrǔ* is widely available everywhere (the Vietnamese version is called *chao*), but there are other variations. In the south of Vietnam, for example, there used to be a huge diversity of tofus reminiscent of French goat cheeses, blue cheeses, and others. These artisanal foods, however, are becoming increasingly scarce, as *chao* is easier to make – whether in factories or at home.

TOFU SKINS

Widely used in Chinese communities in Southeast Asia, the film that forms on the surface of heated soy milk, called *yuba* in Japanese and *fǔpí* in Mandarin, is generally not integrated into the eating habits of the rest of the population. Vietnam is an exception. Locally called *tàu hǔ ky*, this "soy skin" is very common in various dried forms that are rehydrated before going into the pan. It is eaten fried, braised, stuffed – the uses are many and varied.

There is a very wide variety of tofu in Southeast Asia: puffed tofu (1), tofu pudding (2), silken tofu (3), pressed tofu (4) and firm tofu (5).

LEMONGRASS
TOFU
(Đậu hũ xào sả ớt)

Prepared this way, tofu can find its place on your plate alongside all sorts of side dishes, or it can garnish a Vietnamese sandwich (*bánh mì* – see page 204), a vegetarian rice noodle bowl (known Stateside as *bún* – see page 202), or really any salad. You can choose to add Sriracha sauce or not, depending on your taste – or dislike – for spicy chiles. In any case, this recipe is very simple, requires no effort, but will transform plain tofu by giving it tangy flavors and a crisp texture.

🕑 prep **10 min**   🕑 cook **5 min**   🌿 vegan   🍴 **4 servings**

- 14–16 oz firm tofu • 1½ Tbsp minced lemongrass (tender inner white bulb only)
- 1½ Tbsp garlic • 2 tsp Sriracha sauce (optional) • 2 tsp lime juice
- 2 tsp sugar • ½ tsp salt • ½ tsp pepper • 4 Tbsp vegetable oil

Cut the block of tofu crosswise into slices ¼ inch thick. Place them on a few paper towels while you prepare the marinade.

Mix the lemongrass, garlic, Sriracha sauce (if using), lime juice, sugar, and salt and pepper. Add 2 tablespoons of the oil and mix again. Blot the tofu dry with paper towels and place it in a deep plate with this marinade, covering the tofu completely.

In a large frying pan over medium heat, heat the remaining 2 tablespoons oil. Add the tofu slices and brown them for 2–3 minutes on each side. Use the flavored tofu as desired.

Note   For an even more flavorful tofu, which absorbs the marinade especially well, cut it into slices as indicated in this recipe, freeze it for 24 hours in a bag, then take it out of the bag and let it thaw in the refrigerator for 24 hours on a plate covered with several layers of paper towel. Then proceed with the recipe above as directed.

TOFU TERRINE,
VIETNAMESE STYLE
(Chả hấp chay)

They love their pork terrine in Vietnam, but a vegan version made with tofu actually exists. The texture and appearance are very similar to the meaty recipe: dotted with black mushrooms and carrots, as well as mung bean noodles (also called cellophane noodles or glass noodles), it's a great starter to share with family or friends. It can be eaten dipped in a mixture of soy sauce and lime juice, or with the dipping sauce that accompanies spring rolls (see page 208).

🕐 prep **15 min** (+ soak **20 min**)　🕐 cook **20 min**　🌱 vegan　🍽 4 servings

For 1 small terrine
- ½ handful mung bean noodles • 1 Tbsp dried black mushrooms • 7 oz firm tofu
- ½ carrot, grated • 1 tsp fermented tofu, crushed • 1 small shallot thinly sliced
- 1 tsp + 1 Tbsp cornstarch, potato starch, or tapioca • ¼ tsp sugar • ¼ tsp salt
- ¼ tsp pepper • 1 Tbsp water • 1 Tbsp achiote oil

In separate bowls, rehydrate the noodles and the black mushrooms in lukewarm water until they are tender. Drain both, and roughly chop the mushrooms. Set aside.

Drain the firm tofu and mash or mix it until it becomes a paste. Place it in a clean cloth and squeeze to drain the excess water. In a mixing bowl, combine the mashed firm tofu with the carrots, mushrooms, noodles, crushed fermented tofu, the 1 teaspoon starch, the sugar, and the salt and pepper. Mix by hand until you get a homogeneous texture. Pack this mixture well into a small terrine dish – if you don't have one, a small loaf pan or even a glass butter dish can do the trick. Steam for 20 minutes.

After the terrine has steamed for 20 minutes, prepare a jelly by mixing the water, achiote oil, and the 1 tablespoon starch. Mix this jelly well and pour it over the terrine. Spread it over the entire surface, and continue steaming for 7 minutes more. When the terrine cools, the jelly will set.

Serve the terrine in slices. It can be eaten dipped in a mixture of soy sauce and lime juice, or in the dipping sauce that accompanies the spring rolls (see page 208).

Note　You can buy achiote oil at Latin grocery stores or online, but it's also very easy to make. Pick up achiote seeds (check the ethnic foods aisle of the supermarket), toast them in a dry pan until fragrant, and then mix with a neutral-flavored vegetable oil and leave to infuse for 3 days. The oil will take on a beautiful orange-red color.

VEGETARIAN
NOODLE BOWL
(Bún thịt nướng chay)

In France, they call this "*bò bún*," and in the US it's shortened even more to just "*bún*," but for the Vietnamese, this name doesn't really make sense. The original salad with rice noodles and beef is called *bún thịt nướng bò* – so *bún bò* would be a better shortening of the name. The vegetarian – and even vegan – versions of this dish is just as tasty, especially if you use lemongrass tofu (see page 200).

🕐 prep **30 min** 🕐 cook **5 min** 🌱 vegan 🍽 **4** servings

For the pickled carrots
• 3 carrots, grated • 1 tsp salt • 2 Tbsp sugar • 4 Tbsp rice vinegar

For the sauce
• 6 Tbsp light soy sauce • 6 Tbsp sugar • 3 Tbsp lime juice
• 3 Tbsp rice vinegar • 6 Tbsp water • 4 cloves garlic, minced • 1 red chile, thinly sliced

For the rest
• 7 oz rice vermicelli • 8 escarole leaves, thinly sliced • ½ cucumber, julienned
• 2 small handfuls mung bean sprouts • 4 Tbsp mint leaves, thinly sliced
• 4 Tbsp purple *shiso* leaves, thinly sliced • 14–16 oz lemongrass tofu (see page 200)
• 8–12 small fried vegetable spring rolls (optional)
• 4 Tbsp roasted and crushed peanuts • 4 Tbsp fried shallots • Vegetable oil

Prepare the pickled carrots: in a bowl, mix the carrots with the salt and leave to drain for 10 minutes. Press the carrots by hand to drain them. Add the sugar and vinegar, mix and leave to marinate.

Mix together all the ingredients for the sauce, and set aside.

In a pot of boiling water, cook the rice vermicelli according to package directions. Drain and rinse them thoroughly with cold water. Set aside.

In an oiled pan, brown the spring rolls for a few minutes to heat through, then cut them into two or three pieces. Set aside.

Divide the vermicelli among 4 large bowls or soup plates. Top with the escarole, cucumber, bean sprouts, carrots, herbs, tofu, spring rolls, peanuts, and fried shallots, then drizzle with sauce.

TOFU & VEGGIE
SANDWICH
(Bánh mì chay)

The *bánh mì* sandwich is the ultimate symbol of Franco-Vietnamese fusion, bringing together ingredients from both cultures in a baguette to make a fantastic sandwich. The basic recipe contains pork in several forms, but you can replace this with plain tofu or lemongrass tofu (see page 200) for a vegetarian version – or even vegan, if you use mayonnaise without eggs (see page 326).

🕐 prep **30 min** (+ marinate **24 hr**) 🍃 vegetarian 🍴 4 servings

For the pickled carrot & daikon radish
• ½ daikon radish, grated • 2 carrots, grated • 1 portion sugar
• 1 portion hot water • 1 portion rice vinegar • Salt
For the rest
• 2 baguettes • Mayonnaise • Soy sauce • 1 English cucumber, thinly sliced
• 14–16 oz lemongrass tofu (see page 200) • 1 bunch cilantro
• 2 red chiles, thinly sliced (optional)

Prepare the pickles a day in advance: mix the daikon with 1 teaspoon salt and let it drain for 15 minutes. Squeeze it by hand to drain it. Mix it with the carrots, then pack the vegetables into a jar. Add enough vinegar and water to cover. Dilute sugar in an equal volume of hot water, let cool, and add an equal volume of vinegar and ½ teaspoon of salt. Add this to the jar to cover the vegetables, put on the lid, and refrigerate for 24 hours.

Cut the baguettes in half. Open each half-baguette and brush with mayonnaise mixed with a little soy sauce to your taste. Place a few cucumber slices on top, lemongrass tofu slices, carrot and daikon pickles, cilantro leaves, and a few chili slices, if you like.

BRAISED
YUBA
(Đậu hũ ky kho)

Yuba, which English speakers call "tofu skins," is actually more like "soy milk skin," since it is made before the soy milk is coagulated and turned into tofu. Dried *yuba* is found in Asian grocery stores in various forms, usually yellow in color: it can be large folded sheets, rolls, knots.... Perhaps these products do not inspire us at first sight, but they are fabulous in cooking: easy to prepare, they are rich in protein and vitamins, and can be used in various ways, giving very interesting textures to vegetarian and vegan dishes. Braised *yuba*, a classic of Chinese cuisine adopted in Vietnam and elsewhere in Southeast Asia, is a particularly simple and delicious recipe for lovers of sweet-and-salty flavors.

🕐 prep **5 min** (+ soak **6 hr**) 🕐 cook **10 min** 🌱 vegetarian 🍴 4 servings

• 8 long rolls of dried *yuba* • 2 cloves garlic, minced
• 1 Tbsp minced root ginger • ⅓ cup soy sauce
• 1 Tbsp honey (or vegan agave syrup) • 1½ Tbsp sugar
• ½ tsp chile powder • 5¼ cups water
• 1 tsp ground pepper • Vegetable oil • Steamed rice, for serving • Cilantro leaves, for garnish

Place the dried *yuba* rolls in a suitable container and cover them with water. Let them rehydrate for about 6 hours – the timing may be more or less, depending on their thickness. They have to become completely flexible. Drain and cut into segments about 2 inches long.

In a frying pan over medium-high heat, heat a little oil. Brown the *yuba* segments on all sides. Remove from the pan. Add a little more oil if needed, and sauté the garlic and ginger for 30 seconds, stirring, then add the soy sauce, honey, sugar, chile, and water to the pan. Mix and return the *yuba* to the pan.

Reduce the heat to medium-low and cook, turning occasionally, until the liquid is almost completely gone. Season with pepper, taste and add a little salt if needed, and serve over rice, sprinkled with cilantro leaves.

VEGAN

SPRING ROLLS

(Gỏi cuốn chay)

Making spring rolls for your guests is guaranteed success. It seems very technical, but it really isn't. It seems very complicated, but it really isn't that either. In fact, what keeps us from doing it more often is just laziness. It takes a little space, it takes a little time. But no wizarding skills demanded, I promise. This vegan version is a treat. Accompanied it with the sauce of your choice: the thick version with savory flavors, or the clear and sweetish version.

🕐 prep **45–60 min** 🕐 cook **5 min** 🌱 vegan

For 8 rolls
- 2 oz rice vermicelli • 4 oz mung bean sprouts
- 5 oz firm tofu or lemongrass tofu (see page 200)
- 4 stems Asian chives • 8 spring roll wrappers, 7-inch diameter
- 4 large escarole leaves, cut in half • 4 sprigs mint, leaves picked
- 4 sprigs purple *shiso*, leaves picked • ½ cucumber, juliennes • 1 carrot, grated

For a thick, savory dipping sauce
- 3 Tbsp hoisin sauce • 2 Tbsp peanut butter • 1 Tbsp crushed peanuts
- 8 Tbsp hot water • 1 clove garlic, minced • 1 red chile, thinly sliced (optional)

For a clear, sweetish dipping sauce
- 3 Tbsp light soy sauce • 1 Tbsp rice vinegar • 8 Tbsp hot water • 2–3 Tbsp lime juice
- 2–3 Tbsp brown sugar • 1 clove garlic, minced • 1 red chile, thinly sliced (optional)

In a pot of boiling water, cook the rice vermicelli according to package directions (usually about 5 minutes). Drain and rinse thoroughly with cold water. Set aside.

Blanch the bean sprouts in boiling water for 30 seconds–1 minute. Rinse in cold water and set aside.

Cut the tofu into strips a scant ½ inch wide. Cut the garlic chives in half. Arrange all the prepared ingredients close at hand around you, as well as two plates and a large container of warm water.

(continued)

Immerse a spring roll wrapper very quickly in the warm water. It will soften gradually; the main idea is that the whole wrapper has been in contact with the water. Place the wrapper on a plate and place a half-leaf of escarole on it, then some herbs, 2 tofu strips, a little carrot and cucumber, just a few bean sprouts, and a small amount of rice vermicelli. You don't want to overstuff the wrapper to the point where you won't be able to close it without tearing.

Fold in both sides of the wrapper over the filling, then roll it up away from you, keeping the roll fairly tight. (However, do not make it too tight, or the wrapper might tear.) When it is two-thirds of the way rolled, place a garlic chive lengthwise in the roll, letting it extend pas the edge a bit, and finish rolling. The roll will seal on its own thanks to the moisture. Place this finished roll on the second plate, and repeat this process to use all the wrappers.

Prepare the sauce of your choice – or both, let's go crazy! – by mixing all the ingredients. Eat the rolls dipped in the sauce.

Note It's a bit time consuming and we don't do it every day, so I advise you to take advantage of your spring roll sessions. Don't just do 8, you'll just be hankering for more, and plus it's better to use up all the wrappers, which are sold in very large packages. Do 12, 20, 30. Let yourself go. Get other people involved, if needed. In any case, we all know very well that there can never be too many spring rolls. No matter how big your group, you will eat them all.

TOFU PUDDING
WITH GINGER SYRUP
(Đậu hũ nước đường)

If you like ginger, this is the dessert for you. Tofu pudding, smooth, perfectly silky and tender, brings flan to mind; it forms delicate layers sprinkled with a delicious warm syrup made with fresh gingerroot. This recipe is found in many regions: it is a classic of Cantonese, Vietnamese, and Thai street food among others.

🕐 prep **10 min**   🕐 cook **15 min**   🍃 vegan

For 4 bowls
- 12 oz root ginger, peeled and thinly sliced on the diagonal
- 1 Tbsp confectioners' sugar • ⅓ cup palm sugar
- ¼ cup water • 1 lb tofu pudding • Candied ginger, for garnish

In a bowl, mix the ginger slices and confectioners' sugar. Let sit for 10 minutes. Meanwhile, chop and crush the palm sugar.

In a saucepan over low heat, heat the mixture of ginger and confectioners' sugar, stirring constantly, for about 5 minutes. Add the water and the palm sugar and raise the heat to medium. Melt the sugar, stirring; when it is dissolved, lower the heat again and cook for about 6 minutes, until syrupy. Let cool.

Serve the tofu pudding in bowls, drizzled with warm syrup and garnished with slices of candied ginger.

PHILIPPINE-STYLE
BRAISED TOFU
(Adobong tokwa)

Adobo is one of the iconic recipes of the Philippines, rich in vinegar, garlic, black pepper, soy sauce, and bay leaf. Everything can be prepared this way, including tofu. It will be anything but bland, braised in a sauce with tangy, salty, and spicy flavors. It's a simple, healthful dish that is quick to cook. Philippine vinegars have amazing flavors and strong acidity. The most common for this recipe are cane vinegar, coconut vinegar, palm vinegar, and white vinegar (which, by the way, is available everywhere).

🕐 prep **5 min**   🕐 cook **10 min**   🌱 vegan   🍽 **4** servings

• 14 oz extra-firm tofu • ¼ cup white vinegar
• ½ cup soy sauce • 3–4 Tbsp water • 4 cloves garlic, crushed or thinly sliced
• 1 small red onion, coarsely chopped • 3 bay leaves
• 1 tsp black peppercorns • 1 tsp sugar • Vegetable oil • Steamed rice, for serving

Cut the tofu into cubes about 1 inch square. In wok or a sauté pan over medium-high heat, heat a little oil and brown the drained tofu on all sides. Set the tofu aside on paper towels.

In the same wok, combine the vinegar, soy sauce, water, garlic, onion, bay leaves, and peppercorns. Simmer over medium heat for a few minutes, until the sauce has reduced. Add the tofu and sugar, and cook for 1 minute more, stirring to coat all the tofu with sauce.

Serve with rice – adobo sauce with white rice is one of the great joys of life in the Philippines.

TOFU PUDDING
WITH SYRUP PEARLS
(Taho)

Taho inevitably reminds me of the Quiapo district of Manila, where the same guy has been selling this sweet dish in the midst of the morning rush, behind the church, for years. *Taho* is found everywhere in the Philippines, but this fellow has something special – probably due to the context. Tofu pudding and tapioca or sago pearls form a pretty pattern in the deep brown sugar syrup called *arnibal*; the textures are fun, the flavors are simple and straightforward. A dessert – or a snack – to drink as much as to eat.

🕐 prep **2 min** 🕐 cook **30 min** 🌱 vegan 👥 4 servings

For the pearls
• 6¹⁄₃ cups water • ¼ cup raw sugar • ¼ cup small tapioca or sago pearls
For the syrup
• ½ cup water • ½ cup raw sugar

• 14 oz tofu pudding

First prepare the pearls: in a large saucepan over high heat, bring the water and sugar to a boil. Add the pearls and stir until it boils again. Turn the heat down as low as possible, cover, and cook for 20–30 minutes, stirring occasionally. The pearls should be translucent with a small white dot in the center. Drain, rinse, and drain again. Set aside in the covered pan.

While the pearls are cooking, prepare the syrup: pour the water and sugar into a saucepan and bring to a boil over high heat. Reduce the heat to medium-low and simmer for a few minutes, stirring, until the sugar is completely dissolved. Remove from the heat and let cool.

Steam the tofu in its container for about 15 minutes to warm it up. Divide the tofu and pearls among bowls or glasses in alternating layers, and drizzle generously with syrup.

Note Tofu pudding can be found in the fresh section of well-stocked Chinese and Vietnamese grocery stores – look for "tofu pudding" or "soybean pudding" or "douhua" with glucono-delta-lactone (GDL). You can also prepare it yourself (see pages 34 and 36).

CLEAR SOUP
WITH EGG TOFU
(Tom chuet)

This simple and light Thai broth is not exactly a formal recipe; you can add whatever vegetables you want. From one region to another, and even from one family to another, the results will be quite different – if not entirely different. Sometimes you will find in it slices of "egg tofu," the egg-and-soy-milk custard available in tubes in the fresh section in Asian grocery stores. You can also make this egg tofu yourself (see page 49).

⏱ prep **5 min**   ⏱ cook **10 min**   🌱 vegetarian   🍽 **4** servings

- 2 cloves garlic • 1 small bunch cilantro • 2 green onions
- 14 oz egg tofu • 1 carrot • ¼ napa cabbage • Vegetable oil
- 1 qt water or vegetable stock • 2–4 Tbsp light soy sauce
- ½ tsp ground white pepper • Steamed rice, for serving

Mince the garlic. Pick the cilantro leaves; cut the cilantro stems and the green onion into ¾-inch lengths. Cut the egg tofu into slices a scant ½ inch thick, and the carrot into slices $^{1}/_{16}$ inch thick. Roughly slice the cabbage.

In a large saucepan over medium-high heat, heat a little oil and fry the garlic. Add the water or vegetable broth, cilantro stems, carrot, and cabbage, and bring to a boil. Reduce the heat to a simmer, add the green onions and half the soy sauce, and cook for a few minutes. The vegetables should be tender but not overly soft.

Add the tofu and pepper and simmer for a few more minutes. Add a little more soy sauce if necessary. Add the cilantro leaves, and serve with rice.

Note For a vegan version, replace the egg tofu with soft to medium-firm (flexible) tofu.

EGG TOFU STIR-FRY
WITH THAI VEGGIES
(Taohu song kreung)

This stir-fry dish, topped with a creamy sauce, is focused on egg tofu plus a mix of vegetables. This kind of egg-and-soy-milk custard can be found in the fresh section of Asian grocery stores, in tubes. It can also be prepared at home (see page 49). Don't hesitate to use other vegetables if you do not have the ones called for – this recipe follows the vagaries of the produce market without a problem.

| ⏱ prep **10 min** | ⏱ cook **10 min** | 🌱 vegetarian | 👥 4 servings |

- 4 cloves garlic, thinly sliced • 1 small red or green bell pepper, julienned
- 4 oz baby corn, julienned • 2 small carrots, julienned • 4 oz straw mushrooms, halved
- 2 small tomatoes, cut into thin wedges • 14 oz egg tofu, sliced ½ inch thick
- 4 Tbsp soy sauce • 2 Tbsp vegetarian oyster sauce
- 2 tsp cornstarch, potato starch, or tapioca mixed with ¼ cup water
- Vegetable oil • Steamed rice, for serving

Heat a wok over high heat and pour a little oil in it. Add the garlic and stir-fry it for about 30 seconds, then add the bell pepper, baby corn, and carrots, and continue stir-frying for 30 seconds–1 minute, stirring constantly or almost. Add the mushrooms, stir and toss again for 30 seconds–1 minute, then add the tomatoes, tofu, soy sauce, and oyster sauce. Cook for another 1 minute or so, stirring and avoiding breaking up the tofu into crumbs.

Reduce the heat to medium. Give the starch slurry a quick stir, then pour this mixture into the wok. Mix well so that all the vegetables are coated with sauce. Cook for 1 minute more to thicken, then serve straight away with rice.

Notes As always with the wok (or even the frying pan), for best results, do not prepare 4 portions at once. Limit yourself to 2 servings at a time. You will need to separate the above ingredients cook in 2 batches if there are 4 of you at the table (it goes quickly, you can eat together).

For a vegan version, replace the egg tofu with medium-firm (flexible) tofu. Straw mushrooms are found canned in Asian grocery stores. Vegetarian oyster sauce is easily found in Asian grocery stores. If you don't have any, you can always replace it with soy sauce.

THAI-STYLE STIR-FRIED
RICE NOODLES
(Pad Thai)

This is one of the most famous and appreciated Thai dishes throughout the world, and it's easy to understand why: it is fatty, sweet, salty, and gently spiced, and mixes various textures. In short, it speaks to the child in all of us. Let's grow up a little and prepare our pad Thai ourselves; we can then perceive that it is simple and quick to cook, that it doesn't cost a lot, and that we do not need to go to a restaurant to taste this cherished dish.... Here is a vegetarian version – I didn't use the usual fresh and dried shrimp or the fish sauce, but this dish is still fairly faithful to the original. The recipe is for four, but be sure to prepare each serving individually.

🕐 prep **10 min** (+ soak **40 min**) 🕐 cook **10 min** 🌱 vegetarian 🍴 **4** servings

- 14 oz flat rice noodles • ⅓ cup tamarind juice • ⅓ cup soy sauce • 4 Tbsp palm sugar
- 4 small shallots, thinly sliced • 4 good handfuls mung bean sprouts
- 1 bunch Chinese chives, cut into 2-inch lengths • 4 Tbsp crushed roasted peanuts
- 4 Tbsp fried shallots • 2 Tbsp red chile flakes, or as needed
- 7 oz pressed tofu, cut into small rectangles • 4 small eggs • 2 limes • Vegetable oil

Soak your rice noodles in a good amount of warm water for about 40 minutes, or long enough to soften them without their becoming overly soft. Heat the tamarind juice and soy sauce just enough to let you dilute the palm sugar easily. Reserve half of the vegetables, which will be served raw with the noodles, as well as the peanuts, the fried shallots, and the chile flakes. Have everything else around you at hand – the cooking will go very quickly.

Heat up your wok pretty well and add a little oil. Fry the shallots. When they are just starting to brown, add the tofu and brown it on all sides, stirring constantly or almost. Add the noodles, 3–4 tablespoons of tamarind-soy sauce per serving, and a good pinch of chile flakes if you like, and continue to stir so that the sauce goes everywhere and the noodles do not stick together.

Push the entire contents of the wok to one side and add a little more oil. Break an egg directly into the oil, scramble it very quickly to break up the yolk, and place the noodles on top. Let cook for 15 seconds, then start mixing everything again. Lower the heat, add some bean sprouts and garlic chives, and stir and toss until the vegetables soften.

Serve the noodles at once, surrounded with raw bean sprouts and garlic chive, a sprinkling of peanuts, fried shallots – and chile flakes, if you want more – plus half a lime, for squeezing.

Note The wok does not like large quantities. Even if you have a very large one, you will not be able to prepare four portions well in one go: some of the ingredients will go soggy, others will burn, and the rest will not be properly cooked. In short, be wise and go serving by serving, possibly two servings at a time, never all four at once (especially with noodles, that would be carnage). I give ingredients for four with this in mind; dividing by two or four is very easy. For a vegan pad Thai, don't add the egg. If, like me, you want mild flavor, omit the raw garlic chive and the extra portion of chili.

TOFU, GALANGAL & COCONUT MILK SOUP

(Tom kha taohu)

The legendary Thai soup with chicken, mushrooms, and coconut milk called *tom kha gai* can be transformed into a vegan dish if you replace the meat with tofu and the chicken stock with vegetable stock. It will be just as excellent. You can add chile according to your preference, from barely there to five-alarm fire.

🕐 prep **10 min**   🕐 cook **10 min**   🌱 vegan   🍴 **4** servings

- 1 box straw mushrooms, cleaned • 1 stalk lemongrass • 6 red Thai chiles • 6 Thai lime leaves
- 3 limes • 1 thumb-sized piece galangal root • 2 cups coconut milk
- 2 cups vegetable stock (fairly concentrated) • 14 oz firm to extra-firm tofu (flexible), cubed
- ¼ cup light soy sauce • 1 handful cilantro leaves • Steamed jasmine rice, for serving

Cut the larger mushrooms in half. Cut the lemongrass into 1½-inch lengths and bruise them; bruise the red peppers; tear up the lime leaves or crumple them. Squeeze the limes. Peel and slice the galangal on the diagonal as thinly as possible.

In a large saucepan over low-medium heat, combine the coconut milk, stock, lime leaves, lemongrass pieces, and galangal. Heat and stir until simmering. Add the mushrooms and tofu, and continue cooking for a few minutes without letting it come to a boil.

Add the chiles and turn off the heat. Gradually add the lime juice and soy sauce, tasting as you go: the soup should be tart and salty, then softened by the roundness of the coconut milk. Adjust the amount of lime juice, coconut milk, and soy sauce if needed. Add the cilantro leaves, and serve with jasmine rice.

TOFU STIR-FRY
WITH GREEN PEPPERCORNS
(Pad cha taohu)

This fantastic dish is prepared in no time flat, and brings happiness to your life: it is full of varied colors and flavors, and if you like green peppercorns, it will satisfy you. This recipe is from a food stall in the middle of nowhere in the Thai countryside, between two pepper fields belonging to the local democratic party. I just "veganized" it by replacing the fish sauce with soy sauce.

○ prep **10 min** ○ cook **10 min** ● vegan ♟ 4 servings

- 4 red chiles (or less, or more) • 5-inch piece fresh fingerroot (*krachai*)
- 1 stalk lemongrass • 3 Thai lime leaves • ¹/₃ cup green peppercorns
- 4 white Thai eggplants • 4 ears baby corn
- 14 oz firm to extra-firm tofu (flexible), cut into cubes or rectangles • 4 oz Thai pea eggplants
- 3 Tbsp light soy sauce • Vegetable oil • Steamed jasmine rice, for serving

Stem the chiles and mash them in a mortar until they are shredded, without quite purée-ing them. (Don't get chile in your eyes!) Cut the *krachai* into extra-fine julienne strips – the finest possible – after removing the dry bits. Remove the tough outer leaves from the lemongrass, and mince the tender white heart. Chop the Thai lime leaves as finely as possible. If the green peppercorn bunches are very long, cut them in half or quarters.

Thinly slice the white eggplants. Cut the ears of baby corn in half lengthwise, then in 2 or 3 pieces. Place all your ingredients around you close at hand, the cooking will go very quickly. For optimal results, it is best to proceed in two batches and separate your ingredients in half.

Heat a wok over high heat and pour a little oil into it. Add the tofu and chile at once. Stir almost constantly, browning the tofu for a few moments. Add the *krachai*, green peppercorns, sliced white eggplant, whole pea eggplants, baby corn, and lime leaves, and sauté for 1–2 minutes, stirring and tossing constantly. Add a little water if needed. Season with soy sauce, mix well, and taste and adjust the seasoning. Serve at once with jasmine rice.

Note As always with the wok (or even the frying pan), for best results, do not prepare 4 portions at once. Limit yourself to 2 servings at a time. You will need to separate the above ingredients cook in 2 batches if there are 4 of you at the table (it goes quickly, you can eat together).

RED CURRY
TOFU STIR-FRY
(Pad prik gaeng taohu)

Thai curries can be richly sauced or rather dry, depending on how you use the curry paste. This recipe tends towards dry curries; instead of being diluted with coconut cream, the red curry paste is quickly sautéed with tofu and long beans. These delicious beans, quite thick, very long, crunchy and sweet, are not easy to find everywhere, but they can be replaced by standard green beans. As for curry paste, it will taste better homemade with a mortar and pestle, but there are also excellent ones on the market if you're in a hurry.

🕐 prep **20 min**   🕐 cook **15 min**   🌱 vegan   👥 **4** servings

For the curry paste
• 6 dried red Thai chiles • ½ tsp coriander seeds
• ½ tsp cumin seeds • 7 cloves garlic, peeled • 3 small shallots
• 1 stalk lemongrass, peeled and thinly sliced • 1 coriander root, thinly sliced • 1 Tbsp galangal root, thinly sliced • Zest of ½ Thai lime • 2 tsp white peppercorns • 1 tsp salt

For the rest
• 6 Chinese long beans or 7 oz regular green beans • 14 oz extra-firm tofu, cubed
• 1 Tbsp soy sauce • 1 tsp sugar • 6 Thai lime leaves, bruised • Vegetable oil
• Steamed jasmine rice, for serving

Start by making the curry paste. Rehydrate the chiles in a bowl of warm water for about 10 minutes. In a dry pan over medium heat, toast the coriander and cumin seeds for a few minutes, stirring constantly. Transfer to a mortar, add all the curry paste ingredients, then pound and mix with a pestle until you get a homogeneous red paste. Be careful: the chile can burn your eyes and make you cough!

Cut the beans into bite-sized lengths. Heat a wok over high heat and pour in a little oil. Add the curry paste immediately and fry in the oil, stirring for about 30 seconds. Add the tofu and brown it in the paste for 1–2 minutes, stirring constantly. Add the soy sauce, sugar, and a little water if the mixture seems too dry. Add the beans and lime leaves and cook for 30 seconds–1 minute, stirring constantly. Serve over jasmine rice.

Note Thai lime leaves are ideal when fresh, but can be hard to find. The frozen ones are the best alternative – the dried leaves have significantly less flavor.

COCONUT GREEN CURRY
(Gaeng keow wan taohu)

In Thailand, we tend to be instinctively wary of red – beware, hot chile! But the strongest curry is probably the green one. Considered by Thais to be a soft curry (soft in the sense of "sweet"; they are aware that it "provokes"), *gaeng keow wan* owes its color to green chiles, and is traditionally prepared with small, round white eggplants, coconut milk, Thai basil, and Thai lime leaves (also known as kaffir lime leaves). The curry paste does not have to be homemade, especially if you have trouble finding the necessary fresh ingredients: in that case, better a good store-bought curry paste!

🕐 prep **20 min**   🕐 cook **15 min**   🌱 vegan   🍴 **6** servings

For the curry paste
- 1 tsp coriander seeds • 1 tsp cumin seeds
- 5 oz green Thai chiles • 1 head garlic, peeled • 3 small shallots, peeled
- 1 thumb-sized piece galangal root, thinly sliced • 5 coriander roots, thinly sliced • Zest of 1 Thai lime
- 2 stalks lemongrass, peeled and thinly sliced • 1 Tbsp white peppercorns • 1 tsp salt

For the rest
- 1 cup water • 6 Thai lime leaves, bruised • 21 oz firm to extra-firm tofu (flexible), cubed
- 2½ cups coconut cream • 8 white Thai eggplant, cut into wedges
- 2 red chiles, thinly sliced • 8 sprigs Thai basil, leaves picked • Salt
- Steamed jasmine rice, for serving

Start by preparing the curry paste: in a dry pan over medium heat, roast the coriander and cumin seeds for a few minutes, stirring constantly. Transfer to a mortar, add all the curry paste ingredients, then pound and mix with a pestle until you get a fibrous green paste – it should not be smooth, but the ingredients should be indistinguishable. Be careful: the chile can burn your eyes and make you cough!

In a casserole pan or Dutch oven, combine the water, all the curry paste, the lime leaves, and the tofu. Bring to a boil, stirring occasionally, then add the coconut cream. Bring to the boil again, mixing gently, and salt to taste. Add the eggplant and red chile and let it boil for another 2–3 minutes. Turn off the heat, stir in the basil, and serve hot with jasmine rice.

Notes The best curry pastes are made with a mortar and pestle, which takes time and effort. The food processor is a quick and effortless alternative.

Thai lime leaves are best fresh, but may be hard to find. The frozen version is the best alternative - the dried leaves have significantly less flavor.

BRAISED TOFU WITH PINEAPPLE

(Kho manor tawhou)

This Cambodian recipe is most commonly seen with fish, but the tofu version is to die for. If you like sweet-and-sour, you're going to love it. Plus, it is easy and quick to prepare, and does not require impossible-to-find ingredients. Whether you're dining solo or have guests coming, this delicious dish deserves to be cooked.

⏱ prep 10 min   ⏱ cook 10 min   🌱 vegan   👤 4 servings

- 3 cloves garlic • 2 stalks lemongrass • 1 small pineapple or 1 can pineapple chunks
- 14 oz extra-firm tofu • 1 tsp sugar • 1 Tbsp soy sauce • ¼ cup vegetarian oyster sauce
- ½ tsp ground black pepper • 7 Tbsp water • Vegetable oil• Steamed jasmine rice, for serving
- Cilantro leaves, for garnish

Chop the garlic cloves. Peel the tough outer leaves of the lemongrass and chop the tender white heart. If you are using a fresh pineapple, peel it and remove the hard core in the center, then cut the flesh into cubes. Cut the tofu into cubes or rectangles ¾ inch to 1 inch square, and blot dry with paper towels.

In a wok or frying pan over medium-high heat, heat a little oil. Brown the tofu on all sides, then remove from the pan and set aside. Add a little more oil to the pan if needed, then stir-fry the garlic and lemongrass. Add the golden tofu, the pineapple, and the rest of the ingredients; mix and toss until the pineapple is cooked – the sauce should also have thickened a bit.

Serve over jasmine rice, sprinkled with cilantro leaves.

Note Vegetarian oyster sauce is easily found in Asian grocery stores. If you don't have any, you can always replace it with soy sauce.

MULTICOLOR
INDONESIAN SALAD
(Gado gado)

Gado gado is to Indonesia what salade Niçoise is to Nice: the local salad, composed of many ingredients, which everyone is more than happy to argue about. As Indonesia is a large island chain, it makes sense that *gado gado* has many regional variations; also, Indonesians don't necessarily have to talk about cooking to get into a heated discussion. Whichever ingredients you choose, you will often be told that they should all be blanched or steamed...but that's not true – some are fried, and others can be raw!

🕐 prep **20 min**   🕐 cook **15 min**   🌿 vegetarian   👤 4 servings

- 5 oz firm to extra-firm tofu • 5 oz tempeh • 2 eggs • 4 oz green beans • 4 oz mung bean sprouts
- 7 oz pointed cabbage • ½ English cucumber or 1 small Asian cucumber • 1 carrot
- 7 oz boiled potatoes • 4 Tbsp fried shallots • Vegetable oil

For the sauce
- ⅓ cup peanuts • 3 Tbsp thick sweet soy sauce (*kecap manis*) • 1 Tbsp brown sugar
- 1 clove garlic • 1–2 red chiles • ½–⅔ cup coconut milk • Juice of 1 lime

Cut the tofu and the tempeh into cubes or rectangles ¾ inch to 1 inch square, and blot dry with paper towels. In a wok or frying pan over medium-high heat, heat a little oil. Brown the tofu and tempeh on all sides, then remove from the pan and set aside.

Cook the eggs for 7 minutes in a saucepan of boiling water, then immerse them in cold water to stop cooking. Blanch the beans for 2–3 minutes in a pot of boiling water, then run them under a stream of cold water until they have cooled. Blanch the bean sprouts for 30 seconds in a pot of boiling water, then run them under a stream of cold water until they have cooled.

Shred the cabbage, thinly slice the cucumber, grate the carrots, and roughly slice the potatoes. Peel the eggs and halve or quarter them.

Combine all the ingredients for the sauce in a food processor; add more coconut milk to for a milder flavor, or more lime juice for a more tangy result. Arrange all the salad ingredients flat on a large platter, and serve with the sauce.

Note If you can't find *kecap manis*, you can make it yourself by reducing 2 parts soy sauce to 1 part sugar over low heat.

BALINESE CURRY
WITH TOFU & TEMPEH
(Kare tahu)

While Indonesia is not really a vegetarian country, Bali is the exception; the island being mainly Hindu, they eat more tofu there than anywhere else in the archipelago. Tempeh, another product made from soybeans – fermented, in this case – is a staple ingredient. This delicious yellow curry highlights these two ingredients. If you have trouble finding the ingredients you need to make yellow curry paste, you can buy the ready-made version.

prep **20 min**   cook **15 min**   vegan   **4** servings

For the curry paste
• 2 shallots • 3 cloves garlic • 1 red chile (or more) • 1 candlenut (*kemiri*) or 1 macadamia nut • ½ inch root ginger, freshly minced • ½ inch galangal root, freshly minced • 1 tsp minced turmeric root • 1 tsp coriander seeds • Salt and pepper

For the rest
• 7 oz Chinese long beans or regular green beans • 7 oz firm tofu • 7 oz tempeh • 1 stalk lemongrass, thinly sliced (tender inner white bulb only) • 2 Thai lime leaves • 2 bay leaves • ²/₃ cup vegetable stock • ²/₃ cup coconut milk • Vegetable oil • Steamed jasmine rice, for serving

In a mortar with a pestle (or in a food processor), mash and mix all the ingredients for the curry paste.

Cut the beans into 1- to 1½-inch lengths. Cut the tofu and the tempeh into cubes ¾ inch to 1 inch square. Blot the tofu dry with paper towels. You can also drain it a few hours before cooking, wrapped in paper towels.

In a wok or frying pan over medium-high heat, heat a generous amount of oil. Brown the tofu and tempeh on all sides, then remove from the pan and set aside on paper towels.

Pour off all but 2–3 tablespoons of oil from the wok and sauté the curry paste, lemon-grass, and bruised lime leaves and bay leaves. Stir-fry for 1–2 minutes. Add the tofu and tempeh, mix well, then pour in the broth and coconut milk. Continue cooking over medium heat until the sauce turns a uniform color. Add the beans, cover, reduce the heat to low, and cook for about 5 minutes. Serve with rice.

BRAISED TOFU & TEMPEH JAVANESE STYLE

(Tahu dan tempe bacem)

This delicious recipe comes from Yogyakarta, on the island of Java, where they love sweet-and-salty combinations. The sweetness of this dish is balanced nicely by the acidity of the tamarind, and perked up by various spices and aromatics; all these elements, assembled in a bath of coconut water, will reduce by simmering slowly with tofu and tempeh. After a final pass in a hot pan for golden color and crispness, the result will be delicious, savory, and most definitely exotic. For those who dread a bland tofu dish, this is one to savor...

⏱ prep **10 min** ⏱ cook **1 hr** 🌱 vegan 🍴 **4** servings

- 10 oz firm to extra-firm tofu • 10 oz tempeh • 3 shallots, finely minced
- 3 cloves garlic, minced • 3–4 Tbsp palm sugar or brown sugar
- 2 bay leaves • 1½ tsp ground coriander • 1 tsp galangal root powder
- 1 Tbsp tamarind juice • 1 qt coconut water • 1 tsp salt
- Vegetable oil • Steamed rice, for serving
- Thinly sliced fresh chile, for serving

Cut the tofu into 2-inch squares that are ¾ inch thick. Cut the tempeh into triangles of similar dimensions. Combine the tofu, tempeh, and all the remaining ingredients except the oil in a Dutch oven or casserole pan. The coconut water should just cover the tofu and the tempeh. If not, add a little plain water.

Bring to a boil over high heat, then reduce the heat and simmer, uncovered, until the liquid is reduced by half. Gently flip all the tofu and tempeh pieces, and continue simmering in the same way until almost all of the liquid is gone. Drain the tofu and tempeh pieces.

In a frying pan over medium-high heat, heat a little oil. Brown the tofu and tempeh on both sides. Serve hot with rice and thinly sliced chile (if you like spiciness).

TOFU STIR-FRY
WITH BALINESE SAUCE
(Tahu goreng bumbu Bali)

Despite its name, this recipe does not come from the island of Bali, but from the eastern side of Java. Balinese sauce, as the Indonesians call it, is popular all over the country. It is commonly associated with hard-cooked eggs, but also goes very well with tofu (fried or not) or tempeh.

🕐 prep **10 min** 🕐 cook **10 min** 🌱 vegan 🍽 **4 servings**

- 14–16 oz firm to extra-firm tofu • 1 Tbsp tamarind juice
- 1 stalk lemongrass, crushed and tied in a knot • 2 bay leaves
- 2 Thai lime leaves, bruised • ½ tsp salt • 2 tsp palm sugar or brown sugar
- 2 Tbsp thick sweet soy sauce (*kecap manis*) • Vegetable oil • Steamed rice, for serving

For the spice paste
- 8 shallots • 2–3 red chiles (or more, or less) • 2 cloves garlic • ¾-inch piece root ginger
- 5 candlenuts (*kemiri*) or 5 macadamia nuts • ¾-inch piece galangal root

---

Cut the tofu into 1½-inch cubes. In a mortar with a pestle (or in a food processor), mash and mix all the ingredients for the spice paste.

In a frying pan over medium-high heat, heat a little oil. Sauté the spice paste, stirring for about 5 minutes. Add the tamarind juice, lemongrass, bay and lime leaves, salt, and sugar. Mix well. Add the tofu and mix again. Stir-fry for 2 minutes, then add the sweet soy sauce and stir-fry again.

Remove the lemongrass and bay and lime leaves, and serve hot with rice.

Note Before cooking the tofu in the sauce, you can fry it. For this, season the cubes with salt and pepper, dredge with flour, and deep-fry in hot oil until they are golden brown. Drain on paper towels before adding them to the recipe.

SAVORY SPIRAL
COOKIES
(Xiàng ěrduǒ)

Depending on the region of the world where they live, Chinese speakers do not all call these cookies by the same name. In Malaysia and Indonesia, they say "elephant ear" cookies. In Taiwan, they mention "pig ears," elsewhere "cow ears".... They don't agree on the animal, but at least they all agree that it's the ear. Spiral-shaped, these savory cookies – or crackers, or biscuits, whatever you want to call them, even "bear ears" if you like – are common wherever there is a large Chinese community. They're flavored with fermented tofu, fried, and pretty easy to make.

🕐 prep **20 min**   🕐 cook **15 min** (+ freeze **30 min**)   🌱 vegan

For 20–30 cookies
• Oil for deep-frying
For the white dough
• ²/₃ cup flour • 3 Tbsp water • 1 pinch baking soda • 1 pinch salt
For the brown dough
• ¾ cup flour • 2 Tbsp water • 2½ Tbsp raw sugar
• 2 Tbsp vegetable oil • 1½ tsp white fermented tofu (*dòufuru*), puréed
• 1 tsp five-spice powder • 1 pinch baking soda • 2 pinches salt

In separate bowls, combine the ingredients for each of the two doughs. One at a time, roll them out ¹/₁₆ inch thick with a rolling pin, giving each dough a rectangular shape of the same size.

Brush water over the brown paste just to moisten. Place the white dough on top. Brush the white dough with water just to moisten, and roll the two doughs together lengthwise to make a thick roll. Wrap it in plastic wrap and leave it in the freezer for 30 minutes so that you can cut it more easily.

Heat oil for deep-frying to 340°F and cut the roll into slices about ¹/₁₆ inch thick. Place them on parchment paper as you go, without touching, as the dough can be sticky. In several batches, slide the dough slices into the hot oil and fry until the cookies are golden. Let drain and cool on a wire rack before serving. You can also keep them in an airtight container.

TOFU PUFFS
WITH CRUNCHY VEG & SPICED SAUCE
(Tau pok rojak)

In Malaysian, the term *rojak* means "mixture" and designates in generic fashion several types of amazing salads. In Indonesia, these contain mainly uncooked fruits and vegetables, while in Malaysia and Singapore, they are enriched with crackers, puffed tofu, calamari, and pieces of fried dough. *Rojak* street vendors in Singapore often offer small puffed tofu cubes (*tau pok*) filled with raw vegetables to dip in a "*rojak* sauce" of chile, tamarind, and peanuts. This playful recipe, both fresh and delicious, is perfect we a pre-dinner drink.

🕐 prep **10 min**   🕐 cook **5 min**   🌱 vegan

For 20 pieces
- 4 Tbsp palm sugar • 2 Tbsp white sugar • 4 Tbsp tamarind juice
- 1 Tbsp chile powder or chile paste
- 1 torch ginger flower bud (*bunga kantan*), thinly sliced or 1 tsp freshly minced root ginger
- ¾ cup crushed roasted peanuts • Juice of 2 calamansi lemons or 1 lime
- 2 Tbsp thick sweet soy sauce (*kecap manis*)
- 20 cubes puffed tofu (*tau pok*) • ½ cucumber, julienned • 4 oz mung bean sprouts

Chop the palm sugar and mix it with 2 tablespoons of water; heat the mixture in a small saucepan until the sugar is dissolved. Add the white sugar, tamarind juice, chili powder or paste, torch ginger flower bud or ginger, peanuts, citrus juice, and sweet soy sauce. Mix well and place this sauce in a serving bowl.

Slice the puffed tofu cubes in half without going all the way though, as if making mini sandwich rolls. Stuff them with a mixture of julienned cucumber and bean sprouts. Broil these little cubes under the broiler or in a hot oiled frying pan just to brown them on both sides and warm them, without cooking the vegetables. Serve with the sauce.

Note   Puffed tofu cubes are found in the fresh section in Chinese, Vietnamese, Thai groceries.... These are fairly common products within the Chinese community and therefore readily available, even outside of Asia.

TOFU & TEMPEH SATAY
WITH PEANUT SAUCE
(Tahu dan tempe sate bumbu kacang)

In the West, we speak of satay or saté in reference to the famous Indonesian peanut sauce; this is actually a mistake. In Indonesian, the term *sate* designates marinated skewers that are grilled and then served with various sauces. The one that Westerners have focused on is a thick peanut sauce, delicious and rich, hence the association between the word satay and this peanut preparation – which is actually called *bumbu kacang*. Here is the recipe for these delicious skewers, in their tofu and tempeh version, with their fabulous peanut sauce.

🕐 prep **20 min** (+ marinate **1–12 hr**) 🕐 cook **10–20 min** 🌱 vegan 🍽 4 servings

• 7 oz firm or extra-firm tofu • 7 oz tempeh • 4 Tbsp fried shallots
• 4 calamansi lemon or 2 limes • Steamed rice, for serving • Vegetable oil

For the marinade
• 4 cloves garlic • 2 Tbsp chopped palm sugar or brown sugar • 2 Tbsp tamarind juice
• 1 Tbsp soy sauce • 1 Tbsp ground coriander • 3 Tbsp thick sweet soy sauce (*kecap manis*)

For the sauce
• 3 cloves garlic • 3–5 red Thai chiles (or more) • Boiling water, as needed
• ¾ cup unsalted roasted peanuts • 2 Tbsp chopped palm sugar or brown sugar • 2 Tbsp tamarind juice • 7 Tbsp water • 1 Tbsp thick sweet soy sauce (*kecap manis*) • 1 tsp salt

If you are using firm tofu, wrap it in several layers of paper towels and press it between two plates to drain for at least 1 hour. Cut the tofu and tempeh into cubes or 1-inch squares.

In a large bowl, combine the garlic with all the other marinade ingredients. Add the tofu and tempeh and mix to coat all the pieces. Cover and let marinate in the fridge for at least 1 hour or up to overnight, to marry the flavors. Soak bamboo skewers in water during this time, so they won't burn when grilled.

To make the sauce, start by placing the garlic and chiles in a heatpoof bowl and cover them with boiling water. Let steep for about 10 minutes, then drain. In a food processor, purée them and add the remaining sauce ingredients, continuing to purée until you get a creamy consistency. Adjust the amount of water if necessary.

Preheat a grill or broiler. Thread about 4 pieces of tofu and tempeh onto each skewer. Brush the skewers with oil and place on the grill for 5–8 minutes per side or under the broiler for about 10 minutes per side, or until you get a nice golden brown color.

Serve with the sauce, fried shallots, and citrus, as well as rice.

Note If you want the tofu to really absorb the flavors of the marinade, use extra-firm tofu, cut it into cubes as indicated in the recipe, and place it in the freezer in a bag for 24 hours. Take it out of the bag and leave it to thaw in the refrigerator for 24 hours on a plate covered with several layers of paper towel. Then continue with the recipe as directed.

SPICY
TOFU SAMBAL
(Sambal goreng taukwa)

Sambal is a chili sauce or paste found in Indonesia, Malaysia, Sri Lanka, Singapore, and Brunei. There are dozens of regional variations – with fermented shrimp paste, garlic, sugar, ginger, tomatoes, or lime juice, for example. This simple and well-spiced version gives a kick to extra-firm or pressed tofu, whose dense texture will make you forget that it is a vegan product.

🕐 prep **10 min**   🕐 cook **15 min**   🌱 vegan   👥 **4 servings**

- 14 oz extra-firm or pressed tofu • 5 cloves garlic, minced
- 3 shallots, thinly sliced • 1 small tomato, coarsely chopped
- 2 Tbsp chile paste • 1 Tbsp thick sweet soy sauce (*kecap manis*)
- Vegetable oil • Salt • Steamed rice, for serving

Cut the tofu into cubes or rectangles. In a wok over medium-high, heat ½–¾ inch of oil and fry the tofu until it is browned on all sides. Drain the tofu on paper towels, and pour off all but 2 tablespoons of oil from the wok.

Mash the garlic, shallots, tomato, and chile paste in a mortar or food processor until you have a coarse paste. Heat the remaining oil in the wok and sauté this chile paste for about 10 minutes, stirring, until the smell of garlic and raw chili disappears. Add the fried tofu, stir, and cook for another 1–2 minutes. Serve hot with rice.

LAOTIAN
TOFU SALAD
(Larb taohu)

The *larb*, *laap*, *lahb* – I'll pass along all the possible transcriptions – is in itself a symbol of Laotian cuisine. There are variations of this salad of herbed meat in Thailand, Burma, and Yunnan; in Laos, it is prepared with lots of fresh herbs and eaten with sticky rice and raw vegetables. Traditionally, this is not a vegetarian dish at all, but tofu larb is found in some restaurants these days. And it's super good.

🕐 prep **15 min**   🕐 cook **10 min**   🍃 vegan   ♨ **4** servings

- 14–16 oz firm tofu, cut into 1-inch cubes • 2½ Tbsp sticky rice (uncooked)
- 3 Tbsp soy sauce • 2 Tbsp lime juice • ½ tsp pepper
- 2 green onions, thinly sliced (green part only) • 3 Tbsp minced mint leaves
- 3 Tbsp minced cilantro leaves • 2 red chiles, thinly sliced
- 2 shallots, very thinly sliced • Vegetable oil
- Cooked sticky rice, cucumber slices, tomato wedges and/or lettuce leaves, for serving

Blot the tofu dry with paper towels. Heat a good layer of oil in a wok or frying pan over medium-high heat and fry the tofu on all sides. Drain on paper towels and let cool.

Meanwhile, toast the sticky rice in a dry frying pan over medium heat, until it smells fragrant and turns a pretty golden brown color. Then crush the coarse grains of rice to a powder in a mortar or in a blender. Set aside.

Coarsely chop the tofu with a knife or hand chopper. Place it in a bowl and add the soy sauce, lime juice, and sticky rice powder. Mix thoroughly by hand. Add the pepper, green onion, herbs, and chile. Separate the shallot into rings and add them too.

Mix well, add a little soy sauce or lime juice if needed, and serve with hot sticky rice, cucumber slices, tomato wedges, and/or lettuce leaves.

Note   You can opt for a raw version, and not fry the tofu before chopping it.

Burma

တိုဖွား
Thai
ပဲ့ပြား

Tofu fabrication in Burma.

If one tries to classify Burma conventionally among the countries of Southeast Asia, it is another world. Wedged between India, China, and Thailand, covering almost half the coast of the Bay of Bengal and reaching the Himalayas, Burma presents a disconcerting geographical, climatic, and ethnic variety. Its cuisine (or its cuisines) includes many elements typical of Southeast Asia, but it is equally rich in ingredients that we associate more with the Indian subcontinent. Above all, this nation has its own culture, and dishes that cannot be found elsewhere. In short, it is exceptional enough to deserve a dedicated chapter, especially when we talk about tofu.

Soybean tofu exists in Burma. They call it *pè bya*. It is very firm to extra-firm, and mainly consumed by the Chinese community. The rest of the population does not eat it, and so remains fairly marginal. The tofu that is seen everywhere, the true tofu for the Burmese, called *tohpu*, is a completely different product that does not have the same appearance, taste, or texture, and is not prepared in the same way. It is usually made with pigeon peas in the Shan State, and made with so-called Indian chickpeas (the desi type, small with a yellow interior) in the rest of the country – and sometimes the two are mixed. Unless you are very knowledgeable about peas, you will have trouble distinguishing pigeon peas from Indian chickpeas once they are shelled, peeled, and split: they are bright yellow, about the same size, and exactly the same shape.

BRIGHT YELLOW TOFU

Shan yellow tofu and Burmese tofu are also almost indistinguishable, visually or flavor-wise. These two products are both bright yellow (more or less, depending on which peas are used and whether or not turmeric is added), have a perfectly smooth texture, and are extremely pleasant. They are flexible and dense, while offering fabulous unctuousness on the palate. Marvelous! Their flavors are very similar; they are so rich and buttery, they bring to mind nuts, more than chickpeas. If you are into chickpeas, you should fall in love with Burmese pea tofu. By the way, they have absolutely nothing to do with soy tofu. It's possible to remain completely indifferent to the huge variety of soy tofus that exists in the Far East, find them all completely useless and uninteresting, and simultaneously devote yourself to the cult of yellow Shan tofu.

I specify "yellow" Shan tofu because there is yet another similar product in the same region, which is simply called Shan tofu (*hsan tahpo*). It is white, rice-based, firm and supple, and very much like the "rice tofu" from southwestern China, called *mi dòufu* – it's almost exactly the same. Similarly, the regions bordering Burma in China also have a yellow pea "tofu" called *jīdòu liángfěn*. Culinary traditions don't stop at borders. Often, Burmese tofu will be called Shan tofu, and vice versa. Even if it is actually Shan yellow tofu. Often yellow tofu will be made with a mixture of chickpeas and pigeon peas, and we won't even know what to call it. The basic thing to remember to simplify all this is that in Burma, the tofu is yellow, very good, and made from local peas. Let's not try to classify things too rigidly, especially in a country of such diversity, where more or less everything in the kitchen is artisanal and informal.

TOFU TYPES & USES

YELLOW TOFU

Yellow tofu can be made from pigeon peas or Indian chickpeas, or a mixture of both. Its great distinction, beyond the raw material not being soybeans, is that it does not need to be curdled and pressed. It is obtained by soaking ground or peeled and split peas to hydrate and soften them. They then grind the peas if needed (not needed if they are already ground) with water, and filter the mixture to get a kind of raw pea milk. They add a little salt and a pinch of turmeric to heighten the yellow color if desired, and simply cook this "milk" by shaking it vigorously. When it has thickened up, they pour it into a mold and let it set. This preparation is very similar to that of Provençal *panisses*, but the result obtained is of incomparable delicacy.

Yellow tofu can be eaten in a salad – it's excellent this way – or stir-fried, fried, twice fried, fried in chips. As it is very dense and flexible, it can also be cut into extremely thin slices, dried, and then fried to make puffed crackers. Finally, it can be served still hot, before it sets, when it is wonderfully smooth. It can then coat other ingredients – generally noodles – and form a kind of very rich sauce. It is also common to combine this "cream" with fried yellow tofu.

Tofu + tofu = love.

SOYBEAN TOFU

Classic soybean tofu is made by blending and filtering soaked soybeans to extract "milk." This soy milk is curdled by adding magnesium chloride, calcium sulfate, or a mixture of the two, and the curds are finally pressed to obtain a block of tofu. It is a product that exists in Burma, but it is found only within the Chinese community. It is very firm to extra-firm, which helps it keep longer. Other Chinese tofu foods, such as puffed tofu or fermented tofu, are also available – but marginal. Burma is extremely rich in legumes of all kinds, which overshadow soybeans. And the product that the Burmese call tofu (*tohpu*) is made only with other legumes.

Burmese yellow tofu (4) is generally made from pigeon peas (3). It is excellent fried (1)
or cut into thin strips and dried (2) then fried to make puffed crackers.

SHAN COUNTRY
YELLOW TOFU
(Won tahpo)

This recipe was shown to me by Ma Kyi Kyi Khawg, a nice lady who prepares her tofu every morning at home to sell it on her little cart. It's not very complicated, although it may seem impressive. It's above all a good workout – it'll keep your arms in shape. When you have done it once, you gain confidence and you can repeat the process without a problem. What's more, yellow Shan tofu is so good that you'll want to try it again. And since you basically can't buy it outside of Burma, it is homemade or nothing! The split pigeon peas needed for this recipe are available in Indian grocery stores, and even Asian grocery stores in general. You can replace them with Indian split chickpeas (*chana dal*) if you can't find them.

🕐 prep **20 min** (+ soak **24–48 hr**) 🕐 cook **15 min** 🌱 vegan

Makes about 21 oz tofu (4–5 portions)
- **7 oz split pigeon peas (*toor dal*)**
- **½ tsp salt • 1 pinch ground turmeric**

In a large container, soak the peas in five times their volume of water for 24–48 hours. Rinse them several times with clean water, drain, then measure their volume again. Add twice their volume of water. Blend everything (with an immersion blender, ideally) as finely as possible. Pass this mixture through a sieve lined with cheesecloth. When the cloth is full of solid residue, pour a little water on it and squeeze it to collect as much juice as possible. Add the salt and turmeric.

In a cast-iron wok or casserole pan over medium heat, heat 10 cups of water. When it comes to a simmer, pour the pea "juice" into it and stir vigorously and continuously with a wooden spatula. After about 8 minutes, the dough will start to thicken. Continue cooking and don't stop stirring – otherwise it will spatter, and not only will it burn, but it will get all over the walls. When the dough is almost too thick to be pourable, it is ready.

(continued)

Pour it as quickly as possible into a heatproof glass or ceramic mold – a small rectangular baking dish or gratin dish is ideal. Smooth the surface with wet fingers. Let cool to room temperature, then place in the refrigerator for a few hours. Unmold the tofu by placing a plate over it and turning over the mold and the plate together. If it does not come out immediately, you can run the wet blade of a knife along the sides of the dish. Store the tofu on a plate in the refrigerator, wrapped in paper towels or a clean cloth. It will release water over time and become firmer, which is ideal for cooking. I recommend elsewhere to let it drain like this for at least 1 hour before using it in any recipe.

Note If you are kind of useless, a little lazy, or a complete faker, refer to the next recipe, faster, identical at the end, but much simpler at the beginning.

BURMESE TOFU
(Tohpu)

For those who like shortcuts, here is the recipe for Burmese tofu, which is simpler and faster to make than Shan yellow tofu, but with basically identical results. You will only get the characteristic supple, fine, and incredibly smooth texture by using Indian chickpea flour (*chana besan* or *gram* flour), which is easy to find in Indian grocery stores, and even Asian groceries in general – for example, I've bought it from a Vietnamese grocery in Antibes and a Philippine market in Cannes! If you use classic Mediterranean chickpea flour, you will end up with something very like the Provençal specialty *panisse*. Very similar to Burmese tofu, *panisses* have a much grainier and less supple texture – more "rustic," so to speak.

⏱ prep **5 min** (+ soak **2–12 hr**)   ⏱ cook **15 min**   🌱 vegan

Makes about 21 oz tofu (4–5 portions)
• 1 cup extra-fine Indian chickpea flour • 2²/₃ cups water • ½ tsp salt
• 1 pinch ground turmeric

In a mixing bowl, combine the chickpea flour with 1¼ cups of water. Whisk or blend if there are any lumps. Pass through a sieve covered with cheesecloth to get an extra-fine consistency. If the flour is fine, this operation will be very quick. Squeeze the cheesecloth to collect all the juice. Add the salt and turmeric, blend, and let stand for 2–12 hours. Sediment will form at the bottom of the bowl.

In a cast-iron wok or casserole pan over medium heat, heat 1¹/₃ cups of water. Meanwhile, stir the flour mixture to incorporate the sediment and get a kind of pancake batter. When the water simmers, pour the mixture into it and mix vigorously and continuously with a wooden spatula. After about 8 minutes, your arms will hurt, but the dough will suddenly start to thicken. Continue cooking and keep stirring. When the dough is almost too thick to be pourable, it is ready.

Pour it as quickly as possible into a heatproof glass or ceramic mold – a small rectangular baking dish or gratin dish is ideal. Smooth the surface with wet fingers. Let cool to room temperature, then place in the refrigerator for a few hours.

Unmold the tofu by turning placing a plate on top and turning over the mold and plate together. If it does not come out immediately, you can run the wet blade of a knife along the sides of the dish. Store the tofu on a plate in the refrigerator, wrapped in paper towels or a clean cloth. It will release water over time and become firmer, which is ideal for cooking. I recommend elsewhere to let it drain like this for at least 1 hour before using it in any recipe.

BURMESE
TOFU & NOODLE SALAD
(Hsan tohpu thohk)

This salad from the Shan State is a more complete and substantial dish than the basic Burmese tofu salad because it contains rice noodles. Apart from that, we find the same typical flavors – tangy, sweet, salty – and a delightful mixture of textures. This recipe never disappoints and can be arranged to suit anyone's taste. A treat at any time of day, from breakfast to dinner.

🕐 prep **15 min** 🌱 vegan 🍴 **4** servings

- 14 oz Burmese tofu (see page 253) • 14 oz rice vermicelli • Boiling water, as needed
- 4 tsp brown sugar • 4 tsp water • 8 tsp peanut oil
- 2 tsp ground turmeric • 4 tsp tamarind juice
- 8 tsp soy sauce • 3 Tbsp crushed peanuts
- 3 Tbsp crushed white sesame • 4 Tbsp minced cilantro • 4 tsp fried garlic

Cut the Burmese tofu into irregular strips about 1½–2 inches long and ¼–½ inch thick. Place the rice vermicelli in a heatproof container and cover it with boiling water. Stir from time to time until the noodles soften. After a few minutes, they should be cooked but not mushy; taste to check, then drain and rinse with cold water, shaking them in the colander.

Meanwhile, make a brown sugar syrup by briefly heating the sugar and water in a small saucepan over low heat until the sugar is completely dissolved. Let cool. Prepare a turmeric oil by very briefly heating the peanut oil in a small saucepan over low heat with the turmeric until the oil has a uniform color.

In 4 bowls or soup plates, divide the tofu strips, rice vermicelli, sugar syrup, turmeric oil, tamarind juice and soy sauce, then nicely arrange all the rest of the herbs and condiments. Everyone should mix their bowl of salad before devouring it.

BURMESE
TOFU SALAD
(Tohpu thokh)

This delicious salad is sold all over Burma, prepared quickly in street stands. It is very colorful and perfectly representative of Burmese taste: it includes yellow tofu – rich, pleasantly smooth, and not bland at all – as well as crunchy raw cabbage and fresh cilantro in a slightly spicy, tangy, sweet salty sauce, finished with turmeric oil. Fried shallots are essential and give it crispness and character. The cabbage is not always involved, but it would be a shame to skip it, both for taste and texture.

🕐 prep **15 min** 🌱 vegan 🍽 **4** servings

- 1 lb Burmese tofu (see page 253) • 4 tsp brown sugar • 4 tsp water • 3 Tbsp peanut oil
- 2 tsp ground turmeric • 4 tsp chickpea flour • 4 oz sweet cabbage, thinly shredded
- 4 Tbsp minced cilantro • 2 tsp red chile flakes • 8 tsp soy sauce
- 4 tsp tamarind juice or lime juice • 4 Tbsp fried shallots

Cut the Burmese tofu into irregular strips about 1½–2 inches long by ¼–½ inch thick.

Make a brown sugar syrup by briefly heating the sugar and water in a small saucepan over low heat until the sugar is completely dissolved. Let cool. Prepare a turmeric oil by very briefly heating the oil in a small saucepan over low heat with the turmeric until the oil has a uniform color. Let cool. Quickly toast the chickpea flour in a dry pan over medium heat, stirring so that it colors without burning.

Mix the tofu strips with the shredded cabbage, cilantro, chili flakes (skip these if you don't like it spicy), soy sauce, brown sugar syrup, tamarind or lime juice, turmeric oil, toasted chickpea flour, and fried shallots. Divide among 4 bowls or soup plates.

You can prepare a little more of each of the condiments and serve them at the table so diners can adjust the seasoning of their salads to their taste.

BURMESE
TOFU CURRY
(Tohpu gyet)

A Burmese breakfast favorite, this very quick curry is quite simple but rich in flavor. Not a cacophony of various spices, but just a few easy-to-find fresh ingredients are enough to quickly make a healthy and nutritious dish that will appeal to as many people as possible. The amount of chili can obviously be adjusted according to individual preferences. Serve with basmati or jasmine rice. Guaranteed success! And for food lovers who don't mind an extra step, the tofu can be panfried before being added to the curry.

prep **10 min**   cook **10 min**   vegan   **4** servings

- 3 shallots • 3 cloves garlic • 2 tsp minced root ginger
- 6 Roma tomatoes • A few sprigs of cilantro • 2 green onions
- 1 green chile • 1 lb Burmese tofu (see page 253)
- 1 tsp chile powder • 1 tsp ground turmeric • Peanut oil
- Salt • Sugar, if needed • Steamed rice, for serving

Finely chop the shallots, garlic, and ginger. Dice the tomatoes. Cut the tofu into rectangles or squares about 1½ inches square, ½ inch thick. Coarsely chop the cilantro, including the stems, and chop the green onion and chile.

Heat a wok or large frying pan over medium-high heat, heat a little oil. Sweat the shallots until they are translucent, stirring almost all the time. Add the garlic, ginger, the white part of the green onions, the chile powder, and the turmeric, and stir-fry for a few more minutes, continuing to mix and toss.

Add the tomatoes and green chile, season with salt, mix well and continue stir-frying in the same way for a few minutes. Taste: if the tomatoes seem too acidic, you can add a little sugar. Add the tofu and cook for about 2 minutes more, stirring. Taste and adjust the seasoning if needed. Serve the curry with rice, sprinkled with cilantro and the green part of the green onions.

Note   I recommend Roma tomatoes for this recipe, as they are similar to the varieties used in Burma.

FRIED TOFU,
BURMESE STYLE
(Tohpu gyaw)

Anyone who likes fried *panisses* will be absolutely crazy about fried Burmese tofu. The crispy crust contrasts even more with the light and silky interior, with its characteristic taste of butter and hazelnut. It's hard not to buy a truckload of them when you pass a stand on a Burmese street. But you have to elbow your way in, the fans are legion...and it's not hard to see why.

🕐 prep **2 min** + (soak **1–12 hr**) 🕐 cook **10–20 min** 🌱 vegan

For 12 pieces
• 14 oz Burmese tofu (see page 253) • 2 tsp sugar • 2 Tbsp water
• 2 Tbsp soy sauce • 1 red chile, thinly sliced
• 1 clove garlic, minced • 2 Tbsp tamarind juice or citrus juice
• 2 Tbsp minced cilantro (optional) • Oil for deep-frying

For best results, you need a very firm tofu. Wrap your block of tofu in several layers of paper towel and place it on a plate, weighted down with another plate. Leave it in the fridge for at least 1 hour and up to overnight or even 24 hours.

You can prepare the sauce in advance: heat the sugar with the water in a small saucepan until it is dissolved. Mix it with soy sauce, chile, garlic, tamarind juice, and cilantro. If you don't like chile, don't use it; ditto with cilantro. You can, optionally, replace the tamarind with lime or lemon juice.

Cut your tofu into rectangles 3½–4 inches long by 1–1½ inches wide and about ¾ inch thick. In the middle of each rectangle, make a notch or two about 2 inches long. Place the tofu rectangles on paper towels and gently blot them with another sheet to remove excess moisture.

Heat 1¼ inch of oil in a large sauté pan or wok to about 350°F. Add half of the tofu rectangles and fry on each side for about 2 minutes, until they are golden brown. Place on a wire rack and repeat to fry the rest of the tofu. Serve hot and eat with your fingers, dipped in the sauce.

BURMESE
TWICE-FRIED TOFU
(Hnapyan gyaw)

This very crispy fried tofu is the perfect accompaniment to an aperitif. Admittedly, it is not the most diet-conscious, but boy is it good! Accompanied with a tangy and spicy sauce, these little golden triangles go down very easily. Be careful, however, not to gobble down to many – they are quite dense – or you won't have room for the rest of the meal.

⏱ prep **2 min** (+ soak **1–12 hr**) ⏱ cook **10–20 min** 🌱 vegan

For 15–20 triangles
• 14 oz Burmese tofu (see page 253) • 2 tsp sugar • 2 Tbsp water
• 2 Tbsp soy sauce • 1 red chile, thinly sliced • 1 clove garlic, minced
• 2 Tbsp tamarind juice or citrus juice • 2 Tbsp minced cilantro (optional) • Oil for deep-frying

For best results, you need a very firm tofu. Wrap your block of tofu in several layers of paper towel and place it on a plate, weighted down with another plate. Leave it in the fridge for at least 1 hour and up to overnight or even 24 hours.

You can prepare the sauce in advance: heat the sugar with the water in a small saucepan until it is dissolved. Mix it with soy sauce, chile, garlic, tamarind juice, and cilantro. If you don't like chile, don't use it; ditto with cilantro. You can, optionally, replace the tamarind with lime or lemon juice.

Cut the pressed tofu into 1- to 1½-inch triangles about ½ inch thick. Place the triangles on paper towels and gently blot them with another sheet to remove excess moisture.

Heat 1¼ inches of oil in a large frying pan or wok to around 340°F for relatively slow frying. Place half of the triangles in the oil and let them fry for about 2 minutes on each side, until they are golden. They should not brown. If they do, the oil is too hot.

Drain the triangles on paper towels and place them on a rack. Repeat to fry the rest of the triangles. When they are ready, fry the first half a second time in the same way. Again, the tofu should color nicely and become crisp without browning. Do the same with the rest of the tofu. Serve hot and eat with your fingers, dipped in the sauce.

SHAN NOODLES
WITH WARM TOFU CREAM
(Tohpu nwe)

They do gladly eat this dish for breakfast in the Shan State – it makes a great start to the day – but it's not the sort of venture you begin the minute you wake up. It is not very complicated to make, but a little time-consuming, and it's best to be wide awake for it. So, tackle it for a weekend brunch, lunch, or dinner, and you will not regret it: it is a wonderful dish. There are so many textures, from meltingly soft to the crunchy, so many flavors, from sweet to salty, it's fabulously comforting without being heavy, it sticks to the ribs but it's also digestible.... Absolutely worth a try.

⏱ prep **20 min** (+ soak **2 hr**) ⏱ cook **20 min** 🍃 vegan 👥 **4** servings

- 1¼ cups extra-fine Indian chickpea flour (*chana besan* or *gram* flour) • ½ tsp salt
- ¼ tsp ground turmeric • 3 shallots • 3 cloves garlic • 2 tsp minced root ginger
- 4 Roma tomatoes • 14 oz rice vermicelli (or thin, flat rice noodles) • Boiling water, as needed
- 4 tsp brown sugar • 4 tsp water • 4 Tbsp fried shallots or 4 tsp fried garlic
- 1 tsp ground paprika • 4 tsp crushed toasted sesame seeds • 4 tsp crushed toasted peanuts
- 4 pinches red chile flakes • 4 Tbsp soy sauce • 4 Tbsp mustard pickles, thinly sliced
- 2 green onions, thinly sliced • 1 lime • Peanut oil • Salt

In a mixing bowl, combine the chickpea flour with 2 cups of water. Whisk or blend if there are any lumps. Add the salt and turmeric, blend, and let stand for 2 hours. Sediment will form at the bottom of the bowl.

Finely chop the shallots, garlic, and ginger. Dice the tomatoes. Place the rice vermicelli in a heatproof container and cover with boiling water. Stir them from time to time until they soften. After a few minutes, they should be cooked but not mushy; taste to check, then drain and rinse with cold water, shaking them in the colander. Divide them among 4 large bowls or soup plates, and set aside.

(continued)

Make a brown sugar syrup by briefly heating the sugar and water in a small saucepan over low heat until the sugar is completely dissolved. Set aside.

In a wok or large frying pan over medium-high heat, heat a little peanut oil. Sweat the shallots until they are translucent, stirring almost continuously. Add the garlic, ginger, paprika, and turmeric, and stir-fry for a few moments. Add the tomatoes and salt and continue tossing and stirring for a few moments. Remove from the heat, cover to keep warm, and set aside.

In a cast-iron wok or casserole pan over medium heat, pour in half the chickpea flour batter without mixing it first. Stir vigorously and continuously with a wooden spatula while it heats. When it begins to thicken, stir the rest of the batter in the bowl to loosen the sediment that has formed at the bottom. Add the remaining batter and continue to stir for a few moments. When it has a nice consistency of heavy cream, immediately pour it over the noodles in each of the bowls.

Quickly top with the tomato mixture and all other ingredients: sesame seeds, peanuts, chile flakes, brown sugar syrup, soy sauce, green onion, fried shallots, mustard pickles, and a dash of lime juice per bowl. Serve at once. Everyone will mix the contents of their bowl while the tofu is warm and still creamy. It will coat the noodles deliciously and bind all the ingredients. The longer you wait, the more it will stiffen up. It's good that way too, but much better warm.

Notes Mustard pickles are found in Chinese and Vietnamese groceries; they are sold in brine in bags.

You can add a few vegetables to add more crunch to this dish: raw mung bean sprouts or shredded sweet green cabbage, some blanched bok choy leaves...

BURMESE
TOFU CRACKERS
(Tohpu gyauk kyaw)

Watch out! Here's the snack to end all snacks: Burmese tofu, made into puffed crackers or chips. Honestly, if you don't like them, that's because you don't like life. You can buy these little snacks at street stands in Burma, or eat them at a table in tea shops. They have the advantage of being very good cold, and can therefore theoretically be kept on hand, but do not expect to keep them long. You'll eat them all. And then you will start again, and you will eat them all again.

🕐 prep **10 min** (+ optional drying **12 hr**) 🕐 cook **10 min** 🌱 vegan

For 1 large bowl of crackers
• 10 oz Burmese tofu (see page 253) • 2 tsp sugar • 2 Tbsp water • 2 Tbsp soy sauce
• 1 red chile, thinly sliced • 1 clove garlic, minced • 2 Tbsp tamarind juice or citrus juice
• 2 Tbsp minced cilantro (optional) • Oil for deep-frying

For best results, you need a very firm tofu. Wrap your block of tofu in several layers of paper towel and place it on a plate, weighted down with another plate. Leave it in the fridge for at least 1 hour and up to overnight or even 24 hours.

Cut the tofu into slices, as thinly as possible. If you want to make ultra-crisp and lightly puffed crackers, place the tofu slices on a wire rack and let them dry in the sun or near a heater until they are completely dry, about 12 hours. They will curl nicely. If you want to make chips, skip this step.

You can prepare the sauce in advance: heat the sugar with the water in a small sauce-pan until it dissolves. Stir in the soy sauce, chile, garlic, tamarind juice, and cilantro. If you don't like chili, don't use it; ditto with cilantro. You can, optionally, replace the tamarind with lime or lemon juice.

Heat oil for deep-frying to 340–350°F and fry your tofu slices, dried or not, like chips. Do this in several batches to prevent crowding, and keep a sharp eye out: it goes very quickly – it only takes about 30 seconds. When the tofu is nicely browned and crisp (for the chips), or well puffed, golden, and crispy (for the crackers), use a skimmer to scoop it out of the oil and let drain on paper towels or a wire rack. Serve with the sauce alongside, and dip the chips in them before gobbling them up.

India

टोफू

டோஃபு

SO MANY PEAS, BUT NO SOYBEANS

China and India may share a border, but their cultures are decidedly different. South Asia produces huge amounts of legumes – chickpeas, lentils, and more – but became interested in soybeans only very recently. While soybeans were probably introduced to India around 1,000 years ago and adopted on a small scale by a few northern populations, the country really started producing soybeans only about 40 years ago. Until recently, therefore, there was no tofu in South Asia. It was found, of course, in Chinese communities, but it did not break out – just like in Europe.

In the 1970s, things changed. Seeing the potential of soybeans – this "miraculous" legume, according to farmers in the United States – India, Sri Lanka, and Nepal started growing it in large quantities. Their goal was to use it to resolve the food crisis of their poorest populations. However, they had to find uses for these unknown beans that appealed to the public. What seemed most promising to them at first was soy milk, which they intended to use to enrich the diet of babies and children. New soy products targeting the large vegetarian and vegan populations in South Asia were also developed, but their popularity only spread among the most wealthy and educated classes.

While South Asians saw the potential of soybean oil, soybean flour, and soy milk, they struggled with tofu. Soybean curd posed two major problems: it could not compete with paneer, fresh cheese made from cow's or buffalo's milk, since these two foods were very similar, but tofu seemed almost blasphemous to Indians. There was something insulting about the claim that tofu could replace a precious product made from sacred animals.

"SOY PANEER"

For the past thirty years, tofu, or "soy paneer" as it is often called, has been presented as the vegetable alternative to cow's milk cheese. In many recipes, it is a perfect substitute: they are the same color, have similar consistency and flavors, can be cut into cubes.... The Western desire to make tofu a substitute for meat, and in particular in steak, seems much more far-fetched.

Tofu production will probably never outpace that of paneer in South Asia, but this alternative has its advantages and potential for development. Soybean cultivation is easier and more profitable than cattle farming, and the transport of soybeans is less constrained than that of milk. In just a few decades, India has become the world's fifth largest producer of soybeans. For the time being, tofu is mainly produced for an affluent urban clientele; the main selling points are the 100 percent plant-based aspect of the product, health, and thinness, tofu being much less fatty than paneer. Soybeans, which were envisioned in South Asia as a solution to provide much-needed calories for the poor, have become a weight loss solution for the rich.

Tofu is found more and more often in place of paneer in mass-distributed food products. Many curries sold in India for reheating in the microwave now contain tofu. As elsewhere, we can assume that the growth of the South Asian tofu market will continue in the years to come. On the following pages you will find some delicious recipes that substitute tofu for paneer, such as those offered by a growing number of Indian bloggers and culinary authors.

In India, tofu is increasingly replacing paneer made from milk.

SPICED TOFU
PAKORA
(Tofu pakora)

Pakora is a delicious fritter that can be found under various names across the Indian subcontinent. They usually have vegetables encased with a chickpea dough, but can also be found with paneer filling. Tofu replaces this fresh cheese to perfection in this recipe, which is by no means bland, boring, or austere: on the contrary, it is festive, delicious, and rich in spice – without setting your mouth on fire. Serve with a green chutney.

🕐 prep **15 min** 🕐 cook **15 min** 🌢 vegan 🍴 4 servings

- 7 oz flexible medium to firm tofu or firm to extra-firm tofu
- Oil for deep-frying

Pakora batter
- ½ cup + 1 Tbsp Indian chickpea flour (*chana besan* or *gram* flour) • ½ tsp chile powder
- ¼ tsp ground turmeric • 1 tsp puréed root ginger
- 1 tsp garlic purée • 1 Tbsp hot oil
- 2 Tbsp minced cilantro • 1 pinch baking powder • 1 pinch salt

Spiced tofu seasoning
- ¼ tsp ajwain seeds • ½ tsp chile powder • ½ tsp garam masala
- ¼ tsp ground cumin • ¼ tsp ground coriander
- ½ tsp dried mango powder (*amchur*) • ¼ tsp ground turmeric
- ½ tsp *chaat masala* • Salt

In a large bowl, combine all the ingredients for the batter. Add 5¼ cups of water and mix until you get a homogeneous mixture. Set aside.

In a small bowl, combine the ingredients for the spiced tofu seasoning.

Cut the tofu into 1-inch cubes or rectangles, blot dry with paper towels, and mix them gently with the spiced tofu seasoning. You can also lay the tofu cubes flat and sprinkle them on all sides if you are afraid of breaking them.

Heat oil for deep-frying to about 350°F. Dip each spiced tofu cube in the batter and drop it in the oil. Do this in batches without crowding, and let the fritters fry until browned on all sides. Let them drain on a rack or paper towels. Serve warm.

TOFU CURRY
WITH BELL PEPPERS
(Kadai tofu)

Curries can be rather dry or more saucy; this one is on the dry side. It is close enough to its model, *kadai paneer*, that the two could be confused – except that this unorthodox version is vegan. Rich with juicy peppers, onions, and tomatoes, it doesn't require such an insane variety of spices as some other Indian recipes – and all the ingredients in it are extremely easy to find pretty much everywhere. You can, of course, adjust the amount of chile for a less spicy version.

🕐 prep **5 min** 🕐 cook **25 min** 🌱 vegan 🍴 **4 servings**

- 1½ Tbsp coriander seeds • 2–3 dried red chiles • 14 oz crushed tomatoes (fresh or canned)
- 1 large red onion, minced • 1 tsp puréed root ginger • 1 tsp puréed garlic
- 1 large green bell pepper, julienned • 1 green chile, split • ½ tsp garam masala
- 12 oz firm to extra-firm tofu, cubed • 2 Tbsp cilantro leaves, minced • Vegetable oil • Salt
- Steamed basmati rice, naan, and/or roti, for serving

Mash or blend the coriander seeds and the dried chiles until you get a coarse powder. Mix in the crushed tomatoes. Set aside.

In a frying pan or sauté pan over medium heat, heat a little oil. Sweat the onions until they are translucent. Add the ginger and garlic purées and brown them for a few moments, stirring, then add the spiced tomatoes. Fry, stirring, until the mixture looks like a paste and the oil begins to separate.

Add the bell pepper and continue cooking for 3–4 minutes, then add the green chile and about ½ cup of water. Mix well. When the bell pepper is halfway cooked, add some salt and the garam masala. Stir in the tofu. Cook for about 2 minutes more, then remove from heat and add the minced cilantro. Serve with basmati rice, naan, and/or roti.

VEGETARIAN BUTTER CHICKEN
(Tofu makhani)

The original version of this Punjabi dish, called *murgh makhani*, is better known as "butter chicken" outside of India. This is the Indian curry that everyone loves: its rich, creamy sauce is very mild, and appeals to both adults and children. Its looks might deceive you: it is mouthwateringly gorgeous, but surprisingly easy to make. Here is a vegetarian version based on *paneer makhani*, but with tofu as a cheese substitute.

🕐 prep **15 min** 🕐 cook **25 min** 🌱 vegetarian 👥 **4 servings**

For the sauce base
- 1 Tbsp butter • ¼ tsp cumin seeds • ½ tsp puréed root ginger
- ½ tsp puréed garlic • 1 large red onion
- 6 large cashew nuts (or 10 medium) • 1 tomato, diced • 1 green chile, minced (optional) • Salt

For the rest
- 2 Tbsp butter • ½ tsp cumin seeds • 2 cardamom pods • 2 or 3 cloves
- 2 bay leaves • ½ tsp puréed garlic • ½ tsp puréed root ginger
- 10 oz tomato purée • 1 tsp red chile powder • ½ tsp ground turmeric • 1 tsp garam masala
- 1 tsp ground coriander • 12 oz firm to extra-firm tofu, cubed • ¼ cup cream
- A few cilantro leaves • Salt • Steamed basmati rice, naan, and/or roti, for serving

Start with the sauce base: in a frying pan or casserole pan over medium heat, melt the butter. Sauté the cumin seeds and the ginger and garlic purées. Add the onion and cashews and brown. Add the tomato and green chile and continue cooking until the tomato is tender. Remove from the heat, let cool, stir to get a smooth paste, and set aside.

In the same pan, melt the butter and add the cumin, cardamom, cloves, and bay leaf, then the garlic and ginger purées. Sauté for 1–2 minutes, stirring, then add the sauce base and the tomato purée and mix well, cooking for 2 more minutes. Add the chile powder, turmeric, garam masala, ground coriander, and salt to taste and cook for a few more minutes, stirring. Pour about ¼ cup of water into the mixture to get a nice consistency of a slightly-too-runny sauce. Mix well, bring briefly to a boil, then add the tofu and cream and cook for another 3–4 minutes.

Serve sprinkled with cilantro leaves – you can also add a dash of cream – with basmati rice, naan, and/or roti.

TOFU & SPINACH
CURRY
(Palak tofu)

As unavoidable as chicken tikka masala in Indian restaurants in Europe or Stateside, *palak paneer*, or puréed spinach with fresh cheese, is a refuge for vegetarians. Only guess what: the restaurant version we are served is quite remote from the original, which is very spicy as it is full of fresh green chiles. Add them or don't, according to your preferences. I have, of course, replaced the paneer with tofu, making it a vegan dish.

🕐 prep **10 min**　🕐 cook **20 min**　🌿 vegan　👥 **4 servings**

- 1 large bunch spinach • 3 green chiles (or more, or less) • 1 tomato, peeled • 2 sprigs cilantro
- 12 oz firm to extra-firm tofu, cubed • 1 onion, thinly sliced • ½ tsp puréed root ginger
- ½ tsp puréed garlic • ½ tsp ground cumin • ½ tsp ground coriander
- ½ tsp ground turmeric • Vegetable oil • Salt
- Steamed basmati rice and/or Indian breads, for serving

Rinse your spinach well. In a frying pan over medium-high heat, heat 2 tablespoons of oil, add the green chiles, and sauté for 1 minute. Add the spinach, reduce the heat to medium-low, and stir and cook until completely wilted. Let cool, and then use a food processor to blend the spinach, tomato, and cilantro sprigs until you get a fairly smooth paste. Add a little water if needed.

Blot the tofu cubes dry with paper towels. In a frying pan over medium-high heat, heat a little oil. Brown the tofu cubes on all sides, then remove from the pan and set aside. Add more oil if needed and sweat the onion until it is translucent. Add the ginger and garlic purées, mix well, and cook for 1 minute. Add the ground cumin and coriander, and let cook for 1 minute more while mixing.

Add the spinach purée, turmeric, and salt to taste and mix well. Add a little water and cook, covered, for 4–5 minutes over low heat. Add the tofu cubes and mix to coat them with sauce. Cover again and cook for a few minutes, until you get a thick sauce. Serve hot with basmati rice and/or naan, roti, paratha...

TOFU CURRY
WITH GREEN PEAS
(Matar tofu)

Matar paneer, a curry of fresh cheese with peas, is, like *palak paneer* (with spinach), a typical safety dish for vegetarians in Indian restaurants. You can make dry or more saucy versions; it is rich in a very creamy sauce. Here, the paneer has been replaced with tofu and the recipe does not contain cream, making a vegan dish, but you can always add a few spoonfuls at the end of cooking for an even more delectable curry. It will still be vegetarian, along the same lines as tofu *makhani* (see page 274).

🕐 prep **10 min**   🕐 cook **25 min**   🌱 vegan   🍽 **4** servings

For the sauce base
- 1 tsp minced root ginger • 3 cloves garlic, minced • 1 large onion, minced
- 2 large tomatoes, diced • ¼ tsp ground turmeric
- 6 large cashew nuts (or 10 medium) • A few cilantro leaves • Vegetable oil • Salt

For the rest
- 1 small cinnamon stick • 2 cardamom pods • 1 small bay leaf • 1 tsp chile powder
- 1 tsp garam masala • ½ tsp ground coriander • 5 oz peas, blanched fresh or frozen
- 10 oz firm to extra-firm tofu, cubed • Vegetable oil • Salt
- Steamed basmati rice and/or Indian breads, for serving

Start with the sauce base: in a casserole pan or sauté pan over medium-high heat, heat a little oil. Sauté the ginger and garlic for 1 minute. Add the onions and sauté them until they start to brown. Add the tomatoes, turmeric, and salt to taste; sauté for 2–3 minutes, then lower the heat, cover, and cook until the tomatoes are tender. Add the cashews, remove from the heat, let cool, and then mix everything thoroughly. Set aside.

In the same casserole pan, sauté the cinnamon, cardamom, and bay leaf in a little oil. Add the sauce base, chile powder, garam masala, and ground coriander, and sauté, mixing until the oil separates from the sauce. Add the peas and 1 cup of water; mix well to get a nice loose sauce. Add a little more water if needed. Simmer to thicken, stirring constantly. Season with salt to taste. Add the tofu, cook for 2 minutes, covered, and serve with basmati rice or Indian breads.

BLACK PEPPER
TOFU CURRY
(Tofu kalimirch)

This recipe is little known outside India, although it's pretty great – at least, if you like pepper. That is the dominant spice in this well-spiced curry. Pepper has the advantage of waking up paneer, and it does the same for tofu. Thrills guaranteed! You can adjust the amount of pepper according to your tolerance and preferences.

🕐 prep **10 min**   🕐 cook **20 min**   🌱 vegan   🍴 **4** servings

Roasting spice blend
• ¼ tsp fennel seeds • ¼ tsp cumin seeds
• 2 cloves • 1 star anise pod • 1 cardamom pod
• 1 small cinnamon stick • 1 bay leaf

For the rest
• 1 large red onion, thinly sliced • 1 tsp minced root ginger
• 2 cloves garlic, crushed • 1 green chile, split • ¼ tsp ground turmeric
• 1 Tbsp coarsely ground pepper • 1 small tomato, puréed
• 12 oz firm to extra-firm tofu, cubed • A few cilantro leaves, thinly sliced
• Vegetable oil • Salt • Steamed basmati rice and/or Indian breads, for serving

In a dry small frying pan, roast the spice blend, then grind it in a mortar or spice grinder. Set aside.

In a sauté pan or casserole pan over medium-high heat, heat a little oil. Brown the onions until golden. Add the ginger, garlic, and green chile, and sauté for a few moments. Add the turmeric, roasted and ground spice mixture, half of the black pepper, and salt to taste, and sauté for a few minutes.

Add the tomato purée, mix well, cook for a few moments, then add the tofu cubes. Let them simmer for about 5 minutes, turning them regularly so that they brown on all sides. When the tofu is coated with spices, add the rest of the pepper, mix, and garnish with cilantro leaves. Serve hot with basmati rice or Indian breads.

TOFU
TIKKA MASALA

Chicken tikka masala, darling of Indian restaurants worldwide, has uncertain origins. It may have been invented in Britain in the 1960s by a Bangladeshi or Pakistani cook. There is not one recipe, but thousands of variations; their only common point is generally to contain chicken tikka. Here is a vegetarian version of this dish, using tikka tofu instead of chicken.

🕐 prep **15 min**   🕐 cook **20 min**   🍴 vegetarian   🍴 **4 servings**

- 1 tsp cumin seeds• 1 large red onion, minced
- 1½ tsp puréed garlic • 1½ tsp puréed root ginger
- 3 tomatoes, diced • 1 tomato, puréed • 1 tsp chile powder or ground paprika
- ¼ tsp ground turmeric • 1 tsp ground coriander
- 1 tsp ground cumin • A few cilantro leaves, minced
- 1 tsp garam masala • 10 oz tofu tikka (see page 282) • Vegetable oil
- Salt • Steamed basmati rice and/or Indian breads, for serving

In a sauté pan or casserole pan over medium-high heat, heat a little oil. Sauté the cumin seeds, then add the onion and sauté until golden. Add the garlic and ginger purées, and sauté for another minute.

Add the diced tomatoes and a pinch of salt, lower the heat, and cook, covered, until the tomatoes are tender. Add the tomato purée, chile powder, turmeric, coriander, cumin, and ½ cup of water; mix, cover, and cook for about 4 minutes, until oil separates from the sauce.

Add the cilantro leaves and garam masala and cook for a few more minutes, then add the tofu, mix well, and let heat through for a few moments. Serve with basmati rice or Indian breads.

Note   For the smooth and creamy sauce served in restaurants, add a little cream to the curry and stir it on before adding the pieces of tofu.

TOFU
TIKKA

Chicken tikka is undoubtedly the Indian recipe that is most integrated into worldwide eating habits. These pieces of marinated and skewered meat can be replaced by paneer for vegetarians, and paneer can be replaced by tofu, without anyone being the wiser. There are an infinite number of variations on this recipe; here is a general version for everyone, grilled in the oven.

🕐 prep **15 min** (+ marinate **2 hr**) 🕐 cook **20 min** 🌱 vegetarian 🍽 **4** servings

- 1 red bell pepper • 1 green bell pepper • 1 red onion • 10 oz firm to extra-firm tofu, cubed
- 8 oz Greek yogurt • ¼ cup Indian chickpea flour (*chana besan* or *gram* flour)
- 1 tsp puréed root ginger • 1 tsp puréed garlic • 1 tsp ajwain seeds
- 1–3 tsp chile powder • ½ tsp ground turmeric
- 1½ tsp ground coriander • 1½ tsp ground cumin
- ½ tsp garam masala • 1½ tsp dried mango powder (*amchur*)
- 1½ tsp *chaat masala* • 1½ Tbsp oil • 1 lemon or lime • Salt • Mint chutney or sauce of choice

Cut the bell peppers and half of the onion into squares the same size as the tofu cubes. Reserve the rest of the onion. Mix the yogurt, chickpea flour, and all the aromatics and spices in a bowl. Add the tofu and vegetable squares to the marinade. Mix well using your hands. Let marinate for at least 2 hours in the refrigerator.

Take the mixture out of the fridge and let come to room temperature, then arrange the vegetables and tofu on skewers. Preheat the oven to 425–450°F – you can also choose to use the broiler or grill.

Place the skewers on a broiler pan or grill rack and brush with oil. Let them cook for 15–20 minutes, turning them halfway through cooking so that all the sides are golden brown.

Serve the vegetables and tofu with freshly squeezed lemon, the rest of the thinly sliced raw onion, and a mint chutney or sauce of your choice. You can also use this tofu to make tikka masala tofu (see page 281).

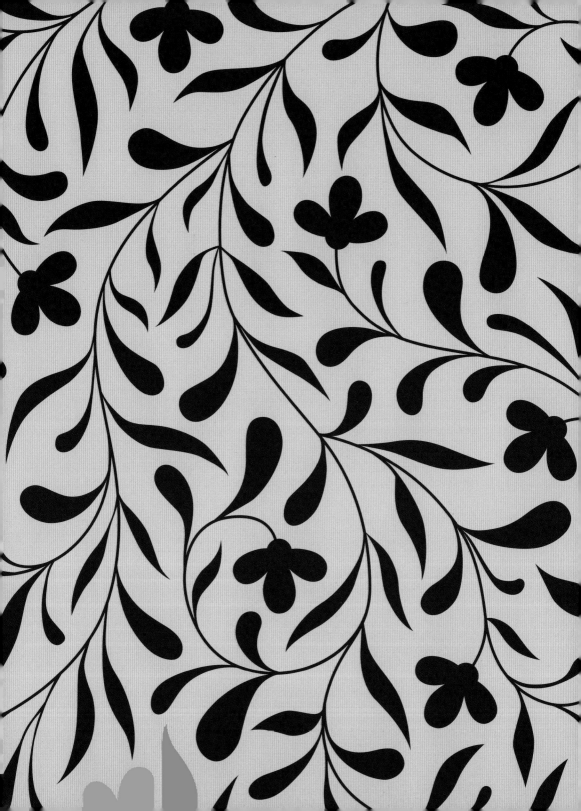

Elsewhere

AN ANCIENT ENCOUNTER

Europeans encountered tofu very early on. Since the sixteenth century, they saw this product – which they often qualified as "cheese" – during travels in Asia. Those who tasted it were pleasantly surprised. Italian traveler Domingo Navarrete reported in 1665 during his stay in China: "It is eaten raw, but more often boiled and garnished with herbs, fish, and other things. Eaten on its own, it is tasteless, but very good embellished as described, and excellent fried in butter. There is also dried and smoked [tofu], or tofu mixed with caraway seeds, which is best of all. [...] If I am not mistaken, the Chinese in Manila make it, but no European eats it because they have never tasted it..." Here is the rub. Aside from a few curious explorers, most Europeans who settled in Asia, in trading posts, colonies, and the like, had no desire to become familiar with tofu.

The Western reception of tofu has been chilly, and we have continued to snub tofu for several centuries. Several attempts to present this product to French, British, and other audiences were generally unsuccessful. It was not until the end of the twentieth century that tofu really began to establish itself in Western markets. The taste for Far Eastern cuisines and vegetarian dishes has enabled tofu to be taken a little more seriously, even if it still suffers from a bad image. Some see it as an immutable, tasteless white block with nothing to teach us in the kitchen; it is often reserved for vegetarians, implying that the only reason to eat tofu is because you're forced to do so by a specific diet.

A VEGETARIAN PRODUCT

It was with the hippie revolution that the vegetarian movement began in the West. The latter has been more successful in the United States and Britain than in my native France. For us, it was still difficult to find vegetarian options in restaurants even a short time ago. And despite the presence of Asian communities, especially in Paris, tofu has remained an unusual food. It didn't really catch on outside of these communities; some vegetarians consumed it, marginally, but the general public certainly did not want to eat it – at least those who knew of its existence. Until the late 1990s, there were few organic and health food stores, and few Asian grocery stores and restaurants. Tofu was not everywhere; far from it. And the one we sold in French shops was pretty bad, creating a lasting image of an inedible product.

Quite suddenly, in the early 2000s, tofu became much more common. The craze for Japanese cuisine in France made it known thanks to one dish in particular: miso soup with wakame and tofu. It is certainly not the most interesting use of tofu, but this soup became so popular and common in France that it has had the credit of making this ingredient known to the masses. At the same time, the number of vegetarians and vegans exploded, as did the market for organic and health food. Today, tofu is easily found everywhere, but not everyone eats it, and few people know what to do with it. It is still, for a large part of the population, "a vegetarian thing" that one mainly uses as a substitute for meat, instead of taking proper advantage of its innate characteristics. This is a mistake: it is the best way to be frustrated while eating tofu, and never learning its value in the kitchen. Tofu can be a source of joy, even for inveterate carnivores – I have seen them amazed and ecstatic while trying an *agedashi tōfu* (see page 114), or a *shēng cài bāo* (see page 52)...

In carrying out a small survey just among people around me, I realized that in France, tofu was even more closely associated with meatless diets than in Asia. It is still rare here that it is served in restaurants that don't specialize in Asian or "Asiatic" cuisines. But the fact that it is widely present in numerous organic markets and ordinary supermarkets has finally given it an image as a French product. Many people who consume tofu in France do not even think of going to Asian grocery stores to buy it.

GOOD TOFUS?

The quality of tofu available in France is better than it used to be, at least as far as firm tofu is concerned. The selection is much wider than it was twenty or even ten years ago, bringing a greater diversity of products and pushing quality up. Prices have come down. Nowadays, there is no longer any reason to make tofu at home, except for pleasure. As an activity it can be fun, but it takes time and space and is definitely not profitable. It's a little like making your own bread: you can do it if you like, but it will require a lot of effort for a result that may not be equivalent to the products made by professionals. Some specific tofus, on the other hand, are not easily found, especially outside large cities. Tofu pudding and Japanese-style silken tofu, for example, are much more difficult to find than firm tofu, so there are good reasons to want to make them yourself.

Although we find some very well-made tofus in regular shops today, not all are good. Firm tofu should always be sold in the refrigerated section, bathing in its whey inside a tray; unfortunately, you can also find a shelf-stable version. This tofu, which keeps for a very long time without any refrigeration, is as far from the real tofu as is cheese that can be kept for six months out of the fridge. It is generally abnormally rigid, with a strange coarse texture and an equally suspect color tending towards beige, even light brown. The texture is unpleasant on the palate, the taste is nonexistent at best, unpleasant at worst, and there is not much to do with it in the kitchen.

But that's not surprising, when you think about it: just as you wouldn't expect to find world-class croissants in a supermarket in a random Chinese village, you can't expect to find the best tofu in a Western supermarket. A mass-produced product in a country that doesn't have the generational know-how, the culture, or the raw material to do it properly will never compete with the achievements of small specialized artisans, born into the culture that invented it, with access to the best ingredients available. It's not even the same thing. It's such a different product that you can't compare them. An artisanal tofu in China or Japan and an industrial French tofu are a world apart – literally.

TOFU TYPES & USES

Most US supermarkets will carry at least one or two types of tofu, usually Chinese-style block tofu and Japanese-style silken tofu. Block tofu will be found in refrigerated cases near the produce or dairy, while silken tofu is more likely found in the Asian foods aisle. Although tofu is made from cooked soybeans and is pasteurized before sale, "raw" tofu should be kept refrigerated for freshness. Many stores also offer marinated cooked tofu.

Towns and cities with an Asian population will have supermarkets and Asian markets with much wider options: seasoned or flavored tofu, tofu skins and sheets, tofu noodles, ready-fried tofu in cubes or slabs, pressed and baked slices of tofu, and so on. Small jars of fermented tofu are also available, usually in red or white varieties, which are used more as a condiment thanks to their intense flavors.

Since tofu is so widely seen as a meat substitute in the West, our markets will also carry an array of soy-based "meat substitutes" that are sometimes designed and flavored to look and taste like meat products.

BLOCK TOFU

Block tofu is widely available and familiar. It comes in several textures: soft, medium, firm, and extra-firm.

Soft block tofu has a mild, milky flavor and a delicate texture similar to Jell-O. Pressing it is not recommended, as it is easily crushed. Its texture, so reminiscent of desserts, makes it a good vehicle for sweet flavors. It may be blotted dry and used raw, or puréed, or it can be deep-fried for an interesting texture contrast (think deep-fried ice cream).

Medium tofu is the next step up in firmness. It still has a relatively high water content and visible curds, and will break if handled roughly. Medium tofu is well suited to gentle cooking methods such as braising or baking.

Firm tofu is the basic, standard tofu used in many Western recipes. It is more flexible and holds up better to handling. It can be pressed to drain, sliced, battered or crusted, and will stand up to all kinds of frying, from deep-frying to panfrying or stir-frying. It's also a good choice for baking and boiling.

Extra-firm tofu is compact, with tight curds and a lower water content. It has a chewy texture that works well in hearty savory dishes. When you're hankering for crispy fried tofu, choose extra-firm tofu.

SILKEN TOFU

The next most common form of tofu in the West, silken tofu can also be found in a range of styles. Not as many as in Japan! But it is widely sold in soft, firm, and extra-firm versions.

The variety of tofu available in the West is immense: silken tofu (1), tofu in sausage form (2), tofu flavored with herbs (3), firm tofu (4), and smoked tofu (5).

Soft silken tofu is droopy and smooth. It's perfect for making dressings, sauces, and smoothies. It may appear in vegan recipes as an egg or yogurt substitute.

Firm or extra-firm silken tofu is firm only in comparison to soft silken tofu. They are made from more concentrated soy milk, and still retain a puddinglike texture. More forgiving than soft silken tofu, they may be handled enough to batter and lightly fry. They also give creamy body to desserts.

FLAVORED TOFU

Five-spice tofu, also known as dry tofu or tofu gan, is a dry, dense tofu that has been coated with seasonings (usually Chinese five-spice blend) and baked, giving its surface a dark brownish-purple color. It requires no prep, working well in dishes where you want a chewy texture and flavorsome taste, like a noodle dish or curry.

Another common extra-firm flavored tofu is smoked tofu, which is wrapped in tea leaves before smoking, giving it a caramel-brown color and evocative flavor. Like dry tofu, it requires no prep and can simply be sliced and tossed into your stir-fry or other preparation.

As interest in tofu grows, we Westerners are seeing more flavored baked tofus appear on the market: teriyaki, sesame ginger, tamarind, and Sriracha, to name a few. My best advice is to taste and see what you prefer!

LACTO-FERMENTED TOFU

From its name, you might think that lacto-fermented tofu has something to do with milk. This is not the case! It simply means tofu that has been fermented with probiotic microorganisms that then produce lactic acid. It's a process akin to making sauerkraut, or cheese. The fermentation adds flavor and supports gut health. However, the cultured tofus that we find here in the West are often a pale reflection of Asian fermented tofu. They do not have a suspicious appearance or a strong smell, and they barely taste different from fresh tofu... Here, these products are often presented as a vegan alternative to cheese, without going any further, and it is recommended to use them as is, in salads.

ABURAAGE & INARI

Inari are sweet- and-salty fried tofu pockets, made of deep-fried tofu called *aburaage*. These are cousins of Japanese *atsuage*: the big difference is that *atsuage* is fried as a block and not in thin slices. *Aburaage* and *inari* are both sold pressed flat, and may be cut and stuffed with rice to make a simple style of sushi called *inarizushi*. They also make a nice addition to soups.

TOFU-BASED PRODUCTS

Sausages, steaks, and other meat substitutes that are tofu based are common in organic stores. Since this is the role tofu is often relegated to – that of a substitute, and not an ingredient in its own right – this is not surprising. Some of these products are quite good and original, others are much less successful. In any case, they have little to do with the meat they are supposed to replace, other than their appearance.

ASIAN TOFUS

In Chinese, Japanese, Korean, Vietnamese, and other Asian groceries, you will
find all the other products described in
the corresponding pages of this book.
Some have no equivalent among domestic brands – like puffed tofu, flexible
tofu, tofu pudding, yuba, and so on. So
you have to go seek them out, and it's an
opportunity to get to know other types
of tofu, other textures, and other plea-
sures even within the realm of tofus that
we already know, such as block tofu and
silken tofu. You will see that a firm Vietnamese tofu is not at all the same as its
Japanese counterpart. That a Japanese
puffed tofu is decidedly different from
its Chinese equivalent. All this is great
fun and opens up many possibilities in
the kitchen. Armed with this book, you
should not lack inspiration to accommodate all of these varied products.

TOFU-OLIVE
CANAPÉS

To accompany an aperitif, you could just serve olives, or you could do something else with them. This slightly more elaborate preparation hardly takes ten minutes; tofu softens the strong flavors of olives and capers, and gives them a creamy texture, perfect for spreading. You can use green or black olives according to your taste, as well as the bread of your choice.

🕐 prep **10 min** 🌱 vegan

For about 12 pieces
- ²/₃ cup pitted green olives • 1 Tbsp capers • 4 oz firm tofu
- 1 Tbsp dried basil • 1 tsp red wine vinegar • 1 Tbsp olive oil
- 12 small slices whole-wheat baguette • 5 pitted green olives, cut into rounds, for garnish

In a food processor, coarsely chop the olives and capers, then add the cubed tofu, half of the dried basil, the vinegar, and the olive oil; blend again, briefly or for longer, depending on your desired texture.

Toast the bread slices and spread them with the olive mixture. Sprinkle with the remaining dried basil, and garnish each with an olive round.

CRISPY DEEP-FRIED TOFU

These little fritters, ideal for serving with an aperitif, will disappear quickly. They aim to please: super crispy on the outside, soft inside, richly flavored, and very tasty; it's hard to stop eating them. Served with sauce that can be more spicy or less so, tangy or sweet, they can also be served as kid's snack, or used to garnish a salad.

🕐 prep **10 min** 🕐 cook **20 min** 🌱 vegan 🍽 **4** servings

- 1¼ cups oatmeal flakes • 10 oz medium-firm to firm tofu (flexible)
- 1 tsp puréed garlic • 1 tsp puréed root ginger • ½ cup water
- ½ cup chickpea flour • Salt and pepper • Oil for deep-frying
- Lemon juice, ketchup, Sriracha sauce, or other sauce of choice

In a food processor, in batches, coarsely blend the oats. The goal is not to reduce them to a powder, but crushed flakes. Spread on a plate and set aside.

Cut the tofu into rectangles ¾ inch by 1¼ inches. Sprinkle with a little salt and pepper. You can also add ground spices of your choice, if desired.

In a bowl, mix the garlic, ginger, water, and chickpea flour; season with salt to taste. Dip each piece of tofu in this paste, coating generously. Then roll them one by one in the oatmeal.

Heat oil for deep-frying, and in batches to prevent crowding, fry the tofu until golden brown on all sides. Drain on a rack or paper towels, and serve hot or warm with lemon, ketchup, Sriracha, or your favorite sauce.

VEGAN TZATZIKI

Replacing Greek yogurt with blended tofu is super easy, and may even go unnoticed! This simple trick allows you to put together an excellent vegan tzatziki for anyone who consumes no milk.

🕐 prep **15 min** (+ salt **30 min**) 🌱 vegan

For 1 large bowl
- 1 Lebanese cucumber or ½ cucumber • 2 cloves garlic
- 4 Tbsp olive oil • 1 bunch dill • A few sprigs of mint, leaves picked
- 1 lb medium-firm or tender (flexible) tofu or extra-firm silken tofu
- Juice of 1 lemon • Salt

Scrub or peel your cucumber, slice it in half lengthwise, and scoop out the seeds with a spoon. Coarsely grate it, add ½ teaspoon of salt, and mix by hand. Let drain for at least 30 minutes in the fridge.

Finely chop or grate the garlic and combine it in a bowl with the olive oil steep. Roughly chop the dill. Finely chop the mint leaves.

In a food processor, blend the tofu until quite smooth. If you find its texture too thick compared to that of Greek yogurt, gradually add very small amounts of water, continuing to blend until you find the ideal consistency. Add half of the lemon juice, the garlic olive oil, and the herbs and blend.

Firmly but gently squeeze the grated cucumber over a colander to extract excess moisture. You can also squeeze it in a clean cloth, that's even easier. Add it to the prepared tofu. Season with salt to taste, adjust the flavor with a little lemon juice or oil if needed, and serve chilled.

WHEAT-FREE
TABBOULEH

Since tofu is considered an alternative to meat by Westerners, they often use it as a substitute for meat, simply swapping it into a dish to make a vegan version. However, do not hesitate to try something different. For example, leftover minced extra-firm tofu reminded me of crushed bulgur. So even though I don't like to simply consider tofu as a substitute for other things, it did work very well to create a wheat-free tabbouleh, perfect for anyone avoiding gluten.

prep 15 min • **vegan** • **4 servings**

- 4 oz extra-firm tofu • 1 bunch flat-leaf parsley, leaves picked
- A few mint leaves or ½ tsp dried mint
- 2 spring onions • 2 medium tomatoes, finely diced
- 2 Tbsp lemon juice • 1½–2 Tbsp olive oil • Salt

With a hand chopper (it's really better!), chop the tofu, parsley leaves, and mint leaves. Chop or slice the spring onions. In a deep plate, mix all these ingredients with the tomatoes, lemon juice, olive oil, and salt to taste.

TOFU
WITH CHILLED
APPLE-MUSHROOM BROTH

Tofu, especially when tender, is always good in broth – at least that's my opinion. This broth doesn't need to be hot; it can even be iced and the dish can almost play the role of a salad. Silken tofu, smooth and melting, seems right at home in this clear little soup, tangy, slightly sweet, and rich in mushrooms with nicely varied textures and flavors. Serve very fresh as a starter.

🕐 prep **10 min**   🕐 cook **5 min**   🌢 vegan   👤 **4** servings

- 1¼ cups vegetarian dashi (see miso soup recipe, page 116) or mushroom-soaking water
- ¾ cup apple juice • 3 Tbsp light soy sauce • ½ bunch *shimeji* mushrooms
- ½ bunch enoki mushrooms • 11 oz extra-firm silken tofu • A few leaves frisée lettuce
- A few leaves radicchio • 1–2 slices dried porcini mushroom
- 2 very fresh button mushrooms, thinly sliced
- 1 Tbsp sesame oil • Salt and pepper

Combine dashi, apple juice, and soy sauce. Taste and season this broth with salt to taste. Place in the fridge or freezer to cool.

Separate the *shimeji* and cut off the ends of the stems; roughly separate the enoki and cut off the bottoms of their stems as well. Blanch the enoki for about 1 minute in a pot of lightly salted boiling water. Drain, run them under cold water, and drain again. Blanch the *shimeji* for about 4 minutes in a pot of lightly salted boiling water. Drain, run them under cold water, and drain again.

Gently unmold the tofu onto a plate and cut into slices about ¼ inch thick. Arrange 3 or 4 slices in each of 4 bowls. Add the *shimeji*, enoki, and a few hand-torn leaves of frisée and radicchio to the bowls.

In a mortar with a pestle or in a spice grinder, blend or grind the dried porcini mushrooms to a powder.

Ladle the chilled broth into the bowls over the tofu. Add a few slices of raw button mushroom; finish each with a dash of sesame oil, a little salt and pepper, and a few pinches of dried porcini powder.

PINK RADISH
VELOUTÉ

This velouté is eaten hot or well chilled, depending on the season – both are excellent. It is a healthful and light starter, and is easy and quick to make. Recommended after a period of excess, whether you ate like a glutton for a few days or have a wicked hangover.

⏱ prep 20 min 🌱 vegetarian 👥 4 servings

- 2 bunches pink radishes • 1 spring onion
- 1 knob butter • 7 oz boiled potatoes
- ¾ cup water • 7 oz firm silken tofu
- Salt and white pepper

Trim and clean the radishes. Reserve two of them for the garnish. Roughly chop the white part of the spring onion. In a frying pan over medium heat, melt the butter. Add the radishes and onion, season with salt, and stir and roll them in the butter for about 3 minutes. Stir constantly so that they soften without browning. If necessary, you can lower the heat, cover the pan, and cook a little longer.

Mix the radishes and onion, the potatoes, the water, and the silken tofu. Season with pepper and additional salt if needed. If you want a chilled velouté, let it sit in the fridge or freezer for a few moments. If you want it hot, reheat it over low heat in a saucepan.

Serve sprinkled with some chopped green part of the spring onion and a few radish slices.

Note For a gourmet version, add 1 teaspoon of fresh cream per bowl. For a vegan version, replace the butter with vegetable oil.

WHITE ASPARAGUS, CRÈME FRAÎCHE & TOFU

This recipe was completely inspired by a wonderful dish created by Tatiana Levha at Le Servan restaurant. It was very beautiful, all white with its asparagus, *tosazu* cream, and small cubes of tender tofu. It was mild but its flavor was incredibly deep, thanks to the dashi and *katsuobushi*; he was delicious, well-balanced, so good. And above all, it was a smart dish: tofu was not used as a substitute for anything else or placed there for no obvious reason. It was perfectly in place in this mixture of French and Japanese flavors and textures. Here's something close to this inimitable dish.

🕐 prep **10 min** 🕐 cook **15 min** 🍴 vegetarian

For 4 starters
- 2 bunches white asparagus
- 10 oz flexible medium tofu • Salt and pepper • 1 tsp kombu powder

For the sauce
- ¼ cup crème fraîche • 2 tsp rice vinegar • 2 tsp mirin rice wine
- 1 tsp soy sauce • 1 tsp light soy sauce

Peel the asparagus spears and cut off the bases of their stems. Cook them in boiling salted water for 10–15 minutes, depending on their size, until they are tender but not mushy. While they are cooking, combine all the sauce ingredients in a saucepan with ½ teaspoon of kombu powder and heat over low heat, stirring until the sauce simmers.

Cut the tofu into ½-inch cubes. Drain the asparagus and cut into 1–1¼ inch pieces. Mix them with the sauce and the tofu. Season with salt and pepper to taste and sprinkle with additional kombu powder. Serve warm (it's good cold too).

LACTO-FERMENTED
TOFU

There are many methods of fermenting tofu, but most of them are quite tricky because they require the step of spontaneous fermentation in the open air. By immersing the tofu in brine (just like feta), you take much less risk. The transformation is not as radical as that of Chinese fermented tofu (*dòufuru*), but home-made lactofermented tofu is slightly salty and tangy, and its texture changes over time; it's a good way to flavor it to your liking.

🕐 prep **5 min** (+ press **1 hr**) 🕐 ferment **10 days+** 🌱 vegan

For one 12-oz jar
- 7 oz firm tofu, plain, herbed, or smoked
- ²/₃ cup 6% brine (²/₃ cup water + 1 tsp coarse salt)
- Aromatics of choice: lemon zest, rosemary, bay, chile... • Fine salt

Wrap the tofu in paper towels and drain it between 2 plates for 1 hour. Blot dry with paper towels. Cut it into cubes or slices and sprinkle them lightly with fine salt. Place the aromatics and spices of your choice at the bottom of a 12-oz jar, then add the tofu. If it is sliced, place it in the jar vertically. If it's in cubes, pack it in well.

Prepare your brine by dissolving the salt in the water. Pour it over the tofu and place a weight (a small glass or porcelain dish, or a plastic food bag filled with brine...) on the tofu and other ingredients to keep them immersed in the brine. Be careful not to fill the jar completely; Keep an inch or more free, because the brine may overflow during fermentation. You can use a larger size jar if it seems easier. Leave to ferment in a cool place, away from light, for 10 days. If mold forms on the surface of the liquid after 1 week, you can gently remove it with a clean spoon – since the tofu is submerged below, it will not be touched. Sprinkle a little salt on the area that seems problematic.

You can start taste-testing your tofu after 1 week, and continue the fermentation if you wish.

Note   The container and all utensils used must be clean and perfectly dry. Work with clean hands or wear sterile gloves. If in doubt – if you detect an unpleasant odor, a pungent taste, mold on the surface of the tofu, etc. – do not consume your tofu. For faster fermentation, you can add a little sauerkraut or kimchi juice to the brine; their bacteria will kick-start the fermentation process.

SOY-GINGER
LACTO-FERMENTED
TOFU

When tofu is fermented in brine, the change in its appearance and texture is not dramatic, but add a little soy sauce and it will be! Under the effect of a classic soy sauce (such as Kikkoman), the tofu turns brown and takes on a meltingly soft texture in no time. It also absorbs more salt, and therefore becomes a condiment to be used sparingly, rather than an ingredient to be used in large quantities. Mashed into a purée, it can add flavor to rice, salad dressings, and stir-fried vegetables, just like *dòufuru*.

🕐 prep **5 min**   (+ press **1 hr**)   🕐 ferment **10 days+**   🌱 vegan

For one 16-oz jar
- 10 oz plain firm tofu • ²/₃ cup 6% brine (²/₃ cup water + 1 tsp coarse salt)
- 3–4 Tbsp soy sauce • 3 thin slices root ginger

Wrap the tofu in paper towels and drain it between 2 plates for 1 hour. Blot dry with paper towels and cut it into cubes. Place the ginger at the bottom of the jar, then pack in the diced tofu.

Prepare your brine by dissolving the salt in the water. Stir in the soy sauce, then pour this mixture over the tofu and place a weight on its surface to keep it immersed in the brine (a small glass or porcelain dish, or a plastic food bag filled with brine...). Be careful not to fill the jar completely. Keep an inch or more free, because the brine may overflow during fermentation. Leave to ferment in a cool place, away from light, for 10 days. If mold forms on the surface of the liquid after 1 week, you can gently remove it with a clean spoon – since the tofu is submerged below, it will not be touched. Sprinkle a little salt on the area that seems problematic.

You can start taste-testing your tofu after 1 week, and continue the fermentation if you wish.

> **Note**   The container and all utensils used must be clean and perfectly dry. Work with clean hands or wear sterile gloves. If in doubt – if you detect an unpleasant odor, a pungent taste, mold on the surface of the tofu, etc. – do not consume your tofu. For faster fermentation, you can add a little sauerkraut or kimchi juice to the brine; their bacteria will kick-start the fermentation process.

VEGAN
GREEK SALAD

This would be sacrilege in Greece, but visually, you don't notice a thing. All the ingredients for the authentic Greek salad are here, except the sheep's milk feta, which has been replaced with fermented tofu. It has a texture quite similar to that of feta, although less creamy. Served sliced atop the salad, as is done in Greece, it's a perfect imposter for the famous cheese.

prep **15 min** | vegan | **4** servings

- 3 tomatoes • 1 medium red onion • 1 small bell pepper
- 1 Lebanese cucumber • 1 handful Kalamata olives
- 3–4 Tbsp olive oil • 1 Tbsp red wine vinegar
- 7 oz lacto-fermented tofu, plain or herbed (see page 303)
- 1 tsp dried oregano • Salt

Cut the tomatoes into quarters. Chop the red onion, seed and chop the bell pepper, and cut the cucumber into half-moons ¼ inch thick. In a large, deep plate or salad bowl, combine the tomatoes, onion, bell pepper, cucumber, and olives. Season with salt to taste, then drizzle with 3 tablespoons each of olive oil and vinegar. Toss.

Serve the salad topped with slices or cubes of fermented tofu, sprinkled with dried oregano, and finished with a drizzle of olive oil.

SESAME-BREADED
TOFU

To give tofu flavor and a crisp texture, nothing like breading it. It remains tender in its golden envelope, and it can be flavored at will: add spices, herbs, seeds, or nuts of your choice to the breading...I used pepper and sesame, but don't hesitate to change up this recipe and invent your own flavor profile. You can also use this breaded tofu to garnish wraps (see page 310) or a tasty mango and avocado salad (see page 312).

🕐 prep **10 min** 🕐 cook **10 min** 🌱 vegetarian 🍴 4 servings

- 1 lb medium-firm to firm tofu • 3 Tbsp cornstarch or potato starch
- 1 large egg, or 2 small • 3 Tbsp panko or other bread crumbs
- 2 tsp black sesame seeds • 2 tsp white sesame seeds
- ½ tsp onion powder • ½ tsp garlic powder
- Salt and pepper • Vegetable oil • Lemon juice or sauce of choice

If you're not in a hurry, you can start by draining the tofu for 30 minutes–1 hour, or soaking it in a bath of hot salt water for 15 minutes. Cut it into cubes or slices and blot dry with paper towels.

Spread the starch on a plate. In a deep plate, beat the egg(s) and season with salt and pepper. Spread the bread crumbs mixed on another plate and mix in the two sesame seeds.

Sprinkle the tofu cubes or slices with salt, pepper, onion powder, and garlic powder. Be generous. Dredge each piece in the starch, then dip it in the egg and coat with bread crumbs. Heat a frying pan over medium-high heat, add a generous splash of oil, and brown the breaded tofu pieces on all sides.

Serve at once with lemon juice or the sauce of your choice.

SUMMER VEGGIE & SESAME-BREADED TOFU WRAP

Wraps became common in France quite suddenly; these large wheat pancakes rolled up with various fillings are nothing more than burritos or *dürüm*, even if they are not presented as such. They are as practical to pack as a lunch and eat on the go as sandwiches, and can also be a nice accompaniment to an aperitif: if you cut the roll into slices, like Japanese maki sushi roll, you get cute bites to share. Here's a simple and delicious idea for stuffing your wraps: sautéed summer vegetables and breaded tofu.

🕐 prep **20 min**   🕐 cook **10 min**   🖖 vegetarian

For 4 rolls
• 1 red bell pepper • 1 yellow bell pepper • 1 zucchini
• 4 green onions or 2 spring onions • 4 large wheat tortillas or other wraps
• 8 strips of tofu breaded with sesame (¾ inch by 3 inches) • Vegetable oil • Salt and pepper
• Dipping sauce of choice (optional)

Cut the peppers lengthwise into strips a scant ¼ inch thick. Do the same with the zucchini. Remove the outer leaves from the green onions, and cut them in half lengthwise. If you are using spring onions, quarter them in the same way. The goal is to get strips to garnish the wrap.

In a frying pan over medium-high heat, heat a little oil. Sauté the green onions or spring onions briefly. Season with salt and pepper and set aside on a large plate. Do the same with the zucchini, the yellow pepper, and the red pepper.

On a wheat tortilla, arrange the breaded tofu on the side closer to you, a third of the way up the tortilla. Add 2 strips of green onion, a few strips of zucchini, and a few strips of bell pepper. Do not put too much, or the roll will not hold, and compact this filling well to form a large strip that occupies only the first third of the tortilla.

If you plan to eat these rolls like sandwiches, leave a few inches of space on the sides to fold up the edges of the patty (just like rolling a spring roll). Fold the sides of the patty over the filling, then roll forward, tightening the filling securely. Cut the rolls in half, or keep them whole and wrap them to pack and eat later.

If you plan to cut the roll into slices, no need to fold the sides, but you will have to roll even tighter. Cut the roll with a sharp knife into ¾-inch pieces, and serve on a plate with the sauce of your choice (they are also very good on their own).

MANGO-AVOCADO SALAD
WITH SESAME-BREADED TOFU & CHIMICHURRI

Sesame-breaded tofu goes with everything. Its crispness, reminiscent of croutons, makes it a perfect addition to salads, like this one. Super tasty, sweet-and-salty, and perked up with a delicious South American–style herb sauce, it's a real treat.

🕐 prep **10 min** 🌱 vegetarian 👥 **4 servings**

For the sauce
- 2 Tbsp red wine vinegar • 2 Tbsp thinly sliced cilantro
- 1 Tbsp thinly sliced flat-leaf parsley • 1 tsp thinly sliced fresh oregano
- 3 Tbsp olive oil • A few drops of Tabasco • Salt

- 1 head romaine lettuce • 2 avocados, diced
- 1 large mango, pitted and cubed • ½ red bell pepper, cut into strips
- 1 spring onion, thinly sliced • 10 oz sesame-breaded tofu (see page 308), cut into cubes

In a bowl, combine all the ingredients for the sauce.

Slice the romaine leaves into ¾-inch strips. Place them in a salad bowl and add all the other ingredients. Place the breaded tofu cubes last to keep them crisp. Just before serving, pour the sauce over the salad and toss.

VEGAN
POTATO SALAD

Here's an excellent potato salad for summer meals or picnics, and it's 100 percent vegan. No one will notice this if you don't talk about it; it is as good and delicious as a classic one studded with bacon. This dish is proof that tofu is not boring in itself: it all depends on what you make of it!

🕐 prep **10 min** 🕐 cook **20 min** (+ rest **30 min**) 🌱 vegetarian 🍴 **4–6** servings

- 5 oz vegan mayonnaise (see page 326) • 21 oz waxy potatoes
- A few sprigs of dill • A few cornichons
- 2 green onions or 1 spring onion • 1½ Tbsp cider vinegar
- 1 tsp whole-grain Dijon mustard • Salt and pepper

Start by preparing the vegan mayonnaise. Keep refrigerated while you make the rest of the salad.

In a saucepan, cover the potatoes with salted water; bring to a boil, then simmer for about 20 minutes, until they are tender. Drain and leave them in the colander, covered with a clean cloth, to steam for 10–15 minutes. Then uncover and let cool for another 15 minutes.

Meanwhile, prepare the rest of the salad: coarsely chop the dill, cut the cornichons into rounds, and chop the green onions.

In a salad bowl, combine the mayonnaise, vinegar, mustard, dill, pickles, and green onions. Season with pepper and mix. Set aside in the refrigerator.

When the potatoes are cool enough to handle, cut them into 1-inch pieces. Add them to the salad bowl, and mix the potatoes with the sauce. Taste and adjust the seasoning if needed, and place in the refrigerator again for at least 1 hour. Mix again before serving.

MEDITERRANEAN-MARINATED TOFU

This very simple marinade is just one example of the countless possibilities that tofu offers. Freezing the tofu beforehand helps it absorb the flavors especially well. The neutral flavor of tofu lends itself to all types of marinades, whether you're looksing for something spicy, sweet-salty, Asian, Indian... In summertime, this Mediterranean version is particularly pleasant in salads.

🕐 prep **30 min** (+ freeze **12 hr**)   🌱 vegan

For 1 block tofu
- 10 oz firm tofu • 1 Tbsp balsamic vinegar
- 1 Tbsp brewer's yeast • 3 Tbsp olive oil
- 1 tsp tomato paste • 1 tsp salt
- ¼ tsp pepper

A day ahead, drain the block of tofu and wrap it in cheesecloth or a clean towel. Place it on a plate in your freezer, and let freeze for at least 12 hours.

The next day, place the tofu under a stream of hot water to peel off the cloth, and immerse it in a pan of boiling salted water for about 10 minutes, or until completely thawed.

Drain it carefully, then wrap it in paper towels to blot dry. Let drain for at least 15 minutes, then unwrap it and cut into ½-inch cubes.

Mix the vinegar, yeast, oil, tomato paste, and salt and pepper to make the marinade and place the diced tofu in it, making sure all the pieces are coated. Leave to marinate for 5 minutes. Your tofu is ready be used in a salad, grilled, sautéed, etc.

WATERMELON SALAD
WITH MARINATED TOFU

Watermelon salad makes everyone happy in summer. To wake up this watery and very sweet fruit, nothing works so well as green onion and mint – a marriage that has become classic. Mediterranean-marinated tofu, with its balsamic vinegar and tomato flavor, is just what you need to perfect this refreshing starter.

⏱ prep 10 min 🌱 vegan 🍴 4 servings

- 1 lb cubed watermelon • 1 small red onion
- 10 oz Mediterranean-marinated tofu (see page 315)
- A few sprigs of fresh mint, leaves picked
- Olive oil • Salt and pepper

If needed, cut the watermelon into generous pieces that are still small enough to take a bite. Finely chop the onion. Place the watermelon pieces in a bowl with the onion, marinated tofu, and coarsely chopped mint leaves. Season with salt and pepper, drizzle with olive oil, and toss.

Note You can use the marinated tofu raw, or fry it for a few moments in its marinade.

TOMATO & TOFU
SALAD
WITH DATE DRESSING

This sweet-and-savory date sauce goes perfectly with small tangy tomatoes, and semi-firm tofu has a consistency reminiscent of mozzarella; this salad is an ideal starter for the middle of summer. If you hate cilantro – it happens – you can replace it with fresh basil.

🕐 prep **10 min** | 🌱 vegan | 🍴 **4** servings

- 2 dates • 14 oz mixed-variety tomatoes
- 10 oz flexible medium-firm tofu • 1 shallot
- A few sprigs of cilantro • 1 Tbsp balsamic vinegar
- 1 Tbsp soy sauce • 3 Tbsp olive oil

Soften the dates by letting them soak in a bowl of hot water while you prepare the other ingredients. Cut the tomatoes into quarters and dice the tofu. Chop the shallot, pick the cilantro leaves, and divide all these ingredients among 4 plates.

Drain the dates and combine them in a food processor with the vinegar, soy sauce, and olive oil. Blend until you get a smooth sauce. If it seems too thick, you can thin it with a little oil or water. Drizzle it over the plates.

ENDIVE SALAD

WITH
MISO-FERMENTED TOFU

Fermenting tofu in miso (*tōfu no misozuke*, see page 128) gives an astonishing result: like a cheese, tofu changes texture and taste over time, becoming more and more tender, salty, and strong. You can eat it with bread or rice and use it as a condiment, but it also works in salads. Endives complement this tofu like nothing else, with nuts and a little whole-grain mustard sauce as a bonus.

🕐 prep **10 min**   🌱 vegan   👤 4 servings

- 4 endives • 4 oz miso-fermented tofu (see page 128) • 1 Tbsp cider vinegar
- 1 tsp whole-grain Dijon mustard • 1 Tbsp water • 2 tsp brewer's yeast
- Salt and pepper • 3 Tbsp olive oil • ¼ cup shelled walnuts

Cut the endives as desired: some prefer large pieces, others like very thin slices, or you can leave the leaves whole as "boats." Cut the fermented tofu into small cubes. Coarsely crush the nuts, and place everything in a bowl.

Separately, mix the vinegar, mustard, salt (a few pinches, taking into account that the ripened tofu is already salted), water, brewer's yeast, and pepper to taste. Add olive oil in a thin stream while whisking, to create an emulsion. Pour this dressing over the salad, and toss just before serving.

Note You can adjust the quantities according to your taste and add a sliced or diced apple, always a welcome addition to an endive salad!

ARUGULA, FIG & SMOKED TOFU SALAD

Oh, beautiful salad! Freshness, a touch of bitterness, smokiness, sweetness, and a tangy counterpoint.... This very quick and simple starter is a delight. One hundred percent vegetable, it has a rich range of flavors and textures, but it is also a mine of minerals, vitamins, and protein. You can prepare it all year round by replacing the figs with other seasonal fruits (grapes, pears, plums, etc.).

⏱ prep **10 min**   🌱 vegan   🍴 **4** servings

- 6 purple figs • 7 oz smoked tofu
- 2 Tbsp balsamic vinegar • 5 Tbsp olive oil
- Salt and pepper • 4 oz arugula • 2 oz watercress
- 2 oz mâche

Cut the figs into quarters and the tofu into thin slices. Mix the vinegar and salt, then add the oil, beating for a moment with a fork to make a quick emulsion. Season with pepper to taste.

In a salad bowl, combine the arugula, watercress, and mâche (obviously well rinsed and spun dry), then the tofu and the figs. You can also arrange the salad flat on a large, shallow platter. Drizzle with dressing, and toss at the last minute.

WARM SALAD

OF BUCKWHEAT, ROASTED CARROTS & LACTO-FERMENTED TOFU

This main-course salad is not complicated to make, does not require ingredients that are difficult to find, and constitutes a healthy and balanced meal on its own. You can eat it warm or cold, prepare it in advance and take it on a picnic or to work, try it with different dressings if you are inspired.... All kinds of variations are possible.

prep **10 min** · cook **35 min** · vegan · **4** servings

- 3 carrots (orange, yellow, purple...) • 2 tsp cumin seeds
- 2 shallots, thinly sliced • 1½ cups kasha (toasted buckwheat groats)
- 7 oz lacto-fermented tofu (homemade, page 303, or store-bought)
- 2 Tbsp pomegranate molasses or lemon juice
- 3 Tbsp olive oil • 4 oz baby spinach leaves
- Vegetable oil • Salt and pepper

Preheat the oven to 350°F. Cut the carrots into strips; put them in a bowl and mix with a little salt, a little vegetable oil, the cumin seeds, and the thinly sliced shallots. Spread them in a single layer on a parchment-lined baking sheet and cook for about 35 minutes, turning them halfway through cooking. Check from time to time; depending on the vegetables, cooking time may take longer or shorter.

Meanwhile, cook the kasha: bring a pan of salted water to a boil and cook the grain for about 5 minutes, until it is tender. Drain, and cover if you want to keep the kasha warm.

Cut the tofu into cubes. Prepare the dressing by mixing pomegranate molasses and a little salt and pepper, then lightly emulsify with olive oil, pouring it in gradually while you whisk.

In a large bowl, combine the spinach, tofu, roasted carrots, and kasha. Drizzle with dressing, toss, and it's ready.

VEGAN MAYONNAISE

Containing no eggs, this mayonnaise will necessarily taste a little less rich than the traditional kind, but it looks very much like it. Lovers of American- or Japanese-style white mayonnaise won't even realize the subterfuge. Very firm, it has a perfect texture, a discreet color, and a familiar taste.

🕐 prep **10 min**   🌱 vegan

For 1 bowl
- 4 oz firm silken tofu • 2 tsp lemon juice
- 1 tsp mustard • 1 cup vegetable oil • Salt

In a food processor, blend the tofu, lemon juice, and mustard until the mixture is nice and smooth. Continue to blend while gradually adding the oil, little by little. The mixture should thicken like a classic mayonnaise. Season with salt, and mix again.

VEGAN TARTAR SAUCE

There are many variations on tartar sauce; the ingredients are not always the same, and it is assembled in different ways. While the traditional emulsion in a mortar has its charm, the version I offer is less technical. It's simply a mayonnaise base, enriched with fresh herbs and condiments.

🕐 prep **10 min**   🌱 vegan

For 1 bowl
- 2 cornichons • 2 tsp capers • 3 sprigs chervil • 3 sprigs parsley
5 leaves tarragon • 3 chives • 1 bowl vegan mayonnaise (see above)

Chop the pickles and the capers, and mince the herbs. Gradually add the herbs and condiments to the mayonnaise, mixing gently.

TOFU
NUGGETS

There are countless ways to fry tofu. This tofu nugget recipe is very simple and will appeal to food lovers. The corn flour fritter dough is light and well flavored with spices and herbs, making delicious little tofu bites that are both crisp and tender.

🕐 prep **10 min**   🕐 cook **15 min**   🌱 vegan   🍴 **4** servings

- 1 lb firm or extra-firm tofu • 1 scant cup corn flour
- 2½ Tbsp + 3 Tbsp cornstarch • ²⁄₃ cup water
- 1 tsp salt • 1 tsp sugar • ½ tsp powdered garlic
- ½ tsp pepper • ¼ tsp paprika • ¼ tsp ground ginger
- ¼ tsp mustard • Oil for deep-frying • Salt • Dipping sauce(s) of choice

Tear the tofu block in half with your hands, then in half again, and so on until you get pieces that are about 1–1½ inches square and about ½ inch thick. Blot dry them with paper towels and sprinkle them with a little salt.

Mix the corn flour, the 2½ tablespoons of cornstarch, the water, the salt, the sugar and all the spices and herbs. The dough should be very thick. Place the 3 spoonfuls of cornstarch on a plate.

Heat oil for deep-frying to 350°F. Roll the tofu pieces in the starch, then dredged them in the fritter dough, and fry them in the oil (in batches without crowding) until they are golden. Drain them on a rack and serve hot with the sauces of your choice.

VEGAN
PISSALADIÈRE

Pissaladière is my passion – like most people in Nice. This onion tart has a sweet flavor, due to the very slow cooking of the onions, which caramelize without turning brown. It also normally has a salty and strong, almost spicy side, which comes from *pissala*, the sauce of fermented anchovies that we add to it. Chinese fermented tofu (*dòufuru*), is an amazing substitute. And so as not to lose the taste of the sea, you can even use a piece of seaweed. Yes, it's a funny idea. But it works.

🕐 prep **30 min**   🕐 cook **2 h 45**   🌱 vegan

For 1 tart (14 inches in diameter)
• 8 oz bread dough • Flour, as needed • ¹/₃ oz (10 g) kombu • 2 lb cipolline or yellow onions
• 1 Tbsp sugar • 2–4 cubes fermented tofu (*dòufuru*) • A few dried thyme sprigs
• 1 bay leaf • 10–15 Niçoise olives • Olive oil • Salt and pepper

Add 1 tablespoon of olive oil to your bread dough by kneading it on a floured surface. Let sit, covered with a cloth, while the onions are being prepared.

In a mortar or small food processor, grind the kombu to a powder.

Thinly slice the onions. In a sauté pan or casserole pan over medium heat, heat 5 tablespoons of olive oil. Sweat the onions, uncovered. When their liquid has evaporated, season with pepper and sugar and add the fermented tofu, kombu powder, thyme sprigs, and bay leaf. Mix well. Add salt carefully: kombu and fermented tofu are already quite salty.

Cook over very low heat (as gently as possible!), covered, stirring occasionally. The onions should not brown at all, but form pretty light blond compote.

When the onions seem almost ready, after 1½–2 hours, preheat the oven to 425°F. Roll out the dough thinly with a rolling pin, so that you can fill your tart mold and form a small rim. Place the dough in the oiled and floured mold, and pierce here and there with a fork.

Remove the bay leaf, kombu, and thyme sprigs. Place the hot onion mixture on the dough. Spread in an even layer with the back of a spoon, and sprinkle with black olives. Put in the oven, lower the oven temperature to 400°F, and cook for 35–45 minutes, until the dough is golden and the onions nicely caramelized on the sides.

There are as many pissaladière dough recipes as there are families from Nice. Some people prefer an olive oil bread dough, others like pie dough; some like it thin, others thick, crisp, or brioche-like.... Store-bought bread dough has the advantage of requiring no effort. Rolled out thin and cooked in a very hot oven, it gives a very respectable result, I find. In a bread – or pizza – oven, it's even better!

EGGPLANT
STUFFED WITH SMOKED TOFU

This recipe is largely inspired by the eggplants that my mother prepares among *les petits farcis* - a Niçoise specialty of meat-stuffed vegetables like squash, tomatoes, mushrooms, eggplants, even onions. By replacing the ham from the original recipe with smoked tofu, we lose nothing, in my opinion; we even gain something, as the smoky flavor of the tofu blends perfectly with the eggplants.

prep **30 min** (+ drain **1 hr**) ⏱ cook **45 min** 🌱 vegetarian 👥 **4** servings

• 4 small Italian eggplants • 1 tomato • ¾ cup fresh bread crumbs • 3½ Tbsp milk
• 2 cloves garlic • 1 spring onion • 2½ Tbsp pine nuts
• 1 egg • 4 oz smoked tofu • A few basil leaves • ⅓ cup grated Parmesan
• Dried bread crumbs • Olive oil • Vegetable oil • Salt and pepper

Cut the eggplants in half lengthwise, salt them, and steam, skin side down, for 5–10 minutes depending on their thickness. Place them, face down this time, on a cutting board that is raised on one side so that they drain for at least 1 hour.

Seed the tomato and chop it coarsely, collecting the juices. Soak the bread crumbs in the juices, adding a little milk to completely soak the bread.

Mince the garlic and the onion. In a frying pan over medium heat, heat a little vegetable oil and sauté the garlic and onion for about 3 minutes. Transfer to a mixing bowl and set aside. Toast the pine nuts and add them to the onions.

Carefully scoop out the cooked eggplant flesh with a spoon, leaving about ¼ inch of flesh along the skin. Roughly chop the scooped-out flesh, the tofu, and the drained bread crumbs and add them to the onion bowl, along with the diced tomatoes, the egg, a few chopped basil leaves, and the cheese. Season with salt and pepper to taste and mix well. Add a little milk to bind the stuffing if necessary.

Preheat the oven to 400°F. In an oiled dish, place the eggplant shells, skin side down, and fill them generously with the stuffing. Sprinkle with a few more bread crumbs, drizzle with a little olive oil, and cook for about 35 minutes. Lower the oven temperature to 350°F and continue cooking for 10–20 minutes.

Note For a vegan version, omit the Parmesan, and replace the egg with 3 ounces of silken tofu and the milk with nondairy milk like soy, almond, or oat.

VEGAN
LEEK TART

When I was little, my mother's leek pie was everyone's favorite. However, we had very disparate tastes. Her recipe was vegetarian, but I wondered if a vegan version with tofu could come close. I was amazed. No one would guess that this tart does not contain milk, eggs, or cheese.

🕐 prep **10 min**   🕐 cook **1 h**   🌱 vegan

For 1 tart (11-inch diameter)
- 3 leeks • 1 onion • ¼ cup cashew nuts
- 7 oz firm or extra-firm tofu • ½ cup water • Salt and pepper

For the dough
- ¼ cup olive oil • ¼ cup sunflower oil
- ½ glass hot water • 1¼ cups flour • ½ tsp salt

Remove the tough outer leaves from the leeks, cut them in half lengthwise and rinse them well. Slice them into ¾-inch lengths, keeping a good portion of the pale green (it's good, the green!). Cut the onion in half and cut into ¼-inch slices. Combine the onion and leeks and steam them together for about 20 minutes.

Preheat the oven to 350–400°F and prepare your dough by blending all the ingredients in a food processor. Spread it by hand in a greased and floured tart mold. Prick with a fork, and bake for 5 minutes in the center of the oven.

In the food processor, blend the cashews and tofu to a very fine meal, and add the water. Blend again. Combine this mixture with the steamed onions and leeks. Take the dough-lined tart mold from the oven, and pour the tofu and leek mixture into it, spreading it evenly over the dough. Return to the oven and bake for about 35 minutes, until golden.

VEGAN
SHAKSHUKA

There are many variations on this comforting dish in North Africa and the Near East; the general idea remains that of simmered vegetables, generally peppers, tomatoes, and onions, with a poached egg served in the center. My vegan version of this recipe is simple: the eggs are just an optical illusion, replaced with tender tofu and olive oil. It's very good, with the tofu bringing a little sweetness to this boldly flavored dish.

🕐 prep **10 min** 🕐 cook **45 min** 🌱 vegan 🍴 **4** servings

- 3 Tbsp peanut oil • 1 onion, diced • 4 cloves garlic, thinly sliced
- 2–3 red bell peppers, diced • 3 very ripe large tomatoes, diced
- 1–2 sugar cubes • 2 Tbsp tomato paste • 1 Tbsp harissa
- 1 tsp cumin seeds • 10 oz medium-firm tofu
- 4 tsp olive oil • A few parsley leaves • Salt and pepper

In a shallow casserole pan or cast-iron skillet over medium heat, heat the peanut oil and sweat the onions. Add the garlic, then the peppers, and brown them for a few minutes. Add the tomatoes, sugar, tomato paste, harissa, cumin seeds, and salt and pepper to taste, and simmer for at least 30 minutes, stirring occasionally.

Blend the tofu until you get a smooth, thick texture, like Greek yogurt. Season with salt to taste.

When the vegetables have melted together and start to caramelize, use the back of a spoon to make 4 small wells and place the tofu in these hollows. Then make a small well in each pile of tofu, and pour in the olive oil. Let it heat another 2–3 minutes on low heat, then serve hot, sprinkled with a little pepper with a few parsley leaves.

ORANGE-BRAISED
TOFU & FENNEL

Tofu is delicious when braised, and fennel is too; all that remained was to put them together. I added oranges – fennel and citrus fruits always go well together – as well as almonds and pistachios, just to be greedy. Served with rice or polenta, it's a complete dish, packed with vitamins and very tasty.

○ prep **10 min**   ○ cook **25 min**   ♥ vegetarian   ♣ **4** servings

- 2 oranges • 4 small bulbs fennel • 1 red onion • 1 lb firm tofu
- 1–2 Tbsp potato starch • ½ cup dry white wine
- 2 Tbsp honey or brown sugar • 2 Tbsp pistachios, blanched and peeled
- 2 Tbsp almonds, blanched and peeled • Vegetable oil • Salt and pepper

Supreme the oranges: Slice off the peels with a knife, then cut along the inner walls of the membranes to free the segments. When all the segments are removed, squeeze the remaining membrane over a bowl to collect the juice.

Cut off the fennel stems and reserve the fronds, if available. Cut the bulbs in half length-wise, then each half into 4 wedges. Do the same for the onion. In a large frying pan over medium-high heat, heat the oil, then brown the fennel and onion on all sides. Season with salt and pepper, add about ½ cup of water, cover, and simmer over low heat for 15 minutes. Stir from time to time and check the water level; it must evaporate gradually. If it is not evaporating, remove the lid from the pan. If it evaporates too quickly, add a little more water.

While the fennel and onions are cooking, cut the tofu into ¾-inch cubes and blot dry with paper towels. Sprinkle them with a little salt and cover them with a light dusting of starch. In another oiled frying pan, brown the tofu on all sides.

Uncover the fennel and onion; if necessary, continue cooking until tender. If there is still a little water left, turn up the heat to dry out the pan. Deglaze with the wine, stirring to scrape up any brown bits from the pan bottom, then add the orange juice and honey. Add the tofu cubes, season with salt and pepper again as needed, and stir. Braise gently over medium heat. When the liquid has largely disappeared, the fennel should be very tender. Add the pistachios and almonds, and stir again. Serve hot, scattered with the orange supremes and a few fennel fronds.

ROASTED BUTTERNUT
WITH SAGE, TOFU, PECANS & COFFEE

Anne Caron, voted best coffee bean roaster in France in 2017, made me love coffee. With her and the excellent chef Marion Bouillot, we seriously thought about interesting ways to use coffee in the kitchen, and they notably proposed using good ground coffee beans like a spice, to jazz up some dishes. The combination proves particularly magical with some ingredients, such as chestnut or butternut squash. So, here's a vegan dish combining coffee, squash, and tofu – it sounds incongruous but actually not at all, it's delicious.

🕐 prep **10 min** 🕐 cook **35–45 min** 🌿 vegan 👤 **4** servings

- 1 butternut squash • Salt • 2 cloves garlic, minced
- A few sprigs of fresh sage, leaves picked or torn • A few pinches ground coffee
- 20 pecans • 7 oz firm or medium tofu • 2 Tbsp olive oil • Zest of 1 lemon • Sunflower oil

Preheat the oven to 375°F. Peel the squash and scoop out the seeds, then cut it into slices about ½ inch thick. Coat these slices with salt, garlic, sunflower oil, and fresh sage leaves. Arrange them in a single layer on a parchment-lined baking sheet and roast for 20 minutes. Turn the slices over and continue roasting until they are tender, 15–25 minutes. Sprinkle with a little freshly ground coffee just before they are finished cooking.

While the squash is cooking, break the pecans in two or three pieces and toast them quickly in a dry pan. Crumble the tofu with a fork and mix it with the olive oil. Season with salt to taste.

Serve the warm squash sprinkled with the tofu in its oil, pieces of pecan, and lemon zest.

GREEN PEAS
WITH SMOKED TOFU

Smoked tofu is so rich in flavor that it cannot sneak by unnoticed. I personally prefer to use it in small quantities, as one would use bacon, because otherwise it could overpower the other aromas in a dish. We often associate the smoky taste of cured pork with peas, lentils, beans, or sauerkraut, and this tofu naturally finds its place with these ingredients.

🕐 prep **25 min** 🕐 cook **5 min** 🌱 vegan 🍴 **4** servings

- 4 oz smoked tofu • 2 hearts of Little Gem lettuce• 2 shallots
- 1 lb peas, fresh or frozen • A few mint leaves • 1 cup water or vegetable stock
- Vegetable oil • Salt and pepper

Cut the tofu into thin slices; you can keep them like this, or cut them into smaller squares. Cut the lettuce hearts lengthwise into quarters or eighths. Thinly slice the shallots.

In a casserole pan over medium heat, heat a little oil and sauté the shallots. Add the lettuce hearts and the tofu, and brown them on all sides. Add the peas, mint, salt and pepper to taste. Stir and add the stock; bring to a boil then lower the heat, cover, and cook for 15–20 minutes, until the peas are tender.

Note Frozen peas require less water and cook faster, especially if they are petite peas. Adjust the amount of water or stock and taste after 10 minutes. As soon as they are tender, it's ready!

VEGAN
STUFFED MUSHROOMS

A beloved classic, revisited in a vegan version. The aroma of smoked tofu and its firm texture lend themselves perfectly to this recipe. Add the mushroom umami, and you get a delicious result; there is actually no need for cheese or meat. It's also a dish that is very rich in protein. Eat as a starter or main course, accompanied with a full salad, for example.

⏱ prep **20 min**   ⏱ cook **35 min**   🌱 vegan   🍴 **4** servings

- 8 mushrooms for stuffing • Juice of ½ lemon • 2 shallots
- 2 cloves garlic • Thyme
- 1 bay leaf • 4 oz smoked tofu • 4 oz firm silken tofu
- Bread crumbs • Vegetable oil • Olive oil • Salt and pepper

Preheat the oven to 350°F. Slice off the mushroom stems and coarsely chop them. Bring a pan of salted water to a boil, add the lemon juice, and blanch the mushroom caps for 3 minutes. Drain and place them gill sides down on a cutting board raised on one side to let them drain completely.

Chop the shallots and garlic. In a frying pan over medium heat, heat a little vegetable oil. Add the shallots and garlic and sweat them without browning, about 3 minutes. Add the chopped mushroom stems, thyme, bay leaf, and salt to taste, and cook until the the mushrooms have released their liquid and it has almost completely evaporated. Remove from the heat. To the pan, add the smoked tofu and the silken tofu. Mix well, and season with pepper and with salt again if needed.

If the mushroom caps are still very damp, wrap them in several layers of paper towel for a few minutes.

Oil an overproof dish, place the mushroom caps on it gill sides up, and fill them with the stuffing. Sprinkle with bread crumbs and drizzle with olive oil. Put in the oven and bake for about 35 minutes, until the stuffed mushrooms are golden.

PANFRIED TOFU WITH BARBECUE SAUCE

This recipe starts off in an odd fashion, since it asks you to freeze the main ingredient. The tofu will spend a night in the freezer, a technique similar to that of "thousand-layer" tofu (see page 56), except that it is then boiled – the Japanese call it "overnight tofu," or *ichiyadōfu*. Once thawed in a boiling water bath and well drained, the tofu absorbs sauces admirably well. So it will do wonders in a pan with barbecue sauce. I'll let you choose the one you like: most store-bought barbecue sauces are completely vegan and do not contain ethically scandalous ingredients. It would therefore be a shame to deprive yourself of them.

prep **10 min** (+ freeze **1 night**) ⏲ cook **25 min** 🌱 vegan 🍽 **4 servings**

- 21 oz firm tofu • 8 Tbsp barbecue sauce
- ¼ cup water • Vegetable oil

The night before, drain the block of tofu and wrap it in cheesecloth. Place it in your freezer on a plate and let it freeze for at least 12 hours.

The next day, place the tofu under a stream of hot water to peel off the cloth and immerse it in a pan of boiling water for 15 minutes for a large block, or until completely thawed.

Drain it carefully, then wrap it in several layers of paper towel. Let it sit for at least 15 minutes, then unwrap it and cut it into slices the size of a cutlet. Blot them dry with paper towels and brown them in an oiled pan over medium heat on both sides.

Add the barbecue sauce and water to the pan and braise the tofu for a few moments, turning it over and making sure it is completely coated with sauce.

Note You can leave the tofu in the freezer this way for up to 2 weeks. You can also use firm tofu without freezing it first, but it won't be quite as good.

TOFU BURGER WITH BARBECUE SAUCE

Tofu simmered with barbecue sauce is the ideal centerpiece for a vegetarian burger. A little crisp lettuce, juicy tomato, melted cheese, a few pickle rings, sesame bun, and voilà, you have a complete sandwich, very hot and quite delicious. Much less fatty and caloric than the original, it would be almost a healthy dish ... if it were not served with a (essential) mountain of fries.

prep 10 min **cook 5 min** **vegetarian**

For 4 burgers
- ½ red onion • 1 large tomato • 4 lettuce leaves (any type)
- 1 large dill pickle
- 4 pieces panfried tofu with barbecue sauce (see page 343)
- 8 slices cheese (Emmental, Cheddar...)
- 4 hamburger buns • Ketchup

Thinly slice the red onion. Separate the rounds and put them to soak in a bowl of cool water.

Cut the tomato into ¼-inch-thick slices. Coarsely slice or quarter the lettuce leaves. Thinly slice the pickle.

Prepare the panfried tofu with barbecue sauce, turn off the heat, and cover each piece of tofu with 2 slices of cheese, directly in the pan. Let them melt slightly with the residual heat. Meanwhile, briefly toast the buns.

To assemble the burgers, place the bottom bun on a plate, add a splash of ketchup, the lettuce, the panfried tofu with barbecue sauce covered with cheese, the pickle slices, 2–3 onion rings, 2 tomato slices, and finish with the top bun.

PASTA
WITH VEGETARIAN BOLOGNESE

For some strange reason, the French decided to associate spaghetti with Bolognese sauce. Traditionally, this is not done in Italy: Bologna is known for its wide-cut fresh egg pasta, such as tagliatelle and pappardelle. The famous ragù alla bolognese suits them well, it must be admitted. In its original meaty version, however, this dish remains particularly heavy. You get amazing results by swapping out the meat for tofu – and your stomach will say thank you...

🕐 prep **10 min** 🕐 cook **45 min** 🌱 vegetarian 👥 4 servings

- 7 oz plain extra-firm tofu (or 4 oz plain tofu + 4 oz smoked tofu)
- 1 onion, diced • 2 cloves garlic, thinly sliced • 1 carrot, diced
- 1 small celery rib, diced • 3½ Tbsp red wine • 14 oz Pomi tomato passata or tomato purée
- 3 Tbsp tomato paste • 2 bay leaves • ½–²/₃ cup vegetable stock
- 1 lb fresh pappardelle (or 12 oz dried pasta of choice)
- A few parsley leaves • Olive oil • Salt and pepper • Parmesan

Roughly chop the tofu with a knife, hand chopper, or food processer. Keep some texture. In a heavy-bottomed Dutch oven or casserole pan over medium heat, sweat the onion in a little oil. Add the garlic, carrot, and celery, season with salt, and continue cooking for a few moments, turning very often. Add the minced tofu, mix well, then pour in the red wine. Cook uncovered, stirring, until there is no more liquid.

Add the tomato passata or purée, tomato paste, bay leaf, and stock, season with salt and pepper to taste, and continue cooking over very low heat. From now on, the sauce will start to spit – the magic of the sizzling tomato. It's messy, it hurts, so partially cover your pot with a lid but leave it ajar. Uncover and mix from time to time.

After 30 minutes, check the seasoning; add salt and pepper if necessary. After 45 minutes, the sauce should have reduced and taken on a thick consistency. Add a little olive oil, mix well, and keep warm.

Cook your pasta according to package directions in a large amount of salted water. Drain and serve covered in a ladleful of sauce with a little minced parsley and grated Parmesan.

SPINACH & TOFU
LASAGNA

Lasagna, those sheets of pasta dough that are baked in the oven, are usually made with eggs. However, it is possible to find eggless durum wheat lasagna sheets. The dried version is available everywhere, while the fresh version can be more difficult to find. No problem: the dry pasta works very well in this recipe. Just thin out the béchamel sauce to give the pasta enough water to cook. The tofu replaces the typical ricotta – they look very similar – and the béchamel used here is vegan.

🕐 prep **15 min** 🕐 cook **45 min** 🌱 vegan 🍴 **4** servings

- 1 lb fresh spinach • 10 oz medium-firm tofu • 2 Tbsp olive oil
- 10–12 sheets lasagna, fresh or dried • Salt and pepper

For the béchamel
- 5 Tbsp olive oil • 2 Tbsp flour
- 2 cups soy milk • Salt, pepper, and nutmeg

Blanch the spinach in boiling salted water for 1 minute. Drain and squeeze it in the colander to extract excess water. Coarsely chop on a cutting board. In a food processor or blender, blend the tofu to get a thick cream, and mix it with the spinach and olive oil. Season with salt and pepper.

In a saucepan over medium-low heat, heat the olive oil, then add the flour. Stir quickly with a wooden spoon for about 1 minute, until you get a thick and homogeneous roux. Gradually add the soy milk while stirring; work out any lumps. Season with salt and pepper and add a good sprinkling of nutmeg. Continue stirring over low heat until the mixture thickens, about 5 minutes. Taste and adjust the seasoning if needed. This is your béchamel.

Preheat the oven to 350–400°F. Grease a rectangular lasagna pan and pour a thin layer of béchamel over the bottom. Add a layer of lasagna sheets, a layer of spinach tofu, then a layer of béchamel. Do this three to four more times: the last layer of lasagna sheets should be covered with spinach tofu and béchamel sauce. Bake for 30 minutes. Then turn off the oven and bake the lasagna in the residual heat for 10 minutes more.

SPAGHETTI
WITH
TOFU-ARTICHOKE CREAM

Blended tofu is great for sauces because it provides a texture close to that of cream (when it is tender) or ricotta (when it is firm). So it is very welcome in vegan pasta recipes. Paired with baby artichokes of spring and autumn, it is a real pleasure. Digestible, low in fat, and rich in protein, here is a spaghetti dish that is richly sauced, but surprisingly healthy.

🕐 prep **10 min** 🕐 cook **35–45 min** 🌱 vegan 👤 **4 servings**

- 6 baby artichokes • 1 lemon • 2 cloves garlic, halved
- 5 oz firm silken tofu • 3 Tbsp olive oil
- 12 oz spaghetti • Vegetable oil • A few parsley leaves • Salt and pepper

Trim the artichokes: cut the stems, remove the tough outer leaves, then cut off the leaf tips halfway down the artichoke to keep only the tender part of the remaining leaves. Pass the blade around the base to cut away any hard bits. Quarter each artichoke, remove the fuzzy choke, and immediately immerse them in a pot of boiling salted water to which you have added the juice of half the lemon.

With a skimmer, remove half of the artichokes from the water after 2 minutes. Place them in a cold water bath with a dash of lemon juice, drain, and set aside.

Drain the rest of the artichokes after 6–8 minutes of cooking, when they are tender. Just before removing them from the water, add the halved cloves of garlic to quickly blanch them – unless you like the taste of raw garlic. Mix the tender artichokes and garlic with the silken tofu, olive oil, and the rest of the lemon juice. Season with salt and pepper to taste, and add a little more oil or lemon if desired.

Heat a very large pot of salted water for cooking pasta (the only way to cook it right is to use 1 quart for every 4 ounces of pasta). Cook the pasta according to package directions.

While they cook, cut the reserved parboiled artichokes into slices. In a frying pan over medium heat, heat a little oil and brown the artichoke slices on both sides.

Briefly heat the tofu and artichoke sauce, stirring. Drain the pasta and mix it with this sauce. Serve sprinkled with the golden artichoke slices and the parsley leaves.

LENTILS
WITH SMOKED TOFU

There's nothing really surprising about marrying lentils and smoked tofu; they go very well together. Just add a few little onions and carrots to get a nourishing dish that is very good for vegetarians and vegans: it is rich in iron and other minerals, protein, vitamins, antioxidants, fiber...in fact, it is good for everyone. And particularly appropriate for diabetics and athletes, thanks to the very low glycemic index of lentils.

🕐 prep **10 min**   🕐 cook **30 min**   🌱 vegan   👤 **4** servings

- 1 large carrot • 6–8 pearl onions or 1 large onion
- 7 oz smoked extra-firm tofu • 8 oz green Puy lentils
- 1 clove • 1 bouquet garni • Vegetable oil • Salt and pepper

Cut the carrot into rounds a scant ¼ inch thick. Thinly slice the onion; if you are using pearl onions, you can cut them in half or keep them whole. Cut the tofu into little chunks, like bacon lardons.

In a frying pan over medium-high heat, heat a little oil. Brown the onions and tofu. In a casserole pan, combine the lentils with three times their volume of cold water. Add the carrots, onions, tofu, clove, and the bouquet garni, cover, and bring to a boil. Lower the heat to maintain a good simmer and cook for 20–25 minutes, stirring from time to time.

When the lentils are tender, season with salt and pepper to taste, stir, and serve hot.

Notes   To make a bouquet garni, tie together a handful of flat-leaf parsley, thyme sprigs, and a bay leaf or two. You can also wrap them in a cheesecloth bundle. Remove at the end of cooking.

Always salt the lentils at the end of cooking; if salt is added too early, their skins toughen up.

STRAWBERRY
PROTEIN SMOOTHIE

Smoothies are a trap: they are sold as healthy drinks, when it would be healthier to just eat fruit. By blending fruit, we lose the benefit of insoluble fiber, and what remains in the glass is water, some vitamins, and a lot of fructose. For anyone who wants to consumer more fruit without eating it, here's what a truly healthy smoothie looks like. And no, no need to put spinach in it for it to be healthy...

🕐 prep **5 min**   🌱 vegan

For 4 glasses
- 1 lb strawberries • 7 oz extra-tender silken tofu (*sundubu*)
- 1 dash lemon juice • 1 pinch salt • 2 tsp agave syrup or sweetener of choice

In a blender, combine all the ingredients except the agave syrup and blend. Taste and adjust the sweetness if needed, then blend again. Thin the smoothie with a little cool water if necessary. Drink right away; fruits don't hold, especially not in the fridge. If you like your smoothies very cold, add a few ice cubes.

PEAR-MATCHA SMOOTHIE

Commercial smoothies are very rich in fructose and low in vitamins. And truth be told, even homemade smoothie recipes are often incredibly caloric and absurd from a dietary viewpoint. It is possible to limit the devastation, however. This drink made with extra-tender Korean tofu (*sundubu*) is a perfectly reasonable smoothie, rich in protein, relatively unsweetened, and loaded with antioxidants thanks to matcha tea. It contains as much caffeine as a cup of coffee, so swap it in at breakfast.

🕐 prep **5 min**   🌱 vegan

For 4 glasses
- 2 organic pears • 1 organic green apple • 5 oz extra-tender silken tofu (*sundubu*)
- 1 dash lemon juice • 1 pinch salt • 2 tsp matcha tea
- 2 tsp agave syrup or sweetener of choice (optional)

Core the pears and the apple, but keep the skins on. In a blender, combine them with the rest of the ingredients, except the agave syrup, and blend. Gradually add about 1/3 cup of cool water to thin the very thick drink. Sweeten to taste as needed, and blend again. You could also add a few ice cubes.

Note You can replace the *sundubu* with soft silken tofu and add a little water.

TOFU
FRENCH TOAST

Tofu panfried with egg is a common dish in Asia, but it is always salty. I wanted to make a sweet version, more along the lines of French toast. With "normal" tofu, whose surface is rather smooth, you need potato starch if you want the sweet coating to stick; with previously frozen tofu (see thousand-layer tofu recipe, page 56), that's another story. Riddled with tiny holes like the crumb of good country bread, it absorbs the liquid, for a delicious result.

🕐 prep **5 min** (+ drain **30 min**) 🕐 cook **10 min** 🌱 vegetarian 🍴 **4** servings

- 1 lb thousand-layer tofu (see page 56) • ¼ cup milk
- 2 eggs, beaten • ½ cup sugar • ½ tsp salt
- 4 tsp butter • Confectioners' sugar

Wrap the thousand-layer tofu with paper towels and let it drain for at least 30 minutes. Cut it into slices ¼ inch–½ inch thick. Blot dry with paper towels.

Stir together the milk, beaten eggs, sugar, and salt. Pour this mixture into a deep plate.

Place the tofu slices in the egg mixture to soak them. In a frying pan over medium-high heat, melt the butter. Add the tofu slices, in batches to prevent crowding, and panfry until golden brown on both sides. Serve hot, sprinkled with confectioners' sugar.

HAZELNUT, CHOCOLATE & SILKEN TOFU
TART

Firm silken tofu lets you to make amazing desserts. This is the case with this tart, rich in chocolate and hazelnuts. The dough is crisp, the chocolate filling is melting, and the combination is quite delicious. Turns out, vegan cuisine and tofu are not synonymous with austerity.

🕐 prep **20 min** (+ chill **12–24 hr**) 🕐 cook **30 min** 🌱 vegan

For 1 large tart
• 12 oz extra-fine firm silken tofu • 12 oz dark chocolate • ½ cup hazelnut butter
• ½ cup almond milk • Fleur de sel sea salt

For the dough
• ½ cup + 1 Tbsp margarine • 2 Tbsp water
• 1¼ cups ground hazelnuts • 1 cup flour
• 3 Tbsp sugar • 1 pinch salt

Preheat the oven to 350°F. Prepare the dough: in a saucepan, heat the margarine and the water. Turn off the heat and add the ground hazelnuts, flour, sugar, and salt. Mix until you get a homogeneous dough. Grease a tart mold and spread the dough in it by hand. Pierce here and there with a fork and bake for about 30 minutes, until the dough is cooked and golden. Remove from the oven and let cool.

Meanwhile, prepare the chocolate filling: put the tofu in a food processor and blend it into a homogeneous cream. Melt the chocolate in the top of a double boiler or in the microwave, then stir in the hazelnut purée, almond milk, and tofu. Mix well.

Fill the tart shell with the chocolate mixture and place in the refrigerator for 12–24 hours to set the chocolate filling. Serve sprinkled with a little fleur de sel.

VEGAN
CARAMEL FLAN

This vegan caramel flan is very easy to make and really looks like its counterpart made with eggs and milk. Thanks to silken tofu and agar-agar, the texture is perfect. Be careful, however, to choose extra-firm (or at least firm) silken tofu – the softer versions won't give you a proper flan consistency.

---

prep 5 min (+ chill 2 hr) · **cook 5 min** · **vegan**

For 4–6 ramekins
• 2 cups soy milk • 1 Tbsp agar-agar powder
• 5 oz extra-firm silken tofu • 2 Tbsp sugar • 1 pinch salt
For the caramel
• ½ cup sugar

Pour the soy milk into a bowl and sprinkle it with the agar-agar. Mix with a whisk and let stand for 10 minutes.

Meanwhile, get your ramekins ready and close at hand. In a small saucepan, melt the sugar for the caramel over low heat, stirring until it begins to take on an amber color. Pour it immediately into the ramekins – do this quickly, it solidifies quickly when you stop heating it. Let cool.

Return to your soy milk: heat it over medium heat, stirring, until it comes to a boil, then reduce the to low and continue stirring for 5 minutes, until the agar-agar is completely dissolved. Remove from the heat.

In a food processor, combine the soy milk with the tofu, sugar, and salt, and blend until you get a perfectly smooth texture. Pour into the ramekins on top of the caramel. Cover with plastic wrap and refrigerate at least 2 hours.

To unmold the flans, immerse the bottom of each ramekin in boiling water for 30 seconds, place a dessert plate over it, then turn the ramekins and plates over together.

ALMOND "TOFU"
WITH CHERRIES &
BLACK PEPPER

Cherries and almonds go well together, everyone knows. We think less about combining cherries and black pepper, and yet it's a happy marriage. The pepper brings out both the sweetness and the acidity of the fruit; add to that the sweet bitterness of almond tofu, and you have a light, amazing dessert, perfect for celebrating the brief cherry season. You can also use frozen cherries, provided they are really good quality.

🕐 prep **15 min**   🕐 cook **5 min**   🌿 vegan   ♟ **4** servings

- 7 oz cherries • ¼ cup sugar • 2 Tbsp water
- 1 tsp lemon juice
- ¼ tsp freshly ground black pepper
- 14–16 oz almond tofu (see page 95)

Cut the cherries in half and remove the pits. Combine the sugar, water, and lemon juice in a small saucepan and heat over low heat, stirring until the sugar is dissolved. Add the cherries and the pepper, mix then turn off the heat. Let cool or chill.

Cut the almond tofu into small cubes and place in cups or dessert bowls. Top with cherries and sprinkle with syrup.

VEGAN
LEMON CAKE

In some recipes, silken tofu is the ideal ingredient to replace eggs. This is the case with this lemon cake, which seems very traditional except that it is entirely vegan. The substitution does not prevent it from rising, baking perfectly normally, and tasting like cake. No, it's true!

🕐 prep **15 min** 🕐 cook **45–55 min** 🌱 vegan

For 1 loaf cake
• 4 oz firm silken tofu • ²/₃ cup nondairy milk • ²/₃ cup sugar
• 5 Tbsp oil • 3 Tbsp lemon juice • Zest of 1 lemon
• 1½ cups flour • ²/₃ cup cornstarch • 2¼ tsp baking powder • 1 pinch salt
Icing
• 1 scant cup confectioners' sugar • 2 Tbsp hot water
• 1–2 Tbsp lemon juice

Preheat the oven to 350°F. Grease and flour a loaf pan. In a food processor, blend the tofu until you get a smooth paste, and add the vegetable milk, sugar, oil, lemon juice, and lemon zest. Mix until the sugar is dissolved. Add the rest of the ingredients and mix until you get a smooth batter.

Pour the batter into the prepared pan and cook for 45–55 minutes, until the cake is golden and a knife blade inserted in the center comes out clean.

Let cool and turn out the cake. Prepare the icing by mixing the icing sugar with the hot water. Add the lemon juice, mix again, and pour over the cake.

LIGHT COFFEE MOUSSE

Originally, my idea was to make a vegan coffee cream. But when I blended silken tofu, magic occurred: its texture become aerated, resulting in an amazing mousse. It is not firm like egg-rich chocolate mousse, and contains fewer small air bubbles; it is delicate, very light, very fresh. The hazelnuts give it a little crunch, and the chocolate is an indulgent touch.

🕐 prep **5 min** (+ chill **3 hr**) 🌱 vegan 🍽 4 servings

- 12 oz extra-fine firm silken tofu
- 1 Tbsp instant coffee or 2 Tbsp freeze-dried coffee • 3 tsp agave syrup

For decoration
- 16 crushed toasted hazelnuts • 1–2 oz dark chocolate, grated

In a food processor, blend all the ingredients until you get a perfectly homogeneous mixture. You can also whip the preparation after mixing it: if you use a hand blender, you can incorporate as much air as possible for a light and fluffy mousse. Pour into 4 ramekins and refrigerate for at least 3 hours.

Serve sprinkled with hazelnuts and grated chocolate.

VEGAN
APRICOT CLAFOUTIS

Frankly, I didn't think this clafoutis could work. Silken tofu subs in well for creamy desserts, but I wasn't sure if it would make a batter that would hold together while remaining meltingly tender, without turning into flan, cake, or porridge. Above all, I was afraid that it would not be a clafoutis that was good enough for real foodies. I was wrong. I ate it all.

🕐 prep **20 min**   🕐 cook **50 min**   🌱 vegan

For one 11-inch diameter plate
- 1 lb apricots • 6 Tbsp flour • 3 Tbsp ground almonds
- 1 pinch salt • ¼ cup brown sugar • 1 Tbsp almond paste
- 5 oz firm silken tofu • 2 Tbsp almond cream • ½ cup nondairy milk

Preheat the oven to 400°F. Grease and flour a baking dish. Cut your apricots in half and remove the pits.

In a large mixing bowl, combine the flour, almond powder, salt, and sugar. In a mixer or food processor, blend the almond paste, tofu, almond cream, and nondairy milk. Add the liquid mixture to the dry ingredients little by little, mixing until you have a homogeneous batter. Add a little milk if necessary.

Place the apricots in the prepared baking dish and pour the batter over them. Bake for 20 minutes at 400°F, then reduce the heat to 350°F and continue cooking for 30 minutes more.

TOFU PUDDING
WITH RED FRUIT COULIS

Tofu pudding is eaten with a lot of different accompaniments in Asia, from ginger syrup to herb jelly, but all are a far cry from the flavors we are used to in France. For a more typical French flavor profile, I've paired a tangy and sweet red fruit coulis with this extremely delicate, smooth and tender type of tofu, for a delicious "fusion" dessert. The coulis also works well with silken tofu, although its texture will be less refined than that of tofu pudding.

⏱ prep **5 min**   ⏱ cook **30 min**   🌱 vegan   🍽 **4 servings**

- 8 oz fresh or frozen red fruits (gooseberries, strawberries, blackberries, raspberres, red currants)
- 3–4 Tbsp water • ⅓ cup brown sugar • 28 oz tofu pudding

Combine the berries with the water in a saucepan and heat over low heat for 15 minutes, stirring regularly. When the fruit is cooked, strain the juice by passing it through a chinois or other fine-mesh strainer, using a spatula to press and squeeze out the last drop of juice.

Cook this juice with the sugar in a small saucepan over medium heat, stirring for about 15 minutes, until it has thickened.

Serve the tofu pudding in bowls, covered with hot or chilled coulis.

Note   You can find tofu pudding in the refrigerator case section of Chinese groceries – look for "tofu pudding," "tofu flan," or "*douhua*" made with glucono-delta-lactone (GDL) – or, prepare it yourself (see pages 34 and 36).

VEGAN CHOCOLATE MOUSSE

This mousse contains only three ingredients – all vegan, if you can believe it – and yet it is rich and creamy. This miracle is made possible by dark chocolate and silken tofu, which, used together, can make sinful desserts. This one, extremely easy and quick to prepare, is the simplest version of the concept.

🕐 prep **15 min** (+ chill **1 hr**) 🌱 vegan ♟ **4** servings

- 4½ oz dark chocolate
- 14 oz extra-firm silken tofu
- 3 Tbsp maple syrup

Melt the chocolate in the top of a double boiler or in the microwave. In a mixer or food processor, blend the silken tofu and maple syrup until you get a smooth cream, then stir in the chocolate and continue blending until the mixture is perfectly homogeneous. Pour into ramekins or bowls and refrigerate for at least 1 hour. Serve chilled.

Note You can add all kinds of yummy toppings to the mousse: chocolate shavings or coconut flakes, toasted sesame seed, rounds of sliced banana…

Bibliography

WORKS IN FRENCH

Joseph FAVRE, *Dictionnaire universel de cuisine. Encyclopédie illustrée d'hygiène alimentaire*, Librairie-imprimerie de la Bourse de commerce, Paris, 1883

Shao Bei HU, *Tofu & soja*, La Plage, Paris, 2006.

WORKS IN ENGLISH

Akiko AOYAGI & William SHURTLEFF, *History of Soybeans and Soyfoods in Korea, and in Korean Cookbooks*, Soyinfo Center, Lafayette, California, 2014

Akiko AOYAGI & William SHURTLEFF, *History of Tofu and Tofu Products (965 CE to 2013)*, Soyinfo Center, Lafayette, California, 2013

Akiko AOYAGI & William SHURTLEFF, *The Book of Kudzu*, Avery, Garden City, New York, 1985

Akiko AOYAGI & William SHURTLEFF, *The Book of Tofu: Food for Mankind, Volume 1*, Autumn Press, Inc., Brookline, Massachusetts, 1975

Akiko AOYAGI & William SHURTLEFF, *Tofu & Soymilk Production: A Craft and Technical Manual*, Soyinfo Center, Lafayette, California, 2000

Teresa M. CHEN, *A Tradition of Soup: Flavors from China's Pearl River Delta*, North Atlantic Books, Berkeley, 2009

Dorothy CULLOTY, *Food from Northern Laos: The Boat Landing Cookbook*, Galangal Press, Bang Sare, Thailand, 2010

Katarzyna Joanna CWIERTKA, *Modern Japanese Cuisine: Food, Power and National Identity*, Reaktion Books, London, 2006

Christine M. DU BOIS, Chee-Beng TAN & Sidney Wilfred MINTZ (eds.), *The World of Soy*, University of Illinois Press, Urbana, 2008

Cathy ERWAY, *The Food of Taiwan: Recipes from the Beautiful Island*, Houghton Mifflin Harcourt Publishing Company, New York, 2015

Georgia FREEDMAN, *Cooking South of the Clouds: Recipes and Stories From China's Yunnan Province*, Kyle Books, London, 2018

Y. H. HUI, Frank SHERKAT et al. *Handbook of Food Science, Technology, and Engineering*, Volume 4, CRC Press, Boca Raton, Florida, 2005

KeShun LIU, *Soybeans: Chemistry, Technology and Utilization*, Springer, New York, 1997

Andrea NGUYEN, *Asian Tofu: Discover the Best, Make Your Own, and Cook It at Home*, Ten Speed Press, Berkeley, 2012

Shanta NIMBARK SACHAROFF, *Flavors of India: Vegetarian Indian Cuisine*, Book Publishing Company, Summertown, Tennessee, 1996

Sasaki SANMI, *Chado: The Way of Tea: A Japanese Tea Master's Almanac*, Tuttle Publishing, North Clarendon, Vermont, 2005

Nina SIMONDS, *Classic Chinese Cuisine, Revised and Updated Edition*, Houghton Mifflin Harcourt Publishing Company, New York, 2003

Mei WEI, *Fujian Cuisine*, Deeplogic, London, 2019

WORKS IN JAPANESE

Hitsujun KA, *Tōfu hyakuchin*, Yamazaki Kinbē, Edo, 1782

ARTICLES IN ENGLISH

W. BAI, C. WANG & C. REN, "Intakes of Total and Individual Flavonoids by U.S. Adults," *International Journal of Food Science and Nutrition*, no. 65 (2014)

O. K. CHUN, S. J. CHUNG & W. O. SONG, "Estimated Dietary Flavonoid Intake and Major Food Sources of U.S. Adults," *Journal of Nutrition*, Vol. 137, Issue 5 (2007)

Shun-Tang GUO & Tomotada ONO, "The Role of Composition and Content of Protein Particles in Soymilk on Tofu Curding by Glucono-δ-lactone or Calcium Sulfate," *Journal of Food Science*, no. 70 (2005)

Nayu IKEDA, Hidemi TAKIMOTO, Shino IMAI, et al. "Data Resource Profile: The Japan National Health and Nutrition Survey (NHNS)," *International Journal of Epidemiology*, Vol. 44, Issue 6 (2015)

Jun Ho LEE & Han San JUNG, "Physicochemical and Consumer Acceptance of Tofu Supplemented with Licorice Powder," *Preventive Nutrition and Food Science*, no. 22 (2017)

Xuanxia MAO, Xiuhua SHEN, Wenjing TANG, Ye ZHAO, "Prevalence of Vegetarians and Vegetarian's Health Dietary Behavior Survey in Shanghai," *Journal of Hygiene Research*, no. 44 (2015)

P. A. MURPHY, T. SONG, G. BUSEMAN, et al. "Isoflavones in Retail and Institutional Soy Foods," *Journal of Agricultural and Food Chemistry*, no. 47 (1999)

C. NAGATA, "Factors to Consider In the Association Between Soy Isoflavone Intake and Breast Cancer Risk," *Journal of Epidemiology*, no. 20 (2010)

Y. SOMEKAWA, M. CHIGUCHI, T. ISHIBASHI & T. ASO, "Soy Intake Related to Menopausal Symptoms, Serum Lipids, and Bone Mineral Density in Postmenopausal Japanese Women," *Obstetrics & Gynecology*, no. 97 (2001)

Taebum YOO & In-Jin YOON, "Becoming a Vegetarian in Korea: The Sociocultural Implications of Vegetarian Diets in Korean Society," *Korea journal*, no. 55 (2015)

ONLINE ARTICLES IN ENGLISH

Catherine HU, "Stinky Tofu," Science and Food, 2015, URL: https://scienceandfooducla.wordpress.com/2015/12/08/stinky-tofu/

"Straight Talk About Soy," Harvard T. H. Chan School of Public Health, URL: https://www.hsph.harvard.edu/nutritionsource/soy/

INGREDIENT INDEX

Almond/Bitter Almond
Orange-Braised Tofu & Fennel 336
Almond Tofu 95

Apple
Pear-Matcha Smoothie 354

Apricot
Vegan Apricot Clafoutis 366

Artichoke
Spaghetti with Tofu-Artichoke Cream. 350

Asparagus
White Asparagus, Crème
Fraîche & Tofu 302

Avocado
Mango-Avocado Salad with Sesame-
Breaded Tofu & Chimichurri 312

Azuki Bean
Tofu Pudding with Adzuki Beans 92

Bamboo Shoots
Steamed Stuffed Yuba 76
Sichuan-Style Braised Tofu 82

Bean Sprouts
Mushroom & Tofu Hot Pot 184
Vegetarian Noodle Bowl (Bún) 202
Vegan Spring Rolls 208
Thai-Style Stir-fried
Rice Noodles (Pad Thai) 218
Multicolor Indonesian Salad 230
Tofu Puffs with Crunchy Veg
& Spiced Sauce 238

Bell Pepper
Sweet & Sour Tofu 66
Red-Cooked Tofu 80
Egg Tofu Stir-fried with Thai Veggies .. 217
Tofu Curry with Bell Peppers 273
Tofu Tikka 282
Vegan Greek Salad 306
Summer Veggie & Sesame-Breaded
Tofu Wrap 310
Mango-Avocado Salad with

Sesame-Breaded Tofu & Chimichurri . 312
Vegan Shakshuka 334

Black Beans, Fermented
Sichuan-Style Mapo Tofu 70

Bok Choy
Bok Choy & Tofu Soup 60
Mung Bean Noodles Braised
with Tofu & Veggies 68

Buckwheat
Warm Salad of Buckwheat, Roasted
Carrots & Lacto-Fermented Tofu 324

Butter
Vegan Butter Chicken 274
Pink Radish Velouté 300
Tofu French Toast 356

Cabbage
Everyday Fried Rice 48
Tofu Pot Stickers 72
Clear Soup with Egg Tofu 216
Burmese Tofu Salad 256

Carrot
Steamed Stuffed Yuba 76
Zen Salad with Tofu Sauce 112
Buddhist Broth 120
Tofu Fritters with Vegetables 126
Okara with Vegetables 144
Deep-Fried Stuffed Chiles 162
Veggie Tofu Cakes 174
5-Color Rice Bowl (Bibimbap) 176
Sushi Rolls with Tofu &
Crunchy Veggies 179
Mushroom & Tofu Hot Pot 184
Little Tofu Pockets with
Multicolor Rice 186
Tofu Terrine, Vietnamese Style 201
Vegetarian Noodle Bowl (Bún) 202
Tofu & Veggie Sandwich (Bánh Mi) .. 204
Vegan Spring Rolls 208
Clear Soup with Egg Tofu 216
Egg Tofu Stir-fried with Thai Veggies 217
Multicolor Indonesian Salad 230
Warm Salad of Buckwheat, Roasted

Carrots & Lacto-Fermented Tofu 324
Pasta with Vegetarian Bolognese 346
Lentils with Smoked Tofu 352

Celery
Pasta with Vegetarian Bolognese 346

Cherry
Almond "Tofu" with Cherries
& Black Pepper 361

Chinese Long Beans
Red Curry Tofu Stir-fry..................... 224
Balinese Curry with Tofu & Tempeh.. 232

Coconut Milk
Tofu, Galangal & Coconut Milk Soup.. 220
Coconut Green Curry 226
Balinese Curry with Tofu & Tempeh 232

Coconut Water
Braised Tofu & Tempeh
Javanese Style................................. 234

Coffee
Light Coffee Mousse 364
Roasted Butternut with Sage, Tofu,
Pecans & Coffee.............................. 338

Cucumber
Sushi Rolls with Tofu &
Crunchy Veggies................................ 179
Iced Noodle Soup with Soy Milk...... 188
Vegetarian Noodle Bowl (Bún) 202
Tofu & Veggie Sandwich (Bánh Mi) . 204
Vegan Spring Rolls 208
Multicolor Indonesian Salad........... 230
Tofu Puffs with Crunchy Veg
& Spiced Sauce 238
Vegan Tzatziki 296
Vegan Greek Salad 306

Daikon Radish
Melting Fried Tofu 114
Miso Soup with Fried Tofu & Daikon 118
Buddhist Broth 120
Little Tofu Pockets with
Multicolor Rice 186
Tofu & Veggie Sandwich (Bánh Mi) . 204

Dates
Tomato & Tofu Salad with
Date Dressing 318

Edamame
Sautéed Tofu in Lettuce Cups............ 52
Tofu Honeycomb Soup 58
Edamame Tofu................................ 146
Iced Noodle Soup with Soy Milk...... 188

Egg
Egg Tofu....................................... 49
Cold Tofu with Century Eggs 54
Sweet & Sour Tofu 66
Tofu Rice Bowl with Scrambled Eggs 140
Deep-Fried Stuffed Chiles............... 162
Herbed Tofu Canapés 164
Veggie Tofu Cakes 174
5-Color Rice Bowl (Bibimbap) 176
Sushi Rolls with Tofu &
Crunchy Veggies.............................. 179
Thai-Style Stir-fried Rice Noodles
(Pad Thai) 218
Multicolor Indonesian Salad........... 230
Sesame-Breaded Tofu 308
Eggplant Stuffed with
Smoked Tofu.................................. 330
Tofu French Toast 356

Egg Tofu
Clear Soup with Egg Tofu 216
Egg Tofu Stir-fried with
Thai Veggies 217

Eggplant
Tofu Stir-fry with
Green Peppercorns 222
Coconut Green Curry 226
Eggplant Stuffed with Smoked Tofu. 330

Fennel
Orange-Braised Tofu & Fennel 336

Fermented Fava Bean Paste
Sichuan-Style Mapo Tofu.................. 70
Sichuan-Style Braised Tofu............... 82

Figs
Arugula, Fig & Smoked Tofu Salad.. 322

Flour, Chickpea
Burmese Tofu................................. 253
Burmese Tofu Salad 256
Shan Noodles with Warm
Tofu Cream.................................... 264
Crispy Deep-Fried Tofu 294
Vegan Tzatziki 296

Flour, Rice
Tofu Mochi... 152
Panfried Tofu with Egg...................... 166
Veggie Tofu Cakes 174

Flour, Wheat
Herbed Tofu Canapés...................... 164
Panfried Tofu with Egg................... 166
Veggie Tofu Cakes 174
Savory Spiral Cookies 236
Hazelnut, Chocolate &
Silken Tofu Tart............................... 358
Vegan Lemon Cake 362
Vegan Apricot Clafoutis.................. 366

Fried Tofu Pockets
Sushi in Tofu Pockets 132
Noodle Soup with Fried Tofu........... 134

Galangal
Tofu, Galangal & Coconut
Milk Soup 220
Tofu Stir-fry with Green
Peppercorns................................... 222
Red Curry Tofu Stir-fry 224
Balinese Curry with Tofu
& Tempeh....................................... 232
Braised Tofu & Tempeh
Javanese Style............................... 234

Garlic Chives
Everyday Fried Rice 48
Cold Tofu with Green Onion 50
Sautéed Tofu in Lettuce Cups........... 52
Cold Tofu with Century Eggs........... 54
Tofu Honeycomb Soup 58
Sweet & Sour Tofu........................... 66
Mung Bean Noodles Braised
with Tofu & Veggies......................... 68
Sichuan-Style Mapo Tofu................. 70
Tofu Pot Stickers 72
Crispy Salt & Pepper Tofu................. 75
Steamed Stuffed Yuba 76
Spicy Tofu with Peanuts 78
Red-Cooked Tofu.............................. 80
Sichuan-Style Braised Tofu.............. 82
Rice Porridge with Sweet Potato....... 84
Pressed Tofu with Garlic Chives........ 90
Cold Tofu with Ginger
& Green Onion................................ 108
Miso Soup with Tofu & Wakame 116
Miso Soup with Fried Tofu & Daikon.. 118
Noodle Soup with Fried Tofu........... 134

Kyoto-Style Tofu Hot Pot.................. 138
Soba Noodles with Fresh Yuba........ 142
Deep-Fried Stuffed Chiles............... 162
Spiced Stew with Very Tender Tofu.. 169
Steamed Tofu with Sautéed Kimchi... 170
Broth with Potatoes & Tofu.............. 172
Veggie Tofu Cakes 174
Spicy Braised Tofu 182
Korean Miso Stew........................... 183
Zucchini-Tofu Dumplings 190
Vegan Spring Rolls 208
Clear Soup with Egg Tofu 216
Thai-Style Stir-fried
Rice Noodles (Pad Thai).................. 218
Laotian Tofu Salad (Larb) 243
Burmese Tofu Curry 258
Vegan Potato Salad......................... 314

Green Beans
Okara with Vegetables 144
Tofu Stir-fry with
Green Peppercorns 222
Balinese Curry with Tofu
& Tempeh....................................... 232

Hazelnut
Hazelnut, Chocolate &
Silken Tofu Tart............................... 358
Light Coffee Mousse 364

Hijiki Seaweed
Sushi in Tofu Pockets 132

Kombu Seaweed
Melting Fried Tofu 114
Miso Soup with Tofu & Wakame 116
Miso Soup with Fried Tofu & Daikon 118
Buddhist Broth 120
Salty-Sweet Fried Tofu Pockets 130
Kyoto-Style Tofu Hot Pot................. 138
Okara with Vegetables 144
White Asparagus, Crème Fraîche
& Tofu 302
Vegan Pissaladière 328

Konjac
Zen Salad with Tofu Sauce............... 112
Buddhist Broth 120

Kudzu
Edamame Tofu................................ 146
Walnut Tofu 147
Sesame Tofu 150

Leek
Vegan Leek Tart 332

Lemon
Lemongrass Tofu 200
Vegan Spring Rolls 208
Tofu, Galangal & Coconut
Milk Soup 220
Tofu Puffs with Crunchy Veg
& Spiced Sauce 238
Laotian Tofu Salad (Larb) 243
Burmese Tofu Salad 256
Shan Noodles with Warm Tofu Cream ...
264
Tofu Tikka 282
Vegan Tzatziki 296
Wheat-Free Tabbouleh 297
Vegan Mayonnaise 326
Roasted Butternut with Sage, Tofu,
Pecans & Coffee............................. 338
Vegan Stuffed Mushrooms.............. 342
Spaghetti with Tofu-Artichoke
Cream 350
Strawberry Protein Smoothie 354
Pear-Matcha Smoothie 354
Almond "Tofu" with Cherries
& Black Pepper 361
Vegan Lemon Cake 362

Lentils
Lentils with Smoked Tofu 352

Longan Fruit
Almond Tofu with Longan Fruit 96

Matcha Tea
Pear-Matcha Smoothie 354

Mint
Vegetarian Noodle Bowl (Bún) 202
Vegan Spring Rolls 208
Laotian Tofu Salad (Larb) 243

Miso
Zen Salad with Tofu Sauce.............. 112
Miso Soup with Tofu & Wakame 116
Miso Soup with Fried Tofu & Daikon 118
Grilled Miso Tofu............................ 122
Tofu Fermented in Miso 128

Mushroom
Sautéed Tofu in Lettuce Cups........... 52
Red-Cooked Tofu............................. 80

Zen Salad with Tofu Sauce.............. 112
Spiced Stew with Very Tender Tofu. 169
Mushroom & Tofu Hot Pot 184
Tofu Terrine, Vietnamese Style 201
Egg Tofu Stir-fried with Thai Veggies 217
Tofu, Galangal & Coconut Milk Soup . 220
Tofu with Chilled
Apple-Mushroom Broth................... 298
Vegan Stuffed Mushrooms.............. 342

Natto (Fermented Soybeans)
Cold Tofu with Natto 110

Noodles, Mung Bean
Mung Bean Noodles Braised
with Tofu & Veggies.......................... 68
Tofu Terrine, Vietnamese Style 201

Noodles, Soba
Soba Noodles with Fresh Yuba........ 142

Noodles, Udon
Noodle Soup with Fried Tofu........... 134

Noodles, Wheat
Iced Noodle Soup with Soy Milk...... 188
Nouilles de riz
Breakfast Noodles............................ 86
Thai-Style Stir-fried
Rice Noodles (Pad Thai)................. 218

Nori Seaweed
Panfried Tofu with Nori 136
Soba Noodles with Fresh Yuba........ 142
5-Color Rice Bowl (Bibimbap) 176
Sushi Rolls with Tofu & Crunchy Veggies . 179

Okara
Okara with Vegetables 144

Okra
Cold Tofu with Natto 110

Peanut
Spicy Tofu with Peanuts 78
Tofu Pudding Yunnan Style 83
Breakfast Noodles............................ 86
Peanut Tofu 145
Vegetarian Noodle Bowl (Bún) 202
Vegan Spring Rolls 208
Multicolor Indonesian Salad............ 230
Tofu Puffs with Crunchy Veg
& Spiced Sauce 238

Tofu & Tempeh Satay with
Peanut Sauce 240
Burmese Tofu & Noodle Salad 254
Shan Noodles with Warm
Tofu Cream....................................... 264

Pear
Pear-Matcha Smoothie 354

Peas
Tofu Curry with Green Peas 278
Green Peas with Smoked Tofu........ 340

Peppercorn, Green
Tofu Stir-fry with Green
Peppercorns...................................... 222

Peppercorn, Sichuan
Sichuan-Style Mapo Tofu................... 70
Crispy Salt & Pepper Tofu 75

Persimmon
Walnut Tofu with Persimmon............ 148

Pineapple
Sweet & Sour Tofu 66
Braised Tofu with Pineapple........... 228

Pink Radish
Pink Radish Velouté 300

Potato
Tofu Fritters with Vegetables 126
Broth with Potatoes & Tofu.............. 172
Multicolor Indonesian Salad........... 230
Pink Radish Velouté 300
Vegan Potato Salad 314

Rice
Everyday Fried Rice 48
Rice Porridge with Sweet Potato........ 84
Sushi in Tofu Pockets 132
Tofu Rice Bowl with
Scrambled Eggs 140
5-Color Rice Bowl (Bibimbap) 176
Little Tofu Pockets with
Multicolor Rice 186
Laotian Tofu Salad (Larb) 243

Sesame Seeds
Zen Salad with Tofu Sauce............... 112
Grilled Miso Tofu............................. 122
Tofu Fritters with Vegetables 126

Sushi in Tofu Pockets 132
Sesame Tofu 150
Caramelized Sesame Tofu............... 168
Steamed Tofu with Sautéed Kimchi.. 170
5-Color Rice Bowl (Bibimbap) 176
Little Tofu Pockets with
Multicolor Rice 186
Iced Noodle Soup with Soy Milk...... 188
Burmese Tofu & Noodle Salad 254
Shan Noodles with
Warm Tofu Cream............................ 264
Sesame-Breaded Tofu 308

Shiitake Mushrooms
Everyday Fried Rice 48
Sautéed Tofu in Lettuce Cups............ 52
Tofu Honeycomb Soup 58
Mung Bean Noodles Braised
with Tofu & Veggies 68
Steamed Stuffed Yuba 76
Buddhist Broth 120
Tofu Fritters with Vegetables 126
Okara with Vegetables 144
Spiced Stew with Very Tender Tofu. 169
5-Color Rice Bowl (Bibimbap) 176
Mushroom & Tofu Hot Pot 184

Shiso Leaf
Vegetarian Noodle Bowl (Bún) 202
Vegan Spring Rolls 208

Soy Milk
Firm Tofu..27
Silken Tofu 30
Silken Tofu with Citrus.....................31
Peau de soja....................................32
Tofu Pudding (method 1) 34
Tofu Pudding (method 2) 36
Egg Tofu.. 49
Soba Noodles with Fresh Yuba........ 142
Vegan Caramel Flan 360

Spinach
Zen Salad with Tofu Sauce............... 112
5-Color Rice Bowl (Bibimbap) 176
Sushi Rolls with Tofu &
Crunchy Veggies...............................179
Tofu & Spinach Curry...................... 276
Warm Salad of Buckwheat, Roasted
Carrots & Lacto-Fermented Tofu 324
Spinach & Tofu Lasagna 348

Squash, Summer
Deep-Fried Stuffed Chiles............... 162
Veggie Tofu Cakes 174
5-Color Rice Bowl (Bibimbap)......... 176
Korean Miso Stew........................... 183
Zucchini-Tofu Dumplings 190

Squash, Winter
Roasted Butternut with Sage, Tofu,
Pecans & Coffee.............................. 338

Strawberries
Strawberry Protein Smoothie 354
Tofu Pudding with Red Fruit Coulis . 368

Sweet Potato
Rice Porridge with Sweet Potato........ 84

Tempeh
Multicolor Indonesian Salad............ 230
Balinese Curry with Tofu & Tempeh.. 232
Braised Tofu & Tempeh
Javanese Style................................ 234
Tofu & Tempeh Satay with Peanut Sauce
240

Tofu, Extra-Firm
Sautéed Minced Tofu 139
Zucchini-Tofu Dumplings 190
Philippine-Style Braised Tofu 212
Tofu, Galangal &
Coconut Milk Soup 220
Tofu Stir-fry with Green
Peppercorns 222
Red Curry Tofu Stir-fry 224
Coconut Green Curry 226
Braised Tofu with Pineapple............ 228
Multicolor Indonesian Salad............ 230
Braised Tofu & Tempeh
Javanese Style................................ 234
Tofu Stir-Fry with Balinese Sauce 235
Tofu & Tempeh Satay with
Peanut Sauce 240
Spicy Tofu Sambal 242
Vegan Butter Chicken..................... 274
Tofu & Spinach Curry...................... 276
Tofu Curry with Green Peas............. 278
Black Pepper Tofu Curry 280
Tofu Tikka 282
Wheat-Free Tabbouleh 297
Tofu Nuggets................................. 327
Vegan Leek Tart 332
Pasta with Vegetarian Bolognese 346

Tofu, Extra-Soft (Sundubu)
Mung Bean Noodles Braised
with Tofu & Veggies........................ 68
Tofu Pot Stickers 72
Steamed Stuffed Yuba 76
Red-Cooked Tofu............................. 80
Sichuan-Style Braised Tofu............... 82

Tofu Stir-fry with Black Beans........... 88
Five-Spice Pressed Tofu................... 94
Spiced Stew with Very Tender Tofu. 169
Strawberry Protein Smoothie 354
Pear-Matcha Smoothie 354

Tofu, Fermented
Chinese Cabbage Sautéed with
Fermented Tofu 62
Rice Porridge with Sweet Potato........ 84
Tofu Terrine, Vietnamese Style 201
Savory Spiral Cookies 236
Vegan Greek Salad......................... 306
Warm Salad of Buckwheat, Roasted
Carrots & Lacto-Fermented Tofu 324
Vegan Pissaladière 328

Tofu, Firm
Sautéed Tofu in Lettuce Cups........... 52
"Thousand-Layer" Tofu 56
Tofu Honeycomb Soup 58
Sweet & Sour Tofu........................... 66
Mung Bean Noodles Braised
with Tofu & Veggies........................ 68
Crispy Salt & Pepper Tofu 75
3-Cup Tofu 77
Red-Cooked Tofu............................. 80
Tofu Stir-fry with Black Beans........... 88
Five-Spice Pressed Tofu................... 94
Zen Salad with Tofu Sauce.............. 112
Very Simple Fried Tofu 113
Buddhist Broth 120
Grilled Miso Tofu........................... 122
Grilled Tofu 124
Tofu Fritters with Vegetables 126
Tofu Fermented in Miso 128
Panfried Tofu with Nori 136
Deep-Fried Stuffed Chiles............... 162
Herbed Tofu Canapés 164
Panfried Tofu with Egg................... 166
Caramelized Sesame Tofu............... 168
Steamed Tofu with Sautéed Kimchi.. 170
Broth with Potatoes & Tofu............. 172
Veggie Tofu Cakes 174
5-Color Rice Bowl (Bibimbap)......... 176

Sushi Rolls with Tofu &
Crunchy Veggies................................179
Spicy Braised Tofu...........................182
Korean Miso Stew.............................183
Mushroom & Tofu Hot Pot...............184
Lemongrass Tofu...............................200
Tofu Terrine, Vietnamese Style.......201
Vegan Spring Rolls..........................208
Tofu, Galangal & Coconut
Milk Soup...220
Tofu Stir-fry with Green
Peppercorns.....................................222
Coconut Green Curry........................226
Multicolor Indonesian Salad............230
Balinese Curry with
Tofu & Tempeh.................................232
Braised Tofu & Tempeh
Javanese Style..................................234
Tofu Stir-Fry with Balinese Sauce....235
Tofu & Tempeh Satay with
Peanut Sauce...................................240
Spicy Tofu Sambal...........................242
Spiced Tofu Pakora..........................272
Tofu Curry with Bell Peppers..........273
Vegan Butter Chicken......................274
Tofu & Spinach Curry.......................276
Tofu Curry with Green Peas............278
Black Pepper Tofu Curry.................280
Tofu Tikka..282
Lacto-Fermented Tofu......................303
Soy-Ginger Lacto-Fermented Tofu......304
Sesame-Breaded Tofu......................308
Mediterranean-Marinated Tofu.......315
Tofu Nuggets....................................327
Vegan Leek Tart...............................332
Orange-Braised Tofu & Fennel........336
Roasted Butternut with Sage, Tofu,
Pecans & Coffee...............................338
Panfried Tofu with Barbecue Sauce.343

Tofu, Grilled
Cold Tofu with Green Onion.............50
Cold Tofu with Century Eggs............54
Bok Choy & Tofu Soup......................60
Sweet & Sour Tofu.............................66
Sichuan-Style Mapo Tofu...................70
Crispy Salt & Pepper Tofu.................75
Red-Cooked Tofu................................80
Miso Soup with Tofu & Wakame......116
Kyoto-Style Tofu Hot Pot.................138
Veggie Tofu Cakes...........................174
Korean Miso Stew.............................183
Mushroom & Tofu Hot Pot...............184

Spiced Tofu Pakora..........................272
Crispy Deep-Fried Tofu....................294
Vegan Tzatziki..................................296
White Asparagus,
Crème Fraîche & Tofu......................302
Sesame-Breaded Tofu......................308
Vegan Shakshuka..............................334
Roasted Butternut with Sage, Tofu,
Pecans & Coffee...............................338
Spinach & Tofu Lasagna..................348

Tofu, Medium-Firm
Cold Tofu with Green Onion.............50
Cold Tofu with Century Eggs............54
Bok Choy & Tofu Soup......................60
Sweet & Sour Tofu.............................66
Sichuan-Style Mapo Tofu...................70
Crispy Salt & Pepper Tofu.................75
Red-Cooked Tofu................................80
Miso Soup with Tofu & Wakame......116
Kyoto-Style Tofu Hot Pot.................138
Veggie Tofu Cakes...........................174
Korean Miso Stew.............................183
Mushroom & Tofu Hot Pot...............184
Spiced Tofu Pakora..........................272
Crispy Deep-Fried Tofu....................294
Vegan Tzatziki..................................296
White Asparagus,
Crème Fraîche & Tofu......................302
Sesame-Breaded Tofu......................308
Vegan Shakshuka..............................334
Roasted Butternut with Sage, Tofu,
Pecans & Coffee...............................338
Spinach & Tofu Lasagna..................348

Tofu, Pressed
Everyday Fried Rice...........................48
Tofu Noodle Salad.............................64
Spicy Tofu with Peanuts...................78
Pressed Tofu with Garlic Chives........90
Egg Tofu Stir-fried
with Thai Veggies............................217

Tofu Pudding
Tofu Pudding Yunnan Style...............83
Breakfast Noodles.............................86
Tofu Pudding with Adzuki Beans.......92
Tofu Pudding with Ginger Syrup.....211
Tofu Pudding with Syrup Pearls......214
Tofu Pudding with Red Fruit Coulis.368

Tofu, Silken
Cold Tofu with Green Onion.............50

Cold Tofu with Century Eggs 54
Breakfast Noodles 86
Cold Tofu with Ginger
& Green Onion 108
Cold Tofu with Natto 110
Melting Fried Tofu 114
Tofu Mochi 152
Tofu with Chilled
Apple-Mushroom Broth 298
Pink Radish Velouté 300
Vegan Mayonnaise 326
Vegan Stuffed Mushrooms 342
Spaghetti with Tofu-Artichoke
Cream 350
Hazelnut, Chocolate &
Silken Tofu Tart 358
Vegan Caramel Flan 360
Vegan Lemon Cake 362
Light Coffee Mousse 364
Vegan Apricot Clafoutis 366
Vegan Chocolate Mousse 369

Tofu Skin (see Yuba)

Tofu, Smoked
Arugula, Fig & Smoked Tofu Salad .. 322
Eggplant Stuffed with Smoked Tofu . 330
Green Peas with Smoked Tofu 340
Vegan Stuffed Mushrooms 342
Lentils with Smoked Tofu 352

Tofu, Soft
Cold Tofu with Green Onion 50
Cold Tofu with Century Eggs 54
Sichuan-Style Mapo Tofu 70
Miso Soup with Tofu & Wakame 116
Vegan Tzatziki 296

Tomato
Iced Noodle Soup with Soy Milk 188

Spicy Tofu Sambal 242
Burmese Tofu Curry 258
Shan Noodles with
Warm Tofu Cream 264
Tofu Curry with Bell Peppers 273
Vegan Butter Chicken 274
Tofu & Spinach Curry 276
Tofu Curry with Green Peas 278
Black Pepper Tofu Curry 280
Tofu Tikka Masala 281
Wheat-Free Tabbouleh 297
Vegan Greek Salad 306
Mediterranean-Marinated Tofu 315
Tomato & Tofu Salad with
Date Dressing 318
Eggplant Stuffed with
Smoked Tofu 330
Vegan Shakshuka 334
Tofu Burger with Barbecue Sauce 344
Pasta with Vegetarian Bolognese 346

Umeboshi (Pickled Plums)
Cold Tofu with Natto 110

Wakame Seaweed
Miso Soup with Tofu & Wakame 116

Walnut
Walnut Tofu 147

Watermelon
Watermelon Salad with
Marinated Tofu 316

Yogurt
Tofu Tikka 282

Yuba (Tofu Skin)
Steamed Stuffed Yuba 76
Braised Yuba 206

•••

RECIPE INDEX

A

Almond "Tofu" with Cherries
& Black Pepper 361
Almond Tofu.................................. 95
Almond Tofu with Longan Fruit 96
Arugula, Fig & Smoked Tofu Salad .. 322

B

Balinese Curry with Tofu
& Tempeh.. 232
Black Pepper Tofu Curry 280
Bok Choy & Tofu Soup...................... 60
Braised Tofu & Tempeh
Javanese Style................................. 234
Braised Tofu with Pineapple............ 228
Braised Yuba 206
Breakfast Noodles............................ 86
Broth with Potatoes & Tofu............. 172
Buddhist Broth 120
Burmese Tofu.................................. 253
Burmese Tofu & Noodle Salad 254
Burmese Tofu Crackers................... 267
Burmese Tofu Curry 258
Burmese Tofu Salad 256
Burmese Twice-Fried Tofu.............. 262

C

Caramelized Sesame Tofu............... 168
Chinese Cabbage Sautéed with
Fermented Tofu 62
Clear Soup with Egg Tofu 216
Coconut Green Curry 226
Cold Tofu with Century Eggs............ 54
Cold Tofu with Ginger &
Green Onion................................... 108
Cold Tofu with Green Onion 50
Cold Tofu with Natto....................... 110
Crispy Deep-Fried Tofu................... 294
Crispy Deep-Fried Tofu................... 294
Crispy Salt & Pepper Tofu................ 75

D

Deep-Fried Stuffed Chiles.............. 162

E

Edamame Tofu............................... 146
Egg Tofu....................................... 49
Egg Tofu Stir-fried with
Thai Veggies 217
Eggplant Stuffed with
Smoked Tofu.................................. 330
Endive Salad with
Miso-Fermented Tofu 320
Everyday Fried Rice 48

F

Firm Tofu....................................... 27
5-Color Rice Bowl (Bibimbap)......... 176
Five-Spice Pressed Tofu.................. 94
Fried Tofu, Burmese Style 260

G

Green Peas with Smoked Tofu........ 340
Grilled Miso Tofu........................... 122
Grilled Tofu 124

H

Hazelnut, Chocolate & Silken Tofu Tart 33
Herbed Tofu Canapés 164

I

Iced Noodle Soup with Soy Milk...... 188

K

Korean Miso Stew........................... 183
Kyoto-Style Tofu Hot Pot................ 138

L

Lacto-Fermented Tofu.................... 303
Laotian Tofu Salad (Larb) 243
Lemongrass Tofu 200
Lentils with Smoked Tofu 352
Light Coffee Mousse 364

Little Tofu Pockets with
Multicolor Rice 186

M

Mango-Avocado Salad with
Sesame-Breaded Tofu
& Chimichurri................................. 312
Mediterranean-Marinated Tofu 315
Melting Fried Tofu 114
Miso Soup with Fried Tofu
& Daikon.. 118
Miso Soup with Tofu & Wakame 116
Multicolor Indonesian Salad............ 230
Mung Bean Noodles Braised
with Tofu & Veggies......................... 68
Mushroom & Tofu Hot Pot 184

N

Noodle Soup with Fried Tofu........... 134

O

Okara with Vegetables 144
Orange-Braised Tofu & Fennel 336

P

Panfried Tofu with
Barbecue Sauce 343
Panfried Tofu with Egg................... 166
Panfried Tofu with Nori 136
Pasta with Vegetarian Bolognese 346
Peanut Tofu 145
Pear-Matcha Smoothie 354
Philippine-Style Braised Tofu 212
Pink Radish Velouté 300
Pressed Tofu with Garlic Chives........ 90

R

Red Curry Tofu Stir-fry 224
Red-Cooked Tofu.............................. 80
Rice Porridge with Sweet Potato........ 84
Roasted Butternut with Sage, Tofu,
Pecans & Coffee.............................. 338

S

Salty-Sweet Fried Tofu Pockets 130
Sautéed Minced Tofu 139
Sautéed Tofu in Lettuce Cups........... 52

Savory Spiral Cookies 236
Sesame Tofu 150
Sesame-Breaded Tofu 308
Shan Country Yellow Tofu............... 250
Shan Noodles with Warm
Tofu Cream.................................... 264
Sichuan-Style Braised Tofu 82
Sichuan-Style Mapo Tofu 70
Silken Tofu 30
Silken Tofu with Citrus.................... 31
Soba Noodles with Fresh Yuba........ 142
Soy Milk & Okara............................. 24
Soy-Ginger Lacto-Fermented Tofu .. 304
Spaghetti with Tofu-Artichoke
Cream 350
Spiced Stew with Very
Tender Tofu 169
Spiced Tofu Pakora 272
Spicy Braised Tofu 182
Spicy Tofu Sambal 242
Spicy Tofu with Peanuts 78
Spinach & Tofu Lasagna 348
Steamed Stuffed Yuba 76
Steamed Tofu with
Sautéed Kimchi............................... 170
Strawberry Protein Smoothie 354
Summer Veggie &
Sesame-Breaded Tofu Wrap............ 310
Sushi in Tofu Pockets 132
Sushi Rolls with Tofu &
Crunchy Veggies............................. 179
Sweet & Sour Tofu............................ 66

T

Thai-Style Stir-fried
Rice Noodles (Pad Thai)................. 218
"Thousand-Layer" Tofu.................... 56
3-Cup Tofu 77
Tofu & Spinach Curry...................... 276
Tofu & Veggie Sandwich (Bánh Mi) . 204
Tofu Burger with Barbecue Sauce.... 344
Tofu Curry with Bell Peppers 273
Tofu Curry with Green Peas............ 278
Tofu Fermented in Miso 128
Tofu French Toast 356
Tofu Fritters with Vegetables 126
Tofu Honeycomb Soup 58

Tofu Mochi....................................... 152
Tofu Noodle Salad 64
Tofu Nuggets 327
Tofu Pot Stickers 72
Tofu Pudding (method 1) 34
Tofu Pudding (method 2) 36
Tofu Pudding with Adzuki Beans....... 92
Tofu Pudding with Ginger Syrup 211
Tofu Pudding with Red Fruit Coulis . 368
Tofu Pudding with Syrup Pearls 214
Tofu Pudding Yunnan Style 83
Tofu Puffs with Crunchy Veg
& Spiced Sauce 238
Tofu Rice Bowl with
Scrambled Eggs 140
Tofu Skins.. 32
Tofu Stir-Fry with Balinese Sauce 235
Tofu Stir-fry with Black Beans........... 88
Tofu Stir-fry with Green
Peppercorns 222
Tofu Terrine, Vietnamese Style 201
Tofu Tikka 282
Tofu Tikka Masala............................ 281
Tofu with Chilled
Apple-Mushroom Broth.................... 298
Tofu-Olive Canapés 292
Tofu, Galangal & Coconut
Milk Soup 220
Tomato & Tofu Salad with
Date Dressing 318

V
Vegan Apricot Clafoutis.................. 366
Vegan Butter Chicken...................... 274
Vegan Caramel Flan 360
Vegan Chocolate Mousse 369
Vegan Greek Salad.......................... 306
Vegan Leek Tart 332
Vegan Lemon Cake 362
Vegan Mayonnaise 326
Vegan Pissaladière 328
Vegan Potato Salad......................... 314
Vegan Shakshuka 334
Vegan Spring Rolls 208
Vegan Stuffed Mushrooms.............. 342
Vegan Tartar Sauce 326
Vegan Tzatziki 296
Vegetarian Noodle Bowl (Bún) 202

Veggie Tofu Cakes 174
Very Simple Fried Tofu 113

W
Walnut Tofu 147
Walnut Tofu with Persimmon........... 148
Warm Salad of Buckwheat, Roasted
Carrots & Lacto-Fermented Tofu 324
Watermelon Salad with
Marinated Tofu 316
Wheat-Free Tabbouleh 297
White Asparagus, Crème Fraîche
& Tofu 302

Z
Zen Salad with Tofu Sauce.............. 112
Zucchini-Tofu Dumplings 190

weldon**owen**

Weldon Owen International
1150 Brickyard Cove Road
Richmond, CA 94801
www.weldonowen.com

Originally published in French as *Tofu: l'anthologie*, © 2019 Hachette-Livre (Éditions La Plage)
English translation © 2020 Weldon Owen International

Author: Camille Oger
Graphic Designer: David Cosson
Photographer: Christophe Girard
Translator: Sarah Putman Clegg

ISBN: 978-1-68188-584-1

10 9 8 7 6 5 4 3 2 1

Printed and bound in China.